Papers in Experimental Economics

VERNON L. SMITH

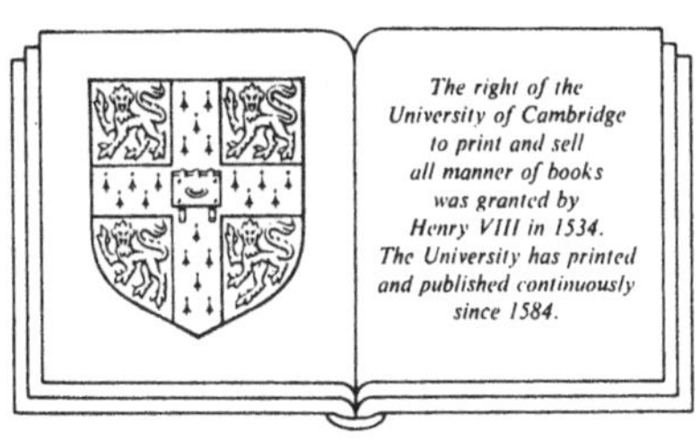

CAMBRIDGE UNIVERSITY PRESS

Cambridge
New York Port Chester Melbourne Sydney

CAMBRIDGE UNIVERSITY PRESS
Cambridge, New York, Melbourne, Madrid, Cape Town, Singapore, São Paulo

Cambridge University Press
The Edinburgh Building, Cambridge CB2 2RU, UK

Published in the United States of America by Cambridge University Press, New York

www.cambridge.org
Information on this title: www.cambridge.org/9780521364560

First published 1991
This digitally printed first paperback version 2006

A catalogue record for this publication is available from the British Library

Library of Congress Cataloguing in Publication data
Smith, Vernon L.
Papers in experimental economics / Vernon L. Smith.
p. cm.
ISBN 0-521-36456-6
1. Economics – Methodology. 2. Economics – Experimental methods
3. Economics – Research. I. Title. II. Title: Experimental
economics.
HB131.S6 1991
330 – dc20 91–3789
CIP

ISBN-13 978-0-521-36456-0 hardback
ISBN-10 0-521-36456-6 hardback

ISBN-13 978-0-521-02465-5 paperback
ISBN-10 0-521-02465-X paperback

This is remembrance – revisitation; and names are keys that open corridors no longer fresh in the mind, but nonetheless familiar in the heart.

Beryl Markham,
West with the Night

Contents

Part V. Industrial Organization

Part VI. Perspectives on Economics

Preface

Since midcentury the use of laboratory experimental methods in economics has developed into a major field of inquiry within microeconomics. The slow but steady development of the 1950s and 1960s was superseded by accelerated development in the 1970s and 1980s. *Development,* not *growth,* is the right word because the methodological purpose and function of experiments in economics has undergone in-depth inner change as well as quantitative growth. The idea that an experiment might be described as a "simulation" – a word used in my first (1962) paper before that word had become clearly associated with a different meaning – has yielded to the realization that in an experiment we create a certain type of controlled market or nonmarket allocation process that is real in the sense of rewards, people, and institutional rules of exchange in which all trades are binding. The issue of parallelism, or the transferability of results from laboratory to other environments, which is of ever-present interest to experimentalists, is most constructively viewed as an empirical question applying to *any* particular data set whether in the laboratory or in the field. Thus data from one field environment may or may not have relevance to another field environment. All data are specific to particular conditions and there is no means by which one can bootstrap finite data sets into a theory or generalization of any kind without falling prey to the fallacy of induction. But through laboratory replication and control and, ultimately, parallel field studies, one can increase the credibility of theory and pretheoretical empirical regularities as informative properties of the economic processes we study. Although the individual and his/her behavior is paramount in these processes, the primary lesson of experimental economics is that the individual and his/her rational behavior cannot be meaningfully separated from other individuals through the interactive process mediated by the rules that govern exchange in particular market institutions.

This collection includes all my experimental papers with the exception of (1) five authored or coauthored by me that appear in *Schools of Economic Thought: Experimental Economics,* edited by V. L. Smith (London: Edward Elgar Publishing, 1989); (2) survey papers that did not report new experimental results; (3) brief reports of incompleted research; (4) my entries, "Auctions" and "Experimental Methods in Economics," in *The New Palgrave,* edited by J. Eatwell, M. Milgate, and P. Newman (London: Macmillan and Co., 1987); and (5) miscellaneous rhetorical pieces related to experimental economics. If I had thought I was as good a rhetor as was Jimmie Savage, I might have included the latter. But the reader will find enough rhetoric in the present volume. Don McCloskey is right: good rhetoric is inseparable from good science. Both facts and theories are mute; they never speak for themselves.

My debt is heavy indeed to many. My machinist father for inspiring in me a curiosity about how things work and my socialist mother for providing a dream of better things (their eighth-grade educations were more than enough for these accomplishments); Dick Howey at the University of Kansas from whom I learned what scholarship meant; long-time personal friends like John Hughes from whom one learns much about what it really means to be human, and Stan Reiter, still the most thoughtful economist I have known; Em Weiler, the Dean who invested to the brim in people and lived to see its enormous return; and finally, and especially important, my many coauthors and critical referees who enlightened my way and created for me a contesting intellectual community in experimental methods before experimentalists could benefit from the extended community we now enjoy.

Acknowledgments

''An Experimental Study of Competitive Market Behavior'' was first published in the *Journal of Political Economy,* April 1962, © 1962 by the University of Chicago. It is reprinted here with permission.

''Effect of Market Organization on Competitive Equilibrium'' was first published in the *Quarterly Journal of Economics,* May 1964, © 1964 by the President and Fellows of Harvard College. Reprinted by permission of John Wiley & Sons, Inc.

''Nature, the Experimental Laboratory, and the Credibility of Hypotheses'' was first published in *Behavioral Science,* July 1964, © 1964 by *Behavioral Science.* It is reprinted here with permission.

''Experimental Auction Markets and the Walrasian Hypothesis'' was first published in the *Journal of Political Economy,* August 1965, © 1965 by the University of Chicago. It is reprinted here with permission.

''Experimental Studies of Discrimination versus Competition in Sealed-Bid Auction Markets'' was first published in the *Journal of Business,* January 1967, © 1967 by the University of Chicago. It is reprinted here with permission.

''Experimental Economics: Induced Value Theory'' was first published in the *American Economic Review,* May 1976, © 1976 by the American Economic Association. It is reprinted here with permission.

''Bidding and Auctioning Institutions: Experimental Results'' was first published in *Bidding and Auctioning for Procurement and Allocation,* edited by Yakov Amihud (New York: New York University Press, 1976), © 1976 by New York University. It is reprinted here with permission.

''Intertemporal Competitive Equilibrium: An Empirical Study of Speculation'' was first published in the *Quarterly Journal of Economics,* November 1977, © 1977 by the President and Fellows of Harvard College. Reprinted by permission of John Wiley & Sons, Inc.

''Experimental Economics at Purdue'' was first published in *Essays in Contemporary Fields of Economics,* edited by G. Horwich and J. P. Quirk (West Lafayette: Purdue University Press, 1981), © 1981 by Purdue Research Foundation, West Lafayette, Indiana 47907. Reprinted with permission.

''On Nonbinding Price Controls in a Competitive Market'' was first published in the *American Economic Review,* June 1981, © 1981 by the American Economic Association. It is reprinted here with permission.

"An Experimental Comparison of Alternative Rules for Competitive Market Exchange" was first published in *Auctions, Bidding, and Contracting: Uses and Theory,* edited by Richard Englebrecht-Wiggans, Martin Shubik, and Robert M. Stark (New York: New York University Press, 1983), © 1983 by New York University. It is reprinted here with permission.

"Competitive Market Institutions: Double Auctions vs. Sealed Bid-Offer Auctions" was first published in the *American Economic Review,* March 1982, © 1982 by the American Economic Association. It is reprinted here with permission.

"Markets as Economizers of Information: Experimental Examination of the 'Hayek Hypothesis' " first appeared in *Economic Inquiry,* April 1982, © 1982 by the Western Economic Association. It is reprinted here with permission.

"The Effect of Rent Asymmetries in Experimental Auction Markets" was first published in the *Journal of Economic Behavior and Organization,* June–September 1982, © 1982 North-Holland. It is reprinted here with permission.

"Microeconomic Systems as an Experimental Science" was first published in the *American Economic Review,* December 1982, © 1982 by the American Economic Association. It is reprinted here with permission.

"Experimental Economics (Reply to R. Heiner)" was first published in the *American Economic Review,* March 1985, © 1985 by the American Economic Association. It is reprinted here with permission.

"A Comparison of Posted-Offer and Double-Auction Pricing Institutions" was first published in the *Review of Economic Studies,* October 1984, © 1984 by The Society for Economic Analysis Limited. It is reprinted here with permission.

"Hypothetical Valuations and Preference Reversals in the Context of Asset Trading" first appeared in *Laboratory Experimentation in Economics,* edited by Alvin Roth (Cambridge: Cambridge University Press, 1987), © 1987 by Cambridge University Press.

"Bubbles, Crashes, and Endogenous Expectations in Experimental Spot Asset Markets" was first published in *Econometrica,* September 1988, © 1988 by The Econometric Society. It is reprinted here with permission.

"The Principle of Unanimity and Voluntary Consent in Social Choice" was first published in the *Journal of Political Economy,* December 1977, © 1977 by the University of Chicago. It is reprinted here with permission.

"Incentive Compatible Experimental Processes for the Provision of Public Goods" was first published in *Research in Experimental Economics,* Vol. 1, (Greenwich, Conn.: JAI Press, 1979), © 1979 by JAI Press, Inc. It is reprinted here with permission.

"An Experimental Comparison of Three Public Good Decision Mechanisms" was first published in the *Scandanavian Journal of Economics,* 81(2), © 1979 by the Department of Economics, University of Stockholm, Sweden. It is reprinted here with permission.

"Experiments with a Decentralized Mechanism for Public Good Decisions" was first published in the *American Economic Review,* September 1980, © 1980 by the American Economic Association. It is reprinted here with permission.

"Experimental Tests of an Allocation Mechanism for Private, Public or Externality Goods" was first published in the *Scandanavian Journal of Economics* 86 (4), © 1984 by the Department of Economics, University of Stockholm, Sweden. It is reprinted here with permission.

"Incentives and Behavior in English, Dutch and Sealed-Bid Auctions" was first published in *Economic Inquiry,* January 1980, © 1980 by the Western Economic Association. It is reprinted here with permission.

"Theory and Behavior of Single Object Auctions" was first published in *Research in Experimental Economics,* Vol. 2 (Greenwich, Conn.: JAI Press, 1982), © 1982 by JAI Press Inc. It is reprinted here with permission.

"A Test that Discriminates Between Two Models of the Dutch-First Auction Non-Isomorphism" was first published in the *Journal of Economic Behavior and Organization,* June–September 1983, © 1983 by Elsevier Science Publishers B.V. (North-Holland). It is reprinted here with permission.

"Theory and Behavior of Multiple Unit Discriminative Auctions" was first published in the *Journal of Finance,* September 1984, © 1984 by the *Journal of Finance.* It is reprinted here with permission.

"Theory and Individual Behavior of First-Price Auctions" was first published in the *Journal of Risk and Uncertainty,* March 1988, © 1988 by Kluwer Academic Publishers, Boston. It is reprinted here with permission.

"A Combinatorial Auction Mechanism for Airport Time Slot Allocation" was first published in the *Bell Journal of Economics,* Autumn 1982, © 1982 by AT&T. Reprinted from the *Bell Journal of Economics* with permission of The RAND Corporation.

"Designing 'Smart' Computer-Assisted Markets" was first published in the *European Journal of Political Economy* 5 (1989), © 1989 by Elsevier Science Publishers B.V. (North-Holland). It is reprinted here with permission.

"An Empirical Study of Decentralized Institutions of Monopoly Restraint" was first published in *Essays in Contemporary Fields of Economics,* edited by G. Horwich and J. P. Quirk (West Lafayette: Purdue University Press), © 1981 by Purdue Research Foundation, West Lafayette, Indiana 47907. Reprinted with permission.

"Natural Monopoly and Contested Markets: Some Experimental Results" was first published in the *Journal of Law and Economics,* April 1984, © 1984 by the University of Chicago. It is reprinted here with permission.

"In Search of Predatory Pricing" was first published in the *Journal of Political Economy,* April 1985, © 1985 by the University of Chicago. It is reprinted here with permission.

"Theory, Experiment and Economics" was first published in the *Journal of Economic Perspectives,* Winter 1989, © 1989 by the American Economic Association. It is reprinted here with permission.

"Experimental Economics: Behavioral Lessons for Microeconomic Theory and Policy" was given as the 1990 Nancy L. Schwartz Memorial Lecture at the J. L. Kellogg Graduate School of Management at Northwestern University on May 9, 1990. It is reprinted here with permission.

PART I

The Formative Years

Introduction

Experimental market economics began with a burst of papers and books from 1959 to 1963: Hoggatt (1959), Sauermann and Selten (1959, 1960), Siegel and Fouraker (1960), Fouraker, Shubik, and Siegel (1961), Smith (1962), Fouraker and Siegel (1963), Suppes and Carlsmith (1962), and Friedman (1963). Many of us were unaware of the parallel research being conducted almost simultaneously by others. E. H. Chamberlin's (1948) precursory study of an informal exchange market had directly influenced the first experiments I conducted in the period 1956–60. This constitutes the published background to the nine papers appearing in the first part of this collection.

The unpublished background includes my significant encounter with Sidney Siegel, reported in my essay "Experimental Economics at Purdue" (1981). One can only speculate as to the course of experimental economics in the last quarter century had it not been for Sid Siegel's untimely death in the autumn of 1961. My opinion is that his energy and towering intellectual competence and technique as an experimental scientist would have accelerated greatly the development of experimental economics. Had he lived there would have been a sustained effort in experimental economics at another institution besides Purdue University. It appears that he has no intellectual descendants in psychology, but many in economics, although few of the latter may be fully aware of their heritage. Also part of the unpublished background is my experience (discussed in paper 9) in the revision and final acceptance for publication of my first experimental paper. My referees did not understand (nor did I at the time) the significance of what I was attempting to do in that paper, and their questions forced me to begin thinking about how we come to know what we think we know, and why one might do laboratory experiments. This experience strengthened my resolve to do several follow-up studies (papers 2–5) and, as it developed, to work out a methodology of experiment for economics. In the meantime I had to make a living and during these formative years I was writing and publishing on other topics – capital and investment theory, corporate finance theory and the economics of uncertainty, and natural resource economics. Compared with the experimental work, this other research was much easier to do and easier to publish. The ballistics of investment and bioeconomics was just undergraduate physics with a flair for modeling in a particular economic context. The profession was hungry for new theory in these areas, indeed, *any* area that employed recognizable methods; it was not hungry for evidence, and certainly not laboratory evidence, because theory provided all the requisite understanding. One had to justify one's interest in experimental inquiry with each new effort. This had a disciplinary and salubrious effect on the development of my thinking as to what economic inquiry was about. I would have been insulated from that influence if I had adhered to more familiar professional paths, comfortably supported by cultures that did not reason why. Other experimentalists have had similar experiences. Experimentation in economics owes much of its development to the challenge to reexamine continually everything we do – our procedures, our empirical interpretation of theories, the replicability and robustness of results, and the implications of experiment for new and better theory. But other areas of empirical research, notably economic history, have evolved under a somewhat similar discipline.

I began teaching a graduate seminar, annually, in experimental economics at Purdue in the spring of 1963. My students that year were Robert Brennen, Jerry Dake, Carter Franklin, Clarke Johnson, Thomas Muench, James Murphy, John Powers, Donald Rice, Hugo Sonnenschein, James Streamo, Peter Stroth, Norman Weldon, and John Wertz. My paper with Don Rice, "Nature, the Experimental Laboratory, and the Credibility of Hypotheses" (1963), grew out of that seminar. It was our first methodological effort, and dealt exclusively with the issue I later would call *parallelism,* a term I got from reading some work of the astronomer Harlow Shapley. His use of the term was with reference to biological parallelism, but I thought it was a term worth generalizing. I never liked the phrase *external validity* as used in psychology because the problem of the comparability of data sets applies to any two environments whether they are both naturally occurring, both experimental, or one is experimental and the other naturally occurring. All environments are relevant sources of data on some aspect of human behavior, perceptions, or thought processes. I think the conceptual approach that Don Rice and I used in this paper to analyze models, data from nature, and data from experiment is still useful. The particular Bayesian formalism we develop has never, to my knowledge, been implemented. But informally, I think it captures the essential elements of the scientist's prior and posterior beliefs about theory and the relevance of different kinds of evidence to testing theory. That framework includes the case in which one's a priori belief is that a particular kind of experimental data is of no relevance to theory or field observations. An example, perhaps, for some economists is the Kahneman-Tversky hypothetical assessment of attitudes toward risk. For those who distrust hypothetical assessments no number of replications will change such a person's posterior beliefs about the credibility of the theory. A less subjective example is the following: the fact that a stone falls when dropped does not verify Newton no matter how many times the experiment is replicated. The observation is consistent with all inverse laws of attraction and is irrelevant to testing the inverse square law.

My "Experimental Studies of Discrimination versus Competition in Sealed-Bid Auction Markets" (paper 5) became part of a series of developments related to the design of market institutions. This development is reported in the introduction to Part V.

The idea that laboratory methods in economics are driven by what I called "induced value theory" was developed in lecture-discussion notes for my experimental seminar at Purdue in the period 1963–67. This theory was originally designed to explicate the role of rewards in defining the private characteristics ("circumstances of time and place") of each subject and thus the market supply and demand environment (known by the experimenter, not the subjects) in my early experiments. It also sought to explain, in terms of "other things in the utility function" (that is, other motivations than money) why some experiments might be consistent with some theory in the absence of monetary rewards, and why some experiments might fail because of inadequate motivation. The objective was to provide some structured guidelines for designing and interpreting the results of experiments. In thinking through the implications of "other things in the utility function," I found Sid Siegel's paper on the two-choice uncertain outcome situation particularly helpful (Siegel 1961). In this binary choice situation, the interpretation of over twenty years of psychology literature had been that people were not rational; specifically, they failed to maximize. Since monetary payoffs had not been used, Siegel hypothesized that subjects did not maximize because there was nothing of value worth maximizing, and that the observed matching behavior of subjects was due to "monotony, both kinesthetic and cognitive" (Siegel 1961, p. 768). Accordingly, he developed an additive model of utility with two terms: the first was the utility of reward, the second the utility of variability, diversification, or monotony relief. The model predicted that subjects would be drawn away from matching toward maximizing by introducing monetary payoffs, and that the greater the payoff levels the nearer would be the response to the maximizing response. The data confirmed the prediction. Then Siegel's ingenuity was turned to a procedure for raising the utility of variability as a treatment. I leave it to the reader to find out how this was accomplished. The data confirmed the prediction. This work was, in my view, of fundamental methodological importance, and I think it is unfortunate that it was not more widely known among experimentalists in both economics and psychology. Perhaps it was not possible for this work to be widely known in either of these two cultures, if economists were willing to accept the premise of the paper without evidence and if psychologists were unwilling to accept the premise with evidence.

In my experimental classes induced value theory was soon generalized to choice in "commodity space," and by 1965 it had provided the basis for a general equilibrium "Edgeworth box" experiment for a student's (George Hill's) project in my seminar class. The results of that experiment turned out to be inexplicable, not because of problems with induced valuation but because none of us was yet fully sensitive to the institution as a variable also driving behavior. We had used a uniform price sealed bid-offer auction for the first time and this, as it became clear to me much later, was the source of the inexplicable behavior.

I discussed these ideas in the late 1960s and early 1970s with Charles Plott, who prevailed upon me to get "something written up" that could be cited. This led to the two 1976 papers on induced valuation and bidding and auctioning institutions. This also led to two joint papers with Plott and with Miller and Plott that were priceless first collaborations for me. The second is reprinted here, the first in *Schools of Economic Thought: Experimental Economics,* cited in the Preface. During this period M. Fiorina and Plott were using the concept to induce individual preferences on a two-commodity public good space (X_1, X_2). The institution they used was Robert's Rules of Order, including majority rule, while the message space consisted of amendments and votes. M. Levine and Plott collaborated to add the agenda to this institution and to manipulate it as a treatment variable. In these papers, Fiorina, Levine, and Plott were instrumental in creating the complementary field of experimental political economy.

References

Chamberlin, Edward. 1948. "An Experimental Imperfect Market." *Journal of Political Economy* 56 (April).

Fouraker, Lawrence, Martin Shubik, and Sidney Siegel. 1961. "Oligopoly Bargaining: The Quantity Adjuster Models." Research Bulletin 20, Department of Psychology, Pennsylvania State University.

Fouraker, Lawrence, and Sidney Siegel. 1963. *Bargaining Behavior.* New York: McGraw-Hill.

Friedman, James. 1963. "Individual Behavior in Oligopolistic Markets: An Experimental Study." *Yale Economic Essays,* vol. 3.

Hoggatt, Austin. 1959. "An Experimental Business Game." *Behavioral Science* (July).

Sauermann, Heinz, and Richard Selten. 1960. "An Experiment in Oligopoly." *General Systems Yearbook of the Society for General Systems Research,* vol. 5, edited by Ludwig von Bertalanffy and Anatol Rappoport. Ann Arbor: Society for General Systems Research. Translation of "Ein Oligopolexperiment," *Zeitschrift für die Gesamete Staatswissenschaft,* number 115 (1959).

Siegel, Sidney. 1961. ''Decision Making and Learning Under Varying Conditions of Reinforcement.'' *Annals of the New York Academy of Science* 89.

Siegel, Sidney, and Lawrence Fouraker. 1960. *Bargaining and Group Decision Making*. New York: McGraw-Hill.

Smith, Vernon L. 1962. ''An Experimental Study of Competitive Market Behavior.'' *The Journal of Political Economy* 70 (April).

Suppes, P., and J. M. Carlsmith. 1962. ''Experimental Analysis of a Duopoly Situation.'' *International Economic Review* 3 (January).

AN EXPERIMENTAL STUDY OF COMPETITIVE MARKET BEHAVIOR[1]

VERNON L. SMITH
Purdue University

I. INTRODUCTION

RECENT years have witnessed a growing interest in experimental games such as management decision-making games and games designed to simulate oligopolistic market phenomena. This article reports on a series of experimental games designed to study some of the hypotheses of neoclassical competitive market theory. Since the organized stock, bond, and commodity exchanges would seem to have the best chance of fulfilling the conditions of an operational theory of supply and demand, most of these experiments have been designed to simulate, on a modest scale, the multilateral auction-trading process characteristic of these organized markets. I would emphasize, however, that they are intended as simulations of certain key features of the organized markets and of competitive markets generally, rather than as direct, exhaustive simulations of any particular organized exchange. The experimental conditions of supply and demand in force in these markets are modeled closely upon the supply and demand curves generated by the limit price orders in the hands of stock and commodity market brokers at the opening of a trading day in any one stock or commodity, though I would consider them to be good general models of received short-run supply and demand theory. A similar experimental supply and demand model was first used by E. H. Chamberlin in an interesting set of experiments that pre-date contemporary interest in experimental games.[2]

[1] The experiments on which this report is based have been performed over a six-year period beginning in 1955. They are part of a continuing study, in which the next phase is to include experimentation with monetary payoffs and more complicated experimental designs to which passing references are made here and there in the present report. I wish to thank Mrs. Marilyn Schweizer for assistance in typing and in the preparation of charts in this paper, R. K. Davidson for performing one of the experiments, for me, and G. Horwich, J. Hughes, H. Johnson, and J. Wolfe for reading an earlier version of the paper and enriching me with their comments and encouragement. This work was supported by the Institute for Quantitative Research at Purdue, the Purdue Research Foundation, and in part by National Science Foundation, Grant No. 16114, at Stanford University.

[2] "An Experimental Imperfect Market," *Journal of Political Economy*, LVI (April, 1948), 95–108. For an experimental study of bilateral monopoly, see S. Siegel and L. Fouraker, *Bargaining and Group Decision Making* (New York: McGraw-Hill Book Co., 1960).

Chamberlin's paper was highly suggestive in demonstrating the potentialities of experimental techniques in the study of applied market theory.

Parts II and III of this paper are devoted to a descriptive discussion of the experiments and some of their detailed results. Parts IV and V present an empirical analysis of various equilibrating hypotheses and a rationalization of the hypothesis found to be most successful in these experiments.

Part VI provides a brief summary which the reader may wish to consult before reading the main body of the paper.

II. EXPERIMENTAL PROCEDURE

The experiments discussed in Parts III and IV have followed the same general design pattern. The group of subjects is divided at random into two subgroups, a group of buyers and a group of sellers. Each buyer receives a card containing a number, known only to that buyer, which represents the maximum price he is willing to pay for one unit of the fictitious commodity. It is explained that the buyers are not to buy a unit of the commodity at a price exceeding that appearing on their buyer's card; they would be quite happy to purchase a unit at any price below this number—the lower the better; but, they would be entirely willing to pay just this price for the commodity rather than have their wants go unsatisfied. It is further explained that each buyer should think of himself as making a pure profit equal to the difference between his actual contract price and the maximum reservation price on his card. These reservation prices generate a demand curve such as *DD* in the diagram on the left in Chart 1. At each price the corresponding quantity represents the maximum amount that could be purchased at that price. Thus, in Chart 1, the highest price buyer is willing to pay as much as $3.25 for one unit. At a price above $3.25 the demand quantity is zero, and at $3.25 it cannot exceed one unit. The next highest price buyer is willing to pay $3.00. Thus, at $3.00 the demand quantity cannot exceed two units. The phrase "cannot exceed" rather than "is" will be seen to be of no small importance. How much is actually taken at any price depends upon such important things as how the market is organized, and various mechanical and bargaining considerations associated with the offer-acceptance process. The demand curve, therefore, defines the set (all points on or to the left of *DD*) of possible demand quantities at each, strictly hypothetical, ruling price.

Each seller receives a card containing a number, known only to that seller, which represents the minimum price at which he is willing to relinquish one unit of the commodity. It is explained that the sellers should be willing to sell at their minimum supply price rather than fail to make a sale, but they make a pure profit determined by the excess of their contract price over their minimum reservation price. Under no condition should they sell below this minimum. These minimum seller prices generate a supply curve such as *SS* in Chart 1. At each hypothetical price the corresponding quantity represents the maximum amount that could be sold at that price. The supply curve, therefore, defines the set of possible supply quantities at each hypothetical ruling price.

In experiments 1–8 each buyer and seller is allowed to make a contract for the exchange of only a single unit of the commodity during any one trading or market period. This rule was for the sake of simplicity and was relaxed in subsequent experiments.

Each experiment was conducted over a sequence of trading periods five to ten minutes long depending upon the number of participants in the test group. Since the experiments were conducted within a class period, the number of trading periods was not uniform among the various experiments. In the typical experiment, the market opens for trading period 1. This means that any buyer (or seller) is free at any time to raise his hand and make a verbal offer to buy (or sell) at any price which does not violate his maximum (or minimum) reservation price. Thus, in Chart 1, the buyer holding the $2.50 card might raise his hand and shout, "Buy at $1.00." The seller with the $1.50 card might then shout, "Sell at $3.60." Any seller (or buyer) is free to accept a bid (or offer), in which case a binding contract has been closed, and the buyer and seller making the deal drop out of the market in the sense of no longer being permitted to make bids, offers, or contracts for the remainder of that market period.[3] As soon as a bid or offer is accepted, the contract price is recorded together with the minimum supply price of the seller and the maximum demand price of the buyer involved in the transaction. These observations represent the recorded data of the experiment.[4] Within the time limit

CHART 1

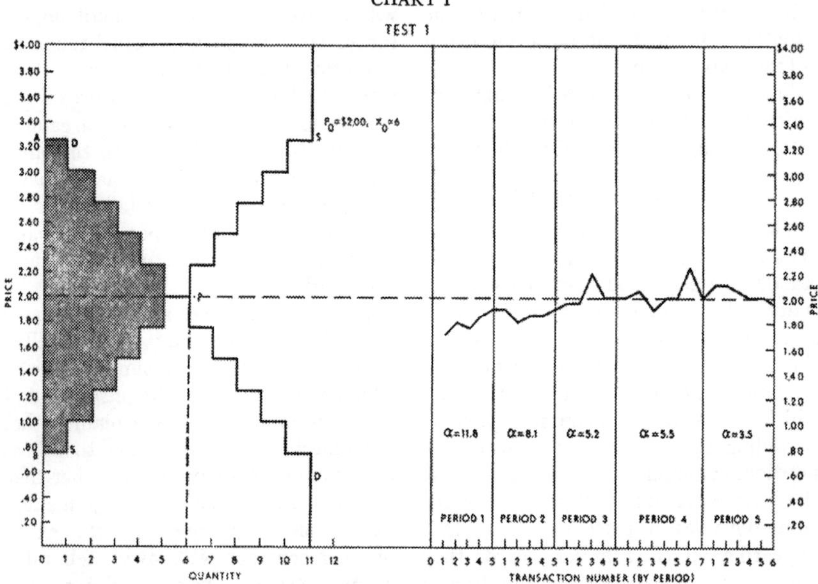

[3] All purchases are for final consumption. There are no speculative purchases for resale in the same or later periods. There is nothing, however, to prevent one from designing an experiment in which purchases for resale are permitted if the objective is to study the role of speculation in the equilibrating process. One could, for example, permit the carry-over of stocks from one period to the next.

[4] Owing to limitations of manpower and equipment in experiments 1–8, bids and offers which did not lead to transactions could not be recorded. In subsequent experiments a tape recorder was used for this purpose.

of a trading period, this procedure is continued until bids and offers are no longer leading to contracts. One or two calls are made for final bids or offers and the market is officially closed. This ends period 1. The market is then immediately reopened for the second "day" of trading. All buyers, including those who did and those who did not make contracts in the preceding trading period, now (as explained previously to the subjects) have a renewed urge to buy one unit of the commodity. For each buyer, the same maximum buying price holds in the second period as prevailed in the first period. In this way the experimental demand curve represents a demand per unit time or per trading period. Similarly, each seller, we may imagine, has "overnight" acquired a fresh unit of the commodity which he desires to sell in period 2 under the same minimum price conditions as prevailed in period 1. The experimental supply curve thereby represents a willingness to supply per unit time. Trading period 2 is allowed to run its course, and then period 3, and so on. By this means we construct a prototype market in which there is a flow of a commodity onto and off the market. The stage is thereby set to study price behavior under given conditions of normal supply and demand.[5] Some buyers and sellers, it should be noted, may be unable to make contracts in any trading period, or perhaps only in certain periods. Insofar as these traders are submarginal buyers or sellers, this is to be expected. Indeed, the ability of these experimental markets to ration out submarginal buyers and sellers will be one measure of the effectiveness or competitive performance of the market.

The above design considerations define a rejection set of offers (and bids) for each buyer (and seller), which in turn defines a demand and a supply schedule for the market in question. These schedules do nothing beyond setting extreme limits to the observable price-quantity behavior in that market. All we can say is that the area above the supply curve is a region in which sales are feasible, while the area below the demand curve is a region in which purchases are feasible. Competitive price theory asserts that there will be a tendency for price-quantity equilibrium to occur at the extreme quantity point of the intersection of these two areas. For example, in Chart 1 the shaded triangular area APB represents the intersection of these feasible sales and purchase sets, with P the extreme point of this set. We have no guarantee that the equilibrium defined by the intersection of these sets will prevail, even approximately, in the experimental market (or any real counterpart of it). The mere fact that, by any definition, supply and demand schedules exist in the background of a market does not guarantee that any meaningful relationship exists

[5] The design of my experiments differs from that of Chamberlin (*op. cit.*) in several ways. In Chamberlin's experiment the buyers and sellers simply circulate and engage in bilateral higgling and bargaining until they make a contract or the trading period ends. As contracts are made the transaction price is recorded on the blackboard. Consequently, there is very little, if any, multilateral bidding. Each trader's attention is directed to the one person with whom he is bargaining, whereas in my experiments each trader's quotation is addressed to the entire trading group one quotation at a time. Also Chamberlin's experiment constitutes a pure exchange market operated for a single trading period. There is, therefore, less opportunity for traders to gain experience and to modify their subsequent behavior in the light of such experience. It is only through some learning mechanism of this kind that I can imagine the possibility of equilibrium being approached in any real market. Finally, in the present experiments I have varied the design from one experiment to another in a conscious attempt to study the effect of different conditions of supply and demand, changes in supply or demand, and changes in the rules of market organization on market-price behavior.

between those schedules and what is observed in the market they are presumed to represent. All the supply and demand schedules can do is set broad limits on the behavior of the market.[6] Thus, in the symmetrical supply and demand diagram of Chart 1, it is conceivable that every buyer and seller could make a contract. The $3.25 buyer could buy from the $3.25 seller, the $3.00 buyer could buy from the $3.00 seller, and so forth, without violating any restrictions on the behavior of buyers and sellers. Indeed, if we separately paired buyers and sellers in this special way, each pair could be expected to make a bilateral contract at the seller's minimum price which would be equal to the buyer's maximum price.

It should be noted that these experiments conform in several important ways to what we know must be true of many kinds of real markets. In a real competitive market such as a commodity or stock exchange, each marketer is likely to be ignorant of the reservation prices at which other buyers and sellers are willing to trade. Furthermore, the only way that a real marketer can obtain knowledge of market conditions is to observe the offers and bids that are tendered, and whether or not they are accepted. These are the public data of the market. A marketer can only know his own attitude, and, from observation, learn something about the objective behavior of others. This is a major feature of these experimental markets. We deliberately avoid placing at the disposal of our subjects any information which would not be practically attainable in a real market. Each experimental market is forced to provide all of its own "history." These markets are also a replica of real markets in that they are composed of a practical number of marketers, say twenty, thirty, or forty. We do not require an indefinitely large number of marketers, which is usually supposed necessary for the existence of "pure" competition.

One important condition operating in our experimental markets is not likely to prevail in real markets. The experimental conditions of supply and demand are held constant over several successive trading periods in order to give any equilibrating mechanisms an opportunity to establish an equilibrium over time. Real markets are likely to be continually subjected to changing conditions of supply and demand. Marshall was well aware of such problems and defined equilibrium as a condition toward which the market would move *if* the forces of supply and demand were to remain stationary for a sufficiently long time. It is this concept of equilibrium that this particular series of experiments is designed, in part, to test. There is nothing to prevent one from passing out new buyer and/or seller cards, representing changed demand and/or supply conditions, at the end of each trading period if the objective is to study the effect of such constantly changing conditions on market behavior.

[6] In fact, these schedules are modified as trading takes place. Whenever a buyer and a seller make a contract and "drop out" of the market, the demand and supply schedules are shifted to the left in a manner depending upon the buyer's and seller's position on the schedules. Hence, the supply and demand functions continually alter as the trading process occurs. It is difficult to imagine a real market process which does not exhibit this characteristic. This means that the intra-trading-period schedules are not independent of the transactions taking place. However, the *initial* schedules prevailing at the opening of each trading period are independent of the transactions, and it is these schedules that I identify with the "theoretical conditions of supply and demand," which the theorist defines independently of actual market prices and quantities. One of the important objectives in these experiments is to determine whether or not these initial schedules have any power to predict the observed behavior of the market.

In three of the nine experiments, once-for-all changes in demand and/or supply were made for purposes of studying the transient dynamics of a market's response to such stimuli.

III. DESCRIPTION AND DISCUSSION OF EXPERIMENTAL RESULTS

The supply and demand schedule for each experiment is shown in the diagram on the left of Charts 1–10. The price and quantity at which these schedules intersect will be referred to as the predicted or theoretical "equilibrium" price and quantity for the corresponding experimental market, though such an equilibrium will not necessarily be attained or approached in the market. The performance of each experimental market is summarized in the diagram on the right of Charts 1–10, and in Table 1. Each chart shows the sequence of contract or exchange prices in the order in which they occurred in each trading period. Thus, in Chart 1, the first transaction was effected at $1.70, the second at $1.80, and so on, with a total of five transactions occurring in trading period 1. These charts show contract price as a function of transaction number rather than calendar time, the latter of course being quite irrelevant to market dynamics.

The most striking general characteristic of tests 1–3, 5–7, 9, and 10 is the remarkably strong tendency for exchange prices to approach the predicted equilibrium for each of these markets. As the exchange process is repeated through successive trading periods with the same conditions of supply and demand prevailing initially in each period, the variation in exchange prices tends to decline, and to cluster more closely around the equilibrium. In Chart 1, for example, the variation in contract prices over the five trading periods is from $1.70 to $2.25. The maximum possible variation is from $0.75 to $3.25 as seen in the supply and demand schedules. As a means of measuring the convergence of exchange prices in each market, a "coefficient of convergence," α, has been computed for each trading period in each market. The α for each trading period is the ratio of the standard deviation of exchange prices, σ_0, to the predicted equilibrium price, P_0, the ratio being expressed as a percentage. That is, $\alpha = 100\ \sigma_0/P_0$ where σ_0 is the standard deviation of exchange prices around the equilibrium price rather than the mean exchange price. Hence, α provides a measure of exchange price variation relative to the predicted equilibrium exchange price. As is seen in Table 1 and the charts for all tests except test 8, α tends to decline from one trading period to the next, with tests 2, 4*A*, 5, 6*A*, 7, 9*A*, and 10 showing monotone convergence.

Turning now to the individual experimental results, it will be observed that the equilibrium price and quantity are approximately the same for the supply and demand curves of tests 2 and 3. The significant difference in the design of these two tests is that the supply and demand schedules for test 2 are relatively flat, while the corresponding schedules for test 3 are much more steeply inclined.

Under the Walrasian hypothesis (the rate of increase in exchange price is an increasing function of the excess demand at that price), one would expect the market in test 2 to converge more rapidly than that in test 3. As is evident from comparing the results in Charts 2 and 3, test 2 shows a more rapid and less erratic tendency toward equilibrium. These results are, of course, consistent with many other hypotheses, including the

TABLE 1

Test	Trading Period	Predicted Exchange Quantity (x_0)	Actual Exchange Quantity (x)	Predicted Exchange Price (P_0)	Average Actual Exchange Price ($\bar{P}$)	Coefficient of Convergence [$\alpha = (100\ \sigma_0)/(P_0)$]	No. of Submarginal Buyers Who Could Make Contracts	No. of Submarginal Buyers Who Made Contracts	No. of Submarginal Sellers Who Could Make Contracts	No. of Submarginal Sellers Who Made Contracts
1.......	1	6	5	2.00	1.80	11.8	5	0	5	0
	2	6	5	2.00	1.86	8.1	5	0	5	0
	3	6	5	2.00	2.02	5.2	5	0	5	0
	4	6	7	2.00	2.03	5.5	5	1	5	1
	5	6	6	2.00	2.03	3.5	5	0	5	0
2.......	1	15	16	3.425	3.47	9.9	4	2	3	1
	2	15	15	3.425	3.43	5.4	4	2	3	1
	3	15	16	3.425	3.42	2.2	4	2	3	0
3.......	1	16	17	3.50	3.49	16.5	5	1	6	2
	2	16	15	3.50	3.47	6.6	5	0	6	1
	3	16	15	3.50	3.56	3.7	5	0	6	0
	4	16	15	3.50	3.55	5.7	5	0	6	0
4*A*......	1	10	9	3.10	3.53	19.1	None	None	None	None
	2	10	9	3.10	3.37	10.4	None	None	None	None
	3	10	9	3.10	3.32	7.8	None	None	None	None
	4	10	9	3.10	3.32	7.6	None	None	None	None
4*B*......	1	8	8	3.10	3.25	6.9	None	None	None	None
	2	8	7	3.10	3.30	7.1	None	None	None	None
	3	8	6	3.10	3.29	6.5	None	None	None	None
5*A*......	1	10	11	3.125	3.12	2.0	7	0	7	0
	2	10	9	3.125	3.13	0.7	7	1	7	0
	3	10	10	3.125	3.11	0.7	7	1	7	0
	4	10	9	3.125	3.12	0.6	7	0	7	0
5*B*......	1	12	12	3.45	3.68	9.4	4	0	3	2
	2	12	12	3.45	3.52	4.3	4	0	3	0
6*A*......	1	12	12	10.75	5.29	53.8	5	3	None	None
	2	12	12	10.75	7.17	38.7	5	3	None	None
	3	12	12	10.75	9.06	21.1	5	2	None	None
	4	12	12	10.75	10.90	9.4	5	0	None	None
6*B*......	1	12	11	8.75	9.14	11.0	4	1	None	None
	2	12	6	8.75	....	....	4	1	None	None
7.......	1	9	8	3.40	2.12	49.1	3	1	None	None
	2	9	9	3.40	2.91	22.2	3	0	None	None
	3	9	9	3.40	3.23	7.1	3	1	None	None
	4	9	8	3.40	3.32	5.4	3	0	None	None
	5	9	9	3.40	3.33	3.0	3	0	None	None
	6	9	9	3.40	3.34	2.7	3	0	None	None
8*A*......	1	7	8	2.25	2.50	19.0	5	0	4	0
	2	7	5	2.25	2.20	2.9	5	0	4	0
	3	7	6	2.25	2.12	7.4	5	0	4	0
	4	7	5	2.25	2.12	7.0	5	0	4	0
8*B*......	1	7	6	2.25	2.23	7.8	5	0	4	0
	2	7	6	2.25	2.29	6.1	5	0	4	0
9*A*......	1	18	18	3.40	2.81	21.8	6	3	None	None
	2	18	18	3.40	2.97	15.4	6	2	None	None
	3	18	18	3.40	3.07	13.2	6	2	None	None
9*B*......	1	20	20	3.80	3.52	10.3	4	3	2	0
10.......	1	18	18	3.40	3.17	11.0	4	2	None	None
	2	18	17	3.40	3.36	3.2	4	1	None	None
	3	18	17	3.40	3.38	2.2	4	0	None	None

CHART 2

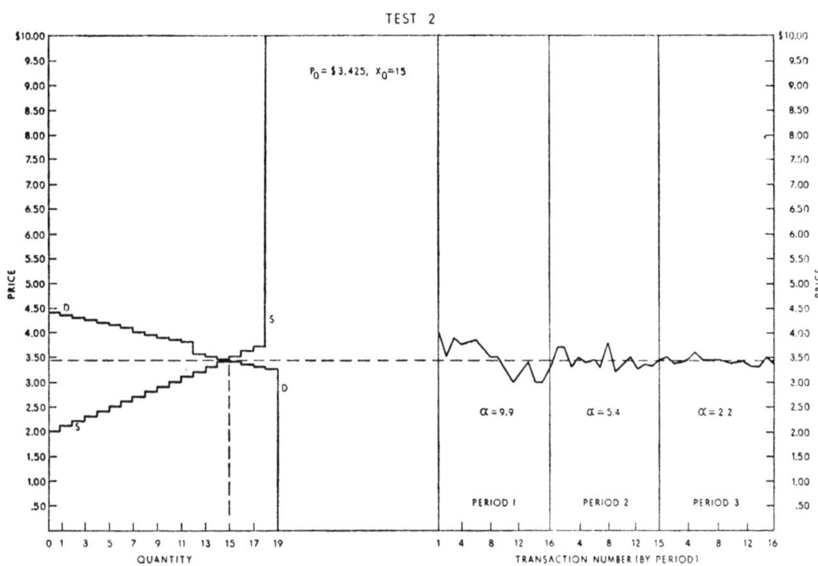
TEST 2
P_0 = $3.425, X_0=15
PRICE
D
S
α = 9.9
α = 5.4
α = 2.2
PERIOD 1
PERIOD 2
PERIOD 3
QUANTITY
TRANSACTION NUMBER (BY PERIOD)

CHART 3

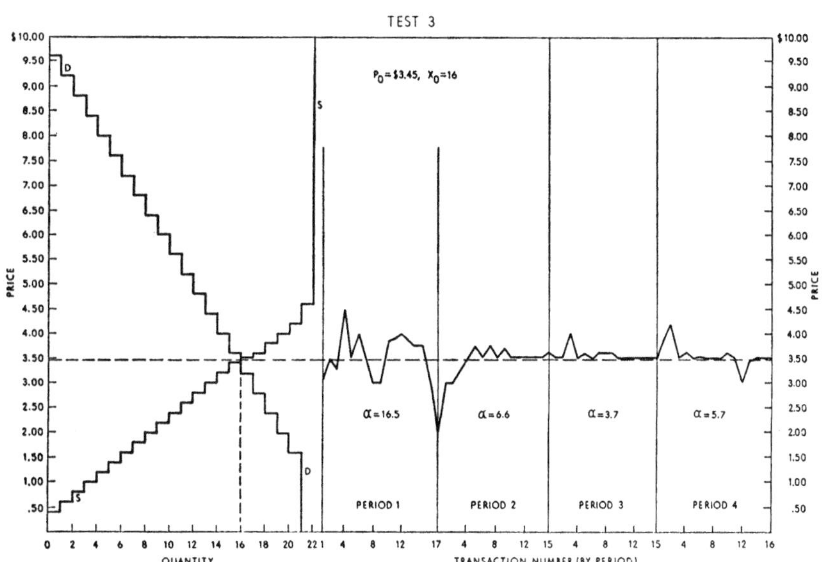
TEST 3
P_0=$3.45, X_0=16
PRICE
D
S
α=16.5
α=6.6
α=3.7
α=5.7
PERIOD 1
PERIOD 2
PERIOD 3
PERIOD 4
QUANTITY
TRANSACTION NUMBER (BY PERIOD)

excess-rent hypothesis, to be discussed later.[7]

The tests in Chart 4 are of special interest from the point of view of the Walrasian hypothesis. In this case the supply curve is perfectly elastic—all sellers have cards containing the price $3.10. Each seller has the same lower bound on his reservation price acceptance set. In this sense, there is no divergence of attitude among the sellers, though there might be marked variation in their bargaining propensities. According to the Walrasian hypothesis this market should exhibit rapid convergence toward the equilibrium since there is a considerable excess supply at prices just barely above the equilibrium price. From the results we see that the market is not particularly slow in converging, but it converges to a fairly stable price about $0.20 above the predicted equilibrium. Furthermore, in test 4*B*, which was an extension of 4*A*, the interjection of a decrease in demand from *DD* to *D*′*D*′ was ineffective as a means of shocking the market down to its supply and demand equilibrium. This decrease in demand was achieved by passing out new buyer cards corresponding to *D*′*D*′ at the close of period 4 in test 4*A*. As expected, the market approaches equilibrium from above, since contracts at prices below equilibrium are impossible.

CHART 4

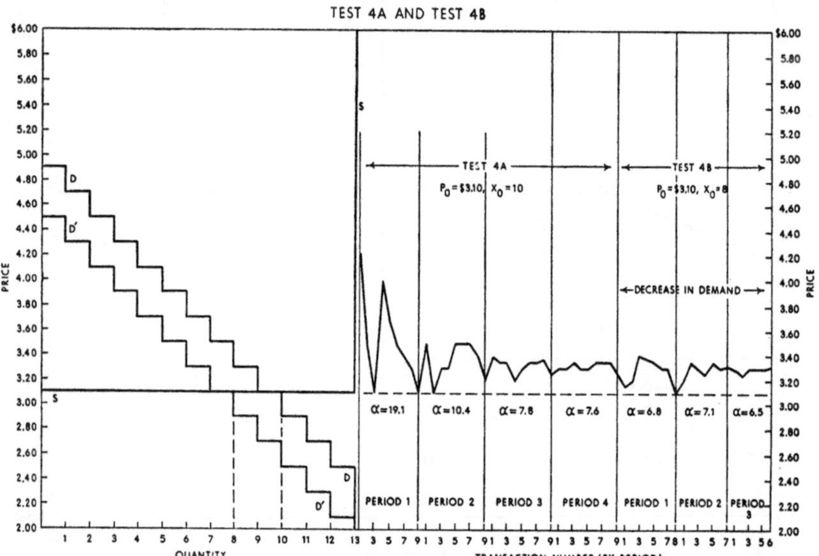

The sellers in this market presented a solid front against price being lowered to "equilibrium." In the previous mar-

[7] The results are inconsistent with the so-called Marshallian hypothesis (the rate of increase in quantity exchanged is an increasing function of the excess of demand price over supply price), but this hypothesis would seem to be worth considering only in market processes in which some quantity-adjusting decision is made by the marketers. The results of a pilot experiment in "short-run" and "long-run" equilibrium are displayed in the Appendix.

kets there was a divergence of seller attitude, so that only a very few marginal and near-marginal sellers might offer serious resistance to price being forced to equilibrium. And this resistance tended to break down when any of the stronger intramarginal sellers accepted contracts below equilibrium.

From these results it is clear that the static competitive market equilibrium may depend not only on the intersection of the supply and demand schedules, but also upon the shapes of the schedules. Specifically, I was led from test 4 to the tentative hypothesis that there may be an upward bias in the equilibrium price of a market, which will be greater the more elastic is the supply schedule relative to demand.[8] For example, let A be the area under the demand schedule and above the theoretical equilibrium. This is Marshall's consumer surplus, but to avoid any welfare connotations of this term, I shall refer to the area as "buyers' rent." Let B be the area above the supply schedule and below the theoretical equilibrium (Marshall's producer surplus) which I shall call "sellers' rent." Now, the tentative hypothesis was that the actual market equilibrium will be above the theoretical equilibrium by an amount which depends upon how large A is relative to B. Similarly, there will be a downward bias if A is small relative to B.

Test 4 is of course an extreme case, since $B = 0$. In test 3, A is larger than B, and the trading periods 3 and 4 exhibit a slight upward bias in the average actual exchange price (see Table 1). This provides some slight evidence in favor of the hypothesis.

[8] Note that the Walrasian hypothesis might lead one to expect a downward bias since excess supply is very large at prices above equilibrium if supply is very elastic relative to demand.

As a consequence of these considerations, test 7 was designed specifically to obtain additional information to support or contradict the indicated hypothesis. In this case, as is seen in Chart 7 (see below), buyers' rent is substantially smaller than sellers' rent. From the resulting course of contract prices over six trading periods in this experiment, it is evident that the convergence to equilibrium is very slow. From Table 1, the average exchange prices in the last three trading periods are, respectively, \$3.32, \$3.33, and \$3.34. Average contract prices are still exhibiting a gradual approach to equilibrium. Hence, it is entirely possible that the static equilibrium would eventually have been attained. A still smaller buyers' rent may be required to provide any clear downward bias in the static equilibrium. One thing, however, seems quite unmistakable from Chart 7, the relative magnitude of buyers' and sellers' rent affects the speed with which the actual market equilibrium is approached. One would expect sellers to present a somewhat weaker bargaining front, especially at first, if their rent potential is large relative to that of buyers. Thus, in Chart 7, it is seen that several low reservation price sellers in trading periods 1 and 2 made contracts at low exchange prices, which, no doubt, seemed quite profitable to these sellers. However, in both these trading periods the later exchange prices were much higher, revealing to the low-price sellers that, however profitable their initial sales had been, still greater profits were possible under stiffer bargaining.

A stronger test of the hypotheses that buyer and seller rents affect the speed of adjustment and that they affect the final equilibrium in the market would be obtainable by introducing actual monetary payoffs in the experiment. Thus, one might offer to pay each seller the difference between his contract price and his reservation price and each buyer the difference between his reservation price and his contract price. In addition, one might pay each trader a small lump sum (say $0.05) just for making a contract in any period. This sum would represent "normal profits," that is, a small return even if the good is sold at its minimum supply price or purchased at its maximum demand price. The present experiments have not seemed to provide any motivation problems. The subjects have shown high motivation to do their best even without monetary payoffs. But our experimental marginal buyers and sellers may be more reluctant to approach their reservation prices than their counterparts in real markets. The use of monetary payoffs, as suggested, should remove any such reluctance that is attributable to artificial elements in the present experiments.[9]

The experiment summarized in Chart 5 was designed to study the effect on market behavior of changes in the conditions of demand and supply. As it happened, this experiment was performed on a considerably more mature group of subjects than any of the other experiments. Most of the experiments were performed on sophomore and junior engineering, economics, and business majors, while test 5 was performed on a

CHART 5

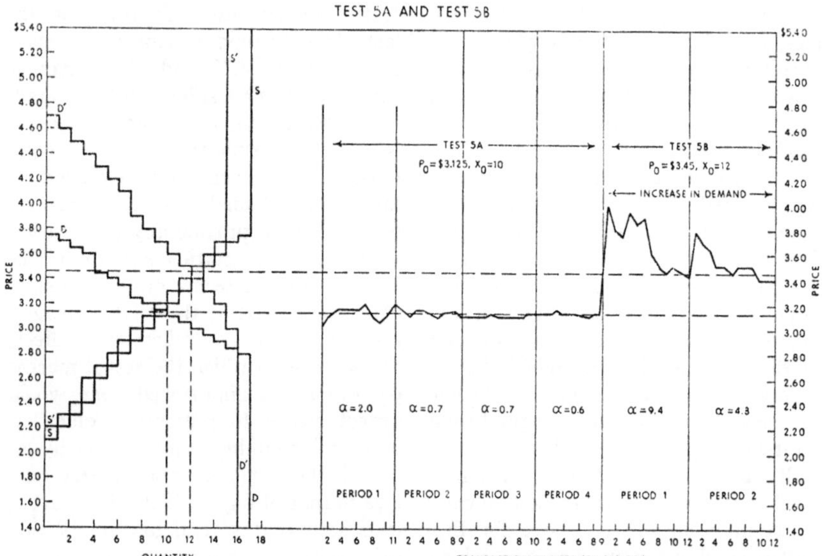

[9] Since this was written, an experiment has been tried using monetary payoffs and the same supply and demand design shown in Chart 4. The result, as conjectured in the text, was to remove the reluctance of sellers to sell at their reservation prices. By the second trading period the market was firmly in equilibrium. In the third period all trades were at $3.10! Apparently $0.05 per period was considered satisfactory normal profit.

graduate class in economic theory. In view of this difference, it is most interesting to find the phenomenally low values for α exhibited by test 5*A*. The coefficient of convergence is smaller for the opening and later periods of this market than for any period of any of the other tests. Furthermore, trading periods 2–4 show α's of less than 1 per cent, indicating an inordinately strong and rapid tendency toward equilibrium. In this case, no offers or bids were accepted until the bidding had converged to prices which were very near indeed to the equilibrium. Contract prices ranged from \$3.00 to \$3.20 as compared with a possible range from \$2.10 to \$3.75.

At the close of test 5*A* new cards were distributed corresponding to an increase in demand, from *DD* to *D′D′*, as shown in Chart 5.[10] The subjects, of course, could guess from the fact that new buyer cards were being distributed that a change in demand was in the wind. But they knew nothing of the direction of change in demand except what might be guessed by the buyers from the alteration of their individual reservation prices. When trading began (period 1, test 5*B*), the immediate response was a very considerable upward sweep in exchange prices with several contracts being closed in the first trading period well above the new higher equilibrium price. Indeed, the eagerness to buy was so strong that two sellers who were submarginal both before and after the increase in demand (their reservation prices were \$3.50 and \$3.70) were able to make contracts in this transient phase of the market. Consequently, the trading group showing the strongest equilibrating tendencies exhibited very erratic behavior in the transient phase following the increase in demand. Contract prices greatly overshot the new equilibrium and rationing by the market was less efficient in this transient phase. In the second trading period of test 5*B* no submarginal sellers or buyers made contracts and the market exhibited a narrowed movement toward the new equilibrium.

Test 6*A* was designed to determine whether market equilibrium was affected by a marked imbalance between the number of intramarginal sellers and the number of intramarginal buyers near the predicted equilibrium price. The demand curve, *DD*, in Chart 6 falls continuously to the right in one-unit steps, while the supply curve, *SS*, becomes perfectly inelastic at the price \$4.00, well below the equilibrium price \$10.75. The tentative hypothesis was that the large rent (\$6.75) enjoyed by the marginal seller, with still larger rents for the intramarginal sellers, might prevent the theoretical equilibrium from being established. From the results it is seen that the earlier conjecture concerning the effect of a divergence between buyer and seller rent on the approach to equilibrium is confirmed. The approach to equilibrium is from below, and the convergence is relatively slow. However, there is no indication that the lack of marginal sellers near the theoretical equilibrium has prevented the equilibrium from being attained. The average contract price in trading period 4 is \$10.90, only \$0.15 above the predicted equilibrium.

At the close of trading period 4 in test 6*A*, the old buyer cards corresponding to *DD* were replaced by new cards

[10] Note also that there was a small (one-unit) decrease in supply from *SS* to *S′S′*. This was not planned. It was due to the inability of one subject (the seller with the \$2.10 reservation price) in test 5*A* to participate in test 5*B*. Therefore, except for the deletion of this one seller from the market, the conditions of supply were not altered, that is, the sellers of test 5*B* retained the same reservation price cards as they had in test 5*A*.

CHART 6

TEST 6A AND TEST 6B

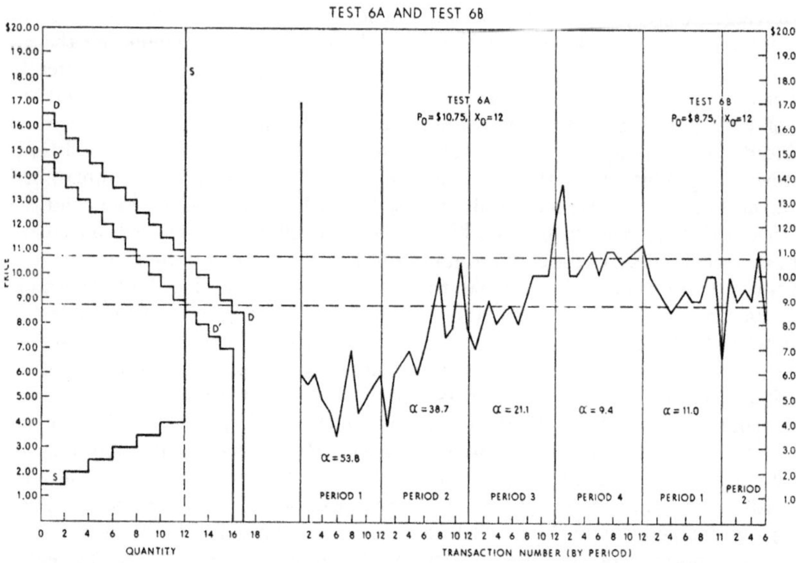

CHART 7

TEST 7

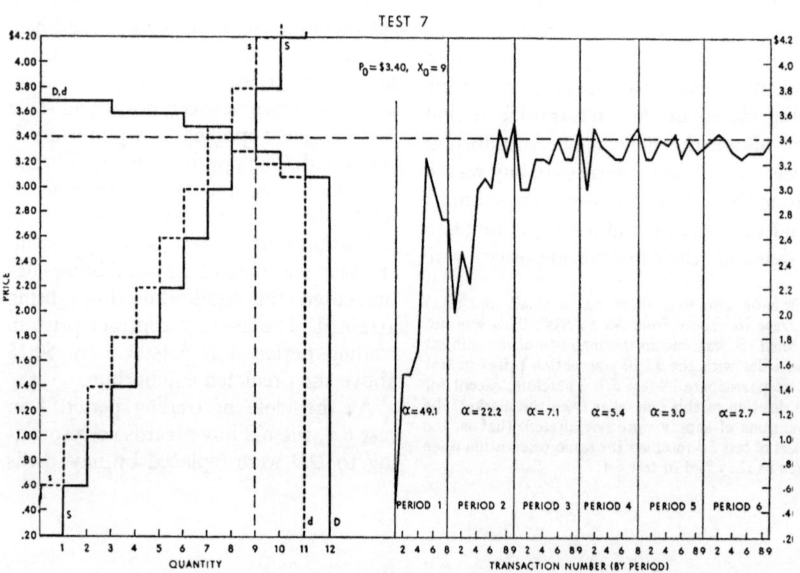

corresponding to $D'D'$ in Chart 6. Trading was resumed with the new conditions of decreased demand (test 6*B*). There was not sufficient time to permit two full trading periods of market experience to be obtained under the new demand conditions. However, from the results in Chart 6, it is evident that the market responded promptly to the decrease in demand by showing apparent convergence to the new equilibrium. Note in particular that there occurred no significant tendency for market prices to overshoot the new equilibrium as was observed in test 5*B*.

All of the above experiments were conducted under the same general rules of market organization. Test 8 was performed as an exploratory means of testing the effect of changes in market organization on market price. In the first four trading periods of this experiment (test 8*A*), only sellers were permitted to enunciate offers. In this market, buyers played a passive role; they could either accept or reject the offers of sellers but were not permitted to make bids. This market was intended to simulate approximately an ordinary retail market. In such markets, in the United States, sellers typically take the initiative in advertising their offer prices, with buyers electing to buy or not to buy rather than taking part in a higgling and bargaining process. Since sellers desire to sell at the highest prices they can get, one would expect the offer prices to be high, and, consequently, one might expect the exchange prices to show a persistent tendency to remain above the predicted equilibrium. The result was in accordance with this crude expectation in the first market period only (test 8*A*, Chart 8). Since sellers only were making

CHART 8

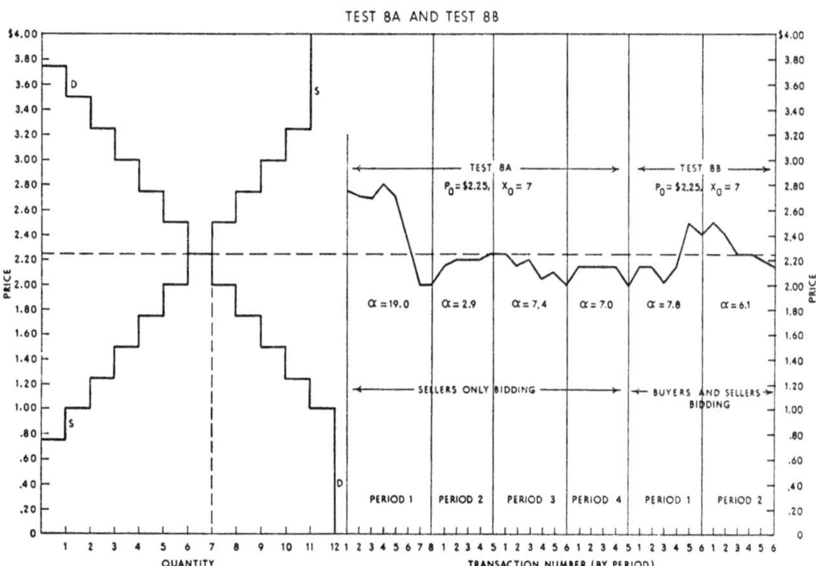

offers, the price quotations tended to be very much above equilibrium. Five of these offers were accepted at prices ranging from $2.69 to $2.80 by the five buyers with maximum reservation prices of $2.75 or more. This left only buyers with lower reservation prices. The competition of sellers pushed the offer prices lower and the remaining buyers made contracts at prices ($2.35, $2.00, and $2.00) near or below the equilibrium price. The early buyers in that first market period never quite recovered from having subsequently seen exchange prices fall much below the prices at which they had bought. Having been badly fleeced, through ignorance, in that first trading period, they refrained from accepting any high price offers in the remaining three periods of the test. This action, together with seller offer price competition, kept exchange prices at levels persistently below equilibrium for the remainder of test 8*A*. Furthermore, the coefficient of convergence increased from 2.9 per cent in the second trading period to 7.4 and 7.0 per cent in the last two periods. At the close of the fourth trading period, the market rules were changed to allow buyers to make quotations as well as sellers. Under the new rules (test 8*B*) two trading periods were run. Exchange prices immediately moved toward equilibrium with the closing prices of period 1 and opening prices of period 2 being above the equilibrium for the first time since period 1 of test 8*A*.

It would seem to be of some significance that of the ten experiments reported on, test 8 shows the clearest lack of convergence toward equilibrium. More experiments are necessary to confirm or deny these results, but it would appear that important changes in market organization—such as permitting only sellers to make quotations—have a distinctly disturbing effect on the equilibrating process. In particular the conclusion is suggested that markets in which only sellers competitively publicize their offers tend to operate to the benefit of buyers at the expense of sellers.

Turning to tests 9*A* and 10 (shown in Charts 9 and 10), it should be noted that the buyers and sellers in these tests received the same cards as their counterparts in test 7. The only difference was that the former entered the market to effect two transactions each, instead of one. Thus the three buyers with $3.70 cards could each buy two units at $3.70 or less in tests 9 and 10. This change in the design of test 7 resulted in a doubling of the maximum demand and supply quantities at each hypothetical price.

By permitting each buyer and seller to make two contracts per period, twice as much market "experience" is potentially to be gained by each trader in a given period. Each trader can experiment more in a given market—correcting his bids or offers in the light of any surprises or disappointments resulting from his first contract. In the previous experiments such corrections or alterations in the bargaining behavior of a trader had to await the next trading period once the trader had made a contract.[11]

[11] This process of correction over time, based upon observed price quotations and the actual contracts that are executed, is the underlying adjustment mechanism operating in all of these experiments. This is in contrast with the Walrasian *tâtonnement* or groping process in which "when a price is cried, and the effective demand and offer corresponding to this price are not equal, another price is cried for which there is another corresponding effective demand and offer" (see Leon Walras, *Elements of Pure Economics*, trans. William Jaffe [Chicago: Richard D. Irwin, Inc., 1954], p. 242). The Walrasian groping process suggests a centralized institutional means of trying different price quotations until the equilibrium is discovered. In our experiments, as in real markets, the groping process is decentralized, with all contracts binding whether they are at equilibrium or non-equilibrium prices.

Comparison of the results of the three trading periods in test 9*A* with the first three trading periods of test 7 shows that the tendencies toward equilibrium (as measured by α) were greater in test 9*A* during the first two periods and smaller in the third period. The same comparison between tests 7 and 10 reveals a stronger tendency toward equilibrium in test 10 than in the first three periods of trade increased to the new equilibrium rate of twenty units per period. Note that the equilibrium tendency in the trading period of test 9*B* was greater than in any of the perious periods of test 9*A*. The increase in demand, far from destabilizing the market as was the case in test 5*B*, tended to strengthen its relatively weak equilibrium tendencies.

CHART 9

TEST 9A AND TEST 9B

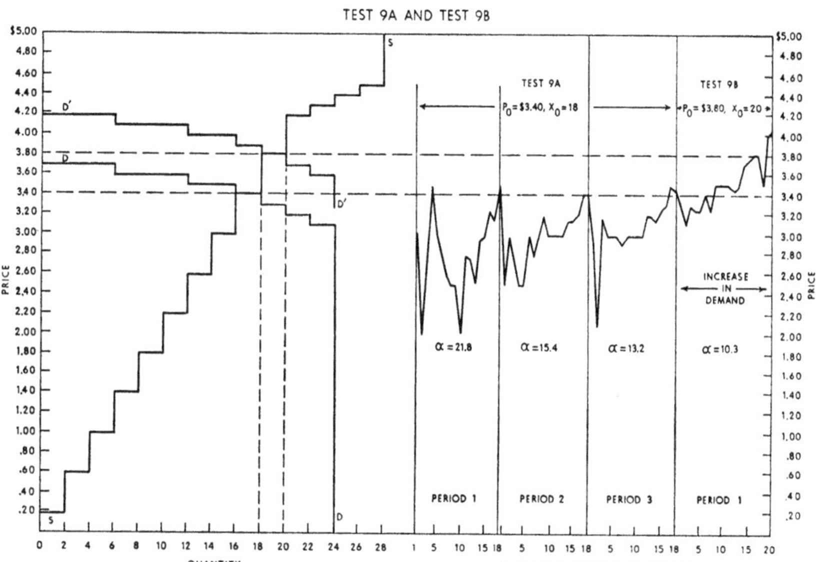

of 7. Hence an increase in volume appears to speed the equilibrating process. Indeed, the three trading periods of test 10 are roughly equivalent to the six trading periods of test 7, so that doubling volume in a given period is comparable to running two trading periods at the same volume.

In test 9*B* the consequences of an increase in demand were once again tested. Contract prices responded by moving upward immediately, and the volume

IV. EMPIRICAL ANALYSIS OF EXPERIMENTAL DATA: THE "EXCESS-RENT" HYPOTHESIS

The empirical analysis of these ten experiments rests upon the hypothesis that there exists a stochastic difference equation which "best" represents the price convergence tendencies apparent in Charts 1–10. The general hypothesis is that

$$\Delta p_t = p_{t+1} - p_t = f[x_1(p_t), x_2(p_t), \ldots] + \epsilon_t, \tag{1}$$

where the arguments $x_1, x_2, \ldots$ reflect characteristics of the experimental supply and demand curves and the bargaining characteristics of individual test groups, and ϵ_t is a random variable with zero mean. For a given experimental test group, under the so-called Walrasian hypothesis $x_1(p_t)$ might be the excess demand prevailing at p_t, with $f = 0$ when $x_1 = 0$.

My first empirical investigation is concerned with the measuremet of the equilibrating tendencies in these markets and the ability of supply and demand theory to predict the equilibrium price in each experiment. To this end note that equation (1) defines a stochastic phase function[12] of the form $p_{t+1} = g(p_t) + \epsilon_t$. An equilibrium price P_0 is attained when $P_0 = g(P_0)$. Rather than estimate the phase function for each experiment, it was found convenient to make linear estimates of its first difference, that is,

$$\Delta p_t = a_0 + a_1 p_t + \epsilon_t .$$

The corresponding linear phase function has slope $1 + a_1$. The parameters a_0 and a_1 were estimated by linear regression techniques for each of the ten fundamental experiments and are tabulated in column 1 of Table 2.[13] Confidence

[12] See, for example, W. J. Baumol, *Economic Dynamics* (New York: Macmillan Co., 1959), pp. 257–65.

[13] The least squares estimate of a_1 in these experiments can be expected to be biased (see L. Hurwicz, "Least-Squares Bias in Time Series," chap. xv, in T. Koopmans, *Statistical Inference in Dynamic Economic Models* [New York: John Wiley & Sons, 1950]). However, since in all of the basic experiments there are twenty or more observations, the bias will not tend to be large.

CHART 10

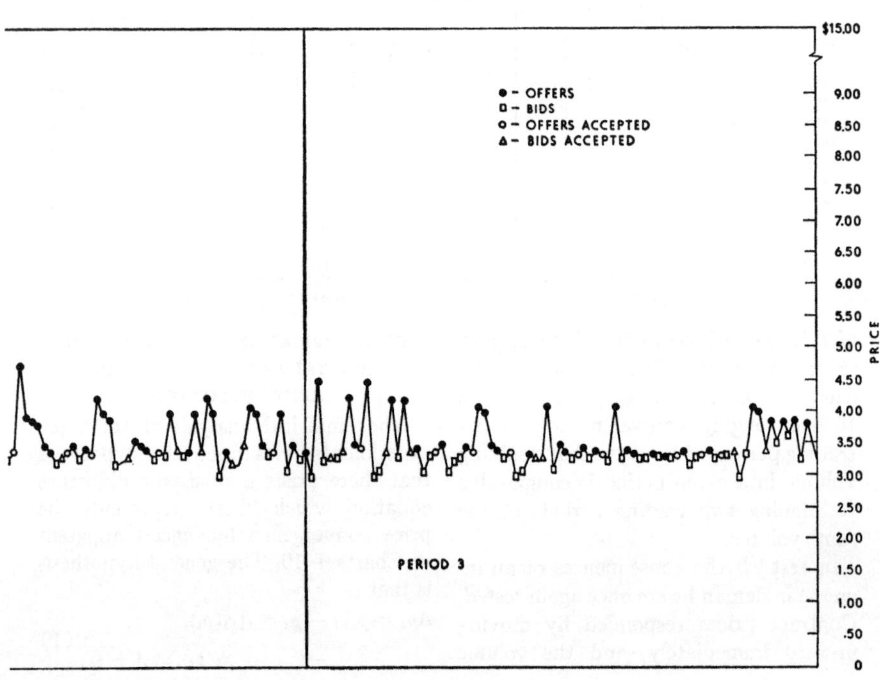

TABLE 2

Experiment	$(\Delta p_t = \alpha_0 + \alpha_1 p_t)$	Walrasian $(\Delta p_t = \beta_{01} + \beta_{11} x_{1t})$	Modified Walrasian $(\Delta p_t = \beta_{03} + \beta_{13} x_{1t} + \beta_{33} x_{3t})$	Excess Rent $(\Delta p_t = \beta_{02} + \beta_{22} x_{2t})$	Modified Excess Rent $(\Delta p_t = \beta_{04} + \beta_{24} x_{2t} + \beta_{34} x_{3t})$
1	$0.933 - 0.474\ p_t$ (± 0.329)	$-0.026 + 0.070\ x_{1t}$ (± 0.042)	$-0.027 + 0.068\ x_{1t} - 0.0056\ x_{3t}$ $(\pm 0.015)\ (\pm 0.0220)$	$-0.028 + 0.486\ x_{2t}$ (± 0.322)	$-0.031 + 0.491\ x_{2t} - 0.0054\ x_{3t}$ $(\pm 0.104)\ (\pm 0.0215)$
2	$1.904 - 0.560\ p_t$ (± 0.250)	$.002 + .035\ x_{1t}$ $(\pm .015)$	$-.170 + .042\ x_{1t} - .0693\ x_{3t}$ $(\pm .006)\ (\pm .0311)$	$.008 + .141\ x_{2t}$ $(\pm .067)$	$-.070 + .152\ x_{2t} - .0313\ x_{3t}$ $(\pm .024)\ (\pm .0649)$
3	$2.275 - 0.647\ p_t$ (± 0.292)	$.157 + .107\ x_{1t}$ $(\pm .045)$	$.093 + .105\ x_{1t} + .0042\ x_{3t}$ $(\pm .014)\ (\pm .0317)$	$.071 + .227\ x_{2t}$ $(\pm .097)$	$-.022 + .225\ x_{2t} + .0064\ x_{3t}$ $(\pm .031)\ (\pm .0315)$
4*A*	$2.852 - 0.849\ p_t$ (± 0.287)	$.761 + .168\ x_{1t}$ $(\pm .057)$	$.794 + .169\ x_{1t} - .0007\ x_{3t}$ $(\pm .018)\ (\pm .0564)$	$.145 + .129\ x_{2t}$ $(\pm .049)$	$.139 + .130\ x_{2t} + .0017\ x_{3t}$ $(\pm .016)\ (\pm .0641)$
5*A*	$2.448 - 0.784\ p_t$ (± 0.302)	$-.031 + .023\ x_{1t}$ $(\pm .009)$	$-.035 + .023\ x_{1t} - .0029\ x_{3t}$ $(\pm .003)\ (\pm .0043)$	$-.007 + .205\ x_{2t}$ $(\pm .098)$	$-.009 + .204\ x_{2t} + .0015\ x_{3t}$ $(\pm .032)\ (\pm .0048)$
6*A*	$1.913 - 0.220\ p_t$ (± 0.174)	$-.675 + .243\ x_{1t}$ $(\pm .175)$	$.010 + .285\ x_{1t} + .0211\ x_{3t}$ $(\pm .057)\ (\pm .0847)$	$-.309 + .038\ x_{2t}$ $(\pm .037)$	$.305 + .034\ x_{2t} + .0146\ x_{3t}$ $(\pm .013)\ (\pm .0906)$
7	$1.216 - 0.368\ p_t$ (± 0.116)	$-.102 + .074\ x_{1t}$ $(\pm .049)$	$-.070 + .075\ x_{1t} + .0063\ x_{3t}$ $(\pm .009)\ (\pm .0738)$	$.007 + .051\ x_{2t}$ $(\pm .021)$	$.058 + .053\ x_{2t} + .0096\ x_{3t}$ $(\pm .007)\ (\pm .0750)$
8*A*	$0.225 - 0.121\ p_t$ (± 0.226)	$-.040 + .020\ x_{1t}$ $(\pm .030)$	$-.027 + .025\ x_{1t} - .0462\ x_{3t}$ $(\pm .011)\ (\pm .0487)$	$-.036 + .051\ x_{2t}$ $(\pm .094)$	$-.022 + .064\ x_{2t} - .0396\ x_{3t}$ $(\pm .035)\ (\pm .0505)$
9*A*	$1.653 - 0.554\ p_t$ (± 0.273)	$-.450 + .061\ x_{1t}$ $(\pm .036)$	$-.447 + .085\ x_{1t} + .0198\ x_{3t}$ $(\pm .012)\ (\pm .0423)$	$-.209 + .071\ x_{2t}$ $(\pm .029)$	$-.065 + .094\ x_{2t} + .0222\ x_{3t}$ $(\pm .009)\ (\pm .0356)$
10	$1.188 - 0.356\ p_t$ (± 0.233)	$-0.039 + 0.020\ x_{1t}$ (± 0.014)	$-0.028 + 0.020\ x_{1t} + 0.0008\ x_{3t}$ $(\pm 0.004)\ (\pm 0.0199)$	$-0.022 + 0.055\ x_{2t}$ (± 0.032)	$-0.008 + 0.056\ x_{2t} + 0.0011\ x_{3t}$ $(\pm 0.014)\ (\pm 0.0194)$

intervals for a 95 per cent fiducial probability level are shown in parentheses under the estimate of α_1 for each experiment. With the exception of experiment 8*A*, the 95 per cent confidence interval for each regression coefficient is entirely contained in the interval $-2 < \alpha_1 < 0$, which is required for market stability. Hence, of these ten experiments, 8*A* is the only one whose price movements are sufficiently erratic to prevent us from rejecting the null hypothesis of instability, and of the ten basic experiments this is the one in which the trading rules were altered to permit only sellers to quote prices.[14]

The regressions of column 1, Table 2, and associated computation provide a means of predicting the adjustment pressure on price, Δp_t, for any given p_t. In particular, we can compute

$$t = \frac{a_0 + a_1 P_0}{S(a_0 + a_1 P_0)}$$

for the sample estimates on the assumption that $\Delta p_t = 0$ when $p_t = P_0$ in the population. These t-values are shown in column 1, Table 3, for the ten primary and the five "*B*" auxilary experiments. Low absolute values of t imply that, relative to the error in the prediction, the predicted equilibrium is close to the theoretical. The four lowest absolute t-values are for experimental designs with the smallest difference between equilibrium buyers' and sellers' rent. These results provide some additional evidence in favor of our conjecture in Part III, that the equilibrium is influenced by the relative sizes of the areas *A* and *B*. However, from the t-values it would seem that the influence is small except for test 4, where $B = 0$. In this case, the null hypothesis ($\Delta p_t = 0$ when $p_t = P_0$) is rejected even at a significance level below .005.

Four specific forms for the difference equation (1) were studied in detail and tested for their ability to predict the

TABLE 3

Experiment	$t=(a_0+a_1P_0)/[S(a_0+a_1P_0)]$ (1)	Walrasian			Excess Rent			Degrees of Freedom (8)
		$\lvert\beta_{01}\rvert$ (2)	$S(\beta_{01})$ (3)	$t=\beta_{01}/S(\beta_{01})$ (4)	$\lvert\beta_{02}\rvert$ (5)	$S(\beta_{02})$ (6)	$t=\beta_{02}/S(\beta_{02})$ (7)	
1..........	−0.673	0.026	0.019	−1.36	0.028	0.021	−0.66	21
2..........	0.460	.002	.029	0.08	.008	.030	0.25	42
3..........	1.008	.157	.055	2.88	.071	.046	1.56	57
4*A*.........	4.170	.761	.137	5.57	.145	.048	3.05	30
4*B*.........	3.219	.391	.284	1.37	.161	.052	3.08	16
5*A*.........	−0.333	.031	.008	−3.72	.007	.006	−1.16	33
5*B*.........	−0.230	.002	.034	0.05	.013	.026	−0.51	20
6*A*.........	−1.412	.675	.362	−1.87	.309	.311	−0.99	42
6*B*.........	2.176	.299	.314	0.95	.179	.290	0.62	13
7..........	−0.740	.102	.057	−1.78	.007	.045	0.15	44
8*A*.........	−1.597	.040	.029	−1.40	.036	.032	−1.13	18
8*B*.........	−0.140	.010	.042	−0.24	.016	.043	−0.37	8
9*A*.........	−0.647	.450	.151	−2.99	.209	.065	−3.21	49
9*B*.........	−0.021	.012	.112	0.11	.016	.071	−0.23	17
10..........	−0.731	0.039	0.033	−1.19	0.022	0.028	−0.80	47

[14] Three of the five auxiliary "*B*" experiments demonstrated a similar instability (in the fiducial probability sense), but the samples were considerably smaller than their "*A*" counterparts, they represented considerably fewer trading periods, and they had different and varying objectives. The unstable ones were 4*B*, 8*B*, and 9*B*.

theoretical equilibrium price. These will be referred to as the Walrasian, the excess-rent, the modified Walrasian, and the modified excess-rent hypotheses, respectively. The Walrasian hypothesis is $\Delta p_t = \beta_{01} + \beta_{11}x_{1t}$, where x_{1t} is the excess demand prevailing at the price, p_t, at which the tth transaction occurred. Because of the conjecture that buyers' and sellers' rent might have an effect on individual and market adjustment, an excess-rent hypothesis was introduced. This hypothesis is $\Delta p_t = \beta_{02} + \beta_{22}x_{2t}$, where x_{2t} is the algebraic area

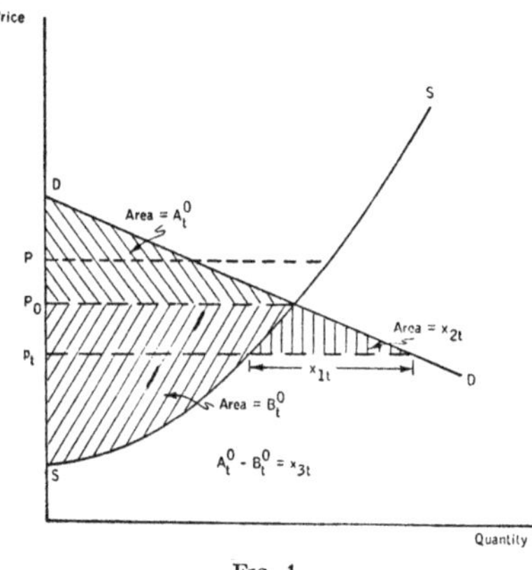

FIG. 1

between the supply and demand curves, and extends from the equilibrium price down to the price of the tth transaction, as shown in Figure 1. The modified Walrasian hypothesis is $\Delta p_t = \beta_{03} + \beta_{13}x_{1t} + \beta_{33}x_{3t}$, where $x_{3t} = A_t^0 - B_t^0$, the algebraic difference between the equilibrium buyers' rent, A_t^0, and the equilibrium sellers' rent, B_t^0. The motivation here was to introduce a term in the adjustment equation which would permit the actual equilibrium price to be biased above or below the theoretical equilibrium, by an amount proportional to the algebraic difference between buyers' and sellers' rent at the theoretical equilibrium. It was believed that such a general hypothesis might be necessary to account for the obvious price equilibrium bias in experiment 4 and the slight apparent bias in experiments 3, 6*A*, 7, and 9*A*. A similar motivation suggested the modified excess-rent hypothesis, $\Delta p_t = \beta_{04} + \beta_{24}x_{2t} + \beta_{34}x_{3t}$.

Since the trading process in these experiments was such that transactions might and generally did take place at non-equilibrium prices, the supply and demand curves shift after each transaction. Hence, in generating observations on x_{1t}, x_{2t}, and x_{3t}, the supply and demand curves were adjusted after each transaction for the effect of the pairing of a buyer and a seller in reducing their effective demand and supply. Thus, in Chart 7, the first transaction was at \$0.50 between the seller with reservation price \$0.20 and a buyer with reservation price \$3.50. Following this trasaction the new effective demand and supply curves become *Dd* and *ss* as shown. The next transaction is at \$1.50. Our hypothesis is that the increase in price from \$0.50 to \$1.50 is due to the conditions represented by *Dd* and *ss* at the price \$0.50. Thus, for the first set of observations $\Delta p_1 = p_1 - p_0 = \$1.50 - \$0.50 = \$1.00$,. $x_{11} = 11$, $x_{21} = 20.10$, and $x_{31} = -9.60$ as can be determined from Chart 7. The second transaction paired a \$3.70 buyer and a \$0.60 seller. The next set of observations is then obtained by removing this buyer and seller from *Dd* and *ss* to obtain x_{12}, x_{22}, and x_{32} at $p_2 = 1.50$, with $\Delta p_2 = p_2 - p_1 = 0$, and so on.

Using observations obtained in this manner, regressions for the four different equilibrating hypotheses were computed for the ten fundamental experiments as shown in Table 2, columns 2–5. A 95 per cent confidence interval is shown in parentheses under each regression coefficient. With the exception of experiment 8*A*, the regression coefficients for every experiment are significant under both the Walrasian and the excess-rent hypotheses. On the other hand, β_{33} in the modified Walrasian hypothesis is significant only in experiment 2. In none of the experiments is β_{34} significant for the modified excess-rent hypothesis. These highly unambiguous results seem to suggest that little significance can be attached to the effect of a difference between equilibrium buyers' and sellers' rent in biasing the price equilibrium tendencies.

On this reasoning, we are left with the closely competing Walrasian and excess-rent hypotheses, showing highly significant adjustment speeds, β_{11} and β_{22}. In discriminating between these two hypotheses we shall compare them on two important counts: (1) their ability to predict zero price change in equilibrium, and (2) the standard errors of said predictions. Since $x^0_{1t} = x^0_{2t} = 0$, in equilibrium, this requires a comparison between the absolute values of the intercepts of the Walrasian and the excess-rent regressions, $|\beta_{01}|$ and $|\beta_{02}|$, and between $S(\beta_{01})$ and $S(\beta_{02})$. Under the first comparison we can think of $|\beta_{01}|$, shown in column 2, Table 3, as a "score" for the Walrasian hypothesis, and $|\beta_{02}|$, shown in column 5, as a "score" for the excess-rent hypothesis. A low intercept represents a good score. Thus, for experiment 1, in equilibrium, there is a residual tendency for price to change (in this case fall) at the rate of 2.6 cents per transaction by the Walrasian and 2.8 cents by the excess-rent regressions. A casual comparison of columns 2 and 5 reveals that in most of the experiments $|\beta_{01}| > |\beta_{02}|$, and in those for which the reverse is true the difference is quite small, tending thereby to support the excess-rent hypothesis. A more exact discrimination can be made by applying the Wilcoxon[15] paired-sample rank test for related samples to the "scores" of columns 2 and 5. This test applies to the differences $|\beta_{01}| - |\beta_{02}|$, and tests the null hypothesis, H_0, that the Walrasian and excess-rent alternatives are equivalent (the distribution of the differences is symmetric about zero). If applied to all the experiments, including the "*B*'s" ($N = 15$), H_0 is rejected at the $< .02$ significance level. The difference between our paired series of "scores" in favor of the excess-rent hypothesis is therefore significant. It is highly debatable whether all the experiments should be included in such a test, especially 4, which did not tend to the predicted equilibrium, 8, which represented a different organization of the bargaining, and possibly the "*B*" experiments, where the samples were small. Therefore, the test was run omitting all these experiments ($N = 8$), giving a rejection of H_0 at the .05 level. Omitting only 4 and 8 ($N = 11$) allowed H_0 still to be rejected at the $< .02$ level.

If we compare the standard errors $S(\beta_{01})$ and $S(\beta_{02})$ in Table 3, columns 3 and 6, we see that again the excess-rent hypothesis tends to score higher (smaller standard errors). Applying the Wilcoxon test to $S(\beta_{01}) - S(\beta_{02})$ for all the experiments ($N = 15$), we find that this difference, in favor of the excess-rent hypothesis, is significant at the $<.01$ level. The difference is still significant at the $<.01$ level if we omit 4 and 8 from the test, and it is significant at the .05 level if we also eliminate all the "*B*" experiments.

The *t*-values for the two hypotheses

[15] See, for example, K. A. Brownlee, *Statistical Theory and Methodology in Science and Engineering* (New York: John Wiley & Sons, 1960), pp. 196–99.

are shown in columns 4 and 7 of Table 3. They tend also to be lower for the excess-rent hypothesis.

Bearing in mind that our analysis is based upon a limited number of experiments, and that revisions may be required in the light of further experiments with different subjects or with monetary payoffs, we conclude the following: Of the four hypotheses tested, the two modified forms show highly insignificant regression coefficients for the added explanatory variable. As between the Walrasian and the excess-rent hypotheses, the evidence is sharply in favor of the latter.

V. RATIONALIZATION OF THE EXCESS-RENT HYPOTHESIS

Having provided a tentative empirical verification of the hypothesis that price in a competitve (auction) market tends to rise or fall in proportion to the excess buyer plus seller rent corresponding to any contract price, it remains to provide some theoretical rationale for such a hypothesis. From the description of the above experiments and their results, the excess-rent hypothesis would seem to have some plausibility from an individual decision-making point of view. Given that a particular contract price has just been executed, it is reasonable to expect each trader to compare that price with his own reservation price, the difference being a "profit" or rent which he considers achievable, and to present a degree of bargaining resistance in the auction process which is greater, the smaller is this rent. Such resistance may tend to give way, even where the rents on one side or the other are very small, if it becomes clear that such rents are unattainable. Thus, if equilibrium buyers' rent exceeds sellers' rent, any early tendency for contract prices to remain above equilibrium (and balance the rents achieved on both sides) might be expected to break down, as it becomes evident that the "paper" rents at those prices may not be attainable by all of the sellers. By this argument, it is suggested that the propensity of sellers to reduce their offers when price is above equilibrium is related to their attempts to obtain some—even if a "small"—amount of rent rather than to a direct influence of excess supply.

A particularly interesting aspect of the excess-rent hypothesis is that it leads naturally to an interesting optimality interpretation of the static competitive market equilibrium. The principle is this: in static equilibrium a competitive market minimizes the total virtual rent received by buyers and sellers. By "virtual rent" I mean the rent that would be enjoyed if all buyers and sellers could be satisfied at any given disequilibrium price. To see this optimality principle, let $D(p)$ be the demand function and $S(p)$ the supply function. At $p = P$, the sum of buyer and seller virtual rent is

$$R = \int_P^\infty D(p)\,dp + \int_0^P S(p)\,dp$$

and is represented by the area from DD down to P and from SS up to P in Figure 1. R is a minimum for normal supply and demand functions when

$$\frac{dR}{dP} = -D(P) + S(P) = 0,$$

that is, when demand equals supply with $P = P_0$. Note particularly that there is nothing artificial about this conversion of the statement of an ordinary competitive market equilibrium into a corresponding minimum problem. Whether one desires to attach any welfare significance to the concepts of consumer and producer surplus or not, it is completely plausible to require, in the interests of strict market efficiency, that no trader be imputed more rent than is absolutely necessary to perform the exchange mechanics. Hence, at price P in Figure 1, virtual rent exceeds equilibrium rent, and if this price persists, some sellers get more rent than they "should."

It should perhaps be pointed out that the excess-rent and Walrasian hypotheses are close analogues in that both deal with virtual, unattainable quantities. Thus, under the Walrasian hypothesis the "virtual" excess supply at P in Figure 1 is unattainable. Indeed, it is this fact that presumably causes price to fall. Similarly, at P, the excess rent area above S and D is unattainable, and leads to price cutting. Also note that the Walrasian hypothesis bears a gradient relationship, while the excess-rent hypothesis shows a global adjusting relationship, to the rent minimization principle. At $P > P_0$ the Walrasian hypothesis says that price tends to fall at a time rate which is proportional to the marginal rent, dR/dP, at that price. The excess-rent hypothesis states that price tends to fall at a time rate which is proportional to the global difference between total rent at P and at P_0.

Samuelson has shown how one may convert the Cournot-Enke problem of spatial price equilibrium into a maximum problem.[16] The criterion to be maximized in a single market would be what he calls social payoff, defined as the algebraic area under the excess-demand curve. In spatially separated markets the criterion is to maximize net social payoff, defined as the sum of the social payoffs in all regions minus the total transport costs of all interregional shipments. But, according to Samuelson, "this magnitude is artificial in the sense that no competitor in the market will be aware of or concerned with it. It is artificial in the sense that after an Invisible Hand has led us to its maximization, we need not necessarily attach any social welfare significance to the result."[17] I think the formulation of competitive market equilibrium as a rent minimization problem makes the "Invisible Hand" distinctly more visible and more teleological.[18] It also has great social (though not necessarily welfare) significance in relation to "frictionless" market efficiency. Rent is an "unearned" increment which literally cries out for minimization in an efficient economic organization. Furthermore, as we have seen with the excess-rent and Walrasian hypotheses, both the abstract teleological goal of the competitive market and the dynamics of its *tâtonnement* process are branches of the same market mechanism.

In view of the electrical circuit analogue so often mentioned in connection with spatially separated markets, a final bonus of the minimum rent formulation is the fact that it represents a more direct analogy with the principle of minimum heat loss in electric circuits.[19] Nature has devised a set of laws to govern the flow of electrical energy, which, it

[16] P. A. Samuelson, "Spatial Price Equilibrium and Linear Programming," *American Economic Review*, XLII (June, 1952), 284–92.

[17] *Ibid.*, p. 288.

[18] The discovery of the excess-rent hypothesis draws me nearer to the camp of "Invisible Hand" enthusiasts, but only because of the greater visibility of the Hand. I cannot quite carry my market metaphysics as far as does Samuelson. It is well known that any problem in economic equilibrium can be converted into a maximum (or minimum) problem, but I question the value of such a transformation (beyond technical advantages) if it is purely artificial without any meaningful interpretation; and if we work at it, such a meaningful transformation may often be found.

[19] Samuelson, *op. cit.*, p. 285.

can be shown, minimizes the inefficient, wasteful loss of heat energy from electrical systems. Similarly, the market mechanism provides a set of "laws" which minimizes the "wasteful" payment of excessive economic rent.

VI. SUMMARY

It would be premature to assert any broad generalizations based upon the ten experiments we have discussed. Yet conclusions are important for purposes of specifying the exact character of any findings, whether those findings are ultimately verified or not. In this spirit, the following tentative conclusions are offered concerning these experiments:

1. Even where numbers are "small," there are strong tendencies for a supply and demand competitive equilibrium to be attained as long as one is able to prohibit collusion and to maintain absolute publicity of all bids, offers, and transactions. Publicity of quotations and absence of collusion were major characteristics of these experimental markets.

2. Changes in the conditions of supply or demand cause changes in the volume of transactions per period and the general level of contract prices. These latter correspond reasonably well with the predictions of competitive price theory. The response to such changes may, however, produce a transient phase of very erratic contract price behavior.

3. Some slight evidence has been provided to suggest that a prediction of the static equilibrium of a competitive market requires knowledge of the shapes of the supply and demand schedules as well as the intersection of such schedules. The evidence is strongest in the extreme case in which the supply curve is perfectly elastic, with the result that the empirical equilibrium is higher than the theoretical equilibrium.

4. Markets whose institutional organization is such that only sellers make price quotations may exhibit weaker equilibrium tendencies than markets in which both buyers and sellers make price quotations—perhaps even disequilibrium tendencies. Such one-sided markets may operate to the benefit of buyers. A possible explanation is that in the price-formation process buyers reveal a minimum of information concerning their eagerness to buy.

5. The so-called Walrasian hypothesis concerning the mechanism of market adjustment seems not to be confirmed. A more adequate hypothesis is the excess-rent hypothesis which relates the "speed" of contract price adjustment to the algebraic excess of buyer plus seller "virtual" rent over the equilibrium buyer plus seller rent. This new hypothesis becomes particularly intriguing in view of the fact that a competitive market for a single commodity can be interpreted as seeking to minimize total rent.

APPENDIX

In the course of this experimental study and its analysis several additional or peripheral issues were investigated, a discussion of which would not fit clearly into the main body of this report. Three such issues will be discussed briefly in this appendix for the benefit of readers interested in some of the numerous additional lines of inquiry that might be pursued.

I. EVIDENCE OF INTER-TRADING-PERIOD LEARNING

In testing the various equilibrating hypotheses under investigation in this paper, no attempt was made to distinguish the effects of different trading periods. The sample of observations for each experiment embraced all the trading periods of that experiment with transactions running continuously from the first trading period through the last. It would appear, however, that learning occurs as the experiment progresses in such a way as to alter the parameters of each equilibrating hypothesis from one trading period to the next. To obtain some idea of the extent of these alterations, regressions for the excess-rent hypothesis were computed by individual trading period for tests 6*A*, 9*A*, and 10. These regression equations are summarized in Table 4. It is evident that there is a tendency for the intercepts of these regressions to converge toward zero as the number of trading periods increases. Convergence of the intercepts suggests that the later trading period regressions may be better equilibrating equations (better predictors of zero price change when excess rent is zero) than the earlier period regressions.

II. CONVERGENCE OF BID, OFFER, AND CONTRACT PRICES

In experiments 9 and 10 a tape-recorder was used for the first time to obtain a record of all bid and offer prices as well as the contract prices. No analysis has as yet been attempted with these additional data. However, a graph of the bid, offer, and contract prices in their serial sequence of occurrence is suggestive. Such a sample graph is shown in Chart 11 for experiment 10. Perhaps the most interesting fact revealed in this

TABLE 4

EXCESS-RENT REGRESSIONS $\Delta p_t = \beta_{02} + \beta_{22}x_{2t}$ BY TRADING PERIOD

Trading Period	Experiment 6A	Experiment 9A	Experiment 10
1	$-2.769+0.101\,x_{2t}$	$-0.335+0.078\,x_{2t}$	$-0.160+0.087\,x_{2t}$
2	$-2.876+0.216\,x_{2t}$	$-0.148+0.061\,x_{2t}$	$-0.053+0.408\,x_{2t}$
3	$0.273+0.029\,x_{2t}$	$-0.191+0.093\,x_{2t}$	$0.007+0.349\,x_{2t}$
4	$0.121+0.391\,x_{2t}$		

CHART 11

BIDS, OFFERS, AND TRANSACTIONS ON TEST 10

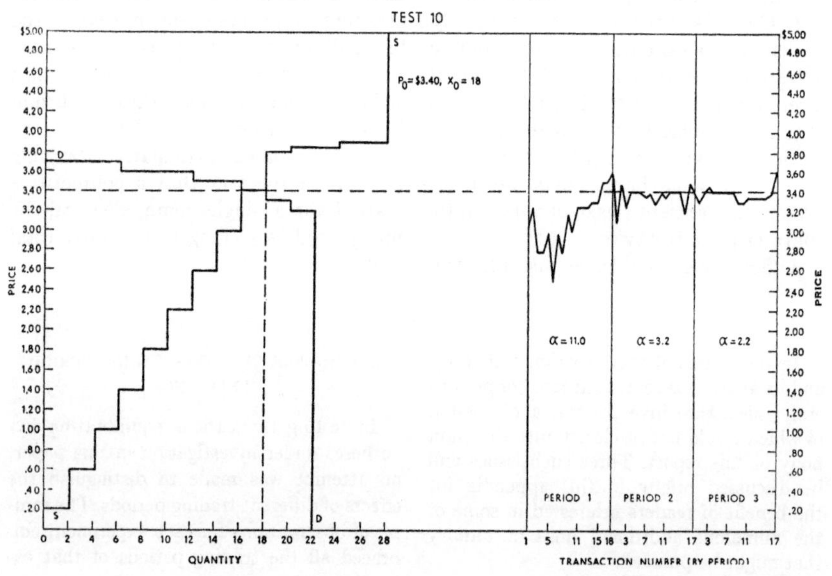

chart is the apparent tendency for the variance of the bids and offers to stabilize early, with the contract prices continuing to converge within this variation in bids and offers. Thus it is at the beginning of period 1, up to about the eighth transaction, that the bids and offers seem to show the most pronounced variation. This variation then remains reasonably steady to the very end of the last trading period. Contract prices converge, but the traders continue to attempt to get better terms by making repeatedly high offers and low bids. In this connection note that the unaccepted offers are further above the contract prive level than the unaccepted bids are below the contract price level. Similar results were evident in a corresponding chart (not shown) for experiment 9. This, apparently, is the auction market's way of compensating for the fact that, in this particular experiment, sellers were in a "softer" (higher rent) position than buyers.

CHART 12

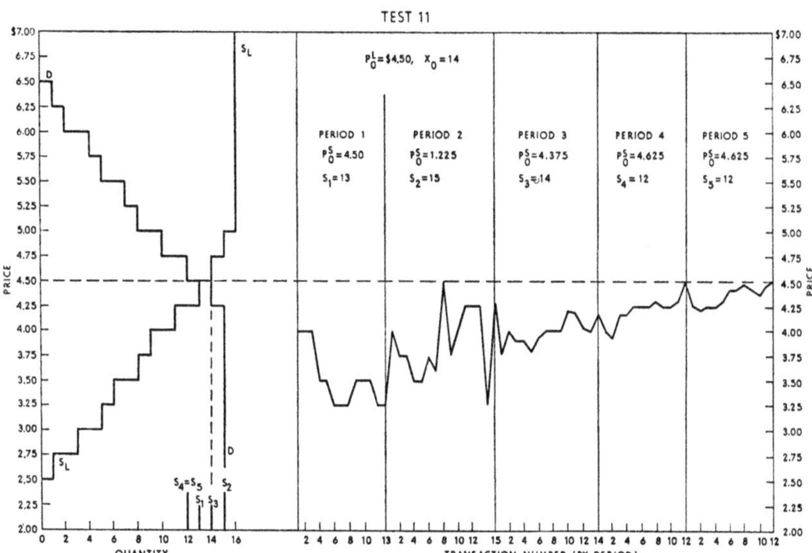

III. A PILOT EXPERIMENT IN "SHORT-RUN" AND "LONG-RUN" EQUILIBRIUM

An important characteristic of the ten experiments discussed in this paper was the absence of any quantity-adjusting decision-making behavior on the part of either buyers or sellers. Such experiments represent the simulation of markets for commodities which do not have to be delivered or even produced until after the sale contract is executed. Hence, the possibility of distress sales, leading to losses by sellers, is ruled out by experimental design. In long-run price theory we think of producers entering or leaving an industry in response to the profits or losses they expect to make. The results of one pilot experiment to simulate this process is shown in Chart 12. The significant new element in this experiment was giving all sellers the option at the beginning of each trading period of entering the market or remaining "out of production." It was understood that if they entered the market it was at a cost equal to the price on their card, and this cost was a net loss to any seller failing to make a sale. Also in this experiment some sellers were producers of two units and some of one unit. Specifically, there were six sellers with one unit and five with two units. Similarly, some buyers were two-unit buyers and some were one-unit buyers. It was not known to the traders generally how many or who were traders in one or in two units. This procedure was employed primarily to prevent traders from having exact knowledge of short-run supply by simply counting the number of sellers in the market in any trading period. Buyers in particular were thereby faced with some uncertainty to temper their knowledge that sellers were under strong selling pressure once they entered the market.

The experiment was conducted over five trading periods. In period 1 two sellers with a capacity to produce three units (the $4.75 and $3.00 sellers in Chart 12) elected to remain out of production. They were market observers only. Therefore the period 1 short-run theoretical supply was perfectly inelastic at $S_1 = 13$. In period 2 only the $4.50 seller, who sold at a loss the first time, remained out, giving $S_2 = 15$. In period 3 the $5.00 and $4.50 sellers remained out giving $S_3 = 14$, and in periods 4 and 5 production stabilized with the $5.00, $4.50, and $4.25 producers out of the market, giving $S_4 = S_5 = 12$.

From the results is it clear that this market approaches its "long-run" equilibrium price, $4.50, more slowly than was the case in the previous experiments. The approach is from below as might be expected by the "distress sale" characteristic of the market. The pressure on producers to sell seems to have had its strongest effect in period 1, in which market prices tended to decline from their opening. Prices moved erratically in period 2, and in the remaining periods climbed steadily in the direction of equilibrium.

EFFECT OF MARKET ORGANIZATION ON COMPETITIVE EQUILIBRIUM *

VERNON L. SMITH

I. INTRODUCTION

Since the use of laboratory experimental techniques in the testing of economic hypotheses seems to have become reasonably well established in recent years, this paper will not attempt to provide any general methodological justification for its existence.[1] A previous study [2] presented the results of ten exploratory pilot experiments in competitive (multitrader auction) market behavior. The major methodological purposes of that study were to (i) test the feasibility of experimental techniques, (ii) synthesize one or more standard experimental designs, and (iii) provide the foundation for a more rigorous empirical examination of several specific hypotheses. The conclusions suggested in that paper were based in part upon hypotheses whose tests and theoretical rationalization were developed after the experimental data had been obtained. The results of such a posteriori testing and theorizing based largely upon un-

* The research reported in this paper was supported by National Science Foundation Grant No. G-24199 to Purdue University. I am indebted to Richard Swensson and John Wertz for computational assistance, and William Starbuck for valuable suggestions and comments.

1. S. Siegel and L. E. Fouraker, *Bargaining and Group Decision Making* (New York: McGraw-Hill, 1960). L. E. Fouraker and S. Siegel, *Bargaining Behavior* (New York: McGraw-Hill, 1963). P. Suppes and J. M. Carlsmith, "Experimental Analysis of a Duopoly Situation. . . ," *International Economic Review*, Vol. 3 (Jan. 1962).

2. V. L. Smith, "An Experimental Study of Competitive Market Behavior," *Journal of Political Economy*, LXX (April 1962).

replicated experiments should be considered highly tentative until such results have been confirmed by further experiments designed specifically to test the particular hypotheses in question.

This paper will report on the results of a series of experiments designed exclusively for the purpose of testing various hypotheses concerning the price equilibrium and adjustment behavior of markets whose organization permits either sellers or buyers, but not both, to engage actively in the higgling and bargaining process. Most retail markets, at least in this country, are characterized by an organization in which sellers post their offers competitively while buyers passively choose among such offers to form exchange contracts. With minor exceptions in such markets, custom precludes buyers from making counter bids in establishing contract prices.

The motivation for the present study stems largely from a pilot experiment [3] in which sellers only were permitted to make quotations. The results of that experiment suggested that although the initial contracts tended to be above the theoretical equilibrium price, all subsequent contracts tended to be executed at prices persistently below the theoretical equilibrium. After the fact, such behavior appeared reasonable. Sellers, desiring to maximize trading profit, should offer to sell at the highest prices they might hope to obtain. Buyers, perhaps fearing that they may be unable to do better, might be expected to accept some of these initial high offers. But as trading proceeds, and buyers learn that by waiting they can take advantage of the competitive pressure on sellers, contract prices may be lowered, possibly to a stable level below the theoretical equilibrium. Such a market has two forms of asymmetry which may operate to the benefit of buyers: the active competitive pressure is on the offers being quoted by sellers, and, in this process, sellers are revealing more information about the prices at which they are willing to sell than are buyers.[4] Buyers either remain silent or passively accept certain of the offers that are tendered. If this reasoning is correct, the results of the pilot experiment should be confirmed by replication of an experiment designed for this purpose. Furthermore, it is to be expected, a priori, that these results will be reversed in an experimental market in which buyers only are allowed to make price quotations.

3. *Ibid.*, pp. 124, 125, 134.

4. My referee notes that the reasoning in this paragraph contradicts the common assertion that administered pricing reacts to the disadvantage of the buyer and that administered purchase pricing (as in labor markets) reacts to the disadvantage of the seller. Also, that the reasoning is reminiscent of the idea that, in von Neuman-Morgenstern terminology, the price-quoter plays a minorant game.

II. The Hypotheses

We define the following trading rule conditions for subsequent reference:

R_S — Sellers are permitted to make offers; buyers are free to accept offers, but are not permitted to make bids.

R_{SB} — Sellers are permitted to make offers and are free to accept bids; buyers are permitted to make bids and are free to accept offers.

R_B — Buyers are permitted to make bids; sellers are free to accept bids, but are not permitted to make offers.

As a consequence of the pilot experimental outcome and speculation thereon, but prior to performing the experiments to be reported here, the following hypotheses were formulated:

H_1: Initial contract prices (defined in advance as those contracts executed in the first trading period) will tend to be ordered

$$P_t^S > P_t^{SB} > P_t^B,\ t = 1,2,\ .\ .\ .\ ,N_1$$

H_2: All remaining contract prices (defined in advance as those contracts executed in trading periods 2, 3, 4 and 5) will tend to be ordered

$$P_t^S < P_t^{SB} < P_t^B,\ t = N_1 + 1,\ N_1 + 2,\ .\ .\ .\ ,\ N$$

where N_1 = number of contracts in trading period 1,

$N - N_1$ = number of contracts in trading periods 2, 3, 4 and 5 combined,

P_t^S = contract price on the tth transaction under condition R_S,

P_t^{SB} = contract price on the tth transaction under condition R_{SB},

P_t^B = contract price on the tth transaction under condition R_B.

Observe that H_1 and H_2 refer to an ordering of the individual contract prices. A third hypotheses, not entirely independent of H_1 and H_2, refers to the ordering of expected equilibrium prices.

H_3: Expected prices in equilibrium will be ordered

$$E(P^S) < E(P^{SB}) < E(P^B).$$

As before, the superscripts refer to the three indicated trading rule conditions. The hypothesis H_3 will be tested in two ways. An ordinary analysis of variance test will be applied to the contract prices in trading periods 4 and 5 (defined in advance as the equilibrium trading periods). Then a first order stochastic difference equation will be estimated for each trading rule condition, using all contract prices occurring under each condition. The expected equilibrium prices implied by these difference equations will then be used to test H_3. The regression coefficients in these equations will provide a measure of the speed at which contract prices converge, and will be employed to test H_4.

H_4: The speed of convergence to equilibrium will be greater under condition R^{SB} than either R^S or R^B.

Hypotheses H_1 through H_4 will be tested by classical statistical procedures in Section IV. In Section V a Bayesian subjective probability analysis will be used to determine the degree of confidence to be attached to the hypotheses that the ordering relation $P_t^S < P_t^{SB} < P_t^B$ holds for the contract prices in trading periods 4 and 5 (equilibrium).

III. Subjects and Experimental Procedure

The above hypotheses will be tested using data from six experimental sessions consisting of two sessions under each of the three conditions R_S, R_{SB} and R_B. The two replications under R_{SB} served as controls on the R_S and R_B sessions. A total of 144 male students enrolled in three sections of each of two sophomore level courses in economics (which we will call course A and course B) provided the subjects for these sessions.[5] Table I illustrates the over-all experimental design and indicates the combination of experimental condition, course, and number of subjects associated with each experiment session. No subject participated in more than one of the experimental sessions. The sessions were run separately in each of two series separated by several months (one semester).

As a means of controlling on information transfer from earlier to later sessions the following procedures were employed:

1. Every session was performed with "captive" subjects. I never used volunteers. Volunteers were more likely to have heard something about "those experiments conducted by the economics department," and were more likely to have superior motivation, which was not necessary for these experiments.

2. The subjects were given no advance warning of an experimental session. I cleared with the instructor in charge and then appeared on a specified date with equipment, payoff money, and

5. Experimental session 2, shown in Table I, had to be repeated on a second group of Course B subjects at a later date to obtain data under adequate controls. In the first run of session 2 a subject executed a contract in violation of the limit price rules specified in the instructions below. This provided false, uncontrolled public information to the experimental market, and it was decided to invalidate the session. Detailed tests were not performed on the data from this invalidated session, but casual examination revealed that the general results were similar to those obtained from the validated session.

TABLE I

NUMBER OF SUBJECTS AND EXPERIMENTAL CONDITION FOR EACH SESSION

Experimental Session Number	Condition			
	R_S	R_{SB}	R_B	Total Subjects
Course A (20 subjects)	1	3	5	60
Course B (28 subjects)	2	4	6	84
Total Subjects	48	48	48	144

materials prepared. The objective was to control as much as possible the amount of pre-game speculation and information-seeking that could occur. This was important where substantial cash payoffs were employed. (The individual subject payoffs in these experiments ran as high as $6.50 for about 40 minutes of participation).

3. The results and all information concerning the constants of the experiments were suppressed until the design block of six sessions was completed.

4. The experimental sessions discussed in this paper were intermingled with sessions for two entirely different studies involving a variety of different experimental designs, conditions, and information. In this way even if a subject had heard something about a previous session, there was very little chance that the session was identical to the one in which he was to participate.

Each session was begun with a general statement that the group was being asked to participate in a decision-making experiment; that they would not be subjected to any unpleasant stimuli or experiences; and furthermore, that they would have an opportunity to earn real money during their participation. Copies of instructions, printed as an appendix to this paper, were then passed out, and read out loud to the entire group.

After reading the second paragraph of these instructions an assistant passed out the indicated yellow and white limit price cards. Then the remaining instructions were read. Paragraphs 5S and 6S were read in the sessions under condition R_S, 5SB and 6SB under conditions R_{SB}, and 5B and 6B under condition R_B. Each session consisted of a series of five trading periods. In order to provide some control over end effects, this information was not given to the subjects. In one session — number 5 — a sixth trading period was run as an additional check on the assumption that periods 4 and 5 represented equilibrium behavior. As a means of assuring an orderly trading process, the subjects were asked to raise their hand when they desired to make a bid or offer. I would then skip around calling upon those with raised hands for their bids or offers. I would then repeat each price bid or offer before calling for another. Each quotation was an outstanding bid or offer that could not be withdrawn, until a new quotation had been made, at which time the previous quotation was no longer outstanding. In this way, one quotation at a time was before the group. The subjects were free to alter previous bids and offers in any way they pleased [6] provided that their limit price conditions were not violated. The subjects were given no information as to the number of buyers and sellers, possible prices at which the commodity might, should, or could sell, and so on — no information beyond that provided by the instructions and the limit prices.

Unknown to the subjects the limit buy prices generated the demand schedules, while the limit sell prices formed the supply schedules shown in Figure I. In experiments 1, 3 and 5, 20 subjects were available in each of three sections of course A (Table I). The supply and demand designs are given by *SS′* (10 sellers) and *DD′* (10 buyers). In experiments 2, 4 and 6, 28 subjects were available, and the supply and demand designs are given by *SS* (14 sellers) and *DD* (14 buyers). Symmetrical demand and supply designs were used throughout the six experiments as a control on other variables, not of interest in the present investigation, that might explain the expected equilibrium biases under the study conditions R_S and R_B. Thus, in each session:

1. The number of buyers is equal to the number of sellers.

2. Equilibrium buyer's rent (consumer surplus) equals equilibrium seller's rent (producer surplus). Differences in these rents

6. In their bilateral bargaining experiments, Siegel and Fouraker require "bargaining in good faith." That is, any bid turned down by a rival may be subsequently accepted by him (see instruction 5, p. 20, in *Bargaining and Group Decision Making, op. cit.*). I have elected to give the trading subjects in these experiments the greatest possible freedom to alter previous bids and offers that were not accepted. This is another aspect of market organization — whether bargaining in good faith, in the above sense, is or is not required — that would be of interest to investigate experimentally.

might affect either the equilibrium level of contract prices or the convergence process.[7]

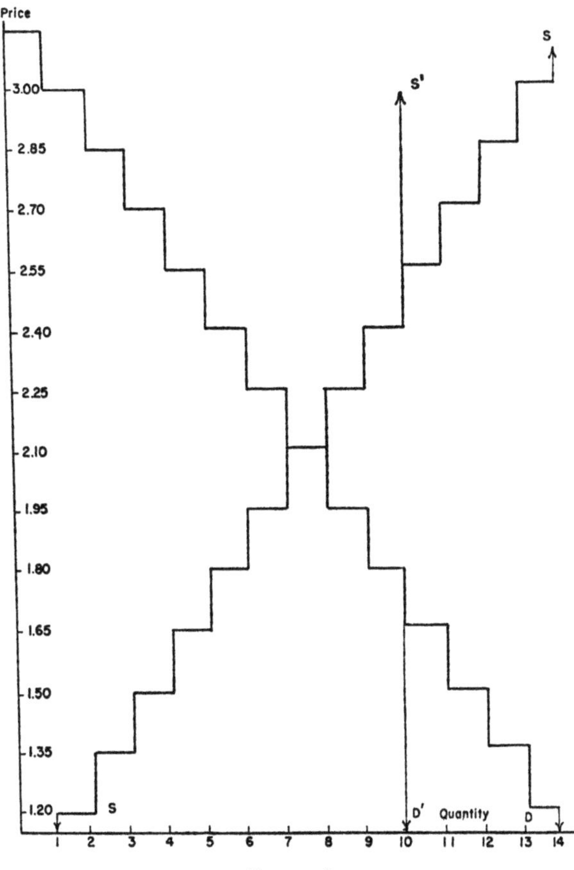

FIGURE I
Experimental Supply and Demand Schedules

IV. EXPERIMENTAL RESULTS AND CLASSICAL TESTS OF HYPOTHESES

Charts 1 through 6 provide a complete series of contract prices in the order in which they were executed in the five trading periods of each session (six trading periods of session 5).

(a) Test of H_1

H_1 will be tested by applying the Jonckheere k-sample test[8]

7. See Smith, *op. cit.*, pp. 119, 120, 130, 134.
8. A. R. Jonckheere, "A Test of Significance for the Relation Between m

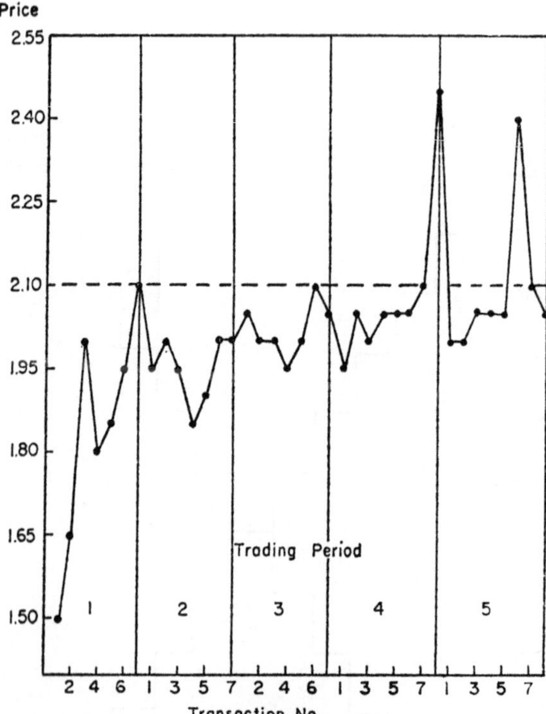

CHART 1
Condition: R_B

against ordered alternatives to the first period contract prices under the three trading rule conditions. The Jonckheere procedure provides a nonparametric test of the null hypotheses that the sample observations $\hat{P}^B_t$, $\hat{P}^{SB}_t$, and $\hat{P}^S_t$ were drawn from three identical populations against the alternative that they came from populations that are in an expected order of increasing value. In this application we have three categories, with 14 observations in the first category (the 14 contract prices in trading period 1 of sessions 5 and 6 under R_B), 15 in the second and 16 in the third. The results are not significant.[9] Hence, we are unable to reject the null hypotheses

Rankings and k Ranked Categories," *The British Journal of Statistical Psychology*, VII, Part II (Nov. 1954), 93–100. Also see A. R. Jonckheere, "A Distribution — Free k-Sample Test Against Ordered Alternatives," *Biometrika*, Vol. 41 (June 1954), pp. 133–45.

9. Using the notation in Jonckheere, "A Test of Significance for the Relation. . . ," pp. 94–97, we have $n = 45$, $m = 1$, $k = 3$, $l_1 = 14$, $l_2 = 15$ and $l_3 = 16$. The test statistic is $P = 268$, with mean $\chi_1(P) = 337$ and variance

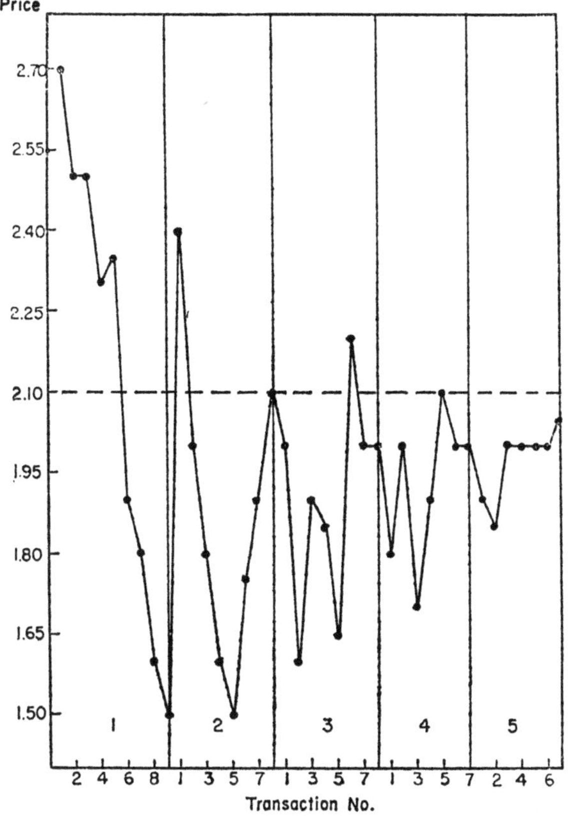

CHART 2
Condition: R_S

that the first period transactions under condition R_S, R_{SB}, and R_B came from the same or identical populations. The failure of the data to support H_1 is evident in sessions 1 and 2, where it would appear that under R_S the initial contracts are as likely to be below as above the theoretical equilibrium.

(b) Test of H_2

H_2 was tested by applying the Jonckheere test to the contract prices in all trading periods beyond the first under the three trading rule conditions. The test is highly significant.[1] The null hypotheses

$\chi_2(P) = 2304$. The unit normal deviate $Z = \dfrac{P - \frac{1}{2} - \chi_1(P)}{\sqrt{\chi_2(P)}} = 1.45$ is definitely not significant.

1. Continuing with the notation of the previous footnote, we have $n =$

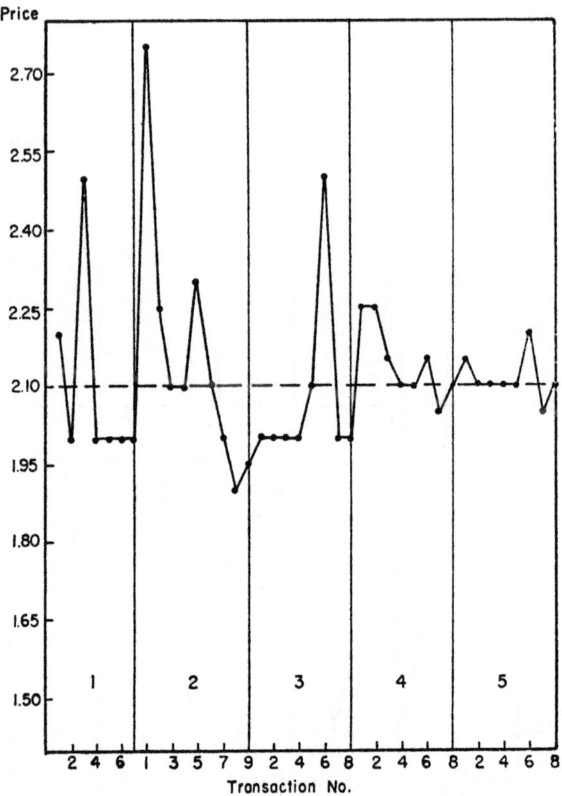

CHART 3
Condition: R_{SB}

that these contract prices came from the same population is rejected at $\alpha < 0.001$.

Since the null complement of H_1 failed to be rejected while the null complement of H_2 was rejected at a very high level of significance, a more general hypothesis than H_2 is suggested by the data, viz,

$$P_t^S < P_t^{SB} < P_t^B, \ t = 1,2, \ldots ,N.$$

That is, the ordering relationship is expected to hold for all contract prices in all trading periods, with an extremely low probability that its null complement would be rejected if it is true.

It might be reasonable to conjecture that the tendencies implied by this ordering relationship are influenced by the first

190, $m = 1$, $k = 3$, $l_1 = 59$, $l_2 = 62$, $l_3 = 69$, $P = 8731$, $\chi_1(P) = 6003$, and $\chi_2(P) = 17000$. Hence, $Z = 20.9$, which is significant at $\alpha < 0.001$.

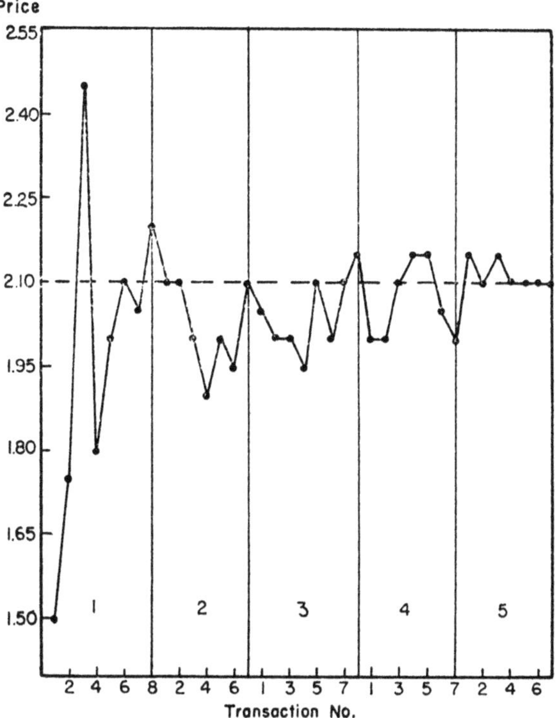

CHART 4
Condition: R_{SB}

contract. For example, if the first contract is below equilibrium, prices might tend to remain below equilibrium. These effects would of course be random in these experiments since no attempt was made to control on the first contract. However, it is of interest to note that the first contract in sessions 1, 4 and 6 happens to have been executed at $1.50 (See Charts 1, 4 and 6). Thus the first contract was the same in one session under each trading condition, yet this fact clearly did not disturb the fundamental tendencies expected under this ordering hypothesis.

(c) Tests of H_3

In testing H_3 by an analysis of variance applied to the contract prices of trading periods 4 and 5, we note from Table I, that a 2 x 3 factorial design is appropriate. Our primary a priori interest is in testing for the effect of trading condition. However, because of differences in the number of subjects available, the two replications

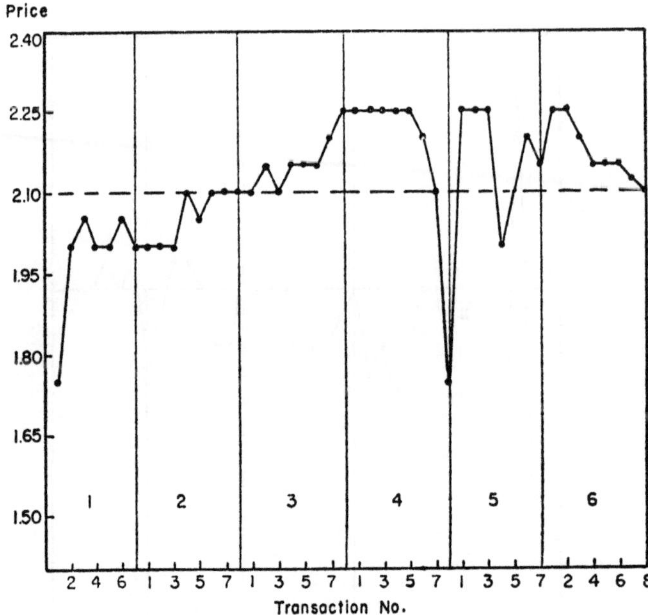

CHART 5
Condition: R_B

under each condition could not be matched. Therefore, the experimental design was deliberately balanced in a way that would permit us also to test for the effect of subject group. The result of our analysis of variance is summarized in the standard form for 2 x 3 designs shown in Table II.

TABLE II

ANALYSIS OF VARIANCE

Source of Variance	Sums of Squares	Degrees of Freedom	Mean Square	F Value
Subject groups	1098.065	1	1098.065	10.894**
Trading rule effect	2706.666	2	1353.333	13.427**
Interaction	465.616	2	232.808	2.310*
Error	8466.637	84	100.793	

** Significant at $\alpha < 0.001$. * Not significant.

Table III shows the mean contract price in trading periods 4 and 5 for each subject group and trading condition. From the components

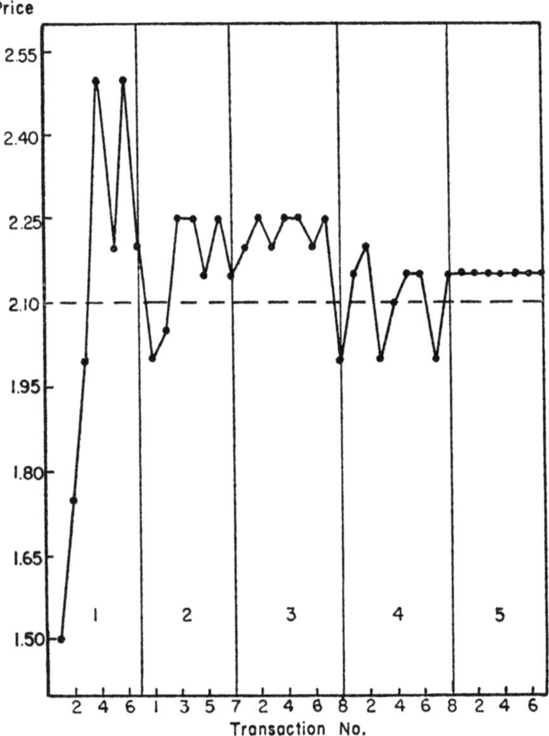

CHART 6
Condition: R_B

of variance shown in Table II, we conclude that there is no significant interaction between the subject group variable and the trading condition variable. Their separate effects are additive. However, both subject group and trading condition are highly significant variables

TABLE III

MEAN CONTRACT PRICE IN TRADING PERIODS 4 AND 5 BY SUBJECT GROUP AND TRADING CONDITION

	R_S	R_{SB}	R_B	Marginal Means
Group A 20 Subjects	208	213	217	213
Group B 28 Subjects	195	209	213	206
Marginal means	202	211	215	209

($\alpha < 0.001$). The effect of trading conditions H_S, R_{SB} and R_B are in the direction indicated a priori by H_3 (Table III). We therefore conclude in favor of H_3 by the analysis of variance test. However, from Table III we also note that the mean equilibrium contract prices were lower for the 28 member subject groups than for the 20 member subject groups. This consistent difference is highly significant, by the analysis in Table II, but neither the difference nor its direction were predicted a priori. Since I have no explanation as to why equilibrium contract prices under all trading conditions should be lowered by the addition of 4 submarginal sellers and 4 submarginal buyers (See Figure I), I attribute this result to unanticipated differences in the subject groups.

The second test of H_3 was obtained from least square estimates of the first order stochastic difference equation:

$$p_{t+1} = ap_t + a_0 + \epsilon_{t+1}, \ |a| < 1, \ t = 0,1,2. \ . \ . \ . \tag{1}$$

where $p_t = P_t - P^0$, P_t is the tth contract price, and P^0 is the theoretical equilibrium price. The general expression for p_t is given by

$$p_t = a^t p_0 + \frac{a_0(1 - a^t)}{1 - a} + \sum_{s=1}^{t} a^{t-s} \epsilon_s. \tag{2}$$

If ϵ_t has mean zero and variance σ^2, then the mean and variance of p_t is given by

$$E(p_t) = \frac{a_0(1 - a^{t+1})}{1 - a} \tag{3}$$

$$S^2(p_t) = \frac{1 - a^{2t}}{1 - a^2} \sigma^2 . \tag{4}$$

If we define $\lim_{t\to\infty} E(P_t)$ as the equilibrium price implied by equaation (1), then the expected deviation of this empirical equilibrium from the theoretical equilibrium is

$$E(p_\infty) = \lim_{t\to\infty} E(p_t) = \frac{a_0}{1 - a} \tag{4}$$

with variance

$$S^2(p_\infty) = \lim_{t\to\infty} V(p_t) = \frac{\sigma^2}{1 - a^2} . \tag{5}$$

The least squares estimates of a_0 and a in equation (1) for the combined experiments under each trading condition are shown in Table IV. The standard errors are shown in parenthesis. All price deviations are measured in cents.

TABLE IV

STOCHASTIC DIFFERENCE EQUATION PARAMETERS FOR EXPERIMENTAL SESSIONS

Trading Condition	Experimental Session	a	a_0	Correlation Coefficient	Standard Error of Estimate	Number of Observations
R_S	1	0.38 (0.13)	−4.8	0.45	12.3	36
	2	0.47 (0.13)	−8.9	0.52	21.5	38
R_{SB}	3	0.03 (0.16)	+1.7	0.03	16.8	39
	4	0.00 (0.14)	−4.3	0.00	11.9	36
R_B	5	0.42 (0.12)	+1.8	0.48	9.3	45
	6	0.34 (0.12)	+4.6	0.44	12.0	36
R_S	1 and 2	0.46 (0.09)	−6.6 (2.3)	0.51	17.6	74
R_{SB}	3 and 4	0.06 (0.11)	−1.0 (1.7)	0.07	14.7	75
R_B	5 and 6	0.38 (0.08)	+3.1 (1.2)	0.46	10.6	81

The estimates of $E(p_\infty)$ and $S(p_\infty)$ from (4) and (5) are

$$E(p^S_\infty) = -12.2, \; S(p^S_\infty) = 19.8$$
$$E(p^{SB}_\infty) = -1.1, \; S(p^{SB}_\infty) = 14.8$$
$$E(p^B_\infty) = +5.0, \; S(p^B_\infty) = 11.4 .$$

From these estimates of $E(p_\infty)$ it is clear that $E(p^S_\infty) < E(p^{SB}_\infty) < E(p^B_\infty)$. The null hypothesis that these means came from a common population is rejected by an F test at $a < 0.001$, which supports H_3. The importance of this test is that the estimate of $E(p_\infty)$ under each trading condition utilizes all the information in the samples, as opposed to the previous test which utilized only the a priori assumed equilibrium transactions in periods 4 and 5. The estimates of $E(p_\infty)$ provide predictions of the deviations from the theoretical equilibrium based upon the convergence tendencies reflected in the entire data. If H_3 had not been supported by this calculation then there would be serious question as to the validity of the assumption that trading periods 4 and 5 represented a sufficiently close approximation to equilibrium.

(d) Test of H_4

Examination of the a coefficients in Table IV reveals that a is greater under conditions R_S and R_B than under R_{SB}, as predicted. An F test of the null hypothesis that the three a coefficients shown in the last three rows of column 3, Table IV, came from a common population is rejected at $a < 0.001$. Rejection of the null hypothesis in favor of differences as predicted confirms hypothesis H_4.

The distinct effect of trading condition on the parameters of the stochastic difference equations summarized in Table IV, suggests the possibility of comprehending these results and those of the previous analysis of variance in a more general nonlinear regression hypothesis in which the trading condition variables are treated explicitly. For this purpose we introduce the binary variables S, B and SB, where

$$S = \begin{cases} 1, & \text{Sellers making quotations} \\ 0, & \text{Sellers not making quotations} \end{cases}$$

$$B = \begin{cases} 1, & \text{Buyers making quotations} \\ 0, & \text{Buyers not making quotations.} \end{cases}$$

Thus, when both sellers and buyers are making quotations $SB = 1$, otherwise $SB = 0$. The general nonlinear (in B, S and p_t) or "interaction" hypothesis is

$$(1') \qquad p_{t+1} = a_{00} + a_{0S}S + a_{0B}B + (a_S S + a_B B + a_{SB}SB)\, p_t + \epsilon_{t+1}$$

in which $a_0 = a_{00} + a_{0S}S + a_{0B}B$ and $a = a_S S + a_B B + a_{SB}SB$, from (1) and (1′). The empirical results of this regression are contained in Table V.

TABLE V

Coefficient	Least Squares Estimate	Standard Error	t Ratio	F Ratio
a_{00}	−2.5	0.63	−4.01	16.0
a_{0S}	−4.1	2.35	−1.73	3.0
a_{0B}	5.6	2.54	2.20	4.8
a_S	0.46	0.07	6.15	37.8
a_B	0.38	0.11	3.37	11.4
a_{SB}	−0.77	0.17	−4.55	20.7

a_{0S} is significant at approximately the .04 level. The remaining coefficients are significant at the .01 level or lower. The significance of a_{0S} and a_{0B} implies that the organization variables B and S have an important effect on the *equilibrium states* toward which these markets are tending. The high significance levels of a_S, a_B and a_{SB}

implies that these organization variables have an even more reliable effect on the *speed* with which our experimental markets converge.

V. A Bayesian Subjective Probability Analysis

In this section a Bayesian analysis[2] will be developed for the following hypothesis:

H: In the population of competive market equilibrium transactions (defined as trading periods 4 and 5) contract prices are ordered $P_t^S < P_t^{SB} < P_t^B$. Based upon certain a priori specified probabilities, and the outcome of the experiments, the objective will be to compute the posterior probability that H is true.

In comparing corresponding equilibrium transactions under the conditions R_S and R_{SB}, let O_S be the sample outcome $\hat{P}_t^S < \hat{P}_t^{SB}$ on the tth transaction, and $\bar{O}_S$ be the outcome $\hat{P}_t^S \geqq \hat{P}_t^{SB}$. Similarly under the conditions R_{SB} and R_B, let O_B be the sample outcome $\hat{P}_t^{SB} < \hat{P}_t^B$, and $\bar{O}_B$ be the outcome $P_t^{SB} \geqq P_t^B$. Before performing the experiments two kinds of prior probability assignments must be, and were, specified:

(i) The a priori degree of belief or probability that the hypothesis is true, $P(H)$, and the probability that the hypothesis is false $P(\bar{H}) = 1 - P(H)$. My assignments were

$$P(H) = 0.6$$

$$P(\bar{H}) = 0.4.$$

Thus, from the pilot experiment and my experience with these kinds of experiments generally, I was prepared to give odds of 1.5 to 1 that the ordering relation in H represented the true state of nature.

(ii) The a priori degree of confidence in the ability of observations from the six experimental sessions to confirm or disconfirm the hypothesis if it is true, or if it is false. These conditional prior probabilities can be written

$$P(O_S \cap O_B|H) = p_1 \qquad P(O_S \cap O_B|\bar{H}) = q_1$$

$$P(O_S \cap \bar{O}_B|H) = p_2 \qquad P(O_S \cap \bar{O}_B|\bar{H}) = q_2$$

$$P(\bar{O}_S \cap O_B|H) = p_3 \qquad P(\bar{O}_S \cap O_B|\bar{H}) = q_3$$

$$P(\bar{O}_S \cap \bar{O}_B|H) = 1 - p_1 - p_2 - p_3 \qquad P(\bar{O}_S \cap \bar{O}_B|\bar{H}) = 1 - q_1 - q_2 - q_3$$

2. See e.g., L. J. Savage, "Bayesian Statistics" in R. E. Machol and Paul Grey (eds.), *Recent Developments in Information and Decisions Processes* (New York: MacMillan, 1962).

where $P(O_S \cap O_B|H)$ is the a priori probability that the relation $\hat{P}^S_t < \hat{P}^{SB}_t < \hat{P}^B_t$ would hold on the $t\overset{th}{-}$ transaction if the hypothesis were known to be true. It represents the degree of confidence in the ability of the experimental sessions, under both the deviant conditions R_S and R_B, to confirm the hypothesis if it is true. Similarly, $P(O_S \cap \bar{O}_B|H)$, is the probability that the ordering relation $\hat{P}^S_t < \hat{P}^{SB}_t \geqq \hat{P}^B_t$ would hold on the $t\overset{th}{-}$ transaction if H were true, i.e., the left half of the ordering relation in H would be confirmed, but not the right half. Again, $P(O_S \cap O_B|\bar{H})$ is the probability that the ordering relation in H would be confirmed by the $t\overset{th}{-}$ transaction though H were false. This is, of course, entirely likely due to experimental error — the effect of random elements not controlled in the experiment.

My prior assignments were

$$\begin{aligned} p_1 &= 0.55 & q_1 &= 0.25 \\ p_2 &= 0.15 & q_2 &= 0.25 \\ p_3 &= 0.15 & q_3 &= 0.25 \\ p_4 &= 0.15 & q_4 &= 0.25. \end{aligned}$$

I was prepared to believe that if H were true, a conservative estimate of 55 out of 100 trials of transactions under R_S, R_{SB} and R_B, would be consistent with H. I guessed that 15 per cent of the transactions would violate either the left, right, or both halves of the ordering relation, if H were true. If H were false, then I felt there was no reason to expect any sample outcome to be more likely than any other ($q_1 = q_2 = q_3 = q_4$). If, for example, the condition R_S does not introduce a downward bias in equilibrium prices then I would expect $\hat{P}^S_t$ to be as likely above as below $\hat{P}^{SB}_t$.

Now let E_{n,n_i} be the event that of the total number, n, of equilibrium transactions, $O_S \cap O_B$ (both the left and right halves of the ordering relation in H is confirmed by the sample outcome) occurs n_1 times, $O_S \cap \bar{O}_B$ occurs n_2 times, $\bar{O}_S \cap O_B$ occurs n_3 times, and $\bar{O}_S \cap \bar{O}_B$ occurs $n - n_1 - n_2 - n_3$ times. Hence, if the observations are independent (equilibrium), the conditional distribution of the n_i are given by the multinomials

$$(6) \quad P(E_{n,n_i}|H) = \frac{n!p_1^{n_1}p_2^{n_2}p_3^{n_3}(1 - p_1 - p_2 - p_3)^{n-n_1-n_2-n}}{n_1!n_2!n_3!(n - n_1 - n_2 - n_3)!}$$

$$(7) \quad P(E_{n,n}|\bar{H}) = \frac{n!q_1^{n}\,q_2^{n}\,q_3^{n}\,(1 - q_1 - q_2 - q_3)^{n-n\,-n\,-n}}{n_1!n_2!n_3!(n - n_1 - n_2 - n_3)!}$$

From Bayes theorem, we can now write the posterior densities

$$(8) \qquad P(H|E_{n,n_i}) = \frac{P(E_{n,n_i}|H)\,P(H)}{P(E_{n,n_i}|H)\,P(H) + P(E_{n,n_i}|\bar{H})\,P(\bar{H})}$$

$$= \frac{p_1^{n_1} p_2^{n_2} p_3^{n_3} (1 - p_1 - p_2 - p_3)^{n-n_1-n_2-n_3} P(H)}{p_1^{n_1} p_2^{n_2} p_3^{n_3} (1 - p_1 - p_2 - p_3)^{n-n_1-n_2-n_3} P(H) + q_1^{n_1} q_2^{n_2} q_3^{n_3} (1 - q_1 - q_2 - q_3)^{n-n_1-n_2-n_3} P(\bar{H})}$$

$$(9) \qquad P(\bar{H}|E_{n,n_i}) = 1 - P(H|E_{n,n_i}).$$

From the data of our six experimental sessions (see Charts 1–6), we have[3] $n = 31$, $n_1 = 14$, $n_2 = 10$, $n_3 = 3$, $n_4 = 4$. Applying (8) and (9) to these results and the prior probabilities specified above we compute $P(H|E_{n,n_i}) = 0.94$, $P(\bar{H}|E_{n,n_i}) = 0.06$.

I now stand 94 per cent sure that H is true.

Appendix

Instructions for Market Experiment

1. This is an experiment in the economics of market decision-making. The National Science Foundation has provided funds for the conduct of this research. The instructions are simple, and if you follow them carefully and make good decisions you may earn a considerable amount of money which will be paid to you in cash at the end of the experiment.

2. In this experiment we are going to simulate a market in which some of you will be buyers and some of you will be sellers in a sequence of trading periods or market days. Two kinds of cards will now be passed out — a set of white cards and a set of yellow cards. Those of you who receive a white card will be sellers, and only sellers. Those of you who receive a yellow card are buyers, and only buyers. These cards have an identification number, which you are to ignore, on the side facing up. On the side facing down appears a figure or price in dollars and cents. You are not to reveal this price to anyone. It is your own private information.

3. If you have received a white card you are a seller of at most one unit of the fictitious commodity being sold in each trading

3. In sessions 1, 3 and 5 forming one trial set of observations, there are 16 transactions in periods 4 and 5 in sessions 1 and 3, and 15 transactions in session 5. I considered this set as representing 16 "trials," and counted the "missing" observation in session 5 against the hypothesis. Similarly there are 14 transactions in sessions 2 and 4, and 15 in session 6, giving 15 more trials for a total of 31. The missing observation in sessions 2 and 4 were counted against the hypothesis.

period. The price on the underside of your white card is the lowest price at which you are to sell your unit of this commodity in any trading period. If you have received a yellow card, you are a buyer of at most one unit of the commodity being sold in each trading period. The price on your yellow card is the maximum price at which you are to buy a unit of this commodity per trading period.

4. The payoffs are as follows: If you are a seller, and you were able to make a sale, you will receive 5 cents for having made a sale plus the difference between the price at which you sold and the price on your white card. Think of the price on your white card as your cost of production. Your profits depend directly upon your ability to sell above this cost, but you should be prepared to sell at this cost, and receive your 5 cent commission, if you can do no better. If you are a buyer, and make a purchase, you will receive a 5 cent commission plus the difference between the price on your card and the price at which you bought. Think of the price on your yellow card as the price you can get by reselling the unit in an entirely separate market, while the price at which you buy in this market is your cost. Your profits depend directly upon your ability to buy at a cost below the price on your card, but you should be prepared to buy at that price, and collect your 5 cents, if you cannot do better. The payoffs for each subject will be accumulated over several trading periods, and the total amount paid in cash at the very end of the experiment. You are not to reveal your profits to anyone until the experiment is completed. There is no penalty except the profits you lose from failing to make a contract.

5S. The market for this commodity is organized as follows: We open the market for a trading day. Any seller is free at any time to raise his hand and make a verbal offer to sell at any price which is *not below* the price on his white card. Any buyer is free to accept the offer of any seller but no buyer is to buy at a price above the price on his yellow card. As soon as an offer is accepted, a binding contract has been closed and the buyer and seller making the deal are to drop out of the market, making no more offers or contracts for the remainder of that trading period. This process continues for a period of several minutes, depending upon the volume of trading. You will be warned when the market is to close and a few more offers will be called for before actually closing. This completes a trading "day." We will then reopen the market for a new trading period, and so on, for a sequence of several periods.

6S. Some of you may be unable to make a purchase or sale in any trading period. Some of you will be able to make a purchase or sale in some trading periods, but not in others. There are likely to be many offers that are not accepted. You are to keep trying and you are to feel free to earn as much cash as you can. Except for the offers you are not to speak to any other subject until the experiment is completed.

5SB. The market for this commodity is organized as follows: We open the market for a trading day. Any buyer is then free at any time to raise his hand and make a verbal bid to buy at any price which *does not exceed* the price on his yellow card. Likewise, any seller is free at any time to raise his hand and make a verbal offer to sell at any price which is *not below* the price on his white card. Any seller is free to accept the bid of any buyer, and any buyer is free to accept the offer of any seller. As soon as a bid or offer is accepted, a binding contract has been closed and the buyer and seller making the deal are to drop out of the market, making no more bids, offers, or contracts for the remainder of that trading period. This process continues for a period of several minutes, depending upon the volume of trading. You will be warned when the market is to close and a few more bids and offers will be called for before actually closing. This completes a trading "day." We will then reopen the market for a new trading period, and so on, for a sequence of several periods.

6SB. Some of you may be unable to make a purchase or sale in any trading period. Some of you will be able to make a purchase or sale in some trading periods, but not in others. There are likely to be many bids and offers that are not accepted. You are to keep trying and you are to feel free to earn as much cash as you can. Except for the bids and offers you are not to speak to any other subject until the experiment is completed.

5B. The market for this commodity is organized as follows: We open the market for a trading day. Any buyer is free at any time to raise his hand and make a verbal bid to buy at any price which does *not exceed* the price on his yellow card. Any seller is free to accept the bid of any buyer but no seller is to sell at a price below the price on his white card. As soon as a bid is accepted, a binding contract has been closed and the buyer and seller making the deal are to drop out of the market, making no more bids or contracts for the remainder of that trading period. This process continues for a period of several minutes, depending upon the volume of trading. You will be warned when the market is to close and a few more bids will be called for before actually closing. This completes a trading "day." We will then reopen the market for a new trading period, and so on, for a sequence of several periods.

6B. Some of you may be unable to make a purchase or sale in any trading period. Some of you will be able to make a purchase or sale in some trading periods, but not in others. There are likely to be many bids that are not accepted. You are to keep trying and you are to feel free to earn as much cash as you can. Except for the bids you are not to speak to any other subject until the experiment is completed.

7. Are there any questions?

CRITIQUE AND COMMENT

Experiments at Ann Arbor indicate that rat life expectancy increases with a diet of ecstasy. Raffish rats live as long as eight years, the tests show, while puritan rats, on love-free and otherwise grim and grubby diets, succumb at five. The autobiographical parallel is tempting, but though "love" is said to be a good metabolizer, and though bacchanals have been recommended for the circulation, whether my two-and-fourscore years have been sustained by my devotion to both, or whether I am still here in spite of them, is only a lay opinion—and a "philosophy of life." The facts are rat facts.

—Igor Stravinsky

Extrapolation from rat to man, or from game simulations to the market-place or the summit conference, is done by the student of men and groups of men, not because he prefers to, but because he must. For how can the scientist inflict on Mr. Stravinsky or on U.S. Steel the rigid controls and intense, sustained observation necessary to obtain useful data? On the other hand, how can he be sure that his carefully designed laboratory experiments are valid tests of hypotheses about the natural world? This dilemma is explored in the present paper, and a framework for testing hypotheses is presented.

NATURE, THE EXPERIMENTAL LABORATORY, AND THE CREDIBILITY OF HYPOTHESES

by Donald B. Rice and Vernon L. Smith

Purdue University

INTRODUCTION

Hypothesis formulation and testing has been the primary means of extension of scientific knowledge in every discipline. Both the natural and social sciences have employed testing in the experimental laboratory to provide evidence as to the validity of hypotheses. In recent years, the classical techniques of experimental social psychology have been adapted for testing hypotheses in economic models of bilateral bargaining (Siegel & Fouraker, 1960), oligopoly (Fouraker & Siegel, 1961; Suppes & Carlsmith, 1962; Hoggatt, 1959), and large-group competitive-price formation (Smith, 1962). Since the data normally available to the economist are gathered for nonscientific purposes under uncontrolled and often incompletely specified conditions, it has been extremely difficult to construct satisfactory tests of economic propositions. For this reason the potential contribution of experimental methodology to economic knowledge is of unique importance. Yet these new developments raise a challenging question which is germane not only to economic applications but to the experimental method generally. What is the relevance of a laboratory experiment to the phenomena of nature or commerce, which is of primary interest to the scientist? The economist has no interest, as such, in sophomores playing game simulations of a duopoly[1] situation for money, unless the behavior of these subjects corresponds in some way to general economic behavior in similar decision situations. Though the economist's data from the actual business world are far from ideal, they are nonetheless from the world in which he is directly interested. When another, perhaps different, world is studied because the data

[1] Monopoly, duopoly, . . . oligopoly are markets consisting of one, two, . . . few competing sellers.

are better, the problem of the connection between the two worlds injects a new dimension of uncertainty. Since all laboratory experiments abstract in some degree from the natural environment of the phenomena under study, the problem is of universal extent.

This paper will attempt to clarify this problem by extending Bayesian subjective probability concepts to the testing of hypotheses in situations in which evidence is available from both a "natural" world and an experimental world. Within this framework the experimenter is provided with a systematic means of utilizing his a priori beliefs about the reliability and relevance of his experimental design, the reliability of his natural-world data, and the truth or falsity of the hypotheses under investigation. (For a fascinating and informative polemical discussion of the application of subjective probability concepts to hypothesis testing, see Savage [1962].)

MODELS AND THE TWO KINDS OF EVIDENCE

There are three event sets of interest to the experimenter: the set of events (outcomes) in the natural world (denoted by N), the set of outcomes predicted by the theoretical model under test (denoted by M), and

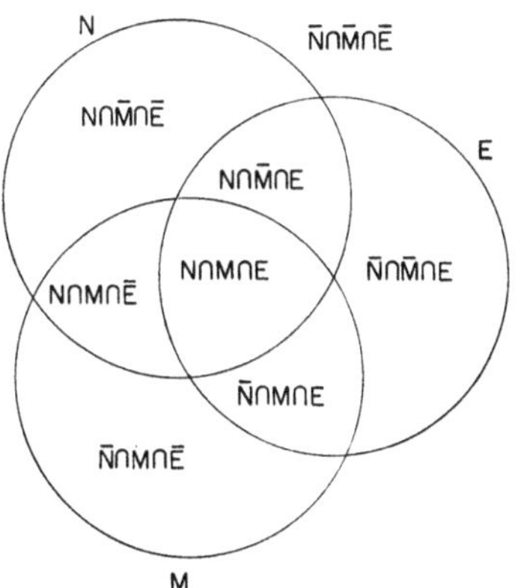

FIG. 1. Schematic Representation of Event Sets N (in the Natural World), M (Predicted by the Theoretical Model), and H (Experimental Outcomes).

the set of outcomes of the experiment being used to test the model (denoted by E). Figure 1 gives a schematic representation of these three sets.

Using the sets as denoted in Figure 1, the experimenter's first objective is to build his theoretical model such that $M \subset N$. Since theoretical models by their nature involve assumptions that simplify and abstract from reality, M will seldom be fully contained in N. The experimenter's second objective is to set $E \equiv M$. Because of the impossibility of perfectly duplicating in the laboratory the environment assumed in the model, this perfect equality will never exist.

The set $[(N \cap M \cap E) \cup (\bar{N} \cap M \cap E)] = (M \cap E)$ constitutes the "validity" of the experiment but $(\bar{N} \cap M \cap E)$ is a part of this validity which contains bias due to M not being fully contained in N. Furthermore, $(N \cap \bar{M} \cap E)$ represents experimental outcomes which correlate with events in the natural world but which do not correlate with outcomes predicted by the model. The set $(\bar{N} \cap M \cap \bar{E})$ represents bias in the model which the experiment does not measure and which hence will not hurt the predictive power of the experiment. The set $(\bar{N} \cap \bar{M} \cap E)$ represents experimental data which do not correlate with either the events observed in the natural world or with the predictions of the model because of the discrepancies discussed above. We suggest that the experimenter must be aware of the existence of all of these possible event sets in order to make rational statements about his beliefs concerning the model he has tested.

AN EXTENSION OF BAYESIAN FORMALISM

More specifically, suppose we have a theoretical model with perhaps several implications, one of which has been selected as a specific hypothesis to be tested. We introduce the following definitions:

- *H:* A set of events corresponding to the particular hypothesis being true. Referring to the previous section we have $H \subset M$.
- *$\bar{H}$:* A set of events corresponding to the hypothesis being false.
- *N:* A set of events in the natural world

which are consistent with or confirm the prediction of the hypothesis.

$\bar{N}$: Not N.

E: A set of events in the experimental laboratory which are consistent with or confirm the prediction of the hypothesis.

$\bar{E}$: Not E.

It is assumed that we can obtain joint observations on the phenomenon of interest in both the natural world and the experimental laboratory. These observations yield different evidence on the validity of the hypothesis. In each case the observations are subject to error (i.e., the effect of variables which cannot be controlled). Thus, economic theory predicts that a *ceteris paribus* increase in demand will increase price. In the natural world, when prices rise, this may be due to an increase in demand, a decrease in supply, or some combination of changes in supply and demand. We cannot control demand or supply in the natural world. However, we do "control" the environment in the sense that we know it is real. In the experimental laboratory, when prices increase with a controlled increase in demand and a controlled stationary supply, this may be due to the increase in demand, but also it could be due to the artificial character of the experimental environment. We can only imperfectly duplicate the natural world environment in an experimental laboratory.

A good example from recent experimental work concerns the hypothesis that there is a greater tendency toward tacit co-operation (joint profit maximization) than toward competition in oligopoly price determination. The experimental work so far tends to disconfirm this hypothesis, by demonstrating a strong tendency of subjects to reach or approach a competitive solution in simple duopoly and triopoly price-decision games (Fouraker & Siegel, 1961). Yet it is quite plain that such results may not hold in the business world, in which the price-making environment is different from that of the laboratory. Indirect evidence from the business world gives the surface impression of conflicting with these experimental results. Price stability and high profits are sometimes cited as indirect evidence of tacit if not formal co-operation in industries composed of a small number of firms. But such evidence is not conclusive. Price stability may be due to stable demand-cost relationships, and high profits may be necessary to induce even a few firms to produce if the risks are large. The evidence from the natural world is therefore tenuous, while the experimental work, though it provides highly consistent results which cannot be lightly swept aside, is open to the charge of having abstracted too much from the real situation.

Figure 2 is a representation of the sets H, N, and E as defined above. Consider the intersection of H, N, and E, viz. $(H \cap N \cap E)$. The event or events in $(H \cap N \cap E)$ correspond to the following: the hypothesis is true, the evidence from the natural world confirms the hypothesis, and the evidence from the laboratory confirms the hypothesis. In terms of the supply and demand example: It is true that a *ceteris paribus* increase in demand increases price, and in the natural world, supposed increases in income are correlated with increases in price (which, according to theory, provides evidence favoring the hypothesis), and in the experimental laboratory controlled increases in demand are followed by increases in contract prices (imperfect evidence favoring the hypothe-

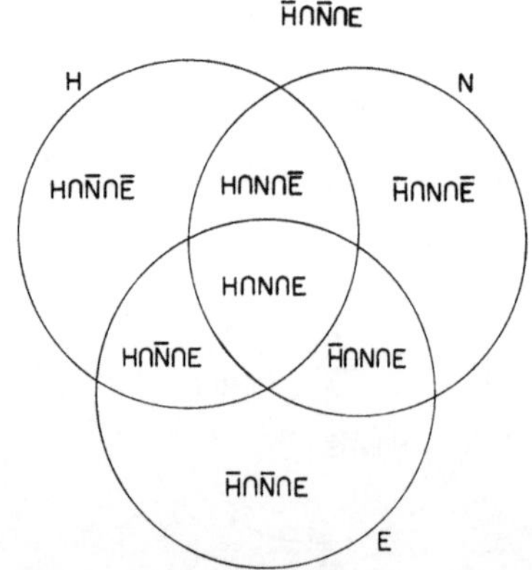

FIG. 2. Schematic Representation of Event Sets H (the Hypothesis is True), N (Natural Events Confirm the Hypothesis), and E (Experimental Events Confirm the Hypothesis).

sis). Similarly $(\bar{H} \cap N \cap E)$ corresponds to the hypothesis actually being false, and yet being confirmed by evidence in the natural world and in the experimental laboratory. This is, of course, a possible event because the evidence is subject to uncertainty.

In fact, everything is uncertain. It is uncertain whether the hypothesis is true or false, and our evidence from both the natural world and the experimental world provides uncertain confirmation or nonconfirmation of the hypothesis. Yet, we must make a judgment, based on the evidence, as to the validity of the hypothesis. What we should like to do, given this uncertainty, is to be able to make probability statements like:

$P(H \mid E \cap N)$ = the probability that the hypothesis is true given that the evidence from both the natural world and the experimental laboratory supports the hypothesis.

$P(H \mid E \cap \bar{N})$ = the probability that the hypothesis is true given that the evidence from the experimental laboratory supports, while the evidence from the natural world fails to support, the hypothesis.

And so on.

Furthermore, it is unreasonable to suppose that we can expect anyone to make such statements on the basis of the observed evidence alone. In addition to the evidence, such statements will and should be influenced by: (a) how strongly we really believe in H or $\bar{H}$, (b) how reliable we think the evidence from the natural world is and (c) how reliable we think the experimental evidence is including how relevant the experiment is to the issues being studied.

So we assume that the scientist can provide (in fact we require him to provide) the following a priori probability assignments:

(a) $P(H)$, $P(\bar{H})$. These represent his a priori degree of belief in the truth or falsity of the hypothesis.

(b) $P(E \cap N \mid H)$, $P(E \cap \bar{N} \mid H)$,
$P(\bar{E} \cap N \mid H)$, $P(\bar{E} \cap \bar{N} \mid H)$
$P(E \cap N \mid \bar{H})$, $P(E \cap \bar{N} \mid \bar{H})$,
$P(\bar{E} \cap N \mid \bar{H})$, $P(\bar{E} \cap \bar{N} \mid \bar{H})$
These represent his a priori degree of belief in the reliability and relevancy of the two kinds of evidence.

Note that since

$$P(E \cap N \cap H) + P(E \cap \bar{N} \cap H) + P(\bar{E} \cap N \cap H) + P(\bar{E} \cap \bar{N} \cap H) = P(H),$$

we have

$$\frac{P(E \cap N \cap H)}{P(H)} + \frac{P(E \cap \bar{N} \cap H)}{P(H)} + \frac{P(\bar{E} \cap N \cap H)}{P(H)} + \frac{P(\bar{E} \cap \bar{N} \cap H)}{P(H)} = 1,$$

or,

$$P(E \cap N \mid H) + P(E \cap \bar{N} \mid H) + P(\bar{E} \cap N \mid H) + P(\bar{E} \cap \bar{N} \mid H) = 1.$$

Similarly,

$$P(E \cap N \mid \bar{H}) + P(E \cap \bar{N} \mid \bar{H}) + P(\bar{E} \cap N \mid \bar{H}) + P(\bar{E} \cap \bar{N} \mid \bar{H}) = 1$$

Thus a consistency requirement on the assignments in (b) is that the unit measure must be distributed among the assignments in the first row, and likewise for the second row.

Given these assignments required of the scientist, we then invoke Bayes' Theorem to compute the probability that the hypothesis is true (false) given the observed evidence from the natural and experimental worlds as follows:

$$(1) \quad P(H \mid E \cap N) = \frac{P(E \cap N \mid H)\, P(H)}{P(E \cap N)}$$

and

$$(2) \quad P(\bar{H} \mid E \cap N) = 1 - P(H \mid E \cap N)$$

$$(3) \quad P(H \mid E \cap \bar{N}) = \frac{P(E \cap \bar{N} \mid H)\, P(H)}{P(E \cap \bar{N})}$$

and

$$(4) \quad P(\bar{H} \mid E \cap \bar{N}) = 1 - P(H \mid E \cap \bar{N})$$

$$(5) \quad P(H \mid \bar{E} \cap N) - \frac{P(\bar{E} \cap N \mid H)\, P(H)}{P(\bar{E} \cap N)}$$

and

$$(6)\quad P(\bar{H} \mid \bar{E} \cap N) = 1 - P(H \mid \bar{E} \cap N)$$

$$(7)\quad P(H \mid \bar{E} \cap \bar{N}) = \frac{P(\bar{E} \cap \bar{N} \mid H)\, P(H)}{P(\bar{E} \cap \bar{N})}$$

and

$$(8)\quad P(\bar{H} \mid \bar{E} \cap \bar{N}) = 1 - P(H \mid \bar{E} \cap \bar{N})$$

where

$$\begin{aligned} P(E \cap N) &= P(E \cap N \mid H)\, P(H) + P(E \cap N \mid \bar{H})\, P(\bar{H}) \\ P(E \cap \bar{N}) &= P(E \cap \bar{N} \mid H)\, P(H) + P(E \cap \bar{N} \mid \bar{H})\, P(\bar{H}) \\ P(\bar{E} \cap N) &= P(\bar{E} \cap N \mid H)\, P(H) + P(\bar{E} \cap N \mid \bar{H})\, P(\bar{H}) \\ P(\bar{E} \cap \bar{N}) &= P(\bar{E} \cap \bar{N} \mid H)\, P(H) + P(\bar{E} \cap \bar{N} \mid \bar{H})\, P(\bar{H}) \end{aligned}$$

The experimenter need not assign the conditional probabilities given H or $\bar{H}$ for the occurrence of the joint events $E \cap N$, $E \cap \bar{N}$, $\bar{E} \cap N$, and $\bar{E} \cap \bar{N}$ if he is willing to assume that N is independent of E, $\bar{N}$ of E, N of $\bar{E}$, and $\bar{N}$ of $\bar{E}$. That is, if the observations from the natural world support the hypothesis, and this knowledge does not change the probability that the experimental outcomes will or will not support the hypothesis and vice versa, then the task of making a priori assignments may be lightened. Under this assumption, which may be plausible, the scientist must specify the following simpler conditional probabilities:

$$\begin{aligned} &P(E \mid H),\ P(\bar{E} \mid H) \\ &P(N \mid H),\ P(\bar{N} \mid H) \\ &P(E \mid \bar{H}),\ P(\bar{E} \mid \bar{H}) \\ &P(N \mid \bar{H}),\ P(\bar{N} \mid \bar{H}) \end{aligned}$$

Again, the unit measure must be distributed on each row. Then the assignments required in (b) above may be calculated as follows:

$$\begin{aligned} P(E \cap N \mid H) &= P(E \mid H) \cdot P(N \mid H) \\ P(E \cap \bar{N} \mid H) &= P(E \mid H) \cdot P(\bar{N} \mid H) \\ P(\bar{E} \cap N \mid H) &= P(\bar{E} \mid H) \cdot P(N \mid H) \\ P(\bar{E} \cap \bar{N} \mid H) &= P(\bar{E} \mid H) \cdot P(\bar{N} \mid H) \\ P(E \cap N \mid \bar{H}) &= P(E \mid \bar{H}) \cdot P(N \mid \bar{H}) \\ P(E \cap \bar{N} \mid \bar{H}) &= P(E \mid \bar{H}) \cdot P(\bar{N} \mid \bar{H}) \\ P(\bar{E} \cap N \mid \bar{H}) &= P(\bar{E} \mid \bar{H}) \cdot P(N \mid \bar{H}) \\ P(\bar{E} \cap \bar{N} \mid \bar{H}) &= P(\bar{E} \mid \bar{H}) \cdot P(\bar{N} \mid \bar{H}) \end{aligned}$$

The unit measure will be distributed on these as previously required and Bayes' Theorem is then applied as before.

The prior probability assignments required in (a) are well known and have received considerable discussion by Bayesian statisticians (Savage, 1962, p. 165). The conditional priors in (b) extend somewhat the usual treatment and call for additional comment. They express the scientist's a priori degree of belief in the reliability of the observations in the laboratory and in the natural world; they also express his degree of belief in the relevance of each kind of evidence to the hypothesis under study. In particular, the relevance of an experiment to real-world situations may be an important issue here. Drawing on our previous example, suppose you believe that an experimental game in oligopoly pricing, played by sophomores for small sums of money, has nothing to do with real oligopoly tendencies to a co-operative price equilibrium. If the hypothesis of co-operative tendencies is true, then regardless of the objective outcome of a gaming experiment, you would consider the result to neither confirm nor deny the hypothesis. This condition of indifference is reflected in the a priori specification $P(E \cap N \mid H) = P(\bar{E} \cap N \mid H)$, and $P(E \cap \bar{N} \mid H) = P(\bar{E} \cap \bar{N} \mid H)$. That is, if H is true, the occurrence of believable experimental outcomes that are consistent with H are as likely as outcomes that are inconsistent with H. Similar statements hold conditional upon $\bar{H}$. If such extreme conditions are imposed, then from the Bayesian transformation (1)–(8), we get a posteriori probability conditions like $P(H \mid \bar{E} \cap N) = P(H \mid E \cap N), P(H \mid \bar{E} \cap \bar{N}) = P(H \mid E \cap \bar{N})$ and so on, which state that experimental observations will not affect the investigator's belief in H. Only natural-world observations will alter this belief. This is an extreme example, but it may help to clarify the manner in which a disproportionate confidence in one type of evidence formally influences the relationship between observation and scientific belief in our extension of the Bayesian scheme.

A THEOREM ON REPEATED OBSERVATIONS

In the previous section we assumed that the hypothesis was to be tested by making a 2-element observation, consisting of an observation in the laboratory and one in the natural world. Let the conditional prior probabilities of each of the four possible outcomes of such a compound observation be

$$\begin{aligned} P(E \cap N \mid H) &= p_1 & P(E \cap N \mid \bar{H}) &= q_1 \\ P(E \cap \bar{N} \mid H) &= p_2 & P(E \cap \bar{N} \mid \bar{H}) &= q_2 \\ P(\bar{E} \cap N \mid H) &= p_3 & P(\bar{E} \cap N \mid \bar{H}) &= q_3 \\ P(\bar{E} \cap \bar{N} \mid H) &= p_4 & P(\bar{E} \cap \bar{N} \mid \bar{H}) &= q_4 \end{aligned}$$

where $\sum_{i=1}^{4} p_i = 1$ where $\sum_{i=1}^{4} q_i = 1$

Now suppose that we can make repeated observations, and let $S_n = S_n(n_1, n_2, n_3)$ be the event that of n observations, the outcome $E \cap N$ is observed n_1 times, $\bar{E} \cap \bar{N}$ occurs n_2 times, $\bar{E} \cap N$ occurs n_3 times, and $\bar{E} \cap \bar{N}$ occurs $n - n_1 - n_2 - n_3$ times. If the observations are independent, the joint distribution of the n_i is the multinomial

$$P(S_n \mid H) = \frac{n!\, p_1^{n_1} p_2^{n_2} p_3^{n_3} p_4^{n-n_1-n_2-n_3}}{n_1!\, n_2!\, n_3!\, (n - n_1 - n_2 - n_3)!} \tag{9}$$

Similarly

$$P(S_n \mid \bar{H}) = \frac{n!\, q_1^{n_1} q_2^{n_2} q_3^{n_3} q_4^{n-n_1-n_2-n_3}}{n_1!\, n_2!\, n_3!\, (n - n_1 - n_2 - n)_3!} \tag{10}$$

The conditional posterior probabilities, given the evidence from these n observations, are

$$P(H \mid S_n) = \frac{P(S_n \mid H)\, P(H)}{P(S_n)}$$

$$P(\bar{H} \mid S_n) = 1 - P(H \mid S_n).$$

Hence, the a posteriori odds of the event H (i.e. the odds that the hypothesis is true as against its being false), are

$$\frac{P(H \mid S_n)}{P(\bar{H} \mid S_n)} = \frac{p_1^{n_1} p_2^{n_2} p_3^{n_3} p_4^{n-n_1-n_2-n_3} P(H)}{q_1^{n_1} q_2^{n_2} q_3^{n_3} q_4^{n-n_1-n_2-n_3} P(\bar{H})}. \tag{11}$$

Intuitively we would expect that as the number of observations is increased, the a priori odds of the event H, viz. $P(H)/P(\bar{H})$ should have a decreasing influence on our belief in the truth or falsity of the hypothesis, and in the limit as $n \to \infty$ we should be certain whether H or $\bar{H}$ holds. We show this by proving the following theorem

If $p_i \neq q_i$, for some $i = 1, 2, 3, 4$, $P(H) \neq 0$, $P(\bar{H}) \neq 0$, then $\lim_{n\to\infty} P[L_n < C \mid H] = 0$, for any $C > 0$, if H is true, where L_n is the random variable defined by

$$\begin{aligned} L_n &= \log \frac{P(H \mid S_n)}{P(\bar{H} \mid S_n)} \\ &= \sum_{i=1}^{3} n_i \log\left(\frac{p_i q_4}{q_i p_4}\right) + n \log \frac{p_4}{q_4} \\ &\qquad + \log \frac{P(H)}{P(\bar{H})}. \end{aligned} \tag{12}$$

The proof is a multinomial extension of a proof by K. J. Arrow[2] using the binomial for one kind of evidence.

The conditional multinomial densities in (9) and (10) have means, variances, and covariances given by

$$\begin{cases} E(n_i \mid H) = np_i, \\ \sigma_{ii}(n_i, n_i \mid H) = np_i(1 - p_i), \\ \sigma_{ij}(n_i, n_j \mid H) = -np_ip_j \end{cases} \quad i, j = 1,2,3,4 \tag{13a}$$

$$\begin{cases} E(n_i \mid \bar{H}) = nq_i, \\ \sigma_{ii}(n_i, n_i \mid \bar{H}) = nq_i(1 - q_i), \\ \sigma_{ij}(n_i, n_j \mid H) = -nq_iq_j \end{cases} \quad i, j = 1,2,3,4 \tag{13b}$$

Taking the expectation of (12), conditional upon H being true, and substituting the means from (13a) gives

$$\begin{aligned} E(L_n \mid H) &= n \sum_{i=1}^{4} [p_i \log p_i - p_i \log q_i] \\ &\qquad + \log \frac{P(H)}{P(H)}. \\ &= an + h \end{aligned} \tag{14}$$

where a and h are constants.

We next show that a is positive by showing that the function

$$f(q_1, q_2, q_3, q_4) = \sum_{i=1}^{4} p_i \log q_i \tag{15}$$

[2] Personal communication, 1961.

reaches a unique maximum at $q_i = p_i$. (15) is maximized subject to $\sum_{i=1}^{4} q_i = 1$ by forming the Lagrangian $\phi = \sum_{i=1}^{4} p_i \log q_i - \lambda\left(\sum_{i=1}^{4} q_i - 1\right)$. Necessary conditions for a maximum are $p_j/q_j = \lambda$. Since $\sum_{i=1}^{4} q_i = \sum_{i=1}^{4} p_i = 1$, it follows that $\lambda = 1$. Hence, the necessary conditions become

$$p_j = q_j, \qquad j = 1,2,3,4. \tag{16}$$

Since the following determinant of second partial derivatives of the Lagrangian function,

$$\begin{vmatrix} & & & & \phi_{\lambda 1} \\ & & & & \phi_{\lambda 2} \\ & \phi_{ij} & & & \phi_{\lambda 3} \\ & & & & \phi_{\lambda 4} \\ \phi_{\lambda 1} & \phi_{\lambda 2} & \phi_{\lambda 3} & \phi_{\lambda 4} & \phi_{\lambda\lambda} \end{vmatrix} = \begin{vmatrix} -\frac{p_1}{q_1^2} & 0 & 0 & 0 & 1 \\ 0 & -\frac{p_2}{q_2^2} & 0 & 0 & 1 \\ 0 & 0 & -\frac{p_3}{q_3^2} & 0 & 1 \\ 0 & 0 & 0 & -\frac{p_4}{q_4^2} & 1 \\ 1 & 1 & 1 & 1 & 0 \end{vmatrix},$$

is positive with its principal minors alternating in sign, the conditions (16) define a unique maximum of f. Therefore,

$$a = \sum_{i=1}^{4} [p_i \log p_i - p_i \log q_i] > 0$$

if $p_j \neq q_j$ for some j. Hence, as n increases in (14) the a priori odds, h, recede in importance. But note that the *rate* at which h becomes unimportant depends upon a. If the p_i are almost equal to the q_i, indicating a very low level of confidence in both kinds of evidence, then a will be small, and n must be correspondingly larger in order to render h negligible.

From (12) and the variances in (13a), the conditional variance of L_n can be written

$$\sigma^2(L_n \mid H) = n\left[\sum_{j=1}^{3} p_i(1 - p_i) \log^2\left(\frac{p_i q_4}{q_i p_4}\right) - 2\sum_{j=1}^{3}\sum_{i=1}^{3} p_i p_j \log\left(\frac{p_i q_4}{q_i p_4}\right) \log\left(\frac{p_i q_4}{q_i p_4}\right)\right] = bn \tag{17}$$

where b is a constant.

Now, if $L_n < C$, then $L_n - E(L_n \mid H) < C - an - h$. And if n is sufficiently large so that $an + h > C$, then $C < E(L_n \mid H)$, and the event $|L_n - E(L_n \mid H)| > an + h - C$ contains the event $[L_n < C]$ as its left tail. It follows that

$$\begin{aligned} P(L_n < C \mid H) &\le P[\,|L_n - E(L_n \mid H)| > an + h - C] \\ &\le \frac{\sigma^2(L_n \mid H)}{(an + h - C)^2} = \frac{bn}{(an + h - C)^2} \to 0, \end{aligned}$$

as $n \to \infty$, by Tchebysheff's inequality, which proves the theorem (Lindgren, 1962, p. 61).

The multinomial analysis of repeated observations reduces to the conventional binomial analysis if we have no confidence in one of the two kinds of evidence. For example, if we do not believe in the experimental method for testing some particular hypothesis, then $p_1 = p_3$, $p_2 = p_4$, $q_1 = q_3$, $q_2 = q_4$, and the a posteriori odds of H in n trials are

$$\frac{P(H \mid S_n)}{P(\bar{H} \mid S_n)} = \frac{p_1^{n_1+n_3} p_2^{n-(n_1+n_3)} P(H)}{q_1^{n_1+n_3} q_2^{n-(n_1+n_3)} P(\bar{H})} = \frac{p^{n_1+n_3}(1-p)^{n-(n_1+n_3)} P(H)}{q^{n_1+n_3}(1-q)^{n-(n_1+n_3)} P(\bar{H})}$$

where $p = 2p_1$, $q = 2q_1$. The binomial model would also be appropriate if data were available from only one source, i.e., either the natural world or the experimental laboratory.

In summary, as long as we have some a priori degree of belief in the hypotheses, $P(H) \neq 0$, $P(\bar{H}) \neq 0$, and some a priori confidence in the discriminatory ability of the evidence, $p_j \neq q_j$, for some j[3], then by replication we can become as sure as we like which event H or $\bar{H}$ is actually true.

REFERENCES

Fouraker, L. E., & Siegel, S. *Bargaining behavior: II. Experiments in oligopoly.* University Park, Pa.: Pennsylvania State Univ., 1961.

Hoggatt, A. An experimental business game. *Behav. Science*, 1959, 4, 192–203.

Lindgren, B. W. *Statistical theory.* New York: Macmillan, 1962.

Savage, L. J. Bayesian statistics. In R. E. Machol & P. Grey (Eds.), *Recent developments in information and decision processes.* New York: Macmillan, 1962. Pp. 161–194.

Siegel, S., & Fouraker, L. E. *Bargaining and group decision making.* New York: McGraw-Hill, 1960.

Smith, V. L. Experimental studies of competitive market behavior. *J. polit. Econ.*, 1962, 70, 111–137.

Suppes, P., & Carlsmith, J. M. Experimental analysis of a duopoly situation. *Internat. econ. Rev.*, 1962, 3, 60–78.

[3] Note, for example, that if $p_j = q_j$, for all j then $P(E \cap N \mid H) = P(E \cap N \mid \bar{H})$, $P(E \cap \bar{N} \mid H) = P(E \cap \bar{N} \mid \bar{H})$, etc. Each possible outcome is as likely to be observed if H is true as if H is false. If this is our belief about the two kinds of evidence, then no amount of observation can change our degree of belief in the hypothesis. It is useless to look at either kind of evidence as our prior beliefs would not be altered by what we observed.

The actions of men are so various and uncertain, that the best statement of tendencies, which we can make in a science of human conduct, must needs be inexact and faulty. This might be urged as a reason against making any statements at all on the subject; but that would be almost to abandon life. Life is human conduct, and the thoughts and emotions that grow up around it. By the fundamental impulses of our nature we all—high and low, learned and unlearned—are in our several degrees constantly striving to understand the courses of human action, and to shape them for our purposes, whether selfish or unselfish, whether noble or ignoble. And since we *must* form to ourselves some notions of the tendencies of human action, our choice is between forming those notions carelessly and forming them carefully. The harder the task, the greater the need for steady patient inquiry; for turning to account the experience, that has been reaped by the more advanced physical sciences; and for framing as best we can well thought-out estimates, or provisional laws, of the tendencies of human action.

ALFRED MARSHALL, *Principles of Economics*

EXPERIMENTAL AUCTION MARKETS AND THE WALRASIAN HYPOTHESIS[1]

VERNON L. SMITH

Krannert Graduate School of Industrial Administration, Purdue University

THIS study reports on a block of experimental market sessions designed primarily to provide (1) the severest test yet attempted of the equilibrating forces operating in competitive auction markets and (2) a more rigorously controlled test of the Walrasian hypothesis.[2] Some data are also supplied which show the effect of cash payoffs on the equilibrating behavior of such markets; in particular, the effect of full cash payoffs to all successful trading subjects as against payoffs to a subset of such subjects chosen at random.

EXPERIMENTAL DESIGN AND SUBJECTS

The supply and demand conditions underlying the experimental design in this study were intentionally unconventional. In each experimental session, each of eleven subject buyers could purchase at most one unit of the fictitious commodity per trading period at a price not to exceed the limit price \$4.20. Therefore, the demand per unit of time, or trading period, was perfectly elastic at \$4.20 up to the maximum demand quantity of eleven units. In each session each subject seller could sell at most one unit of the commodity at any price not below the given minimum reservation price \$3.10. There were thirteen such sellers in two experimental sessions, sixteen in two additional experimental sessions, and nineteen in the final two markets. Therefore, the supply per trading period was perfectly elastic up to the maximum supply quantities of thirteen, sixteen, and nineteen units, respectively, in the three experimental treatments.

Each session was begun with a general statement that the group was being asked to participate in a decision-making experiment; that they would not be subjected to any unpleasant stimuli or experiences; and, furthermore, that they would have an opportunity to earn real money during their participation. Copies of instructions were passed out and read aloud to the entire group.[3] The payoff formula for each buyer in each trading period was \$0.05 for making a contract plus the difference between his limit buy price and his contract price. Each seller received \$0.05 for making a contract plus the difference between his contract price and his limit sell price.

Each subject trader had initial information only on his own limit price.[4] The additional information provided in the course of the market sessions consisted of the ordered public bids and offers announced by the individual traders. Since the public acceptance of a bid or offer constituted a contract, each trader knew which bids and offers were

[1] The research reported in this paper was supported by National Science Foundation grants G-24199 and GS-370 to Purdue University.

[2] An earlier paper (V. L. Smith, "An Experimental Study of Competitive Market Behavior," *Journal of Political Economy*, LXX [April, 1962], 126–34) seemed to provide sufficient evidence to warrant the tentative conclusion that a linear version of the well-known Walrasian hypthesis of competitive market-adjustment behavior was inferior to a linear test alternative called the "excess-rent hypothesis."

[3] The printed instructions given to each subject were reproduced in the Appendix to V. L. Smith, "Effect of Market Organization on Competitive Equilibrium," *Quarterly Journal of Economics*, LXXXVII (May, 1964), paragraphs 1–4, 5SB, 6SB, 199–201.

[4] The same subjects held the same limit price cards in all trading periods, and this fact was evident to all the subjects. They did not know that all buyers had the same limit prices, and all sellers had the same limit prices. They were not told the number of buyers or the number of sellers, but they soon became aware, in successive trading periods, that there was excess supply at the end of each trading period.

accepted and which were not. Under these information conditions it is difficult to imagine a test of the equilibrium tendencies in auction markets that would be more severe than the design described above. In equilibrium, with these supply and demand conditions, the entire rent in this market, (\$4.20–\$3.10)11 = \$12.10 per trading period, must be allocated to buyers! In full competitive equilibrium, each seller would receive only his "normal profit" commission of \$0.05 per transaction, while buyers receive \$1.15 per transaction. Under such cash-payoff conditions one would expect sellers to be very resistant to contract prices being forced down to the \$3.10 equilbrium. Thus, suppose each subject is assumed to have a utility function for additional income which is concave from below, and that an individual's bargaining resistance is proportional to marginal utility. Then the nearer is price to the \$3.10 equilibrium, the greater is seller resistance to a further reduction in price and the weaker is buyer resistance to an increase in price. The question is whether the competition created by excess sellers will produce equilibrium even under this condition of exaggerated imbalance in the rental rewards to bargaining.

The 162 subjects participating in these experiments were Sophomore and Junior students enrolled in three sections each of two undergraduate courses in economics. One course was introductory economics, the other introductory economic theory. Two replications were run under each of the three values, 2, 5, and 8 for the "treatment" variable, e = excess supply. Table 1 illustrates the over-all experimental design and indicates the combination of experimental conditions, course, and number of subjects associated with each session. No subject participated in more than one of the sessions. The sessions were run separately in each of two series separated by several months. Subjects were given no advance warning that an experiment was going to be performed in their class, and the experimental sessions discussed in this paper were intermingled with sessions for entirely different experiments. This procedure was used to minimize information transfer between subject groups.[5]

TABLE 1

NUMBER OF SUBJECTS AND EXPERIMENTAL CONDITION FOR EACH SESSION

Experimental Session No.	Condition			
	$e=2$	$e=5$	$e=8$	Total Subjects
Course 1	1 ($N=24$)	3 ($N=27$)	5 ($N=30$)	81
Course 2	2 ($N=24$)	4 ($N=27$)	6 ($N=30$)	81
Total subjects	48	54	60	162

EXPERIMENTAL DATA

Figures 1*A*–1*F*, corresponding to experimental sessions 1–6, provide complete series of contract prices in the order in which they were executed in the four trading periods of each session (six trading periods of session 1). Cash payoffs for the six sessions totaled \$342 of which \$281.70 represented the earnings of buyers, the remainder being earned by sellers. Motivation was excellent.

In spite of the extreme asymmetry in buyer and seller rent, it is seen that contract prices show a strong tendency to converge to the theoretical competitive equilibrium. It is also clear from these charts that the tendency to equilibrium is an increasing function of e (a precise measure of this tendency is discussed later in Table 2). In sessions 1 and 2 (e = 2), only six contracts were at equilibrium in trading periods 1–4;

[5] See Smith, "Effect of Market Organization on Competitive Equilibrium," *op. cit.*, pp. 184–86.

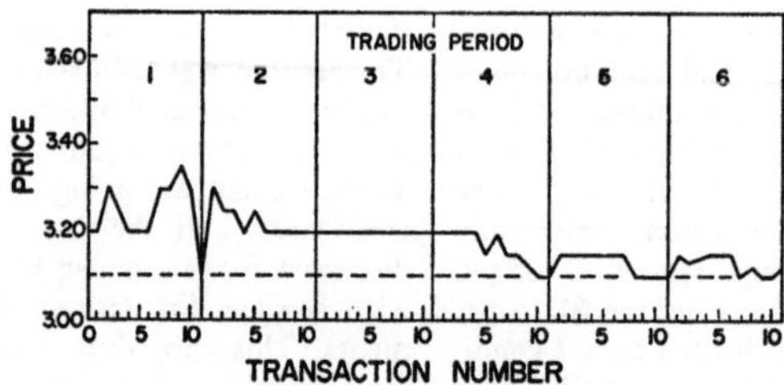

FIG. 1A.—Experimental session 1, $e = 2$

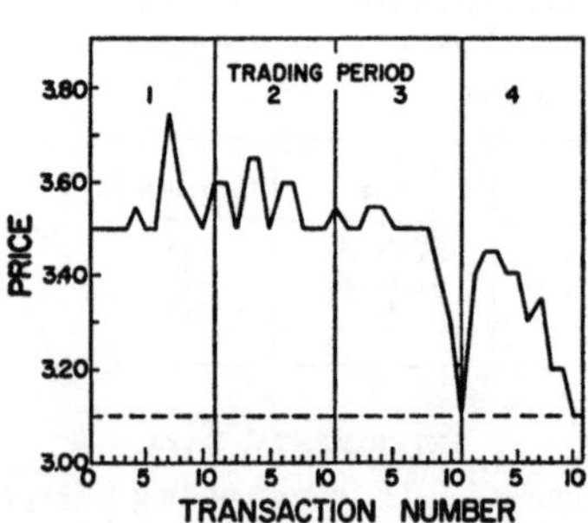

FIG. 1B.—Experimental session 2, $e = 2$

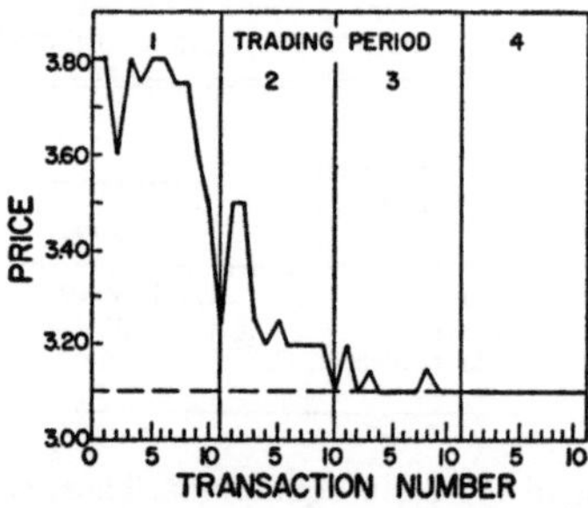

FIG. 1D.—Experimental session 4, $e = 5$

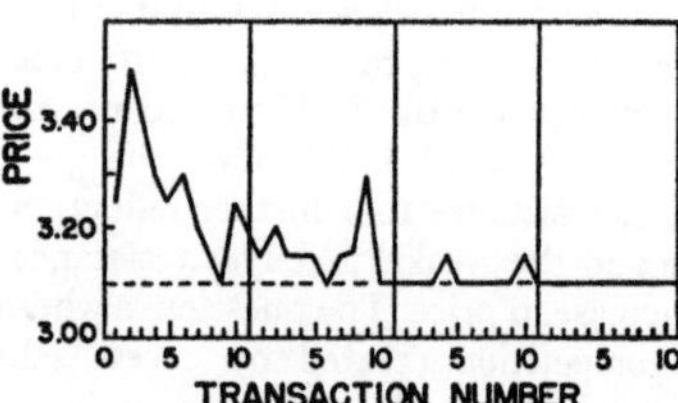

FIG. 1E.—Experimental session 5, $e = 8$

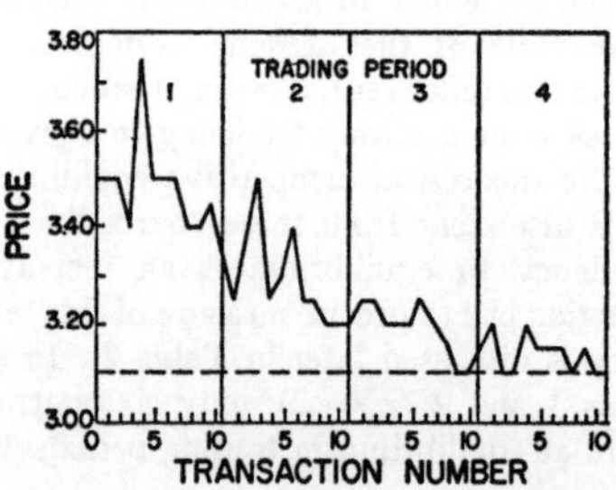

FIG. 1C.—Experimental session 3, $e = 5$

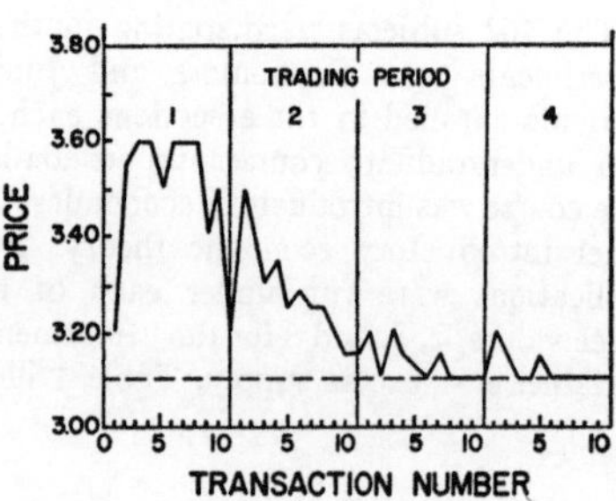

FIG. 1F.—Experimental session 6, $e = 8$

in sessions 3 and 4 ($e = 5$), twenty-seven contracts were at equilibrium; in sessions 5 and 6 ($e = 8$) there were thirty-seven such contracts. Two additional trading periods were run in experiment 1 to see if the added trading experience would produce equilibrium under the weak equilibrating condition, $e = 2$. From Figure 1*A* the convergence tendencies continue in evidence, though weakly, in trading periods 5 and 6.

Session 2 shows the degree to which it may be possible for sellers to maintain prices above equilibrium for comparatively long series of transactions when there are only two excess sellers in the market. In this session a form of temporary tacit co-operation among sellers produced a minimum price line of $3.50 until transaction 9 in period 3. This co-operative set was then broken by the seller who sold at $3.75 (yielding a cash payoff of $0.70) in period 1 and then failed to make a contract in period 2. Rather than fail again in period 3, he sold at $3.40. This, of course, alerted all buyers to the possibility of making contracts below $3.50, with the result that all remaining contracts in periods 3 and 4 were at prices below $3.50. In the absence of formal collusion and side payments, which were prohibited in these sessions, such tacit co-operation is extremely difficult to maintain. One "nervous" seller may be sufficient to break the co-operative set, and the probability of having at least one increases with e. Thus, with $e = 5$ and $e = 8$ in sessions 3–6, we see no such extensive "price lines" being established above $3.10.

From Figures 1*A* and 1*B* one might be tempted to conjecture that the initial contract price was highly significant in determining the course of the market. The initial contract in experiment 1 was at $3.20, and thereafter most contract prices were not far from this level. Experiment 2 began at $3.50 and did not fall below this level for some time. But experiment 6, as it happens, also began at $3.20 and rose much above this level for several transactions in spite of the large excess supply of eight units. Similarly, experiment 3 began at $3.50 but prices behaved differently than in experiment 2. First-period contracts tend to be very erratic and sensitive to subtle differences in the dynamics of different subject groups. The main trends that can be related to more traditional economic variables emerge more clearly after the first-period learning experience is completed.

TESTS OF THE WALRASIAN HYPOTHESIS

The major analytical purpose of this paper is to test the Walrasian hypothesis (WH) against a test alternative, the excess rent hypothesis (ERH). As we use them here, WH refers to the hypothesis that price tends to fall (rise) at a rate which is proportional to the excess supply (demand) at any given price and ERH refers to the hypothesis that price tends to fall (rise) at a rate proportional to excess economic rent at any given price, where excess rent is measured by the area between the supply and demand curves from the price in question down (or up) to the equilibrium price. In the present design, at the price p_t and an excess supply e, excess rent is $e\,(p_t - 310)$. The significance of this design is that e becomes a design constant under experimental control at all feasible contract prices. Furthermore, e is independent of which particular buyers and sellers are paired in each contract.

We should note that no a priori commitment to ERH is intended. It is WH which has a long, and by frequency of reference, perhaps a distinguished history. You cannot test any hypothesis except by reference to a competing test alternative, and ERH represents such a plausible alternative. In this experimental design, ERH turns out to have a distinct intuitive appeal. To see this, imagine price being temporarily "established" at p_t. If this price were to persist in further contracts, any seller failing to make a contract at p_t stands to forego a profit (rent) equal to $p_t - 310$ cents. If $e = 2$, so that we must have two sellers failing to make contracts, the total potential loss at p_t is $2(p_t - 310)$. Under ERH the assumption is that price-cutting occurs at a rate proportional to this potential monetary loss and is influenced both by the number of excess sellers *and* their individual potential losses. Thus, under ERH, the rate of price-cutting diminishes as p_t falls and the potential loss decreases. In other words, if you have a lot to lose by failing to make a contract, you are quick to undercut your competitors in order to increase your chances of making a sale; if you have little to lose by failing to make a contract, you are slower to undercut your competitiors. Under WH, price-cutting is independent of such potential trading losses, depending only on the constant excess supply on the market.

Mathematically, WH implies an adjustment equation of the following form:

$$\Delta p_{t+1} = p_{t+1} - p_t = \begin{cases} \beta e + u_{t+1}, \text{ if } p_t > p^0 - \beta e \\ u_{t+1}, \text{ if } p^0 \leq p_t \leq p^0 - \beta e, \ \beta < 0, \end{cases} \tag{1}$$

while ERH implies

$$\Delta p_{t+1} = p_{t+1} - p_t = \alpha e(p_t - p^0) + v_{t+1}, \quad \alpha < 0, \tag{2}$$

where $p^0 = 310$ is the theoretical equilibrium in cents, β is the adjustment speed coefficient under WH, α is the adjustment speed coefficient under ERH, and p_t is the contract price on the tth transaction. With this experimental design it is evident that the two hypotheses have quite distinct empirical implications. Phase lines for each of the two hypotheses are shown in Figure 2 for two levels of the control variable, e_1 and e_2, where $e_1 < e_2$. Under WH the phase lines all have a slope of unity, and increases in e simply shift these lines parallel to the right. Under ERH, the phase line has a slope less than unity and this slope is a decreasing function of e as shown. It is seen that our peculiar experimental supply and demand design provides a relatively crucial test of WH as opposed to ERH.

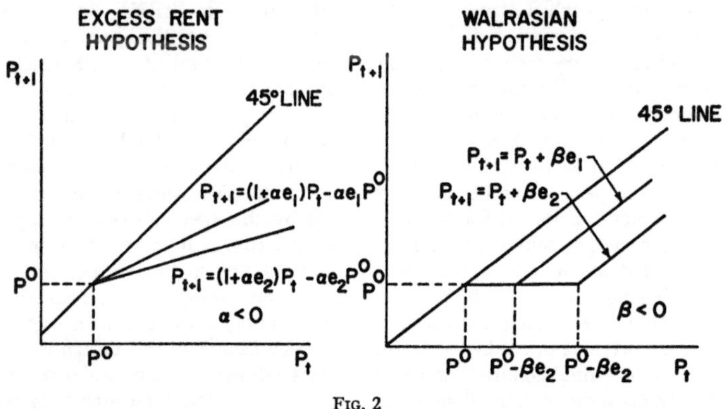

FIG. 2

Using this analysis and the data from the six experiments reported in the last section the test of WH against ERH is based upon the stochastic process defined by

$$\Delta p_{t+1} = p_{t+1} - p_t = \alpha_{01} + \alpha_1(p_t - p^0)e + \beta_1 e + \epsilon_{1,\,t+1}, \tag{3}$$

which is a general linear hypothesis containing both WH and ERH as special polar cases.

Table 2 shows the results of least-squares regression estimates of the coefficients of equations (1)–(3). Because of the "kink" in the phase line at $p_t = p^0 - \beta e$ (see Fig. 2) implied by WH, the regressions were performed using all the observations from the six experiments and again with the observations $0 \leq \hat{p}_t < 0.05$ omitted. The second regression reduces bias in favor of ERH by eliminating observations in the flat region of the kink. Under classical significance tests we see in either case, from the standard errors of $\hat{a}_1$ and $\hat{\beta}_1$, that $\hat{a}_1$ is quite significantly different from zero, whereas $\hat{\beta}_1$ is not.[6]

EFFECT OF CASH REWARDS ON CONVERGENCE

Before conducting the six experiments discussed above, two pilot experimental sessions were run. In the pilot sessions instead of paying every buyer (seller) who made a contract the difference between his contract price and his limit price plus $0.05, this amount was paid to four subjects selected at random at the end of each trading period. This reinforcement formula was made known to the subjects at the beginning of each of the pilot sessions. Expected rewards in these sessions would, of course, be much lower than with full cash payoffs to all trading subjects. The objective was to provide a low-cost means of testing the mechanics of the experimental technique prior to performing the six analysis sessions and to provide two control sessions with weak payoffs to determine the effect of reinforcement condition on convergence.

TABLE 2

REGRESSION ESTIMATES: WH VERSUS ERH

Observation Subsets	$p_{t+1}-p_t=a_{01}+a_1(p_t-p^0)e+\beta_1 e+\epsilon_{1,t+1}$*			$p_{t+1}-p_t$ $=a_{02}+a_2(p_t-p^0)e+\epsilon_{2,t+1}$		$p_{t+1}-p_t$ $=a_{03}+\beta_3 e+\epsilon_{3,t+1}$	
	$\hat{a}_{01}$	$\hat{a}_1$	$\hat{\beta}_1$	$\hat{a}_{02}$	$\hat{a}_2$	$\hat{a}_{03}$	$\hat{\beta}_3$
With all observations . ($N=259$)	−0.6134 (1.108)	−0.0226 (0.0051)	0.2198 (0.1952)	0.3419 (0.597)	−0.0213 (0.0050)	−1.3317 (0.507)	0.0258 (0.1972)
With $0\leq\hat{p}_t<0.05$ omitted.... ($N=189$)	−0.7216 (1.618)	−0.0204 (0.0073)	0.1595 (0.3008)	−0.2191 (0.873)	−0.0185 (0.0064)	−0.9868 (1.328)	−0.2469 (0.2679)

* Standard errors are shown in parentheses.

Table 3 provides least-squares estimates of the parameters of equation (4):

$$\pi_{t+1} = a_0 + \beta_0 \pi_t + \epsilon_{t+1}\,, \qquad (4)$$

where $\pi_t = p_t - p^0$. If we define

$$\lim_{t\to\infty} E(\pi_t) = E(\pi_\infty)\,,$$

as the expected deviation in experimental equilibrium price from the theoretical equilibrium, then it is readily shown that[7] $E(\pi_\infty)$

[6] Bayesian Report: If we assume a uniform joint prior distribution of a_1, β_1, μ, and $\log \sigma^2$, where $\mu = a_{01} + a_1(p_t - p^0)e + \beta_1 e$, in equation (3), then, under the assumptions of normal regression theory, the joint posterior distribution of a_1 and β_1 is bivariate normal, conditional on σ^2 with parameters

$$\hat{a}_1 = -0.0204\,, \qquad \hat{\beta}_1 = 0.1595\,,$$

$$\sigma(\hat{a}_1) = 0.073\,, \qquad \sigma(\hat{\beta}_1) = 0.3008\,,$$

$$\sigma = 0.2109\,,$$

for the regression with $N = 189$.

From these parameters and tables of ordinates and cumulative probabilities for the normal distribution we compute, using Bayes's theorem, the following posterior experimental odds favoring ERH as against WH:

$$\frac{P(\text{ERH})}{P(\text{WH})} = \frac{P\left(\frac{2}{e} < a_1 < 0,\ \beta_1 = 0\right)}{P(\beta_1 < 0,\ a_1 = 0)}$$

$$= \frac{P\left(-\frac{2}{e} < a_1 < 0 \,\middle|\, \beta_1 = 0\right) P(\beta_1 = 0)}{P(\beta_1 < 0 \mid a_1 = 0) P(a_1 = 0)} > 300\,.$$

The odds favoring ERH are over 300 to 1.

[7] Cf. "Effect of Market Organization," *op. cit.*, p. 194.

$= \alpha_0/(1 - \beta_0)$. Estimates of $E(\pi_\infty)$ are also contained in Table 3. It is seen that under the full payoff condition the experimental market equilibrium is only 4.5 cents below the theoretical, for $e = 2$, and 4.3 cents above it for $e = 5$, as compared with a discrepancy of 26.4 and 13.8, respectively, under weak payoffs. A t-test on the $\hat{\alpha}_0$ for weak payoffs shows $\hat{\alpha}_0$ to be significantly above zero for $e = 2$, $t(2) = 1.95$, but not for $e = 5$, $t(5) = 0.99$. With full payoffs under neither condition of excess supply is $\hat{\alpha}_0$ significantly different from zero, $t(2) = -0.087$, $t(5) = 0.40$. An F-test comparison of the estimates $\hat{\sigma}^2$ under weak and full cash payoffs shows the differences to be highly significant ($\alpha < 0.005$) for $e = 2$, but insignificant for $e = 5$. We conclude that there exist some conditions under which experimental results are likely to be biased to an important degree by the substitution of random for full cash payoffs. Consequently, the use of random payoffs cannot generally be defended as a compromise between no payoffs and full cash payoffs.

TABLE 3

COMPARISON OF FULL VERSUS WEAK (RANDOM) PAYOFFS

Excess Supply, E	Experiment	$\hat{\alpha}_0$*	$\hat{\beta}_0$	$\hat{\sigma}^2$	No. Observations	$E(\pi_\infty)$
2	1, 2; full payoff	−0.188 (2.435)	0.9584 (0.0367)	6.207	100	− 4.52
	A; weak payoff	5.753 (2.960)	0.7820 (0.0939)	12.885	58	26.4
5	3, 4; full payoff	0.528 (1.329)	0.8769 (0.0461)	8.801	79	4.29
	B; weak payoff	2.079 (2.110)	0.8491 (0.0676)	8.455	50	13.8

* Standard errors are shown in parentheses.

SUMMARY

The results of our six experimental sessions tend to support the view that the auction-market mechanism produces strong competitive equilibrating tendencies, even under conditions of extreme imbalance in the rental rewards to buyers as opposed to sellers. These tendencies are weakest when excess supply is small, strongest when excess supply is large. This conclusion, and the results on which it is based, assume the information conditions under which our experimental markets were operated and should not be assumed without further inquiry to hold under different information conditions.[8]

A test of WH as against ERH yields strong support for the latter. The credibility of this conclusion is strengthened by the fact that the experimental design was determined by the objective of providing good discrimination between the competing hypotheses.

The experimental sessions under full cash payoffs to all subjects were compared with two pilot sessions under full cash payoffs to only a subset of subjects chosen at random. The results show enough difference in market behavior to suggest that one should not arbitrarily substitute random payoff rewards for full payoff rewards, on the assumption that the results will not be significantly altered.

[8] See L. Fouraker and S. Siegel, *Bargaining Behavior* (New York: McGraw-Hill Book Co., 1963), pp. 142–51, 184–93, for a discussion of the effect of amount of information on oligopoly bargaining behavior.

EXPERIMENTAL STUDIES OF DISCRIMINATION VERSUS COMPETITION IN SEALED-BID AUCTION MARKETS*

VERNON L. SMITH†

I. INTRODUCTION

IN THIS study, attention focuses on the behavior of a class of auction markets where formal organization requires the individual competing bidders to submit one or more written "sealed bids" specifying the quantity and price at which they are committed to buy (or sell) units of the item being traded.

In many such markets only a single unit, such as a contract for the construction of a bridge or building, is involved. The experimental designs and theory underlying this study assume that many units of the item are to be offered for sale (or are required to be purchased). Perhaps the most important continuing market having this structure is the auction market for new Treasury bills with maturities of 91 and 182 days. Other examples might be the letting of contracts for transportation service, where the service requirements are in excess of the capacity of any single firm, or the letting of material contracts, say for cement, where the requirements exceed the capacity of any one producer.

Our primary purpose is to study individual bidding behavior and price determination under two alternative forms of market organization: (1) price discrimination, under which successful individual bids are filled at their bid prices, and (2) pure competition, under which successful individual bids are filled at the same market-clearing price. The methodology is that of the controlled laboratory experiment, in which the major "treatment" variables are the instructions defining the rules for accepting subject bids under the two forms of market organization.

II. INSTITUTIONAL EXAMPLES: THE TREASURY-BILL AUCTION

For institutional background we discuss briefly some mechanics of the Treasury-bill auction. This auction is an ideal example because its organization and functioning are known in considerable detail, and it has been proposed that the discriminative practice of the Treasury be replaced by a competitive procedure.[1] However, the bill auction,

* This research was supported by National Science Foundation Grant No. GS-370 to Purdue University. I wish to thank Mr. Meyer W. Belovicz for conducting one of the experimental sessions.

† Professor of economics and administrative science, Purdue University.

[1] Andrew Brimmer, "Price Determination in the United States Treasury Bill Market," *Review of Economics and Statistics*, XLIV, No. 2 (May, 1962), 178–83; Deane Carson, "Treasury Open Market Operations," *Review of Economics and Statistics*, Vol. XLI, No. 4 (November, 1959); Henry Goldstein, "The Friedman Proposal for Auctioning Treasury Bills," *Journal of Political Economy*, LXX, No. 4 (August, 1962), 386–92; Joint Economic Committee, Congress of the United States, "Constructive Suggestions for Reconciling and Simultaneously Obtaining the Three Objectives of Maximum Employment, and Adequate Rate of Growth, and Substantial Stability of the Price Level," *Hearings: Employment, Growth and Price Levels* (86th Cong., 1st sess., October, 1959), Part 9A, pp. 3023–26; Milton Friedman, *A Program for Monetary Stability* (New York: Fordham University Press, 1960), pp. 63–65; and Michael Rieber, "Collusion in the Auction Market for Treasury Bills," *Journal of Political Economy*, LXXII, No. 5 (October, 1964), 509–12.

as such, has no dominating interest for this study. Our interest is in the general characteristics of the sealed-bid auction and the effect of price discrimination and pure competition on behavior, whether the commodity be securities or potatoes.

The bill auction is a weekly phenomenon beginning each Wednesday when the Treasury releases an announcement, through the Reserve Banks, inviting tenders for a specified amount of 91-day and 182-day issues. The weekly offering of 91-day issues amounts to around one billion dollars, that of the longer issue about half a billion. The resulting bids are normally tendered the following Monday to each Reserve Bank by the bill investors in each Federal Reserve district. Delivery is made to the successful bidders on the following Thursday. Before 1947, all bids had to be entered at a specified price. Since 1947, investors have had the option of submitting non-competitive bids for limited amounts of bills. The successful competitive bids are filled at their individual-bid prices, while the non-competitive bids are filled at a quantity-weighted average of the accepted competitive bids. (Incidentally, "competitive" as used in the Treasury-auction literature does not mean "competitive" as we shall employ the term in contrast to the term "discriminative.")

To illustrate price determination, suppose that the net offering of ninety-one-day bills to the competitive bidders is Q_O in Figure 1. Q_O would be the total offering minus the amount of non-competitive bids. The array of competitive bids from highest to lowest forms an effective demand, *dd*, for the offering. The lowest accepted bid would be at P_L, the highest at P_H.

In this illustration, the gross receipts from the offering are given by the area under *dd* and to the left of Q_O in Figure 1. Thus, with respect to the effective demand curve, *dd*, the seller acts as a perfect price discriminator, receiving all the buyer's rent or surplus under the demand curve. By contrast, if this market were operated to simulate a perfectly competitive auction, and *if* we assume the same bids to have been submitted as in the example for price discrimination, the result would have been the uniform market-clearing price, P_L, for

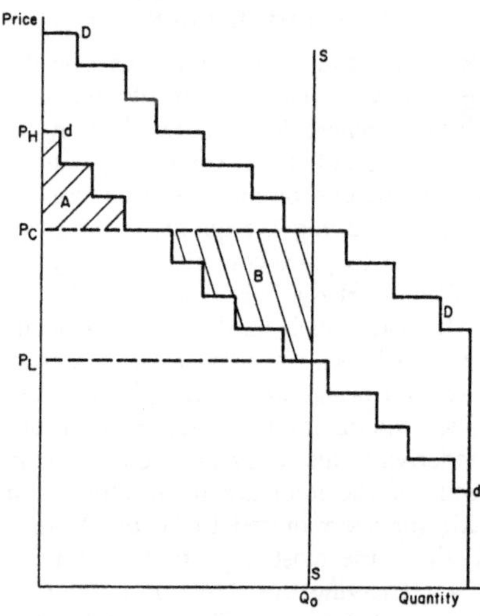

FIG. 1.—Price determination in the bill auction

all successful bidders. Under these assumptions, the Treasury receives greater revenue as a consequence of practicing price discrimination. However, as is demonstrated in the bidding theory outlined in Appendix I, it is not necessarily the case that the bids will be the same under price discrimination as under a purely competitive market organization.[2]

For illustration, suppose each bidder, *i*, in the market has a firm reservation price, P_i, that he is willing to pay for a unit of the item traded. Then the "po-

[2] Also cf. Goldstein, *op. cit.*, pp. 391–92.

tential" demand, or limit-price set, is determined by the ordered set $[P_i]$ arrayed in descending order from highest to lowest. Such a set is illustrated by DD in Figure 1 and corresponds to the demand curve of ordinary price theory. As is shown in Appendix I, under price discrimination the optimal-price bid for any buyer is not in general equal to his reservation limit, P_i. Intuitively, when a buyer knows that a successful bid will be filled at his bid price, it is evident that he will bid more conservatively than if he knows it will be filled at the marginal bid price of all the buyers. If the limit-price set is DD under a purely competitive organization, then the effective demand under price discrimination might be as shown by dd in Figure 1. It follows that for a given DD, and a single auction, price discrimination might yield a seller, such as the Treasury in the bill auction, more or less revenue than a simulated purely competitive auction. A seller gets *less* revenue under price discrimination if area A < area B. Over time, with repeat bidding in successive (daily, weekly, etc.) discrimination auctions, if the DD and SS conditions were constant, it is clear that the unsuccessful bidders in earlier auctions would tend to raise their bids, while the successful bidders would tend to lower their bids. Consequently, area B would approach zero, as dd (to the right of SS) rose toward DD. But in any real market, and most certainly in the bill auction, both DD and SS change from one auction to another. Hence the price uncertainties which lead one to expect dd to be below DD may persist indefinitely over time.[3] An important objective of our experimental design will be to capture the essence of this uncertainty in a laboratory setting.

The above considerations arise in an auction conducted by a single buyer, except that in this case the demand curve is vertical at the desired quantity and the purely competitive supply curve is formed from the ordered set of offer-limit prices. Under discrimination the supply-price bids would tend to exceed the limit-supply prices. The effective supply function would therefore be to the left of that prevailing in a competitive auction. If the difference were sufficiently great a buyer might pay more for the purchase under discrimination than in a competitive auction.

III. THE EXPERIMENTAL PARADIGM

In designing an experimental paradigm for the study of behavior in the sealed-bid auction market it will not be our objective, even if it were possible, to simulate the institutional details of any particular market such as the Treasury-bill auction. We shall be concerned, rather, with creating a group task situation that reflects the essential economic characteristics of such a market. These characteristics seem to be three in number:

1. The individual participants in such a market can be expected to place (*a*) different and (*b*) uncertain subjective valuations on the commodity being exchanged.
2. The price at which units of the commodity can be purchased in the auction cannot be known with certainty at the time the participants tender their irrevocable bids.
3. The rules for determining who pays how much for the commodity might be either of the discriminative form or the purely competitive form.

These characteristics are incorporated into the experimental design by requiring

[3] There is even uncertainty as to SS in the bill auction since the Treasury announcement always invites tenders for $\$X$ billion, *or thereabouts*. The Treasury is thereby in a position to cut the bid array with its own reservation sale price if the bids are unusually thin or thick. In practice, there seems to be negligible deviation between the announced offering and the actual volume of bids accepted.

the subjects to submit irrevocable bids for units of an abstract commodity, offered inelastically in specified quantity, for resale at a price that is a random variable with a specified mass or frequency function. The subjects are paid in U.S. currency a sum equal to the algebraic difference between selling price and purchase price. Since the subjects may be presumed to have different subjective valuations (utility functions) for money, this paradigm satisfies condition 1(*a*). Condition 1(*b*) is satisfied by making resale price a random variable. The fact that it is a known random variable corresponds roughly in a real market to the knowledge and judgmental ability that the participants gain from experience. Condition 2 is satisfied by prohibiting communication among the subjects. Hence, no individual subject can have certain knowledge, in advance, of purchase price or selling price. Of course Condition 3 is satisfied by varying the bidding rules as between two experimental groups.

In the Treasury-bill market this experimental paradigm corresponds most directly to the dealer participants who buy in the primary auction for purposes of resale in the secondary, existing-asset market. Dealer profits are squeezed from below by uncertainty as to the lowest accepted bid that will prevail in the Treasury auction and from above by uncertainty as to the price at which they can resell the bills in the existing-asset market. The assumption that "resale price" is uncertain may also correspond indirectly to the behavior of some non-dealer bidders in the Treasury auction. Thus, although a participant may not be buying for resale, he may still be influenced, in placing his bids, by his estimate of the expected future price of bills in the secondary market at the time of delivery of new bills acquired in the auction. If he wishes to minimize his opportunity cost of buying in the primary market, when he might have bought in the secondary at a more favorable price, such behavior would be formally equivalent to that of a dealer bidding to maximize some utility function of profit.

IV. THE HYPOTHESES

Prior to conducting the experiments reported in this paper several specific hypotheses were formulated, which helped to govern the experimental design. In each case we will state the research hypothesis, it being understood that the classical null alternative is the negative of the research hypothesis. The use of a C will refer to "competitive treatment," a D to "discriminative treatment."

The basic hypothesis, labeled H_2, grows directly out of the intuitive arguments in the previous section and the bidding theory in Appendix I:

> H_2: In the tth auction period, the bids, B^t_C, tendered by subjects in a C group will exceed[4] the bids, B^t_D, tendered by subjects in the corresponding D group, that is, $B^t_C > B^t_D$, $t = 1, 2, 3, \ldots$

When we come to test H_2 it will be necessary to select a test procedure. The obvious classical test is a simple one-tailed t-test on the means of the bids. However, the t-test requires the assumption that the two samples being compared are from populations with the same variance. Therefore, before H_2 can be tested, it is necessary to formulate a hypothesis as to the behavior of the variance of bids tendered under the two

[4] The precise meaning of "exceed" is defined implicitly by the bid-test statistic used in the comparison. The use of a t-test would imply that the *mean* B^t_C and B^t_D would satisty the inequality $B^t_C > B^t_D$. The use of a rank-order non-parametric test would imply that the sum, mean, or other function of the ranks assigned to bids satisfied the hypothesized inequality.

treatments. Such a hypothesis will be of intrinsic interest in that, if true, it will reflect a behavioral difference caused by the different treatments. What in fact can we expect? Will the variance of the bids under condition C be greater, equal, or less than the variance of the bids under condition D? The following argument suggests that the variance will be greater:

The individual bidder in a discriminative auction is uncertain as to whether a given bid will be successful, but if it is successful he is certain about the purchase price—his purchase price, by definition, will be his bid price. He has little incentive to bid "high," for although it will increase the certainty that a bid will be accepted it raises his purchase price and lowers his profit. But in a competitive auction the individual bidder faces uncertainty both as to whether a given bid will be accepted and as to what his purchase price will be. If he bids high this increases his chance of success, and, provided that others bid low, his purchase price is low, and he makes a profit. The individual is not penalized no matter how much his bid exceeds the lowest accepted bid. But if others bid high it raises the purchase price to all, and all suffer losses. This implies greater risk under condition C, and, if attitudes toward risk vary among individual subjects, some will "gamble" with high bids, others will play it safe with more conservative bids. Hence, the variance of bids under C should exceed that of bids under D.

H_1: In the tth auction period, the variance of bids tendered by subjects in a C group, $V(B_C^t)$, will exceed the variance of bids tendered by subjects in the corresponding D group, $V(B_D^t)$, that is, $V(B_C^t) > V(B_D^t)$, $t = 1, 2, 3, \ldots$

It is instructive to consider the rationale for H_1 and H_2 from the point of view of a game matrix. Consider the following highly simplified illustration: Suppose an individual subject can enter one of three bids, 1, 2, or 3, and that resale price is 1, 2, or 3, with equal probability. Also assume that when a subject ties with others for low bids he has a $\frac{1}{2}$ chance of having his bid accepted. Now imagine that a typical subject is concerned with what he should bid on the assumption that others bid (or the low bid is) a 1, 2, or 3. Under the D or C conditions our subject might perceive the payoffs given in Table 1.

TABLE 1

SUBJECT'S PAYOFF

If Subject Bids	Hypothetical D Payoff Matrix			Hypothetical C Payoff Matrix		
	If Others Bid (or the Low Bid Is):			If Others Bid (or the Low Bid Is):		
	1	2	3	1	2	3
1	$\frac{1}{2}$	0	0	$\frac{1}{2}$	0	0
2	0	0	0	1	0	0
3	-1	-1	$-\frac{1}{2}$	1	0	$-\frac{1}{2}$

In D, if he bids 1 and others bid 1, his bid is accepted $\frac{1}{2}$ the time, giving a profit of 0, 1, or 2 with chances $\frac{1}{3}$ each. Hence, payoff averages $\frac{1}{2}$. If he bids 1 and others a 2 or 3, he gets nothing. If he bids 2 and others 1, his bid is accepted but at an average profit of 0. If he bids 2 and others 2 he still averages 0, while if others bid 3 his bid is never accepted, giving 0, and so on. In D it is best to go low, while a high bid never pays. Some might try bids of 2 since it still involves fair odds, and one could "get lucky." Hence, bids of 1 are most likely, with perhaps a few at the resale mean, 2. Note that a bid of 1 is both the co-operative (joint maximizing) and the selfish course of action.

The same payoff vector accrues in C for a bid of 1. If our hypothetical subject bids 2 and others 1, his bid is always accepted and filled at 1, the lowest accepted bid, giving an average profit of 1 $(= \frac{1}{3} \cdot 0 + \frac{1}{3} \cdot 1 + \frac{1}{3} \cdot 2)$. If he bids 2 and others 2, he averages 0, and so on. In C it is best to bid 2. However, if a subject is anxious to co-operate he might bid 1, which cannot generate a loss. If he hopes to intimidate others into making low bids he will bid rivalistically at 3, risking a loss of $\frac{1}{2}$ but also inflicting a loss of $\frac{1}{2}$ on all others who bid 3. The "right" course of action is less evident in C than in D.

From this example it is clear that the bids would tend to be higher in C than in D (H_2). Given that subject attitudes toward risk and toward punishing versus co-operative strategies are likely to vary, it is seen that the C bids would tend to have a higher variance than D bids (H_1).

Given the validity of H_2, it is conjectural whether the bids will be high enough in the C group to yield a monopolistic seller greater revenue under competition than discrimination. This prospect was considered sufficiently likely to assert the following hypothesis:

H_3: In the tth auction period the total revenue to a seller in a C group, R_C^t, will exceed that in the corresponding D group, R_D^t, that is, $R_C^t > R_D^t$, $t = 1, 2, 3, \ldots$

Although the classical experimental methodology calls for independent subject groups to be exposed to the treatment conditions whose effects are to be compared, there is an important sense in which such a procedure is artificial in the present context. In any actual institutional form of the sealed-bid auction, such as the Treasury-bill auction, the participants have a long-standing experience with the discriminative form of organization. If market organization is changed to the competitive form, will the previous history and experience have an important effect on behavior under the new conditions? If one is concerned with the Carson-Friedman policy proposal, namely, to change from discriminative rules to competitive rules,[5] then the relevant experiment is to expose the same group of subjects initially to the discriminative treatment for a series of bid periods, then to the competitive treatment. Although some "hystereses" (or path-dependent) phenomena may be detectable, it is expected that the above propositions will be valid when the same experimental group is exposed first to the D, then to the C, conditions. The above three hypotheses will be labeled H_1', H_2', and H_3' when applied to comparable bid periods under the D and C conditions for the same experimental group.

Although we are prepared to predict that the bids will be lower and the seller's receipts lower under discrimination, it is apparent that such results are not likely to be independent of market conditions, in particular the relative number of rejected bids. *Ceteris paribus*, it would appear that the greater the volume of rejected bids the higher would tend to be the bids under either the C or D condi-

[5] Carson, *op. cit.*; Joint Economic Committee, *op. cit.*

tion. However, since we expect the bids to be higher, and therefore the trading gains thinner, under C (as opposed to D), we will expect the volume of excess bids to have its most pronounced effect under condition D. Indeed, at some point, as the number of bidders is increased in successive experimental groups, with the offering quantity constant, the differential effect of the C and D conditions on seller revenue may disappear. These expectations will be tested via hypotheses H_4 and H_5.

H_4: With a fixed offer quantity, in corresponding auction periods, bids tendered by subjects in D groups, B_D^t, will be higher the greater the number of rejected bids, that is, $B_D^t(NR_1) > B_D^t(NR_2) > B_D^t(NR_3) > \ldots, t = 1, 2, 3, \ldots,$ if $NR_1 > NR_2 > NR_3 > \ldots$

H_5: Same as H_4 applied to C groups, that is, $B_C^t(NR_1) > B_C^t(NR_2) > B_C^t(NR_3) > \cdots,$ $t = 1, 2, 3, \ldots,$ if $NR_1 > NR_2 > NR_3 > \ldots$

V. EXPERIMENTAL DESIGN

A total of seventy-seven subjects, all in undergraduate courses in economics and industrial management at Purdue, participated in a design block of six experiments conducted in five groups or sessions. No subject participated in more than one session. The relevant experimental conditions for each session are designated in Table 2. Roman numerals I through V refer to the five subject groups in the chronological order in which the experiments were conducted.

The instruction sheets given each subject in the D experiments, and read aloud to the entire group, are reproduced in Appendix II. Appendix II also contains the C instructions.

Group III participated in two experiments conducted in sequence. In the first experiment (IIID), the D instructions were read, followed by a trial auction, then by eight auctions for money. Then without advance warning the C instructions were read followed by eight more auctions (experiment IIIC). The other four experiments were conducted on independent groups of subjects.

TABLE 2

EXPERIMENTAL-DESIGN CONDITIONS

Experiment	Purchase-Price Rules	No. of Subjects	No. of Rejected Bids	No. of Bid Periods
ID.......	Discriminative	15	12	5
IIC.......	Competitive	15	12	5
IIID......	Discriminative	13	8	8
IIIC......	Competitive		8	8
IVD......	Discriminative	17	16	10
VC.......	Competitive	17	16	10

Group III consisted of an entire student class, whereas the other groups were randomized out of much larger classes. As a means of controlling on pregame conditions the classes were given no advance warning that they would serve as captive subjects in an experiment. End effects were controlled by withholding information on the number of auction periods.

As indicated in the instructions, in each experiment the number of bids that could be submitted by a subject was arbitrarily set at two. The quantity offered, X, was announced at the beginning of each auction period. This offering was eighteen units in all periods of all experiments, but the subjects discovered this only through the sequential announcements. Hence, in experiments ID

and IIC, a total of thirty bids (fifteen subjects) was submitted of which twelve were rejected. Similarly in III*D* and III*C* eight bids were rejected out of twenty-six, and in IV*D* and V*C* we have sixteen bids rejected out of thirty-four.

In each auction of each experiment a subject's profit on a successful bid was (selling price) − (purchase price), zero otherwise, this sum to be added to or subtracted from his $1.00 starting capital. In both the *D* and *C* auctions the lowest successful bid was determined by arraying the bids from highest to lowest and accepting the first *X* bids. In the *C* auctions "purchase price" was determined by the lowest successful market bid, while in the *D* auctions it was determined by the bid price on each individual accepted bid. In both auctions

TABLE 3

BID FREQUENCIES BY AUCTION PERIOD[a]

Bids	Auction 1	2	3	4	5
	Experiment I*D*				
≤$0.45.....					
0.55.....					
0.65.....					
0.75.....	2				
0.85.....	2	1			
0.95.....	12	4			
1.05.....	7	11	3	2	1
1.15.....	2	9	22	10	1
1.25.....	4	5	4	14	19
1.35.....	1		1	4	9
1.45.....					
1.55.....					
1.65.....					
1.75.....					
1.85.....					
1.95.....					
≥ 2.05.....					
	Experiment II*C*				
≤$0.45.....	1	1			1
0.55.....	0	0			0
0.65.....	0	1			0
0.75.....	1	0			0
0.85.....	0	0		1	0
0.95.....	2	2	2	1	0
1.05.....	2	1	0	0	0
1.15.....	5	2	3	2	3
1.25.....	4	3	3	2	1
1.35.....	6	6	4	5	4
1.45.....	2	4	7	5	6
1.55.....	3	4	5	9	6
1.65.....	0	3	2	1	3
1.75.....	3	2	2	2	4
1.85.....	1	0	1	1	0
1.95.....		1	1	0	2
≥ 2.05.....				1	

Bids	Auction 1	2	3	4	5	6	7	8
	Experiment III*D*							
≤$0.45.....								
0.55.....								
0.65.....	1	1						
0.75.....	3	0						
0.85.....	6	2						
0.95.....	9	11	1					
1.05.....	1	7	11	2	1			
1.15.....	4	3	12	11	2		2	1
1.25.....	0	0	2	12	17	8	9	9
1.35.....	0	2		1	6	16	15	16
1.45.....	2					2		
1.55.....								
1.65.....								
1.75.....								
1.85.....								
1.95.....								
≥ 2.05.....								
	Experiment III*C*							
≤$0.45.....								
0.55.....								
0.65.....								
0.75.....	2							
0.85.....	2							
0.95.....	2							
1.05.....	0							
1.15.....	1	1		2				
1.25.....	6	4	2	3	3	3		
1.35.....	5	7	3	4	3	5	6	8
1.45.....	3	6	8	6	11	9	10	10
1.55.....	2	6	3	6	5	5	7	6
1.65.....	2	0	2	1	0	3	0	0
1.75.....	0	0	2	0	0	0	0	0
1.85.....	0	1	3	2	4	1	3	2
1.95.....	1	1	3	2				
≥ 2.05.....								

[a] Bids between the rules = accepted bid range.

"selling price" was determined by independent drawings from a rectangular distribution over the nine prices, \$1.15, \$1.25, \$1.35, . . . , \$1.95. Each auction began with an announcement that eighteen units were being offered for sale and ended with an announcement of the highest accepted bid, the lowest accepted bid, and the result of the drawing to determine "resale price." All data were written on the blackboard at the time of announcement and left there in tabular form for the duration of the experiment.

Each session began with a trial auction which did not count toward the computation of the subject's cash rewards. Following the trial auction further questions concerning the mechanics of the auction were invited. The same

TABLE 4

BID FREQUENCIES BY AUCTION PERIOD[a]

BIDS	AUCTION 1	2	3	4	5	6	7	8	9	10
					Experiment IV*D*					
≤\$0.45										
0.55										
0.65										
0.75										
0.85										
0.95	2	1								
1.05	3	2								
1.15	7	4	2	1			1			
1.25	12	9	8	2	3	2	2	1	1	
1.35	8	17	11	15	11	12	4	4	3	3
1.45	2	1	13	14	20	17	26	26	26	27
1.55				2		3	1	3	4	4
1.65										
1.75										
1.85										
1.95										
≥ 2.05										
					Experiment V*C*					
≤\$0.45		1	1	1	4	2	2	2	2	3
0.55		1	1	1	0	0	0	0	0	0
0.65	2	1	0	0	0	0	0	0	0	0
0.75	1	1	0	0	0	0	0	0	0	0
0.85	4	1	0	0	0	0	0	0	0	0
0.95	5	1	1	1	0	0	0	1	1	1
1.05	3	3	2	0	1	0	1	2	0	0
1.15	3	5	2	1	2	5	3	2	1	0
1.25	2	6	3	4	1	2	3	3	3	3
1.35	2	1	7	3	1	4	7	5	6	5
1.45	1	1	3	6	8	5	2	2	4	3
1.55	2	1	4	3	4	3	3	4	4	7
1.65	0	1	0	0	0	0	0	0	1	1
1.75	1	1	3	3	4	3	5	4	4	2
1.85	0	1	0	3	0	0	0	2	1	0
1.95	1	0	3	1	1	1	2	1	3	2
≥ 2.05	7	8	4	7	8	9	6	6	4	7

[a] Bids between rules = accepted bid range.

random sequence of resale prices was used in all experiments (except III*D*, since it was the same subject group as III*C*) as a control on the effect of particular sequences.

VI. RESULTS, TESTS OF HYPOTHESES

The data to be analyzed from the five experiments are compiled in Tables 3 and 4. Complete protocols of bids by individual subjects are reported in Appendix III. Tables 3 and 4 contain the frequency of each bid tendered in each auction period. The highest and lowest of the accepted bids, by auction period, are indicated by the rules. Except for ties at the low-bid price which were randomly assigned to the acceptance and

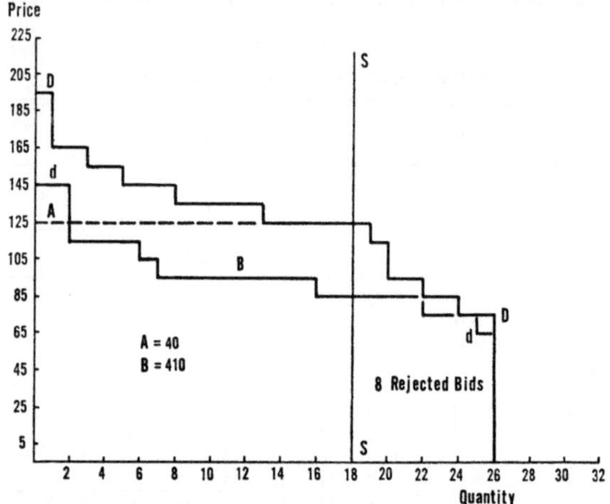

FIG. 2.—Experiments III*D* and III*C*, auction period 1

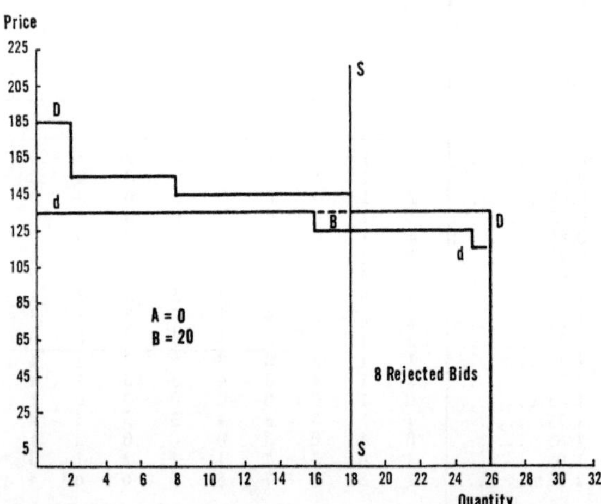

FIG. 3.—Experiments III*D* and III*C*, auction period 8

rejection sets, the bids between these rules constitute the acceptance set of bids. For example, in auction period 3, experiment II*C*, eighteen bids were between $1.45 and $1.95, and therefore all were accepted. In auction 4 of the same experiment, nineteen bids fell in the $1.45–$2.05 range. Hence, one of the $1.45 bids was randomly selected for rejection.

It should be noted that five auctions in addition to the trial auction were run in the first two experiments, I*D* and I*C*. Since the bid frequencies, the lowest accepted bid, and seller total revenue appear not to have stabilized, the number of auctions was increased to eight in experiments III*D* and III*C* and to ten in experiments IV*D* and V*C*. Actually the question of equilibrium over time is a moot one. In a real market, conditions are not likely to remain constant long enough to achieve a static equilibrium. On the other hand, the participants in

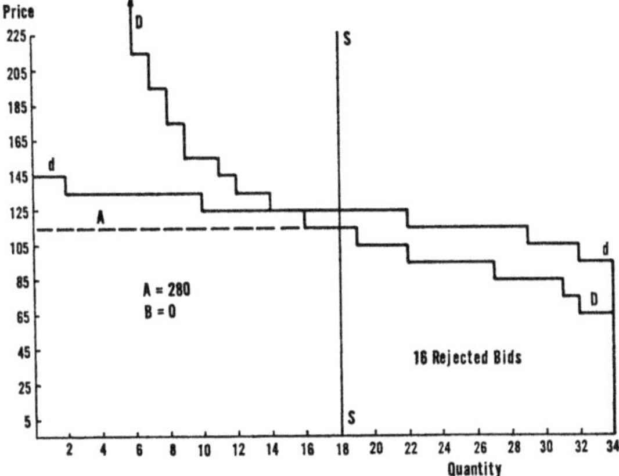

FIG. 4.—Experiments IV*D* and V*C*, auction period 1

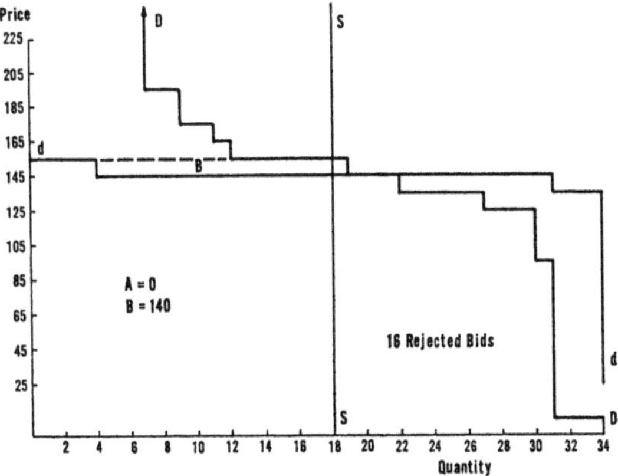

FIG. 5.—Experiments IV*D* and V*C*, auction period 10

real markets are more experienced than subjects in laboratory experimental markets, and the behavior of the latter may be more comparable to that of the former only after several trials of learning experience.

The sample demand curves generated by the bid arrays in the first and last auction periods of experiments III*D*, III*C*, IV*D*, and V*C* are provided in Figures 2–5. These charts convey some idea of the variation in the demand curves is the ratio of the variance of bids tendered under *C* to those tendered under *D*. Only two of the twenty-three compared variances fail to be significantly different in the predicted direction at α probability levels of less than .001. In the experiment V*C*, the bid variance in every period was several thousand times as large as in IV*D*. In IV*D* and V*C* nearly half of the bids were rejected in each auction, putting the maximum pressure (relative to the other experiments) on subjects

TABLE 5

F-Ratio Test of H_1 and H_1'

$V(B_C) > V(B_D')$

F-Ratio $= V(B_C')/V(B_D)$			Auction Period									
Paired Experiments[a]	Degrees of Freedom f_C	Degrees of Freedom f_D	1	2	3	4	5	6	7	8	9	10
ID-II*C*........	29	29	4.3	9.5	15.3	9.4	25.4	......	......	......	......	......
III*D*-III*C*......	25	25	2.3**	1.5*	9.8	9.8	6.6	5.7	5.2	5.3	......	......
IV*D*-V*C*........	31	31	7,582	b	b	b	b	b	b	b	b	28,500

[a] In order of predicted increasing level of bids.
[b] All these *F*'s are very large.
* Significant at $\alpha = .10$.
** Significant at $\alpha = .025$. All other *F*-values significant at $\alpha < .001$.

as between the two treatment conditions in different experimental groups. Generally, demand *dd* (under discrimination) tended to rise and flatten relative to the price axis in successive auction periods. *DD* (under competitive rules) tended to rise but not necessarily flatten, expecially in group V*C*, in successive auctions.

A comparison of the distributions of bids under the *C* and *D* conditions for corresponding auction periods (Tables 3 and 4) leaves little doubt that the variance of bids is much higher under *C* than *D*. The results of an *F*-test of H_1 (and H_1') is shown in Table 5. Each *F* entry to bid high if they hoped to tender successful bids. However, much of this extreme variation may be attributable to the effect of a single subject in V*C* who entered two bids of over $100.00 in the trial auction and in most of the auctions thereafter. This seems to have induced subsequent bids (up to nine) at very high levels by subjects seeing that (1) very high bids guaranteed success and (2) that enough other subjects entered cautious low bids to yield reasonably low purchase prices. By the fifth auction three subjects were entering bids at $0.05 or 0 (see Appendix III), apparently to be certain of limiting their losses to a single bid in the event that the number of exorbitant bids should exceed the eighteen-unit offering. Many of the very high and very low bids are perhaps therefore attributable to the high bids submitted, and then advertised in the subsequent announcement, by a single subject. Hence, the group variance of bids under *C* may vary sharply in different groups depending upon whether a group contains a subject willing to bid almost without limit to be sure of success. Such a bid is analogous to orders to "buy at market" on the organized stock exchanges. An order "buy at market" placed with a stock broker instructs him to obtain title to the security on whatever terms are required. There is no upper limit to the purchase price.

Since H_1 is very strongly confirmed it is clear that the testing of H_2 and H_2' cannot be based upon the assumption that the *C* and *D* populations of bids have a common variance. Therefore, instead of a *t*-test on bid means, our fundamental hypothesis, H_2, will be tested by the Jonckheere procedure,[6] which is a non-parametric (rank-order) test of the hypothesis that *k* random variables have been ordered a priori so that each is stochastically larger than those appearing on its left in the order sequence. The test statistic *P* is formed by taking each bid tendered by a *D* group, starting with the lowest and counting the number of bids in the corresponding *C* group that are greater. If for the *i*th bid in a *D* group there are N_i larger bids in the parallel *C* group, then

$$P = \sum_i N_i .$$

As the sample sizes increase, the distribution of *P* converges rapidly to the normal.[7]

TABLE 6

JONCKHEERE TEST OF H_2 AND H_2'

$B_C' > B_D'$

Z, Unit Normal Deviate		Auction Period									
Paired Experiments[a]	No. of Rejected Bids	1	2	3	4	5	6	7	8	9	10
III*D*-III*C*.........	8	3.3	6.0	6.1	4.5	4.6	2.8	4.5	3.8	......	......
I*D*-II*C*...........	12	3.6	3.9	4.3	4.1	4.0	......	......	......	......	......
IV*D*-V*C*..........	16	−1.0	−0.7	0.5	1.4	1.4	0.4	0.0	0.0	0.1	0.6

[a] In order of predicted increasing level of bids. Entries in first two rows significant in predicted direction at $\alpha < .001$. Entries in bottom row not significant in predicted direction.

Table 6 contains the values of the unit normal deviate, *Z*, computed for each auction period, on the a priori hypothesis that bids under condition *C* would have higher ranks than those under *D*. In the first two sets of paired groups, corresponding to eight and twelve rejected bids, the *Z* values are significant at $\alpha < .001$. H_2 and H_2' are

[6] A. R. Jonckheere, "A Test of Significance for the Relation between *m* Rankings and *k* Ranked Categories," *British Journal of Statistical Psychology*, VII (November, 1954), 93–100, and *idem*, "A Distribution-Free *k*-Sample Test against Ordered Alternatives," *Biometrika*, XLI (June, 1954), 133–45.

[7] Jonckheere, "A Distribution-Free *k*-Sample Test against Ordered Alternatives," p. 140.

confirmed under these conditions. However, in the third pair of experiments, with sixteen rejected bids, H_2 is not confirmed. The Z values are small, and even negative in the first two auctions. Negative Z here means that the bids under C tend to be lower in rank than under D—the reverse of the order predicted by H_2. These results suggest that we can expect bids under the C treatment to exceed those under D when the proportion of rejected bids is small or moderate. But this ordering relationship is reversed when the proportion of rejected bids approaches half the number of bids tendered.

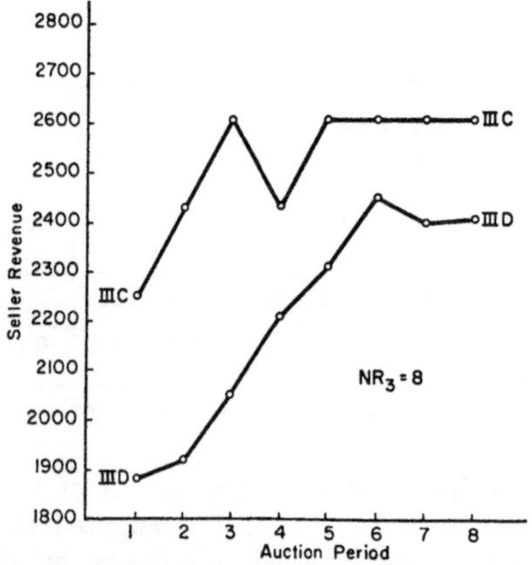

FIG. 6.—Seller revenue by auction period; test of H'_3, $R^t_C > R^t_D$.

Data relevant to the testing of H_3 and H'_3 are contained in Figures 6, 7, and 8, showing the total revenue accruing to a monopolistic seller, in each auction period, under the C and D conditions. H_3 is supported by every observation in the experimental groups in which twelve bids were rejected (Fig. 7). However, H_3 is supported only in the tenth auction, where sixteen bids are rejected in each auction period (Fig. 8). H'_3 is also supported by every observation (Fig. 6).

The results of Jonckheere tests of H_4 and H_5 are shown in Table 7. As suggested in our discussion of these hy-

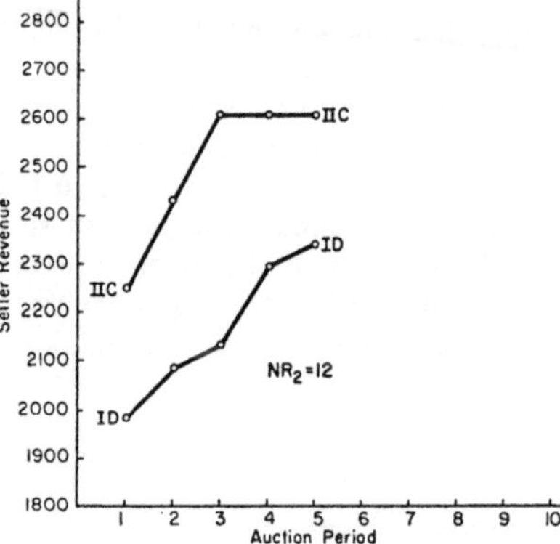

FIG. 7.—Seller revenue by auction period; test of H_3, $R^t_C > R^t_D$.

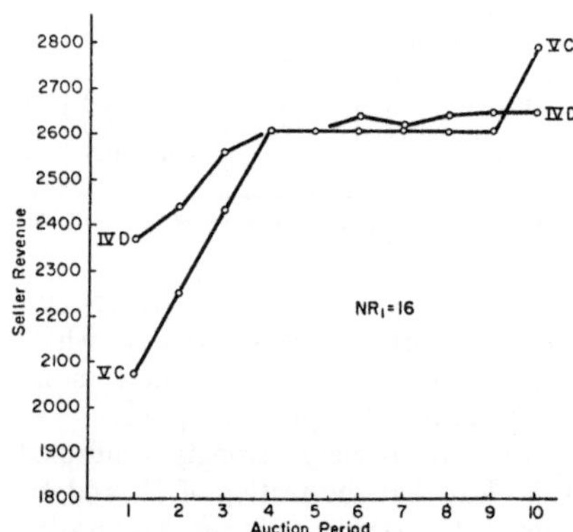

FIG. 8.—Seller revenue by auction period; test of H_3, $R^t_C > R_D$.

potheses, the ordering relation B^t_D (16) $> B^t_D$ (12) $> B^t_D$ (8) holds for discrimination, but the ordering B^t_C (16) $> B^t_C$ (12) for competition is not confirmed. It is suspected that, under condition D, increasing the number of rejected bids beyond sixteen would not significantly increase the level of bids tendered, but this was not tested. (In Fig. 5 it is seen that the discrimination bids are crowding the mean, \$1.55, of the resale-price-density function.)

Therefore, under condition *C*, increasing the number of rejected bids does not raise the level of bids tendered. This simply means that the effect of the *C* condition completely dominates the effect of the number of rejected bids. These results suggest that the outcome of a discrimination auction may depend crucially upon the number of bidders, whereas the outcome of the same offering under competition may be relatively independent of the number of bidders. This is further confirmed by comparing the seller-revenue curves for III*D*, I*D*, and IV*D* and for III*C*, II*C*, and V*C* in Figures 6, 7, and 8. Under the *D* condition we have R^t_D (16) > R^t_D (12) > R^t_D (8) for all auction periods. But under *C*, seller revenue is not unambiguously larger the greater the number of rejected bids.

In Appendix I it is shown that an expected-profit maximizer (utility linear in money) would submit bids $p_1^* = p_2^* < \bar{P}$ in a *D* auction, and $p_1^{**} = p_2^{**} = \bar{P}$ in a *C* auction, where $\bar{P}$ (= \$1.55 in the experiments) is the mean of the resale-price density. Since it has often been assumed or claimed that the stakes involved in laboratory experiments are small enough to approximate subject utility with a linear function, these theorems provide us with a test of this assumption. Examination of the data in Appendix III reveals that in the *D* auctions only three subjects approached consistency in tendering equal bids: number 7 in III*D*, 17 and 28 in IV*D*. In the *C* auctions only two subjects tendered both bids at \$1.55: number 4 in II*C* and 9 in III*C*. Five out of seventy-seven subjects tendered bids consistent with the postulate that utility is linear in money!

TABLE 7

JONCKHEERE TEST OF H_4 AND H_5

$B^t_D(16) > B^t_D(12) > B^t_D(8)$, $B^t_C(16) > B^t_C(12)$

Z, UNIT NORMAL DEVIATE	AUCTION PERIOD				
Compared Experiments[a]	1	2	3	4	5
H_4: III*D*-I*D*-IV*D*	6.1	5.4	5.9	5.0	3.6
H_5: II*C*-V*C*	−1.3[b]	−0.8[b]	−0.5[b]	0.6	−0.1[b]

[a] In order of (1) increasing proportion of rejected bids and (2) predicted increasing level of bids.

[b] Negative values indicate that level of bids *decreases* as proportion of rejected bids *increases* in *C* treatment, contrary to prediction. All other *Z* values are significant at $\alpha < .001$ in the predicted direction.

In terms of utility theory, these rather negative results could have any of several interpretations: (1) Subjects may tend to be expected-utility maximizers, where utility is linear in money, but with "noise" in their decision behavior or perceived utilities. (2) Subjects may tend to be expected-utility maximizers, but utility is nonlinear in money. (3) Subjects may tend to be expected-utility maximizers but with other variables, besides money, in the utility function. One obvious such variable is bid variety—it may be boring, tedious, or just "uninteresting" to enter the same two bids auction after auction. Some utility may therefore be derived from bid variety, and the lower the cash rewards the greater the relative strength of the urge to diversify.[8] A test for such effects might be obtained by replication of the above experiments, with double the cash rewards, as a means of reducing the relative importance of bid variety in determining bid behavior.

VII. SUMMARY AND DISCUSSION

This paper has initiated an experimental investigation of the effect of discrimination, competition, and the relative number of rejected bids on the level of bids tendered by subjects and the receipts of a monopolistic seller. The experimental paradigm is one in which subjects tender bids for an abstract commodity offered inelastically at a stated quantity. Purchase price to the individual is determined by his bid (if it is accepted) in the discriminative auction. It is determined by the lowest of all the accepted bids in the competitive auction. The abstract commodity is then sold at a price determined by a rectangular-mass function. The essence of the decision task is to determine at what levels to tender two bids, with knowledge only of the results of the previous auctions (the high and low accepted bids) and of the rectangular distribution of resale price.

The results of six experiments lend tentative support to the following conclusions:

1. The variance of competitive bids is consistently greater than the variance of discriminative bids. This discrepancy in bid variance tends to widen as the proportion of rejected bids increases.

2. For proportions of rejected bids that are low or moderate, competitive bids tend to stochastically dominate discriminative bids, that is, the probability of any bid Y or less being received tends to be greater for the discriminative auction than for the competitive auction. The proposition fails for a high proportion of rejected bids, where "high" seems to be in the neighborhood of 50 per cent.

3. The total receipts of a monopolistic seller are greater in a competitive auction than in a discriminative auction when the proportion of rejected bids is low or moderate. The proposition fails when there is a high proportion of rejected bids.

4. Discriminative auctions with a high proportion of rejected bids tend to stochastically dominate discriminative auctions with a lower proportion of rejected bids. The proposition does not hold in competitive auctions.

5. The total receipts of a monopolistic seller are greater, the greater the proportion of rejected bids in a discriminative auction. The proposition does not hold in competitive auctions.

6. The bids of only five out of seventy-seven subjects can be considered reasonably consistent with the postulate of a linear utility for money. However, the bids of the remaining seventy-two subjects do not necessarily imply utility functions that are non-linear in money if bid diversity itself is an argument of the utility function.

This study does not claim to be definitive. Only the surface is scratched. For given values of the treatment variables—market organization and proportion of rejected bids—the variability due to different subject groups has not been

[8] Sidney Siegel ("Decision-Making and Learning under Varying Conditions of Reinforcement," *Annals of the New York Academy of Science*, LXXXIX [January 28, 1961], 766–83) has employed a similar utility interpretation of differential behavior, under various reward conditions, in the binary-choice probability experiment.

determined: some of the experiments should be replicated with different subjects to see if our results are confirmed. The constraint that no more than two bids are to be submitted by each subject is arbitrary and should be relaxed in later studies. The interesting set of experiments in which the number of bids to be submitted is also a decision variable are yet to be performed. In our experiments several subjects entered at least one of their two bids at levels so low that it was almost sure not to be accepted. Presumably such subjects would not have tendered additional bids, or at least not at effective levels. However, other subjects consistently risked two high bids and no doubt would have been tempted to tender additional high bids if given the opportunity. The result might render all auctions relatively independent of the number of bidders, with the number of bids submitted per subject varying inversely with the number of subjects for a given quantity offering.

It would be of interest to develop a more specific experimental simulation of the Treasury auction, with subjects permitted to enter either "competitive" or "non-competitive" bids in the D auction. Instead of a rectangular mass for resale price, samplings could be made from the actual historical frequency distribution $f(P_D - P_B)$, where P_D is price in the existing-asset market at the time of delivery of new bills and P_B is price in the existing-asset market at the time bids are tendered. In this paradigm, the subjects would be given P_B (since such information is available to bidders in the bill market), as well as the quantity offering, at the beginning of each auction.

These are but a few of many possible variations on the present experiments that could sharpen or broaden the conclusions.

APPENDIX I

BIDDING THEORY

In this Appendix we develop static expected-utility models of individual decision behavior in discriminative and competitive auction markets. In the first model, Section A, we assume that the individual buyer has a fixed resale or limit price above which he will not bid for a unit of the commodity. This case provides the theory for the illustration in Figure 1 and, under the simplest set of assumptions, gives some analytical foundation for the intuitive conjecture that an individual may bid lower in a discriminative than in a competitive auction. This first model would apply in a situation in which the individual bidders had fixed limit prices above which they would or could not bid for units of the commodity or had certain known prices at which they could resell units of the commodity.

The second model, B, provides a static theory of bidding behavior for subject behavior in the several experiments reported in this paper in which the subjects buy units of an abstract commodity for resale at a price whose frequency distribution is known. Thus, the value of the traded item (resale price) is uncertain at the time bids are submitted.

A. LIMIT OR RESALE PRICE FIXED

For a typical buyer we assume the following:

1. A utility function of money, $U(m)$, with $U(0) = 0$.

2. A subjective density function $f(x)$ for the minimum successful bid, x, in a discriminative auction, and $g(x)$ in a competitive auction; that is, for the discriminative

case, the cumulative distribution function $F(t) = \int_0^t f(x)dx$ is the subjective probability that the minimum successful bid in a particular auction will be t or less.

3. Expected-utility-maximization bidding behavior.

In a price-discrimination auction, the payoff to an individual will be $\pi = P - p$, if $p \geq x$ (his bid is successful), and $\pi = 0$, if $p < x$ (his bid is unsuccessful), where P is the individual's limit or resale price and p is his bid price for a single unit or fixed lot of the item. Therefore, given $U(m)$ and $f(x)$ for such an auction, a subject who is a von Neumann-Morgenstern-Savage, subjective-expected-utility maximizer, should $\max_p$ $E_D(U)$, where

$$E_D(U) = \int_0^p U(P-p)f(x)dx,$$

for an individual entering a single bid. $E_D(U)$ is maximum at p^* if

$$\frac{\partial E_D}{\partial p} = U(P-p^*)f(p^*) - U'(P-p^*)F(p^*) = 0. \quad \text{(A1)}$$

For an interior maximum at p^*, one must also have

$$\frac{\partial^2 E_D}{\partial p^2} = U(P-p^*)f'(p^*) - 2U'(P-p^*)f(p^*) + U''(P-p^*)F(p^*) < 0. \quad \text{(A2)}$$

The inequality in (A2) can be taken as a postulate, or, if we assume diminishing marginal utility, $U'' < 0$, and a unimodal density $f(p)$, then the inequality necessarily holds for solutions p^* above the mode, since in that region $f'(p) < 0$. Geometrically, the condition (A2) requires the function $U(P - p)f(p)$ to cut $U'(P - p)F(p)$ from above at p^*. Hence, if $U'(P - p) > 0$, $F(p) > 0$ (as seems reasonable), the solution $p^* < P$ will be at point D, as illustrated in Figure 9.

In a competitive auction, by contrast, since all bids are filled at the uniform market-clearing price, the payoff to an individual for a successful bid is independent of his bid, namely, $\pi = P - x$, if $p \geq x$, and $\pi = 0$, if $p < x$. Expected utility in such an auction is therefore

$$E_C(U) = \int_0^p U(P-x)g(x)dx$$

for a single bid. We assume $g(x)$ to be different from $f(x)$, since the individual bidders will expect the minimum successful bid to be different, presumably lower, under dis-

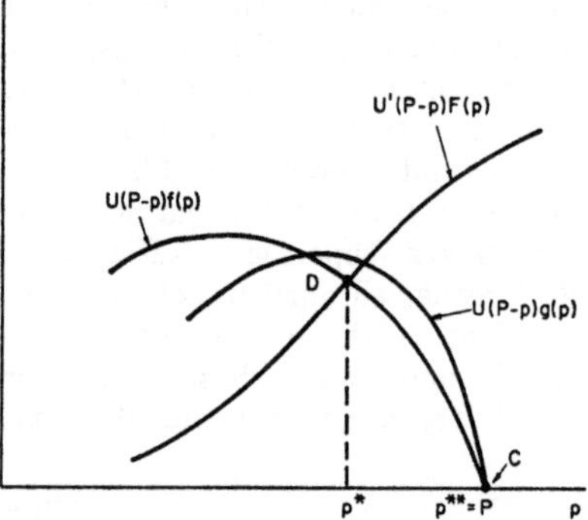

FIG. 9.—Optimal price bids under discrimination and competition.

crimination than under competition. That is, we would expect

$$F(t) = \int_0^t f(x)dx \geq G(t) = \int_0^t g(x)dx$$

for all t. For $\max_p E_C(U)$ at p^{**} we must have

$$\frac{\partial E_C}{\partial p} = U(P-p^{**})g(p^{**}) = 0. \quad \text{(A1')}$$

But if $U(P - p) > 0$, and $f(p) > 0$ on $0 \leq p < P$, and $U(P - p) = 0$, when $p = P$, the equality can only be satisfied at $p^{**} = P$. That is, the theorem requires the individual to have a positive utility for money and to believe that there is at least some small probability that the minimum successful bid will be as high as his limit, P. Hence, as is intuitively obvious, in competitive auctions the expected-utility maximizer will bid his full limit or resale price, P. There is no penalty for winning the bid at a price above the market-clearing price, so the bidding problem reduces to the obvious one of maximizing the chance of success. This is accomplished by bidding the maximum possible, at P, as illustrated in Figure 9 at point C (competition).

Hence, under the above assumptions, we conclude that a maximizer would bid lower under discrimination than under competition.

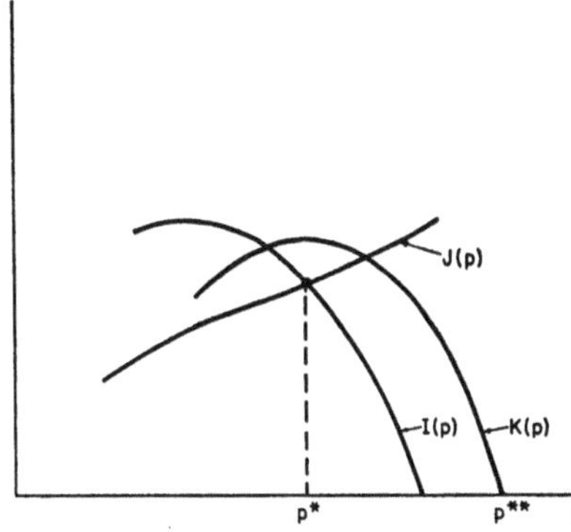

FIG. 10.—Optimal price bids under discrimination and competition.

B. LIMIT OR RESALE PRICE UNCERTAIN

Where the individual is to submit a single bid to buy a single unit or fixed lot of the item, we again assume a utility function $U(P - p)$ if the bid is successful, $U(0) = 0$ otherwise. In addition, for the discriminative auction we assume a subjective joint density $f(x, P)$, where x is the lowest accepted bid and P the resale price. Similarly, for the competitive auction we assume a subjective joint density $g(x, P)$.

In the discriminative auction, expected utility is now

$$E_D(U) = \int_0^\infty \int_0^p U(P-p) f(x, P)\, dx\, dP .$$

Expected utility is maximum at p^* if

$$\frac{\partial E_D}{\partial p} = I(p^*) - J(p^*) = 0 \qquad \text{(B1)}$$

and if

$$\frac{\partial^2 E_D}{\partial p^2} = I'(p^*) - J'(p^*) < 0 , \qquad \text{(B2)}$$

where

$$I(p^*) = \int_0^\infty U(P - p^*) f(p^*, P)\, dP ,$$

$$J(p^*) = \int_0^\infty \int_0^{p^*} U'(P - p^*) \times f(x, P)\, dx\, dP .$$

In a competitive auction, expected utility for the same bidder would be

$$E_C(U) = \int_0^\infty \int_0^p U(P - x) g(x, P)\, dx\, dP .$$

A maximum at p^{**} requires

$$\frac{\partial E_C}{\partial p} = K(p^{**}) = 0 , \qquad \text{(B3)}$$

and

$$\frac{\partial^2 E_C}{\partial p^2} = K'(p^{**}) < 0 , \qquad \text{(B4)}$$

where

$$K(p^{**}) = \int_0^\infty U(P - p^{**}) \times g(p^{**}, P)\, dP .$$

The condition (B2) requires $I(p)$ to cut $J(p)$ from above at p^*, as shown in Figure 10. In order for p^{**} to exceed p^* we see from Figure 10 that it is sufficient for $K(p)$ to lie above $I(p) - J(p)$ in the region above p^*. That we may have $p^{**} > p^*$ is readily demonstrated. For example, consider the case in which utility is linear in money, $U(m) \equiv m$. Then (B1) can be written

$$\int_0^\infty (P - p^*) f(p^*, P)\, dP - \int_0^\infty \int_0^{p^*} f(x, P)\, dx\, dP = 0 .$$

The second term is the cumulative marginal-probability function $F_1(p^*)$. Substituting $f(p^*, P) = f(P\,|\,p^*)f_1(p^*)$ we get

$$f_1(p^*)\,[E_f(P\,|\,p^*) - p^*] = F_1(p^*)\,. \quad \text{(B1}'\text{)}$$

Similarly, (B3) becomes

$$g_1(p^{**})\,[E_g(P\,|\,p^{**}) - p^{**}] = 0\,. \quad \text{(B2}'\text{)}$$

If we make the reasonable assumption that expected resale price in the discriminative auction cannot be greater than that in the competitive auction, that is,

$$\bar{P}(p^*) \equiv E_f(P\,|\,p^*) \leq E_g(P\,|\,p^{**}) \equiv \bar{P}(p^{**})\,,$$

then from (B1′) and (B2′)

$$p^* = \bar{P}(p^*) - \frac{F_1(p^*)}{f_1(p^*)} < \bar{P}(p^*) \leq \bar{P}(p^{**}) = p^{**}\,.$$

This assumption surely holds in the experimental design in this paper, since the (rectangular) distribution of resale price is identical in the C and D auctions.

The conclusion is that a bidder submitting a single bid *may* (and we predict that he will) bid lower in a discriminative auction than in a corresponding competitive auction.

In our experiments the subjects are permitted to submit up to two bids each. We will therefore extend the above bidding theory to this case.

Let $0 \leq p_1 \leq p_2$ be the two bids to be submitted. In the discriminative auction expected utility would be

$$E^D(U) = \int_0^\infty \int_0^{p_1} U(2P - p_1 - p_2) \times f(x, P)\,dx\,dP + \int_0^\infty \int_{p_1}^{p_2} U(P - p_2)\,f(x, P)\,dx\,dP\,, \quad \text{(B5)}$$

where the utility is $U(2P - p_1 - p_2)$ if both bids are successful, $U(P - p_2)$ if only the high bid is successful, and 0 if neither bid is accepted. A relative maximum occurs at (p_1^*, p_2^*) if

$$\frac{\partial E^D}{\partial p_1} = \int_0^\infty U(2P - p_1^* - p_2^*) \times f(p_1^*, P)\,dP - \int_0^\infty \int_0^{p_1} U'(2P - p_1^* - p_2^*) \times f(x, P)\,dx\,dP - \int_0^\infty U(P - p_2^*)\,f(p_1^*, P)\,dP = 0\,, \quad \text{(B6)}$$

$$\frac{\partial E^D}{\partial p_2} = -\int_0^\infty \int_0^{p_1} U'(2P - p_1^* - p_2^*) \times f(x, P)\,dx\,dP + \int_0^\infty U(P - p_2^*)\,f(p_2^*, P)\,dP - \int_0^\infty \int_{p_1}^{p_2^*} U'(P - p_2^*) \times f(x, P)\,dx\,dP = 0\,. \quad \text{(B7)}$$

and if

$$\begin{vmatrix} E_{11}^D & E_{12}^D \\ E_{21}^D & E_{22}^D \end{vmatrix} > 0\,, \quad E_{11}^D < 0\,.$$

If utility is linear in money, (B6) and (B7) can be written

$$f_1(p_1^*)\,[E_f(P\,|\,p_1^*) - p_1^*] - F_1(p_1^*) = 0\,,$$

and

$$f_1(p_2^*)\,[E_f(P\,|\,p_2^*) - p_2^*]\,F_1 - (p_2^*) = 0\,,$$

where

$$E_f(P\,|\,p_i^*) = \int_0^\infty P f(P\,|\,p_i^*)\,dP\,.$$

Hence $\bar{P}(p_1^*) = \bar{P}(p_2^*) > p_1^* = p_2^*$. If utility is linear in money the theory implies that an individual submitting two bids should enter them at the same price and at a price below the mean of the subjective density of resale price.

Expected utility in a competitive auction is

$$E^C(U) = \int_0^\infty \int_0^{p_1} U(2P-2x) \times g(x,P)\,dx\,dP + \int_0^\infty \int_{p_1}^{p_2} U(P-x) \times g(x,P)\,dx\,dP. \tag{B8}$$

Necessary conditions for a minimum can be written

$$\frac{\partial E^C}{\partial p_1} = \int_0^\infty U(2P-2p_1^{**}) \times g(p_1^{**},P)\,dP - \int_0^\infty U(P-p_1^{**}) \times g(p_1^{**},P)\,dP = 0 \tag{B9}$$

and

$$\frac{\partial E^C}{\partial p_2} = \int_0^\infty U(P-p_2^{**}) \times g(p_2^{**},P)\,dP = 0\,. \tag{B10}$$

And for a relative maximum,

$$\begin{vmatrix} E_{11}^C & E_{12}^C \\ E_{21}^C & E_{22}^C \end{vmatrix} > 0,\ E_{11}^C < 0\,.$$

If $U(m) \equiv m$, we can write (B9) and (B10) in the form

$$\frac{\partial E^C}{\partial p_1} = \int_0^\infty (P-p_1^{**})\,g(P\mid p_1^{**})\,dP = g(p_1^{**})\,[E_g(P\mid p_1^{**}) - p_1^{**}] = 0$$

and

$$\frac{\partial E^C}{\partial p_2} = \int_0^\infty (P-p_2^{**}) \times g(P\mid p_2^{**})\,g(p_2^{**})\,dP = g(p_2^{**})\,[E_g(P\mid p_2^{**}) - p_2^{**}] = 0\,,$$

and hence $\bar{P}(p_1^{**}) = \bar{P}(p_2^{**}) = p_1^{**} = p_2^{**}$. If utility is linear in money, an individual submitting two bids in a competitive auction will enter both bids at the mean of the subjective density of resale price.

Thus, if expected resale price under competition is not less than its value under discrimination, $p_1^* = p_2^* < \bar{P}(p_1^*) = \bar{P}(p_2^*) \leq \bar{P}(p_1^{**}) = \bar{P}(p_2^{**}) = p_1^{**} = p_2^{**}$, then, for utility that is linear in money, an individual's bids under discrimination will be lower than his bids under competition.

APPENDIX II

INSTRUCTIONS

EXPERIMENTS I*D*, III*D*, IV*D* (DISCRIMINATIVE)

This is an experiment in the economics of market decision-making. The National Science Foundation has provided funds for conducting this research. The instructions are simple, and if you follow them carefully and make good decisions you may earn a considerable amount of money.

1. You will be given a starting capital credit balance of $1.00. Any profit earned by you in the experiment will be *added* to this sum, and any losses incurred by you will be *subtracted* from this sum. Your net balance at the end of the experiment will be calculated and paid to you in real money.

2. This experiment will simulate a certain kind of market in which you will act as buyers in a sequence of trading periods. Each trading period begins with an announcement indicating the quantity of the fictitious commodity that is offered for sale.

3. In each period, your task is to attempt to buy units of the commodity by submitting written bids for it in competition with other buyers. Each unit that you are able to purchase is then resold by you at a price whose determination is explained below in paragraph 5. The procedure for determin-

ing whether a bid for a unit is accepted, and the purchase price of that bid, will be explained in paragraph 6.

4. If a bid is not accepted your profit is zero. If a bid is accepted, you make a profit equal to the difference between your selling price and your purchase price. If this difference is negative, it represents a loss. That is, your profit for each unit is: profit = (selling price) − (purchase price).

5. For all bids that are accepted, the resale price of each unit is determined by a random drawing (using a random-number table) from the following nine numbers: $1.15, $1.25, $1.35, $1.45, $1.55, $1.65, $1.75, $1.85, and $1.95. Each of these prices is *equally likely to be drawn in each market period.* Since there are nine prices, this means that there is a $\frac{1}{9}$ chance that any one price will be drawn in any market period. For example; if $1.25 is drawn in one period, this has no effect on the $\frac{1}{9}$ chance that $1.25 will be drawn in any later market period.

You know the range within which the selling price will fall, $1.15–$1.95, and you know that each price in this range has a $\frac{1}{9}$ chance of occurring. But you do not know in advance, at the time you enter your bids to buy, what the exact selling price will be.

6. Whether a bid is accepted, and at what price, is determined as follows: Suppose X units are offered for sale at the beginning of a market period. Each bidder submits two written bids on cards supplied for this purpose. Each bid specifies a price for a single unit of the commodity. The bid prices must be in dollars and cents and end in the digit 5, for example, $1.35, $0.75, $0.45. These bids will be collected and then arrayed in descending order from the highest to the lowest. With X units offered for sale, the first X of these bids (starting with the highest) will be accepted, and the remaining bids will be rejected. In the case of ties at the lowest accepted bid price, random numbers will be used to determine which bids are to be accepted. The highest and lowest bids will then be announced. Each accepted bid will represent the purchase of one unit of the commodity at a purchase price equal to *your bid price.* Therefore, the higher your bid price the smaller is your potential profit on that bid if it is accepted. But the higher your bid the more likely it will be above the lowest accepted bid and thereby be accepted. You must weigh these considerations carefully in deciding upon each bid price to be submitted. A bid of zero is acceptable and is essentially equivalent to not entering a bid, or "standing pat."

7. Consider a numerical example. Suppose Jones submits two bids—one at $1.45 and another at $0.65. Suppose that the array of bids and the quantity offered are such that the highest accepted bid is $1.55 and the lowest is $0.45. Since both of Jones's bids were above $0.45, they are accepted. He has purchased one unit at $1.45 and another at $0.65. Now assume that the result of the drawing to determine selling price yields a price of $1.35. Then Jones has incurred a profit of $1.35 − $1.45 = −$0.10, a loss on one unit and a profit of $1.35 − $0.65 = $0.70 on the second unit. His net profit is $0.60 on the two bids.

As another example, suppose Jones submits bids at $0.85 and $0.25. Assume that the highest accepted bid is $1.25 and the lowest is $0.55. Then Jones's high bid was accepted while his low bid was not. That is, he has purchased one unit at $0.85. Now let the result of the random drawing be a selling price of $1.65. His profit on the single unit is $1.65 − $0.85 = $0.80.

(Paragraphs 6 and 7 were supplemented with graphical illustrations like Figure 1, without the shaded area, but with the bids indicated in these paragraphs shown on the graphs.)

You are not to reveal your bids, or profits, nor are you to speak to any other subject while the experiment is in process.

Are there any questions?

EXPERIMENTS IIC, IIIC, VC (COMPETITIVE)

The instructions for the competitive treatments were the same as for the discriminative except for paragraphs 6 and 7 as follows:

6. Whether a bid is accepted, and at what price, is determined as follows: Suppose X units are offered for sale at the beginning of a market period. Each bidder submits two written bids on cards supplied for this purpose. Each bid specifies a price for a single unit of the commodity. The bid prices must be in dollars and cents and end in the digit 5, for example, $1.35, $0.75, and $0.45. These bids will be collected and then arrayed in descending order from the highest to the lowest. With X units offered for sale, the first X of these bids (starting with the highest) will be accepted, and the remaining bids will be rejected. In the case of ties at the lowest accepted bid price, random numbers will be used to determine which bids are to be accepted. The highest and lowest bids will then be announced. Each accepted bid will represent the purchase of one unit of the commodity at a purchase price equal to the *lowest accepted bid price, not your bid price.* Therefore, your potential profit is not decreased if your bid is above the lowest accepted bid. The higher your bid the more likely it will be above the low bid and thereby be accepted. But your cost and potential profit are determined by the lowest accepted bid, not your bid. A bid of zero is acceptable and is essentially equivalent to not entering a bid, or "standing pat."

7. Consider a numerical example: Suppose Jones submits two bids—one at $1.45 and another at $0.65. Suppose that the array of bids and the quantity offered are such that the highest accepted bid is $1.55 and the lowest is $0.45. Since both Jones's bids were above $0.45, they are accepted. He has purchased two units at $0.45. Now assume that the result of the drawing to determine selling price yields a price of $1.35. Then Jones has made a profit of $1.35 – $0.45 = $0.90 on each unit, or a total of $1.80 on the two bids.

As another example, suppose Jones submits bids of $0.85 and $0.25. Assume the highest accepted bid is $1.25 and the lowest is $0.55. Then Jones's high bid was accepted while his low bid was not. That is, he has purchased one unit at $0.55. Now let the result of the random drawing be a selling price of $1.65. His profit on the single unit is $1.65 – $0.55 = $1.10.

APPENDIX III

A. Experimental Data, *ID*

Subject No.	Auction 0		Auction 1		Auction 2		Auction 3		Auction 4		Auction 5	
	p_2	p_1	p_2	p_1	p_2	p_1	p_2	p_1	p_2	p_1	p_2	p_1
1	$1.35*	$1.15*	$1.25*	$1.05*	$1.25*	$1.15*	$1.25*	$1.15*	$1.25*	$1.25*	$1.35*	$1.25*
2	1.15*	0.55	1.25*	0.95	1.25*	1.15*	1.25*	1.15*	1.25*	1.25*	1.25*	1.25*
3	0.65	0.45	0.85	0.75	0.95	0.85	1.15*	1.15*	1.25*	1.15	1.35*	1.25*
4	0.95*	0.75	0.95	0.95	1.05	0.95	1.15	1.05	1.25*	1.15	1.25*	1.25*
5	0.55	0.45	1.05*	0.95*	1.15*	1.05*	1.15	1.15	1.35*	1.25*	1.35*	1.25
6	1.35*	0.85*	1.25*	0.95	1.05	1.05	1.15	1.15	1.25*	1.15	1.35*	1.35*
7	0.95*	0.85*	0.95*	0.95*	1.05*	1.05	1.15*	1.15*	1.15	1.15	1.25*	1.25
8	0.65	0.45	1.15*	0.95	1.15*	1.05	1.15*	1.15*	1.15	1.05	1.25*	1.25
9	1.05*	0.75	1.25*	0.95	1.05*	1.05*	1.15	1.05	1.25*	1.05	1.15	1.05
10	1.35*	1.15*	1.05*	1.05*	1.15*	1.05	1.15	1.15	1.25*	1.25*	1.25	1.25
11	1.15*	0.85*	1.05*	0.85	1.15*	0.95	1.15*	1.05	1.25*	1.15	1.35*	1.25*
12	1.05*	0.35	1.05*	0.95	1.25*	1.25*	1.25*	1.25*	1.35*	1.35*	1.35*	1.35*
13	1.05*	0.85	1.05*	0.95	1.15*	1.05	1.15*	1.15*	1.25*	1.15	1.25	1.25
14	1.25*	0.95*	1.15*	0.95*	1.15*	0.95	1.15*	1.15	1.25*	1.15	1.25	1.25
15	1.45*	0.75	1.35*	0.75	1.25*	1.15*	1.35*	1.15*	1.35*	1.15	1.35*	1.25*
Highest accepted bid	$1.45		$1.35		$1.25		$1.35		$1.35		$1.35	
Lowest accepted bid	0.85		0.95		1.05		1.15		1.25		1.25	
Resale price	1.75		1.15		1.95		1.35		1.95		1.45	

* Accept bids.

B. Experimental Data, II*C*

Subject No.	Auction 0		Auction 1		Auction 2		Auction 3		Auction 4		Auction 5	
	p_2	p_1	p_2	p_1	p_2	p_1	p_2	p_1	p_2	p_1	p_2	p_1
1	$1.45*	$0.75	$1.55*	$1.15	$1.95*	$1.35*	$1.95*	$1.45*	$2.05*	$1.55*	$1.95*	$1.45*
2	1.75*	1.35*	1.85*	1.35*	1.65*	1.55*	1.65*	1.45*	1.55*	1.45*	1.65*	1.35
3	1.75*	0.75	1.45*	0.45	1.45*	0.45	1.45*	1.15	1.75*	1.15	1.75*	1.55*
4	1.55*	1.45*	1.55*	1.55*	1.55*	1.55*	1.55*	1.55*	1.55*	1.55*	1.55*	0.45
5	1.15*	0.85	1.35*	0.75	1.15	0.95	1.45*	0.95	1.25	0.95	1.75*	1.35
6	1.75*	1.25*	1.75*	1.25*	1.75*	1.35	1.75*	1.75*	1.45	1.35	1.75*	1.65*
7	1.05	0.35	1.75*	1.05	1.35*	1.05	1.35	1.15	1.45*	1.15	1.45	1.15
8	1.85*	1.75*	1.45*	1.35*	1.45*	1.35*	1.45*	1.45*	1.45*	1.45*	1.45	1.45
9	0.85	0.05	1.15	0.95	0.95	0.65	1.25	0.95	1.25	0.85	1.35	1.15
10	1.65*	1.25*	1.35*	1.25*	1.75*	1.45*	1.55*	1.35	1.75*	1.35	1.75*	1.55*
11	0.65	0.45	1.25*	1.15	1.55*	1.25	1.55*	1.35	1.55*	1.35	1.55*	1.45*
12	1.25*	0.55	1.35*	0.95	1.65*	1.25	1.65*	1.35	1.65*	1.55*	1.65*	1.55*
13	1.45*	1.05*	1.35*	1.15	1.45*	1.35	1.55*	1.45*	1.55*	1.55*	1.55*	1.45*
14	1.15*	1.05*	1.15	1.05	1.35*	1.15	1.25	1.15	1.85*	1.35	1.25	1.15
15	0.95	0.75	1.75*	1.25*	1.65*	1.25	1.85*	1.25	1.55*	1.35	1.95*	1.35
Highest accepted bid	$1.85		$1.85		$1.95		$1.95		$2.05		$1.95	
Lowest accepted bid	1.05		1.25		1.35		1.45		1.45		1.45	
Resale price	1.75		1.15		1.95		1.35		1.95		1.45	

* Accept bids.

C. Experimental Data, III*D*

Subject No.	Auction 0		Auction 1		Auction 2		Auction 3		Auction 4		Auction 5		Auction 6		Auction 7		Auction 8	
	p_2	p_1	p_2	p_1	p_2	p_1	p_2	p_1	p_2	p_1	p_2	p_1	p_2	p_1	p_2	p_1	p_2	p_1
1........	$0.95*	$0.55	$0.95*	$0.85*	$1.05*	$1.05*	$1.15*	$1.15*	$1.15*	$1.15	$1.25*	$1.25*	$1.35	$1.25	$1.35*	$1.25	$1.35*	$1.25
2........	0.55	0.15	0.95*	0.65	1.05*	0.65	1.05*	0.95	1.15*	1.05	1.25*	1.15	1.25	1.25	1.35*	1.25*	1.25	1.25
3........	0.55	0.25	1.45*	1.15*	1.35*	0.95*	1.25*	1.05	1.35*	1.15	1.35*	1.15	1.35*	1.35*	1.35*	1.25	1.35*	1.25*
4........	0.95*	0.75*	0.95*	0.85	0.95	0.85	1.05*	1.05	1.35*	1.15	1.35*	1.15	1.35*	1.35*	1.25*	1.15	1.25	1.25
5........	1.55*	1.15*	1.45*	0.95*	1.35*	0.95	1.25*	1.15*	1.25*	1.25*	1.35*	1.25*	1.35*	1.35*	1.35*	1.35*	1.35*	1.35*
6........	0.75*	0.55	0.85	0.75	0.95*	0.95	1.15*	1.05	1.25*	1.15*	1.25*	1.25	1.45*	1.35*	1.35*	1.25	1.35*	1.35*
7........	0.75*	0.65*	1.15*	0.85	1.15*	0.95*	1.15*	1.05	1.25*	1.15*	1.25*	1.25	1.45*	1.25	1.35*	1.35*	1.35*	1.35*
8........	0.85*	0.65*	0.95*	0.75	0.95	0.85	1.15*	1.05*	1.25*	1.15	1.25*	1.25	1.25	1.25	1.25	1.25	1.35*	1.35*
9........	1.25*	0.55	1.15*	0.95*	1.15*	1.05*	1.15*	1.15*	1.15*	1.15	1.25*	1.25*	1.35*	1.35*	1.25*	1.25	1.25	1.25
10........	1.05*	0.75*	1.05*	0.95*	1.05*	0.95*	1.05*	1.05	1.25*	1.25*	1.25*	1.25	1.35*	1.25	1.35*	1.35*	1.35*	1.25*
11........	1.15*	0.95*	1.15*	0.95*	1.15*	0.95*	1.15*	1.15*	1.25*	1.15	1.35*	1.25*	1.35*	1.35*	1.35*	1.35*	1.35*	1.35*
12........	1.05*	0.65*	0.95*	0.85*	1.05*	0.95*	1.15*	1.15*	1.25*	1.25*	1.35*	1.25*	1.35*	1.35*	1.35*	1.35*	1.35*	1.35*
13........	0.85*	0.45	0.85	0.75	1.05*	0.95	1.05	1.05	1.25*	1.05	1.35*	1.05	1.35*	1.25	1.35*	1.15	1.35*	1.15
Highest accepted bid.....	$1.55		$1.45		$1.35		$1.25		$1.35		$1.35		$1.45		$1.35		$1.35	
Lowest accepted bid.....	0.65		0.85		0.95		1.05		1.15		1.25		1.35		1.25		1.25	
Resale price....	1.75		1.15		1.95		1.35		1.95		1.45		1.15		1.35		1.85	

* Accept bids.

D. EXPERIMENTAL DATA, IIIC

Subject No.	Auction 1		Auction 2		Auction 3		Auction 4		Auction 5		Auction 6		Auction 7		Auction 8	
	p_2	p_1	p_2	p_1	p_2	p_1	p_2	p_1	p_2	p_1	p_2	p_1	p_2	p_1	p_2	p_1
1	$1.25*	$1.25	$1.35	$1.25	$1.35	$1.25	$1.35	$1.25	$1.35	$1.25	$1.35	$1.25	$1.45*	$1.35	$1.45*	$1.35
2	1.55*	1.25*	1.55*	1.25	1.65*	1.45	1.45*	1.15	1.45*	1.25	1.45*	1.45*	1.55*	1.45*	1.55*	1.45*
3	1.35*	1.25*	1.55*	1.35*	1.65*	1.35	1.35	1.25	1.85*	1.45*	1.65*	1.35	1.45*	1.45*	1.45*	1.35
4	1.35*	0.95	1.95*	1.25	1.85*	1.25	1.35	1.15	1.35	1.25	1.35	1.25	1.35	1.35	1.35	1.35
5	1.35*	1.25*	1.55*	1.35*	1.95*	1.75*	1.45*	1.45*	1.45*	1.45*	1.65*	1.45*	1.45*	1.35	1.45*	1.45*
6	1.25*	1.15	1.45*	1.35	1.55*	1.45*	1.55*	1.55*	1.55*	1.45	1.55*	1.45*	1.55*	1.45*	1.55*	1.45*
7	1.45*	1.35*	1.45*	1.45*	1.45*	1.45*	1.55*	1.35*	1.55*	1.45	1.55*	1.45*	1.55*	1.45	1.55*	1.35
8	1.95*	0.75	1.85*	1.25	1.95*	1.95*	1.95*	1.95*	1.45*	1.45*	1.35	1.35	1.85*	1.85*	1.35	1.35
9	1.65*	1.65*	1.55*	1.55*	1.55*	1.55*	1.55*	1.55*	1.55*	1.55*	1.55*	1.55*	1.55*	1.55*	1.55*	1.55*
10	1.45*	0.75	1.45*	1.15	1.85*	1.35	1.85*	1.25	1.85*	1.35	1.85*	1.45*	1.85*	1.35	1.85*	1.45*
12	0.95	0.85	1.35*	1.35	1.45*	1.45	1.45*	1.45*	1.45*	1.45*	1.45*	1.45*	1.45*	1.45	1.45*	1.45*
13	1.45*	1.35*	1.45*	1.45*	1.45*	1.45	1.55*	1.45*	1.55*	1.45*	1.55*	1.45*	1.55*	1.45*	1.55*	1.45
14	1.55*	0.85	1.55*	1.35*	1.85*	1.75*	1.85*	1.65*	1.85*	1.85*	1.65*	1.25	1.55*	1.35	1.85*	1.35
Highest accepted bid	$1.95		$1.95		$1.95		$1.95		$1.85		$1.85		$1.85		$1.85	
Lowest accepted bid	1.25		1.35		1.45		1.35		1.45		1.45		1.45		1.45	
Resale price	1.35		1.45		1.35		1.75		1.95		1.25		1.75		1.35	

* Accept bid.

E. Experimental Data, IV*D*

Subject No.	Auction 0 p_2	Auction 0 p_1	Auction 1 p_2	Auction 1 p_1	Auction 2 p_2	Auction 2 p_1	Auction 3 p_2	Auction 3 p_1
11	$1.45*	$1.25*	$1.45*	$1.25*	$1.45*	$1.25	$1.45*	$1.25
12	1.25*	0.85	1.25	0.95	1.25	1.05	1.45*	1.35
13	1.15*	0.75	1.35*	1.25*	1.25	0.95	1.25	1.35
14	1.25*	1.55*	1.45*	1.25	1.35*	1.25	1.45*	1.25
15	1.65*	1.75*	1.25*	1.15	1.35*	1.35*	1.45*	1.45*
16	1.45*	0.75	1.15	1.05	1.15	1.25	1.35	1.25
17	0.95	0.75	1.35*	1.35*	1.35*	1.35*	1.45*	1.45*
18	0.95	1.35*	1.35*	0.95	1.35*	1.35*	1.45*	1.45*
20	1.05	0.65	1.15	1.25	1.15	1.05	1.45*	1.45*
21	0.85	1.05	1.35*	1.25*	1.35*	1.25	1.35*	1.25
22	1.15*	0.75	1.15	1.15	1.15	1.15	1.35*	1.25
23	1.25*	1.15*	1.25*	1.25*	1.35*	1.25	1.45*	1.35*
24	1.15*	0.95	1.35*	1.15	1.35*	1.35*	1.45*	1.35
25	1.25*	1.35*	1.25*	1.25*	1.35*	1.25	1.35	1.15
26	0.95	0.95	1.05	1.15	1.35*	1.35*	1.25	1.25
27	1.05	1.05	1.25	1.05	1.35*	1.25	1.35	1.15
28	1.45*	1.35*	1.35*	1.35*	1.35*	1.35*	1.35*	1.35*
Highest accepted bid	$1.75		$1.45		$1.45		$1.45	
Lowest accepted bid	1.15		1.25		1.35		1.35	
Resale price	1.75		1.15		1.95		1.35	

Subject No.	Auction 4 p_2	Auction 4 p_1	Auction 5 p_2	Auction 5 p_1	Auction 6 p_2	Auction 6 p_1	Auction 7 p_2	Auction 7 p_1
11	$1.45*	$1.35	$1.45*	$1.35	$1.45*	$1.35	$1.35	$1.45
12	1.45*	1.35	1.45	1.45	1.55*	1.45*	1.45*	1.45*
13	1.55*	1.15	1.45*	1.25	1.35	1.25	1.25	1.25
14	1.45*	1.25	1.35	1.35	1.35	1.35	1.45	1.35
15	1.45*	1.45*	1.45*	1.45*	1.45*	1.45	1.45*	1.45
16	1.35	1.35	1.45*	1.35	1.45*	1.45*	1.45*	1.45*
17	1.45*	1.45*	1.45*	1.35	1.35	1.35	1.45*	1.45*
18	1.45*	1.45*	1.45*	1.45*	1.45*	1.45*	1.45*	1.45*
20	1.35	1.35	1.45*	1.35	1.35	1.25	1.15	1.35
21	1.35*	1.25	1.45*	1.35	1.45*	1.35	1.45*	1.45
22	1.55*	1.35	1.45*	1.45*	1.55*	1.35	1.45*	1.45
23	1.35	1.35	1.45*	1.35	1.45*	1.35	1.45	1.45
24	1.45*	1.45*	1.45*	1.45*	1.45*	1.45*	1.45	1.35
25	1.45*	1.35	1.45*	1.35	1.55*	1.45	1.55*	1.45*
26	1.35*	1.35	1.25	1.25	1.35	1.35	1.45*	1.45*
27	1.45*	1.45*	1.35	1.35	1.45*	1.45*	1.45*	1.45
28	1.35	1.35	1.45*	1.45*	1.45*	1.45*	1.45*	1.45*
Highest accepted bid	$1.55		$1.45		$1.55		$1.55	
Lowest accepted bid	1.35		1.45		1.45		1.45	
Resale price	1.95		1.45		1.15		1.35	

Subject No.	Auction 8 p_2	Auction 8 p_1	Auction 9 p_2	Auction 9 p_1	Auction 10 p_2	Auction 10 p_1
11	$1.45*	$1.45	$1.45*	$1.45*	$1.45*	$1.45
12	1.45*	1.45	1.45*	1.45	1.45*	1.45*
13	1.45*	1.25	1.35	1.25	1.45*	1.35
14	1.35	1.45	1.45*	1.35	1.45	1.35
15	1.45*	1.45	1.55*	1.45	1.55*	1.45
16	1.45*	1.45	1.45	1.45	1.45*	1.45*
17	1.55*	1.55*	1.55*	1.45*	1.55*	1.45*
18	1.45*	1.45*	1.45*	1.45*	1.45	1.45
20	1.35	1.35	1.45*	1.35	1.45*	1.35
21	1.45*	1.45	1.45*	1.45	1.45*	1.45*
22	1.45*	1.45*	1.45*	1.45	1.45*	1.45
23	1.45*	1.45	1.45	1.45	1.45	1.45
24	1.45*	1.35	1.45*	1.45*	1.45*	1.45
25	1.55*	1.45*	1.45	1.45	1.45*	1.45
26	1.45*	1.45	1.45*	1.45	1.45*	1.45
27	1.45*	1.45	1.55*	1.55*	1.55*	1.55*
28	1.45	1.45	1.45*	1.45	1.45	1.45
Highest accepted bid	$1.55		$1.55		$1.55	
Lowest accepted bid	1.45		1.45		1.45	
Resale price	1.85		1.55		1.35	

* Accept bid.

F. Experimental Data, VC

Subject No.	Auction 0		Auction 1		Auction 2		Auction 3		Auction 4		Auction 5	
	p_2	p_1	p_2	p_1	p_2	p_1	p_2	p_1	p_2	p_1	p_2	p_1
11	$ 1.45*	$ 1.05*	$ 1.25*	$ 1.05	$ 1.25*	$ 1.05	$ 1.35	$ 1.25	$ 1.55*	$ 1.45	$ 1.05	$ 0.00
12	1.45*	0.45	1.35*	0.85	1.85*	1.25	1.95*	1.35	1.85*	1.45	2.05*	0.35
13	1.35*	0.55	1.55*	0.65	1.25	0.55	1.25	0.55	2.15*	2.05*	2.05*	1.25
14	1.55*	0.85	1.35*	0.95	1.55*	1.05	1.55*	1.05	1.55*	0.95	1.55*	1.15
15	1.15*	0.35	1.15*	0.65	7.25*	1.25*	10.05*	1.25	11.05*	1.35	10.05*	1.45
16	125.15*	125.15*	255.55*	250.75*	255.55*	225.25*	265.65*	255.55*	255.55*	244.45*	255.55*	244.45*
17	1.65*	1.05*	10.00*	1.95*	1.05	0.85	1.15	1.35	1.85*	1.85*	1.75*	1.55*
18	1.15*	0.55	2.15*	0.75	1.15	0.75	1.55*	1.05	1.25	1.15	1.95*	1.15
19	0.65	0.55	1.15*	0.95	1.15	0.95	1.55*	1.45*	1.25	1.25	1.55*	1.45
20	0.75	0.45	3.75*	1.25*	1.45*	1.25*	1.45*	1.35	5.05*	1.45	1.55*	1.45
21	1.45*	0.75	1.75*	1.05	100.05*	2.55*	1.95*	1.95*	1.95*	1.55*	1.75*	1.45
22	1.05*	0.75	1.15	1.05	10.05*	1.15	1.45*	1.35*	1.45	1.35	1.45	1.35
23	1.75*	0.55	3.55*	0.85	3.55*	0.65	1.75*	0.95	1.75*	0.55	3.75*	0.05
24	1.45*	0.85*	1.45*	0.85	1.75*	0.05	1.75*	0.05	1.75*	0.05	275.75*	0.05
25	2.05*	0.75	10.05*	0.95	105.05*	1.15	1,000.05*	1.15	200.05*	1.25	100.05*	1.75*
26	0.75	0.35	0.95	0.85	1.35*	1.25*	1.35	1.35	1.45*	1.35	1.45*	1.45
27	0.95*	0.45	1.55*	0.95	1.65*	1.15	1.75*	1.55*	1.75*	1.45	1.75*	1.45
Highest accepted bid	$125.15		$255.55		$255.55		$1,000.05		$255.55		$275.75	
Lowest accepted bid	0.85		1.15		1.25		1.35		1.45		1.45	
Resale price	1.75		1.15		1.95		1.35		1.95		1.45	

Subject No.	Auction 6		Auction 7		Auction 8		Auction 9		Auction 10	
	p_2	p_1	p_2	p_1	p_2	p_1	p_2	p_1	p_2	p_1
11	$ 1.45	$1.15	$ 1.45*	$1.35	$1.45	$1.35	$1.55*	$1.45*	$1.55*	$1.45
12	2.05*	1.15	1.95*	1.35	1.85*	1.45*	1.95*	1.35	2.05*	1.35
13	2.15*	2.05*	2.15*	2.05*	2.15*	2.05*	2.15*	2.05*	2.15*	2.05*
14	1.55*	1.15	1.55*	1.05	1.55*	0.95	1.55*	1.25	1.55*	1.25
15	10.05*	1.45*	10.05*	1.35	1.95*	1.35	1.95*	1.35	1.95*	1.35
16	2.25*	2.15*	2.25*	2.15*	2.25*	2.15*	1.85*	1.75*	2.05*	1.95*
17	1.45	1.15	1.35	1.15	1.15	1.05	1.35	1.35	1.35	1.35
18	1.25	1.15	1.25	1.15	1.15	1.05	1.95*	0.95	1.55*	0.95
19	1.35	1.25	1.25	1.15	1.25	1.25	1.25	1.25	1.25	1.25
20	1.75*	1.55*	1.55*	1.45*	1.55*	1.55*	1.65*	1.55*	1.65*	1.55
21	1.75*	1.75*	1.75*	1.75*	1.75*	1.75*	1.75*	1.75*	1.75*	1.55*
22	1.35	1.35	1.35	1.25	1.35	1.25	1.45	1.35	2.05*	1.35
23	3.75*	0.05	3.75*	0.05	3.75*	1.85*	5.75*	0.05	4.75*	0.05
24	285.95*	0.05	1.75*	0.05	1.75*	0.05	1.75*	0.05	1.75*	0.05
25	100.05*	1.45*	1.75*	1.75*	1.75*	0.05	1.45	1.15	1.55*	0.05
26	1.45	1.35	1.35	1.35	1.35	1.35	1.45	1.35	1.45	1.45
27	1.95*	1.55*	1.95*	1.55*	2.05*	1.55*	2.05*	1.55*	2.05*	1.55*
Highest accepted bid	$285.95		$10.05		$3.75		$5.75		$4.75	
Lowest accepted bid	1.45		1.45		1.45		1.45		1.55	
Resale price	1.15		1.35		1.85		1.55		1.35	

* Accepted bid.

Experimental Economics: Induced Value Theory

By VERNON L. SMITH*

It is the premise of this paper that the study of the decision behavior of suitably motivated individuals and groups in laboratory or other socially isolated settings such as hospitals (R. Battalio, J. Kagel, et al., 1973) has important and significant application to the development and verification of theories of the economic system at large. There are two reasons for this.

1. The results of laboratory studies can serve as a rigorous empirical pretest of economic theory prior to the use of field data tests. The state of economic hypothesis testing, as it is sometimes done, can be described roughly as follows: based on casual observation of an economic process and the self-interest postulate, one develops a model, which is then tested with the only body of field data that exists. The results of the test turn out to be ambiguous or call for improvements, and one is tempted to now modify the model in ways suggested by the data "to improve the fit." Any test of significance now becomes hopelessly confused if one attempts to apply it to the same data. Where it is possible and feasible, as in the study of price formation, the data from controlled experiments can be used to test hypotheses stemming from prescientific casual observations of a particular phenomenon. The fact that one can always run a new experiment means that it is never tautological to modify the model in ways suggested by the results of the last experiment. Since economic theories always deal with certain alleged behavioral tendencies in isolation, the experimental laboratory is uniquely well suited for testing the validity of such theories. It provides an exceptionally rigorous discipline of our ability to model elementary situations whether or not field data can be regarded ultimately as having been generated by such elementary models.

2. The results of experiments can be directly relevant to the study and interpretation of field data. Other so-called nonexperimental sciences such as meteorology and astronomy have depended crucially for their development on (a) small-scale laboratory experiments in the physics of mass motion, thermodynamics, and nuclear reactions; and (b) the postulate that such microphysical experimental results apply, with suitable modifications, to the study of the weather, the planets and the stars. This parallelism, "As far as we can tell, the same physical laws prevail everywhere" (Harlow Shapley 1964, p. 43), also has application to the study of social economy. Laboratory experience suggests that all of the characteristics of "real world" behavior that we consider to be of primitive importance—such as self-interest motivation, interdependent tastes, risk aversion, subjective transactions cost (time is consumed), costly information (it takes time to acquire and process information), and so on—arise naturally, indeed inevitably, in experimental settings. Anyone who had begun the study of economics in

* Department of Economics, University of Arizona. Support from NSF grants is gratefully acknowledged. This paper is an articulation of concepts originally developed in the course of several seminars in experimental economics taught at Purdue University, 1964–67.

the laboratory without these concepts would soon find himself inventing them. Furthermore, the process of experimental design forces one to articulate rules and procedures, the collection of which forms an institution, organization, or "body of law" with striking "real world" parallels (cf. Martin Shubik 1974). The laboratory becomes a place where real people earn real money for making real decisions about abstract claims that are just as "real" as a share of General Motors.

I. The Theory of Induced Valuation

Control is the essence of experimental methodology, and in experimental exchange studies it is important that one be able to state that, as between two experiments, individual values (e.g., demand or supply) either do or do not differ in a specified way. Such control can be achieved by using a reward structure to induce prescribed monetary value on actions. The concept of induced valuation (Smith 1973) depends upon the postulate of *nonsatiation:*

> Given a *costless* choice between two alternatives, identical except that the first yields more of the reward medium (usually currency) than the second, the first will always be chosen (preferred) over the second, by an *autonomous* individual, i.e., utility is a monotone increasing function of the monetary reward, $U(M)$, $U' > 0$. [pp. 22–23]

This postulate applies to experiments designed to test price theory propositions conditional upon known valuations. Separate experiments can be designed to test propositions in preference theory.

Example 1. In the experimental study of competitive equilibria in isolated markets it is necessary to induce known (to the experimenter) supply or demand on individual subjects. Let subject buyers $i=1, 2, \ldots, n$ each be given a table listing increasing concave total receipts $R_i(q_i)$ representing the currency redemption or "resale" value of q_i units acquired by subject i in an experimental market. The instructions state that if subject i acquires q_i units at prices $p_1^i, p_2^i, \ldots, p_{q_i}^i$, he will receive cash earnings of $R_i(q_i) - \sum_{k=1}^{q_i} p_k^i$. Neoclassical demand is defined as the quantity that would be purchased as a function of a given hypothetical price p. By this definition, if for a fixed p a subject purchases q_i units, he earns $R_i(q_i) - pq_i$. If his utility for money is $U_i(M_i)$ he will wish to $\max_{q_i} U_i[R_i(q_i) - pq_i]$. We have an interior maximum if and only if

$$(R_i' - p)U_i' = 0,\ U_i' > 0, \qquad \text{or } q_i = R_i'^{(-1)}(p),$$

for the class of functions U_i, R_i such that $(R_i' - p)^2 U_i'' + U_i' R_i'' < 0$. This reward scheme induces arbitrary demand $R_i'^{(-1)}(p)$ on subject i, and the experimentally controlled market demand becomes $Q = \sum_{i=1}^{n} R_i'^{(-1)}(p)$ independent of the U_i.

Similarly, let $j=1, 2, \ldots, m$ subject sellers be given cost functions $C_j(q_j)$, and receive cash earnings $\sum_{k=1}^{q_j} p_k^j - C_j(q_j)$ from selling q_j units at prices $p_1^j, p_2^j, \ldots, p_{q_j}^j$. If utility is $V_j(M_j)$, $V_j' > 0$, then $\max_{q_j} V_j[pq_j - C_j(q_j)]$ implies a supply function $q_j = C_j'^{(-1)}(p)$. The experimentally controlled market supply is $Q = \sum_{j=1}^{m} C_j'^{(-1)}(p)$ independent of the V_j. Such induced supply and demand become flows per period in experiments in which trading is conducted in a sequence of periods.

Example 2: Let subject traders be given a table listing increasing concave currency receipts $M(x_1, x_2)$ to be paid by the experimenter for terminal stocks (x_1, x_2) of each of two abstract experimental commodities exchanged in an experimental general equilibrium market. Then subject i's unknown utility for currency $U_i(M)$ induces the value $U_i[M(x_1, x_2)]$ on terminal stocks (x_1, x_2). Consequently, the experimentally controlled indifference map given by the level contours of $M(x_1, x_2)$ are induced upon subject i independent of his particular U_i. That is, each subject's marginal rate of substitution of x_2 for x_1 is given by $U_i' M_1/U_i' M_2 = M_1/M_2$, $U_i' > 0$. This allows the "Edgeworth Box" representation of general exchange equilibrium to be reproduced experimentally by inducing a given indifference map on each member of one group of subjects, and another indifference map on each of a second group of subjects. With given endowments of the abstract commodities for members of each of the two trading groups, the experimental stage is set for exchange.

II. Some Qualifications

There are three important qualifications to the nonsatiation postulate:

1. There may be subjective costs (or values) associated with market decisions. In a competitive market experiment a subject may find it arduous to monitor and make quotations, and to execute transactions. If such considerations are not negligible, then we lose some control over the process of induced valuation. The effect of boredom and the subjective costs of decision making have been emphasized in the important study by Sidney Siegel (1961). Roger Sherman (1974) has interpreted alleged violations of the Savage axioms in terms of the subjective cost of making the appropriate computations. In terms of the utility interpretation of the previous section, the utility function can now be written $U^i(M_i, E_i)$ where E_i is the "transactional effort" required to obtain reward M_i (cf. Harvey Leibenstein 1969; and implicitly, Ronald Coase 1960). To see the potential implications of costly choice, consider example 1 of the previous section in which demand $R_i'^{(-1)}(p)$ is induced upon i. Utility is now $U^i\{R_i[q_i(E_i)]-pq_i(E_i), E_i\}$ where it is assumed crudely that "bargaining effort," E_i, results in the purchase quantity $q_i(E_i)$. Then $\max_{E_i} U^i$ implies $(R_i'-p)\, q_i' U_1^i + U_2^i = 0$, and now the induced demand is $q_i = R_i'^{(-1)}(p - U_2^i/U_1^i q_i') < R_i'^{(-1)}(p)$, if $U_2^i < 0$, $q_i' > 0$. Hence, if there is a cost (value) to transacting in the experimental task, the induced demand will be smaller (larger).

There are several ways of dealing with this problem:

(a) One is to examine the experimental results to see if the quantity exchanged is less than predicted. If it is, this is consistent with a significant transactions cost. Awareness of such transactions cost may provide valuable clues to understanding why certain experiments may fail to produce predicted results. The process is not tautological as long as one can redesign the experiment and show that such conjectured transactional effects can be reduced.

(b) Another approach is to use a reward structure to compensate for, or offset, the subjective costs of transacting. There are two ways of doing this. (i) One way (Siegel 1961) is to simply raise the reward level. This increases the subjective value relative to the subjective cost of acquiring units q_i. Let α be a scale parameter determining reward level. Then utility becomes $U^i\{\alpha(R_i[q_i(E_i)]-pq_i(E_i)), E_i\}$. Induced demand is now $q_i = R_i'^{(-1)}(p - U_2^i/U_1^i q_i'\alpha) \to R_i'^{(-1)}(p)$ in the limit as α increases provided that the marginal rate of substitution $-U_2^i/U_1^i q_i'\alpha$ decreases with the reward level. (ii) Alternatively, and this is the device used most extensively, subjects are promised a "commission," β, for *each* transaction in addition to their cash trading profits. Now utility is $U^i\{R_i[q_i(E_i)] -(p-\beta)q_i(E_i), E_i\}$, and induced demand is

$$q_i = R_i'^{(-1)}(p - \beta - U_2^i/U_1^i q_i')$$
$$\cong R_i'^{(-1)}(p) \qquad \text{if } \beta \cong -U_2^i/U_1^i q_i' > 0.$$

Compare two experiments (Charles Plott and Smith 1975, pp. 20–21) in which the induced supply and demand conditions were identical but one paid no cash trading commission, only trading profit, while the other paid both: In the one experiment, volume was below (17–18 units) the "theoretical" equilibrium quantity (20 units) in all seven trading periods; in the second experiment, volume was below (19 units) equilibrium in only two of eight trading periods.

2. Individuals may attach game value to experimental outcomes. A profit in "points," $R_i(q_i)-pq_i$, may have subjective value $S_i[R_i(q_i)-pq_i]$. If S_i is monotone increasing then such game utilities create no methodological problems since they reinforce rather than distort the effect of an explicit monetary reward structure. Because of such game utilities it is often possible in simple-task experiments to get satisfactory results without monetary rewards by using instructions to induce value by role-playing behavior (i.e., "think of yourself as making a profit of such and such when . . . "). But such game values are likely to be weak, erratic, and easily dominated by transactions costs, and subjects may be readily satiated with "point" profits.

Qualifications 1 and 2 are illustrated in the convergence behavior of three experimental markets with no cash rewards and seven markets with complete and with random cash rewards. In the first three cases subjects were asked to imagine that trading profits and commissions were real. In each case the market was organized as a continuous double auction. (Buyers could make oral bids and sellers oral offers for a single unit, and any seller could accept a bid, any buyer an offer. Each subject knew only his own demand or supply conditions.) (See Smith 1964, pp. 199–201 for the instructions.) In the first case (Smith 1962, p. 118, Chart 3) subjects trade only one unit per trading period. The absence of cash rewards does not hinder convergence to prices near equilibrium by the third trading period. However, deviations increase in period 4. In the absence of cash rewards this is more likely to occur as gaming boredom follows an initial (pleasant) experience of learning.

In a second experiment (previously unpublished) buyers received multiunit revenue (or resale value) schedules, and sellers multiunit total cost schedules. There were three buyers with one schedule, eight with another; four sellers with one cost schedule, eight with another. Now the task is more difficult and incentives are weak. Price convergence is strong, especially in the second period, since the greater volume when traders are given multiple-unit capacities increases the learning experience within a trading period. But volume is considerably below (24 and 26 units in the first and second periods) the competitive prediction (30 units). This is consistent with the above theory where the task is more difficult (higher transactions cost) and monetary rewards are absent.

Case 3 (Smith 1962, p. 119, Chart 4) illustrates an experiment which fails to reach either the competitive price or quantity although the market stabilizes nicely. In this case equilibrium requires contract prices to fall to the common limit price of all sellers. They are to "imagine" themselves as making a 5-cent commission on

Table 1—Mean Contract Price by Trading Period

Experiment	1	2	3	4	5	6	7
Excess Supply	5	5	5	5	8	8	8
Reward Condition	Complete	Complete	Random	Complete	Complete	Complete	Complete
Information Condition	Incomplete	Incomplete	Incomplete	Complete	Incomplete	Incomplete	Complete
Trading Period 1	3.48	3.67	3.60	3.51	3.26	3.49	3.56
Trading Period 2	3.29	3.26	3.44	3.40	3.15	3.28	3.25
Trading Period 3	3.19	3.12	3.31	3.34	3.11	3.13	3.20
Trading Period 4	3.14	3.10	3.24	3.37	3.10	3.12	3.17

trades at these limit prices, but clearly this is not real enough to induce many contracts at \$3.10 (the theoretical equilibrium). Not even a decrease in demand succeeded in lowering contracts to \$3.10 (Table 1). This contrasts with several experiments (1, 2, 5, 6 in Table 1) using complete cash rewards in which the supply and demand are even more asymmetric than in case 3. In Table 1, markets with an excess supply of five (eight) consisted of eleven buyers with limit prices \$4.20 and sixteen (nineteen) sellers with limit prices \$3.10. A different subject group participated in each double auction experiment. Convergence to the competitive price and quantity by trading period 4 was strong, although at the equilibrium price each buyer receives \$1.15 profit with commission per trade while each seller receives only the 5-cent commission.

A controlled measurement of the effect of complete versus random monetary rewards is shown in Table 1, experiments 1–3. In 1 and 2 all subjects were paid their trading profit plus commission in cash, while in 3 four of the 27 subjects were chosen at random to receive cash profits at the end of each trading period. The weaker random reward structure significantly retards the market's convergence.

Qualifications 1 and 2 lead to a precautionary corollary: with or without monetary rewards, the experimenter may be tempted to add "realism" by giving the abstract experimental commodity a name such as "wheat," or otherwise attempt to use instructions to simulate the alleged circumstances of a particular market. This runs the danger of so enriching induced values that control over valuation is lost. Suppose, as above, that a subject is paid $R_i(q_i) - pq_i$, but also perceives that he must attach instruction-induced value to q_i. Utility may now be $U^i[R_i(q_i) - pq_i, q_i]$, and demand becomes $q_i = R_i'^{(-1)}(p - U_2^i/U_1^i) > R_i'^{(-1)}(p)$. Consequently, it may be preferable *not* to embellish the instructions with well-intentioned attempts at "realism." Let the explicit reward structure be the singular source of valuation, insofar as this is possible.

3. Individuals may not be autonomous own-reward maximizers. Interpersonal utility criteria may qualify the theory of induced valuation. Thus subject i's utility may depend upon both i's and k's reward, $U^i[R_i(q_i) - pq_i, R_k(q_k) - pq_k]$. If this condition prevails, then the demand of i may depend upon that of k. However, this kind of interdependence is effectively controlled by the experimental condition of "incomplete" information, first defined and studied by Lawrence Fouraker and Siegel (1960, 1963) in experimental studies of bilateral bargaining and oligopoly. Under incomplete information subjects only know their own payoff contingencies. With $R_k(q_k)$ unknown to i, it cannot appear as a subjective argument of U^i.

The effect when subjects have complete information on each other's payoff contingencies is seen (Table 1) by comparing 1 (5) and 2 (6) with 4 (7). In 1 (5) and 2 (6) each subject knew only his own limit price. In 4 (7) the only change in the instructions was to add the information that there were eleven buyers, each with a \$4.20 resale value, and sixteen (nineteen in 7) sellers, each with unit cost \$3.10. From the mean price series it is seen that "complete" information of this kind retards the equilibrium tendencies of the double auction. Mean prices, especially in periods 3 and 4, tended to be higher under complete information than under incomplete information. The explanation is that with information on each other's payoffs, the way is open for "equity" considerations to modify self-interest choices. Sellers, believing that it is "fair" for trading profits to be shared between buyers and sellers, try to resist price decreases more vigorously than when they do not know what constitutes such a fair price. Buyers acquiesce in this sharing by accepting many contracts well above $3.10, but since there is an excess of sellers, those holding out for the higher prices are the sellers most likely to fail to make contracts. Consequently, contract prices tend to decline, if slowly, when excess supply is 5, but more rapidly when excess supply is 8. The tendency of prices to be higher under complete information is contrary to the view of those who have argued that "perfect" information is essential for establishing competitive prices. The results are consistent with the game-theoretic proposition that more information increases the prospect of collusion (Shubik 1959, p. 171), and with the results of Fouraker and Siegel (1963, p. 187) in which the tendency of the competitive equilibrium to prevail under duopoly bargaining is reduced under complete information.

REFERENCES

R. Battalio, J. Kagel, J. Winkler, R. Fisher, R. Basmann and L. Krasner, "A Test of Consumer Demand Theory Using Observations of Individual Consumer Purchases," *West. Econ. J.*, Dec. 1973, 411–28.

R. Coase, "The Problem of Social Cost," *J. Law. Econ.*, 1960, *3*, 1–44.

L. Fouraker and S. Siegel, *Bargaining Behavior*, New York 1963.

H. Leibenstein, "Organizational or Frictional Equilibria, X-Efficiency, and the Rate of Innovation," *Quart. J. Econ.*, Nov. 1969, *83*, 600–23.

C. Plott and V. Smith, "An Experimental Examination of Two Exchange Institutions," California Inst. of Tech. 1975.

H. Shapley, *Of Stars and Men*, Boston 1964.

R. Sherman, "The Psychological Difference Between Ambiguity and Risk," *Quart. J. Econ.*, Feb. 1974, *88*, 166–69.

M. Shubik, *Strategy and Market Structure*, New York 1959.

———, "A Trading Model to Avoid Tatonnement Metaphysics," Cowles Foundation disc. pap. no. 368, Feb. 13, 1974.

S. Siegel, "Decision Making and Learning under Varying Conditions of Reinforcement," *Ann. N. Y. Acad. Sci.*, 1961, *89*, 766–83.

——— **and L. Fouraker,** *Bargaining and Group Decision Making*, New York 1960.

V. L. Smith, "An Experimental Study of Competitive Market Behavior," *J. Polit. Econ.*, Apr. 1962, *70*, 111–37.

———, "Effect of Market Organization on Competitive Equilibrium," *Quart. J. Econ.*, May 1964, *78*, 181–201.

———, "Experimental Auction Markets and the Walrasian Hypothesis," *J. Polit. Econ.*, Aug. 1965, *73*, 387–93.

———, "Notes on Some Literature in Experimental Economics," Social Science working pap. no. 21, California Inst. of Tech., Feb. 1973. 1–27.

Bidding and Auctioning Institutions: Experimental Results

Vernon L. Smith

Among the laboratory experimental studies of market price behavior there are numerous experiments designed on the basis of various bidding and auctioning processes of allocation. The theme of this conference will serve as the organizing principle of this paper which presents a summary of several published and previously unpublished experiments in auction and sealed-bid market behavior.

I. VALUES, INSTITUTIONS AND MARKET STRUCTURE AS TREATMENT VARIABLES

In discussing the use of experimental methods to determine the equilibrium and dynamic properties of market price behavior it is helpful to distinguish three classes of experimental market "treatment" variables:

A. *Individual values and their aggregation to form market values.* In isolated single-commodity market experiments such values are defined as the individual supply and demand schedules, or simply the aggregate supply and demand conditions that bound price-quantity behavior.
B. *The institution of contract.* This is defined as the entire set of rules and procedures of an experiment which taken together specify the *process* whereby individual subjects communicate, exchange information, and form *binding* contracts.
C. *Market structure.* This is defined by the number of participants (buyers and sellers) and their relative "power" in the sense of relative demand or supply (cost) capacity.

A complete set of market experiments can be viewed as providing observations on the mapping from values (supply and demand), institutions and market structure into price-quantity outcomes (price levels, price trajectories, quantities exchanged). That is, price-quantity outcome = f (values, institutions, market structure). None of the experiments to be summarized in this report have systematically varied market structure except insofar as changes in the conditions of supply and demand have been effected by changing the number of sellers and buyers. But in each case reported here numbers are large enough and economic power sufficiently dispersed to yield competitive price behavior. However, empirically, "large" in this context typically means only about three or more sellers (and as many buyers)

There are a number of laboratory studies (Hoggatt, 1959; Fouraker and Siegel, 1963; Friedman, 1963; Murphy, 1966) of duopoly and triopoly bargaining in which buyer response is simulated by the experimenter using a pre-specified demand function. This literature will not be treated here since it is only tangentially related to bidding and auctioning, and has been very ably summarized by Friedman (1969).

The institutions of contract that have been studied experimentally, and that will be summarized below, are defined as follows:

(1) *Double Auctions.*

(i) In this market in each trading period of specified duration, any buyer is free at any time to make an oral bid to buy one unit of a homogeneous commodity. Any seller is free at any time to make an oral offer to sell one unit. Any buyer is free to accept the offer of any seller and any seller to accept the bid of any buyer. An accepted bid or offer constitutes a binding contract. A given bid or offer is outstanding until it is either accepted or another bid or offer is made. The new bid or offer does not have to provide better terms than a previous bid or offer. Hence, no "convergence rules" are imposed on bid and offer sequences, and only one (the last) bid or offer is outstanding at a time. Over-the-counter security markets and real estate markets have the feature that a bid or offer not accepted is not binding at a later time unless it is restated.

(ii) A variation on the above institution is to write all bids and offers on a blackboard, visible to all. Following an initial unrestricted bid or offer, any new bid (offer) is admissible only if it is higher (lower) than the last bid (offer) until a contract occurs. When a contract occurs a new "auction" begins with an initial unrestricted bid or offer, and so on. The requirement that a new bid or offer provide better terms than the last is characteristic of organized trading as on the New York Stock Exchange (Leffler and Farwell, 1963, pp. 187, 191).

(2) *Bid Auction.* Buyers are free to make bids and sellers to accept bids as in the double auction, but sellers are not permitted to make offers. This procedure is typical of art auctions and auctions for the sale of farm animals and machinery.

(3) *Offer Auctions.* Sellers make offers and buyers may accept offers, but buyers cannot make bids. As an experimental treatment variable this institution is the negative of the bid auction.

(4) *Posted Pricing.* Under this institution each seller (buyer) independently selects a "take-it-or-leave-it" price offer (bid), i.e. a price is selected without knowledge of the prices being selected by competitors. These prices are then posted on a blackboard where they are visible to all buyers and sellers. Next a buyer (seller), chosen at random, selects a seller (buyer), and makes that seller (buyer) a quantity offer at his posted price. The seller (buyer) then responds with a quantity (any portion of the offer) acceptance which forms a binding contract. If some portion of the quantity offer is not accepted, the buyer (seller) may choose a second seller (buyer) and make a quantity offer, and so on. When the first buyer (seller) has finished his contracts, a second, chosen at random, selects a seller (buyer), makes a quantity offer, and so on, until all buyers (sellers) have completed their contracts.

Most retail markets have the feature that sellers post prices which are not subject to alteration for some considerable period of time. Clothing merchants post selling prices for spring garments, Sears, Roebuck publishes spring-summer and fall-winter catalogues of selling prices, and refiners post price bids at which they are willing to buy crude oil. In the experimental procedure, the fact that a given seller may not satisfy the demand of a buyer corresponds to a stock-out in retail markets. That is, retailers post a price, and normally do not specify a quantity (except perhaps to say "while they last"), but stocks may be exhausted before all buyers are satisfied.

(5) *Discriminative Sealed-bid Auction.* In this institution in each trading period the seller offers a specified quantity, Q, of a homogeneous commodity and invites buyers to tender bids independently at stated prices for stated quantities of the good. The bids are arrayed from highest to lowest, and the first Q bid units are accepted with a random device used for allocating among tie bids at the lowest accepted price. All accepted bids are then filled at their full bid prices. This procedure has been characteristic of the auctioning of U.S. Treasury bills.

(6) *Competitive Sealed-bid Auction.* The rules are the same as in (5) except that all accepted bids are filled at the price of the lowest accepted bid. This is approximately the procedure followed in the

French auctioning of new stock issues (see McDonald and Jacquillat, 1974).

As an experimental treatment variable the institution of contract is specified and controlled in any given experiment through the design of subject instructions. To write the instructions for an experimental task is to define a trading institution in all its mechanical detail. For examples of instructions defining some of the above exchange institutions refer to Smith (1964, pp. 199–201; 1967, pp. 76–78), and Williams (1973, pp. 111–113).

II. INDUCING CONTROLLED SUPPLY AND DEMAND CONDITIONS

If (i) for every experimental subject more currency is better, i.e. if U(M) is a subject's unknown utility of money, with $U'(M) > 0$ for all $M \geq 0$, and (ii) the experimental task required to earn M is simple enough so that the subjective transactions cost (i.e. the disutility of learning, computing, and executing the experimental procedures) is negligible, then actual monetary rewards can be used to induce value in the form of any predesigned demand or supply function on each subject. Aggregate market demand or supply will then be the quantity summation of these individual demand or supply functions.

This is accomplished rather simply. The instructions inform a subject, say a buyer, that at the end of each of a series of trading periods the person will receive a sum of money $R(q) - \sum_{k=1}^{q} p_k$, for units purchased at prices $p_1, p_2, \ldots, p_q$. R(q) is increasing and concave in q, the number of units of an abstract commodity purchased during the period. The classical definition of demand is the number of units that will be purchased as a function of a hypothetical *fixed* price p. Hence subject hypothetical utility is $U[R(q) - pq]$, and for a maximum $U' \cdot (R' - p) = 0$, or $q = R'^{(-1)}(p)$, if $U' > 0$, where $R'^{(-1)}(p)$ is the induced individual demand valuation per trading period independent of the individual U function. The sum over all such buyer valuations defines the experimental market demand schedule (as illustrated on the left of Charts 1–7). A subject seller is instructed that he will be paid $\sum_{k=1}^{q} p_k - C(q)$, for selling q units at prices $p_1, p_2, \ldots, p_q$, where C(q) is increasing and convex in q. For a maximum of $U[pq - C(q)]$, $U' \cdot (p - C') = 0$, or $q = C'^{(-1)}(p)$, if $U' > 0$, where $C'^{(-1)}(p)$ is the induced individual supply valuation. Summing over such individual supply valuations yields the experimental market supply (see Charts 1–7).

By imposing the appropriate reward structure in this way it is possible to effect virtually complete control over the experimental conditions of supply and demand to study the effect of any given configuration on price adjustment behavior. The experimenter always has complete knowledge of the conditions of supply and demand that generated a given sequence of observations. How much knowledge the subjects have is an experimental treatment variable. In the experiment reported here subjects only have knowledge of their own supply or demand functions. A subject is therefore never in a position of having more knowledge of market conditions than any nonlaboratory economic agent.

For experimental markets in which the supply and demand schedules are not too asymmetric (i.e. total producer surplus is not greatly different from consumer surplus) and which are conducted over periods of less than 40–50 minutes, satisfactory results can often be obtained without actual monetary rewards. But motivation is likely to be weak when subjects bargain for "points" so that results are more likely to be effected by boredom and the cost of transacting once the task becomes routine.

Of the twenty experiments summarized here only the five whose results are exhibited in Charts 1–5 were conducted without actual cash profit rewards.

III. DOUBLE AUCTIONS

The motivation for selecting the double auction for extensive experimental study (Smith, 1962) was based on the conjecture that this institution was the one under which classical supply and demand theory had the best chance of being validated. However, I did not seriously expect competitive price theory to be supported by these initial probes; such was the power and influence of the Chamberlin-Robinson revolt against competition. But if competitive theory had validity under the double auction, this would provide the "control case" or reference institution against which other forms of market organization could be compared.

The salient features of the double auction experiments can be listed as follows:

1. No subject is given any information on the cost or revenue schedules provided to the other subjects or on the number of buyers or sellers, or on the level at which contract prices might occur. A subject only has information on his own cost or revenue conditions, the bids or offers being made, and the prices at which contracts are executed.
2. Any buyer (seller) can make an oral price bid (offer) for one unit at

a time. Any seller (buyer) can accept the bid (offer) of any buyer (seller).

3(i). A bid (offer) is outstanding only until it is either accepted or a new bid or offer is made, whether or not the new bid or offer provides better terms than the last. Consequently there is only one quotation (a bid or an offer) outstanding at any one time.

3(ii). A bid (offer) is outstanding until it is either accepted or a new bid (offer) is made. A new bid (offer) is admissible only if it provides better terms, i.e. is higher (lower) than the previous bid (offer). Once a first bid and a first offer have been made, thereafter two quotations (one bid and one offer) will be outstanding at any one time. When a contract is executed a new "auction" begins with a new bid or offer which need not provide better terms than the last.

4. The market is conducted over a sequence of several market periods with constant controlled conditions of supply and demand from period to period.

5. No subject participated in more than one experiment in order to control on previous trader knowledge and experience. This specification provides minimum conditions of knowledge and experience.

The contract price sequences for twelve double auction experiments are shown in Charts 1–7. In each chart the controlled experimental market supply and demand are shown on the left. The presentation and discussion of these results will be organized to illustrate five empirical propositions.

Proposition 1. Contract prices converge to "near" the theoretical (Supply = Demand) equilibrium level usually within the first twenty to thirty transactions. The more slowly converging markets are associated with very asymmetric supply and demand (producer surplus is substantially different from consumer surplus).

The concept of prices being "near" the competitive equilibrium eludes satisfactory, precise, objective definition. The requirement that, beyond some transaction or period, every contract be at the competitive equilibrium price is precise but clearly too strong although such results are obtainable as in the second experiment in Chart 7. All econometric studies of individual markets allow for noise in the competitive price hypothesis. A requirement that contract prices differ from the monopoly and monopsony levels by statistically significant amounts, is precise but much too weak as is evident in the contract price sequences in Charts 1–7. There are few if any trading periods in these sequences for which the monopsony and monopoly price hypotheses would fail to be rejected at high levels of significance. Such tests might be impressive but not very relevant. What is missing in competitive price theory are adequate price adjustment models that permit more definitive statements about the characteristics of equilibrium. The assertion that all of the double auction experiments reported in Charts 1–7 converge to "near" the competitive equilibrium is neither very objective nor precise, but I have found in oral presentations that virtually all observers agree subjectively that convergence is "good" or "remarkable," in these experiments.

The experiment in Chart 1 illustrates a case in which contract prices tend to equilibrium in the sense that every contract price is within the range \$1.75 to \$2.25 between the first intramarginal seller and buyer valuations. The contracts in Chart 2 are relatively more erratic than in Chart 1, but by trading period 3 have converged very closely to the equilibrium price. The two experiments in Charts 3 and 4 illustrate the effect of doubling the supply and the demand of each trader. In Chart 3 each subject could buy (or sell) one unit per trading period, while in Chart 4 two units could be bought (or sold) in each trading period. Consequently, in Chart 4, there is roughly as much convergence in one trading period as there is in two trading periods of Chart 3. This suggests that

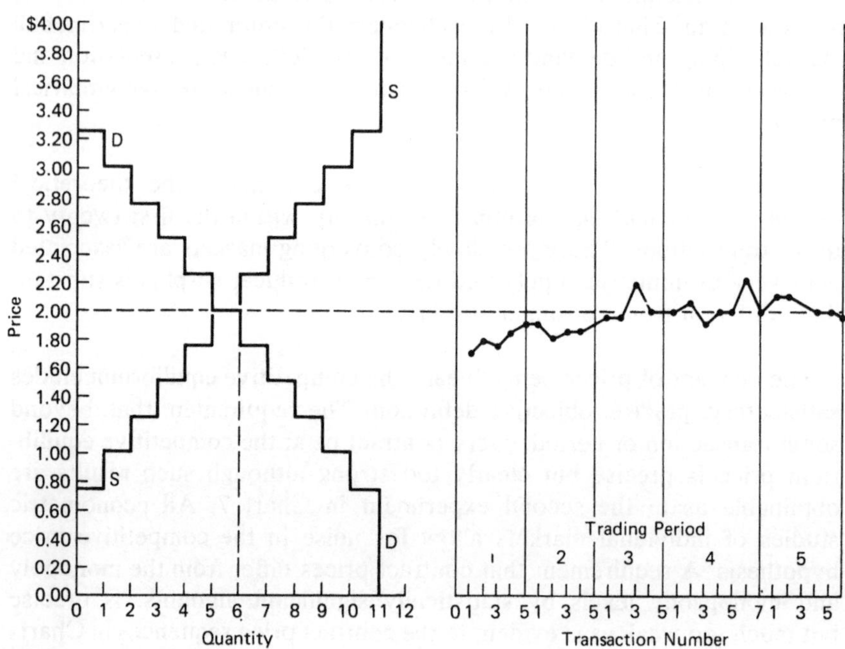

CHART 1

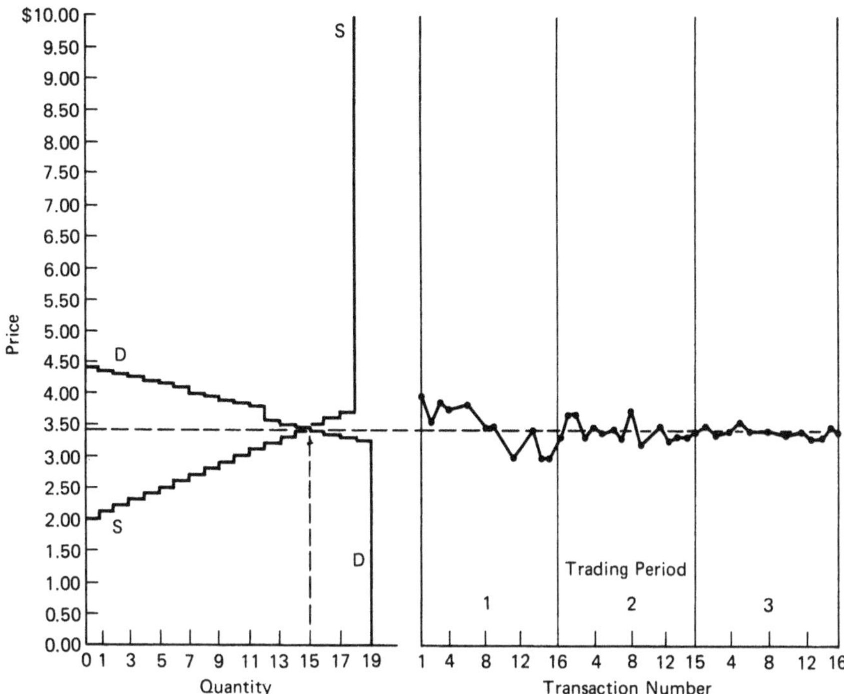

CHART 2

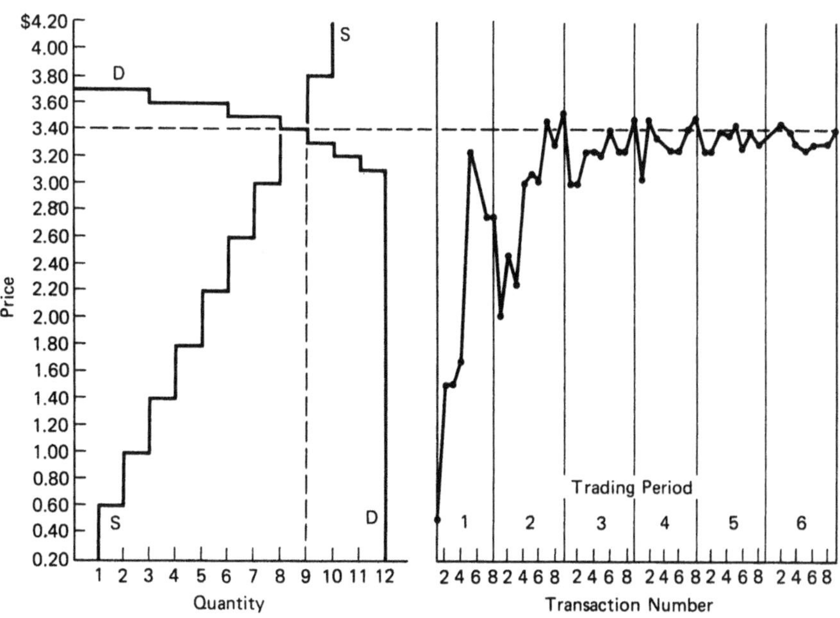

CHART 3

convergence is related to transaction experience, not just to "trading period" experience. Similarly, in Chart 5 each buyer and seller had multiunit revenue and cost schedules, and the larger volume of transactions produced substantial convergence by the end of the first trading period.[1]

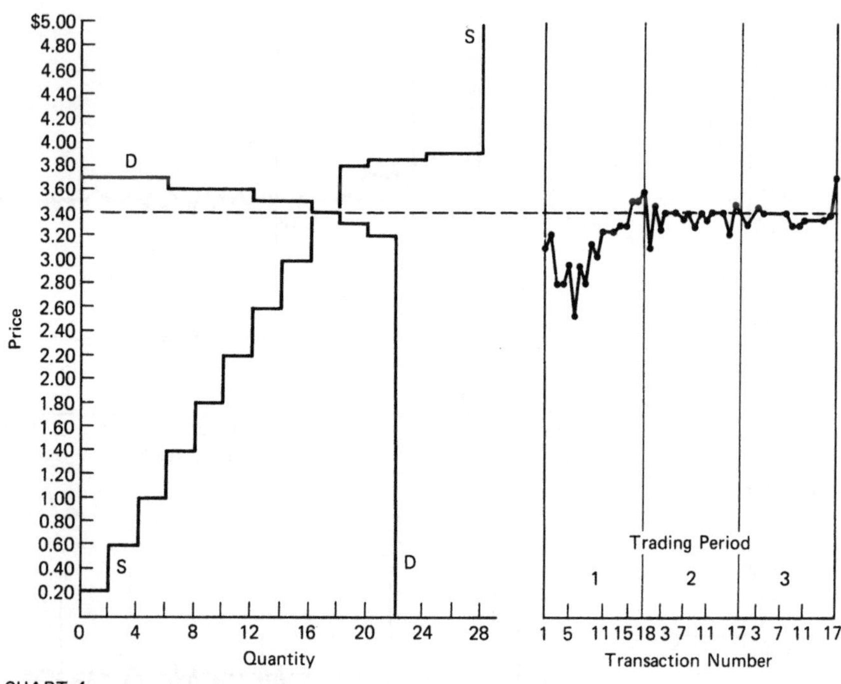

CHART 4

The three experiments in Chart 7 provide the most rigorous test of the equilibrating power of the double auction.[2] In these experiments all rent, or pure profit, is allocated to buyers at the competitive equilibrium price. The eleven buyers each receive $1.10 in trading profit per period plus a 5 cent commission, while eleven of the sixteen successful sellers receive only the 5 cent commission. In all three replications sellers resist the tendency for prices to decline to seller unit cost, but by period 4 most contracts are very near the equilibrium, $3.10.

[1] Charts 1–4 are reproduced from Smith (1962). Chart 5 reports a previously unpublished experiment.

[2] The second and third experiments in Chart 7 are reproduced from Smith (1965), while the first is previously unpublished.

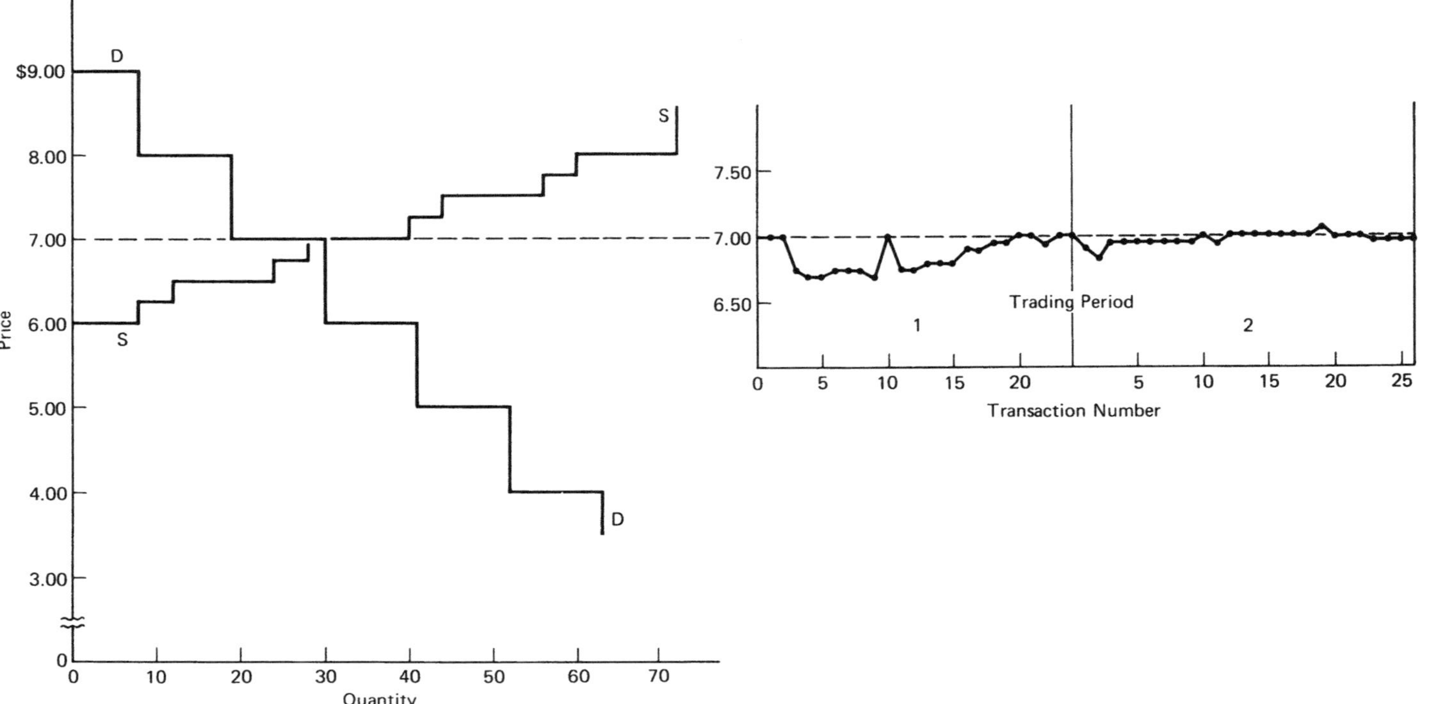

D
$9.00
8.00
7.00
6.00
5.00
4.00
3.00
0
Price
S
S
D
0
10
20
30
40
50
60
70
Quantity
7.50
7.00
6.50
Trading Period
1
2
0
5
10
15
20
5
10
15
20
25
Transaction Number

CHART 5

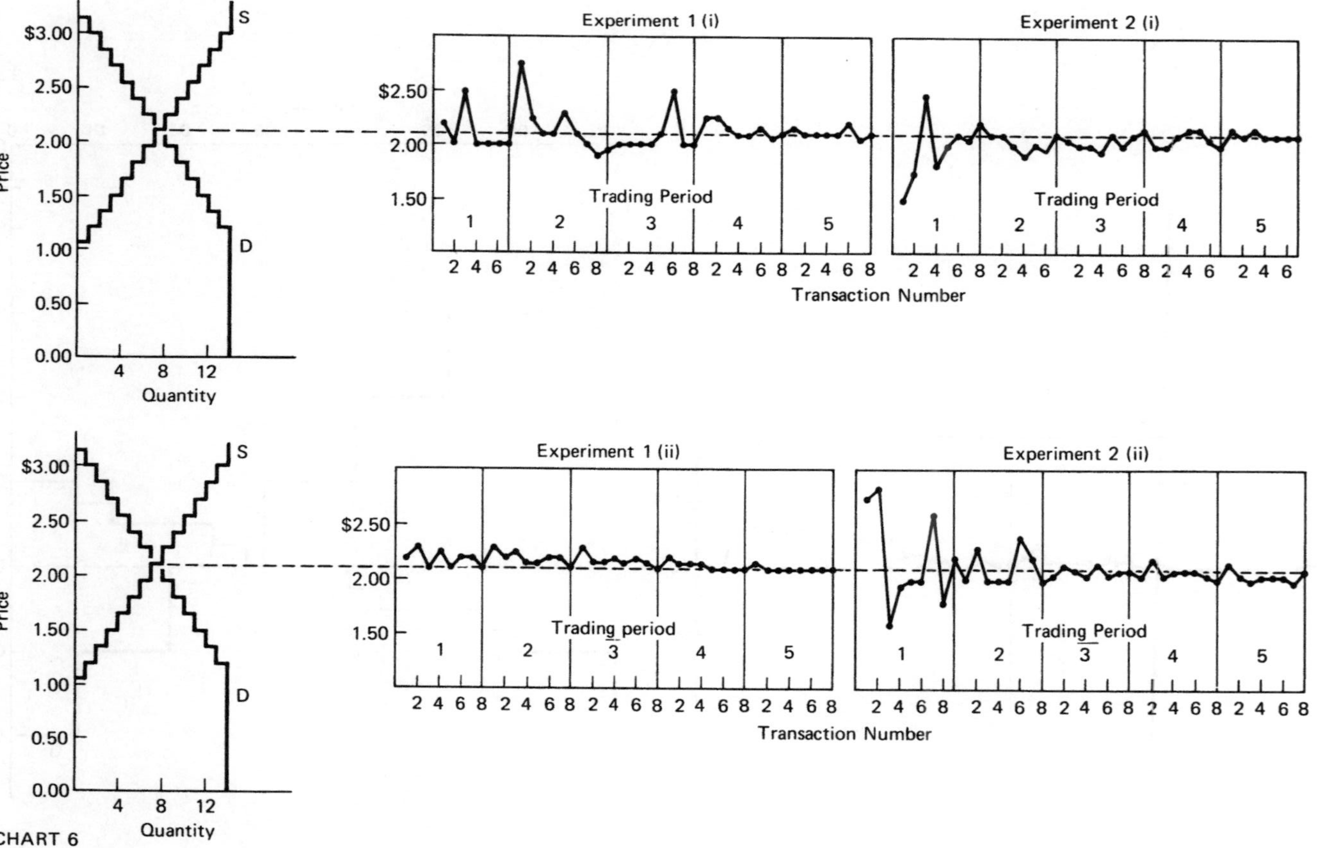

S
D
$3.00
2.50
2.00
1.50
1.00
0.50
0.00
Price
4
8
12
Quantity
Experiment 1 (i)
Experiment 2 (i)
$2.50
2.00
1.50
Trading Period
Transaction Number
Experiment 1 (ii)
Experiment 2 (ii)
Trading period
Trading Period
Transaction Number

CHART 6

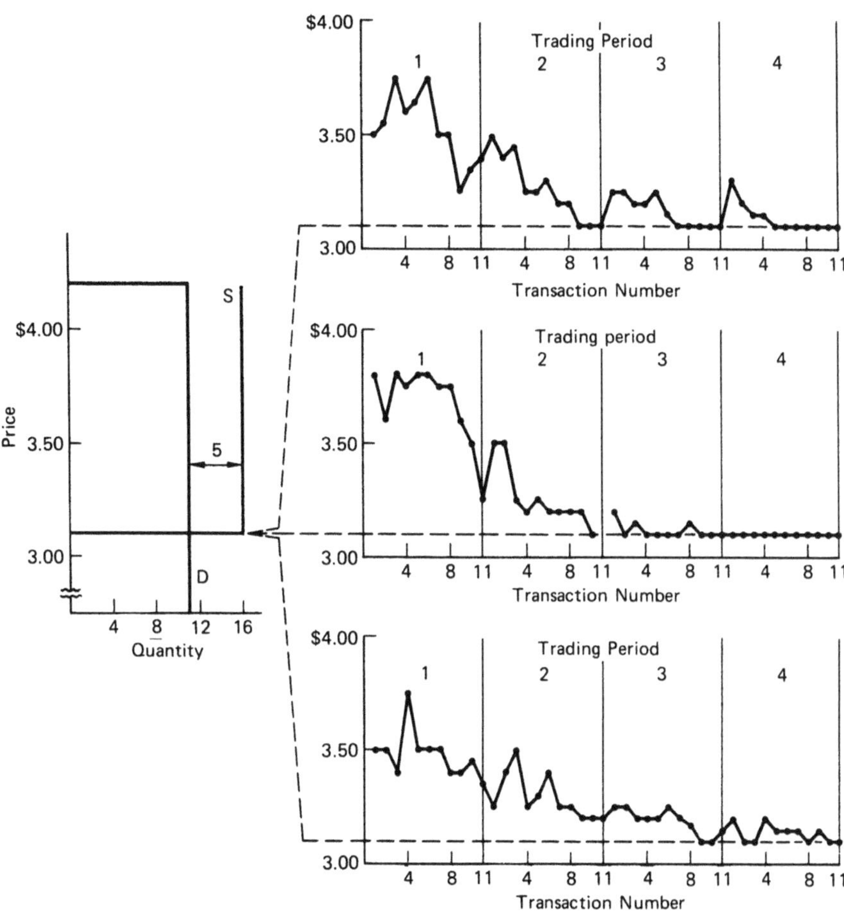

CHART 7

Proposition 2. Quantities exchanged per period rarely differ from the theoretical (S = D) equilibrium by more than a single unit in *any* trading period.

This proposition is supported in every trading period for all the experiments in Charts 1–4, 6, 7. The exception is the multiunit case in Chart 5 in which there were no cash rewards, and the experimental task was made more difficult by giving the subjects multiunit revenue and cost schedules rather than single unit costs and resale prices as in the other experiments. However, other multiunit experiments using cash rewards (Plott and Smith, 1975) and the bid auction institution did not yield a deficient volume of transactions. This suggests that the proposition holds very broadly when motivation is based on cash rewards.

The fact that the quantities exchanged are very close to the theoretical quantity even in the initial period when there is the least amount of information is especially significant. An examination of individual trades reveals that even in the first trading period it is common for submarginal buyers and sellers to be unable to make contracts (cf. Smith, 1962, Table 1, p. 117). Auction markets are therefore quite efficient in excluding submarginal units even before contract prices have converged to their final levels. Consequently the more erratic price variations observed initially have a much greater effect on income distribution than upon allocative efficiency (Plott and Smith, 1975).

Proposition 3. A variation on the double auction rules in which a bid (offer) is not admissible unless it provides better terms than the previous bid (offer) does not appear to provide any significant increase in the convergence rate of contract prices.

This proposition arose from an attempt to test the hypothesis that convergence would be more rapid when the auction rules required a bid or an offer to provide improved terms. Four experiments with identical and symmetrical market supply and demand schedules (Chart 6) were conducted each with a different set of subjects.[3] Two of the experiments, designated 1(i) and 2(i) used the double auction variation (i) above, while two of the experiments designated 1(ii) and 2(ii) used variation (ii) requiring bids and offers to improve. From the contract price sequences alone it is not evident that differences due to the treatment variable (compare the charts vertically) are any greater than differences due to sampling (subject) variation (compare the charts horizontally).

Table 1 compares the variance of contract prices, pooled across subjects, period by period across the two experimental sessions, under the two treatment conditions. In periods 2 through 4 the variance is significantly greater ($\alpha < .10$) under rule (i) than rule (ii), but in periods 1 and 5 the variance ratio is less than unity. These comparisons do not inspire confidence in the hypothesis that rules requiring bids and offers to improve will speed convergence in the sense of reducing period-by-period variance. The hypothesis may be true but the effect too small to be established without a large number of experimental replications.

Proposition 4. The sampling variation (among different subject groups) in market price adjustment paths is considerable, but the variation in equilibrium prices (contract prices in the final period of trading) is minor.

[3] Experiments 1(i) and 2(i) are reproduced from Smith (1964), while 1(ii) and 2(ii) are previously unpublished.

TABLE 1

Trading period	σ^2_{ii}	σ^2_{i}	$F = \sigma^2_{ii}/\sigma^2_{i}$
1	.06344	.10580	0.60
2	.04023	.01542	2.61
3	.01766	.00266	6.65
4	.00506	.00246	2.06
5	.00133	.00138	1.00

The four experiments in Chart 6 tend to support this proposition. All four experiments yield contracts very near the $2.10 equilibrium in periods 4 and 5, yet 1(ii) converges from above, 2(i) converges generally from below, while 1(i) and 2(ii) exhibit greater price variation than the other two experiments. Chart 7 exhibits the results of three double auction experiments using identical supply and demand but different subject groups. The variation in the contract price sequences is entirely attributable to differences among the three subject samples of size 27 each. Thus in the second experiment only one first-period contract is below $3.50, whereas in the third experiment only one is above $3.50. The price paths are markedly different, but fourth period contracts are all very near the $3.10 equilibrium.

Proposition 5. Contract price convergence is more likely to be from below (above) when producer's surplus is greater (less) than consumer's surplus.

Clearly, in Chart 7, such experimental markets must converge from above if sellers are to sell at a positive profit. Less extreme cases, such as in Charts 3 and 4, should rarely if ever converge from above. Chart 6 supports proposition 5 by illustrating the greater variability in convergence mode (from above, below, or random around the equilibrium) when producer's and consumer's surplus are equal.

The empirical evidence summarized in Charts 1–7 provides very strong support for static competitive price theory when markets are organized on the principle of the double auction. It is also clear that *the information requirements for the achievement of competitive equilibrium prices are very weak.* The argument of numerous economists (see Shubik, 1959, pp. 169–171) and of many textbook authors, that "perfect" information is required for establishing competitive prices, is not supported by the experimental evidence. On the other hand Marshall's (1949, pp. 333–334) famous description of market price determination in a hypothetical corn market is not contradicted by this evidence. The position of Hayek (1945) that an important feature of decentralized pricing is that it economizes on information, is also consistent with the results of these double auction experiments. Marshall (p. 334) also notes perceptively that it is not necessary for the competitive price argument "that any dealers should have a thorough knowledge of the circumstances of the market." There are no experimental results more important or more significant than that the information specifications of traditional competitive price theory are grossly overstated. The experimental facts are that no double auction trader needs to know *anything* about the valuation conditions of other traders, or have *any* understanding or knowledge of market supply and demand conditions, or have *any* trading experience (although experience may speed convergence), or satisfy the quaint and irrelevant requirement of being a price "taker" (every trader is a price *maker* in the double auction).

IV. COMPARISON OF BID, DOUBLE AND OFFER AUCTIONS

One-sided oral auctions lead to contracts tending to favor the silent side. If only buyers quote prices (the bid auction), the bids tend to begin much below the competitive equilibrium but thereafter to rise because not all such bids are accepted (there is excess demand). As buyers raise bids competitively to induce sales, sellers learn that it is to their advantage to wait, i.e. the more silent role of sellers is an aid to tacit collusion. Contract prices tend to rise above the competitive equilibrium, but the rise is limited by the fact that the resulting excess supply causes some queuing on the part of sellers to accept bids. This queuing is expressed in the form of ties by two or more sellers to accept a bid. The process is reversed when sellers make offers.

Proposition 6. Let $F_B^t(P)$, $F_D^t(P)$, and $F_O^t(P)$ be the number (or percentage) of contract prices executed at P or greater in trading period $t > 1$ under the bid, double, and offer auctions respectively. Then

$$F_B^t(P) \geqslant F_D^t(P) \geqslant F_O^t(P), \qquad t > 1.$$

That is, prices in the bid auction stochastically dominate prices in the double auction which stochastically dominate prices in the offer auction. Hence, contracts tend to be executed to the *disadvantage* of the side having the price initiative.

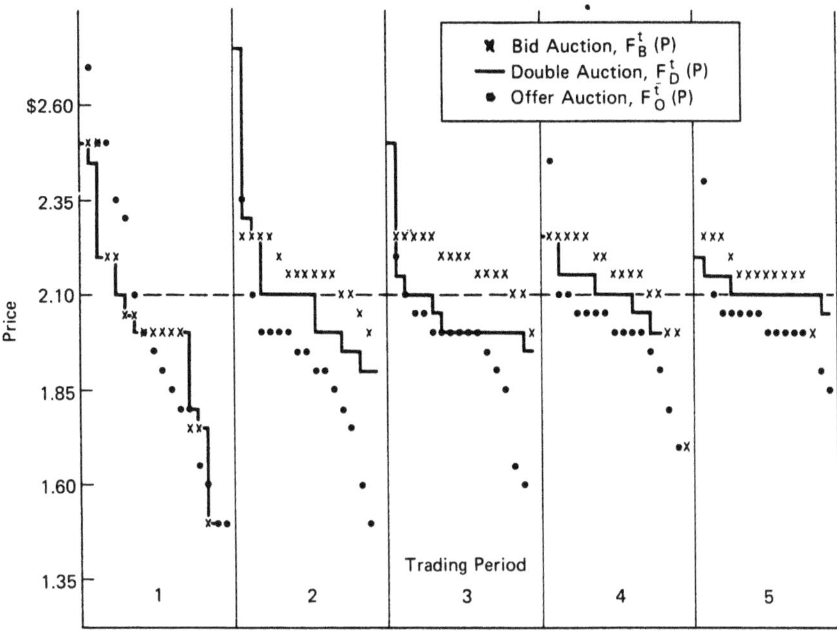

CHART 8

Chart 8 illustrates the empirical distribution of contract prices in successive trading periods for six experiments consisting of two replications under each of these three treatment institutions (see Smith, 1964). The two "control" experiments using the double auction rules are those labeled 1(i) and 2(i) in Chart 6. The supply and demand designs are the same as those appearing on the left of Chart 6. The dominance relation stated in proposition 6 is supported by these data and is statistically significant (Smith, 1964, pp. 189–192). These results suggest that both the dynamic and equilibrium properties of exchange prices may be affected by the institutional rules or practices governing price initiative (Plott and Smith, 1975).

V. POSTED-BID VERSUS POSTED-OFFER INSTITUTIONS

The first experimental investigation of posted pricing and the determination of its effect on competitive equilibrium is due to Williams (1973). Empirically he establishes that when buyers post bids, contract prices are lower than when sellers post offers. This is the reverse of the result from comparing the oral bid and offer auctions; posted pricing operates to the *advantage* of the price initiator. The process of posting a "take-it-or-leave-it" price (for all units to be offered) tends to support collusive coordination among independent traders. The fact that only inter-period price adjustments are possible retards and perhaps prevents equilibrium convergence.

Proposition 7. Let $G_B^t(P)$ and $G_O^t(P)$ be the number (or percentage) of contract prices executed at P or greater in trading period $t > 1$ under the posted-bid and posted-offer institutions respectively. Then

$$G_O^t(P) \geqslant G_B^t(P), \qquad t > 1.$$

That is, prices in the posted-offer institution stochastically dominate prices in the posted-bid institution.

The empirical bid distributions $G_B^t(P)$ and $G_O^t(P)$ are shown in Chart 9 for six trading periods of four experimental sessions reported by Williams (1973, p. 102). The data from two sessions using posted bids are combined period-by-period to generate the distribution $G_B^t(P)$. Two sessions using posted offers are combined to generate $G_O^t(P)$. The dominance relation of proposition 7 is supported by these data, and is statistically significant (Williams, 1973, pp. 104–105). The results of the posted-bid sessions of Williams have been replicated (Plott and Smith, 1975) using a different subject pool and modified instructions. Williams' results appear to be very robust.

VI. SEALED-BID AUCTIONS

Six sealed-bid auction experiments have been reported by Smith (1967). Belovicz (1967) has considerably extended this work in a study consisting of twenty-seven sealed-bid auctions conducted under a variety of different conditions. The experimental paradigm is one in which subjects submit sealed bids for eighteen units of a commodity that can be resold at a price determined by a rectangular distribution over the nine prices $1.15 to $1.95 (Chart 10). The purchase cost is determined as described in either paragraph (5) or (6) of section I.

Using the discriminative rules subjects tend to submit lower bids than when the competitive rules are used. This is because the accepted bids are filled at the full bid price. Under the competitive rules an accepted bid is filled at the lowest accepted bid price, and profit is independent of the bid price submitted. Consequently, there is an incentive to bid higher to assure acceptance with no penalty in the form of higher purchase cost when the bid is above the lowest accepted bid.

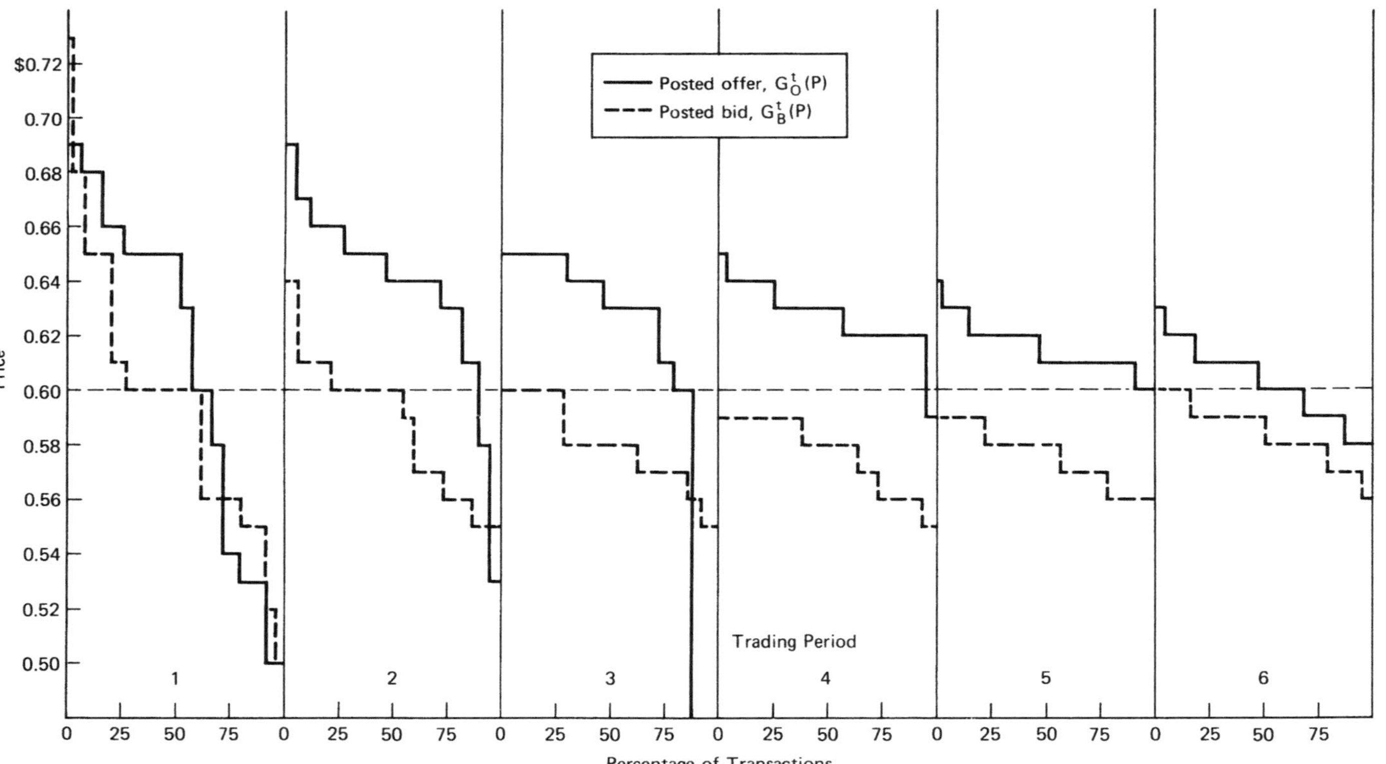

Posted offer, $G_O^t(P)$
Posted bid, $G_B^t(P)$
Price
$0.72
0.70
0.68
0.66
0.64
0.62
0.60
0.58
0.56
0.54
0.52
0.50
Trading Period
1
2
3
4
5
6
0
25
50
75
Percentage of Transactions

CHART 9

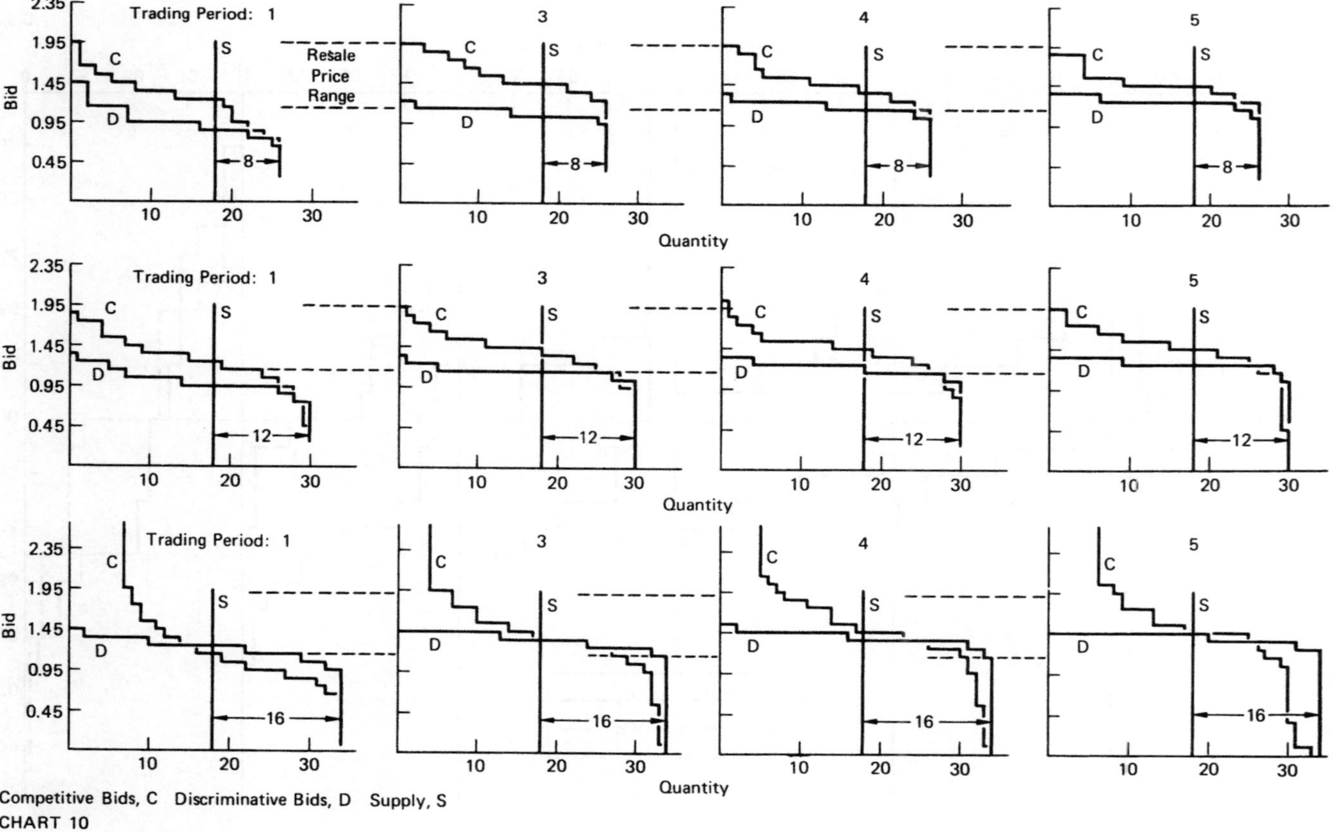

Competitive Bids, C Discriminative Bids, D Supply, S

CHART 10

Proposition 8. Let $H_C^t(B)$ and $H_D^t(B)$ be the number of bids *accepted* at B or greater in trading period $t > 0$ in the competitive and discriminative sealed-bid auctions, respectively. Then

$$H_C^t(B) \geqslant H_D^t(B), \qquad t > 0.$$

That is, accepted bids in the competitive sealed-bid auction stochastically dominate bids in the discriminative sealed-bid auction.

Chart 10 compares the bid distributions $H_C^t(B)$ and $H_D^t(B)$ for three different sets of paired competitive-discriminative experiments. In the top pair, each of thirteen subjects in each experiment submitted up to two bids each per trading period providing eight rejected bids. In the middle pair there were twelve rejected bids (fifteen subjects), and in the last pair there were sixteen rejected bids (seventeen subjects). The dominance relation of proposition 8 is supported in all three comparisons. Belovicz (1967) in a much more comprehensive study establishes that this block of experimental results can be independently replicated.

VII. CONCLUSION

The potential of experimental analysis for the study of bidding and auctioning processes has very wide but as yet undefined bounds. I am not aware of any exchange process that could not be studied experimentally in some simplified form. The value of such studies cannot be fully assessed at this time. Perhaps the most important ultimate value is to provide a rigorous testing of our ability to model elementary behavior before confronting such models with field data. This is partly illustrated in the study of the French sealed-bid auction (McDonald and Jacquillat, 1974) in which the authors build upon the results of competitive sealed-bid auction experiments to test the efficiency of the French marketing of new stock issues. Another possibility is to provide empirical justification and preliminary experience for the design of field experiments. This is especially well illustrated in some of the bond marketing experiments by the U.S. Treasury reported at this conference. Some of these field policy experiments seek to assess the effect of competitive auction rules and were undertaken with knowledge of the laboratory experimental results on competitive versus discriminative auctions. Finally, experimental methodology has potential in exploring the policy implications of new institutions, or alterations in existing institutional rules. Experimental studies of exchange institutions have the potential of increasing our understanding of decentralized allocation processes with implications for antitrust policy and the use of decentralized institutional forms of market regulation and constraint.

BIBLIOGRAPHY

Belovicz, M., "The Sealed Bid Auction: Experimental Studies," Ph.D. Thesis, Purdue University, 1967.

Fouraker, L. and Siegel, S., *Bargaining Behavior*. New York: McGraw-Hill, 1963.

Friedman, J., "Individual Behavior in Oligopolistic Markets: An Experimental Study," *Yale Economic Essays,* vol. 3 (Fall 1963): 359–417.

Friedman, J., "On Experimental Research in Oligopoly," *Review of Economic Studies,* vol. 36(4), no. 108 (October 1969): 399–415.

Hayek, F. von, "The Use of Knowledge in Society," *American Economic Review,* vol. 35 (September 1945): 519–530.

Hoggatt, A., "An Experimental Business Game," *Behavioral Science,* vol. 4 (July 1959): 192–203.

Leffler, G. and Farwell, C. L., *The Stock Market*. New York: Ronald Press, 1963.

Marshall, A., *Principles of Economics*. New York: Macmillan Company, 1949.

McDonald, J. and Jacquillat, B., "Pricing of Initial Equity Issues: The French Sealed-Bid Auction," *Journal of Business,* vol. 47, no. 1 (January 1974): 37–47.

Murphy, J., "Effects of the Threat of Losses on Duopoly Bargaining," *Quarterly Journal of Economics,* vol. 80 (May 1966): 296–313.

Plott, C. and Smith, V., "An Experimental Examination of Two Exchange Institutions." California Institute of Technology, 1975.

Shubik, M., *Strategy and Market Structure*. New York: John Wiley and Sons, 1959.

Smith, V., "An Experimental Study of Competitive Market Behavior," *Journal of Political Economy,* vol. 70 (April 1962): 111–137.

Smith, V., "Effect of Market Organization on Competitive Equilibrium," *Quarterly Journal of Economics*, vol. 78 (May 1964): 181–201.

Smith, V., "Experimental Auction Markets and the Walrasian Hypothesis," *Journal of Political Economy*, vol. 73 (August 1965): 387–393.

Smith, V., "Experimental Studies of Discrimination versus Competition in Sealed-Bid Auction Markets," *Journal of Business*, vol. 40, no. 1 (January 1967): 56–84.

Williams, F., "The Effect of Market Organization on Competitive Equilibrium: The Multiunit Case," *Review of Economic Studies*, vol. 40 (1), No. 121 (1973): 97–113.

INTERTEMPORAL COMPETITIVE EQUILIBRIUM: AN EMPIRICAL STUDY OF SPECULATION

ROSS M. MILLER
CHARLES R. PLOTT
VERNON L. SMITH

In his prologue to the theory of speculation, Samuelson (1966a, p. 947 and passim) deals exclusively with the case of "foreseen changes in future supply and demand" in outlining a theory of intertemporal competitive price-quantity equilibria in markets that are subject to speculation. The analysis was considered to be a preliminary step to the more complicated cases involving uncertainty. Modern extensions of the theory (Mandelbrot, 1971; Samuelson, 1972; Schimmler, 1973) to include uncertainty have been accompanied by such vestiges of this original "perfect knowledge" model (e.g., common, well-defined expectations) as demanded, perhaps by the limitations of mathematical machinery and imagination for restructuring the theory.

Samuelson provides an extension to intertemporal markets of the assumption made by some writers that "perfect" knowledge in the sense of foreknowledge of market supply and demand is a precondition for competitive equilibrium in stationary markets. However, it is now well established by many experimental replications that knowledge of market supply and demand is not a necessary and may not be a sufficient condition for classical competitive equilibria to be achieved when a stationary market is organized under auction rules. Such knowledge is not necessary because in experiments in which subject participants know only their own supply and demand valuations contract prices demonstrably converge to or deviate only slightly from the theoretical equilibrium (Smith, 1974, pp. 7–15); knowledge of supply and demand may not be sufficient because under supply and demand conditions in which the entire exchange surplus is received by buyers (and all subjects are informed of these conditions), equity considerations seem to retard and in some instances may preclude convergence to the classical (i.e., no externalities) competitive equilibrium (Smith, 1975, pp. 11–12).

It appears that necessary and sufficient conditions for a classical competitive stationary equilibrium include the following: (1) each economic agent knows only his own valuation conditions,[1] (2) information on all price bids, price offers, and price contracts is available at approximately zero cost to all agents, and (3) the process is repetitively stationary, i.e., each agent is a buyer or a seller of units in each of several trading periods with individual valuations unchanging from period to period. This permits learning by trial and error from one trading period to the next.

This paper is based upon the conjecture that the information conditions that yield a competitive equilibrium in stationary markets will also yield an intertemporal competitive equilibrium in a seasonal market with cyclical but unknown shifts in demand and a stationary supply. The trading institution will be organized as a double auction and will permit units purchased in the first season to be carried over for resale in the second season.

Theory and Hypotheses

The theory of intertemporal competitive equilibrium (Williams, 1935; Samuelson, 1966a, p. 946) in a two-season market is particularly simple and well known, and is a straightforward extension of spatial price equilibrium theory (Samuelson, 1966b, p. 925). Let $D_1(\cdot)$ be the demand in season 1, $D_2(\cdot)$ be demand in season 2, and $S(\cdot)$ be the supply in each season. Suppose that the theoretical equilibrium price in season i is p_i^* under conditions of autarky (i.e., in the absence of units being carried over from season 1 to season 2). If T is the cost of carrying over a unit from season 1 to season 2 and $p_2^* > p_1^* + T$, then the following conditions define the theoretical intertemporal equilibrium prices p_1^0, p_2^0:

$$p_2^0 = p_1^0 + T \tag{1}$$

$$S_1(p_1^0) - D_1(p_1^0) = D_2(p_2^0) - S_2(p_2^0). \tag{2}$$

These are the familiar conditions that, in equilibrium, prices in the

1. Condition (1) will not seem like a proper sufficient condition, since it means literally that when agents know each others' valuations a classical competitive equilibrium is impossible. What the condition does, empirically, is to protect the postulate of a classical environment with no externalities. When each agent knows only his own valuation, then his behavior cannot be influenced by utility or disutility derived from the rewards received by others. In the experiments cited, and further similar unpublished experiments by Smith, it is clear that when there is extreme asymmetry between producer and consumer surpluses, and subjects have full information on each other's valuations, and therefore profits, the asymmetry always retards, and in some instances seems to prevent, convergence to the equilibrium. Consequently, what condition (1) does is to provide a (strong) sufficient condition for a classical environment, with no external utility effects.

two markets will differ only by the carryover cost (inventory plus transactions cost), and the excess supply at the season 1 equilibrium price (the amount carried over) will equal the excess demand at the season 2 equilibrium price. This equilibrium is illustrated graphically on the left side of Figures I and II, for $T = 0$.

We propose to test the validity of this model for two different forms of speculation, neither of which involves participants who have "foreseen knowledge" of supply and demand. Experiment 1 is a market in which any buyer can purchase season 1 (blue) output in sufficient quantity to satisfy his own season 1 demand as well as some or all of his own, known, future season 2 (yellow) demand. In this market only buyers are allowed to speculate, and each knows at the time of the speculative purchase the future value to him of the purchases, but he does not know the future prices or the future market supply and demand. This corresponds to a market in which flour millers have fixed-price contracts for the future delivery of flour but do not know future wheat prices. Buyers are uncertain whether it is advantageous to purchase in the first or in the second season. In experiment 2 all speculative purchases are made by a subset of subjects designated as "traders," who have the exclusive right to purchase units in season 1 for resale in season 2. These participants have no knowledge of market or any individual supply or demand in either season. This treatment corresponds to a market composed of producers, consumers, and a group of specialists who engage only in speculative purchases for resale. Such speculators are uncertain about their season 2 resale prices at the time of their season 1 purchases.

Our primary hypothesis in experiments 1 and 2 is that in equilibrium (defined as the final trading period) the contract prices in each season constitute samples drawn from normal populations with the same mean.

If this research hypothesis is valid, it means that we shall reject the null alternative that both of the season autarky equilibria prevail under speculation. Specifically, if speculation is an ineffective "treatment" variable, then in equilibrium, the ith season ($i = 1,2$) contracts will represent a sample drawn from a normal population with mean p_i^*, and we shall be unable to reject the null hypothesis that $(\bar{p}_2 - \bar{p}_1) - (p_2^* - p_1^*) = 0$, where $\bar{p}_i$ is the sample mean of prices in season i.

Subjects and Experimental Design

The subjects were undergraduate male and female students at the California Institute of Technology. They were recruited by asking

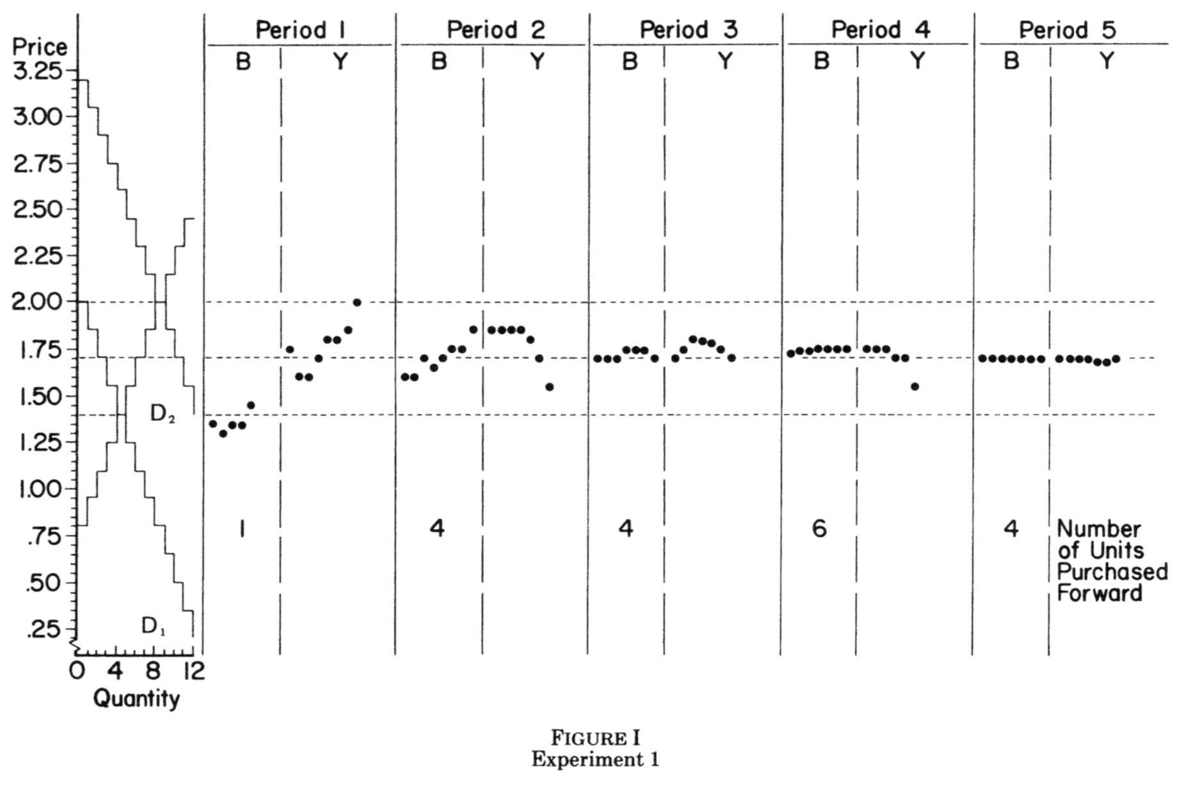

FIGURE I
Experiment 1

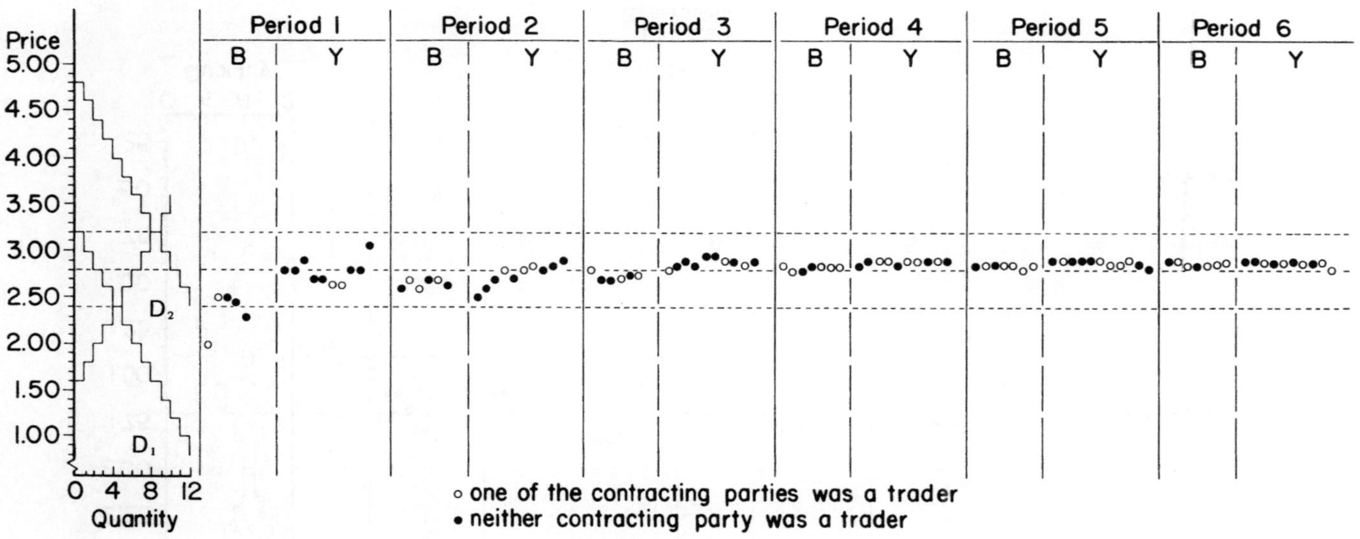

FIGURE II
Experiment 2

for volunteers in the lounges of three student houses. None had participated previously in an experimental speculative market. The role of trader and the individual marginal supply or demand valuations were assigned randomly to the subjects who were spatially seated so that such individual information conditions could be private. Copies of the instructions were distributed (see Appendices 1 and 2) and read aloud by one of the experimenters[2] after which questions were answered.

In both experiments purchases in the blue season could be carried over to the yellow season at zero storage cost. Short sales were not included in the opportunity set, and no purchases could be carried over from a yellow to a blue or any later season. This corresponds to a commodity that is perishable by the end of the summer season, whether produced in the summer or the previous winter.

The demand and supply schedules shown in Figures I and II were constructed in accordance with the theory of induced valuation (Smith, 1973, pp. 22–23; and 1975, pp. 4–6). For example, from Figure I, subject 7 (a buyer in experiment 1) had marginal valuations of $2.00 for his first unit and $1.10 for a second unit in season 1. Similarly, in season 2 his marginal valuations were $2.45 and $1.55. Each buyer received cash payments equal to $0.05 plus the difference between the marginal valuation and purchase price for each unit bought. Each seller received cash payments equal to $0.05 plus the difference between the sales price and the marginal cost for each unit sold. Each trader (experiment 2) received $0.05 plus the difference between selling price and buying price for each unit traded. The purpose of the 5 cent "commission" was to overcome subjective transaction cost and thereby to induce minimally the exchange of marginal units by a buyer or seller and the exchange of the marginal carryover unit by traders (see Smith, 1975, pp. 7–8). Traders each received $3.00 in starting capital to cover potential losses.

Market demand was obtained from the demands of six buyers, each of whom could purchase at most two units, while market supply was derived from the supplies of six sellers, each of whom could produce at most two units. The individual buyers or sellers, identified by subject number and marginal valuations or costs, are shown in Appendix 3. In experiment 1 (Figure I) the autarky price-quantity

2. Miller recruited the subjects, prepared the hand-out materials and conducted both experiments. Using the same experimenter across a given design block of experiments provides some measure of control over experimenter effects. However, the stationary state tendencies of the auction market mechanism do not appear to be sensitive to the particular experimenter. Each of us has conducted such experiments using approximately the same procedure that yielded convergence to the competitive equilibrium.

equilibria were ($1.40, 5 units) and ($2.00, 9 units) for the blue and yellow seasons, respectively, while the intertemporal equilibrium price was $1.70 with 7 units produced in each season and 4 units carried over. In experiment 2 (chart 2) the autarky equilibria were ($2.40, 5 units) and $3.20, 9 units), while the intertemporal equilibrium price was $2.80 with 7 units produced in each season and 4 units carried over. Two subjects in experiment 2 were endowed with trading rights. Neither trader had knowledge of the valuations of any buyer or seller and were not explicitly informed of each other's inventory.

Experimental Results

Figures I and II exhibit the pronounced tendency of contract prices in successive trading periods to converge to values near the intertemporal equilibrium price. Only in the blue season of the first trading period of each experiment, before any significant learning can occur, are contract prices near the autarky equilibrium. The fact that the yellow season of the first trading period in each experiment led to contracts well below the autarky equilibrium is consistent with previous results (Smith 1975, pp. 13–15) in which contract prices tended to lag behind the first two or three successive increases in demand in markets without speculation. Since subjects do not know that demand has increased from the first blue to yellow season, expectations created by these low blue season prices tend to influence contracts in the subsequent season.

The tendency of speculation to narrow the contract prices between seasons is revealed in the difference between the mean blue and mean yellow season contract prices. In the successive trading periods of experiment 1 these differences (in cents) were 40, 11, 3, 5, and 1; in experiment 2 we have 44, 8, 15, 5, 4, and 1. The two seasons in period 5 of experiment 1 give a pooled mean price of $1.6957 compared with the predicted $1.70. The pooled mean price in period 6 of experiment 2 is $2.87 compared with the predicted $2.80. The larger deviation from the predicted intertemporal equilibrium in experiment 2 is explained by the fact that in each of the last three yellow seasons at least one seller (see the data in Appendix 4) failed to sell a unit. In each case the seller quoted offers either too high to be acceptable or if competitive with other offers, the offer lost to another seller. Such intense bargaining, which could lead to unsatisfied sales during the five-minute trading period limit, was entirely within the rules. The result was to hold yellow season prices above the intertemporal equilibrium and permitted speculators to carry over (profitably) an additional unit from the blue season. This additional speculative demand in the blue season had the effect of maintaining prices above the intertemporal competitive equilibrium in that period. Hence, the seller strategy of holding out for above-equilibrium prices in the yellow season tended to raise prices in both seasons. But we attribute this to sampling variation in the behavior strategy of sellers and not to the treatment variable in experiment 2.

The null hypothesis that the prices observed in the blue and yellow seasons of the final period of trading came from populations with means equal to the autarky prices in these seasons is tested using the t-statistic:

$$t(n_1 + n_2 - 2) \sim \frac{\bar{p}_2 - \bar{p}_1 - (p_2^* - p_1^*)}{S\sqrt{(1/n_1) + (1/n_2)}}.$$

$\bar{p}_1$ is the sample mean of n_1 prices in the final blue season. $\bar{p}_2$ is the sample mean of n_2 prices in the final yellow season. p_1^* and p_2^* are the theoretical autarky equilibrium prices in the blue and yellow seasons, respectively. S^2 is the pooled estimate of the population variance for the combined final blue and yellow seasons in each experiment. In experiment 1, $t = -59.5$, and for experiment 2, $t = 59.8$. We reject the null hypothesis in both experiments at significance levels of less than 0.001.

An alternative assessment of experimental market performance is obtained by computing an index of efficiency (Plott and Smith, 1975, pp. 14–19). Inefficiencies occur when extramarginal units (units with marginal supply valuations above, and units with marginal demand valuations below the equilibrium price) are traded, and when intramarginal units (with marginal supply valuations below, and marginal demand valuations above the equilibrium) fail to be traded. No inefficiency occurs if and only if subjects receive the maximum total payments (consumer plus producer surplus). Actual payments as a percentage of the maximum available under perfect intertemporal price equilibrium ($16.40 per period in experiment 1, and $21.40 per period in experiment 2) provide an index of efficiency.

Table I records the inefficient contracts and the index of efficiency by period and season for the two experiments. In the design for experiment 1 a perfect autarky equilibrium would be 92.7 percent efficient and for experiment 2, 92.5 percent efficient. The speculative markets average 98 percent across the five periods of experiment 1 and 96.3 percent across the six periods of experiment 2. Speculation is clearly a more efficient mode of organization than is autarky.

Concepts of stability provide a third means of assessing market performance, and while our experiments were not designed to test theories of stability,[3] our results do shed some light on the subject. Our markets converge to an equilibrium and exhibit none of the properties of instability found in the theoretical literature. In addition, the contracting behavior of speculators seems to have no pronounced "destabilizing" properties. In experiment 2 contracts involving speculators are not noticeably different from contracts involving nonspeculators.[4]

We do observe behavior in these experiments which, in a world of business, might be called speculator-induced "instability," which some may judge as undesirable and a justification for governmental limitations on speculative activities. Speculation does induce a delicate interdependency between markets, and disequilibria are likely to involve sharp "corrections." In both experiments the high prices in the yellow period pulled the blue season prices up "too high" at first and in experiment 1 forced them back down in the final period. In period 3 of experiment 1 the relatively high prices in the yellow period induced a 50-percent increase in carryover (from four units to six units) in period 4. This had the predictable effect of "market collapse" near the end of the yellow season in period 4. Had experiment 2 continued another period or two, we would expect a sharp "market correction" in both yellow and blue periods, as sellers who were withholding units in the yellow season learned that this strategy was not to their individual advantage. When one market gets "out of phase," speculation will cause accommodating adjustments in other markets. This sensitive interdependence is probably recognized in the business community and then properly attributed to speculators. However, whether or not one wants to call it "instability" is another question, and since this interdependence is a natural consequence of the in-

3. The theories summarized by Mandelbrot (1971), Schimmler (1973), and Samuelson (1972) seem to begin where this study ends. They all *presuppose* as a basic postulate that equilibrium in speculative markets means that the distribution of price changes forms a martingale.

4. The average prices for speculators and nonspeculators for each season in experiment 2 are

Period	1		2		3		4		5		6	
Season	B	Y	B	Y	B	Y	B	Y	B	Y	B	Y
Speculators	2.25	2.65	2.67	2.82	2.79	2.85	2.84	2.90	2.84	2.88	2.87	2.86
Nonspeculators	2.45	2.82	2.65	2.72	2.72	2.90	2.83	2.88	2.85	2.88	2.88	2.89

creased efficiency, it should probably be viewed as a desirable feature rather than as an undesirable feature of speculative markets.

CONCLUDING REMARKS

We describe this as an empirical study of speculative markets rather than an experimental test of theories of speculative markets. As such, our title reflects much of what we see to be the role of experimental work in economics and what we think can be learned by means of experimental methods. We do not view these experiments as "approximations" of the real markets that economic theory attempts to explain. For us these laboratory markets *are* real markets in which the principles of economics are just as operative as they are in any other setting. They provide an independent source of empirical data that economic theory should be prepared to predict and explain.

The question we asked was, "Are the intertemporal competitive equilibrium price and quantity accurate predictors of the outcomes of certain speculative markets where participants do not have perfect information about demand and supply?"

Our answer is "yes." It is *not* the case that perfect foreknowledge of demand and supply is a necessary precondition for the application of the intertemporal competitive model. The question of sufficiency remains open. To the extent that applicable theories exist and to the extent that such theories predict something other than the intertemporal competitive equilibrium price and quantity, they are highly suspect if not simply wrong.

Our secondary questions related to market performance. Speculative markets are more efficient than are autarky markets. We also conclude that the presence of speculators is not a sufficient condition to cause instability in markets characterized by cyclical demands.

APPENDIX 1: INSTRUCTIONS FOR MARKET EXPERIMENT 1

1. This is an experiment in the economics of market decision making. The National Science Foundation has provided funds for the conduct of this research. The instructions are simple, and if you follow them carefully and make good decisions, you may earn a considerable amount of money that will be paid to you in cash at the end of the experiment.

2. In this experiment we are going to simulate a two-season market in which some of you will be buyers and some of you will be sellers in a sequence of trading periods. Each trading period will be divided into two parts that we shall refer to as seasons. The first part

TABLE I
INEFFICIENTLY ALLOCATED UNITS IN EXPERIMENTS 1 AND 2

	Season	Limit prices of untraded marginal and intra-marginal demand units	Limit prices of traded extramarginal demand units	Limit prices of untraded marginal and intra-marginal supply units	Limit prices of traded extramarginal supply units	Efficiency measure
			Experiment One			
Theoretical autarky	B	—	1.55; 1.40	1.55; 1.70	—	92.6%
equilibrium	Y	1.85; 1.70	—	—	1.85; 2.00	
Period 1	B	—	1.55	1.55; 1.70	—	95.7%
	Y	1.85; 1.70	—	—	1.85	
Period 2	B	—	—	—	1.85	98.8%
	Y	—	1.55	—	—	
Period 3	B	—	—	—	—	100%
	Y	—	—	—	—	
Period 4	B	1.70	—	—	—	95.7%
	Y	—	—	1.10	—	
Period 5	B	—	—	—	—	100%
	Y	—	—	—	—	

		Experiment Two				
Theoretical autarky equilibrium	B	—	2.60; 2.40	2.60; 2.80	—	92.5%
	Y	3.00; 2.80	—	—	3.00; 3.20	
Period 1	B	3.00	2.40	2.60; 2.80	—	94.9%
	Y	2.80	—	—	3.00	
Period 2	B	—	—	2.80	—	99.5%
	Y	2.80	—	—	—	
Period 3	B	—	—	2.80	—	99.5%
	Y	2.80	—	—	—	
Period 4	B	2.80	—	—	—	94.4%
	Y	2.80	—	2.20; 2.40	—	
Period 5	B	2.80	—	—	—	94.9%
	Y	—	—	1.80	—	
Period 6	B	2.80	—	—	—	94.4%
	Y	2.80	—	2.20; 2.40	—	

SAMPLE RECORD SHEETS, EXPERIMENT 1

TALLY SHEET, SELLER

Trading Period	White Card			
	BLUE SEASON		YELLOW SEASON	
	1st Unit	2nd Unit	1st Unit	2nd Unit
1				
2				
⋮				
8				

TALLY SHEET, BUYER

Trading Period	BLUE CARD		YELLOW CARD	
	1st Unit	2nd Unit	1st Unit	2nd Unit
1				
2				
⋮				
8				

CARRYOVER SLIP

ID # ____________________

Period # ____________________

Units to be carried over ____________________

of each trading period will be the blue season, and the second part will be the yellow season. Three kinds of cards will now be passed out—a set of white cards and a set of blue and yellow cards. Those of you who receive a white card will be sellers, and only sellers. Those of you who receive a blue card and a yellow card will be buyers, and only buyers. These cards have an identification number, which you are to ignore, on the side facing up. On the side facing down appear two prices in dollars and cents, one labeled "First Contract" and the other labeled "Second Contract." These prices will be referred to, respectively, as the "First Contract Price" and the "Second Contract Price." You are not to reveal these prices to anyone. It is your own private information.

Record Sheet, Seller # 4

	Trading year	1		. . .	8	
	Season	B	Y	. . .	B	Y
1	Sale price					
2	Cost of 1st unit	1.60	1.60	. . .	1.60	1.60
3	Profit (row 1 – row 2)					
4	Profit 5¢ commission (row 3 + .05)					
5	Sale price					
6	Cost of 2nd unit	3.80	3.80		3.80	3.80
7	Profit (row 1 – row 2)					
8	Profit + 5¢ commission (row 7 + .05)					
9	Total earnings (row 4 + row 8)					

You will also receive a tally sheet on which you are to record the price at which you make purchases in the case of buyers and sales in the case of sellers.

3. If you have received a white card, you are a seller of at most two units of the fictitious commodity being sold per trading *season*. As each season begins, the First Contract Price represents the lowest price at which you are to sell a unit of this commodity. If you sell this first unit of the commodity, you can then sell a second unit. The Second Contract Price on your white card represents the lowest price at which you are to sell a second unit of the commodity during the season. If you have received a blue card and a yellow card, you are a buyer of at most four units of the commodity being sold in each trading *period*. As the blue season begins, the First Contract Price on both your blue and yellow cards represents the highest price at which you can buy a unit of the commodity. If you buy the first unit on either card, then the Second Contract Price represents the highest price at which you can buy a second unit of the commodity against the Second Contract Price on that card. However, once the blue season ends, you can no longer buy the commodity against the blue card prices. At the end of the blue season, you are to hand a carryover slip to the experimenter indicating in the space labeled "Units to be Carried Over" the number of units you bought during the blue period

Record Sheet, Buyer # 3

	Trading year	1		. . .	8	
	Season	B	Y	. . .	B	Y
1	1st unit redemption value	2.20	4.80	. . .	2.20	4.80
2	Purchase price					
3	Profit (row 1 − row 2)					
4	Profit + 5¢ commission (row 3 + .05)					
5	2nd unit redemption value	1.00	3.60		1.00	3.60
6	Purchase price					
7	Profit (row 5 − row 6)					
8	Profit + 5¢ commission (row 7 + .05)					
9	Total earnings (row 4 + row 8)					

against the prices on your yellow card. It is profitable to buy for the yellow season during the blue season only if you think that the commodity will not be available at a lower price during the yellow season.

4. The payoffs are as follows: If you are a seller, and you were able to make a sale, you will receive 5 cents for having made a sale plus the difference between the price at which you sold and the corresponding price on your white card. Think of the price on your white card as your cost of production. Your profits depend directly upon your ability to sell above this cost, but you should be prepared to sell at this cost and receive your 5 cent commission, if you can do no better. If you are a buyer and make a purchase, you will receive a 5 cent commission plus the difference between the corresponding price on your card and the price at which you bought. Think of the prices on your blue and yellow cards as the prices you can get by reselling the unit in an entirely separate market, while the price at which you buy in this market is your cost. Your profits depend directly upon your ability to buy at a cost below the price on your card, but you should be prepared to buy at that price and collect your 5 cents, if you cannot do better. The payoffs for each subject will be accumulated over several trading

Record Sheet, Trader # 1

Unit		Trading Year	1	. . .	8
1	1	Sale price (Yellow Period)			
	2	Purchase price (Blue Period)			
	3	Profit (row 1 − row 2)			
	4	Profit + 5¢ commission (row + .05)			
⋮			⋮		⋮
4	13	Sale price (Yellow Period)			
	14	Purchase price (Blue Period)			
	15	Profit (row 13 − row 14)			
	16	Profit + 5¢ commission (row 15 + .05)			

periods, and the total amount paid in cash at the very end of the experiment. You are not to reveal your profits to anyone until the experiment is completed. There is no penalty for failing to make a contract.

5. The market for this commodity is organized as follows: We start a trading period by opening the market for the blue trading season. Any buyer is then free at any time to raise his hand and make a verbal bid to buy at any price that *does not exceed* the corresponding price on his blue or yellow card. Likewise, any seller is free at any time to raise his hand and make a verbal offer to sell at any price which is *not below* the price on his white card. Any seller is free to accept the bid of any buyer, and any buyer is free to accept the offer of any seller. As soon as a bid or offer is accepted, a binding contract has been closed, and the buyer and seller making the deal are to enter the price at which they bought or sold the unit on their tally sheet. This process continues for a period of several minutes, depending upon the volume of trading. You will be warned when the market is to close and a few more bids and offers will be called for before actually closing. This completes the blue trading season. The buyers' carryover slips are collected, and then the market is opened for the yellow trading season.

After trading for the yellow season has ended, the period has been completed. We shall then reopen the market for a new trading period, and so on, for a sequence of several periods.

6. Some of you may be unable to sell any or all of your available units in any trading season. Some of you may be able to buy or sell all of your available units in some trading seasons, but not in others. There are likely to be many bids and offers that are not accepted. You are to keep trying, and you are to feel free to earn as much cash as you can. Except for the bids and offers you are not to speak to any other subject until the experiment is completed.

7. Are there any questions?

APPENDIX 2: INSTRUCTIONS

General

This is an experiment in the economics of market decision making. Various research foundations have provided funds for this research. The instructions are simple, and if you follow them carefully and make good decisions, you might earn a considerable amount of money which will be paid to you in cash.

In this experiment we are going to simulate a market in which some of you will be buyers, some of you will be sellers, and some will be traders in a sequence of market years. Each year consists of two seasons, one of which will be called the "blue season" and the other, "yellow season." Attached to the instructions you will find a sheet, labeled buyer, seller, or trader, which describes the value to you of any decisions you might make. *You are not to reveal this information to anyone.* It is your own private information.

Specific Instructions to Buyers

During each market season you are free to purchase up to two units of the commodity. For the first unit that you buy *during a trading season,* you will receive the amount listed in row (1) marked *1st unit redemption value*; if you buy a second unit, you will receive the additional amount listed in row (5) marked *2nd unit redemption value.* The profits from each purchase (which are yours to keep) are computed by taking the difference between the redemption value and purchase price of the unit bought. *Under no condition may you buy a unit for a price that exceeds the redemption value.* In addition to this profit you will receive a 5 cent commission for each purchase. That is,

[your earnings = (redemption value)
− (purchase price) + 0.05 commission].

Suppose, for example, that you buy two units and that your redemption value for the first unit is $200 and for the second unit is $180. If you pay $150 for your first unit and $160 for the second unit, your earnings are

$$\begin{aligned} \$ \text{ earnings for 1st} &= 200 - 150 + 0.05 = 50.05 \\ \$ \text{ earnings for 2nd} &= 180 - 160 + 0.05 = 20.05 \\ \text{total } \$ \text{ earnings} &= 50.05 + 20.05 = 70.10. \end{aligned}$$

The blanks are for recording your profits. The purchase price of the first unit you buy during the first season should be recorded on row (2) *at the time of purchase.* You should then record the profits on this purchase as directed on rows (3) and (4). At the end of the period record the total of profits and commissions on the last row on the page. Subsequent seasons should be recorded similarly. In each season any units purchased *must be used for redemption in that season.*

Specific Instructions to Sellers

During each market season you are free to sell up to two units of the commodity. The first unit that you sell *during a trading season* you obtain at a cost of the amount listed on the attached sheet in the row (2) marked *cost of 1st unit*; if you sell a second unit, you incur the cost listed in the row (6) marked *cost of the 2nd unit.* The profits from each sale (which are yours to keep) are computed by taking the difference between the price at which you sold the unit and the cost of the unit. *Under no condition may you sell a unit at a price below the cost of the unit.* In addition to this profit you will receive a 5 cent commission for each sale. That is

$$[\text{your earnings} = (\text{sale price of unit}) - (\text{cost of unit}) + 0.05 \text{ commission}].$$

Your total profits and commissions for a season, which are yours to keep, are computed by adding up the profit and commissions on sales made during the season.

Suppose, for example, that your cost of the 1st unit is \$140 and your cost of the second unit is \$160. If you sell the first unit at \$200 and the second unit at \$190, your earnings are

$$\begin{aligned} \$ \text{ earnings for 1st} &= 200 - 140 + 0.05 = 60.05 \\ \$ \text{ earnings for 2nd} &= 190 - 160 + 0.05 = 30.05 \\ \text{total } \$ \text{ earnings} &= 60.05 + 30.05 = 90.10. \end{aligned}$$

The blanks on the table are for recording your profits. The sale price of the first unit you sell during the 1st season should be recorded on row (1) *at the time of sale.* You should then record the profits on this sale as directed on rows (3) and (4). At the end of the period record the total of profits and commissions on the last row on the page. Subsequent periods should be recorded similarly.

Specific Instructions to Traders

As a trader you are able to buy units in the blue season for resale in the yellow season. You are free to buy and sell as many units as you desire but you can sell only units that you have already purchased. Units purchased in the blue season of any given year can be "carried over" and sold only in the yellow season of the *same year.* You cannot purchase units during any yellow season or sell units during any blue season, and units carried over from the previous blue season in one year cannot be carried over to the following year. There can be no carryovers between years as there are between the blue and yellow season of a given year. Your earnings are determined by the difference between the price you pay for units and the price you receive upon reselling them. You will also be paid a 5 cent commission for each unit sold. In addition, you are given a $3 capital endowment. Your total earnings then consist of your capital endowment plus any profits on trades plus all commissions minus any losses on trades.

At the time you purchase units during the blue season, you are to record the price you paid for the unit in the row labeled "purchase price (blue season)." The price received for each unit sold during the following yellow season should be entered in the row labeled "sale price (yellow season)" for that unit. At the end of the yellow season of each year all units you have in inventory, that is all units carried over from the blue season but remain unsold, are automatically sold at a price of $0. It is as though the commodity spoils after the end of the yellow season and cannot be carried over to the next year. The profit or loss from each transaction is computed by taking the difference between the sale price and the purchase price. In addition, you receive a 5 cent commission for each unit sold in the yellow season. That is,

[your earnings = (sale price) − (purchase price) + 0.05 commission]

Suppose, for example, that you buy two units in the blue season and you pay $200 for the first unit and $150 for the second unit. If you then sell the first unit for $210 and the second unit for $220 in the yellow season, your earnings are

$$\begin{aligned} \$ \text{ earnings for 1st} &= 210 - 200 + 0.05 = 10.05 \\ \$ \text{ earnings for 2nd} &= 220 - 150 + 0.05 = 70.05 \\ \text{total } \$ \text{ earnings} &= 10.05 + 70.05 = 80.10. \end{aligned}$$

You are to calculate your profits in the space provided on your trading sheet, and at the end of each year you are to record your total profits for that year in the last row of the last page of your trading sheet.

Market Organization

The market for this commodity is organized as follows. The market will be conducted in a series of years each consisting of a blue season followed by a yellow season. Each season lasts for 5 minutes. Anyone wishing to purchase a unit is free to raise his hand and make a verbal bid to buy one unit of the commodity at a specified price, and anyone with units to sell is free to accept or not accept the bid. Likewise, anyone wishing to sell a unit is free to raise his hand and make a verbal offer to sell one unit at a specified price. If a bid or offer is accepted, a binding contract has been closed for a single unit, and the contracting parties will record the contract price to be included in their earnings. Any ties in bids or acceptance will be resolved by random choice. Except for the bids and their acceptance, you are not to speak to any other subject. There are likely to be many bids that are not accepted, but you are free to keep trying. You are free to make as much profit as you can.

APPENDIX 3: SUBJECT INDEX AND LIMIT PRICES

Subject number	Experiment in which participated	Demander or supplier	Blue limit prices 1st unit	Blue limit prices 2nd unit	Yellow limit prices 1st unit	Yellow limit prices 2nd unit
1	1	S	0.80	2.45	0.80	2.45
2	1	S	0.95	2.30	0.95	2.30
3	1	S	1.10	2.15	1.10	2.15
4	1	S	1.25	2.00	1.25	2.00
5	1	S	1.40	1.85	1.40	1.85
6	1	S	1.55	1.70	1.55	1.70
7	1	D	2.00	1.10	2.45	1.55
8	1	D	1.85	0.95	2.60	1.70
9	1	D	1.70	0.80	2.75	1.85
10	1	D	1.55	0.65	2.90	2.00
11	1	D	1.40	0.50	3.05	2.15
12	1	D	1.25	0.35	3.20	2.30
13	2	S	1.60	3.80	1.60	3.80
14	2	S	1.80	3.80	1.80	3.80
15	2	S	2.00	3.40	2.00	3.40
16	2	S	2.20	3.20	2.20	3.20
17	2	S	2.40	3.00	2.40	3.00
18	2	S	2.60	2.80	2.60	2.80
19	2	D	2.20	1.00	4.80	3.60
20	2	D	2.40	1.20	4.60	3.40
21	2	D	2.60	1.40	4.40	3.20
22	2	D	2.80	1.60	4.20	3.00
23	2	D	3.00	1.80	4.00	2.80
24	2	D	3.20	2.00	3.80	2.60
25	2	trader	open		open	
26	2	trader	open		open	

APPENDIX 4: CONTRACTS IN EXPERIMENT 1, AND BIDS, OFFERS, AND CONTRACTS FOR EXPERIMENT 2

CONTRACTS IN EXPERIMENT 1

Period	Season	Buyer	Seller	Price
1	B	9	4	1.35
		7	1	1.30
		8	3	1.35
		10	2	1.35
		7*	5	1.45
1	Y	12	5	1.75
		10	2	1.60
		8	1	1.60
		9	6	1.70
		12	6	1.80
		10	3	1.80
		11	5	1.85
		11	4	2.00
2	B	10	5	1.60
		9	2	1.60
		9*	1	1.70
		7	4	1.65
		11*	6	1.70
		8	3	1.75
		11*	6	1.75
		8*	5	1.85
2	Y	12	2	1.85
		12	1	1.85
		10	6	1.85
		9	4	1.85
		7	6	1.80
		8	3	1.70
		7	5	1.55
3	B	7	6	1.70
		10*	2	1.70
		9	1	1.70
		9*	5	1.75
		10*	4	1.75
		8	6	1.75
		12*	3	1.70
3	Y	8	6	1.70
		12	1	1.75
		11	6	1.80
		11	2	1.79
		9	4	1.78
		7	5	1.75
		8	3	1.70
4	B	9*	1	1.73
		11*	4	1.74
		11*	2	1.74
		8	6	1.75
		8*	5	1.75
		12*	3	1.75
		10*	6	1.75
4	Y	9	6	1.75
		10	5	1.75
		12	2	1.75
		7	6	1.70
		8	1	1.70
		7	4	1.55
5	B	12*	6	1.70
		12*	1	1.70
		7	4	1.70
		9	6	1.70
		8	3	1.70
		11*	5	1.70
		11*	2	1.70
5	Y	10	6	1.70
		8	1	1.70
		8	2	1.70
		9	3	1.70
		10	5	1.67
		7	4	1.67
		9	6	1.70

* Blue period purchases against Yellow period demand.

Bids, Offers and Contracts for Experiment 2

1 Blue

Number	Bid	Offer	Taker
23	1.15		
22	1.20		
21	1.25		
24	1.40		
26	1.50		
22	1.55		
16		4.00	
20	1.65		
15		3.35	
26	2.00		13
14		2.50	
22	2.00		
20	2.10		
22	2.20		
13		3.90	
26	2.50		14
18	3.00		
22	2.50		17
20	2.35		
24	2.45		15
14		4.00	
21	1.80		
23	1.85		
18		2.80	
16		2.50	
20	2.00		
16		2.40	
23	1.95		
20	2.10		
16		2.35	
24	1.90		
23	1.92		
20	2.20		
21	2.25		
20	2.30		16
23	2.25		
20	1.00		
21	2.00		
23	2.10		
21	2.25		
21	2.30		
21	2.50		
14		4.20	
18		2.80	

1 Yellow

Number	Bid	Offer	Taker
18		2.80	19
16		2.80	21
26		3.00	
20	2.90		14
20	2.10		
15		2.95	
14		2.70	19
23	2.70		13
22	2.65		26
22	2.65		26
20	2.80		15
21	2.75		
24	2.80		17
23	2.80		
16		3.50	
21	2.80		
21	2.90		
13		3.90	
17		3.10	
21	3.00		
21	3.05		

2 Blue

Number	Bid	Offer	Taker
24	1.05		
16		3.00	
22	2.00		
23	2.60		13
14		2.70	
20	2.05		
25	2.70		14
26	2.40		
24	2.50		
18		2.75	
16		2.70	
26	2.60		17
24	2.70		18
26	2.50		
22	2.50		
16		2.70	
21	2.55		
22	2.55		

BIDS, OFFERS AND CONTRACTS FOR EXPERIMENT 2 (*continued*)

Number	Bid	Offer	Taker
26	2.60		
22	2.65		
16		2.70	26
22	2.65		
21	2.50		
22	2.65		15
20	2.20		
21	2.50		
18		2.85	
26	2.60		
16		3.50	
21	2.60		
26	2.65		
	2 Yellow		
24	2.00		
13		2.50	20
21	2.60		14
23	2.70		15
19	2.70		
26		2.80	24
17		2.70	19
20	2.80		25
22	2.75		
16		2.85	21
26		3.00	
18		2.90	
24	2.60		
19	2.80		18
22	2.85		26
22	2.85		
16		3.50	
22	2.90		18
24	2.50		
23	2.75		
17		3.10	
24	2.60		
	3 Blue		
20	2.00		
23	2.60		
18		2.80	25
13		2.70	24
26	2.60		
22	2.65		
16		2.85	
14		2.80	
26	2.65		
22	2.70		14
25	2.70		
26	2.71		17
13	2.72		
26	2.75		
16		2.80	
15		2.79	
16		2.80	
26	2.70		
15		2.76	23
20	2.35		
21	2.60		
26	2.70		
16		2.75	25
26	2.70		
	3 Yellow		
15		3.50	
25		2.80	19
14		3.20	
18		2.85	21
16		2.90	21
22	2.85		13
20	2.95		14
22	2.80		
24	2.85		
20	2.95		15
26		2.90	23
22	2.90		18
16		3.50	
24	2.80		
19	2.85		25
24	2.90		17
24	2.60		
23	2.75		
24	2.75		
14		3.00	

BIDS, OFFERS AND CONTRACTS FOR EXPERIMENT 2 (*continued*)

Number	Bid	Offer	Taker
18		2.90	21
25		2.90	24
15		2.91	
16		2.95	
25		2.90	22
19	2.85		14
20	2.90		25
26		2.90	22
18		2.90	
4 Blue			
22	2.65		
25	2.70		
24	2.75		
18		2.85	25
13		2.80	25
24	2.70		
16		2.90	
14		2.80	23
20	2.20		
22	2.75		
18		2.85	24
16		2.90	
26	2.75		
15		2.85	25
22	2.80		
17		2.85	
26	2.82		
26	2.85		16
26	2.80		
17		2.85	
22	2.80		
26	2.81		
26	2.85		17
23	2.85		
4 Yellow			
13		2.90	
21	2.85		13

Number	Bid	Offer	Taker
24	2.75		
14		3.00	
18		2.90	21
25		2.90	24
15		2.91	
16		2.95	
25		2.90	22
19	2.85		14
20	2.90		25
26		2.90	22
18		2.90	
19	2.90		18
26		2.90	20
15		2.90	23
16		2.90	
17		2.90	
16		2.88	
5 Blue			
18		2.85	24
16		2.85	26
22	2.80		
13		2.85	23
15		2.90	
25	2.85		18
17		2.85	25
20	2.30		
21	2.60		
26	2.80		14
22	2.80		
15		2.85	25
26	2.80		
22	2.80		
16		3.50	
26	2.80		
26	2.81		
17		3.05	
16		3.50	
26	2.70		

BIDS, OFFERS AND CONTRACTS FOR EXPERIMENT 2 (*continued*)

Number	Bid	Offer	Taker
22	2.80		
26	2.85		
	5 Yellow		
23	2.90		17
26		2.90	24
20	2.80		
18		2.90	20
13		2.90	21
16		2.90	21
19	2.85		
14		2.95	
25		2.90	20
22	2.86		25
15		2.90	
19	2.85		
22	2.86		25
26		2.90	19
19	2.85		18
14		2.90	
23	2.80		
15		2.86	
14		2.85	
15		2.81	23
16		3.50	
14		2.85	
	6 Blue		
18		2.90	24
16		2.90	25
22	2.80		
26	2.85		14
13		2.85	23
26	2.85		15
25	2.85		
16		3.40	
18		2.90	
26	2.85		
17		2.90	

Number	Bid	Offer	Taker
26	2.85		
25	2.86		18
26	2.85		
25	2.86		
26	2.85		
25	2.86		
26	2.87		17
25	2.88		
16		3.40	
24	2.00		
20	2.40		
26	2.85		
25	2.90		
	6 Yellow		
13		2.90	24
21	2.85		
14		2.90	20
16		2.90	
22	2.86		
23	2.88		25
18		2.88	21
16		2.90	
22	2.88		26
18		2.90	19
20	2.85		
21	2.88		26
22	2.88		15
26		2.89	20
16		2.90	
19	2.85		
25		2.90	
16		2.89	
25		2.88	
16		2.85	
17		2.85	
25		2.80	19
16		2.80	
17		2.70	

References

Mandelbrot, Benoit B., "When Can Price Be Arbitraged Efficiently? A Limit to the Validity of the Random Walk and Martingale Models," *Review of Economics and Statistics*, LIII (Aug. 1971), 225–36.

Plott, Charles R., and Vernon L. Smith, "An Experimental Examination of Two Trading Institutions," California Institute of Technology Social Science Working Paper No. 83, 1975, forthcoming, *Review of Economic Studies.*

Samuelson, Paul A., "Intertemporal Price Equilibrium: A Prologue to the Theory of Speculation," *The Collected Papers of Paul A. Samuelson,* Vol. II, J. E. Stiglitz, ed. (Cambridge: M.I.T. Press, 1966a), 946–84.

——, "Spatial Price Equilibrium and Linear Programming," *The Collected Papers of Paul A. Samuelson,* Vol. II, J. E. Stiglitz, ed. (Cambridge: M.I.T. Press, 1966b), 925–45.

——, "Mathematics of Speculative Price," *Mathematical Topics in Economic Theory and Computation,* R. H. Day and S. M. Robinson, ed. (Philadelphia: S.I.A.M., 1972), pp. 1–42.

Schimmler, Jorg, "Speculation, Profitability, and Price Stability—A Formal Approach," *Review of Economics and Statistics,* LV (Feb. 1973), 110–14.

Smith, Vernon L., "Notes on Some Literature in Experimental Economics," California Institute of Technology Social Science Working Paper No. 21, 1973.

——, "Bidding and Auctioning Institutions: Experimental Results," California Institute of Technology Social Science Working Paper No. 71, 1974. To appear in *Proceedings of Conference on Bidding and Auctioning,* New York University, Y. Amihod, ed. (1976).

——, "Experimental Economics: Some Theory and Results," California Institute of Technology Social Science Working Paper No. 73, January 1975. Published in part, *American Economic Association Papers and Proceedings* (May 1976).

Williams, Fred, "The Effect of Market Organization on Competitive Equilibrium: The Multiunit Case," *Review of Economic Studies,* XL, no. 121 (Jan. 1973), 97–114.

Williams, John, "Speculation and the Carryover," this *Journal,* L (1935), 436–55.

EXPERIMENTAL ECONOMICS AT PURDUE

Vernon L. Smith

This memoir is about many people connected with Purdue and with Em Weiler, but mostly it is about me and a continuing struggle of escape from the prison of conventional patterns of economic thought.

I arrived in West Lafayette in the summer of 1955. I had turned down an offer from Princeton at $3,750 per year, because I was already poor enough, and a good offer from Carnegie Tech, because somehow Carnegie seemed too structured. Whatever Purdue was, it wasn't that! In the next two to three years I found myself in the company of Ed Ames, Lance Davis, George Horwich, Chuck Howe, John Hughes, Jim Quirk, Stan Reiter, Rubin Saposnik, Larry Senesh, and, of course, Em Weiler. Many of us had only one thing in common—a very subverting sense of considerable dissatisfaction with our own graduate education, whether it was at Chicago, Harvard, Stanford, or wherever, and with the state of economic knowledge. This was the glue that bound—that allowed each of us to be encouraged to "do our own thing" (before that phrase became part of the language) by Em Weiler. Em, I think, had no prevision at all as to which direction that collection of renegades should go, but he had an intuition that maybe something would emerge out of a process that did not try to prevent things from happening.

Out of this menagerie many successful (and unsuccessful) cultural experiments emerged: a remarkable graduate program, an honors undergraduate program, the Quantitative Institute Seminars, cliometrics, and—for me—experimental economics.

Experimental economics at Purdue started in the late fall of 1955. In those days it was common to teach twelve hours, and I was teaching four sections of principles—the hardest job I have ever had. Not surprisingly, I had insomnia one night, and for reasons that utterly escape me, in the dead of night I found myself thinking about the classroom demonstration that Ed Chamberlin used to perform with the Harvard graduate students to "prove" the impossibility of pure competition. I didn't take Chamberlin's course, because I decided after sitting in on the first two meetings that I had had a superior course on imperfect competition from Dick Howey at the University of Kansas. But I did observe and participate in Ed Chamberlin's little "experiment." The scuttlebutt among the Harvard graduate students was that the whole exercise was sort of silly; and being at a peer-impressionable age, I recall being in agreement with this rather harsh and, I think in retrospect, inaccurate conclusion.

So there I was, wide awake at 3 a.m., thinking about Chamberlin's "silly" experiment. He gave each buyer a card with a maximum buying price for a single unit, and each seller a card with a minimum selling price for one unit. All of us were instructed just to circulate in the room, engage a buyer (or seller), negotiate a contract, or go on to find another buyer (or seller), and so on. If a buyer and a seller made a contract, they were to come to Chamberlin, reveal the price of the exchange, turn in their cards, and he would post the price on the blackboard for all to see. When it was all over, he would reveal what had been the implicit supply and demand (without-income-effects) schedules, and we would learn the important lesson that supply and demand theory was worthless in explaining what had happened; namely, that prices were not near the equilibrium, and neither was the quantity exchanged.

The thought occurred to me that the idea of doing an experiment was right, but what was wrong was that if you were going to show that competitive equilibria are not realizable operationally under conditions of incomplete information, then you should choose an existing institution of exchange that might be informationally more favorable to yielding competitive equilibria. Then, when such an equilibrium failed to be approached, you had a more powerful result. This led to two ideas: (1) Instead of having the subjects circulate and make bilateral deals, why not use the double oral auction procedure, used on the stock and commodity exchanges? After all, it would seem that these markets would come closest to that which is surely unattainable: competitive equilibria. (2) Since Marshall had talked about a competitive equilibrium as simply a tendency, conditional upon the supply and demand flows remaining stationary for a "long enough" period of time, why not conduct the experiment in a sequence of trading "days" in which supply and demand were renewed to yield functions that were "daily" flows? These two changes seemed to be the appropriate modifications to do a more credible job of rejecting competitive price theory, which after all, was for teaching, not believing (everyone at Harvard knew that, and you just knew, deep down, that those Chicago guys also knew it). So, I thought, in the spring semester (1956), to keep myself from repeating again, four times over, the textbook supply-and-demand song-and-dance, I would first take a class period to run this new experiment. I will run it on the class before they are contaminated by any discussion of supply and demand or of competitive markets.

The following January, I carried through on my insomniacal plan. The experiment I ran is labeled "Chart 1, Test 1" on page 113 of "An Experimental Study of Competitive Market Behavior" in the *Journal of Political Economy* (April 1962). I am still recovering from the shock of the experimental results. The outcome was unbelievably consistent with competitive price theory. If these results were to be believed, what was being knocked down was Chamberlin's hypothesis of the unattainability of supply-and-demand equilibria. But the results *can't* be believed, I thought. It must be an accident, so I will take another class and do a new experiment with different supply-and-demand schedules.

I performed the experiment labeled "Test 2" in the 1962 article. Wham! It converged remarkably fast. How can this be? These subjects do not have knowledge of the market supply-and-demand schedules of the experiment. They do not even know, as yet, what "supply" and "demand" might mean. Then an explanation occurred to me. Why didn't I think of it before? Both of these experiments used symmetrical supply-and-demand curves—consumers' surplus is equal to producers' surplus—these were just special cases! The next semester, I ran an experiment with the asymmetrical design labeled "Test 7" in the 1962 article. It took a little longer, but it converged! This early series of experiments continued until 1960.

Meantime I was doing "serious" research on engineering production functions, their characteristics, and how these characteristics affected investment and production theory. I was also teaching it, and the Purdue graduate students had named it "enginomics." That had all started because I wasn't sure I believed all that stuff about production functions and how there were diminishing returns with all those guys tramping around in the cornfields with their rakes and hoes. I thought that there ought to be a better case for factor substitution, or there was no case at all.

By 1961 I had gotten that bone out of my throat, and thinking I now knew what could be believed about production and investment theory, I published *Investment and Production.* Also in 1961, I went to Stanford as a visitor. There I ran several experiments, received some strong encouragement from Bill Capron and (if my memory serves me) Mo Abramovitz, and I discovered that there was nothing unusual about Purdue students as experimental subjects. I also got convergence with the Stanford students. Although there were some wise guys at Stanford who thought these experiments were trivial, I thought they might be wrong, although it was probably the case that they were smarter than I.

A really important event at Stanford was my meeting Sydney Siegel, who was a fellow that year at the Center for Advanced Study in the Behavioral Sciences. I knew Syd only six weeks before, very inconveniently, he died. (I have never forgiven him. What a great experimental scientist!) I showed him my work. He was skeptical, too, but it was different; his was the skepticism of a scientist, not a wise guy. He had ideas, suggestions, and challenges for me that emanated from a deep commitment to the science of behavior. Through his cutting criticism came excitement and implicit encouragement. I learned much from Syd on what experimental science is all about. I eventually read most of his work. We were both delighted to find someone else thinking along similar lines for economics—although he was doing bilateral bargaining, duopoly, and triopoly experiments with Larry Fouraker, while I was doing larger-group competitive-market experiments and was more interested in studying institutions and market efficiency than in studying the effect of numbers. I often thought how well Syd would have fitted in with the Purdue crowd. I even wondered how come he turned out to be such an individualist without knowing Em Weiler.

Whatever the exact genesis, I got up the courage to write a paper reporting on all the experiments I had done from 1956 to 1960. It wasn't easy. People had been skeptical that there was a trick, some simple reason why the experiments worked that had *nothing* to do with economics or theory or that overused, undefined thing that economists call the "real world." But there were also those who consistently encouraged me—John Hughes and Em Weiler, in particular. I had gotten arrogant enough to give a seminar on the subject at Northwestern, about 1957. I had the feeling that they had no idea what I was up to, that I hadn't articulated very well what I was doing, and that they did not really believe any of it. But the seminar must not have been as bad as I thought, since they later asked if I would entertain an offer to come to Northwestern. I guess they figured, "Well, he does other things too." I didn't go to Northwestern, although I certainly was tempted.

In 1960 I wrote up my results and thought that the obvious place to send it was the *Journal of Political Economy*. It's surely a natural for those Chicago guys, I thought. What have I shown? I have shown that with remarkably little learning, strict privacy, and a modest number, inexperienced traders converge rapidly to a competitive equilibrium under the double oral auction mechanism. The market works under much weaker conditions than had traditionally been thought to be necessary. You didn't have to have large numbers. Economic agents do not have to have perfect knowledge of supply and demand. You do not need price-taking behavior—everyone in the double oral auction is as much a price maker as a price taker. A great discovery, right? Not quite, as it turned out. At Chicago they already knew that markets work. Who needs evidence?

So I shipped two copies of the first draft of "An Experimental Study" off to the *JPE*, soon to be "edited by Harry Johnson in cooperation with other members of the Economics Department of the University of Chicago." (Before the episode initiated by that action was over, I would wonder how appropriate was the word "cooperation.") Harry and I went through three referees (Harry revealed that he had been a fourth, just prior to his becoming the new editor.) I wrote detailed comments on each referee's comments and, in the end, big independent Harry, after a long period of waiting, simply "ran over" a couple of those referees. In a letter to me, dated October 13, 1961, Harry wrote:

If you feel that your paper stands up against their criticisms or that the revisions you suggest are the only concessions that you think it is necessary to make to them, just send the article to me as revised, and I will publish it. If the referees feel strongly enough to write up their criticism as comments, and these comments are worth publishing, you will have the right to rejoin. But somehow, I don't think that we will have much trouble that way. . . . I have learned something about my referees from this experience. As you may suspect, this is a very difficult job inasmuch as one has to keep evaluating everyone, including oneself."

So the paper was published, and I won't forgive Harry for dying either.

There was laughter, there were tears, in all those years—with Em helping us achieve whatever might be our individual aspirations. Me too, Mort. If Em or his representative came and interviewed me again, and said there was a place just like Purdue, I would go. Maybe you can't go home again, but it sure would be worth a try.

PART II

Institutions and Market Performance

Introduction

Soon after I came to the University of Arizona in 1975, I became involved in joint work with several undergraduate and graduate students in the development of interactive software programs that would enable experimental subjects to trade via computer terminals under the rules of alternative exchange institutions. The computer brought a new dimension to experimental economics. This period also initiated my longtime collaboration with Arlington W. Williams, first as a graduate student at the University of Arizona, then as a member of the faculty at Indiana University. Williams has been instrumental in bringing the "machine age" to economic experimentation in the form of a staggering volume of software development and refinement.

With these new tools we undertook a number of studies of comparative institutional performance. We systematically examined the effect of nonbinding price controls under computerized double auction trading rules (paper 10). This work had been motivated by the original discovery by R. Mark Isaac and Charles Plott of the nonbenign dynamic effect of price controls, including nonbinding controls, on convergence to competitive equilibria – a result that was not anticipated by static theory. Williams and I executed a design based on a systematic replication of these unexpected results and measured the quantitative effect of nonbinding controls on price outcomes within this design. Even more surprising is the fact that the same qualitative effects of price controls documented in these papers carries over to posted-offer markets. The latter ware reported in my paper with Don Coursey, omitted here, but reprinted in *Schools of Economic Thought: Experimental Economics.*

Papers 11, 12, 14, and 17 each examines different institutional issues. In 11 we dissect certain key features of New York Stock Exchange rules, and ask what is the marginal effect on performance of the different components of these rules. In 12 we compare real-time continuous double auctions with the sealed bid-offer (sometimes called "clearing house") mechanism. In 14 we ask how asymmetry in buyer-seller surplus is related to the convergence of real-time double auction markets. Finally, in 17 we report an extensive systematic comparison of posted-offer pricing with continuous real-time double auction pricing. Software for the former was originally programmed by Jonathan Ketcham.

Paper 13 interprets the results of a large number of experimental auction markets in terms of the Hayek hypothesis that a primary function of markets and decentralization is to economize on information. Thus market institutions provide a discovery process yielding not just exchange but the information needed for exchange.

Paper 15 is an attempt to restate the purpose and function of experimental methodology based on the perspective of over two decades of research. New perspectives are encountered with each new set of experiences, and old perspectives are transformed into more coherent meaning. In this paper I tried to rearticulate most of the old fragments into a more comprehensive statement. I think the bridge-building in that article between experimental economics and the Reiter-Hurwicz – sometimes called the Northwestern – view of economic theory has been particularly helpful in showing how experiments can be integrated with microeconomic theory when the latter is enriched with extensive-form institutional interpretations. The comment on this paper by Ronald Heiner raised a number of issues, some that had recurrently concerned me, on which the original paper was silent, and my reply (paper 16) took advantage of the welcome opportunity to reflect further on methodological questions and issues of empirical interpretation omitted from the original discussion.

The experiments in stock market trading in the laboratory (paper 19) with G. L. Suchanek and A. W. Williams, which were conducted in the period 1982–86, have assumed new dimensions of significance since the great crash in world security markets on October 19, 1987. Suddenly the idea that subjects in laboratory asset trading, where shares have well-defined commonly shared information on fundamental dividend value, can self-generate price bubbles becomes a credible general characteristic of human behavior. Of course panics have been a recurrent event in markets for centuries, but historical memories are short and one's memory can be refreshed at will with experiments. Often the precipitating "cause" in past panics defies identification. This is clearly the case in our experiments where subjects are unable to forecast a turning point immediately in advance of the trading period where the turn occurs. But in the experimental case prices do have an important predictable component based on bid-offer information generated by the traders, although this information is not assembled in a way that is useful to them.

Some three dozen additional experiments, conducted since this original study was written, have explored potential treatments for extinguishing price bubbles in the laboratory. These include price limit change rules, introducing a short selling capability, homogeneous endowments, and the imposition of transactions fees. None of these policies or changes in the environment eliminates the propensity of inexperienced and once-experienced traders to generate transaction prices away from dividend value. Experience appears to be the most reliable source of rational-expectations trading near fundamental value.

On Nonbinding Price Controls in a Competitive Market

By VERNON L. SMITH AND ARLINGTON W. WILLIAMS*

Interest in the effect of nonbinding price controls on double auction markets stems from two primary considerations. The double auction institution converges to a competitive allocation more rapidly, and with fewer participating agents than any other institution with which it has been compared (see Smith et al.). One way to improve our understanding of this important property is to determine what conditions, if any, can interfere with or retard this convergence process. Nonbinding price controls represent a condition that may affect this convergence process. Hence, if such effects can be documented, they will provide a body of data that any future proposed model of the double auction process should be able to explain. A second reason for studying the effect of nonbinding controls on the double auction is practical: The organized commodity exchanges "...often set limits on price fluctuations during any single day. When prices at any point during a day rise above or fall below the closing prices of the preceding day by more than the amount of the limit, no further trading for that day is permitted" (Walter Labys, p. 162). Consequently, commodity trading frequently occurs at prices near the level of nonbinding price floors or ceilings.

Mark Issac and Charles Plott report the results of twelve exploratory experiments in which various price control constraints are imposed on double auction markets. Their two principal conclusions can be summarized as follows:

1) The hypothesis is rejected that nonbinding price controls, that is, price ceilings above or price floors below the competitive equilibrium (*CE*), will serve as a focal point or signalling price on which sellers and buyers will key their contracts.

2) Inconclusive evidence is presented in support of the hypothesis that nonbinding controls near the *CE* will bias prices *below* *CE* when there is a price ceiling and *above* *CE* when there is a price floor.

Support for this second hypothesis is not conclusive because some experimental markets show a tendency to converge from below and others from above depending upon the relative bargaining strength of buyers as against sellers. Thus sampling variation among subjects can yield a group in which buyers (sellers) are able to make contracts at an average price below (above) *CE* for several periods of trading. Consequently, in an experiment in which there is a price ceiling (floor) five cents above (below) *CE* and in which contract prices are observed to occur below (above) *CE*, one cannot determine conclusively whether the observed effect was due to the nonbinding price control or to the bargaining characteristics of the market participants.

We report below an experimental design developed for the purpose of separating these confounding factors and allowing the effect of nonbinding controls to be isolated. The results of sixteen experiments strongly support the hypothesis that markets with a nonbinding price ceiling (floor) near *CE* will converge from below (above) relative to any otherwise identifiable tendency to converge from below (above). An analysis of the effect of a nonbinding price ceiling (floor) on the distributions of bids and offers reveals the cause of this bias: ceilings limit the bargaining strategies of sellers especially, but also that of buyers, while floors have the opposite effect. Thus, in the absence of price controls, double auction trading is characterized by a process in which sellers typically make concessions from offer prices well above *CE* while buyers most often concede from bid prices well below *CE*. A price ceiling truncates seller offer prices at the ceiling, requir-

*University of Arizona and Indiana University, respectively. Research support by the National Science Foundation is gratefully acknowledged.

ing them to begin their bargaining from a less advantageous position at the ceiling or below. Buyer bids are also effected, but less dramatically, in that the occassional bid above *CE* that might occur in a free market, will be blocked by the ceiling. Also the ceiling, and/or the consequent lower offers by sellers, induces somewhat lower-bidding behavior by buyers.

I. Experimental Design

Since the research task is to isolate the treatment effect of price controls on competitive market dynamics, and since this effect can be obscured by noise and confounding factors, we have devoted considerable care to the development of an appropriate experimental design. The resulting design has the following principal characteristics:

1) All experiments used the PLATO computer version of the double auction exchange mechanism developed by Williams (1980). The computer permits better control over "experimenter" effects by assuring uniform procedures across all experiments, with accurate computerized recording of all bids, offers, contracts, and their time of occurrence. The particular form of the double auction used in the price control experiments employs both the New York Stock Exchange "improvement rule", and a computerized version of the "specialist book." During a particular auction sequence, the improvement rule (rules 71 and 72 on the Exchange; see George Leffler and Loring Farwell, pp. 187–88) requires a bid (offer) to be higher (lower) than an outstanding bid (offer) before it can be announced. When a trade occurs, the "auction" of the unit ends and the market (in our case PLATO) awaits new bids and offers that must provide sequentially improving terms. A bid (offer) that is lower (higher) than the outstanding bid (offer) is entered into a PLATO queue, lexicographically ordered with higher bids (lower offers) having priority, and tied bids (offers) ordered chronologically—the first in having priority over the second, etc.

2) Only subjects who had participated in at least one previous PLATO double auction market, without price controls and defined by different supply and demand parameters, were used in the experiments. (See our earlier paper for a discussion of alternative bidding rules and trading experience as experimental treatment variables in PLATO double auctions.)

3) The induced values and costs or limit prices (see Smith) for a typical experiment are shown in Table 1 for each of four buyers and four sellers. (The theoretical total surplus is \$10.20 per trading period, with commissions of \$3.00 per period for fifteen traded units, giving a total payout of \$198 per experiment.) The corresponding market supply and demand with symmetrical buyer and seller surpluses are shown on the lower left of Figure 1. Each buyer (seller) receives a cash payment equal to the difference between his/her value (selling price) for a unit and his/her purchase price (cost) plus a ten cent commission for each unit traded. Except for the commissions, buyers (sellers) earn the realized consumer's (producer's) surplus. Notice that in this design (Figure 1) there are several intramarginal and submarginal units in the range from five cents above to five cents below the *CE* price. Hence, inefficient submarginal trades can easily occur if there are many contracts away from the *CE* price. Similarly, intramarginal units near the *CE* price are less well motivated to trade than other more profitable units, leading to an increased chance of inefficiency. These features specify a supply and demand design in which efficiency, defined as the ratio of realized to theoretical buyers' plus sellers' surplus, is likely to be sensitive to factors, such as nonbinding price controls, hypothesized to interfere with the trading process. These features were not present in the Issac and Plott (Figure 2) design in which intramarginal and submarginal units were ten cents or more above or below the *CE* price.

4) All experiments consist of three "weeks" of trading, each week consisting of five (or four in some experiments) trading periods. Week 1 provides the baseline set of observations with *no* price control. If a particular group is characterized by relatively strong bargaining buyers, this is measured by the difference between the total surplus realized by buyers and the total surplus obtained

TABLE 1 — UNIT VALUES AND COSTS IN DOLLARS

Subject	Unit 1	2	3	4	5	6	Individual Competitive Equilibrium Surplus
Buyer 1	5.35	5.10	4.70	4.60	4.50	–	1.20
Buyer 2	5.60	4.90	4.80	4.65	4.55	–	1.35
Buyer 3	5.60	4.90	4.80	4.65	4.60	4.50	1.35
Buyer 4	5.35	5.10	4.70	4.65	4.55	–	1.20
Seller 1	3.95	4.20	4.60	4.65	4.75	–	1.20
Seller 2	3.70	4.40	4.50	4.65	4.75	–	1.35
Seller 3	3.95	4.20	4.60	4.70	4.80	–	1.20
Seller 4	3.70	4.40	4.50	4.65	4.70	4.80	1.35
Total Market Surplus							10.20

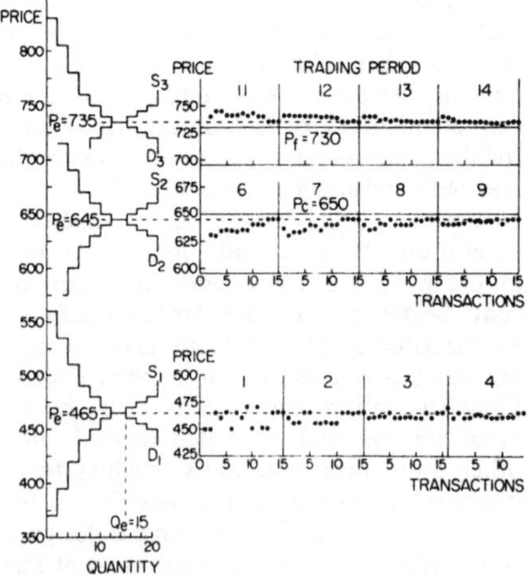

FIGURE 1. EXPERIMENT 2:26

by sellers. Since in our design, differential surplus is zero at the *CE*, this measure should reflect only the relative bargaining strength of buyers in any particular experiment.

5) In each experiment, following the completion of the first week of trading, a prespecified constant is added to each limit price value and cost unit, thereby uniformly shifting the supply and demand schedules up or down relative to Week 1. Also the assignment of unit values (costs) to buyers (sellers), as illustrated in Table 1, is rerandomized by reassigning the shifted buyer (seller) limit price valuations (costs) among the buyers (sellers). Trading is then resumed in Week 2, periods 6 through 9 or 10, under these new conditions. In eight experiments, a price ceiling is also imposed. In four other experiments a price floor is imposed, and in four others no price control is imposed. This procedure is designed to allow any effect of the shift in supply and demand to be separated from the effect of the price controls. Subjects are informed that trading will proceed during Week 2 under a price ceiling (at, for example $6.50 as in Figure 1) by the appearance of the following message on their display screens at the end of Week 1:

SPECIAL ANNOUNCEMENT

> Price controls will be in effect during market Week 2. The MAXIMUM allowed bid or offer price will be $6.50. Any entry which violates the above will be automatically rejected and will generate a descriptive error message.

If a subject attempts to violate the $6.50 price ceiling the following message is generated: "Your entry exceeds the maximum allowed price of $6.50." The announcement of a price floor is made in exactly the same format as given above with "MINIMUM" replacing "MAXIMUM" in the announcement's text.

6) Following the completion of the second week of trading, the valuations (costs) are again shifted and rerandomized. Trading is then resumed in Week 3, period 11 through

TABLE 2—NUMBER OF EXPERIMENTS PERFORMED UNDER EACH TREATMENT CONDITION

Supply and Demand Shift in Week 2 (3)	Price Control Variable		
	No Price Control in Week 2 or Week 3	Week 2 Price Ceiling 5 Cents Above *CE* Week 3 Price Floor 5 Cents Below *CE*	Week 2 Price Floor 5 Cents Below *CE* Week 3 Price Ceiling 5 Cents Above *CE*
Up (Up)	1	2	1
Up (Down)	1	2	1
Down (Up)	1	2	1
Down (Down)	1	2	1

14 or 15, with a price floor in eight experiments, a price ceiling in four experiments, and with no price control in four. The number of experiments conducted under each Week 2–Week 3 shift condition, with or without a price ceiling (floor), is shown in Table 2. It should be noted, however, that the design is still not completely "balanced" in that only four were conducted using a price floor in Week 2 followed by a price ceiling in Week 3. Although it would be scientifically appealing, we thought that it was perhaps not worth the cost (subject earnings are about $200 per experiment) to fill in these additional cells with experimental observations.

Based on this experimental design, we propose two linear models for separating the effect of 1) the differential bargaining strength of buyers relative to sellers, 2) a uniform shift in supply and demand with individual random reassignment of units, 3) a price ceiling just above *CE*, and 4) a price floor just below *CE*. Define:

$B(t)$: Buyer realized surplus (earnings net of commissions) in period t.

$S(t)$: Seller realized surplus in period t.

$D(t) \equiv B(t) - S(t)$: Differential bargaining strength of buyers over sellers.

$$X_i^c = \begin{cases} 1, \text{ if ceiling price is imposed in Week } i. \\ 0, \text{ if no price control is imposed in Week } i. \end{cases}$$

$$X_i^f = \begin{cases} 1, \text{ if floor price is imposed in Week } i. \\ 0, \text{ if no price control is imposed in Week } i. \end{cases}$$

$$Y_i = \begin{cases} 1, \text{ if supply and demand shift down in Week } i. \\ 0, \text{ if supply and demand shift up in Week } i. \end{cases}$$

The proposed linear models are stated:

(1)
$$D(t) = \begin{cases} \alpha_2 D(t-5) + \beta_2 X_2^c + \gamma_2 X_2^f + \delta_2 Y_2 \\ \alpha_3 D(t-10) + \beta_3 X_3^c + \gamma_3 X_3^f + \delta_3 Y_3 \end{cases}$$

If $\alpha_i > 0$ it means that whether buyers are stronger ($D > 0$) or weaker ($D < 0$) in a particular experimental group, this characteristic tends to persist across comparable trading periods (for example, 1, 6, and 11; 2, 7, and 12; etc.) in successive weeks. If $\alpha_3 < \alpha_2 < 1$, this suggests week-to-week learning (in the sense of continued convergence to *CE*) after correcting for the effect of shifts in supply and demand. The principle research hypothesis of this paper is that $\beta_i > 0$, and $\gamma_i < 0$, that is, a nonbinding price ceiling favors buyers by lowering contract prices relative to *CE*, while a nonbinding price floor favors sellers by raising contract prices relative to *CE*. Finally, the effect of a uniform shift in supply and demand could cause prices to overshoot the new equilibrium ($\delta_i > 0$), benefiting buyers (sellers) when there is a downward (upward) shift. Alternatively, following a supply and demand shift, prices might undershoot the new equilibrium ($\delta_i < 0$). If successive shifts in supply and demand have a diminished disequilibrating effect, then we would expect $|\delta_2| > |\delta_3|$.

II. Experimental Results

Table 3 lists the mean deviation of contract prices from the *CE* price, and the ef-

TABLE 3—MEAN DEVIATION OF CONTRACT PRICES FROM *CE* (AND EFFICIENCY) BY WEEKS

Experiment Number	Price Controls	D and S Shift	Week 1	Week 2	Week 3
2:18	Ceiling, Week 2	Up, Week 2	.058	.024	.066
	Floor, Week 3	Up, Week 3	(99.63)	(100.)	(99.51)
2:26	Ceiling, Week 2	Up, Week 2	−.036	−.056	.029
	Floor, Week 3	Up, Week 3	(99.39)	(99.51)	(99.88)
2:27	Ceiling, Week 2	Down, Week 2	−.095	−.113	−.010
	Floor, Week 3	Up, Week 3	(98.90)	(99.26)	(99.02)
2:30	Ceiling, Week 2	Down, Week 2	−.041	−.043	.061
	Floor, Week 3	Up, Week 3	(95.46)	(98.53)	(97.67)
2:35	Ceiling, Week 2	Down, Week 2	−.034	−.112	.020
	Floor, Week 3	Down, Week 3	(99.51)	(99.39)	(99.39)
2:36	Ceiling, Week 2	Up, Week 2	−.021	−.010	.030
	Floor, Week 3	Down, Week 3	(99.75)	(100)	(100)
2:40	Ceiling, Week 2	Up, Week 2	.017	−.003	.069
	Floor, Week 3	Down, Week 3	(99.26)	(99.26)	(99.63)
2:41	Ceiling, Week 2	Down, Week 2	−.031	−.026	.005
	Floor, Week 3	Down, Week 3	(99.63)	(98.65)	(99.88)
2:49	None	Down, Week 2	−.030	−.036	.004
		Up, Week 3	(100)	(99.39)	(100)
2:54	None	Up, Week 2	.042	.040	−.004
		Down, Week 3	(99.14)	(99.39)	(99.51)
2:56	None	Up, Week 2	.113	−.005	−.023
		Up, Week 3	(97.67)	(99.63)	(100)
2:57	None	Down, Week 2	.046	−.008	−.023
		Down, Week 3	(98.16)	(99.51)	(99.51)
3:8	Floor, Week 2	Up, Week 2	−.063	.063	−.069
	Ceiling, Week 3	Up, Week 3	(99.14)	(99.39)	(98.53)
3:10	Floor, Week 2	Down, Week 2	.032	.030	−.093
	Ceiling, Week 3	Up, Week 3	(99.75)	(99.88)	(99.02)
3:12	Floor, Week 2	Down, Week 2	−.142	−.001	−.093
	Ceiling, Week 3	Down, Week 3	(97.67)	(96.32)	(99.35)
3:21	Floor, Week 2	Up, Week 2	−.227	.039	−.134
	Ceiling, Week 3	Down, Week 3	(93.75)	(99.88)	(97.67)

ficiency by weeks for all sixteen experiments. These experiments, which are listed in chronological order, were conducted over a period of nearly two years and were interspersed with a large number of other double auction experiments with quite different research objectives. From the mean price deviations in Table 3 for the sixteen price control experiments, one can discern a strong tendency for prices to be lower (higher) in Week 2 when the nonbinding ceiling (floor) is in effect relative to the baseline Week 1, and higher (lower) in Week 3 when the nonbinding floor (ceiling) is in effect relative to Week 1. Mean price deviations in Week 2 are consistent with this observation for every price control experiment except 2:36, 2:41, and 3:10, while in Week 3 mean price deviations violate this observation only in experiments 3:12 and 3:21.

The effect of the uniform shift in supply and demand on price deviations relative to the baseline week is not obvious by inspection, although there appears to be a tendency for prices to overshoot the new equilibrium. Efficiency, measured by realized buyers' plus sellers' surplus as a percentage of theoretical total surplus, is close to 100 percent under all treatments, which is highly characteristic of PLATO double auction experiments using experienced subjects (see Williams; Smith and Williams). Table 3 shows some tendency for efficiency to improve across the three weeks of trading, regardless of whether there is or is not a price control, and independently of the shift condition. This suggests that week-to-week learning dominates price controls, as well as supply and demand shifts, in affecting market efficiency. A Wilcoxon test of the hypothesis that price controls lead

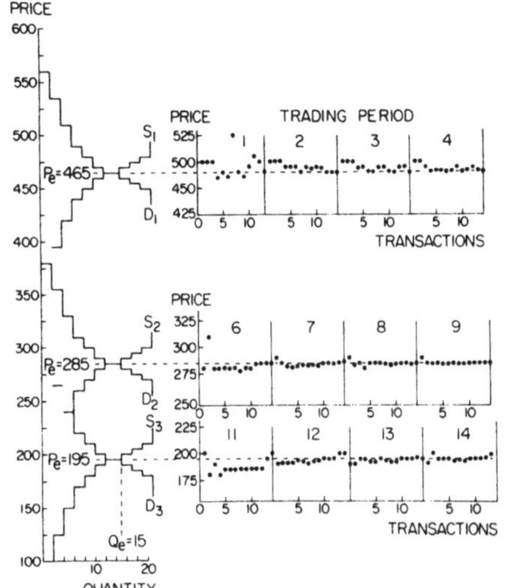

FIGURE 2. EXPERIMENT 2:57

to a relative decrease in efficiency is easily rejected.

Figures 1 and 2 display the contract price sequences by trading period for experiments 2:26 (with price controls), and 2:57 (without price controls).[1] These two experiments illustrate the tendency (measured in the regression estimates reported below) for 1) the price ceiling (floor) to cause contract prices to occur below (above) the *CE* relative to the baseline week; and 2) the shift in supply and demand to cause contract prices to overshoot the new equilibrium relative to baseline. The charts also illustrate the pronounced tendencies to converge to the *CE* under *all treatment conditions*. The effect of price controls is merely to retard this convergence, and to cause convergence to be from below (above) when there is a price ceiling (floor). Nonbinding price controls affect market dynamics, but not static equilibria.

[1]Most of the experiments consisted of five periods of trading in any given week. Figures 1 and 2 display only the contract prices for the first four trading periods of each week. The fifth period results in most all of the experiments produced trades very near the *CE*.

The results of estimating the coefficients in the regression model (1) yield,

$$(2)\quad D(t)= \begin{cases} \underset{(3.41)}{0.236}\, D(t-5) + \underset{(2.08)}{0.464}\, X_2^c - \underset{(-6.03)}{2.02}\, X_2^f \\ \quad + \underset{(4.81)}{1.089}\, Y_2,\ R^2=.55,\ N=70 \\ \underset{(1.94)}{0.111}\, D(t-10) + \underset{(8.47)}{2.315}\, X_3^c - \underset{(-6.54)}{1.190}\, X_3^f \\ \quad + \underset{(1.38)}{.260}\, Y_3,\ R^2=.74,\ N=67 \end{cases}$$

which supports the following conclusions:

1) The price ceiling transfers an average of about 46 cents per period in surplus from sellers to buyers during Week 2 and \$2.32 during Week 3. The floor transfers \$2.02 per period from buyers to sellers during Week 2 and \$1.19 during Week 3. The *t*-values shown in parenthesis indicate that the ceiling and floor regression coefficients are highly significant ($P<.025$, one-tailed test). We reject the hypothesis that nonbinding price controls near the *CE* have no effect on the dynamics of the equilibrating process in favor of the hypothesis that they are effective in the a priori predicted direction.

2) Differential bargaining strength by either buyers or sellers, in particular double auction markets, tends to persist in successive trading periods, and weeks, but with decreasing effect. The differential buyer-seller surplus in Week 2 averages 24 percent of its Week 1 level, and by Week 3 it is only 11 percent of its Week 1 level.

3) A uniform shift, up or down, in demand and supply, and a rerandomization of the assignments of individual supply and demand, causes some overshooting of the new equilibrium. A downshift in Week 2 redistributed \$1.09 of surplus from sellers to buyers relative to an upshift. In Week 3, this redistribution is reduced to about twenty-six cents. This implies that double auction markets show an improved ability to track changes in *CE* with successive changes in supply and demand. Experienced market

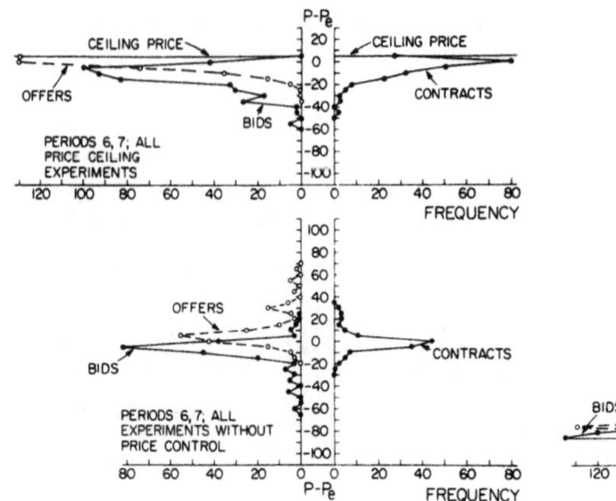

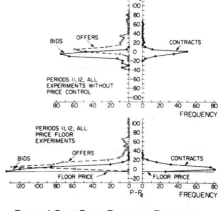

FIGURE 3. PRICE CEILING FREQUENCY DISTRIBUTIONS

FIGURE 4. PRICE FLOOR FREQUENCY DISTRIBUTIONS

participants learn to adapt more quickly, in terms of convergence speed, to shifts in supply and demand so that this further "experience" has an identifiable treatment effect.

III. How Nonbinding Price Controls Interfere with the Double Auction Bargaining Process

Issac and Plott speculate that their conjectured effect of nonbinding price controls in biasing prices away from the equilibrium "may have something to do with information and 'search'." Our PLATO computerization of the double auction institution makes it feasible to examine the effect of price controls on the distributions of bids and offers.

The upper half of Figure 3 plots the distributions of bids and offers on the left, and the distribution of contracts on the right, pooled across all Week 2 price ceiling experiments for trading periods 6 and 7. The lower half of Figure 3 plots the corresponding distributions for periods 6 and 7 across all experiments in which no price control is in effect during Week 2. The most obvious effect of the price ceiling is to truncate the bid and offer distributions above the ceiling. But this truncation is most pronounced with the offer distribution as sellers are required to begin their bargaining with offers at or below the ceiling. One would expect experienced buyers rarely to enter bids as high as the ceiling, even in the absence of the ceiling.

Similarly, a price floor five cents below the *CE* price truncates the bid and offer distributions from below, but it is the bid distribution that is most strongly affected. This is seen in Figure 4 comparing the bid, offer and contract distributions without a floor with the corresponding distributions when a floor is in effect.

Table 4A displays a comparison of the mean price quotations generated under the ceiling (Week 2)–floor (Week 3) treatment sequence with those generated in the experiments with no price controls. The mean bid and the mean offer are lowered by a price ceiling, but the decrease in the mean offer is much larger than for the decrease in mean bid. A price floor reverses this effect, with the mean bid increasing more than the mean offer increases. The Mann-Whitney unit normal deviate (Z_u) indicates rejection of the hypothesis that the period 6–7 offer distributions are identical with and without a price ceiling. This hypothesis is also rejected for the period 6–7 bids, but at a lower significance level. The same qualitative conclusions hold when comparing period 11–12 bids (offers) with and without a price floor.

Table 4B compares mean price quotations generated under the floor (Week 2)–ceiling (Week 3) treatment sequence with those gen-

TABLE 4A—MEAN DEVIATIONS OF QUOTATIONS FROM *CE* AND MANN-WHITNEY TESTS OF SIGNIFICANCE

Price Control Condition	Quotation	
	Bids	Offers
Trading Periods 6–7		
Price Ceiling Experiments	−0.170	−0.015
No Price Control Experiments	−0.110	0.176
Mann-Whitney, Z_u	6.63	11.0
Trading Periods 11–12		
No Price Control Experiments	−0.099	0.113
Price Floor Experiments	0.003	0.137
Mann-Whitney, Z_u	12.2	4.25

TABLE 4B—MEAN DEVIATIONS OF QUOTATIONS FROM *CE* AND MANN-WHITNEY TESTS OF SIGNIFICANCE

Price Control Condition	Quotations	
	Bids	Offers
Trading Periods 6–7		
Price Floor Experiments	.001	.238
No Price Control Experiments	−.110	.176
Mann-Whitney, Z_u	10.43	5.80
Trading Periods 11–12		
No Price Control Experiments	−.099	.113
Price Ceiling Experiments	−.464	−.059
Mann-Whitney, Z_u	13.99	12.22

erated without price controls. As in Table 4A, the values of Z_u indicate rejection of the hypothesis of identical distributions in all cases. However, the Week 3 price ceiling has a much stronger effect on the bid distribution than was the case with the Week 2 ceiling (Table 4A). This can be explained, at least partially, by noting that three of the four experiments run under the floor-ceiling sequence were characterized during Week 1 trading as having relatively "strong" buyers (as indicated by the negative mean price deviations from *CE* given in Table 3). In contrast, three of the four experiments run without price controls display positive mean price deviations during Week 1, indicating that sellers were somewhat stronger than buyers. The comparisons of price quote distributions across only the price control treatment conditions do not control for the relative bargaining strengths displayed by each subject group.

These data show that price ceilings or floors tend to interfere asymmetrically with the double auction bargaining process. Price ceilings limit the bargaining strategies of sellers. With a ceiling price, sellers must learn to refrain from making competitive offer concessions much below the ceiling, or avoid accepting bids until buyers are bidding near the ceiling. But a price ceiling also lowers the bids of buyers, partly because the relatively rare high bids are truncated by the price ceiling, and partly perhaps because the buyers learn that, with the ceiling, they can induce the sellers to accept somewhat lower bids. These considerations also apply when there is a price floor, except that the position of buyers and sellers, and the directional effects are reversed.

REFERENCES

R. M. Issac and C. R. Plott, "Price Controls and the Behavior of Auction Markets: An Experimental Examination," *Amer. Econ. Rev.*, June 1981, *71*, 448–59.

W. C. Labys, "Bidding and Auctioning on International Commodity Markets." in *Bidding and Auctioning for Procurement and Allocation*, New York 1976.

George L. Leffler and Loring C. Farwell, *The Stock Market*, New York 1963.

V. L. Smith, "Experimental Economics: Induced Value Theory," *Amer. Econ. Rev. Proc.*, May 1976, *66*, 274–79.

______ **and Arlington W. Williams,** "An Experimental Comparison of Alternative Rules for Competitive Market Exchange," Yale Univ. Conference on Auctions and Bidding (Dec. 1979), rev. Mar. 1980.

______ **et al.,** "Computerized Competitive Market Institutions: Double Auctions versus Sealed-Bid Auctions," Univ. Arizona, rev. Apr. 1981.

A. W. Williams, "Computerized Double Auction Markets: Some Initial Experimental Results," *J. Bus. Univ. Chicago*, July 1980, *53*, 235–58.

AN EXPERIMENTAL COMPARISON OF ALTERNATIVE RULES FOR COMPETITIVE MARKET EXCHANGE

Vernon L. Smith

Arlington W. Williams

> In short, the argument that we cannot experiment in the behavioral sciences because the problems are too complex is no more than a blanket rationalization of our ignorance as to what experiments to perform, and how to go about performing them (Abraham Kaplan, 1964).

1. INTRODUCTION

Double oral auction trading on the New York Stock Exchange, and on most organized stock and commodity exchanges throughout the world, has evolved over more than two centuries.[1] This evolution has consisted, in part, of a gradual formulation of rules governing the mechanics of "floor" trading. Our scientific curiosity as to why these institutional rules exist has motivated an interest in studying the effect of contracting rules on the convergence and efficiency properties of competitive markets. Does the "specialist book," and the New York Stock Exchange trading post rule requiring admissible bids and offers to narrow the bid-ask range, have identifiable affects on market performance? Our working hypothesis is that the survival value of a rule is manifest in measures of improved market performance.

The 21 experiments reported in this chapter use computerized transformations of the oral double auction that have been programmed by Williams using the PLATO computer system's TUTOR language. Our interest in real-time electronic trading institutions is motivated in part by the gradual evolution of both private and government securities markets into systems based on electronic quotations[2] and in part by the scientific value of the computer in providing closer control over the procedures, and recording of data, in group exchange experiments. Computerized

---

[1] Smith (1976, 1962).

[2] Garbade (1978).

variations on the double-auction are particularly relevant to the continuing debate within the securities industry concerning the design and technological feasibility of implementing an integrated national stock-trading system. (The Cincinnati/NMS pilot project actually tested a fully automated trading system based on the double auction.[3])

Although our primary purpose is to examine questions of institutional design by dissecting certain features of New York Stock Exchange trading, we also examine the effect of subject trading experience on market outcomes. This is important since we want to measure something more than transitory behavior. The first series of PLATO double-auction experiments[4] suggested that alternative bidding rules and subjects' trading experience could significantly affect market behavior. Using inexperienced subjects, PLATO double auctions were much slower to converge toward the competitive equilibrium price than comparable _oral_ double-auctions run "by hand." The implementation of a rule requiring new bids and offers to provide better terms to the other side of the market seemed to improve the convergence properties of the

---

[3]Schorr and Rustin (1978); Crock (1979).

[4]Williams (1980).

computerized mechanism. However, the results appeared to be similar to the oral double auction when subjects had participated in a previous computerized double-auction experiment using different cost and valuation parameters.

2. THE MECHANISM

In the computerized trading procedure employed in the experiments reported below, buyers and sellers enter price quotes by typing in a number on their keysets and then touching a designated area on their display screen. Any buyer (seller) can accept a seller's offer (buyer's bid) by touching a box labelled "ACCEPT." The acceptor must then touch a box labelled "CONFIRM" at which time the contract is logged in both the "maker's" and "taker's" private record sheets. Bids, offers, and subsequent contracts are the only public information.[5]

Two distinct sets of bidding rules, each having an optional electronic queuing scheme, are used in the experiments which follow.

Bidding Rule 1. There is only one (the most recent) bid or offer displayed on the market at any instant. A bid or offer remains displayed until it is either

[5] Williams (1980) describes this mechanism in detail.

accepted or another bid or offer is made. Any price quote is rejected if it is entered before the previous quote has been "standing" open to acceptance in the market for a minimum of three seconds. There are no rules governing the bid-offer sequence.

This institution represents a thin relatively unorganized exchange, with features similar to an over-the-counter telephone market in which a potential buyer or seller has no assurance that successive quotations will provide better prices. Furthermore, a price quotation cannot be entered if the telephone is "busy." Hence, there is a relatively high waiting cost in gaining access to the market for purposes of entering a price quotation.

Bidding Rule 2. Price quotes must progress so as to reduce the bid-ask spread. An outstanding bid to buy and offer to sell are displayed to the entire market and are open to acceptance. Any price quote which does not provide "better" terms is rejected, and an appropriate explanatory message is sent to the individual attempting to make the quotation. When a contract is agreed to, a new auction for one unit of the commodity begins with no established bid-ask spread. This corresponds to rules 71 and 72 of the New York Stock Exchange.[6] Until such time

[6] Leffler and Loring (1963).

as a contract occurs a potential buyer or seller knows that the terms of trade cannot become less favorable. Under our rule 2 "waiting" incurs the risk that a competitor will make the contract. Under rule 1, to this risk is added the further risk that the subsequent quotation will provide less favorable terms.

Bidding Rule 1Q (Time Queue). Each price quote entered stands displayed to the market for a minimum of three seconds as in rule 1. However, if quotes come in more rapidly than this, they are not rejected but are placed in a queue according to the time of entry (that is, first in, first out). After three seconds the standing quote is automatically replaced by the entry at the front of the queue (no. 1) and the xth queued entry becomes the $(x-1)^{th}$. All participants are given continuously updated information on the current queue length and, if queued, their own position in the queue. As in rule 1, there is no restriction on the bid-ask sequence and only the most recent bid or offer is standing in the market open to acceptance.

This institution is entirely artificial in the sense that it provides a queue (type of "specialist's book") without the bid-ask reduction rule. In studying this procedure we attempt to dissect an observed composite institution.

Bidding Rule 2Q (Rank Queues). Price quotes must

progress so as to reduce the bid-ask spread in rule 2. However, if a bid (offer) is entered which is not higher (lower) than the currently standing "best" bid (offer) the entry is placed in a bid queue (offer queue) rather than being rejected. If queued, the maker is given the entry's position in a "rank queue" which continually arrays bids from highest to lowest (offers from lowest to highest). Subjects may have only one entry either queued or standing at any point in time. Queued entries may be withdrawn by pressing a key labelled "-EDIT-." Price quotes standing as the best in the market cannot be withdrawn. However, the maker may "bump" his own best bid (offer) with a still better one. Upon the initiation of a new auction, after a contract has been made, the lowest queued offer to sell and highest queued bid to buy are automatically entered as the new (post-contract) standing bid and offer. This procedure combines the "specialist's book" with the bid-ask spread reduction rule which are features of trading on the New York Stock Exchange. This is the observed institution that is our primary interest to study and which is hypothesized to be superior to the test alternatives mentioned above.

3. EXPERIMENTAL DESIGN

The experiments reported in this study use the structural parameters given in Table 1 which result

TABLE 1

Buyers' Resale Values and Sellers' Costs as Deviation from P^0

	Unit 1	Unit 2	Unit 3
Buyer 1	+.95	-.10	-.25
Buyer 2	+.70	0	-.05
Buyer 3	+.45	0	-.15
Buyer 4	+.25	+.05	-.20
Seller 1	-.95	+.10	+.25
Seller 2	-.70	0	+.05
Seller 3	-.45	0	+.15
Seller 4	-.25	-.05	+.20

in the market supply and demand arrays shown on the left of Figure 1. Trading takes place over a sequence of at least eight 300 second market periods. The competitive equilibrium quantity (Q^0) is seven units per period if both marginal units are traded. The competitive equilibrium price (P^0) is varied by an arbitrary constant across market replications. Participants are paid a 10 cent commission per contract to compensate for subjective transaction costs in addition to the difference between the selling price

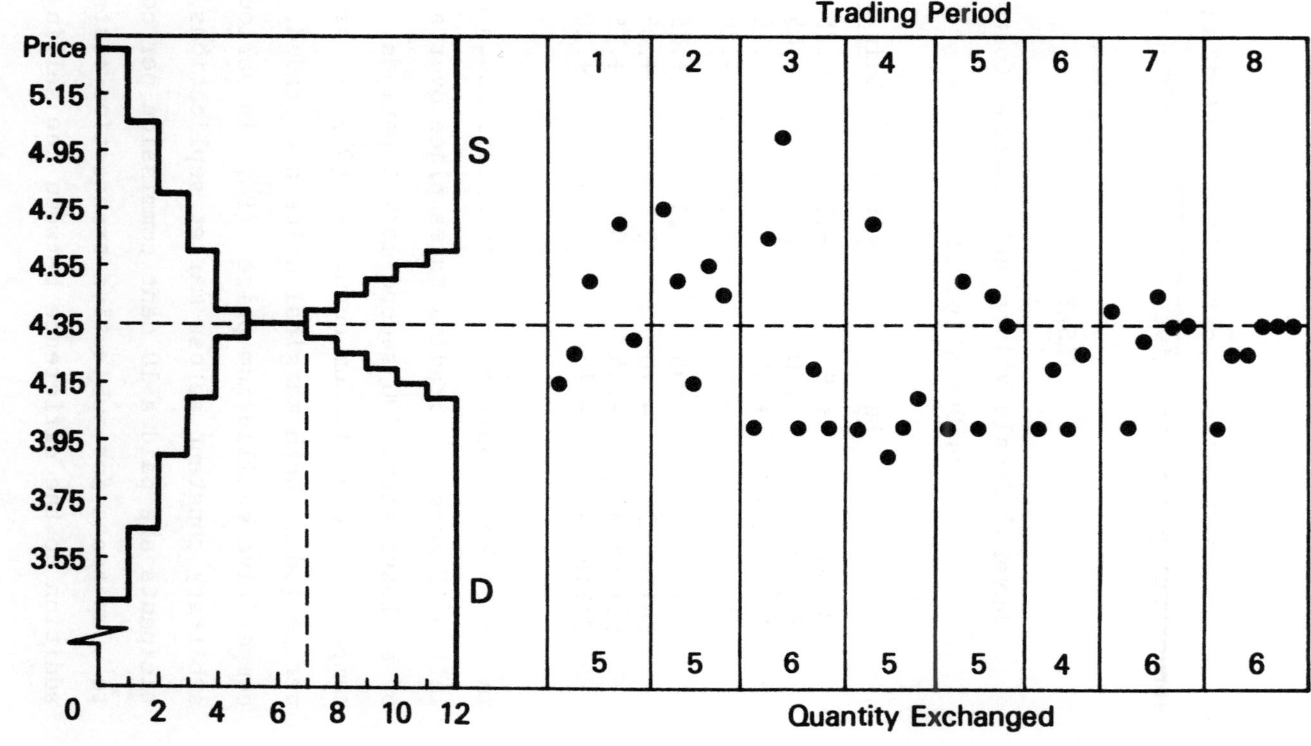

FIGURE 1. Time-queue, Inexperienced Subjects

and the cost (or buyer resale value and purchase price). In equilibrium, the subjects would earn a total of $6.20 per trading period. Note that the supply and demand arrais are constructed so that the monetary rewards from exchange are split equally between the buyers and sellers at P^0 .

Subjects were initially recruited from undergraduate and graduate classes at the University of Arizona. After having participated in any double-auction experiment a subject was considered "experienced." Groups of experienced subjects were generally recruited by phone after they had indicated their willingness to participate in another experiment by leaving their telephone number. (It may be interesting to note that the volunteer rate for experienced subjects was very nearly 100 percent.)

Upon arriving at the PLATO lab each participant was paid $2 for keeping the appointment and randomly assigned to a computer terminal. PLATO then was used to randomize the subjects into individual cost or valuation conditions, present the instructions at an individually controlled speed, and then execute the experiment, strictly enforcing all the institutional rules of the game. At the end of the experiment subjects were paid in cash the amount of their individual earnings over the entire experiment. Using the bid-ask spread reduction rule, electronic queuing, and subjects' trading experience as treatment conditions, the (2×2×2) eight-celled experimental design, shown in Table 2, was employed. A total of 21 experiments were conducted

TABLE 2

Number of Experiments
(and Total Number of Periods of Trading)
Classified by Trading Rule Institution
and Subject Experience

	Institution			
Subjects	Rule 1	Rule 1Q	Rule 2	Rule 2Q
Inexperienced	3 (30)	3 (31)	3 (29)	3 (28)
Experienced	2 (19)	2 (19)	2 (20)	3 (25)

with either two or three experiments under each treatment condition (see Table 2).

4. EXPERIMENTAL RESULTS

The behavior of contract prices over time is illustrated for four experiments in Figures 1 through 4 in which contract prices are plotted in sequence for eight trading periods. In the experiment in Figure 1, inexperienced subjects traded under rule 1Q (time queue) while in Figure 2 inexperienced subjects traded

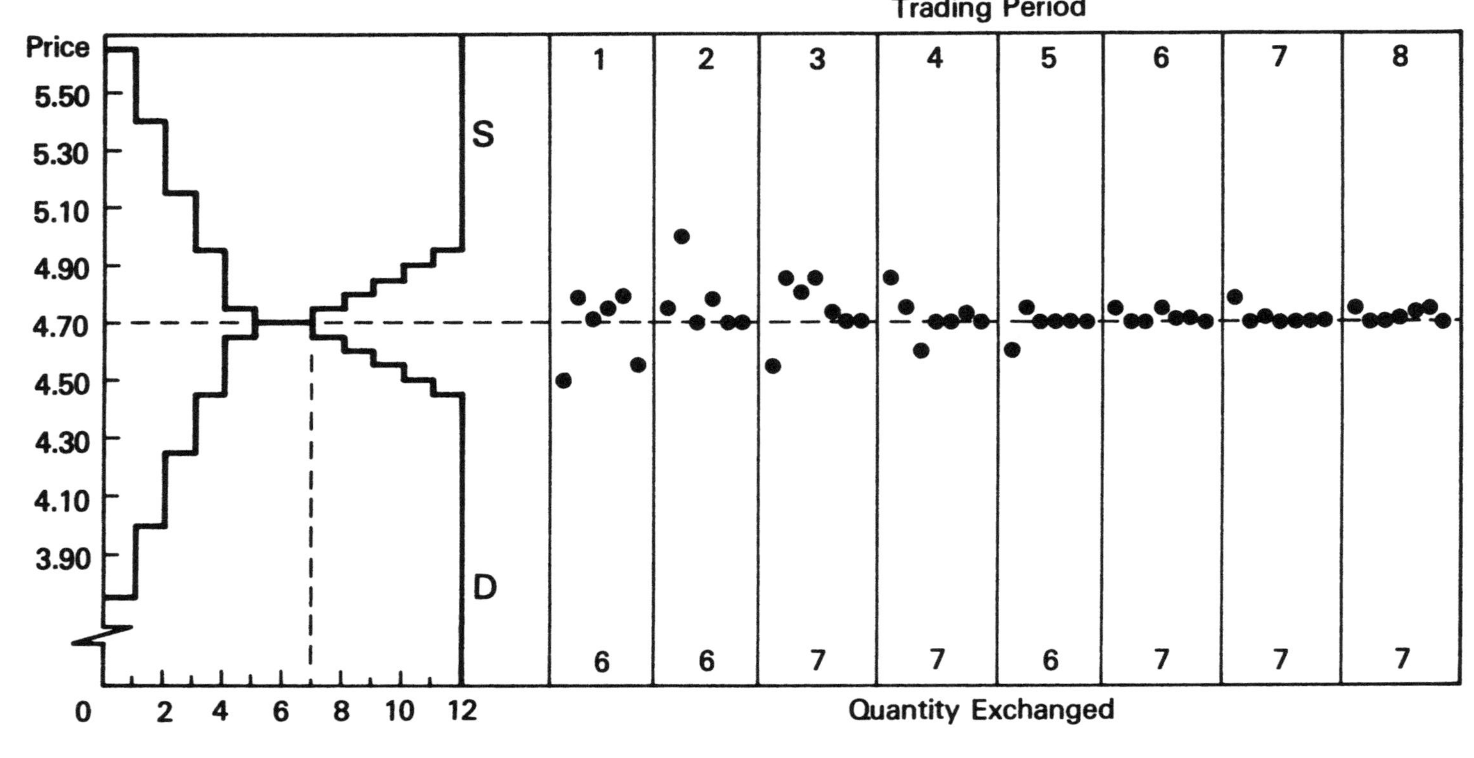

FIGURE 2. Rank-queue, Inexperienced Subjects

under rule 2Q (rank queues). In Figures 3 and 4 exchange occurred between experienced subjects under rules 1Q and 2Q. These four experiments illustrate the range of convergence behavior in the 21 experiments in which experienced subjects using rule 2Q showed the most rapid convergence to the competitive equilibrium and inexperienced subjects using rule 1Q showed the least.

Convergence behavior under each set of trading rules using inexperienced and experienced subjects will be summarized for all the experiments in regression form. Letting $t = 1, 2, \ldots$ be the trading period, we define

$$\alpha^2(t) = \sum_{k=1}^{Q(t)} (P_k - P^o)^2 / Q(t)$$

which equals the variance in the contract price deviations from the theoretical competitive equilibrium price in trading period t, where $P_k = P_k(t)$ is the kth contract price, and $Q(t)$ is the total number of contracts, in period t. The dependent variable $\alpha(t)$ provides a measure of price "distance from the competitive equilibrium which reflects both the variance of prices, and the mean deviation of price from the competitive equilibrium; that is, $\alpha^2(t) = V(t) + (\overline{P}(t) - P^o)^2$. A market is "close" to

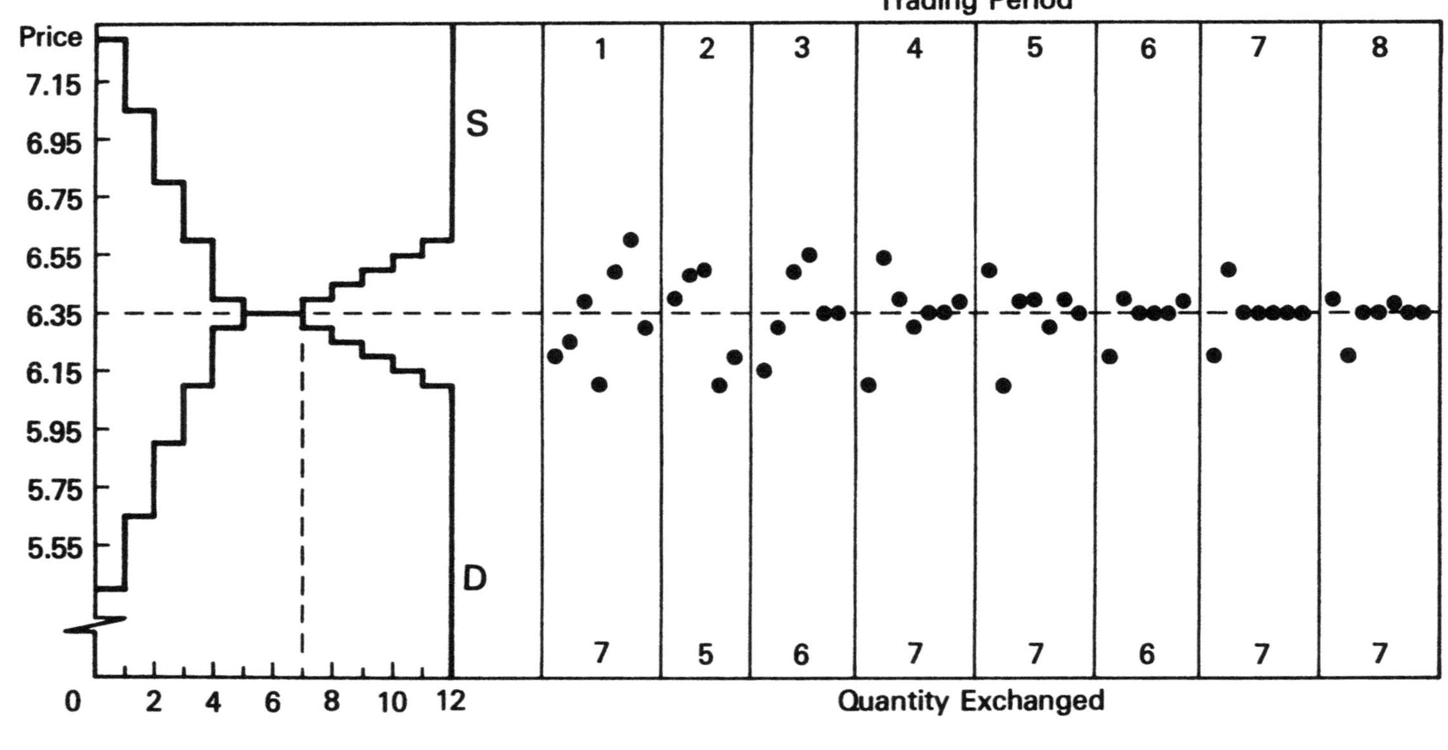

FIGURE 3. Time-queue, Experienced Subjects

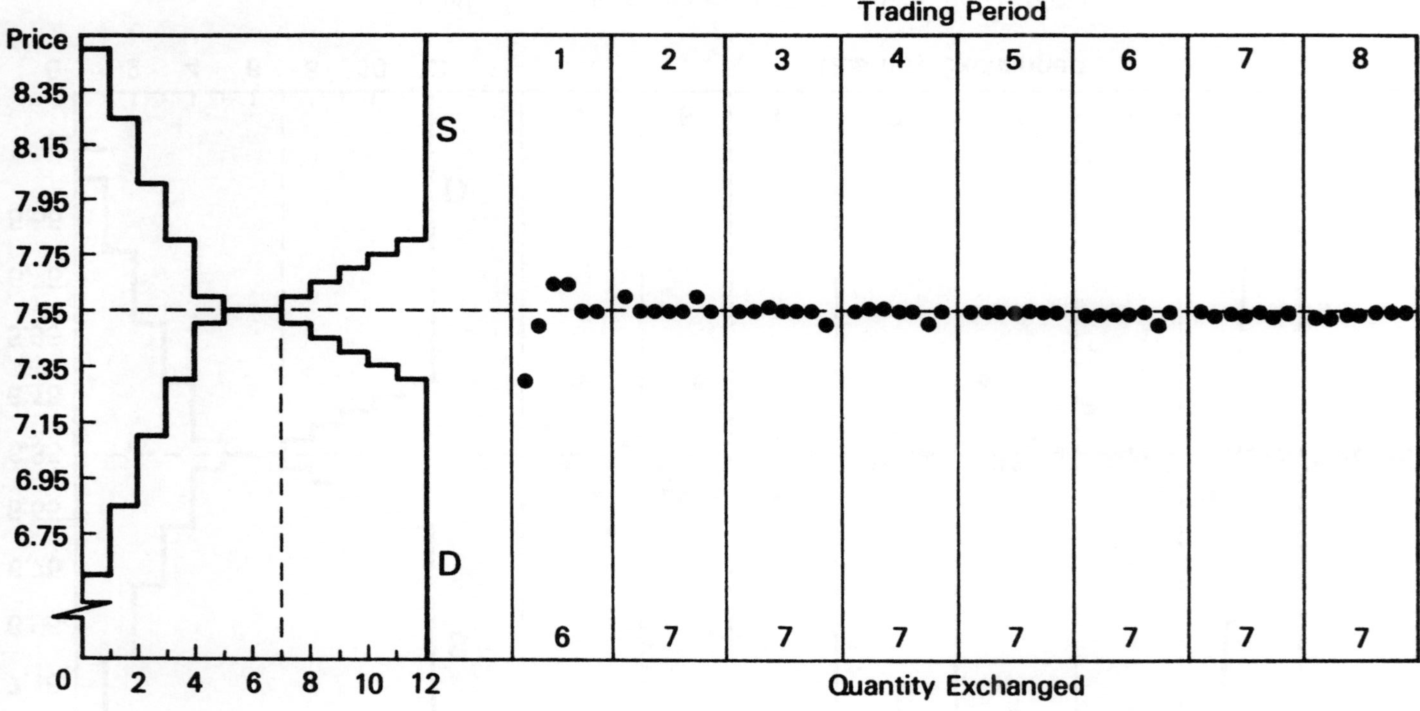

FIGURE 4. Rank-queue, Experienced Subjects

the competitive equilibrium only if the mean price is near the competitive equilibrium and price variability is low.

Table 3 reports the results, for each trading institution, of the least squares regression

$$\ell n\ \alpha(t) = a + bt + cX_s$$

where

$$X_s = \begin{cases} 1, & \text{if experienced subjects} \\ 0, & \text{if inexperienced subjects} \end{cases}$$

All four regressions in Table 3 show a significant exponential convergence rate, with $\alpha(t)$ declining at a rate varying from 8.7 percent per trading period under rule 1Q to 20.5 percent per trading period under rule 2Q. In each institution subject experience has a large and significant effect on convergence.

The exponential decay functions in Table 3 are shown in Figures 5a and 5b. In Figure 5a rule 2 prices are closer to the competitive equilibrium than the rule 1 prices (for $t < 10$), when subjects are inexperienced. With experienced subjects the price convergence behavior of the two institutions is practically indistinguishable. It appears that under rule 1 experienced subjects learn to ignore, that

TABLE 3

Regression Results for Each Trading Institution

Regression Parameter / Institution	a (Constant)	b (Trading Period)	c (Subject Experience)	Adjusted R^2	F for the Regression	Number of Observations
Rule 1	-.817 (-3.42)	-.186 (-5.12)	-1.098 (-5.22)	.51	25.7	49
Rule 2	-1.149 (-7.40)	-.166 (-6.93)	-.875 (-6.35)	.65	45.4	49
Rule 1Q	-1.095 (-8.37)	-.087 (-4.49)	-.736 (-6.35)	.53	28.4	50
Rule 2Q	-1.609 (-7.68)	-.205 (-6.14)	-.872 (-5.01)	.52	28.9	53

All the t-values (shown in parentheses) are significant at $P < .001$.

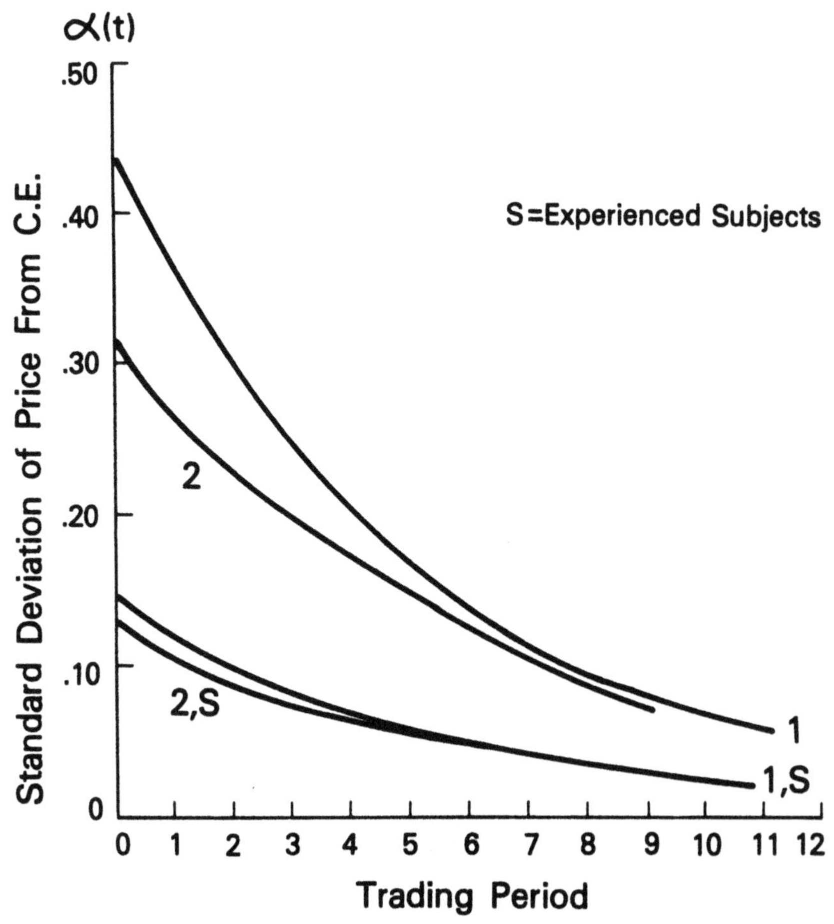

FIGURE 5a. Price Convergence, Rules 1 and 2

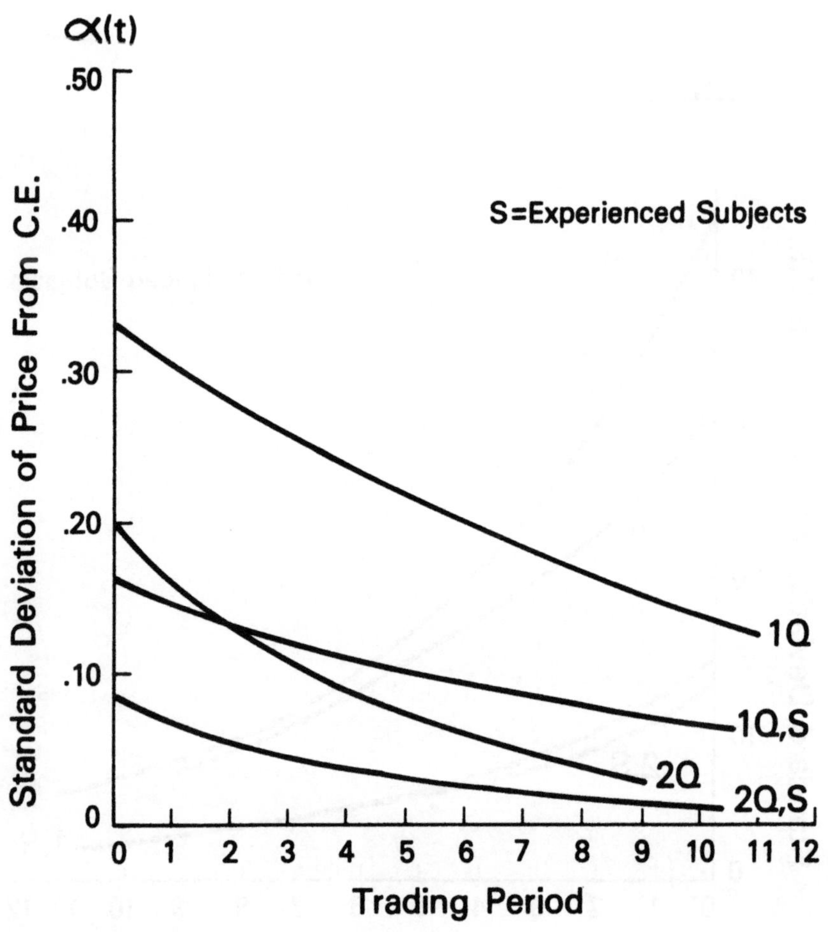

FIGURE 5b. Price Convergence, Rules 1Q and 2Q

is, they do not accept, bids and offers that fail to provide better terms. In effect, subjects impose their own bid-ask reduction rule on their acceptance behavior. However, the higher R^2 and F values for the rule 2 regressions (Table 3) suggest that rule 2 is a more reliable producer of competitive equilibrium prices than rule 1.

From Figure 5b it is seen that the convergence behavior of rules 1Q and 2Q are quite distinct even for experienced subjects. Comparing Figures 5a and 5b rule 1Q provides the least, and rule 2Q the greatest, price convergence behavior. With experienced subjects trading under rule 2Q conditions prices are never very far from the competitive equilibrium.

The comparative effect of adding the queuing condition, or the bid-ask reduction rule, on convergence, while simultaneously correcting for the effect of subject experience is summarized in the following regressions:

$$1.\quad \ell n\ \alpha(t) = \underset{(-7.67)}{-1.16} - \underset{(-6.46)}{0.135t} + \underset{(3.35)}{0.400X_{1Q}} - \underset{(-7.47)}{0.920X_2}$$

$$N = 99\ ,\quad R^2 = 0.51\ ,\quad F = 34.4$$

where

$$X_{1Q} = \begin{cases} 1, & \text{if rule 1Q} \\ 0, & \text{if rule 1} \end{cases}$$

2. $$\ell n\ \alpha(t) = \underset{(-5.99)}{-0.918} - \underset{(-8.11)}{0.175t} - \underset{(-1.13)}{0.138X_2} - \underset{(-7.88)}{0.984X_s}$$

$$N = 98\ ,\quad R^2 = 0.56\ ,\quad F = 42.9$$

where

$$X_2 = \begin{cases} 1, & \text{if rule 2} \\ 0, & \text{if rule 1} \end{cases}$$

3. $$\ell n\ \alpha(t) = \underset{(-7.30)}{-1.05} - \underset{(-9.07)}{0.184t} - \underset{(-5.93)}{0.658X_{2Q}} - \underset{(-7.78)}{0.867X_s}$$

$$N = 102\ ,\quad R^2 = 0.63\ ,\quad F = 57.1$$

where

$$X_{2Q} = \begin{cases} 1, & \text{if rule 2Q} \\ 0, & \text{if rule 2} \end{cases}$$

From regression 1, adding the time queue to the unstructured (rule 1) market causes a significant increase in $\alpha(t)$. The time queue was introduced into the mechanism without the bid-ask reduction rule in an effort to reduce the task requirements involved in entering a price quotation into the market. Without this time queue, bids and offers are rejected if they are entered prior to the expiration of the standing time for the current price quotation. The maker must wait until the outstanding quotation "dies" or is accepted before he can enter a quotation. This procedure proved to be very effort costly for the subjects as each attempted to enter a new quotation, but only one could be first. Consequently, the subjects had an incentive to enter more concessionary quotations under rule 1 than rule 1Q. With the time queue one is assured that any quotation will work down the queue and enter the market. This lowers the opportunity cost of entering less concessionary quotations. These considerations seem to show up very strongly in the positive coefficient of the dummy variable, X_{1Q} , in regression 1. Further support is provided by direct examination of the bid and offer distributions generated by experienced subjects under the two bidding rules. Table 4 displays central tendency measures and a distribution-free test of the research hypothesis that price quotations generated under rule 1Q will tend to be farther from P^o than those generated under rule 1. The Mann-Whitney unit normal deviate, Z_u , indicates that time-queue bids (offers) tend to be lower (higher) than they would be if there was a queue.

From regression 2, the effect of the bid-ask reduction rule is to improve convergence, but it is not statistically significant. (The result is somewhat surprising, given the results of Williams, but consistent with the small sample of evidence presented by Smith using oral double auctions. We suspect that

TABLE 4

Comparisons of Rule 1 and Rule 1Q
Quotations as Deviations from P^o

			Bids	Offers
Periods 1 and 2	Rule 1	mean median	-.3765 (-.15)	.2134 (.09)
	Rule 1Q	mean median	-.8606 (-.30)	.3344 (.25)
	Mann-Whitney	Z_u	5.313[a]	4.752[a]
	Sample Size	Rule 1 Rule 1Q	(121) (126)	(89) (156)
Periods 8 and 9	Rule 1	mean median	-.129 (-.10)	.1131 (.05)
	Rule 1Q	mean median	-.1484 (-.10)	.1448 (.10)
	Mann-Whitney	Z_u	1.324[b]	5.131[a]
	Sample Size	Rule 1 Rule 1Q	(144) (125)	(97) (170)
Periods 1 through 9	Rule 1	mean median	-.2215 (-.14)	.1941 (.05)
	Rule 1Q	mean median	-.3726 (-.15)	.2058 (.10)
	Mann-Whitney	Z_u	4.854[a]	8.877[a]
	Sample Size	Rule 1 Rule 1Q	(593) (575)	(422) (754)

[a]Reject H_0, $p = .01$.

[b]Reject H_0, $p = .1$ (direction predicted).

the 2:1 vs. 1:1 rent split may be the cause of the discrepancy.[7]) This is explained, as indicated above, by the apparent behavior of experienced subjects in imposing their own bid-ask reduction rule when this condition is not part of the formal trading rule mechanism. In regression 3, the effect of adding the electronic "specialist's book" or rank queues is to improve convergence significantly. We think this is due to a form of additional price competition "away from the market" as participants modify their queued bids or offers in an attempt to gain a more favorable position within their respective queues.

5. MARKET EFFICIENCY COMPARISONS

Table 5 displays the mean market efficiency per quartile, for each of the bidding rule treatments, using inexperienced and experienced subjects, and where our index of efficiency = 100 (actual earnings ÷ potential earnings), exclusive of commissions. In these calculations the first eight trading periods are divided into quartiles consisting of two pooled trading periods in each quartile. The figures indicate that all four of the bidding schemes studied

---

[7] Williams (1980); Smith (1976).

TABLE 5

Mean Market Efficiency
Experienced Subjects
(Inexperienced Subjects)

	Rule 1	Rule 2	Rule 1Q	Rule 2Q
Quartile 1	84.90 (86.11)	98.18 (83.33)	89.33 (93.40)	99.31 (86.46)
Quartile 2	98.70 (96.53)	99.74 (95.83)	98.96 (98.44)	99.48 (97.57)
Quartile 3	99.48 (92.71)	95.06 (97.22)	98.70 (98.79)	99.31 (99.65)
Quartile 4	99.22 (99.31)	99.22 (97.22)	94.54 (98.32)	99.58 (99.13)
Overall	97.57 (93.66)	98.05 (93.40)	95.38 (97.22)	99.41 (95.70)

result in highly efficient markets. See Smith, Williams, Bratton and Vannoni for a comparison of efficiency in the double auction with two versions of a uniform price sealed bid-offer auction.[8] Using experienced subjects, the rank queue (rule 2Q) is significantly more efficient than the time queue (rule 1Q) using the Mann-Whitney U-test ($\alpha = .05$). However, none of the other three bidding rule comparisons are significant. Using inexperienced subjects, none of the four bidding treatments are significant ($\alpha = .05$)

---

[8] Smith, Williams, Bratton and Vannoni (1982).

6. SUMMARY

In the context of the supply and demand configuration employed in this study (symmetric exchange surplus, four buyers, four sellers) changes in the double auction's bidding rules have a significant effect on the convergence of contract prices to the competitive equilibrium price. While no significant difference in convergence seems to exist between markets organized under rule 1 compared to rule 2, the introduction of the associated electronic queueing scheme does affect convergence.

The time queue (rule 1Q) acts to destabilize and the rank queue (rule 2Q) acts to stabilize contract prices. We conjecture that by lowering the cost of entering a price quote, the time queue encourages market participants to concede more erratically and slowly in the price bargaining. This increases the risk of waiting for a better quotation, and leads to more erratic contract prices. We further suggest that the rank queue acts to promote additional price competition "away from the market" as participants attempt to gain a favorable position within their respective queues.

The use of subjects with prior experience with the trading mechanism (but not the market parameters) is a powerful treatment variable. Experienced subjects result in a more stable market and appear to be less sensitive to changes in the bidding rules than markets in which inexperienced subjects participate. Market efficiency in the double auction is generally very high. The rank queue combined with experienced subjects yields almost perfectly efficient markets.

We conclude that the rank queue (or "specialist's book"), combined with the rule requiring the bid-ask spread to narrow, provides a trading institution that is superior, in terms of both price stability and market efficiency, to any of the alternative institutions we have studied. Whatever the historical origins of this institution, once established, it appears to have important economic benefits that may help to explain its longevity.

REFERENCES

Crock, S. and R. E. Rustin (1979). "Work on National Stock-Trading System Lags Badly; Some Blame Brokers and SEC," The Wall Street Journal, February 2, p. 32.

Garbade, K. D. (1978). "Electronic Quotation Systems and the Market for Government Securities," F.R.B. N.Y. Quarterly Review, Summer, pp. 13-20.

Kaplan, A. (1964). The Conduct of Inquiry: Methodology for the Behavioral Sciences. Scranton, Pa.: Chandler Publishing Co.

Leffler, G. L. and C. F. Loring (1963). The Stock Market, 3rd edition. New York: The Ronald Press Company.

Schorr, B. and R. E. Rustin (1978). "A Stock-Trading Test Could Presage Future of Securities Industry," The Wall Street Journal, October 3, p. 1.

Smith, V. L. (1962). "An Experimental Study of Competitive Market Behavior," Journal of Political Economy, 70, pp. 111-37.

Smith, V. L. (1976). "Bidding and Auctioning Institutions: Experimental Results," in Y. Amihud (ed.), Bidding and Auctioning for Procurement and Allocation. New York: New York University Press, pp. 43-64.

Smith, V. L. (1980). "Relevance of Laboratory Experiments to Testing Resource Allocation Theory," in Jan Kmenta and James Ramsey (eds.), Evaluation of Econometric Models. New York: Academic Press, pp. 345-377.

Smith, V. L., A. W. Williams, W. K. Bratton, and M. G. Vannoni (1982). "Competitive Market Institutions: Double Auctions versus Sealed Bid-Offer Auctions," American Economic Review, Vol. 72, pp. 58-77.

Williams, A. W. (1980). "Computerized Double Auction Markets: Some Initial Experimental Results," Journal of Business, Vol. 53, pp. 235-58.

Competitive Market Institutions: Double Auctions vs. Sealed Bid-Offer Auctions

By VERNON L. SMITH, ARLINGTON W. WILLIAMS, W. KENNETH BRATTON, AND MICHAEL G. VANNONI*

Consider a market with the following characteristics: 1) privacy, that is, each agent knows only his own valuation (or cost) conditions; 2) exchange follows the rules of the oral double auction, that is, buyers freely announce bids or accept offers and sellers freely announce offers or accept bids; 3) aggregate market supply and demand per trading period is stationary for at least two to three periods; and 4) there are at least four buyers, and as many sellers. The literature reporting the results of a large number of experimental markets with these characteristics documents what appears to be a remarkably rapid convergence to a competitive equilibrium (*CE*).[1] However, any claim of double auction (*DA*) "convergence" to the *CE* can only have meaning in one of three senses:

(i) The *CE* is attained immediately.

(ii) After *T* periods of trading, some measure of the market's state, such as mean price, is nearer, relative to experimental sampling variability, to a *CE* than to some distinct alternative equilibrium such as a monopoly or Nash equilibrium.

(iii) After *T* periods of trading, this measure is nearer to a *CE* in *DA* experimental markets than in markets organized under a different institution of contract, for example, a sealed-bid auction.

Since everything from electrons and the stars to rats and people yield state measures subject to "error" or random variation, the deterministic criterion (i) can have no serious scientific standing. By such criteria any hypothesis can be rejected and there could be no science of physics, biology, or economics.[2] With the exception of certain very simple markets such as single object auctions, or certain idealized markets such as the Cournot quantity adjuster model, economics has only two concepts of equilibrium—monopoly and competitive. The only formal model of *DA* trading that has been proposed (see David Easley and John Ledyard, p. 6) predicts stochastic convergence (in finite time, with probability one) to a *CE*. Hence, the only test alternative to the *CE* research hypothesis in *DA* markets is a monopoly (or monopsony) equilibrium. Experimentalists have not reported statistical tests of the *CE*

*Professor, department of economics, University of Arizona; assistant professor, department of economics, Indiana University; instructor, department of economics, University of Arizona; and Sandia National Laboratories, Albuquerque, NM, respectively. We are indebted to the National Science Foundation for research support, and to Art Denzau and Mort Kamien for helpful comments.

[1]There is an early and recently growing body of experimental evidence for convergence to a competitive equilibrium under double auction rules: the earliest evidence (contained in experiments initiated in January 1956) is reported in Smith (1962, 1964, 1965, 1976). However, these early experiments used between twenty and fifty or so participant buyers and sellers because, in keeping with prevailing professional beliefs, it was thought that a *CE* was unlikely to be approached unless numbers were quite large. Using large numbers was not unreasonable since it is a good beginning procedure to give a theory whatever is believed to be its "best shot." More recent evidence using six buyers, six sellers, and two traders in "speculative" *DA* markets with cyclical demand is reported by R. M. Miller, Charles Plott, and Smith, and Williams (1979). For evidence from a comparison of oral and computerized *DA* experiments with four buyers and four sellers, see Williams (1980). For further evidence in the context of the study of price controls, see M. Isaac and Plott (1981b) and Smith and Williams (1981b); in the context of a conspiracy study see Isaac and Plott (1981a); in the context of comparisons between *DA* and posted offer pricing, see Jon Ketcham, Smith, and Williams; in the context of a study of four variations on *DA* rules, see Smith and Williams (1980). All of these more recent papers report double auction experiments using no more than four buyers and four sellers.

[2]As Frederick Mosteller once noted, if you wanted to reject the inverse square law of attraction, try tossing a sheet of paper out the window.

research hypothesis as against the null monopoly hypothesis because it would be a useless exercise in arithmetic. Savage's informally well-known "interocular trauma test" (just look at the data) is sufficient. For an example look ahead to Figures 3 and 4, which plot *DA* contract prices, and see if you think the monopoly (or monopsony) price receives convincing empirical support as against the *CE* price, or examine any of the data in the references cited in footnote 1. There is even evidence of unexpectedly poor support for the monopoly price hypothesis when there is but *one* seller (Smith, 1981 and Smith and Williams, 1981a). Hence, the data support the static *CE* hypothesis as against the only proffered alternative hypotheses.

The objective of this paper is to explore criterion (iii). Experimentalists happen to have begun their studies of the laboratory behavior of markets with the *DA* institution. They have found this institution to be unexpectedly robust with respect to numbers of agents, design parameters, shifts in parameters and certain variations on the trading rules, in yielding convergence to *CE* outcomes. *Are these properties common to all institutions of contract or are they unique to the DA institution?* This paper reports the results of forty-eight experiments (using 408 subjects) that were designed to provide an answer to this question.[3] The pricing mechanisms used in this paper for comparison with *DA* have been selected either because they have features that are or have been of importance in economic thought or theory, and/or that have been characteristic of some particular ongoing market in the field.

In the next section we discuss briefly the experimental designs and procedures that are common to all the experimental price mechanisms studied. Section II defines each of these price mechanisms in terms of the bid-offer-contract procedures used, summarizes any formal or informal theory that applies, and relates the mechanism, where appropriate, to examples of similar markets in the field.

I. Experimental Design

Most of the experimental results reported in Section IV use the supply and demand design shown in Figure 1(a). Each of the four buyers (sellers) is assigned (privately) the two marginal valuations (costs) indicated by the B1,...,B4 (S1,...,S4) labels in Figure 1(a). The aggregate of these individual demand and supply schedules generates the theoretical (or hypothesized) market demand, *D*, and market supply, *S*, resulting in the *CE* illustrated in Figure 1 (a): $(P^0, Q^0) = (4.90, 6)$. Since these assigned valuations (costs) are repeated in each of a sequence of trading periods, the resulting demand and supply represent flows per trading period. As a means of maintaining a state of incomplete information across different experimental subject groups, the equilibrium price was varied in successive experiments by adding an arbitrary positive or negative constant to each of the individual marginal valuations and costs that pertained to the previous experiment. Note in this design that, at the *CE*, 2/3 of the exchange surplus is captured by the buyers with 1/3 going to sellers. In a few of the experiments to be reported below this property is reversed, that is, the sellers receive 2/3 and the buyers receive 1/3 of the total surplus. We also report the results of some experiments with larger groups using the higher volume supply and demand designs shown on the left in Figures 4 and 6. These latter experiments allow us to determine whether any observed differences among the trading institutions studied are affected by larger markets.

All the experiments reported below use the PLATO computer to display the experimental instructions to each subject trader, administer the rules of the particular pricing institution, compute and display the appropriate private and public information generated by the market, and compute individual subject payoffs. In these experiments we use subject processing procedures which have become standard in all of our PLATO experiments: volunteers are recruited, usu-

[3] Our research builds on six pilot experiments conducted by Bratton (reported in Smith et al., appendix, pp. 35–39), which provided preliminary experience enabling us to develop the PLATO computer programs discussed in Section I.

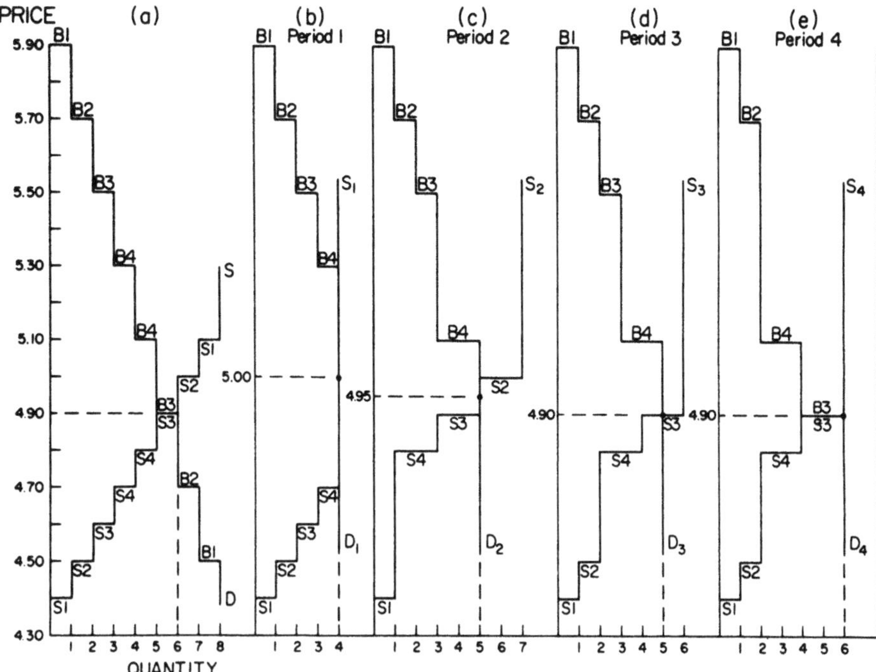

FIGURE 1

ally from business and economics classes, who wish to "earn some money in a decision making experiment." When they arrive at the PLATO room, they are given a number in sequence. When all have arrived, each is paid $3.00 in cash, and randomly assigned to a private computer terminal (or to the nonparticipation condition, since we have to "overbook" volunteers to cover the occasional subject who does not show). PLATO then randomizes each terminal to a buyer or seller experimental condition. When the experiment is completed, each subject is paid (privately) his/her earned consumer's (or producer's) surplus, that is, assigned value minus purchase price for each unit traded by a buyer (purchase price minus assigned cost for each unit traded by a seller), plus a commission (in this case $0.05) for each unit traded. The commission provides a minimal inducement to trade a unit at its assigned value (cost) to compensate for transaction cost and provide incentive for the marginal *CE* units to be exchanged.

II. The Exchange Mechanisms and Hypotheses

A. *Double Auction* (*DA*)

The *DA* experiments reported here follow the procedures described in detail by Williams (1980). He used the PLATO computer system to write a computer program allowing up to fifteen agents, each sitting at a display console with typewriter keyboard to trade under any of four alternative versions of the double auction institution. Subject buyers (sellers), operating privately, enter discretionary quotations by typing a number, verifying it, then tapping a touch sensitive "box" area on their PLATO terminal display screen. Only one bid and one offer are displayed at any one instant. Any buyer (seller) can accept a seller's displayed offer (buyer's bid) by touching a box labelled *ACCEPT*. The acceptor then touches a box labelled *CONFIRM* at which time the contract is logged into both the "makers" and "takers" private record sheets. This screen display touch sensitive bid (offer)—acceptance—confirm procedure is highly functional (not just an "electric train" novelty) in that traders do not have to take their eyes off the data displays to execute contracts. Displayed bids, offers, and contracts in sequence are the only public information.

In the two versions of PLATO double auction that are used in most of the experiments reported below, price quotations must progress so as to reduce the bid-ask spread. Once a bid to buy and offer to sell are displayed to the entire market, they are "standing" for acceptance. Any new price quote that provides better terms (i.e., an offer that is lower than the standing offer or a bid that is higher than the standing bid) will automatically "bump" or displace the standing quote. If a bid (offer) is entered which is *not* higher (lower) than the standing best bid (offer) the entry is either: version 1) rejected and a descriptive error message is generated, or, version 2) placed in a bid queue (offer queue) and the maker is given the entry's position in a "rank queue" which continuously arrays bids from highest to lowest (offers from lowest to highest). In this latter version, tied quotations are assigned queue priority according to the chronological order of entry. Subjects may have only one entry either queued or standing publicly at any point in time. Queued entries may be withdrawn by pressing a key labelled *EDIT* but price quotes standing displayed as the best in the market cannot be withdrawn. However, the maker may bump his own bid (offer) with a better one. Upon the initiation of a new auction, after each contract has occurred, the lowest queued offer to sell and highest queued bid to buy are automatically entered as the new (postcontract) standing bid and offer. This procedure combines an "electronic" version of the specialist's book with the bid-ask improvement rule; both are features of New York Stock Exchange trading.[4] Trading occurs in a sequence of up to fifteen timed market periods or "days." In the experiments reported here, each trading period lasted 300 (360) seconds for the low (high) volume markets.

B. *Shubik's Block Trading, Sealed Bid-Offer Process* (*PQ*)

Our first PLATO sealed bid-offer auction mechanism, *PQ*, uses the following procedure: In each trading period each buyer submits one bid price, and a corresponding maximum quantity he/she is willing to buy at that price or less. Similarly, each seller submits one offer price and a corresponding maximum quantity he/she is willing to sell at that price or more. Next, the bids are ordered from highest to lowest, by bid price; the offers are ordered from lowest to highest, by offer price. If two bids (offers) are tied, the one entered first (chronologically) has priority. Then a selection algorithm generates a single market-clearing price.[5] An example actually used in the PLATO instructions for this bid-offer auction mechanism is shown in Figure 2. In the *PQ* mechanism, all acceptable bids and offers in any period form binding "short-term" contracts for the quantities accepted. Each period ends when the last subject enters his/her *PQ* decision. Such contractual rights and obligations are essentially the same as in *DA* above.

[4] Smith and Williams (1980) have shown that this rank queue version of the PLATO *DA* tends to outperform three other computerized variations of *DA* trading rules in terms of the speed of convergence to the *CE* price. The experiments reported here represent a sampling from all four *DA* variations. We thus give the sealed bid-offer processes (discussed in Section II, parts B and C below) a better chance of matching the *CE* convergence performance of *DA* than if only the *DA* rank queue had been used.

[5] This price, $\bar{P}$, is determined as follows: Define B_Q = Lowest accepted bid $\geqslant B_{Q+1}$ = Highest rejected bid; A_Q = Highest accepted offer $\leqslant A_{Q+1}$ = Lowest rejected offer; Q = Number of accepted bids (accepted offers) = Largest integer such that $B_{Q+1} < A_{Q+1}$, and $B_Q \geqslant A_Q$. Then $\bar{P}$ = Midpoint of the set $\{P \mid ed(p) = 0\}$, i.e., the set of prices such that excess demand is zero. Then $P = [min(B_Q, A_{Q+1}) + max(A_Q, B_{Q+1})]/2$. If the highest bid is below the lowest offer, we have $Q = 0$, and this highest bid and lowest offer is reported to all agents.

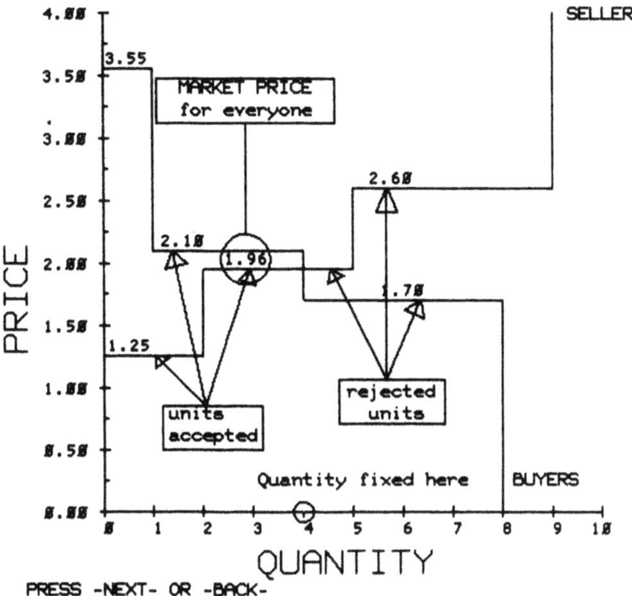

FIGURE 2

The *PQ* process, proposed by Martin Shubik, is an abstract mechanism with no operating field counterpart known to us. We have chosen it for study because of its important theoretical property (incentive compatibility) to be discussed in the next section. For this reason *PQ* is a particularly good calibration standard against which to measure the relative performance of *DA*. As noted above, in the absence of such a calibrating alternative, we are without an objective means of judging how good is the ostensibly "good" performance of *DA*. Since *PQ* has good theoretical incentive properties, its experimental examination provides a test of our ability to design better allocation mechanisms based on hypothesized principles of individual behavior.

A desirable condition for any laboratory price mechanism (or any abstract mechanism such as *PQ*) to satisfy is that of field realizability. Thus if laboratory mechanisms are to be transferable to field environments there must be no aspect of the mechanism that depends on information available only under laboratory conditions. In laboratory *PQ* environments, it is possible to know and therefore to guarantee that each agent has submitted only one price and quantity. Clearly, under field conditions, this might be costly if not impossible to achieve since primary bidders could operate through multiple accounts or agents and avoid the constraint of stating only a single price-quantity demand (supply) point.

C. *A Variable Quantity Sealed Bid-Offer Process* (*P*(*Q*))

Our second PLATO sealed bid-offer auction mechanism, *P*(*Q*), uses the following procedure: In each trading period each buyer submits one bid price for *each unit* that he/she desires to buy except that the buyer cannot submit more bids than the number of units for which he/she has been assigned valuations. Similarly, each seller submits one offer price for each unit which it is desired to sell up to a maximum defined by the number of unit costs assigned to the seller. Next, the bids are ordered from highest to lowest, and the offers from lowest to highest. Tied bids (offers) are ordered chronologically. Hence, $P(Q)$ uses the same lexicographic ordering used in *PQ* and the *DA* rank queue. Finally, a single market-clearing price is generated by the same selection algorithm used in the *PQ* process.

The $P(Q)$ process is important to study not only because the mechanism is incentive *in*compatible (see Section III), but also because the procedure is used daily to provide the opening price for each stock listed on the New York Stock Exchange. (See J. W. Hazard and M. Christie.) Furthermore, its features of simplicity and realizability argue for extending its application to the completely automated computer trading of corporation and government securities (see M. Mendelson, J. W. Peake, and R. T. Williams). But before any such field application is attempted, we should learn more about the behavioral properties of $P(Q)$ and how its performance compares with *DA* which is the dominant securities market-trading institution.

D. *Tâtonnement Versions of PQ and* $P(Q)$

Two additional mechanisms that we study represent tâtonnement versions of the *PQ* and $P(Q)$ pricing procedures. Each of these mechanisms, called *PQv* and $P(Q)v$, respectively, require unanimous consent by all those agents having some portion of their bids and offers accepted. Hence, in *PQv*, following the determination of the price and allocation in each period, PLATO asks each agent who participates in the allocation to vote "yes" or "no" as to whether he/she desires to accept the results of that "trial" period as binding. Any agent whose entire bid (offer) array is rejected on a given trial is disenfranchised on that trial. Consequently, the jurisdiction of voting is defined as consisting of the set of active buyers and sellers. If unanimity prevails following any trial up to the maximum allowed, T, a "long-term" contract is sealed for a multiple of T times the individual bid and offer quantities that were acceptable on that trial. If, after T trials, no unanimity agreement has been reached, the process stops with zero payoff to the subjects, that is, nothing has been earned in exchange.[6] Any *PQv* experiment that stops under this unanimity rule yields the same potential total payoff as any *PQ* experiment programmed to run for T "short-term" contracting periods. The tâtonnement version of $P(Q)$ uses exactly the same voting and long-term contract procedures as in *PQv*.

There is a long history in economic theory concerned with the indeterminacy of equilibrium when transactions occur at disequilibrium prices. Artificial solutions were provided in the form of Walras' tâtonnement exchange and in "recontracting" by Edgeworth who was critical of Walrasian tâtonnement.[7] The voting procedures described for *PQv* and $P(Q)v$ provide a simple operational mechanism for guaranteeing that there will be only one price in the market. Whether this mechanism will strengthen the achievement of *CE* outcomes is one of the empirical questions which we seek to answer. The practical relevance of the procedure is indicated by the fact that the same voting conditions have been used for over fifty years in the London gold bullion market (see H. G. Jarecki). In this market, five gold bullion dealers meet twice daily to determine the price of gold. Various prices are tried by the chairman, and a price is "fixed" such that total reported excess demand is zero, and each dealer has registered his approval. This is the only unanimity tâtonnement market known to us. In this case, apparently no dealer is disenfranchised in the vote count, but, since each is a broker executing orders from a large number of clients, each will normally be involved in an active trade.

[6] On the first three trials, the vote of all agents is counted, with the disenfranchisement rule applying on trials 4 to T. This is to avoid a premature stop caused by inadequate information. For example, on trial 1, if only one bid and one offer is acceptable, the two agents might vote a contract and exclude all other agents before the latter had an opportunity to adjust their bids and offers.

[7] See the papers by Donald Walker (1972, 1973) for a thorough treatment of tâtonnement exchange and "recontracting" in the economics literature. We know of no discussion of unanimity voting as a mechanism for operationalizing the tâtonnement concept.

III. Theory and Hypotheses

Since the primary hypotheses to be tested in this paper are derived from static Nash equilibrium theory, it is appropriate to discuss the basis (if any) for believing that static Nash theory might be relevant to the behavior of the various trading institutions we have described. First, we note what perhaps is obvious, namely, that any concept of economic (market clearing) equilibrium, such as monopoly (market clearing with underrevelation of supply) or a *CE* (market clearing with revelation of demand *and* supply) must be supported by some form of the Nash equilibrium (*NE*) concept, since the latter is our *only concept of noncooperative equilibrium*. Thus if any *CE* is not a *NE*, then, if that *CE* is attained, it will be in the interest of any trader to deviate from *CE* behavior and the *CE* is not sustainable. Second, one should carefully distinguish between a static *NE* property of a mechanism and some hypothesized dynamic process which might (or might not) converge to *NE*. The most prominent example of the latter is the Cournot adjustment or "best reply" hypothesis. It is entirely possible for a market institution to achieve a static *CE* which is also a static *NE* by accident, by random trials, or by some process which has been invisible to articulation and observation. But once a *NE* is stumbled upon there are, by definition, individual incentives which oppose change. We shall argue, providing appropriate documentation, that there is a great deal of evidence supporting static *NE* behavior in laboratory markets, but considerably less than convincing evidence for the Cournot best-reply adjustment dynamics.

A. *Empirical Support for the NE Hypothesis*

The *NE* hypothesis has been examined in a variety of different institutions and group sizes. Our discussion will be limited to a few studies of the following: 1) Price leadership bilateral monopoly; 2) Cournot quantity adjuster duopoly and triopoly; 3) Bertrand price adjuster duopoly and triopoly; and 4) The Groves-Ledyard public good mechanism.

Table 1 summarizes the results of 51 bilateral monopoly (the B1–B5 series), 54 quantity adjuster (the Q7–Q10 series) and 55 price adjuster (the P13–P16 series) experiments reported by L. Fouraker and S. Siegel. Under the pricing institution employed in the price leadership bilateral monopoly and Bertrand price adjuster experiments, each seller chooses (independently) a take-it-or-leave-it price. In the bilateral bargaining experiments, the buyer responds with a quantity choice, while in the price adjuster experiments, buyer response is simulated by choosing a corresponding quantity on a given demand schedule (this procedure assumes demand revelation by an unspecified number of hypothetical buyers). These institutional procedures have been called "posted offer" pricing by Plott and Smith.[8]

With the exception of the B5 series, all the bilateral bargaining experiments provide more support for *NE* (which is also monopoly) than *CE*. In B5, Fouraker and Siegel hypothesize that the combination of 1) complete payoff information, 2) the repeat transaction condition (which provides "communication"), and 3) a parameter design that fixes the equal-split profit point at the surplus maximizing *CE*, will yield outcomes supporting *CE*. Under the quantity adjuster "pricing" condition, the preponderance of support is for *NE* under both incomplete and complete information, except that triopoly yields more support for *CE* than duopoly (Table 1, Q7–Q10). This last result suggests that as the number of sellers, *N*, increases, the *behavioral* tendency to *CE* is greater than predicted by the classic theorem stating that *NE* converges in the limit (as *N* increases) to *CE*. In the price adjuster model (*NE* is also *CE*), *NE* receives overwhelming support (Table 1, P13–P16) in incomplete information duopoly and in triopoly.

Using a version of the Groves-Ledyard mechanism, which yields a *NE* at the Lindahl optimum for a public good, Smith (1979) reports the response behavior of subjects in two groups of public good experiments. The first group of experiments had the design characteristic of rapid convergence to *NE* under Cournot best-reply adjustment dy-

[8]Also see Plott, Smith (1980), and Ketcham, Smith, and Williams.

TABLE 1—SUPPORT FOR ALTERNATIVE EQUILIBRIUM CONCEPTS UNDER VARIOUS INSTITUTIONS

Identification of Experiment (Number of Replications)	Treatment Conditions	Number of Observations Supporting: Nash	Competitive	Monopoly	Probability at Which H_0 is Rejected
B1 (10)	CSE_N	9.5	0.5	Same	.01
B2 (10)	CSE_C	10.0	0.	as	.001
B3 (9)	IRE_C	8.0	1.0	Nash	.02
B4 (10)	CRE_N	6.5	3.5		.38
B5 (12)	CRE_C	5.0	7.0		—
Q7 (16)	IRD	14.0	2.0	0.	0.002
Q8 (11)	IRT	11.0	9.0	0.	0.035
Q9 (11)	CRT	15.0	15.0	3.0	—
Q10 (16)	CRD	12.5	9.5	10.0	—
P13 (17)	IRD	17.	Same	0.	.001
P14 (11)	IRT	11.	as	0.	.001
P15 (10)	CRT	10.	Nash	0.	.001
P16 (17)	CRD	11.		6.	.17

Source: Based on data reported in Fouraker and Siegel, pp. 32–33, 35, 38, 42, 45, 131–32, 134–35, 141–42, 174, 177, 181, 183.
Note: B = Bilateral Monopoly; Q = Quantities Variable; P = Prices Variable; I = Incomplete Information: Each subject knows only his own payoff table; C = Complete Information: Each subject knows each participant's payoff table; S = Single transaction experiment; R = Repeat transaction experiment; D = Duopoly; T = Triopoly; E_N = Equal profit split at NE, E_C = Equal profit split at CE; H_0 = Null hypothesis is the CE in the B and Q experiments, monopoly in the P experiments.

namics, while the second group was divergent under Cournot adjustment behavior. However, empirically, all of the experiments converged under the stopping rules to aggregate outcomes very near the *NE* prediction. Yet, in the convergent design, slightly less than half of the individual responses were best-reply choices,[9] while in the divergent design only about one-quarter of the responses were best replies. These low best-reply frequencies meant that the empirical convergence of the first group of experiments was slower than if all responses had best replies, while in the second group it meant that divergent behavior was avoided.

These results suggest that 1) empirical support for Cournot adjustment dynamics is weak, 2) this does *not* preclude behavioral convergence to the *NE*, and 3) the failure of individuals to follow a best-reply strategy allows "divergent" systems to stabilize near *NE* aggregate outcomes. Hence, the fact that people do not follow a Cournot response pattern may be an important factor in permitting *NE* states to be achieved.[10] These general conclusions are also supported by John Carlson's experimental study of the Cobweb Theorem. Two of Carlson's experiments were Cournot convergent and two were divergent. Yet all four experiments were observed to converge to aggregate outcomes near the *CE*.

B. *Theory and Hypothesis*: *DA vs. P(Q)*

A *CE* under the *DA* rules of exchange is also a static *NE* in the following sense: If it were thought by any buyer (seller) that all other buyers and sellers were going to bid

[9]A check of the individual choices in the Q7 experiments of Table 1 shows that approximately one-half are best replies!

[10]Ledyard analyzed the data from a preliminary draft of the Smith (1979) paper, and offered the following important observation: In the divergent group of experiments, if one adds to the set of Cournot best replies those subject responses which simply repeat the previous choice, the result as a proportion of total responses is similar to the proportion observed in the convergent group. Intuitively, one suspects, or at least may conjecture, that in these low-information uncertain environments the frequent use of the repeat choice strategy may be an intelligent means of imparting needed inertia to group choice in Cournot divergent systems.

and offer all units at a *CE* price, then the remaining buyer (seller) could do no better individually than to bid (offer) at that price. If all agents act on this belief, the market will clear at this price, and the expectation is "rational" in that it is sustained by individual experience. Only a *CE* has this property. Since the *DA* process is in real time with bids (offers) freely announced, and acceptances occurring in a temporal stochastic sequence, it is not clear in any *formal* sense yet articulated, how such self-reinforcing equilibrium expectations are evolved.[11] But the same observation also applies to the simpler processes (Table 1) studied by Fouraker and Siegel.

William Vickrey's classic contribution to the theory of incentive compatible institutions begins with the observation that when buyers and sellers are "too few" in number to ignore their influence on price then "...the normal result in such a case is that less than the optimal quantity will be provided..." (1961, p. 9). That Vickrey has in mind a process like we have described as $P(Q)$ is made clear when he subsequently sets forth his agency for "counterspeculation" beginning with the statement "...what the marketing agency needs, in order to determine the optimum pattern of transactions in its commodity, is an unbiased report of the marginal-cost (= competitive supply) curves of the sellers and of the marginal-value (= competitive demand) curves of the purchasers..." (1961, p. 10). Vickrey then proceeds to articulate his incentive mechanism designed to elicit each individual's undistorted marginal cost (value) schedule, which is then used to establish a single *CE* price.

That the $P(Q)$ mechanism provides an incentive for the individual to bid below his/her marginal willingness to pay is easily demonstrated. Let $E_i(P)$ be individual i's reported excess demand function, where P is the common price resulting from the $P(Q)$ process. Individual i will want to choose $E_i(P)$ so as to maximize $V_i[E_i(P)] - PE_i(P)$ subject to the uniform price constraint $E_i(P) + \Sigma_{j \neq i} E_j(P) = 0$, where V_i' is i's marginal valuation (cost, if $E_i(P) < 0$) function. The first-order conditions for a maximum give $V_i'(E_i) = P - E_i(P)/\Sigma_{j \neq i} E_j'(P) < P(E_i)$ if i believes that $\Sigma_{j \neq i} E_j'(P) < 0$, where $P(E_i) = E_i^{-1}(P)$. Even if i believes that all $j \neq i$ will reveal excess demand, that is, $E_j \equiv V_j'^{(-1)}(P)$, it will still pay i to underreveal demand, since $\Sigma_{j \neq i} V_j'^{(-1)}(P) < 0$. Note that i can deduce that it is optimal to underreveal demand without having to know the $E_j(P)$ functions; all that is required is for i to believe that all $j \neq i$ will report decreasing excess demand functions.

Figure 1(a) illustrates the *CE* price and quantity for one of the two basic experimental designs. This outcome would be obtained under $P(Q)$ pricing if each individual bids (offers) each unit at its assigned value (cost), that is, if B1 bids \$5.90 for his/her first unit and \$4.50 for the second, S3 offers units at \$4.60 and \$4.90, and so on. But suppose each person except B3 reveals demand (supply), then B3 can lower the market price by bidding \$4.70 for his/her second unit. Intuitively it is clear that under $P(Q)$ agents have an incentive to lock in their more valuable (less costly) units with revealing bids (offers) and to underreveal on the remaining units in an attempt to lower (increase) the clearing price. Hence, the theory implies the following hypothesis: *DA will yield outcomes closer to CE than will P(Q).*

C. *Theory and Hypothesis*: *PQ and DA vs. P(Q)*

Shubik, and P. Dubey and Shubik prove that the *PQ* process has the property that each *CE* has corresponding to it a *NE*. In the demand and supply design of Figure 1(a), such an equilibrium, which is also demand revealing (d_r) (or supply revealing (s_r)), is indicated by D4 and S4 in 1(e). Thus, if B1 and B2 (S1 and S2) each bid (offer) their respective marginal valuations (costs) for one unit; if B3 and B4 (S3 and S4) each bid (offer) two units at the marginal valuations (costs) corresponding to their respective sec-

[11] Formally, *DA* trading may be likened to a double price search process with learning. That is, when buyers (sellers) see an offer (bid) they observe a sample from the distribution of potential purchase (sale) prices. But neither side is searching a fixed distribution. That is, buyers (sellers) have motivation to alter their bidding (offering) behavior in response to the offers (bids) and acceptances they observe.

ond units; this would be d_r (s_r) behavior and the result is a *NE*. That this is a *NE* is seen, for example, by noting that if B3 (S3) unilaterally bids lower (offers higher), the bid (offer) is rejected, and his/her earnings are zero. If B3 (S3) bids higher (offers lower), the market-clearing price increases (decreases), and earnings decrease. Similarly, for each of the other agents, if the bid (offer) shown in Figure 1(e) is unilaterally altered, that agent's return is not increased. That there are non-d_r and s_r bids and offers that are *NE*, and that provide a competitive equilibrium is similarly obvious. Thus, if B1 were to bid anything in the range (4.90–5.90), given the other bids and offers shown in Figure 1(e), the result would be a *NE*.

A convergent dynamic scenario for the *PQ* sealed bid-offer mechanism is illustrated in Figure 1(b)–1(e). Assume each agent is a simple Cournot maximizer, that is, on each trial each agent chooses his "best reply" to the choices made by all other agents on the previous trial. Also assume that each agent, not knowing the bids and offers to be tendered by the others, minimizes the risk of being excluded from the market by choosing a d_r (s_r) bid (offer). Finally, let each agent initially follow the cautious strategy of entering a bid (offer) for only one unit with the idea of bidding (offering) on both units if on any trial that choice is his/her best reply. The first period outcome is shown in Figure 1(b). Each agent quotes one unit at the marginal value (cost) of that unit providing the outcome $(P_1,Q_1)=(5.00,4)$. At a price of \$5.00, B4's best reply is to bid \$5.10 for two units; S2's best reply is to offer two units at \$5.00; S3 and S4 each offer two units at \$4.90 and \$4.80, respectively; while the remaining agents repeat their first-period response. This result in $(P_2,Q_2)=(4.95,5)$ with all of S2's offer rejected as shown in Figure 1(c). At the price \$4.95, the best-reply bids and offers are shown in Figure 1(d) giving $(P_3,Q_3)=(4.90,5)$; the best reply to this is the *CE* (4.90,6) in Figure 1(e). Hence, the *CE* allocation is reached in four moves of the game.[12] From our discussion above of *NE* behavior in a wide variety of previous experiments, we do not expect subjects to follow the Cournot dynamic consistently, but this example illustrates the ease and rapidity with which it is possible for equilibrium to occur within the framework of traditional price theory.

In comparing the $P(Q)$ and *PQ* mechanisms, it should be noted that a special case of $P(Q)$ is one in which a fixed quantity of a good is offered in inelastic supply, and the items are discrete with each buyer bidding on at most *one* unit. As noted long ago by Vickrey (1961, 1962), demand revelation is optimal in this case and yields a *NE* (actually, still stronger, it is a dominant strategy to reveal demand) under the highest rejected bid pricing rule. In discussing the second price auction, and the multiple unit case with one unit per bidder, Vickrey observes that

> The essence of these cases that admit of the achievement of a Pareto optimal result seems to be that to the extent that the participants have a choice as to participating or not, it is an all-or-nothing choice. There can be no strategic holding back: for an individual to hold back is to achieve a zero gain for himself. [1976, p.15]

Hence, Shubik's *PQ* bid-offer mechanism can be interpreted as an ingenious way of generalizing this Vickrey intuition by reducing the $P(Q)$ procedure to the case in which each agent bids for only a "single" (price-quantity) unit.

These considerations invite the following hypothesis: *PQ will yield outcomes comparable to DA, that is, closer to CE than will the outcomes under P(Q).*

D. *Effect of Tâtonnement Voting*

Since *PQ* is incentive compatible (each *CE* is a *NE*), we would expect its voting version to perform at least as well. Indeed, in view of Vickrey's all-or-none intuition, *PQv* might

[12] Other initial moves are reasonable in this extensive form game. For example, each agent could choose initially a d_r (s_r) bid (offer) for both units. This case, given our other assumptions, would converge to the *CE* of Figure 1(e) on the second move, with the first move $(P_1,Q_1)=(4.90,4)$.

TABLE 2—DOUBLE AUCTION (*DA*)

Experiment	Number (buyers, sellers)	Final Period, T	Ratio of Buyer's to Seller's Surplus	Mean Price Deviation, Period 7, $P_7 - P^0$	Quantity Deviation, Period 7, $Q_7 - Q^0$	Efficiency, Period 7, E_7	Efficiency, All Periods, E
1	(4,4)	10	2	0.02	0	100.0	96.8
2	(4,4)	10	2	0.12	−1	74.6	89.1
3	(4,4)	9	2	−0.02	0	100.0	90.4
4	(4,4)	8	2	0.04	−1	91.1	94.2
5	(4,4)	9	2	0.14	−1	100.0	98.0
6	(4,4)	10	2	0.10	−2	84.4	87.9
7	(4,4)	10	2	−0.01	−1	100.0	95.1
8	(4,4)	9	2	0.03	0	95.6	97.0
9	(4,4)	8	2	0.	0	100.0	95.3
10′	(4,4)	5	2	(Period 5: 0.08)	(Period 5: −1)	(Period 5: 100.0)	96.9
11	(4,4)	9	2	0.128	−1	91.1	91.6
12	(6,6)	8	2	−0.034	−1	94.9	98.0
13	(6,6)	8	2	−0.019	0	98.7	97.7
14	(7,7)	9	2	0.008	0	97.4	95.4
15	(6,6)	8	1/2	−0.033	−1	100.0	98.2

do better than *PQ* since the stakes are increased by the condition that there will be only one T-period long-term contract. In particular, the disenfranchisement rule greatly increases the incentive for $d_r(s_r)$ behavior at "safe" bid-offer levels that minimize the risk of exclusion. Our hypothesis is: *PQv will yield outcomes at least as close to CE as will PQ.*

Since $P(Q)$ is not incentive compatible, it is not evident what might be the effect of adding the voting tâtonnement conditions. Thus an agent's veto power might be perceived as providing increased incentive to influence price by underrevealing demand (supply). This is easier in $P(Q)v$ than PQv since in the former mechanism one can be assured of not being disenfranchised by $d_r(s_r)$ behavior on the first unit only. However, since every agent has equal veto power this effect could be neutralized. We offer no a priori hypothesis for the *CE* behavior of $P(Q)v$.

IV. Experimental Results

A. *Comparison of DA with PQ, PQv*

The results of fifteen double auction (*DA*) experiments are reported in Table 2. The first four columns identify each experiment by its design characteristics: Sequence number, 1, 2, etc. (col. 1), where the prime on 10′ refers to a group of experienced subjects; number of buyers and sellers (col. 2); number of periods of trading (col. 3); and the ratio of theoretical buyer's to seller's surplus (col. 4). Experiments 1 to 11 used the valuation and cost parameters shown in Figure 1(a), except for the parameter-disguising constant by which all individual valuations and costs differed between successive experiments. In experiments 12–15 using six or seven buyers, and as many sellers, the competitive volume of exchange is twice as large as in experiments 1–11. The supply and demand design shown on the left of Figure 6 applies to experiments 12–14. In experiment 15, this design is altered so that the surplus ratio is 1/2 instead of 2 (see Figure 4).[13]

The fifteen *DA* experiments summarized in Table 2 show results which we have found typical of the PLATO version of the *DA* mechanism. Efficiency is "high" but not as high, nor is convergence as rapid, as for

[13] For an explicit analysis of the effects of variations in the distribution of available market surplus on price convergence in *DA* experiments, see Smith and Williams (1981c).

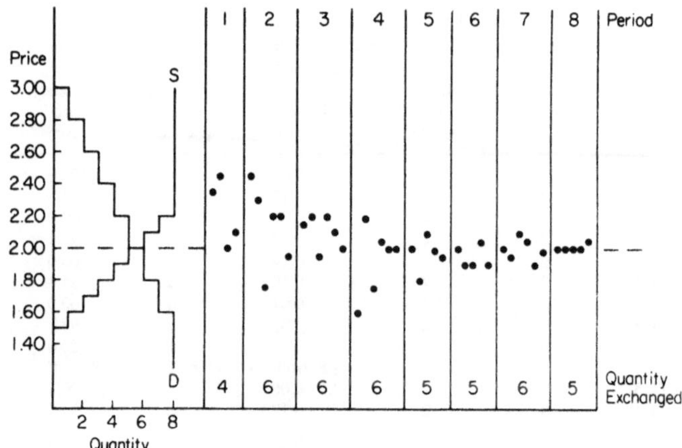

FIGURE 3. *DA* Experiment 9

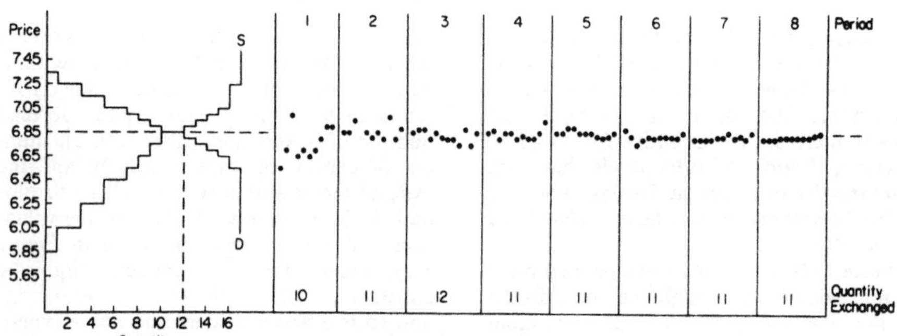

FIGURE 4. *DA* Experiment 15

similarly inexperienced subjects in the oral version of *DA* (Williams, 1980). Since the final trading periods in these experiments vary from 8 to 10 (5 in experiment 10′), we report the period 7 mean price deviation from equilibrium and the quantity deviation from equilibrium in columns 5 and 6. The efficiency for period 7 is shown in column 7, and the efficiency across all *T* periods, for each experiment, is reported in column 8. Efficiency is computed as the ratio of total subject earnings (excluding commissions) to equilibrium consumer's plus producer's surplus, expressed as a percentage. The tendency for the period 7 efficiency to exceed the efficiency across all periods reflects the effect of experience in causing a rise in efficiency.

Figure 3 displays all the contract prices in sequence for each trading period of *DA* experiment 9. This particular experiment shows somewhat more rapid convergence than is typical for inexperienced subjects. The contract results for a higher-volume market, experiment 15, is shown in Figure 4.

Table 3 summarizes the results of eleven *PQ* experiments based on short-term contracting, and Table 4 summarizes five experiments using the tâtonnement long-term contracting rules. Primes on an experiment

TABLE 3—SEALED-BID (PQ) AUCTION; SHORT-TERM CONTRACTS

Experiment	Number (buyers, sellers)	Final Period, T	Ratio of Buyer's to Seller's Surplus	Price Deviation, Period 7, $P_7 - P^0$	Quantity Deviation, Period 7, $Q_7 - Q^0$	Efficiency, Period 7, E_7	Efficiency, All Periods, E
3′	(4,4)	10	2	0.15	−2	77.8	73.3
5′	(3,3)	10	2	0.14	−1	100.0	84.3
6	(4,4)	10	2	0.11	−2	75.6	83.3
7	(4,3)	8	2	0.10	−1	97.8	90.6
7′	(4,3)	8	2	0.04	−2	64.4	76.7
8	(4,4)	8	1/2	−0.10	−1	88.9	76.9
12	(4,4)	10	2	−0.01	−1	100.0	74.9
13	(4,4)	10	2	0.10	−1	91.1	74.9
14″	(7,7)	10	2	0.	0	100.0	85.8
15	(6,6)	10	2	0.05	−5	80.8	73.2
15′	(6,6)	10	2	0.08	−2	97.4	83.0

TABLE 4—SEALED-BID (PQv) AUCTION: LONG-TERM CONTRACTS

Experiment	Number (Buyers, Sellers)	Maximum Number of Trials, T	Ratio of Buyer's to Seller's Surplus	Price Deviation, Period t^*, $P_{t^*} - P^0$	Quantity Deviation, Period t^*, $Q_{t^*} - Q^0$	Agree, A or Veto, V	Contract or Last Trial, t^* (Number Disenfranchised)	Efficiency
8′v	(4,4)	8	2	−0.07	−3	A	8 (3)	53.3
9v	(4,4)	8	2	0.10	−1	A	7 (1)	91.1
10v	(3,3)	8	1/2	−0.15	−2	A	4 (2)	43.3
10′v	(3,3)	8	2	−0.05	−2	A	4 (0)	93.3
12′v	(4,4)	10	2	0.	−1	A	10 (0)	100.0

number indicate that the experiment was the second, "experience" session in a two-experiment sequence (with different marginal values and costs) using the same subjects. An exception was experiment 14″ in which the subjects were very experienced, having been in one or more previous sealed-bid auctions and in other PLATO experiments such as *DA*.

Figures 5 and 6 display the period-by-period contracts for experiments 13 and 15′. These results are typical of the tendency for prices to be above (or below, if the ratio of buyer's to seller's surplus is 1/2) the competitive equilibrium as is indicated by the price deviations in column 5 of Table 3. Similarly, the exchange quantity tends to be one or two units below the competitive allocation, as indicated in column 6 of Table 3. In Figure 5, the reader should note the abrupt reduction in the exchange quantity in period 6. This is not atypical, and appears to be interpretable as a strong attempt by several buyers and sellers to influence the price.

Figure 7 plots the vetoed price-quantity results of trials 1 through 6, and the trial 7 long-term contract outcome of experiment 9v. Again, these results are representative of those voting experiments that reached agreement.

It is obvious from Tables 2 to 4 that support is lacking for the hypothesis that some version of the *PQ* mechanism will outperform *DA*. If we rank order the efficiencies, E, for all periods, using the first eleven *DA* experiments in Table 2 and the comparable first eight *PQ* experiments in Table 3, the Wilcoxen two-sample rank test yields the value $U_p = -3.32$ for the test statistic (asymptotically a unit normal deviate). The hypothesis that the *DA* and *PQ* mechanisms are of equivalent efficiency is rejected ($P =$

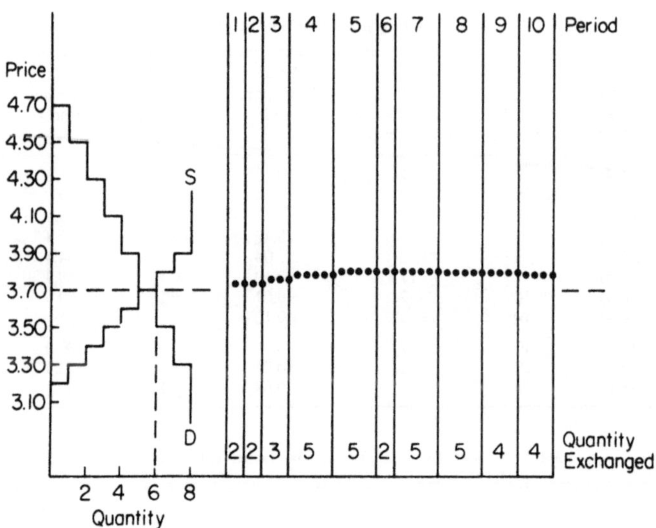

FIGURE 5. *PQ* Experiment 13

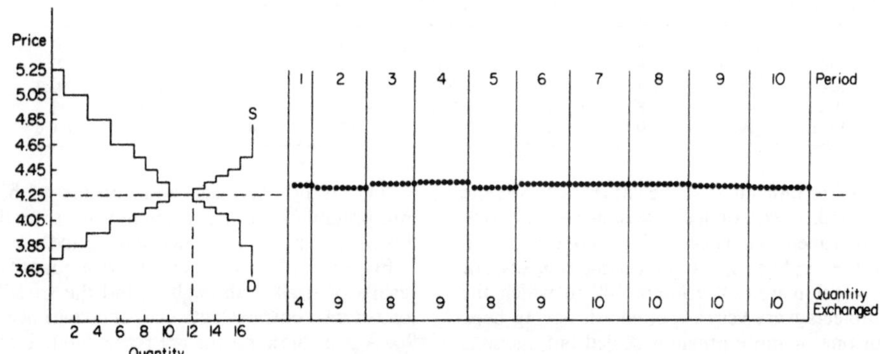

FIGURE 6. *PQ* Experiment 15′

0.00045). The hypothesis does better using the Wilcoxen test on the period 7 efficiencies with $U_p = -1.32$ ($P = 0.09$). This suggests the possibility that over time, with experience, subjects in *PQ* may approach the efficiency manifest in *DA*. Also, the fact that *PQ* experiments 14″ and 15′ (Table 3) showed high efficiency by period 7, suggests that a combination of larger numbers and/or increased experience may cause the *PQ* efficiency to approach that of *DA*.

The efficiency results of the voting (tâtonnement) versions of *PQ* are highly erratic (Table 4). All five of the *PQv* experiments reached a unanimity allocation. Three of these (9*v*, 10′*v*, and 12′*v*) compare favorably with the *DA* experiments, but the remaining two did much worse than any *DA* experiment. Also, somewhat surprisingly, three of these latter experiments (8′*v*, 9*v*, and 10*v*)

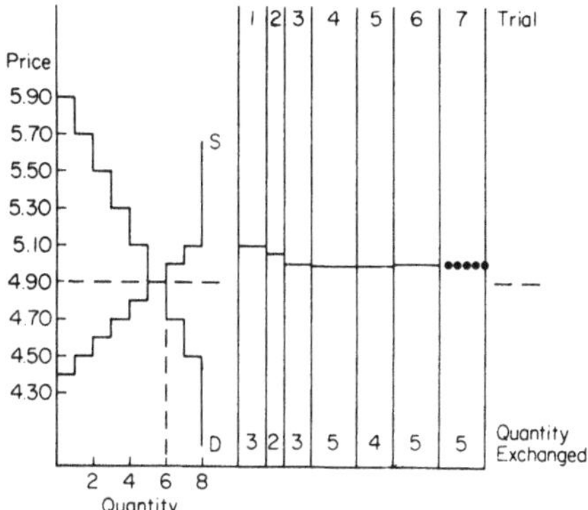

FIGURE 7. *PQ* Experiment 9v

reached unanimity with at least one subject being disenfranchised. We had thought the disenfranchisement rule would create stronger incentives to bid high (offer low) enough to assure nonexclusion from the market.

B. *Further Analysis of PQ: The m-m Hypothesis*

Prices in the *PQ* mechanism show a persistent bias upward when buyers' surplus exceeds that of sellers. In experiment 8 (Table 3) the surplus ratio was reversed and price was biased below the *CE*. We think these results are related to the frequent attempts by both buyers and sellers to influence price to the advantage of their side of the exchange.

If the *PQ* market is not at a *NE* on any particular trial, it is clearly possible for an individual to determine price to his/her advantage. Thus, suppose in period 2, Figure 1(c), that any one of the three sellers, S1, S3, or S4 were to offer $4.99. This would be a best reply, although not a s_r reply, to period 1. This strategy would yield a higher price, providing a benefit to all sellers (except S2). In fact, given the d_r bids of the buyers in period 2, if the sellers can somehow put together a cooperative response in which S2 and S3 give up their second units (which is behaviorally reasonable since the sale of these second units is risky), then any of the sellers could raise the price to $5.09 by offering that amount. If sellers hold to this behavior, it may induce buyers to bid as shown in period 2. This illustrates the strategic possibilities in the *PQ* mechanism. Buyers have similar strategic opportunities if sellers are prone to s_r behavior. A little calculation shows that the monopoly price in Figure 1(a) is $5.30 (achievable if all sellers withhold their second units and all buyers reveal their first unit demands). The monopsony price is $4.70 (achievable if all buyers withhold their second units and all sellers reveal their first unit supply). A monopoly-monopsony price of $5.00 would be achieved if S1–S3 and B1–B3 all withhold their second units, and the group settles on a split-the-difference (5.30–4.70) compromise price of $5.00. However, at this price S4 and B4 can trade their second units without disturbing this equilibrium. These alternative static price-quantity hypotheses are summarized in Table 5.

If we compare the period 7 price deviations in Table 3 with the behavioral hypotheses summarized in Table 5, it is clear that the only serious alternatives are the *CE* and *m-m* hypotheses. Neither the monopoly or the monopsony alternatives is remotely supported by the data. If we let H_0 be the *CE* (null) hypothesis ($P\text{-}P^0=0$), and H_1 be the single *m-m* alternative hypothesis ($P\text{-}P^0=0.1$) to be considered, the results can be reported in the classical α-β (Type I-Type II) error framework. The mean and variance of the price deviations (col. 5) of the first eight experiments in Table 3 are $\bar{p}=0.091$, and $V=0.002755$, respectively.[14] If we choose an α error of 0.01 (the probability of rejecting H_0, and accepting H_1, when in fact this would be incorrect), then the critical value for the price deviation is $p_c=t_\alpha\,(V_p/N)^{1/2}=0.054$. The t-value under H_1 is then $t=(0.054-0.1)/(V_p/N)^{1/2}=-2.48$ corresponding to a β error (the probability of accepting H_0, and rejecting H_1, when this would be incorrect) of less than 0.025. Consequently, the "power" of the test is $1\text{-}\beta>0.975$ (the probability of correctly rejecting

[14] In this calculation we change the sign of $P_7-P^0=-0.10$ for experiment 8 to correspond to the design change that reversed the surplus ratio from 2 to 1/2.

TABLE 5—ALTERNATIVE *PQ* HYPOTHESES USING FIGURE 2 PARAMETERS

	Price	$P-P^0$	Quantity	$Q-Q^0$
Competitive Equilibrium	4.90	0	6	0
Monopoly Equilibrium	5.30	0.40	4	−2
Monopsony Equilibrium	4.70	−0.20	4	−2
m-m Equilibrium	5.00	0.10	4(5)[a]	−2(−1)

[a]The quantity is 5 if B4 and S4 each trade two units.

TABLE 6—SEALED-BID ($P(Q)$) AUCTION; SHORT-TERM CONTRACTS

Experiment	Number (Buyers, Sellers)	Final Period, *T*	Ratio of Buyer's to Seller's Surplus	Price Deviation, Period 7	Quantity Deviation, Period 7	Efficiency, Period 7	Efficiency, All Periods
1	(4,4)	10	2	0.12	−1	97.8	93.1
2	(4,4)	10	2	0.22	−2	75.6	78.2
3	(4,4)	10	2	0.05	−1	100.0	86.0
3′	(4,4)	10	2	0.10	−1	91.1	96.7
4	(4,4)	10	2	0.02	−1	100.0	82.4
5	(4,4)	10	2	−0.04	−2	84.4	89.1
5′	(4,4)	10	2	0.	−1	100.0	97.8

H_0 and accepting H_1). Since, in the sample, $\bar{p}=0.091$ the experimental outcome is well within the region (i.e., above $p_c=0.054$) in which we accept H_1 and reject H_0. The quantity deviation prediction of the *m-m* hypothesis (-1 or -2) is supported by all of the first eight experiments in Table 3. Consequently, it appears that the data can be interpreted as follows: The group of buyers and the group of sellers each attempt to manipulate price to their groups' advantage; this leads to prices that vary randomly around the midpoint between the monopoly and monopsony prices, depending upon whether it is the buyers or the sellers that are the most successful in this effort. At these prices it is usually possible to trade five, but sometimes only four, units.[15] It should be noted that when similar calculations are made using the mean price deviations for the double auction (col. 5, Table 2) the results fail to provide significant support for the *m-m* hypothesis (for example, the mean of the *DA* price deviation is $\bar{p}=0.05$. Furthermore, the larger group *DA* experiments show a negative price deviation, while the large group *PQ* experiments continue to show a positive (but reduced) price bias.

[15]We are indebted to Morton Kamien for suggesting a possible "bilateral bargaining" interpretation of the *PQ* experimental results which led us to formulate the *m-m* hypothesis.

C. *Comparison of DA, PQ, and P(Q)*

The results of seven experiments using the $P(Q)$ mechanism for short-term contracting are listed in Table 6. A priori, we do not expect $P(Q)$ to perform as well as *PQ*, but the results are *contrary* to this hypothesis. The mean price deviation in period 7 for $P(Q)$ is .067, compared with .091 for *PQ*. Similarly, both the period 7 efficiencies and the efficiencies for all periods tend to be greater for $P(Q)$ than for *PQ* (compare Tables 3 and 6). Based on Nash equilibrium theory, we expect the efficiencies for the three institutions to be ranked $E[DA]=E[PQ]>E[P(Q)]$, and the price deviations from the competitive equilibrium to be ranked $p[DA]=p[PQ]<p[P(Q)]$. Neither of these hypotheses are supported. The $P(Q)$ auction comes closer than *PQ* to approximat-

TABLE 7—SEALED-BID ($P(Q)v$) AUCTION: LONG-TERM CONTRACTS

Experiment	Number (Buyers, Sellers)	Maximum Number of Trials, T	Ratio Buyer's to Seller's Surplus	Price Deviation, Period t^*, $P_{t^*}-P^0$	Quantity Deviation, Period t^*, $Q_{t^*}-Q^0$	Agree, A or Veto, V (Number of Vetoes)	Contract or Last Trial, t^* (Number Disenfranchised)	Efficiency
$6v$	(4,4)	10	2	0.02	−1	A	4 (0)	97.8
$6'v$	(4,4)	10	2	0.02	−1	A	3 (0)	100.0
$7v$	(4,4)	10	2	0.17	−1	A	9 (0)	100.0
$8v$	(4,4)	10	2	0.02	−1	V(1)	10 (0)	0 (100.0)
$8'v$	(4,4)	10	2	0.01	−1	A	9 (0)	100.0
$10v$	(4,4)	10	2	−0.01	−2	A	9 (0)	93.3
$11v$	(4,4)	10	2	0.01	−1	V(1)	10 (1)	0 (88.9)
$11'v$	(4,4)	10	2	−0.09	−1	A	6 (0)	100.0
$12v$	(4,4)	10	2	0.04	−1	A	7 (0)	100.0
$12'v$	(4,4)	10	2	0.03	−1	A	2 (1)	91.1

ing the high performance standards of *DA*. It appears that the temptation of buyers (sellers) to raise (lower) their marginal bids (offers) to get these units accepted tends to outweigh the temptation to influence the price level with these marginal bids (offers). This contrasts sharply with *PQ* in which the evidence suggests that the "all-or-nothing" character of the bid-offer mechanism *increases* individual attempts to influence the price level. The hypothesized greater discipline in *PQ* than in $P(Q)$ simply is not supported. These results raise serious questions as to the explanatory power of the Nash equilibrium concept within the context of *these particular experiments.*

D. *Is $P(Q)v$ Better Than DA?*

The results of ten $P(Q)v$ experiments using long-term contracting (voting with disenfranchisement) are shown in Table 7. Five of these ten experiments were 100 percent efficient, and outperformed all the *DA* experiments in Table 2. However, two experiments, $8v$ and $11v$, failed to reach agreement in ten trials. In $8v$ the subject who vetoed the 100 percent efficient outcome (shown in parentheses) on the last trial simply did not realize that a veto at that point meant no payoff. However, both of these experimental groups reached agreement in their second follow-on "experienced" sessions, $8'v$ and $11'v$. Hence we conclude that of the four sealed-bid institutions that have been compared with *DA* only $P(Q)v$ does as well or better than *DA*. Based on Nash theory we expect *DA*, *PQ*, and *PQv* to behave comparably and to approach *CE* allocations more consistently than $P(Q)$ or $P(Q)v$. The opposite behavior is observed. $P(Q)$ performs better than *PQ* though not quite as well as *DA*, while $P(Q)v$ seems clearly to be at least as good as any of the other institutions.

V. Individual Behavior in the Sealed-Bid Mechanisms

In view of the discussion of best-reply strategies in Section III, it will be of interest to examine the trial-by-trial choices of individual subjects in the *PQ*, *PQv*, $P(Q)$, and $P(Q)v$ experiments. A summary of these choices, classified by subject experience, and the number of buyers and sellers that constitute the market, is enumerated in Table 8. The first column of data lists the number of subjects participating in all experiments in a particular classification.

The second column lists the total number of subject-trial replies in all experiments in a given classification. Column three shows the total number (and percent of column 2) of such responses that were simple best replies, while row four lists the total number (and percent of column 3) of responses that were d_r or s_r replies. The best-reply percentages are quite stable (80–83 percent) across all *PQ* treatments, while the d_r (s_r) percentages

TABLE 8—SUMMARY OF INDIVIDUAL CHOICES, *PQ*, *PQv*, *P(Q)*, *P(Q)v* EXPERIMENTS

	Total Subjects	Total Number of Subject Reply Choices in All Trials	Number (%) Choices that were Best Replys	Number (%) of Best Replys that were Demand Revealing
PQ				
6-8 Buyers & Sellers				
Inexperienced	39	321	263 (82%)	26 (10%)
Experienced	21	175	145 (83%)	35 (24%)
12-14 Buyers & Sellers				
Inexperienced	12	108	86 (80%)	9 (10%)
Experienced	26	269	216 (80%)	53 (25%)
PQv				
6-8 Buyers & Sellers				
Inexperienced	14	66	56 (85%)	8 (12%)
Experienced	22	138	128 (93%)	31 (22%)
P(Q)				
8 Buyers & Sellers				
Inexperienced	40	571	459 (80%)	85 (14%)
Experienced	16	230	217 (94%)	111 (51%)
P(Q)v				
8 Buyers & Sellers				
Inexperienced	48	498	424 (85%)	84 (20%)
Experienced	32	272	242 (89%)	74 (31%)

Note: *PQ* and *P(Q)* are short-term contracts; *PQv* and *P(Q)v* are long-term contracts, unanimity, included agents.

approximately double for experienced subjects. Hence, the tendency to make "strategic" choices (defined as the complement of best replies) does not change with any of the treatment conditions, but within the set of best-reply choices the tendency to revelation increases with experience. In *PQv* it is seen that voting causes an increase in best reply choices, particularly with experienced subjects (93 percent).

In the *P(Q)* mechanism, the percent of choices that were best replies (80 percent) is about the same as for *PQ* with inexperienced subjects, but increases (94 percent) for experienced subjects. However, the tendency to d_r (s_r) behavior is greater in *P(Q)* than in either *PQ* or *PQv* for both inexperienced and experienced groups. In *P(Q)v* the best-reply percentages are about the same as in *P(Q)*, but the d_r (s_r) percentages are lower for experienced subjects. These data suggest that the high performance of *P(Q)* and *P(Q)v* relative to *PQ* and *PQv* is not clearly and consistently related to a stronger tendency to make best-reply, or revealing, choices in the former. We would suggest that the poorer performance of *PQ* and *PQv* is due to the block trading feature which increases the number of missed trades. Hence, the *consequences* of a given tendency to behave strategically is more serious in the *PQ* and *PQv* mechanisms.

VI. Summary

Based on the forty-eight experiments comprising the present study our conclusions can be summarized as follows:

1. Prices are nearer to their theoretical competitive equilibrium values in the *DA* than in the *PQ* mechanism. In *PQ*, the price-quantity outcomes are best explained by a monopoly-monopsony equilibrium in which it is hypothesized that buyers withhold demand in an attempt to obtain a monopsony profit; sellers simultaneously withhold supply in an attempt to achieve monopoly profits; and that the two sides settle on a split-the-

difference compromise price half way between the monopoly and the monopsony price.

2. Overall efficiencies are significantly higher under *DA* exchange than under the *PQ* mechanism. However, this efficiency difference is smaller for the period 7 efficiency comparison than for the comparison of overall efficiency. This narrowing of the difference suggests the possibility that with more experience subjects in *PQ* may approach the efficiencies obtained in *DA*.

3. The unanimity tâtonnement version of the sealed-bid mechanism, *PQv*, does not provide an improvement in performance over the *PQ* mechanism with short-term contracting. Efficiency and the price outcomes in *PQv* are as erratic as in *PQ*.

4. The $P(Q)$ mechanism, which allows buyers (sellers) to submit demand (supply) schedules, yields better results in terms of price and efficiency outcomes than is obtained with *PQ*. Although $P(Q)$ does not perform as well as *DA*, it comes closer to the *DA* standard than does *PQ*. This result is contrary to expectations based on Nash equilibrium theory since the competitive equilibria are among the Nash equilibria for *PQ* but not for $P(Q)$ (computed net of commissions).

5. Adding the unanimity tâtonnement feature to this last mechanism, called $P(Q)v$, yields performance at least as good as *DA*. Again, this is not consistent with Nash predictions.

6. An analysis of the mass of individual choices in the *PQ* mechanism indicates that the percentage of strategic responses (those that are not best reply choices) is approximately constant (17–20 percent) whether the trading group is small (6–8) or large (12–14), experienced or inexperienced. However, under *PQv* such responses decline to only 7 percent for experienced groups. Approximately the same incidence of strategic responses in *PQ* occurs in the $P(Q)$ experiments. The same observation applies in comparing *PQv* and $P(Q)v$. It appears that an important advantage of $P(Q)$ and $P(Q)v$ over *PQ* and *PQv* is that the former produces few missed trades attributable to the block trading characteristic of the latter, without causing any significant increase in the incentive to underreveal demand or supply.

REFERENCES

Carlson, John A., "The Stability of an Experimental Market with a Supply-Response Lag," *Southern Economic Journal*, January 1967, *33*, 299–321.

Dubey, P. and Shubik, M., "A Strategic Market Game With Price and Quantity Strategies," *Zeitschrift fur Nationalokonomie*, 1980, *60*, 24–34.

Easley, David and Ledyard, John, "Notes on a Theory of Price Formation and Exchange in Oral Auctions," Northwestern University, November 1980.

Fouraker, L. and Siegel, S., *Bargaining Behavior*, New York: McGraw-Hill Book Co., 1963.

Groves, T. and Ledyard, J., "Optimal Allocation of Public Goods: A Solution to the 'Free Rider Problem'," *Econometrica*, May 1977, *65*, 783–809.

Hazard, J. W. and Christie, M., *The Investment Business*, New York: Harper and Row, 1964, 177–78.

Isaac, M. and Plott, C. R., (1981a) "The Opportunity for Conspiracy in Restraint of Trade," *Journal of Economic Behavior and Organization*, March 1981, *2*, 1–30.

______ **and** ______, (1981b) "Price Control and the Behavior of Auction Markets: An Experimental Examination," *American Economic Review*, June 1981, *71*, 448–59.

Jarecki, H. G., "Bullion Dealing, Commodity Exchange Trading and the London Gold Fixing: Three Forms of Commodity Auctions," Essay 16 in Y. Amihud, ed., *Bidding and Auctioning for Procurement and Allocation*, New York: New York University Press, 1976, 146–54.

Ketcham, Jon, Smith, V. L., and Williams, A. W., "The Behavior of Posted Offer Pricing Institutions," Southern Economic Association Meetings, Washington, D.C., November 5–7, 1980.

Ledyard, John, "Alternatives to the Cournot Hypothesis," presented at the Summer Meeting of the Econometric Society, Boulder, Colorado, June 1978.

Mendelson, M., Peake, J. W., and Williams, Jr., R. T., "Toward a Modern Exchange: The Peake-Mendelson-Williams Proposal for an Electronically Assisted Auction Market," in E. Bloch and R. A. Schwartz, eds., *Impending Changes for Securities Markets: What Role for the Exchanges*, Greenwich: JAI Press, 1979, 53–74.

Miller, R. M., Plott, C. R., and Smith, V. L., "Intertemporal Competitive Equilibrium: An Empirical Study of Speculation," *Quarterly Journal of Economics*, November 1977, *111*, 559–624.

Plott, C. R., "Theories of Industrial Organization as Explanations of Experimental Market Behavior," FTC Staff Seminar on Antitrust Analysis, June 5–6, 1980.

______ **and Smith, V. L.**, "An Experimental Examination of Two Exchange Institutions," *Review of Economic Studies*, February 1978, *65*, 133–53.

Shubik, M., "A Price-Quantity Buy-Sell Market With and Without Contingent Bids," Cowles Foundation Discussion Paper No. 445, May 16, 1977.

Smith, V. L., "An Experimental Study of Competitive Market Behavior," *Journal of Political Economy*, April 1962, *70*, 111–37.

______, "Effect of Market Organization on Competitive Equilibrium," *Quarterly Journal of Economics*, May 1964, *78*, 181–201.

______, "Experimental Auction Markets and the Walrasian Hypothesis," *Journal of Political Economy*, August 1965, *73*, 387–93.

______, "Bidding and Auctioning Institutions: Experimental Results," Essay 6 in Y. Amihud, ed., *Bidding and Auctioning for Procurement and Allocation*, New York, 1976, 43–64.

______, "Incentive Compatible Experimental Processes for the Provision of Public Goods," in his *Research in Experimental Economics*, Vol. 1, Greenwich: *JAI* Press, 1979.

______, "Theory, Experiment and Antitrust Policy," FTC Staff Seminar on Antitrust Analysis, June 5–6, 1980.

______, "An Empirical Study of Decentralized Institutions of Monopoly Restraint," in J. Quirk and G. Horwich, eds., *Essays in Contemporary Fields of Economics in Honor of E. T. Weiler*, West Lafayette: Purdue University Press, 1981.

______ **et al.**, "Competitive Market Institutions: Double Auction Versus Sealed-Bid Auctions," department of economics discussion paper, University of Arizona, November 1980.

______ **and Williams, A. W.**, "An Experimental Comparison of Alternative Rules for Competitive Market Exchange," Yale University Conference on Auctions and Bidding, December 1979; revised March 1980.

______ **and** ______, (1981a) "The Boundaries of Competitive Price Theory: Convergence, Expectations and Transaction Cost," Public Choice Society Meetings, New Orleans, March 13–15, 1981.

______ **and** ______, (1981b) "On Nonbinding Price Controls in a Competitive Market," *American Economic Review*, June 1981, *71*, 467–74.

______ **and** ______, (1981c) "On the Effects of Rent Asymmetries in Experimental Auction Markets," Public Choice Society Meetings, New Orleans, March 13-15, 1981.

Vickrey, William, "Counterspeculation, Auctions, and Competitive Sealed Tenders," *Journal of Finance*, March 1961, *16*, 8–37.

______, "Auctions and Bidding Games," in *Recent Advances in Game Theory*, Princeton University Conference, Princeton: Princeton University Press, 1962, 15–27.

______, "Auctions, Markets, and Optimal Allocation," Essay 2 in Y. Amihud, ed., *Bidding and Auctioning for Procurement*, New York, 1976, 13–20.

Walker, D. A., "Competitive Tâtonnement Exchange Markets," *Kyklos*, 1972, *25*, 345–63.

______, "Edgeworth's Theory of Recontract," *Economic Journal*, March 1973, *83*, 138–49.

Williams, A. W., "Intertemporal Competitive Equilibrium: On Further Experimental Results," in V. L. Smith, ed., *Research in Experimental Economics*, Vol. 1, Greenwich: JAI Press, 1979.

______, "Computerized Double-Auction Markets: Some Initial Experimental Results," *Journal of Business*, July 1980, *53*, 235–58.

MARKETS AS ECONOMIZERS OF INFORMATION: EXPERIMENTAL EXAMINATION OF THE "HAYEK HYPOTHESIS"

VERNON L. SMITH*

I. INTRODUCTION

Economics has tended to be long on theories (Hypotheses) and the use of "logical completeness" as a criterion for judging the value of a theory, but short on technologies for discriminating among theories on the basis of rigorous standards of empirical evidence. Consequently, the body of theory in economics tends to grow from a steady stream of additions, with replacements occurring only occasionally. It is sometimes claimed that our methodology is limited by the fact that economics is complicated and we cannot do experiments, with the result that logical completeness becomes a crucially important test criteria. Caricaturized, it is as if economics had tried to do the work of classical physics by a shortcut that bypassed Galileo and Kepler and started "at the top" with the intellectually more interesting methods of Isaac Newton. The consequences of this confusion of form with substance would be of less import were it not for the fact that as "experts" we have made, or fellow-traveled with, policy prescriptions requiring us to know more than indeed we can demonstrate that we know. This professional process seems to have led us to believe that our Keynesian prescriptions could fine-tune the economy, that regulation would solve the alleged monopoly problem, and that coercive action was implied *ipso facto* by the untested theorem that market institutions will "fail" in the presence of externality and public goods. In all these matters the profession is now undergoing an agonizing reappraisal, which is hopeful, because it carries the prospect that it will expose our illusions. As suggested by Kenneth Boulding, "The Scientific community . . . should be deeply concerned with the images of science that lie outside it and even those that lie within it . . . (and) try to dispel illusions about it, especially by better processes of testing" (1980, p. 833). Hopefully, in this reappraisal we will learn that the fuse between science and policy must be much longer than we have so impatiently believed and that if we are to salvage economics as a science we might have to be prepared to start over by rethinking and testing our most fundamental propositions.[1]

*Department of Economics, University of Arizona. I am grateful to Arlington Williams with whom I have collaborated in conducting most of the experiments presented in this paper, and to the National Science Foundation for research support. As indicated in the citations, this paper draws on several experiments that have appeared as part of larger joint studies on themes different from that developed herein. This paper is a substantially shortened version of an invited paper presented at the 50th Jubilee Congress of the Australian and New Zealand Association for the Advancement of Science, Adelaide, Australia, May 12-16, 1980.

1. I doubt that it will be sufficient to be more eclectic within the current state of the economics literature, which seems to be suggested by R. M. Solow (1980, p. 2).

Although experimental methods in economics had precursors in the papers by Chamberlin (1948), Thurston (1931) and others, it is only in the last two decades that a number of researchers [Hoggatt, 1959; Siegel and Fouraker, 1960; Smith, 1962; Friedman, 1963; Battalio, *et al.*, 1973; Fiorina and Plott, 1978], have started to examine systematically the controlled experiment as a reconstructive vehicle for asking what it is that we can credibly claim to know. These two decades have produced some hard replicable results, including some Keplerian challenges to price theory, and shown that as economists we have not been on the wrong track in emphasizing the significance of individual incentives as an organizing principle in social economy. But there is much that we do not understand about the processes through which incentives do their work. Among our theories there seem to be some credible ones (in particular some of our static theories perform very well), if we will but have the patience and commitment to design experimental or other empirical filters to separate the wheat from the chaff. The need is not for less theory, but for theory inspired by hard evidence (albeit distilled into stylized facts). In the end this is likely to give us new and better theory, but in any case holds forth the possibility that we can be surer, and justifiably more confident, about what it is that we think we know.

II. INFORMATION AND COMPETITIVE EQUILIBRIUM IN PRIVATE GOODS MARKETS

The fundamental proposition of decentralized market theory is that a competitive equilibrium provides allocations that exhaust the gains from specialization and exchange (the allocations are Pareto optimal). But there is far less professional agreement as to the institutional and technical conditions necessary to achieve a competitive equilibrium (C. E.). One view, which has commanded a modest following since the classic work of Adam Smith, suggests that the attainment of C. E. allocations do not require any individual participant to have knowledge of the circumstances of other agents, or to have an understanding either of the market as an allocation system or of his/her role in promoting "and end which was no part of his intention" [Smith, 1937 (1776), p. 423]. Thus Alfred Marshall notes in his famous illustration of price determination in a local corn market, that "it is not indeed necessary for our argument that any dealers should have a thorough knowledge of the circumstances of the market" [Marshall, 1948 (1890), p. 334]. But it was Hayek who put the case more strongly and more influentially in recent decades, by emphasizing that "the most significant fact about this (price) system is the economy of knowledge with which it operates, or how little the individual participants need to know in order to be able to take the right action . . ." [Hayek, 1945, p. 526-527]. The problem which is addressed by the price system "is precisely how to extend the span of our utilization of resources beyond the span of the control of any one mind; and, therefore, how to dispense with the need of conscious control and how to provide inducements which will make the individuals do the desirable things without anyone having to tell them what to do" [Hayek, 1945, p. 527].

But how "little" need be the knowledge of each individual, and yet allow the market to do its work of efficient allocation? How is this relationship between the knowledge of individuals and the achievement of efficient market outcomes affected by the internal (formal or informal) rules of the market? How is it affected by external conditions such as the stationarity or dynamic nature of costs or tastes?

The extreme case of "little" knowledge is the circumstance of strict *privacy* wherein each buyer in a market knows only his/her own valuation of units of a commodity, and each seller knows only his/her own cost of the units that might be sold. Experimental markets have been used to test what we will call the *Hayek Hypothesis:* Strict privacy together with the trading rules of a market institution are sufficient to produce competitive market outcomes at or near 100% efficiency. Of those institutions that have been studied experimentally, the one which has been used most extensively to test the Hayek Hypothesis is the oral double auction characteristic of the organized stock and commodity markets. In this institution buyers and sellers announce price bids and offers subject to specified rules, and contracts are born, sequentially, of those bids and offers that are accepted.

The vast majority of economists in the main stream of British and American economic thought have not accepted, indeed have been openly skeptical of Hayek's claim that decentralized markets are able to function with such an extreme economy of information. In the absence of direct evidence such skepticism is warranted. Two contrary hypotheses have formed the core of main stream economic thought concerning the conditions for a competitive equilibrium. According to the *price taking hypothesis,* which seems to have been articulated first by Cournot (1838), the essential feature of a competitive market is that the number of buyers and sellers is so large that each individual has an imperceptible influence on price and, consequently, takes price as a given constant. This has been the standard textbook treatment of competitive price theory to which young minds have been exposed for many decades. Another theme in price theory specifies even stronger conditions for achieving competitive allocations, namely the *complete knowledge hypothesis* wherein it is asserted that competitive allocations require perfectly "foreseen" conditions of supply and demand [Samuelson, 1966, pp. 947, 949, *passim*].[2] Sometimes a definitional distinction is made between "pure" competition where the price taking hypothesis prevails, and perfect competition, where the complete knowledge hypothesis is assumed to apply.

2. The condition that there be perfect knowledge of the conditions of supply and demand, seems first to have been emphasized by Jevons (1871). See Stigler (1957) for a historical treatment of the concept of perfect competition.

III. EXPERIMENTS WITH STATIONARY ENVIRONMENTS

The design and execution of the experiments that have been used to examine the above hypotheses can be described under the following three headings:

1. *Inducing specified supply and demand conditions.*

In laboratory studies of market behavior a monetary reward system is used to induce whatever supply and demand conditions the experimenter wishes to administer as an experimental treatment. For example, consider the supply and demand schedules shown on the left of the experiment reported in figure 1. This experiment consisted of four buyers and four sellers, each with a capacity to buy or sell three units. Buyer 1 is assigned a value $8.50 for unit 1, $7.45 for unit 2, and $7.30 for unit 3, with the understanding that in each trading period he/she will earn the difference in cash between the assigned value and the purchase price for each unit bought. Consequently, buyer 1's schedule of valuations is a marginal valuation, or induced individual demand schedule. Buyer 1 will exhibit a maximum demand of 1 unit at any price above $7.45, but below $8.50; a demand for two units at prices above $7.30, but below $7.45, and so on. Similarly, seller 1 is assigned costs of $6.60 for unit 1, $7.65 for unit 2, and $7.80 for unit 3, and is guaranteed to pocket the cash difference between the selling price and cost of each unit sold.[3] This defines a marginal cost or induced individual supply schedule. If we array these assigned valuations (costs) for all four buyers (sellers) from highest to lowest (lowest to highest), as indicated on the left of figure 1 (also, see figures 2-7) the resulting schedule corresponds to the demand (supply) schedule of economic theory. Note that demand (supply) is *defined as if* all economic agents were price takers, which perhaps accounts for the widespread professional acceptance of the price-taking hypothesis for competitive markets. It is easy to have the impression that price-taking behavior is inherent in the very concept of market demand (supply).

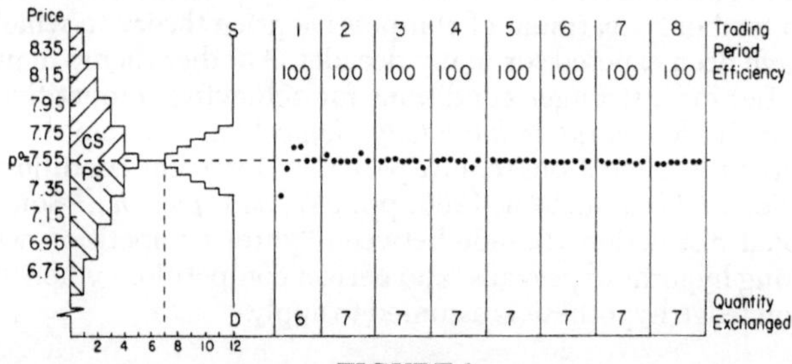

FIGURE 1

3. Buyers and sellers may also receive a small "commission," say 5 cents for making a trade. This provides a minimal inducement to trade a marginal unit at a price equal to its assigned value (or cost). In the experiments reported here subject buyers and sellers typically earn $12-$25 for participating in an experiment requiring two hours or less to complete.

In this experimental design if it should happen that all exchanges take place at the C. E. market-clearing price, P_e, the total earnings of the participants (not counting the commissions paid) is given by the shaded area shown on the left of figure 1. In particular, buyers earn the "consumer's surplus" labeled CS and sellers earn the "producer's surplus" labeled PS in figure 1. This total area, or surplus, provides a monetary measure of the aggregate gains from exchange and therefore, a measure of the ideal value of the market process itself. If the earnings actually realized in the market by all buyers and sellers is divided by the theoretical earnings given by the shaded area in figure 1, this ratio provides a measure of the market's efficiency. If and only if a market is 100% efficient, will the gains from exchange be exhausted.

2. *The double auction as an institution of contract.*

We define an institution of contract as the complete set of rules (or customs) which specify the process through which economic agents communicate, exchange information and negotiate contracts for the exchange of items or services of value. The experiments reported here use a computerized form of some key double auction rules that govern trading on the New York Stock Exchange.[4] This computerized experimental market is a real-time trading institution in which the market is open for a specified interval of time, during which any buyer of the commodity is free to announce at any instant a bid price for the commodity. This bid is admissable to the "floor," i.e., is displayed on each participant's computer terminal, only if it provides a better (higher) price than the outstanding bid. Similarly, sellers are free to announce price offers except that an offer is admissible only if it provides a better (lower) price than the outstanding offer. A bid or offer, once established, is binding until it is either displaced by a better bid or offer, or a bid or offer is accepted to form a contract. Each bid, offer, or contract is understood to refer to a single unit. The "auction" for a unit ends with a contract, and the market (or computer) waits for a new bid or offer. This process continues until the trading period countdown is ended, at which time, after a short pause, the experimental market is reopened for a new "day" of trading on the same terms. The experiment in figure 1 represents a case in which the buyer valuations and seller costs remain unchanged from period to period, corresponding to a well-defined stationary supply and demand environment, i.e., the supply and demand schedules represent flows per period of trading.

Note carefully in this institution that each agent is *not* in a price taking environment. The environment is one of multilateral negotiation in which each agent is as much a *price maker* (who actively announces bids or offers) as a price taker (who accepts bids or offers).

4. For a more complete description see Smith and Williams (1980).

3. *The information state of the experimental market.*

From this description of the market institution it is clear that all bids, offers, and contracts represent public information available to all the participants. This is a characteristic feature of all organized stock and commodity markets. However, if we are to obtain a test of the Hayek hypothesis, all knowledge except this public price information must remain private to individuals. Hence in the experimental market, individual values (costs) are assigned privately, and remain private throughout the experiment. All information pertaining to the market supply and demand condition and the individual values (costs) of other participants is withheld from each agent.

Under these experimental conditions if there is a pronounced tendency for these markets to converge to the competitive equilibrium, the Hayek hypothesis is supported in stationary environments. If these markets fail to converge or if convergence is weak, the Hayek hypothesis must be rejected (or is certainly suspect), and the alternative hypotheses seriously considered. That is, some form of price-taking behavior with a much larger number of buyers and sellers, or more complete participant knowledge of market conditions, may be necessary to produce C. E. states.

The experimental evidence, which at the present writing consists of perhaps 150 to 200 individual experiments conducted by many different investigators [For example, see Smith, 1976; Smith and Williams, 1980; Isaac and Plott, 1981], provides unequivocal support for the Hayek hypothesis. Double oral auctions with either inexperienced or experienced participants converge with astonishing speed to the C. E. price and quantity.[5] Computerized forms of the double auction show similar rapid convergence when *experienced* subjects are used. (i.e., subjects who have participated in a previous double auction experiment that used different supply and demand conditions). The reasons for this difference are due, apparently, to the motor activities that must be learned in computerized trading, and to differences between the auditory and visual information processing ability of people [Williams, 1980]. Figures 1-4 illustrate typical patterns of contract price convergence in computerized double auction experiments. These figures plot contract prices in the order in which bids (or offers) were accepted.

The experiment in figure 1, using eight experienced subjects, converges essentially to the C. E. by the second trading period with very high efficiency in all periods. Figure 2 presents an experiment corresponding to a "thicker" market (six buyers, six sellers, twelve units exchanged at the C. E.), but with inexperienced subjects. Apparently, the slower convergence behavior of inexperienced subjects is offset somewhat, in this case, by the larger trading volume.

5. Of the large number of double auction experiments reported, the only exception to this statement appears to be experiment II reported by Isaac and Plott (1981, p. 452).

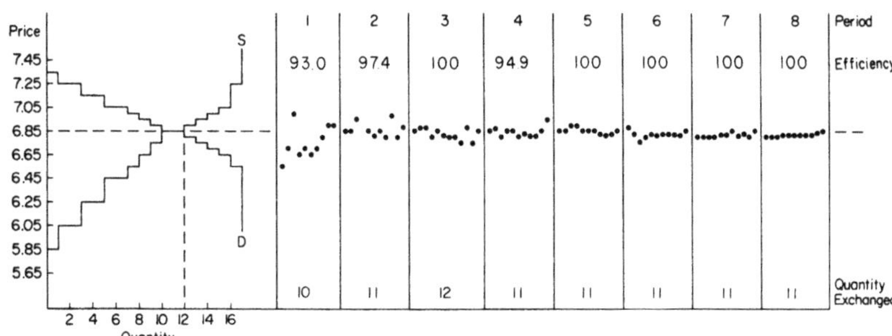

FIGURE 2

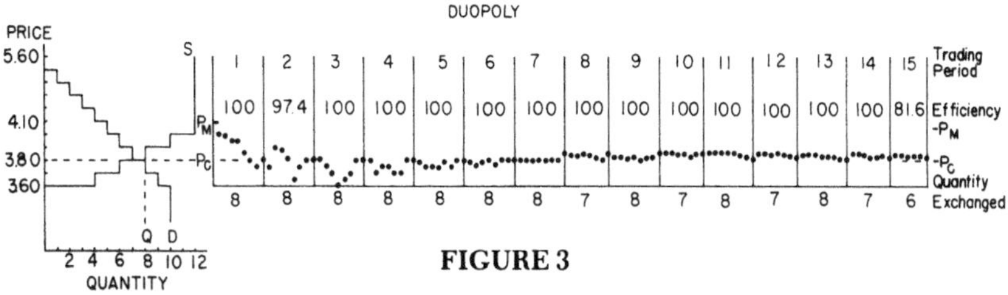

DUOPOLY

FIGURE 3

In figure 3 two sellers constitute the supply schedule shown on the left while five buyers compose the indicated demand schedule. Average price in all but the first period is within five cents of the C. E. price ($3.80). Efficiency is 100 percent in all periods except 2 and 15. Hence the rapid convergence property of double auction trading is robust with respect to a reduction in the number of sellers to only two.[6]

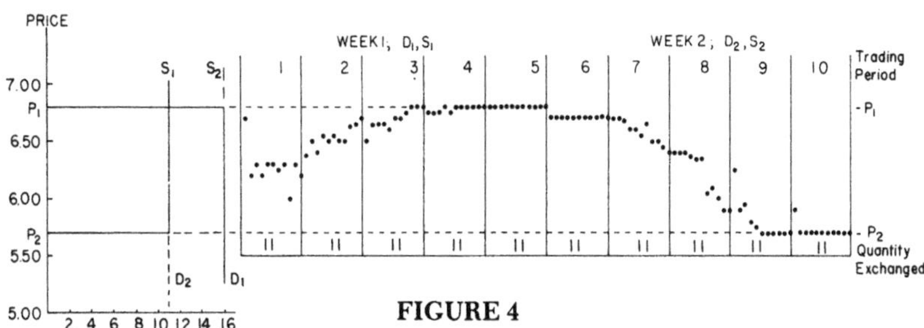

FIGURE 4

6. The large decrease in efficiency in period 15 was due to the failure of buyer 2 (with first and second unit valuations of $4.30 and $3.80) to make a purchase. He entered no bids until near the end of the period. His first bid at $3.80 was "bumped" by an overbid from another buyer. He then re-entered a bid of $3.80 eight seconds before the market close, and seller 2 who had not yet sold his third unit (cost $3.70) refused to accept the bid or make a counter offer. Buyer 2 had followed a similar strategy in previous periods, i.e., holding out with low bids until near the market close, but only in period 15 did this strategy fail to yield a contract.

Figure 4 illustrates an experimental design that provides the most stringent of all reported tests of the equilibrating tendency in double auction trading. In this market four sellers all have identical unit costs ($5.70) and four buyers all have the same unit values ($6.80). In the first week of trading aggregate supply capacity is eleven units, while demand capacity is sixteen units. In the interface between period 5 and period 6, the total capacity of sellers is increased to sixteen units for week 2, while the demand capacity is reduced to eleven units. From the point of view of the participants this change is rather subtle in that their individual value and cost assignments remain constant. But the C. E. price shifts from P_1 = $6.80 in week 1 to P_2 = $5.70 in week 2. At the week 1 C. E. price all the exchange surplus ($12.10 per trading period) is obtained by the sellers, with buyers receiving only the commission (10 percent per transaction). In week 2 at the C. E. price, all surplus goes to the buyers with the sellers receiving commissions only. In this "pathological case" buyers (sellers) in week 1 (in week 2) can be expected to offer exceptionally strong bargaining resistance to contract prices that converge to P_1 (P_2). As shown by the contract price sequence in figure 4, the convergence is slow, but definitive in week 1, with all contracts at P_1 in period 5. In periods 6, 7 and the first half of 8 it is evident that the high price expectations and profit aspirations established in week 1 are slow to extinguish under the new week 2 conditions, but by period 10 all contracts except the first are at P_2. In this design the C. E. is not the unique efficient (Pareto optimal) allocation that exhausts the gains from trade. In fact, *any allocation* and set of prices such that eleven units are exchanged will be 100% efficient. Hence, the C. E. has no special "ethical" appeal in this case, but as an experimental design this case allows the boundary of performance in double auction trading to be tested.

These results provide strong support for the Hayek hypothesis in *stationary* double auction environments with constant repetitive conditions of supply and demand; neither complete information nor price-taking behavior (with its "large number" implications) is necessary for C. E. convergence. But will the Hayek hypothesis receive similar support in other environments? The next section presents experimental data from environments that are either cyclical or subject to irregular shifts in supply and demand.

IV. EXPERIMENTS WITH DYNAMIC ENVIRONMENTS; CYCLIC DEMAND

Many markets are characterized by seasonal changes in demand (or supply). The demand for swimwear is concentrated in the summer; and the daytime demand for electricity exceeds the demand at night. Where the commodity (or service) is nonstorable, or storable only at prohibitive costs, the maximum output level is determined by the peak demand conditions. Where the commodity can be stored economically, substantial savings may be obtained by smoothing output over the cycle and allowing peak demand to be satisfied out of inventories accumulated during off-peak demand periods. An important function of markets is to establish price patterns over time that provide individual incentives for the optimal smoothing of supply responses over time.

The experiments shown in figures 5 and 6 [Williams, 1979, p. 258, 262] deal with the case in which demand cycles alternately between a "low" (B) and a "high" (Y) level. In figure 5 a distinct group of (two) "traders" are given the exclusive right to buy in one period for resale in the subsequent period, but without benefit of any information on demand except that which is revealed publically in the double auction bid-offer process of exchange. In this experiment traders incur a zero cost of storage. At the intertemporal C. E. price ($2.80) sellers should supply seven units per period, traders should buy four units in B for resale in Y, with consumption of three units in B, eleven units in Y. At the C. E. both buyers and sellers received a larger surplus due to the speculative activity of traders.

Referring to figure 5, in period 1B and 1Y the traders made no purchases and therefore no sales. Having observed lower contract prices in the "B season" than in the "Y season," traders purchased two units in period 2B for resale in 2Y. The carryover was expanded to four units in periods 3B and 3Y and in all subsequent periods. By periods 7B and 7Y most contract prices are near the intertemporal C. E. price, and trader's profits have been lowered from 50-60 cents per trade in period 2 to 5-10 cents per trade in period 7. Beginning with period 3 market efficiency is 100% of its theoretical intertemporal C. E. level.

No traders participated in the experiment shown in figure 6. In this autarky (no trade) market the C. E. price should cycle between $2.40 in the B period and $3.40 in the Y period with exchange quantities of five units and nine units respectively. At these prices, the theoretical efficiency would be 92% of the intertemporal C. E. with optimal carry-over. It will be noted that this market is very slow in approaching this cyclical equilibrium. Sellers have no reason to expect prices to change from the B to the Y seasons (their costs do not change) and in the bargaining process tend to negotiate prices above the C. E. price in B and below the C. E. price in Y. Gradually, however, this "hysteresis" effect diminishes with prices approaching their respective seasonal C. E. levels by period 7. Beginning with period 3 market efficiency attained its theoretical autarkic value.

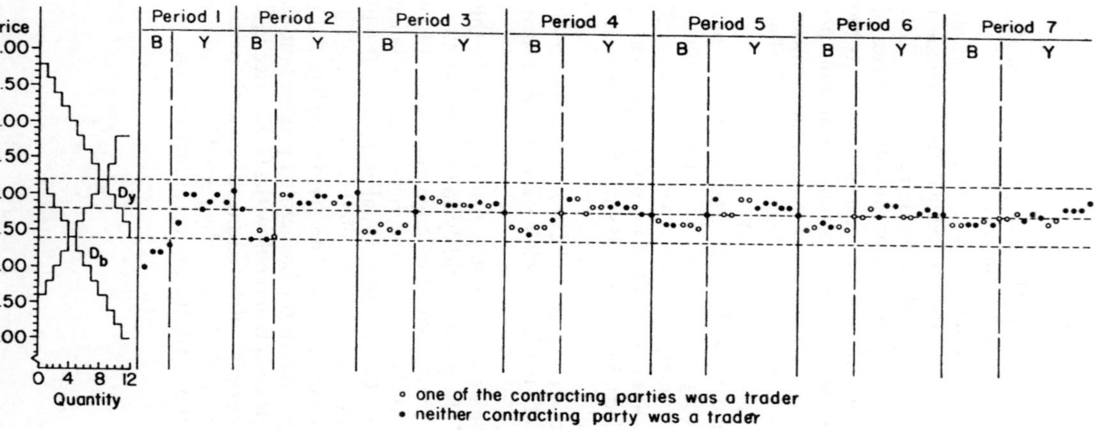

FIGURE 5

Reproduced from Williams, 1979
p. 258 by permission of JAI press

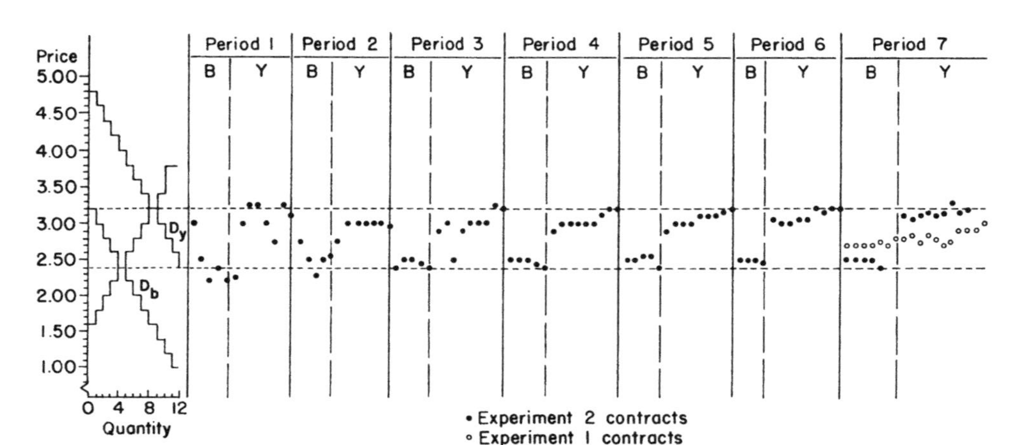

FIGURE 6

Reproduced from Williams, 1979
p. 262 by permission of JAI press

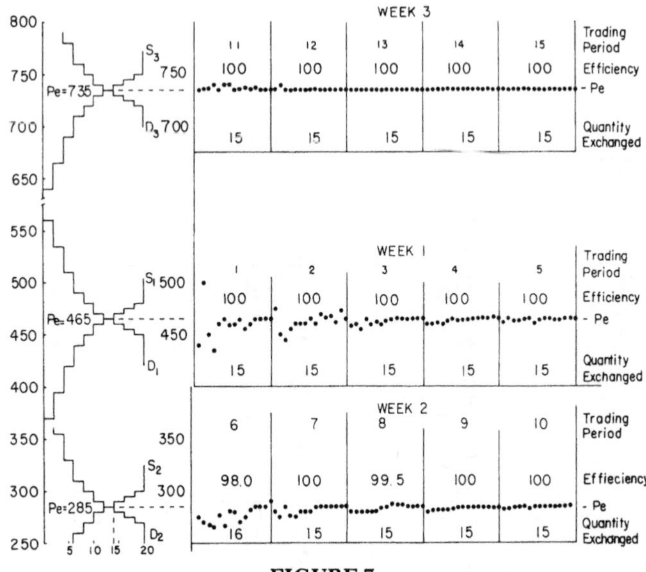

FIGURE 7

V. IRREGULAR SHIFTS IN SUPPLY AND DEMAND

In figure 7 is shown a double auction experiment in which demand and supply were stationary for five periods; then both were shifted down, again remained stationary for five periods; and finally both were shifted up, remaining stationary for the final five periods of the experimental session. In each week of trading this market converged to the temporary C. E. price before a new week brought a shift in the supply and demand schedules. In week 3 convergence was very rapid with all contracts "locked" into the C. E. price in periods 13, 14 and 15. It should be noted that in this environment, consisting of a simultaneous shift in both supply and demand, there is some tendency to overshoot the new C. E. price (see periods 6 and 11).

VI. DISCUSSION

In all three of the double auction environments studied experimentally (stationary, cyclical, and irregular shifts in demand and supply) the evidence is consistent with the Hayek hypothesis and inconsistent with both the "large numbers" price-taking hypothesis and the much stronger complete-information hypothesis. Does this mean that markets will always perform in accordance with competitive price theory under the low information Hayek conditions? Not necessarily — certainly not without more empirical evidence. For example, the Hayek hypothesis performs better under double auction exchange than under some alternative exchange institutions. In experiments with "posted offer" pricing in which sellers independently select prices that are then administered to buyers on a take-it-or-leave-it (not negotiable) basis, price convergence is slower and allocations less efficient than is typical of double auction exchange [See, for example, Williams, 1973]. Also, recent experiments comparing double auction (continuous) trading with various forms of the sealed-bid auction show the former to be more efficient that some forms of the latter [Smith, Williams, *et al.* 1982]. Finally, multiple interdependent double auction markets have been studied in only one exploratory probe [Easly and Ledyard, 1979], and although the reported results are generally consistent with those reported above, they are too tentative to provide hard further evidence on the Hayek hypothesis.

What has been established is, that in the simple environments studied to date, the attainment of C. E. outcomes is possible under much less stringent conditions than has been thought necessary by the overwhelming majority of professional economists. *A priori* these experimental results have not been considered intuitively plausible. In this sense, Hayek's claims concerning the price system as an economizer of information, must be classified as an "outrageous" hypothesis contrary to what the common sense of most scholars had led them to expect. But it is not uncommon in the history of science for an initially "outrageous" hypothesis eventually to become credible — even widely accepted. Two recent examples in geology are the Continental Drift and Greak Spokane Flood hypotheses.[7] The most famous example is probably the hypothesis that all falling bodies, as well as the motion of the planets and the stars are subject to the same inverse square law of attraction. For a sixteenth century natural philosopher it would be difficult to imagine a more outrageous theory.

But even if our Hayek hypothesis continues to outperform its competitors in laboratory experiments, does this mean that it will do comparably well in the "field" environment of the economy? On the assumption of parallelism, namely that the same physical (and behavioral) laws hold everywhere, it is a reasonable working hypothesis, provisionally, to make this extension, but independent field observations, or experiments, are the appropriate vehicle for testing the extended hypothesis. Comparisons of laboratory bidding behavior with that of participants in the market for new issues of U.S. Treasure bond support the assumption of behavioral parallelism in sealed-bid auctions [Tsao and Vignola, 1977], but few such field experiments have been attempted. There is much casual evidence to suggest that the Hayek hypothesis applies to markets in the economy; e.g., prior to the energy department's gasoline allocation program, with its con-

7. For a discussion of these "outrageous" hypotheses in geological science, see Baker (1978).

sequent disruptive misallocations, the right amount of gasoline appears to have been continuously supplied to the right place at the right time. But this evidence is indirect, and based on correlations and is not of the same quality as the experimental evidence. For example, in field environments we can never know whether observed allocations are optimal. However, indirect field evidence acquires added significance when controlled experiments confirm the effectiveness of price mechanisms in coordinating allocations under conditions of privacy. Our confidence in interpreting this field evidence should be increased for the same reason that we have greater confidence in our interpretation of the correlation between lung cancer and cigarette smoking after laboratory experiments establish that rats, injected with cigarette tars, show an increased incidence of tumors. But of course the scientist in us should *always* remain just a little skeptical even of those propositions that appear to receive very convincing, replicable, evidential support.

REFERENCES

Baker, V. R., "The Spokane Flood Controversy and the Martian Outflow Channels," *Science*, 202, (22 December 1978), 1249-1256.

Battalio, R. C., Kagel, J. H., Winkler, R. C., Fisher, E. G., Basmann, R. L., and Krasner, L., "A Test of Consumer Demand Theory Using Observations of Individual Consumer Purchases," *Western Economic Journal, 11* (December 1973), 411-428.

Boulding, K. E., "Science: Our Common Heritage," *Science, 207*, (22 February 1980), 831-836.

Chamberlin, E. H., "An Experimental Imperfect Market," *Journal of Political Economy, 56*, (April 1948), 95-108.

Cournot, A., *Mathematical Principles of the Theory of Wealth*, New York: Kelly, 1960 (originally, 1838).

Easly, D., and Ledyard, J., "Simultaneous Double Oral Auction Markets," Public Choice Society Meetings, March 17-19, Charlestown, S.C. 1979.

Fiorina, M., and Plott, C., "Committee Decisions Under Majority Rule: An Experimental Study," *American Political Science Review*, 72, (June 1978), 575-598.

Friedman, J. E., "Individual Behavior in Oligopolistic Markets: An Experimental Study," *Yale University Essays, 3*, 359-417.

Hayek, F. A., "The Uses of Knowledge in Society," *American Economic Review*, *35*, (September 1945), 519-530.

Hoggatt, A., "An Experimental Business Game," *Behavioral Science, 4*, (July 1959), 192-203.

Isaac, R. M., and Plott, C., "Price Control and the Behavior of Auction Markets: An Experimental Examination," *American Economic Review*, *71*, (June 1981), 448-459.

Jevons, W. S., *Theory of Political Economy*, London: MacMillan, 1st edition, 1871.

Marshall, A., *Principles of Economics*, New York: MacMillan, 1948 (originally, 1890).

Miller, R. M., Plott, C., and Smith, V., "Intertemporal Competitive Equilibrium: An Experimental Study of Speculation," *Quarterly Journal of Economics, 91*, (November 1977), 599-624.

Samuelson, P. A., "Intertemporal Price Equilibrium: A Prologue to the Theory of Speculation," The Collected Papers of Paul A. Samuelson, Vol. II, J. E. Stiglitz, editor, Cambridge, Mass.: M.I.T. Press, 1966, 946-984.

Siegel, S., and Fouraker, L., *Bargaining and Group Decision Making*, New York: McGraw-Hill, 1960.

Smith, A., *The Wealth of Nations*, New York: Random House, Modern Library Edition, 1937 (originally, 1776).

Smith, V. L., "An Experimental Study of Competitive Market Behavior," *Journal of Political Economy, 70*, (April 1962), 111-137.

__________, "Bidding and Auctioning Institutions: Experimental Results," in *Bidding and Auctioning for Procurement and Allocations*, Amihud, editor, New York: New York University Press, 1976, 43-64.

__________, "Relevance of Laboratory Experiments to Testing Resource Allocation Theory," in *Evaluation of Econometric Models*, J. Kmenta and J. Ramsey, editors, New York: Academic Press, 1980, 345-377.

Smith, V. L., and Williams, A. W., "An Experimental Comparison of Alternative Rules for Competitive Market Exchange," University of Arizona, April 1980.

Smith, V. L., Williams, A. W., Bratton, K., and Vannoni, M., "Competitive Market Institutions: Double Auctions vs Sealed Bid-Offer Auctions," to appear *American Economic Review*, 1982.

Solow, R. M., "On Theories of Unemployment," *American Economic Review, 70*, (March 1980), 1-11.

Stigler, G., "Perfect Competition, Historically Contemplated," *Journal of Political Economy, 65*, (February), 1957, 1-17.

Thurston, L., "The Indifference Function," *Journal of Social Psychology*," 2, (May 1931), 139-167.

Tsao, C., and Vignola, A., "Price Discrimination and the Demand for Treasury's Long Term Securities," Preliminary Report; 1977.

Williams, A. W., "Intertemporal Competitive Equilibrium," in *Research in Experimental Economics*, Vol. 1, V. L. Smith, editor, Greenwich, Conn.: J.A.I. Press, 1979, 255-278.

Williams, A. W., "Computerized Double Auction Markets: Some Initial Experimental Results," *Journal of Business, 53*, (July 1980), 235-258.

Williams, F., "Effect of Market Organization on Competitive Equilibrium: The Multi Unit Case," *Review of Economic Studies, 40*, (January 1973), 97-113.

THE EFFECTS OF RENT ASYMMETRIES IN EXPERIMENTAL AUCTION MARKETS*

Vernon L. SMITH

University of Arizona, Tucson, AZ 85721, USA

Arlington W. WILLIAMS

Indiana University, Bloomington, IN 47401, USA

We report the results of twelve 'double-auction' market experiments designed to analyze the effects of asymmetric induced supply and demand configurations on the price convergence path toward a competitive equilibrium. The proposition (convergence bias) that prices tend to approach the competitive equilibrium from above (below) when consumer surplus is greater (less) than producer surplus cannot be rejected. We do, however, reject the proposition (convergence symmetry) that these convergence biases are of equal absolute magnitude. Excesses of producer over consumer surplus are found to have a more pronounced effect on the sequence of contract prices.

1. Introduction

This paper uses experimental methods to examine two questions. Does asymmetry in the relative theoretical surplus of buyers and sellers in single market double auction (DA) exchange affect the convergence path of prices toward the competitive equilibrium (CE)? In particular, do prices tend to converge from above (below) the CE price when buyer surplus is greater (less) than seller surplus? This question is important in establishing the replicable 'stylized facts' that characterize market dynamics.

The second question we examine is whether agent trading behavior, as revealed in the convergence of DA markets, is symmetric with respect to the roles of buying and selling. Specifically, suppose we examine the convergence of DA markets in an asymmetrical supply and demand design in which, at the CE, two-thirds of the total surplus is obtained by buyers, and one-third is obtained by sellers. Now consider a second experimental design which is the mirror reflection of the first design, i.e., one-third of the surplus is

*Research funding from the National Science Foundation is gratefully acknowledged. Don Coursey helped us conduct many of the experiments reported in this paper.

obtained by buyers and two-thirds by sellers, with all other aspects of the design identical to the first. Will the convergence pattern (the period-by-period mean deviation of contract prices from the CE) in the second design be the mirror reflection of that in the first? Alternatively, consider a symmetric supply and demand design with buyers (sellers) receiving one-half of the total surplus. Will the period-by-period deviations in contract prices from the CE be significantly negative (or positive)? The question here is whether the buyer (as compared with the seller) mode of negotiation behavior is a significant treatment variable. This second question is important for two reasons:

(1) Economics traditionally assumes that there is no 'artifactual' bias in the maximizing behavior of agents in exchange. Hence, there should exist no strategic or negotiating advantage in the role of buyer as distinct from seller, after controlling for any differences in the objective circumstances of the two roles. If such a fundamental hypothesis is subject to empirical doubt, we should be aware of this condition.

(2) From a technical point of view in experimental economics, if, for example, subjects assigned randomly to the seller role exhibit a weaker bargaining propensity than those assigned to the buyer role, then the evaluation of any treatment variable which alleges a bias in price deviations must take account of biases inherent in the relative bargaining behavior of buyers and sellers. Laboratory experimental markets have been used to study the effect of trading rules [Plott and Smith (1978)], buyer or seller conspiracies [Isaac and Plott (1981a)] and price ceilings and floors [Isaac and Plott (1981b), Smith and Williams (1981)]. In each of these studies the objective was to determine whether a particular institutional treatment variable — the trading rules, the opportunity for conspiracy, or a price ceiling — had a significant effect in altering the observed deviations from the competitive equilibrium price. Thus if a buyers' conspiracy or a non-binding price ceiling is associated with a negative deviation of contract prices from the CE, this result could be misidentified as due to the conspiracy or price ceiling treatments, when it is actually due to asymmetry in the behavior of buyers and sellers. In such cases the effect of conspiracy or of a price ceiling must be measured relative to the decrease in prices that would have occurred due to the weaker relative bargaining performance of sellers in non-conspiracy markets or in markets without price ceilings. The important implication for experimental design is that in such cases each experimental study must include experiments that establish an empirical baseline reflecting any biases inherent in the subject population, or (for more precise control) any biases in each particular sample of subjects from that population.

We report the results of twelve laboratory experiments using a fully computerized trading environment based on DA exchange rules similar to those employed in floor trading in many major security and commodity exchanges.[1] Smith and Williams (1980) have extended the initial experimental results of Williams (1980) to show that a version of this mechanism which incorporates an electronic limit order file or 'specialist's book' tends to outperform several other computerized variations of DA trading. All of the experiments reported in this study employ this specialist's book or 'rank queue' mechanism.[2]

2. Experimental design

Fig. 1 displays the induced supply and demand configurations used in the experiments reported on in the next section. The 17 total units in each array were distributed evenly among the subjects so that each buyer (seller) had at least 2 and at most 3 units potentially purchased (sold) during each 360 second trading period. Buyers (sellers) were paid in cash the difference between marginal value (sale price) and purchase price (marginal cost) for each unit traded plus a 10¢ commission to cover subjective transaction costs. All subjects had at least one intramarginal unit.

Note that both the design 1 and design 2 parameters are set so that the total consumer plus producer surplus available is extracted after ten trades at

[1]The PLATO computerized trading environment ensures that procedures are standardized across experimental replications, minimizes experimenter–subject interaction thus reducing the possibility of introducing 'experimenter effects', and automatically stores all price quotes and their time of occurrence for later recall and analysis. All of the statistical calculations presented in the following sections were done on PLATO using data transfer and analysis options linked to our double-auction data base. Our interest in electronic trading environments stems from the scientific advantages embodied in the automation of behavioral observation techniques as well as the gradual evolution of securities markets into electronic trading systems such as the Cincinnati Stock Exchange's NMS pilot project. The Commerce Committee of the U.S. House of Representatives has recently criticized the Securities and Exchange Commission for failing to push rapidly enough toward the creation of the national securities market envisioned in 1975 legislation (*Wall Street Journal*, 1980). Our trading mechanism demonstrates a small scale application of a technology which could drive such a geographically dispersed trading system. This paper's primary focus, however, is on an empirical analysis of how asymmetries in induced supply and demand arrays can affect price convergence in an experimental market environment.

[2]Buyers and sellers are free to enter price quotes by typing in a number and then touching a designated rectangle on their display screen. Any buyer (seller) is free to accept any seller's (buyer's) quotation by touching a rectangle labelled 'ACCEPT'. The acceptor must then touch a box labelled 'CONFIRM' at which time the contract is logged in both the maker's and taker's private record sheets. Bids, offers and subsequent contracts are the only public information. The 'rank-queue' mechanism requires price quotes to progress so as to reduce the bid–ask spread. The 'best' (highest) bid and (lowest) offer are displayed to the entire market and are open to acceptance. Any quotation which does not provide better terms is placed in a queue which ranks bids from highest to lowest (offers from lowest to highest). The maker is given the entry's position in the queue and may withdraw a queued entry by pressing a key labelled -EDIT-. After a contract occurs, the lowest queued offer and highest queued bid are automatically entered as the new post-contract bid–ask spread.

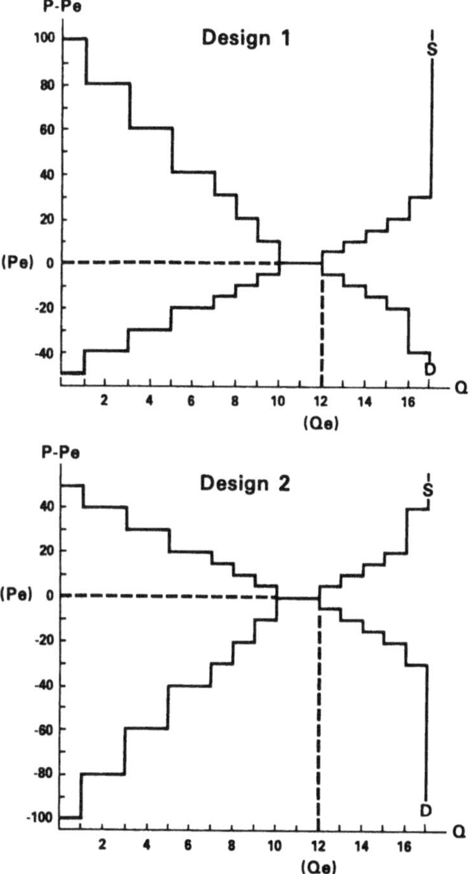

Fig. 1. Induced supply and demand.

prices within four cents of the competitive equilibrium price (P_e). Two marginal units will trade at P_e if the subjects choose to trade at zero profit and receive only their 10¢ commission. The extramarginal supply and demand units begin at $P_e \pm 0.05$ so that even small price deviations away from P_e could result in market inefficiencies. Any extramarginal unit traded will necessarily result in the actual surplus (profit) extracted by the group being less than the potential surplus. Perfect efficiency results only if the actual surplus extracted equals the maximum potential surplus ($E = 100 \times$ actual group profit $\div$ maximum potential profit).

The design feature of main concern is the asymmetry around P_e of the supply and demand arrays in both design 1 and design 2. In design 1 consumer surplus is twice as large as producer surplus (\$5.20; \$2.60); the exact opposite is true of design 2. The symmetry of the S and D step functions *across designs* (e.g., design 1 supply compared with design 2 demand) presents an opportunity to investigate the effects of asymmetric rent conditions on market outcomes.

Table 1 gives information on the number of experiments and trading periods conducted under each rent split condition. The subjects were male and female undergraduate and graduate students from Indiana University in Bloomington and the University of Arizona in Tucson. A '[a]' in table 1 after the experiment number indicates that the experiment was run with subjects participating simultaneously at both locations. The experiment identification numbers given in the first column of table 1 indicate the version of the PLATO Double Auction (PDA) software used and the experiment's position in a sequential list of runs using that version (e.g., 3–41 was the forty-first experiment using PDA version 3 software). The only differences between versions 2 and 3 for the 12 experiments presented here were program efficiency gains which were transparent to subjects. All 76 subjects were volunteers and were inexperienced in the sense that none had participated in a previous double-auction experiment. The twelve experiments reported were run over a two year period and served as training sessions for experimental designs which employed only experienced subjects [e.g., Smith and Williams (1981)]. The results of several of the experiments used in the current study are also used by Smith, Williams, Bratton and Vannoni (1982) to compare double-auction trading with several variations of a computerized bid–offer trading mechanism.

Table 1

Experiment classification and information.

	No. of buyers	No. of sellers	Final period	P_e
Design 1 experiments				
2–37	6	6	8	4.25
2–38	6	6	8	5.60
2–39	7	7	9	6.40
2–55	7	7	9	5.70
3–27[a]	6	6	10	4.25
3–41[a]	6	6	10	4.25
Design 2 experiments				
2–44	6	6	8	6.85
3–26[a]	6	6	9	6.85
3–31[a]	6	6	10	5.55
3–32[a]	6	6	10	7.70
3–38[a]	6	6	10	6.70
3–40[a]	6	6	10	2.40

[a]Indicates a multisite experiment.

3. Experimental results

Our research objectives are to examine empirically the validity of the following propositions:

Proposition 1. Convergence bias — Contract prices will tend to approach the competitive equilibrium from above (below) when consumer surplus is greater (less) than producer surplus.

Proposition 2. Convergence symmetry — The price convergence biases resulting from Proposition 1 above will be of equal absolute magnitude for equal absolute differences in consumer surplus and producer surplus, ceteris paribus.

Proposition 1 was first stated by Smith (1976) for *oral* double auctions. Results presented by Williams (1980) (using a 2:1 consumer–producer surplus ratio) suggested that the proposition would hold for PLATO computerized double auctions as well. Proposition 2 is obviously stronger than Proposition 1 and implies that the average observed upward price bias in design 1 experiments will equal the average observed downward price bias in design 2 experiments.

Fig. 2 presents a charting of the sequence of mean contract prices for the six experiments conducted in each treatment group. Fig. 3 charts the sequence of actual contract prices for two design 1 experiments (2–37 and 3–

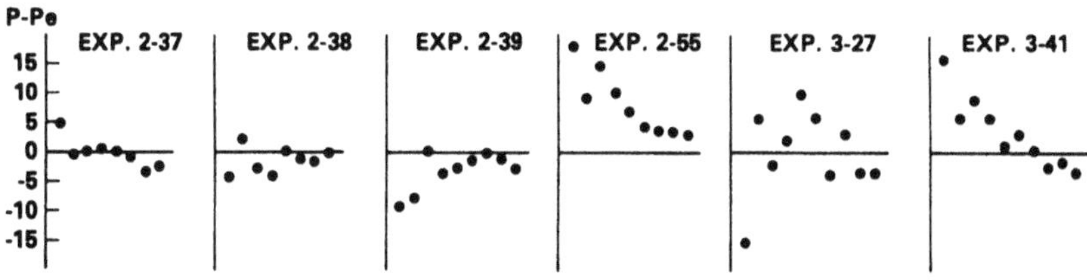

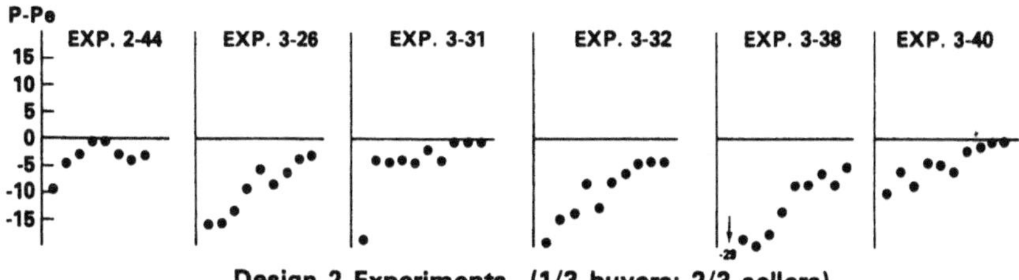

Fig. 2. Sequential mean contract prices.

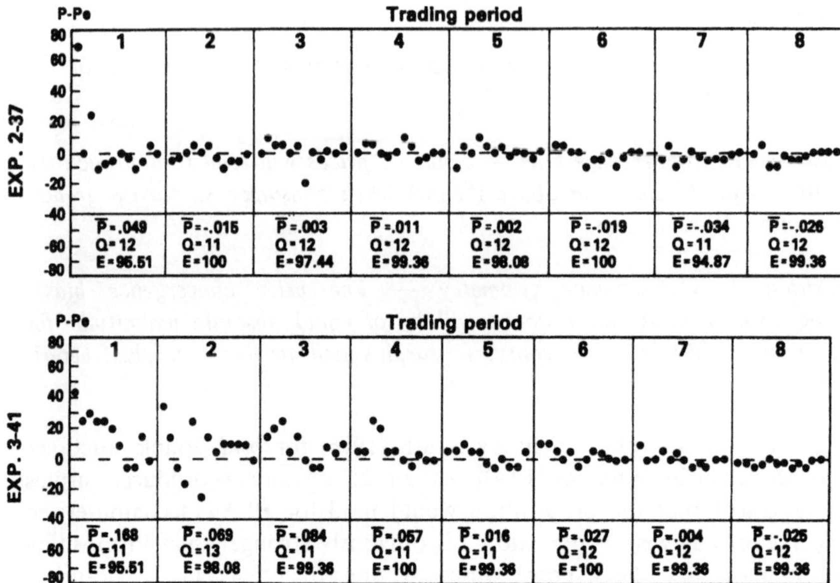

Fig. 3. Sequential contracts, Design 1.

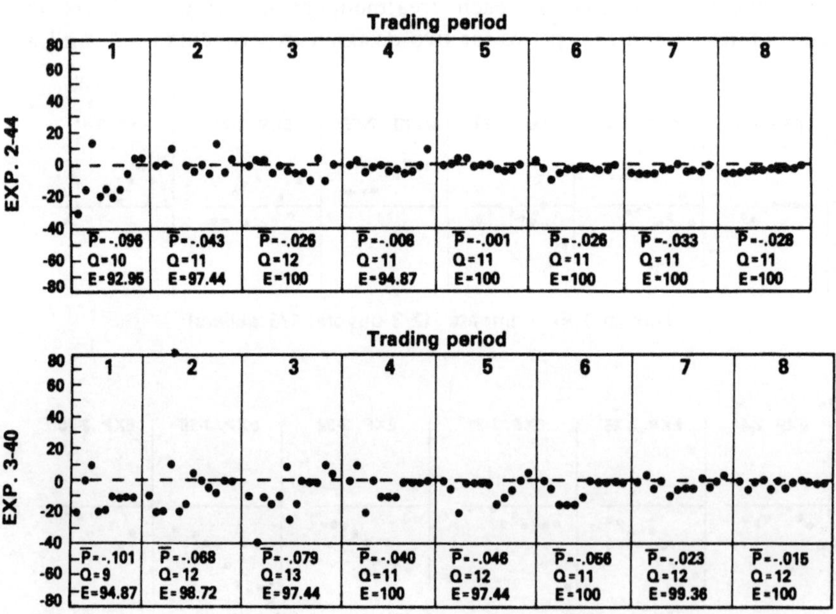

Fig. 4. Sequential contracts, Design 2.

Table 2

Contract price comparisons.[a]

Trading period	Mean $(P-P_e)$		Quantity exchanged		Standard deviation		F	t	Z_u
	Design 1	Design 2	Design 1	Design 2	Design 1	Design 2			
1	0.032	−0.171	58	58	0.203	0.210	1.06	5.29	4.93
2	0.031	−0.107	68	71	0.148	0.206	1.93	4.52	4.18
3	0.030	−0.102	65	74	0.119	0.138	1.34	5.99	5.33
4	0.019	−0.072	71	67	0.106	0.108	1.05	4.96	4.88
5	0.027	−0.069	67	71	0.093	0.121	1.40	5.18	5.46
6	0.012	−0.060	70	68	0.065	0.087	1.79	5.50	5.23
7	−0.005	−0.049	70	70	0.068	0.058	1.43	4.10	4.36
8	−0.003	−0.034	70	69	0.049	0.051	1.10	3.75	3.28
9	−0.012	−0.034	47	59	0.060	0.053	1.26	2.02	1.61
10	−0.033	−0.028	24	47	0.043	0.040	1.10	−0.55	−0.724

[a]Last period common to all experiments was period 8.

41) and fig. 4. charts sequential contract prices from two design 2 experiments (2–44 and 3–40).

From fig. 2 we observe that the price bias postulated in Proposition 1 occurs in all of the design 2 experiments but in only about half of the design 1 experiments. However, figs. 3 and 4 illustrate that fact that actual contract prices are initially quite dispersed around the mean price. Table 2 presents summary statistics for contract price deviations from P_e, pooled across the six experimental replications in each treatment group. The three columns on the far right of table 2 present variance ratios (F) testing homoscedasticity, as well as t-ratios testing the equality of mean $(P-P_e)$ for each period and the non-parametric Mann–Whitney unit normal deviate testing homogeneity of population distributions for each period. These statistics are calculated using pooled individual price observations, not a pooling of period mean prices.

The null hypothesis of equal population means is easily rejected for the eight trading periods common to all twelve experiments. However, rejection of equal means is a rather weak test of Proposition 1's validity since we are concerned with the direction of each sample's deviations from P_e.

Fig. 5 plots the 95% confidence band for the mean contract price deviation from P_e, period by period, for each treatment group. The asymmetry in the convergence paths of the mean price is striking. While contracts will on average be slightly above P_e in the early trading periods of a design 1

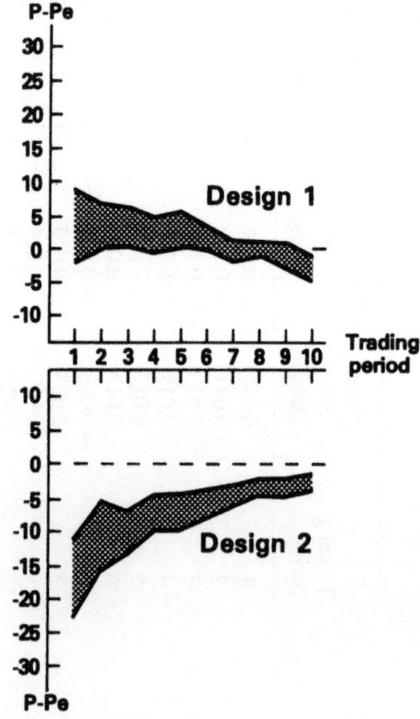

Fig. 5. 95% Confidence bands for mean contract price.

experiment, we cannot state that this will be true with a high degree of certainty since only two of the ten confidence bands lie entirely above P_e. In sharp contrast to this, all ten of the design 2 confidence bands lie below P_e.

The difference between the two treatment groups is further illustrated by the frequency polygons for pooled period 1–8 contract price observations presented in fig. 6. The design 1 sample is skewed upward with mode and median equal to P_e and mean 1.7 cents above P_e. The skewness of the design 2 sample is more pronounced and in the opposite direction with mode equal to P_e, median 5 cents below P_e, and mean 8.1 cents below P_e. A statistical comparison of the two samples yields $F=1.465$, $t=12.86$, and $Z_u=12.87$.

Given these results, we cannot reject Proposition 1 (convergence bias), as worded, but we can state that violations will occur more frequently for cases where convergence is predicted to occur from above (consumer surplus > producer surplus). This implies that Proposition 2 (convergence symmetry) will in general not hold.

A specific test of Proposition 2 can be obtained by a comparison of pooled time series least squares regression estimates of the following exponential decay function:

$\alpha(t)=ae^{bt}$, where

$$\alpha^2(t)=\sum_{i=1}^{Q}(P_i-P_e)^2/Q,$$

$P_i=P_i(t)$ is the ith contract price in trading period t,

$Q=Q(t)$ is the total number of contracts in period t.

Thus, $\alpha^2(t)$ is the mean squared deviation of contract prices from the competitive equilibrium price. Regressions of the above form using the eight trading periods common to all twelve experiments yield

$$\text{design 1, } \ln\alpha = \underset{(12.77)}{-1.63}\underset{(-7.30)}{-0.185t}, \quad (n=48) \tag{1}$$

$$\bar{R}^2=0.526, \quad F=53.23,$$

$$\text{design 2, } \ln\alpha = \underset{(-7.11)}{-1.286}\ \underset{(-6.10)}{-0.2188t}, \quad (n=48) \tag{2}$$

$$\bar{R}^2=0.435, \quad F=37.23,$$

where the numbers in parentheses are t-ratios testing the null hypothesis that

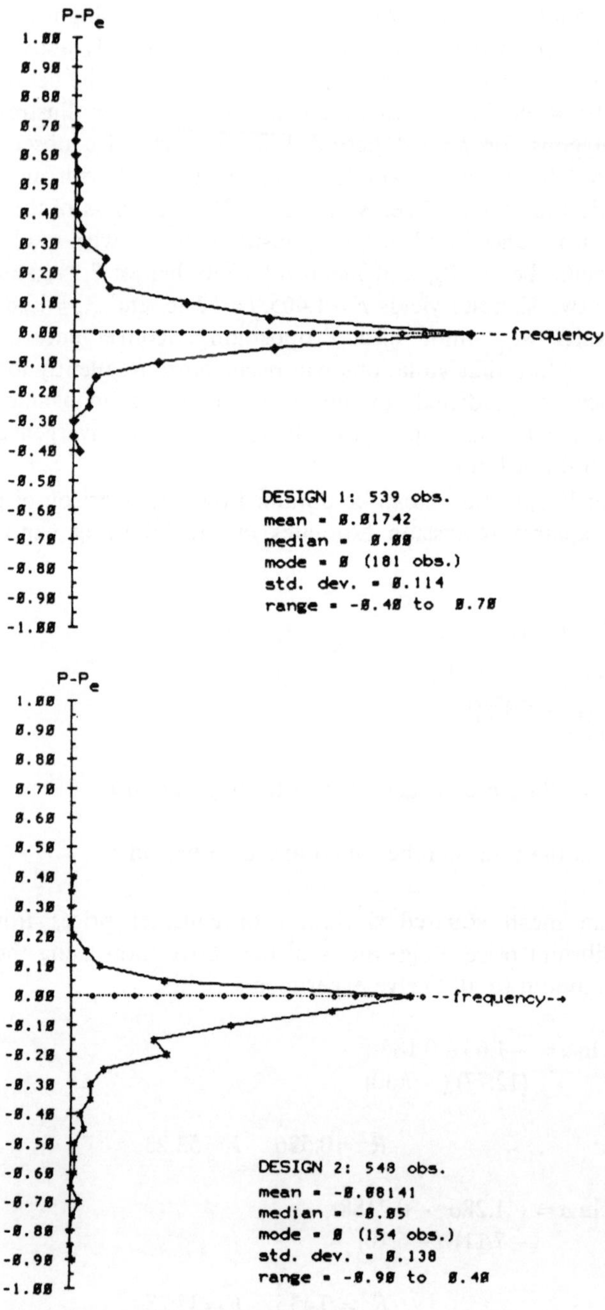

Fig. 6. Contract price frequency polygons.

the regression coefficient equals zero. An F test of the overall homogeneity of regressions (1) and (2) yields $F_{(2,92)}=2.12$. We may reject overall homogeneity at the 87.4% ($p=0.126$) level of confidence.

A pooled regression using all 96 observations and including a design dummy ($d=0$ if design 1, $d=1$ if design 2) yields

$$\ln\alpha = -1.56 - \underset{(-9.21)}{0.202t} + \underset{(1.91)}{0.191d}, \qquad \bar{R}^2 = 0.488, \quad F = 44.24. \tag{3}$$

The dummy is significant at $p=0.06$ indicating that we may reject the general empirical validity of Proposition 2. The inclusion of a $(t\times d)$ interaction term in regression (3) above indicates that the difference in the decay rates of $\alpha(t)$ is not significant ($p=0.437$). Thus the convergence paths of $\alpha(t)$ differ due to different starting points with the rate of convergence being nearly equal across designs. The difference between the two treatment groups is illustrated by fig. 7 which plots the unconstrained decay functions given by regressions (1) and (2).

Additional support for rejecting the validity of Proposition 2 is provided by a two-sample comparison of transformed raw price observations where for each observed contract price (P) we define

$$P' = (-1)^d(P-P_e) \quad \text{for } d=1 \text{ if design 1 contract,}$$
$$d=2 \text{ if design 2 contract.}$$

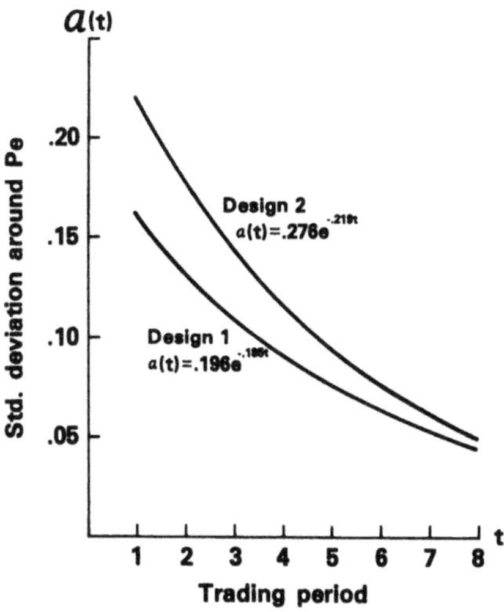

Fig. 7. Price convergence comparison.

Thus the sample distribution of design 1 price deviations from P_e (shown in fig. 6) is 'flipped' relative to P_e. Strict convergence symmetry implies that P' is identically distributed across designs. A comparison of pooled period 1–8 observations of P' from each design treatment yields $Z_u = 9.532$ ($t = 8.326$). The null hypothesis of identically distributed populations is easily rejected.

Another criterion for the comparison of the two treatment groups is trading efficiency (as defined in section 2). Table 3 presents the mean efficiency (E) in periods 1–8 for each treatment group. No significant difference in efficiency exist between the two groups of experiments. The figures in table 3 are consistent with a large body of experimental evidence which indicates that the double auction is an extremely efficient exchange institution in a wide variety of market environments.

A corollary of Proposition 1 is the proposition that in market designs with an equal number of buyers and sellers and *symmetric* consumer–producer surplus we will observe no systematic deviation of contract prices either above or below the CE price across experimental replications using different subject groups. In several previous experimental studies we have, in fact, conducted such experiments using both inexperienced and experienced subjects. An examination of price data from the initial trading periods of a four buyer, four seller, symmetric rent design [described in detail by Smith and Williams (1980)] yields mean prices that are not significantly different from P_e using either all experienced or all inexperienced subject groups. The sample sizes are around 20 observations per period. An examination of price data generated in the initial trading periods of sixteen replications of another symmetric rent design [see Smith and Williams (1981)] which used only experienced subjects (four buyers, four sellers) yields quite different results. Table 4 reveals that the mean price is significantly below the CE price in the

Table 3

Efficiency comparison.

Trading period	Mean efficiency	
	Design 1	Design 2
1	89.85	92.41
2	96.80	95.62
3	97.76	97.75
4	99.57	98.61
5	98.40	97.44
6	99.36	98.29
7	98.40	99.47
8	99.68	99.25
1–8	94.48	97.36

Table 4

Contract price information, symmetric design.

Trading period	Mean $(P-P_e)$	*s.d.*	No. obs.	t
1	−0.038	0.183	221	−3.12[a]
2	−0.029	0.131	228	−3.37[a]
3	−0.013	0.107	239	−1.82[b]
4	−0.014	0.102	240	−2.17[b]

[a]Significantly less than zero, $p=0.01$ (one tailed).
[b]Significantly less than zero, $p=0.05$ (one tailed).

first four trading periods. Note that the statistical significance is a large sample result; the means are only slightly below P_e. This result casts empirical doubt on the validity of assuming away the existence of an 'artifactual' or cultural bargaining bias within our subject population.

4. Parting comments

The empirical analysis reported in the preceding section reveals that rent asymmetries can have a significant effect on the price convergence path in auction market experiments organized under double-auction trading rules.[3] In general, price convergence to the competitive equilibrium will be from below if producer surplus exceeds consumer surplus and from above if consumer surplus exceeds producer surplus. Further, excesses of consumer over producer surplus appear to have less of an effect than excesses of producer over consumer surplus.

An initial step toward probing more deeply into the underlying process which generated these results was to look at the contract price distributions shown in fig. 6 broken down into the distribution of bids accepted by sellers and the distribution of offers accepted by buyers. We are interested in addressing the following empirical questions: (1) Do the distributions of accepted bids (accepted offers) differ significantly across treatment groups? (2) Does the distribution of design 2 accepted bids (accepted offers) differ significantly from the 'flipped' distribution of design 1 accepted bids (accepted offers)? (3) Is the ratio of accepted bids to accepted offers similar in both treatment groups?

Fig. 8 displays frequency polygons and associated descriptive statistics for a period 1–8 pooling of accepted bids in each treatment group. Fig. 9

[3]It is important to note that the double auction is only one of many methods of market organization. While our results clearly document the potential importance of the distribution of CE exchange surplus in determining the observed price convergence path, our specific conclusions should not be assumed to hold for alternative trading institutions in the absence of empirical confirmation. See Smith (1976, 1982) for a discussion of alternative trading rules and a summary of experimental results.

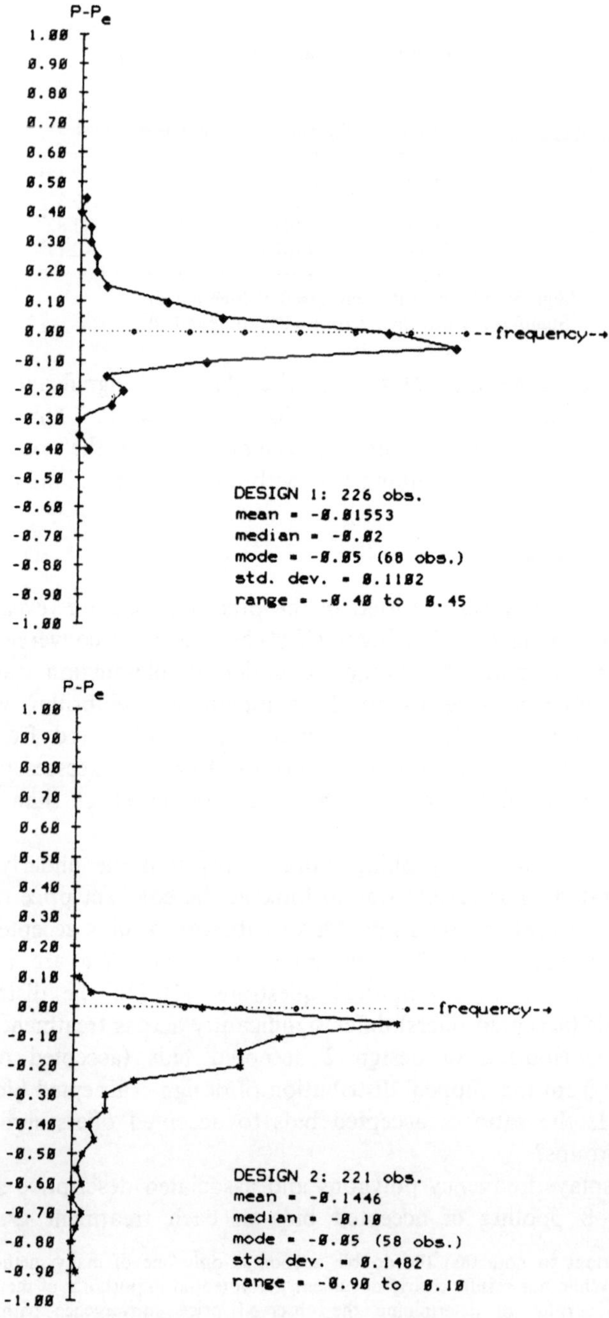

Fig. 8. Frequency polygons for accepted bids.

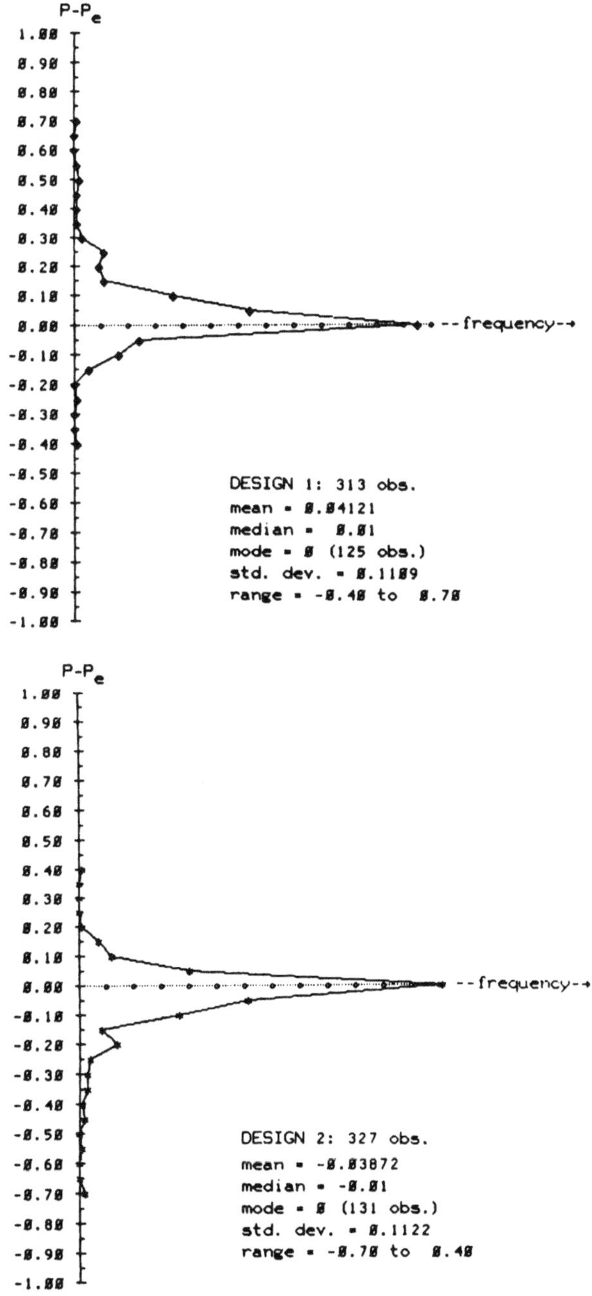

Fig. 9. Frequency polygons for accepted offers.

displays similar pooled frequency polygons and descriptive statistics for accepted offers. Both the accepted-bid and accepted-offer distributions are centered on a significantly lower price in the design 2 experiments ($t=10.46$, $Z_u=10.39$ for accepted bids; $t=9.06$, $Z_u=9.48$ for accepted offers). The distribution of accepted bids is shifted down by about 13 cents and the distribution of accepted offers by about 8 cents. The exchange surplus reversal appears to have a magnified effect on the acceptance behavior of sellers relative to buyers. A comparison of the period 1–8 bid distributions and offer distributions (both accepted and unaccepted quotations) yields similar results. The design 1 mean bid is $P_e-0.2011$ ($n=1539$) compared to a design 2 mean bid of $P_e-0.2708$ ($n=1659$); the difference is statistically significant ($t=4.114$). The design 1 mean offer is $P_e+0.2245$ ($n=1640$) compared to a design 2 mean offer of $P_e+0.0936$ ($n=1515$); the difference is highly significant ($t=9.57$). Thus, the design change affects the price initiative behavior of sellers more than buyers.

A period 1–8 comparison of the design 2 accepted-offer distribution and the design 1 'flipped' accepted-offer distribution yields $t=0.283$ ($Z_u=0.114$). The distributions are incredibly similar; rounding to the nearest penny they have identical means, medians, modes, variances, and ranges! In contrast with this result, a period 1–8 comparison of design 2 accepted bids and design 1 'flipped' accepted bids yields $t=12.98$ ($Z_u=13.24$). This clearly indicates that the invalidity of Proposition 2 (convergence symmetry) is almost entirely due to the relatively 'weak' acceptance behavior of sellers in the design 2 experiments.

58.07% of all design 1 contracts and 59.67% of all design 2 contracts were formed through buyers accepting sellers' offers, an observation which could be explained by the fact that most subjects' day-to-day market experiences are purchases made in retail stores organized under posted-offer pricing.[4] The fact that most subjects have much more experience with the role of a buyer than that of a seller may also explain the relative weakness of the sellers' bargaining behavior in the experiments.

[4]See Ketcham, Smith and Williams (1980) for a description of a PLATO computerized posted-offer pricing mechanism and an empirical comparison of the double-auction and posted-offer trading institutions.

References

Isaac, R. Mark and Charles R. Plott, 1981a, The opportunity for conspiracy in restraint of trade, Journal of Economic Behavior and Organization 2, 1–30.

Isaac, R. Mark and Charles R. Plott, 1981b, Price controls and the behaviour of auction markets: An experimental examination, American Economic Review 71, 448–459.

Ketcham, Vernon L. Smith and Arlington W. Williams, 1980, The behavior of posted-offer pricing institutions, Southern Economic Association Meetings, Washington DC, Nov. 5–7.

Plott, Charles R. and Vernon L. Smith, 1978, An experimental examination of two exchange institutions. Review of Economic Studies 45, 133–153.

Smith, Vernon L., 1976, Bidding and auctioning institutions: Experimental results, in Y. Amihud, ed., Bidding for procurement and allocation (New York University Press, New York).

Smith, Vernon L., 1982, Reflections on some experimental mechanisms for classical environments, in: Leigh McAllister, ed., Research in marketing, Supplement 1: Choice models for buyer behavior (J.A.I. Press, Greenwich, CT).

Smith, Vernon L. and Arlington W. Williams, revised 1980, An experimental comparison of alternative rules for competitive market exchange, to appear in Martin Shubik, ed., Auctions, bidding and contracting: uses and theory (New York University Press, New York).

Smith, Vernon L. and Arlington W. Williams, 1981, On nonbinding price controls in competitive market, American Economic Review 71, 467–474.

Smith, Vernon L., Arlington W. Williams, W. Kenneth Bratton and Michael G. Vannoni, 1982, Competitive market institutions: Double auctions vs. sealed bid-offer auctions, American Economic Review 72, 58–77.

Wall Street Journal 1980 (Sept. 12), SEC Hit by House Unit for Slow progress in Creation of National Securities Market.

Williams, Arlington W., 1980, Computerized double-auction markets: Some initial experimental results, Journal of Business 53, 235–258.

Microeconomic Systems as an Experimental Science

By VERNON L. SMITH*

Study nature, not books...
Louis Agassiz

After studying economics for six years I have reached the conclusion that there is no difference between discovery and creation...
[Graffiti by an unknown student]

The experimental literature contains only a few attempts to articulate a "theory" of laboratory experiments in economics (Charles Plott, 1979; Louis Wilde, 1980; my articles, 1976a, pp. 43–44, 46–47; 1976b; 1980). It is appropriate for this effort to have been modest, since it has been more important for experimentalists to present a rich variety of examples of their work than abstract explanations of why one might perform experiments. Wilde's contribution provides an integration and extension of the earlier papers, and brings a fresh perspective and coherence that invites further examination. This seems to be the time and place to attempt a more complete description of the methodology and function of experiments in microeconomics.

The formal study of information systems in resource allocation theory (Leonid Hurwicz, 1960) and the laboratory experimental study of resource allocation under alternative forms of market organization (Sidney Siegel and Lawrence Fouraker, 1960, Fouraker and Siegel, 1963; my 1962, 1964 articles) had coincident beginnings and, in important respects, have undergone similar, if mostly independent, intellectual developments. The similarity of intellectual development in these two new endeavors is represented by the increasing focus upon the role of institutions in defining the information and incentive structure within which economic outcomes are determined. While the (new)[2] welfare economics (Stanley Reiter 1977) was articulating a formal structure for the design and evaluation of allocation mechanisms (institutions) as *economic variables* (Hurwicz, 1973), experimentalists were comparing the performance of experimental economies in which the rules of information transfer and of contract appeared as *treatment variables* (Plott and myself, 1978; my 1964, 1976a articles). Since it is not possible to design a laboratory resource allocation experiment without designing an institution in all its detail, it was foreordained by the nature of the questions asked, that the work of experimentalists would parallel that of the (new)[2] welfare economics.[1]

In the sequel, the definition of a microeconomic system will be developed. Then the laboratory market or resource allocation experiment will be developed and discussed as an example of a microeconomic system. This framework will be used to provide a taxonomy for laboratory experimentation which allows the methods, objectives and results of such experiments to be interpreted and perhaps extended.[2] An important message of the paper which has been emphasized before (Plott, 1979, p. 141; my 1976b article, p. 275), but was articulated more satisfactorily by Wilde (1980), is that laboratory microeconomies are real live economic systems, which are certainly richer, behaviorally, than

*University of Arizona. I am grateful to the National Science Foundation for research support, and for many significant encounters over the years which have helped to shape my thinking about experimental microeconomy. Although any list is bound to omit some key sources of inspiration, in addition to the many authors cited in the references, I particularly want to mention Sidney Siegel, Jim Friedman, Charlie Plott, Martin Shubik, and Arlie Williams.

[1]Experimental microeconomics includes the study of individual choice behavior. For an excellent description of the methodology and some of the results from the experimental study of human and animal choice behavior, see the survey by John Kagel and Raymond Battalio (1980).

[2]Nothing in this paper will be very helpful to anyone desiring to learn the important techniques and mechanics of conducting experiments. For explanations of experimental procedures, it will be necessary to consult the references. But learning to run experiments is like learning to play the piano—at some point you have to start practicing. The classic model of good experimental technique is still to be found in Fouraker and Siegel (1963).

the systems parameterized in our theories. Consequently, it is important to economic science for theorists to be less own-literature oriented, to take seriously the data and disciplinary function of laboratory experiments, and even to take seriously their own theories as potential generators of testable hypotheses. Since "the discovery of new facts is open to any blockhead with patience and manual dexterity and acute senses" (attributed to Sir William Hamilton in N. R. Hanson, 1971, p. 23), it is equally important that experimentalists take seriously the collective professional task of integrating theory, experimental design, and observation.

I. Microeconomic System Theory

A. *Defining a Microeconomic System*

In defining a microeconomic system two distinct component elements will be identified: an environment and an institution.

1. *The Environment*

The environment consists of a list of N economic agents $\{1,\ldots,N\}$, a list of $K+1$ commodities (including resources) $\{0,1,\ldots,K\}$, and certain characteristics of each agent i, such as the agent's utility function u^i, technology (knowledge) endowment T^i, and a commodity endowment vector ω^i. Hence, the ith agent is characterized by the vector $e^i=(u^i,T^i,\omega^i)$ whose components are assumed to be defined on the $K+1$ dimensional commodity space R^{K+1}. Hence, a microeconomic *environment* is defined by the collection of characteristics $e=(e^1,\ldots,e^N)$. This specification defines the environment as a set of initial circumstances that cannot be altered by the agents or the institutions within which they interact. The reader should appreciate that by appropriate interpretation this definition does not rule out learning, that is, changes in preferences and/or technology. But if learning is to be part of the economic process, then one must specify agent preferences and technology in terms of learning (or sampling or discovery) activities. In this case the fixed environment would specify the limitations and search opportunities for altering tastes and knowledge in an economy with changeable tastes and resources. It should be noted that, in an experimental environment, e will include some circumstances that cannot be altered by the agents because they are control variables fixed by the experimenter—a matter to which I will return later.

A subtle but important feature of the environment deserves emphasis: the superscript i on the characteristic of each agent i means that the initiating circumstances in an economic environment are *in their nature private*. Tastes, knowledge, and skill endowments are quintessentially private: *I* like, *I* know, *I* work, and *I* make.[3]

2. *The Institution*

The above is no less true in societies with weak than in those with strong private property right systems. Whether private tastes matter little or are sovereign; whether or not an idea can be patented, copyrighted, or trademarked as alienable private property; and to what extent one has a property right in the fruits of one's "own" labor; these are all matters of the institution which is itself public in administration. It is the institution which specifies that soliciting for the purpose of prostitution is punishable by fines and imprisonment; that smoking in the hallway is to be allowed; that forms of indentured labor are prohibited (except in professional sports); that patents expire after seventeen years; that Ohm's law is not patentable; that price discrimination is illegal (except in the Treasury bill auction); that trespassers will be prosecuted; and that no one has the right to obstruct free use of the air by airlines above private land (except that, at one time, alcoholic beverages were not to be served in flights over Kansas).

It is the institution that defines the rules of private property under which agents may communicate and exchange or transform commodities for the purpose of modifying

[3] This does *not* mean that an individual's environmental state is autonomous and uninfluenced by others; it means merely that individual skills, knowledge, and willingness to work and buy are not publicly observable —only their consequences are observable.

initial endowments in accordance with private tastes and knowledge. Since all commodity exchange and commodity transformation must be preceded by interagent communication, *property rights in messages are as important as property rights in commodities or ideas*. Thus if stealing can lead to the charge of robbery or burglary, saying "your money or your life" can lead to the charge of attempted robbery. The institution defines the rights of private property which include the right to speak or not speak (you can't say "one hundred" at an auction unless you mean to bid $100), the right to demand payment or delivery, and the right to exclude others from use, that is, to "own." The institution specifies:

a. A *language* $M=(M^1,\ldots,M^N)$ consisting of messages $m=(m^1,\ldots,m^N)$, where m^i is an element of M^i, the set of messages that can be sent by agent i. A message might be a bid, an offer, or an acceptance. The allowable messages M^i for i need not be identical to M^j for j. Thus buyers may tender written bids at an auction, while the seller may have the right to offer or not offer an item for sale, but may not be allowed to bid on his own item or announce a reservation price.

b. A set $H=(h^1(m),\ldots,h^N(m))$ of *allocation rules* for each i. The rule $h^i(m)$ states the final commodity allocation to each i as a function of the messages sent by all agents. Since there may be an exchange of messages which precedes the allocation, m may refer to the final allocation-determining message.

c. A set $C=(c^1(m),\ldots,c^N(m))$ of cost *imputation rules*. The rule $c^i(m)$ states the payment to be made by each agent in numeraire units (money) as a function of the messages sent by all agents. Note that C is redundant in that it could be included in the definition of H, but it will be convenient in many applications (as when there are no income effects) to distinguish between commodity allocations by H and payment imputations by C.

d. A set $G=(g^1(t_0, t, T),\ldots, g^N(t_0, t, T))$ of *adjustment process rules*. In general, these rules consist of a *starting rule* $g^i(t_0,.,.)$ specifying the time or conditions under which the exchange of messages shall begin, a *transition rule* (or rules) $g^i(., t,.)$ governing the sequencing and exchange of messages, and a *stopping rule* $g^i(.,., T)$ under which the exchange of messages is terminated (and allocations are to begin).[4] For example, an English or progressive auction begins with an announcement by the auctioneer identifying the item to be offered for sale and calling for bids. The starting rule might also allow the seller to specify a reservation price. The transition rule requires any new bid to be higher than the previous standing bid. The stopping rule requires that no new overbid is obtained in response to a call from the auctioneer (for example, three calls for a "final" bid). In an unstructured bilateral negotiation, there is a starting "rule" in that bargaining cannot begin until there is a first bid or offer, and stops with an acceptance. Disputes concerning the negotiation process, and its outcome, are settled under the common law of contracts.

Each agent i's *property rights* in communication and in exchange are defined by $I^i=(M^i, h^i(m), c^i(m), g^i(t_0, t, T))$, which specifies the messages that i has the right to send; the starting, transition, and stopping rules which govern these communication rights; and finally the right to claim commodities or payments in accordance with the outcome rules that apply to messages. A microeconomic *institution* is defined by the collection of all these individual property right characteristics $I=(I^1,\ldots,I^N)$.

It should be noted that none of the above rules of an institution need be formal as in a body of written law. A rule can be simply a tradition as, for example, in the Eskimo polar bear hunting party in which the upper half of the bear's skin, prized for its long mane hairs, was awarded to the individual hunter who (at great personal risk) was the first to fix his spear in the dangerous prey (Peter Freuchen, 1961, p. 53.)

[4]Note that the arguments of $g^i(t_0, t, T)$ are public "goods" or characteristics, i.e., the rules governing communication are common to all participating agents. Hence, when comparing the performance of alternative institutions, we are comparing alternative common outcome states.

3. *A Microeconomic System*

A microeconomic environment together with a microeconomic institution defines a *microeconomic system*, $S=(e,I)$.

B. *Agent Behavior*

1. *Outcome Behavior*

A microeconomy is closed by the behavioral actions (choices) of agents in the message set M. In the static description of an economy we are concerned only with the final outcome choices in M. Thus agent i's *outcome behavior* is defined by a function $\beta^i(e^i \mid I)$ which yields the allocation-determining message m^i sent by agent i with characteristic e^i, given the property rights of all agents defined by I. The conditional-on-I notation in β^i is intended to denote that the behavior function β^i depends upon I, that is, is a member of a class indexed by I. The mapping β^i may represent a single message transmission as in a sealed-bid auction, or it may constitute the final result of an exchange of messages in an iterative process such as a negotiation session in the London gold bullion market which stops to yield transactions only when there is agreement (unanimity) (H. G. Jarecki, 1976). Note that the β^i functions generate the message-sending behavior of agents, which need not be based on preference maximization. The latter is a theory (hypothesis) about behavior that could be false.

The branches of the triangle diagram in Figure 1 (compare Stanley Reiter, 1977) illustrate the conceptual process in which, given the institution, the message m^i depends on agent characteristics e^i, and the messages sent by all i in turn determine, via the institution, the outcomes

$$h^i(m)=h^i\big[\beta^1(e^1|I),\dots,\beta^N(e^n|I)\big]$$

and $$c^i(m)=c^i\big[\beta^1(e^1|I),\dots,\beta^N(e^N|I)\big].$$

The import of all this is that agents do *not* choose direct commodity allocations. *Agents choose messages, and institutions determine allocations via the rules that carry messages into allocations.* There is a social process that culminates in exchanges. Every country auction has its own rules and procedures of sale. The New York Stock Exchange specifies the admissible form in which orders to buy or sell shares may be tendered to its broker members by investors—"at the market," limit price, "stop" orders, etc.—and also specifies a detailed list of auction rules governing communication and exchange at each trading post.[5] Within the applicable procedural rules, all markets involve "do-it-yourself" (Robert Clower and Axel Leijonhufvud, 1975) exchange.

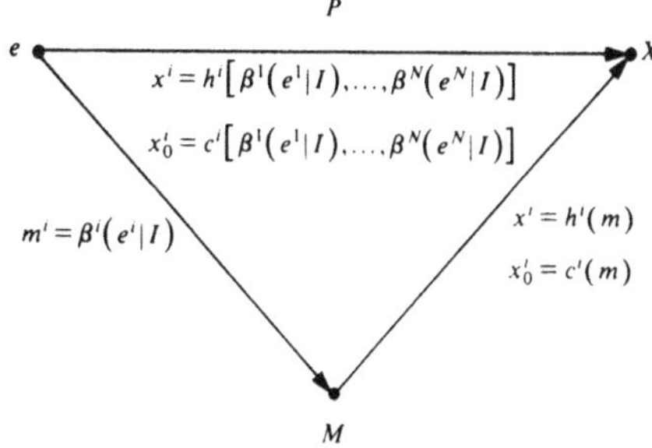

FIGURE 1. A MICROECONOMIC SYSTEM

2. *Response Behavior*

In the dynamic or process description of an economy we are concerned with, the exchange of messages in M that precedes the final allocation-determining messages. Agent i's *response behavior* is defined generically by a function f^i in the equation (compare Reiter, 1977)

$$m^i(t)=f^i\big(m(t-1)|e^i,I\big),$$

[5]In retail markets, sellers post offer prices, buyers respond by saying "I'll take it," but the result need not constitute an exchange as when the retailer has a stockout, or the chair is returned to the store after the customer finds that it does not match the living room rug. Institutions vary in the richness and composition of the message space. In stock and commodity markets, the items exchanged are simply defined and well standardized, but the message space is rich in the conditional bid, offer, and acceptance messages that can be sent. In retail markets, commodities are heterogeneous and rich in qualitative dimensions, which may help to explain why a price negotiation institution is not used.

which gives i's message response $m^i(t)$, at sequence point t, to earlier messages $m(t-1)$ by all agents. This response behavior might follow an optimal decision rule, a "rule of thumb," be random, or simply inexplicable. The starting rule triggers the first iteration of f^i, with subsequent messages given by f^i under the transition rules in I. The process stops with $m^i = m^i(T)$ when the stopping rule in I is actuated.

C. *System Performance*

Theorists view the framework we have been describing as one within which alternative resource allocation mechanisms can be evaluated. The traditional performance criterion is Pareto optimality, that is, the relation between outcomes in X (Figure 1) and microeconomic environments "should" be identical to the one provided by the Pareto correspondence criterion (P in Figure 1). Since utility functions and production possibility sets (technologies) are not observable, the evaluation of outcomes in X in terms of the Pareto criterion only has meaning in terms of the Pareto implications of a particular set of *assumptions* about preferences, technology, agent behavior, and institutions. Thus if certain standard conditions on the environment are satisfied, such as continuity and convexity, and if institutions and agent behavior correspond to those of the competitive mechanism, then the classical welfare theorems establish that the Pareto criterion is satisfied. In this literature, a *mechanism* can be defined as a formal theory or model of agent equilibrium behavior within some institution. Thus, in the competitive mechanism, agents maximize utility and profits given prices, and the "institution" (which is unspecified in the sense defined above) is assumed to produce market-clearing prices. An *adjustment mechanism* can be defined as a formal dynamic theory of a trading process for economic agents within some institution as defined above. Examples are the greed process (Hurwicz, 1960) and a stochastic trading process described by Hurwicz, Roy Radner, and Reiter (1975). In the latter, agents choose offers according to a fixed-probability distribution on the set of feasible trades for which utility will not be decreased. These offers are transmitted to a center where the institutional rules convert those offers which are compatible into binding contracts. The process is then iterated based on the commodity holdings prevailing after this transitional exchange. This process yields probabilistic convergence satisfying the Pareto criterion.

An important concept in the evaluation of a microeconomic system is that of incentive compatibility. In general, an institution's rules are *incentive compatible* if the information and incentive conditions that it provides individual agents are compatible with (i.e., support) the attainment of socially preferred outcomes such as Pareto optimality ($P.O.$). Specifically, in the theoretical literature, an allocation mechanism is incentive compatible if it yields Nash equilibria that are $P.O.$ This means that the *rules* specified in the *institution* in conjunction with the maximizing *behavior* of agents yields a choice of *messages* which constitute a Nash equilibrium whose *outcomes* are $P.O.$

A point which should be emphasized, because it bears on the relationship between laboratory experiments and the model of Figure 1, is the following. The mapping $h^i[\beta^1(e^1|I),\ldots,\beta^N(e^N|I)]$: $e \to m \to x^i$, is generated by any microeconomy, particularly an experimental microeconomy, provided that we have a methodology for systematically varying the elements of E (and also I, if institutions as variables are to be studied) and observing the consequent elements in M and X. This is important because there may *not* exist in all contexts (or in any) a satisfactory theory or hypothesis allowing derivation of the β^i functions. If we can experiment, then we are not bound to study *only theoretical* systems that carry E into X. Experiments permit stable patterns of behavior in relation to institutions to be identified and to motivate more explicit theories.

II. The Microeconomic Experiment

With the above background it is now possible to attempt to say something coherent about the role of the laboratory experiment in the study of microeconomic sysems. Although the concepts in the (new)^2 welfare economics have been used primarily to explicate a class of exercises in normative theory, my particular version of it in the schema of Figure 1 has been developed for the purpose of defining exercises in *measurement*, *hypothesis testing*, and the *comparative performance of institutions*.

A. *Field Observations and the Possibility of a Microeconomic Science*

1. *What is Observable?*

It will be useful as a starting point to ask which of the elements that compose the schema of Figure 1 are observable (in principle) in the field. Among the observable elements of an economy are (*i*) the list of agents, (*ii*) the list of physical commodities and resources, (*iii*) the physical commodity and resource endowments of individual agents, (*iv*) the language and property right characteristics of institutions, and (*v*) outcomes. What is not observable are (*vi*) preference orderings, (*vii*) technological (knowledge, human capital) endowments, and (*viii*) agent message behavior $\beta^i(e^i \mid I)$, $i = 1,2,\ldots,N$. These last elements are not observable because they are not only private, but to a degree *unrecorded*. Willingness to buy (preferences) and willingness to produce (technology and preferences) can at best only be inferred from agent point actions in the message space. Often we cannot even observe point messages, for example, we may know allocations and prices, but not all bids. In any case, we cannot observe the message behavior *functions* because we cannot observe (and vary) preferences.

As already noted, by making assumptions about preferences, technology, and behavior, we can "test" the logical consistency of such assumptions with the Pareto criterion. The empirical content of the assumptions, such as the monotonicity and convexity of preferences, tend to reflect idealizations, if not caricaturizations, of our *introspective* personal experience as economic agents.[6] But logical completeness laid upon a base of casual introspective "observations" cannot be sufficient to give us an understanding of the processes we would like to study. There is a vast difference between coherent conjecture (theory) and "true" (i.e., nonfalsified) knowledge of an observed process. If outcomes should turn out to be *P.O.* in the presence of certain institutions, we would like to know if we have predicted this property for the right reasons. If outcomes are not *P.O*, then it would be scientifically irresponsible not to be curious as to which part(s) of our theory is wrong and how to modify it.

2. *What Would We Like to Know?*

In terms of the schema of Figure 1 we would like to know enough about the economic environment, and about agent behavior in the presence of alternative institutions, to be able to classify institutions according to the mapping they provide from environments into outcomes. Are some institutions dependable producers of *P.O.* allocations? If so, how robust are these results with respect to changes in the environment? Do some institutions perform well for only certain classes of environments? If an institution performs well, are all its property right rules essential to this performance or are some redundant? Are some rules redundant for most environments, but become important under contingency conditions that involve unlikely changes in the environment?[7] These are just the tip of the great iceberg of questions that one would like to pose with some prospect of obtaining answers that are replicable, and (ultimately) insightful due to their theoretical coherence.

3. *Learning by "Listening to the Radio Play"*

Econometrics is and has been the mainstay of our attempts to fashion tools that enable us to learn what we would like to know. These tools have been developed primarily on the premises that (*i*) economics is a nonexperimental, or under certain limited cir-

[6]In this regard, it has not been clear that being an economic agent has had any advantages in the scientific study of economic behavior.

[7]For example, there are discretionary contingency conditions under which trading in a particular security is suspended for a time on the New York Stock Exchange, while on the Chicago Board of Trade, trading in a commodity is closed for the remainder of the day if price rises or falls from the previous day's close by a specified amount.

cumstances a field experimental, science, and (*ii*) preferences and technologies are not directly observable or controllable. It follows immediately from the discussion above that these premises prevent us from answering the most elementary scientific questions. What we can do with the tools of econometrics is the following: (*i*) We can specify a model of a market or markets based upon certain observable characteristics of the operant institution, on certain assumptions about preferences and/or technology, for example, Cobb-Douglas, fixed coefficients, *CES*, translog, etc., and upon some assumption about behavior, for example, static maximization of utility and/or profit. (*ii*) Using one of several different estimation procedures with different statistical properties, provided that the model is at least partially "identified," we can estimate, from data on outcomes, all or a subset of the parameters defined by the particular model that was specified. In other words, we can measure certain preference and/or technology parameters (income and substitution coefficients) and the effect of certain institutional rules (Did state law require or not require licensing? Did it prohibit or allow advertising by optometrists, etc.?). Furthermore, within the specifications of the model (the maintained hypothesis), we can test particular hypotheses about elasticities and income effects. Rarely are we able to obtain a test of the model specification. Hence, an econometric model provides a mapping from specifications into conclusions about preferences, technology, and institutions. Insofar as the conclusions are sensitive to the specifications, we are left with scientific propositions that are open-ended with respect to the environment, institutions, and agent behavior. Furthermore, since parameter identifiability and the properties of estimators depend upon model specification, the particular model chosen inevitably must be influenced partly by the technical requirements of the methodology and not only the scientific objectives of the exercise.

But these limitations of conventional econometric methodology have not foreclosed a positive contribution, which has been to allow us to deduce a great deal more information on economic structure from nonexperimental data than would otherwise be possible. Over twenty-five years ago, Guy Orcutt characterized the econometrician as being in the same predicament as that of an electrical engineer who has been charged with the task of deducing the laws of electricity by listening to a radio play. To a limited extent, econometric ingenuity has provided some techniques for conditional solutions to inference problems of this type.

But the econometric methodology is on particularly thin ice when the following scenario applies: Based on introspection, some casual observations of some process, and a contextual interpretation of the self-interest postulate, a model is specified and then "tested" by estimation using the only body of field data that exists. The results turn out to be ambiguous or call for "improvements" (some coefficients—for example, income—have the "wrong" sign or are embarrassingly close to zero), and now one is tempted to modify the model in ways suggested by these results to improve the fit with "reasonable expectations." Any tests of significance within the new model specification now become hopelessly confused if one attempts to apply it to the same data.[8,9]

The controlled field experiment is a recent development designed to relax some of the limitations of econometric methods when applied to the traditional sources of economic data. But the field experiment does not enable us to study the effect of controlled

[8] In effect, the whole process becomes an exercise in fitting a particular belief system to field data by manipulating model specification and perhaps estimation methods. There is nothing to prevent exactly the same procedure from being applied to experimental data. The difference is that one can always run another set of experiments. Also, the whole process, including the experiments, are subject to replication by another scholar. The skeptic with a different belief system can seek a set of "crucial" experiments that would enable the opposing hypotheses to be tested.

[9] Within professional econometrics, criticism such as this of naive econometric practice stretches back at least three decades, but recently the critique has grown louder, and constructive formal approaches have been offered in which, for example, the reporting procedures delineate the range of inferences that can be drawn from a given range of model specification (see Edward Leamer and Herman Leonard, 1981).

changes in preferences and/or technology. It does, however, provide important forms of control over institutional rules. Thus in a peak-load pricing experiment it is possible to vary pricing parameters and methods over a much larger range, and to sample scientifically a larger range of income and demographic variables than would occur naturally in ordinary consumer data obtained by "listening to the radio play." It is also possible to experiment with new and innovative pricing institutions. But one is still without control over preferences, and still unable directly to observe preferences and therefore behavior as a mapping from preferences to messages. That is, it is still necessary to interpret the data in terms of (*i*) assumptions about preferences, and (*ii*) assumptions about behavior (for example, static or dynamic maximization subject to constraint). Hence, it is *not possible* to evaluate alternative institutions in terms of their ability to produce optimal outcomes. But to the extent that one is interested in observed demand behavior (which may be underrevealing) with improved controls rather than evaluating the performance of institutions under alternative preference configurations, these limitations are not a valid criticism of the field experiment.

B. *Laboratory Experiments with Microeconomic Systems*

The fundamental objective behind a laboratory experiment in economics is to create a manageable "microeconomic environment in the laboratory where adequate control can be maintained and accurate measurement of relevant variables guaranteed" (Wilde, p. 138). "Control" and "measurement" are always matters of degree, but there can be no doubt that control and measurement can be and are much more precise in the laboratory experiment than in the field experiment or in a body of Department of Commerce data.

How laboratory experiments deal operationally with the problems of control, measurement, experimental design, and hypothesis testing is best seen by examining individual experimental studies. Attention here will be confined to a somewhat more abstract discussion of the principles and underlying precepts of experimental economics. In particular, the concept and objectives of a laboratory experiment will be related to the microeconomic model, consisting of an environment, an institution, and agent behavior, illustrated in Figure 1.

Returning to the question of what we would like to know tells us what we want to be able to accomplish with experiments. First we want to be able to control the elements of $S = (e, I) = (u^i, T^i, \omega^i; M^i, h^i, c^i, g^i)$. To control a variable means that we can fix and maintain it at some constant level, or, alternatively, set it at different levels across different experiments or at different points of time in the same experiment. Secondly, we want to be able to observe and measure the message responses of agents, m^i, and the outcomes h^i and c^i resulting from these messages. We want to measure outcomes because we want to be able to evaluate the performance of the system, S. We want to measure messages because we want to identify the behavioral modes, $\beta^i(e^i|I)$, revealed by the agents and test hypotheses derived from theories about agent behavior.

In order to accomplish these objectives, laboratory experiments must satisfy several conditions, which will be referred to as *precepts* of experimental economics. They are *not* to be regarded as self-evident truths, and therefore are not properly to be considered as axioms.[10] However, with the modifications proposed by Wilde, they do constitute a proposed set of sufficient conditions for a valid controlled microeconomic experiment. Applying (or testing) these conditions in the

[10] In reference to the precept parallelism (see subsection 1.f below), this has been misunderstood or misread as follows: "Smith treats this 'parallelism' virtually as an axiom, while Kagel and Battalio go even farther and extend the principle not only beyond the limits of the laboratory but across the boundaries of the human species as well" (John Cross, 1980, p. 403). The word precept rather than axiom was used to guard against any notion that these precepts were self-evident truths, rather than key conditions for experimental validity. The truth of these precepts can only be established empirically. It is hard to find an experimentalist who regards anything as self-evident, including the proposition that people prefer more money to less.

laboratory (and in parallel field studies) requires some skill and thoughtful consideration. The issues that have motivated these precepts are important to have in mind when designing and executing laboratory experiments.

1. *Sufficient Conditions for a Microeconomic Experiment*

Control over preferences is the most significant element distinguishing laboratory experiments from other methods of economic inquiry. In such experiments, it is of the greatest importance that one be able to state that, as between two experiments, individual values (or derivative concepts such as demand or supply) either do or do not differ in a specified way. This control can be exercised by using a reward structure and a property right system to induce prescribed monetary value on (abstract) outcomes.

a. *Precept 1: Nonsatiation*. The concept of induced valuation (see the examples in subsection c below) depends upon (compare my 1976b article):

Nonsatiation: Given a *costless* choice between two alternatives, identical (i.e., equivalent) except that the first yields more of a reward medium (for example, U.S. currency) than the second, the first will always be chosen (i.e., preferred) over the second, by an *autonomous* individual. Hence utility, $U(V)$, is a monotone increasing function of the monetary reward, $U' > 0$, where V is dollars of currency.

b. *Precept 2: Saliency*. In order that subject rewards in a laboratory experiment have motivational relevance such rewards must be associated indirectly with the message actions of subjects. This is called

Saliency: Individuals are guaranteed the right to claim a reward which is increasing (decreasing) in the goods (bads) outcomes, x^i, of an experiment; individual property rights in messages, and how messages are to be translated into outcomes are defined by the institution of the experiment.

This statement of saliency modifies that of Wilde (1980) which relates rewards to the decisions of subjects. This modification is necessitated by the distinction made here between outcomes and messages. *In both the field and the laboratory, value is induced on messages by the institution* whose rules state how messages are to be translated into valuable outcomes. In the field outcomes are valuable because they have "utility" (i.e., agents have preferences). But in the laboratory we also have to induce value on outcomes with a monetary (or other) reward function. Thus in an experiment, in addition to giving a subject certain property rights defined by the institution under study, we must also give the subject a property right to rewards that are related appropriately to the realized experimental outcomes, x^i.[11]

[11]It is sometimes said that the use of currency to induce value on abstract outcomes in a laboratory experiment may be an artificial procedure peculiar to experimental methodology and is not the same thing as having "real preferences." Those who raise this question seem not to realize that all economic systems produce forms of intangible property on which value is induced by specifying the rights of the holder to claim money or goods. All financial instruments, including shares, warrants, and fiat money itself, have value induced upon the instruments by the bundle of rights they convey. Subject rights to claim money in return for their purchase and sale of intangible experimental "goods" are defined by the experimental instructions. This procedure is exactly of the form used by the airlines when, for promotional purposes, they issued travel vouchers to their passengers. These travel vouchers conveyed a legal right to redemption by the bearer as a cash substitute in the purchase of new airline tickets. As a consequence, value was induced on these travel vouchers and they soon commanded an active market price in all busy airports. An airline ticket itself is an abstract claim. It is *not* equivalent to a seat on an airplane. It is a right to *claim* a seat under specified conditions, for example, you can't have a seat if none is available, or if you insist on carrying oversize luggage, or if you want to board with your pet tiger, or if you are carrying a Colt 45, and so on. An important part of the property right rules of any institution is the specification of the conditions under which intangible goods can be redeemed in terms of other intangibles or commodities. Arrangements like these were invented in the context of *field* institutions eons before I or anyone thought of doing laboratory experiments. What we experimentalists have done is to adapt these ingenious institutions to the problem of inducing controlled preferences in experimental microeconomies. Obviously, the reward medium may make a difference, but this is easily studied as a treatment variable by anyone who is haunted by the thought that it is important. But to argue that preferences based on cash-induced value is somehow different than homegrown preferences over commodities is also to argue that preferences among intangible instruments in the field are also somehow different than commodity preferences.

Not all rewards are salient. At the University of Arizona we pay subjects \$3 "up front" for agreeing to participate and arriving at the laboratory in time for the experiment. A second payment equal to a subject's cumulative earnings over the experiment, based on experimental outcomes, is paid when he/she leaves the laboratory. This second payment is a salient reward; the first is not.

c. *Examples and Discussion*. A few examples will be offered to illustrate the application of these precepts, and their role in driving an experimental economy.

Example 1. Suppose each of N subject agents are assigned the values $V_1, V_2, \ldots, V_N$ in dollars representing the currency redemption value of one unit of an abstract commodity to be sold at auction. The instructions to each subject state that the winner of the item at auction, say individual w, will have the unqualified right to claim $V_w - p$ dollars from the experimenter where p is the auction purchase price. Hence each i will have an incentive to pay as little as possible and yet win the item, but in no case pay in excess of V_i. If we assume that agents are numbered so that $V_1 > V_2 > \cdots > V_N$, then this ordered array of values represents the discrete induced (Marshallian) demand for units of the item, the supply of which is inelastic at 1.

Example 2. Consider the problem of inducing specified conditions of demand or supply on individual subjects in an isolated experimental market. Let subject buyers $i = 1, 2, \ldots, n$ each be given reward schedules $V_i(x^i)$ representing the currency redemption value of x^i units of an abstract commodity acquired by subject i in an experimental market. If x^i units are acquired by subject i, he/she has the right to claim $V_i(x^i)$ units of currency less the purchase cost of the x^i units, where $V_i(x^i)$ is increasing and concave in x^i. Demand is defined as the maximum quantity that can be purchased beneficially as a function of a given hypothetical price, p. Hence, if i purchases x^i units at the fixed price p, then i's currency earnings are given by $\pi_i(x^i) = V_i(x^i) - px^i$. If i's utility function for currency is $U_i(\pi_i)$, then from precept 1 subject i will wish to maximize $U_i[V_i(x^i) - px^i]$. An interior maximum results if and only if $(V_i' - p)U_i' = 0$, or $x^i = V_i'^{(-1)}(p)$, since $U_i' > 0$ and $(V_i' - p)^2 U_i'' + U_i' V_i'' = U_i' V_i'' < 0$.

This reward procedure induces the prespecified demand $V_i'^{(-1)}(p)$ on subject i. Hence, the experimentally controlled market demand is $\sum_{i=1}^{n} V_i'^{(-1)}(p)$ independent of the U_i, that is, we do not have to observe or know the U_i functions. In terms of my previous definition of a microeconomic environment, the market consists of two commodities, money x_0^i and one "good," x^i. In outcome space utility has the no-income-effects form $u^i(x_0^i, x^i) = U_i[x_0^i + V_i(x^i)]$ to be maximized subject to a budget constraint $\omega^i = x_0^i + px^i$ where the endowment $\omega^i = 0$, and $u^i = U_i[-px^i + V_i(x_i)]$.

Similarly on the supply side, let $j = n + 1, \ldots, N$ subject sellers be given increasing convex cost functions $C_j(x^j)$, and, assuming x^j units are sold at price p, let j be allowed to claim cash earnings equal to $\pi_j = px^j - C_j(x^j)$. If utility for money is $U_j(\pi_j)$, then j will want to maximize $U_j[px^j - C_j(x^j)]$ which implies the inverse marginal cost supply function $x^j = C_j'^{(-1)}(p)$. Total supply is then $\sum_{j=n+1}^{N} C_j'^{(-1)}(p)$, and is controlled by the experimenter through the choice of the C_j functions.

The induced total demand $\sum_{i=1}^{n} V_i'^{(-1)}(p)$ and total supply $\sum_{j=n+1}^{N} C_j'^{(-1)}(p)$ become flows per period in experiments conducted over a sequence of periods in which the valuation and cost schedules for each individual are repeated in each period. If p is a competitive equilibrium ($C.E.$) price, then the cash reward per period for each buyer (seller) is the "consumer's" ("producer's") surplus for each buyer (seller). Consequently, each experimental subject has the monetary equivalent of the motivation that we interpret as applying to economic agents in any market outside the laboratory.

Example 3. Let each subject i be given an increasing quasi-concave function (in tabular form) specifying currency receipts, $V^i(x_1^i, x_2^i)$, that can be claimed by i for terminal quantities of two abstract goods (x_1^i, x_2^i). Then i's unknown utility for currency $U_i(\pi_i)$ induces utility $u^i = U_i[V^i(x_1^i, x_2^i)]$ on the Euclidean point (x_1^i, x_2^i). These claim rights induce on subject

i the experimentally controlled indifference map given by the level contours of $V^i(x_1^i, x_2^i)$, independent of i's utility of money. That is, if $U_i' > 0$, i's marginal rate of substitution of x_2^i for x_1^i is given by[12]

$$dx_2^i/dx_1^i = -U_i'V_1^i/U_i'V_2^i = -V_1^i/V_2^i.$$

These examples all apply to classical environments (no externalities), but this should not be misread to mean that the methodology is similarly restricted.[13] Thus in example 3, the induced value function for i might be $V^i(x_1^i, X_2)$ where X_2 is a public good (common outcome) for all individuals (see my 1979 article); or induced value could be $V^i(x_1^i, x_2^i, x_2^j)$ if j's holding of good 2 is an externality to i; or induced value might be $V^i(x_1^i, \Sigma_{k=1}^N x_2^k)$ if the total quantity of good 2 is an externality for i. One's ability to induce any arbitrary pattern of valuation (including "altruistic" interdependence) is limited only by the imagination in inventing the appropriate set of claim conditions.

Three qualifications to the nonsatiation precept have been discussed by myself elsewhere (1980) under the heading of *complexity*. These qualifications arise because the subjects in an experiment are drawn from the population of economic agents and therefore can be expected to have all the characteristics of such agents. Two of these qualifications stem from the adjectives "costless" and "autonomous" in Precept 1, and provide the justification for introducing Precepts 3 and 4 below.

The first qualification, which could sever the link between monetary rewards and control over preferences in a laboratory experiment, is the possibility that economic agents may attach nonmonetary subjective cost (or value) to the process of making and executing individual decisions. The subjective cost of transacting, that is, the cost of thinking, calculating, and acting (compare Jacob Marschak, 1968), need not be inconsequential. In example 1, suppose the values $V_1, V_2, \ldots, V_N$ are drawn from a probability distribution known by the subjects. Suppose subject k receives a value V_k which almost certainly is among the lowest values drawn. This individual is very unlikely to win the item auctioned, and may be poorly motivated to take the auction seriously. If there is a cost to thinking and calculating one's bidding strategy, this effort may not be expended when a "low" value is assigned. Similarly, if it is arduous for an individual to monitor quotations, make counteroffers, and execute transactions in a continuous auction, then willingness to pay may not be measured by the marginal induced value function. Note that this description of the problem suggests that transactional effort is more naturally related to agent messages, m^i, than to institutionally determined outcomes, x^i.

These considerations can be illustrated in terms of the example 2 above. Suppose that subject buyer i who receives a monetary reward π_i must send m^i messages (for example,

[12]As noted in my 1973 paper, this induced-value procedure could be used to study general pure exchange equilibrium between two trading groups with or without a medium of exchange ("stage" money). For example, one could give $N/2$ subjects the endowments $\omega^i = (\omega_1^i, 0)$, $i = 1, 2, \ldots, N/2$, and the remaining $N/2$ subjects the endowments $\omega^j = (0, \omega_2^j)$, $j = (N/2)+1, \ldots, N$, and thus set up "Edgeworth Box" trading between two groups each with homogeneous tastes within the group. To quote from my 1973 paper, "Production and a producers market could be added by introducing production function tables and trading in claims on labor input endowments.... But note that in such a general equilibrium model one would not have to introduce profit tables for producer subjects, as in partial equilibrium oligopoly experiments.... The (payoff) functions of 'consumer' subjects would be the entire driving force of the economy, inducing value, through production, upon artificial labor input endowments" (p. 23).

[13]As, for example, when it is incorrectly claimed that an important assumption by experimentalists is that "individuals are motivated by self-interest" (John Chamberlin, 1979, p. 162), and, consequently, experiments "exclude important parts of 'political reality' in order to achieve internal validity" (p. 164). Nonsatiation requires people to prefer more money to less, whether they want to spend it, burn it, or give it to charity. Given nonsatiation, if we want to study the effect of preferences with the property that A gets positive (negative) satisfaction out of B's consumption, then we simply induce that preference property on A. When great care is used in an experiment to make induced value be the primary source of motivation, it is *not* for the purpose of making sure that subjects have a self-interested motivation; it is for the purpose that we *know* what were the preference patterns of the subjects in the experiment. It is not only fitting, but mandatory, that such preferences be interdependent if that is the purpose of the experiment.

bids) to obtain the reward π_i. The reward is commodious, but messages require discommodious effort. Assume the utility of money-with-effort is $U^i(\pi^i, m^i)$ where U^i is increasing in π_i but decreasing in m^i. Now let the purchase quantity depend on the messages sent according to the institutional rules, so that $x^i = h_i(m^i)$. Individual i now makes a costly choice by choosing m^i to maximize $U^i\{V_i[h_i(m^i)] - ph_i(m^i), m^i\}$. At a maximum we have $(V_i' - p)h_i'U_1^i + U_2^i = 0$, and the expression for induced demand becomes

$$x^i = V_i'^{(-1)}(p - U_2^i/U_1^i h_i') < V_i'^{(-1)}(p)$$

if $U_2^i < 0$, $h_i' > 0$. It follows that if there is a disutility associated with messages in the experimental task (i.e., with transacting through the institution to obtain outcomes), the induced demand is lower than in the absence of such a cost.[14]

d. *Precept 3: Dominance.* A condition sufficient to guarantee that we have not lost control over preferences has been suggested by Wilde (1980), namely,

> *Dominance*: The reward structure dominates any subjective costs (or values) associated with participation in the activities of an experiment.

This precept is suggested by the fact that the most common means of rendering nonmonetary task utilities inconsequential is to use payoff levels that are judged to be high for the subject population. The principle here can be seen by letting α be a scale parameter that determines reward level in the induced demand example. Then utility becomes $U^i\{\alpha V_i[h_i(m^i)] - \alpha ph_i(m^i), m^i\}$ and the resulting demand is $x^i = V_i'^{(-1)}\{p - U_2^i/U_1^i h_i'\alpha\}$. As α increases demand approaches $x^i = V_i'^{(-1)}(p)$ provided that $lim_{\alpha \to \infty} U_2^i/U_1^i h_i'\alpha = 0$. A sufficient condition for the latter is that the marginal rate of substitution U_2^i/U_1^i be nonincreasing in α.[15]

But high payoff levels are not the only means of satisfying the dominance precept. A second procedure is to pay a small "commission," say five or ten cents, for each subject's transaction.[16] For example, in the induced demand illustration if the "commission" is β, utility is $U^i\{V_i[h_i(m^i)] - (p - \beta)h_i(m^i), m^i]$, and demand is $x^i = V_i'^{(-1)}(p - \beta - U_2^i/U_1^i h_i') \cong V_i'^{(-1)}(p)$ if $-\beta \cong U_2^i/U_1^i h_i'$. Actually β can be thought of as a type of "nonsalient" reward in which the objective is to compensate for transactions cost and thus allow theories which abstract from transactions cost to be tested.[17]

e. *Precept 4: Privacy.* The second qualification to the nonsatiation precept which carries a potential for losing control over

[14] This suggests a kind of "principle of indeterminacy of induced preference," i.e., we know what are the induced preferences in a given experiment only within a margin of error which is determined by the subjective costs of individual choice in the message space. Although experimentalists have devised various ways of finessing this margin of error, one should always have the question of dominance (see below) in mind when designing and running experiments. Since these subjective costs are part of the cost of operating an institution, they should be viewed, not as a nuisance, but as part of the problem of comparative institutional analysis.

[15] An early path-breaking experimental study of the binary choice, or Bernoulli trials, game by Siegel (1961) systematically varied reward level. The results showed an increase in the proportion of reward maximizing choices when the reward level was increased for a constant task complexity. Furthermore, when the task complexity was increased holding reward level constant, this treatment reduced the proportion of reward maximizing choices.

[16] Plott and I (1978, pp. 143–44) report two experiments with identical induced supply and demand conditions but one experiment paid a commission in addition to earned surplus, while the second paid only earned surplus. In the first experiment (#3, p. 143), volume was always below (17–18 units) the competitive equilibrium quantity (20 units) while in the second experiment (#4, p. 144) volume was 19 units in one, and 20 units in seven of eight trading periods. An alternative to commissions has been used by myself and Arlington Williams (1981b) in which the design permits a range of *C. E.* prices to be defined. Within this range, trades with positive gains between all intramarginal buyers and sellers are possible, and each individual reveals his/her supply price of transacting.

[17] A third procedure can be directly inferred from the Siegel (1961) results, namely to design the procedures, displays and computing aids of an experiment so as to make the experimental task as simple and transparent for the subject as is possible without, of course, compromising the essential features of the institution under study. That is, task complexity may be an important part of the *difference* between two institutions in which case such features must be preserved. But if a computing or display aid is used to simplify the subject's task in experiments comparing two institutions, one should use the same aid in both institutional treatments.

preferences is the fact that individuals may not be autonomous own-reward maximizers. Interpersonal utility considerations may upset the achievement of well-defined induced valuations. Thus subject i's utility may depend upon both i and j's reward, or $U^i[\pi_i, \pi_j] = U^i[V_i(x^i) - px^i, V_j(x^j) - px^j]$ in the induced demand example. If this "consumption" externality condition prevails, then i's induced demand will not be independent of j's demand. However, this kind of interdependence is effectively controlled by the experimental condition of "incomplete" information, first defined and studied by Siegel and Fouraker (1960) in experimental studies of bilateral bargaining. Under incomplete information subjects are informed only as to their own payoff contingencies. This leads to a precept that, following Wilde (1980), I call

Privacy: Each subject in an experiment is given information only on his/her own payoff alternatives.

Induced value privacy would be an important experimental condition to reproduce in the laboratory quite apart from the technical requirement of controlling interagent payoff externalities. This is because privacy is a pervasive characteristic, in varying degrees, of virtually all market institutions in the field. Keep in mind that monetary rewards for nonsatiated subjects in the laboratory have the same function that commodity utility indicators (preferences) serve in field microeconomies. In field microeconomies we never observe the preferences of others.[18]

A third qualification to the nonsatiation precept causes no difficulties in inducing value. As with their counterparts in the economy, experimental subjects may attach "game value" to experimental outcomes (as to messages). Thus winning the item at auction may be joyful quite apart from the satisfaction obtained from possessing or consuming the item. Consequently, in an experiment a make-believe "point" profit $V_i(x^i) - px^i$ may have subjective value $S_i[V_i(x^i) - px^i]$. If S_i is monotone increasing in "points," then such gaming utilities reinforce rather than distort the effect of any explicit reward structure. This qualification would hardly merit mentioning except that it explains why results consistent with maximizing behavior are sometimes obtained in experiments with no monetary rewards. Some evidence indicating that experimental results are less consistent under replication over time, when no rewards or only random rewards are used, is provided in my article (1976b, pp. 277–78).[19]

f. *Precept 5: Parallelism.* Nonsatiation and saliency are sufficient conditions for the existence of an experimental microeconomy, that is, motivated individuals acting within the framework of an institution, but they are not sufficient for a *controlled* microeconomic experiment. For this we also must have dominance and privacy, since individuals may experience important subjective costs (or values) in transacting, and may bring invidious, egalitarian, or altruistic cannons of taste to the laboratory from every day social economy. Precepts 1–4 permit us to study laboratory microeconomic environments in which real economic agents exchange real messages through real property right institutions that yield outcomes redeemable in real money.

Insofar as we are only interested in testing hypotheses derived from theories, we are done, that is, Precepts 1–4 are sufficient to provide rigorous controlled tests of our abil-

[18]It might be thought that privacy should not apply where subjects function as firms in a market experiment in which they are assigned cost functions since costs can be observed from corporate published records in the field. But this is not a correct interpretation because assigned (marginal) cost functions in an experiment represent well-defined willingness-to-sell schedules, and subject earnings (exclusive of "commissions") exactly measure realized producer's surplus. Corporate records yield accounting costs and accounting profits which differ for different purposes (stockholder reporting, income taxation, regulatory reporting); the relation between such measures and willingness to sell is obscure if not misleading.

[19]If gaming utilities are associated with messages instead of outcomes, the problem may be more serious and is formally equivalent to the problem of subjective transaction cost discussed above, i.e., messages may yield subjective utility rather than disutility and this may compromise our control over induced valuation. Of course, the same phenomena are evident in nonlaboratory economies when people enjoy their jobs, like trading futures, or prefer Dutch to English auctions because of the "suspense" experience in Dutch auctions.

ity as economists to model elementary behavior. Microeconomic theory abstracts from a rich variety of human activities which are postulated not to be of relevance to human economic behavior. The experimental laboratory, precisely because it uses reward-motivated individuals drawn from the population of economic agents in the socioeconomic system, consists of a far richer and more complex set of circumstances than is parameterized in our theories. Since the abstractions of the laboratory are orders of magnitude smaller than those of economic theory, there can be no question that the laboratory provides ample possibilities for falsifying any theory we might wish to test.

Once replicable results have been documented in laboratory experiments, one's scientific curiosity naturally asks if these results also apply to other environments, particularly those of the field. Since economic theory has been inspired by field environments, we would like to know, if we were lucky enough to have a theory fail to be falsified in the laboratory, whether our good luck will also extend to the field. Even if our theories have been falsified, or if we have no theory of certain well-documented behavioral results in the laboratory, we would like to know if such results are transferable to field environments.

A sufficient condition for this transferability of results can be summarized as a final precept (compare my 1980 article).

Parallelism: Propositions about the behavior of individuals and the performance of institutions that have been tested in laboratory microeconomies apply also to nonlaboratory microeconomies where similar *ceteris paribus* conditions hold.

Harlow Shapley (1964, p. 67) has applied the term "parallelism" to the similarity of evolutionary steps and attained ends in earth animals, but I use the term more comprehensively to generalize the important conjecture that "as far as we can tell, the same physical laws prevail everywhere" (Shapley, p. 43). The data of astronomy and meteorology, like those of economics, fall into the category of "listening to the radio play," but scientific progress in both astronomy and meteorology has depended on the maintained hypothesis that the physics of mass motion and the thermodynamic properties of gases studied in laboratory experiments have application to the stars and the climate. The abundance of opportunities to make nonexperimental measurements in astronomy and meterology that have not yet contradicted these physical laws means that this maintained hypothesis is yet to be falsified.

In biology, parallelism means that if tobacco smoke, or injected tobacco tars, produce more cancer tumors in treatment group rats than in control group rats, then the likelihood is increased that the greater incidence of lung cancer in human cigarette smokers is due to the cigarette smoke and not to some spurious characteristic of cigarette smokers. Obviously parallelism does not state that all mammals are subject to the same maladies; that hydrogen atoms exhibit the same excitation state in the sun's interior as on the earth's surface; or that Northern Hemisphere storms are indistinguishable from Southern Hemisphere storms. In each of these cases the appropriate proposition requires narrower *ceteris paribus* conditions. Only man, chimpanzees, and monkeys are susceptible to Type 1 polio virus infection; the excitation state of hydrogen atoms depends on temperature; and Northern Hemisphere meteorological conditions differ from those of the Southern Hemisphere. *Which kinds of behavior exhibit parallelism and which do not can only be determined empirically by comparison studies.*

What parallelism hypothesizes in microeconomy is that if institutions make a difference, it is because the rules make a difference, and if the rules make a difference, it is because incentives make a difference. That is, whatever the context of the particular microeconomy—the laboratory (using induced values), the primary market for U.S. Treasury bills, or the auctioning of scarce job interview slots among Chicago Business School graduates whose bids are denominated in "points," and constrained by a fixed endowment of such points—parallelism says that the incentive effects of different bidding rules are qualitatively the same;

if rule A produces lower bids than rule B in one market, it will do so in other markets.[20] Will these incentive effects be the same quantitatively? The answer is likely to be "no" unless the different microeconomies are comparable in terms of the types of bidders, the stakes involved, and so on. The more narrowly defined is the alleged parallelistic phenomena, the more narrowly defined must be the *ceteris paribus* conditions across the different microeconomies. If one is interested in parameter estimation, as in a field experiment with the negative income tax, with the idea of applying the estimates to a population, then the representativeness of the sample is of obvious importance. But if one is testing a theory which assumes only that economic agents are motivated to bid so as to maximize expected utility, any sample of agents not likely to be saturated in money is sufficient to initiate a program of research. If the theory is not falsified in several replications, then one can begin to ask whether the results generalize to different subject pools and to field environments. But what is most important about any particular experiment is that it be relevant to its purpose. If its purpose is to test a theory, then it is legitimate to ask whether the elements of alleged "unrealism" in the experiment are parameters in the theory. If they are not parameters of the theory, then the criticism of "unrealism" applies equally to the theory and the experiment. If there are field data to support the criticism, then of course it is important to parameterize the theory to include the phenomena in question, and this will affect the design of the relevant experiments.

The appropriate way to falsify parallelism with respect to some particular aspect of behavior is to show that some replicable property of a theory or institution in a laboratory microeconomy is falsified with field data. A few parallel studies have been reported by John Ferejohn, Robert Forsythe, and Roger Noll (1979), Michael Levine and Plott (1977), and myself (1980). In these cases the results are reassuring in the sense that there are several laboratory findings that appear also to characterize nonlaboratory microeconomies. But more such studies are welcome, and are necessary, if answers of substance are to be provided to questions of parallelism.

In terms of the evidential standards and precedents that have been established in this literature, it is not appropriate to list reasons (unencumbered by documentation) why experimental situations might be different from what one imagines might be important about "real world" behavior (Cross, p. 404). Speculation about a list of differences between two microeconomies (laboratory or nonlaboratory) is not the same thing as showing empirically that the microeconomies exhibit different behavior and that this is because of factors appearing in the list. Nor is it likely that experimentalists will be diverted from their work by "an approach to research in economics alternative to experiments... called the phenomenological approach" in which the leading example cited is that of the discredited[21] "Phillips curve a simple empiri-

[20]Parallelism has been criticized because it "specifies *ceteris paribus* conditions without naming the variables which are required to be held constant" (Cross, 1980, p. 404). The answer is that the variables to be held constant are those that were constant in the laboratory experiments whose results are alleged to apply to nonlaboratory microeconomies. Such a list is always well defined in advance by the initiating studies and therefore it is ingenuous to conclude that "Given such broad residual powers to restrict the applicability of the principle, counter-examples to the proposition would certainly be hard to defend" (p. 404). Thus, in experiments that compare the incentive effects of discriminative and competitive auctions (Propositions 3 and 14 below), subjects are drawn from the same subject pools, and induced values are drawn from the same distribution under the same information conditions. Clearly, if preferences and/or the population of bidders is different in two nonlaboratory (or any) environments, these differences may swamp any incentive differences due to the different auction rules. But many experiments have established that some behavioral laws are robust with respect to changes in preferences and the type of subjects, in which case this fact would become the (less restrictive) working hypothesis to be tested in nonlaboratory environments. In the context of parallelism, *ceteris paribus* means the same thing that it does in demand theory when we say that the effect of price on the demand quantity may be dominated by the effect of income if the latter is allowed to vary.

[21]See Robert Lucas (1981) for a discussion of the status of the Phillips curve doctrine. The Phillips curve

cal regularity" (Frank Stafford, 1980, p. 408). It is this type of example that motivated some of us long ago to begin exploring experimental methods.

2. *An Example of a Microeconomic Experiment: Two Sealed-Bid Auction Institutions*

An example of a simple laboratory experiment will be used to illustrate the definition of a microeconomic system developed in Section I. As noted above nonsatiation and saliency are sufficient to allow such an experiment to be defined.

a. *An Experimental Microeconomy with Two Institutional "Treatments."* Consider experiments in which a single unique item is to be sold in a sealed-bid auction organized under the alternative first and second price sealed-bid auction rules (William Vickrey, 1961).

(*i*) Environment: There are $N>1$ subject agents. The unique item is offered for sale (by the experimenter) at zero cost (i.e., is offered inelastically). Each i knows that the values V_k for all k are independent drawings from the uniform density $(\bar{V})^{-1}$ on $[0,\bar{V}]$. Initially, each i knows his/her own V_i but does not know V_j, for all $j \neq i$. Hence $e^i = (V_i, \bar{V}, N)$.

(*ii*) Agent property rights in message space: The language M consists of bids in dollars for the unique item. One and only one bid is admissible by each individual. Thus $m^i = b_i$ is i's bid in dollars, $0 \leqslant b_i < \infty$, $i = 1,\dots,N$. Let the bids be numbered so that $b_1 > b_2 \dots > b_N$ (assuming no ties). Then $m = (b_1,\dots,b_N)$ is the set of messages sent by N agents.

(*iii*) Agent property rights in outcome space: I identify two distinct institutions.

The first price auction. Define $I_1 = (I_1^1,\dots,I_1^N)$, where $I_1^1 = [h^1(m)=1;\ c^1(m) = b_1]$, $I_1^i = [h^i(m)=0;\ c^i(m)=0]$, $i>1$, that is, the item is awarded to the first (highest) bidder and all other i get nothing; the first bidder pays what he/she bid and all other i pay nothing.

The second price auction. Define $I_2 = (I_2^1,\dots,I_2^N)$, where $I_2^1 = [h^1(m)=1;\ c^1(m) = b_2]$, $I_2^i[h^i(m)=0;\ c^i(m)=0]$, $i>1$, that is, the item is awarded to the first bidder at a price equal to the amount bid by the second highest bidder. All others receive and pay nothing.

(*iv*) Agent property rights in rewards: If $i=1$, the experimenter guarantees the payment $V_1 - b_1$ (or b_2) to agent 1. If $i>1$, the payment is 0 to i.

b. *Agent Behavior.* Agent behavior carries the environment e^i into bids b_i depending upon the institution I_i. If i is assigned value V_i, then $e^i = [V_i, \bar{V}, N]$ and agent behavior *as observed* is

$$b_i = \hat{\beta}^i[e^i \mid I] = \begin{cases} \hat{\beta}_1^i[e^i], & \text{if } I = I_1, \quad \forall i. \\ \hat{\beta}_2^i[e^i], & \text{if } I = I_2, \quad \forall i. \end{cases}$$

The information state of the environment also allows a Nash equilibrium (*N.E.*) *theory* of agent behavior to be specified. If i has constant relative risk aversion r_i (unobserved by the experimenter), that is, the utility of money to i is $[V_i - b_i]^{r_i}$, then individual i's *N.E.* bid is (see Cox, Roberson, and myself, 1982) given by

$$b^i = \beta^i[e^i \mid I] = \begin{cases} \dfrac{(N-1)V_i}{N-1+r_i}, & \text{if } I = I_1, \quad \forall i. \\ V_i, & \text{if } I = I_2, \quad \forall i. \end{cases}$$

In the first price auction, the *N.E.* strategy is to bid a constant proportion of one's value

literature is a good example of the incredible life that an economic system of belief can enjoy in the absence of a rigorous methodology of falsification. The methodology of curve fitting with data which do not change much from year to year elevated the Phillips curve to an "empirical regularity" that would still be riding the crest of "fine-tuned" policy were it not for the fact that "nature" (perhaps aided by such policy) finally gave us the "crucial" national experiment in which both inflation and unemployment were so outrageously high that belief in the tradeoff doctrine was no longer sustainable outside of a coterie of devout disciples. For me, the doctrine expired its last gasp in 1971 when in a lecture by a prominent economist it was concluded that the Phillips curve had shifted and that we now had to accept a higher inflation rate to achieve the targeted unemployment rate. At that point it became clear that the whole doctrine was like that of the earth-centered universe which could accommodate any new observation by a Ptolemic juggling of the epicycle via the device of introducing a "movable eccentric" (Arthur Koestler, 1963, p. 67).

depending upon N and r_i. In the second price auction the $N.E.$ strategy (also a dominant strategy equilibrium) is to submit a bid equal to value, that is, to fully reveal demand independent of N and r_i.

c. *System Performance*. Suppose the experimental economy consists of T trials $t = 1,\ldots,T$. One measure of performance might be the percentage of all awards which were to the highest value bidder (the percentage of $P.O.$ awards), T_P/T, where T_P is the number of auctions in which the highest bidder also had the highest value.

Efficiency can be defined as $V_w(t)/V_h(t)$ where $V_w(t)$ is the value drawn by the winning bidder and $V_h(t)$ is the highest value in auction t. A second measure of performance is mean efficiency across T auctions, $\bar{E} = T^{-1}\Sigma_{t=1}^{T} V_w(t)/V_h(t)$.

III. Types of Microeconomic System Experiments

There are many ways of classifying experiments (Abraham Kaplan, 1964, pp. 147–54). I propose to keep things straightforward in this section by considering only two broad classifications—functional and methodological. The functional classification of experiments follows directly from my definition of a microeconomic system. The methodological classification will be limited to only a few very comprehensive categories which can be readily identified in the experimental economics literature.

A. *A Functional Classification of Experiments*

The universe of "interesting" experiments is defined naturally by the set of all possible or feasible elements of a microeconomic system (i.e., if S_e is the set of all environments, and S_I the set of all institutions, this universe is the product of S_e and S_I). Since an experiment yields observations on elements in X and in M, what classes of experiments can we conduct? We can do experiments in which (A) the environment is a variable or (B) the institution is a variable. Within either of these classes, we can compare system performance (outcomes) or individual behavior (messages). For any environment and institution, we can do experiments which (C) compare outcomes (or messages) with a theory or theories. Essentially hypothesis testing directed at theory falsification is a type of comparison in which one or more sets of outcomes (or messages) in the comparison are predicted by theory(ies). Consequently, in all experimental studies we are in some sense making comparisons—comparing observed outcomes arising from different environmental or "institutional treatment" conditions, or comparing observed with theoretical predicted outcomes.

Examples of experimental studies in which the environment is varied include (i) the extensive oligopoly studies by Fouraker and Siegel (1963), and James Friedman and Austin Hoggatt (1980) in which the number of participants and the cost or demand conditions are varied, (ii) the speculation experiments of Miller, Plott, and myself (1977), and Williams (1979) in which demand is varied in a cyclical "seasonal" pattern, and (iii) the committee decision experiments reported by Morris Fiorina and Plott (1978) in which the committee size and induced preferences were varied. Experiments comparing different institutions of contract include (i) studies of the effect of discriminative versus uniform pricing (see Section IV.C) on the bids (messages) submitted and the outcomes in sealed-bid auctions (my 1967 article), (ii) a comparison of outcomes in Dutch and English auctions (V. Coppinger, myself, and J. Titus, 1980), and (iii) studies of the effect of binding or nonbinding price ceilings or floors in continuous double auction trading (see Section IV.B) (R. Mark Isaac and Plott, 1981a; myself and Williams 1981a).

Studies in which both the environment and the institution are varied include (i) a comparison of markets with and without speculation under cyclical demand (Williams, 1979), (ii) comparisons of discriminative versus uniform price rules under alternative induced demand conditions (Miller and Plott, 1980), and (iii) comparisons of first and second price sealed-bid, and Dutch auctions using different numbers of bidders (Cox, Roberson, and myself, 1982).

Experiments comparing observed outcomes with theoretical outcomes or predictions include (i) the bilateral bargaining experiments of Fouraker and Siegel (1963) comparing observed outcomes with the Bowley-Nash theory predictions, (*ii*) the public good experiments reported in my 1979 article comparing observed outcomes with the Lindahl and free-rider theories, and (*iii*) the asset market experiments of Plott and Shyam Sunder (1982) comparing experimental outcomes with the predictions of rational expectations theory.

B. *Methodological Classification of Experiments*

Philosophers of science (see, for example, Karl Popper 1959; Hanson 1969, 1971; Kaplan 1964) have written extensively on scientific methodology, particularly experimental methodology. Although most of this work relates to the physical sciences, the main features apply to any experimental effort. An insightful perspective is provided by considering various kinds of microeconomic experiments in terms of their methodological objectives (compare Kaplan, pp. 147–54).

1. *Nomothetic Experiments — Establishing the "Laws" of Behavior*

These are the law-giving experiments that employ replication and rigorous control to reduce error in testing well-defined hypotheses. Nomothetic experiments provide the most compelling and objective means by which each of us, as scientists, comes to see what others see, and by which, together, we become sure of what it is that we think that we know. It is useful to distinguish between nomo-theoretical experiments, concerned with establishing laws of behavior through a process of testing theories, and nomo-empirical experiments designed to test propositions about behavior that are suggested by observed empirical regularities in field data or pilot experiments.

a. *The Importance of Theory*; *When does the Priest Wear Robes*? Theory is fundamental to scientific methodology for three reasons:

(*i*) Theory economizes on the statement of behavioral regularities. It is a shorthand way of summarizing more detailed and complex descriptions. Thus Newton's theory (the inverse square law of attraction) provides a much simpler statement than defining an ellipse and explaining that this is the orbit of a planet around the sun, explaining that the distance traversed by a falling body is proportional to the square of the time of descent, and so on. These and many more terrestrial and solar system observations were shown to be deducible from the simple inverse square law.

(*ii*) Theory brings a coherence—an underlying pattern or rationale—that integrates otherwise diverse observations and phenomena into a single whole. Wo(men) experience this result as a liberating understanding (Eureka!) of the whole that is easier to comprehend, to appreciate, to impart to the uninitiated. Thus plate tectonic theory provides an explanation of the worldwide pattern of earthquake activity, and of volcanic activity; explains why the geology of the continents differ from that of the ocean floor; provides one rather than a hierarchy of anecdotal explanations of mountain formation; and also accounts for geophysical data on the earth's interior. In the space of twenty years, this new (general equilibrium?) theory has ignited a renaissance of interest and research in the geological sciences (see, for example, C. L. Drake and J. C. Maxwell, 1981).

(*iii*) Theory can chart the path to new observations based upon predictions of phenomena or events for which there was previously no special motivation or search. Thus the theory that the late Pleistocene wave of large animal extinctions was due to paleo hunter cultures (Paul Martin, 1967) has accelerated the search for evidence that early man may have predated these extinctions in North America. Similarly, a variety of new particles have been predicted by theory, then discovered, in modern physics.

The crowning success of theory in the physical sciences, which is associated so dramatically with Newtonian physics, has elevated theory to the pinnacle of respect, and theorists to an undeclared priesthood in most of the sciences. Yet theory achieves its scientific importance only when closely allied with observation (and, ultimately, vice versa).

Newtonian mechanics created a scientific revolution, not because of the aesthetic beauty of the inverse square law, but because it acccounted for two distinct bodies of observation: Galileo's experimental law of falling bodies, namely that the distance traversed was proportional to the square of the time of fall; and Kepler's three laws of planetary motion distilled from a lifetime of study of the mass of astronomical observations recorded with astonishing accuracy by Tycho Brahe (Koestler, 1963, pp. 496–509). Newton showed that these (and other) empirical laws were derivable from one theoretical gravitational law of attraction—an intellectual triumph which easily established him as the founder of theoretical physics. But it was Galileo who is associated with the necessity of investigating the *how* of things before attempting to explain the *why* of things, and who thereby was enshrined as the founder of modern physics. "The introduction of this point of view really marks the beginning of modern science, and it is to it that the remarkable scientific developments since the sixteenth century have been largely due" (Millikan, Roller and Watson, 1937, p. 3). That this is a metaphorical image of Galileo has been made clear by modern historians of science. However, as noted by Robert Butts, "It also seems to me true that although Galileo did not invent experimentation, he did most importantly modify the epistemological point of doing experiments" (1978, p. 59).

The Galileo-Kepler laws contained the same information as did Newton's law. What was missing in the former was the nifty but insightful interpretation of the latter.

b. *The Necessity for Replicable Empirical Laws—Would You Scale a Mountain Without a Rope?* The priority importance of Galileo's experimental law to the Newtonian system is evidenced by the countless experiments which later confirmed Newton's theory. Indeed, perturbations in the planet Mercury were inconsistent with the Newtonian system so that it was actually the evidence from experimental mechanics that made Newton credible. Only later was the Mercury puzzle explained by Einstein's relativity theory extending the Newtonian mechanics. Ultimately, sophisticated experiments have confirmed that Newton's theory was only an approximation, albeit a good one at "ordinary" velocities small relative to the speed of light. Hence new ropes have made it possible for physics to scale new heights. But, it is the rope that allows the new position to be sustained, lays the basis for a new ascension, and occasionally sparks a totally new transformation (for example, the influence of the Michaelson-Morely experiment on Einstein).

The history of science by no means implies that rigorous observation must precede theoretical speculation. But it is difficult to get off the ground in the absence of a stable pattern of observations and a frank recognition of the ecclesiastical pretense of theory unsupported by measurement. The genius often attributed to Galileo was the revolutionary idea that if you were curious about how a stone falls, then the thing to do was to try it. From the observation that a stone, dropped from the mast tip of a moving ship, shares the ship's forward motion, he inferred that if the earth moved, surface objects would share the earth's momentum, and would not be left behind as claimed by received (ecclesiastical) theory. It is often said that it was the failure to combine controlled systematic observation with rigorous reasoning that accounts for the failure of science to develop more fully in ancient Greece, China and India (Kaplan, 1964, p. 144–45).

In Section IV below is provided a summary, in proposition form, of some of the candidates for the list of nomothetic results from experimental microeconomy. Any such list must of course be subject to further replication or modification by new experimental evidence.

2. *Heuristic Experiments*

Heuristic or exploratory experiments are used to provide empirical probes of new topics of inquiry. Such experiments are less likely to follow a rigorous design pattern than nomothetic experiments because (a) the objectives may not be as sharply defined by theory or by a hypothesized pattern which is thought to characterize previous experimental results, and (b) the procedural mechanics of the experiment may be new and untested. Heuristic experiments may provide nomotheoretical contributions because they may be fortuitously adequate for distinguishing between two or more hypotheses with very distinct, widely separated, outcome implications; but they may be conducted for no better articulated reason than to just "see what will happen." Although there is widespread scientific prejudice against this latter type of "grubbing in the facts," I think this view is much too rigid and purist, and carries the prospect of needlessly discouraging an important source of new discoveries. Science needs the wings of heuristic experiments as much as the foundational support of nomothetic experiments. It is through exploratory probes of new phenomena that attention may be redirected, old belief systems may be reexamined, and new scientific questions may be asked. The early oligopoly (Hoggatt, 1959) and competitive market (my 1962 article) experiments were of this tentative, exploratory character. An excellent recent example is provided by the Plott and Wilde (1982) experiments dealing with products or services requiring seller diagnosis and recommendation (for example, physicians and repairmen) based on uncertain information.

3. *Boundary Experiments*

Whenever a theory or an empirical regularity has received replicable support from several independent experimental or other empirical studies, and is thereby established as a behavioral law with some claim to generality, it is natural to ask whether one can design experiments that will test for those extreme or boundary conditions under which the law fails. Kaplan (1964, p. 150) refers to such inquiries as boundary experiments. These experiments have an obviously important function in establishing the limits of generality of a theory, and setting the stage for important new extensions in theory.

A few examples of boundary experiments in economics will help to illustrate the concept. The double auction (see Section IV.B below) is a remarkably robust trading institution for yielding outcomes that converge to the *C.E.* It achieves these results with a small number of agents, under widely different supply and demand conditions, with each individual agent having strict privacy, that is, the agent only knows his/her own value or cost conditions. Several sets of experiments have been conducted to test the boundary of application of these conditions. One set of experiments (my 1981a article; myself and Williams 1981b) used only one or two sellers (Propositions 5 and 8 below). Only in the one-seller experiments is there a failure to arrive consistently at *C.E.* outcomes, thus establishing "one" as the limiting number of sellers at which competitive price theory fails under double auction trading.

A one-seller experiment can also be viewed as a boundary experiment testing the limits of applicability of cartel theory. A cartel may fail to achieve monopoly outcomes because of incentive failure or "chiseling" incentives by cartel members; because of internal cartel enforcement problems; or because of external demand uncertainty or strategic countervailing behavior by buyers. An experiment using only one seller controls for all the internal circumstances that can cause a breakdown in cartel agreements. Hence single seller behavior provides the extreme boundary of behavior for a cartel. If one individual has difficulty achieving monopoly outcomes when demand is unknown, within a given exchange institution, then one expects a group of cartel conspirators to have even more difficulty in achieving a monopoly result (Propositions 8 and 9 below).

Another type of boundary experiment is represented by the supply and demand schedules shown in Figure 2. This experimental design has been used to test whether the *C.E.* tendencies of double auction would continue to hold under rent asymmetries so extreme that at the *C.E.* all the exchange surplus is earned by the buyers. This was a boundary experiment that failed, that is, the design in Figure 2 yields rapid convergence to the *C.E.* for an excess supply quantity ($Q_s - Q_d$) of 5 or 8 units (see my 1965; 1976a articles).

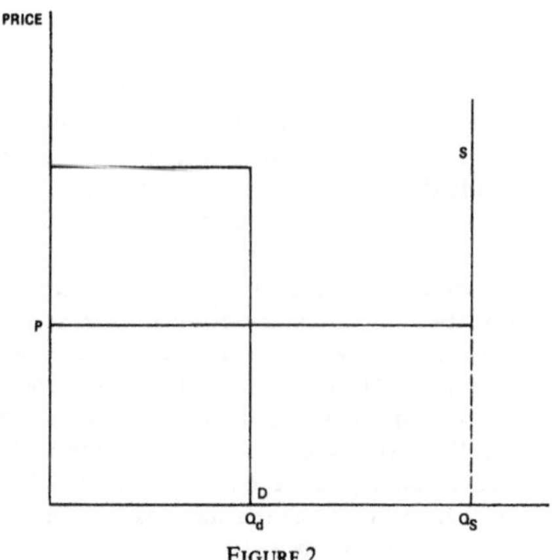

FIGURE 2

IV. Some Institutions and Some Corresponding Experimental "Stylized Facts"

In what follows each of several institutions that have been studied experimentally will be described very briefly, and some of the principal "stylized facts" from these experiments will be summarized in the form of brief empirical propositions. Reference to the original studies will be necessary for readers desiring more comprehensive detail.

There are two basic kinds of auctions—continuous or "oral" auctions, and sealed-bid auctions. In *continuous auctions* an agent may alter his/her bid in response to the bids of others or the failure of a bid to be accepted, that is, an exchange of messages occurs according to specified rules of negotiation prior to each contract. In *sealed-bid auctions* each agent submits one message to a center, which then processes the messages according to publicized rules, and announces aggregate or summary information describing the outcome. The important difference between the two kinds of auctions is the greater information content of the continuous as compared with sealed-bid auctions. Either auction may of course be repeated over time which generates a history of outcome information, but in addition the continuous auction provides a message history between successive contracts. In the experiments reported below the contracting process is repeated sequentially sometimes for as many as twenty or more consecutive periods.

A. *Auctions for a Single Item*

From the long history and great variety of auctions (Ralph Cassady, 1967) for the sale of a single item offered by a seller, two continuous auctions, the English and Dutch, and two sealed-bid auctions, the first and second price auction, have been identified for experimental investigation.

English. The process begins with a call for a bid. Once a bid is announced it remains standing until it is displaced by a new bid, which is required to be higher. The process stops with an irrevocable award of the item to the standing bidder when, in the auctioneer's judgment, no new overbid can be elicited. Anonymity is easily preserved by working out a signalling code with the auctioneer (Cassady, 1967, pp. 150–51).

Dutch. The seller's offer price starts at a level judged to be well in excess of what the highest bidder is likely to pay, then lowered in increments by an auctioneer or clock device until one of the buyers accepts the most recent offer to form an irrevocable contract.

First Price. The process begins with a request for bids to be tendered. Privately each bidder submits a bid price. When all the bids have been received by the center, or by the seller, the award is made to the highest bidder at a price equal to the highest bid.

Second Price. This auction is identical to that of the first price, except that the award is made to the highest bidder at a price equal to the second highest bid.

PROPOSITION 1: *Using the subscripts e(English), d(Dutch), 1(First), and 2(Second), and letting E_e, E_d, E_1, and E_2 be measured either by the mean efficiency or the proportion of P.O. awards, then $E_e \cong E_2 > E_1 > E_d$.*[22]

[22] Propositions 1–3 are based on the theoretical analysis and the experimental results (from a total of about 1,000 auctions) reported by Coppinger, myself, and Titus (1980) and Cox, Roberson and myself (1982). Both of these studies were stimulated by the prior theoretical work of Vickrey (1961).

These measures of E vary somewhat depending upon the particular procedure for inducing demand (random from an announced distribution, random from an unannounced distribution, random level of linear demand), but the efficiency ordering appears not to be affected by this procedure.

PROPOSITION 2: *English and second price auctions which are theoretically isomorphic, that is, are subject to the same analysis and which predict identical allocations, appear to be equivalent behaviorally. Dutch and first price auctions which are theoretically isomorphic are not equivalent behaviorally.*

Although English auction prices are higher and the awards slightly more efficient than in the second price auction the difference is not significant. Contract prices in first price auctions are significantly higher, and are more efficient, than in Dutch auctions. This behavioral difference between first price and Dutch auctions can be explained either by a model which postulates a nonmonetary utility for the "suspense of waiting" in the real time Dutch auction or by a model which postulates a systematic underestimate of the Bayes' Rule risk of loss in not stopping the Dutch price decline (Cox, Roberson, and myself, 1982). The second model is consistent with the results of independent experiments testing Bayes' Rule (David Grether, 1980), while the first model is consistent with the reported impression of subjects that they enjoy the "suspense of waiting" in the Dutch auction. Given two theories each predicting prices to be lower in Dutch than in first price auctions, one naturally asks if there is a "crucial"[23] experiment that will discriminate between the two theories. In this case a simple such experiment is to replicate an existing set of Dutch and first price auction experiments with all parameters unchanged except that the monetary reward level is doubled. The reported difference between Dutch and first price auction behavior should narrow if the "suspense of waiting" model is correct, while the differences should not narrow if the "Bayes rule underestimation" model is correct.

PROPOSITION 3: *Prices, allocations, and individual bids in the first price auction require the rejection of Nash equilibrium models of bidding behavior based on the assumption that all bidders have the same concave utility function. But the experimental results for $N > 3$ bidders are consistent with a Nash equilibrium model based on the assumption that bidders have power utility functions with different coefficients of constant relative risk aversion.*

All models which achieve tractability by assuming that bidders share the same risk neutral or risk averse utility function flounder on the rocks of predicting that individual bids will be ordered the same as individual values. Consequently, these models predict *P.O.* allocations, whether or not bidders are risk averse, which is not what we observe.

B. *Double Auctions*

The institution most extensively studied by experimentalists has been some version of the double auction (*DA*) rules that characterize trading on the organized security and commodity exchanges. This is because *DA* was one of the first institutions to be studied experimentally, and from the beginning demonstrated "surprising" competitive properties. These properties of *DA* especially recommended its use in testing propositions based on competitive price theory. It is an

[23] The quotation marks are used because Hanson shows convincingly that the so-called "crucial" experiment can yield deceptive results. For example, the experiments of Fresnel, Young, and Foucault rejected the hypothesis that the velocity of light in water should be greater than its velocity in air, which was interpreted as implying a rejection of "Hypothesis I," that light consists of particles (rather than waves). As noted by Hanson, the experimental result means either that "light does not consist of high-speed particles, or the assumptions required to give Hypothesis I teeth are (in part or completely) false. One of these assumptions would be... that light must be either wavelike or corpuscular, but not both.... Every experiment tests, not just an isolated hypothesis, but the whole body of relevant knowledge that is involved by the logic of the problem, the experiment, and the hypothesis" (1969, pp. 253–54).

example of a continuous auction and was probably an outgrowth and generalization of the English auction with origins in Babylon and Rome (Cassady, 1967, pp. 26–29). The following description of *DA* applies to only one of the versions that has been used extensively in experiments. In this description each contract is for a single unit.[24]

Double Auction (Leffler and Farwell, 1963, pp. 186–92). After the market opens an auction for a unit begins with the announcement of a price bid by any buyer or a price offer by any seller. Any subsequent bid (offer) must be at a higher (lower) price to be admissible. Once a bid (offer) has been made public, that is, is "standing", it cannot be withdrawn. A binding contract occurs when any buyer (seller) accepts the offer (bid) of any seller (buyer). The auction ends with a contract. If the standing bid (offer) was not part of the contract (for example, if a buyer other than the one with the standing bid accepted the standing offer), the maker of that bid (offer) is no longer bound to it unless the bid (offer) is now re-entered. Following a contract a new auction begins when a new price bid (offer) is announced. The new bid (offer) may be at any level, and may involve "signalling." This process continues until the market "day" comes to an end.

Although different studies report the use of alternative versions of these *DA* rules, the experimental results do not differ in terms of their equilibrium properties.[25] These propositions are based on the results of perhaps 100 to 150 *DA* experiments reported in the literature.

PROPOSITION 4: *Allocations and prices converge to levels near the competitive equilibrium (C.E.) prediction. This convergence is rapid, occurring in three to four trading periods or less when subjects are experienced with the institution (but not the particular induced values).*[26]

Even in the first period of trading, the allocations and price tendencies are generally such as to reject monopoly (monopsony) behavior in favor of the *C.E.* (Isaac and Plott, 1981; my 1962, 1964, 1965, 1976a articles; myself and Williams, 1981a, b; 1982). Repeated "signalling" with high (low) offers (bids) is common, but ineffective.

PROPOSITION 5: *Convergence to C.E. prices and allocations (Proposition* 4) *occurs with as few as six to eight agents (most experiments have used eight), and as few as two sellers (Smith and Williams,* 1981b).

Many economists express surprise, if not discomfort, when presented with the evidence for Proposition 4 and particularly Proposition 5. The idea that a *C.E.* is an ideal "frictionless" state not likely to be approached in any observable market—and certainly not without a "large" number of agents with its assumed concomitant "price-taking" behavior—is a deeply ingrained belief based on untested theory going back to Cournot. Since Cournot's theory does not specify an institution, it is unclear in what context the theory is supposed to have relevance. As for price-taking behavior, note that every agent in *DA* is as much a price maker (announcing bids or offers) as a price taker (announcing acceptances). Empirically it is now thoroughly documented that this institution exhibits strong *C.E.* tendencies.

PROPOSITION 6: *Complete information on the theoretical supply and demand conditions*

[24] On the New York Stock Exchange there are also trading post rules governing multiple unit contracts.

[25] The *DA* trading procedure has been programmed for the PLATO computer system (Williams, 1980; myself and Williams, 1982). This program allows subjects in an experiment to negotiate and trade with each other entirely through individual computer terminals. In a comparison of oral with computerized *DA* trading, differences appear to disappear with the use of experienced subjects (Williams, 1980). A comparison of experimental results using four variations on the computerized *DA* rules is reported by myself and Williams (1982). These different rules yield different price dynamics, but do not affect equilibrium or efficiency.

[26] This proposition applies to environments in which supply and demand are stationary over all the periods of an experiment. Work in process suggests that this result may not generalize to environments with period-by-period shifts in demand (Glenn Harrison, Williams, and myself).

of a market (i.e., agent knowledge of the induced values and costs of all agents) is neither necessary nor sufficient for the rapid convergence property in Proposition 4.

That complete information is not necessary is established by the large number of *DA* experiments that have shown rapid convergence when such information was withheld. That complete information is not sufficient follows from the results of eight experiments, using the "swastika" design of Figure 2. In four of these experiments complete information was withheld; in two, complete information was provided; and in two, the information was incomplete for the first two to three trading periods, and then switched to complete for two additional trading periods. In these experimental comparisons, the incomplete information condition yielded more rapid convergence than the condition of complete information (my 1980 article, p. 357 ff).[27]

PROPOSITION 7: *Price convergence tends to be from above (below) the C.E. price when consumer's surplus is greater (smaller) than producer's surplus (my* 1962, 1965, 1976a *articles*; *myself and Williams*, 1982).

PROPOSITION 8: *Experiments with one seller and five buyers do not achieve monopoly outcomes, although some replications achieve the C.E. outcome. Buyers tend to withhold purchases (and repeatedly signal with low bids) giving the seller a reduced profit, especially at the higher prices. This encourages contracts near the C.E. price, but normally at a loss in efficiency due to the withheld demand (my* 1981a *article*).

This "counterintuitive" result runs roughshod over most belief sysems. But if *C.E.* theory (as conventionally taught) is questionable, monopoly theory is more seriously questionable: The *DA* institution yields the *C.E*: even if the "large" number story is not right, but with *DA* (also see Propositions 19 and 20 below) monopoly theory goes begging for evidential support.[28]

PROPOSITION 9: *Experiments with four buyers and four sellers in which the sellers (or the buyers) are allowed to "conspire" (i.e., engage in premarket, and between market conversation about pricing strategies) do not converge to the monopoly (or monopsony) outcome; neither do they seem to converge dependably to the C.E. Furthermore, the conspiring group often makes* less *than the C.E. profit (Isaac and Plott*, 1981a; *my* 1981b *article*).

PROPOSITION 10: *Binding price ceilings (floors) yield contract price sequences which converge to the ceiling price from below*

[27]In this supply and demand design (Figure 2), complete information means that both buyers and sellers are aware of the extreme asymmetry in the gains from exchange at prices near the *C.E.* Consequently, sellers hold out for higher prices under complete rather than under incomplete information. Similarly, buyers bid higher or accept higher offers, perhaps because of egalitarian motives or because they do not want to risk failing to make a contract if sellers succeed in their effort to maintain prices above unit cost.

[28]Before rejecting the experimental outcomes as "unrealistic," i.e., contrary to your belief system, consider the following points: (A) There is perhaps a tendency to think casually in terms of the perfect information textbook monopoly diagram in which the monopoly outcome seems transparent. But remember that the subject monopolists in Proposition 8 do *not* know their demand curves except as demand is revealed by real subject buyers. (B) Implicit perhaps in monopoly thinking is the assumption of a large number of buyers. Here we have only five buyers, which of course is more than enough to yield the *C.E.* if there are at least two sellers (Proposition 5). Hence, if you say, "Oh, the result follows because there are only a few buyers," then you have to tell me why a large number is necessary for monopoly but not for a *C.E.* (C) There is *no* institution in textbook monopoly theory, but there is an implicit assumption that buyers reveal 100 percent of demand, while the seller optimally underreveals supply. Hence, implicit in monopoly theory is an asymmetric processless assumption from which the conclusion is unassailable but trivial.

Proposition 8 is consistent with monopoly theory under random demand, but since this theory predicts either a higher or a lower price than if demand were certain (Leland, 1972, p. 289), this fact is not very satisfying. Also, it is not clear how these "uncertainty" models are related to experiments in which demand is *unknown* by all agents but is stationary. Does the appropriate uncertainty involve randomness in behavior, or sampling theory?

(above). If the price ceiling (floor) is nonbinding, i.e., if it is above (below) the C.E. price, prices converge to the C.E., but along a path which is below (above) the price path in a market without a price ceiling (floor). If a binding price ceiling (floor) is removed, this causes a temporary explosive increase (decrease) in contract prices before the C.E. price is approached (Isaac and Plott, 1981a; *myself and Williams,* 1981a).

The significance of this proposition for price theory is that a binding price control does *not* quickly freeze prices at the control level, and a nonbinding control has demonstrable effects on the dynamics of market price behavior. Neither of these characteristics is part of conventional price theory. My article with Williams (1981a) presents data on the bid and offer distributions, with and without price controls, which show clearly that nonbinding controls affect the bargaining-contracting process, although convergence to the *C.E* price ultimately occurs. The explosive price changes that Isaac and Plott (1981a) show can follow the removal of a price control is reminiscent of the similar behavior of field observations. However, the latter phenomenon is sometimes explained as due to "pent-up" demand, that is, an accumulation of unsatisfied demand. This cannot be the explanation in the cited experimental markets because all sales are for immediate current period demand. Hence, the observed price dynamics must be due to expectations as they affect current bargaining strategies in the *DA* institution. Also rejected by the experimental data on nonbinding controls is the hypothesis that the control price will provide a collusive "focal point" for price determination.

PROPOSITION 11: *Asset markets with eight or nine agents converge slowly (eight or more two-period trading cycles) toward the C.E. (rational expectations) price and efficiency determined by the cumulative two-period dividend value of the asset. Convergence is greatly hastened by introducing a first-period "futures" market in second-period holdings, which enables second-period dividend values to be reflected in (or discounted by) period* 1 *asset prices more quickly (Forsythe, Palfrey, and Plott,* 1982).

PROPOSITION 12: *Asset markets with nine or twelve agents in which the asset yields an uncertain state-contingent dividend, known in advance only by a subset of insiders* (3 *or* 6), *converges toward the C.E. (rational expectations) price and efficiency (Plott and Sunder,* 1982).

Propositions 11 and 12 break new experimental ground in studying asset markets under the *DA* intitution, and demonstrating that the competitive properties of this institution extend to asset markets. The results provide qualified support for the rational expectations theory. In Proposition 11, market replication over time is sufficient to allow private information on divergent induced dividend values across periods to be reflected in asset prices. In Proposition 12, full information on dividend state contingencies by a subset of agents is sufficient to allow asset prices to reflect these dividend values.

Perhaps the most important general feature of the experimental results summarized in all the above *DA* propositions is the support they provide for what might be termed the Hayek hypothesis: *Markets economize on information in the sense that strict privacy together with the public messages of the market are sufficient to produce efficient C.E. outcomes.* This statement is offered as an interpretation in hypothesis form of what Hayek meant in emphasizing that "the most significant fact about this (price) system is the economy of knowledge with which it operates, or how little the individual participants need to know in order to be able to take the right action..."(Hayek, 1945, p. 35).

C. *Sealed-Bid Auctions*

There are two types of sealed-bid auctions which apply when there is a single seller offering a specified quantity of a homogeneous commodity in inelastic supply (i.e., without specification of a reservation price).

Discriminative Auction. The process begins with the seller announcing the quantity,

Q, to be offered and requesting that bids be tendered. Each buyer submits a bid (or bids) stating price(s) and corresponding quantity(ies). When the last bid has been received, all bids are arrayed from highest to lowest by price, and the first Q bid units in this ordering are accepted at prices equal to the bid price stated by each successful buyer. A random or proportionality rule is normally used for allocation among tie bids at the lowest accepted price. The process ends with a private communication of the outcome of each individual bid and a public announcement of a truncated summary of the results (as in the auctioning of U.S. Treasury securities); the highest and lowest accepted bid, and the total quantity of bid units that were tendered.

Competitive (or Uniform-Price) Auction. The procedure in this auction is identical to that of the discriminative auction except that the highest Q bid units are all accepted at a *uniform* price equal to the bid price specified by the $Q+1$th (in some versions, the Qth) bid unit.

The discriminative and competitive auctions are multiple-unit generalizations of the first and second price auctions, respectively. A large number of discriminative and competitive auction experiments, conducted under various conditions of induced demand, number of bidders, and quantity offering, have been reported in the literature. These studies form the empirical basis for the following propositions:

PROPOSITION 13: *When all individual values are identical and based on a single draw from a rectangular distribution (made after all bids have been entered) the following results obtain:*[29]

(a) *If $F_C^t(p)$ and $F_D^t(p)$ are the proportions of accepted bids specifying a price of p or higher in auction period t under competitive and discriminative auction rules, respectively, then $F_C^t(p) \geqq F_D^t(p)$ for all t, that is, within the acceptance sets, bids in competitive auctions are at prices at least as high as those in discriminative auctions.*

(b) *Seller revenue in the final ("equilibrium") auction in a sequence is greater in competitive than in discriminative auctions in eight of fourteen paired experiments.*[30]

Proposition 13 is based on thirty-three experiments reported by M. W. Belovicz (1979, p. 314) and myself (1967), with the number of bidders varying from thirteen to thirty-four and each bidder submitting either one, two, or an unspecified number of unit bids.

PROPOSITION 14: *When aggregate induced demand is linear and fixed, but individual private assignments are random (i.e., the assignments are without replacement) and are made prior to the submission of bids, the bids satisfy Proposition 13(a). However, if the slope of the linear induced demand is sufficiently low (i.e., steep) seller revenue is greater in discriminative than in competitive auctions; if the slope of induced demand is increased seller revenue becomes smaller in discriminative than in competitive auctions (Miller and Plott, 1980).*[31]

The ordering property of the bids in Propositions 13 and 14 is consisent with theories showing that when each bidder is a buyer of at most one unit, bidders have an incentive to bid their "true" (or induced) value in competitive auctions but to bid less than this value in discriminative auctions (Vickrey, 1961, 1962).[32]

[29]This environment was designed to capture the essential features of the market faced by dealers in U.S. Treasury bills who buy in the primary auction for resale in the secondary market. Dealers buy under bid acceptance uncertainty for resale at an uncertain post-auction price.

[30]Reported incorrectly as 5 in 15 in my 1980 paper, Table 2.

[31]The higher revenue from the discriminative rules when demand is sufficiently steep can be explained as follows: The highest value intramarginal bidders face a high opportunity cost of failing to have their bid accepted. Consequently, they bid more, and the discriminative treatment increases seller rent relative to the case in which demand is less steep and valuations less diverse.

[32]However, it should be noted that in some of the experiments of Proposition 13 and in all of the experiments of Proposition 14, bidders could submit more than a single unit bid.

Since new Treasury security offerings at auction are small relative to the outstanding stock of Treasury securities and the large stock of closely competing private securities, it seems credible to conjecture that the demand for Treasury securities is highly elastic. This suggests the likelihood that the revenue from primary auctions of Treasury securities would be greater in a competitive than in a discriminative auction.

Sealed Bid-Offer (Double) Auctions. Bids are tendered by buyers and offers are tendered by sellers. Experimental markets have examined two different bid-offer rules. (A) $P(Q)$: Each buyer (seller) submits a demand (supply) schedule, that is, specifies a bid (offer) price for each unit demanded (supplied). (B) PQ: Each buyer (seller) submits a single bid (offer) price and corresponding quantity. Under either $P(Q)$ or PQ the bids are then arrayed from highest to lowest by price, and the offers from lowest to highest. A selection algorithm, which incorporates a rule for handling tied bids (offers), determines a single market-clearing price and corresponding quantity. Except for excluded tie bids (offers), bids equal to or greater (offers equal to or less) than this price are accepted. The process ends with a private communication of the outcome resulting from each individual's bid (offer), and a public announcement of the market-clearing price and quantity.

The institution which I call $P(Q)$ above is used on the New York Stock Exchange to obtain the opening price each day in each stock based on the accumulation of buy and sell orders after the previous day's close (J. Hazard and M. Christie, 1964, pp. 177–78). Also it has been proposed that the $P(Q)$ procedure be used in the development of a completely computerized national market for trading all securities (Mendelson, Peake, and Williams, 1979). However, $P(Q)$ has a theoretical "defect," namely it provides an incentive for each agent to underreveal demand (supply), and therefore its outcomes are not *P.O.* The institution which I call PQ corrects this defect. This institution, proposed by Pradeep Dubey and Martin Shubik (1980), has been shown by them to have the property that each *C.E.* is also a Nash equilibrium and is therefore incentive compatible. Intuitively the all-or-nothing feature of PQ compared with $P(Q)$, enables PQ to neutralize the incentive to strategically "hold back," and is thereby similar to the second price auction (compare Vickrey, 1976, p. 15).

Three institutions, DA with "good" *C.E.* behavioral properties (Propositions 4 and 5); $P(Q)$ with theoretically "poor" incentive properties; and PQ with theoretically "good" incentive properties, have been compared experimentally under conditions in which the environment is held constant while the institutional treatment is varied (my article with Williams, Bratton, and Vannoni, 1982). The results are summarized in the following:

PROPOSITION 15: *Based on the prior empirical performance of DA and theory pertaining to P(Q) and PQ, we expect the efficiency of allocations in these three institutions to be ranked* $E[DA] \cong E[PQ] > E[P(Q)]$ *and the deviation of prices from the C.E. to be ranked* $p[DA] \cong p[PQ] < p[P(Q)]$. *The experimental results suggest the contrary observed ordering* $E[DA] > E[P(Q)] > E[PQ]$ *and* $p[DA] < p[P(Q)] < p[PQ]$.

In terms of the observed experimental outcomes, DA performs (somewhat) better than $P(Q)$, and $P(Q)$ better than PQ. The poor performance of PQ is accounted for by what appears to be a persistent tendency of subject agents to raise their offers (lower their bids) in an attempt to influence price. By comparison with $P(Q)$, this leads to a higher proportion of missed trades because of the block-trading characteristic of PQ. Even with the use of experienced subjects this property of PQ persists, whereas with experience the DA and $P(Q)$ institutions show improved performance.

Sealed Bid-Offer (Double) Auctions: Unanimity Tatonnement. A variation on the $P(Q)$ and PQ institutions called $P(Q)v$ and PQv is the following: After the market-clearing price and quantity has been determined, a *conditional* allocation in the form of accepted bids and offers is made. Each agent, some portion of whose bid (offer) was accepted, is then asked to vote "yes" or "no" as to whether the allocation should be finalized, that is, only the active traders on a given trial are enfranchised. If all such traders vote yes, the process stops and each individual executes a long-term contract for T times the outcome of that trial. Otherwise the process proceeds to another repeat bid-offer trial with a maximum of T trials.

Unanimity voting in the above sense provides a procedure for operationalizing the concept of tatonnement in which contracts are not binding until a final exchange of messages triggers a market outcome. The London Gold Bullion Exchange appears to be the only ongoing market that uses unanimity voting as a message exchange stopping rule (Jarecki, 1976).

PROPOSITION 16: *Measured in terms of efficiency and deviations from the C.E. price, PQv provides no improvement over PQ. P(Q)v performs better than P(Q) and appears to be the equal of DA (Smith et al.* 1982).

Propositions 15 and 16 (which are based on forty-eight experiments) are important in confirming our expectation that the rules ought to make a difference as to what we observe in a market. These propositions also make clear that not just any institution one might wish to define has *C.E.* properties as good as *DA*. Finally, although there are many experimental studies which provide empirical support for the static Nash equilibrium hypothesis (compare Smith et al., 1982, Section III.A), the hypothesis fails to receive support in the context of the sealed bid-offer auction. Something else, perhaps having to do with lumpiness, is driving the results.

D. *Posted Pricing*

Our experience as economic agents does not normally include any of the institutions discussed so far. The ordinary retail markets of daily life use what has been called the posted offer institution (Plott and myself, 1978) in which sellers display take-it-or-leave-it price offers to buyers. With only a few exceptions (such as "big ticket" items like automobiles and houses) the buyer does not bargain with the seller over price. Less well known, but important, is the existence of markets in which buyers post the bid prices at which they are willing to buy. Thus refiners post bids for crude oil, and canners post bids for produce and other foods.

Posted Offer (Bid) Pricing. The process begins with each seller (buyer) privately selecting a take-it-or-leave-it price offer (bid). These prices are then publicly posted so that they are visible to each buyer and seller. Next a buyer (seller), selected at random, chooses a seller to whom a quantity response or offer is made. The seller (buyer) then responds with an acceptance of all or any part of the buyer's (seller's) quantity offer which forms a binding contract. (However, the seller must accept at least one unit, i.e., the seller may not post an offer price and then refuse to sell any units at that price.) If any part of the quantity offer is not accepted the buyer (seller) may choose a second seller (buyer) and make a quantity response, and so on. When the first buyer (seller) has finished trading, a second, selected at random (without replacement) proceeds to choose a seller (buyer), makes a quantity offer, and so on. This process stops when the last buyer (seller) has completed the exchange cycle. The trading period ends without any further public announcement.[33] Note that under posted offer (bid) pricing, only the sellers (buyers) can "signal" by raising (lowering) their price quotations.

Several experimental studies have investigated the properties of this institution. A few of these properties are summarized below.

PROPOSITION 17: *If $G_o^t(p)$ and $G_b^t(p)$ are the proportions of contract prices at p or higher in trading period t under the posted offer and*

[33] In the PLATO computerized version of "posted offer," seller prices are displayed on each buyer's and seller's terminal screen. Besides a price, each seller also selects the maximum number of units that he/she is willing to deliver, but this information is not public. When a buyer purchases the last unit from a seller, the message "stock out" replaces that seller's price on each buyer's screen. This procedure preserves the privacy of sales and "stockage" for each seller as in the typical, retail market. Also, the computerized version has options requiring buyers to pay a fixed fee, corresponding to shopping cost, to obtain a seller's price quotation. Alternatively, the seller may be charged a fee, corresponding to price advertising.

posted bid institutions, respectively, then $G_o^t(p) \geqq G_b^t(p)$ *for all* $t > 1$ *(W. Cook and E. Veendorp,* 1975; *Plott and myself,* 1978; *my* 1976a *article; F. Williams,* 1973).

This proposition establishes the empirical characteristic that posted pricing operates to the advantage of the side with the posting initiative. If sellers post offers convergence is from above the *C.E.* price.

PROPOSITION 18: *Experiments with single seller posted-offer pricing, in both increasing and decreasing cost environments, yield convergence to the monopoly price. This convergence appears to be faster with increasing cost (my* 1981a *article) than with decreasing cost (Don Coursey, Isaac, and myself,* 1981). *The slow convergence (at least fifteen periods) in three of four replications under decreasing cost appears to be attributable to the fact that buyer withholding of purchases (more likely in earlier periods at the higher posted-price offers) impacts the seller's most profitable units.*

This proposition supports monopoly theory, but only within the institutional context of posted-offer pricing, which from Proposition 17 operates to the advantage of sellers. If single sellers achieve monopoly outcomes under the seller-favored posted-offer institution, how well would they fare under the unfavorable posted-bid institution? If buyers post bids to a single seller will this provide a form of decentralized institutional restraint of monopoly power?

PROPOSITION 19: *In a market with one seller and five buyers using posted-bid pricing, prices tend to converge to the C.E. price, but volume and efficiency are somewhat below the C.E. levels (my* 1981a *article, pp.* 96–99).

Consequently posted-bid pricing does serve to severely limit monopoly power, but the resulting market falls short of achieving *C.E.* outcomes. However, the average efficiency (three replications) exceeds that which would have prevailed at the monopoly equilibrium.

PROPOSITION 20: *In decreasing cost environments in which demand is insufficient to support more than a single seller, but the market is "contested" by two sellers with identical costs, there is a strong tendency (six experimental replications, each with fifteen to twenty-five trading periods) for posted-offer prices to decay to the C.E. price range (Coursey, Isaac, and myself,* 1981).

This proposition provides empirical support for the contested market hypothesis (Elizabeth Bailey and John Panzar, 1980), and for the effect of "bidding to supply a market" in disciplining market power (Harold Demsetz, 1968).

In all of the experimental studies summarized above, it should be noted that institutions are being examined in their *pure* form, without the modifications that might result from attaching supplemental secondary institutions sometimes observed in the field. Thus, if an award fails to be *P.O.* at an organized Dutch auction, there may be an additional "aftermarket" exchange in which the successful Dutch bidder resells the item to the highest value agent. Similarly, "first-cut" inefficiency in posted-offer retail markets may be corrected by the end-of-season "sale" or via the Sears Roebuck special discount catalogue. But studying institutions in their purest form enables one to better understand why some institutions develop secondary correctional procedures and others do not. Also, an institution that makes efficient allocations saves the cost of running secondary markets.

In Section II.B it is stated that one of the scientific objectives of experimental microeconomy is to "measure messages because we want to identify the behavioral modes, $\beta^i(e^i|I)$, revealed by the agents and test hypotheses derived from theories about agent behavior." The reader should note that only Proposition 3 in the above list directly addresses this particular objective. This paucity of experimental results reflects the limited extent to which economic theory has dealt directly with institutional specifications and agent message behavior within these specifications. Bidding and auctioning theory is one of the few exceptions to this generalization. It follows that if future experimental research is to test theories of the message behavior of agents, it is essential that more such theory be developed. In the absence of such theory, experimental research is likely to be directed to comparisons between observed outcomes, and the standard static competitive, monopoly or Nash models of final outcome allocations. This means that all those messages in an experiment, which did not also represent allocations, will be subjected to very limited, if any, analysis, and what analysis is provided will not be guided by explicit theory.

V. Epilogue

At the heart of economics is a scientific mystery: How is it that the pricing system accomplishes the world's work without anyone being in charge? Like language, no one invented it. None of us could have invented it, and its operation depends in no way on anyone's comprehension or understanding of it. Somehow, it is a product of culture; yet in important ways, the pricing system is what makes culture possible. Smash it in the command economy and it rises as a Phoenix with a thousand heads, as the command system becomes shot through with bribery, favors, barter and underground exchange. Indeed, these latter elements may prevent the command system from collapsing. No law and no police force can stop it, for the police may become as large a part of the problem as of the solution. The pricing system—How is order produced from freedom of choice?—is a scientific mystery as deep, fundamental, and inspiring as that of the expanding universe or the forces that bind matter. For to understand it is to understand something about how the human species got from hunting-gathering through the agricultural and industrial revolutions to a state of affluence that allows us to ask questions about the expanding universe, the weak and strong forces that bind particles, and the nature of the pricing system, itself. But what can we as economists say for sure about what we know of the pricing system? It would appear that after 200 years, we know and understand very little. Incredibly, it is only in the last 20 of these 200 years that we have seriously awakened to the hypothesis that property right institutions might be important to the functioning of the pricing system!

Laboratory research in microeconomics over the past two decades has focused on the simplest and most elementary questions—some might say simple-minded questions. This is because the premises of this research are that we possess very little knowledge that can be demonstrated; that the roots of our discipline require a complete reexamination; that we are only just at the beginning. Above all, we need to develop a body of knowledge which clarifies the difference between what we have created (theory as hypothesis) and what we have discovered (hypothesis that, to date, is or is not falsified by observation).

REFERENCES

Bailey, Elizabeth and Panzar, John, "The Contestability of Airline Markets During the Transition to Deregulation," mimeo., May 6, 1980.

Belovicz, M. W., "Sealed-Bid Auctions: Experimental Results and Applications," in Vernon Smith, ed., *Research in Experimental Economics*, Vol. 1, Greenwich: JAI Press, 1979, 279–338.

Butts, Robert E., "Some Tactics in Galileo's Propaganda for the Mathematization of Scientific Experience," in his and J. C. Pitts, eds., *New Perspectives on Galileo*, Dordrecht: Reidel, 1978, 59–85.

Cassady, Ralph, *Auctions and Auctioneering*, Berkeley: University of California Press, 1967.

Chamberlin, John, "Comments on The Application of Laboratory Experimental Methods to Public Choice," in Clifford Russell, ed., *Collective Decision Making*, Washington: Resources for the Future, 1979, 161–66.

Clower, Robert and Leijonhufvud, Axel, "The Coordination of Economic Activities: A Keynesian Perspective," *American Economic Review Proceedings*, May 1975, *65*, 182–88.

Cook, W. D. and Veendorp, E. C. H., "Six Markets in Search of an Auctioneer," *Canadian Journal of Economics*, May 1975, *8*, 238–57.

Coppinger, Vicki, Smith, Vernon and Titus, John, "Incentives and Behavior in English, Dutch and Sealed-Bid Auctions," *Eco-*

nomic Inquiry, January 1980, *18*, 1–22.

Coursey, Don, Isaac, R. Mark and Smith, Vernon, "Natural Monopoly and the Contestable Markets Hypothesis: Some Experimental Results," department of economics discussion paper, University of Arizona, July 1981.

Cox, James, Roberson, Bruce and Smith, Vernon, "Theory and Behavior of Single Object Auctions," in V. Smith, ed., *Research in Experimental Economics* Vol. 2, Greenwich: JAI Press, 1982.

Cross, John, "Some Comments on the Papers by Kagel and Battalio and by Smith," in Jan Kmenta and James Ramsey, eds., *Evaluation of Econometric Models*, New York: New York University Press, 1980, 403–06.

Demsetz, Harold, "Why Regulate Utilities?," *Journal of Law of Economics*, April 1968, *11* 55–65.

Drake, C. L. and Maxwell, J. C., "Geodynamics —Where Are We and What Lies Ahead?," *Science*, July 3, 1981, *213*, 15–22.

Dubey, Pradeep and Shubik, Martin, "A Strategic Market Game with Price and Quantity Strategies," *Zeitschrift fur Nationalokonomie*, No. 1-2, 1980, *40*, 25–34.

Ferejohn, John, Forsythe, Robert and Noll, Roger, "An Experimental Analysis of Decision Making Procedures for Discrete Public Goods," in Vernon Smith, ed., *Research in Experimental Economics*, Vol. 1, Greenwich: JAI Press, 1979, 1–58.

Fiorina, Morris and Plott, Charles, "Committee Decisions Under Majority Rule: An Experimental Study," *American Political Science Review*, June 1978, 575–98.

Forsythe, R., Palfrey, Thomas and Plott, Charles, "Asset Valuation in an Experimental Market," *Econometrica*, May 1982, *50*, 537–67.

Fouraker, Lawrence and Siegel, Sidney, *Bargaining Behavior*, New York: McGraw-Hill, 1963.

Freuchen, Peter, *Book of the Eskimos*, Cleveland: World Publishing, 1961.

Friedman, James and Hoggatt, Austin, *An Experiment in Noncooperative Oligopoly*, Supplement 1 to Vernon Smith, ed., *Research in Experimental Economics*, Vol. 1, Greenwich: JAI Press, 1980.

Grether, David, "Bayes Rule as a Descriptive Model: The Representativeness Heuristic," *Quarterly Journal of Economics*, November 1980, *95*, 537–57.

Hanson, N. R., *Perception and Discovery*, San Francisco: Freeman, 1969.

______, *Observation and Explanation*, New York 1971.

Harrison, Glenn, Smith, Vernon and Williams, Arlington, "Learning Behavior in Experimental Auctions Markets," University of California-Los Angeles, November 1981.

Hayek, Friedrich A., "The Use of Knowledge in Society," *American Economic Review*, September 1945, *35*, 519–30.

Hazard, J. and Christie, M., *The Investment Business*, New York 1964.

Hoggatt, Austin, "An Experimental Business Game," *Behavioral Science*, July 1959, *4*, 192–203.

Hurwicz, Leonid, "Optimality and Informational Efficiency in Resource Allocation Processes," in Kenneth Arrow et al., eds., *Mathematical Methods in the Social Sciences*, Stanford: Stanford University, 1960, 27–46.

______, "The Design of Mechanisms for Resource Allocation," *American Economic Review Proceedings*, May 1973, *63*, 1–30.

______**, Radner, Roy, and Reiter, Stanley,** "A Stochastic Decentralized Resource Allocation Process: Part I," *Econometrica*, March 1975, *43*, 187–221; "Part II," May 1975, 363–93.

Isaac, R. Mark and Plott, Charles R., (1981a) "Price Control and the Behavior of Auction Markets: An Experimental Examination," *American Economic Review*, June 1981, *71*, 448–59.

______ **and** ______, (1981b) "The Opportunity for Conspiracy in Restraint of Trade: An Experimental Study," *Journal of Economic Behavior and Organization*, March 1981, *2*, 1–30.

Jarecki, Henry G., "Bullion Dealing, Commodity Exchange Trading and the London Gold Fixing: Three Forms of Commodity Auctions," in Y. Amihud, ed., *Bidding and Auctioning for Procurement and Allocation*, New York: New York University 1976, 146–54.

Kagel, John and Battalio, Raymond, "Token

Economy and Animal Models for the Experimental Analysis of Economic Behavior," in Jan Kmenta and James Ramsey, eds., *Evaluation of Econometric Models*, New York: Academic Press, 1980, 379–401.

Kaplan, Abraham, *The Conduct of Inquiry*, New York: Chandler Publishing, 1964.

Ketcham, Jon, Smith, Vernon, and Williams, Arlington, "The Behavior of Posted Offer Pricing Institutions," paper presented at the Southern Economic Association Meeting, November 5–7, 1980.

Koestler, Arthur, *The Sleepwalkers*, New York 1963.

Leamer, Edward and Leonard, Herman, "An Alternative Reporting Style for Econometric Results," discussion paper no. 145, University of California-Los Angeles, June 1981.

Leffler, George and Farwell, C. Loring, *The Stock Market*, New York: Ronald, 1963.

Leland, Hayne, "Theory of the Firm Facing Uncertain Demand," *American Economic Review*, June 1972, *62*, 278–91.

Levine, Michael and Plott, Charles, "Agenda Influence and Its Implications," *Virginia Law Review*, May 1977, *63*, 561–604.

Lucas, Robert E., Jr., "Tobin and Monetarism: A Review Article," *Journal of Economic Literature*, June 1981, *19*, 558–67.

Marschak, Jacob, "Economics of Inquiring, Communicating, Deciding," *American Economic Review Proceedings*, May 1968, *48*, 1–18.

Martin, Paul, "Prehistoric Overkill," in his and H. E. Wright, Jr., eds., *Pleistocene Extinctions*, New Haven: Yale University, 1967.

Mendelson, M., Peake, J. and Williams, R. Jr., "Toward a Modern Exchange: The Peake-Mendelson-Williams Proposal for an Electronically Assisted Auction Market," in E. Blochand and R. Schwartz, eds., *Impending Changes for Securities Markets*, Greenwich: JAI Press, 1979, 53–74.

Miller, Gary and Plott, Charles "Revenue Generating Properties of Sealed-Bid Auctions," Social Science Working Paper No. 234, California Institute of Technology, September 1980.

Miller, Ross, Plott, Charles and Smith, Vernon, "Intertemporal Competitive Equilibrium: An Empirical Study of Speculation," *Quarterly Journal of Economics*, November 1977, *91*, 599–624.

Millikan, R. A., Roller, D. and Watson, E. C., *Mechanics, Molecular Physics, Heat and Sound*, Boston 1937.

Plott, Charles R., "The Application of Laboratory Experimental Methods to Public Choice," in Clifford S. Russell, ed., *Collective Decision Making*, Washington: Resources for the Future, 1979.

______ **and Smith, V. L.,** "An Experimental Examination of Two Exchange Institutions," *Review of Economic Studies*, February 1978, *45*, 133–53.

______ **and Sunder, Shyam,** "Efficiency of Experimental Security Markets with Insider Information," *Journal of Political Economy*, August 1982, *90*, 663–98.

______ **and Wilde, Louis,** "Professional Diagnosis vs. Self-Diagnosis: An Experimental Examination of Some Special Features of Markets with Uncertainty," in Vernon Smith, ed., *Research in Experimental Economics*, Vol. 2, Greenwich: JAI Press, 1982.

Popper, Karl R., *The Logic of Scientific Discovery*, London 1959.

Reiter, Stanley, "Information and Performance in the $(\text{New})^2$ Welfare Economics," *American Economic Review Proceedings*, February 1977, *67*, 226–34.

Shapley, Harlow, *Of Stars and Men*, Boston 1964.

Siegel, Sidney, "Decision Making and Learning Under Varying Conditions of Reinforcement," *Annals of the New York Academy of Science*, 1961, 766–83.

______ **and Fouraker, Laurence,** *Bargaining and Group Decision Making*, New York: McGraw-Hill, 1960.

Smith, Vernon L., "An Experimental Study of Competitive Market Behavior," *Journal of Political Economy*, April 1962, *70*, 111–37.

______, "Effect of Market Organization on Competitive Equilibrium," *Quarterly Journal of Economics*, May 1964, *78*, 181–201.

______, "Experimental Auction Markets and the Walrasian Hypothesis," *Journal of Political Economy*, August 1965, *73*, 387–93.

______, "Experimental Studies of Discrimination versus Competition in Sealed-Bid Auction Markets," *Journal of Business*, January 1967, *40*, 58–84.

______, "Notes on Some Literature in Experimental Economics," Social Science Working Paper no. 21, California Institute of Technology, February 1973.

______, (1976a) "Bidding and Auctioning Institutions: Experimental Results," in Y. Amihud, ed., *Bidding and Auctioning for Procurement and Allocation*, New York: New York University, 1976, 43–64.

______, (1976b) "Experimental Economics: Induced Value Theory," *American Economic Review Proceedings*, May 1976, *66*, 274–79.

______, "Incentive Compatible Experimental Processes for the Provision of Public Goods," in his *Research in Experimental Economics*, Greenwich: JAI Press, 1979, 59–168.

______, "Relevance of Laboratory Experiments to Testing Resource Allocation Theory," in Jan Kmenta and James B. Ramsey, *Evaluation of Econometric Models*, New York 1980, 345–77.

______, (1981a) "An Empirical Study of Decentralized Institutions of Monopoly Restraint," G. Horwich and J. Quirk, eds., *Essays in Contemporary Fields of Economics*, W. Lafayette: Purdue University, 1981.

______, (1981b) "Theory, Experiment and Antitrust Policy," in S. Salop, ed., *Strategy, Predation, and Antitrust Analysis*, Washington: FTC, September 1981.

______ **and Williams, Arlington W.**, (1981a) "On Nonbinding Price Controls in a Competitive Market," *American Economic Review*, June 1981, *71*, 467–74.

______ **and** ______, (1981b) "The Boundaries of Competitive Price Theory: Convergence, Expectations and Transaction Cost," paper presented at the Public Choice Society Meetings, New Orleans, March 13–15, 1981.

______ **and** ______, "Effect of Rent Asymmetries in Competitive Markets," *Journal of Economic Behaviour and Organization*, forthcoming.

______ **and** ______, "An Experimental Comparison of Alternative Rules for Competitive Market Exchange," in Martin Shubik, ed., *Auctions, Bidding and Contracting: Uses and Theory*, New York: New York University Press, 1982.

Smith, Vernon et al., "Competitive Market Institutions: Double Auctions versus Sealed Bid-Offer Auctions," *American Economic Review*, March 1982, *72*, 58–77.

Stafford, Frank, "Some Comments on the Papers by Kagel and Battalio and by Smith," in Jan Kmenta and James Ramsey, eds., *Evaluation of Econometric Models*, New York: Academic Press, 1980, 407–410.

Vickrey, William, "Counterspeculation, Auctions and Competitive Sealed Tenders," *Journal of Finance*, March 1961, *16*, 8–37.

______, "Auctions and Bidding Games," in *Recent Advances in Game Theory*, Princeton: Princeton University, 1962, 15–27.

______, "Auctions, Markets, and Optimal Allocation," in Y. Amihud, ed., *Bidding and Auctioning for Procurement and Allocation*, New York: New York University, 1976, 13–20.

Wilde, Louis, "On the Use of Laboratory Experiments in Economics," in Joseph Pitt, ed., *The Philosophy of Economics*, Dordrecht: Reidel, 1980.

Williams, Arlington, "Intertemporal Competitive Equilibrium: On Further Experimental Results," in Vernon Smith, ed., *Research in Experimental Economics*, Vol.1, Greenwich: JAI Press, 1979, 225–78.

______, "Computerized Double Auction Markets: Some Initial Experimental Results," *Journal of Business*, July 1980, *53*, 235–58.

Williams, Fred, "Effect of Market Organization on Competitive Equilibrium: The Multiunit Case," *Review of Economic Studies*, January 1973, *40*, 97–113.

Experimental Economics: Reply

By VERNON L. SMITH*

More than in any particular method of inquiry, I think the hallmark of science is to be found in a constructively skeptical attitude toward knowledge.[1] The more fundamental are the concepts and assumptions of a science, the easier it is to take them for granted and to abandon this skepticism. In this spirit, Ronald Heiner (1985) is correct in emphasizing that the "knowledge" obtained from the study of the performance of experimental markets is only as secure as the classical preference model used to induce prespecified value structures on the agents in such markets. If the purpose of an experiment is to test a theory (for example, supply and demand), and the theory is not "falsified" by the test, this in no way supports any premise of the theory which was also a premise of the experimental design. When we falsify a theory, the implication is that one or more of its assumptions about the behavior of economic agents (maximization of expected utility, commonly shared (homogeneous) expectations, risk aversion, zero subjective costs of transacting, etc.) is in question, and the immediate task is to modify the suspected behavioral assumptions of the original theory. Other assumptions—such as that agents have well-defined preferences, or know the probability distribution from which other agent values were drawn—are not brought into question by the experiment because the experimental design reproduced (or should have) the environment posited by the theory being tested. When testing formal market theories in this way, we should always be aware of the fact that *we are studying behavior within the context of our representations of the economic environment.* If any of these representations is wrong, then our studies have only increased our self-knowledge, not our knowledge of things (natural economic processes).

If we are to increase our knowledge of things, then our ultimate aim should aspire to more than discovering that the behavioral

*Department of Economics, University of Arizona, Tucson, AZ 85721.

[1]The principal contribution of Popper's falsificationist methodology is, I believe, the influential attempt to develop a formal logic of skeptical inquiry. That the attempt has failed, in the sense that it has produced no defensible codified set of procedures that yield a science of scientific method (happily it would appear that all such attempts will fail), should not detract from the disciplinary value of the falsificationist perspective in approaching scientific questions. Its value to the experimentalist is to force him to ask "How can I design an experiment with the property that the set of potentially observable outcomes can be partitioned into those that are consistent with one (or a given) theory and those that are consistent with other theory(ies) (or inconsistent with the given theory)?" That experimental life is such that his effort is about as likely to fail as to succeed by no means detracts from the value of the exercise. Its value to the theorist (if he will just forgo the career-advancing primeval incentive to publish yet another technically tractable extension of the existing theory literature) is to force him to ask "How can I model this question so as to suggest (as Martin Shubik would say) a do-able experiment, and so as to yield observable implications that do not exhaust the set of possible outcomes?" That this effort will often fail does not detract from the value of the exercise. Having said this I would not want to leave the impression that experiments that are fishing expeditions in the laboratory to see what will happen are of no value; seeing what happens can be essential in defining an analytical-empirical research program. Similarly, when a theorist builds (as Buz Brock would say) castles in the air, this is not necessarily useless, for it may lead to more operational forms of theory. We should impute some nonzero probability to the proposition that Feyerabend's "anything goes" posture is right. But at this stage I think it has become pretty obvious where our professional weaknesses are concentrated. Economists, while spouting the rhetoric (Donald McClosky, 1983) of the falsificationist, are in fact verificationist to the core. We all do it. We take a proposition, conjecture, or theory, then search for supportive historical or empirical examples. As everyone ought to know, seek and ye are likely to find, whether one is a "Keynesian" or a "supply sider." What is not sufficiently appreciated is that this verificationist grubbing is a prescientific exercise in which one asks whether there is *any* supporting evidence, and how difficult it is to find; if there is none or if it is pretty hard to uncover, it suggests abandonment in the prescientific womb.

properties of our own creations are consistent with controlled experimental evidence, although the attempt to falsify these creations may be a necessary step in acquiring the conditional knowledge that can improve our theorizing ability. This is why empirical investigations of all aspects of parallelism between laboratory and field behavior are important. Similarly, our experimental and other investigations should not be *confined* to testing formal theory (for example, nomothetic experiments) since this objective requires us to impose more structure on the free play of decision making than ultimately may be justified. Finally, our research methodology should not be too rigid in testing only the market implications of a theory (or in testing only the assumptions of a theory).

Thus, John Kagel et al. (1981) have addressed direct tests of the observable implications of preference theory. This literature reports results consistent with standard preference theory (i.e., with Hicks-Slutzky income-compensated demand theory), but also with the *ad hoc* widely assumed law of demand, which Heiner (1983) is able to deduce from his model of adaptive uncertain choice.[2] As noted by Kagel et al., the convergence tendency reported in auction market experiments "depends critically on the fact that subjects behave in a way which is consistent with utility-maximizing principles underlying consumer demand theory and that negatively sloped demand curves have been induced in the market" (p. 13). I do not wish to suggest that these studies have put to rest the issues raised by Heiner whose emphasis is on the inadequacy of standard theory when preferences are uncertain. Indeed, both the animal and especially the human preference studies of Kagel et al. exhibit "dynamic" effects or lagged responses that are not even supposed to exist in received preference theory, and which may reflect the "insecure preference beliefs" suggested by Heiner (1983). It would seem that lagged responses are inconsistent with a cognitive, calculating interpretation of preference theory, but consistent with some sort of adaptive response interpretation. Even if preference theory accounts for many agents' stationary state choices in certain experimental situations, it tells us nothing about the *processes* that yield these "good" predictions or why some agents' behavior is not consistent with the theory. The failure of animal studies to falsify demand theory can be interpreted as lending support to Heiner's (1983) emphasis on rule-governed behavior although here the "rules" are apparently programmed into the instincts (genes), unless we are prepared to accept the proposition that species other than ours have cognitive decision-making powers.

Furthermore, the numerous direct studies of individual decision making under uncertainty, over the past 25 years (see the recent papers by David Grether, 1980; Grether and Charles Plott, 1979; and especially the survey and evaluation by Paul Slovic and Sarah Lichtenstein, 1983), suggest that our theories of decision under uncertainty are in several respects inconsistent with controlled evidence. The results of these experiments are robust under replication, and various artifactual explanations of the results (that might have rescued the theory) have been systematically eliminated. The results are not to be idly dismissed by anyone with the slightest interest in evidence. What I want to suggest is that (so far as we are able to tell) experimental methods are entirely competent

[2] Since it seems that no one has ever produced any rigorous evidence for the existence of a price inferior good (Sir Giffen was just speculating, and had no controls on his "experiment"), its prediction by textbook theory is a curiosity (which was recognized as such by Alfred Marshall who started it all), that should have counted against the theory, just as the failure to find a planet "Vulcan" between Mercury and the sun (there was no shortage of claimed sightings), that would account for the advance of Mercury's perihelion, ultimately counted against Newtonian theory (David DeVorkin, 1983, p. 1058). In more mature sciences this might have sparked analytical interest in producing a theory consistent with the law of demand, but having other falsifiable implications. Contrarily, in economics such a theory might even be considered unpublishable because of its "lack of generality," and the Giffen good curiosity has sparked an endless preoccupation with examples of "multiple" and "unstable" equilibria based on the Walrasian adjustment mechanism, which is itself devoid of any institutional evidence. These have been good analytical exercises, but so far as I can see all this self-knowledge is good only for teaching the defenseless and uninitiated students who will form the next generation of automata.

to examine these important issues. New theory, such as that proposed by Heiner (1983) and Soo Hong Chew (1983) (also see Don Coursey, 1982) are particularly welcome at this stage in research programs using, or directly concerned with testing, preference theory under uncertainty.

However, among those who take these experimental results as a serious challenge to existing theory, not all may interpret them in the same way. In the following I will try to state some of my interpretations, and relate them, where it seems appropriate, to Heiner's work.

1) The state of experimental research on decision under uncertainty has produced many unresolved anomalies. Experimental tests of *market* theories, which explicitly assume expected utility (or value) maximization, have *not* falsified many of these theories (for example, James Cox, Bruce Roberson and myself, 1982; Plott and Louis Wilde, 1982). Yet, as indicated above, the results of direct tests are inconsistent with the expected utility hypothesis (*EUH*). Some, but not all (for example, violation of simple dominance), of these anomalies are resolved by Chew's weighted expected utility hypothesis (*WEUH*). Although at this stage I think it would be premature to abandon *EUH*, and especially its extensions, it is not premature to work on the resolution of these anomalies. (One did not reject Newton's inverse square law of attraction because the planets failed to move in perfect ellipses, nor because of the highly inconsistent observed advance in the perihelion of Mercury.)

2) One route to such a resolution may be to recognize, and to elaborate more formally, the hypothesis that subjects are more rational (in the sense of received decision theory under uncertainty) in the context of laboratory markets, than when responding to questionnaire choices among prospects, because of Heiner's conjecture that "Exchange environments also enable agents to interact with each other in an organized and often repeated fashion. Markets thus provide agents with additional feedback that may help guide their behavior" (1985, p. 263). From the study of experimental markets, I have long thought that markets may induce greater "rationality" in behavior because they force or promote a response to, or discovery of, opportunity cost conditions, that need not be readily forthcoming when agents merely think about the choices they make. What I have in mind may be close to Armen Alchian's (1977, pp. 27–32) imitative and trial-and-error forms of conscious adaptive behavior, except that I would deemphasize the "conscious" element.[3]

Different forms of market organization have been found to differ in their power to induce or extract neoclassical rational behavior. Thus the English auction is slightly more efficient (97 percent of the allocations are Pareto optimal), and prices are consistently closer to the predicted second highest value among the bidders, than is the Second price sealed-bid auction (94 percent Pareto optimal allocations) (see Cox, Mark Isaac, and myself, 1983, pp. 73–75). An explanation is simple. In the English auction it is a dominant strategy to raise the standing bid if it is less than your value, and to never raise your own bid. Behaviorally, the temptation to use this strategy is irresistable, and made transparent (without thinking) by the sequential complete bid information properties of the process. In terms of Heiner's model (1983), subjects easily (I would say at low cost)

[3] In writing this reply, I found myself reminiscing that Adam Smith did not begin his economic analysis, as does mainstream economics, with preferences as the primeval cause of the phenomena we study. He began with a deeply insightful *observation* qua *axiom*, which states that man is unique among all animal species in exhibiting "the propensity to truck, barter and exchange one thing for another." (Man is not unique in revealing preferences.) After some speculation that this might be a consequence of man's ability to use language (I would speculate that man's development of language may have been in part due to the specialization and affluence made possible by markets), Smith deduced the important result that it is this power of exchanging that gives rise to wealth creating specialization, which in turn is limited by the extent of the market. Markets thus lead agents to promote ends which are no part of their intention. Except for modern scholars such as Hayek, the idea that we are studying processes that contain major elements that are *not* consciously or cognitively purposive has been lost in the pyrotechnics of straightening out Smith's little paradoxes of value. No wonder that Kenneth Boulding will tell you flat out that Smith was the first great post-Newtonian scientist.

perceive, perhaps quite unconsciously, the opportunity cost of "nonoptimal" behavior. In the Second price sealed-bid auction it is a dominant strategy to submit a bid equal to your value. But this requires *reasoning* which is in fact *very subtle*, although, as with all puzzles, it is obvious or "trivial" once you understand it.[4] One must perceive that if one's own bid is the highest, the price paid is the amount of the next highest bid, and therefore one's surplus to be gained is independent of the amount bid. So the "rational" bid is to maximize your chance of winning by bidding your value. About a third of the subjects recruited out of campus classrooms to participate in a sequence of Second price auctions (with values assigned independently from a distribution to all bidders in each auction), bid "as if" they perceive the implied dominant strategy from the beginning. About one-third appear to "learn" asymptotically from their success-failure experience that this is the "best" strategy. Another third do not clearly converge to the dominant strategy—some hit it irratically, some rarely, if ever, and some bid just below value. An examination of the bids that are less than value reveals that many occur at values so low that the prospect of having the winning bid is remote. These can be interpreted as "throw-away" bids, and if in the strict sense they are "irrational," at least they are only marginally so.[5]

3) The wide variety of different experimental studies of decision making under uncertainty, yielding results inconsistent with *EUH*, are subject to different interpretations in terms of the damage they inflict on *EUH*. I think a key element in these interpretations is what Jacob Marschak (1968) long ago called the cost of thinking, calculating, deciding, and acting, which are all part of what I have called the subjective cost of transacting (*SCT*) (see my 1982 article, p. 934 and passim). Of course, one could argue that *EUH* and its Chew-Machina-type extensions are on the face of it inadequate theories because they leave *SCT* out of the formal apparatus. But this is much too harsh. Considerations of *SCT* are hard to formalize within a framework as general as that attempted in *EUH* and *WEUH*, that allow the latter to be deduced as limiting cases when *SCT* goes to zero, or when outcome values get large relative to a fixed *SCT*. But the modification of standard *EUH* theory by introducing *SCT* elements in particular decision-making contexts (Sydney Siegel, 1961), or in illustrative examples (my 1982 article, p. 934), point to the untapped potential of imbedding standard theories in larger (and more "rational") frameworks. How important are the *SCT* elements in the various decision contexts which yield violations of *EUH*?

(a) I think the class of violations which are due to Kahneman-Tversky framing effects (see Slovic and Lichtenstein, and the references therein), do relatively low level damage to *EUH*. The typical case here is that the options are identical in two situations except that in one the outcomes are stated in terms of what will be lost (deaths), the other in terms of what will be gained (lives saved). It seems to me that these are like elementary optimal illusions, which the individual, at comparatively low cost, can learn to recog-

[4] Richard Thaler once reported in a seminar that, informally, he had gone around polling economists as to how they would bid, after describing the Second price auction procedure. This was before William Vickrey's discussion of this auction had become so well-known. He reported that very few got it "right." Most thought one should bid at least a "little" under value. The early polling of economists on Allais, Ellsberg, Second price, and other such "paradoxes" makes it clear that economists will get it "wrong" about as often as the sophomore subject (who of course we pay a monetary reward) until he or she has had considerable time to think and analyze. Incidentally, this observation provides an answer for that somewhat mythical businessman who asks, "If you're so smart why ain't you rich?" My classmate, Otto Eckstein, didn't get rich by equating price to marginal cost.

[5] An outstanding young economist once asked me why I was bothering to do Second price sealed-bid auction experiments since the dominant strategy property was so trivial. I encounter statements in this spirit so regularly that it has become a permanent way of life. They reveal two things: 1) how quickly, easily and matter of factly as economists we are prepared to believe our own propaganda (theorems), and to use these beliefs to insulate ourselves from evidence; and 2) how the use of experimental methods leads one to think about the world of economic knowledge in a fundamentally different way.

nize as such (for example, the individual can be taught that the death rate is one minus the survival rate. If it is hard to teach this, as it may be, then I am wrong in interpreting it as a low-cost recognition problem). We all learn that when the sun is low, the pond in the highway ahead is just a reflection, and we do not risk a rear-end collision by jamming on the brakes. In saying this, I do *not* mean to suggest that the study of framing effects is of no interest. On the contrary, these examples show how bad we can be at intuitive problem solving, and why it is important to examine a decision from alternative perspectives. Also, these examples vary in transparency. I find the second example cited by Slovic and Lichtenstein (p. 597) to involve more *SCT* than the first. I think the equivalence of the two situations in the first example could be conveyed to the uninitiated much more easily than the second. So some of these "optical" illusions may be more costly to expose than others.[6] Note that this *SCT* interpretation blurs the distinction often made between positive and normative economic theory, but I have never been convinced that such a distinction was very helpful.

(b) The preference reversal examples may represent still more sophisticated "optical" illusions, and may require rather more *SCT* to yield consistency of choice. However, the fact that they seem to be moderated (although they do not disappear) when the motivation is increased (Werner Pommerehne et al., 1982) is consistent with the hypothesis that subjects do seek to increase benefits net of *SCT*, even where the latter are relatively large. A preference reverser is of course vulnerable to a con game (money pump) in which a sequence of decisions will produce a loss in assets. Will a person discover his decision inconsistencies and learn the appropriate corrections in a money pump sequence? In this context *EUH* is being tested in a more market-like framework. J. E. Berg et al. (1984) report results showing that although the frequency of preference reversals is *not* reduced, the total value (dollar magnitude) of preference reversals *is* reduced. Apparently, there is positive interaction between the stakes, and the money pump treatment. They also report that the preference reversal phenomena tends to decline across experiments with the same subjects.

4) The results of direct laboratory tests of *EUH* have been used to explain the apparent failure of *EUH* in insurance, securities and futures markets (see Kenneth Arrow, 1982; Heiner, 1983). Although this appears to be evidence of parallelism in behavior between laboratory and field, I think we have to be particularly careful in drawing this parallel. There is first a question of the comparability of the quality of the evidence in the two environments, and second a question of whether *EUH* is failing for the same reason in the two environments. In the laboratory experiments, the situations are carefully controlled and structured, the states of nature are well-defined, and so are the outcomes. Consequently, the results are much more clearly interpretable as inconsistent with *EUH*, even if the cause of the inconsistency is an inappropriate carryover to the laboratory of Heiner's rule-governed agent whose habits have been developed in the more unstructured uncertainty environments of the field; or if, as I have suggested, the results can be interpreted in terms of *SCT*, and *EUH* is considered to be just a limiting case of a more general economic problem.

[6] In studies of science learning it is found that both weak and strong learners come to their first science classes with extensive "naive" theories about how the world works. They use these naive theories to explain physical events and tend, even after instruction in the new concepts and the scientific support for them, to resort to their prior theories to solve problems that differ from the textbook examples (Lauren Resnik, 1983). Of course with *EUH* we have the difficult problem of deciding when the subject is making a "mistake" (an "optical" illusion) which she can at more-or-less cost recognize as such, and when the theory is a mistake, or not relevant to the actual problem faced by the subject (which, for example, might be better represented by *WEUH* than *EUH*). The fact that about one-third of the subjects in sequential Second price sealed-bid auctions "learn" to make dominant strategy choices has been interpreted as analogous to learning that a certain mirage is an optimal illusion and the self-interest is not served by taking such a phenomenon at its face value (Vicki Coppinger et al., 1980, p. 20). Also see Thaler (1983) for a discussion of cognitive illusions and mirages in decision making.

An example may help to clarify one type of ambiguity in interpreting field observations in terms of *EUH*. Suppose you have had a sore rib for many weeks that hasn't healed. Your doctor sends you to the lab for an x-ray to "see if it is fractured." It is not fractured, and she tells you, "Well, a hairline fracture might not show, but it doesn't much matter since the treatment is the same whether it is a fracture or a contusion." You think, "This violates the Savage axioms!" Does it? How do you (or does she) know that there are only two states of nature, rib fractured or rib bruised, given that it is sore? Could a carcinoma behind the rib make it sore? There may be hundreds of causes of sore ribs, and it may not be worth anyone's trouble to list them all, or even to invest time in thinking about any significant fraction of them. A host of past experiences may have programmed your doctor to acquire information that appears to be redundant in this particular case, and she may be unable to organize these experiences into an articulate case for her actions because such a detailed cognitive treatment of every decision is neither a necessary nor a desirable feature of her modus operandi.

As a second example, take the reported reluctance of people to insure against rare disasters even though, since 1969, the government has offered subsidized flood insurance rates that are *below* actuarial value. Is it a fact that this violates *EUH*? If it is a fact, then I like Heiner's explanation that there is a tradeoff between the greater setup costs (these are part of what I call *SCT*) of insuring against more events of small probability, and the expected loss from failing to insure, and it is hardly economical to insure against everything. Hence, in the field situation *EUH* is failing because it formulates the *wrong economic choice problem*, by leaving out *SCT*. But it is not clear from the evidence that this is an example of the violation of *EUH*. Arrow tells us that the reason the government offered the subsidized insurance "was to relieve the pressure for the government to offer relief when floods occurred" (p. 2). If I have built a house on a flood plane, if flood planes sometimes flood (we call them 100-year floods in Arizona), and if it is standard political procedure for the governor to declare it a disaster area, and the federal government to respond with relief when a flood occurs, then I might not buy insurance even at rates below actuarial value. (This need not be a conscious decision with people able to state that the failure to buy insurance was due to the expectation of government relief.) Without better controls on the experimental treatment variable, I don't know how to interpret the observations. This problem does not reflect on the quality of these excellent studies cited by Arrow, but on the difficulty of doing field experiments with the most desirable controls. Similar considerations apply when asking whether interest rates or stock prices vary "too much" (see the studies by Cagan and Shiller cited in Arrow). It is unclear what is to be concluded when the falsifying "facts" are no more than "an impression which many students of these markets and practitioners in them seem to have" (Arrow, p. 4).

But Stewart's finding that unprofessional speculators lose money in grain futures is cited by Arrow as "especially surprising," and he asks "why did they enter the market at all?" (p. 3). I would suggest that they do it for the same reason that people go to Las Vegas to play roulette, buy tickets in the Arizona Lottery, and play bingo at the local church on Thursdays. I don't see any way to understand these phenomena with *EUH* (it is well known that convex, risk-preferring, utility doesn't explain repetitive small stakes wagering) nor any way to understand them with Heiner's theory. I find it necessary, if not entirely satisfactory in terms of seeking a universal theory, to accept the idea that some people just simply like to gamble (ancient hunter cultures did it) and that it has commodity value, or perhaps that some people have "pathological" expectations, whether it is roulette, grain futures or stock investment. (See my 1971 article.)[7]

[7]If in all markets with uncertainty there is a subclass of participants with these "irrational" characteristics, this lowers the insurance cost of hedging and lowers the cost of capital to firms. The gamblers lose money volun-

I have no disagreement with Heiner's critique of classical preference theory, which is among the roots that should be reexamined. However, I would register disagreement with Heiner's interpretation of "privacy" as an experimental condition. As noted in my article (1982, p. 933, fn. 13; p. 935) the purpose of privacy is to maintain control over preferences. Privacy does not deny the existence of interpersonal externalities. The latter is achieved under controlled conditions by simply inducing the appropriate interdependent preferences if that is the topic of investigation. If one wishes to study the effect of "utility information" on behavior, one publicizes information on commodity allocations, or token earnings (which is analogous to income in the field), but not subject cash payoffs since these are to induce utility on allocations and indirectly on token income. The idea is to preserve the natural uncertainty about other's subjective value of allocations, and of the exchange medium.

tarily, the economy benefits and perhaps only *EUH* suffers as a predictive theory for some types of agents. But the existence of such agents in futures, stock, and option markets will cause such markets to appear to be irrational by our definitions, whereas actually these markets may be performing with high allocative efficiency, given the environment, by taking wealth away from the gamblers and giving it to the hedgers, investors, and rational expectationists. Isn't Las Vegas an exchange market between gamblers (customers) and rational expectationists (casinos)? The question may be not "Why are certain markets inefficient?," but "What is wrong with our interpretation of markets?" An important technical difference between casinos and financial markets is that in the former the agent learns immediately the outcome of her investment. But the more variable are the prices of financial instruments, the more will they have this casino characteristic, and the more attractive they will be to this type of investor. Hence, the alleged "fact" that security prices vary "too much" may be both the effect and the cause of its appeal to these kinds of investors.

I suspect that Adam Smith would wonder why there is so much modern professional interest in the internal efficiency or "perfection" of particular markets, and so little interest in what determines the extent of markets, and how this in turn may create social gains that are more important and significant than the "imperfections" in particular markets that are suggested by our theory of "rational" preferences.

REFERENCES

Alchian, Armen, "Uncertainty, Evolution and Economic Theory," in *Economic Forces at Work*, Indianapolis: Liberty Press, 1977.

Arrow, Kenneth, "Risk Perception in Psychology and Economics," *Economic Inquiry*, January 1982, *20*, 1–9.

Berg, J. E., Dickhaut, J. W. and O'Brien, J. R., "Preference Reversal and Arbitrage," in V. Smith, ed., *Research in Experimental Economics*, Vol. 3, Greenwich: JAI Press, 1984.

Chew, Soo Hong, "A Generalization of the Quasilinear Mean with Applications to the Measurement of Income Inequality and Decision Theory Resolving the Allais Paradox," *Econometrica*, July 1983, *51*, 1065–92.

Coppinger, Vicki, Smith, Vernon and Titus, John, "Incentives and Behavior in English, Dutch and Sealed-Bid Auctions," *Economic Inquiry*, January 1980, *18*, 1–22.

Coursey, Don L., "Hierarchical Preferences and Consumer Choice," unpublished doctoral dissertation, University of Arizona, 1982.

Cox, James, Roberson, Bruce and Smith, Vernon, "Theory and Behavior of Single Object Auctions," in V. Smith, ed., *Research in Experimental Economics*, Vol. 2, Greenwich: JAI Press, 1982.

______**, Isaac, Mark and Smith, Vernon,** "OCS Leasing and Auctions: Incentives and the Performance of Alternative Bidding Institutions," *Supreme Court Economic Review*, July 1983, *2*, 43–87.

DeVorkin, David H., "Review of N. T. Roseveare, *Mercury's Perihelion from Le Verrier to Einstein*," *Science*, March 4, 1983, *219*, 1058.

Grether, David, "Bayes Rule as a Descriptive Model: The Representativeness Heuristic," *Quarterly Journal of Economics*, November 1980, *95*, 537–57.

______ **and Plott, Charles,** "Economic Theory of Choice and the Preference Reversal Phenomenon," *American Economic Review*, September 1979, *69*, 623–38.

Heiner, Ronald A., "The Origin of Predictable Behavior," *American Economic Review*, September 1983, *73*, 560–95.

———, "Experimental Economics: Comment," *American Economic Review*, March 1985, *75*, 260–63.

Kagel et al., John H., "Demand Curves for Animal Consumers," *Quarterly Journal of Economics*, February 1981, *96*, 1–16.

Marschak, Jacob, "Economics of Inquiring, Communicating, Deciding," *American Economic Review Proceedings*, May 1968, *58*, 1–18.

McClosky, Donald N., "The Rhetoric of Economics," *Journal of Economic Literature*, June 1983, *21*, 481–517.

Plott, Charles and Wilde, Louis, "Professional Diagnosis vs. Self-Diagnosis: An Experimental Examination of Some Special Features of Market With Uncertainty," in *Research in Experimental Economics*, Vol. 2, Greenwich: JAI Press, 1982, 63–112.

Pommerehne, Werner W., Schnieder, Frederick and Zweifel, Peter, "Economic Theory of Choice and the Preference Reversal Phenomenon: A Reexamination," *American Economic Review*, June 1982, *72*, 569–74.

Resnik, Lauren, B., "Mathematics and Science Learning: A New Conception," *Science*, April 29, 1983, *220*, 477–78.

Siegel, Sydney, "Decision Making and Learning Under Varying Conditions of Reinforcement," *Annals of the New York Academy of Science*, 1961, *89*, 766–83.

Slovic, Paul and Lichtenstein, Sarah, "Preference Reversals: A Broader Perspective," *American Economic Review*, September 1983, *73*, 596–605.

Smith, Vernon L., "Economic Theory of Wager Markets," *Western Economic Journal*, September 1971, *9*, 242–55.

———, "Microeconomic Systems as an Experimental Science," *American Economic Review*, December 1982, *72*, 923–55.

Thaler, Richard H., "Illusions and Mirages in Public Policy," *Public Interest*, Fall 1983, *73*. 60–74.

A Comparison of Posted-Offer and Double-Auction Pricing Institutions

JON KETCHAM
University of Arizona

VERNON L. SMITH
University of Arizona

and

ARLINGTON W. WILLIAMS
Indiana University

This paper presents an experimental study of a computerized "posted-offer" pricing mechanism that captures many of the basic institutional features of retail exchange in the U.S. Posted-offer market performance is evaluated relative to "double-auction" market performance using two supply and demand designs. Subject experience with the trading mechanism is explicitly considered as an experimental treatment variable. The market data suggest that prices tend to be higher and efficiency lower under posted-offer pricing relative to double auction. However, the institutional effect appears to interact with other design conditions. When feasible, the predictive power of competitive, Nash, and limit-price theoretic equilibria are empirically evaluated.

1. INTRODUCTION

The institution of posted-offer pricing is defined (Smith, 1976*b*; Plott and Smith, 1978) as a market mechanism in which each seller "posts" a selling price at the beginning of each trading period. Once prices have been displayed to all buyers and sellers, buyers then proceed in random order to purchase the quantity each desires. Viewed as an extensive form (minorant) game, sellers move first by sending price messages, buyers respond with quantity messages disclosing how much each will buy from some seller. Each seller involved in a trade moves last by indicating when no further units will be delivered (a "stock out" occurs). Although this pricing institution dominates almost all retail markets in the United States, it is a comparatively new pricing mechanism whose ascendency is associated with the retail innovations of R. H. Macy and F. W. Woolworth in the last half of the nineteenth century. These new mass retailers replaced the small owner-operated general store, with an organization which separated the clerical, management, and ownership functions. Since sales were made by large numbers of clerks, the take-it-or-leave-it posted price replaced the "haggling" that had characterized pricing in the general store (Marburg (1951), p. 527). By the 1930's this form of pricing was being referred to as "administered" pricing and was associated with anti-competitive practices in the economics literature.

This paper provides a systematic study of the performance characteristics of posted-offer pricing. Since the performance of an institution can be meaningfully evaluated only by using some alternative empirical standard as a base line, we compare the relative performance of the posted-offer and "double-auction" market institutions. In the double auction, both buyers and sellers are free to enter price quotes into the market. Any buyer (seller) is free to accept any sellers' (buyers') quotation and form a binding contract. This pricing institution characterizes floor trading on many organized stock and commodity exchanges throughout the world. Past experimental examinations of double-auction markets have shown that these markets exhibit two important characteristics: (1) "Rapid" convergence of prices to the theoretical competitive equilibrium (C.E.), and (2) highly efficient allocations (see, for example, Smith (1976*b*), Smith and Williams (1983*a*), Smith, Williams, Bratton and Vannoni (1982)). Consequently, the double auction provides a natural calibration standard against which posted-offer markets can be compared. From previous experimental investigations, it appears that posted-offer markets exhibit a tendency to produce contract prices above the C.E. price. In addition, posted-price markets appear to converge more slowly and be less efficient than oral auctions and negotiated pricing (Hong and Plott (1982), Plott and Smith (1978), Smith (1982*a*), F. Williams (1973)). For several reasons these summary statements can represent only very tentative conclusions: the total number of reported posted-price experiments is too small to permit meaningful significance tests (wherein each experiment is treated as a unit observation); these experiments did not examine the effect of subject experience; and none consisted of as many as 25 trading periods. It is an open question whether a C.E. will be approached and sustained in longer trading sequences. Since a C.E. under posted pricing is not typically a Nash equilibrium (see Alger, 1979, for an analysis of posted pricing), the behaviour of this important pricing institution acquires heightened significance.

2. THE PLATO POSTED-OFFER MECHANISM

All the experiments reported here were conducted using the PLATO computer system as the passive medium of public-information transfer and private-information display. The PLATO posted-offer program allows buyers and sellers sitting at individual PLATO computer terminals to make exchanges over a maximum of 25 trading periods. Each subject is shown a record sheet that contains a number of units of an abstract homogeneous commodity. Subjects may have up to five units to buy (sell) each period. For each unit, the buyer (seller) has a marginal valuation (cost) which represents the value (cost) to him of consuming (producing) that unit. These controlled unit valuations yield aggregate market supply and demand schedules (Smith (1976*a*)). During the experiment, buyers (sellers) may earn cash rewards by purchasing (selling) a unit at a price which is lower (higher) than the unit's marginal value (cost). Profits can only be made as a result of trading between buyers and sellers. In addition, buyers (sellers) are neither penalized nor rewarded for any unit(s) which they do not purchase (sell).

Offer procedure for sellers

Figure 1 illustrates the screen display for a seller in a PLATO posted-offer experiment. In this illustration the seller's capacity is three units per trading period. Initially, in each trading period, buyers are placed in a "waiting loop" and each seller is asked to submit a price offer. To enter an offer, a seller types a price on his/her computer terminal keyset; the offer is displayed on the seller's screen as the "selling price" as shown in Figure 1. After a seller's price is entered, PLATO compares that price with the seller's unit costs to determine the minimum and maximum number of units that can be offered. The seller is then asked to submit a quantity offer which must be between this specified minimum and maximum.

The maximum number of units a seller can offer corresponds to the number of the last unit whose cost is less than or equal to the price which the seller offers. This constraint prevents a seller from selling his last units at a loss. The minimum number of units a seller can offer corresponds to the number of the first unit whose cost is less than or equal to the seller's price offer. The seller is required to offer at minimum the first unit for which he covers his cost. This restriction serves to insure that a seller bargains in good faith; that is, he/she cannot post an offer and refuse to sell at least one of his/her units at that price. Only when a seller's price offer fails to cover any of the unit costs is a seller able to enter a quantity offer of zero. In this case, however, buyers will simply receive an "Out of Stock" message instead of the seller's price (see Figure 2).

The minimum and maximum quantity constraints have different implications depending on whether a seller faces rising or declining marginal costs. In the case of rising costs, the seller will be prevented from making a negative profit on any unit he sells. Where the seller faces declining marginal costs, these quantity constraints make it possible for him to lose money on the first units he sells. A seller who loses money on his/her first units because of declining costs has the possibility of making up that loss with the profits earned on later units.

Because it may be difficult for a seller to calculate the profit that a particular offer may yield (especially under declining costs), PLATO always informs the seller of the potential profit if all offered units are sold. If a seller has no possibility of earning a positive profit, PLATO displays a warning to this effect.

If a seller is satisfied with the selected price and quantity, he/she presses the touch sensitive "OFFER BOX" displayed on the screen (see Figure 1). The effect of this action is to place that seller's offer into the market. Before touching this box, a seller may change the price and/or quantity offer as many times as desired. Once an offer is entered into the market, the seller cannot change that offer for the duration of the trading period.

Seller 1	TRADING PERIOD →	*1	2	3	4	5
	Selling Price					
UNIT 1	Production Cost	2.45	2.45	2.45	2.45	2.45
	Profit + $.10 comm.					
	Selling Price					
UNIT 2	Production Cost	3.15	3.15	3.15	3.15	3.15
	Profit + $.10 comm.					
	Selling Price					
UNIT 3	Production Cost	3.20	3.20	3.20	3.20	3.20
	Profit + $.10 comm.					
	Gross Profit					

SELLING PRICE $3.50
UNITS in STOCK >
maximum stock 3
minimum stock 1

OFFER BOX

Type in the number of units you want to offer to the market at $ 3.50. The number you choose must not be greater than the "maximum stock" given above, nor less than the "minimum stock". Press -NEXT- when you're done. Press -SHIFT/EDIT- to change your SELLING PRICE.

FIGURE 1
Seller display, PLATO posted-offer market

Acceptance procedure for buyers

A typical screen display for a buyer is illustrated in Figure 2. In this example the buyer's capacity is three units and there are four sellers in the market.

When all of the sellers have entered their offer price and quantity, all prices are displayed to each buyer, as shown in Figure 2. PLATO then places the sellers in a "waiting loop" and randomly orders the buyers to determine the sequence in which they will make purchases. Only one buyer at a time is allowed to purchase units and a buyer has as much time to make purchases as is needed. To purchase a seller's unit, the buyer touches the display screen box containing the seller's offer price (see Figure 2), and then presses a key on the keyset to confirm the purchase. Upon confirming the acceptance of a seller's price offer, the seller is informed of this fact by PLATO and the contract information is automatically logged in both the buyer's and seller's record sheet. A buyer is allowed to purchase up to his/her capacity of units, and to purchase those units from any seller desired. In all purchases, however, buyers are subject to the following two restrictions:

Buyer 4	TRADING PERIOD →	*1	2	3	4	5
	Resale Value	3.40	3.40	3.40	3.40	3.40
UNIT 1	Purchase Price					
	Profit + $.10 comm.					
	Resale Value	3.20	3.20	3.20	3.20	3.20
UNIT 2	Purchase Price					
	Profit + $.10 comm.					
	Resale Value	2.95	2.95	2.95	2.95	2.95
UNIT 3	Purchase Price					
	Profit + $.10 comm.					
	Gross Profit					

SELLER 1	SELLER 2	SELLER 3	SELLER 4
3.50	3.30	OUT of STOCK	3.40

You may now begin to purchase units. To buy a unit, touch the box of the SELLER whose unit you want to buy. If you touch the wrong box, press -BACK-. Otherwise, to confirm the purchase, press -DATA-. You may buy as many units as you can. WHEN YOU ARE DONE, PRESS -LAB-.

FIGURE 2

Buyer display, PLATO posted-offer market

(1) A buyer cannot purchase a unit whose price is greater than the unit's marginal valuation, and would therefore yield a negative profit.

(2) A buyer cannot purchase a unit from a seller who has sold all of the units offered. When a seller has no more units to sell, the box on the buyer's screen is replaced with the message "Out of Stock" (see Figure 2).

After the first buyer has finished making purchases, the next buyer in random order is permitted to make purchases. This process is repeated until each buyer has had a chance to purchase units. After the last buyer finishes, the current trading period is closed and a new trading period is begun. In each trading period, buyers and sellers follow the same procedures with sellers posting offers and the randomly ordered buyers purchasing units.

A point to emphasize is that buyers and sellers are given only a limited amount of information. The unit values given to each individual are strictly private, known only to the subject and the experimenter. Each buyer can see all of the sellers' price offers but not their quantity offers. Only when an "Out of Stock" message is encountered does the buyer know that a seller has no units left to sell. Aside from the units he/she buys, a buyer has no information about the contracts made by others during a trading period. Unlike buyers, sellers may or may not be able to see the prices which other sellers offer. This important treatment variable is controlled by the experimenter and will be the subject of a separate report. The PLATO computer program also allows one to conduct experiments in which buyers are charged to see any seller's price (costly search) or in which sellers must pay to display a price (advertising). Like buyers, sellers know only their own transactions.

3. A COMPARISON OF DOUBLE-AUCTION AND POSTED-OFFER TRADING INSTITUTIONS

Experimental design

The institution used in this comparison is the PLATO computerized double auction developed by A. Williams (1980). The double auction experimental results used in this section are taken, in part, from results reported in Smith and Williams (1983*a*). Six previously unreported double-auction experiments are included in the analysis that follows.

The particular version of the PLATO double auction used as a basis for comparison with posted offer is that found by Smith and Williams (1983*a*) to produce the most rapid convergence and the highest efficiency. This version incorporates both a "bid-ask spread reduction rule" and a "rank queue". According to the bid-ask spread reduction rule, a new price quote is admissible for market (public) display only if it serves to reduce the gap between the outstanding bid and offer. Price quotes that do not satisfy the bid-ask spread reduction rule are placed in a queue that ranks bids (offers) in ascending (descending) order as they wait for possible entry into the market after a contract occurs. The rank queue is an electronic version of the "specialist's book" in the New York Stock Exchange.

Since buyers and sellers in the double-auction market can see all bids and offers that satisfy the bid-ask reduction rule, the posted-offer market used in these comparisons will allow sellers (as well as buyers) to see all prices offered in both the current and the previous trading period. The range of information given buyers and sellers in both markets will therefore be similar.

The market comparisons in this study were made using two different experimental designs. Table I gives the (normalized) buyers' resale values and sellers' costs for Design I. One of the resulting supply and demand arrays is illustrated on the left of Figure 3. The C.E. exchange quantity is seven units. The equilibrium price is varied across experiments by adding some arbitrary constant to all buyer and seller valuations. Note

TABLE I

Design I Subjects' unit valuations as deviations from P_c

	Unit 1	Unit 2	Unit 3
Buyer 1	0·95	−0·10	−0·25
Buyer 2	0·70	0	−0·05
Buyer 3	0·45	0	−0·15
Buyer 4	0·25	0·05	−0·20
Seller 1	−0·95	0·10	0·25
Seller 2	−0·70	0	0·05
Seller 3	−0·45	0	0·15
Seller 4	−0·25	−0·05	0·20

that these supply and demand conditions yield equal amounts of consumer and producer surplus at the C.E. (the total is \$6·20 per trading period). In addition, to compensate for any subjective costs of trading, each subject is paid a \$0·10 commission on each unit traded. This provides a small inducement for any unit to exchange at a price equal to its value or cost.[1]

In Design I under posted pricing the C.E. is not a Nash equilibrium (N.E.). Thus from Table I, or the supply and demand schedule in Figure 3, if all sellers except i post $P_C = 4{\cdot}70$, then the revealed C.E. supply is $S(P_C) = 5$ if $i \neq 1$, and $S(P_C) = 6$ if $i = 1$. Under these conditions, if the deviant seller is $i = 2$, 3 or 4, that seller can increase profit at prices above P_C. For example seller 2 makes a profit of \$0·70 (plus commissions of \$0·20) by posting P_C along with the remaining sellers. Now let seller 2 post $P_2 = \$5{\cdot}15$. Then with probability 3/4, buyer 1 or 2 or 3 will purchase last in sequence, and any of these events leads to the sale of one unit by seller 2, resulting in an average profit of (3/4) (5·15 − 4·00) = \$0·8625 (plus commissions of \$0·075). Consequently, seller 2 is better off. This assumes of course that buyers fully reveal demand and that the subjective cost of transacting is not greater than the commission for any agent. We do not know whether Design I has many or no Nash equilibria. But from this example showing that a C.E. is not a N.E. the reader can appreciate the large number of combinatorial possibilities to be examined in identifying any N.E.

Under the double-auction rules, the C.E. in Design I is also a N.E. in the sense that if all but one participant (a buyer or a seller) were to bid (offer) each profitable unit at the C.E. price, then the remaining person could do no better than to bid (offer) each profitable unit at the price.

In contrast to the symmetrical supply and demand arrays of Design I, Design II gives each of the three sellers constant costs, and *no* subject is paid a commission. Table II gives the unit valuations for this design. An example of the resulting supply and

TABLE II

Design II Subject's unit valuations as deviations from P_C

	Unit 1	Unit 2	Unit 3	Unit 4	Unit 5
Buyer 1	0·77	0·12	−0·08	−0·28	—
Buyer 2	0·67	0·17	−0·03	−0·23	—
Buyer 3	0·57	0·27	0·02	−0·18	—
Buyer 4	0·47	0·37	0·07	−0·13	—
Seller 1	−0·13	−0·13	−0·13	−0·13	−0·13
Seller 2	−0·03	−0·03	−0·03	−0·03	−0·03
Seller 3	0·07	0·07	0·07	0·07	0·07

demand arrays is shown on the left in Figure 8. As before, these valuations are varied across experiments by adding some arbitrary constant. The market structure in Design II is a variation of triopoly where the highest cost seller is cut out of the market above the C.E. price. In this design, we can define two prices toward which the market might converge. The lower price corresponds to a C.E. price. Since several prices clear the market in this design, "the" C.E. price is taken to be the midpoint of this set, rounded to the nearest cent (labeled P_C in Figure 8). Alternatively, the market might approach a "limit-price" equilibrium where the highest cost seller is just excluded from the market (labled P_L in Figure 8). With constant costs, this limit price will equal the unit cost of the highest cost seller. At P_C, the two lower cost sellers can sell all 10 of their units. At P_L, these two sellers will be able to sell at most 9 units. Subjects will earn a total of $4·30 per trading period at P_C and $0·05 to $0·15 less at P_L, depending on whether the marginal unit trades. Although in this design no commissions are paid, the range of C.E. prices at a quantity of ten allows a positive return to the marginal units supplied or demanded.

In Design II we can identify a N.E. that is distinct from the C.E. and near the limit-price equilibrium. To show this suppose we assume that no buyer (seller) will buy (offer) a unit at a price which is not at least $0·01 below (above) the value (cost) of the unit. This implies that the cost of transacting is positive but less than $0.01. Under these conditions a N.E. posted-price vector (normalized on the C.E. price) for Design II is $(P_1, P_2, P_3) = (0{\cdot}05, 0{\cdot}06, 0{\cdot}08)$ and the corresponding quantities sold are $(Q_1, Q_2, Q_3) = (5, 4, 0)$, where the subscripts 1, 2 and 3 refer to the lowest, middle and highest unit cost sellers, respectively. This is shown in Table III, which lists the profits of sellers 1 and 2

TABLE III

Expected profit of sellers 1 and 2 (π_1, π_2) for price offers of $AC_3 = P_C + 0{\cdot}07$ and below, Design II

		P_2 = Price offer of Seller 2 ($AC_2 = P_C - 0{\cdot}03$)			
	π_2 / π_1	0·07	0·06*	0·05	0·04
P = Price offer of Seller 1 ($AC_1 = P_C - 0{\cdot}13$)	0·07	0·40 0·80	0·45 0·70	0·40 0·70	0·35 0·70
	0·06	0·35 0·95	0·41 0·86	0·40 0·76	0·35 0·76
	0·05*	0·35 0·90	0·36 0·90	0·36 0·81	0·35 0·72
	0·04	0·35 0·85	0·36 0·85	0·32 0·85	0·32 0·77

Note: * Indicates N.E. price offers.

as a function of the prices P_1 and P_2, on the assumption that $P_3 = 0{\cdot}08$. To see that this is a N.E., note first that seller 3 can do no better than to post $P_3 = 0{\cdot}08$ (4·76 in Figure 8), given that P_1 and P_2 are at $0·08 or below. So all the action is between sellers 1 and 2 at prices strictly below $P_3 = 0{\cdot}08$ (otherwise sellers 1 and 2 make profits below the potential shown in Table III). The calculations shown in Table III are straightforward given our assumptions about transactions cost and buyer choice of quantities. Thus, at normalized prices $(P_1, P_2, P_3) = (0{\cdot}07, 0{\cdot}07, 0{\cdot}08)$ (i.e. (4·75, 4·75, 4·76) in Figure 8) eight units are sold regardless of the order in which buyers make their purchases. Hence, sellers 1 and 2 each deliver 3, 4 or 5 units depending upon how buyers divide their purchases between these two sellers. If this is random, each seller has expected sales of 4 units, giving an expected profit of \$0·80 per period to seller 1 and \$0·40 per period to seller 2 as shown in Table III. At prices $(P_1, P_2, P_3) = (0{\cdot}06, 0{\cdot}07, 0{\cdot}08)$ seller 1 delivers 5 units per period for a profit of \$0·95 per period, but seller 2 delivers either 3 units or 4 units depending upon whether buyer 4 is third or fourth in the buyer purchase queue or in first or second position. Thus, if buyer 4 buys in the third or fourth position, his/her last unit must be purchased from seller 2, and at $P_2 = 0{\cdot}07$ buyer 4 will buy no more than 2 units. Then total sales will be 8 units with only 3 units delivered by seller 2. But if buyer 4 is in either the first or second buying position, he/she will be able to purchase 3 units from seller 1 at $P_1 = 0{\cdot}06$, total sales will be 9 units, and 4 units will be delivered by seller 2. Consequently, seller 2 will have expected sales of 3·5 units and a profit of \$0·35 per period.[2] The same reasoning applies in calculating the remaining cells in Table III. At the normalized prices $P_1 = 0{\cdot}05$ and $P_2 = 0{\cdot}06$ in Table III neither seller 1 nor seller 2 can improve their respective profits given the other seller's price, thereby yielding the N.E. $(P_1, P_2, P_3) = (0{\cdot}05, 0{\cdot}06, 0{\cdot}08)$.

All subjects were recruited from economics classes at the University of Arizona, or in the case of "multisite" experiments, subjects were recruited from both the University of Arizona and Indiana University. (There are over 100 PLATO sites in the United States connected by telephone line to a central computer at the University of Illinois which permits subjects at more than one site to trade.)

Each subject who reports to the PLATO lab is paid \$3·00 for keeping the appointment. When all subjects have arrived, each is randomly assigned to a computer terminal. PLATO then gives each subject a randomly chosen buyer/seller designation and a set of unit valuations/costs. Subjects are then presented with a set of appropriate instructions which each can read individually. When all subjects have completed their instructions, PLATO executes the experiment, monitoring the progress of each subject and enforcing all rules of the market institution. At the experiment's conclusion, each subject is paid in private his/her accumulated earnings during the course of the experiment.

Experimental results

The results in this section are based on twenty-four experiments as follows:

Design I.
- Double Auction (DA).
  - Inexperienced subjects: Three experiments (2DA17, 2DA21, 2DA24).
  - Experienced subjects: Three experiments (2DA20x, 2DA47x, 2DA53x).
- Posted Offer (PO).
  - Inexperienced subjects: Three experiments (PO7i, PO12i, PO19i).
  - Experienced subjects: Three experiments (PO27ix, PO32ix, PO17ixs).

Design II.
- Double Auction (DA).
  - Inexperienced subjects: Three experiments (3DA16, 3DA18, 3DA19).
  - Experienced subjects: Three experiments (3DA28x, 3DA30x, 3DA36x).
- Posted Offer (PO).
  - Inexperienced subjects: Four experiments (PO4i, PO5i, PO11i, PO22i).
  - Experienced subjects: Two experiments (PO14ix, PO25ix).

An "i" in the name of a posted-offer experiment means that sellers have complete information on all price offers, while an "x" in a double-auction or posted-offer experiment refers to experienced subjects. Subjects were "experienced" if each had participated in at least one previous experiment using the same trading rules. However, a subject who had been a buyer (seller) in a previous experiment would not necessarily be a buyer (seller) in an "x" session (except in PO17ixs reported below).

Contract prices are charted in sequence as solid circles for a sample of four Design I experiments in Figures 3–6, and two Design II experiments in Figures 8 and 9. The open circles in the PO experiments are unaccepted price offers. The DA Design I experiments were not continued beyond ten trading periods because the convergence

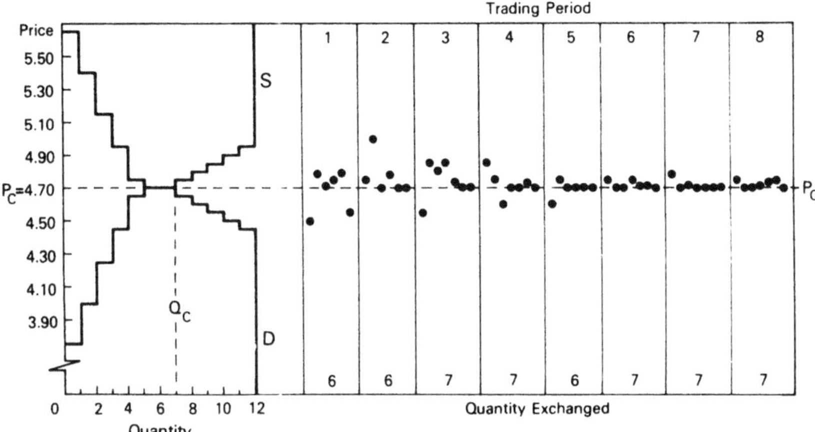

FIGURE 3
Double auction 2DA 24

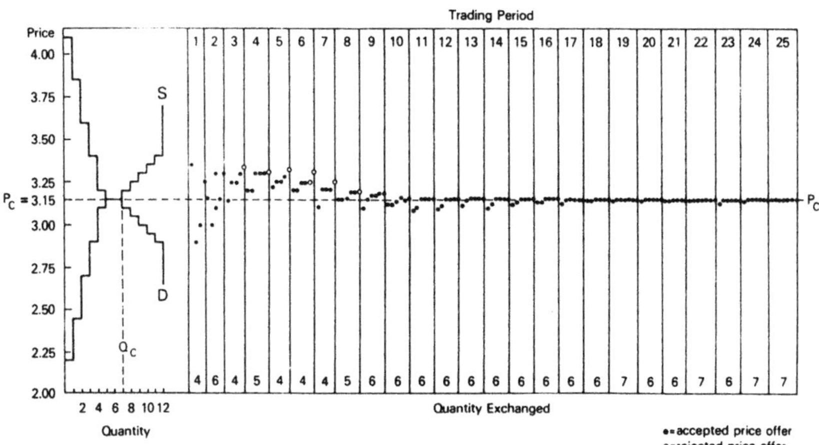

FIGURE 4
Posted offer PO7i

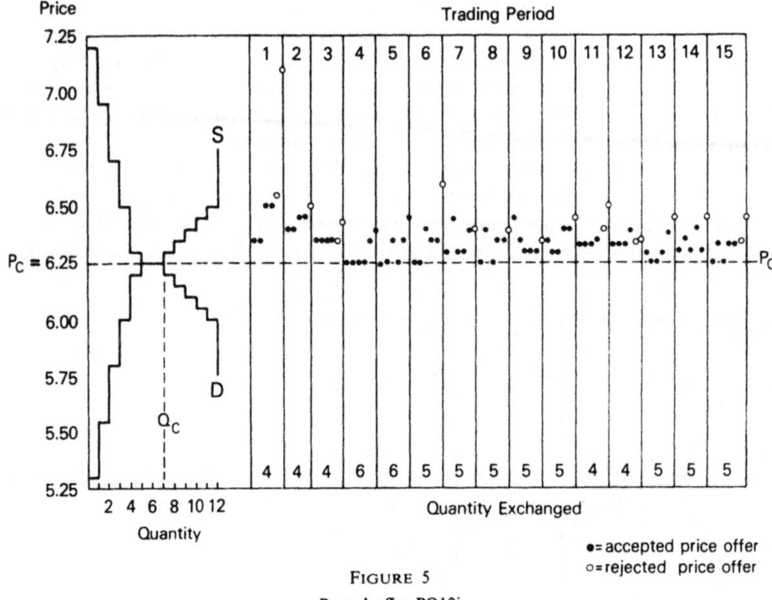

FIGURE 5
Posted offer PO12i

properties of this institution are well established. In the posted-offer experiments we conducted as many trading periods as were possible (usually 25) within the two-hour sessions. Figures 7 and 10 respectively, chart the mean deviation of contract prices from the C.E. price by trading period for all the Design I and Design II experiments.

In addition to these summary and individual charts, which we invite the reader to study, we will suumarize the effect of the various treatment variables on price convergence using linear regression estimates. In each regression one of three dependent variables is used to measure "nearness" to the C.E. As indicated below, more than one measure of distance between the observations and the predictions of C.E. theory is used because there exists no single quantity that is sufficient. Also, an experiment consists of a sequential series of observations on any particular chosen measure. Therefore, if an experiment is the basic unit of observation subject to random sampling error (due to sampling variations from the population of participant buyers and sellers), it is necessary to transform the appropriate set of observations from each experiment into a single number, and the rule of transformation must be the same in all experiments if biasedness is to be minimized. Based on these considerations the following three measures will be employed:

(1) The asymptotic root mean square error (RMSE) deviation in contract prices from the C.E. price, is given by

$$r^0 = \lim_{t\to\infty} r(t) = \frac{a}{1-b} \tag{1}$$

where a and b are least squares estimates of the first-order difference equation in $r(t)$,

$$r(t) = a + br(t-1) + \varepsilon_t, \qquad |b| < 1, \qquad t = 2, \ldots, T. \tag{2}$$

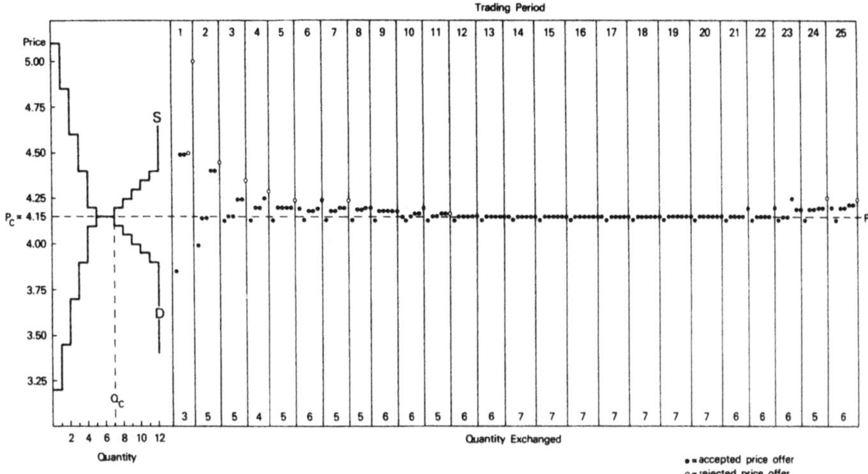

FIGURE 6
Posted offer PO17ixs

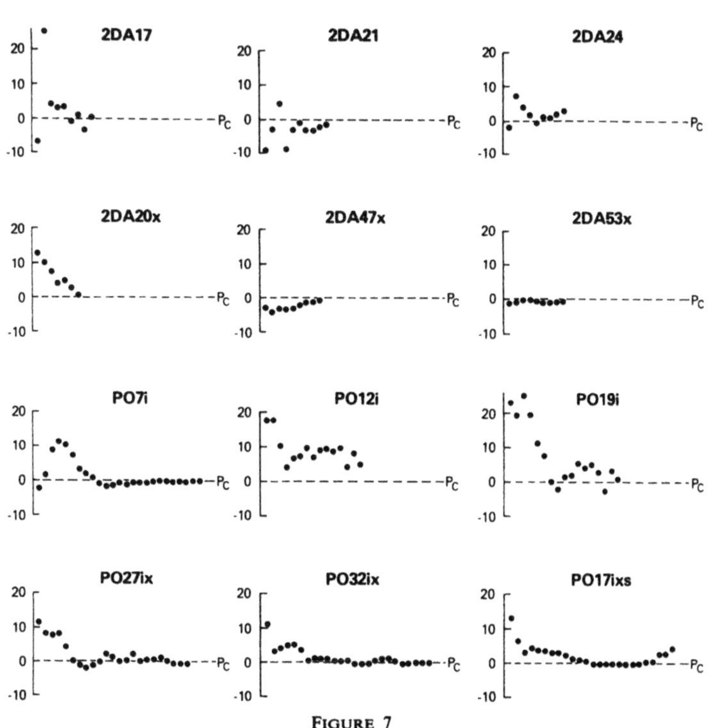

FIGURE 7
Mean deviation from C.E. price, Design I

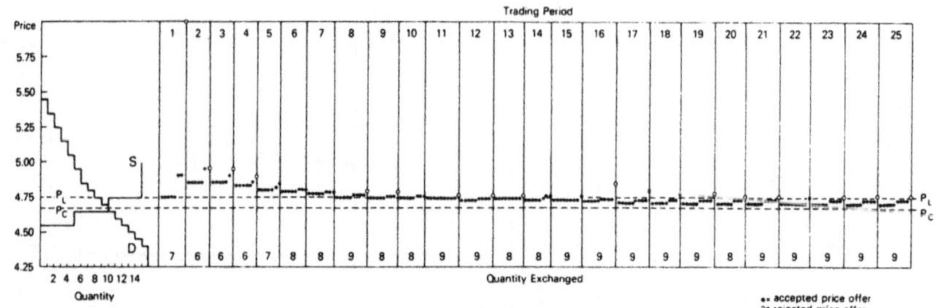

FIGURE 8
Posted offer PO5i

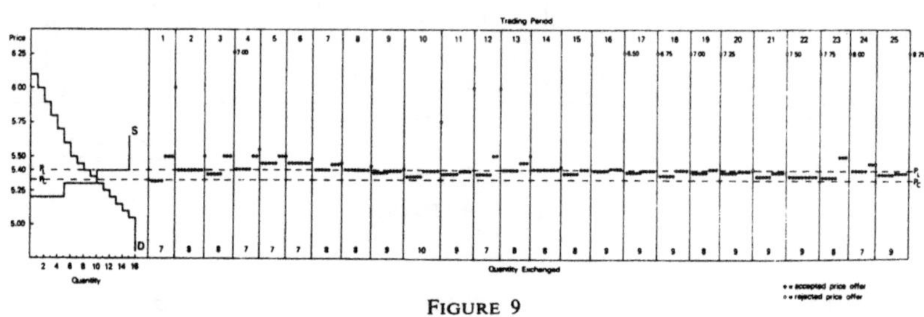

FIGURE 9
Posted offer PO14ix

In (2), $r(t)$ is the RMSE of contract prices in period t; i.e.

$$r^2 = \frac{1}{Q(t)} \Sigma_{q=1}^{Q(t)} [P_q(t) - P_C]^2 = \frac{1}{Q(t)} \Sigma_{q=1}^{Q(t)} [P_q(t) - \bar{P}]^2 + [\bar{P}(t) - P_C]^2 \tag{3}$$

where $P_q(t)$ is the q-th contract price in period t, and $Q(t)$ is the total number of contracts in period t. Note in (3) that RMSE depends upon both the variance of prices and the deviation in mean price from the C.E. Of the three measures to be used, r^0 is the only measure of revealed price convergence behavior based on all the price information in each experiment.

In Design II the Nash and limit price concepts of equilibrium differ from the C.E., and corresponding values of r^0 can be computed for these alternative equilibria. Since a Nash equilibrium (given our assumptions about subjective cost) is $(P_1, P_2, P_3) = (0{\cdot}05, 0{\cdot}06, 0{\cdot}08)$; $(Q_1, Q_2, Q_3) = (5, 4, 0)$ it follows that the Nash asymptotic RMSE is $r_N^0 = \{[5(0{\cdot}05)^2 + 4(0{\cdot}06)^2 + 0(0{\cdot}08)^2]/9\}^{1/2} = \$0{\cdot}055$. Similarly the limit price asymptotic RMSE is $r_L^0 = \{[5(0{\cdot}07)^2 + 5(0{\cdot}07)^2 + 0(0{\cdot}07)^2]/10\}^{1/2} = \$0{\cdot}07$. If we observe $r^0 \neq 0$ (the C.E. prediction, since r^0 is normalized on the C.E. price) these values of r_N^0 and r_L^0 allow us to ask if the data support the Nash or limit price predictions.

(2) The mean error (ME) deviation in contract price from the C.E. price in period t is

$$\delta(t) = \frac{1}{Q(t)} \Sigma_{q=1}^{Q(t)} (P_q(t) - P_C). \tag{4}$$

Our measure of "equilibrium" ME, δ^0, will be the average $\delta(t)$ for periods 7, 8 and 9. In Design II, the Nash ME is $\delta_N^0 = [5(0{\cdot}05) + 4(0{\cdot}06) + 0(0{\cdot}08)]/9 = \$0{\cdot}054$, while the limit price ME is $\delta_L^0 = \$0{\cdot}07$.

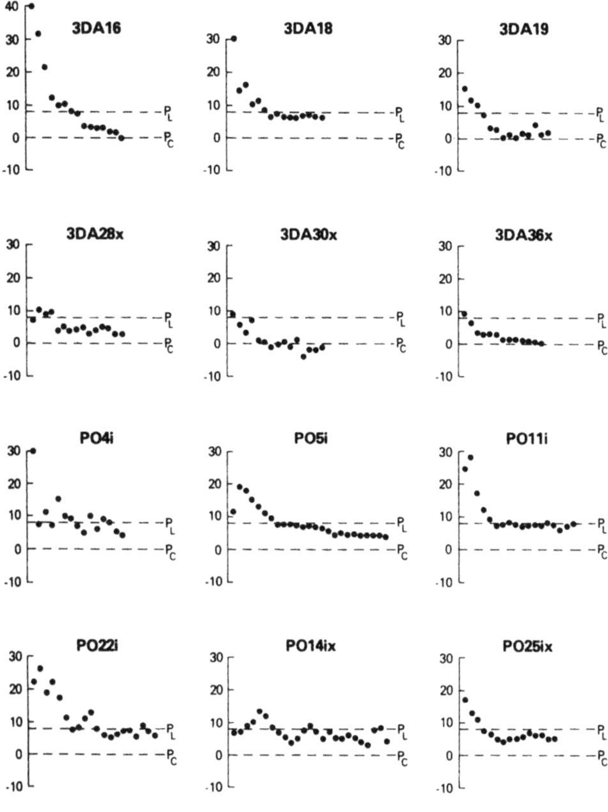

FIGURE 10
Mean deviation from C.E. price, Design II

(3) Efficiency in period t is

$$E(t)=\frac{\sum_{i=1}^{N}\pi_i(t)}{\sum_{i=1}^{N}\pi_i^C(t)} \tag{5}$$

where N is the number of agents, $\pi_i(t)$ is the realized profit (excluding commissions) of agent i, and $\pi_i^C(t)$ is the C.E. profit of agent i. We take as our measure of "equilibrium" efficiency, E^0, the average $E(t)$ for periods 7, 8 and 9. In Design II, efficiency of the N.E. is $E_N^0=98{\cdot}8$, and at the limit price equilibrium is $E_L^0=96{\cdot}5$.

Each of the three quantities, r^0, δ^0 and E^0 measures something distinct. Differences in the variability of prices for a given mean price is reflected in r^0, but not in δ^0. Neither r^0 nor δ^0 provides any indication of how effectively the gains from exchange are exhausted. Efficiency is 100% if and only if all possible gains from exchange are realized. Also, if posted-offer prices are biased above P_C in comparison with double-auction prices, this property will be more adequately reflected in δ^0 than in r^0.[3]

The first six data columns of Table IV report the regression results for the first order difference equation (2) applied to the data of all 24 experiments. Most of the regressions are highly significant, the exceptions occurring in only three inexperienced groups (2DA17, 2DA21, and PO4i). Column 7 contains the asymptotic RMSE price deviations from equation (1), while columns 8 and 9 provide the average ME price deviations and efficiencies averaged over periods 7–9 in each experiment. Generally, the price measures r^0 and δ^0 are closer to zero and E^0 is closer to 100% for experienced than for inexperienced subjects. Similarly, these measures appear to be nearer their C.E. predictions in the double-auction mechanism than in posted-offer pricing.

TABLE IV

Measures of convergence

Experiment	(1) a	(2) b	(3) R^2	(4) F	(5) $d.w.$	(6) $T-1$	(7) r^0	(8) δ^0	(9) E^0
Design I:									
2DA17	0·0813	0·0277	0	0·47	1·00	8	0·1125	−0·009	99·65
2DA21	0·0678	0·1178	0	0·12	1·44	9	0·0769	−0·029	97·92
2DA24	0·0001	0·8496	0·84	44·4	1·01	9	0·0006	0·019	93·40
2DA20x	−0·0124	0·9487	0·96	134·2	2·25	6	0	0·003	100·00
2DA47x	0·0019	0·8701	0·44	6·58	1·97	8	0·0145	−0·016	99·31
2DA53x	0·0126	0·0964	0·14	2·12	2·82	8	0·0139	−0·008	100·00
PO7i	0·0032	0·7411	0·87	149·8	1·76	24	0·0124	0·019	89·24
PO12i	0·0477	0·4614	0·29	6·36	2·41	14	0·0886	0·085	86·46
PO19i	0·0191	0·7117	0·55	19·4	2·29	16	0·0662	−0·002	92·71
PO27ix	0·0049	0·7039	0·71	52·1	2·40	22	0·0166	−0·015	100·00
PO32ix	0·0092	0·3835	0·71	58·2	1·04	24	0·0149	0·012	92·02
PO17ix	0·0123	0·4683	0·85	129·4	1·87	24	0·0232	0·027	97·92
Design II:									
3DA16	0·0207	0·6878	0·93	183·9	1·45	14	0·0662	0·060	97·29
3DA18	0·0345	0·5226	0·73	36·7	2·96	14	0·0722	0·066	94·57
3DA19	0·0111	0·6534	0·80	48·9	2·37	13	0·0319	0·007	98·84
3DA28x	0·0147	0·7393	0·45	11·5	2·28	14	0·0563	0·044	98·84
3DA30x	0·0114	0·5901	0·46	11·9	2·25	14	0·0279	−0·003	89·54
3DA36x	0·0074	0·4918	0·88	78·7	0·98	12	0·0146	0·018	96·90
PO4i	0·0767	0·0958	0	0·54	2·08	14	0·0848	0·070	96·89
PO5i	0·0027	0·9210	0·86	145·4	1·04	24	0·0338	0·081	94·19
PO11i	0·0094	0·7694	0·81	76·3	2·17	14	0·0409	0·078	96·51
PO22i	0·0127	0·8194	0·75	53·7	2·09	19	0·0705	0·092	90·31
PO14ix	0·0331	0·5300	0·25	8·86	1·65	24	0·0705	0·070	97·29
PO25ix	0·0183	0·6440	0·91	139·2	1·29	14	0·0515	0·048	97·29

A more precise determination of the marginal (linear) effect of each treatment variable is obtained from the regressions

$$y_k^0 = K + \alpha X_k + \beta P_k + \gamma D_k + \varepsilon_k \tag{6}$$

where for experiment $k = 1, 2, \ldots, N$,

$$y_k^0 = \begin{cases} r_k^0 \\ \delta_k^0 \\ E_k^0 \end{cases}, \quad X_k = \begin{cases} 0, & \text{if subjects in } k \text{ are inexperienced,} \\ 1, & \text{if subjects in } k \text{ are experienced.} \end{cases}$$

$$P_k = \begin{cases} 0, & \text{if } k \text{ uses double-auction rules,} \\ 1, & \text{if } k \text{ uses posted-offer rules.} \end{cases} \quad D_k = \begin{cases} 0, & \text{if } k \text{ uses Design I,} \\ 1, & \text{if } k \text{ uses Design II.} \end{cases}$$

The OLS estimates of the coefficients $(K, \alpha, \beta, \gamma)$ in (6) with separate estimates of (K, α, β) for Designs I and II are shown in Table V. The results of earlier experiments

TABLE V

Regression estimates

Dependent variable	Data set	Coefficients of independent variables: Constant	Subject experience X	Pricing institution P	Supply-demand design D	Regression measures: Adjusted R^2	F Statistic	Number of experiments N
r^0, asymptotic root mean square error in prices	All Experiments	0·049 (4·11)	−0·029* (−2·49)	0·005 (0·409)	0·013 (1·09)	0·186	2·76	24
	Design I, D=0	0·059 (3·56)	−0·046* (−2·38)	0·001 (0·030)		0·249	2·82	12
	Design II, D=1	0·050 (4·55)	−0·011 (−0·843)	0·012 (0·935)		0·175	0·95	12
δ^0, mean error in prices, periods 7, 8 and 9	All Experiments	0·000 (0·002)	−0·019* (−1·92)	0·033* (3·44)	0·044* (4·59)	0·614	13·2*	24
	Design I, D=0	0·000 (0·000)	−0·013 (−0·837)	0·028 (1·74)		0·135	1·85	12
	Design II, D=1	0·044 (4·24)	−0·023* (−1·91)	0·037* (3·13)		0·559	7·98*	12
E^0, mean efficiency, periods 7, 8 and 9	All Experiments	95·83	2·52 (1·69)	−2·74* (−1·85)	0·196 (0·132)	0·144	2·29	24
	Design I, D=0	95·89	4·98* (2·73)	−5·32* (−2·92)		0·640	8·00*	12
	Design II, D=1	95·81	0·368 (0·186)	−0·522 (−0·267)		0·000	0·063	12

Note: * Significant at 0·05 level or below.

suggest that a priori, we can expect subject experience to decrease the deviation of prices from the C.E., and to increase efficiency. Also we can expect posted-offer pricing (relative to double-auction pricing) to increase the deviation of prices from the C.E., and to decrease efficiency. Finally, in Design II, since there are only two active competitors at the limit price and below, we can expect that the effect of Design II (relative to Design I) is to weaken competition; i.e. to increase price deviations from the C.E., and to decrease efficiency. Since these are *a priori* sign predictions (indeed we wrote them down before running the regressions) one-tailed significance tests are appropriate for the dummy variable coefficients in Table V. All of these sign predictions are supported by the results listed in Table V except that efficiency increases slightly (instead of decreasing), but not significantly, with the design variable, *D*. The effect of experience and the pricing institution conform with these expectations in all of the regressions including those run separately for each of the two designs.

However, it should be noted that the *significance levels* (*t* values are shown in parentheses) of the various treatment effects are *not stable* across the different measures of "nearness" to the C.E.; nor are they stable between Designs I and II. Thus subject experience has a significant effect on the RMSE price measure and efficiency in Design I but not in Design II. This is consistent with the general hypothesis that competition is weaker in Design II. Similarly, the pricing institution and the design treatment has quite significant effects on the ME price measure but insignificant effects on the asymptotic RMSE price measure. This difference in the behaviour of the RMSE measure and the ME measure reflects two information differences. First, the intraperiod variability of prices affects RMSE but not ME. Thus if posted-offer contract prices tend to be higher, but *less* variable, than double-auction prices, then the RMSE price index will not be affected by the institution as much as the ME index. Second, since RMSE measures the asymptotic equilibrium tendencies implied by the observations across all the trading periods of an experiment, it contains more (though not unbiased) information than ME. Consequently, it is of some interest that by the RMSE measure neither the design nor the institution contributes significantly to the convergence tendency, after correcting for the effect of subject experience. But we are not dealing here with robust effects since the *F* value for the RMSE regression is low.

Previous studies (Hong and Plott (1982), Plott and Smith (1978), F. Williams (1973)) suggesting that ME will be higher and efficiency lower in posted-offer markets than in double-auction markets receive confirmation in Table V. However, the price biases of the posted-offer institution are much weaker in the symmetrical Design I, with four sellers, than in the asymmetrical Design II with three sellers, only two of which are intramarginal competitors. This suggests that the effect of the institution interacts with other design conditions. This is consistent with previous reports of monopoly experiments (Smith (1981), (1982*a*)) in which one posted-offer monopoly was far more effective than any of several directly comparable double-auction monopoly experiments.

4. SIGNALLING AND TACIT COLLUSION

The double-auction and posted-offer institutions of exchange provide quite different opportunities for signalling and for tacit collusion. In double auctions, the signalling opportunity for buyers is the same as for sellers; buyers are free to signal with low bids, just as sellers are free to signal with high offers. A bid or an offer is for a single unit, and if not accepted, can always be revised. The opportunity cost of signalling is thus insignificant. Consequently, signaling occurs frequently, but it has not been apparent that this phenomena is effective in yielding collusive outcomes for either buyers or sellers. The only clear exception to this is under monopoly, where buyers signal vigorously and are effective (Smith (1982*a*), Smith and Williams (1983*b*)) in restraining the power of the monopolist.

In posted-offer pricing, buyers have no opportunity to signal. A buyer may accept or refuse to accept any offer, but such acts are private and unknown to other buyers. Any seller is free to signal with an increase in his posted price. Since only sellers can signal, this favors the possibility of tacit collusion among sellers to coordinate an increase in prices. Since a posted price cannot be revoked during a trading period, the act of signalling with a higher price is costly in terms of foregone sales. This reduces the incentive of the individual seller to signal, and may promote "free riding"; each seller will want other sellers to signal. However, this costliness makes a signal more credible, or meaningful, when it does occur and this may increase the prospect that signalling will be effective.

In view of these opposing considerations it is especially significant to find that signalling is quite common among posted-price sellers. In the contract price chart for PO12i (Figure 5) note the repeated attempts by one or more sellers to signal a price increase with high unaccepted price offers (plotted as open circles) in periods 6, 10, 11 and 13–15. Comparing Figure 4, in which sellers engaged in no significant signalling, with Figure 5 it is clear that although signalling was effective in raising contract prices, this effect tended to erode over time as reflected in the observed decline in the average contract price. From the regression results reported in Table V it is clear that over all experiments posted-offer price signalling could not have been effective in yielding a significant increase in ME prices in Design I.

In Design II signalling was more common and more dramatic in posted-offer pricing, and more effective in both institutions than in Design I. In Design II, the existence of a third seller with constant cost at P_L increases the opportunity for tacit collusion in that, once prices stabilize at or below P_L, this seller typically engages in price signalling by raising his/her posted offer. By such action this seller has nothing to lose! Furthermore, because of the privacy of cost information, the other two sellers do not know that this action is costless to the third seller. This is illustrated in experiment 14ix (Figure 9) in which the highest cost seller engaged in such price signals in periods 10, 11, 12, 15–19, 21–23 and 25 (see the open circles, representing unaccepted price offers, in Figure 9). This high frequency of signalling is followed by temporary increases in contract prices in periods 11–13, 16, 19 and 23–24, however, these collusive efforts are unstable. In every case, contract prices tend to erode back to P_L or below. In experiment PO5i (Figure 8) the highest cost seller engaged in no significant signalling (a modest signal to increase first occurs in period 16). Consequently, in this experiment contract prices had fallen to P_L by periods 10–13, and subsequently drifted downward through period 25. We would suggest that these dramatic signalling efforts to raise price in Design II explain the regression results in Table V in which the posted-offer institution has a significant effect on ME prices in Design II but not in Design I. It is clear, however, from the regression using all three dummy variables that the effect of Design II on ME prices is both positive and significant after correcting for the effect of experience and the pricing institution. This is indicated in Figure 10 in which ME prices persist at levels above the C.E. in one-third of the double-auction experiments for both experienced and inexperienced subjects. The only previously reported double-auction duopoly experiments (Smith and Williams (1983*b*)) did not exhibit a comparable effect on the ME price measure. Since seller unit costs were increasing in these earlier experiments it would appear that the effects reported here are due to the constant cost conditions of each seller.

The chart for PO17ixs in Figures 6 and 7 is of special interest because the subjects were both experienced and selected. In conducting the Design II experiments and other experiments to be reported separately, we encountered three experimental groups in which the three sellers were able to effect a collusive increase in their price offers on one or more trials (see for example the chart for PO22i in Figure 10). The resulting sample of nine sellers who revealed tacit collusive tendencies provided an opportunity to conduct an experiment in which the "treatment" was the preselection of sellers with this collusive "trait". We recruited four subjects from these nine experienced sellers and assigned them at random to the four seller positions in the symmetrical Design I experiment, PO17ixs. The buyers in PO17ixs were "experienced" in the sense applying to all other "x" sessions, namely each had participated in at least one previous posted-offer experiment either as a buyer or a seller. Our objective in this experiment was to create what we thought were conditions highly favourable to tacit collusion—posted-offer pricing by sellers screened for their collusive tendencies. Experiment 17ixs, charted in Figures 6 and 7, cannot be counted as an observation favourable to this objective. Except in period 4, the mean price declined in all but the final five periods. Since these were all experienced subjects who had reason to believe that the experiment would end by period 25, the somewhat modest collusive tendencies in periods 21–25 might be attributable to "end effects".

5. TENDENCIES TOWARD COMPETITIVE, NASH OR LIMIT-PRICE EQUILIBRIA

Table VI reports the observed mean (computed across experiments from Table IV) for each of the three measures of performance ($\bar{r}^0$, $\bar{\delta}^0$, $\bar{E}^0$), and each treatment condition. In the double auction the C.E. is also a N.E., and in Deisgn I all three measures of performance are very close (prices within one cent and efficiency within 1%) to their C.E. (and N.E.) predictions with experienced subjects. Double auction experienced subjects in Design II deviate more from these predictions than in Design I, but all three measures are closer to the C.E. (and N.E.) predictions than to the limit-price equilibrium. Under posted-offer pricing the C.E. is not a N.E., but in Design I all three measures are reasonably near (prices within two cents and efficiency within four percent) their C.E. predictions with experienced subjects. Posted offer experienced subjects in Design II

TABLE VI

Mean performance measures and alternative equilibria by treatment

Treatment conditions			Mean performance (from Table IV) and alternative equilibria								
			RMSE			ME			Efficiency		
Subjects	Institution	Design	$\bar{r}^0$	r_N^0	r_L^0	$\bar{\delta}^0$	δ_N^0	δ_L^0	$\bar{E}^0$	E_N^0	E_L^0
NX	DA	I	0·063	0	—	−0·006	0	—	97·0	100	—
X	DA	I	0·009	0	—	−0·007	0	—	99·8	100	—
NX	PO	I	0·056	?	—	0·034	?	—	89·5	?	—
X	PO	I	0·018	?	—	0·024	?	—	96·6	?	—
NX	DA	II	0·057	0	0·07	0·044	0	0·07	96·9	100	96·5
X	DA	II	0·033	0	0·07	0·020	0	0·07	95·1	100	96·5
NX	PO	II	0·058	0·055	0·07	0·080	0·054	0·07	94·5	98·8	96·5
X	PO	II	0·061	0·055	0·07	0·059	0·054	0·07	97·3	98·8	96·5

Note: NX, Inexperienced. DA, Double auction. X, Experienced. PO, Posted offer.

produce outcomes as close or closer to their N.E. predictions than either the C.E. or limit-price predictions. These results can be interpreted as providing tentative support for the N.E. hypothesis of individual behavior; i.e. outcomes are nearest to the C.E. when this is also a N.E. and when the N.E. is distinct from the C.E., outcomes deviate from the C.E. in the direction of those predicted by the N.E. Of course, in no case do we get errorless support for any theoretical prediction.

6. SUMMARY OF EXPERIMENTAL RESULTS

Our experimental data support the conclusion that prices tend to be higher and efficiency lower in posted-offer markets relative to double-auction markets. This institutional effect appears to interact with other design parameters; the effect is much weaker in the Design I experiments relative to Design II. Subject experience tends to increases both efficiency and the speed of price convergence toward the competitive equilibrium. However, this effect is stronger in the Design I experiments than in Design II.

Price signaling, indicating attempts at tacit collusion, is rather common among sellers in posted-offer markets. Both the frequency and effectiveness of price signalling among sellers is higher in Design II compared with Design I. Even in Design II, however, the attempts at tacit collusion are unstable.

In both the Design I and Design II double auctions (the competitive theoretic equilibrium is also a Nash theoretic equilibrium), market outcomes approach the competitive-Nash prediction. In the Design II double auctions, deviations from the competitive prediction are somewhat larger than under Design I, but the competitive prediction receives more empirical support than the limit-price equilibrium. In the Design I posted-offer markets (the competitive equilibrium is not a Nash equilibrium and no Nash equilibrium is identified), outcomes tend to approach the competitive prediction. In the Design II posted-offer markets (the competitive equilibrium is not a Nash equilibrium and a Nash equilibrium is identified), outcomes are as close or closer to the Nash prediction than to either the competitive or limit-price predictions.

We gratefully acknowledge research support from the National Science Foundation and helpful comments from Daniel Alger and Glenn Harrison on earlier drafts. This is a revised version of a paper reporting many other experiments that was first presented at the Southern Economic Association Meetings, November 5–7, 1980. A separate paper will report the experiments in the larger study that are not included herein. The instructions presented to subjects prior to the experiments are available from the authors upon request.

NOTES

1. Smith and Williams (1983*b*) have conducted experiments designed to reveal the minimum profit per transaction required to induce exchange in the double-auction institution; this minimum profit appears to be in excess of 5 cents but less than 10 cents.

2. There is a strong tradition in economics going back to Cournot to base the computation of N.E. states on two assumptions: (1) All agents trade as if the cost of transacting were zero. (2) All buyers (and sellers) enter the market simultaneously and all trades are either at the same price, or, if sellers quote different prices, each seller's demand is contingent upon the prices quoted by other sellers but not upon the order in which individual buyers make their purchases. [But see Shubik (1959), pp. 82–91, and Alger (1979) for a correct treatment of contingent demand.] These examples for Design II and the one above for Design I illustrate the sensitivity of the N.E. calculation to these assumptions. Also in these examples, note that the N.E. strategy choices (if they exist) occur directly in the message space (seller posted prices), with the consequent payoff outcomes depending upon the rules by which the institution converts the messages into realized allocations (Smith (1982*b*), pp. 926–927, 938). Under posted-offer pricing buyers arrive in random order during the trading period; this gives rise to probability distributions on allocations, payoffs, and the exchange quantitites at the posted prices.

3. The reader should note that the regression estimates of equation (2) are subject to a small sample bias and that the sample size for the regressions are generally smaller for the DA experiments than the PO experiments.

REFERENCES

ALGER, D. (1979), "Markets Where Firms Select Both Prices and Quantities" (Ph.D. dissertation, Northwestern University).

HONG, J. T. and PLOTT, C. (1982), "Rate Filing Policies for Inland Water Transportation: An Experimental Approach", *The Bell Journal of Economics*, **13**, 1–19.

MARBURG, T. (1951), "Domestic Trade and Marketing", Chapter 26 in H. Williamson (ed.) *Growth of the American Economy* (Englewood Cliffs: Prentice-Hall, Inc.) 511–533.

PLOTT, C. R. and SMITH, V. L. (1978), "An Experimental Examination of Two Exchange Institutions", *The Review of Economic Studies*, **45**, 113–153.

SHUBIK, M. (1959) *Strategy and Market Structure* (New York: John Wiley and Sons).

SMITH, V. L. (1976*a*), "Induced Value Theory", *American Economic Review*, **66**:2, 274–279.

SMITH, V. L. (1976*b*), "Bidding and Auctioning Institutions: Experimental Results", in Y. Amihud *Bidding and Auctioning for Procurement and Allocation* (New York: New York University Press).

SMITH, V. L. (1982*a*), "Reflections on Some Experimental Market Mechanisms for Classical Environments", in L. McAlister (ed.) *Choice Models for Buyer Behavior Research in Marketing, Supplement* (Greenwich, CN: JAI Press).

SMITH, V. L. (1982*b*), "Microeconomic Systems as an Experimental Science", *American Economic Review*, **72**, 923–955.

SMITH, V. L. and WILLIAMS, A. W. (1983*a*), "An Experimental Comparison of Alternative Rules for Competitive Market Exchange", in R. Engelbrecht-Wiggans, M. Shubik and R. Stark (eds.) *Auctions, Bidding and Contracting: Uses and Theory* (New York: New York University Press).

SMITH, V. L. and WILLIAMS, A. W. (1983*b*), "The Boundaries of Competitive Price Theory: Convergence, Expectations and Transaction Cost" (paper presented at the Public Choice Society Meetings, New Orleans, 13–15, 1981, revised).

SMITH, V. L., WILLIAMS, A. W., BRATTON, W. K. and VANNONI, M. G. (1982), "Competitive Market Institutions: Double Auctions Versus Sealed Bid-Offer Auctions", *American Economic Review*, **72**, 58–77.

WILLIAMS, A. W. (1980), "Computerized Double-Auction Markets: Some Initial Experimental Results", *Journal of Business*, **53**, 235–258.

WILLIAMS, F. (1973), "Effect of Market Organization on Competitive Equilibrium: The Multiunit Case", *Review of Economic Studies*, **40**, 97–113.

Hypothetical valuations and preference reversals in the context of asset trading

MARC KNEZ AND VERNON L. SMITH

5.1 Background and setting

Several studies soliciting willingness-to-pay (WTP) and willingness-to-accept (WTA) responses for a variety of goods have found a large disparity between these "buying price" and "selling price" measures of value (see Knetsch and Sinden, 1984, for a summary of these studies). Although utility theory is consistent with some disparity between them, scholars generally have argued that the empirical disparity in these responses is much larger than is expected from the theory. Indeed, the mean WTA values obtained in this way are frequently several times greater than the mean WTP values so obtained. These empirical results are very robust under investigations designed to determine the effect of monetary incentives, experience, and other factors on the disparity. These results cast serious doubt on the validity of utility (or demand) theory as a calculating, cognitive model of individual decision behavior.

Another related series of experimental results have established what is commonly referred to as the preference reversal phenomenon (see the survey by Slovic and Lichtenstein, 1983). This refers to the large proportion of subjects who report that they prefer item A to item B (or B to A) but whose WTP or WTA is smaller for A than for B (or larger for A than for B if they said they preferred B to A). Often A and B are prospects or gambles, but they can be any items of value to the individual. Again, these preference reversal results are robust under careful controls designed to provide good incentives for reporting "true" subjective preferences. Although such preference reversals have been interpreted as violating transitivity, Karni and Safra (1985) show that they may violate independence rather than transitivity and are not inconsistent with non-expected utility models of decision making. However, the preference reversal phenomenon clearly violates expected utility theory (EUT).

However, other experimental studies based on choices in repetitive, revealed demand, market, or marketlike settings have shown high consistency with standard demand utility theory. Thus the consumption–leisure revealed demand behavior of mice, rats, monkeys, pigeons, and people in repeat-purchase environments yields steady-state results consistent with the Slutsky–Hicks demand model of maximizing behavior. Similarly, many studies of individual and market behavior based on expected utility models of market decision making yield results consistent with these models (for references see Smith, 1985; Knez, Smith, and Williams, 1985).

Coursey, Hovis, and Schulze (forthcoming) have challenged the conventional interpretation of this WTA–WTP disparity by allowing individuals to bid in a repetitive series of second price auctions for entitlements to an item. The resulting bids provide revealed measures of WTP (or WTA), which are then compared with hypothetical measures of WTA and WTP. Coursey, Hovis and Schulze found that the WTA–WTP disparity in hypothetical measures is also observed in an initial auction market but that it tends to disappear after a series of such auctions.

All these studies taken together appear to support the proposition that utility theory and demand theory do very poorly as cognitive calculating models of single-choice decision behavior but relatively well in the learning-feedback environment of a repetitive market. Why is it important to study the theory of individual choice in the context of markets in particular and institutions in general? We suggest three reasons:

1. Markets are the distinguishing forte of the economist. Indeed, professional economics was born in the context of the attempt by Adam Smith and his forerunners to understand the broad social significance of the universal human "propensity to truck, barter and exchange." Only later, after articulating the demand (supply) theory of market price, did economists turn to the derivation of demand from hypotheses about individual behavior and the additivity of this behavior across individuals.

2. The efficiency and social significance of markets does not depend on the validity of any particular theory of individual demand. Theory asserts that markets are efficient if they yield market clearing prices under the appropriate property right arrangements, even if the given demand behavior is inconsistent with individual "rationality" in the sense of utility theory. Hence, the empirical validity or falsity of efficient markets theory is a proposition that is entirely distinct from

the empirical validity or falsity of theories of individual demand in markets. The economic theory of market behavior may be empirically sound, whereas the economic theory of individual behavior is not, or vice versa. Distinguishing between individual choice behavior and individual behavior in markets is justified for the same reason that distinguishing between the psychology and sociology of individual behavior is justified.

3. The institutions in which individuals function can directly, and may indirectly, impinge on individual rationality in the sense of demand theory. Thus in the Treasury bill auction and on the New York Stock Exchange, individuals may want to submit a multiple bid order, for example, a maximum of 20,000 units at price 96 and a maximum of an additional 20,000 units at price 97. Demand theory hypothesizes that the individual's ordering of these bids should be reversed, that is, up to 20,000 at 97, and 20,000 more at 96. But these trading institutions operate under rules *requiring* any bid stating a higher price to have exchange priority over any other bid stating a lower price. In effect, the market rules impose diminishing returns on the submitted multiple bids of any individual. Indirectly, markets may impinge on individual rationality because of emulative behavior and/or learning.

This chapter reports the results of a series of six experiments. In each experiment the objects of value are two assets (gambles), each conveying the right to a dividend drawn from each of two distinct probability distributions. In the next section we discuss briefly some related earlier experiments that conditioned the designs we chose for the new series of experiments reported here.

5.2 Related earlier experiments

This study was directly motivated by an earlier article (Knez et al., 1985) that was confined to the study of WTP–WTA responses and trading behavior for units of an asset with a given dividend structure. Figure 5.1 charts the detailed results of one of these earlier experiments (reported in very abbreviated form as experiment 37, series II, in Knez et al., 1985).

In this experiment, nine subjects were given the opportunity to trade an asset in a sequence of trading periods in which all individual endowments of cash and shares are *reinitialized* at the beginning of each period. Thus except for individual learning, these trading periods represent pure replications under the same treatment conditions. In particular, this design controls for trading effects due to capital gains

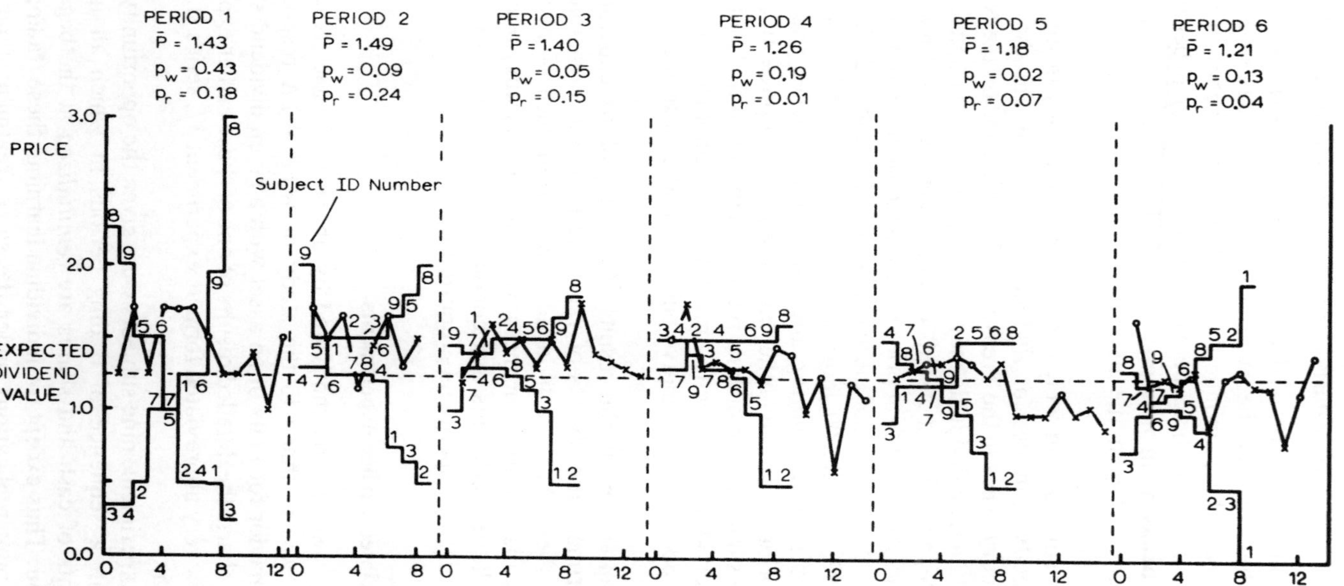

Figure 5.1. Experiment 37. Key: $\overline{P}$, mean price; P_w, hypothetical competitive price: $P_w = |P_w - \overline{P}|$; $p_r = |1.25 - \overline{P}|$; x, accepted bid; o, accepted offer.

expectations across periods, although not, of course, for such expectations within a period. A single draw at the end of each trading period is made from a binary probability distribution of dividends $(p_1, d_1; p_2, d_2) = (\frac{1}{2}, \$0.50; \frac{1}{2}, \$2.00)$. The expected holding value of the asset is therefore \$1.25. Letting E_i = (cash, shares) be the endowment vector for subject i, each experiment has three agent classes, $E_1 = (\$4.50, 1)$, $E_2 = (\$3.25, 2)$, and $E_3 = (\$2.00, 3)$, with three subjects assigned randomly to each class (nine subject traders). Note that the expected value of each agent's endowment is \$5.75 in each of the independently initialized trading periods of an experiment. The instructions fully inform the subjects about the dividend distribution and state that this dividend structure means that "on average" a share has a "holding value" of \$1.25. Each subject is informed only of her own endowment vector. After completing the instructions (which are devoted largely to explaining the rules of double-auction trading) but before the countdown to the first (timed) period of trading, the following two questions are put to each of the subjects (the blanks are filled in with the applicable numbers):

(1) Given your endowment of \$________ cash (i.e., working capital) and ________ asset units, what would be the minimum price you would be willing to accept in order to sell one unit of your inventory in the trading period about to begin? (2) Given your endowment of \$________ cash (i.e., working capital) and ________ asset units, what would be the maximum price that you would be willing to pay in order to buy one unit of this asset in the trading period about to begin?________

After each trading period, each subject is logged into a new one-period asset trading experiment identical to the one described above. Before the countdown to the opening of trade, the questionnaire is filled in again. This cycle of endowment initialization, questionnaire administration, followed by trading was conducted six times, as shown in Figure 5.1.

Each of the six panels in Figure 5.1 graphs the hypothetical demand represented by the individual WTP_i responses arrayed from highest to lowest and the hypothetical supply represented by the WTA_i arrayed from lowest to highest. For example in period 1, before trading, subject 8 reported WTP_8 = \$2.25 and WTA_8 = \$3.00. Subject 9 reported WTP_9 = \$2.00 and WTA_9 = \$1.95. Since the maximum possible dividend was \$2.00, neither of these responses can be described as inspiring confidence in any known concept of individual rationality. However, before trading in period 2, subject 8 is providing responses that are not inconsistent with EUT, and by period 3, subject 9 is no longer claiming to be willing to pay \$2.00 for a 50–50 chance of receiving $0.50 or $2.00. In each period note that the hypothetical demand and supply schedules yield a competitive market clearing price P_w (= $1, e.g., in period 1). We can think of this price as the *market's* hypothetical value for the asset. Each panel also plots the contract prices in the sequential order in which the exchanges occurred. In period 1 the first contract occurred when some seller accepted the standing bid (shown as an x) of some buyer at $1.25. In the second contract a buyer accepted a standing offer (shown as a circle) at $1.70, and so on.

Several features of the results illustrated in Figure 5.1 should be emphasized. Although there are numerous instances of individually "irrational" reported values for the asset, the social valuation represented by the hypothetical market price P_w is not inconsistent with EUT. In period 1, although two subjects (8 and 9) report WTPs equal to or larger than maximum payoff, and three (2, 3, and 4) report WTAs less than or equal to the minimum payoff, the market value based on these WTP–WTA schedules is P_w = $1.00, which is a reasonable risk-averse adjusted value for a one-shot draw with a 50–50 chance of yielding $0.50 or $2.00. "Irrationally" high WTPs (or low WTAs) do not imply irrational market clearing prices since the latter are determined by the marginal WTP–WTA valuations. To be sure, this hypothetical market value rises to $1.40 in period 2, but that is a reasonable response to the observation that 11 of the 12 trades in period 1 were at prices at least as high as $1.25. Subjects' stated WTPs or WTAs are not independent of what they think the market price will be. Although in the first three periods prices are at levels consistent with risk-preferring behavior, there is a general downtrend, with the frequency of risk-averse (or neutral) valuations predominating in the last two periods.

Individual traders repeatedly reveal selling prices below their reported WTA and buying prices above their reported WTP. For example, in period 2 the fourth contract occurred at a price below the stated WTA of any seller, and in period 3, the third, fifth, seventh, and ninth contracts occurred at prices in excess of the stated WTP of any buyer. Across all three experiments of this type, Knez et al. (1985) reported that for 34% of the subjects the lowest offer made was below their stated WTA_i, whereas for 47% the highest submitted bid exceeded the reported WTP_i. The impunity with which subjects violate their own reported values suggests that these responses may serve (at best) only as pretrade bargaining objectives from which deviations are made contingent on events experienced in the trading process.

Capital gains expectations may not have been controlled sufficiently by restricting the trading horizon to a single period. This is suggested in Figure 5.1 by the observance of multiple trades by individuals and a trading volume in every period that was many times larger than the hypothetical volume based on single-unit (per subject) buying and selling prices. Also, the downtrend of prices within each period and across successive periods may be due to the failure of initial capital gains expectations to be realized, leading to a sell-off.

5.3 Preferences, valuation, and double-auction asset trading

A new series, consisting of six experiments, was designed with the following features. Several groups of subjects who participated in other double-auction market experiments unrelated to the six reported in this section were asked to respond to a questionnaire before leaving the laboratory but after completing the experiment for which they had been recruited. This questionnaire described two gambles (situations) using the pie charts (Grether and Plott, 1979) that are standard in this research: Asset A provides a probability distribution of dividends given by $(p_1, d_1; p_2, d_2) = (\frac{1}{36}, -\$1.00; \frac{35}{36}, +\$4.00)$. Asset B provides a probability distribution of dividends given by $(p_1, d_1; p_2) = (\frac{25}{36}, -\$1.50; \frac{11}{36}, +\$16.00)$. If the individual had been a seller in the experiment in which she had just participated she was asked which situation, A, B, or "don't care," she preferred. Then she was asked, if she were in situation A, "What is the lowest price that you would accept for one unit of that particular asset?" Similarly, she reported her WTA for asset B. If the individual had been a buyer, his preference was solicited in the same manner, and he was asked to state the highest price that he would pay for each of the two assets A and B. These responses were used to classify subject sellers and buyers as to whether they were preference reversers [e.g., A preferred or indifferent to B, but WTP_A $(\text{WTA}_A) < \text{WTP}_B$ (WTA_B)] or nonreversers. Because of the difficulty of getting a large pool of preference-reversing subjects in this way, we supplemented the pool with questionnaires given to individuals who were on our sign-up lists for participation in experiments. Our total pool of 118 subjects consisted of 66 nonreversers and 52 reversers (44%).

From this subject pool we recruited groups of buyers and groups of sellers to return for our asset-trading experiment. The subjects were logged into an asset-trading experiment describing the rules of trading and the characteristics of the asset to be traded, which was asset A as just described. They were also informed that, when the trading period for asset A was completed, they would be logged into an experiment in which they would have the opportunity to trade asset B for one period. Those subjects who had been buyers in their original double-auction experiment and who responded to the questionnaire for buyers were constrained to be buyers only in the new experiment for assets A and B. These buyer subjects were given the endowment vector E^B_A = (cash, shares) = ($5.50, 0) for asset A and E^B_B = (cash, shares) = ($5.50, 0) for asset B. In the trading period for asset A, each buyer could buy no more than a single unit of A. Similarly, in trading asset B, each buyer was constrained to buy no more than a single unit of asset B. Those subjects who originally had been sellers and responded to the seller questionnaire were constrained to be sellers only in the new experiment. These sellers were given the endowment E^S_A = (cash, shares) = ($1.65, 1) for asset A and the endowment E^S_B = (cash, shares) = ($1.65, 1) for asset B. Note that the expected value of all the endowments for both buyers and sellers and for both asset A and B is $5.50. All trading was constrained to one unit per buyer (seller) for the purpose of controlling for expectations of capital gains from resale within a trading period.

After the subjects completed the instruction for asset trading and were assigned their endowments, but before the commencement of the first trading period for asset A, the buyers and sellers were given questionnaires similar to the original screening questionnaire. However, in this case the questionnaires were endowment specific (see appendixes A and B): that is, situations A and B not only specified the (dividend) outcomes and probabilities, but also specified the endowments in each situation. Both preferences and the WTP for buyers (WTA for sellers) were therefore "framed" in terms of the endowments that would constrain actual trading.

Each experiment (except experiment 60) consisted of questionnaire response 1, trading 1 (asset A, then asset B); response 2, trading 2; response 3, trading 3; response 4. Thus the questionnaire was administered before and after each two-period trading sequence in asset A followed by B.

5.3.1 Hypothetical supply and demand, and trade realizations over time

Figures 5.2 and 5.3 chart the market results from experiments 73 and 87, respectively. In each figure the hypothetical supply and demand schedules, based on subject WTA–WTP responses, are drawn for each interrogation, and the contract realizations from trade are plotted for the subsequent markets in asset A and asset B.

As in Figure 5.1 we note several obvious violations of simple dominance; in Figure 5.2, response 1, buyer 1 claims to be willing to pay $5 for asset A, which cannot possibly yield more than $4, whereas buyers 2 and 5 state WTPs of $4, an outcome that is probable but not certain. In the subsequent market we observe two trades at "reasonable" prices below expected value ($3.85). As in Figure 5.1, the line connecting x's (accepted bids) or O's (accepted offers) represents contracts. An x or O at the end of a period indicates the closing bid and offer when they existed. Over time in markets A.1 through A.3 the price of asset A rises, with all contracts reflecting slight risk-preferring behavior in period 3. Similarly, the market price of asset B rises over time, except that in period 1 the contracts are near the risk-neutral level and rise to modest risk-preferring levels. However, a comparison of the hypothetical supply and demand schedules with price realizations reveals that, except for period 1, prices tend frequently to be outside the predicted WTA–WTP bounds.

In Figure 5.3 we see more violations of simple dominance in WTP responses: buyer 3 in responses A.1 and A.2, and buyer 4 in response A.2. As in Figure 5.2 the price of asset A rises but hovers near expected value in periods 2 and 3. Except for the first trade in asset B, the price of B is fairly steady, near expected value, across all three trading periods. As in Figure 5.2, several of the trades are outside the bounds predicted by the hypothetical supply and demand schedules. These schedules do not appear to be reliable predictors of the range of contract prices.

Figure 5.4 charts only the contracts for experiments 60, 70, 98, and 101. Across all six experiments we count 3 in 76 contracts (4%) that represent clear violations of EUT. In each case a buyer purchased a unit of asset A at a price of $4 or more. This contrasts with 14 instances in which a buyer's *reported* WTP was $4 or more. In experiment 101, involving experienced subjects, contract prices for both A and B are more stable than in any of the other experiments. Prices are consistent with risk aversion in both markets. Prices for A tend to exceed prices for B, revealing an overall preference for A over B.

5.3.2 Effect of trading experience on reported preference reversals

Figure 5.5 plots the percentage of all subject buyers and sellers who exhibit preference reversals. The results of the initial screening response questionnaire is recorded as response 0: 63% reversals for buyers, 52% for sellers. After subjects return for the asset market experiment, buyer reversals fall to 42% whereas seller reversals remain

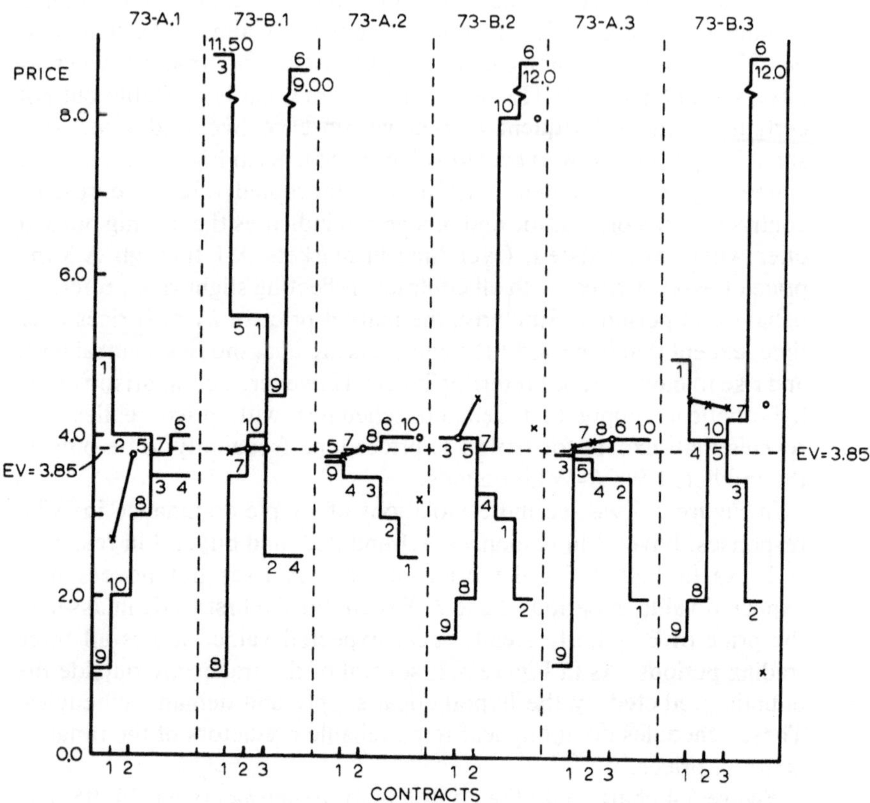

Figure 5.2. Experiment 73. Key: x, bid; o, offer. Subjects: 1–5, buyers; 6–10, sellers.

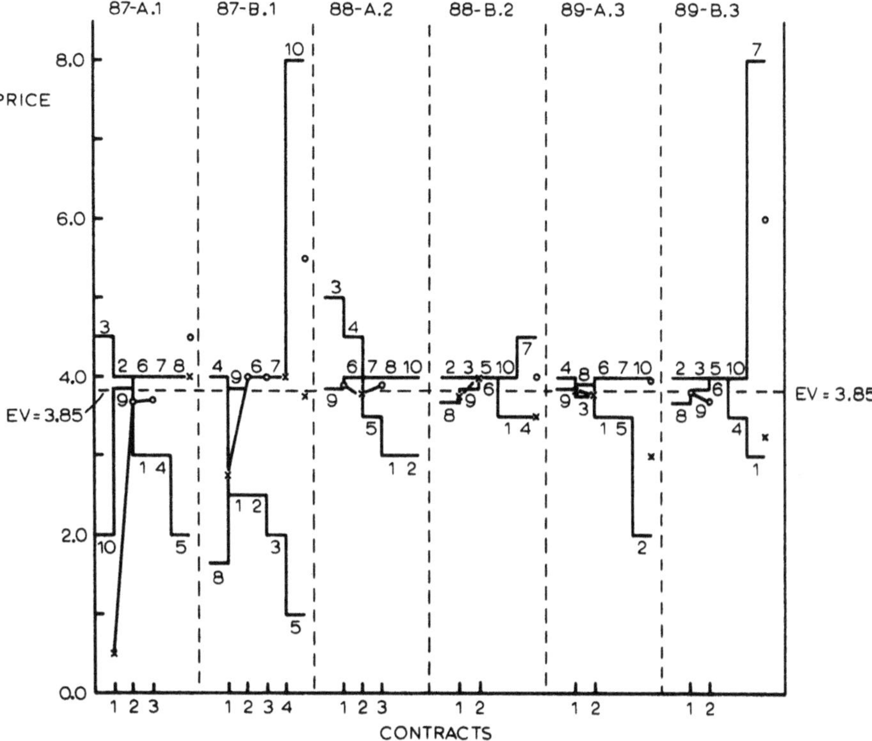

Figure 5.3. Experiment 87. Key: x, bid; o, offer. Subjects: 1–5, buyers; 6–10, sellers.

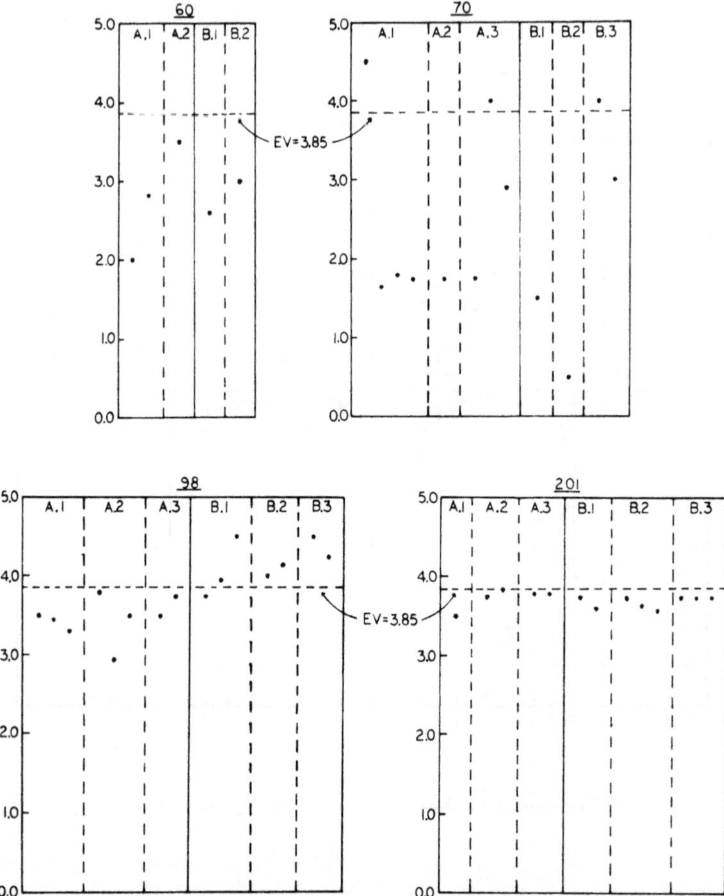

Figure 5.4. Contract prices in experiments 60, 70, 98, and 101.

at 52%. After three trading periods, each followed by a new interrogation, reversals decline to 38% for sellers and 35% for buyers, but the decline is not monotonic. Also plotted in Figure 5.5 are the results for the small sample (nine) of buyers and sellers who repeated the experimental sequence a second time. It seems clear that there is a hard core of 35 to 38% reversals that continue to be exhibited by the reported preferences and values of these subjects.

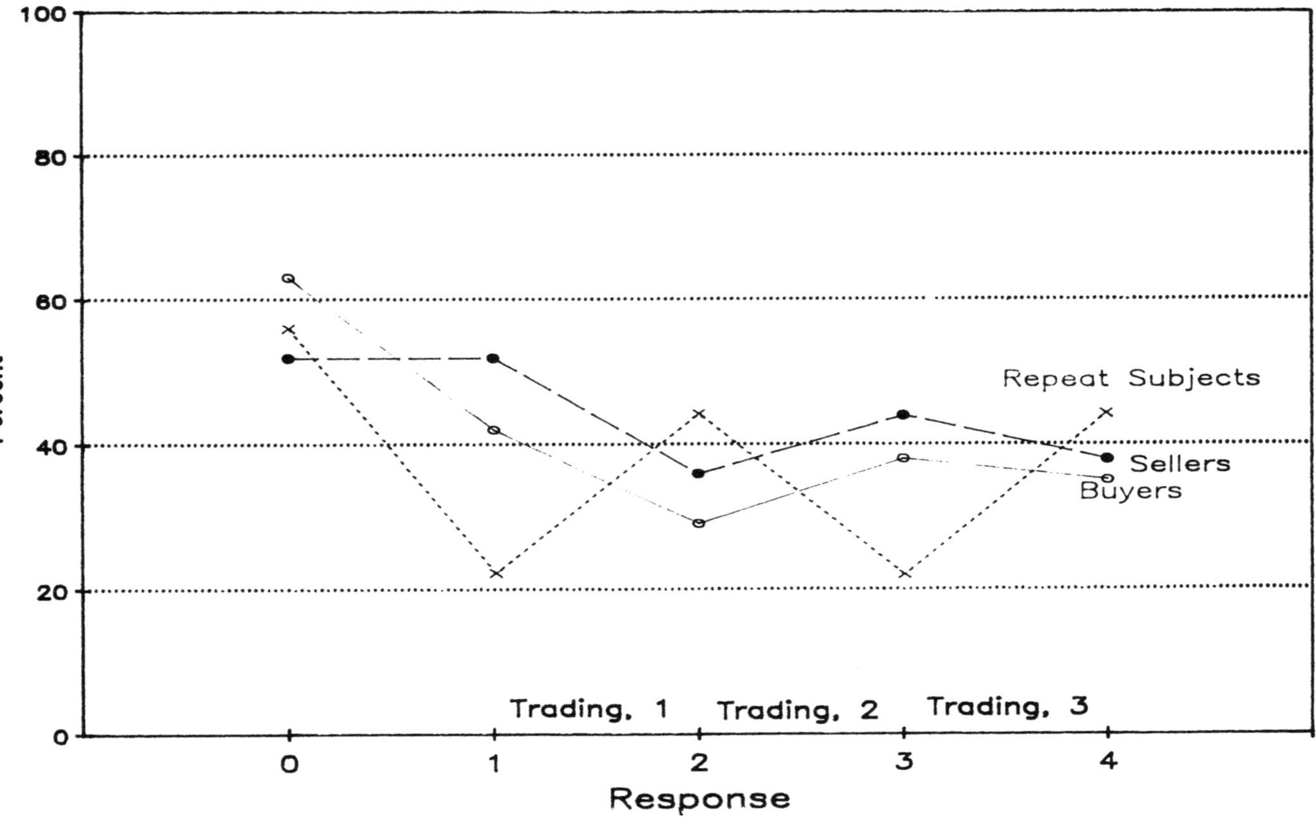

Figure 5.5. Percentage of subjects exhibiting preference reversal.

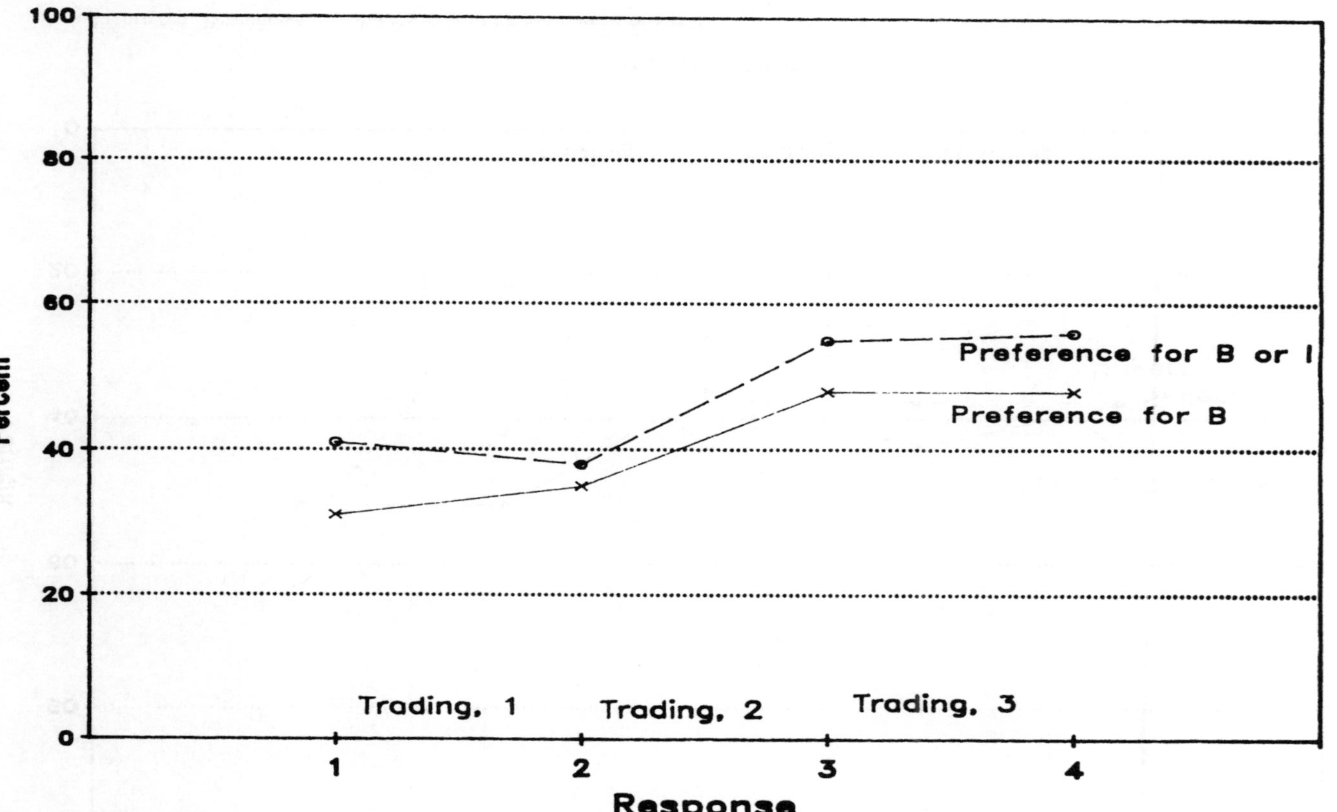

Figure 5.6. Percentage of sellers' preferences favoring asset B, related to trading.

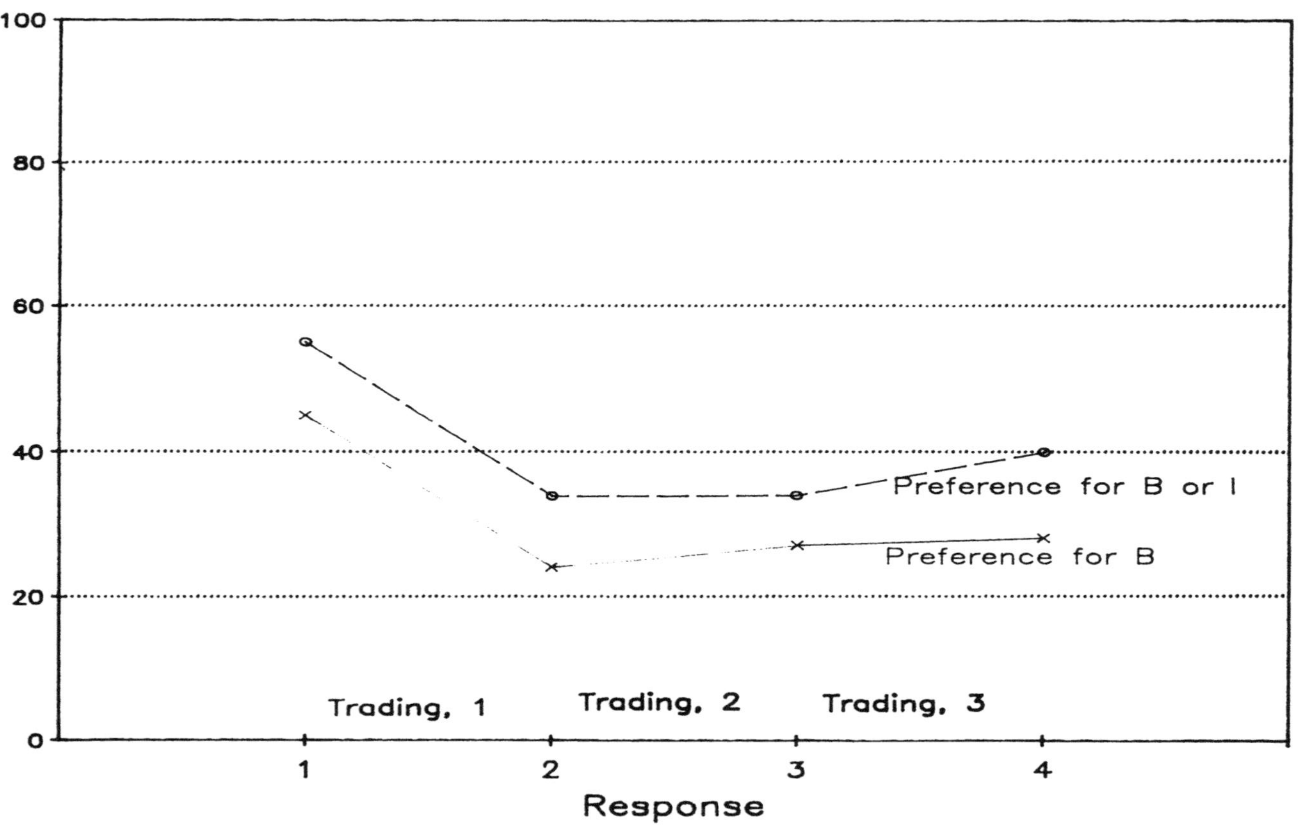

Figure 5.7. Percentage of buyers' preferences favoring asset B, related to trading.

5.3.3 Effect of trading on stated asset preferences

The change in subject seller and buyer reported asset preferences over time can be seen in Figures 5.6 and 5.7. The percentage of sellers strictly favoring asset B over A rose from 31 to 48%; among buyers this percentage fell from 45 to 28%. Thus "learning" took the form of increasing preference for B by sellers but decreasing preference for B by buyers. Asset B was much riskier than A, and sellers apparently learned from experience the advantages of cashing out at prices that ranged from $0.50 to $4.50 across all six experiments instead of holding for the dividend draw with large chances of a $1.50 loss and small chances of a $16 gain. Buyers, who were the providers of this largess to the sellers, increasingly expressed a dispreference for B over A. Their experience was a loss of $1.50 on units for which they paid as much as $4.50. This is perhaps an illustration of the old adage about "learning from the school of hard knocks." In any case, stated asset preferences are unstable and not independent of one's market experience with the assets. Figures 5.6 and 5.7 also plot the percentage of subjects either preferring asset B over A or expressing indifference. The latter category remains approximately constant over time for both buyers and sellers.

5.3.4 Discrepancies between reported and market-revealed asset values

Each subject buyer reports his or her maximum WTP for assets A and B just before the commencement of trading in A (followed by trading in B). Each buyer is free to enter no bid or to enter one or more sequential bids in each of these markets. Buyers are also free to accept at any time the standing best offer price of any seller. Most buyers either enter one or more bids or accept a seller's offer, or both. Hence, except for buyers who are voluntarily inactive in any market, in each market we observe a buyer's highest submitted bid and/or her acceptance of a seller's offer. For each buyer i, let HB_{im} be the highest bid entered, or the offer price accepted, whichever is the largest in market m. Then HB_{im} is subject i's revealed WTP in market m. If in any market we have $HB_{im} > WTP_{im}$ (where WTP_{im} is i's stated WTP for the asset to be traded in market m), we have a discrepancy (or violation) between the individual's stated and revealed WTP values. In Table 5.1 we list the relative frequency of these violations, pooling across all experiments and markets in asset A, and similarly for asset B; that is, $N(HB_{im} > WTP_{im})$ is the number of such discrepancies for each asset.

Table 5.1. *Incidence of discrepancy between reported and market-revealed asset value, all experiments*

Subjects	Asset A	Asset B	Asset A and B
Buyers $\frac{N(HB_{im} > WTP_{im})}{\text{trade opportunities}}$	$\frac{30}{83} = 36\%$	$\frac{37}{83} = 45\%$	$\frac{67}{166} = 40\%$
Sellers $\frac{N(WTA_{im} > LO_{im})}{\text{trade opportunities}}$	$\frac{28}{83} = 34\%$	$\frac{28}{83} = 34\%$	$\frac{56}{166} = 34\%$
Buyers and sellers	$\frac{58}{166} = 35\%$	$\frac{65}{166} = 39\%$	$\frac{123}{332} = 37\%$

For sellers we have a violation if $WTA_{im} > LO_{im}$; that is, a seller's lowest offer (or acceptance price of a buyer's standing bid) is below his prior stated lowest WTA.

From Table 5.1 we see that the incidence of these discrepancies exceeds one-third under all four classifications. Seller violations are the same (34%) for both A and B, but buyer violations are more frequent for B (45%) than for A (36%).

Table 5.2 answers a different question: How large are these violations? To answer this we sum over all instances in which $HB_i - WTP_i > 0$ for buyers and over all the $(WTA_i - LO_i) > 0$ cases for sellers. We see that the dollar magnitude of seller discrepancies is larger than it is for buyers, especially for asset B, in which seller discrepancies are 50% larger than buyer discrepancies. The magnitude of these discrepancies is also larger for asset B than asset A for both buyers and sellers and roughly two-thirds larger for buyers and sellers combined. Clearly, both buyers and sellers have more difficulty living up to their valuation estimates for asset B than for A, and sellers exhibit more such difficulty than buyers for both assets. This is consistent with the results reported by Coursey et al. (1984) in which sellers' hypothetical valuations are much larger relative to revealed value than is the case for buyers.

5.3.5 *Examples of individual responses to discrepancies between hypothetical and revealed valuations*

The high incidence with which subjects' bid (offer) behavior violates their previous WTP (WTA) responses raises the following question.

Table 5.2. *Magnitude ($) of discrepancy between reported and market-revealed asset value, all experiments*

	Asset		
Agent	A	B	A and B
Buyers $\Sigma_{i \in P} (HB_i - WTP_i)$	28.44	40.22	68.66
Sellers $\Sigma_{i \in P} (WTA_i - LO_i)$	30.15	60.53	90.68
Total, buyers and sellers	58.59	100.75	159.34

Note: Here P is the set of subjects for whom $HB_i - WTP_i$ or $WTA_i - LO_i$ is positive; i.e., the WTP_i or WTA_i limits are violated by the subsequent revealed measures.

How do subjects respond to these discrepancies? There are many types of responses – too many, we think, to suggest a useful classification scheme, and in any case such a scheme would contain subjective elements of judgment. However, we can identify three types of behavior that illustrate the polar cases. One type of subject never bids (offers) in violation of her stated WTP (WTA). Of the subjects who exhibit such a discrepancy in an earlier trading period (for either asset A or B or both), there are two polar response cases: Those who show a persistent discrepancy across market replications and those who respond to the discrepancy either by correcting their market behavior or by correcting their stated valuations.

In Figure 5.8, seller 5 in experiment 70 entered slight upward adjustments in reported WTA after each trading period, but the lowest offer made in each period was never below the previously stated WTA. In Figure 5.9 buyer 3 in experiment 87 always entered highest bids below the previously stated WTP. The latter rose from response 1 to response 2, then stabilized in the third and fourth responses. Seller 3 in experiment 98 and buyer 2 in experiment 73 provide examples of subjects who repeatedly violated their own WTA–WTP by factors of 2 or more. Their behavior suggests that they attach no value whatsoever to consistency between their actions and their statements. Seller 2 (Figure 5.8) offered less than WTA(1) in period 1, drastically lowered the WTA(2), then submitted a higher LO(2), adjusted WTA(3) upward, again made a consistent offer, and finally raised WTA(4) to a level consistent with the offers in periods 2 and 3. Buyer 3 (Figure 5.9) performed in a similar manner after exhibiting discrepancies in the first two trading periods.

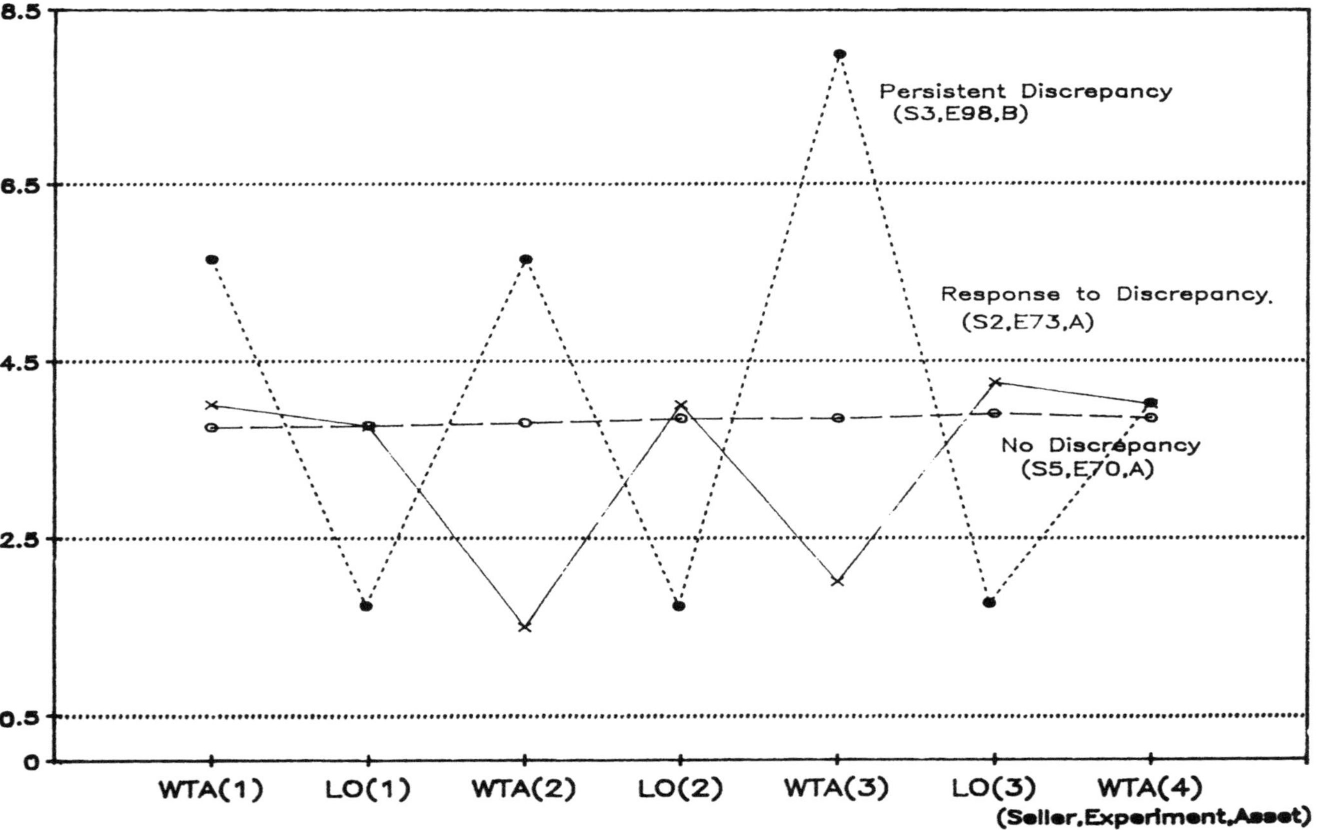

Figure 5.8. Sample of sellers.

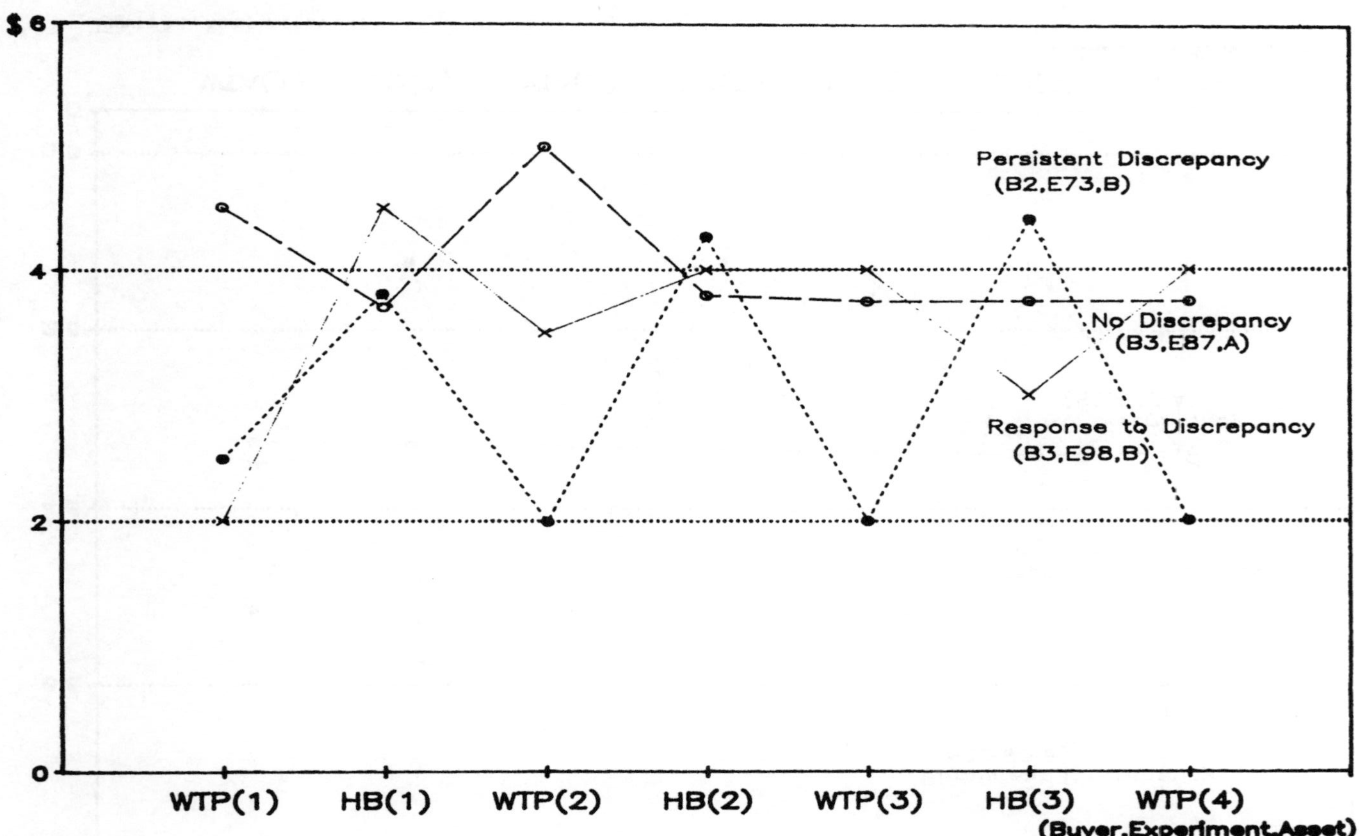

Figure 5.9. Sample of buyers.

5.3.6 Summary

Our results and conclusions can be summarized briefly as follows. From a pool of 118 subjects, buyers, 63% of whom were preference reversers, and sellers, 52% consisting of preference reversers, were recruited to engage in markets for the two assets A and B used in the initial questionnaire instrument to partition the subjects into four categories (buyer, seller), (reverser, nonreverser). Subjects who were asked for their WTP responses for A and B would be buyers; those asked for their WTA responses would be sellers.

After arriving for the market experiments, reading the instructions for double-auction asset trading, and learning their (cash, shares) endowments, each subject was again asked for his or her preference for A and B and corresponding WTP or WTA responses. Buyer reversals decline to 42%, whereas seller reversals remain at 52%.

Pooling the hypothetical response data and trading data across all markets, we find 14 instances in which a buyer's reported WTP violates dominance, but only 3 cases in which contracts occur at *prices* that violate dominance. Some 73 contracts (96%) are consistent with EUT. "Rationality," in the expected utility sense, as revealed in repeat-experience market outcomes is clearly greater than rationality as revealed in individual response measures.

Reported preference for asset A or B changes across trading periods 1 through 3. At the end of period 3 the percentage of buyers strictly favoring asset B over A falls from 45 to 28%, but among sellers this percentage rises from 31 to 48%. Since asset B was much riskier than A, sellers apparently learned from trading the advantages of cashing out at positive prices (from \$0.50 to \$4.50) instead of risking the dividend draw with high probability of a \$1.50 loss, whereas the buyers who paid these prices and risked the loss learned the disadvantages of incurring this gamble. These data illustrate how market experience may produce a socializing effect on individual values as measured by the response questionnaire.

Reported WTP and WTA measures of asset value are frequently violated by individual subjects' subsequent highest bid or lowest offer in double-auction trading. The incidence of such buyer or seller discrepancies across the two assets varies from 34% (for sellers of both A and B) to 45% (for buyers of B). However, the size of these discrepancies is larger for sellers across A and B [$\Sigma(WTA_i - LO_i) =$ \$91] than for buyers [$\Sigma(HB_i - WTP_i) =$ \$69].

How are subjects' hypothetical WTP–WTA responses altered by these discrepancies? There are three polar cases: (1) the subject who never bids or offers in violation of her reported WTP or WTA, (2) the subject who persists in this discrepancy across repeated interrogations and market trading periods, and (3) the subject who responds to the discrepancy either by correcting his market behavior or correcting his stated valuations. These results show the great variability in the importance that individual subjects attach to maintaining consistency between reported and revealed valuation behavior.

The results of this study call into question the interpretation, reliability, and robustness of preference reversal phenomena in the joint context of repetitive responses and market trading. However, we would not suggest that the phenomena have significance only in such contexts. They are obviously of potential importance in interpreting the rationality of nonmarket or nonrepetitive market decision making. However, even in these contexts there are institutional elements that may impinge on the phenomena, such as the use of "expert advice," in the case of large infrequent transactions and the use of committees and other social processes in nonmarket decision making.

Appendix A: seller questionnaire

Seller ____________

Suppose you are confronted with the following two situations:

A. You are given a cash endowment of \$1.65 and one asset unit, which you may sell. This particular asset unit will pay a dividend of either −\$1.00 (a loss) with probability $\frac{1}{36}$ or \$4.00 (a gain) with probability $\frac{35}{36}$.

B. You are given a cash endowment of \$1.65 and one asset unit, which you may sell. This particular asset will pay a dividend of either −\$1.50 (a loss) with probability $\frac{25}{36}$ or +\$16.00 (a gain) with probability $\frac{11}{36}$.

Note that in both A and B the only source of reward from holding a unit of the asset is the prospective dividend it will pay. So your decision in both A and B is made up of the following two choices: (1) Hold onto your cash endowment and keep your one asset unit and collect whatever dividend you receive from it. (2) Hold onto your cash endowment and sell your one asset unit, and keep all the money you receive from the sale.

Please answer the following questions:

1. Suppose you have the opportunity to be in situation A or B; which would you prefer? Check one:

A______
B______
Don't care______

2. (a) Suppose now you are in situation A. What is the lowest price that you would accept for one unit of that particular asset?______
   (b) Suppose now you are in situation B. What is the lowest price that you would accept for one unit of that particular asset?______

Appendix B: buyer questionnaire

*Buyer*____________

Suppose you are confronted with the following two situations:

A. You are given a cash endowment of $5.50, which you may use to buy one asset unit. This particular asset unit will pay a dividend of either −$1.00 (a loss) with probability $\frac{1}{36}$ or $4.00 (a gain) with probability $\frac{35}{36}$.
B. You are given a cash endowment of $5.50, which you may use to buy one asset unit. This particular asset unit will pay a dividend of either −$1.50 (a loss) with probability $\frac{25}{36}$ or $16.00 (a gain) with probability $\frac{11}{36}$.

Note that in both A and B the only source of reward from holding a unit of the asset is the prospective dividend it will pay. So your decision in both A and B is made up of the following two choices: (1) Hold onto your cash endowment and not buy an asset unit. (2) Use some part of your cash endowment to buy a unit of the asset and keep whatever is left of your cash endowment after adjustment for the dividend you receive.

Please answer the following questions:

1. Suppose you have the opportunity to be in situation A or B; which would you prefer? Check one:

   A______
   B______
   Don't care______

2. (a) Suppose now you are in situation A. What is the highest

price that you would pay for one unit of that particular asset?______

(b) Suppose now you are in situation B. What is the highest price that you would pay for one unit of that particular asset?______

References

Coursey, Don, Hovis, John, and Schulze, William, "On the Supposed Disparity Between Willingness-to-Accept and Willingness-to-Pay Measures of Value." *Quarterly Journal of Economics*, forthcoming.

Grether, David, and Plott, Charles, "Economic Theory of Choice and the Preference Reversal Phenomenon," *American Economic Review*, *69*, September 1979, 623–38.

Karni, Edi, and Safra, Svi, "Preference Reversal and the Observability of Preferences by Experimental Methods." Johns Hopkins University, Department of Political Economy, November 1985.

Knetsch, Jack, and Sinden, J. A., "Willingness to Pay and Compensation Demanded: Experimental Evidence of an Unexpected Disparity in Measures of Value," *Quarterly Journal of Economics*, *99*, August 1984, 507–21.

Knez, Peter, Smith, Vernon, and Williams, Arlington, "Individual Rationality, Market Rationality, and Value Estimation." *American Economic Review*, *75*, May 1985, 397–402.

Slovic, Paul, and Lichtenstein, Sarah, "Preference Reversals: A Broader Perspective." *American Economic Review*, *73*, September 1983, 596–605.

Smith, Vernon L., "Experimental Economics: Reply." *American Economic Review*, *75*, March 1985. 265–72.

BUBBLES, CRASHES, AND ENDOGENOUS EXPECTATIONS IN EXPERIMENTAL SPOT ASSET MARKETS[1]

BY VERNON L. SMITH, GERRY L. SUCHANEK, AND ARLINGTON W. WILLIAMS

Spot asset trading is studied in an environment in which all investors receive the same dividend from a known probability distribution at the end of each of $T = 15$ (or 30) trading periods. Fourteen of twenty-two experiments exhibit price bubbles followed by crashes relative to intrinsic dividend value. When traders are experienced this reduces, but does not eliminate, the probability of a bubble. The regression of changes in mean price on lagged excess bids (number of bids minus the number of offers in the previous period), $\bar{P}_t - \bar{P}_{t-1} = \alpha + \beta(B_{t-1} - O_{t-1})$, supports the hypothesis that $-\alpha = E(\tilde{d})$, the one-period expected value of the dividend, and that $\beta > 0$, where excess bids is a surrogate measure of excess demand arising from homegrown capital gains (losses) expectations. Thus, when $(B_{t-1} - O_{t-1})$ goes to zero we have convergence to rational expectations in the sense of Fama (1970), that arbitrage becomes unprofitable. The observed bubble phenomenon can also be interpreted as a form of temporary myopia (Tirole, 1982) from which agents learn that capital gains expectations are only temporarily sustainable, ultimately inducing common expectations, or "priors" (Tirole, 1982). Four of twenty-six experiments, all using experienced subjects, yield outcomes that appear to the "chart's eye" to converge "early" to rational expectations, although even in these cases we get $\hat{\beta} > 0$, and small price fluctuations of a few cents that invite "scalping."

KEYWORDS: Rational expectations, stock market trading, price bubbles, experimental markets.

1. INTRODUCTION

A LONG STANDING THEORY of common stock valuation holds that a stock's current market value tends to converge to the (risk adjusted) discounted present value of the rationally expected dividend stream. If markets are efficient, then, *in equilibrium*, stock prices should change only when there is new information that changes investors' dividend expectations. We examine this rational expectations model in a laboratory environment in which we can control the dividend distribution, and traders' knowledge of it in a market with a finite trading horizon. From rational expectations theory we hypothesize that although deviations from risk adjusted dividend value might be temporarily sustainable by divergent individual expectations, such deviations cannot persist because of the uncertain profits that can be earned by arbitraging the asset's price against its expected dividend value. Consequently, individual adjustments will occur until any risk differences are compensated, and expectations become common and coincide with dividend value. However, current theory makes no prediction as to how long this will take, and whether, or in what form, this process can be characterized.

Three adjustment dynamics can be distinguished: the process that describes changes in the asset's dividend value, the evolution of agents' price expectations, and the asset's price adjustments. Unless agents' expectations are common

[1]We are grateful for support from the National Science Foundation to Indiana University (A. Williams, PI) and to the University of Arizona (V. Smith, PI), and for the research assistance of Shawn LaMaster. Hard copies of the experimental instructions are available at cost upon request.

and correspond to dividend value, the three dynamics will not coincide. Any differences may be due to a lack of common, not irrational, expectations. An important issue is whether the three dynamics converge as expectations become more homogeneous. Fama's (1970) criterion for market efficiency is that there exist no systematic price patterns that allow arbitrage to yield a positive expected net profit, while in the rational bubble literature agents are assumed to have common priors about the value of the asset. For example in Tirole (1982, p. 1163), "... we investigate the possibility of speculative behavior when traders *have* rational expectations. The general idea is fairly simple: *unless* traders have different priors about the value of a given asset... (the)... market does not give rise to gains from trade. Thus *speculation relies on inconsistent plans and is ruled out by rational expectations* (all italics ours)." But how do traders come to "have" rational expectations: i.e. "consistent plans": i.e. common priors? In an experiment we *cannot* control expectations when the theory provides no explicit implementable model of expectations,[2] but we can control the dividend structure and trader knowledge of it. Consequently, we *can* ask whether common knowledge of a common dividend payout is sufficient to induce common expectations. But there is no a priori basis for *assuming* that *initially* all traders will expect other traders to react in the same way to the same information. Each trader may be uncertain as to the *behavior* of others with the same information. Operationally, then, in testing market efficiency or rational expectations in multiperiod asset environments, the important issue is whether through learning within and across (experimental or natural) markets agents will come to "have" rational common expectations and thus produce a no-arbitrage equilibrium.

The objectives of this study, as it developed, were to answer the following questions: (i) Will economic agents trade an asset whose dividend distribution is common knowledge? (ii) If so, can we characterize (empirically) the price adjustment process, and interpret it in terms of convergence to dividend value? (iii) Will we observe price bubbles and crashes as part of the adjustment process occurring in any or some of the experiments?

Before discussing the background for these questions we state briefly our principal finding: expectations (as measured by forecasts) and price adjustments

[2]Bidding theory articulates an explicit Nash version of rational expectations. Thus, an equilibrium bid function $b_i = \beta(v_i|I)$ relates agent i's message b_i to his environment (the item's value, v_i), and the institution, I. This is an equilibrium bid function if each agent i expects his $N-1$ rivals to also use this behavioral decision rule. In the case of the first price auction institution, and constant relative risk averse agents (with CRRA parameter $1-r_i$), we have $\beta(v_i|I_i) = (N-1)v_i/(N-1+r_i)$, with, say, $r_i \in (0,1]$. In this theory one can "control" expectations in an experimental implementation by letting each individual, i, bid against $N-1$ computerized bidders, and *informing* the subject that each computerized bidder bids a fixed fraction of his value $b_j = \hat{\beta}_j v_j$, where the v_j are drawn from the same distributions as v_i in each auction, and each $\hat{\beta}_j$ is drawn once for all auctions from some distribution on the interval $[(N-1)/N, 1)$. Here we "control" expectations by giving each bidder complete information on the bidding behavior of his rivals, where that behavior is defined by the Nash model of *equilibrium* bidding (Walker, Smith, and Cox, 1986). In the absence of a corresponding micro model of the individual agent in bubble theory, the experimenter cannot know what it means to induce common expectations.

are both adaptive, but the adaptation over time across experiments with increasing trader experience tends to a risk adjusted, rational expectations equilibrium.

In the next section we summarize previous experiments that are related to the asset trading environment described in Section 3. The design parameters and the interplay between market performance and the sequence of experiments are discussed in Section 4.

2. PREVIOUS EXPERIMENTS

Several double auction market studies have been characterized by some form of asset trading over time (Miller, Plott, and Smith, 1977; Williams, 1979; Plott and Agha, 1982; Williams and Smith, 1984). In a typical experiment, a constant stationary supply is induced on five agent sellers ("producers") and a two-period cyclically stationary demand is induced on five agent buyers. A third group of agents, who are asset "traders," have the exclusive right to buy in one period and sell in the next. Thus the environment is represented by cyclically stationary flow supply and demand conditions, with agent traders empowered to make asset carryover decisions.

With the exception of Williams and Smith (1984), in all of these experimental markets a pure replication of the environment is imposed by the experimental design. For example in Miller, Plott, and Smith (1977) and in Williams (1979), in addition to demand repeating a two-period cycle, traders can only buy in the low-price period and sell in the high-price period, and are required to close out their inventory positions by the end of each two-period cycle. In Williams and Smith (1984) traders can carry units across market cycles and the rate of convergence is retarded. All of these experimental studies report a significant treatment effect from the speculative action of traders: i.e. in the final market period, contracts tend to be nearer the intertemporal competitive equilibrium price than to either of the cyclical autarky theoretical equilibrium prices, or to the observed contracts in paired comparison cyclical autarky experiments. These results, and all of the many experimental studies of double auction markets without asset trading (see the summary by Smith, 1982) can be interpreted as supporting rational expectations theory as originally defined by Muth (1961, p. 316).

Experiments in which the item traded is an asset proper, in the sense that the environment generates dividends for asset holders at the end of each trading period, were originated by Forsythe, Palfrey, and Plott (1982) and continued in Plott and Sunder (1982), and Friedman, Harrison, and Salmon (1984). Although these important contributions shifted the experimental environment to that of pure asset trading, they maintained two characteristics of the earlier cited "speculation" studies: (i) A two-period A-B cycle (three-period A-B-C cycle in the Friedman, Harrison, and Salmon, 1984, experiments) in private (dividend) values is induced on the item traded, which is repeated over a trading horizon of several cycles. These dividend values differ for different groups of agents creating the same type of (induced value) gains from exchange as in the earlier experiments. (ii) The inventories (shares and money) of traders are *reinitialized* at the beginning of each cycle as a means of achieving a pure replication of the cyclical environment. Within this framework, these asset market experiments are interpreted as yielding prices tending to converge over time toward levels consistent with the rational expectations hypothesis. This is because agents bid for assets initially in period A on the basis of their private information, but slowly learn, across replicating cycles, to adjust their contracting to account for additional information concerning the period B *market* value of the asset. In these experiments agents are observed to engage in very little trading for capital gains in spite of the repetitive pattern of price increases. This may be a consequence of the short capital gains horizon.

Our immediate objective in the present series of experiments was to determine whether agents would actively trade an asset when all investors faced identical uncertain dividend payout schedules. The previous cited asset experiments pay different dividends to different investors on the grounds that investors have different opportunity costs. But if this is so, subject agents ought to have their own homegrown differences in opportunity cost (as in field environments). Consequently it is an open question whether artificially inducing different dividend values on subject investors is a *necessary* condition for observing trade. If our agents are not observed to trade this supports the strong version of the theory in which risk neutral agents have common initial expectations (induced, presumably, by contemplating the implications of a common dividend distribution). Our second objective, given that agents are observed to trade in this environment, is to characterize the observed price adjustments. Do we observe convergence to the rational expectations equilibrium as in previous asset market experiments? Do subjects' forecasts of the mean price (collected in nine experiments), taken as a measure of their price expectations at the time of interrogation, reveal adaptive or rational expectations?

Because of our concern that there might be insufficient divergence in subjective expected values to observe trading, and/or that the finiteness of our market horizon might frustrate any possibility of observing bubbles, we introduced a random valued buyout condition in the first series of experiments in an effort to enhance the possibility of a bubble. As it happens, these ex ante concerns were not supported. Bubbles (relative to the dividend value of the asset) are observed in most of our experiments with inexperienced and to a lesser extent experienced subjects. Moreover, eliminating the random buyout does not eliminate bubbles.

3. THE ASSET MARKET MECHANISM

The trading procedure employed in this study is an enhanced version of the PLATO computerized double-auction mechanism described by Williams and Smith (1984) for commodity markets with intertemporal speculators. The basic trading mechanics for asset-market speculators are identical to those for the commodity-market speculators in the Williams and Smith study. Figure 1 pro-

WEEK 1

RECORD SHEET for TRADER 3	TRADING PERIOD (columns) 1	2	3	4	5
Unit 1 selling price	3.00		2.40		2.50
Unit 1 purchase price	0.00		0.00		0.00
Profit	3.00		2.40		2.50
Unit 2 selling price					2.50
Unit 2 purchase price					0.00
Profit					2.50
Unit 3 selling price					2.50
Unit 3 purchase price					2.00
Profit					0.50
Unit 4 selling price					
Unit 4 purchase price					
Profit					
Unit 5 selling price					
Unit 5 purchase price					
Profit					
Dividend Earnings	0.80	2.00	0.48	0.48	
Total Earnings for Period	3.80	2.00	2.88	0.48	

Period purchased	1	3	3
Purchase price	2.45	2.30	2.35

Inventory= 3, Working capital=$10.84, Dividend per unit=$?????

BUYER 2 BIDS $2.48 SELLER 8 OFFERS $2.60

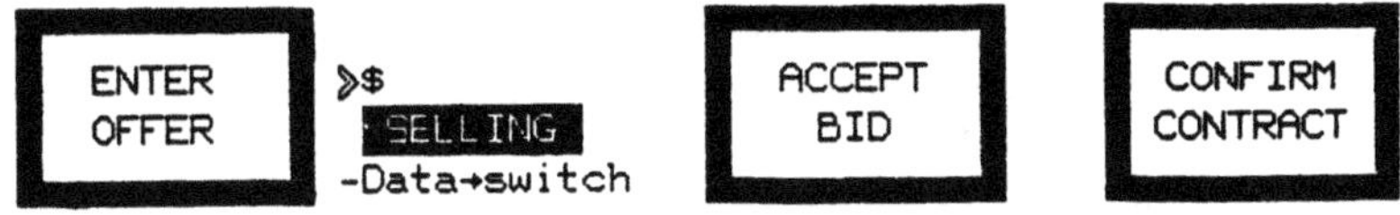

Last 9 contracts: 2.50,2.50,2.50,2.55,2.60,2.61,2.40,2.65,2.53
Trading Period 5 now in progress. SECONDS REMAINING: 108
0 of 12 people have voted to end period 5: -LAB→ vote to end

FIGURE 1.—Screen display for asset market trader.

vides a participant's screen display for our asset market. All agents (referred to as traders) are able to switch between buying mode and selling mode by pressing a key labeled DATA. Traders are free to enter a price quote to buy (or sell) one asset unit by typing their entry and then touching the rectangular area on their screen display labeled "ENTER BID" (or "ENTER OFFER"). Traders are likewise free to accept any other trader's bid to buy (or offer to sell) by touching a screen area labeled "ACCEPT BID" (or "ACCEPT OFFER"). The acceptor must then touch an area labeled "CONFIRM CONTRACT" at which time a binding contract is formed and the exchange information is recorded in the buyer's and seller's private record sheets.

Price quotes must progress so as to reduce the bid-ask spread. Only the highest bid to buy and the lowest offer to sell are displayed to the entire market and are open to acceptance. Price quotes that violate this rule are placed in a "rank queue"; after a contract occurs the rank queue automatically enters the best (highest) queued bid and best (lowest) queued offer as the new bid-ask spread. Smith and Williams (1983) have shown that this version of the double auction tends to outperform three alternative versions in terms of allocative efficiency and the speed of convergence to a competitive equilibrium.

Trading occurs over a sequence of 15 (or 30) market periods, each lasting a maximum of 240 seconds. Market participants can bypass this stopping rule by unanimously voting to end a period. Registering a vote to end a period does not affect a trader's ability to participate actively in the market. The number of seconds remaining and the current vote to end the period are presented as shown at the bottom of the Appendix display. Screen displays are updated approximately every second.

At the beginning of the experiment, each trader is given an asset endowment and a cash endowment. A trader's cash holding (referred to as "working capital") at any point will differ from his/her cash endowment by: (i) accumulated capital gains (or losses) via market trading, and (ii) accumulated dividend earnings via asset units held in inventory at the end of each trading period. At the experiment's conclusion, participants are paid in cash the amount of their final working capital. It is worth re-emphasizing that traders' asset and cash holdings are endogenous to the experiment beyond the beginning of trading period 1. We do not "reinitialize" the market at any time as has been done in the cited studies of experimental asset markets, with the exception of Williams and Smith (1984).

Traders are informed in the instructions of the probabilistic nature of the dividend structure that they will encounter and the total number of trading periods in the experiment. Specifically, they know all the possible (per-unit) dividend values that might be drawn (i.i.d.) and the probability associated with each potential dividend value. They do not, however, know the actual dividend that will be awarded at the end of any trading period until that period's conclusion, at which time they are informed of their dividend earnings for that period. Prior to *each* period, traders are reminded of the dividend distribution, and informed of the "average," minimum, and maximum possible dividend earnings for each unit held in their inventory for the remainder of the experiment. All participants are verbally informed that the dividend structure and actual dividend draws are the same for everyone in the market. At the end of each period, market participants are also given access to a table displaying the average, maximum, and minimum contract price, as well as the dividend awarded in all previous periods.

When a trader buys an asset unit the price and the period purchased are recorded in the trader's inventory table (see the Appendix). (Endowed asset units are recorded as being purchased in period 0 at a price of 0.) Traders can continue to buy asset units as long as their working capital is sufficient to cover the purchase price. There is also a (rarely binding) maximum inventory size of seven units due to the horizontal space limitations of the display screen. Traders can sell off inventory units at any time. However, short sales are not permitted. For record-keeping purposes, inventories are automatically maintained on a *first in first out* basis. When a unit is sold, the sale price, purchase price, and resulting capital gain or loss are recorded in the trader's record sheet.

In some of the experiments reported below, all asset units were automatically purchased by the experimenters at the market's conclusion. (The default mode is to award only the period 15 dividend.) The "buy-out price" equals the sum of the dividend draws over all 15 periods plus or minus a constant (each with .5 probability). The buy-out option keeps the expected value of an asset unit from falling to the expected value of a single dividend draw during the final trading period. When the buy-out option is utilized, the information presented to subjects regarding the maximum, expected, and minimum dividend earnings associated with holding an asset unit for the remainder of the market is automatically adjusted to account for the buy-out.

4. OVERVIEW OF DESIGN PARAMETERS, MARKET PERFORMANCE, AND THE SEQUENCE OF EXPERIMENTS

We report the findings from 27 experiments using the design parameters listed in Table I. In every experiment there were three endowment classes of agents (see columns 2–4), each consisting of three (four) subjects in the nine (twelve) trader experiments. This design permits pure expansions in the size of a market to be effected without altering its per capita structure. Designs 1 and 3 were used mostly for inexperienced subjects. All subjects had participated in a previous double auction experiment with induced flow supply and demand conditions. Consequently, all experiments with an "x" suffix in Table I and charted in the figures used subjects who had been in at least two previous experiments.

Many of the experiments we report were directly motivated by questions and puzzles posed by the results of earlier experiments. The research program developed as a continuing dialogue between hypothesis and empirical results in an effort to increase our understanding of the trading patterns that emerged in these markets. This historical theme allows the reader to appreciate the experiments we scheduled at each stage in the development of our tentative conclusions. The reader is cautioned that this narrative, and the associated price charts, may give the initial impression that rationality is "grossly" violated. The empirical analysis in Section 5, however, reveals that the predominating characteristic of these experiments is the tendency for expectations and price adjustments to converge to intrinsic value across experiments with increasing subject experience.

Our first pilot experiments (not reported) used subjects with no previous double auction experience of any kind, and the expected dividend or holding value of a share was computed and reported to the subjects only for the first period. Because prices in these experiments deviated by a wide margin from $E(\tilde{D}_t^T)$, we decided to increase the experience level and information state of our subjects to eliminate the possibility that our results were sensitive to these factors.

TABLE I

Design	Endowment[a] Class I	Class II	Class III	Dividend $\tilde{d}$, cents ($p = 1/4$)[b]	Expected Dividend per Period, $E(\tilde{d})$, cents	Intrinsic (Dividend) Value per Share Period 1, $E(\tilde{D}_1^T)$[c]	Experiments[d]
1	($2.80; 4)	($7.60; 2)	($10.00; 1)	(0, 4, 8, 20)	8	$2.40 (Including Buyout)	(5; 12) (7; 12) (12xn; 9, 3c) (17; 12) (23pc; 12)
2	($2.25; 3)	($5.85; 2)	($9.45; 1)	(0, 4, 14, 30)	12	$3.60 (Including Buyout)	(6x; 9) (9x; 9) (10; 9) (16; 9) (18; 9) (19x; 9) (20xpc; 9)
3	($2.80; 4)	($7.60; 2)	($10.00; 1)	(0, 8, 16, 40)	16	$2.40	(26; 12) (41f; 12)
4	($2.25; 3)	($5.85; 2)	($9.45; 1)	(0, 8, 28, 60)	24	$3.60	(25x; 9) (28x; 9) (30xsf; 9) (36xx; 9) (39xsf; 9) (43xnf; 9) (46f; 9) (48xnf; 9) (49xnf; 9) (50xxf; 9) (90f; 9) (124xxf; 9)
5[e]	($2.25; 3)	($5.85; 2)	($9.45; 1)	(0, 8, 28, 60)	24	$7.20	(42xf; 9)

[a] In experiments with 9(12) traders, 3(4) traders are assigned to each class.
[b] Each dividend outcome occurs with probability 1/4 in each period.
[c] Each period's expected dividend value, $E(\tilde{D}_t^T)$, $t = 1, 2, \ldots, T$, is computed and displayed to each trader before the beginning of the period. In designs 3–5 (no buyout), $E(\tilde{D}_t^T) = E(\tilde{d})(T - t + 1)$, $t = 1, 2, \ldots, T$. In designs 1–2 (with buyout), $E(\tilde{D}_t^T) = \Sigma_{\tau=1}^{t}\hat{d}_\tau + 2E(\tilde{d})(T - t + 1)$, since the buyout at T is $\Sigma_{t=1}^{T}\hat{d}_t \pm 0.50$, probability 1/2, in design 1 ($\Sigma\tilde{d}_t \pm 1.00$, probability 1/2 in design 2), $\hat{d}_\tau$ refers to the realized dividend at the end of τ.
[d] (5; 12) means experiment number 5 using 12 subjects. x means experienced. xx means superexperienced. s means subjects were trained in a sequence of independent single period asset markets. n means some novice (inexperienced) subjects were combined with experienced subjects. f means subjects were asked to forecast next period's mean price. pc means price controls were set at $E(\tilde{D}_t^T) \pm 0.10$ for $t = 1, 2, 3$. In experiment (12xn; 9, 3c), 3 of the 12 traders were confederates.
[e] $T = 30$ in experiment (42xf; 9): otherwise $T = 15$.

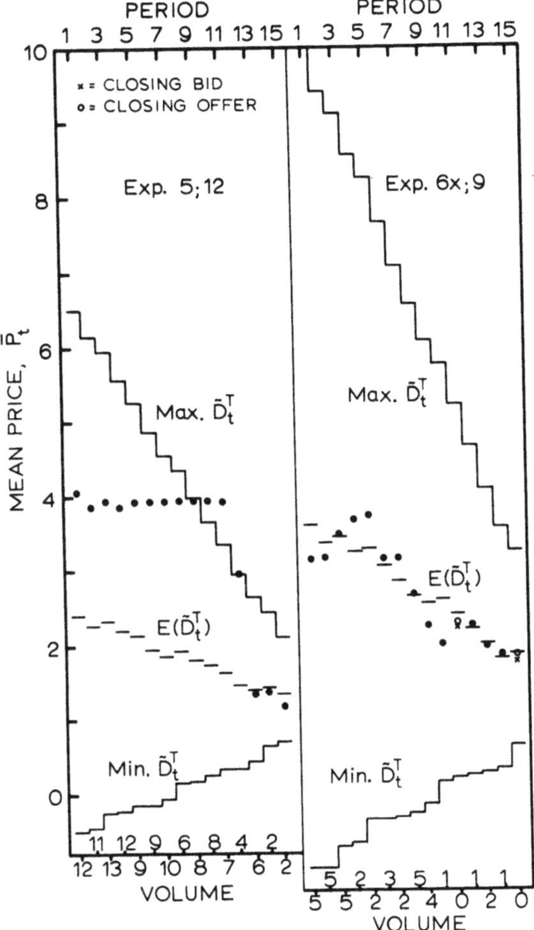

FIGURE 2

Our first two experiments, 5 and 6x, are charted in Figure 2.[3] The nine traders in 6x were a subset of the twelve who participated in 5. Because of the large volume of transactions we chart only the mean price by period. Experience appeared to be an important determinant of trading patterns. Both inexperienced and experienced subjects had a sense of the asset's intrinsic worth. For example, subjects in the inexperienced group asked the experimenters "why the buying panic?" and "shouldn't it sell near dividend value?" However, the subject who perceived a "buying panic" accumulated net inventory through period 11 and suffered a capital loss in period 12! Indeed, if you expected prices to hold steady

[3]Under the influence of RE theory and the strong previous experimental evidence favoring it in replicated environments, we hypothesized initially that allowing asset holdings to float (without reinitialization) might not be sufficient to yield observations that deviated much from the intrinsic value (dividend) rational expectations hypothesis, $E(\tilde{D}_t^T)$, over the ostensibly "short" horizon of $T = 15$ trading periods.

for many periods, it was rational to buy (or hold), collect the dividends, and plan to sell later at the inflated price. The top earning subject approximated this strategy. Experiments 6x, and 9x using experienced subjects from experiment 7, appeared to confirm our conjecture that with experience and full (calculated) information, prices would converge to the intrinsic value, $E(\tilde{D}_t^T)$, although 9x (Figure 3) suggests that behavior consistent with risk aversion may be observed in the first several periods.

In each of the first four experiments (5, 6x, 7, 9x) the mean price in period 2 was "close" to the mean in period 1. Therefore, we conjectured that expectations might be sensitive to the initial contracts, and that if we could induce initial trading at prices near $E(\tilde{D}_t^T)$, then the market might follow this path. We tested this conjecture by recruiting seven experienced subjects and two inexperienced subjects at Indiana University for experiment 12xn. Three experimenters at the University of Arizona participated as confederate "insiders" in a 12 trader market (most experiments were conducted multisite). Our plan was for the insiders to trade so as to maintain the price in a range within 10 cents of $E(\tilde{D}_t^T)$ for two trading periods, using period 3 to adjust the total insider share inventory to the level of the initial endowment, and then become inactive. Since both previous experienced trader markets had opened below $E(\tilde{D}_t^T)$, we guessed that insider activity in experiment 12xn would have to concentrate on buying support. Hence, the strategy was for the two insiders with the largest cash endowments (7.60 and 10.00) each to enter opening bids at 2.30, and for the trader with the largest share endowment (4 units) to enter an opening offer at 2.50. If the standing bid was accepted, it was backed by a new bid at the same price. If the standing offer was accepted the strategy was to immediately replace it with a new offer at 2.50. The insiders encountered unanticipated buying strength, and they were able to contain the surge in demand only by allowing some contract prices in excess of $E(\tilde{D}_t^T) + 0.10$ during the first three periods. As shown in Figure 3, this effort partially succeeded in that prices did not rise by very much in periods 4 and 5 before converging to near $E(\tilde{D}_t^T)$. Based on experiment 12xn we tentatively rejected the hypothesis that these markets are robustly sensitive to the "accident" of where they start. Strong endogenous expectations and behavioral uncertainty appear to determine the starting level as well as the subsequent course of prices, and these expectations are not easily neutralized even when 25% of the market is controlled by a confederate attempt to impose $E(\tilde{D}_t^T)$ expectations.

Since our first markets with experienced traders were yielding less than complete convergence to $E(\tilde{D}_t^T)$ share values, we continued to run paired experiments consisting of a 12 trader asset market followed by a market using a 9 trader subset of the first group (Figures 4–7). In two of these experiments (20x in Figure 5, and 23 in Figure 6) we imposed a computer enforced price ceiling at $E(\tilde{D}_t^T) + 0.10$ and a price floor at $E(\tilde{D}_t^T) - 0.10$ for the first two trading periods. These price controls would have the effect of forcing the market to trade within 10 cents of $E(\tilde{D}_t^T)$, which was the objective in experiment 12xn, but with the potentially important difference that it would be common knowledge that prices in this range would be the result of an externally imposed constraint. In

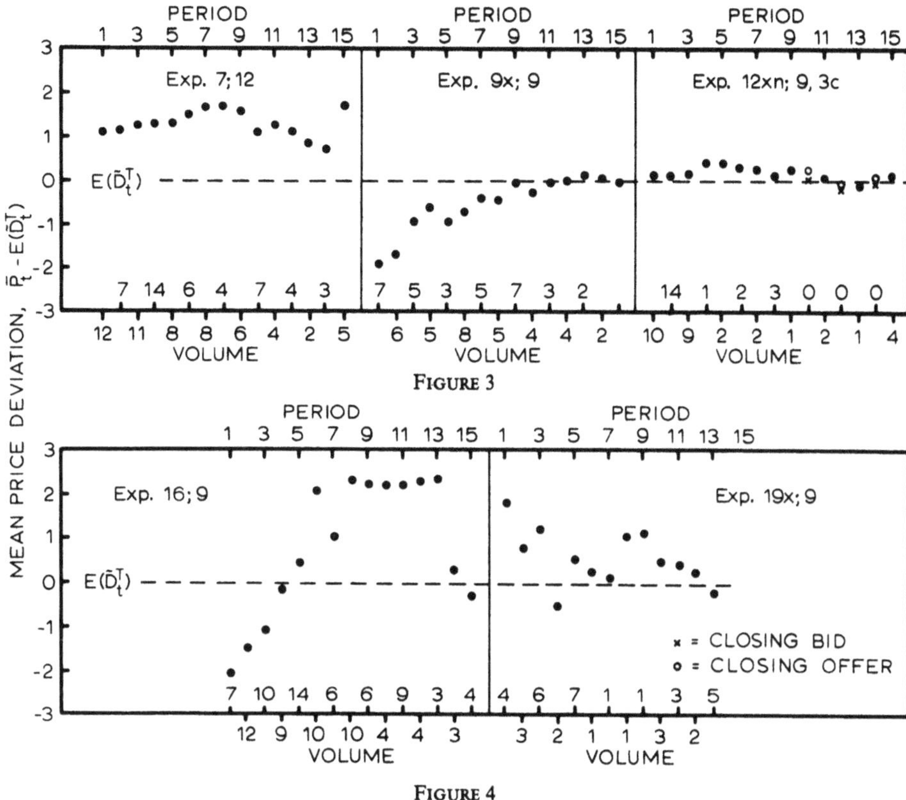

FIGURE 3

FIGURE 4

experiment 12xn we had sought surreptitiously to create the belief that such prices had occurred "naturally."

In experiment 16 (Figure 4) we observed our first full scale market bubble—a boom followed by a market crash. Replication of this experiment (19x) with experienced subjects failed to extinguish a boom-bust pattern of trading. In experiment 17 we observe a relatively smooth bell-shaped pattern of mean prices over time. A subset of these subjects returned to participate in experiment 20x which imposed a price ceiling and floor in periods 1 and 2 designed to see if such a constraint could induce $E(\tilde{D}_t^T)$ price expectations. This treatment worked as predicted, showing that an intrinsic value rational expectations price pattern could be approximated by combining experience (even bubble experience) with two initial periods of trading at controlled prices near $E(\tilde{D}_t^T)$. Would the same result be produced with inexperienced traders, and, if so, would it carry over into a subsequent market (without price controls) using a subset of these "conditioned" traders? From the chart of experiments 23 and 25x in Figure 6, we see that the answer is emphatically no. In experiment 23 the market traded near the ceiling price for the first two periods. Upon the removal of the price controls the market price increased by about one-third, with increased volume, then held

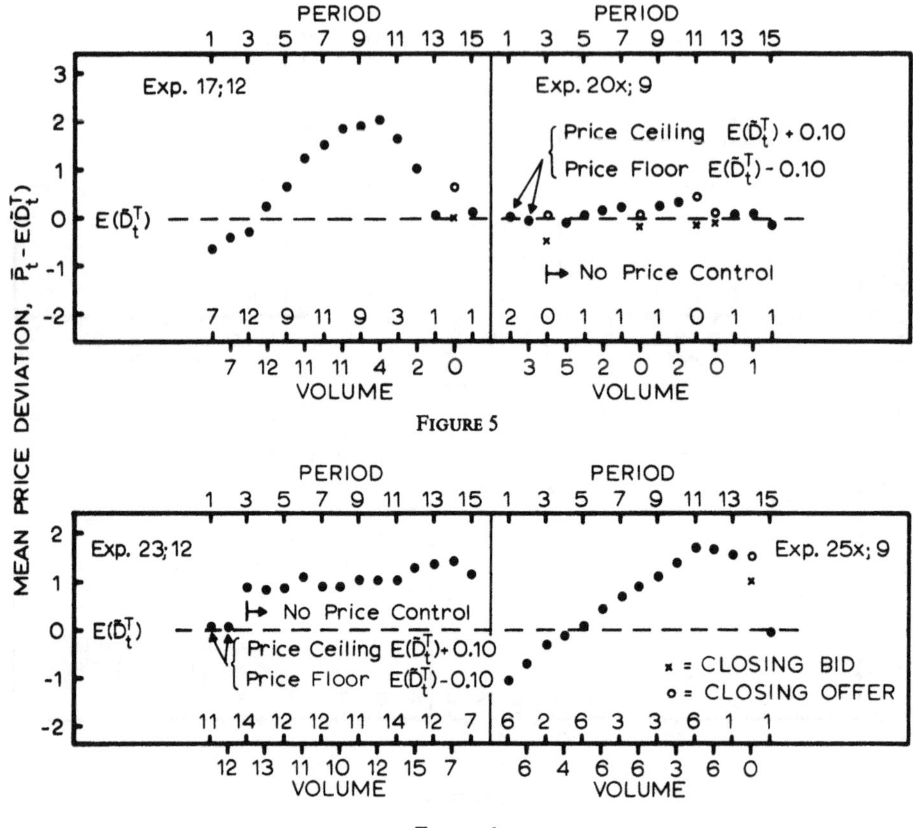

FIGURE 5

FIGURE 6

approximately steady until the last period. But the nine member subset of this group who participated in experiment 25x produced a substantial bull market measured relative to $E(\tilde{D}_t^T)$. This demonstrates the potential for endogenous expectations to dominate the objective underlying parameters of a market. Experiment 25x marked the beginning of our series of experiments with no end-of-horizon buyout at $T = 15$, and demonstrated that our use of such a buyout to enhance the volatility of expectations was unnecessary.

The two experiments in Figure 7 provide back-to-back market bubbles in which the first experiment (26) appears to have produced an expectation of a bubble in the replication (28x) causing the second bubble to rise faster, and break sooner than the first. (As subjects were arriving for 28x, one commented to an experimenter that he expected this market to "crash," which of course implied that he also expected it to first "boom.") This appears to be an excellent example of self-fulfilling expectations.

Experiment 10 (Figure 8) is noteworthy because of its use of professional and business people from the Tucson community, as subjects. This market belies any notion that our results are an artifact of student subjects, and that businessmen who "run the real world" would quickly learn to have rational expectations. This

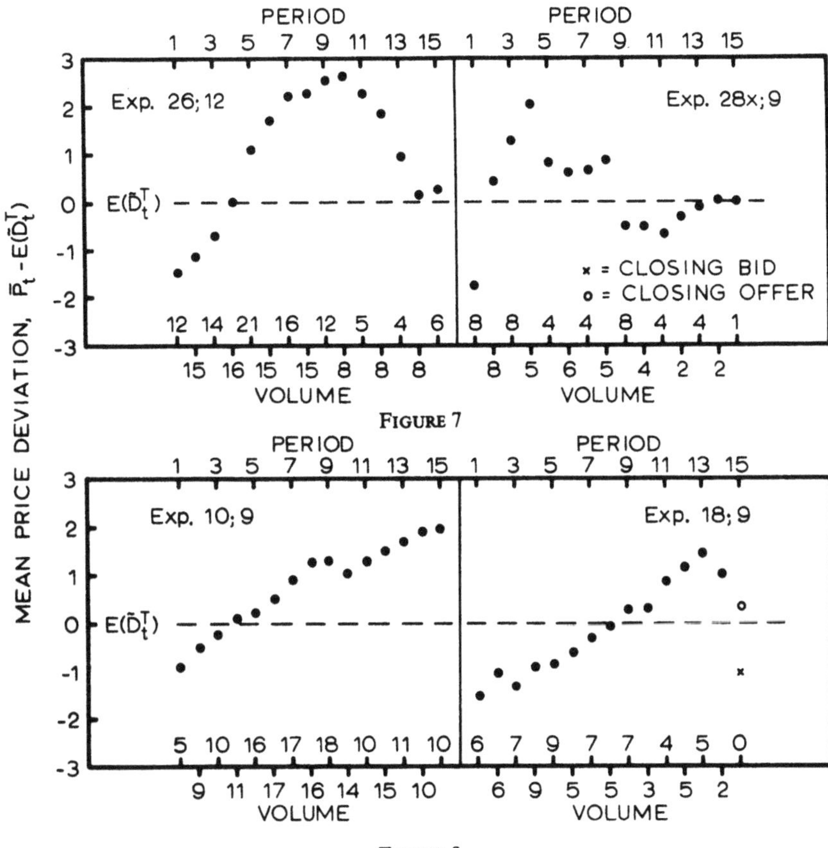

FIGURE 7

FIGURE 8

is the only experiment we conducted that closed on a mean price higher than in all previous trading periods. Of interest is the fact that because this experiment was conducted in the evening hours (9–11 pm CST), it had to be interrupted shortly (about 10 minutes) for the regular 10 pm CST PLATO shutdown for servicing. We informed subjects that they would be logged back in for period 10 at the same asset position each had at the end of period 9. In spite of our assurances that things would proceed as if there had been no interruption, the market steadied in anticipation of the interruption at the end of period 9, sold off in period 10 after restarting, then recovered to resume the steady-growth trend of periods 1–8. This result illustrates the sensitivity of an asset market to external sources of subjective uncertainty even when the experimenter uses instruction to attempt to neutralize their possible significance; it also corroborates the widely held belief that stock markets are vulnerable to "psychological" elements (factors other than "fundamentals" that create common expectations).

An empirical regularity in those markets that experience a price bubble is for the collapse in market prices to occur on a trading volume that is smaller than the average volume in the periods preceding the collapse. This is illustrated in

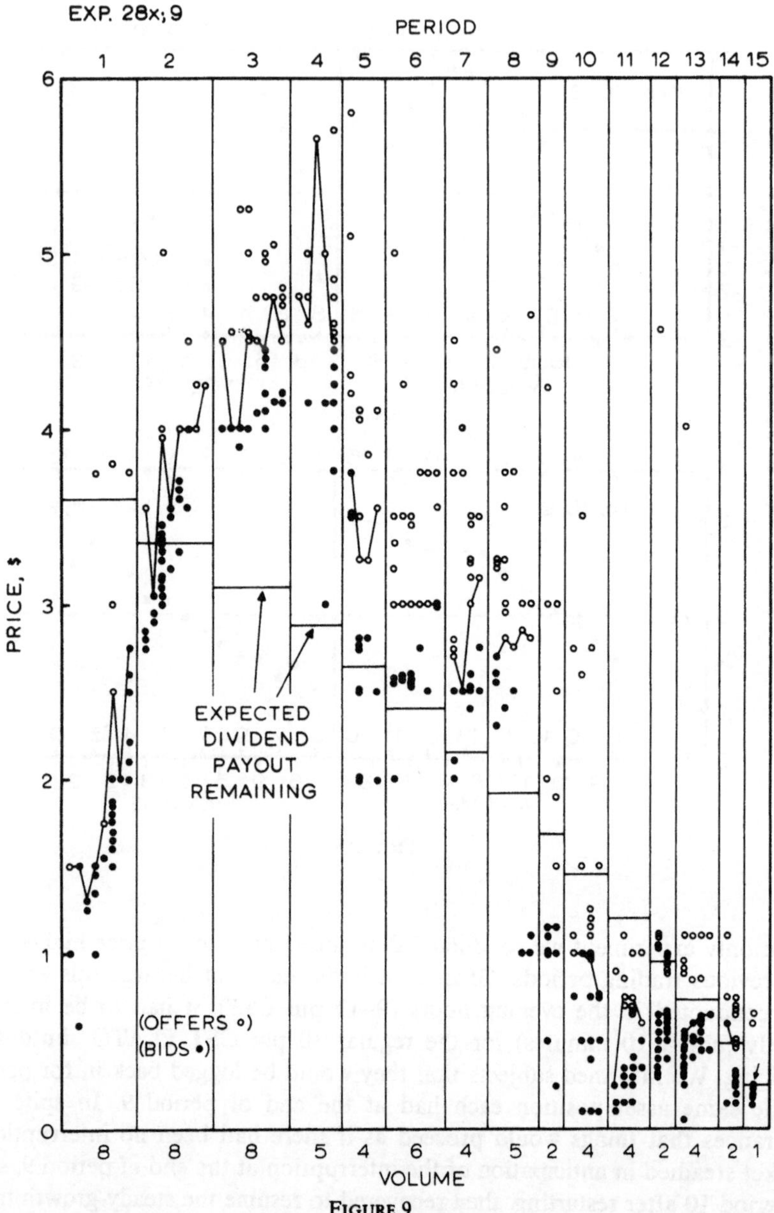

FIGURE 9

experiments 16 (periods 7 and 14), 17 (periods 11–15), 26 (periods 11–15), 28x (period 5), and 18 (periods 14–15). Even more telling is the tendency for volume to shrink in the period just *prior* to the collapse in prices.

Figure 9 provides a chart of all bids and offers and the resulting contract prices (joined by line segments) in sequence for experiment 28x, and illustrates the dynamics of price behavior both within and across trading periods in one market bubble. This market rose from an intraperiod low of $1.30 in period 1 to an intraperiod high of $5.65 in period 4. The significance of the changing pattern of bid-offer activity will be discussed in Section 5.2.

At this juncture in our research we posed the following questions. Are our results influenced artifactually by the confounding condition that when subjects participate in their first asset market experiment they simultaneously acquire training in the mechanics of asset trading *and* form expectations about the price behavior of such markets over time? In particular could it be that the price bubbles and market crashes with first-time asset traders are due to their inexperience, with similar bubble and crash phenomena repeated with second-time traders because of expectations created in the first market? To resolve these questions, in experiments 30xsf and 39xsf (Figure 10) subjects were experienced, but they did *not* acquire experience from a previous 15 period asset market. Their experience was obtained by participating in a sequence of single-period asset trading markets in which each trader's endowment was reinitialized at the beginning of each period, and no inventories of shares purchased in any earlier period could be carried over to any later period. Thus subjects were trained in an asset trading market in which no capital gains (or losses) were possible across trading periods. This treatment allowed subject experience in trading mechanics to be acquired while controlling for bubbles and crashes. The results charted in Figure 10 for experiments 30xsf and 39xsf show that bubbles and crashes can indeed occur in markets with experienced subjects who have not been inadvertently conditioned to expect bubbles and crashes in the process of acquiring experience. Although the trading patterns are quite different in 30xsf and 39xsf, each corresponds to one of the two major performance patterns identified in the earlier experments.

Experiment 36xx was designed to see if the "superstar" traders in our previous experiments would yield intrinsic value market prices. These nine subjects had all participated in at least two previous asset markets (in addition to the basic supply and demand trainer). Also they had been screened for profit performance, so that eight of the subjects had been among the top earning subjects in all previous experiments. (One subject who was an exception to this screening rule earned the third highest profits in 36xx.) As indicated by the chart in Figure 10, experiment 36xx yielded a substantial (but very low volume) price bubble.

The single period horizon experiments ($T = 1$) used to train subjects for experiments 30xsf and 39xsf produced no intraperiod price bubbles. Yet we often observe bubbles when $T = 15$. (One of us has observed bubbles when $T = 3$ using inexperienced subjects.) This suggests the extra theoretical hypothesis that bubble effects should be intensified if we double the horizon from 15 to 30 periods, since this would increase the scope for capital gains expectations to swamp intrinsic value. In experiment 42xf, we set $T = 30$ using a nine member subset of the subjects in 41f (Figure 11). Contrary to this view, experiment 42xf (charted in Figure 11) appears to converge quickly to intrinsic dividend asset value (but see Section 5 for qualifications) in spite of the trading group's experience with a sharp price bubble and collapse in 41f. We interpret this result as strengthening the interpretation that these markets are sensitive to group endogenous expecta-

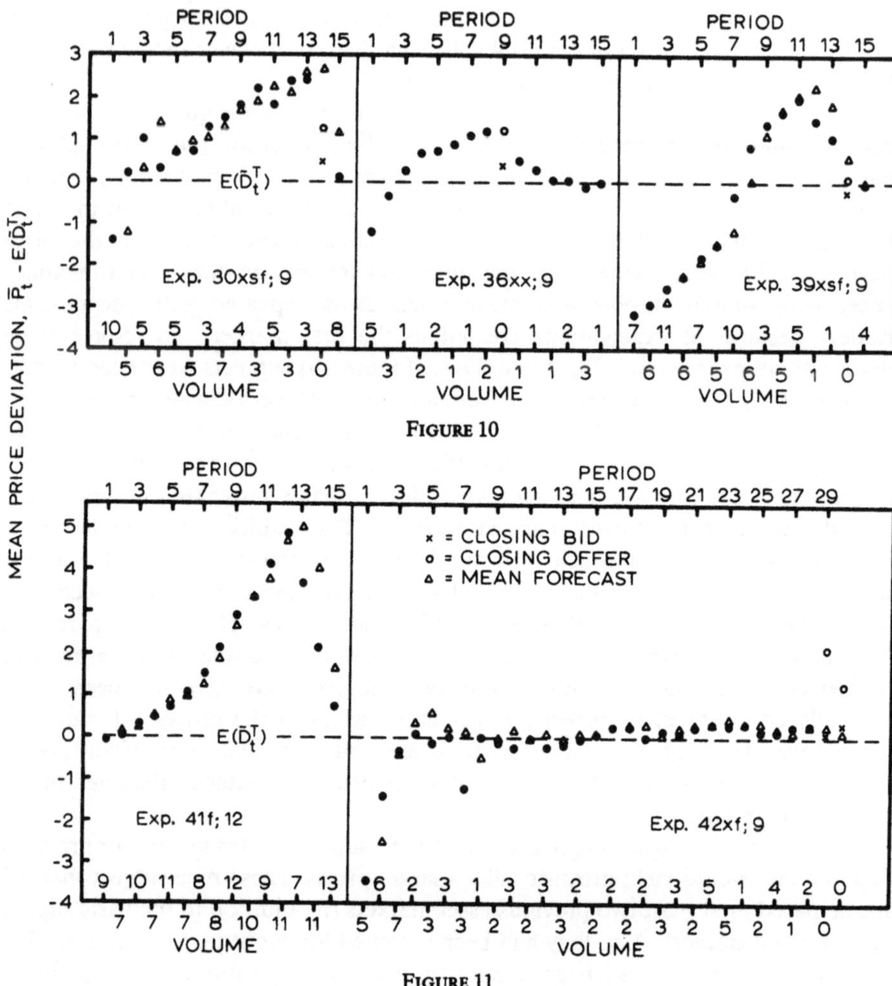

FIGURE 10

FIGURE 11

tional factors that are not reliably manipulated by such controllable treatment variables as experience, information, and horizon length.

Experiments 43xnf, 48xnf, and 49xnf represent an effort to mix experienced traders who had yielded intrinsic value equilibrium prices with traders who either had no experience or who had a bubble experience. This treatment was motivated by the conjecture that if the stock market was dominated only by professional traders, one might observe intrinsic value asset prices, but that the presence of uninformed novices who lose money, leave the market, and are replaced by new novices, prevents such equilibria from occurring. In 43xnf, six subjects were recruited from the "professionals" who had participated in experiment 42xf. The remaining three subjects in 43xnf were novices in the sense that one had no previous asset trading experience and two had experience only in a bubble

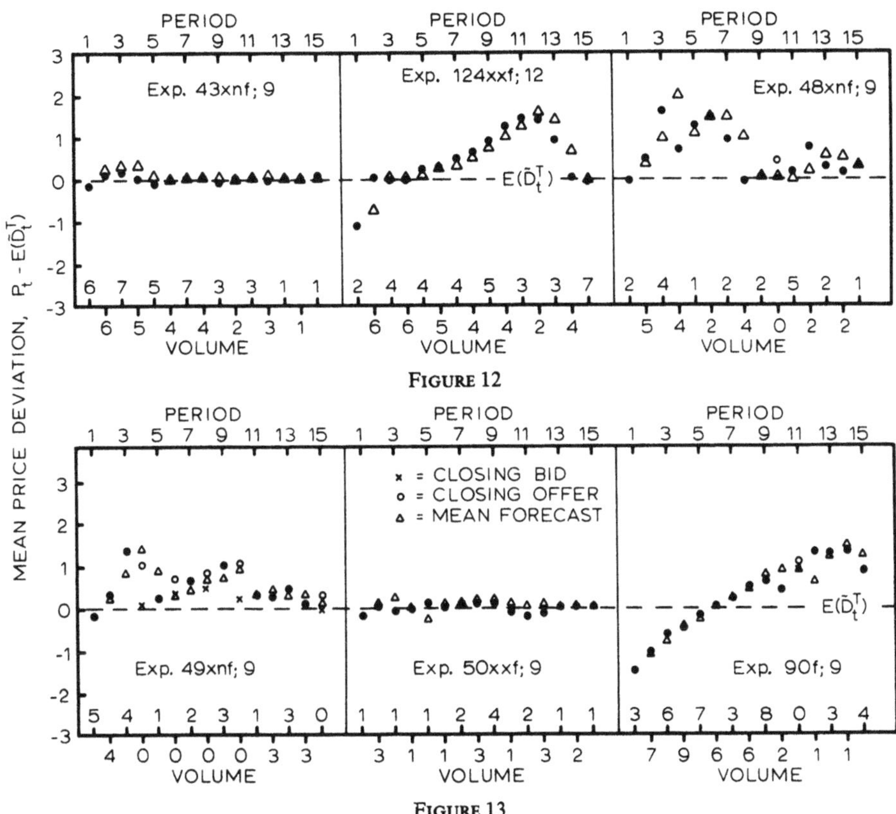

FIGURE 12

FIGURE 13

market (experiment 41f). From the chart of mean prices for 43xnf in Figure 12 it is seen that with two-thirds of the market made by "professionals," we observe convergence. But experiment 48xnf, with only three "professionals," four with bubble experience, and two inexperienced subjects, provided an erratic bubble for the first six periods. These results do not contradict a conjectured "professional effect" such that, if there are enough such experienced traders, they will dampen any bubble tendency. This conjecture is further supported by experiments 49xnf and 50xxf. In 49xnf we had a mixture of four "professionals" and five subjects with bubble, or no experience; these subjects created a small bubble (Figure 13). We then recruited these same subjects for a replication (one was replaced with a highly experienced subject), and the new market, experiment 50xxf, traded near intrinsic value. It appears that *replication with essentially the same subjects* eventually will create a "professional" market with common expectations in which bubble tendencies are extinguished and replaced by intrinsic value pricing. In this regard experiment 124xxf is of special significance in that the subjects were sophisticated graduate students with experience in at least two previous asset markets, but it was their first 15 period time horizon. Their previous experience was with the Forsythe et al. (1982) and Friedman et al. (1984) environments in which they converged to the rational expectations equilibrium. As shown in Figure 12, this market converged temporarily on dividend value then exhibited a bubble before crashing back to dividend value. These subjects clearly understood the dividend structure, but "played" the bubble.

Beginning with experiment 30xsf, at the end of each trading period each subject was asked to forecast the mean contract price in the next trading period. The forecasting exercise followed the procedures utilized in Williams (1987). The subject with the smallest cumulative absolute forecasting error over periods 2 to 15 earned an additional $1. Individual forecasts were private information, and to avoid providing an incentive to manipulate price in a "close" forecasting race no subject was informed how their own forecasts compared with those of others. While entering forecasts, subjects' screens displayed the entire history of their own forecasts, mean price, and absolute forecast errors. Williams (1987) provided evidence that $1 is sufficient incentive for serious forecasting, but not so large as to motivate strategic manipulation of the mean price in an effort to win the forecasting prize.

In Figures 10–13 are plotted the mean of these individual forecasts on the same scale with the mean contract prices realized in each period. These charts reveal several characteristics of the mean forecasts: (1) in many periods the mean forecast appears not to be a bad predictor of the mean price; (2) forecasts tend to be good when the mean price is approximately constant (as in 90f, periods 13–14), exhibits a small trend (as in 41f, periods 2–6), or follows intrinsic value (as in 42xf): (3) the forecasts lag behind larger changes or trends in price (as in 30xsf, periods 2–4, and 49xnf periods 2–10); (4) the forecasts invariably fail to predict turning points (as in 30xsf, period 4, 39xsf, period 12, and 41f, period 13). In short our subject's forecasting ability in these markets is similar to that of professional forecasters in the field.[4] Characteristics (3) and (4) are particularly interesting since experimental market prices, including price jumps and turning points, are determined entirely by the endogenous actions of the same individuals who are making the forecasts!

5. PRICE FORECASTS AND PRICE DYNAMICS: HYPOTHESES AND EMPIRICAL RESULTS

In formulating some hypotheses implied by alternative models of forecasting behavior and price adjustments, we will distinguish between *rational expectations in the sense of Muth* (REM) and *rational expectations in the sense of Nash* (REN). In Muth's (1961) well known treatment the REM hypothesis is "...that expectations of firms (or, more generally, the subjective probability distribution of outcomes) tend to be distributed, for the same information set, about the

[4]Such characteristics of professional forecasters have a long history. For example, "...forecasters tend to rely heavily on the persistence of trends in spending, output, and the price level. To the extent that inertia prevails in the economy's movement, their predictions turn out to be roughly right...but...such forecasts suffer from missing business cycle turns and underestimating recessions and recoveries..." (Zarnowitz, 1986, pp. 17–18).

predictions of the theory (or the 'objective' probability distribution of outcomes)." However, it is perhaps less well known that many years earlier Nash (1950, p. 158) defined the concept less restrictively by stating that "... since our solution should consist of *rational* expectations of gain..., these expectations should be realizable." Thus REN implies only that expectations are sustained (or reinforced) by outcomes, while REM implies that expectations are sustained by outcomes that in turn support the predictions of some theory.[5]

5.1. *Are Subject Price Forecasts Accurate, Valuable, Adaptive?*

We begin our analysis with the experiments (designated with an "f" under the listing "design 4 experiments" in Table I and displayed in Figures 10–13) in which traders submitted forecasts of the mean price in the next trading period. The question of forecast accuracy is examined using OLS estimation of the equation

$$\text{(1)} \qquad \bar{P}_{t,e} = \alpha_1 + \beta_1 F_{t,e,i} + \varepsilon_{t,e,i},$$

where $\bar{P}_{t,e}$ is the mean price in trading period t $(t = 3,\ldots,15)$ of experiment e; $F_{t,e,i}$ is the forecast of the period t mean price in experiment e entered by trader i $(i = 1,\ldots,9)$; and $\varepsilon_{t,e,i}$ is the random error term. Forecasts are "accurate" if they are unbiased predictors of the mean price. The REN hypothesis implies the inability to reject the joint null hypothesis $(\alpha_1, \beta_1) = (0,1)$. REN is the correct interpretation here since we are not asking whether prices correspond to some specific theoretical prediction but simply whether prices and forecasts are mutually supportive.

The OLS estimation of equation (1) yields

$$\text{(1')} \qquad \bar{P}_{t,e} = \underset{(5.98)}{.208} + \underset{(-8.25)}{.844}\ F_{t,e,i}, \qquad R^2 = .823,\ N = 852.$$

The numbers in parentheses are t ratios associated with the null hypotheses $\alpha_1 = 0$ and $\beta_1 = 1$. Both indicate rejection at any standard level of significance as does the test of the joint null hypothesis $(\alpha_1, \beta_1) = (0,1)$ which yields $F_{(2,850)} = 38.9$. Clearly, there is a systematic tendency for forecasts to deviate from the observed mean price.[6]

We also estimated equation (1) for each of the ten forecasting experiments and for each individual subject in three forecasting experiments (39xsf, 41f, and

[5] When testing REM using field survey data, investigators assume implicitly that observed prices are randomly distributed about some theoretical equilibrium price. It should be emphasized that unless this assumption is satisfied, these investigations are testing REN. No distinction between REM and REN is possible without experimental control of dividends.

[6] Estimation of (1′) using the opening price as the dependent variable rather than the mean price does not alter this result. The coefficient estimates and test statistics are very similar to those using the mean price. The coefficient of correlation between the mean and opening price is $r = .97$. Forecast accuracy was also evaluated using the change in the observed mean price $(\bar{P}_t - \bar{P}_{t-1})$ as the dependent variable and the predicted change in the mean price $(F_t - \bar{P}_{t-1})$ as the independent variable. The results indicate that the null hypothesis $(\alpha, \beta) = (0,1)$ must be rejected $(F_{2,779} = 93.8)$.

TABLE II

REGRESSION ESTIMATES: PROFIT VERSUS ABSOLUTE FORECASTING ERROR

Experiment	N (Subjects)	Forecast Error Regression Coefficient
30xsf	9	−4.4
39xsf	9	−3.0
41f	12	−2.55**
42xf	9	−1.1*
43xnf	9	−0.058
48xnf	9	−0.83
49xnf	9	−1.4**
50xxf	9	−0.43*
90f	9	−1.1
124xxf	9	−0.74

*Significant Pr $\leq$ 0.05.
**Significant Pr $\leq$ 0.01.

124xxf). The results strongly parallel those shown in equation (1′). It is clear, however, that some subjects were much better forecasters than others. Furthermore, there was a tendency for the better forecasters to earn more money. We established this by regressing profit on absolute forecasting error across individual subjects in each of the ten forecasting experiments. Table II lists the coefficient estimate for the forecast error variable. The coefficient is negative in all ten regressions with four estimates being significant at the 95% level. Greater accuracy in forecasting is associated with greater profit. This is consistent with, but does not prove, the proposition that the better forecasters *acted* on their forecasts to earn higher profits.

Figure 14 summarizes the accuracy of subject price forecasts using the forecast error frequency polygon ($F_t - \overline{P}_t$ rounded to the nearest .05 node) generated by a pooling of all individual forecasts across trading periods 3–15. The sample distribution is not abnormal in appearance but is slightly skewed toward positive forecast errors with mean, median, and modal error of .049, −.01, and −.05, respectively. The vast majority of the forecasts are within one standard deviation of the mean. Can the forecast errors depicted in Figure 14 (pooled across time and subjects) be characterized as a sample of independent draws from a single random variable? We address this question by formally testing the null hypotheses: (i) serial independence of forecast errors, and (ii) no systematic relationship between forecast errors and changes in the forecasting objective.

Serial independence of forecast errors implies the inability to reject the null hypothesis $\beta_2 = 0$ in the equation

$$(2) \qquad (F_t - \overline{P}_t) = \alpha_2 + \beta_2(F_{t-1} - \overline{P}_{t-1}) + \varepsilon_t,$$

where indexing over experiments (e) and individuals (i) is implied. Our alternative hypothesis, based on evidence presented in Williams (1987) and inspection of the charts of the forecasting experiments, is that forecast errors are positively autocorrelated implying $\beta_2 > 0$. OLS estimation of equation (2) for $t = 3, \ldots, 15$

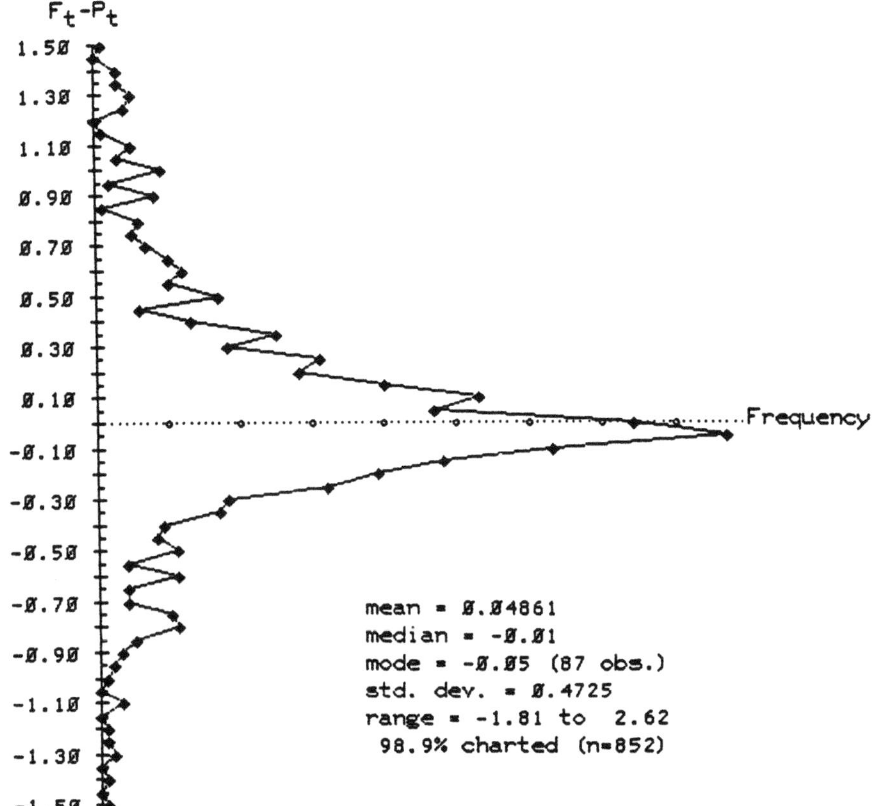

FIGURE 14.—Forecast error frequency polygon.

yields:

$$(2') \qquad (F_t - \bar{P}_t) = \underset{(3.03)}{.046} + \underset{(8.66)}{.282}\,(F_{t-1} - \bar{P}_{t-1}), \qquad R^2 = .089,\ N = 769.$$

The t ratio shown in parentheses under the slope coefficient estimate indicates that the null hypothesis of serial independence is rejected.

Given that forecast errors tend to persist over time, we now ask how forecast errors are linked to changes in the forecasting objective. Figure 14 shows that the distribution of forecast errors is fairly symmetric with a slight tendency for subjects to over-predict the mean price. However, inspection of the charts of the forecasting experiments with bubbles clearly indicates a tendency for the mean forecast to under-predict the mean price during booms ($F_t < \bar{P}_t$) and over-predict the mean price ($F_t > \bar{P}_t$) during crashes. Thus, forecast errors appear to be inversely related to changes in the forecasting objective. More formally, for the equation

$$(3) \qquad (F_t - \bar{P}_t) = \alpha_3 + \beta_3(\bar{P}_t - \bar{P}_{t-1}) + \varepsilon_t$$

TABLE III

STATISTICS FOR THE DISTRIBUTION OF $x_{i,t} = F_{i,t} - E(D_t^T)$

Group[a]	N	Mean[b]	Median	Range	Variance	F_{12} ratio[c]	F_{23} ratio[c]	F_{13} ratio[c]
x^1: 30xsf, 39xsf, 41f, 90f, 124xxf	672	0.93	0.86	−3.36 +5.70	2.5953			
						5.04		
x^2: 42xfa, 43xnf, 48xnf, 49xnf	504	0.32	0.22	−3.66 +2.87	0.5155			37.27
							7.40	
x^3: 42xfb, 50xxf	251	0.14	0.14	−2.63 +0.76	0.0696			

[a] x^1, experiments in which subjects had not previously participated in a 15 period asset market. kx^2, experiments in which some (all in 42xfa) subjects had participated in a previous 15 period asset market. (Experiment 42xfa represents periods 1–15 of 42xf.) x^3, experiments in which all subjects had been in the same two previous 15 period asset markets. (Experiment 42xfb represents periods 16–30 of 42xf.)

[b] Each of these means is significantly different from each other using either a t test or a rank sum test.

[c] F_{ij}, the F statistic for groups i, j.

this implies rejection of the null hypothesis $\beta_3 = 0$ in favor of the alternative hypothesis $\beta_3 < 0$. Estimation of equation (3) yields

$$(3') \qquad (F_t - \overline{P}_t) = \underset{(-7.30)}{-.077} \; \underset{(-33.4)}{-.824} \, (\overline{P}_t - \overline{P}_{t-1}), \qquad R^2 = .589,\ N = 781.$$

The null hypothesis $\beta_3 = 0$ is easily rejected in favor of the one-tailed alternative $\beta_3 < 0$, and we see a pronounced tendency to under-predict in expansions and over-predict in contractions. This lagged updating of forecasts relative to movements in the mean price combined with positively autocorrelated forecast errors suggests that forecasts were being formed adaptively.

Expectations are considered adaptive if $0 < \beta_4 < 1$ and $\alpha_4 = -E(\tilde{d}_t)$ (if all agents are risk neutral) in the equation

$$(4) \qquad (F_t - F_{t-1}) = \alpha_4 + \beta_4(\overline{P}_{t-1} - F_{t-1}) + \varepsilon_t.$$

The adaptive expectations model states that the current forecast updates the previous forecast by subtracting the expected single period dividend and adding a fraction of the previous period's forecast error. OLS estimation of equation 4 for $t = 3, \ldots, 15$ yields

$$(4') \qquad (F_t - F_{t-1}) = \underset{(12.11)}{-.117} + \underset{(38.16)}{.815} \, (\overline{P}_{t-1} - F_{t-1}), \qquad R^2 = .632,\ N = 850$$

The t ratios shown in parentheses under the coefficient estimates indicate rejection of the null hypotheses $\alpha_4 = -.24$ and $\beta_4 = 0$, respectively. The null hypothesis $\beta_4 = 1$ is also rejected ($t = -8.66$). These results indicate that forecasts are adaptive in the sense that $0 < \beta_4 < 1$; however, there is a persistent forecasting bias with $\alpha_4 > -E(\tilde{d}_t)$. As will be shown below, this bias is consistent with agents being risk averse in dividends.[7]

[7] If agents utilize the most recent price information to formulate their forecasts, this implies that the right-hand side of equation (4) should utilize the closing price in period $t-1$ rather than the mean price. This change yields qualitatively similar results to the estimates reported in (4′): $\hat{\alpha}_4 = -.136$, $\hat{\beta}_4 = .628$, $R^2 = .491$ with strong rejection of the null hypotheses $\alpha_4 = -.24$, $\beta_4 = 0$, and $\beta_4 = 1$.

5.2. *Do Subjects' Forecasts Converge to REM with Experience?*

Table IV provides statistics for the distribution of $x_{i,t} = F_{i,t} - E(D_t^T)$ for three different poolings of experiments according to subject experience. All subjects in the x^1 grouping were inexperienced. Those in x^3 had all participated in two previous 15 period markets, while only some of the subjects in x^2 had been in such previous asset market experiments. These groups show clearly that as the experience level increases across experiments, both the mean deviation and the variance of forecasts relative to the dividend value decline significantly. Consequently, with increasing experience our subjects tend to acquire common intrinsic value expectations as behavioral uncertainty decreases.

5.3. *Price Adjustment Dynamics*

The empirical analysis of Section 5.1 distinguishes forecast (expected) prices, F_t, and observed prices $\overline{P}_t$. According to equation (4′), the linear adaptive forecast error dynamic characterizes the adjustment of forecasts over time, and provides a link between forecast prices and observed prices. In this section we consider a (mean) price adjustment hypothesis, H, for characterizing the intertemporal behavior of observed prices. This hypothesis includes the risk neutral and risk adjusted REM hypotheses as special equilibrium cases.

H: Walrasian adaptive, expected capital gains adjusted, REN,

$$\overline{P}_t - \overline{P}_{t-1} = -E(\tilde{d}) + K + \beta(B_{t-1} - O_{t-1}), \qquad \beta > 0. \tag{5}$$

The mean price change from one period to the next is separable into (at most) three components: a term expressing the decline in expected dividend value, $-E(\tilde{d})$; an adjustment term for risk, K; and a measure of the revealed excess demand for shares arising from capital gains expectations. We postulate that excess demand is positively correlated with excess bids (number of bids entered minus number of offers) in those markets which spontaneously self-generate an expectation of capital gains (losses).[8] This hypothesis was formulated after

[8] The first two terms are easily derived assuming constant absolute risk aversion (CARA). Applying the Arrow-Pratt measure of the risk premium (or charge if the agent is risk preferring), the value of a share is given by

$$V_t = E(\tilde{D}_t^T) - \sigma^2(\tilde{D}_t^T)U''[E(\tilde{D}_t^T)]/2U'[E(\tilde{D}_t^T)].$$

Since $\tilde{D}_t^T = \Sigma_{\tau=t}^T \tilde{d}_\tau$, and $\tilde{d}_\tau = \tilde{d}$ (independent dividend realizations), it follows that $E(\tilde{D}_t^T) = \Sigma_{\tau=t}^T E(\tilde{d}) = (T-t+1)E(\tilde{d})$, and $\sigma^2(\tilde{D}_t^T) = \Sigma_{\tau=t}^T \sigma^2(\tilde{d}) = (T-t+1)\sigma^2(\tilde{d})$. Hence

$$V_t = (T-t+1)E(\tilde{d}) + (T-t+1)\sigma^2(\tilde{d})\frac{U''[(T-t+1)E(\tilde{d})]}{2U'[(T-t+1)E(\tilde{d})]}.$$

If we have CARA, then $U''(m)/U'(m) = -a$, and

$$V_t = (T-t+1)[E(\tilde{d}) - a\sigma^2(\tilde{d})/2].$$

Now assume that market prices average the effect of individual risk attitudes in such a way that the mean price equation has the same form as the typical individual's valuation of a share. Then if capital gains expectations are nil, we have $\overline{P}_t = (T-t+1)(E(\tilde{d}) - K)$ and $\overline{P}_t - \overline{P}_{t-1} = -E(\tilde{d}) + K$, as in (5).

TABLE IV

ESTIMATION OF EQUATION $\overline{P}_t^e - \overline{P}_{t-1}^e = \alpha^e + \beta^e(B_{t-1}^e - O_{t-1}^e) + \beta_t^e$

Experiment	$E(\bar{d}^e)$	$\hat{\alpha}^e$	$\hat{\beta}^e$	R^2	dw[c]
Group I, Stable Price Markets					
5	0.08	−0.22	0.014	0.06	1.6
		(−1.04)	(0.88)		
7	0.08	−0.10	−0.013	0.09	1.6
		(−0.21)	(−1.1)		
42xf	0.24	−0.18	0.025[b]	0.23	2.2
		(+0.62)	(2.8)		
43xnf	0.24	−0.22	0.0044	0.20	1.9
		(+0.56)	(1.7)		
50xxf	0.24	−0.23	0.006	0.11	2.0
		(+0.29)	(1.2)		
Group II, Growing Price Markets					
9x	0.12	0.027[a]	−0.00038	0.0004	2.3
		(+2.6)	(−0.07)		
10	0.12	0.20[a]	−0.010	0.26	1.7
		(+5.4)	(−2.1)		
90f	0.24	−0.053[a]	0.0063	0.02	1.6
		(+2.2)	(0.50)		
Group III, Bubble-Crash Markets					
6x	0.12	−0.16	0.014[b]	0.49	2.1
		(−0.74)	(3.4)		
16	0.12	0.058	0.038[b]	0.28	3.0
		(+0.76)	(2.2)		
17	0.08	−0.23	0.035[b]	0.63	2.9
		(−1.6)	(4.5)		
18	0.12	−0.17	0.029[b]	0.21	1.4
		(−0.40)	(1.8)		
25x	0.24	−0.47[a]	0.033[b]	0.60	1.6
		(−2.2)	(4.3)		
26	0.16	−0.082	0.039[b]	0.46	1.3
		(+0.66)	(3.2)		
28x	0.24	−0.12	0.063[b]	0.56	2.5
		(+0.74)	(3.9)		
30xsf	0.24	−0.32	0.073[b]	0.63	2.5
		(−0.57)	(4.5)		
36xx	0.24	−0.20	0.012	0.04	0.5
		(+0.35)	(0.71)		
39xsf	0.24	−0.28	0.044[b]	0.57	2.6
		(−0.32)	(4.0)		
41f	0.16	−0.58	0.049[b]	0.32	0.7
		(−1.5)	(2.4)		
48xnf	0.24	−0.31	0.031	0.17	2.6
		(−0.45)	(1.6)		
49xnf	0.24	−0.37	0.030	0.12	2.3
		(−0.74)	(1.3)		
124xxf	0.24	−0.31	0.025[b]	0.25	1.3
		(−0.50)	(2.0)		

[a] Intercept is significantly different from $-E(\bar{d}^e)$ (two-tailed test, $p < 0.05$).
[b] Walrasian coefficient of adjustment speed is significantly positive (one-tailed test, $p < 0.05$).
[c] dw: Durbin-Watson statistic.

examination of the data from two experiments suggested that there might be a tendency for the number of bids (as a measure of demand intensity) to thin relative to the number of offers in the period (or periods) prior to a crash in contract prices. Our interest in this potential regularity in the data was heightened when we realized that it might be expressed as a lagged Walrasian adjustment hypothesis in which excess bids are a surrogate for excess (capital gains) demand. We conjectured that excess bids might be correlated with excess demand because at a price below that which is market clearing there are more willing buyers than willing sellers, and this might be revealed in the context of the double auction institution by the simple numerical excess of bids over offers.

Concerning the interpretation of H, three remarks are appropriate.

1. If we interpret the capital gains component of the price change in H as a price change that is literally *expected* by the traders, then why do rational traders not act on that expectation in period $t-1$ and drive this component of the price change to zero? The answer is contained in a different interpretation of H in which it is proposed that traders *do not expect* the price that occurs in period t; they expect the price they forecast, which is adaptively error prone. In particular, traders fail to predict large price changes and turning points. By this interpretation what the excess bids variable does is to predict trader excess demand in the next period; i.e. excess bids measures *potential* excess demand, with that excess demand impinging on subsequent price realizations. These price realizations *then* produce or reinforce new price expectations. This scenario is consistent with the behavior of price forecasts, and with the excess bids hypothesis. The behavioral mechanism postulated by this interpretation is as follows. In the market's bull phase, if bidding activity is strong in t, with many bids not being accepted, this signals a strong willingness-to-pay and presages an *incentive* induced increase in bid levels in the next period; i.e. traders experience rejection (nonacceptance) of their bids and are motivated to bid higher. Similarly, a thinning of bids, even though at a higher contract price level in t, with few bids failing to be accepted, presages an incentive induced decline in bid levels in the subsequent period. A symmetrical argument would also apply to offers. Traders do not expect this change in prices either because they fail to be aware of excess bid activity, or fail to anticipate the incentive response to high levels of bid rejection. Figure 9 for experiment 28x, illustrates changes in the bid-offer activity over the course of a bubble which are consistent with this interpretation. Notice that the large volume of excess bids in periods 1 and 2 are followed by jumps in bid levels in periods 2 and 3. In periods 3 and 4, when excess bids become negative, there follows a reduction in bid levels in periods 4 and 5, and so on. We have no insight concerning the deeper homegrown source of the endogenous expectations that give rise to positive or negative excess bids. It is not evident that the ultimate "cause" or source of such expectations can be formulated in terms of a traditional dynamic.[9]

[9]What we have in mind has been articulated by Coleman (1979, p. 280) in his discussion of "a panic of the sort that sometimes occurs in a crowded theater. The most puzzling question here is not why panics occur, but why their occurrence is so uncertain. In one situation, a panic will occur,... In

2. We regard H as directly representing rational expectation in the sense of Nash because capital gains (losses) expectations, if they persist, must be sustained by the subsequent observation of rising (falling) prices. Thus in Figure 9, an expectation of rising prices is sustained by the price outcomes in periods 1–4. The price decline in period 5, although presaged by the relative thinning of bids in periods 3 and 4 but not anticipated (forecast) by the traders, induces an adaptive reversal of trader price expectations which are then sustained by falling observed prices. However, in an equilibrium sense, H represents rational expectations in the sense of Muth, since it implies convergence to risk-neutral or risk-adjusted intrinsic dividend value if, and when, excess bids stabilize at zero. This interpretation of H is not inconsistent with the view articulated by Lucas (1986), which is supported by the examples he cites and the experiments reported by Williams (1987), in which adaptive expectations may be part of a transient (learning) process that culminates in a rational expectations equilibrium.

3. The risk-neutral and risk-adjusted REM hypotheses are special cases of H. Thus, risk neutral REM (H1) yields

$$(5.1)\qquad \bar{P}_t - \bar{P}_{t-1} = -E(\tilde{d}),$$

risk adjusted REM (H2) yields

$$(5.2)\qquad \bar{P}_t - \bar{P}_{t-1} = -E(\tilde{d}) + K.$$

We propose to test H, and its special cases H1 and H2, by estimating for each experiment the equation

$$(5.3)\qquad \bar{P}_t - \bar{P}_{t-1} = \alpha_5 + \beta_5(B_{t-1} - O_{t-1}) + \varepsilon_t.$$

If we reject the null hypothesis $\beta_5 \leqq 0$ this supports H.[10] If we are unable to reject $\beta_5 = 0$, but we reject $\alpha_5 = -E(\tilde{d})$, with $\hat{\alpha}_5 > -E(\tilde{d})$, this supports a risk averse interpretation of H2, while if we reject $\alpha_5 = -E(\tilde{d})$ with $\hat{\alpha}_5 < -E(\tilde{d})$, this supports the risk-preferring interpretation of H2. Finally, if we are unable to reject the null hypotheses $\beta_5 = 0$ and $\alpha_5 = -E(\tilde{d})$ this supports H1. We were somewhat skeptical, a priori, that α would be statistically very close to $-E(\tilde{d})$.

---

other apparently similar situations, a panic fails to take place. Why? Another observation is that training, such as fire drills, is effective for panics… initiated by fire." Our market bubbles project this same kind of uncertainty. Two groups seem to have similar experiences (e.g. 28x and 42xf), but one path is "near" intrinsic value, the other yields a bubble. Yet it appears that if most of the members of any group return repeatedly (42xf, 43xnf and 50xxf), this will produce "near" intrinsic value pricing, much like the effect of fire drills on the propensity to panic in the face of fire.

[10] The research (Walrasian) hypothesis is that $\beta_5 > 0$, so a one-tailed test of the null alternative, $\beta_5 \leqq 0$, is appropriate. We should note, however, that the statistical meaning of coefficient tests will be compromised for this particular sample of experiments in an imprecise way by the fact that casual examination of two experiments (25x, 26) was a key factor leading to the formulation of H. This is not a significant problem for experimental methodology since one can always run new experiments. In the field, one cannot rerun the world, and all tests suggested by the data are questionable, if not irrelevant. A conservative way to report on the present sample is to exclude the two experiments where data were examined in advance.

From previous double auction experiments with induced supply and demand arrays we have observed that different subject groups confronted with the same market parameters vary considerably in terms of the number of price quotations entered by each side. Such group asymmetry need not reduce the *relative* effect of excess bids on price changes but price changes might disappear with nonzero excess bids yielding a contribution to the intercept that is unrelated to the expected dividend.

Pooling across all 12 experiments with $E(\tilde{d}) = .24$, OLS estimation of equation (5.3) for $t = 2, \ldots, 15$ yields

$$(5.3') \qquad (\bar{P}_t - \bar{P}_{t-1}) = \underset{(0.29)}{-.230} + \underset{(7.55)}{.027}\,(B_{t-1} - O_{t-1}), \qquad R^2 = .240,\ N = 182.$$

The t-values indicate that the null hypothesis $\alpha_4 = -.24$ cannot be rejected but the null hypothesis $\beta_5 = 0$ can be rejected at the 95% confidence level. This result generally supports the risk-neutral interpretation of H but since α_5 is estimated to be greater than $-E(\tilde{d}) = -.24$ there is weak evidence that subjects tend, on average, to display risk aversion.

Our application of H to *interperiod* mean price adjustments might be compromised if excess bids are positively correlated with *intraperiod* price movements. That is, $(\bar{P}_t - \bar{P}_{t-1})$ may be at least partially generated by price changes within period $t-1$ that are related to $(B_{t-1} - O_{t-1})$. To test for this *intraperiod* effect of excess bids on prices we estimate, for the same sample of twelve experiments used in equation (5′),

$$(6) \qquad (P^C_{t-1} - P^O_{t-1}) = \alpha_6 + \beta_6(B_{t-1} - O_{t-1}) + \varepsilon_{t-1}$$

where P^C_{t-1} and P^O_{t-1} are the closing and opening price in period $t-1$. Rejection of the null hypothesis $\beta_6 = 0$ in favor of the one-tailed alternative $\beta_6 > 0$ would indicate a significant *intraperiod* excess bids effect which tends to confound our interpretation of equation (5′). The null hypothesis $\alpha_6 = 0$ implies that intraperiod price trends will tend to be absent when the number of bids is equal to the number of offers. OLS estimation of (6) for $t = 2, \ldots, 15$ yields

$$(6') \qquad (P^C_{t-1} - P^O_{t-1}) = \underset{(1.19)}{.045} + \underset{(2.71)}{.010}\,(B_{t-1} - O_{t-1}), \qquad R^2 = .039.$$

The null hypothesis $\alpha_6 = 0$ cannot be rejected. However, the null hypothesis $\beta_6 = 0$ can be rejected confirming the existence of a small intraperiod excess bids effect. This result suggests that a more rigorous test of the ability of excess bids to predict *interperiod* price movements is provided by the regression specification

$$(7) \qquad (P^C_t - P^C_{t-1}) = \alpha_7 + \beta_7(B_{t-1} - O_{t-1}) + \varepsilon_t$$

since changes in the closing price from period $t-1$ to period t cannot be due to price adjustments within period $t-1$. OLS estimation of equation (7) yields

$$(7') \qquad (P^C_t - P^C_{t-1}) = \underset{(0.55)}{-.219} + \underset{(5.09)}{.020}\,(B_{t-1} - O_{t-1}), \qquad R^2 = .126,$$

which is quite consistent with equation (5′) although the predictive power of the model and the significance of the excess bids coefficient are somewhat diminished. Our conclusion that the data are generally supportive of a weakly risk-averse version of H is unchanged.[11]

The regression results for equation (5.3) are listed in Table IV for each of the 22 (of 26) experiments in which there were no interventionist treatment conditions (price controls, computer crashes, or the use of confederates). Table IV groups the experiments into a "stable markets" (group I) class, "growing markets" (group II), and "price bubble—crash markets" (group III). This classification was made on the basis of the charts, Figures 2–13, in advance of the regression estimates. Group I consists of those markets in which prices appeared to follow dividend value, or were constant or followed approximately parallel with dividend value over most of the horizon. Group III consisted of markets that produced price bubbles that collapsed sometime *before* the final period. Group II consisted of the experiments not in I and III, and are called "growing price" markets. Group II includes experiment 9x which grew asymptotically from below to dividend value, and thus seems to suggest risk-averse REM.

From Table IV it is seen that the support for H in Group III markets is exceptionally strong. The adjustment speed coefficient, $\hat{\beta}_5$, is positive in every experiment in this group. Furthermore, we reject the null hypothesis, $\beta_5 \leqq 0$, in 11 of the 14 experiments in Group III.[12] As we interpret it the strong support for H in Group III is because (a) lagged excess bids is indeed a consistent and, in eleven cases, a strong predictor of price changes, and (b) this group is rich in price jumps as well as turning points, thereby allowing any potential predictive power of excess bids to swamp the noise in price adjustments. We think that excess bids is a good leading indicator of stock price changes because in the period prior to a jump in contract price traders fail to be aware of the greater relative intensity (number) of bids being entered (and not all accepted) or fail to anticipate that this portends an increase in bid prices the next period. Hence, their forecasts under-predict price increases, but excess bids is relatively accurate. Similarly, just prior to a downturn in prices in a bull market, traders fail to be aware that bids are relatively thinner even though contract prices are still increasing (their forecasts at the end of the period will now over-predict realizations), and that this portends lower prices in the future. But these characteristics are only tendencies obscured by much noise, with our traders having to rely on their perceptions unreinforced by data analysis. *We* were not aware of it until after studying our data.

[11] We also estimated equations (5), (6), and (7) for a pooling of the six experiments (with no experimenter intervention) where $E(\tilde{d}_t) = .12$. The results are qualitatively similar to those shown in (5′), (6′), and (7′).

[12] It is natural to conjecture that capital gains expectations, and therefore price adjustments, are heavily influenced by end effects, but if we add $T - t + 1$ as a presumed "independent" variable in the regressions of Table IV we get no important improvement. The coefficient of the added variable, $T - t + 1$, is significant in only two experiments (90f and 39xsf). The dynamics associated with the horizon time remaining is already adequately taken into account by excess bids.

In groups I and II there is also some support for H, namely, 5 of the 8 experiments in these two groups yield $\hat{\beta}_5 > 0$, and $\beta \leqq 0$ is rejected in favor of $\beta > 0$ in one case, 42xf. But this case is of particular interest because the chart for this experiment (Figure 11) appears to the eye to show early and strong convergence to REM. But $\hat{\beta}_5$ is significantly positive suggesting that the small changes in mean price constitute a pattern of fluctuation (mini-booms and busts) which were, on average, anticipated by lagged excess bids. One is reminded of what commodity traders call "scalping"—trading on small price movements of only a few cents. Similarly, experiments 43xnf and 50xxf exhibit positive (if not significant) coefficients of adjustment speed, although the charts of mean prices for these experiments (Figures 12 and 13) suggest that the market trades very near to the REM price from beginning to end. These cases show that in a macromarket sense one might have "close" support for rational expectations, but within the interval of "close" there may be a subtle trading dynamics fed by expectations of modest capital gains. In experiments 42xf, 43xnf, and 50 xxf, we estimate $\hat{\alpha}^e > -E(\tilde{d}^e)$, but in none of these experiments can we reject the null hypothesis that $\alpha^e = -E(\tilde{d}^e)$. Experiment 9x is the only market providing strong support for a risk averse adjusted REM. Pooling the four experiments (9x, 42xf, 43xnf, and 50xxf) which exhibit the strongest support for REM we estimated (5.3) as follows:

$$\bar{P}_t^e - \bar{P}_{t-1}^e = \underset{(0.99)}{-0.15} + \underset{(3.1)}{0.013}\left(B_{t-1}^e - 0_{t-1}^e\right), \qquad R^2 + 0.12,\ n = 71.$$

Thus across all "REM experiments" the Walrasian coefficient of adjustment speed is significantly positive. Although the intercept shows risk aversion $\hat{\alpha} = -0.15 > -E(\tilde{d})$ $(= -0.21)$ across the four experiments, the difference is not significant.

Only 4 of 22 experiments yield $\hat{\alpha}_5$ estimates significantly different from $-E(\tilde{d}^e)$ (experiments 9x, 10, 25x, and 90), and across all 22 experiments 11 show $\hat{\alpha}^e > -E(\tilde{d}^e)$ and 11 show the reverse, suggesting no consistent tendency toward either risk aversion or risk preferring. We think this is because any adjustment for risk is small, relative to price variability due to capital gains expectations.

6. SUMMARY: WHAT HAVE WE LEARNED?

Our conclusions will be summarized under four headings:

6.1. *General Conclusions*

1. Inducing different private dividend values on different traders, as has characterized previous asset market experimental designs, is not a necessary condition for the observance of trade. Exchanges, sometimes in large volume,

occur when identical probabilistic dividends are to be paid on share holdings at the end of each period, and this fact is common knowledge. Consequently, it appears that there is sufficient homegrown diversity in agent price expectations and perhaps risk attitudes to induce subjective gains from exchange. This is not inconsistent with the rational bubble literature which assumes that traders have common priors. Our subject traders tend, with experience, to acquire common, intrinsic dividend value, rational expectations.

2. Previous studies that reinitialize and replicate a two or three period dividend environment all report convergence toward REM prices in successive replications. All of our experiments with experienced traders, and most of those with inexperienced traders converge to "near" the REM price prior to the last trading period. Thus our results, and those of the more structured markets reported in previous asset market studies all support the view that expectations *are adaptive*, and the adaptation over time is to *REM equilibrium outcomes* when asset value "fundamentals" remain unchanged over the horizon of trading.

3. Of the 22 experiments that did not involve experimenter intervention or inadvertent disruptions, the modal outcome (14 experiments of which 9 used experienced subjects) was a market characterized by a price bubble measured relative to dividend value.

4. Four experiments, all using experienced subjects, provide the strongest support for the REM model of asset pricing.

5. Regardless of the pattern of price movements the volume of exchange tends to be less for experienced than for inexperienced subjects. Although the divergence in agent price expectations tend to persist with experience, this divergence is attenuated, and markets become thinner.

6. None of the above conclusions are inconsistent with the Fama (1970) criterion for REM (no arbitrage profits), or with the Tirole (1982) model (agents have common priors). Here is what we learn from these experiments, their immediate predecessors, most of experimental economics, and from the examples cited in Fama (1970) and Lucas (1986). Real people in any environment usually do not come off the stops with common expectations; they usually do not solve problems of maximization over time by ex ante reasoning and backward induction, nor is this irrational when there is insufficient reason to believe that expectations are common.[13] What we learn from the particular experiments reported here is that a common dividend, and common knowledge thereof is insufficient to induce initial common expectations. As we interpret it this is due to agent uncertainty about the behavior of others. With experience, and its lessons in trial-and-error learning, expectations tend ultimately to converge and yield an REM equilibrium.

[13]Other experimental evidence supports our interpretation, namely that it is the failure of the assumption of common expectations, not backward induction incompetence by subject agents that explains bubbles. Thus, Cox and Oaxaca (1986) find that subject behavior is strongly consistent with the predictions of a job search model, requiring maximization over time using backward induction, but their subjects are making decisions in a game against nature which requires them to form expectations only about their own future behavior. Behavioral uncertainty is thus minimized.

6.2. *Forecasting Behavior*

1. In every (ten) forecasting experiment agent forecasts fail to be unbiased predictors of the mean contract price in period t.

2. The forecasts fail to predict abrupt increases and decreases in price and consistently fail to predict both upper and lower turning points. Both the mean forecast and the individual forecasts show a tendency to over-predict the mean price. However, in the bubble experiments the forecasts under-predict in the boom phase and over-predict in the crash.

3. Individual agents vary in their prediction accuracy with some agents being better forecasters than others. Furthermore, the better forecasters tend to earn more money.

4. The forecasts are highly adaptive: i.e. the change in forecasts from one period to the next is significantly and positively related to the forecasting error in the previous period. Also, the forecasting errors are autocorrelated.

5. Both the mean deviation and the variance of individual forecasts relative to dividend value decline significantly with increasing subject experience across experiments. With experience subjects tend to converge to common dividend value expectations as behavioral uncertainty decreases.

6.3. *Empirical Characteristics of Market Bubbles*

1. Experienced subjects frequently produce a market bubble, but the likelihood is smaller than for inexperienced subjects. When the same group returns for a third market, the bubble disappears (except that we do observe "scalping" on small price fluctuations).

2. In every market bubble experiment (Group III, Table IV), the mean price in the first period was below $E(\tilde{D}_t^T)$. This suggests the possibility that risk aversion plays a role in market bubbles by depressing prices at first, with the subsequent recovery (after such preferences are satisfied) helping to create or confirm expectations of capital gains.

3. The crash in market prices following a boom, whether with experienced or inexperienced subjects, occurs on a trading volume that is smaller than the volume during the bubble phase.

4. The collapse of price bubbles tends to be presaged by a thinning of bid relative to offer activity, as measured by excess bids (number of bids minus number of offers), in the period or periods immediately before the collapse. Similarly, a subsequent recovery or stabilizing of prices tends to be presaged by an increase in excess bids. Thus the change in mean price in all bubble-crash experiments is positively related with lagged excess bids, and the null hypothesis that this adjustment speed coefficient is nonpositive is rejected in 11 of 14 cases.

5. The tendency for experienced traders to produce price bubbles is not eliminated if we first "train" subjects in a sequence of single-period asset markets that controls for interperiod capital gains by initializing the asset holdings prior to trading in each period. This result is contrary to the conjecture that bubbles

with experienced subjects are caused by expectations of a bubble created in the markets in which the subjects acquired their experience.

6.4. *Characteristics of Markets That Most Strongly Support REM*

1. All four markets providing the strongest support for REM yield intercepts in the regression equation (5.3) that exceed the risk neutral prediction, $-E(\tilde{d})$. This supports the risk-averse adjusted version of REM. In only one of the four cases can we reject the null hypothesis that the intercept is $-E(\tilde{d})$. Also this null hypothesis cannot be rejected if we pool all four experiments in estimating equation (5.3). We conclude that there is weak support for the risk averse model of REM.

2. The three experiments (42xf, 43xnf, and 50xxf) that appear to converge to $E(\tilde{D}_t^T)$ in the first 1–3 periods, and to follow closely the path of $E(\tilde{D}_t^T)$ thereafter, all yield a positive coefficient of adjustment speed in equation (5.3). In one experiment (42xf) we reject the null hypothesis that this coefficient is nonpositive; we also reject the null hypothesis when the three experiments are pooled to estimate equation (5.3). Thus the Walrasian adaptive capital gains adjustment hypothesis receives support even in those experiments which appear to provide the strongest support for REM. We conclude that even these experiments are not an exception to the general conclusion that the REM model of asset pricing is supported only as an *equilibrium concept* underlying an adaptive capital gains price adjustment process.

College of Business Administration, University of Arizona, Tucson, AZ 85721, U.S.A.

and

Department of Economics, Indiana University, Bloomington, IN, U.S.A.

REFERENCES

COLEMAN, JAMES S. (1979): "Future Directions for Work in Public Choice," in *Collective Decision Making*, ed. by C. S. Russell. Baltimore: The Johns Hopkins University Press.

COX, JAMES, AND RONALD OAXACA (1986): "Laboratory Research with Job Search Models," Western Economic Association Meetings, July.

FAMA, EUGENE F. (1970): "Efficient Capital Markets: A Review of Theory and Empirical Work," *Journal of Finance*, 25, 383–417.

FORSYTHE, ROBERT, THOMAS PALFREY, AND CHARLES PLOTT (1982): "Asset Valuation in an Experimental Market," *Econometrica*, 50, 537–567.

FRIEDMAN, DANIEL, GLENN HARRISON, AND JON SALMON (1984): "The Informational Efficiency of Experimental Asset Markets," *Journal of Political Economy*, 92, 349–408.

LUCAS, ROBERT (1986): "Adaptive Behavior and Economic Theory," *Journal of Business*, 59, S401–S426.

MILLER, ROSS M., CHARLES R. PLOTT, AND VERNON L. SMITH (1977): Intertemporal Competitive Equilibrium: An Empirical Study of Speculation," *Quarterly Journal of Economics*, 91, 599–624.

MUTH, JOHN F. (1961): "Rational Expectations and the Theory of Price Movements," *Econometrica*, 29. 315–355.

NASH, JOHN F. (1950): "The Bargaining Problem," *Econometrica*, 18, 315–335.

PLOTT, CHARLES R., AND SHYAM SUNDER (1982): "Efficiency of Experimental Security Markets with Insider Trading," *Journal of Political Economy*, 90, 663–698.

PLOTT, CHARLES R., AND GUL AGHA (1982): "Intertemporal Speculation with a Random Demand in an Experimental Market," in *Aspiration Levels in Bargaining and Economic Decision Making*, ed. by R. Tietz. Berlin: Springer-Verlag.

SMITH, VERNON L. (1982): "Microeconomic Systems as an Experimental Science," *American Economic Review*, 72, 923–955.

SMITH, VERNON L., AND ARLINGTON W. WILLIAMS (1983): "An Experimental Comparison of Alternative Rules for Competitive Market Exchange," in *Auctions, Bidding and Contracting: Uses and Theory*, ed. by R. Engelbrecht-Wiggans, M. Shubik, and R. Stark. New York: New York University Press.

TIROLE, JEAN (1982): "On the Possibility of Speculation Under Rational Expectations," *Econometrica*, 50, 1163–1181.

WALKER, JAMES M., VERNON L. SMITH, AND JAMES C. COX (1986): "Bidding Behavior in First Prize Sealed Bid Auctions: Use of Computer-Nash Competitors," Indiana University, November, 1986.

WILLIAMS, ARLINGTON W. (1979): "Intertemporal Competitive Equilibrium: On Further Experimental Results," in *Research in Experimental Economics*, Vol. 1, ed. by Vernon L. Smith, Greenwich, Conn.: JAI Press.

——— (1987): "The Formation of Price Forecasts in Experimental Markets," *Journal of Money, Credit and Banking*, 19, 1–18.

WILLIAMS, ARLINGTON W., AND VERNON L. SMITH (1984): "Cyclical Double-Auction Markets With and Without Speculators," *Journal of Business*, 57, 1–33.

ZARNOWITZ, VICTOR (1986): "The Record and Improvability of Economic Forecasting," NBER Working Paper No. 2099, December, 1986.

PART III

Public Goods

Introduction

My interest in applying experimental methods to the study of public goods was inspired by my prepublication knowledge of the proposed Groves-Ledyard "solution to the free rider problem." Consequently, we have the rare circumstance in which an economic theory and experimental tests of it are published fairly close together in time. Public goods was a natural for experimentation: one had a hypothesized problem in incentive failure and an incentive-compatible solution. It was necessary to establish, empirically, that there was a free rider problem in the first place and that, in the second place, the proposed solution improved matters. Ultimately, what emerged was: (1) there is a free rider problem but it is not as severe, empirically, as the strong version of the theory predicts; (2) the "solution" works quite well, but so do other "solutions" (such as the auction mechanism) with much less attractive static theoretical equilibrium properties (they have a blizzard of static equilibria); (3) all group-decision procedures require a stopping rule, and this has its own incentive effects whatever the nature of the static model; and (4) our theories are woefully weak on dynamic process analysis.

Why do not "free rider" mechanisms perform more poorly than they do? The answer, I think, may be related to the question of why opportunistic behavior is not more common in private contracting, why there is not more crime – at least petty crime – since it appears to pay, why property rights tend to be respected in the absence of continuing enforcement and why tipping is commonplace even in restaurants people are unlikely to visit again, and so on. What is clear from both the experimental and the field evidence is that private incentives matter importantly in varying degrees, but that it is not true that *only* private incentives matter. There appears to be something to the proposition that ideology (to use Douglas North's term) matters. Because ideology matters, enforcement is relatively inexpensive in cultures that reinforce the value of human rights, including the right to property and the right to recognition and respect by others. These things create community, or, at least, this is the underlying hypothesis we have to work with. Whether they are derived from our culture, genetic endowment, reciprocity considerations, or all three, is yet to be understood.

The Auction Mechanism was originally intended as a generalization of certain features of private-contribution or fund drives by churches, museum associations, universities, and so on. I still find it helpful to keep that model in mind when interpreting laboratory results. A recent study by Banks, Plott, and Porter (1988) finds that the efficiency of the Auction Mechanism does not persist under sequential replication. It starts out with high efficiency in the first round but then decays toward zero. Perhaps this result explains why the United Fund Organization pools the budgets of a large number of eleemosynary institutions into a single large fund drive each year. The alternative is to have a large number of organizations attempting to obtain contributions almost weekly. Apparently, back-to-back attempts to raise money soon lead people to be saturated both in the field and in the laboratory.

There is now a large and growing literature on experimental public goods allocation. For a summary of the literature on pure contribution mechanisms the reader is referred to Isaac and Walker (1987) in addition to the bibliographical references in Banks, Plott, and Porter (1988).

References

Banks, Jeffrey S., Charles R. Plott, and David P. Porter. 1988. ''An Experimental Analysis of Unanimity in Public Goods Provision Mechanisms.'' *Review of Economic Studies* 55 (April).

Isaac, R. Mark, and James M. Walker. 1987. ''Success and Failure of the Voluntary Contributions Process: Some Evidence from Experimental Economics.'' Discussion Paper No. 87-1, Department of Economics, University of Arizona.

The Principle of Unanimity and Voluntary Consent in Social Choice

Vernon L. Smith

University of Arizona

A discrete version of the author's incentive-compatible Auction Mechanism for public goods is applied to the problem of social choice (voting) among distinct mutually exclusive alternatives. This Auction Election is a bidding mechanism characterized by (1) unanimity, (2) provision for the voluntary compensation of voters harmed by a winning proposition, and (3) incentives for "reasonable" bidding by excluding members of a collective from maximal increase in benefit if they fail to agree on the proposition with largest surplus. Four of five experiments with six voters, bidding privacy, monetary rewards, and cyclical majority rule structure choose the best of three propositions.

Solutions to the problem of specifying incentive-compatible mechanisms for the provision of public goods have been proposed by Thompson (1965), Groves (1969, 1973), Clarke (1971), Drèze and de la Vallée Poussin (1971), Groves and Ledyard (1975), and Smith (in press *a*, in press *b*). Tideman and Tullock (1976) have applied the Clarke-Groves "demand revealing process" to the problem of social choice among discrete alternatives. Several laboratory and field experimental studies of these mechanisms, and of the so-called free-rider problem in public goods, have been conducted by Bohm (1972), Scherr and Babb (1975), the Public Broadcasting Service (reported by Ferejohn and Noll 1976), and Smith (in press *b*). These studies provide strong support for the proposition that practical decentralized mechanisms exist for the provision of public goods.

The sequel will briefly review the incentive-compatible Auction Mechanism (Smith in press *b*) for a public good whose size is variable. A

Research support by the National Science Foundation is gratefully acknowledged. I am indebted to R. Auster and G. Tullock for stimulating my interest in the application of the Auction Mechanism to the social choice problem and to an anonymous referee for helpful, clarifying suggestions.

special case of this mechanism consists of a mutually exclusive and exhaustive set of discrete alternatives. This is the familiar problem of social choice in the sense of voting among discrete alternatives to choose the "preferred" social state. The resulting voting mechanism, which we will call the Auction Election,[1] can be interpreted as an implementation of Wicksell's (1896) "principle of unanimity and voluntary consent in taxation." It is a pleasure to acknowledge Wicksell by plagiarizing the title to section 4 of his great paper.[2] In Section V the results of five voting experiments based on the Auction Election will be reported. The experimental design chosen is one for which the majority rule outcome is indeterminate, but for which there is a unanimously preferred alternative achievable with the automatic compensation features of the Auction Election.

I. The Auction Mechanism for Public Goods

Consider a collective composed of I members. Using a partial equilibrium framework,[3] let $V_i(X)$, with measurement normalized so that $V_i(0) = 0$, be the dollar value of a quantity X of the public good to member i and let q be the dollar price of the public good. Although q is assumed constant, the mechanism is easily modified for cases of increasing or decreasing returns (Smith in press *a*). Assume that collective decision must abide by the following rules or institution:

(1) Let each agent i submit a two-tuple (b_i, X_i) consisting of a bid and a proposed quantity with the understanding that his share of cost is $(q - B_i)\bar{X}$, where

$$B_i = \sum_{j \neq i} b_j, \qquad \text{and } \bar{X} = \sum_{k=1}^{I} X_k/I.$$

(2) Each agent has the unqualified right to veto or agree to the cost share $(q - B_i)\bar{X}$ allocated to him by all other agents. He sends the message "agree" by choosing $b_i = q - B_i$, and $X_i = \bar{X}$. He sends the message "veto" if he chooses $b_i \neq q - B_i$ and/or $X_i \neq \bar{X}$.

[1] Auster (1976) has proposed the use of "Compensating Elections" to resolve conflicts in social choice. The Auction Election, the Tideman-Tullock "Clarke Tax" Election, and Auster's proposal are identical in purpose although they represent distinct mechanisms.

[2] Also see Buchanan (1959) who, almost alone among modern scholars, has examined and extended Wicksell's ideas on public choice.

[3] More precisely it is assumed that there are no income effects. A general equilibrium two-good (one private, one public) version of the Auction Mechanism using Cobb-Douglas payoff (induced value) functions and a linear production possibility frontier underlies an experimental design currently in research process. This more sophisticated experiment uses the PLATO computer system to program subjects through the decision process. The results of the first several experiments suggest that introducing income effects does not reduce the ability of collectives to reach public good decisions, but the decision outcomes appear to exhibit more sampling variation (across replications with different groups of subjects) than the partial equilibrium experiments reported in Smith (in press *b*).

(3) Group equilibrium prevails if and only if agreement is signaled by every agent i. If such unanimity obtains, $\hat{X}$ units of the public good are purchased with agent i paying $b_i\hat{X} = (q - B_i)\hat{X}$.

Under these rules, i's net benefit is

$$v_i = \begin{cases} V_i(\hat{X}) - (q - B_i)\hat{X}, & \text{if } b_i = q - B_i, \quad \text{and} \\ \quad X_i = \hat{X} = \left(X_i + \sum_{j \neq i} X_j\right)\Big/ I & \text{or} \\ \quad X_i = \left(\dfrac{1}{I-1}\right)\sum_{j \neq i} X_j, & \text{for all } i \\ V_i(0) = 0, & \text{otherwise.} \end{cases} \tag{1}$$

Conditions on (b_i, X_i) to maximize v_i, assuming concavity of V_i, are

$$V_i'\left[\left(X_i + \sum_{j \neq i} X_j\right)\Big/ I\right] = q - B_i, \tag{2}$$

$$b_i = q - B_i, \tag{3}$$

$$X_i = \hat{X}, \qquad \text{for all } i. \tag{4}$$

Each i will try to satisfy (2) where the marginal private benefit from his proposal, X_i, is equal to the net private price allocated to him by the "market," while if (3) and (4) are not satisfied, the rules require each i to accept the inferior outcome $V_i(0) = 0$. The rules exclude i unless he agrees to accept the unit cost $q - B_i$, and the group's proposal $\hat{X}$. This is very similar to the incentive of an economic agent to "meet the market" in a competitive auction to avoid "exclusion." The difference is that under the above rules if any i is excluded, then all are excluded. Whether this difference leads to more extensive strategic gaming and signaling that prevents equilibrium is an empirical question which so far, in the literature cited, has not been an important problem.

Equations (2)–(4) yield the Lindahl equilibrium.[4] Summing (2) over all i, and using (3),

$$\sum_{i=1}^{I} V_i'(X_i) = \sum_{i=1}^{I} V_i'(\hat{X}) = \sum_{i=1}^{I} b_i = b_i + B_i = q.$$

Hence $\hat{X}$ must be the Lindahl optimal quantity of the public good.

[4] These conditions also define one of many local Nash equilibria. As shown in Smith (in press *b*) the Auction Mechanism provides multiple local Nash equilibria among which is the Lindahl equilibrium. This is easy to see from eq. (1). If X^o is the Lindahl equilibrium, then any $X \neq X^o$ yielding $V_i(X) - (q - B_i)X > 0$ for each i is better than nothing and each i has at least some incentive to agree, i.e., to set $b_i = q - B_i$, $X_i = X$. Empirically (Smith, in press *b*) across experiments with different subjects, the final outcome bids are tightly distributed around the Lindahl prices, $V_i'(X^o)$, so that there is a clear tendency for the Lindahl optimal Nash equilibrium to prevail. But in *every* case the Lindahl (and Pareto) optimal *quantity* is chosen. Hence, empirically, the Auction Mechanism allows for a fair degree of variability in the ex post distribution of wealth while preserving Pareto efficiency.

Observe that if X is a public "bad" for any i, then V_i and V_i' are negative, his bid b_i must be negative, and in equilibrium each member harmed by X is compensated. It is in the interest of all harmed agents to agree as soon as their compensation is "adequate" (what this means theoretically is that marginal Lindahl rent is zero).

II. The Auction Election

In social choice group decision produces a common outcome. Thus a referendum legalizing marijuana either passes or fails, and all citizens experience the resulting state. This is just a discrete public good (or bad) to which the Auction Mechanism applies if X is restricted to assume only the values zero or one. Under unanimity i receives net benefit $v_i = V_i(1) - (q - B_i) = V_i(1) - b_i > V_i(0) = 0$. In the problem of pure "political" choice the proposition has a zero resource price. Thus if the proposal is to make daylight saving time official across the United States, then $q = 0$ for that common outcome. Presumably this issue involves only private valuations. Of course q could be negative, for example, legalizing marijuana saves enforcement costs.

Consider first the case of a choice between two alternatives, proposition A or $\bar{A}$ (not A), that is, if A fails to be approved the status quo continues. In the Auction Election ($q = 0$) the social choice problem is solved by allowing each i to submit a bid $b_i \gtreqless 0$ "on" or "for" the proposition. Proposition A wins if $\sum_{i=1}^{I} b_i \geq 0$, otherwise it loses. As in (1), net benefit for voter i is

$$v_i = \begin{cases} V_i(A) - b_i, & \text{if } b_i \geq -B_i, \quad \text{for all } i \\ V_i(\bar{A}), & \text{otherwise.} \end{cases} \tag{5}$$

A transparent theorem is the following: If

$$\sum_{i=1}^{I} V_i(A) > \sum_{i=1}^{I} V_i(\bar{A})$$

(A yields a larger rent to the collective than $\bar{A}$), then there exists a bid b_i^* for each i such that proposition A will win, that is,

$$\sum_{i=1}^{I} b_i^* \geq 0,$$

and no i will be made worse off, that is, $v_i^* = V_i(A) - b_i^* \geq V_i(\bar{A})$. Formally, each voter i will rationally bid no more than his personal valuation of A, $V_i(A)$, net of the *opportunity cost* of A, $V_i(\bar{A})$, that is, $b_i \leq V_i(A) - V_i(\bar{A})$. Hence, if

$$\sum_{i=1}^{I} [V_i(A) - V_i(\bar{A})] > 0,$$

TABLE 1

VOTER VALUATIONS

Voter	Alternative: A	$\bar{A}$
1	30	0
2	0	60
3	40	0
Total	70	60

there exists an $\varepsilon_i \geq 0$ for each i such that if we set $b_i^* = V_i(A) - V_i(\bar{A}) - \varepsilon_i \leq V_i(A) - V_i(\bar{A})$, then

$$\sum_{i=1}^{I} b_i^* = \sum_{i=1}^{I} [V_i(A) - V_i(\bar{A}) - \varepsilon_i] \geq 0 \text{ (proposition } A \text{ wins)},$$

and $v_i^* = V_i(A) - b_i^* = V_i(A) - [V_i(A) - V_i(\bar{A}) - \varepsilon_i] = V_i(\bar{A}) + \varepsilon_i \geq V_i(\bar{A})$.[5]

An example, borrowed from Tideman and Tullock (1976), will help to illustrate the process. Table 1 exhibits the valuations of A and $\bar{A}$ for each of three voters. Proposition A might be a proposed change in a land zoning ordinance. Voter 1, now holding valueless property, would enjoy a capital gain of 30. Voter 2, owning land worth 60, would be wiped out. Voter 3, owning land worth nothing, would receive a gain of 40. In an Auction Election for A voter 1 will bid no more than 30, voter 2 no more than -60, and voter 3 no more than 40. Proposition A yields 10 units more collective rent than $\bar{A}$. Voters can submit bids for A yielding an aggregate net benefit up to 10 without causing A to lose. Thus if $\varepsilon_i = 3$ for each i, then

$$\sum_{i=1}^{3} b_i^* = 1,$$

proposition A wins, and each voter is 3 units better off. Each has a competitive incentive to bid enough to ensure passage of A to avoid

[5] Clearly there is an infinite number of imputations of the surplus

$$\sum_{i=1}^{I} [V_i(A) - V_i(\bar{A})]$$

among I voters, and each imputation represents a possible equilibrium outcome. Any particular equilibrium outcome may depend upon the strategic or "bluffing" behavior of agents, the utility of the outcome relative to the perceived subjective costs of "strategizing," and so on. The situation is analogous to the so-called indeterminacy in the classical bilateral bargaining problem. Indeterminacy simply means that we do not have as yet a sufficiently sharp behavioral theory to account for particular outcomes within the set of Pareto superior points.

"exclusion" from A and thereby being forced to accept a less desirable alternative.

Obviously, proposition A will fail to win if one or more voters is "too greedy." If voter 1 bids less than 20, thus holding out for more than a 10 unit improvement over his present position, he will block passage and get nothing. If voter 2 bids less than -70, hoping for an improvement in excess of 10, he will get no improvement. And so each voter has an incentive to yield sufficiently to ensure that proposition A wins.

III. The "Clarke Tax" Election

Using this example the Auction Election can be compared instructively with the "Clarke Tax" election proposed by Tideman and Tullock (1976). Under their scheme A would also win over $\bar{A}$. Assuming that each voter responds to the Tideman-Tullock incentive to bid his full valuation, then voter 1 pays a tax of $60 - 40 = 20$, the amount necessary to bring the bids for A up to equality with the bids for $\bar{A}$. Similarly, voter 3 pays a tax of 30, but voter 2 pays no tax because his bids do not change the outcome, that is, A would win over $\bar{A}$ if 2 did not bid at all. Hence, voter 1 ends with a benefit net of his tax, 10; voter 3 with a net benefit, 10; but voter 2, who pays no tax and gets zero from proposition A, has had his property (worth 60 under $\bar{A}$) confiscated without due process. As noted by Tideman and Tullock (1976, p. 1149), "It may seem that a person who sustains a large loss when his preference is not followed deserves compensation, but this cannot be given without motivating an excessive statement of differential value. . . . In regard to the uncompensated losses that are produced, the demand revealing process is similar to majority rule." In the Auction Mechanism, agreement requires those who would gain to compensate those who would lose. Both types of voters have motivation to not ask for an excessive share of the rent, that is, to bid sufficiently high to avoid a less favorable outcome. Any mechanism that does not exploit this competitive-like exclusion characteristic (or in some other manner maintains incentive compatibility) and does not require unanimity seems likely to be inefficient or confiscatory or both (as with majority rule). But these criticisms of the "Clarke Tax" should not detract from the innovative contribution of Clarke, Tideman, and Tullock. It should be expected that any of the several new mechanisms of public choice now in only their formative stages will be subjected to a variety of improvements.[6]

[6] The Auction, "Clarke Tax," and Auster "Compensating" elections differ primarily in terms of how each would allocate the consumer surplus from an issue among the electorate.

IV. Multiple Choice Auction Elections: An Experimental Design

The Auction Election extends readily to multiple options. Let there be N discrete alternatives, $p = 1, 2, \ldots, N$, with option p having value V_i^p normalized so that the status quo null alternative to the N options has value zero for all i. Each i submits a bid b_i^p for option p. A winning option is one for which the algebraic sum of the bids is nonnegative and no smaller than the algebraic sum of the bids for any other option. Tied options are considered equivalent and a winner selected by an equal probability random device. The expression for net benefit is then[7]

$$v_i = \begin{cases} V_i^p - b_i^p & \text{if } 0 \leq b_i^p + B_i^p \geq b_i^q + B_i^q, \\ & \qquad \text{for all } i \text{ and all } q \neq p, \\ 0, & \text{otherwise,} \end{cases} \tag{6}$$

where

$$B_i^p = \sum_{j \neq i} b_j^p, \qquad B_i^q = \sum_{j \neq i} b_j^q.$$

If there is a winning option p it has the property

$$0 \leq \sum_{i=1}^{I} b_i^p \geq \sum_{i=1}^{I} b_i^q$$

for all $q \neq p$. If there is no winning option, that is, $b_i^r + B_i^r < 0$ for all $r = 1, 2, \ldots, N$ the status quo is maintained.

The example in table 2 applying to six voters and three options provides the subject valuations in dollars used in the experiments to be discussed in the next section. The entries in table 2 are measured relative to the status quo, or the null proposition (not shown). Thus if proposition 3 wins, voter 1's wealth state is \$20 lower than if none of the three propositions wins. Propositions 2 and 3 are both highly attractive with aggregate rents of \$105 and \$45, respectively, but the Auction Election can be expected to choose 2. Under a majority rule decision process the outcome is intransitive. Proposition 2 beats 1 by a vote of 4 to 2, proposition 3 beats 2 by 4 to 2, and 1 beats 3 by 4 to 2. As is well known and typical of majority rule, (1) it leads to an inefficient outcome unless the "right" agenda is followed, and there is no way (to my knowledge) that an appropriate agenda can be selected on the basis of objective voting data, and (2) even if the optimal choice is selected by majority rule it produces an involuntary redistribution of wealth. The Auction Election redistributes relative wealth voluntarily.

[7] Note that an Auction Election with N options is just the Auction Mechanism with N discrete, mutually exclusive alternatives, i.e., N different public goods $X = 1, 2, \ldots, N$, one and only one of which can be chosen.

TABLE 2

VOTER VALUATIONS ($)

PROPOSITION	VOTER 1	2	3	4	5	6	TOTAL
1	5	−30	−30	25	25	0	−5
2	60	5	5	−10	−10	55	105
3	−20	45	45	0	0	−25	45

V. Experiments and Results

Thirty subjects participated in five experimental sessions, each consisting of six-member voter collectives using the induced value payoffs[8] in dollars shown in table 2. The instructions printed in the Appendix were distributed and read aloud to the six subjects in each session who had been recruited from large sections of business and economics courses at Arizona State and the University of Arizona. No subject participated in more than one session. Each subject also received a copy of a recording form, a sample of which (for voter 1 in table 2) is included in the Appendix. The three propositions, as defined by the vector of subject valuations, were reordered (i.e., renumbered 1, 2, 3) randomly for each experiment. In each experiment the subjects were assigned randomly to the six valuation conditions and seated so that the privacy of such information could be maintained. This right of privacy included a provision for separately paying each subject his cash earnings after each experiment was completed. It was then each subject's choice whether such information was to be revealed to any other person.

In each experiment a maximum number of trials was specified. The first trial was a "practice trial" that did not count in the determination of a winning proposition. Experiments 1 and 2 (see fig. 1) consisted of a maximum of 10 trials, while experiments 3, 4, and 5 allowed up to six trials. The trial maximum was reduced after the first two experiments as it became evident that a very few trials were sufficient to allow collectives to reach a decision. It seems possible that more trials may even make group agreement less likely. Only one of the five experiments (experiment 2) failed to produce a winning proposition, and it was a 10-trial session.

Figure 1 exhibits the trial sequence of individual subject bids for the superior proposal (proposition 2, table 2) in each experiment. The subject identification numbers correspond to the voter numbers, with associated

[8] Subjects were paid $V_i^p - b_i^p + \$2$ if proposition p won, $V_i^o = \$2$ if no proposition won, where the induced values V_i^p were as given in table 2. A total of $464 was paid to the 30 subjects under these rules.

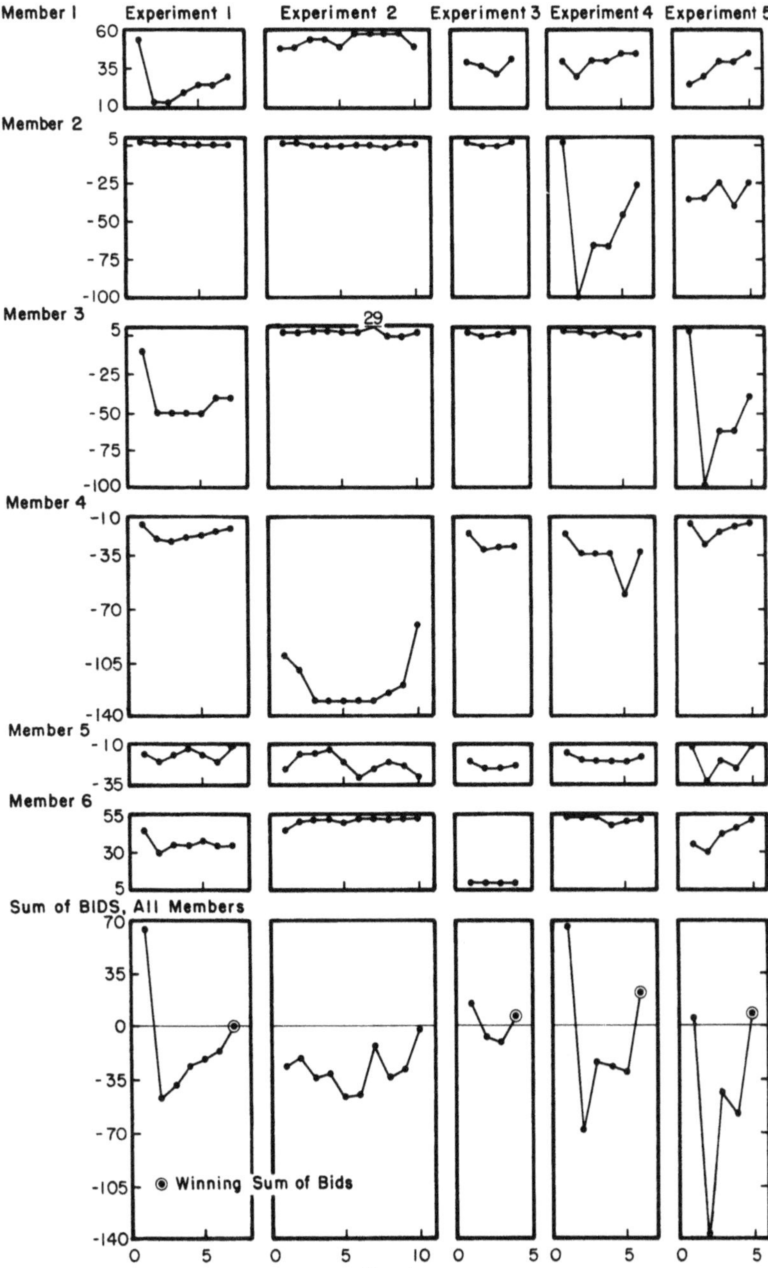

Member I
Experiment I
Experiment 2
Experiment 3
Experiment 4
Experiment 5
Member 2
Member 3
Member 4
Member 5
Member 6
Sum of BIDS, All Members
Winning Sum of Bids

Fig. 1

proposition values, shown in table 2. The panel at the bottom of figure 1 plots the bid sum for each trial.

The practice trial, besides providing familiarity with the procedure, was of considerable importance in yielding information, however imperfect, on the potential surplus available among the three proposals. In every experiment the best proposition received the largest bid sum on the first trial. This first-trial bid sum was positive in all sessions except experiment 2 and (especially in experiments 1 and 4) revealed to members of the collective that the total surplus available from the best proposition was substantial. Consequently, on the second trial the bids tended to fall sharply as subjects generally attempted to "game" for an increased share of the surplus (23 of the 30 subjects reduced their bids on trial 2). The question or hypothesis at issue, as in previous public good experiments (Smith, in press *b*) is *not* whether members will "game" for a personal advantage in the Auction Election, but whether the mechanism is sufficiently effective to guide the collective to the optimal choice. Obviously some, perhaps many, members will "game"; and obviously, in figure 1, they do "game." But the mechanism also confronts each member of the collective with the discipline of exclusion if each does not, by the final trial, at least match the "market price," $-B_i$, presented to him by the other members. Four of the five experimental collectives reached agreement on the optimal proposition. In experiment 2 the group failed by $2,

$$\sum_{i=1}^{6} b_k = -2,$$

on trial 10 to elect the best proposition. If we take these results literally, the sample evidence suggests that an Auction Election choice among three propositions (four, counting the null proposition or status quo) with parameters as defined in table 2 would select the optimal proposition in 80 percent of the elections. (And remember, under majority rule *none* of these propositions can prevail by pairwise voting.) The robustness of these results can only be established with more experiments. Experiment 2 was very close to producing agreement in spite of unusually aggressive, and ineffective, play by subject 4. This subject expressed puzzled disappointment with the outcome, suggesting that failure experiences might mitigate such aggressive bidding in subsequent elections. Experience may be an important treatment variable and deserves systematic study. However, the failure of experiment 2 may be due to the fact that subject 3's bid (29) on trial 7 exceeded his valuation (5), producing unrealistic profit expectations in the other subjects.

In previous public good experiments (Smith, in press *b*) using the Auction Mechanism it was hypothesized that equilibrium bids across

TABLE 3

Trial	$\hat{\beta}$	$t_{\beta-1}$	$\hat{\beta}_o$	$t_{\beta o}$	R^2	SE	$F(1,28)$
1	0.92	−0.678	−12.0	−3.01	.674	18.71	60.87
$t^* - 1$	1.105	−0.767	−24.18	−4.59	.630	24.72	50.38
t^*	0.998	−0.019	−16.33	−4.39	.737	17.46	82.29

individual subjects would tend to the theoretical Lindahl prices for those subjects. Formally this took the form of testing the research hypothesis $\beta_o = 0$ and $\beta = 1$ in the regression equation

$$y_{ij} = \beta_o + \beta x_{ij} + \eta_{ij}, \tag{7}$$

where y_{ij} is the observed final equilibrium bid of subject j in experiment i and x_{ij} is the (experimentally controlled) Lindahl price for subject j in experiment i. In the present Auction Election experiments there are no Lindahl prices where marginal Lindahl rents are zero because the public outcome of an election is discrete. However, the individual valuations x_{ij} of subject i in experiment j for the best proposition do represent Lindahl price upper bounds on subject equilibrium bids. In the Auction Election these valuations should explain much of the variation in the final outcome bids. In the above regression for the Auction Election the research hypothesis becomes $\beta_o < 0$, $\beta = 1$. If $\beta = 1$ the estimate $-\hat{\beta}_o$ is a measure of the equilibrium surplus ($x_{ij} - y_{ij} = -\beta_o$) obtained by the average subject. In the Auction Election the hypothesis that $\beta = 1$ follows from the expectation that the surplus obtained by a subject on a winning proposal will not depend on his valuation, that is, those able to pay z dollars more will on the average pay z dollars more.

The regression results using the data shown in figure 1 for the first, penultimate, and final (t^*) trials are shown in table 3. For each of these trials $\hat{\beta}$ is very close to unity with very low t-values, particularly on the final trial. The estimates of $\hat{\beta}_o$ indicate that the average voter's initial demand for net surplus, \$12, is below his final earnings, \$16. On the penultimate trial the extent of "bluffing" is indicated by an average demand for \$24 of surplus. The R^2 values show that subject valuations account for 63 percent or more of the variation in subject bids. However, the final trial R^2 of .74 is below the final trial R^2 in three different sets of public good experiments (Smith 1976*b*), in which the Lindahl prices accounted for 82 percent, 97 percent, and 99 percent of the variation in subject bids. A reasonable conjecture might be that the mechanically simpler Auction Election invites more strategic bluffing and signaling by members of the collective.

VI. Conjecture, Impossibility Theory, and the Evidence

In 1896, Wicksell conjectured that if the utility of a public outcome exceeded its cost then it was theoretically possible to find a distribution of costs so that all members of the collective would approve the outcome unanimously. In 1955, Samuelson first conjectured the "fatal inability" of any decentralized mechanism to determine optimal public choices, a view that was later (Samuelson 1969) reasserted even more emphatically. Neither Wicksell nor Samuelson actually specified decentralized mechanisms which could provide theoretical foundations for their respective conjectures. The Auction Election solves the Arrow (1963) problem in somewhat the same sense that a competitive private goods economy solves the problem of resource allocation: the competitive economy provides a Pareto optimal outcome for a given distribution of primary resources and has nothing to say about the optimal distribution of such resources. Actually, the mechanism does a little more than this by providing for some voluntary redistribution of wealth whenever a winning proposition is produced.

Hurwicz (1972), for pure exchange private goods economies, and Ledyard and Roberts (1974), for economies with public goods, have proved that it is impossible to find a mechanism that provides individually rational Pareto optima and which is simultaneously individually incentive compatible. Obviously, the above mechanisms do not contradict these theorems which postulate a much broader range of strategic behavior by economic agents than Nash equilibrium competitive behavior. But why do real people making real decisions for real money, in the experiments reported here and in the cited experimental public good literature, behave predominantly in accordance with the competitive postulate? Why do they not exhibit the more "sophisticated," "strategic" behavior postulated by Hurwicz and Ledyard-Roberts? I think it is because there are significant direct (and indirect opportunity) costs of thinking, calculating, and signaling which make strategizing uneconomical. In the Auction Election the opportunity cost of failing to reach agreement is the loss of the more valuable best proposition. Strategizing not only consumes costly time and thought, it increases the risk of group disagreement. Disagreement means exclusion from better wealth states on the sobering principle that nobody gets more if there is not more available to get.

Can all the hard scientific evidence from experiments to date be dismissed as irrelevant, too simplistic, or based on particular experimental parameters? I think not, for the reason that such results are consistent with a great deal of field evidence. Thousands of buildings have been purchased by religious organizations, clubs, art associations, and private societies through member voluntary contributions having the exclusionary characteristic of the Auction Mechanism and the Auction Election: if contributions do not cover the cost of the proposed project, the project dies. Numerous universities meet specific capital needs from contributions and gifts by alumni and associates. We tend to explain these phenomena, while holding on to our enshrined belief in the impossibility of decentralized public good decision, by attributing them to atypical "altruism." The theory discussed here suggests that such behavior is entirely consistent with self-interest motivation since the decision procedure is the same as that of the Auction Mechanism for public goods.

But it is not my intention to argue that either the present state of evidence or the present state of theory is satisfactory. There is no theory, only conjecture, to support the assertion above that competitive behavior may be a rational response when signaling, thinking, and calculating are costly. Nor can we be confident of the empirical results until new experiments are conducted and old experimental results replicated with different subjects and different experimenters. In future experiments I intend to explore the effect of larger collectives, experience, and balanced budget versions of the Auction Election in which aggregate overbids are rebated in proportion to individual bids.[9]

Appendix

Instructions

This is an experiment in the economics of group decision making. The instructions are simple, and if you follow them carefully and make good decisions you may earn a considerable amount of money which will be paid to you in cash at the end of the experiment. Various research foundations have provided funds for this research.

You are a member of a group that must decide which one of 3 proposals is to be selected. The group will decide by bidding which proposal will be chosen. The value to you of each alternative proposal is shown in column (1) (under each

[9] In earlier experiments (Smith, in press *b*) it was found that the stopping requirement under which each member must *exactly* match his share of cost was needlessly demanding on group agreement. A better rule is to require $b_i \geq q - B_i$ and to distribute any overbid as a rebate to each member in proportion to his bid. Letting

$$B = \sum_{k=1}^{I} b_k = b_i + B_i > q,$$

each i is assigned a new lower bid

$$b_i' = b_i - \frac{b_i(B - q)}{B}.$$

Then

$$B' = \sum_{i=1}^{I} b_i' = \sum_{i=1}^{I} \left[b_i - \frac{b_i(B - q)}{B} \right] = q.$$

The budget is balanced with the new bids (b_i'), and since $b_i' < b_i$ every agent is better off. In any case any agent can still veto the arrangement and reject the new calculated bid. This procedure makes group agreement mechanically easier, i.e., compliance cost is lower for the group stopping rule.

TRIAL 1			
PROPOSITION	(1) MY VALUE	(2) MY BID	(3) MY NET VALUE
1	5		
2	60		
3	-20		
4			
5			

TRIAL 2			
PROPOSITION	(1) MY VALUE	(2) MY BID	(3) MY NET VALUE
1	5		
2	60		
3	-20		
4			
5			

TRIAL 3			
PROPOSITION	(1) MY VALUE	(2) MY BID	(3) MY NET VALUE
1	5		
2	60		
3	-20		
4			
5			

TRIAL 4			
PROPOSITION	(1) MY VALUE	(2) MY BID	(3) MY NET VALUE
1	5		
2	60		
3	-20		
4			
5			

TRIAL 5			
PROPOSITION	(1) MY VALUE	(2) MY BID	(3) MY NET VALUE
1	5		
2	60		
3	-20		
4			
5			

TRIAL 6			
PROPOSITION	(1) MY VALUE	(2) MY BID	(3) MY NET VALUE
1	5		
2	60		
3	-20		
4			
5			

FIG. A1

trial), on your record sheet. Net value, which will be paid to you in cash on the final decision, is computed by subtracting your bid from your value for the winning proposal.

The decision process consists of a series of trial bids as follows (refer to your record sheet): On each trial each member privately selects and writes a bid in column (2), expressed in whole dollars, for each of the proposals. For example, 20, 0, − 15. A negative bid means that you are asking for compensation from the other members. *A bid should not exceed your proposal value if you want to make money.* On each trial, I will go to each member and record his bids, compute the algebraic sum of all member bids for each proposal, and post these sums on the blackboard. The proposal with the largest positive bid sum will be the winner. On each trial compute your potential net value, column (1) minus column (2), for each proposal and write it in column (3). If and when a proposal wins, draw a circle around your net value for the winning proposal. You will have a maximum of 6 trials to determine the winning proposal. The first trial will be for practice to familiarize you with the procedure and will not count in determining a winning proposition.

If a proposal wins we will stop on that trial, and you will be paid $2 plus your net value. Otherwise, you will be paid $2. The proposition values on your record sheets are not the same for all members. They represent your own private information and are not to be revealed to any other member. Feel free to earn as much cash as you can. Do not speak to any other participant.

References

Arrow, K. *Social Choice and Individual Values.* 2d ed. New York: Wiley, 1963.

Auster, R. "Renting the Streets." *Proceedings of the Conference on American Re-Evolution.* Tucson: Dept. Econ., Univ. Arizona, in press.

Bohm, P. "Estimating Demand for Public Goods: An Experiment." *European Econ. Rev.* 3 (1972): 111–30.

Buchanan, J. "Positive Economics, Welfare Economics, and Political Economy." *J. Law and Econ.* 20 (October 1959): 124–38.

Clarke, E. "Multipart Pricing of Public Goods." *Public Choice* 11 (Fall 1971): 17–33.

Drèze, J., and de la Vallée Poussin, D. "A Tâtonnement Process for Public Goods." *Rev. Econ. Studies* 38 (April 1971): 133–50.

Ferejohn, J., and Noll, R. "An Experimental Market for Public Goods: The PBS Station Program Cooperative." *A.E.R. Papers and Proceedings* (May 1976): 267–73.

Groves, T. "The Allocation of Resources under Uncertainty: The Informational and Intensive Roles of Prices and Demands in a Team." Technical Report no. 1, Univ. California Berkeley, Center Res. Management Sci., August 1969.

———. "Incentives in Teams." *Econometrica* 41 (July 1973): 617–33.

Groves, T., and Ledyard, J. "Optimal Allocation of Public Goods: A Solution to the 'Free-Rider Problem.'" Discussion Paper no. 144, Northwestern Univ., Center Math. Studies Econ. and Management Sci., September 1975.

Hurwicz, L. "On Informationally Decentralized Systems." In *Decision and Organization,* edited by R. Radner and B. McGuire. Amsterdam: North-Holland, 1972.

Ledyard, J., and Roberts, J. "On the Incentive Problem with Public Goods." Discussion Paper no. 116, Northwestern Univ., Center Math. Studies Econ. and Management Sci., 1974.

Samuelson, P. "Diagrammatic Exposition of a Theory of Public Expenditure." *Rev. Econ. Statis.* 37 (November 1955): 350–56.

———. "Pure Theory of Public Expenditure and Taxation." In *Public Economics,* edited by J. Margolis and H. Guitton. New York: St. Martins, 1969.

Scherr, B., and Babb, E. "Pricing Public Goods: An Experiment with Two Proposed Pricing Systems." *Public Choice* (Fall 1975): pp. 35–48.

Smith, V. "Mechanisms for the Optimal Provision of Public Goods." *Proceedings of the Conference on American Re-Evolution.* Tucson: Dept. Econ., Univ. Arizona, in press. (*a*)

———. "Incentive Compatible Experimental Processes for the Provision of Public Goods." NBER Conference on Decentralization, April 23–25, 1976. Forthcoming in *Research in Experimental Economics,* edited by V. Smith. Greenwich, Conn.: JAI Press, in press. (*b*)

Thompson, E. "A Pareto Optimal Group Decision Process." *Papers in Non-Market Decision-Making* 1 (1965): 133–40.

Tideman, T., and Tullock, G. "A New and Superior Process for Making Social Choices." *J.P.E.* 84 (December 1976): 1145–59.

Wicksell, K. "A New Principle of Just Taxation." Translated by J. Buchanan. In *Classics in the Theory of Public Finance,* edited by R. Musgrave and A. Peacock. New York: St. Martins, 1967.

INCENTIVE COMPATIBLE EXPERIMENTAL PROCESSES FOR THE PROVISION OF PUBLIC GOODS

Vernon L. Smith, UNIVERSITY OF ARIZONA

> After providing ... [public expenditure] ... theory with its ... optimal conditions, I went on to demonstrate the fatal inability of any decentralized market or voting mechanism to attain or compute this optimum [Samuelson, (1955), p. 35].
>
> ... to say that market mechanisms are non-optimal, and that there are difficulties with most political decision processes, does not imply that we can never find new mechanisms of a better sort [Samuelson (1958), p. 334].
>
> Providing the [public] expenditure in question holds out any prospect at all of creating utility exceeding costs, it will always be

> theoretically possible, and approximately so in practice, to find a distribution of costs such that all parties regard the expenditure as beneficial and may therefore approve it unanimously [Wicksell (1896), pp. 89–90].
>
> How much of this [the principle of unanimity and voluntary consent in taxation]... may be of practical use in the near future, men of affairs may decide [Wicksell (1896), p. 73].

I. INTRODUCTION

The theory of public goods has, in the space of 20 years, revolutionized teaching and research in public finance, had a major impact on the content of microeconomic theory in general, and has provided, for many, the analytical foundation for an economic justification for the state. The most widely accepted proposition in contemporary public finance is the "fatal inability" of decentralized market or voting institutions to attain a Pareto-optimal allocation of resources when there are public goods. This proposition has been called into question by a series of important new contributions based on a variety of different behavioral assumptions. The first proposed mechanism for revealing marginal willingness to pay for public goods seems to be Earl Thompson's (1965) "D-Process," based on risk-averse behavior, in which demand is revealed by individual purchases of government-offered insurance against relatively unfavorable public outcomes. Two proposals based on minimax choice behavior are those of Drèze and Vallée Poussin (1971) and Malinvaud (1971). Contributions based on Nash equilibrium (or competitive) behavior, include the "demand revealing process" developed independently by Clarke (1971) and Groves (1969, 1973), analyzed further by Groves and Ledyard (1974, 1977) under the title of the "abstract" government (G*), and the simpler quadratic tax mechanism, or "optimal" government (O).

A remarkable precursor of Clarke, Groves and Groves-Ledyard is Vickrey's (1961) "counterspeculation" process, and the "second price" sealed bid auction developed to induce revelation of demand for private goods,[1] but having the essential behavioral features of the Clarke, Groves and Groves:Ledyard (G*) mechanisms. But, as indicated in Smith (1977), the most promising of these recent mechanisms appears to be the Groves-Ledyard (O) quadratic tax rule under which economic agents have a particularly simple maximum problem and are required only to communicate messages in Euclidean space. The "demand revealing" or G* process requires agents to communicate functions reporting marginal willingness to pay.

This study reports the results of 21 (exclusive of pilot experiments)[2] laboratory experiments using 118 subjects to test hypotheses about the performance characteristics of three different processes for the provision of public goods. The experimental methods are based on the use of nontrivial monetary rewards to induce controlled valuations on abstract goods or decisions (Smith, 1975). The treatment variable in these experiments is the public good cost allocation mechanism together with the supporting institution defining information transfer, agreement, and process outcome. The term "mechanism" will be used to denote a formal mathematical theory, while "process" will be used to denote a procedure for arriving at a collective decision. Thus, each of the three institutions of public choice to be studied are based on a mechanism of cost allocation and maximization, but we propose no adjustment mechanisms, i.e., formal dynamic theory, for these institutions. But the adjustment process for each institution is specified rather carefully to facilitate the possible articulation of formal adjustment mechanisms. For those interested in resource allocation adjustment mechanisms, but unfamiliar with laboratory experimental methods, it will become evident (cf. Hurwicz, 1973) that it is impossible to design a group decision experiment without designing an institution in all its structural detail (Shubik, 1974).

Section 2 and 3 discuss the Groves-Ledyard (G-L) tax rule and the experimental process using their mechanism. Since the G-L mechanism purports to solve the free-riding problem, it is necessary to design a control experimental process to establish that there is a problem to be solved. The scientific requirement must be to establish an evidential basis for free-riding that is comparable to the evidence supporting any proposed solution to the problem. The experimental control process is defined by a "Lindahl pricing procedure" in section 4 which attempts to reproduce the circumstances that scholars have in mind when discussing the free-rider phenomenon. Since such discussions do not typically involve the specification of a process, the control experiment is based on a process interpretation of public goods theory. Based largely on the Nash equilibrium properties of the G-L mechanism, section 5 offers some hypotheses concerning the comparative results to be expected from the Lindahl control and G-L research experiments. Section 6 presents the experimental designs and the results of four Lindahl and three G-L experiments. These results tend to support the hypothesis that the Lindahl process is not incentive compatible while the G-L process is. Section 7 replicates the G-L experiments with different design parameters.

Incentive incompatibility in the Lindahl mechanism is explained by the noncompetitive condition that each economic agent is placed in a position of exercising effective control over his own price. The G-L mechanism is incentive compatible because it removes such control over price from the individual. These considerations suggest still another mechanism, called the Auction Mechanism (section 8), in which each agent's share of cost is determined by the bids of the other agents. He may signal agreement only by matching his share of cost with his bid, and by matching the group's mean quantity proposal with his own proposal. This yields incentive compatibility, and has certain advantages such as simplicity and a balanced budget at all levels of the public good. Section 9 describes an experimental design and the results of 12 experiments based on the Auction Mechanism. These results tend to support the hypothesis that the Auction process leads to the Lindahl optimal provision of public goods.

This study suggests that the conventional wisdom, emphasizing the inevitability of the underprovision of public goods by decentralized institutions, is much too pessimistic. This conclusion receives evidential support in field and laboratory experiments reported by Bohm (1972), Ferejohn and Noll (1976) and Sherr and Babb (1975). Thus, Bohm reports that his experiments "indicate that the well-known risk for misrepresentation of preferences (for public goods)... may have been exaggerated" (Bohm, 1972, p. 111). Of course in field experiments it is not possible to know the Lindahl optimum. Only in laboratory environments, where Lindhal prices and quantities are well defined, can we make more percise judgments about the optimality characteristics of different processes.

What emerges from this paper, and finds support in the cited experimental studies, is that practical decentralized processes exist for the provision of public goods. Some of these processes lead to optimal or approximately optimal allocations. If there are a few such processes there must be thousands—some better, some worse, some cheaper, some dearer.

If these studies are corroborated by further investigation, the unanimity rule in public choice, endorsed in Wicksell (1896) and in the comprehensive work of Buchanan and Tullock (1962), will have empirical support far in excess of the weight of contemporary professional opinion.

2. THE G-L INCENTIVE COMPATIBLE TAX RULE

There are several possible forms for the G-L tax rule (Groves and Ledyard, 1974; 1977), and we shall use one of the simpler versions as a basis for the research (R) experiments to be reported here.

Consider a collective of I economic agents choosing a public good that can be produced in the amount X at constant unit cost q. Let $\Delta X_i = x_i \gtrless 0$, be an increment to the quantity of the public good that is proposed by agent i, where $i = 1,2,\ldots,I$, and $X = \sum_{i=1}^{I} x_i$ is defined as the group's proposed quantity of the public good. Also define $S_i = \sum_{j \neq i} x_j$ as the sum of the increments proposed by all members of the group except i. Then the G-L tax rule allocates to agent i a total tax cost, C_i, depending on his choice of x_i and conditional upon S_i, given by

$$C_i(x_i \mid S_i) = -\left(IS_i - \frac{q}{I}\right)\left(x_i + S_i\right) + \left(\frac{I-1}{2}\right)\left(x_i + S_i\right)^2 \tag{2.1}$$

The marginal tax to agent i is

$$C_i'(x_i \mid S_i) = -\left(IS_i - \frac{q}{I}\right) + (I-1)(x_i + S_i). \tag{2.2}$$

Since $X = x_i + S_i$, summing over the marginal tax levels of all I agents gives

$$\begin{aligned} \sum_{i=1}^{I} C_i'(x_i \mid S_i) &= \sum_{i=1}^{I} \left[-I(X - x_i) + \frac{q}{I} + (I-1)X \right] \\ &= -I^2X + IX + q + I(I-1)X = q. \end{aligned} \tag{2.3}$$

It follows that if agent i has a marginal willingness to pay for X given by $M_i(X)$, and if agent i chooses x_i^0 to maximize his net benefit, then $M_i(x_i^0 + S_i^0) = C_i'(x_i^0 \mid S_i)$, and

$$\sum_{i=1}^{I} M_i(X^0) = q. \tag{2.4}$$

$X^0 = \sum_{i=1}^{I} x_i^0$ is the group's Pareto optimal amount of the public good. Under the G-L tax rule, if each agent maximizes his net benefit, then in equilibrium his marginal willingness to pay is revealed by his marginal tax level easily calculated from (2.2) for any given S_i.

It should be noted that this version of the G-L tax rule does not balance the budget for the public good for every X. That is,

$$\sum_{i=1}^{I} C_i(x_i \mid S_i) \neq qX,$$

for all X. Other versions of the G-L tax rule (Groves and Ledyard, 1977) guarantee a balanced budget for every $X \geq 0$.

3. AN EXPERIMENTAL ALLOCATION PROCESS BASED ON THE G-L TAX RULE

This section presents an experimental design in which the G-L tax rule is imbedded in one of numerous conceivable elementary adjustment processes for group choice of a public good.

Environment

The experimental environment specifies a very simple *technology:* An abstract public good can be produced at constant unit cost, q, only for integer values X, no larger than $\tilde{X}$, i.e., $0 \le X \le \tilde{X}$. Each experiment is conducted with a group of $I \ge 2$ subject agents. Utility is induced on units of the abstract public good by *privately* specifying functions $V_i(X)$, (increasing in X), and endowing subject i with the unabridged right to claim $V_i(X)$ dollars in U.S. currency net of his allocated share of the cost of the good, C_i, *if* the group agrees on the quantity X under the process stopping rules. If the group fails to reach agreement under the rules, each subject is to receive a "modest wage" small in comparison with the net dollar earnings, $v_i = V_i(X) - C_i(x_i | S_i)$.

Proposition 1. If each subject derives a strictly monotone increasing utility from U.S. currency, $U_i(v_i)$, and chooses x_i to maximize this utility of money, the reward rule $v_i = V_i(X) - C_i(x_i | S_i)$ induces the controlled marginal willingness to pay function $M_i = V_i'(X)$ on units of the abstract public good, which in turn implies a Lindahl group equilibrium.

Each i seeks to

$$\max_{x_i} U_i[V_i(x_i + S_i) - C_i(x_i | S_i)]$$

where $C_i(x_i | S_i)$ is given by (2.1). For U_i, V_i such that U_i is concave in x_i, it is necessary and sufficient for a maximum that

$$\{V_i'(x_i^0 + S_i) - C_i'(x_i^0 | S_i)\} U_i' = 0. \tag{3.1}$$

But if $U_i' > 0$, (3.1) implies

$$V_i'(X) = C_i'(x_i^0 | S_i). \tag{3.2}$$

Hence, $V_i'(X)$ is i's marginal willingness to pay for X. Since (3.1) and (3.2) must hold for all $i = 1,2,\ldots,I$, then we have from (2.3) the *Lindahl equilibrium* $[X^0, V_1'(X^0), \ldots, V_1'(X^0)]$, such that

$$\sum_{i=1}^{I} V_i'(X^0) = q, \tag{3.3}$$

for the experimental environment.

Adjustment Process

The experimental procedure (see the instructions in Appendix I) involves a dialogue between the subject agents and the experimenter in which the *language* consists of *private* messages (incremental proposals), $x_i(t) \gtreqless 0$, $i = 1,2,\ldots, I$ chosen from the integers $\tilde{x}, \tilde{x}+1, \ldots, 0, 1, 2, \ldots, \tilde{X}$, and a *public* message (the group proposal), $X(t) = \sum_{i=1}^{I} x_i(t)$, on each "trial" $t = 1,2,\ldots$ The process consists of the following iterative procedure:

(*i*) *Starting rule.* On trial t each subject independently, and privately, chooses an integer $\tilde{x} \leq x_i(t) \leq \tilde{X}$, and records $x_i(t)$ on a prescribed record sheet. (Appendix I).

(*ii*) *Transition rules.*

(*ii*.a) The experimenter records each $x_i(t)$, computes $X(t) = \sum_{i=1}^{I} x_i(t)$, and posts X(t) on a blackboard, the posting to remain until the end of the process.

(*ii*.b) Each subject records X(t), then computes and records $S_i(t) = X(t) - x_i(t)$.

(*ii*.c) Each subject determines his private net valuation of $[x_i(t), S_i(t)]$, from a pre-computed $(\tilde{X} - \tilde{x})^2$ table (Appendix I, Table 3) of the values

$$v_i = \begin{cases} V_i(x_i + S_i) - C_i(x_i \mid S_i), \text{ if } 0 < x_i + S_i \leq \tilde{X} \\ 0, \text{ if } x_i + S_i \leq 0 \text{ or } x_i + S_i > \tilde{X} \end{cases}$$

The resulting $v_i(t)$ is recorded on his record sheet. This completes trial t.

(*ii*.d) Each subject then proceeds to trial t + 1 and chooses $x_i(t+1)$ as in (*i*).

(*iii*) *Stopping rule.*

(*iii*.a) The process stops on trial t* if

$$x_i(t^* - 2) = x_i(t^* - 1) = x_i(t^*), \forall i, \text{ and } t^* \leq T;$$

(*iii*.b) Otherwise, the process stops on trial t = T.

(*iv*) *Outcome rule.* If the process stops by (*iii*.a) the group has reached *equilibrium* (agreement), and each subject is paid $v_i(t^*)$ in cash. Otherwie, he receives a small cash payment.

Discussion

Certain features of the above process deserve special emphasis:

(1) Each subject agent at all times is assured the right of privacy with respect to his total valuation, V_i, cost allocation, C_i, net valuation, v_i, incremental proposal, x_i, and the sum of all other such proposals, S_i. The only public information consists in the elements of the set $(I, q, X(1), X(2) \ldots X(t) \ldots)$. The publicity of such elements is *realizable* in any field application of the procedure. But the valuations $V_i(X)$ are subjective in field applications, and their publicity is therefore not credibly realizable, even if considered desirable.

(2) In addition to field realizability the condition of privacy in the laboratory experiments also has the important function of protecting the postulate of a neoclassical environment (no externalities in consumption). If agent i does not know V_j, C_j, or x_j for any $j \neq i$ then

the earnings and decisions of other agents cannot enter as arguments of i's utility function.[3] Thus, privacy helps to insure that U_i will depend predominantly on v_i only.

(3) The stopping rule requires every agent to send the same message on three successive trials. Hence agreement requires *unanimity* on any proposed X. Furthermore any agent who signals a desire to reach agreement by repeating his previous message may still veto the proposal by altering his subsequent message. This effectively precludes "accidental" agreement.

(4) The process has the desirable property that no transactions occur unless and until equilibrium obtains. This outcome rule is particularly important where, as in the case of public goods, the group decision pertains to the construction of durable capital. This is in accordance with one of the desiderata suggested by Hurwicz (1973, p. 26), but contrasts with the process examined by Drèze and de la Vallée Poussin (1971) which was an instantaneous utility criterion rather than a final-outcome utility criterion. The above outcome rule also contrasts with that of most of the experimental adjustment literature based on oral auction (Smith, 1964), sealed-bid auction (Smith, 1967), and posted-price (Williams, 1973; Plott and Smith, 1975) institutions of contract. In this literature, utility is derived from the flow of per period exchanges. Disequilibrium contracts are binding, and therefore agent "endowments" are altered by such contracts. But the final-outcome utility rule presents behavioral hazards in that it is pretty well established experimentally that the exchange of information under costless (no payoff) conditions differs from that under costly conditions. Strategic bluffing, inattentive decisions, and gaming utilities may make process convergence more difficult when utility is based on final outcomes instead of the flow of intermediate outcomes. But we have no choice except to confront these issues, since it is final-outcome utilities that are relevant to the public good decision.[4]

4. A CONTROL PROCESS BASED ON THE LINDAHL PRICING PROCEDURE

The control experiment is based on an interpretation of the "conventional" description of the free-riding problem in public good decisions (e.g., Samuelson, 1955). The alleged problem is that if each agent's allocation of cost for the public good is determined by his stated willingness to pay, then he will have an incentive to understate his willingness to pay thereby gaining an advantage by letting other members of the group carry a larger burden of the cost.

Environment

The technology and induced utility functions are the same as in the previous experimental process. However, agent i's share of unit cost is now determined by his bid for the marginal (proposed) unit of the public good. If his bid for unit X is $b_i(X)$, then his net reward is

$$v_i = V_i(X) - b_i(X)X,$$

if the group reaches agreement under the stopping rules, otherwise he receives a modest wage. The instructions (Appendix II) require the subjects to submit noncreasing lists of bids $b_i(1), b_i(2) \ldots b_i(\tilde{X})$ on each trial. Therefore (assuming differentiability), $b_i'(X) \leq 0$, for all i. The group proposal rule in the experiment is $X \geq 0$ such that $q = \sum_{k=1}^{I} b_k(X)$ (We ignore the trivial case in which $q > \sum_{k=1}^{I} b_k(0)$).

Proposition 2. If each subject derives a strictly monotone increasing utility from U.S. currency, $U_i(v_i)$, then maximizing this utility under the reward rule, $v_i = V_i(X) - b_i(X)X$ requires each subject's optimal bid function to be not greater than his marginal willingness to pay function, i.e., $b_i(X) \leq V_i'(X)$.

Agent i seeks to $\max_{b_i(X)} U_i[V_i(X) - b_i(X)X]$ subject to the group proposal rule that $q - \sum_{k=1}^{I} b_k(X) = 0, X \geq 0$. But since $q = b_i(X) + \sum_{j \neq i} b_j(X)$, this is equivalent to the problem

$$\max_{X} U_i\{V_i(X) - [q - \sum_{j \neq i} b_j(X)]X\}. \tag{4.1}$$

If U_i concave in X, and $U_i' > 0$ it is necessary and sufficient for a maximum that

$$V_i' = q - \sum_{j \neq i} b_j(X) - X \sum_{j \neq i} b_j'(X). \tag{4.2}$$

That is, through his choice of the bid function, $b_i(X)$, i implicitly chooses X so that his marginal willingness to pay equals his marginal net cost. His net total cost is the residual $[q - \sum_{j \neq i} b_j(X)]X$ left to be paid after netting out the contributions of all other agents $j \neq i$. Substituting from (4.2) into the group proposal rule,

$$b_i(X) = q - \sum_{j \neq i} b_j(X) = \tag{4.3}$$

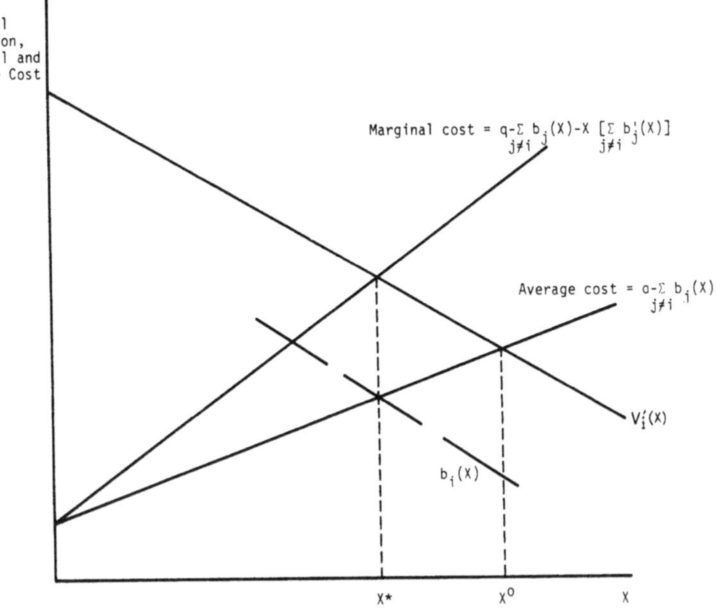

Figure 1.

$$V_i'(X) + X\sum_{j\neq i} b_j'(X)\begin{cases} < V_i'(X), X > 0, & \text{if } b_j'(X) < 0 \text{ for some j.} \\ = V_i'(X), X > 0, & \text{if } b_j'(X) = 0, \forall j \end{cases}$$

Consequently, if i believes that $b_j(X)$ will be decreasing for some j, and therefore $q - \sum_{j\neq i} b_j(X)$ will be increasing, he will bid less than $V_i'(X)$. This is because his net average unit cost, $q - \sum_{j\neq i} b_j(X) = b_i(X)$ is less than his net marginal cost, $q - \sum_{j\neq i} b_j(X) - \sum_{j\neq i} b_j'(X)$. If i believes that $b_j(X) \equiv b_j$ will be constant for every j, then his net average and marginal costs are the same, $q - \sum_{j\neq i} b_j$, and his optimal bid function is $V_i'(X)$. This property is exploited by the adjustment procedure to be discussed in section 8.[5]

But in the Lindahl procedure note that even if i is very optimistic about the bids to be submitted by $j \neq i$, and believes each will bid his marginal willingness to pay, then $b_j(X) \equiv V_j'(X)$. Therefore $b_j'(X) = V_j''(X) < 0$ and i will bid $b_i(X) < V_i'(X), X > 0$. Figure 1 illustrates the Free-Rider equilibrium quantity X^*, which is below the Lindahl equilibrium quantity, X^0.

Adjustment Process

The *language* of the Lindahl process consists of *private* bid messages $b_i(X,t), i = 1,2,\ldots,I; X = 1,2,\ldots\tilde{X}$, and a *public* message (the group proposal),

X(t) defined implicitly by

$$q \begin{cases} \leq \sum_{k=1}^{I} b_k(X,t), & X \leq \hat{X}(t) \\ > \sum_{k=1}^{I} b_k(X,t), & X > \hat{X}(t) \end{cases}$$

for each trial t. As in the research experiment, the process uses an iterative procedure as follows:

(*i*) *Starting rule.* On trial t, each subject independently and privately selects a vector of bids $[b_i(1,t), \ldots, b_i(\tilde{X},t)]$ that are written in non-increasing order on a bid submission form.

(*ii*) *Transition Rules*

(*ii*.a) The experimenter collects the bid forms, computes the sum $\sum_{k=1}^{I} b_k(X,t)$ for $X = 1, 2, \ldots, \hat{X}$ where $\hat{X}(t)$ is the largest integer X such that $\sum_{k=1}^{I} b_i(\hat{X},t)$ is not larger than q. Then $\hat{X}(t)$ is posted on the blackboard where it remains until the end of the experiment.

(*ii*.b) Each subject records $\hat{X}(t)$ on a prescribed record sheet (Appendix II), determines $V_i(\hat{X}(t))$ from his valuation table, and enters this value on his record sheet.

(*ii*.c) The experimenter then privately communicates to each subject the subject's lowest accepted bid, $b_i(\hat{X}(t),t)$. In some experiments each subject obtained this from his own records.

(*ii*.d) Each subject then computes his share of facility cost $\hat{X}(t)b_i(\hat{X}(t),t)$, and subtracts it from gross value $V_i(\hat{X}(t))$ to determine net value, $\hat{v}_i = V_i(\hat{X}(t)) - \hat{X}(t).\, b_i(\hat{X}(t),t)$, and records it on his record sheets.

(*ii*.e) Each subject then proceeds to trial t + 1, choosing a new bid vector $[b_i(1,t+1), \ldots, b_i(\hat{X}(t+1),t+1)]$ as in (*i*).

(*iii*) *Stopping Rule*

(*iii*.a) The process stops if each subject's lowest accepted bid is the same on three succesive trials, i.e. on trial t* if $b_i(\hat{X}(t^*-2), t^*-2) = b_i(\hat{X}(t^*-1), t^*-1) = b_i(\hat{X}(t^*), t^*)$, for all i where $t^* \leq T$;

(*iii*.b) Otherwise, the process stops on trial t = T.

(*iv*) *Outcome rule.* The subjects are paid $v_i(t^*)$ in cash if the process stops by (*iii*.a) otherwise a small cash payment for their time. In some variations this small payment was also added to $v_i(t^*)$.

Discussion

It is commonly asserted that the free rider problem is due to agents failing to report "truthfully" their marginal willingness to pay. But the issue is better stated as one in which the agent has a conflict of interest between *revealing* his marginal willingness to pay and enjoying a *low share* of the cost. It is unlikely that agent resolution of this conflict of interest will yield the same decision as would obtain in the absence of such a conflict. In the typical nonlaboratory group decision problem in which willingness to pay is subjectively and perhaps very vaguely defined, "truthfulness" (an objective concept) is not well defined.

It is because of these considerations that in the above interpretation of the Lindahl paradigm we do not request of subject-agents that they "truthfully" report their willingness to pay for successive units of X. We ask rather (in a more neutral manner) that they simply submit bids for successive units of the public good with the understanding that their private unit cost is determined by the lowest of their accepted bids. Some might think this is too bland a directive, and that subjects should be exhorted to be "very honest" and write down their "true" willingness to pay schedules. But this would be quite the wrong approach. To see why, suppose in the experimental situation that one could use such moral suasian to induce fairly consistent bid sequences at or near $V_i'(X)$. Such results would be nontransferable to field environments because in nonlaboratory environments we *cannot know* what are the "true" valuations. The proper approach, therefore, is to design a procedure, such as the one based on the G-L tax rule, that allegedly removes the conflict between theself-interest and the desired revelation. Then one designs a second "Lindahl" procedure, as outlined above, in which the alleged confict is given the opportunity to be expressed. Neither procedure should use forms of persuasion that could only have objective meaning in laboratory environments.

5. THEORY AND HYPOTHESES

The research experimental mechanism described above yields a static Lindahl equilibrium characterized by the important Nash property. It is this property that provides the motivation for our prediction of the experimental outcomes and the hypotheses to be tested. If we let $U_i[V_i(x_i \mid S_i)]$ be the utility derived by subject i when he chooses x_i given that all $j \neq i$ choose x_j, and let $\max U_i[V_i(x_i \mid S_i)] = U_i[v_i(x_i^0 \mid S_i^0)]$, for all i, $S_i^0 = \sum_{j \neq i} x_j^0$, then $(x_1^0, x_2^0, \ldots, x_1^0)$ is a Nash equilibrium: $U_i[V_i(x_i^0 \mid S_i^0)] \geq U_i[V_i(x_i \mid S_i^0)]$, for all i, and all $x_i \neq x_i^0$ From Proposition 1, each i chooses x_i^0 so that his implicit bid is his marginal willingness to pay $V_i'(X^0)$, while from Proposition 2 we expect subjects in the Lindahl bid procedure to bid less than $V_i'(X)$. We propose the following specific hypotheses for the first series of research (R1) experiments and a series of control experiments (C).

Hypothesis 1. In R1 experiments reaching equilibrium under the stopping rule (*iii*a) in section 3, the proposed quantities of the public good on the final trial will be distributed with mean X^0.

Hypothesis 2. In C experiments reaching equilibrium under the stopping rule (*iii*a) in section 4, the proposed quantity of the public good will be distributed with mean $< X^0$.

Hypothesis 3. Whether or not C experiments reach equilibrium, the C experiment bids for the marginal unit, X^0, of the public good will tend to be below the marginal willingness to pay for X^0, i.e. $b_i(X_0(t),t) < V_i'(X^0)$.

Hypothesis 4. Whether or not the C or R1 experiments reach equilibrium, the proposals, $X(t)$, in the R1 experiments will tend to exceed those in the C experiments, $\hat{X}(t)$.

6. EXPERIMENTS AND TESTS OF HYPOTHESES

Subjects and Design Parameters

Thirty-five subjects participated in two sets of experiments consisting of three R1 and four C experiments using five subjects in each experiment. No subject participated in more than one of the seven sessions. Volunteers were solicited for a "group decision making experiment in which participants will have an opportunity to receive payments in cash depending upon their decisions." The subjects were obtained from graduate or undergraduate economics classes at the University of Southern California, University of Arizona, Stanford University, and University of California (Berkeley).

The marginal valuation functions, $V_i'(X)$, for the C experiments are shown in Figure 2. The price of the public good is $q = \$45$ and the Lindahl equilibrium is $(X^0; V_1^i, V_2', V_3', V_4', V_5') = (5 \text{ or } 6; 3, 3, 8, 13, 18)$. For R1, Tables (1.1–1.4) in Appendix I exhibit the individual total and marginal valuation schedules $V_i(X)$, $V_i'(X)$. The form of the G-L tax rule used in the R1 experiments $(I = 5, q = 45)$ is $C_i(x_i | S_i) = -(5S_i - 9)(x_i + S_i) + 2(x_i + S_i)^2 + k_i(S_i)$ where

$$k_1(S_1) \equiv 2.5(S_1 - 1)S_1 - 3$$
$$k_2(S_2) \equiv 2.5(S_2 - 1)S_2 - 3$$
$$k_3(S_3) \equiv 2.5\,S_3(S_3 + 1) - 3$$
$$k_4(S_4) \equiv 2.5\,S_4(S_4 + 1) + 22$$
$$k_5(S_5) \equiv 2.5\,S_5(S_5 + 1) + 42$$

The tabulations of $C_i(x_i | S_i)$ provided to the subjects are exhibited in Tables (2.1–2.4), Appendix I. These parameters of C_i produce a balanced budget for the public good at $X^0 = 6$. The resulting net valuations

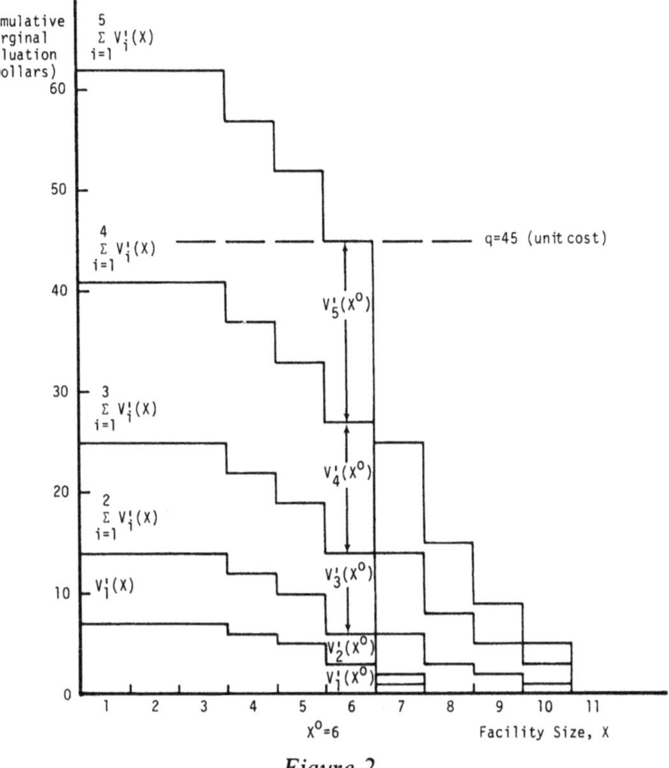

Figure 2.

$v_i = V_i(x_i + S_i) - C_i(x_i | S_i)$ are shown in Tables (3.1–3.4), Appendix I. A copy of the form used by each subject to record each decision and its consequence is also contained in Appendix I.

Appendix II contains the instructions and forms used in the C experiments including the bid submission form (Table 2), and the record form used by each subject to compute his net membership value on each trial.

The marginal valuation functions and Lindahl prices in Figure 2 were selected with two objectives. First, these design parameters correspond with a collective having very diverse preferences for a public good. Consequently, the Lindahl equilibrium is clearly distinct from an egalitarian equilibrium—such as an equal sharing of the cost burden. Second, it will be noted in Figure 2 that the marginal valuations are constant for $X \leq 3$, with \$51 worth of consumer's surplus available at $X = 3$ (compared with \$70 at the Lindahl equilibrium). It was thought that this design would, if anything, tend to favor the C experiments. With this experimental design, if free riding is not too extensive, there might appear to be a reasonable possibility that group agreement could occur for at least three units of the public good. Except for the values of $X \leq 4$ the marginal valuations used in R1 and C were the same, and the LE was the same.

Experimental Results, Discussion

Charts R1.1–R1.3 graph the sequence of choices, $x_i(t)$, for each subject, and the group proposal, $X(t)$, for the three G–L "treatment" experiments. Charts C.1–C.4 graph the sequence of lowest accepted bids, $b_i(\hat{X}(t), t)$ (or the first bid, on trials for which $\hat{X} = 0$), and the group proposal, $\hat{X}(t)$, for the four Lindahl control experiments. The numbers corresponding to selected observations represent trial earnings, $v_i(t)$, for each subject (or total group earnings, $\sum_{i=1}^{I} v_i(t)$, in bottom panel). For example, in Chart R1.1, trial 1, subject 1 chose $x_1(1) = 0$, with $S_1(1) = \sum_{j \neq i} x_j(1) = 2$, $v_1(1) = v_1(x_1(1) \mid S_1(1)) = -\$2$. In chart C.1, trial 1, the group proposal under the Lindahl procedure was $\hat{X}(1) = 2$, and the lowest accepted bid for subject 1 (his second bid) was $b_1(2(1), 1) = \$4$, with $v_1(1) = \$6$.

Experiments R1.1 and R1.3 reached the Lindahl quantity, $X(t^*) = X^\circ = 6$ under the stopping rules on trial $t^* = 16$, and R1.2 attained this quantity at $t^* = 29$. Two of the control experiments reached agreement: C.1 stopped on trial $t^* = 26$, with the null proposal $X(t^*) = 0$, and C.4 stopped on trial $t^* = 24$ with $\hat{X}(t^*) = 2$. Free riding was so extensive in C.1 that it was decided that if in C.2 and C.3 equilibrium did not obtain by trial 15, then on trial 16 a bid sequence identical with the marginal valuation schedule for each subject would be imposed privately. Following this the sequence of trials, with free choice of individual bids, would continue as before. This was accomplished by an announcement, following trial 15 in C.2 and C.3, that the experiment was being interrupted, and each member would be given a bid decision for trial 16. Each member was then approached independently and that member's sequence of marginal valuations was copied onto his or her bid form for trial 16. This procedure was used to provide a test of the *static stability* of the Lindahl equilibrium, if attained, although that equilibrium might be unattainable by the dynamic procedure. As evidenced in Charts C.2 and C.3, this Lindahl equilibrium was not stable as the subjects tended to lower their bids on trial 17 and thereafter. In both C.2 and C.3, four of the five subjects reduced their bids for the sixth unit.

Experiment C.2 was terminated on trial 21 by the unanimous consent of the somewhat frustrated subjects. In C.2, member 2 sent repeated cooperative signals (high bids) which seemed to have the primary effect of inviting others to free-ride. Experiment C.3 was terminated on trial 28 when it was indicated that not all bids would be repeated to yield equilibrium. Member 2 was unwilling to accept a zero imputation of the surplus, and reduced his bid from (7,7,7,6,5,3) on trial 27 to (7,7,6,0,0,0) on trial 28. However, member 3 did not alter his bids in spite of his zero imputation and indicated (after the experiment) willingness to receive nothing to assure better prospects of reward for the other subjects.

It was more difficult to maintain order in the C than in the R1 experiments as subjects in the former tended to express their frustration by breaking the silence rule. From postexperimental comments of the subjects it seemed apparent that they perceived the task of group agreement to be very difficult if not impossible in the C experiments.

Although in each R1 session group agreement produced the Lindahl quantity, only R1.2 resulted in Lindahl equilibrium (LE) incremental proposals (corresponding to implicit Lindahl prices) for every subject. In Chart R1.1, subject 5 was below his LE proposal by one unit, $x_5(t^*) = 2$ ($x_5^0 = 3$) and subject 2 was above his LE by one unit, $x_2(t^*) = 1(x_2^0 = 0)$. In R1.3, $x_2(t^*) = 1(x_2^0 = 0)$ and $x_4(t^*) = 1(x_4^0 = 2)$. In each case, of course, the low (high) member received a payoff greater (less) than his Lindahl surplus, or rent: In R1.1, $v_5(t^*) = \$22 > \$12 = v_5^0$, while in R1.3, $v_2(t^*) = \$12 < \$17 = v_2^0$. Two considerations make deviations from individual Lindahl (and therefore Nash) equilibria possible and perhaps likely: (*i*) The payoff structure provides limited rewards to game strategic behavior, i.e., if player i chooses $x_i < x_i^0$, and one or more players j make accommodating choices $x_j > x_j^0$, then i can gain at the "expense" (the game is nonzero sum) of j. (*ii*) There are subjective transactions costs inherent in the procedure (*any* procedure), and a risk of opportunity loss implicit in the stopping rule. Neither consideration can be illustrated better than in the play of subjects 2 and 5 in Chart R1.1. Only once, on trial 5, did subject 5 choose x_5 as high as his Lindahl (Nash) choice ($x_5^0 = 3$). Unable to turn a positive payoff on trials 7–10, the subject's proposal was lowered from 2 to -3 on trials 11–13. This "punishing" message produced zero or negative net benefits for all members, but subjects 1 and 3 increased their choices by 1 unit on trial 13, while subject 5 returned to his choice of $x_5 = 2$ on trial 14, yielding him \$22. Subject 2 (who had made the accommodation to 5's choice), when asked later why he or she did not lower from $x_2 = 1$ to 0, since it provided an increase in conditional payoff, replied, "Oh yes, but to change at that point would require us to continue at least three more trials, risking failure to agree, and the extra \$3 (from \$12 to \$15) wasn't worth it." There it is, the time cost of more trials, and the increased risk to group agreement when anyone changes his message—these may combine to make it entirely rational for a subject to accept an "unfavorable" deviation from his Nash choice.

Experimental Results, Tests of Hypotheses

Hypotheses 1 and 2 are not contradicted by the results summarized above and the charts; we shall consider them as tentatively confirmed. Hypothesis 3

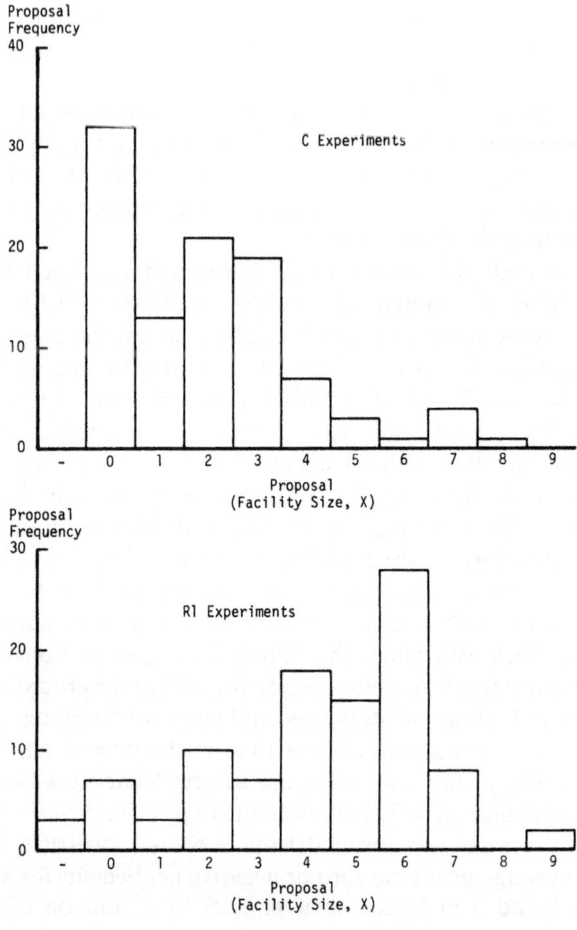

Figure 3.

is supported by the following calculation: Of the 495 total subject bids for the 6th unit in the four control experiments, 29 percent were equal to or larger, and 71 percent below, the Lindahl equilibrium prices (20 percent were zero). Using the binomial test, the null hypothesis that the probability of bids below the Lindahl prices is one half (and the probability of bids equal to or above the Lindahl prices is one half) is rejected at a significance level $p < .001$. Comparing the group proposals in the R1 and C experiments using the two-sample t–test, the null hypothesis that the proposals in C experiments exceed these in R1 experiments is rejected with $p < .001$. This calculation should be taken with the usual grain of salt as there is no a priori case for successive trial proposals to be statistically independent. Histograms of the distribution of proposals in the C and R1 experiments are shown in Figure 3. These data leave little doubt that the experimental results support hypothesis 4.

7. REPLICATION OF THE G-L EXPERIMENT WITH DIFFERENT PARAMETERS

The following unique features of the experimental design used in the R1 experiments suggest the need for further experiments to study the robustness of the G-L mechanism with respect to various parameter variations:

1. In R1 the experimental "joint facility" was a public good for every subject agent. However, the G-L mechanism can be applied to taste configurations in which the common outcome is a "bad" for some agents. If the public good harms an economic agent, the G-L tax rule allocates that agent a subsidy such that the person receives a net benefit depending upon the total surplus available from the public good, and the parameters of the tax rule.
2. The parameters I, $k_i(S_i)$, and q appearing in the tax allocation rule were chosen with the objective of balancing the budget at the LE and providing "reasonable" net dollar outcomes ($12 and $17) for the subjects. These choices resulted in net value (payoff) matrices $v_i(x_i, S_i)$ for each subject with the property that a relatively small number of row choices (x_i) provided some positive payoffs. Thus, in Appendix I, Tables 3.1–3.4, the choices $\langle -3, -2, -1, 0, 1, 2\rangle$ for subjects 1 and 2, $\langle -2, -1, 0, 1, 2\rangle$ for subject 3, and so forth, provide some positive payoffs.
3. The version of the G-L tax rule used in R1 does not balance the budget for every proposal. Consequently, there are strategies and group proposals that yield group payoffs in excess of the aggregate LE surplus. An example is represented by the play of experiment R1.1 which stopped with an aggregate surplus payment of $75.

Experimental Design

The first two of these features were eliminated in the design of a second research experiment (R2) based on the G-L mechanism. The design applies to a collective of I = 8 agents, with the joint facility a marginal "bad" at all levels of X for subject 1, and a "bad" in total at the LE quantity ($X^0 = 4$). Again, the budget was balanced only at the LE. The valuation and cost functions are the quadratics,

$$V_i(X) = (A_i - B_i X)X + \alpha_i, \tag{7.1}$$

$$C_i(X) = -(0.1\, IS_i - q/I)X + (0.05)(I - 1)X^2 + K \tag{7.2}$$

Table 1. Parameter and Lindahl Equilibrium Values

Paramter *Subject*	A_i	B_i	α_i	x_i^0	v_i^0
1	−2.6	0	10	−4	$10
2	11.8	1.50	0	−1	24
3	11.8	1.50	0	−1	24
4	12.6	1.50	0	0	24
5	7.4	0.75	0	1	12
6	10.2	1.00	0	2	16
7	11.0	1.00	0	3	16
8	9.8	0.75	0	4	12
		Total		4	$138

where $I = 8$, $q = 8$, and $K = 5.6$. Table 1 lists the values of (A_i, B_i, α_i) and the equilibrium choices (x_i^0), and rents (v_i^0), by subject. The G-L tax rule allocates subject # 1 a subsidy such that his value net of the "disutility" of $X^0 = 4$ is $10. The design corresponds to a collective with quite diverse tastes and for which the cost of the public good is small in relation to its value. At the LE total cost, $qX^0 = 8 \cdot 4 = \$32$, total value is $170, and the net LE surplus is $138. For instructions, cost and valuation tables see Appendix III.

By comparison with R1, the net value matrices in R2 yield payoffs that are considerably less sensitive to deviations from the LE. Consequently, it is expected that the R2 experiments will exhibit greater deviations from this equilibrium than the R1 experiment.

Experimental Results

The trial sequence of choices, $x_i(t)$ for each subject, and the resulting group proposals, $X(t)$, are exhibited in Charts R2.1 and R2.2. Both experiments stopped under the agreement rule with the quantity proposal, 3. As expected, in comparison with the R1 experiments the relatively large surplus, and insensitivity of surplus imputations to individual choices, produces considerable deviation in equilibrium agreement choices from the LE values. No peculiarities seem to have arisen because the common outcome was a bad for one subject.

8. A DECENTRALIZED AUCTION PROCESS

Corollaries of the G-L and Lindahl Mechanisms

The unanimity feature of the stopping rule used in the above research and control experiments together with corollaries of the G-L and Lindahl cost allocation mechanisms may be combined to suggest a "new" adjustment procedure.

Consider the following bid interpretation of the G-L tax rule:

From (2.2) a maximizing agent choosing x_i^0, conditional on S_i, implicitly reveals the following bid message

$$b_i(x_i^0 \mid S_i) = -\left(IS_i - \frac{q}{I}\right) + (I-1)(x_i^0 + S_i)$$

$$= Ix_i^0 - X + \frac{q}{I} \tag{8.1}$$

Given x_i^0, and the collective's proposal, X, we can always compute $b_i(x_i^0 \mid S_i)$. Similarly, for all agents $j \neq i$, their bid message is $b_j(x_j^0 \mid S_j)$. Summing over these bids, define

$$B_i = \sum_{j \neq i} b_j(x_j^0 \mid S_j) = IS_i - (I-1)X + \left(\frac{I-1}{I}\right)q = -Ix_i^0 + X + \left(\frac{I-1}{I}\right)q \tag{8.2}$$

But rearranging (8.2),

$$Ix_i^0 - X + \frac{q}{I} = q - B_i,$$

and from (8.1) $b_i(x_i^0 \mid S_i) = q - B_i$. Consequently, the G-L tax mechanism guides agent i to bid exactly the difference between public marginal cost and the sum of all other bids. The implicit private marginal cost to i is $q - B_i$, and his implicit cost allocation is $(q - B_i)(x_i + S_i)$. In effect, agent i has chosen x_i to maximize

$$U_i[V_i(x_i + S_i) - (q - B_i)(x_i + S_i)] \tag{8.3}$$

Under this interpretation (and nothing more is claimed for the above arithmetic) we have

Corollary 1. Maximizing (8.3) is equivalent to maximizing $U_i[V_i(x_i + S_i) - C_i(x_i \mid S_i)]$ in Proposition 1.

This corollary provides some additional insight into why the ingenious G-L tax rule is incentive compatible. The rule presents each agent with a "price", $q - B_i$, determined by the actions (bids) of all other agents, over which i has no "significant" control. (Since $B_i = \sum_{j \neq i} b_j(x_j \mid S_j)$, and x_i is a component of S_j, agent i may indirectly, but diffusely, have an effect on $q - B_i$). Agent i is then essentially in the position of an agent in any competitive market, and, from the experimental evidence, he responds in the expected manner.

This bid interpretation of the G-L tax rule is also suggested by the Lindahl cost allocation mechanism. In the proof and discussion of Proposition 2 we have already made note of the following special case:

Corollary 2. From (4.3) if agent i believes that $b_j(X) \equiv b_j$ will be constant for every j, then his net average and marginal costs are the same, $q - \sum_{j \neq i} b_j - B_i$, and his optimal bid function is $V_i'(X)$.

Hence, i's net reward is $v_i = V_i(X) - (q - B_i)X$ as in Corollary 1, and his competitive response in the Lindahl process would be to send the bid message $b_i(X) = V_i'(X)$.

An Alternative Decentralized Mechanism

Consider the following institution for collective public good decision:

(1) Let each agent i submit a bid and a proposed quantity (b_i, X_i) with the understanding that his share of unit cost is $(q - B_i)$, and his share of total cost is $(q - B_i)X_i$.

(2) Give each agent the right to veto or agree to the unit cost, $q - B_i$, allocated to him by all other agents. He signals agreement by choosing $b_i = q - B_i$ and a veto by choosing $b_i \neq q - B_i$. Also give each agent i the right to veto or signal agreement by choosing $X_i = \bar{X} = \sum_{k=1}^{I} X_k/I$ (agree), or $X_i \neq \bar{X}$ (veto).

(3) Group agreement prevails if and only if agreement is signaled by every agent $i = 1, 2, \ldots, I$, in which case $\bar{X}$ units of the public good are purchased, with each agent paying the unit cost share $q - B_i$.

Environment

In the experimental paradigm for this institution, member i receives net reward $v_i = V_i(X_i) - (q - B_i)X_i$, if the collective reaches agreement, and a small payment, v_0, otherwise.

Hence, utility is

$$u_i = \begin{cases} U_i[V_i(X_i) - (q - B_i)X_i], & \text{if } b_i = q - B_i, \text{ and } X_i = \bar{X} \text{ for all i.} \\ U_i[v_0], & \text{otherwise.} \end{cases} \tag{8.4}$$

Proposition 3. If $U_i' > 0$ and each subject i chooses (b_i, X_i) to maximize u_i in (8.4), this implies a Lindahl group equilibrium.

At a maximum for u_i,

$$[V_i'(X_i) - (q - B_i)]U_i' = 0, \tag{8.5a}$$

$$b_i = q - B_i, \tag{8.5b}$$

$$X_i = \bar{X}, \text{ for all i.} \tag{8.5c}$$

From (8.5a) and (8.5c) $X_1 = X_2 = \ldots = X_I = \bar{X}$, and $V_i'(\bar{X}) = q - B_i$.[6] Therefore from (8.5b) $q = \sum_{i=1}^{I} b_i = \sum_{i=1}^{I} V_i'(X^0)$, giving the LE.

In the sequel the mechanism defined by the institution (1)–(3) which leads to proposition 3 will be called the *auction mechanism*, or when combined with a dynamic procedure, an *auction* process. This identification is used because the mechanism can be interpreted (Smith, 1977) as a variation on the following well-known auction principle for markets in private goods (Vickrey, 1961; Smith, 1967): Each bidder in a market has an incentive to bid his marginal willingness to pay if his purchase cost is independent of his bid, and if his success in obtaining the good requires his bid to be not smaller than the cost. Thus, in the above public good auction mechanism any subject who bids less than his marginal willingness to pay increases the risk of excluding himself (along with the entire collective) from the benefits of the good.[7]

Adjustment Process

The *language* of the auction process consists of *private* messages $(b_i(t), X_i(t))$, and the *public* messages $B(t) = \sum_{i=1}^{I} b_i(t), \bar{X}(t) = \sum_{i=1}^{I} X_i(t)/I$ on each trial $t = 1, 2, \ldots$ The iterative procedure is as follows:

(*i*) *Starting rule.* On trial t, each subject independently and privately selects two integers $(b_i(t), X_i(t))$, each confined to specified intervals, and records these choices on a prescribed record sheet (Appendix IV).

(*ii*) *Transition rules.*

(*ii*.a) The experimenter records each $(b_i(t), X_i(t))$, computes, then posts $B(t)$, and $\bar{X}(t)$ on a blackboard, the posting to remain until the end of the process.

(*ii*.b) Each subject records $B(t)$, and $\bar{X}(t)$, then computes, and records, $B_i(t) = B(t) - b_i(t)$ and $q - B_i(t)$.

(*ii*.c) Each subject determines his private net valuation of $(q - B_i(t), X_i(t))$ from a pre-computed table (Appendix IV, Tables 2.1–2.4) of the values $v_i = V_i(X_i) - (q - B_i)X_i$. The resulting $v_i(t)$ is recorded on his record sheet. This completes trial t.

(*ii*.d) Each subject then proceeds to trial $t + 1$ and chooses $(b_i(t + 1), X_i(t + 1))$ as in (*i*).

(*iii*) *Stopping rule.*

(*iii*.a) The process stops on trial t^* if $b_i(t^* - 1) = q - B_i(t^* - 1) = b_i(t^*) = q - B_i(t^*), X_i(t^*) = \bar{X}(t^*)$, for all i, and $t^* \leq T$;

(*iii*.b) Otherwise the process stops on trial $t = T$.

(*iv*) *Outcome rule.* If the process stops by (*iii*.a) the group has reached *equilibrium* (agreement), and each subject is paid $v_i(t^*)$ in cash. Otherwise he receives a modest wage. In some experimental sessions this outcome was modified so that each i received $v_i(t^*) + \$2$ if (*iii*.a) occurs, otherwise \$2.

DISCUSSION

In section 5 it was seen that the G-L mechanism yields Lindahl equilibria that are Nash equilibria. This same property characterizes the Auction mechanism. However, because of the discontinuity in (8.4) the Auction Mechanism provides multiple local Nash equilibria among which are to be found the Lindahl equilibria. From (8.4) if I agents choose *any* (b_i, X_i), $i = 1,2,\ldots, I$ such that (1) $q = \sum_{k=1}^{I} b_k$, (2) $X_i \neq X^0$ and/or $b_i \neq V_i'(X^0)$ for some i, and (3) $V_i(X) - (q - B_i)X > v_0$ for all i, then unanimous agreement is individually rational, and the equilibrium is locally Nash stable. That is, if any agent deviated from (b_i, X_i) by choosing, say (b_i^0, X^0), where $b_i^0 = V_i'(X^0) \neq q - B_i$, then this constitutes a veto and the agent receives v_0 making him worse off. This is illustrated in Table 2a for a collective of I = 2 members with valuation schedules given by $V_3(X)$ and $V_4(X)$ in Figure 2, and with $q = 21$, $v_0 = 0$. The LE is given by $[X^0; V_3'(X^0), V_4'(X^0)] = [5 \text{ or } 6; 8, 13]$. Clearly, the set of choices ($b_3 = 8$, $X_3 = 5$; $b_4 = 13$, $X_4 = 5$) is a Nash equilibrium, but so also are all the choices with positive payoffs in Table 2a.

Table 2a. Auction Process Payoff Matrix

b_3 \ b_4		12				13				14			
	X_3 \ X_4	4	5	6	7	4	5	6	7	4	5	6	7
7	4									7 / 15	0	0	0
	5									0	7 / 17	0	0
	6		0				0			0	0	6 / 18	0
	7									0	0	0	0 / 15
8	4					11 / 11	0	0	0				
	5					0	12 / 12	0	0				
	6		0			0	0	12 / 12	0		0		
	7					0	0	0	7 / 8				
9	4	15 / 7	0	0	0								
	5	0	17 / 7	0	0								
	6	0	0	18 / 6	0		0				0		
	7	0	0	0	14 / 1								

Table 2b. G–L Process Payoff Matrix

$x_3(t^*-1)$	$x_4(t^*-1)$ →	3			4			5		
	$x_3(t^*)$ \ $x_4(t^*)$	2	3	4	3	4	5	4	5	6
1	0	0	0	0	0	0	0	0	0	0
	1	0	• \ •	0	0	12 \ 1	0	0	• \ •	0
	2	0	0	0	0	0	0	0	0	0
2	1	0	0	0	0	0 \ 0	0	0	0	0
	2	0	2 \ 11	0	0 \ 0	12 \ 12	0 \ 0	0	21 \ 7	0
	3	0	0	0	0	0 \ 0	0	0	0	0
3	2	0	0	0	0	0	0	0	0	0
	3	0	• \ •	0	0	7 \ 21	0	0	• \ •	0
	4	0	0	0	0	0	0	0	0	0

It should be noted that the discontinuity in (8.4) is directly a consequence of the stopping rule requiring each i to avoid a veto by "matching" $b_i = q - B_i$, $X_i = \bar{X}$. The lesson here is that the *process* (complete with stopping rule) in which a mechanism is imbedded interacts with and alters the Nash equilibrium properties of the static payoff conditions of the mechanism. The same considerations apply to the G-L mechanism when we take account of a process stopping rule. For example suppose our stopping rule is that the choice of x_i must be repeated once, i.e., we stop on trial t* where $x_i(t^*) = x_i(t^* - 1)$ for all i. Now consider the same illustration used in Table 2a. The choice $(x_3 = 2,\ x_4 = 4)$ is a static Nash equilibrium. But due to the stopping rule, the payoff matrix appears as in Table 2b, and this particular Nash equilibrium is achieved only if $(x_3 = 2,\ x_4 = 4)$ is repeated on the next trial. Hence, the G–L mechanism together with the stopping process also yields multiple local Nash equilibria among which are to be found the Lindahl equilibria.

9. AUCTION PROCESS; HYPOTHESES, EXPERIMENTS AND RESULTS

Hypotheses

The auction procedure of section 8 defines a new experimental research process (A). Since the auction process is incentive compatible, we expect it to yield quantities and cost shares corresponding to the LE. Specifically, we propose

Hypothesis 5. The sample quantities and prices determined by those A experiments reaching equilibrium under stopping rule (*iii.a*) in section 4, may be regarded as having been drawn from populations with means equal to the Lindahl equilibrium $[X^0;V_1'(X^0),\ldots,V_1'(X^0)]$.

Two groups of experiments (A2 and A3), which will be described in the next section, are identical in the structure (i.e., distribution) of member valuations and in the Lindahl optimal quantity of the public good, but in the second group I and q are each double their respective values in the first group. The variability of price and quantity outcomes is expected to increase with increased collective size since the maximum feasible surplus that can be captured by any one agent is increased.

Hypothesis 6. Replication of A experiments with the parameters I and q increased in the same proportion will increase the variance of equilibrium price-quantity outcomes.

Subjects and Experimental Design

Sixty-seven subjects participated in twelve different sessions within a design block of three series of auction process experiments (A1,A2,A3). Table 3 lists the design parameters, consisting of the LE prices, quantity,

Table 3. Auction Experimental Design Parameters

LE Prices, V_i'	*Experiment A1*	*Experiment A2*	*Experiment A3*
	Number of Subjects with LE Price V_i'		
−5	0	1	2
3	2	1	2
8	1	1	2
13	1	1	2
18	1	0	0
Number in Collective, I	5	4	8
LE Quantity, X^0	5 (or 6)	6 (or 7)	6 (or 7)
LE Total Surplus	$70	$69	$138
Public Good Price, q	$45	$19	$ 38
Number of Ex-perimental Sessions	3	5	4
Total Subjects	15	20	32

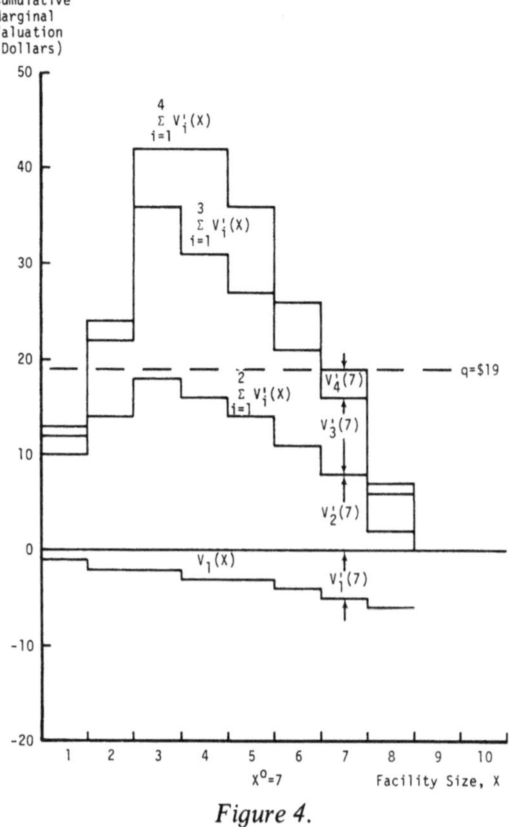

Figure 4.

and total surplus, the number of members in each collective, the price of the public good, and the number of experimental sessions and participating subjects for each set of design parameters. The marginal valuation functions, $V_i'(X)$, used in A1 are identical with those illustrated in Figure 2 for the C experiment. The A1 experiments are thus directly comparable to the R1 and C experiments.[8] Figure 4 illustrates the $V_i'(X)$ functions for the A2 experiments. Figure 4 also applies to the A3 experiments if each $V_i'(X)$ is vertically doubled, i.e., replaced with two identical $V_i'(X)$ functions. A3 differs from A2 only by the scale change from doubling the number of members with each configuration of tastes, $V_i'(X)$, and doubling the unit cost of the public good. This provides replication control over the effect of I on collective outcomes for the purpose of testing Hypothesis 6.

Experimental Results, Discussion

Charts A1.1–A1.3, A2.1–A2.5, and A3.1–A3.4 provide the sequence of bid-quantity choices $b_i(t)$, $X_i(t)$, and the resulting cost shares $q - B_i(t)$ and mean quantity proposals, $\bar{X}$, for all experimental sessions. The numbers corresponding to the last five cost share observations represent trial earnings, $v_i(t)$.

The following modifications were made in the transition rules, the stopping rules, and the outcome rule at various points in the chronological sequence in which these twelve experiments were performed:

(1) In the four experiments A1.1–A1.3, and A2.1, the group average proposal was not computed and made public until subject trial bids had converged nearly to their unit cost shares. In all subsequent experiments, average proposals were posted with the bid sums on every trial.

(2) In experiments A1.3, A2.1–A2.3, and A3.1–3.3 the stopping rule in the written instructions was supplemented by the verbal specification that the experiment would be terminated on trial 15 if by that trial the sum of the bids had not reached to within one dollar of the price, q. This instruction was introduced to discourage subjects from waiting until trial 20 or later to make realistic bids, causing coordination difficulties as trial 30 approached. This coordination difficulty first emerged in A1.2 which failed to reach stopping rule agreement when the bids overshot unit cost on trial 29. On trials 27 and 28 the bids were just one dollar below unit cost. On trial 29 three subjects attempted to make the agreeing bids, making it then impossible to satisfy the stopping rule before trial 30. Although the 15th-trial modification caused the bids to increase more rapidly, it did not solve all coordination problems. Thus, in experiment A2.1 all subjects repeated their bids, one dollar short of unit cost share, on trials 24–29, as each waited for another to increase his bid. Subject 3 at first raised his bid to \$7 on trial 29 then changed it back to \$6 fearful, as he indicated after the experiment, that another member would also raise causing an overshoot.[9] As a consequence of this experience the stopping rule was further modified to allow random choice among two or more subjects who, in attempting to produce agreement, cause an overshoot. But other, probably superior modifications might resolve these coordination difficulties among agreeing members. One possibility is to relax the lumpiness of the requirement that all bids be in whole dollar amounts, and give a bid rebate if the bid total exceeds cost.

(3) In experiments A2.4, A2.5 and A3.4, the outcome rule paid each subject an amount

(a) $v_i(t^*) + \$2$, if group agreement occurred
(b) \$2, otherwise.

Essentially, the purpose of the lump-sum payment, v_0, is to compensate for time and transactions cost which exist whether or not agreement occurs (Smith, 1975). If this sum is paid only as a small "consolation prize," and does not also supplement the Lindahl rents, a disincentive to agreement is provided any subject who finds, near the end of the trial sequence, that his choices have cornered him with a net value $v_i \leq v_0$.

The results of experiments A1.1–A1.3 demonstrate that the auction process possesses properties of incentive compatibility comparable to those in the G-L process for experiments R1.1–R1.3. Experiments A1.1 and A1.3 yielded stopping rule agreement at the LE quantity, 5, while the failure of A1.2 to produce agreement was influenced by coordination problems that can occur under the extremely exacting requirements of the stopping rule. On trials 26–30 in A1.2, subject choices are not in violation of incentive compatibility since the bids overshoot unit cost share on three of these trials. Table 5 compares final trial choices by subjects in the R1 and A1 experiments. The R1 session "prices" are the bids implicit in each subject's incremental proposal, x_i, given S_i computed using the $C_i'(x_i \mid S_i)$ applying to R1. It is clear that equilibrium quantities are as invariable in the Auction process as in the G–L process. The higher equilibrium quantity in the R1 experiments merely reflects the sharp Nash equilibrium and balanced budget at $X^0 = 6$, and is not significant. The Lindahl rents are the same at $X^0 = 5$ or 6 and the Auction process provides no incentive for collectives to choose the larger quantity.[10] In fact at the larger quantities individual earnings are more sensitive to unit cost shares, and it appears significant that (except for A2.5) the experimental groups for $I = 4$ and 5 always agreed on the smallest X that maximizes the total Lindahl rent available.

The more rapid convergence of the R1 experiments may be of significance although the sample is much too small to be sure. The lower dimensionality of the choice space in the G-L process may favor convergence. At this stage

Table 4. Equilibrium Price-Quantity Outcomes, Experiments A2 and A3

	A2 Sessions, Prices						*A3 Session, Prices*				
Subject	$V_i'(7)$	*A2.1*	*A2.2*	*A2.3*	*A2.4*	*A2.5*	$V_i'(7)$	*A3.1*	*A3.2*	*A3.3*	*A3.4*
1	−5	−5	−6	−6	−4	−6	−5	−4		−4	−3
2	13	13	12	14^+	13	14	13	14		13^+	14
3	8	7^+	8	7	7	6	−5	−6	no	−5	−3
4	3	4	5	4	3	5	13	13	agree-	10	14
5							3	1	ment	4	4
6							8	9		5	8
7							3	0		5	2
8							8	11		10	2
Equilibrium	Quantity	6	6	6	6	7		6	7	6	7
Final trial	t*	29	26	29	19	15		28		29	16

$^+$Simulated bid increase by subject chosen at random among those demonstrating willingness to increase.

one can only speculate on the dynamic behavioral differences between the two processes. Hypotheses concerning such detail must be sharply enough fomulated to allow the appropriate testing experiments to be designed.

Selected results of the A2 and A3 experimental sessions are summarized in Table 4. Briefly, the following characteristics of the results of these experiments may be noted:

(1) In most of the A2 and A3 sessions the collective attained a stable equilibrium quantity proposal before the bids and cost shares reached agreement (A2.2, A2.3, A2.4, A3.1, A3.2, A3.3, A3.4). It was easier to agree on the quantity that maximized the total surplus to be divided, than on the cost shares that determine the distribution of that surplus. The Auction process provides motivation for efficiency in the sense of the Lindahl optimal quantity.

(2) Although the A2 collectives largely agree on the smallest quantity that maximizes total surplus, the A3 collectives do not. Perhaps the greater adjustment freedom provided by an increase in the size of the collective from 4 to 8 generates less member resistance to agreeing on the larger quantity.

(3) There appears to be no empirical support for a relationship, positive or negative, between collective size and price convergence speed. All groups, whether $I = 4$ or 8, tend to resist price agreement until somewhere near the trial bound, T.

(4) Experiment A3.2 is the only session failing to reach agreement under the stopping rule in a manner that can be interpreted as consistent with incentive incompatibility. The reasons for the failure to reach agreement are clear from chart A3.2. Subjects 2 and 4 held to bids substantially below their LE prices. Each had an LE price of 13, and their final trial bids were $b_2(29) = 6$ and $b_4(29) = 7$, implying a demand for net earnings $v_2(29) = \$69$ and $v_4(29) = \$62$. Since the maximum total surplus was \$138 these were unrealistic demands although, of course, the subjects had no way of knowing this. It happened in this experiment that the random assignment of member valuations to subjects gave the two largest marginal valuation schedules to the two most intransigent subjects. Together, at the LE, subjects 2 and 4 accounted for a \$26 share of the \$38 unit price of the public good, and there was just not enough slack among the remaining members to permit an accommodation to these choices. However, such an accommodation might have been obtained (although not likely) if the group had converged to the quantity 6 instead of 7, for then the final trial bids would have produced the net values, $v_2(29) = \$62$, $v_4(29) = \$56$ leaving a residual surplus of \$20 for the remaining six subjects.

(5) Comparing the results of the A1 sessions with those of A2 and A3, there is no evidence to suggest that the Auction process is unable to handle

public good decisions which are "bads" for one or more members of the collective.

(6) Experiment A2.1 was the only session using carefully selected experienced subjects. All four subjects had participated previously in one of the A1 (I = 5) collectives, and by their responses had shown quick ability to master the procedures. From Chart A2.1 it is seen that each member's bids converged asymptotically (but \$1 short) to member cost share. Experience seemed to yield a smoother, quicker, play of the game, but did not guarantee equilibrium for the reasons discussed previously.

Experimental Results, Tests of Hypotheses

From Table 5 both the R1 and the A1 sessions produced Lindahl equilibrium quantities (5 or 6). The sample variance of deviations in final prices from the Lindahl optimal prices is $S_A^2 = 6.07$ for the A1 experiments and $S_R^2 = 7.14$ for the R1 experiments. These variances are not significantly different from each other and we are unable to reject the hypothesis that the variability of price outcomes is the same in the Auction and G–L mechanisms.

Hypothesis 5 was tested by estimating the parameters β_0, β in the equation

$$y_{ij} = \beta_0 + \beta x_{ij} + \varepsilon_{ij} \tag{9.1}$$

where y_{ij} is the observed final equilibrium bid of subject j in experiment i, and x_{ij} is the Lindahl optimal price for subject j in experiment i. According to hypothesis 5, $\beta_0 = 0$ and $\beta = 1$, i.e. the mean final equilibrium bids are not significantly different from the theoretical Lindahl prices. Least squares estimates $(\hat{\beta}_0, \hat{\beta})$ were obtained using the method proposed by McGuire, Farley, Lucas and Ring (1968), pp. 1207–1208) when dependent variables

Table 5. Final Trial Price-Quantity Outcomes, G-L and Auction Process Experiments

		R1 Sessions, Prices			*A1 Sessions, Prices*		
Subject	$V_i(X^0)$	*R1.1*	*R1.2*	*R1.3*	*A1.1*	*A1.2*	*A1.3*
1	3	3	3	3	4	6	4
2	3	8	3	8	6	2	4
3	8	8	8	8	10	9	3
4	13	13	13	8	9	13	15
5	18	13	18	18	16	15^+	19
Equilibrium Quantity		6	6	6	5	5	5
Final Trial, t*		16	29	16	30	30	29

$^+$Simulated bid increase by subject chosen at random among those demonstrating willingness to increase.

Table 6

Statistic	$\hat{\beta}_0$	$t(\hat{\beta}_0 - 0)$	$\hat{\beta}$	$t(\hat{\beta} - 1)$	R^2	*Var. Error*
A1 Sessions	1.761	1.635	0.812	− 1.80	0.82	4.458
A2 Sessions	− 0.005	− 0.17	1.001	0.03	0.97	1.200
A3 Sessions	0.246	0.46	0.948	0.78	0.99	4.131

are subject to add-up constraints (in this case, the stopping rule defining equilibrium requires the final bids to add up to the experimentally defined price of the public good). Using observations from the A1, A2 and A3 sessions shown in Tables 4 and 5, the regression results are summarized in Table 6. The low t-values (especially for the A2 and A3 sessions) under the "null hypotheses," $\beta_0 = 0$, $\beta = 1$, are consistent with hypothesis 5. From the R^2 calculations, approximately 90 percent of the variation in equilibrium bids is explained by the controlled Lindahl price variable in each experiment. The F-values for the three regressions are all highly significant ($P < 0.001$).

From Table 6 the variance of error about the regression line is greater for $I = 8$ (A3) than for $I = 4$ (A2). An F-test of this variance ratio is significant at $P < .05$. This supports hypothesis 6 that replication of a public good economy holding the structure of tastes and costs constant, but increasing (doubling) the number of agents will increase the variability of equilibrium bids.

10. ON SUBJECT ADAPTIVE RESPONSE BEHAVIOR

The research in this paper did not propose any a priori hypotheses regarding the dynamic response behavior of subjects over successive experimental trials. With the large number of subject-trial observations contained in the experiments reported, it is tempting to do some a posteriori analysis in an attempt to obtain some characterizations of subject dynamic behavior in the G-L and Auction Mechanism experiments. Such "fishing" in the data are justified only as a means of suggesting plausible hypotheses about subject dynamic behavior that might be tested by further experiments. In what follows some simple models of subject adaptive response behavior are explored using data from R1 and R2 for the G-L mechanism and data from A1, A2 and A3 for the Auction mechanism.

Adaptive Response in the G-L Experiments

The simplest and most obvious model of subject responses in the G-L experiment is that of Cournot adjustment behavior, i.e., each subject is assumed to choose $x_i(t)$ to maximize $v_i[x_i(t)]$ on the assumption that $S_i(t) = S_i(t-1)$. Thus, the subject's response on trial t is his best reply to trial $t-1$. Since there is little reason a priori to expect such a decision rule to yield group equilibrium for any given experimental design, it is instructive to examine the designs in R1 and R2 for Cournot stability. These two designs yield very different Cournot stability properties.

The payoff matrices in the R1 experiments imply very rapid convergence to the Nash equilibrium (Lindahl optimum) under the Cournot adjustment dynamic from any of a large number of "reasonable" initial choices. An examination of the "Net Membership Value" tables 3.1–3.4 in Appendix I suggests that for subjects 1 and 2 a reasonable initial choice is any element of $\langle -1,0,1 \rangle$, while for subjects 3, 4 and 5 any element of $\langle -1,0,1,2 \rangle$ is appealing. Furthermore, if all five subjects choose 0 or 1 initially the Cournot dynamic converges to the Lindahl optimum in one iteration; if the five subjects start at the point (0,1,1,2,2) or (0,1,1,1,3) in the choice space they converge in two iterations.

In contrast, I have not found any similar initial points, using the R2 payoff matrices in Tables 3.1–3.7 (Appendix III), that map into the Nash equilibrium. If one plays out the Cournot dynamic assuming initial choices equal to the actual final choices in R2.1, $(-3,0,-2,2,1,1,2,2)$, and in R2.2, $(-4,3,-1,1,-1,3,0,2)$, in each case the Cournot process diverges to the boundaries of the subject payoff matrices in two iterations.

Consequently, the R1 design appears to be strongly Cournot convergent, while the R2 design appears strongly Cournot divergent. Yet the subject collectives in R2 reached stopping rule equilibrium about as easily as the R1 collectives. Although the R2 collectives missed the Lindahl optimal quantity by one unit, this did not represent a large sacrifice in economic rent. The decision makers in these experiments seem to perform poorly compared with Cournot simple maximizers in experiments strongly Cournot convergent, but superior to Cournot simple maximizers in experiments strongly Cournot divergent! This suggests a form of gestalt, global, or nonmyopic response behavior that permits collectives to reach agreement where none is possible or likely under a Cournot dynamic. In this respect it is interesting to examine the data from the two sets of expriments for Cournot responses. Of the 230 total subject responses in the R1 experiments 123 were Cournot "best reply" choices. Of the 288 subject responses in the R2 experiments only 67 were Cournot choices. This difference is significant at $P < 0.0001$. Our experimental decision makers appear to use the Cournot rule rather frequently when it will work, and to abandon it when it will not work! However, in both the R1 and R2 experiments there was a smaller number of Cournot responses in the first half of the trials ($56\frac{1}{2}$ in R1, 26 in R2), than in the second half ($66\frac{1}{2}$ in R1, 41 in R2).

"Strategy" Evaluation in the G-L Experiments

One can classify subjects according to whether (i) half or more of their incremental proposal choices, $x_i(t)$, for $t < t^*$, were equal to or greater than their final (equilibrium) choice, $x_i(t^*)$, or (ii) half or more of their $x_i(t)$ were equal to or less than their $x_i(t^*)$ choice. If subjects in the first group are called "cooperative," and subjects in the second group are called "competitive," do "competitive" subjects earn a larger fraction of their Lindahl optimal rent than "cooperative" subjects? (No judgmatic significance should be attached to these labels as one might send "cooperative" responses with the intention of underbidding near the end.) Are these fractional earnings more variable for "competitive" subjects than "cooperative" subjects? The answer to both questions is in the negative based on a t-test comparison of the mean earnings fractions ($t = 0.854$), and an F-test comparison of the variance ($F = 0.694$), in the two classifications.

Adaptive Response in the Auction Mechanism

With the exception of A3.2 all the Auction mechanism experiments exhibit strong tendencies to converge to the Lindahl optimal quantity and to bids (cost shares) distributed tightly around means equal to the Lindahl optimal prices. In this section we report the results of an attempt to "explain" or characterize the dynamic adjustment of subject bids in the twelve Auction experiments by means of the linear bid equation,

$$\Delta b_i(t) = \alpha_i[q - B_i(t-1)] + \beta_i \Delta B_i(t-1) + \gamma_i t + \delta_i, \text{ where} \qquad (10.1)$$
$$\Delta b_i(t) = b_i(t) - b_i(t-1), \text{ and } \Delta B_i(t-1) = B_i(t-1) - B_i(t-2).$$

Hence, $\Delta b_i(t)$ is the change in subject i's bid from trial $t-1$ to trial t, $q - B_i(t-1)$ is subject i's cost share on trial $t-1$, and $\Delta B_i(t-1)$ is the change in the sum of all bids by subjects $j \neq i$ from trial $t-2$ to $t-1$. The coefficients α_i and γ_i measue the adaptive response, respectively, of bid changes to cost share, and to the passage of "time", i.e., the using up of maximum allowable trials. If $\alpha_i > 0$ then the greater is cost share the larger the adaptive bid increase, while $\gamma_i < 0$ implies a smaller increase in bids as the trial limit approaches. β_i measures the "strategic" response of bid changes to the aggregate of all other bids. If $\beta_i > 0$ then i will (tit for tat) increase his bid if, on balance, there is an increase in the bids of all others.

Least squares estimates of $\hat{\alpha}_i$, $\hat{\beta}_i$, $\hat{\gamma}_i$ and $\hat{\delta}_i$ were computed for 66 of the 67 subjects participating in the three series of Auction experiments. (For subject 5 in A3.4 all coefficients were zero since for $t > 1$ all his bids were identical.)

The results of these regressions provide minimal encouragement for the

Table 7

Experiment Series	*Number of Regressions (Subjects)*	*Number (Percentage) of Significant (P < 0.05) Coefficients*		
		$\hat{\alpha}_i$	$\hat{\beta}_i$	$\hat{\gamma}_i$
A1	15	1 (7%)	3 (20%)	0 (0%)
A2	20	1 (5%)	0 (0%)	1 (5%)
A3	31	3 (10%)	3 (10%)	1 (3%)
Total	66	5 (8%)	6 (11%)	2 (3%)

prospect of explaining very much of the dynamics of subject behavior. Of the 66 regressions only 12 of the F statistics were significant at $P < 0.05$. (This means that about 18 percent of the regressions were significant at a 5 percent level of confidence.) Table 7 lists the number (percentage) of coefficients, excluding the constants, that were significant ($P < 0.05$) for each of the three series of Auction experiments. Across all experiments 8 percent of $\hat{\alpha}_i$ coefficients were significant, 11 percent of the $\hat{\beta}_i$ and 3 percent of the $\hat{\gamma}_i$. This suggests a weak tendency for the typical subject to relate his bid changes to his cost share, and to make bid changes in response to the bid changes of other subjects. Number of trials has no significant effect on bid response.

In view of these weak quantitative results, Table 8 provides an enumeration of the number of coefficient estimates that were positive or negative. This enables us to test qualitatively whether the positivity of the coefficients is significant. Using the binomial test we reject the hypothesis that α_i is as likely to be positive as negative ($P < 0.0001$) in the population of subjects. Similarly do we reject the equally likely hypothesis for the signs of β_i ($P < 0.02$). But for γ_i we cannot reject this null hypothesis ($P < 0.16$). We

Table 8

Experiment	*Number of Regressions (Subjects)*	*Number of Coefficients with Indicated Signs*					
		$\hat{\alpha}_i$		$\hat{\beta}_i$		$\hat{\gamma}_i$	
		+	−	+	−	+	−
A1	15	13	2	10	5	9	6
A2	20	13	7	13	7	11	9
A3	31	26	5	18	13	16	15
Total	66	52	14	41	25	36	30

conclude that $\alpha_i > 0$, $\beta_i > 0$ for the typical subject, but that the magnitude of our estimate of these coefficients is quite small relative to their sampling variability.

11. OTHER EXPERIMENTS IN PUBLIC GOOD DECISIONS

Three previous papers (Bohm, 1972; Scherr and Babb, 1975; Ferejohn and Noll, 1976) report the results of experiments in public good decisions.

Bohm Experiment

In the Bohm (1972) experiment consumers (who had volunteered to come to a TV studio for a payment of Kr. 50) were randomly assigned to six different groups and asked to state how much they were willing to pay under six different cost-sharing rules, to watch a particular TV program that had not yet been shown to the public. The sixth group made hypothetical choices while for the remaining five the program would be shown if and only if the aggregate of the amounts offered were sufficient to cover the cost. However, this outcome rule was not "real" in the sense that each group was led to believe that there were parallel groups in other rooms whose responses were to be merged with theirs. In this way a group, for example of size 23 (treatment I) would find it credible that with offers of only several Kr. each the program cost (Kr. 500) was covered. Unknown to the subjects, the program was to be shown whatever the amount of the offer.

Among the various experimental groups the amounts each consumer paid were as follows (the mean offer in Kr. appears in parenthesis):

I. The amount stated (Kr. 7.61).

II. A percentage of the amount stated, normalized so that cost is just covered (Kr. 8.84).

III. Either the amount stated, a percentage of this amount, Kr. 5, or nothing to be determined by a lottery (Kr. 7.29).

IV. Kr. 5 (Kr. 7.73).

V. Nothing. The costs would be paid by the broadcasting company i.e. out of general taxes (Kr. 8.78).

VI. Nothing. The response was hypothetical (Kr. 10.19).

According to Bohm's analysis only treatment VI led to offers which differed to any (classically) significant degree from the others. Several interpretations and observations seem relevant to this experiment:

1. Treatment I corresponds to the Auction Mechanism applied to an indivisible public good. The theory discussed in section 9 suggests that there are strong incentives for revealing demand under this mechanism and from our experiments we have evidence that in the context of an iterative process

this mechanism produces incentive compatible outcomes. Consequently, Bohm's treatment I should not be expected to yield strong free-rider tendencies unless this is a peculiarity of single trial responses. The theory that has maintained that free-riding will occur in this context has not taken account of the opportunity losses incurred by failure to cover cost.

2. Irrespective of these considerations, if treatment I is regarded as the "free-rider" control experiment against which comparisons are made then the effect of each of the treatments II, IV, V and VI is to raise the average offer, in what might be considered the expected direction. That is, subjects might be expected to offer more in II than in I in the expectation that their share of cost in II is unlikely to exceed that in I. Similarly, IV provides a modest fixed imputation of the cost regardless of one's offer, and similarly for V and VI. If the pre-experimental hypothesis had been that these were the directions in which the treatment outcomes would diverge, then irrespective of the significance tests by classical standards, one would have to conclude that the experimental results increased to some degree the credibility of the hypothesis.

3. The lower offers elicited under treatment III are not in accordance with expectations based upon the above arguments. However, treatment III is by far the most complex or ambiguous, psychologically. The lower average offer in III is consistent with the "ambiguity hypothesis" which would assert that where outcomes are defined by psychologically "rich" (complicated, mysterious, uncertain) processes, subjects are more conservative, or cautious, in their responses. This phenomenon is suggested in a somewhat different context (Ellsberg, 1961; Sherman, 1974) but may have application in the Bohm experiment.

4. The seemingly "high" offers by customer groups across all treatments is consistent with the following "mixed motive" hypothesis: It appears reasonable from the instructions to assume that, since the investigation by the "Research Department" was aimed "... at finding out what viewers think about various TV programs" (Bohn, 1972, p. 127), the subjects may have felt some responsibility for seeing to it that the program was shown, particularly since it was made by the two best-known humorists in Sweden. Consequently, the showing may have been perceived as having private and perhaps broader public values than the immediate utility from the viewing at the TV studio.

5. Each subject was asked for a single response. Although the subjects "accepted the question as ... posed and [most] ... gave their responses in a matter of a minute or less" (p. 126), the result is not likely to be the same as would obtain if the subjects arrived at a final decision through a process involving many response-outcome iterations. There are many examples of treatment variables, such as price contracting rules in a market (Smith, 1964; Plott and Smith, 1975) in which the effects of the treatment variable

are not felt in the first (or first sequence of) observations, but only in the character of the entire path, or in the final observations.

All the above interpretations, or alternative hypotheses, are conjectures suggested in part by the data of the Bohm experiment or by experience in entirely different experiments. They are not in any scientific sense confirmed by that data. But a source of power in this methodology is the fact that new experiments can always be run to test hypotheses suggested, in part, by previous experiments (Smith, 1975). It is in this spirit that the above comments may be relevant.

Scherr-Babb Experiment

The Scherr-Babb (1975) laboratory experiment was designed to have subjects in collectives of size two (each subject was led to believe that he was paired with one other) reveal demands under the Clarke, Loehman-Whinston (total cost shared equally among agents) and a voluntary contribution plan. Each subject received $10.00 for his participation, and could contribute up to $.50 to each of 14 pricing situations involving an allegedly real Library Fund and a Concert Fund. None of the three pricing methods elicited responses significantly different from the others.

1. As in the Bohm experiment, the single response character of the decisions does not permit reconsideration on the basis of iterative experience although the fact that there were 14 decision situations would have permitted learning to affect decisions later in the sequence. However, the randomization of sequences meant that such effects were averaged across observations so as to not produce systematic bias.

2. The "mixed motive" problem may be particularly severe in this experiment. The highest demands were revealed under the voluntary system. To the extent that subjects perceived fund contribution as having private (altruistic) value, the voluntary system might appear to be the simplest, least mysterious, method of making "donations." Indeed, the use of the word "donations" in the instructions may have suggested a certain congruence between the purpose of the exercise and the voluntary system.

3. The pairing of subjects into two-element collectives may have elicited behavior special to that case. It is well-known in noncooperative oligopoly experiments (Fouraker and Siegel, 1963; Shubik, 1975) that the step from two to three or more is considerable. All the cited experiments, and those reported in this paper, involved larger collectives.

The PBS Station Program Cooperative

In 1974 the Public Broadcasting Service began a three-year experiment to develop a decentralized process for the selection of programs to be broadcast over the noncommercial television network. Some results of the first two seasons of experience with this Station Program Cooperative (SPC) have been reported by Ferejohn and Noll (1976). Approximately 150 participating stations made actual selections from 93 programs in the first experiment, and 136 in the second. The process consisted of 12 iterations (with each station manager communicating through his teletypewriter) and converged rapidly (in seven iterations) to 25 produced programs the first year and (in ten iterations) to 38 produced programs the second year. The cost of program j for station i on trial t was

$$C_j\left[\frac{0.8b_{ij}(t)}{B_j(t)}+\frac{0.2n_{ij}(t)}{N_j(t)}\right]$$

where C_j was the producer's cost of program j, b_{ij} is the budget and n_{ij} the population served for any station i selecting program j, and B_j is the aggregate budget and N_j the aggregate population served for all stations selecting program j.

This cost-sharing rule has the essential features of the Auction Mechanism, i.e., (1) each manager risks forfeiting his private net benefit if he fails to "vote for" a program, and (2) he has veto power over the cost allocated to him by the choices of all other stations. However, it has the undesirable characteristic that stations can only accept or reject a program at a bid determined mechanically by the above formula. A station willing to pay some amount for a particular program but less than the formula allocation must perforce decline to select the program, while a station willing to pay more than its formula allocation has no way of signaling this intensity by increasing its bid. It is conjectured that one way to correct these "flaws" is to let each station manager bid whatever he desires on any program irrespective of budget and viewing population, but with the understanding that if equilibrium is not reached by round T his (along with every other) station will not receive the program. This Auction system is incentive compatible is simple and easy to understand, and there is empirical evidence in laboratory settings that it yields bids distributed with means equal to the Lindahl optimum. It would seem that a PBS Auction Mechanism experiment might "work" for essentially the same reasons that the present SPC system is working but with increased flexibility. But the fact that the Ferejohn-Noll-PBS experiment is working to produce decisions in a large collective is an exciting and path-breaking development. Alleged or conjectured improvements in a system, which the station managers themselves find attractive, must be thoroughly tested under suitable controls, bearing in mind that it is a long way from an idea to an operating institution.

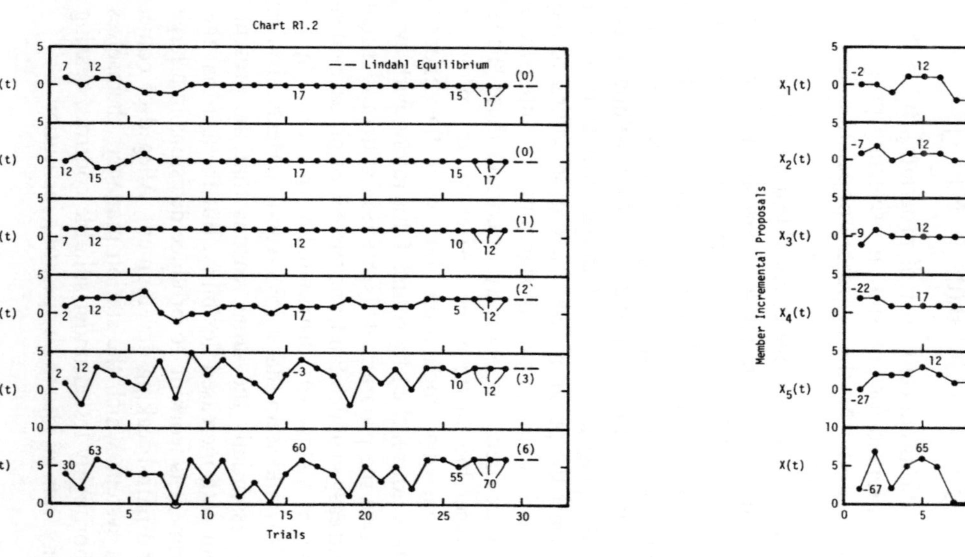
Chart R1.2
— — Lindahl Equilibrium
Member Incremental Proposals
$X_1(t)$
$X_2(t)$
$X_3(t)$
$X_4(t)$
$X_5(t)$
X(t)
Trials
Chart R1.1
— — Lindahl Equilibrium
Member Incremental Proposals
$X_1(t)$
$X_2(t)$
$X_3(t)$
$X_4(t)$
$X_5(t)$
X(t)
Trials

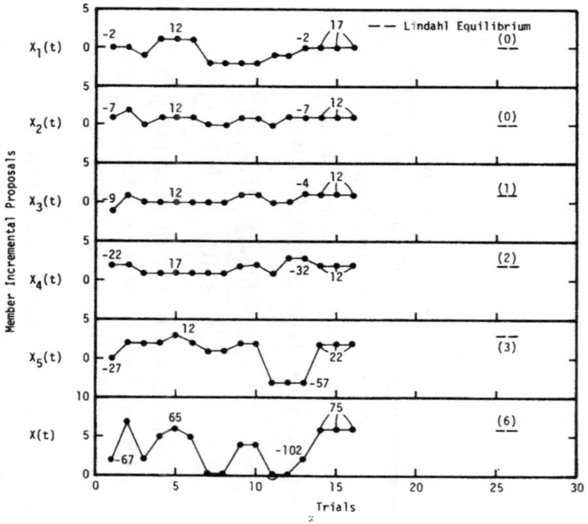

Chart R1.3

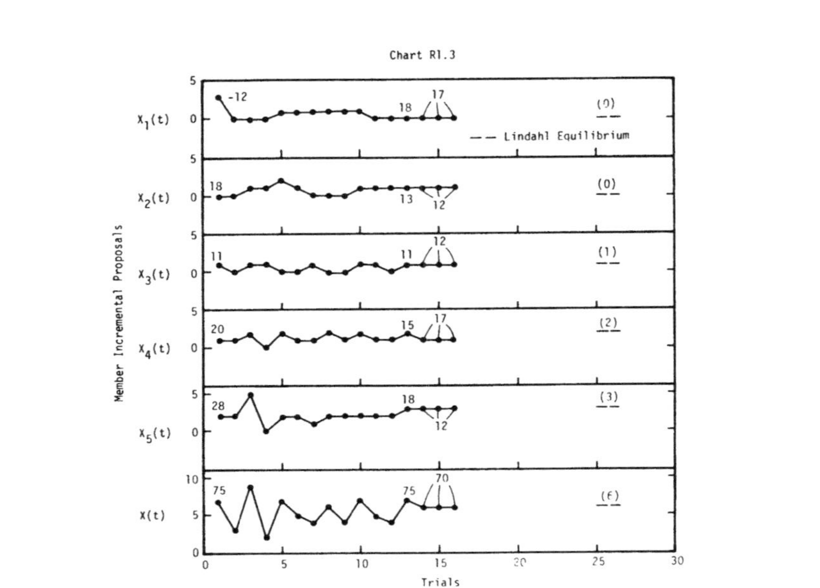

Member Incremental Proposals
$X_1(t)$
$X_2(t)$
$X_3(t)$
$X_4(t)$
$X_5(t)$
$X(t)$
-- Lindahl Equilibrium
Trials

Chart C.1

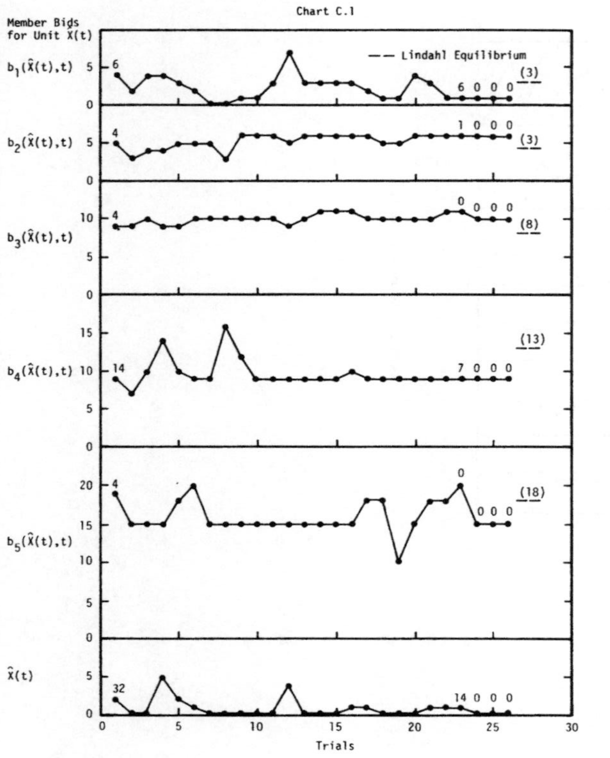

Chart C.2

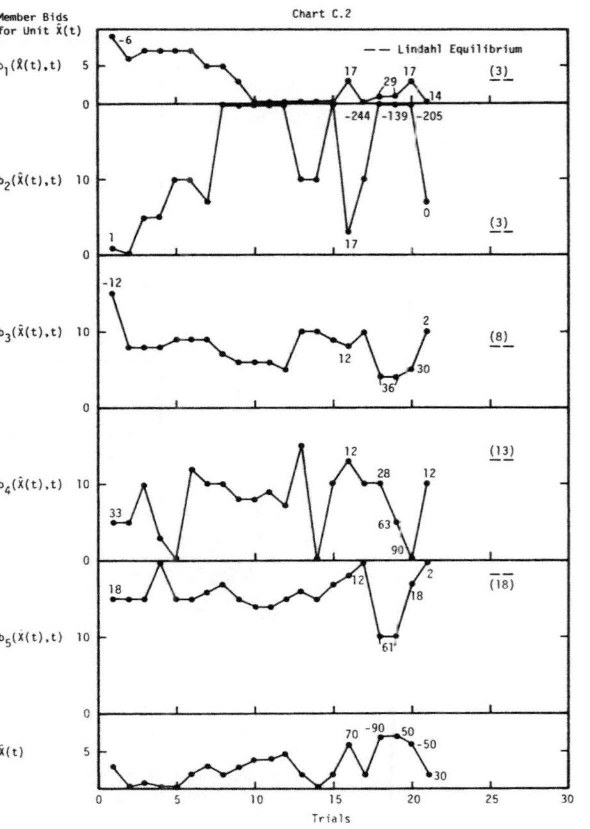

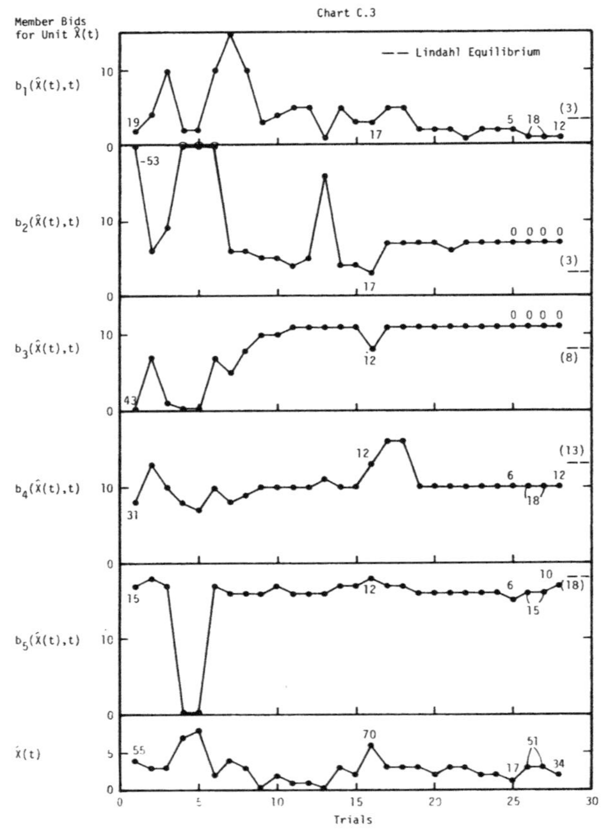

Chart C.3
Member Bids for Unit $\hat{X}(t)$
— — Lindahl Equilibrium
$b_1(\hat{X}(t),t)$
$b_2(\hat{X}(t),t)$
$b_3(\hat{X}(t),t)$
$b_4(\hat{X}(t),t)$
$b_5(\hat{X}(t),t)$
$\hat{X}(t)$
(3)
(3)
(8)
(13)
(18)
Trials

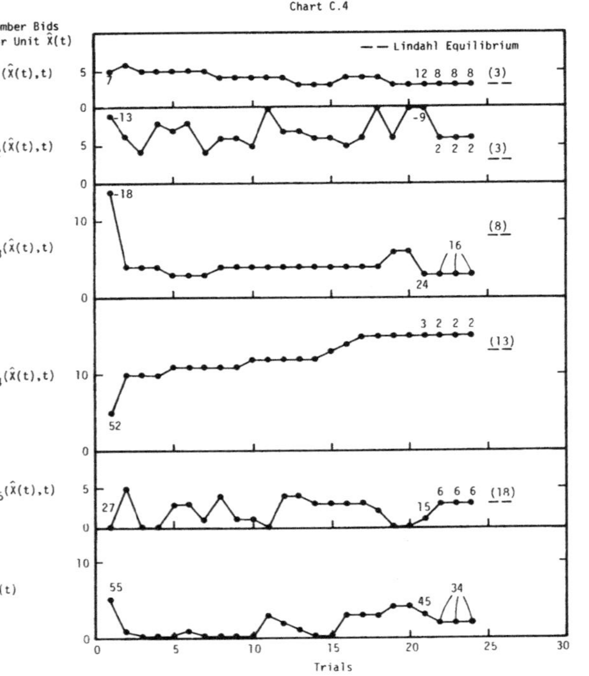

Chart C.4
Member Bids for Unit $\hat{X}(t)$
— — Lindahl Equilibrium
$b_1(\hat{X}(t),t)$
$b_2(\hat{X}(t),t)$
$b_3(\hat{X}(t),t)$
$b_4(\hat{X}(t),t)$
$b_5(\hat{X}(t),t)$
$\hat{X}(t)$
(3)
(3)
(8)
(13)
(18)
Trials

Chart R2.1

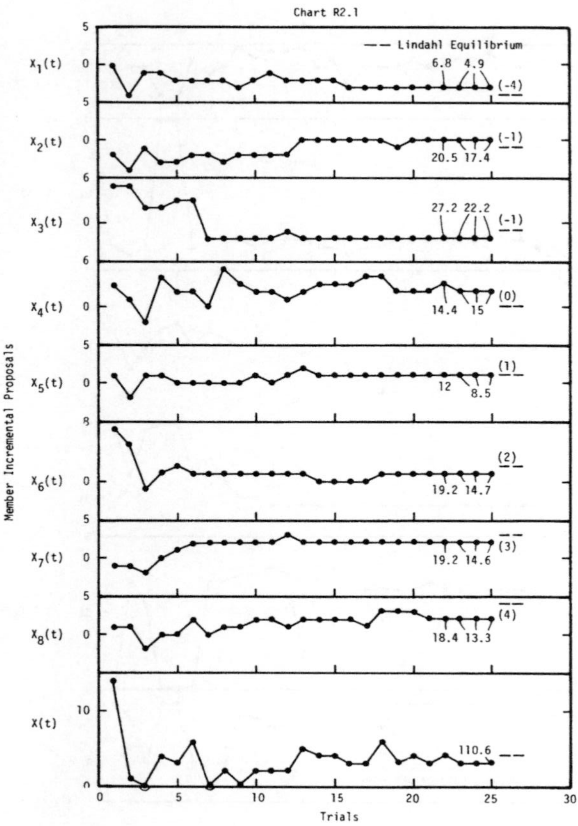

Chart R2.2

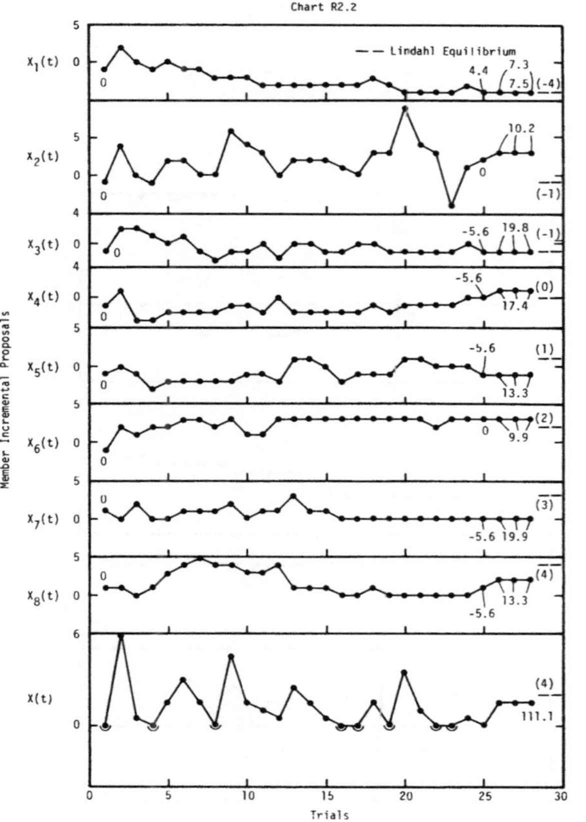

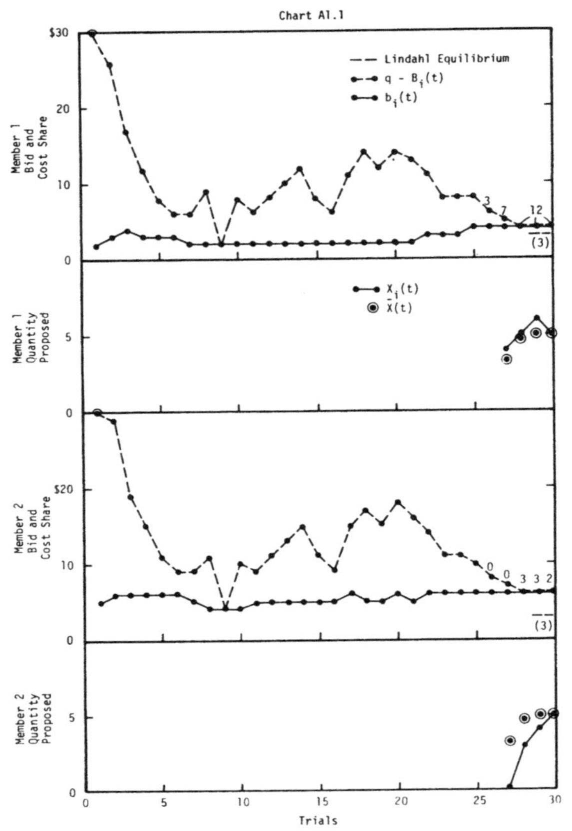
Chart A1.1
Lindahl Equilibrium
q - B_i(t)
b_i(t)
X_i(t)
X̄(t)
Member 1 Bid and Cost Share
Member 1 Quantity Proposed
Member 2 Bid and Cost Share
Member 2 Quantity Proposed
Trials

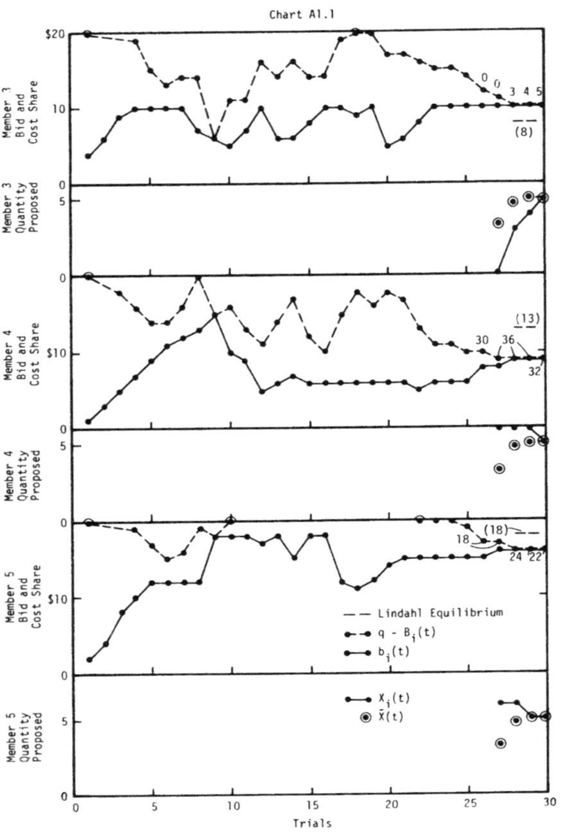
Chart A1.1
Member 3 Bid and Cost Share
Member 3 Quantity Proposed
Member 4 Bid and Cost Share
Member 4 Quantity Proposed
Member 5 Bid and Cost Share
Member 5 Quantity Proposed
Lindahl Equilibrium
q - B_i(t)
b_i(t)
X_i(t)
X̄(t)
Trials

Chart A1.2

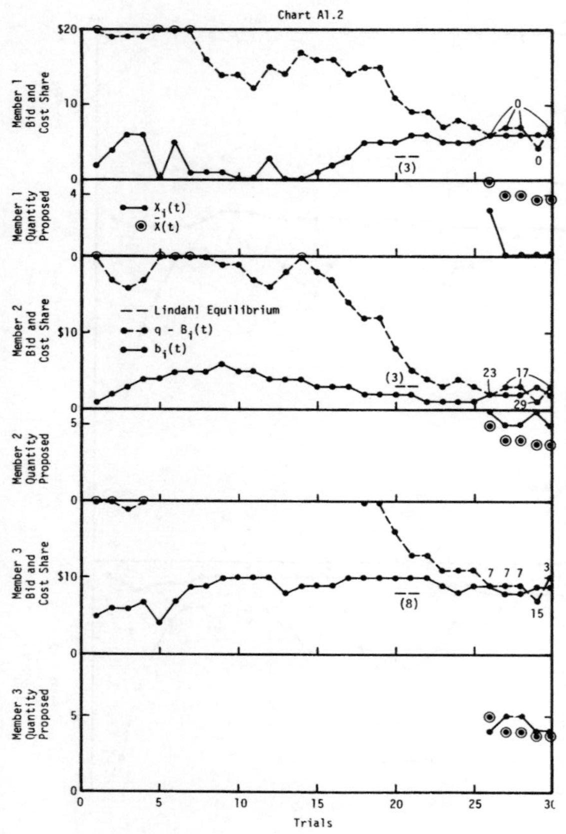

Chart A1.2

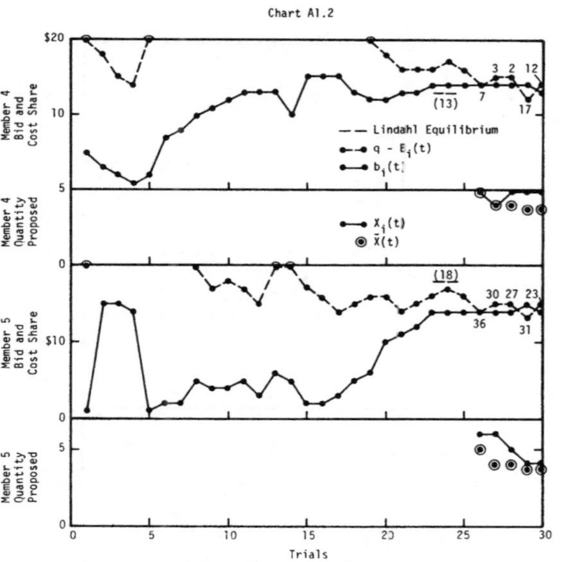

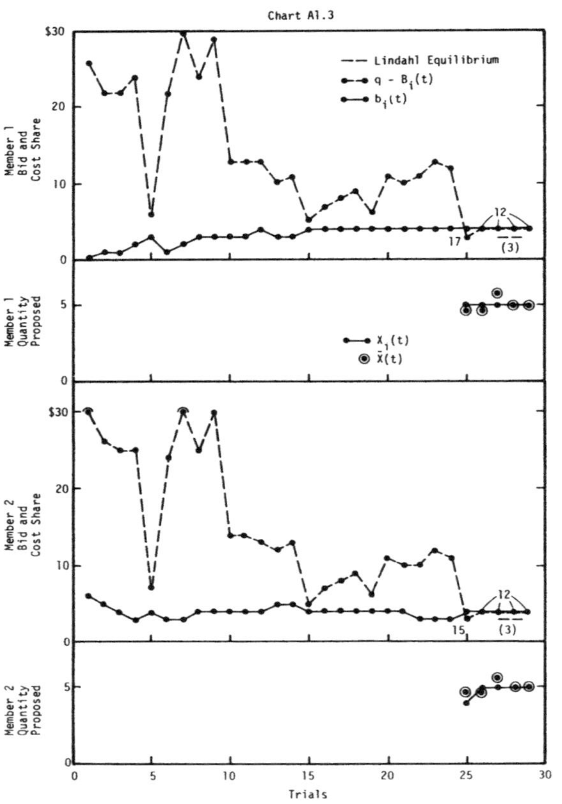
Chart A1.3
Lindahl Equilibrium
q - B_i(t)
b_i(t)
Member 1 Bid and Cost Share
Member 1 Quantity Proposed
X_1(t)
X̄(t)
Member 2 Bid and Cost Share
Member 2 Quantity Proposed
17
12
(3)
15
12
(3)
Trials

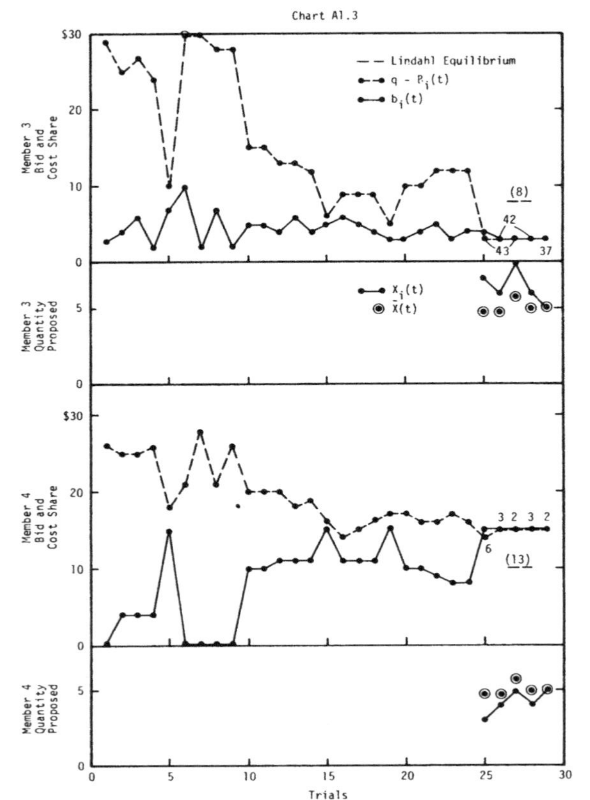
Chart A1.3
Lindahl Equilibrium
q - B_i(t)
b_i(t)
Member 3 Bid and Cost Share
Member 3 Quantity Proposed
X_i(t)
X̄(t)
Member 4 Bid and Cost Share
Member 4 Quantity Proposed
(8)
42
43
37
3 2 3 2
6
(13)
Trials

Chart A1.3

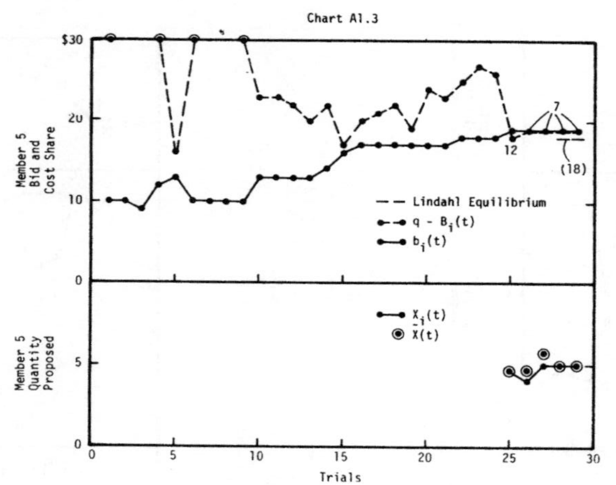

Member 5
Bid and
Cost Share
Member 5
Quantity
Proposed
$30
20
10
0
5
0
0
5
10
15
20
25
30
Trials
Lindahl Equilibrium
$q - B_i(t)$
$b_i(t)$
$X_i(t)$
$\bar{X}(t)$
12
7
(18)

Chart A2.1

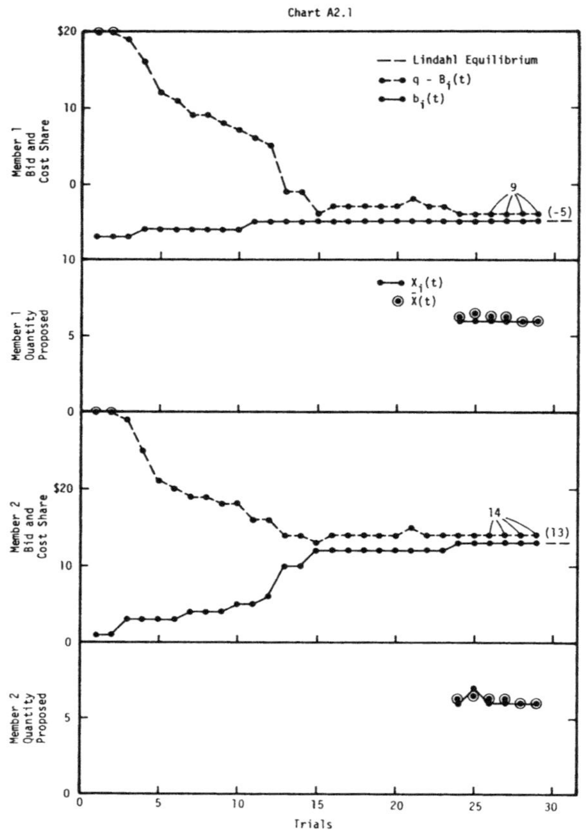

Chart A2.1

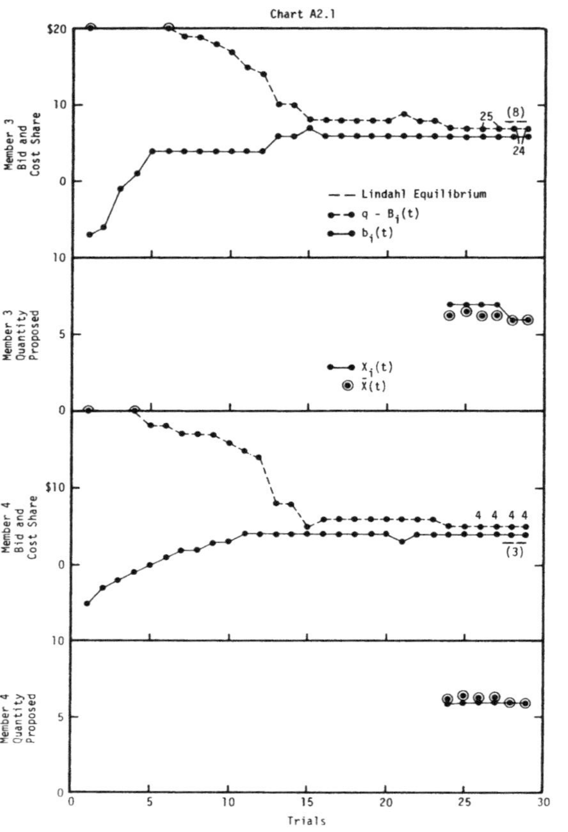

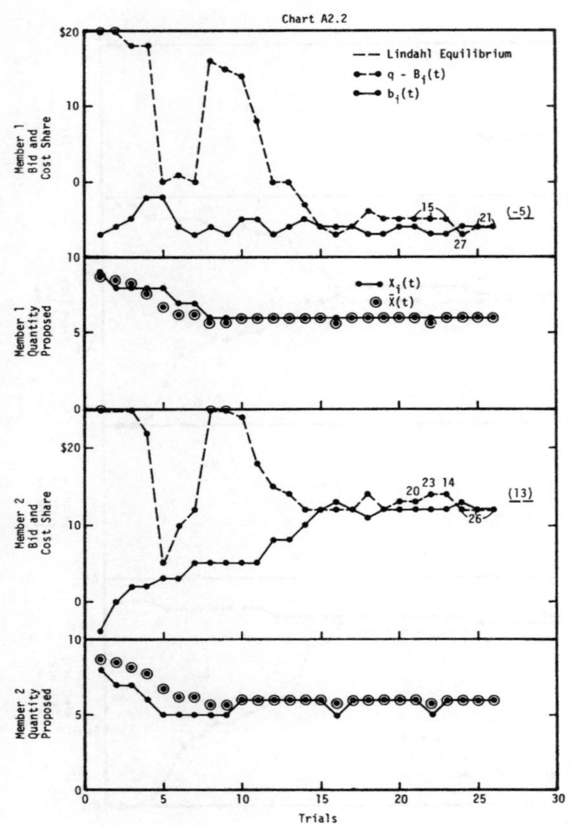
Chart A2.2
Lindahl Equilibrium
q - $B_i(t)$
$b_i(t)$
$X_i(t)$
$\bar{X}(t)$
Member 1 Bid and Cost Share
Member 1 Quantity Proposed
Member 2 Bid and Cost Share
Member 2 Quantity Proposed
$20
10
0
10
5
0
$20
10
0
10
5
0
15
21
27
(-5)
20
23
14
26
(13)
0
5
10
15
20
25
30
Trials

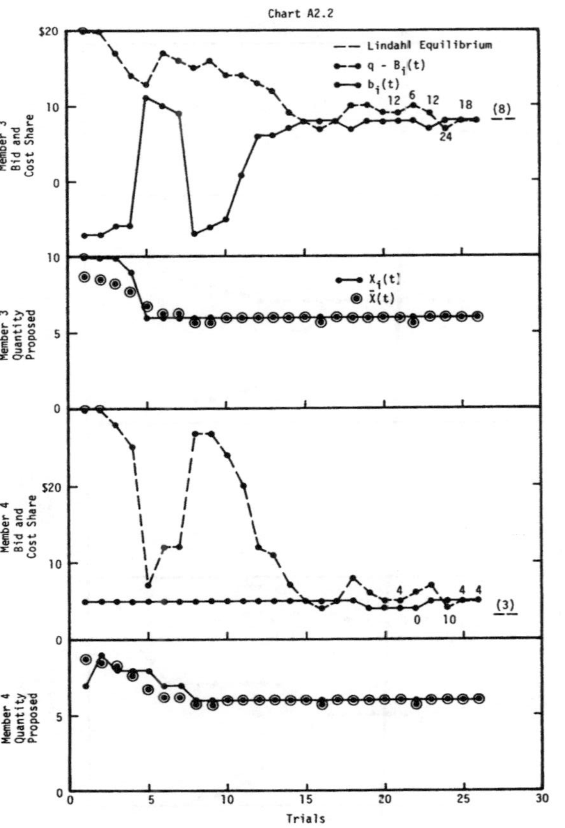
Chart A2.2
Lindahl Equilibrium
q - $B_i(t)$
$b_i(t)$
$X_i(t)$
$\bar{X}(t)$
Member 3 Bid and Cost Share
Member 3 Quantity Proposed
Member 4 Bid and Cost Share
Member 4 Quantity Proposed
$20
10
0
10
5
0
$20
10
0
5
0
12
6
12
18
24
(8)
4
4
4
0
10
(3)
0
5
10
15
20
25
30
Trials

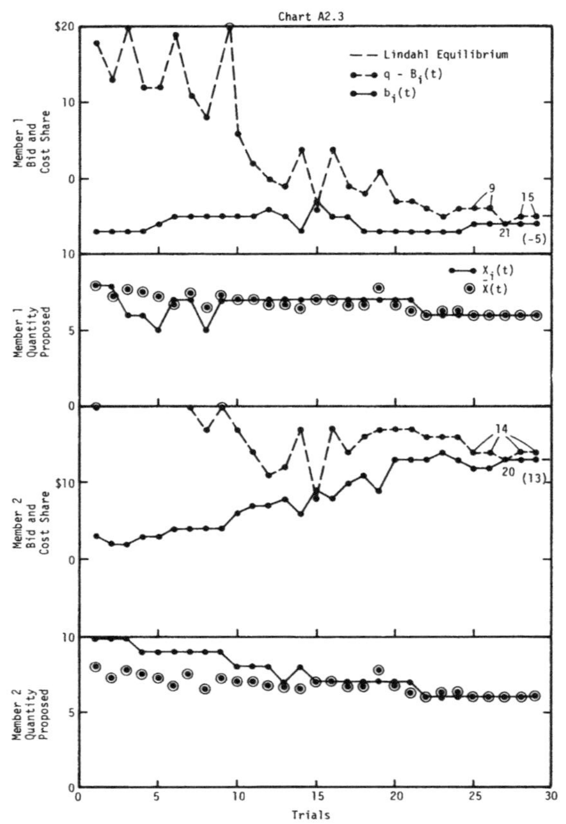
Chart A2.3
Lindahl Equilibrium
q - B_i(t)
b_i(t)
X_i(t)
X̄(t)
Member 1 Bid and Cost Share
Member 1 Quantity Proposed
Member 2 Bid and Cost Share
Member 2 Quantity Proposed
$20
$10
9
15
21
(-5)
14
20
(13)
Trials

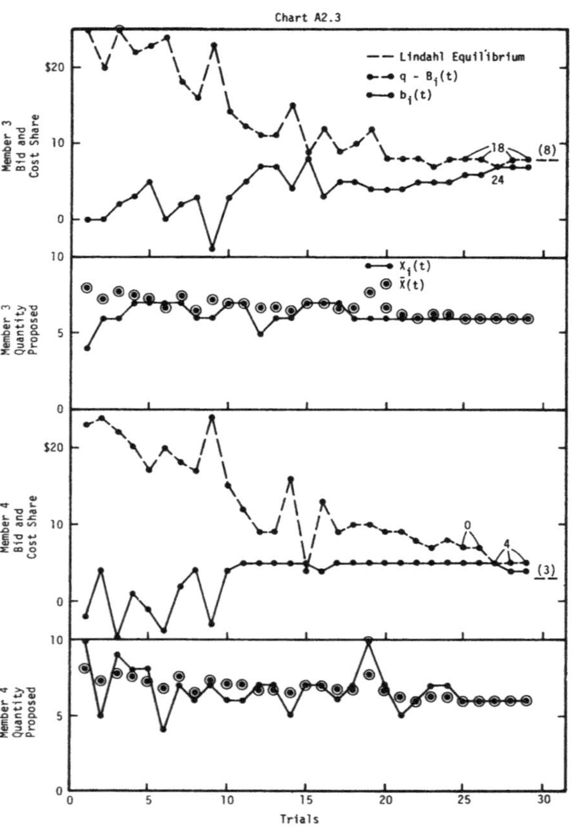
Chart A2.3
Lindahl Equilibrium
q - B_i(t)
b_i(t)
X_i(t)
X̄(t)
Member 3 Bid and Cost Share
Member 3 Quantity Proposed
Member 4 Bid and Cost Share
Member 4 Quantity Proposed
$20
18
24
(8)
0
4
(3)
Trials

Chart A2.4

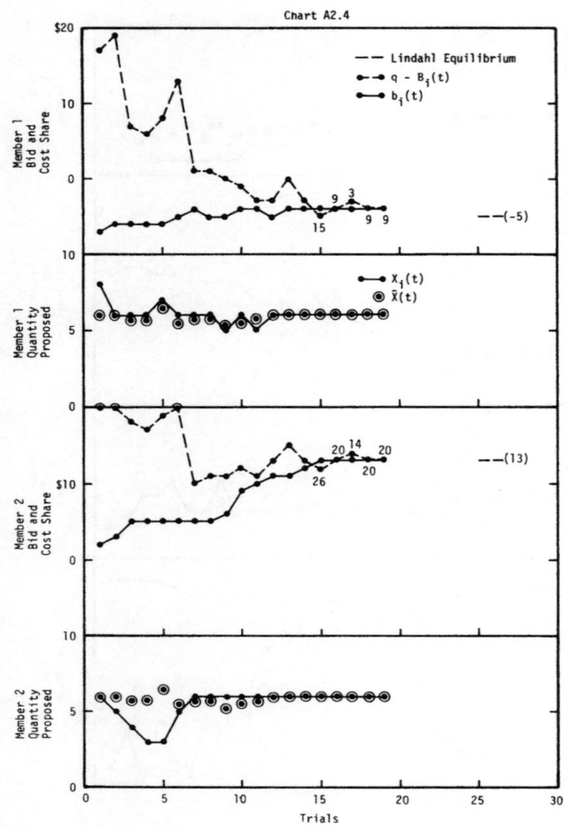

Chart A2.4

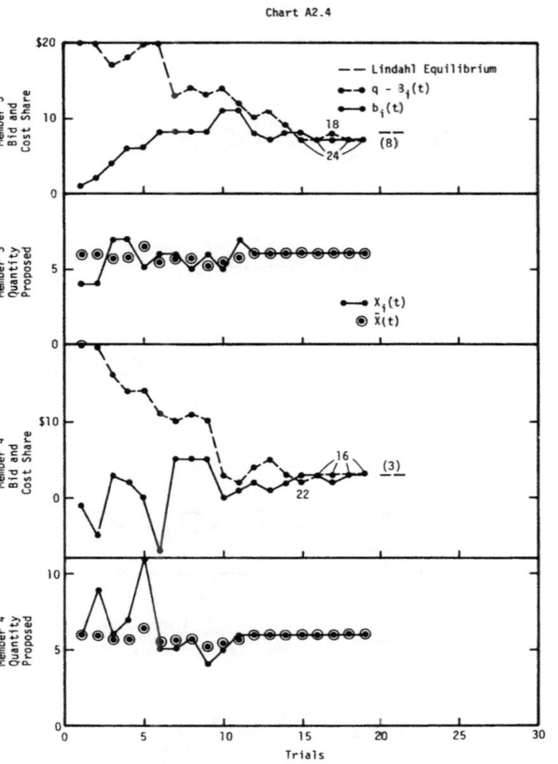

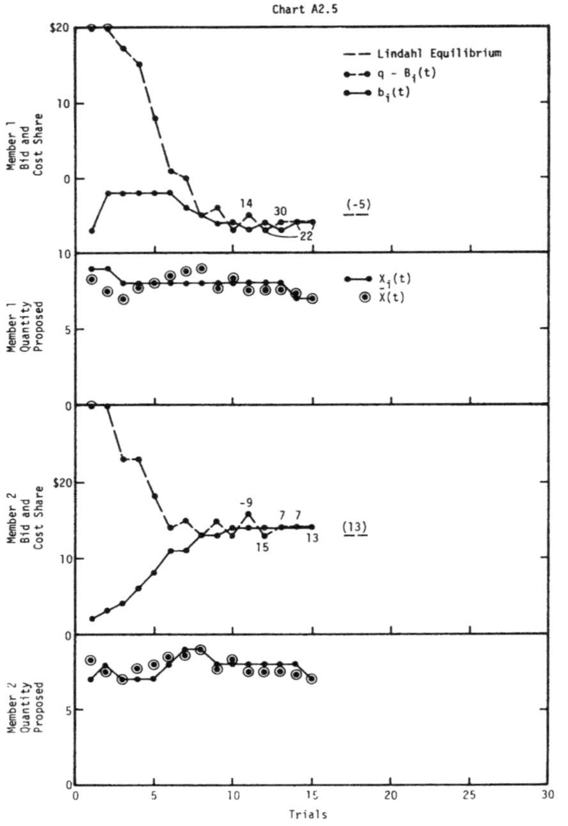
Chart A2.5
Lindahl Equilibrium
q - $B_i(t)$
$b_i(t)$
$X_i(t)$
$\bar{X}(t)$
(-5)
(13)
Member 1 Bid and Cost Share
Member 1 Quantity Proposed
Member 2 Bid and Cost Share
Member 2 Quantity Proposed
Trials

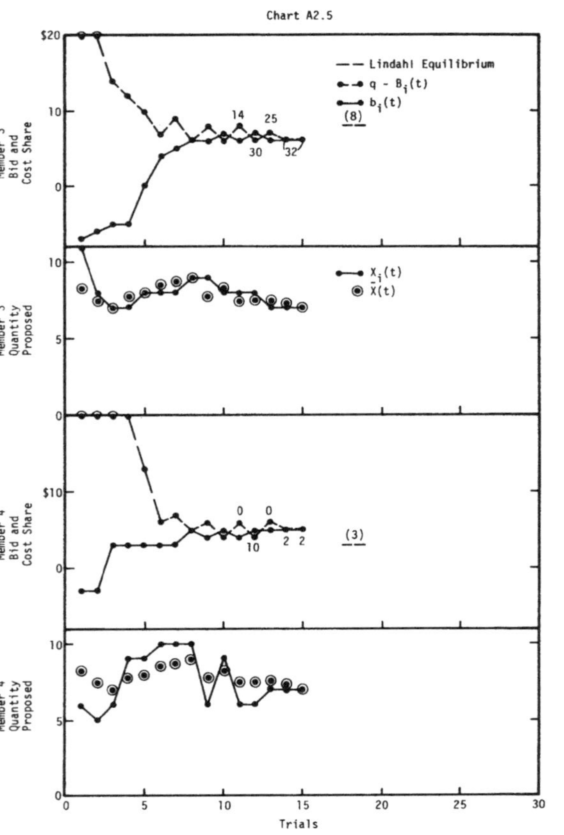
Chart A2.5
Lindahl Equilibrium
q - $B_i(t)$
$b_i(t)$
$X_i(t)$
$\bar{X}(t)$
(8)
(3)
Member 3 Bid and Cost Share
Member 3 Quantity Proposed
Member 4 Bid and Cost Share
Member 4 Quantity Proposed
Trials

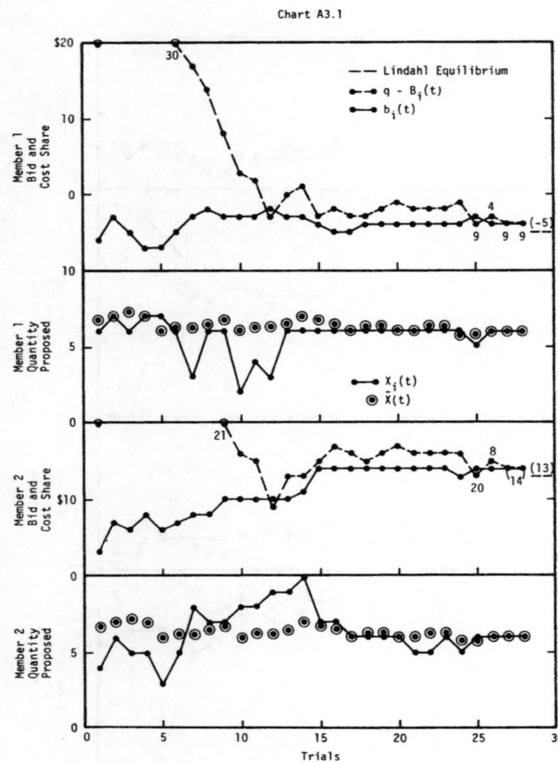
Chart A3.1
Lindahl Equilibrium
q - $B_i(t)$
$b_i(t)$
$X_i(t)$
$\bar{X}(t)$
Member 1 Bid and Cost Share
Member 1 Quantity Proposed
Member 2 Bid and Cost Share
Member 2 Quantity Proposed
$20
10
0
10
5
0
$10
0
5
0
30
4
9
9
9
(-5)
21
8
20
14
(13)
0
5
10
15
20
25
30
Trials

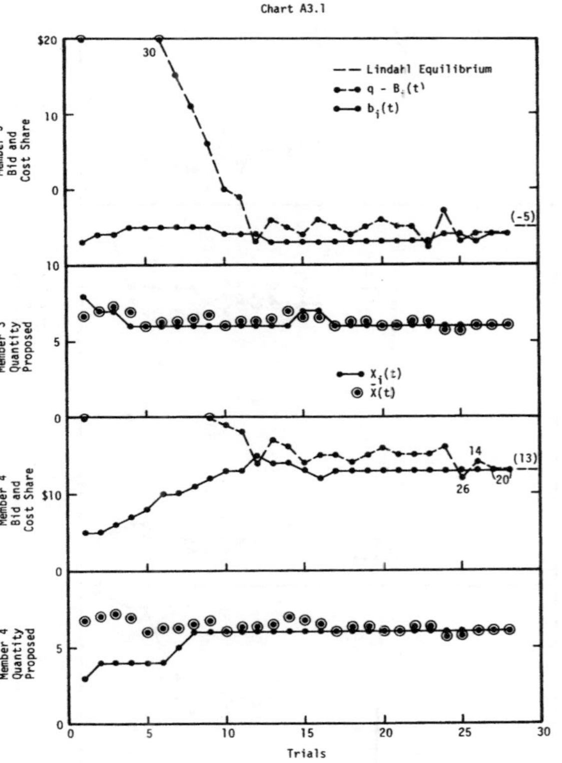
Chart A3.1
Lindahl Equilibrium
q - $B_i(t)$
$b_i(t)$
$X_i(t)$
$\bar{X}(t)$
Member 3 Bid and Cost Share
Member 3 Quantity Proposed
Member 4 Bid and Cost Share
Member 4 Quantity Proposed
$20
10
0
10
5
0
$10
0
5
0
30
(-5)
14
26
20
(13)
0
5
10
15
20
25
30
Trials

Chart A3.1

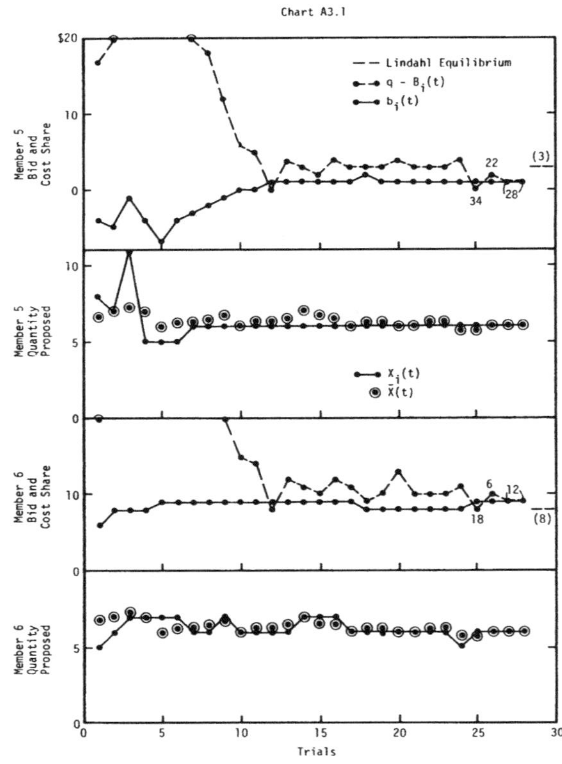

Chart A3.1

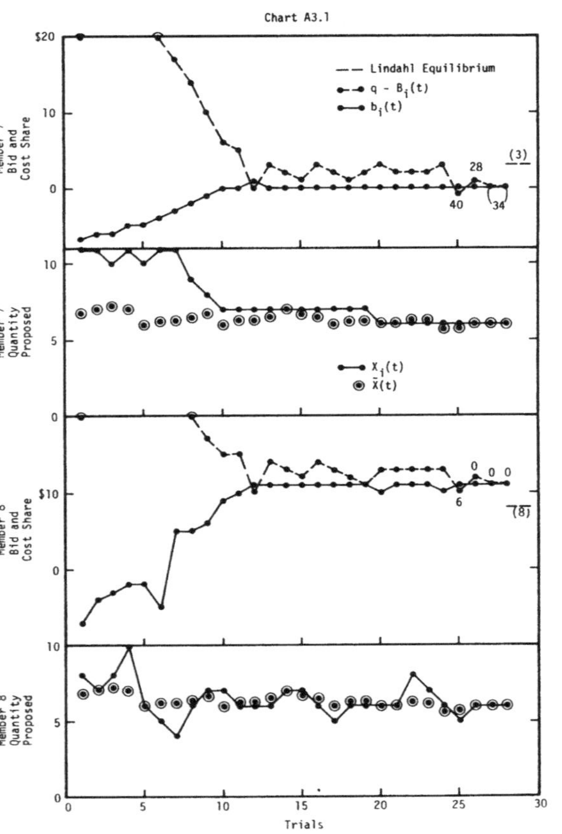

Chart A3.2

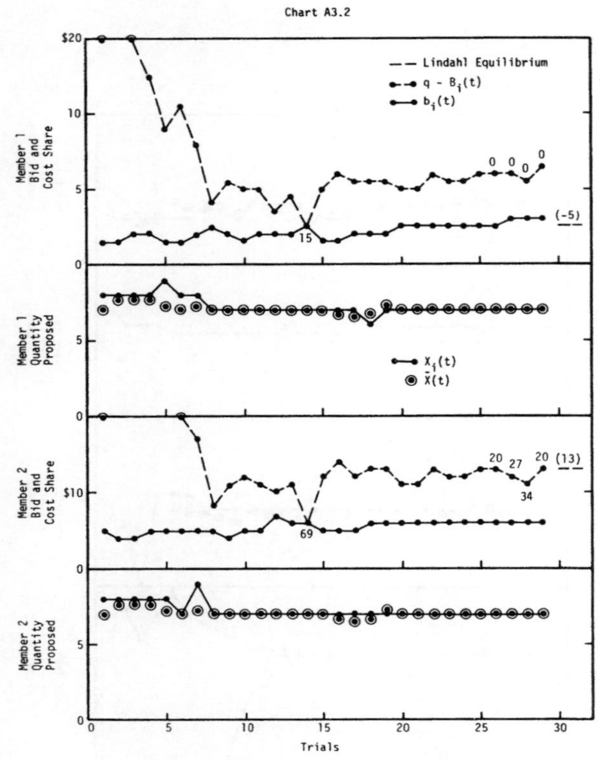

Chart A3.2

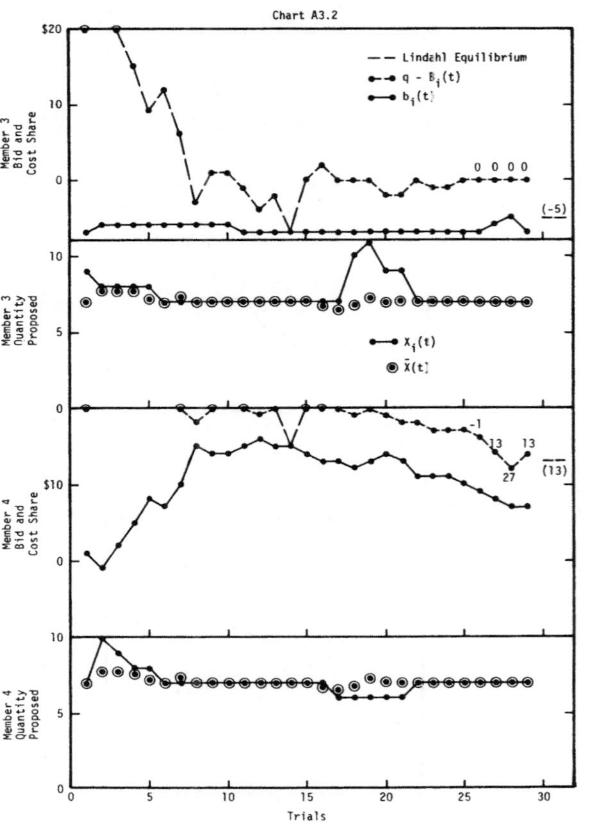

Chart A3.2

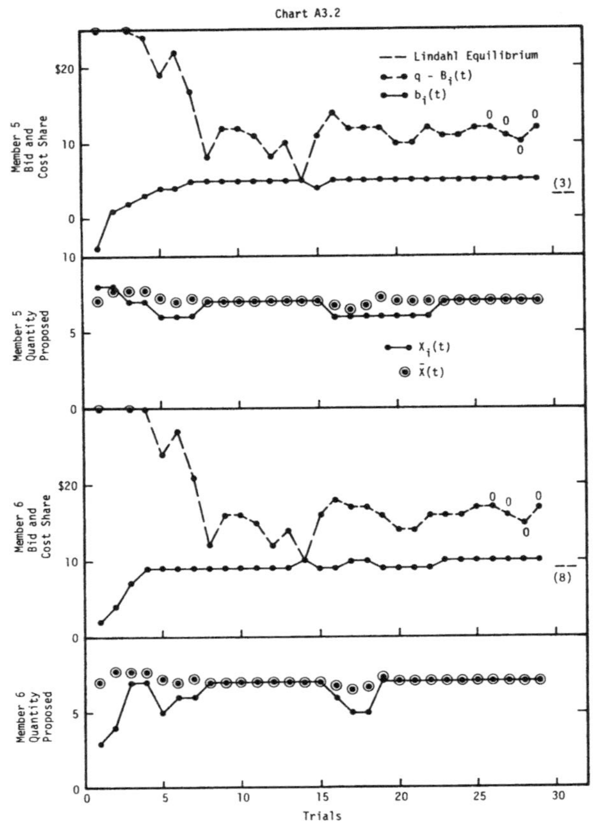

Chart A3.2

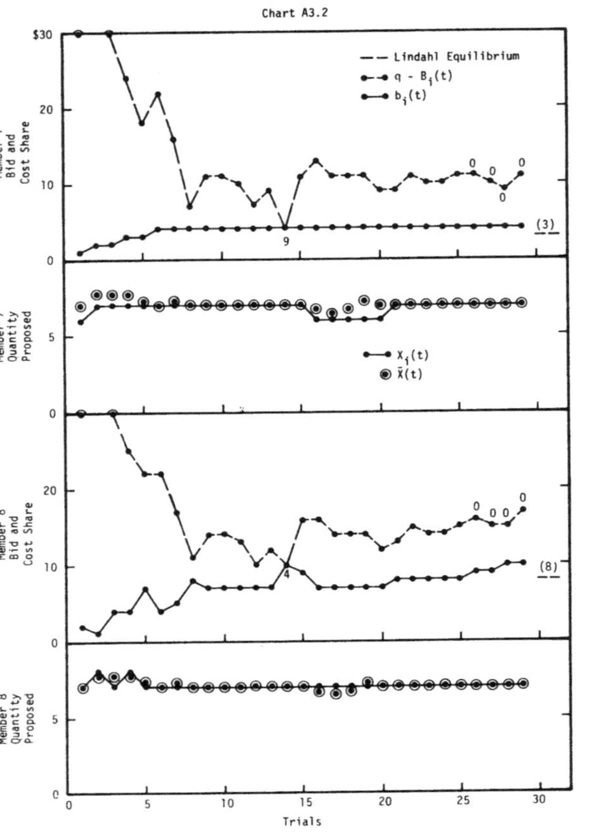

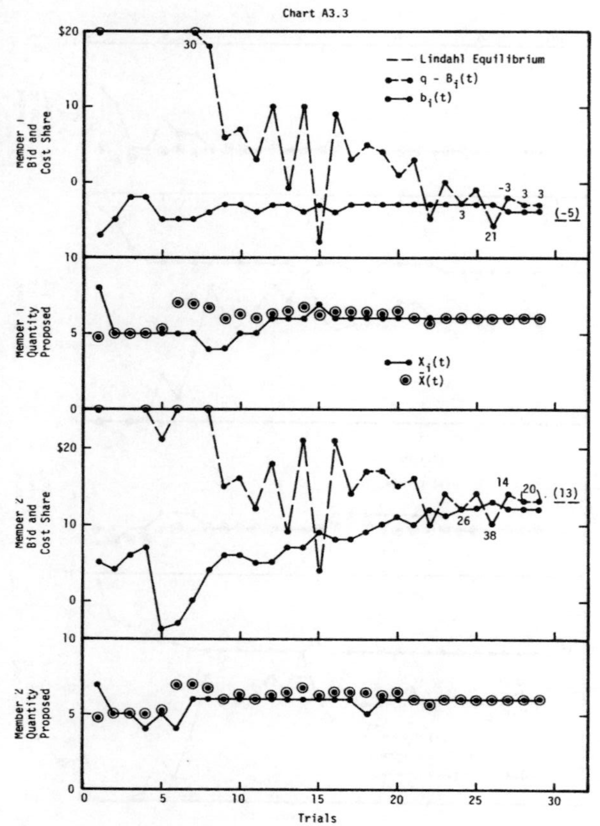
Chart A3.3
Lindahl Equilibrium
$q - B_i(t)$
$b_i(t)$
$X_i(t)$
$\bar{X}(t)$
Member 1 Bid and Cost Share
Member 1 Quantity Proposed
Member 2 Bid and Cost Share
Member 2 Quantity Proposed
$20
10
0
5
30
-3
3
3
3
21
(-5)
14
20
(13)
26
38
Trials
15
25

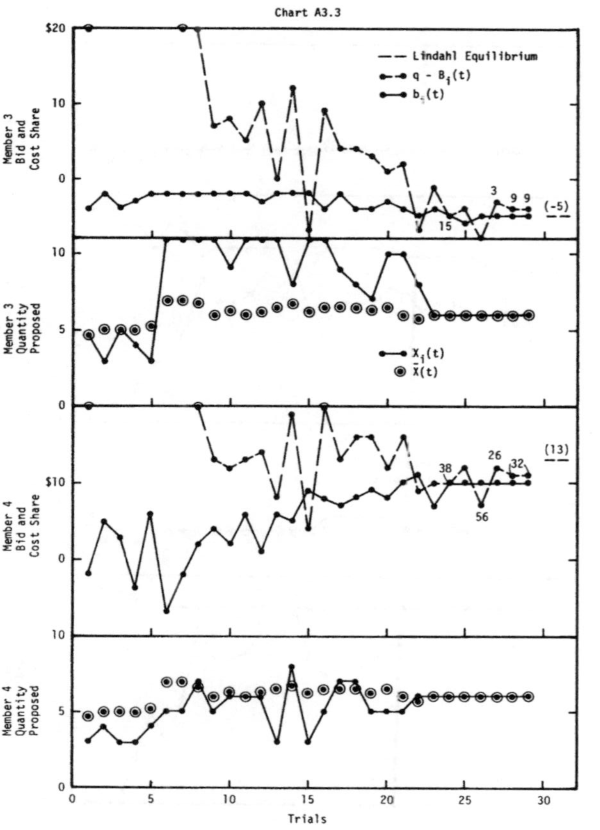
Chart A3.3
Lindahl Equilibrium
$q - B_i(t)$
$b_i(t)$
$X_i(t)$
$\bar{X}(t)$
Member 3 Bid and Cost Share
Member 3 Quantity Proposed
Member 4 Bid and Cost Share
Member 4 Quantity Proposed
$20
$10
10
0
5
3
9
9
15
(-5)
38
26
32
56
(13)
Trials
20
25
30

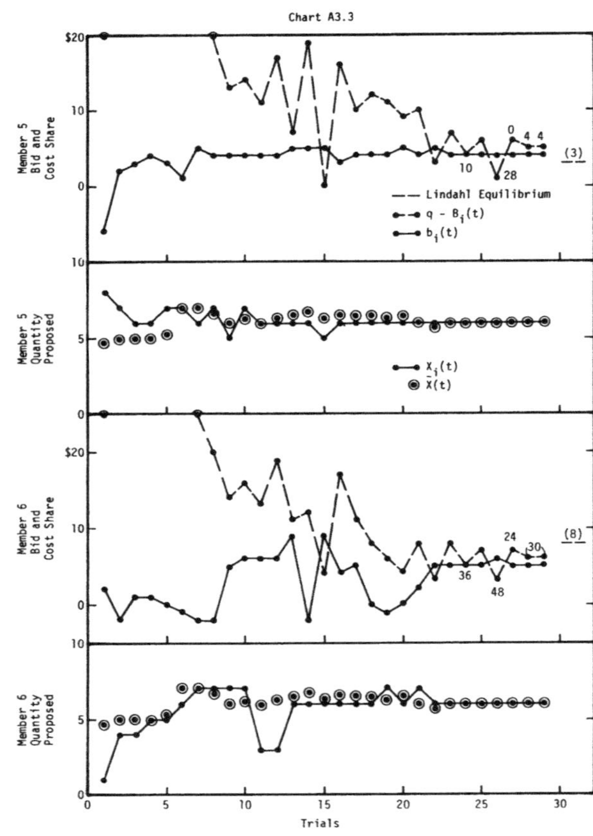
Chart A3.3
Member 5 Bid and Cost Share
$20
10
0
Lindahl Equilibrium
q - $B_i(t)$
$b_i(t)$
0 4 4
10
28
(3)
Member 5 Quantity Proposed
10
5
0
$X_i(t)$
$\bar{X}(t)$
Member 6 Bid and Cost Share
$20
10
0
24
30
36
48
(8)
Member 6 Quantity Proposed
10
5
0
0 5 10 15 20 25 30
Trials

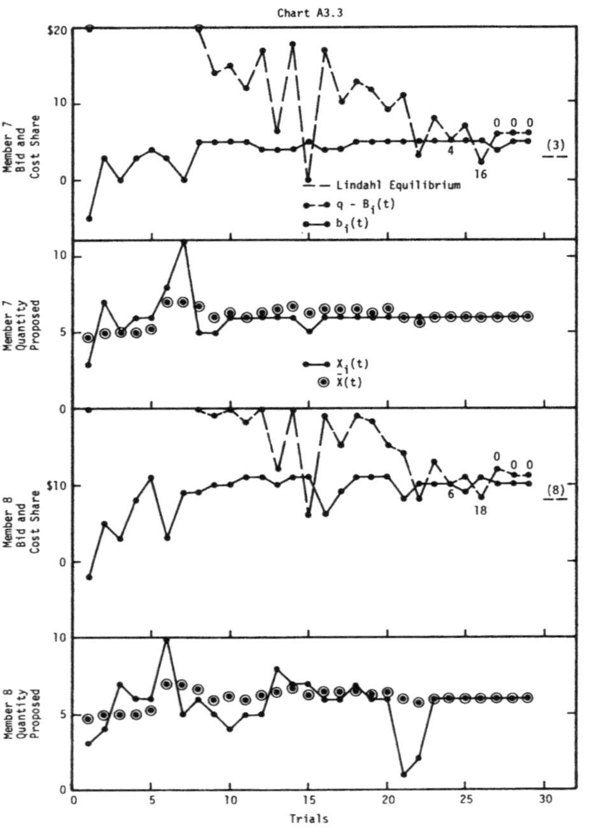
Chart A3.3
Member 7 Bid and Cost Share
$20
10
0
Lindahl Equilibrium
q - $B_i(t)$
$b_i(t)$
0 0 0
4
16
(3)
Member 7 Quantity Proposed
10
5
0
$X_i(t)$
$\bar{X}(t)$
Member 8 Bid and Cost Share
$10
0
0 0 0
6
18
(8)
Member 8 Quantity Proposed
10
5
0
0 5 10 15 20 25 30
Trials

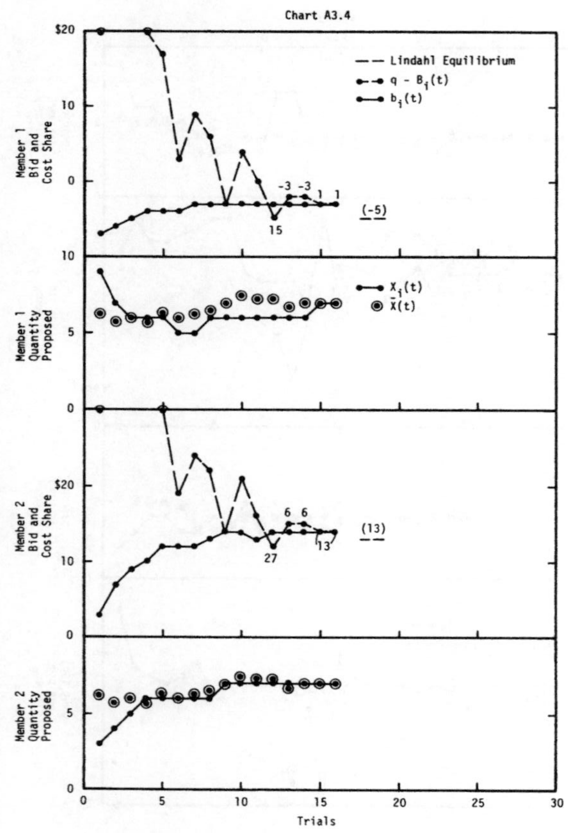

Chart A3.4
Member 1 Bid and Cost Share
Member 1 Quantity Proposed
Member 2 Bid and Cost Share
Member 2 Quantity Proposed
Lindahl Equilibrium
q - B_i(t)
b_i(t)
X_i(t)
X̄(t)
(-5)
(13)
Trials

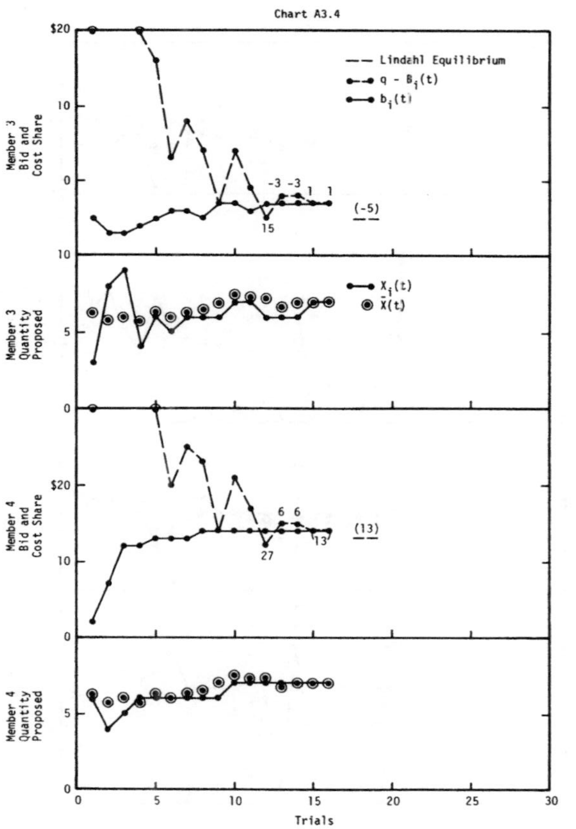

Chart A3.4
Member 3 Bid and Cost Share
Member 3 Quantity Proposed
Member 4 Bid and Cost Share
Member 4 Quantity Proposed
Lindahl Equilibrium
q - B_i(t)
b_i(t)
X_i(t)
X̄(t)
(-5)
(13)
Trials

Chart A3.4

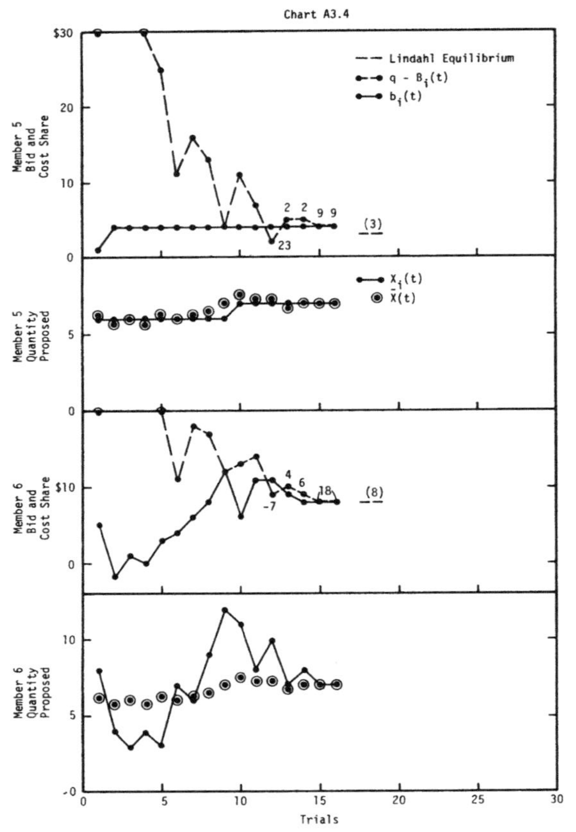

Chart A3.4

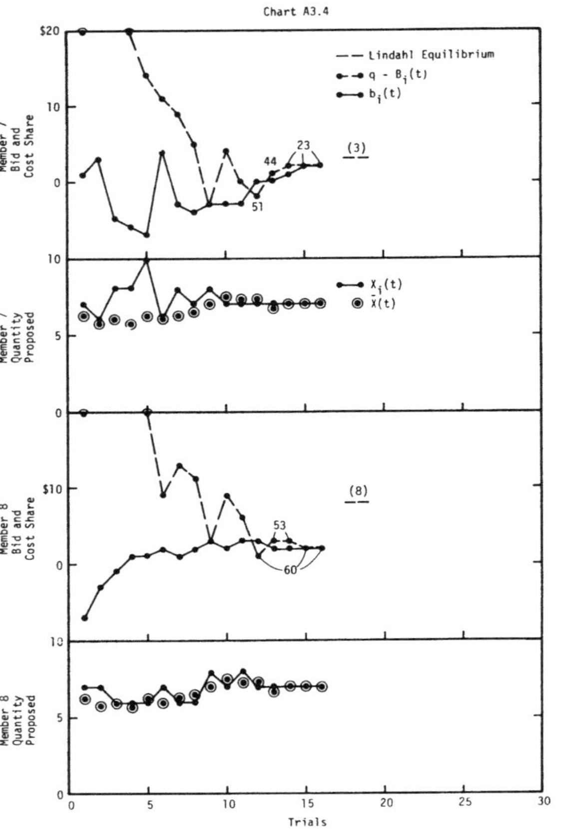

FOOTNOTES

I am happy to acknowledge my indebtedness to S. Reiter for first directing my attention to the path-breaking work of Groves and Ledyard (1974) before the first draft of their work was available for distribution; to T. Groves for inviting me to speak at Northwestern on another topic, but allowing me to use the visit to learn more about the "solution to the free-rider problem"; to T. Groves and J. Ledyard for stimulating my interest in public good experiments; to C. Plott for helping to re-ignite 1973–1974, my long-standing interest in experimental economics; to the dozen or more faculty members at USC, Berkeley, Stanford, Northwestern, and the University of Arizona who allowed me to recruit experimental subjects from their classes; to the 150 or more students who volunteered to participate in some 29 pilot and final experiments; to K. Boles, M. Rached, and S. Wade for computing and charting assistance; to the National Science Foundation for support of a research methodology that does not inspire enthusiasm in every referee, but in enough to be cheering. A preliminary version of this paper, reporting the first two series of experiments discussed below, was presented at the ORSA-TIMS conference in Las Vegas, November 17–19, 1975.

1. In the "second price" auction sealed-bids are tendered (for a single item offered for sale) with the understanding that the highest bidder will be awarded the item, but at a price determined by the second highest bid. Since the price paid is independent of one's bid, each bidder is motivated to bid his full willingness to pay thereby minimizing the chance of "excluding" himself from the award. Actually, the essence of the second price rule in providing an incentive for demand revelation was suggested earlier by Jacob Marschak. I had forgotten the incident until I read Vickrey (1961) recently for the first time. In 1953 Jacob Marschak visited briefly at Harvard. He held informal office hours for the graduate students during that visit. In the course of one of these discussions he noted that there was a very simple device for getting a buyer to reveal what he was willing to pay for anything. The seller privately writes a price on a card and puts it face down on the table. The buyer then makes his bid with the understanding that he is awarded the item at the seller's price if, and only if, his bid exceeds the seller's price. This, of course, is just Vickrey's "second price" auction in which the seller is allowed to bid, and to retain the item if his bid is the highest. This version of the Marschak-Vickrey mechanism does not even depend upon there being two or more buyers. See Marschak (1968) for an "honest asking price" version of the rule.

2. Four pilot experiments with the G-L and Lindahl processes were required before the instructions, tables, recording forms, language, and computing task of the subjects were simple enough to be comprehended by the subjects in a reasonable period of time, and to permit orderly conduct of the experiments. Similarly, four pilot experiments with the Auction Mechanism were run. Numerous revised drafts of the instructions were used in the course of these pilot experiments.

3. Empirically, the condition of privacy may not be sufficient in all cases to control on consumption externalities. A possible example occurred with subject # 3 in experiment A2.1 (see footnote 9).

4. This guarded statement accurately reflects my pre-experimental belief state, but turns out to have been overly cautious. The reason why the ennumerated possible difficulties were not of commanding importance is now clearer. There are differences between experiments without monetary rewards, those with rewards on each trial following a series of no-reward practice trials, and those with a final-outcome reward. The absence of monetary rewards may invite inattentive decisions, and extraneous gaming utilities. Practice trials, to be followed by reward trials, may produce exaggerated forms of strategic bluffing, i.e., the sending of diversionary messages from which one may hope to gain. Final-outcome reward invokes quite serious choices, especially as the end

approaches and subjects become aware of the need for group coordination to trigger the stopping rule. The opportunity costs of bluffing are high in these final-reward experiments, while bluffing is "free" in pre-reward practice trial experiments. None of these considerations are peculiar to laboratory experiments—they would be directly relevant to any field applications because the behavioral issues are the same.

5. This property explains why the television field experiment reported by Bohm (1972) does not fail because of free-riding. In this application the public good in question is indivisible, bids are therefore constant, and the Lindahl process is not distinguishable from the Auction process in section 8. The same considerations apply to the PBS field experiment reported by Ferejohn and Noll (1976) except that the members of the PBS collective are not free to vary their own bids, only to accept or reject the formula cost imputed to them. This argument suggests that the conventional wisdom which asserts that free-riding will occur in these cases, was wrong from the beginning, and based upon failure to specify a decision mechanism.

6. Obviously, there are many variations on the rule $X_i = \bar{X}$ for obtaining agreement on a common quantity of the public good. Statically equivalent alternatives include $X_i = \max\{X_1, \ldots, X_I\}$, $X_i = \min\{X_1, \ldots, X_I\}$, $X_i = \text{median}\{X_1, \ldots, X_I\}$ and $X_i = \text{mode}\{X_1, \ldots, X_I\}$, but these alternatives may have different dynamic implications.

7. Apparently it has occurred to several scholars that the free-rider "problem" is moderated, or perhaps rendered nonexistent, if economic agents are put in the position either of "filling the cost gap" or losing all utility derivable from the public good. E.g., Kihlstrom (1973, pp. 30, 31) states "From one point of view, the incentives which operate in the (Kihlstrom's) legislative economy ... are the same as ... in the competitive process. ... The consumer has an incentive to reveal the truth to avoid ... (accepting) a non-optimal consumption bundle" [Brubaker, 1975, pp. 150–155]. expresses the idea in his concept of "pre-contract group excludability" although his "golden rule of revelation" seems to rely more than is needed on altruistic considerations. Also, when I visited Berkeley to conduct a Lindahl experiment, D. McFadden questioned what might be the effect of making each subject's share of cost depend upon the bids of all other subjects.

8. Except that the $V_i(X)$ were not the same in C and R1 for those values of $X \leq 4$.

9. However, this subject's motives were somewhat mixed for he also indicated after the experiment that he suspected someone in the group must be "cleaning up." When I corrected this impression and reminded him that the instructions state that not all the Tables are the same, he asked if he could participate again in one of the experiments. This interrogation suggests that although privacy keeps each subject from knowing the decisions and payoffs of others during the experiment, it may not keep subjects from having conjectures and suspicions about other's payoffs, with possible external effects.

10. This incentive could be provided by paying a small commission for each unit agreed upon. This commission would then induce a nonzero demand for the marginal unit.

REFERENCES

Bohm, P. (1972), "Estimating Demand for Public Goods: An Experiment,", *European Economic Review* 3: 111–130.

Brubaker, E. R. (April 1975), "Free Ride, Free Revelation, or Golden Rule?", *Journal of Law and Economics* 18, No. 1: 147–161.

Buchanan, J. and Tullock, G. (1962), *The Calculus of Consent*, Ann Arbor: University of Michigan Press.

Clarke, E. H. (Fall 1971), "Multipart Pricing of Public Goods," *Public Choice* 11: 17–33.

Drèze, J. and de la Vallée Poussin, D. (1971), "A Tâtonnement Process for Public Goods," *Review of Economic Studies* 38, No. 2: 133–150.

Ellsberg, D. (November 1961), "Risk, Ambiguity and the Savage Axioms," *Quarterly Journal of Economics* 75: 643–669.

Ferejohn, J. A. and Noll, R. (1976), "An Experimental Market for Public Goods: The PBS Station Program Cooperative," *American Economic Review Papers and Proceedings*: 267–273.

Fouraker, L. and Siegel, S. (1963), *Bargaining Behavior*, New York: McGraw-Hill.

Groves, T. (August 1969), "The Allocation of Resources Under Uncertainty: The Informational and Intensive Roles of Prices and Demands in a Team," Technical Report # 1, Centre for Research in Management Science, University of California, Berkeley, Chapter IV, pp. 71–73.

———. (July 1973), "Incentives in Teams," *Econometrica* 41: 617–33.

Groves, T. and Ledyard, J. (1974), "An Incentive Mechanism for Efficient Resource Allocation in General Equilibrium with Public Goods," Discussion Paper No. 119, The Center for Mathematical Studies in Economics and Management Science, Northwestern University.

——— and ———. (May 1977), "Optimal Allocation of Public Goods: A Solution to the 'Free Rider Problem'," *Econometrica*, 45: 783–809.

Hurwicz, L. (May 1973), "The Design of Mechanisms for Resource Allocation," *American Economic Review, Paper and Proceedings*: 1–30.

Kihlstrom, R. (1974), "A Legislative Mechanism for Achieving Lindahl Equilibrium in a Public Goods Economy," NSF-SSRC Conference on Individual Rationality, Preference Revelation and Computation Cost in Models of General Economic Equilibrium, University of Massachusetts, July 1973. Revised, State University of New York, April 1974.

Loehman, E. and Whinston, A. (Autumn 1971), "A New Theory of Pricing and Decision-Making for Public Investment," *The Bell Journal of Economics and Management Science* 2, No. 2: 606–625.

Malinvaud, E. (March 1971), "A Planning Approach to the Public Good Problem," *Swedish Journal of Economics* 73, No. 1: 96–112.

Marschak, J. (1968), "Decision Making: Economic Aspects," *International Encyclopedia of the Social Sciences*, Vol. 4, New York: Macmillan and Free Press, pp. 42–53.

McGuire, T., Farley, J. Lucas, R. and Ring, L. (December 1968), "Estimation and Inference for Linear Models in which Subsets of the Dependent Variable are Constrained," *Journal of the American Statistical Association*: 1201–1213.

Plott, C. and Smith, V. (April 1975), "An Experimental Examination of Two Exchange Institutions," Social Science Working Paper No. 83, Cal Tech. To appear in *Review of Economic Studies*.

Samuelson, P. (November 1955), "Diagrammatic Exposition of a Theory of Public Expenditure," *The Review of Economic Statistics* 37, No. 4: 350–356.

———. (November 1958), "Aspects of Public Expenditure Theories," *The Review of Economics and Statistics* 40, No. 4: 332–338.

Scherr, B. and Babb E. (Fall 1975), "Pricing Public Goods: An Experiment with Two Proposed Pricing Systems," *Public Choice*: 35–48.

Sherman, R. (February 1974), "The Psychological Difference Between Ambiguity and Risk," *Quarterly Journal of Economics* 88: 166–169.

Shubik, M. (1974), "A Trading Model to Avoid Tatonnement Metaphysics," *Conference on Bidding and Auctioning*, Y. Amihud (ed.), New York: New York University Press, 1976.

———. (May 1975), "Oligopoly Theory, Communication, and Information," *American Economic Review* 65: 280–283.

Smith V. L. (May 1964), "Effect of Market Organization on Competitive Equilibrium," *Quarterly Journal of Economics*: 181–201.

———. (January 1967), "Experimental Studies of Discrimination versus Competition in Sealed-Bid Auction Markets," *Journal of Business* 40: 56–84.

———. (May 1975), "Experimental Economics: Induced Value Theory," *American Economic Review, Papers and Proceedings*: 274–279.

———. (1977), "Mechanisms for the Optimal Provision of Public Goods." *American Re-Evolution/Papers and Proceedings*, R. Auster and B. Sears (eds.), (Tucson: University of Arizona).

Thompson, E. (1965), "A Pareto Optimal Group Decision Process," *Papers in Non-Market Decision-Making* I: 133–140.

Vickrey, W. (March 1961), "Counterspeculation, Auctions and Competitive Sealed Tenders," *Journal of Finance*: 8–37.

Wicksell, Knut (1896), "A New Principle of Just Taxation," translated by J. M. Buchanan, in R. A. Musgrave and A. T. Peacock, *Classics in the Theory of Public Finance*, New York: St. Martin's Press, 1967.

Williams, F. (January 1973), "Effect of Market Organization on Competitive Equilibrium: The Multi-unit Case," *Review of Economic Studies* 40: 97–113.

AN EXPERIMENTAL COMPARISON OF THREE PUBLIC GOOD DECISION MECHANISMS

*Vernon L. Smith**

University of Arizona, Tucson, Arizona, USA

Abstract

Three public good mechanisms, all sharing the characteristics of collective excludability, unanimity and budget balance, are compared: The mechanisms differ in ways that are hypothesized to effect free-riding behavior with the Auction mechanism expected to show the least, and the Free-Rider and Quasi Free-Rider mechanisms showing the greatest such behavior. All three mechanisms yield mean quantities of a public good that are significantly greater than the free-rider quantity. However, the Auction mechanism provides a mean quantity of the public good which is significantly larger than that of the other two procedures, and closer to the Lindahl optimal quantity.

I. Introduction

Coinciding with the recent theoretical contributions of incentive compatible mechanisms for the provision of public goods, e.g. Clarke (1971), Groves (1973), Groves & Ledyard (1977), several experimental studies have tested various propositions in public goods theory; see Bohm (1972), Sweeny (1973), Marwell & Ames (1977), Ferejohn, Forsythe & Noll (1979), and Smith (1979*a*, *b*). All of these widely differing studies tend to support the proposition that decentralized mechanisms exist that allow a collective to choose and finance optimal or near-optimal quantities of a public good. Three of these studies, Ferejohn, Forsythe & Noll (1979), and Smith (1979*a*, *b*), have assumed implicitly, if not explicitly, that collectives cannot be expected to provide optimal quantities of a public good unless a decision mechanism is used that provides explicit individual incentives that favor the optimal provision of the public good. In other words, it is assumed that free-riding will occur in the absence of incentives designed to prevent free-rider behavior. One study, Bohm (1972), tested several alternative cost imputation rules for the provision of a discrete

* I am grateful to the National Science Foundation for providing research support, and to Michael Vannoni for writing the PLATO programs for all three public good mechanisms.

public good. The mean contributions to the public good under the alternative methods did not differ significantly from each other or from a "free-rider" control method; these results led to the conclusion that the free-rider problem may have been exaggerated. However, as noted in Smith (1979*a*), it is possible to interpret Bohm's alternative methods as representing versions of the Auction Mechanism in Smith (1979*a*), which excludes members of a collective from enjoying the surplus from a public good if the cost of the good is not covered. This exclusion characteristic may provide a disincentive to free-ride. Two experimental papers, Sweeny (1973) and Marwell & Ames (1977), provide evidence for only a very weak version of the free-rider hypothesis in the context of experimental paradigms that appear to provide strong free-riding incentives. Consequently, if a particular incentive compatible mechanism is found to produce no significant free-rider behavior, it is uncertain as to how much of these "good results" are attributable to the mechanism and how much to a residual core of non free-rider behavior.

Smith (1979*a*) compared three public good mechanisms under the condition of no income effects: (1) The Groves–Ledyard quadratic cost allocation Mechanism, (2) The Auction Mechanism (which are both incentive compatible in the sense that Pareto optimal allocations are among the set of Nash equilibria), and (3) The incentive incompatible Lindahl Mechanism. Under the experimental conditions studied the Groves–Ledyard and Auction Mechanisms produced comparable, and approximately optimal, quantities of the public good, whereas the Lindahl Mechanism seriously underprovided the public good. However, there are other, and simpler, "free-rider" mechanisms than the Lindahl mechanism studied in Smith (1979*a*). In the analysis to follow we compare the Auction Mechanism and a Free-Rider Mechanism of similar structure with the objective of isolating the incremental effect of the alleged incentive properties of the Auction Mechanism. We also provide the results of several experiments with a Quasi Free-Rider Mechanism which combines features from both the Auction and Free-Rider mechanisms in an attempt to further delineate the forces at work in these different institutions.

The three public good mechanisms studied here all share the following characteristics: Collective excludability, unanimity,[1] and budget balance. All three exploit the fact that prior to the actual provision of a pure public good a collective, and thus each member, can be excluded from the benefits of the good by not providing it. If the unanimity–excludability feature is a prominent element in discouraging free-rider behavior, then with none of these procedures should we observe strong free-riding, i.e. sample public good quantities should be significantly greater than the theoretical free-rider quantity of the public good. Also common to all three public good mechanisms is the following experimental context: The economy consists of one private and one public good.

[1] This unanimity feature is reminiscent of Wicksell's (1896) views on the possibility of the voluntary provision of public goods.

Each consumer agent i ($i=1, 2, \ldots, I$) has an endowment ω_i of the private good, and a payoff function (known privately) $V^i(y_i, X)$, increasing and quasi-concave in (y_i, X), yielding V^i dollars if i retains $y_i (0 \leqslant y_i \leqslant \omega_i)$ units of the private good and the collective of I members chooses to produce X units of the public good. A unit of the public good can be produced with q units (a constant) of the private good.

The three mechanisms differ only in terms of the bid-proposal decisions of the members, and the public and private information reported to each member of the collective after each decision trial. We describe these differences in the three sections to follow.

II. The Auction Mechanism

In the Auction Mechanism each individual chooses a 2-tuple (B_i, X_i), where $B_i = \omega_i - y_i$ is the bid in private good units that i contributes to the production of the public good and X_i is the quantity of the public good proposed by i. We define:

(*a*) The collective's proposed quantity of the public good is the mean proposal $\bar{X} = \sum_{\forall k} X_k / I$.

(*b*) The partial mean proposal (excluding i) is $\bar{X}_i = \sum_{\forall j \neq i} X_j / (I-1)$.

(*c*) The partial sum of bids (excluding i) is $\hat{B}_i = \sum_{\forall j \neq i} B_j$.

(*d*) The residual unit cost of the public good to i is $q - \hat{B}_i / \bar{X}_i$, and his share of the cost of the collective's proposal is $(q - B_i / \bar{X}_i)\bar{X}$.

(*e*) Collective agreement requires each i to accept his share of cost by bidding that amount and to accept the collective's proposed quantity of the public good as his personal proposal, i.e. agreement occurs when there is unanimity in the sense that $B_i = (q - \hat{B}_i / \bar{X}_i)\bar{X}$ and $X_i = \bar{X} \forall i$. The process by which these conditions can be met will be discussed below.

The payoff to i is then

$$v_i = \begin{cases} V^i[\omega_i - (q - \hat{B}_i/\bar{X}_i)\bar{X}, \bar{X}], & \text{if } B_i = (q - \hat{B}_i/\bar{X}_i)\bar{X}, \quad X_i = \bar{X}, \forall i. \\ V^i[\omega_i, 0], & \text{if } B_i \neq (q - \hat{B}_i/\bar{X}_i)\bar{X} \quad \text{or } X_i \neq \bar{X}, \quad \text{for any } i, \end{cases} \tag{1}$$

where we assume $V^i[\omega_i, 0] < V^i(y_i, X) \forall y_i < \omega_i, X > 0$.

If each i chooses (B_i, X_i) to maximize v_i, the resulting conditions correspond to those of a Lindahl equilibrium, which is also a Nash equilibrium. However, (1) defines a great many Nash equilibria that are not Lindahl equilibria. A maximum of v_i requires agreement as defined above and

$$-(q - \hat{B}_i/\bar{X}_i)(1/I)\, V_1^i + (1/I)\, V_2^i = 0$$

or

$$B_i = (q - \hat{B}_i/\bar{X}_i)\bar{X}, \quad \forall i \tag{2}$$

$$X_i = \bar{X}, \quad \forall i \tag{3}$$

$$\frac{V_2^i}{V_1^i} = q - \hat{B}_i/\bar{X}_i, \quad \forall i \tag{4}$$

Since (3) implies $\bar{X}_i = \bar{X}$, from (2)

$$B_i + \hat{B}_i = q\bar{X} \tag{5}$$

and from (4), (2) and (5)

$$\sum_{\forall k} \frac{V_2^k}{V_1^k} = \sum_{\forall k} (q - \hat{B}_k/\bar{X}_k) = \frac{\sum_{\forall k} B_k}{\bar{X}} = \frac{B_i + \hat{B}_i}{\bar{X}} = q. \tag{6}$$

Equations (4) and (6) define an interior Lindahl equilibrium $(y_1^0, \ldots, y_I^0, X^0)$. This is also a Nash equilibrium since if all $j \neq i$ bid $B_j^0 = \omega_j - y_j^0$, and propose $X_j = X^0$, agent i's best choice is $B_i^0 = \omega_i - y_i^0$ and $X_i = X^0$; otherwise he prevents agreement and receives payoff $V^i(\omega_i, 0) < V^i(y_i^0, X^0)$.

That there are numerous Nash equilibria that do not satisfy (4) and (6) is seen by considering any $(y_1^*, \ldots, y_I^*, X^*)$ such that $V^i(y_i^*, X^*) > V^i(\omega_i, 0)$ $\forall i$ and $\sum_{\forall i} \omega_i = \sum_{\forall i} y_i^* + qX^*$. Then if $\forall j \neq i$ $B_j = \omega_j - y_j^*$, $X_j = X^*$, agent i's best choice is to agree to the arrangement by setting $B_i = \omega_i - y_i^* = -\sum_{j \neq i} \omega_j + \sum_{i \neq j} y_j^* + qX^*$, and $X_i = X^*$.

All the experiments to be reported below used the PLATO computer system with visual display consoles to program subjects through an iterative decision process. Such a system is particularly effective in standardizing procedures, eliminating possible discretionary experimenter effects, recording subject choices, performing routine calculations, and displaying the appropriate private or public information to the subjects. The appendix records a summary of the instructions for the Auction Mechanism as they were presented to each subject by PLATO.

In the Auction Mechanism process each trial begins with each subject entering the choice (B_i, X_i) into his or her terminal. PLATO then computes $(\sum_{\forall i} B_i, \bar{X})$, and transmits this message to each subject. If $\sum_{\forall i} B_i < q\bar{X}$ PLATO computes each individual's share of cost $(q - B_i/\bar{X}_i)\bar{X}$ which is received as a private message by each i, and then PLATO proceeds to the next trial. If $\sum_{\forall i} B_i = q\bar{X}$, each agent's share of cost is set equal to his bid $q\bar{X} - \sum_{j \neq i} B_j = B_i$, this fact is reported to each i, and PLATO goes into a voting mode in which each agent is asked to type "yes" or "no" indicating whether he wishes to accept or not accept as final the arrangement resulting from that trial. If $\sum_{\forall i} B_i > q\bar{X}$, before the voting mode is entered, PLATO modifies the collective decision $(\sum_{\forall i} B_i, \bar{X})$ so that the "center" retains none of the bid surplus. This is achieved by giving each individual a "rebate" as follows: The outcome $(\sum_{\forall i} B_i, \bar{X})$ is adjusted to give $(\sum_{\forall i} B_i', \bar{X}')$ where the vector from $(\sum_{\forall i}(\omega_i - B_i), \bar{X})$

to $\sum_{\forall i} (\omega_i - B_i'), \bar{X}')$ is orthogonal to the production possibility frontier and the point $(\sum_{\forall i} (\omega_i - B_i'), \bar{X}')$ lies on the frontier. Consequently, the adjusted quantity of the public good, and the adjusted bid of i are

$$\bar{X}' = \frac{\bar{X} + q \sum_{\forall k} B_k}{1+q^2}, \qquad B_i' = \frac{B_i q \bar{X}'}{\sum_{\forall k} B_k}. \tag{7}$$

The process stops on trial $t^* \leqslant T$ if the arrangement resulting from trial t^* is brought to a vote, and all i vote "yes". Otherwise the process stops on trial T. In the unanimity case subject i receives $V^i[\omega_i - B_i'(t^*), \bar{X}']$ dollars in cash. Otherwise he receives $V^i[\omega_i, 0]$.

The above description of the Auction Mechanism has two conditions that will be varied in the alternative experimental "control" mechanisms to be discussed below:

(1) Each i chooses on each trial a desired or proposed quantity of the public good, and the collective's proposal is defined as the mean of these individual proposals.

(2) After each trial for which the aggregate of the bids are insufficient to cover the cost of the mean proposal, each individual receives an imputation or share of the cost $(q - \hat{B}_i/\bar{X}_i)\bar{X}$ where the "price" $(q - \hat{B}_i/\bar{X}_i)$ to each i depends only on the choices of all $j \neq i$. It is hypothesized that this imputation gives each i an incentive to "meet the market" by adjusting his responses as if in an ordinary private goods market in which each agent faces a competitive price determined by the actions of other agents; see Smith (1979*a*).

A Free-Rider Mechanism, described in the next section eliminates both of these conditions, while a Quasi Free-Rider Mechanism, described in Section IV, retains condition (1) but alters (2).

III. A Free-Rider Mechanism

In the Free-Rider Mechanism each i chooses a bid only, $B_i = \omega_i - y_i$. The collective's proposed quantity of the public good is $X' = \sum_{\forall k} B_k/q$, and the payoff to i is simply

$$V_i = V^i[\omega_i - B_i, (B_i + \hat{B}_i)/q]. \tag{8}$$

If each i chooses B_i to maximize v_i, this results in the free-rider equilibrium $(y_1', y_2', \ldots, y_I'; X')$ defined by the conditions

$$\frac{V_2^i}{V_1^i} \leqslant \frac{\sum_{\forall i} (\omega_i - y_i')}{X'} = q, \tag{9}$$

where $y'_i = \omega_i$ if $<$ holds for any i. Conditions (9) allow for boundary solutions $y'_i = \omega_i$ since they occur in the experimental design reported in Section V.

In the PLATO experimental process using the Free-Rider Mechanism, on each trial each i chooses B_i. PLATO then computes the group's proposal $X = \sum_{\forall k} B_k/q$, reports the result to each subject, and proceeds directly into the voting mode described in the previous section. If the arrangement is unanimous "yes", the process stops and each i is paid $V^i(\omega_i - B_i, \sum_{\forall k} B_k/q)$ dollars in cash. Otherwise, the process proceeds to another trial, with a maximum of T trials. If by trial T no group proposal has received unanimous approval, the process stops and each i receives $V^i(\omega_i, 0)$.

IV. A Quasi Free-Rider Mechanism

This mechanism retains condition (1) in Section II, requiring each i to state a desired quantity of the public good, but alters the cost imputation procedure in condition (2). In the Quasi Free-Rider Mechanism each i chooses a 2-tuple (B_i, X_i) on each trial. If $\sum_{\forall i} B_i \geqslant q\bar{X}$ each member votes on whether to accept the allocation as final after receiving a rebate of any overbid of cost.[1] If $\sum_{\forall i} B_i < q\bar{X}$ PLATO computes each individual's share of cost as simply $q\bar{X} = \hat{B}_i = q\bar{X} - \sum_{\forall j \neq i} B_j$.

Hence, the payoff to i is

$$v_i = \begin{cases} V^i[\omega_i - (q\bar{X} - \hat{B}_i), \bar{X}], & \text{if } B_i = q\bar{X} - \hat{B}_i,\ \bar{X}_i = \bar{X},\ \forall_i. \\ V^i[\omega_i, 0], & \text{if } B_i \neq q\bar{X} - \hat{B}_i \quad \text{or } X_i \neq \bar{X}, \quad \text{for any } i. \end{cases} \tag{10}$$

If v_i is at a maximum with respect to (B_i, X_i) then we must have $B_i = q\hat{B} - \hat{B}_i$, $X_i = \bar{X}$ and $-q(1/I)_1^{vi} + (1/I)_2^{vi} \leqslant 0$, and therefore the free-rider condition (9) above must be satisfied.

V. Experimental Design and Results

The instructions for the Free-Rider and Quasi Free-Rider PLATO experiments are the same as those reported in the appendix for the Auction Mechanism with appropriate changes to allow for the different cost imputation and rebate rules in the Quasi Free-Rider experiments and for the fact that each i chooses only a bid on each trial in a Free-Rider experiment.

If the cost imputation information and procedure in the Auction Mechanism is effective in reducing Free-Rider behavior, then experimental outcomes with

[1] In this rebate procedure PLATO first rounds $\bar{X}$ to the nearest integer, then determines if the overbid is sufficient to allow an integer increase in the size of the public good, i.e. the largest $n = 0, 1, 2, \ldots$ such that $\sum_{\forall i} B_i \geqslant q(\bar{X} + n)$ was computed. Any remaining bid surplus is then rebated to each i in proportion to i's bid. Hence, if agent i's bid was B_i the adjusted bid becomes $B'_i = B_i q(\bar{X} + n)/\sum_{\forall k} B_k$ where $\bar{X} + n$ is the adjusted proposed size (an integer) of the public good. Results reported in Smith (1979b) find no significant difference between this rebate procedure and that described in Section II.

Table 1. *Experimental design*

$I = 6$, $q = 2$, $X^0 = 9$, $X' = 3.33$

Parameter	Parameter class		
	I	II	III
α_i	0.24	0.96	0.8
β_i	0.96	0.24	0.8
a_i	1.5	1.5	1.5
ω_i	5	10	6
y_i^0, LE Private quantity	1	8	3
y_i', Free-Rider Private quantity	1.67	10	6

this mechanism should provide larger quantities of the public good than the Free-Rider Mechanism. The Quasi Free-Rider Mechanism retains the Auction Mechanism condition (1) but alters the cost imputation condition (2) so as to encourage Free-Rider behavior. If condition (1) is an important feature tending to discourage free-riding even though the cost imputation rule does not, then the Quasi Free-Rider Mechanism should yield public good quantities somewhere between those yielded by the other two mechanisms. If condition (1) is not an important feature inhibiting free-riding then public good quantities provided by the Free-Rider and Quasi Free-Rider Mechanisms should not be distinguishable from each other, but should be significantly less than public good quantities provided by the Auction Mechanism. All three mechanisms use the exclusionary unanimity stopping rule. If this Wicksellian unanimity condition is of importance in inhibiting free-rider behavior, then all three mechanisms should yield public good quantities that are greater than the free-rider quantity.

These hypotheses will be tested using data from three series of PLATO experiments, each series corresponding to one of the three mechanisms described above. Prior to the commencement of each PLATO experiment it is initialized by specifying numerical values for $(I, T, q, \omega_i, a_i, \alpha_i, \beta_i)$ where I is the number of subjects in an experimental collective, T is the maximum number of trials, q is the unit cost of the public good, ω_i is the endowment of subject i, and the payoff function in dollars for i is $V^i \equiv a_i y_i^{\alpha_i} X^{\beta_i}$. For all the experiments reported here, $q = 2$ and $I = 6$, with two subjects in each of three payoff-endowment parameter classes. Table 1 lists the payoff and endowment parameters, the Lindahl equilibrium private quantities, y_i^0, and the free-rider private quantities, y_i', corresponding to each of the three parameter classes used in the experiments. With these parameters the Lindahl equilibrium quantity of the public good from (4) and (6) is $X^0 = 9$; the free-rider equilibrium quantity from (9) is $X' = 3.33$. In order that the effect of endowment not be

Table 2. *Bid-quantity outcomes, PLATO. Auction Mechanism experiments*

$I=6$, $q=2$, $X^0=9$, $X'=3.33$, $T=10$. Figures within parentheses denote final trial choices in experiments failing to reach agreement

Subject ...	1	2	3	4	5	6		
Parameter class ...	I $\omega_1=5$	II $\omega_2=10$	III $\omega_3=6$	I $\omega_1=5$	II $\omega_2=10$	III $\omega_3=6$		
Lindahl Equilibrium bids, ω_i-y_i' ...	4	2	3	4	2	3	X^*, Final quantity	t^*, Final trial
Final bids, B_i^*								
A1	3	3	3	2	1	3	7.5	9
A1′	2.98	4.96	2.98	2.98	0.99	0.99	7.93	10
A2	(1.5)	(4)	(4)	(0)	(6)	(1)	(8.83)	(10)
A3	3.92	3.92	2.94	3.92	2.94	0.98	9.3	7
A3′	1.97	1.97	1.97	1.97	4.93	1.97	7.4	9
A4	3.61	4.51	3.61	0.90	4.51	4.51	10.83	1
A4′	3.81	4.76	4.76	1.90	0	4.76	10	8
A5	(0.99)	(9.88)	(3.95)	(3.95)	(1.98)	(1.98)	(11.37)	(10)
A5′	3	1	1	4	10	3	11	10
A6	3.73	7.47	0.93	2.8	0	2	8.87	9

confounded with preference for the public good, the parameters in Table 1 were chosen so that the low endowment condition ($\omega_1=5$) is associated with a relatively large Lindahl equilibrium bid ($\omega_1-y_1^0=4$), while the high endowment condition ($\omega_2=10$) is associated with a relatively small Lindahl equilibrium bid ($\omega_2-y_2^0=2$). That is "rich" subjects have a weak preference, while "poor" subjects have a strong preference for the public good relative to the private good.

A total of 102 subjects, enrolled in undergraduate and graduate courses in economics or business, participated in 27 experiments (10 Auction, 8 Free-Rider and 9 Quasi Free-Rider Mechanism experiments). The subjects were invited to participate in a decision making experiment, for which they would receive \$2 when they arrived and would be paid whatever they earned in the experiment when they finished. The total amount earned under these conditions was approximately \$2 400. Whenever there was sufficient time a 6-member experimental group participated in a series of two sequential experiments in which the second was considered an "experience" session. At the beginning of each experiment the subjects were randomly assigned to each parameter-endowment class, and to each computer terminal.

Tables 2, 3 and 4 list the final-trial bids for each subject (B_i^*), the final-trial quantity of the public good (X^*), and the number of the final trial (t^*) for each of the 27 experiments. Each experiment is identified by a letter indicating the institutional treatment and a number indicating the sequential order in which an experimental session in the series occurred. A prime by the number indicates

Table 3. *Bid-quantity outcomes PLATO. "Free-Rider" Mechanism experiments*

$I = 6$, $q = 2$, $X^0 = 9$, $X' = 3.33$, $T = 10$

Subject ...	1	2	3	4	5	6		
Parameter	I	II	III	I	II	III		
class ...	$\omega_1 = 5$	$\omega_2 = 10$	$\omega_3 = 6$	$\omega_4 = 5$	$\omega_5 = 10$	$\omega_6 = 6$	X^*,	t^*,
Free-Rider							Final	Final
bids, $\omega_i - y_i'$ ...	3.33	0	0	3.33	0	0	quantity	trial
Final bids, B_i^*								
F1	2	1	1	2	0	1	3.5	8
F2	3	3	2	3	5	2	9	1
F3	3	7	1	3	1	2	8.5	8
F3′	1	7	1	2	7	1	9.5	1
F4	4	2	1	2	4	1	7	10
F5	3	7	1	1	3	2	8.5	1
F5′	3	7	3	3	0	0	8	7
F6′	0	4	0	2	0	3	4.5	10

an experiment with experienced subjects, i.e. the second experiment in a session with the same subjects. Thus A4 is the first experiment in the fourth Auction Mechanism session; F5′ is the second experiment in the fifth Free-Rider Mechanism session. The only exception to this pattern is F6′ which followed A6 using the same 6 subjects.

Two of the Auction Mechanism experiments, A2 and A5, failed to reach agreement. Based on the results of thirty-eight Auction Mechanism experiments reported in Smith (1979*b*), it appears that approximately 10 per cent

Table 4. *Bid-quantity outcomes. Quasi Free-Rider Mechanism experiments*

$I = 6$, $q = 2$, $X^0 = 9$, $X' = 3.33$, $T = 15$

Subject ...	1	2	3	4	5	6		
Parameter	I	II	III	I	II	III		
class ...	$\omega_1 = 5$	$\omega_2 = 10$	$\omega_3 = 6$	$\omega_4 = 5$	$\omega_5 = 10$	$\omega_6 = 6$	X^*,	t^*,
Free-Rider							Final	Final
bids, $\omega_i - y_i'$ ...	3.33	0	0	3.33	0	0	quantity	trial
Final bids, B_i								
Q1	1	3	3	1	4	2	7	1
Q1′	2.8	5.6	1.867	1.867	0.933	0.933	7	2
Q2	1.882	1.882	1.882	0.941	6.588	2.824	8	11
Q3	3	2	2	2	1	2	6	15
Q3′	1	4	3	3	1	4	8	2
Q4	1	6	3	5	0	4	9	9
Q4′	3.76	2.82	2.82	2.82	0	3.76	8	3
Q5	4	0	2	3	1	2	6	15
Q5′	0.93	6.53	0	0	0.93	5.6	7	12

Table 5. *Mean provision of the public good*

Mechanism	Inexperienced subjects	Experienced subjects	Pooled
Free-Rider	7.3	7.3	7.3
Quasi Free-Rider	7.2	7.5	7.3
Auction	9.12	9.08	9.10[a]

[a] This mean is 7.9 if the two disagreement experiments are counted at the free-rider quantity (3.33).

fail to reach agreement under this institution. None of the experiments using the alternative mechanisms failed to reach agreement.

The mean quantity of the public good provided by each of the three institutions in inexperienced and experienced collectives is shown in Table 5. Experience is clearly not an effective treatment variable for any of the institutions. This result is also reported in Smith (1979*b*) for the Auction Mechanism using different payoff-endowment parameters, and collectives of size 3, 6 and 9. The pooled (across experience) means in Table 5 show that the Auction Mechanism provides larger quantities of the public good in those experiments reaching agreement than is provided by the alternative institutions.

Table 6 records the α (Type I error) and $1-\beta$ (power) probabilities, where the null hypothesis, H_0, is that the sample means for each mechanism came from a population with mean equal to the theoretical free-rider quantity (3.33), and the alternative hypothesis, H_1, is that the sample means came from a population with mean equal to the Lindahl equilibrium quantity (9). The first row of selected α probabilities is used to calculate the critical values, X_c (for each mechanism), above which we reject H_0 (accept H_1) if the sample mean exceeds X_c. The calculations are based on the t-distribution with sample sizes shown in Table 6 and sample variances computed from the X^* observations in Tables 2, 3 and 4. These critical values are then used to compute the $1-\beta$

Table 6. *Error and power probabilities for Free-Rider* (H_0) *and Lindahl Equilibrium* (H_1) *hypotheses*

Institution	Free-Rider mechanism $N_f = 8$	Quasi Free-Rider mechanism $N_q = 9$	Auction mechanism $N_a = 8$
α = probability of rejecting H_0 (accepting H_1) when H_0 is true	0.001	0.001	0.001
$1-\beta$ = probability of accepting H_1 (rejecting H_0) when H_1 is true	0.93	0.91	0.93
Critical value, X_c	6.8	4.8	5.6

Table 7. *Mean bids by parameter class and mechanism*

	Parameter class		
Mechanism	I $\omega_1 = 5$	II $\omega_2 = 10$	III $\omega_3 = 6$
Free-Rider	2.31	3.62	1.38
Quasi Free-Rider	2.17	2.63	2.59
Auction	2.91	3.50	2.65
Lindahl equilibrium bids	4	2	3

probabilities or the so-called "power" of the test. For example, for the free-rider mechanism (Column 2, Table 6), $X_c = 3.33 + t_\alpha \sqrt{V_f/N_f} = -6.8$ corresponding to a Type II error $\beta < 0.07$, and hence $1 - \beta > 0.93$. For each mechanism the sample mean (Column 4, Table 5) exceeds the critical value shown in Table 6 and we reject H_0 in favor of H_1. However, the outcomes in the Auction Mechanism provide significantly stronger support for H_1 then either of the other mechanisms. This is indicated by a t-test comparison of the Auction Mechanism mean with the pooled mean of the other two mechanisms, giving a t-value of 2.14 with $\alpha < 0.05$, i.e., we reject the hypothesis of no difference between the Auction and the alternative mechanisms. However, the "better" results in the Auction Mechanism seem to be achieved at the cost of a somewhat higher failure to reach unanimity than in the alternative institutions.

Table 7 shows the mean bids of subjects in each parameter class for each institution. These results are generally consistent with those reported in Smith (1979*b*) for the Auction Mechanism. In all three institutions the mean bids differ from the corresponding Lindahl equilibrium bids. Consequently, although the Auction Mechanism provides public good quantities that approximate the Lindahl equilibrium quantity the private good allocations do not approximate the Lindahl equilibrium quantities. As is seen in Table 7 this is because subjects with low endowment (5 or 6) tend to contribute less, while subjects with high endowment (10) contribute more, than is required for a Lindahl allocation.[1]

VI. Summary

The Auction Mechanism is compared with two mechanisms in which conventional analysis implies that free-riding will occur in the provision of a pure public good. However, all three mechanisms employ a unanimity stopping rule so that the condition of group excludability is present in each institution. The principal conclusions are:

[1] See Smith (1979*b*) for a regression model test of the hypothesis that these deviations from the Lindahl allocation are within the Pareto optimal set for collectives of size 3.

1. The Auction Mechanism yields public good quantities that are significantly greater than the theoretical free-rider quantity, but that are not significantly different from the theoretical Lindahl equilibrium quantity of the public good.

2. In the Auction Mechanism there appears to be a somewhat greater tendency of groups to fail to reach unanimity on a final allocation. If these "no agreement" sessions are included in the calculations the Auction Mechanism does not produce significantly larger quantities of a public good than the alternative mechanisms.

3. Both of the free-rider mechanisms yield public good quantities significantly larger than the theoretical free-rider quantity. Hence, under unanimity, it appears that empirical support for the free-rider hypothesis is very weak. This result is consistent with that reported by Bohm (1972) Sweeny (1973) and Marwell–Ames (1977) using quite diverse experimental paradigms.

4. The bidding pattern in all three institutions reveals a central tendency of subjects with small endowments to contribute less, and subjects with large endowments to contribute more, to the provision of a public good, than is predicted by the theoretical Lindahl equilibrium allocation.

An unresolved question is whether the absence of strong free-rider behavior in all three mechanisms is due to the exclusionary unanimity stopping rule employed. It is proposed that an aswer to this question be attempted by replication of the Free-Rider experiments without the voting mode, i.e., the group decision is defined as whatever outcome prevails on trial T following $T-1$ practice trials.

References

Bohm, P.: Estimating demand for public goods: An experiment. *European Economic Review 3*, 111–130, 1972.

Clarke, E.: Multipart pricing of public goods. *Public Choice 2*, 17–33, Fall 1971.

Ferejohn, J., Forsythe, R. & Noll, R.: An experimental analysis of decision making procedures for discrete public goods: A case study of a problem in institutional design. In *Research in experimental Economics* (ed. V. Smith). JAI Press, Greenwich, 1979, in press.

Groves, T.: Incentives and teams. *Econometrica 41*, 617–33, July 1973.

Groves, T. & Ledyard, J.: Optimal allocation of public goods: A solution to the free-rider problem. *Econometrica 45*, 783–809, May 1977.

Marwell, G. & Ames, R.: Experiments on the provision of public goods. I. Resources, interest, group size, and the free-rider problem. Social Behavior Research Center, Working Paper 77-1, 1977.

Smith, V.: Incentive compatible experimental processes for the provision of public goods. In *Research in experimental economics* (ed. V. Smith). JAI Press, Greenwich, 1979*a*, in press.

Smith, V.: Experiments with a decentralized mechanism for public good decision. Forthcoming in *American Economic Review*, 1979*b*.

Sweeny, J.: An experimental investigation of the free-rider problem. *Social Science Research 2*, 277–292, 1973.

Wicksell, K.: Ein neues Prinzip der gerechten Besteuerung. In *Finanztheoretische Untersuchungen*, Jena 1896. Translated by J. M. Buchanan, "A new principle of just taxation", in *Classics in the theory of public finance*, 72. Musgrave and Peacock Rd., 1958.

Appendix

INSTRUCTIONS

This is an experiment in the economics of group decision making. The instructions are simple, and if you follow them carefully and make good decisions you may earn a CONSIDERABLE AMOUNT OF MONEY which will be paid to you in cash at the end of the experiment. Various research foundations have provided funds for this research.

You are a member of a group that must decide upon, and bear the cost of, a jointly shared facility (like, for example, a neighborhood swimming pool.) The group must decide on the size, X, of the commonly shared facility. Each member has a specified number of work days available to divide between private use and a contribution to building the joint facility. The value to you if the group decides on a facility of size X, and if you use "y" days for your own use is given in your personal pay- off table.

Each unit of the joint facility requires 2 mandays of work. Hence the total workdays required is 2X if the group agrees on a facility of size X. Your share of total facility work requirements is determined from a series of trial bids.

The following will be an example based on your personal payoff table. However, your available workdays MAY NOT apply to you in the experiment. Take as much time with the instructions as you feel you need.

PRESS NEXT TO CONTINUE

Number of days available=9 EXAMPLE!

x \ y	1	2	3	4	5	6	7	8	(9)	10	11	12
1	1.00	3.38	4.93	6.11	7.08	7.90	8.61	9.25	9.83	10.36	10.85	11.30
2	3.38	6.11	7.90	9.25	10.36	11.30	12.12	12.86	13.52	14.13	14.69	15.21
3	4.93	7.90	9.83	11.30	12.50	13.52	14.41	15.21	15.93	16.59	17.20	17.76
4	6.11	9.25	11.30	12.86	14.13	15.21	16.16	17.00	17.76	18.46	19.10	19.70
5	7.08	10.36	12.50	14.13	15.46	16.59	17.58	18.46	19.26	19.99	20.66	21.29
6	7.90	11.30	13.52	15.21	16.59	17.76	18.79	19.70	20.53	21.29	21.99	22.63
7	8.61	12.12	14.41	16.16	17.58	18.79	19.85	20.79	21.64	22.42	23.14	23.81
8	9.25	12.86	15.21	17.00	18.46	19.70	20.79	21.76	22.63	23.44	24.18	24.86
9	9.83	13.52	15.93	17.76	19.26	20.53	21.64	22.63	23.53	24.35	25.11	25.81
10	10.36	14.13	16.59	18.46	19.99	21.29	22.42	23.44	24.35	25.19	25.96	26.68
11	10.85	14.69	17.20	19.10	20.66	21.99	23.14	24.18	25.11	25.96	26.75	27.48
12	11.30	15.21	17.76	19.70	21.29	22.63	23.81	24.86	25.81	26.68	27.48	28.23

At the beginning of each trial you independently select a bid representing your contribution of work days for the joint facility,and a proposed facility size x. (The facility size YOU propose will be referred to with a small-case x. The average proposal size of the group will be referred to with a capital X. Your number of workdays available is the circled number on the y-column of your chart. Your bid is a deduction from your workdays available; this determines your desired workdays for your own use (y).) Your bid and facility size choices are to be typed in after the arrow when requested. If you make a mistake or change your mind, press the ERASE key to erase one digit at a time. When you are finished typing your decision in a trial, press the NEXT key. PRESS NEXT TO CONTINUE

Now let's see how the process works. Suppose you are member number 1. Further suppose you choose to bid 3 days of work and propose a facility size of 5. PLATO will record the bids and proposals of all members. PLATO will then compute the sum of all work bids, your share of the facility cost, and the average proposal size. Press NEXT to see the mechanics of this process or BACK to review what you have covered.

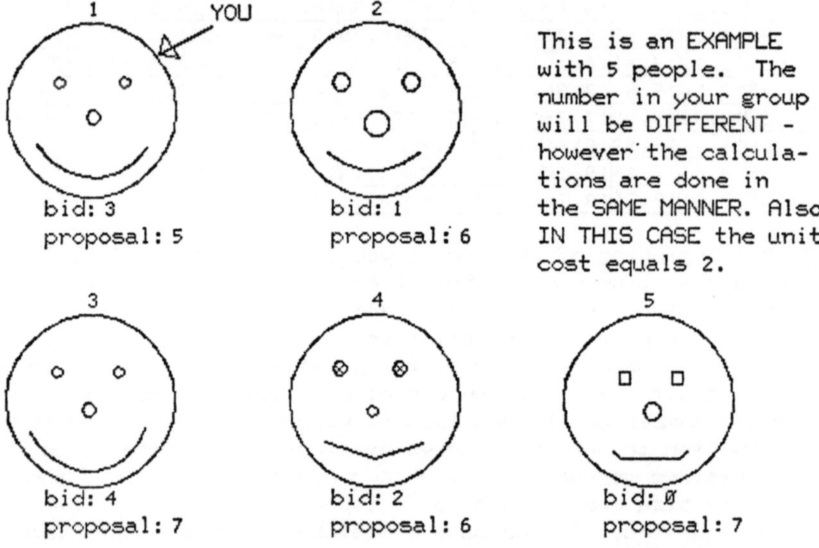

This is an EXAMPLE with 5 people. The number in your group will be DIFFERENT - however the calculations are done in the SAME MANNER. Also, IN THIS CASE the unit cost equals 2.

These are the five members. Remember in this example you are number 1. Press NEXT to enter their bids and proposals.

The sum of the bids is 1Ø. The average proposed size is 6.2

The sum of the bids of all other members is 7. (1Ø-3)

Your share of facility cost is: (unit cost - sum of bids of all others/average proposal of others) × (the average group proposal). In this case,
(2 - 7/6.5) × 6.2 = 5.72

The value to you of the trial decision is obtained from your personal payoff table by finding the row for X (average proposal size) and the column for y (the number of workdays left for your own use). The resulting dollar value can be found at their intersection. Press NEXT to see how this would look in the example.

EXAMPLE!

X \ y	1	2	3	4	5	6	7	8	9	10	11	12
1	1.00	3.38	4.93	6.11	7.08	7.90	8.61	9.25	9.83	10.36	10.85	11.30
2	3.38	6.11	7.90	9.25	10.36	11.30	12.12	12.86	13.52	14.13	14.69	15.21
3	4.93	7.90	9.83	11.30	12.50	13.52	14.41	15.21	15.93	16.59	17.20	17.76
4	6.11	9.25	11.30	12.86	14.13	15.21	16.16	17.00	17.76	18.46	19.10	19.70
5	7.08	10.36	12.50	14.13	15.46	16.59	17.58	18.46	19.26	19.99	20.66	21.29
6	7.90	11.30	13.52	15.21	16.59	17.76	18.79	19.70	20.53	21.29	21.99	22.63
7	8.61	12.12	14.41	16.16	17.58	18.79	19.85	20.79	21.64	22.42	23.14	23.81
8	9.25	12.86	15.21	17.00	18.46	19.70	20.79	21.76	22.63	23.44	24.18	24.86
9	9.83	13.52	15.93	17.76	19.26	20.53	21.64	22.63	23.53	24.35	25.11	25.81
10	10.36	14.13	16.59	18.46	19.99	21.29	22.42	23.44	24.35	25.19	25.96	26.68
11	10.85	14.69	17.20	19.10	20.66	21.99	23.14	24.18	25.11	25.96	26.75	27.48
12	11.30	15.21	17.76	19.70	21.29	22.63	23.81	24.86	25.81	26.68	27.48	28.23

Your bid = 3

Your proposal = 5

NOTICE: PLATO will adjust for fractional values!!

Your share of cost = 5.72

Average proposal size = 6.2

Work days for personal use = 3.28

Value of decision to you = $14.23

Total bid = 10

This process will be repeated for at most 10trials. In order that the process stop, TWO events must occur.

1. On any single trial each member's bid must be equal to his share of cost. If the sum of all bids exceed the cost of the average facility size, all members get a rebate such that the bid of each is equal to his share of cost. Note in the previous example that the total bid (10) was less than the cost of the average facility size (2×6.2 = 12.4).

2. Each member must vote to accept his share of cost and accept the group's average proposal. Hence, the vote must be unanimous for the decision to be finalized. If not, the group will go to the next trial and will have to meet condition (1) over again

You will be given additional instructions about the voting procedure on any trial that satisfies (1).

PRESS -NEXT- TO CONTINUE OR -BACK- TO REVIEW

If the process stops by these rules, then you will receive a cash payment equal to the value of your final decision. Otherwise you will receive nothing

The personal payoff table and number of days available are NOT the same for all members. It is your own private information. Do not speak to any other participant. Feel free to earn as much cash as you can. Press NEXT to begin the experiment or BACK to review the stopping rules.

P.S.
If you forget some portion of the instructions, HELP will be available during the experiment.

INSTRUCTIONS PROVIDED WHEN THERE IS AN

OVERBID OF TOTAL COST:

The group has overbid the total cost by the amount - - . This amount is divided between an increase in the facility size and a total rebate of work time in the ratio of . to . . Each member's share of this rebate is proportional to that member's bid.

You have 1 trial left.

The group has reached a tentative joint decision. It is now the group's job to decide whether or not to finalize it. You will vote "yes" if you want to accept your current bid and the group's average proposal size, or "no" to veto the decision. The decision vote must be unanimous to be valid. If it is unanimous, you will be done and the current value of the group decision paid to you in cash. You have the option to veto the joint solution and go for additional trials if you think you can improve your position.

EXAMPLE:

Your current bid = 2.5 Your share of cost = 2.5

Your current proposal = 2 Average proposal size = 2.5

The current value to you of this decision = $ 4.50

Enter your vote on whether or not to accept the current group decision and press NEXT.

>

Experiments with a Decentralized Mechanism for Public Good Decisions

By VERNON L. SMITH*

Public goods theory, as articulated by Paul Samuelson (1954), Mancur Olson, and many others, has maintained that the distinguishing characteristic of nonexcludability, inherent in public goods, implies the impossibility of optimal public good provision by decentralized (voluntary) mechanisms. Since no one can be excluded from the benefits of the public good, each has an incentive to "free ride"; that is, contribute less than his marginal valuation to the cost of the public good. Consequently, public goods theory has suggested two hypotheses.

H_F: *The free rider hypothesis.*

H_I: *The impossibility of decentralized public good provision.*

Traditional public goods theory has not viewed H_F and H_I as independent hypotheses. The assumption of free rider behavior has led to the conclusion that all decentralized mechanisms would lead to the nonprovision of public goods (for example, Earl Brubaker refers to this as a consequence of the strong free rider hypothesis), or at least to suboptimal quantities of public goods.

Precursory and recent contributions by William Vickrey, Edward Clarke (1968, 1971), Theodore Groves (1969, 1973), and Groves and John Ledyard, while accepting the logic of free riding behavior, have sought solutions to the problem in the form of cost-sharing mechanisms that would give each individual an incentive to contribute to the cost of a public good an amount equal to his marginal private valuation of the public good. Consequently, such mechanisms are incentive compatible, that is, individual's acting out of self-interest support outcomes (Pareto optimality) judged to be desirable by the collective. The idea is to find procedures that harness the self-interest to produce optimal *common* outcomes, just as the traditional theory of private goods exchange has argued that action in the self-interest is like an invisible hand guiding collectives to specialize, then cooperate through market exchange, to provide optimal *private* outcomes. The Clarke-Groves-Ledyard (hereafter, C-G-L) research denies H_I, and hypothesizes:

H_p: *The possibility of designing decentralized adjustment mechanisms for optimal public good decision.*

Traditional public goods theory, while asserting H_F and H_I, has not questioned similarly the invisible hand hypothesis in the provision of private goods. In fact the argument for H_I has leaned on a sharp contrast between private goods, where there is no presumed problem of decentralized decision, and public goods, where the problem is assumed to be inevitable. As noted by Samuelson, there is a fundamental technical difference between private and public goods: by departing from the rule of preference revelation, "... any one person can hope to snatch some selfish benefit in a way not possible under the self-policing competitive pricing of private goods" (1954, p. 389).

It might be supposed from the above discussion that the "new" conventional wisdom in public goods is acceptance of the proposition that although there are very important technical differences between public and private goods, it is nevertheless possible, by applying C-G-L types of ingenuity, to design incentive-compatible decentralized pricing systems for public goods. But such a simplified reduction of these important new contributions is not warranted. Leonid Hurwicz, for private goods, and Ledyard and John Roberts, for public goods, have proved that it is impossible to find a mechanism that provides individually rational

*University of Arizona. Research support by the National Science Foundation is gratefully acknowledged. I am indebted to Michael Vannoni for programming the PLATO version of the Auction Mechanism.

Pareto optima and which is also individually incentive compatible. These results assume a broader range of (costless) strategic behavior than the Nash competitive behavior postulated by C-G-L. In summary the current state of theory on these issues appears to be as follows: *Depending upon what one assumes about the strategic behavioral modes of economic agents, the attainment of optimal resource allocation by decentralized pricing systems may be either possible or impossible, but in either case this result does not depend on whether goods are private or public.*

There are many lessons in the literature that have brought us full circle to this state, but none more important than the necessity of learning much more about the behavior of people in institutions that attempt to operationalize the significant concept of incentive compatibility. But abstract theory has done more than simply return to where it started, dramatizing its own dead end in the absence of a better understanding of behavior. Together, the above theoretical contributions have brought a glimpse of possibility, of operational forms as in Vickrey for private goods, and Groves and Ledyard for public goods, and a better understanding of the scientific questions that require investigation.

I. Empirical Tests of Public Goods Theory

There is much casual evidence to suggest that mechanisms exist for the voluntary provision of public goods. Thousands of churches, music halls, libraries, scientific laboratories, art museums, theatres, and other such facilities have been financed by voluntary contributions to fund drives conducted by private societies. If such observations are dismissed as evidence contrary to H_I on the grounds that these are instances of atypical altruism, then there is a serious question as to whether public goods theory consists of any refutable hypotheses. If observations contrary to a theory are to be ruled out on the basis of special explanations not part of the original theory, then we are indeed dealing only with Galbraithian systems of belief, not with scientific propositions.

A more substantive objection to these observations of successful private society fund drives might be that they represent "small" groups, whereas the public good problem is a "large" group problem. But regardless of the size of any finite group, one can always imagine a larger collective, and conclude that the hypothesis has not been disproven. Even in a collective of size two there is incentive to free ride, and underprovide the joint outcome. Consequently, if size is claimed to be a critical parameter in public goods theory, the nature of its effect must be well specified before examining the observations. But suppose we grant that action by private societies is not compelling evidence rejecting H_I; that although the distinction between small and large is not precise, private societies are "clearly" too small to represent a valid test of H_I. Then we must look for examples of voluntary action by larger collectives. Such an example is voting in national elections, which, unlike Australia, is not yet required by law in the United States. The problem of voting is often described as a public goods problem: since no individual voter can have any perceivable effect on the common outcome, and since the act of voting involves some cost (going to the polls, reading and marking the ballot, etc.), it follows, allegedly, that one should observe little or no voting activity. In fact, "remarkably large" numbers of people vote. Is this judged to be evidence contrary to H_I by political economists? No, it is a "paradox," and there is a great literature on the paradox of voting with many distinguished contributions (see Gordon Tullock; George Stigler; J. Ferejohn and M. Fiorina). Once again, a cherished belief remains unshaken, and the observation is explained anecdotally.

I am not arguing that H_I is disproved by the fact that people vote, or the observation that private societies are sometimes successful in building-fund drives; I am arguing for clearer standards of evidence. These field observations are clearly inconsistent with the strong free rider hypothesis; large numbers of people vote, and public goods are being provided by private societies. What we do not know and cannot know from field observation is the optimal quantity of the given public good that was provided. Some fund drives succeed, and the facility is built; others fail. In terms of optimality, should some of the latter have succeeded, or should some of the former have provided larger or better facilities? We cannot know what was optimal without independent information on individual valuations.

This problem appears to be inherent in field studies, but not in controlled laboratory experiments which can provide a unique source of empirical data for testing hypotheses about resource allocation mechanisms. It appears that in field studies the best we can do is to compare mechanism A with mechanism B. Suppose theory suggests that A is incentive compatible, while B is not. Then we can test the hypothesis that observations on mechanism A come from distributions over a larger quantity of the public good than do observations on mechanism B. But we cannot test the hypothesis that observations from A come from a distribution whose central tendency is the optimal quantity of the public good. This last hypothesis (as well as the former) can be tested using appropriate laboratory experiments because we can, to a close approximation, induce known preferences or values on decision outcomes (see my 1979 and forthcoming papers), and thereby compute the theoretically optimal quantity of the public good.

A. *Laboratory Experiments*

In my previous experimental research using a partial equilibrium design (no income effects), I found that collectives composed of four, five, or eight members are able, in most replications, to reach agreement to produce optimal or near optimal amounts of a public good under either a version of the Groves-Ledyard mechanism or the auction mechanism (see my 1979 paper). However, under the Lindahl mechanism which (unlike the Groves-Ledyard and auction mechanism) is *not* incentive compatible (i.e., Pareto optimal allocations are not among the set of points that are Nash equilibria), I found that experimental collectives did much worse; specifically, in three replications none of the public good was produced, while in one, a positive quantity equal to one-half the optimum was provided. Hence, the Lindahl mechanism experimental results provided evidence in support of H_F, while the results from the two incentive-compatible mechanisms support H_P by demonstrating that operational procedures exist for the solution of the free rider problem.

The auction mechanism, which will be reviewed in greater detail in Section II, is characterized by collective excludability, unanimity, and budget balance. It exploits the fact that prior to the actual provision of a pure public good, a collective, and therefore each of its members, can be excluded from the good by not providing it. Therefore, the stopping rule requires that (a) the sum of individual bids (contributions) cover the cost of the proposed public good, and, if this occurs, (b) the collective *then* agree unanimously to accept this result. I once thought this was a new mechanism, but actually it is just an extension, generalization, and formalization of the age-old "fund drive" procedure used by many private societies and eleemosynary institutions.

It is my conjecture that it is this "pre-contract, group excludability" (see Brubaker) feature that derives these earlier experimental results (see my 1979 paper) and the results to be reported below. But this is not a certainty, as is suggested, perhaps, by the results of J. Sweeney and G. Marwell and R. Ames.

Sweeny reports the results of experiments in which an individual subject pedaled a bicycle connected to an electric generator. Each individual thought she was in a group of size six with the group goal (public good) to maintain the bright illumination of a "group light" for at least ten minutes and thereby receive partial course credit for her participation. In fact, the experimenter regulated the group light with a rheostat, as well as the subject's six individual lights which enabled her to perceive the contributions of other supposed members of her group. Average pedalling speed (revolutions per minute) was used to measure the individual's contribution to the public good. The results showed that subjects in a large group (where perceived individual effectiveness is nil) withhold a statistically significant part of their contributions in comparison to a small group (perceived effectiveness is large). This supports H_F in the context of a situation in which (it may be presumed) subjects believed they would be excluded from course credit if the group light was not kept sufficiently bright. However, two points must be emphasized: 1) of great significance is the fact that contributions were quite large under all experimental conditions. Mean contributions differed from zero far more significantly than from each other, even where the group light was bright and independent of subject speed and other subjects were contributing very little. Thus mean contributions (across six different treatment conditions) varied from speeds of 170.45 to 203.61, while standard errors varied from 26.12 to 58.89. 2) The conditions of excludability were imprecise, that is, there was no exact measurement which indicated to the subject when the group light was adequately bright to meet the group goal. These considerations suggest that H_F is supported only in a *very weak* form, and perhaps only because there was vagueness as to the conditions under which group excludability would occur. Indeed, given the high mean contributions under all treatment conditions, it seems that the results (a) are consistent with those reported in my 1979 paper for an entirely different experimental paradigm, and (b) do not support the generally held belief that free riding is a serious problem in the provision of public goods.

A more recent experimental study by Marwell and Ames also concludes that only a weak version of H_F is supported. The Marwell-Ames results are of particular interest because traditional public goods theory applied to their experimental paradigm provides a clear incentive to free ride. Each subject allocated an endowment of "tokens" (225 in the equal distribution case) between a "private exchange," yielding a well-defined constant private marginal rate of return in money, and a "group exchange" yielding a well-defined marginal rate of return in money that varied with the group's total contribution. The group exchange required an average contribution of 100 tokens per subject to yield a return better than that in the private exchange, and an average of 200 per subject to yield an optimal allocation. It would appear that the incentive to contribute nothing to the public good is very high. Using collectives of size four and eighty, the mean contribution was 127.6, well below the optimum, but remarkably large by conventional reasoning. Since subjects in the Marwell-Ames experiment made only one investment, it is possible to argue that learning effects in a repeat-play version would produce greater (or why not less?) support for H_F. But the Marwell-Ames results do not contradict those in other experiments (see my 1979 paper) that used repeat play. Hence, it seems that these empirical results are robust under replication and call into question the traditional model of public good decision behavior.

B. *Field Experiments*

Beginning in 1974, approximately 150 station managers in the American network of noncommercial television stations have used a computer-based decentralized mechanism called the Station Program Cooperative (*SPC*) to produce and allocate a substantial portion (nearly half in the 1974–75 season) of the programs broadcast by these stations. The *SPC* procedure uses a series of up to twelve trials, and has selected from 25 to 38 programs from menus of over 200 in each of its operating seasons.

Unlike the laboratory experiments reported above, and the field experiment reported below, the *SPC* (inefficiently, in theory) selectively excludes members who do not contribute their share of cost to a given program. On each trial, each station agent votes "yes" or "no" on each program, based on the cost share allocated to him on the previous trial. For the first trial an initialization procedure is followed. At present, the cost borne by station i for program j is simply

$$C_j B_i / \sum_{k \in S_j} B_k$$

where C_j is the production cost of program j, B_i is the budget (measured by the Community Service Grant awarded the station) of station i, and S_j is the set of stations voting for program j on the previous trial. With a little (but not much) discretionary intervention by the center over the twelve-trial sequence, the process converges in ten to twelve trials.

It is not illegitimate to question the correctness, that is, efficiency, of this process. But it is much more interesting to ask if it works, why it works, and whether it can be improved upon using well-defined criteria. It works in the sense that the participants seem heartily to approve of the process, but think it can be improved. It seems to work in the sense of rapid convergence because of strong individual exclusionary features, but in view of the good results from other experiments (less rich in number of commodities) that do not depend on individual exclusion, it is not certain that this is a necessary feature. Ferejohn, Robert Forsythe, and Roger Noll (pp. 43–57) have investigated some of these issues in a series of laboratory experiments comparing the *SPC* procedure with a "*B* procedure" based on a mechanism proposed by Jerry Green and Jean-Jacques Laffont. The termination condition for both procedures was that either 1) the same selections were made by all subjects on two consecutive trials (after the third), or 2) the trial exceed a "secret" number (always ten). The *SPC* terminated under 1) in every case (five experiments), while the *B* procedure terminated under 2) in every case (eight experiments). In terms of efficiency, neither procedure was clearly superior to the other. Hence, for multiple discrete public goods where individual exclusion is possible, the *SPC* stands as the operational mechanism that would-be designers must beat: It makes allocations no worse, and terminates earlier, than the only other mechanism with which it has been compared.

Peter Bohm has reported the results of a significant Swedish television field experiment which provides no support for H_F even in its weak form. The results are significant because they were particularly unexpected in November 1969 when the experiment was conducted. This was well before any of the ideas in the recent literature on incentive compatibility had become known. But Bohm's data gave him no recourse but to conclude "that the well-known risk for misrepresentation of preferences in this context may have been exaggerated" (p. 111). In retrospect the results are not unexpected because the conditions of the Bohm experiment effectively introduce the collective excludability characteristic of the auction mechanism, and, as I have argued elsewhere (1979), the results were actually to be expected because what was wrong was the theory that predicted free riding in the first place.

In summary, the empirical evidence from laboratory experiments, controlled field experiments, and actual field experience (*SPC*) overwhelmingly supports H_P. Not only is it true that incentive-compatible public good mechanisms are possible, and that there exist operational forms for such mechanisms; it is also true that such mechanisms are fairly easy to invent, they are not complicated and difficult to understand, and they are easy to computerize for large-scale decisions. Furthermore, there is some evidence (see Marwell and Ames) to suggest that the problem of free riding is not severe —in fact, pretty weak—even where there are strong and fairly obvious incentives to withhold contributions to a public good. In those mechanisms that are incentive compatible, perhaps this undercurrent of non-free-rider behavior by some agents helps to offset the effect of strategic manipulation (always potentially present) by other agents.

II. The Auction Mechanism for Public Goods

Consider an economy consisting of one private and one public good. Let consumer agent $i(i=1,2,\ldots,I)$ have an endowment ω_i of private good, and a utility function $u^i(y_i, X)$, increasing and concave in (y_i, X) yielding utility u^i if i retains y_i units of the private good for himself and the collective of I agents chooses to produce X units of the public good. A unit of the public good can be produced from q units (a constant) of the private good.

Let each agent choose a 2-tuple (B_i, X_i) where $B_i = \omega_i - y_i$ is the bid in private good units that i contributes to the production of the public good, and X_i is the quantity of the public good proposed by i. Define:

The collective's proposed quantity of the public good is the mean, $\bar{X} = \Sigma_{\forall k} X_k / I$, of the individual proposals.

The mean of all proposals excluding i is $\bar{X}_i = \Sigma_{\forall j \neq i} X_j/(I-1)$.

The sum of all bids excluding i is $\hat{B}_i = \Sigma_{\forall j \neq i} B_j$.

The net (residual) price of the public good to i is $q - \hat{B}_i/\bar{X}_i$, and his share of the cost of the collective's proposal is $(q - \hat{B}_i/\bar{X}_i)\bar{X}$.

Collective agreement (equilibrium) requires each i to accept his share of cost by bidding that amount and to accept the collective's proposed quantity of the public good as his personal proposal, that is, agreement occurs when there is unanimity in the sense that $B_i = (q - \hat{B}_i/\bar{X}_i)\bar{X}$ and $X_i = \bar{X}, \forall i$. A procedure for operationalizing these conditions is contained in the process described in the next section.

Assume $u^i(\omega_i, 0) < u^i(y_i, X) \forall y_i < \omega_i, X > 0$. Then i receives utility

(1)

$$W_i = \begin{cases} u^i\left[\omega_i - \left(q - \hat{B}_i/\bar{X}_i\right)\bar{X}, \bar{X}\right], & \\ \quad \text{if } B_i = \left(q - \hat{B}_i/\bar{X}_i\right)\bar{X}, X_i = \bar{X}, \forall i & \\ u^i[\omega_i, 0], \quad \text{if } B_i \neq \left(q - \hat{B}_i/\bar{X}_i\right)\bar{X} & \\ \quad \text{or } \bar{X}_i \neq \bar{X} \text{ for any } i & \end{cases}$$

It will be shown that if each i chooses (B_i, X_i) to maximize W_i, the resulting conditions correspond to a Lindahl equilibrium which is also a noncooperative or Nash equilibrium. However, (1) defines many Nash equilibria which are not Lindahl equilibria.

Assuming differentiability, a maximum of W_i requires "agreement" as defined above, and $-(q - \hat{B}_i/\bar{X}_i)(1/I)u_1^i + (1/I)u_2^i = 0$, or

$$B_i = \left(q - \hat{B}_i/\bar{X}_i\right)\bar{X}, \forall i \tag{2}$$

$$X_i = \bar{X}, \forall i \tag{3}$$

$$\frac{u_2^i}{u_1^i} = q - \hat{B}_i/\bar{X}_i, \forall i \tag{4}$$

From (2), since (3) implies $\bar{X}_i = \bar{X}$,

$$B_i + \hat{B}_i = q\bar{X}, \forall i \tag{5}$$

and, from (4), (2), and (5)

$$\sum_{\forall k} \frac{u_2^k}{u_1^k} = \frac{\sum_{\forall k} B_k}{\bar{X}} = \frac{B_i + \hat{B}_i}{\bar{X}} = \frac{\sum_{\forall k}(w_k - y_k)}{\bar{X}} = q \tag{6}$$

which defines an interior $(0 < y_i^0 < \omega_i)$ Lindahl equilibrium, $(y_1^0, \ldots, y_I^0, X^0)$. This is also a Nash equilibrium since if all $j \neq i$ bid $B_j^0 = \omega_j - y_j^0$, and propose $X_j = X^0$, agent i's best choice is $B_i^0 = \omega_i - y_i^0$ and $X_i = X^0$; otherwise he prevents agreement and receives utility $u^i(\omega_i, 0) < u^i(y_i^0, X^0)$.

That there exist Nash equilibria that do not satisfy (4) and (6) is seen by considering any $(y_1^*, \ldots, y_I^*; X^*)$ such that $u^i(y_i^*, X^*) > u^i(\omega_i, 0) \forall i$ and

$$\sum_{\forall i} \omega_i = \sum_{\forall i} y_i^* + qX^*$$

Then if $\forall j \neq i$, $B_j = \omega_j - y_j^*$, $X_j = X^*$, agent i's best choice is to agree to the arrangement by setting

$$B_i = \omega_i - y_i^* = -\sum_{j \neq i} \omega_j + \sum_{j \neq i} y_j^* + qX^*$$

and $X_i = X^*$.

It is well known that a Lindahl equilibrium is among the set of Pareto optimal arrangements, where the latter must satisfy (6). The Lindahl equilibrium defined by (4) and (6) and the Pareto optimal set defined by (6) can be contrasted with the free rider solution. To obtain this solution, assume that each agent i chooses y_i on the assumption that X is determined by whatever budget $\Sigma_{\forall i}(\omega_i - y_i)$ results from these choices. Thus if each i chooses y_i, $0 \leqslant y_i \leqslant \omega_i$, then $X = \Sigma_{\forall i}(\omega_i - y_i)/q$. Each i is then assumed to $\max_{y_i} u^i(y_i, \Sigma_{\forall i}(\omega_i - y_i)/q)$. Hence, at a maximum, $(y_1', y_2', \ldots, y_1'; X')$, we have

$$(7) \qquad \frac{u_2^i}{u_1^i} \leqslant \frac{\sum_{\forall i}(\omega_i - y_i')}{X'} = q$$

where $y_i' = \omega_i$ if $<$ holds for any i. In (7) we allow for boundary solutions $y_i' = \omega_i$ since they occur in the experimental design reported in Section III below.

The auction mechanism experiments reported in my 1979 paper correspond to the model stated above if we set $u_1^i \equiv 1$, $\forall i$. The utility function is then $u^i(y_i, X) \equiv y_i + u_i(X)$ and $u_2^i = u_i'(X)$. Consequently, the set of Pareto optimal allocations defined by (6) is simply the quantity of the public good X^0 satisfying $\Sigma_{\forall i} u_i'(X^0) = q$, which is also the Lindahl equilibrium quantity if this equation has a unique solution. The Lindahl prices $b_i = u_i'(X^0)$ are given by (4) with b_i representing agent i's bid in numeraire units per unit of the public good. The budget constraint is necessarily satisfied since $X^0 \Sigma_{\forall i} b_i = qX^0$ identically.

III. PLATO Public Good Experiments

The experiments to be reported here used a computerized iterative decision process to operationalize the mechanism of the preceding section. The computations in this process are too complex to have been executed effectively without computer aid. The PLATO computer system with visual display consoles was programmed to execute the procedures that guide subject groups through the decision process. Such a system has enormous advantages over manually executed experiments in standardizing procedures, eliminating possible experimenter or "auctioneer" effects, recording subject choices, performing routine calculations, and displaying the appropriate private or public information to the subjects.

Prior to the commencement of an experiment it must be initialized by the experimenter. For initialization PLATO requires numerical values for $(I, T, q, \omega_i, a_i, b_i, \alpha_i, \beta_i)$, where I is the number of subject agents who will participate in the experiment, T is the maximum number of decision trials, q is the unit cost of the public good, ω_i is the private good endowment of subject i, and the payoff function in dollars to i is $V^i(y_i, X) \equiv a_i y_i^{\alpha i} X^{\beta i} - b_i$ for all (y_i, X) such that $V^i \geqslant 0$.

The language of the process consists of private messages $(B_i(t), X_i(t))$ sent by agent i on trial t to PLATO, and private messages $(q - \hat{B}_i/\overline{X}_i)\overline{X}$ and public messages $(\Sigma_{\forall i} B_i, \overline{X})$ sent by PLATO to each i on each trial. The process uses the following iterative procedure:

(i) *Starting rule*: On trial t each agent, using his or her typewriter keyboard, independently and privately types a 2-tuple $(B_i(t), X_i(t))$ where $B_i(t) \in [0, \omega_i]$ and $X_i(t) \in [0, 12]$. Agent i, at his discretion, then presses a key that actually transmits his selection to the "center," that is, a memory space in PLATO.

(ii) *Transition rules*:

(a) After the last subject-agent has entered his choices, PLATO computes $(\Sigma_{\forall i} B_i, \overline{X})$. In sixteen of the experiments below, this message was transmitted to each agent, while in thirteen experiments, $\overline{X}$ was first rounded to the nearest integer before the message was sent.

(b) If $\Sigma_{\forall i} B_i \geqslant q\overline{X}$, the collective has reached tentative agreement. If $\Sigma_{\forall i} B_i = q\overline{X}$, each agent's share of cost is set equal to his bid $q\overline{X} - \Sigma_{\forall j \neq i} B_j = B_i$. This fact is reported to each i, and PLATO goes into a voting mode in which each agent is asked to type "yes" or "no" indicating whether he wishes to accept or not accept as final the arrangement resulting from that trial. If $\Sigma_{\forall i} B_i > q\overline{X}$, PLATO modifies the collective's decision $(\Sigma_{\forall i} B_i, \overline{X})$ so that the center retains none of the bid surplus. Two procedures were used in this modification:

1. Rebate rule 1: PLATO first determines if the overbid is sufficient to allow an integer increase in the size of the public

good, that is, the largest $n=0,1,2,\ldots$ such that $\Sigma_{\forall i} B_i \geq q(\bar{X}+n)$ was chosen. Any remaining bid surplus is then rebated to each agent in proportion to his bid. Thus, if agent k's bid was B_k the adjusted bid becomes

$$(8) \qquad B_k' = B_k\left[1 - \frac{\sum_{\forall i} B_i - q(\bar{X}+n)}{\sum_{\forall i} B_i}\right] = \frac{B_k q(\bar{X}+n)}{\sum_{\forall i} B_i}$$

where $\bar{X}+n$ is the adjusted proposed size of the public good.

2. Rebate rule 2: PLATO adjusted the outcome $(\Sigma_{\forall i} B_i, \bar{X})$ to give $(\Sigma_{\forall i} B_i', \bar{X}')$ where the vector from $(\Sigma_{\forall i}(\omega_i - B_i), \bar{X})$ to $(\Sigma_{\forall i}(\omega_i - B_i'), \bar{X}')$ is orthogonal to the production-possibility frontier and the point $(\Sigma_{\forall i}(\omega_i - B_i'), \bar{X}')$ lies on the frontier. Consequently, the adjusted quantity of the public good and the adjusted bid of agent k are

$$(9) \qquad \bar{X}' = \frac{\bar{X} + q\sum_{\forall k} B_k}{1+q^2}$$

$$B_k' = \frac{B_k q \bar{X}'}{\sum_{\forall i} B_i}$$

(c) If $\Sigma_{\forall i} B_i < q\bar{X}$, PLATO computes each agent's share of cost $(q - \hat{B}_i/\bar{X}_i)\bar{X}$, which is received as a private message by each i. In this case PLATO bypasses the voting mode, goes to trial $t+1$, and again each agent selects a 2-tuple $(B_i, \bar{X}_i)$ to be transmitted to the center.

(iii) *Stopping rule*:

(a) The process stops on trial $t^* \leq T$ if the arrangement resulting from trial t^* is brought to a vote, and all i vote yes.

(b) Otherwise the process stops on trial T.

(iv) *Outcome rule*:

(a) If the process stops by (iiia) the collective has reached an equilibrium agreement, and each agent is paid $V^i[\omega_i - B_i(t^*), \bar{X}(t^*)]$ dollars in cash. If $U_i(\cdot)$ is i's (unobserved) utility of money with $U_i' > 0$, then the final outcome to i from equation (1) in Section II is

$$W_i(t^*) = u^i\left[y_i(t^*), \bar{X}(t^*)\right] = U_i\left\{V^i\left[\omega_i - B_i(t^*), \bar{X}(t^*)\right]\right\}$$

(b) Otherwise (i.e., if the process stops by (iiib)) each agent receives $W_i(T) = u^i(\omega_i, 0) = U_i[V^i(\omega_i, 0)]$.

IV. Experimental Design and Results

If subject i has a monotone increasing utility $U_i(V^i)$ for V^i dollars, where $V^i = a_i y^{\alpha_i} X^{\beta_i} - b_i$ is i's payoff function, then the Lindahl equilibrium quantities of the private and public good are independent of the U_i, and given by

$$(10) \qquad y_i^0 = \frac{\alpha_i \omega_i}{\alpha_i + \beta_i}$$

$$X^0 = \left(\frac{1}{q}\right)\sum_{\forall_i}\left(\frac{\beta_i \omega_i}{\alpha_i + \beta_i}\right)$$

Table 1 exhibits the individual experimental design parameters for the basis set of three classes of subject agents, and Lindahl equilibrium private quantities, bids, and payoffs. The PLATO version of the auction mechanism is designed to replicate the basis economy in multiples of three. That is, there are three classes of individuals identified by endowment and payoff function parameters. An experimental collective consists of k subjects in each class, $k=1,2,3,\ldots$, corresponding to collectives of size $I=3,6,9,\ldots$, in which the unit cost of the public good is $q, 2q, 3q, \ldots$. The public design parameters applying to the experimental collectives and number of experiments conducted under each condition are listed in Table 2. Whenever the available time was adequate, an experimental session consisted of two back-to-back experiments in which the second experiment was a second play with the same "experienced" subjects. The total number of

TABLE 1—EXPERIMENTAL DESIGN, INDIVIDUAL PARAMETERS

Parameter	Parameter Class I	II	III
α	0.2	0.4	0.1
β	0.2	0.1	0.4
a	16	7	14
b	15	6	13
ω	8	10	5
y_i^0, *LE* Private Quantities	4	8	1
$\omega_i - y_i^0$, *LE* Bids	4	2	4
$V^i(y_i^0, X^0)$	\$14.14	\$12.89	\$13.65

Note: *LE* refers to Lindahl equilibrium.

TABLE 2—EXPERIMENTAL DESIGN, COLLECTIVE PARAMETERS

Collective Size I	3	6	9
q, Unit Cost Public Good	2	4	6
X^0, Lindahl Optimal Quantity	5	5	5
X', Free Rider Quantity	2.89	1.67	1.42
Number Experiments:			
Inexperienced Subjects	8	3	4
Experienced Subjects	7	3	4
Total Experiments	15	6	8
Total Subjects	45	36	72

experiments classified by collective size and experience treatment is shown in Table 2. The free rider quantities of the public good listed in Table 2 are computed using (7), which for Cobb-Douglass payoff functions leads to the solution

(11)

$$y_i' = \min\left[\omega_i, \frac{\alpha_i q X'}{\beta_i}\right], X' = \frac{1}{q}\sum_{\forall_i}(\omega_i - y_i')$$

Tables 3, 4, and 5 contain the final trial bids by subject parameter class, and the quantity of the public good provided in each experiment for collectives of size three, six, and nine, respectively. Each experiment is code numbered in the first column of each table. For example in Table 3, PA3.3 refers to PLATO auction, collective size three, session three, in that order. Experiments without a prime designation on the last digit were the first "inexperienced" play while those with a prime were the second "experienced" play. Thus PA3.3 was the first of two experiments in the third session with three subjects, while PA3.3′ was the second experiment using the same subjects. The only difference (besides experience) between two such experiments is that the subjects are rerandomized among the three parameter classes in the second experiment. Experiment PA9.1 aborted due to a program error, but the second experiment in that session PA9.1′ was completed and counted as an experience play. Out of a total of twenty-nine experiments, one collective of size three (PA3.1) and one of size nine (PA9.3) failed to reach agreement to provide units of the public good.

The mean quantity of public good provided by the experimental collectives in each size and experience class is shown in Table 6. Excluded from these calculations are the zero outcomes in the two experimental groups that failed to reach agreement. The pooled overall mean is 5.3 if these two observations are included. From Table 6 it will be seen that there appears to be no systematic effect of collective size or experience on the quantity of public good provided. This is borne out more precisely by a regression of X^* on 1) collective size, 2) a dummy variable for experience, and 3) a dummy variable for the rebate rule. None of these variables are significant: the largest value for the t-statistic for any of these three independent variables is 0.285, with $R^2 = .005$. I must conclude that none of the alleged "treatment" variables has any credible effect on the provision of the public good. Collectives of all sizes provide much larger quantities of the public good than is predicted by the free rider hypothesis, and mean quantities slightly larger than is predicted by the Lindahl quantity. Figure 1 plots all twenty-nine experimental final trial outcomes $(\Sigma_{V_i} y_i^*, X^*)$ along the production-possibility frontier. All twenty-seven experi-

TABLE 3—BID-QUANTITY OUTCOMES, PLATO AUCTION MECHANISM EXPERIMENTS, $I=3$

Subject	1	2	3	X^*, Final Quantity[a]	t^*, Final Trial[c]
Parameter Class	$\omega_1=8$	$\omega_2=10$	$\omega_3=5$		
LE Bid, $w_i-y_i^0=B_{i0}$	4	2	4		
Final Bids, B_i^*					
Rebate Rule 1					
PA3.1[b]	(3)	(1)	(2)	0 (5)	15
PA3.2	4.55	1.8	3.6	5	6
PA3.2′	5	5	4	7	2
PA3.3	2	8	0	5	12
PA3.3′	5	2	1	4	11
PA3.4	3.67	3.67	4.58	6	3
PA3.4′	4.58	6.42	0.92	6	14
Rebate Rule 2					
PA3.5	1.95	3.89	3.89	4.87	12
PA3.5′	3.69	5.54	1.85	5.53	12
PA3.6	3.95	5.92	4.93	7.4	14
PA3.6′	2.94	4.42	4.91	6.13	4
PA3.7	2.85	1.9	2.85	3.8	14
PA3.7′	1	2	3	3	10
PA3.8	3.94	6.89	1.97	6.4	1
PA3.8′	4.89	7.82	1.96	7.33	4

Note: See Table 1.
[a]The *LE* quantity is $X^0=5$, in all experiments.
[b]Bids and quantities in parentheses are the final trial outcomes for experiments failing to reach agreement.
[c]Maximum number of trials, $T=15$.

TABLE 4—BID-QUANTITY OUTCOMES, PLATO AUCTION MECHANISM EXPERIMENTS, $I=6$

Subject	1	2	3	4	5	6	X^* Final Quantity[a]	t^*, Final Trial	T, Maximum Trials
Parameter Class	I $\omega_1=8$	II $\omega_2=10$	III $\omega_3=5$	I $\omega_1=8$	II $\omega_2=10$	III $\omega_3=5$			
LE Bid, $w_i-y_i^0=B_i^0$	4	2	4	4	2	4			
Final Bids, B_i^*									
Rebate Rule 1									
PA6.1	5.76	2.88	2.88	3.83	5.75	2.88	6	3	15
PA6.1′	5.4	3.6	0.9	2.73	4.5	2.73	5	6	15
Rebate Rule 2									
PA6.2	3.92	6.86	0	6.86	8.83	1.9	7.1	8	10
PA6.2′	0	5.99	3.99	3.99	8.98	1.4	6.08	7	10
PA6.3	5.87	6.85	3.91	6.85	3.91	4.89	8.07	8	10
PA6.3′	2.99	4.99	3.99	1	5.98	3.99	5.74	6	10

Note: See Table 1.
[a]See Table 3.

ments reaching agreement produced quantities of the public good in excess of the relevant free rider quantity.

Table 7 records the α (Type I error) and $1-\beta$ (power) probabilities, where the null hypothesis H_0 is that the sample quantities of the public good for each collective size came from a population with mean equal to the theoretical free rider quantities (Table 2), and the alternative hypothesis H_1 is that the sample quantities came from a population with mean equal to the Lindahl quan-

TABLE 5—BID-QUANTITY OUTCOMES, PLATO AUCTION MECHANISM EXPERIMENTS, $I=9$

Subject	1	2	3	4	5	6	7	8	9			
Parameter Class	I $\omega_1=8$	II $\omega_2=10$	III $\omega_3=5$	I $\omega_1=8$	II $\omega_2=10$	III $\omega_3=5$	I $\omega_1=8$	II $\omega_2=10$	III $\omega_3=5$	X^*, Final	t^*, Final	T, Maximum
LE Bid, $w_i-y_i^0=B_i^0$	4	2	4	4	2	4	4	2	4	Quantity[a]	Trial	Trials
Final Bids, B_i^*												
Rebate Rule 1												
PA9.1′	6.22	3.56	1.78	0.89	7.11	4.44	5.4	2.67	3.56	6	10	15
PA9.2	7.47	2.79	3.71	5.57	1.86	1.76	5.57	8.36	4.64	7	11	15
PA9.3[b]	(1.25)	(6)	(5)	(4)	(1)	(5)	(6)	(7)	(4)	0(7)	(15)	15
PA9.3′	0.97	1.94	3.89	3.89	9.72	1.94	3.89	5.84	3.89	6	14	15
Rebate Rule 2												
PA9.4	3.99	3.99	2.99	4.99	4.99	0	2.99	1	3.99	4.82	8	15
PA9.4′	3	6	1	0	4	1	4	4	2	4.17	12	15
PA9.5	3	5	3	2	1	3	5	7	3	5.33	7	10
PA9.5′	4.99	3.99	0	5.99	4.99	1	5.99	3.99	0	5.16	9	10

Note: See Table 1.
[a]See Table 3.
[b]Bids (quantities) in parenthesis are the final trial bids (quantities) for experiments failing to reach agreement.

tity (5). The first row of selected α probabilities is used to calculate the critical value X_c (for each collective size I), above which we reject H_0 (accept H_1) if the sample mean exceeds X_c. The calculations are based on the t-distribution with sample sizes equal to the number of experiments, and variances computed from the X^*, as listed in Tables 3, 4, and 5. These critical values are then used to compute the $1-\beta$ power probabilities of the test. For example, under H_0 for $I=3$ (col. 1, Table 7), $X_c=2.89+t_\alpha(V_f/N_f)^{1/2}=3.5$ corresponding to a power of $1-\beta=0.7$ (i.e., $t_\beta=(3.5-5)(V_f/N_f)^{1/2}=-0.528$).

Examples of the trial-by-trial "moves" by experimental collectives are illustrated in Figures 2 and 3 for collectives of size three and nine, respectively. In Figure 2 on trial 1, the collective proposed $\bar{X}(1)=8$, and bid $\Sigma_{i=1}^3 B_i(1)=\Sigma_{i=1}^2[\omega_i-y_i(1)]=23-10=13$; on trial 2, $(\bar{X}(2),\Sigma B_i(2))=(8,10)$; and so on. Trials 4 and 11 were voting trials as indicated by the asterisks. On trial 4, the collective overbid the cost of the proposal, i.e., $2\bar{X}=6<\Sigma B_i=8$, and under the integer-increase Rebate Rule 1, the collective's proposal was increased (dashed arrow) to 4. This outcome was vetoed and the collective proceeded to trial 5. Finally, on trial 11 the collective proposed 4, bid 8 and approved

TABLE 6—MEAN PROVISION OF PUBLIC GOOD
$I=3,6,9$; $X^0=5$

Collective Size I	Mean Quantity of Public Good Chosen: Inexperienced Collectives	Experienced Collectives	Pooled
3	5.50	5.57	5.53
6	7.06	5.61	6.33
9	5.72	5.33	5.50
Pooled	5.91	5.51	5.7[a]

[a]Based on the twenty-seven "agreement" experiments. The overall mean is 5.3 for all twenty-nine observations.

TABLE 7—ERROR AND POWER PROBABILITIES FOR FREE RIDER (H_0) AND LINDAHL EQUILIBRIUM (H_1) HYPOTHESES

Collective Size	3	6	9
$\alpha=$ Probability of Rejecting H_0 (Accepting H_1) when H_0 is True	0.5	.05	.05
$1-\beta=$ Probability of Accepting H_1 (Rejecting H_0) when H_1 is True	.70	.85	.83
Critical Value X_c	3.5	2.6	2.1

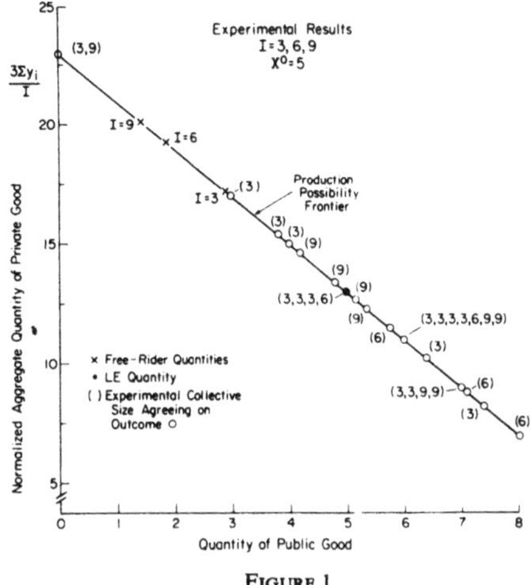

FIGURE 1

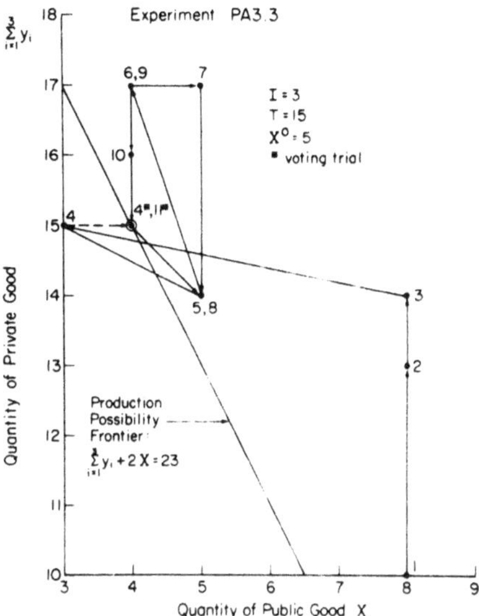

FIGURE 2

the outcome unanimously. Figure 3 illustrates one of the nine-member collectives under the orthogonal rebate rule. Thus on trials 4, 5, and 7, the collective overbid the mean proposal, and in each case a new proposal and bid sum was computed by PLATO based on the orthogonal adjustment (dashed arrows), under Rebate Rule 2, to the boundary of the production-possibility set.

It will be noted that the public good quantity proposals in Figure 3 are less variable than those in Figure 2. This was typical of the larger collectives which, because of this "law of large numbers" effect, were less interactive than the smaller collectives. The variance of final quantities of the public good in three-member collectives was 1.82; in six-member collectives, 1.36; in nine-member collectives, 0.82. This result supports the hypothesis that larger groups are less interactive than smaller groups, but using the Bartlett test, I am unable to reject the null hypothesis that the three population variances are equal.

Since subjects in an auction mechanism experiment are free to bid zero, it is of interest to examine the data of Tables 3–5 for instances of such behavior on the final (equilibrium or boundary) trial. In Table 3,

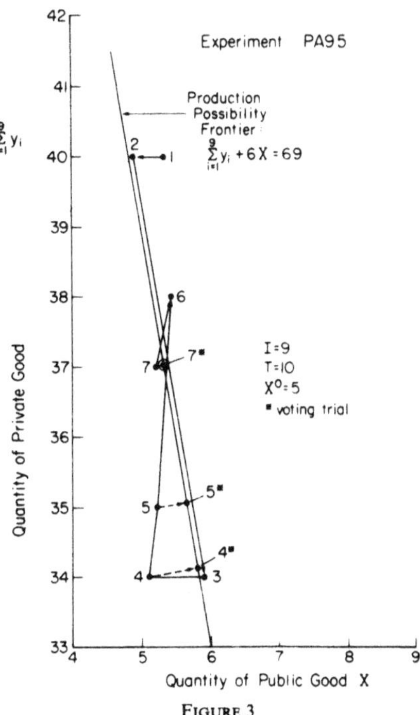

FIGURE 3

TABLE 8—FRACTION OF SUBJECTS BIDDING ZERO OR THEIR ENDOWMENT ON THE FINAL TRIAL

Collective Size	Fraction of Subjects Bidding 0	Fraction of Subjects Bidding ω_i
3	$\frac{1}{45}=.022$	$\frac{3}{45}=.067$
6	$\frac{2}{36}=.056$	$\frac{1}{36}=.028$
9	$\frac{4}{72}=.056$	$\frac{6}{72}=.083$
All Collectives	$\frac{7}{153}=.046$	$\frac{10}{153}=.065$

it is seen that in only one three-member collective did an individual bid zero (subject 3 in PA3.3) on the final trial. At the other extreme, three individuals (subject three in PA3.4, PA3.6, and PA3.6′) bid their entire endowments (before rebate) on the final trial. Normally there was an overbid on a final (agreement) trial with a corresponding rebate that prevented such bids from yielding a zero payoff. Table 8 provides a summary, classified by collective size, of the fraction of subjects bidding zero or their entire endowments. All twenty-nine sessions were included in this determination. If zero bidders represent free rider behavior, and endowment bidders represent anti-free rider behavior, the results in Table 8 suggest that these two extremes are represented about equally in the population of subjects. Furthermore, Table 8 shows no credible increase in free rider bidding behavior as collective size increases in the range from $I=$ 3–9.

V. On the Pareto Optimality of Experimental Outcomes

The previous section tested experimental public good outcomes against the free rider and Lindahl optimal quantities of the public good. However, as has been emphasized by Samuelson (1969), the Lindahl equilibrium (LE) (when there are income effects) provides merely one of many Pareto optimal allocations, and has no special ethical appeal. Since our experimental collectives typically reached agreement on public good quantities that deviated from the Lindahl optimal quantity, it is natural to ask whether these deviations fell within the Pareto optimal set.

The Pareto optimal set is defined by (6). For $I=3$ and Cobb-Douglas utility functions (6) becomes

$$(6') \qquad \sum_{i=1}^{3}\frac{\beta_i y_i}{\alpha_i X}=q=\frac{\Sigma(\omega_i-y_i)}{X}$$

This suggests a linear regression hypothesis among any three of the four quantities (y_1, y_2, y_3, X) depending upon which quantities are arbitrarily selected as the dependent and independent variables. If y_2 and y_3 are regarded as the independent variables with X being the dependent variable, then the Pareto-regression hypothesis is

$$(12) \quad X=\left[\frac{\gamma_2-\gamma_1}{q(1+\gamma_1)}\right]y_2 + \left[\frac{\gamma_3-\gamma_1}{q(1+\gamma_1)}\right]y_3+\frac{\gamma_1\sum_{i=1}^{3}\omega_i}{q(1+\gamma_1)}$$

where $\gamma_i=\beta_i/\alpha_i$. Based on the experimental design parameters listed in Table 1, the Pareto-prediction hypothesis is

$$(12') \quad X=-0.1875y_2+0.75y_3+5.75$$

Using the fourteen observations on collectives of size three to estimate the coefficients of equation (12′) gives

$$X=\underset{(-3.915)}{-0.546y_2}-\underset{(-9.728)}{0.497y_3}+\underset{(5.648)}{9.533}$$

$$R^2=.74$$

The t-statistics shown in parentheses under each coefficient are computed on the null hypothesis that the population value is given by the corresponding coefficient in (12′). It is clear that these coefficients differ very significantly from their Pareto-predicted values. Hence, we reject the hypothesis that collectives of size three, using the auction

TABLE 9

Parameter Class	I $\omega_1=8$	II $\omega_2=10$	III $\omega_3=5$
LE Bid, $\omega_i - y_i^0$	4	2	4
Mean Bid, All Collectives	3.94	4.86	2.63

Note: See Table 1.

mechanism, tended to provide Pareto optimal allocations.

An examination of mean bids by subjects in the three parameter classes (Table 9) provides some insight into the nature of subject deviations from the Lindahl optimum. Subjects in class I having an endowment of 8, and a theoretical *LE* bid of 4, bid on average very close to 4. However, class II subjects with an endowment of 10 and a theoretical *LE* bid of 2, have a mean bid of 4.86. These subjects much prefer the private good to the public good, but apparently because of their relatively large endowments tend to "overcontribute" to the public good. Similarly, class III subjects with an endowment of 5 and a *LE* bid of 4, tend to "undercontribute" with a mean bid of only 2.63. Hence, the "rich" give more and the "poor" give less than is predicted by the *LE* bids. In this design, such a pattern of deviation is not consistent with Pareto optimality.

These results contrast sharply with my 1979 paper reporting the results of twelve auction mechanism experiments based on designs with no income effects. In these previous experiments, subject i received a payoff table $V_i(X)$ mapping quantities of the common quantity X into private dollars. Subject bids b_i were in dollars per unit of the public good, and the stopping rule required $b_i = q - \Sigma_{\forall j \neq i} b_i$, $\forall i$, on two successive trials with $X_i = \bar{X}$, $\forall i$, on the second trial (see my 1979 paper for a complete discussion). All but one of these partial equilibrium experiments converged to the unique Pareto and Lindahl optimal quantity of the public good given by $\Sigma_{\forall i} V_i'(X^0) = q$. Furthermore, a linear regression of final trial bids b_i^* on the *LE* prices $V_i'(X^0)$ using data on individual subjects across three series of experimental replications yielded intercepts insignificantly different from zero, slopes insignificantly different from one and R^2 values between 0.82 and 0.99. Hence, with no income effects, experimental outcomes are very accurately predicted by the *LE* quantity of the public good and the *LE* price. In the current series of experiments with income effects, the *LE* quantity of the public good is a fair predictor, and the *LE* bids a very poor predictor of experimental outcomes.

VI. Effect of Parameter Changes: How Robust Are the Experimental Results?

It is always appropriate to ask whether particular experimental results are due to artifacts unrelated to the theory one purports to test. In this context, it will be noted that subject payoffs were presented as 12 × 12 tables listing $V^i(y_i, X)$ for the integer values $y_i, X = 1, 2, \ldots, 12$. Hence, the median value of X in a subject's payoff table is 6.5. From Table 6 the pooled mean provision of the public good is 5.7 which is about as close to this median as it is to the theoretical *LE* quantity (5). Also, look at Table 9 listing mean bids. On average subjects contribute approximately one-half their endowments to the public good and retain one-half for private use. With total endowment 23 and $q = 2$ in a collective of three members, under the one-half rule the total bid is 11.5, providing budget support for 5.7 units of the public good. In such low-information games as the auction mechanism, it is not unreasonable to conjecture that subjects are drawn to median quantity proposals, or a simple

TABLE 10—EXPERIMENTAL DESIGN: $I=6, q=2, X^0=9, X'=3.33, T=10$

Parameter	Parameter Class I	II	III
α	.24	.96	.8
β	.96	.24	.8
a	1.5	1.5	1.5
b	0	0	0
ω	5	10	6
y_i^0, *LE* Private Quantities	1	8	3
$\omega_i - y_i^0$, *LE* Bids	4	2	3

Note: See Table 1.

TABLE 11—BID-QUANTITY OUTCOMES, PLATO AUCTION MECHANISM EXPERIMENTS; $I=6, q=2, X^0=9, X'=3.33, T=10$

Subject	1	2	3	4	5	6		
Parameter Class	I $\omega_1=5$	II $\omega_2=10$	III $\omega_3=6$	I $\omega_1=5$	II $\omega_2=10$	III $\omega_3=6$	X^*, Final Quantity	t^*, Final Trial
LE Bid, $\omega_i-y_i^0=B_i^0$	4	2	3	4	2	3		
Final Bids, B_i (Rebate Rule 2)								
PA1	3	3	3	2	1	3	7.5	9
PA1′	2.98	4.96	2.98	2.98	0.99	0.99	7.93	10
PA2	(1.5)	(4)	(4)	(0)	(6)	(1)	(8.83)	10
PA3	3.92	3.92	2.94	3.92	2.94	0.98	9.3	7
PA3′	1.97	1.97	1.97	1.97	4.93	1.97	7.4	9
PA4	3.61	4.51	3.61	0.90	4.51	4.51	10.83	1
PA4′	3.81	4.76	4.76	1.90	0	4.76	10	8
PA5	(.99)	(9.88)	(3.95)	(3.95)	(1.98)	(1.98)	(11.37)	10
PA5′	3	1	1	4	10	3	11	10

Note: See Table 1.

TABLE 12—MEAN BIDS AND MEAN PROVISION OF PUBLIC GOOD

Parameter Class	I $\omega_1=5$	II $\omega_2=10$	III $\omega_3=6$
LE Bid $\omega_i-y_i^0=B_i^0$	4	2	3
Mean Bid	2.85	3.46	2.81
Mean Provision of Public Good 9.14			

Note: See Table 1.

50–50 division of endowment between the public and private expenditure alternatives.

These arguments suggest the desirability of replicating the experiments with a different set of parameters. Table 10 lists the parameters used in a second series of nine experiments. For variation on the previous design, this design uses parameters $\alpha_i+\beta_i>1$ yielding only quasi-concave $V^i(y_i, X)$ functions. Two subject classes in the present design retain the same endowments (5 and 10) and *LE* bids (1 and 8) that characterized the previous design.

The final trial bids and quantities of the public good are shown in Table 11. Seven of the nine experimental collectives reached agreement. The mean provision of public good and the mean bids by parameter class are listed in Table 12. A t-test of the null hypothesis that the population mean quantity is the *LE* 9 cannot be rejected ($t_L=0.24$), whereas the free rider hypothesis is rejected ($t_F=10.1$). It is also clear that collectives are not providing quantities of the public good near the artifactual median X in their payoff tables. Comparing the mean bids of class III and class II subjects in Table 9 with the mean bids of class I and class II subjects in Table 12 (endowments 5 and 10, respectively), note a modest increase in the bids of subjects with endowments of 5 and a considerable decrease in the mean bid of subjects with endowments of 10. This is not consistent with the artifactual one-half endowment bidding rule.

I conclude that the auction mechanism results reported in Section IV are robust with respect to parameter changes. Both sets of experimental results support a slight over-provision of public goods relative to the Lindahl optimum. However, individual bids do not support Lindahl optimal bids, with the deviation of actual from Lindahl optimal bids being explained by a consistent tendency for endowment-rich subjects to overcontribute, and endowment-poor subjects to undercontribute, in relation to the Lindahl optimum.

REFERENCES

P. Bohm, "Estimating Demand for Public Goods: An Experiment," *Euro. Econ. Rev.*, No. 2, 1972, *3*, 111-30.

E. Brubaker, "Free Ride, Free Revelation, or Golden Rule?," *J. Law Econ.*, Apr. 1975, *18*, 147-61.

E. Clarke, "Multipart Pricing of Public Goods," *Pub. Choice*, Fall 1971, *2*, 17-33.

______, "A Market Solution to the Public Goods Problem," Urban Econ. Repts., Univ. Chicago, 1968.

J. Ferejohn and Fiorina, "The Paradox of Not Voting: A Decision Theoretic Analysis," *Amer. Polit. Sci. Rev.*, June 1974, *68*, 525-36.

______, **R. Forsythe, and R. Noll,** "An Experimental Analysis of Decision Making Procedures for Discrete Public Goods: A Case Study of a Problem in Institutional Design," in Vernon Smith, ed., *Research in Experimental Economics*, Greenwich 1979.

J. K. Galbraith, "Economics as a System of Belief," *Amer. Econ. Rev. Proc.*, May 1970, *60*, 469-78.

J. Green and J.-J. Laffont, "Characterization of Satisfactory Mechanisms for the Revelation of Preferences for Public Goods," *Econometrica*, Mar. 1977, *45*, 427-38.

T. Groves, "Incentives and Teams," *Econometrica*, July 1973, *41*, 617-33.

______, "The Allocation of Resources Under Uncertainty: The Information and Incentive Roles of Prices and Demands in a Team," tech. rept. no. 1, Center Res. Manage. Sci., Univ. California-Berkeley, Aug. 1969, ch. 4, 71-73.

______ **and J. Ledyard,** "Optimal Allocation of Public Goods: A Solution to the Free-Rider Problem," *Econometrica*, May 1977, *45*, 783-809.

L. Hurwicz, "On Informationally Decentralized Systems," in Roy Radner and C. Bart McGuire, eds., *Decision and Organization*, Amsterdam 1972.

J. Ledyard and J. Roberts, "On the Incentive Problem with Public Goods," disc. paper no. 116, Center Math. Stud. Econ. Manage. Sci., Northwestern Univ. 1974.

G. Marwell and R. Ames, "Experiments on the Provision of Public Goods I: Resources, Interest, Group Size, and the Free Rider Problem," *Amer. J. Sociol.*, May 1979, *84*, 1335-60.

Mancur Olson, *The Logic of Collective Action: Public Goods and the Theory of Groups*, New York 1968.

P. Samuelson, "The Pure Theory of Public Expenditure," *Rev. Econ. Statist.*, Nov. 1954, *36*, 387-89.

______, "Pure Theory of Public Expenditure and Taxation," in Julius Margolis and Henri Guitton, eds., *Public Economics*, London 1969.

V. Smith, "Incentive Compatible Experimental Processes for the Provision of Public Goods," in his *Research in Experimental Economics*, Greenwich 1979.

______, "Relevance of Laboratory Experiments to Testing Resource Allocation Theory," in Jan Kmenta, ed., *Evaluation of Econometric Models*, forthcoming.

G. Stigler, "Economic Competition and Political Competition," *Publ. Choice*, Fall 1972, *13*, 91-109.

J. Sweeney, "An Experimental Investigation of the Free-Rider Problem," *Soc. Sci. Res.*, 1973, *2*, 277-92.

Gordon Tullock, *Toward a Mathematics of Politics*, Ann Arbor 1967, ch. 7.

W. Vickrey, "Counterspeculation, Auctions and Competitive Sealed Tenders," *J. Finance*, Mar. 1961, *16*, 8-37

Experimental Tests of an Allocation Mechanism for Private, Public or Externality Goods*

Don L. Coursey
University of Wyoming, Laramie, WY, USA

Vernon L. Smith
University of Arizona, Tucson, AZ, USA

Abstract

The results of eleven three-part experiments provide data on the performance of a voluntary, unanimity, bidding mechanism (EXTERN) for private, public and externality goods. The important feature of this mechanism is that *all* of its information requirements are endogenous. All of the private and externality good experiments reached unanimity agreement; nine of the public good experiments reached agreement. Measures of demand revelation tended to be lower for the private good than the public good. This tendency carried over into the private and public components of the externality experiments which lowered allocative efficiency.

I. Introduction

In this paper we propose and test experimentally a decentralized mechanism, called EXTERN, for allocating a good whose aggregate production (= consumption) yields an external benefit (or cost) for each agent. Examples of such goods include commons models such as cattle grasslands or fisheries where aggregate consumption affects individual consumption, information models such as advertising or mineral exploration where individual and pooled information is valuable to each firm, and pollution models where aggregate consumption of a commodity creates a classic external diseconomy.

The classical correctional procedure for externalities is for a central authority to use taxes (or subsidies) to internalize the costs (or benefits) due to external effects. More recently, as a means of reducing the administrative burden of regulation, marketable pollution licenses have been proposed for industrial emissions and transferable catch quotas for ocean fisheries.

---

* We are grateful to the National Science Foundation for research support. A longer version of this paper, including a more detailed theoretical analysis, a description of the functional forms used for the payoff functions, and the experimental instructions, is available from Don Coursey upon request.

However, none of these procedures are closed with respect to the private information required to implement them. Where such information is unknown, attempts to correct for externality may reduce rather than increase welfare. Even the new incentive compatible mechanisms for public good decision, such as the Groves–Ledyard (1977) mechanism, require a central authority to impose certain parameters of the quadratic cost allocation rule. These parameters are therefore public goods chosen exogenously, and there is no guarantee that they will be set at levels that will avoid bankruptcy. EXTERN operates on the basis of the endogenous messages (bids) submitted by individual agents, and does not require a central authority to possess any information exogenous to the process. Since EXTERN operates entirely with preprogrammed information processing and allocation rules, no central authority is necessary beyond that which is required for enforcing property rights in ordinary market exchange.

The purpose of this paper is to report the results of an initial set of experiments designed to study operational forms of this mechanism. When any new mechanism, such as EXTERN, is proposed, the objective of applied "institutional engineering" is to find a *system* of institutions which reinforce the behavioral assumptions of the mechanism. A point developed at some length in Smith (1979*a*) is that all public good allocation mechanisms with "strong" theoretical properties lose those properties and take on a sea of Nash equilibria the moment they are imbedded in an information exchange process with an unanimity stopping rule. Generally then the problem of designing externality mechanisms whose information requirements are endogenous is inherently difficult and any solution found is not likely to be unique. EXTERN opens up analysis of mechanisms which specify a fully articulated allocation process and stopping rule and are based upon variations of procedures used in the field. This paper provides a first step in the experimental examination of this complex allocation problem.

EXTERN combines a pure private good mechanism—the competitive or uniform price sealed bid auction—with a pure public good mechanism, called the auction mechanism. Both of these procedures have been studied extensively in previous experimental research. For private goods, the discriminative auction, in which each accepted bid is charged a price equal to the amount bid, had been compared with the competitive auction, in which all accepted bids are charged a common price equal to the highest rejected bid (or, in some versions, the lowest accepted bid); cf. Belovicz (1979), Cox et al. (forthcoming), Miller & Plott (forthcoming) and Smith (1967). In both auctions, if X is the supply offered, the X highest bids are accepted. These studies have established that the competitive auction provides much better incentives for demand revelation, and higher market allocative efficiency, than does the discriminative auction. The high efficiency and demand (supply) revelation properties of the competitive sealed-bid auction have been shown to extend to the case of a uniform price sealed bid-offer auction in which buyers submit bids, and sellers submit offers, for each unit demanded or supplied; cf. Smith et al. (1982).

For pure public goods, the unanimity auction mechanism has been used in several experimental papers to obtain results in which near, or on average, optimal quantities of a public good are provided by groups with up to nine members; cf. Smith (1979*a*, 1979*b*, 1980).

Since EXTERN contains a pure private good and a pure public good mechanism as special cases of an externality mechanism, it is convenient in the experimental design to have each experiment consist of three parts: a private good sealed bid auction experiment, followed by a public good experiment, and finally an experiment in which a private good causes external effects. This three-part sequence allows subjects to obtain experience with the component private and public good mechanisms before attempting the more complex bidding procedure for the externality case in Part 3.

II. Theory

Consider an economy with two private goods (y, x) and I agents, let y be the numeraire good. Each agent i has a differentiable concave utility function $u^i(y_i, x_i, X)$ increasing in (y_i, x_i), with aggregate consumption $X = \Sigma_{k=1}^{I} x_k$ entering each u^i as a positive, negative or zero externality. This formulation can be interpreted as a pollution model if x is a commodity such as gasoline whose aggregate consumption creates an external diseconomy. The formulation is a commons model if, for example, x is grass consumed by cattle in a commons grassland, and aggregate grass consumption X affects individual meat production, $z_i = f(x_i, X)$. Then $u^i(y_i, x_i, X) = U^i(y_i, f(x_i, X))$ if (y, z) gives utility $U^i(y_i, z_i)$. Alternatively, x_i could be interpreted as test drilling by oil company i which yields valuable information to i. But total drilling activity, X, in the same geographical area is also of value to each i if information is pooled.

There are two special cases. In the first case $u^i(y_i, x_i, X) \equiv u^i(y_i, x_i, \cdot)$, and we have two pure private goods with no external effects. In the second case $u^i(y_i, x_i, X) \equiv u^i(y_1, \cdot, X)$, and we have a pure public good.

Consider first the general externality case. Let an institution, EXTERN, for allocating externality goods be defined as follows:

(i) on each of a series of not more than T trials let each i choose a $(x_i + 2)$–tuple $(b_i(1), \ldots, b_i(x_i); c_i, X_i)$ where $b_i(x_i)$ is i's bid b_i in numeraire units for the x_ith unit of the good, c_i is i's proposed per unit contribution (or bribe, if X provides a negative externality) and X_i is i's personal proposal for group aggregate consumption of the good.

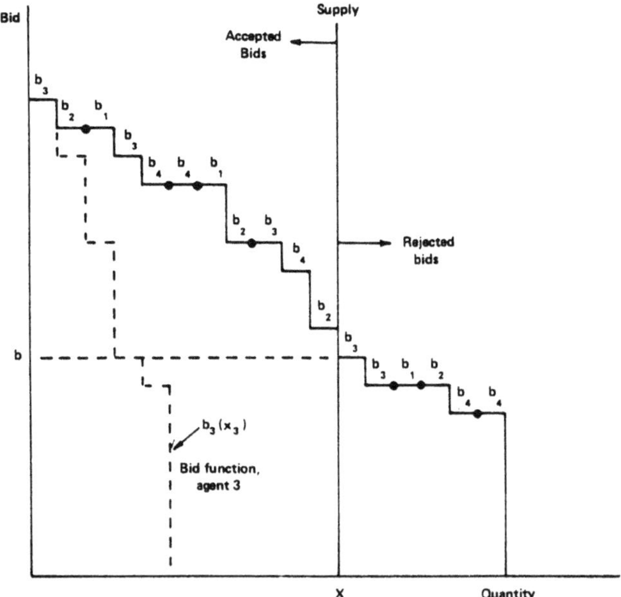

Fig. 1. Price determination from sealed bids.

(ii) The collective's proposed aggregate consumption of the externality good is $\bar{X}=\Sigma_{k=1}^{I}X_k/I$.

(iii) Let each of the unit bids of all agents be pooled and arrayed in descending (nonincreasing) order, i.e., $b_i(1)\geqslant b_j(2)\geqslant\ldots\geqslant b_k(\bar{X})\geqslant b_m(\bar{X}+1)\geqslant\ldots$, where i, j, k, m are any of the (not necessarily distinct) I agents. Note that if any i submits an increasing bid function this procedure reorders each agent's bids so that each bid function is nonincreasing.

(iv) The ruling price is the bid for the $(\bar{X}+1)$th unit in descending order, i.e., $b=b_m(\bar{X}+1)$, where the $(\bar{X}+1)$th highest bid is submitted by agent m. Hence, the $\bar{X}$ highest bids are accepted. If two or more agents are tied for the $\bar{X}$th accepted bid, e.g., $b_k(\bar{X})=b_m(\bar{X}+1)$, then k is determined by a random draw from the set of tied agents. This procedure is illustrated in Figure 1 for an example with four bidders.

(v) If agent i has x_i^a bids accepted, we have $b_i(x_i^a)\geqslant b$ (since $b_i(x_i)$ is nonincreasing we necessarily have $b_i(1)\geqslant b_i(2)\geqslant\ldots\geqslant b_i(x_i^a)$), and i is charged total cost bx_i^a for x_i^a privately consumed units. If q is the constant marginal rate of transformation of y into x, then unit social benefit (cost) is $(q-b)>0(<0)$ of which $\Sigma_{j\neq i}c_j$ is financed by positive (negative) contributions from all others. Therefore each i's net share of unit social benefit (cost) is $q-\Sigma_{j\neq i}c_j-b>0(<0)$. Total private plus social benefit (cost) in numeraire units is $bx_i^a+(q-\Sigma_{j\neq i}c_j-b)\bar{X}$. With endowment w_i of good y, the budget constraint for i is $w_i = y_i + b\,x_i^a + (q - \Sigma_{j \neq i} c_j - b)\bar{X}$. Note that the rule for accepting only the $\bar{X}$ highest bids assures closure with respect to private consumption, i.e. $\Sigma_{k=1}^{I} x_k^a = \bar{X}$.

(vi) At the end of each trial each agent votes as to whether he/she is satisfied with the trial outcome (price, quantity and share of benefit) and desires to stop the process. The stopping rule (agreement) requires unanimous consent.

We hypothesize that agent i will not want to stop this iterative process unless:

(a) $x_i^a = x_i^b$, where x_i^b is optimal for i at price b, i.e., if $x_i^a < x_i^b$, i will want to increase his/her bid for the units x_i^a, $x_i^a+1, \ldots, x_i^b$ to at least b. Implicit in this hypothesis is that i behaves as if b is independent of i's decisions.[1] A major purpose of the experiments reported below is to test this price-taking or demand-revealing hypothesis when only the *final* agreed upon outcome determines the utility of the agents.

(b) $c_i = q\Sigma_{j \neq i} c_j - b$, i.e., the net share of cost imputed to i is equal to an amount, c_i, that i is willing to contribute.

(c) $X_i = \bar{X}$, i.e., the group's proposed aggregate consumption is acceptable to i. If these hypotheses hold then optimality conditions for equilibrium will be satisfied when all agents vote "yes" on a given trial.

III. The Extern Experimental Design

EXTERN defines a more complex decision task than is represented by most previous experiments in economics. If the results of experiments based on this mechanism are to be meaningful it will be important to simplify and streamline the procedures as much as possible, and to program the experiment so that the learning requirements of the task are facilitated. This simplification is attempted by conducting the experiment in three separate parts corresponding to the case of a pure private good in Part 1, a pure public good in Part 2, and the externality good in Part 3. In addition, the condition $u_0^i \equiv 1$ is imposed in equation (2) to provide a utility function of

---

[1] If there are no ties at the highest rejected bid, b is determined uniquely by one of the bidders, and that bidder might lower the unit cost of his/her x_i^a accepted bids by reducing the bid for the (x_i^a+1)th unit. For example, in Figure 1, b would be less if agent 3 were to lower his/her bid for unit four. If agents are aware of this strategic possibility then the optimality conditions below do not apply. Dubey & Shubik (1980) have proposed a solution to this problem in which each bidder submits a single (b_i, x_i) pair. In this mechanism every competitive equilibrium is also a Nash equilibrium. Since all units bid for must be bid at the same price, this undercuts the theoretical incentive to underbid marginal units to influence price. Our first version of EXTERN was designed to use this single price-quantity bidding systems, but research reported by Smith et al. (1982) offered evidence showing that the Dubey–Shubik procedure yielded less efficient allocations than when bidders could submit bid schedules.

the form $u^i = y_i + f^i(x_i, X)$. Operationally this is achieved by giving experimental subject i a monetary payoff function $V^i(x_i, X)$. If $U_i(\cdot)$ is i's (increasing) utility of money, then the effect is to induce a utility $U_i[V^i(x_i, X)]$, corresponding to $u^i - y_i$, on outcomes (x_i, X). In the experiments reported below $V^i(x_i, X)$ is additively separable.

In Part 1 payoff is $V^i \equiv V^i(x_i, \cdot)$ and the experimental procedure corresponds to the special case of a pure private good offered in fixed inelastic supply. This experiment gives subjects experience in choosing x_i-tuples, $b_i(1), \ldots, b_i(x_i)$, and in price determination by the highest-rejected-bid rule. Furthermore, this experiment provides observations on a competitive sealed bid auction using a strong unanimity stopping rule. Part 2 is a pure public good experiment with payoff $V^i \equiv V^i(\cdot, X)$, where units of X can be purchased at constant unit cost q. Experiments of this form have already been performed; see Smith (1979*a*). Part 2 not only gives subjects experience in choosing 2-tuples (c_i, X_i) for financing and determining the quantity of a public good, but also provides an opportunity to replicate these earlier experiments. Given the experience with the pure private and pure public good components of EXTERN the subjects proceed (in one sitting) to Part 3 dealing with the general externality case.

In Part 1 of the experiment each of I subjects is given (marginal) valuation tables derived from payoff functions $v_i(x_i)$ for a maximum of nine units of private commodity x. A fixed total supply of units X_1 is announced as the supply for Part 1. On each trial t, each agent i submits a vector of bids $(b_i(1), \ldots, b_i(9))$ for each of nine units with the restriction that each bid $b_i(x_i)$ does not exceed the marginal valuation $v_i(x_i)$ for x_i units. All individual bids are collected, pooled, and arrayed in order from highest to lowest. A single market price b_1 is determined for all agents as the value of the $(X+1)$th highest bid. If $\hat{X}_1 \leqslant X_1$ bids are strictly greater than b_1, all such bids are accepted. If $\delta > (X_1 - \hat{X}_1)$ bids are equal to b_1, the δ bids are placed in a random sequence, and the first $(X_1 - \hat{X}_1)$ bids in this sequence are accepted. Hence, for each i, x_i^a bids are accepted such that $\Sigma_{i=1}^{I} x_i^a = X_1$. Finally, potential trial profits are computed as $\pi_i^1(x_i^a) = v_i(x_i^a) - b_1 x_i^a$ and reported to each i. Each i then votes on whether to finalize the results of trial t. If the group is unanimous "yes" for all I agents, then Part 1 ends and each i realizes the profit $\pi_i^1(x_i^a)$ in cash. If at least one agent votes "no" to reject the results of trial t, then a new trial begins with each i submitting a new vector of bids unless the maximum number of trials (T_1) allowed in Part 1 has been reached in which case Part 1 ends and each i receives *zero payoff*.

In Part 2 of the experiment each of the I agents is given (marginal) valuation tables derived from payoff functions $V_i(X)$ for a maximum of eight group units of a public good. The unit price, q_2, of X is announced at the beginning of Part 2. On each trial t, each i submits a 2-tuple (c_i, X_i) which is i's proposed per unit contribution c_i and proposed quantity of public good X_i. The group proposal is then computed (and defined) as the rounded average of the I individual proposals, $\bar{X}_2 = \Sigma_{i=1}^{I} X_i/I$, where $\bar{X}_2$ is rounded to the nearest integer. The total per unit group contribution is $C = \Sigma_{i=1}^{I} c_i$. If $C < q_2$ then unit cost is not covered, and each i receives a report of the profit $\pi_i^2(\bar{X}_2) = V_i(\bar{X}_2) - (q_2 - \Sigma_{j \neq i} c_j)\bar{X}_2$ that would be realizable if i were to contribute $c_i = q_2 - \Sigma_{j \neq i} c_j$, and if all other contributions and the group proposal remained unchanged on the next trial.[2] Hence, each i is informed of the potential opportunity cost if i fails to close the gap between unit cost and the contributions by all others. The purpose of this procedure is to emphasize the private cost of group exclusion which is incurred if the group fails to reach agreement. Following this report of the trial outcome the group proceeds to the next trial, and chooses a new 2-tuple (c_i, X_i), unless the maximum number (T_2) of allowable trials has been reached. If $C \geqslant q_2$ then each i receives a unit rebate, $r_i = (C - q_2)c_i/C$, which is proportional to i's contribution. Each i's per unit cost share is then recomputed as $c_i - r_i = c_i - (C - q_2)c_i/C = q_2 c_i/C$ so that total unit contributions, $\Sigma_{k=1}^{I} q_2 c_k/C = q_2$, are exactly equal to the unit cost of the public good. This procedure assures each agent that an overbid does *not* result in a loss of surplus to the center. Furthermore, the greater the overbid by any individual agent the greater is that agent's rebate. Based on this rebate, potential profit

$$\pi_i^2(\bar{X}_2) = V_i(\bar{X}_2) - \left[q_2 - \sum_{j \neq i} (c_j - r_j) \right] \bar{X}_2 = V_i(\bar{X}_2) - (q_2 c_i/C)\bar{X}_2$$

is computed and reported to each i. Each i then votes "yes" or "no" on whether to accept the group proposal and cost share for that trial. If the vote is unanimous, i.e., all agents vote "yes", then Part 2 ends and each i realizes the profit $\pi_i^2(\bar{X}_2)$ in cash.[3] If at least one agent votes "no" to reject the results of trial t, then the group proceeds to the next trial and chooses a

[2] Note, however, that the instructions do not actually "coach" a subject to raise his/her contribution in this manner.

[3] It should be noted that the unanimity stopping rule has the effect of making any individually rational allocation a Nash equilibrium on the final trial. As discussed in Smith (1979*a*) this property is shared by any mechanism, such as that of Groves and Ledyard (1977), which uses this stopping rule. An important result reported by Smith (1979*a*) was that the auction mechanism did as well as the Groves–Ledyard mechanism in public good allocation, and both mechanisms yielded very efficient allocations in spite of the proliferation of Nash equilibria in each; cf. also Smith (1979*b*, 1980). Other stopping rules, such as a random stop, may be more benign in terms of their effect on the static Nash property of the underlying mechanism, but they have not been studied experimentally and in view of the good results already reported it is clear that there is room for only marginal improvements. A random stop has two important deficiencies not shared by our unanimity stopping rule: First, it may stop the process before the agents feel that there has been sufficient information exchange. Second, a random stop cannot guarantee against involuntary bankruptcy.

new 2-tuple (c_i, X_i) unless the maximum number (T_2) of allowable trials has been reached. If the last trial has been reached each i receives *zero payoff*.

In Part 3 of the experiment care is taken to make the combined private and public decision process similar to that of the corresponding separate processes experienced in Parts 1 and 2. Each of the I agents is given a (marginal) valuation table for nine units of private consumption, x_i. Each agent is also given a public good (marginal) valuation table for a maximum of twenty "group" units of aggregate consumption. These tables are derived from an additively separable payoff function $v_i(x_i)+V_i(X)$. The constant per unit cost, q_3, of producing units of x is announced at the beginning of Part 3. On each trial t, each i submits an (x_i+2)-tuple consisting of a vector of bids $b_i(1), \ldots, b_i(x_i)$, a proposed per unit contribution, c_i, and a proposed level of aggregate consumption, X_i. Group proposed consumption is defined as the average of the individual proposals, $\bar{X}_3=\Sigma_{i=1}^{I} X_i/I$ rounded to the nearest integer. The private market price b_3 is then computed as in Part 1 as the $(\bar{X}_3+1)$th highest bid, with the x_i^a highest bids of subject i accepted such that $\bar{X}_3=\Sigma_{i=1}^{I} x_i^a$. Hence, the private good is allocated exactly as in Part 1 except that the total amount offered, $\bar{X}_3$, is determined endogenously by the individual proposals. Total unit contributions $C=\Sigma_{i=1}^{I} c_i$ are determined as in Part 2. If $C<q-b_3$ the public unit consumption cost, $q-b_3$, is not covered. In this case each i receives a report of the profit,

$$\pi_i^3(x_i^a, \bar{X}_3) = v_i(x_i^a)+V_i(\bar{X}_3)-\left(q_3-\sum_{j\neq i} c_j-b_3\right)\bar{X}_3-b_3 x_i^a$$

that would be realizable if i were to contribute $c_i=q_3-\Sigma_{j\neq i} c_j-b_3$, and if all other contributions, the group proposal, and the market price remained unchanged on the next trial. Each i then proceeds to the next trial unless the maximum number of trials for Part 3 has been reached. If $C\geqslant q_3-b_3$ then public unit consumption cost is covered and each i receives a proportional rebate $r_i=[C-(q_3-b_3)]c_i/C$. Hence, each i's per unit cost share is recomputed as $c_i-r_i=c_i-[C-(q_3-b_3)]c_i/C=(q_3-b)c_i/C$. Potential profit,

$$\begin{aligned}\pi_i^3(x_i^a, \bar{X}_3) &= v_i(x_i^a)+V_i(\bar{X}_3)-\left[q_3-\sum_{j\neq i}(c_j-r_j)-b_3\right]\bar{X}_3-b_3 x_i^a \\ &= v_i(x_i^a)+V_i(\bar{X}_3)-[(q_3-b_3)\,c_i/C]\,\bar{X}_3-b_3 x_i^a\end{aligned}$$

is computed and reported to each i. Each i then votes on whether to accept the group proposal, cost share, and market price for that trial. If the vote is "yes" for all i, then Part 3 ends and each i realizes the computed profit $\pi_i^3(x_i^a, \bar{X}_3)$ in cash. If at least one subject votes "no" and rejects the results of trial t, then the collective proceeds to the next trial and chooses a new

Table 1

Experiment number (1)	Number of agents (2)	Part 1: private good Supply (3) X_1	Price Observed (4) b_1	Price Comp. Equil. (5) b_1^o	Efficiency (6) E_1	Trials Observed (7) $\hat{T}_1$	Trials Maximum (8) T_1	Part 2: public good Unit cost (9) q_2	Quantity Observed (10) $\bar{X}_2$	Quantity P.O. (11) X_2^o	Quantity Free rider (12) X_2^f	Contributions (13) Σc_i	Efficiency (14) E_2	Trials Observed (15) $\hat{T}_2$	Trials Maximum (16) T_2
2.1.4	4	19	0.22	0.54	98	4	6	1.0	5	7	2	1.26	97	3	6
2.2.4	4	19	0.56	0.57	99	1	6	1.0	4	7	2	1.17	92	4	6
2.3.4	4	19	0.30	0.57	95	3	6	1.0	7	7	2	1.00	100	6	6
5.1.4	4	18	0.40	0.90	90	3	6	1.7	7	7	0	1.72	100	8	8
5.2.4	4	18	0.75	0.90	100	1	6	1.7	6	7	0	1.74	99	5	8
5.3.4	4	18	0.32	0.90	92	6	6	1.7	6	7	0	1.83	99	6	8
5.1.8[a]	8	36	0.25	0.90	90	2	6	3.4	7	7	0	3.27	(100)	8	8
5.2.8[b]	8	36	0.58	0.90	99	5	6	3.4	6	7	0	2.93	(99)	8	8
5.3.8	8	36	0.22	0.90	91	1	6	3.4	6	7	0	3.53	99	8	8
5.4.8	8	36	0.50	0.90	98	3	6	3.4	6	7	0	4.16	99	8	8
5.5.8	8	36	0.10	0.90	91	2	6	3.4	6	7	0	4.17	99	4	8

[a] In Experiment (5.1.8), Part 2, cost was not covered in trial 8. The results reported are for trial 7. Trial 7 was vetoed by subject 1 with a realizable profit of \$3.57.
[b] In experiment (5.2.8), Part 2, cost was not covered on trial 8. Trial 7 results are reported. Trial 7 was vetoed by subject 6 with potential profit \$0.42 and by subject 8 with potential profit \$0.00.

Table 2

Experiment number (1)	Number of agents (2) I	Part 3: externality good Unit cost (3) q_3	Quantity (4) $\bar{X}_3$	Quantity (5) X_3^o	Quantity (6) X_3^f	Price (7) b_3	Price (8) b_3^o	Contributions (9) Σc_i	Contributions (10) Σc_i^o	Efficiency (11) E_3	Trials (12) $\hat{T}_3$	Trials (13) T_3
2.1.4.	4	1.0	9	18	8	0.59	0.60	0.63	0.40	72	6	6
2.2.4	4	1.0	11	18	9	0.83	0.64	0.59	0.36	85	2	8
2.3.4	4	1.0	13	18	9	0.69	0.64	1.78	0.36	93	8	8
5.1.4	4	1.7	11	17	7	1.25	1.00	1.38	0.74	84	3	8
5.2.4	4	1.7	12	17	7	1.15	1.00	1.03	0.74	88	2	8
5.3.4	4	1.7	8	17	7	0.80	1.00	2.06	0.74	72	5	8
5.1.8	8	3.7	9	13	0	1.95	1.70	3.28	2.00	85	2	8
5.2.8	8	3.7	8	13	0	2.21	1.70	2.79	2.00	85	3	8
5.3.8	8	3.7	12	13	0	1.75	1.70	2.14	2.00	96	4	8
5.4.8	8	3.7	11	13	0	1.65	1.70	2.51	2.00	94	7	8
5.5.8	8	3.7	10	13	0	1.75	1.70	2.00	2.00	91	6	8

vector of bids, contributions and proposals unless the maximum number of allowable trials has been reached, in which case each i receives *zero payoff* for Part 3.

The above procedures for each of the three parts of the experiment were programmed on the PLATO computer system. All the experiments reported in the next section used either four or eight subjects. Individual marginal valuation tables for units of private and public good were obtained from linear logarithmic functions modified to yield more peaked profit functions at integer values for the theoretical equilibrium points. This modification insures that theoretically optimal allocations in Parts 2 and 3 actually occur at integer values of the public good. Column (1) in Tables 1 and 2 identify each experiment by series number, experiment number, and number of subject agents. Thus 5.1.8 refers to series 5, experiment 1, with eight subjects. Columns (3) and (5) in Table 1 exhibit the theoretical competitive equilibrium quantity and price (X_1, b_i^0) for each (Part 1) private good experiment. Columns (9), (11) and (12) in Table 1 show the unit cost (announced), Lindahl optimal quantity and free rider quantity (q_2, X_2^0, X_2^f) for each (Part 2) public good experiment. Columns (3), (5), (6) and (8) in Table 2 provide the unit cost (announced), optimal quantity, free rider quantity and competitive equilibrium price ($q_3, X_3^0, X_3^f\, b_3^0$) for each (Part 3) externality experiment. Columns (8) and (16) in Table 1 and column (13) in Table 2 indicate the maximum number of trials allowed for each experiment.

Figure 2 provides a graph of the aggregate market conditions that apply to the four-member groups in series 5 (experiments 5.1.4–5.3.4). Quadrant IV graphs aggregate demand for the pure private good experiment in Part 1. With $X_1=18$ units offered, the competitive equilibrium price is \$0.90 under the highest rejected bid rule. Quadrant I graphs the pure public good experiment of Part 2. With $q_2=\$1.70$, the Lindahl optimal quantity is $X_2^0=7$. By imposing the Pareto condition (for a discrete good) $\Sigma_{i=1}^{I} V_i(X_3^0) \geq q_3 - b_3^0$, Figure 2 graphs[4] the optimal allocation under the externality conditions of Part 3. With $q_3=\$1.70$, we have a discrete externality equilibrium at $b_3^0=1.00$, $X_3^0=17$.

The experiments with eight subjects (5.1.8–5.5.8) use four distinct valuation functions that are identical to those used in the experiments (5.1.4–5.3.4) using four subjects. The eight-person experiments differed from the four-person experiments in that (1) two subjects were assigned each of the four distinct valuation functions; (2) in Part 1 the inelastic offer quantity was doubled, i.e., $X_1=18$ in the four-person experiments and

[4] Note in Figure 2 that quadrants II and III impose graphically the Pareto condition that $\sum_{i=1}^{4} V_i'(17) = 0.74 > q - b = 1.70 - 1.00 = 0.70$.

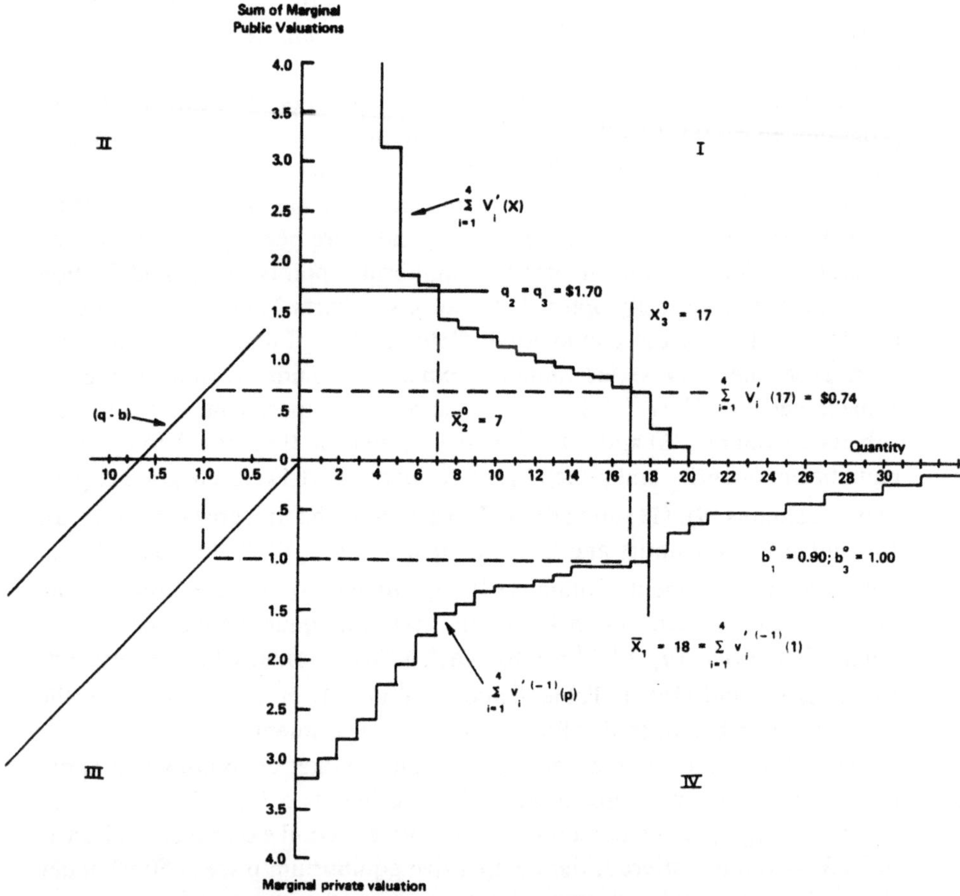

Fig. 2. Market equilibrium: four agents, series 5.

X_1=36 with eight bidders; (3) in Part 2 the unit cost of the public good was doubled from q_2=1.7 with four persons to q_2=3.4 with eight subjects. Consequently there was no structural difference between the four-person and the eight-person experiments in Parts 1 and 2. Since pure private good and pure public good allocations are invariant with a scalar increase in the number of agents in each valuation (utility and endowment) class, and the same scalar increase in pure private good supply, or in pure public good unit cost, this experimental design allows one to examine the effect of *ceteris paribus* changes in market size on performance. However, this is not possible in Part 3 of our experiments since external effects introduce a nonhomogeneity into the equilibrium conditions. In general doubling the number of agents in each valuation class and doubling unit cost does not double optimal output.

All the subjects who participated in the experiments reported below were

University of Arizona undergraduate and graduate students. They were relatively sophisticated in that they had previously participated in at least one, and in most cases several, PLATO programmed private market experiments. Although generally experienced with decentralized market mechanisms, none had previously participated in EXTERN.

IV. Experimental Results

A summary of the final trial results of each experiment is shown in Tables 1 and 2. Figures 3–5 chart the trial-by-trial outcomes for three illustrative experiments (5.1.4, 5.2.8, and 5.3.8).

Part 1: Private Good

Column (4) in Table 1, reporting observed market clearing prices for the private good shows a strong tendency to be much below the demand revealing competitive equilibrium prices (column 5). However, column (6), reporting the corresponding efficiency in these markets, shows that at least 90 percent of the potential surplus is realized in every auction (five auctions are at least 98 percent efficient). Consequently, although under-revelation substantially lowers the price and therefore the surplus to the seller, allocative efficiency is not reduced to a corresponding extent. This is because agents do not differ greatly in the degree to which demand is under revealed. This conclusion appears to hold with equal force in both the 4 and the 8 agent markets. There is evidence (see Figures 3 and 4) that price (and efficiency) is likely to increase (or not decrease) in successive trials as agents tend to increase their bids on rejected bid units in an attempt to increase their private purchases. This process is arrested early by the unanimity stopping rule. In only three of the eleven experiments did the private market continue beyond the third trial. This suggests that, under unanimity, allocative efficiency might be improved by requiring a minimum as well as a maximum number of trials.

Part 2: Public Good

Two of the eleven public good experiments failed to reach agreement under unanimity. Most of the remaining nine experiments (compare columns 10–12 in Table 1) reached agreement at or very near the Pareto optimal quantity of the public good, but all were well in excess of the free rider quantity. In this comparison the free rider quantity is defined as the maximum quantity, X_2^f, of the public good that would be purchased privately by any agent. All other agents are assumed to free ride on that agent's purchase. From column (14) in Table 1 public good efficiency is very high; on average efficiency is higher in Part 2 than in Part 1. These results are consistent with the pattern of outcomes reported in previous public good

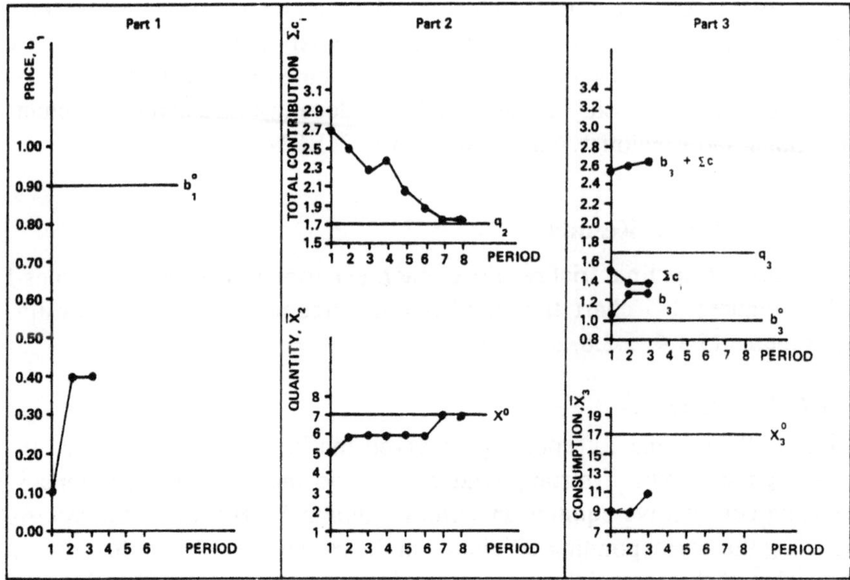

Fig. 3. Experiment 5.1.4.

experiments using the unanimity auction mechanism; cf. Smith (1979*a*, 1979*b*, 1980). The center panel in each of the Figures 3–5 exhibits the group decisions in successive trials for three illustrative experiments. In experiments (5.1.4) and (5.3.8) each group's proposed quantity of the public good

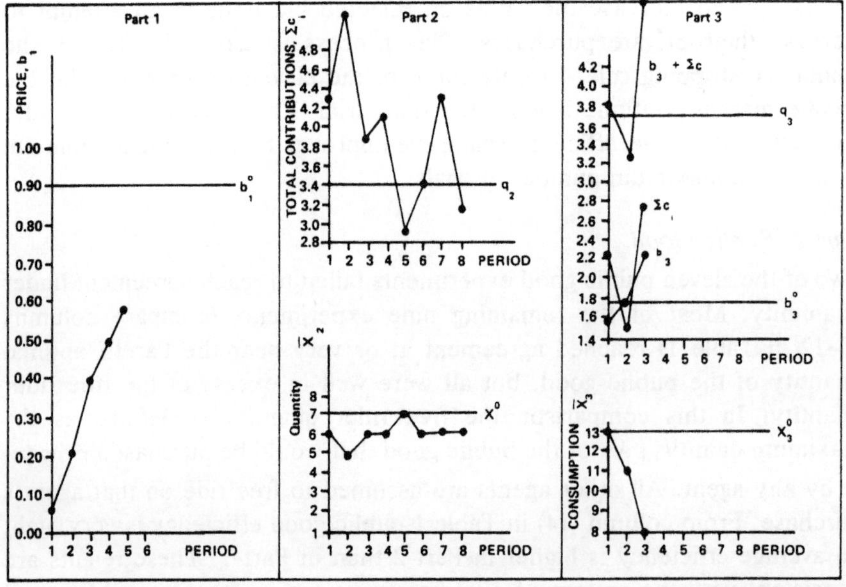

Fig. 4 Experiment 5.2.8.

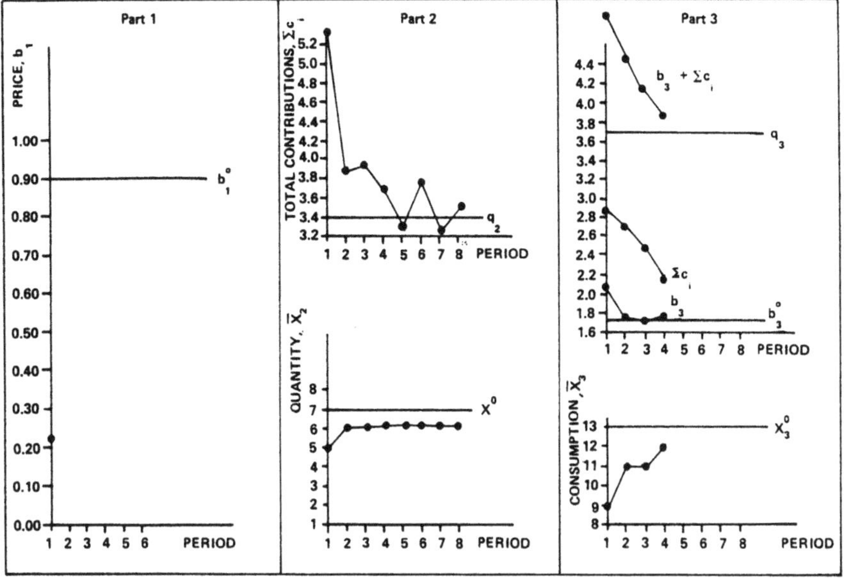

Fig. 5. Experiment 5.3.8.

tended to rise or hold constant over time, while total gross contributions (before the normalizing proportional rebate) tended to decline. In Part 2 of experiment (5.2.8), the collective failed to reach agreement in the eight allowable trials (see Figure 4). The anatomy of failure in this case illustrates a fairly common pattern observed in the 10–15% of the auction mechanism experiments that have failed to reach agreement, i.e., the penultimate trial was vetoed, and the final trial contributions failed to cover cost; cf. Smith (1979*b*, 1980).

The most significant empirical property of the comparative results in Parts 1 and 2 is the marked tendency toward greater under-revelation of demand in the private good mechanism than in the public good mechanism. The unanimity feature induced relatively good demand revelation for public goods, as indicated in Table 1, columns (9) and (13), by the fact that in most of the experiments total unit contributions are well in excess of the announced unit cost to be covered. But the unanimity (and/or the multiple unit bidding) feature of the private good mechanism provides poor demand revelation in the sense that the market clearing prices tend to be much below the competitive prices. This result is directly contrary to the conventional view that underrevelation of demand is inherently a more serious problem with public goods than with private goods. These experiments are consistent with the hypothesis that demand revelation is related more closely to the incentive properties of the mechanism than to the private versus public classification of the good.

Part 3: Externality Good

As in Part 1 for private goods, all eleven externality experiments reached unanimity agreement. Comparing columns (4)–(6) in Table 2, it will be observed that the agreed quantity of the externality good was always greater than the free rider quantity but consistently below the Pareto optimal quantity. Columns (7) and (8) show that in eight of the eleven experiments the market clearing price was above the theoretical competitive equilibrium price. Hence, even though there was some tendency to under-reveal bid demand as in Part 1 for the pure private good, the level of group aggregate proposed consumption (equal to supply) was reduced enough to raise most of the observed prices above the theoretical price. As in Part 2, contributions to cover the external benefits of aggregate consumption tended to exceed the value of such benefits. Hence, market price plus total contributions $(b_3+\Sigma c_i)$ in Part 3 exceeded unit cost by a substantial margin in most experiments. Yet subjects were content to accept large rebates on their unit contributions rather than propose, and finance, larger levels of aggregate consumption. This may have been a means of minimizing the risk of failing to cover unit cost, which would have precluded agreement under the stopping rule. What is not evident is why such behavior characterizes the externality good but not the public good. Thus in Figure 3, Part 2, the group gradually lowers unit contributions until unit cost is just barely covered, and increases the group proposal to the Pareto optimal quantity. But in Part 3 price plus unit contributions remain well above unit cost, while aggregate quantity was adjusted upward but incompletely toward the optimal level. The group in Figure 4, Part 3, started at the Pareto optimal quantity with cost covered, reduced both quantity and contributions, failed to cover cost, then voted to accept trial 3 at a still lower quantity, but one for which unit cost was covered by a large margin. Figure 5 charts the group that achieved the highest efficiency in Part 3 by moving within one unit of the Pareto optimal quantity on trial 4 while maintaining price and contributions high enough to cover unit cost.

V. Summary and Conclusions

This paper reports the results of eleven experiments, each providing data on the performance of a voluntary, unanimity, bidding mechanism (EXTERN) for private, public and externality goods. The distinguishing feature of the EXTERN mechanism is that its information requirements are endogenous. Although EXTERN incorporates a more complex set of institutional rules than normally used in laboratory experiments, it ran successfully when compared to other public good experiments. All of the eleven experiments reached unanimity agreement under the pure private and externality good versions of the EXTERN mechanism; nine experiments reached agreement under the pure public good version of the mechanism. Demand revelation (measured by efficiency and price for the private good, and measured by efficiency and total contributions for the public good) tended to be lower for the private good than for the public good.

Since previously reported experiments using the uniform price sealed-bid auction provided better demand revelation properties than the private good experiments reported here, we attribute this difference to either or both of the two new conditions added to the private good version of EXTERN studied in this paper: These are unanimity contracting and multiple unit individual demand. In the private good experiments the prospect of a veto does not introduce an excludability incentive because tentative allocations in the auction already exclude potential buyers. What it does is to reinforce the "cooperative" incentive to bid low in the following manner. Over time each bidder finds that some units are being excluded and raises his/her bids. Other bidders do the same and the surplus actually starts to fall over successive trials. Rather than continue to let things worsen, the typical group votes to stop early. Thus, since realizable or potential efficiency did tend to improve and some of the low realized (final trial) efficiency occurred in experiments which reached agreement within the first three trials, it is possible that efficiency could be improved by requiring a minimum number of trials, say 3 or 4.

The pure public good version of EXTERN is the same as the auction mechanism for public goods studied in previous experiments. The results reported here replicate the results reported previously: Among those experiments reaching unanimity agreement, the auction mechanism tends to provide public good quantities that are near the P.O. level.

The tendency to under reveal the demand for the private good carries over into the externality experiments. This characteristic, coupled with a tendency to propose aggregate consumption levels (= supply) that are below the P.O. level, causes efficiency in the externality experiments to be below the efficiency achieved in both the private and the public good experiments. This occurs even though the market price plus total contributions tends to be considerably in excess of the unit cost of the externality good even when the experiments terminate early. It appears then that the "cooperative" incentives may carry over from the pure private good auction to the externality experiments. It is less clear why this should occur in Part 3 since in some of the experiments surplus had been increasing at the time the process stopped. This is why, again, we suggest that there should be a minimum as well as a maximum number of trials (which, of course, we recognize could change the incentives). We could eliminate voting in Part 1 altogether, but *a priori*, we thought voting should occur since it was essential for those aspects of Part 3 which subsume Part 1.

Consideration of other members of the system of institutions which reinforce the behavior of the theoretical EXTERN mechanism is left for future research. New experiments which are designed to measure the relative importance of unanimity rules and the existence of multiple units per bidder in determining relative private market efficiency are called for. This extension ought to be conducted both in the context of no minimum and a minimum number of trials as discussed above. In the present set of experiments we have deliberately chosen group sizes which correspond to previous private and public auction experimental research. Our experiments need to be replicated for larger group sizes. Again, the role and relative importance of the unanimity rule will have to be considered. Although we feel that the assumption of induced additive separability of preferences is appropriate (at least as a good first approximation) to many field externality situations, a final important topic for future research is a test of EXTERN's institutional robustness with respect to this assumption.

References

Belovicz, M.: Sealed-bid auctions: Experimental results and applications. In *Research in experimental economics* (ed. V. Smith), Vol. 1, pp. 279–338. Greenwich, 1979.

Cox, J., Smith, V. & Walker, J.: Expected revenue in discriminative and uniform price sealed bid auctions. In *Research in experimental economics* (ed. V. Smith), Vol. 3, Jai Press, Greenwich (forthcoming).

Dubey, P. & Shubik, M.: A strategic market game with price and quantity strategies. *Zeitschrift für Nationalokonomie 40*, 25–34, 1980.

Groves, T. & Ledyard, J.: Optimal allocation of public goods: A solution to the free rider problem. *Econometrica 45*, 783–809, May 1977.

Miller, G. & Plott, C.: Revenue from sealed-bid auctions: Experiments with competitive and discriminative processes. In *Research in experimental economics* (ed. V. Smith), Vol. 3, Jai Press, Greenwich (forthcoming).

Smith, V.: Experimental studies of discrimination versus competition in sealed-bid auction markets. *Journal of Business 40*, 58–84, Jan. 1967.

Smith, V.: Incentive compatible experimental processes for the provision of public goods. In *Research in experimental economics* (ed. V. Smith), Vol. 1, pp. 59–168. Greenwich, 1979*a*.

Smith, V.: An experimental comparison of three public good decision mechanisms. *Scandinavian Journal of Economics 81*, No. 2, 1979*b*.

Smith, V.: Experiments with a decentralized mechanism for public good decisions. *American Economic Review 70*, 584–599, September 1980.

Smith, V., Williams, A., Bratton, K. & Vannoni, M.: Competitive market institutions: Double auctions vs. sealed bid-offer auctions. *American Economic Review 72*, 58–77, March 1982.

PART IV

Auctions and Institutional Design

Introduction

In an important sense, auction theory represents one of the most significant developments in economics and game theory in the second half of the twentieth century. Much of game theory, as with general equilibrium theory, is stillborn, unable to guide meaningful empirical investigation because of its failure to come to grips with exchange institutions and thus with process. But the modeling of auctions is predicated directly upon the allocation and message rules of alternative auction institutions. The distinction between agent messages and agent allocations, the effect of the environment (the number of bidders, parameters defining the probability distributions of values or cost, etc.), and assumptions about agent expectations and agent maximizing behavior are all explicit and clearly specified. In environments in which alternative auction institutions are equivalent, this institution-free property is derived as a theorem instead of being an implicit assertion. Auction theory does more than begin with the extensive form of a game, it begins with the various extensive forms we observe in the economy (with the exception, perhaps, of the Dutch auction, as discussed below). Consequently, it is able to guide empirical testing programs with a minimum overlay of empirical interpretation, or what Lakatos calls "initial conditions" and *ceterus paribus* clauses. Where the theory fails under experiment, which inevitably it will do with sufficiently rigorous "boundary" experiments, it is easier to see which part of the theory has failed and to see where theory needs improvement. It is for these reasons that the path of inquiry initiated by William Vickrey in 1961 is of such unusual significance; its research potential has only begun to be developed.

In the papers appearing in this Part, I and my coauthors report the results of experiments initiated in 1977 and which are continuing as I write. Paper 25 was the first and only report to examine all of the four basic auctions. During the whole of this period there has been an ongoing interaction between "measurement" or testing in the laboratory and the development of theory, particularly with respect to first-price single-object auctions and discriminative multiple-unit auctions. An important building block in this development was provided when John Ledyard proposed to us an equilibrium bid function for constant-relative-risk-averse (CRRA) agents in first-price auctions, where values are drawn from a rectangular distribution: $b_i = (N-1)\, v_i/(N-1 + r_i)$. This laid the foundation for the first noncooperative equilibrium model of bidding in strategic auctions that allowed for heterogeneous bidders – a property that the data had demanded of the theory beginning with our first experiments in 1977. We subsequently showed that this bid function applied only to that part of its nonnegative support below $\bar{v}_i$ corresponding to the maximum bid, $\bar{b}$, that would be made by the least risk-averse bidder in the population of bidders. If the least risk-averse bidder is risk-neutral, then $\bar{b} = (N-1)\, \bar{v}/N$. This theory and many new experiments are reported in paper 26. We subsequently extended the CRRA noncooperative model to multiple-unit auctions in which each of N bidders desires at most one of the $Q < N$ units offered for sale in a discriminative auction. This model and a large number of multiple-unit auctions are reported in paper 28. In these cases ($N > Q > 1$), the bid function is nonlinear in an environment with rectangularly distributed values, and we no longer observed linear bidding behavior by subjects. This result effectively falsifies the hypotheses, sometimes informally proffered, that linear bidding behavior somehow arises as a form of ''bounded rationality'' in bidders. (Obviously ''rationality'' is bounded; the real issue is how and in what ways that yield well-defined testable predictions.) In paper 30 we generalized the CRRA model for $Q = 1$ to the class of log concave utility functions in which the individual is characterized by $M-1$ parameters (in addition to his value, v_i). Because of our finding in this paper that the homogeneity property of linear predicted-bid functions was rejected for 22 percent of our subjects, we extended the CRRA model to include a (nonmonetary) utility of winning and a threshold utility effect. Some of the empirical implications of this new model were tested with new experiments.

Quite early in this auction research program we found evidence that the Dutch and first-price auctions were not equivalent (papers 25 and 26). We formalized two models designed to account for this nonequivalence (papers 26 and 27). In paper 27 we proposed, and conducted, a test to discriminate between the two models. The failure of the Dutch and first-price auctions to be isomorphic for the *particular* parameters we studied should not come as a surprise. The Dutch auction institution requires two free parameters of the Dutch clock to be chosen: the initial starting price offered on the clock, and the rate at which this offer price descends in real time. Dutch auction theory ignores these parameters, in effect assuming that they are irrelevant. Our finding that mean prices tend to be less in the Dutch than they are in the first-price auction might be reversed if the speed of the Dutch clock were increased sufficiently. Actual Dutch auctions have very fast clocks so that there is some uncertainty as to the exact price at which anyone stops the clock. In fact

Boulding's original conjecture (see paper 25), that the highest-value bidder should stop the Dutch clock as soon as it drops to, or just below, his demand price, may have predictive power for very fast Dutch clocks.

Like languages, exchange institutions and their supporting property-right institutions are not the product of one mind or of someone's logical experimental design, but are the product of thousands of minds over many generations of trial-and-error filtering, combined with a societal memory for those arrangements that are in some sense best, or good enough, in competition with other arrangements. Can we consciously design new and better property-right exchange systems? There is good reason to be skeptical about whether any of us as professionals knows or understands enough about the elements of institutional success to allow an affirmative answer to this question. But it is also true that we have made significant progress in the last quarter of a century in our abstract and empirical understanding of incentives in institutions. What we have tended to lack is the understanding that comes from practice, from trying, failing, and learning from the consequences. (This practice allows one to acquire what N. R. Hanson calls understanding the "go" of things.) More important perhaps than imperfections in our analysis is the fact that we may be reluctant to let our designs be reshaped by the opportunity-cost challenges that operate in less structured, unplanned environments.

Can laboratory experiments help us to design new and better exchange systems? The answer is yet to be determined. Since laboratory experiments allow us to study the incentive and performance characteristics of exchange institutions, it is reasonable to hypothesize that they can provide part of the means of giving us the needed practice at low cost. There have been several attempts to use experiments to help evaluate new institutions leading to mixed, uncertain, and sometimes unanticipated results. I describe three early such attempts in the chronological order in which they arose.

In 1967 I reported the results of several multiple-unit sealed-bid auction experiments comparing the usual discriminative form of this auction with the competitive (uniform-price) auction procedure proposed by Milton Friedman. These results provided some empirical support for Friedman's argument that the competitive auction would yield greater revenue to the seller than the discriminative auction. Henry Wallich, while he was a consultant to the U.S. Treasury, used these experiments to help convince Treasury officials of the merits of their running some field experiments in the two types of auctions. The results of sixteen long-term bond auctions (ten under discriminative and six under competitive rules) in the early 1970s suggested the conclusion that Treasury revenue was increased by the competitive treatment. This did not lead to a change in policy (I would not argue that it necessarily should have), and for several years Treasury officials were unwilling to allow the results of the study to be published. However, the idea of selling securities in competitive or uniform-price auctions (Wall Street misleadingly calls them Dutch auctions) spread quickly to the private sector. The mechanism was simple: an Under Secretary of the Treasury during the period when the Treasury was experimenting with competitive auctions later became a vice president of Exxon and introduced the procedure in some bond offerings by the company beginning in 1976. The procedure has been used weekly since 1978 by Citicorp to auction commercial paper, and Salomon Brothers has applied an extension of the procedure (the uniform-price sealed bid-offer auction) for regularly resetting the dividend on variable-rate preferred stock issues. In this case experiments played a role in introducing a new institution, but the focus and extent of its adoption were not a direct consequence of the original policy objectives.

A "success" story in institutional design is that of the Station Program Cooperative (SPC), suggested by Roger Noll and used by the American network of noncommercial television stations. The SPC was initiated (as a field experiment) in 1974 and was continued with relatively minor alterations thereafter. Under the SPC, member-station managers participate in a sequential computerized decision mechanism. At each round the PBS center sends information to each station about the identity and prices of active (nonexcluded) programs, and receives the list of programs each station desires to purchase at prices (cost shares) determined by the ratio of the station's "ability to pay" (a weighted average of its budget and the population it serves) to that of the sum of all other stations that elected the program on the previous round. Programs are dropped when no station desires to purchase it at the last quoted price. The first several SPC's converged in about twelve rounds. Theoretically, the procedure is neither efficient nor demand-revealing. But in practice the procedure converges rapidly, and misrevelation strategies are difficult to identify and execute successfully so that generally satisfactory allocations are achieved.

In the late 1970s Robert Forsythe, John Ferejohn, and Roger Noll conducted a series of experiments designed to replicate the SPC procedure in the laboratory and compare it with two alternative institutions representing attempts to improve the efficiency of SPC. Although efficiency averaged only 40 percent of the potential surplus available in the SPC treatment, neither of the alternatives did any better, and they took longer to terminate than did the SPC experiments.

A third example of experimental institutional design has had an uneven history and impact on public policy. With airline deregulation it became apparent that the allocation of airport access rights – runway rights for takeoff and landing – needed to be reevaluated. David Grether, Mark Isaac, and Charles Plott (GIP) applied laboratory experiments to the study of alternative methods for allocating runway rights, including the method of assignment by committee under unanimity rules that had been used prior to deregulation.

They recommended selling such rights in simultaneous competitive (uniform-price) sealed-bid auctions of each airport's available quantity in each time slot, as in the Treasury and laboratory experiments discussed above. Then an aftermarket open-book bid-offer mechanism would allow each airline to trade for the flight-compatible packages of different airport slots needed to support their multiple-city service schedules. Building upon the GIP institutional design, we (Steven Rassenti, myself, and Robert Bulfin) proposed and tested experimentally a "combinatorial auction" scheme (paper 30). We were struck by the unusual character of runway slot rights as commodities: they were worthless in use as independent commodities, and were in natural demand only in those package combinations that served feasible flight routes. We invented a "smart" computer-assisted auction in which buyers submitted bids for the desired packages (bidders could specify linear restrictions on such packages if there were budget, "either *X* or *Y* but not both," or "*X* only if *Y*" constraints on the desired package combinations). The computer then solved an integer programming problem that allocated elemental slots in fixed supply among the package bids so as to maximize the (revealed-bid) market value of all slots. Our mechanism priced each package at the sum of the marginal values ("shadow" prices) of the component elements. Consequently, bidders generally paid less than they bid and had some incentive to reveal demand. The experimental results showed that in fact demand revelation was good (efficiencies approached 99 percent with experienced subjects).

These latter efforts at institutional design in allocating airport rights have not progressed beyond the stage of academic exercises in spite of their promising showing in laboratory tests. For many years there were political obstacles to creating a cash market for runway slots even under the stipulation that the airlines be given grandfather rights to their initial holdings. Although this restriction was lifted for a time, what has been acceptable has been direct slot-for-slot(s) exchange. Charles Plott has worked with the carriers in implementing these slot exchanges and building upon the original GIP "aftermarket" experimental procedures. But a full-blown unconstrained market using a computer-assisted examination of the combinatorial aspects of the exchange problem has not yet developed. Runway rights are a strategic capital asset likely to be desired for long-term holding. Consequently, the market for them may remain for some time too dispersed and thin to take full advantage of the combinatorial possibilities in a thick continuous market. But the slot-trading concept is now firmly implanted in industry and government thinking. In the future, new airports and new airport capacity expansions have the option of financing their capital needs from direct sales of the additional runway rights. Also, combinatorial auctions are generic to a large number of commodities with the characteristic that combination value exceeds the sum of elemental values, and other applications may develop by extrapolation.

The combinatorial auction appears to be the first example of a "smart" computer-assisted exchange institution. In these institutions the computer executes algorithms designed to maximize "surplus," or the gains from exchange, conditional upon willingness-to-pay bids and/or willingness-to-accept offers submitted to a dispatch center by economic agents. The center bears a relationship to the industry similar to that of the New York Stock Exchange with the securities industry. The efficiency, price, and dynamic performance of these institutions is then evaluated with laboratory experiments by comparison with alternative institutions. Other examples of "smart" computer-assisted markets are being explored by Stephen Rassenti, Kevin McCabe, and me. One is an auction market for the pricing and allocation of electric power in a deregulated and decentralized electric power networks. Another is an auction for natural gas pipeline networks (paper 31). In the gas network application wholesale buyers submit location-specific bid schedules for delivered gas, wellhead owners submit location-specific offer schedules for produced gas, and pipeline owners submit leg-specific offer schedules of transportation capacity. The computer solves a linear program that yields surplus maximizing nondiscriminatory prices and gas flows for each source, each delivery point, and each transportation segment. In all these cases agents do what they are best qualified to do: provide to the dispatch center dispersed information on their private circumstances as reflected in their willingness-to-pay and willingness-to-accept schedules. The computer responds by doing what it is best qualified to do: solve the coordination problem so as to maximize efficiency using nondiscriminatory and nondiscretionary (and in this sense fair) procedures. The objective is to combine the information advantages of decentralization with the coordination advantages of centralization.

McCabe, Rassenti, and I are also exploring a number of exchange institutions that are new generalized forms of the ancient Dutch and English auction procedures for a single item. For example, the multiple-unit English and Dutch clock auctions are one-sided generalizations of their single-object counterparts in which all contracts are executed at a single nondiscriminating price. Further generalizations of these synthetic institutions are to two-sided multiple-unit auctions in which both buyers and sellers are active in the price-making exchange process: the double Dutch and double English institutions, each using two price change clocks and yielding multiple-unit exchange at nondiscriminative prices.

INCENTIVES AND BEHAVIOR IN ENGLISH, DUTCH AND SEALED-BID AUCTIONS

VICKI M. COPPINGER, VERNON L. SMITH, and JON A. TITUS*

The Pareto optimality and price behavior of English and Dutch oral auctions, and First-Price and Second-Price sealed-bid auctions are compared under various procedures for assigning valuations among cash motivated bidders. The Vickrey propositions with respect to the mean and variance of prices under the English, Dutch and Second-Price auctions are not falsified by the data. Individual behavior and prices in the First-Price auction deviates considerably from Vickrey's Nash postulate. Behaviorly, the English and Second-Price auctions appear to be isomorphic, but the Dutch and First-Price auctions may not be isomorphic.

Evidence for the existence of auctions is recorded in the histories of ancient Babylon and Rome (Cassady (1976, pp. 26-29)), and auctioning institutions continue today as important mechanisms for the exchange of a very large variety of commodities (Cassady (1967, pp. 16-19)). Yet there seems to have been only rare empirical or theoretical studies of the behavioral properties of alternative auction techniques. The unusual variety of different methods of auctioning goods suggests that the method of auctioning is believed to effect the transaction cost or the price of an exchange. We propose to use laboratory experimental methods for a fairly extensive study of the common forms of oral and sealed-bid (or written-bid) auctioning. The present paper reports the first series of experiments in this exploration.

I. ENGLISH AND DUTCH AUCTIONS: THEORY AND HYPOTHESES

The two most common forms of the oral auction are the English "ascending bid" procedure and the Dutch "descending bid" scheme.[1] It appears from the small amount of literature available, that there is general agreement as to the price outcome expected in an English auction, but a disparity of agreement as to what can be expected in the Dutch auction. In discussing the English system, Boulding (1948, p. 41), Vickrey (1961, p. 14) and Cassady (1967, p. 67) all suggest that an article will be awarded to the bidder placing the highest value on it, at a price

*Arizona State University, University of Arizona, and Arizona State University. Support by the National Science Foundation is gratefully acknowledged.

1. It seems likely that the English ascending bid auction was the most important in Roman history, since as noted by Cassady (1967, p. 28) the word auction is derived from the Latin root auctus, meaning "an increase".

just above the second highest value among the values of all potential purchasers of the article. This result, it is argued, follows because bids are freely announced until no potential buyer wishes to make a higher bid. Consequently, the article is "knocked down" to the most eager buyer at a price just above the demand price of the second most eager buyer. As noted by Vickrey (1961) in his incisive analysis of auctions, this is Pareto-optimal.[2]

In the Dutch system the bidding starts at a price certain to be above what any buyer would be willing to pay, and is lowered by an auctioneer (or a mechanical clock device) in increments until one of the bidders accepts the last price offer. Boulding (1948, p. 42) argues that in this auction we may expect the article to be sold to "the most eager buyer at a price which is just about the highest he is willing to pay, for in this case the most eager buyer does not know what prices the other buyers are willing to give," and ". . . each buyer fears that someone may slip in ahead of him." Similarly, Cassady (1967, p. 67) suggests that in the Dutch system ". . . if the bidder with the highest demand price really wants the goods, he cannot wait too long to enter his bid lest he endanger his chance of gaining the award. He thus may bid at or near his highest demand price." Vickrey (1961, pp. 14-15) observes that such full value bidding maximizes the probability of obtaining the object while guaranteeing a zero gain. Optimality requires the individual to balance the increased risk of losing the article with the increased gain if obtained, as the price is lowered. Hence, the Dutch auction is technically a game, and the price outcome depends on each bidder's knowledge or assessment of the valuations and behavior of the other buyers. The Dutch auction price must be below the highest valuation among the bidders, but need not be above the valuation of the second, or third, etc. most eager buyers. In fact the result need not be Pareto-optimal as, for example, would occur if the most eager buyer allowed the offer price to fall below the second highest valuation, continued to wait, and lost the item to this second most eager buyer.

Based on the assumption of Nash equilibrium behavior, expected gain maximization and symmetrical expectations in which each bidder assumes that the valuations of all bidders can be regarded as having been generated by a rectangular density, Vickrey (1961, pp. 14-20, 29-37) compares the English and Dutch auctions: In this special case the mean prices are the same in the two auctions, but the variance of prices in the English auction is larger than the variance of prices in the Dutch auction. Specifically, Vickrey shows that the mean price in Dutch and English auctions is $m = \dfrac{N-1}{N+1}$, where N is the number of bidders each of whose values were drawn from a rectangular density on the interval $[0,1]$. Simi-

2. Also see Loeb (1977) for a discussion of the important lineage of Vickrey's article with the reçent literature on incentive compatible resource allocation mechanisms.

larly, the variance of Dutch auction prices is $V_d = \dfrac{(N-1)^2}{N(N+1)^2(N+2)}$ and of English auction prices is $V_e = \dfrac{2(N-1)}{(N+2)(N+1)^2}$.

We are motivated by the above considerations to state the following hypotheses for experimental testing. Let P_e be the price in an English auction, P^o be the "optimal" price (defined as the second highest valuation among the buyers), and P_d be the price in a comparable Dutch auction. Then, if $p_e = P_e - P^o, p_d = P_d - P^o$, we state

H_0: $p_d^* = 0, \quad p_e^* = 0, \quad$ where $p_e^* = E(P_e - P^o), p_d^* = E(P_d - P^o)$.

H_1: $P_d^* = P_e^* = m$ where $P_d^* = E(P_d), P_e^* = E(P_e)$,

H_2: $\text{Var}\, P_d = V_d < V_e = \text{Var}\, P_e$ where m, V_d and V_e are as defined above.

If the Dutch and English auctions are equivalent institutions, and both are able to approximate Pareto-optimal results, then we will be unable to reject the null hypothesis, H_0, that in each institution deviations in prices from the second highest valuation came from a distribution with zero mean. This will serve as the general hypothesis to be tested in all experiments whatever the procedure used to assign valuations to individual subjects.

If Vickrey's assumptions and analysis hold (i.e., linear utility, homogeneous expectations and a rectangular distribution of individual valuations) we will be unable to reject the null hypothesis, H_1, that Dutch and English prices came from distributions with the same mean, m. If H_0 (or H_1) is rejected with $p_d^* > p_e^*$ (or $P_d^* > P_e^*$) the Dutch auction is more favorable to the seller than the English auction, which supports the position articulated above by Boulding and Cassady. If H_0 (or H_1) is rejected and $p_d^* < p_e^*$ (or $P_d^* < P_e^*$), the Dutch auction is less favorable to the seller than the English auction, which contradicts both the Vickrey and the Boulding-Cassady positions. However, a finding that $p_d^* > p_e^*$ (or $P_d^* > P_e^*$) would not be inconsistent with a risk averse version of the Vickrey model. Thus, if bidders in a Dutch auction maximize expected (concave) utility of gain then to compensate for risk they would enter somewhat higher acceptance bids (seeking lower, more certain gains) than if they maximize expected gain. This would raise the relative Dutch auction price, p_d^*. Risk aversion in the English system would have no effect on the expected price, p_e^*, because the second highest value is a dominant strategy equilibrium (Loeb, 1977). Finally, if we fail to reject the hypothesis H_2, this supports the Vickrey theory, otherwise his theory is not supported by the variance characteristics of the experimental observations.

Frahm and Schrader (1970) have compared the English and Dutch auction procedures using experimental methods. Their experimental paradigm was the more complicated multiple unit successive auction (Vickrey (1967, pp. 24-26)) in which buyers have private induced

TABLE 1

Number of Auctions Performed, by Session and Auction Type

Session \ Auction Type (in sequence)	Dutch	English	Dutch	English
1		10		
2		5	5	5
3	10			
4	5	5	5	
5		12	12	12
6	12	12	12	

demand schedules for units of a homogeneous commodity, and the quantity offered for sale is put up for bidding one unit at a time. Frahm and Schrader found the variance of prices in the English auction significantly greater than in the Dutch auction thereby supporting the Vickrey hypothesis. They also found $p_e^* > p_d^*$, which was statistically significant in one paired comparison but not in a second comparison.

II. ENGLISH AND DUTCH AUCTIONS: EXPERIMENTAL DESIGN

We propose here to examine the oral auction for only a single unit of a commodity. A total of 48 subjects participated in a design consisting of six experimental sessions each with eight buyers. Table 1 exhibits the sequence of "treatment" (auction type) conditions for each session. Session 1 consisted of 10 English auctions to be compared with session 3 consisting of ten Dutch auctions. In session 2, five English auctions were followed by five Dutch auctions, and then five more English auctions. In session 4 the sequence was five Dutch, five English, and five Dutch auctions. Employing such "switch treatment" sequences is a powerful experimental technique for rendering more credible the proffered finding that measured effects are due to the treatment condition, and not just to sampling variation or other unidentifiable factors. One controls on effects due to differences in subject groups by exposing the same group to both treatments. One examines learning or other "hysteresis" effects by switching away from, then back, to the initial treatment; and by replication with a different sequencing of treatment application (cf. Battalio, et al (1973, pp. 421, 426)). In each session a demand for one unit was induced on subject i by promising him a cash payment of $V_i(t)$ less the price in auction t (plus 5 cents) if i was the winning bidder. In every auction these values (referred to as "resale values" in the instructions), when arrayed in descending order, were separated by increments of $1.50. However, these arrays differed by a parameter-disguising constant from one auction to the next and the individual valuation sequences were assigned randomly to the eight subjects in each session. By using the same valuation sequences we obtain some control over any potential influence of particular sequences. Each experimental subject received a copy of the instructions and a record sheet.[3] Each subject's earnings were accumulated over all auctions and paid in cash at the end of the experiment. Subjects were given information only on their own valuation parameters and were seated so that such information would remain private.[4]

All auctions were conducted orally. Each auction began with the experimenter specifying a predetermined starting price. To stimulate active bidding among the participants each English auction was started at $1.50 below the lowest valuation. Each Dutch auction was started at a price of $2.00 above the highest resale value, and the price descended in $0.50 steps at seven second intervals. A coin toss was used to determine the winner when there was a tie. Of course both starting prices and price change increments must be supposed to be treatment variables. Whatever effects they have must either be randomized or held constant across experiments. We chose to keep them constant.

For purposes of testing the more specific Vickrey hypotheses, H_1 and H_2, and exploring the robustness of the results from sessions 1-4, we replicated sessions 2 and 4 using different subjects, a rectangular distribution, and longer auction sequences. Session 5 replicated 2 but the sequence consisted of twelve English auctions followed by twelve Dutch, followed by twelve English. Similarly, session 6 replicated 4, but with twelve Dutch followed by twelve English, then twelve more Dutch auctions. In sessions 5 and 6 each of the eight subjects were assigned values at random from the 100 element set ($0.10, $0.20, . . . $9.90, $10.00). We also omitted the 5 cent commission for making a purchase that was paid in sessions 1-4.

3. Interested readers may write V. Smith to obtain copies of an Appendix consisting of the valuations, instructions and recording forms used in representative experiments.

4. We regard the privacy of individual valuations as an important characteristic of many if not most markets using oral auction institutions. Cassady (1976, p. 150-151) reports some particularly dramatic examples that support this. Thus, in the auction of Rembrandt's "Titus", Norton Simon wrote out an elaborate agreement with the auctioneer presumably to prevent other bidders from knowing when and how much he was bidding. When "Mr. Simon is sitting down he is bidding. If he bids openly he is bidding. When he stands up he has stopped bidding. If he sits down again he is not bidding unless he raises his finger . . ." and so on (Cassady (1976, p. 151)). As can be appreciated the auctioneer got lost in the procedure, and awarded the painting to another bidder before being challenged by Mr. Simon who was actually the high bidder.

TABLE 2

Means and Variances of Differences, $p = P(t) - P^{o}(t)$, by Session and Auction Type.

Session	Auction Type, in sequence	Dutch	English	Dutch	English
1	Mean		0.106		
	Variance		0.0295		
2	Mean		−0.10	−1.40	0.45
	Variance		0.6437	0.30	0.1375
3	Mean	−0.80			
	Variance	0.6778			
4	Mean	−1.50	−0.50	−1.20	
	Variance	1.875	0.9688	1.575	
5	Mean		0	0.233	0.038
	Variance		0.0036	1.5988	0.0160
6	Mean	0.383	0.017	−0.050	
	Variance	3.19	0.0320	0.7645	

III. ENGLISH AND DUTCH AUCTIONS: EXPERIMENTAL RESULTS

A. Sessions 1-4. Charts 1-2 plot the difference $P(t)$-$P^{o}(t)$ for each of the four experimental sessions, where $P(t)$ is the English or Dutch auction price resulting from auction t, and $P^{o}(t)$ is the second highest valuation (the theoretical English auction price) for auction t. Inspection of these data points leaves little doubt that with our particular experimental design parameters, a) English and Dutch auctions are distinct pricing institutions, and b) the Dutch auction produces a lower selling price than the English auction. Table 2 lists the means and the variances of the differences $P(t)$-$P^{o}(t)$ for each session and auction type. On the average Dutch auction prices occur from \$.80 to \$1.50 below the second highest valuation (recall that the assigned valuations are separated by \$1.50 steps). Consequently, Dutch auction prices are closer to the *third* highest valuation than to the second highest valuation. English auction prices average from \$.45 above to \$.50 below the second highest valuations.

The pooled mean of the price differences in the four sets of Dutch auctions is $\bar{p}_d = -1.14$, while the pooled mean for the English auctions is $\bar{p}_e = .0124$. A t-test of H_0 gives $t_d = -5.09$, and $t_e = 0.096$, requiring us to reject the null hypothesis that Dutch auction prices do not

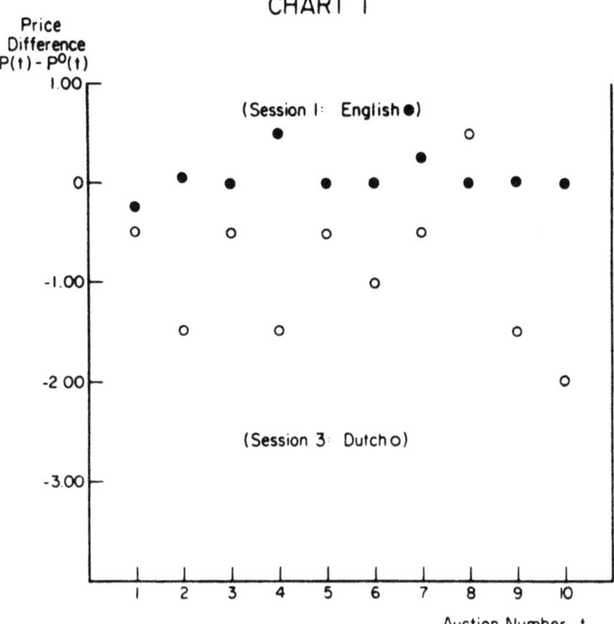
CHART 1
Price
Difference
P(t) - P°(t)
1.00
0
-1.00
-2.00
-3.00
(Session 1: English ●)
(Session 3: Dutch o)
1
2
3
4
5
6
7
8
9
10
Auction Number, t

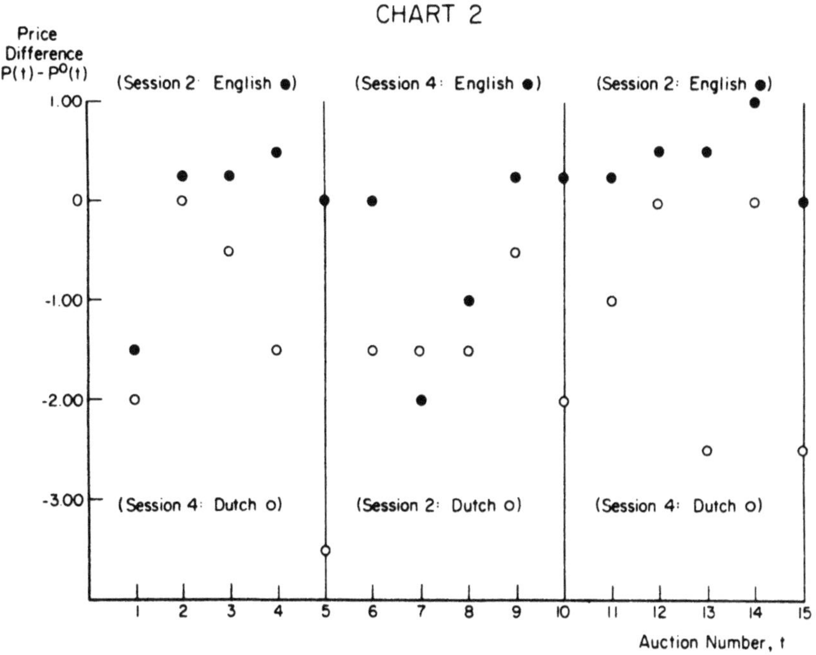
CHART 2
Price
Difference
P(t) - P°(t)
(Session 2: English ●)
(Session 4: English ●)
(Session 2: English ●)
1.00
0
-1.00
-2.00
-3.00
(Session 4: Dutch o)
(Session 2: Dutch o)
(Session 4: Dutch o)
1
2
3
4
5
6
7
8
9
10
11
12
13
14
15
Auction Number, t

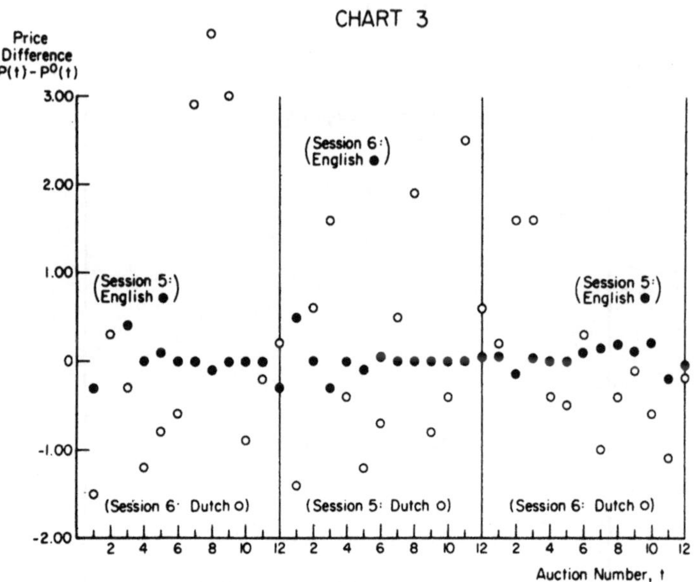

differ from the optimal price, but to accept this null hypothesis for English auction prices.

A total of 50 auctions were conducted in the four experimental sessions. All but 5 of these auctions were Pareto optimal, i.e., the sale was made to the highest value buyer in 45 auctions. The five non-Pareto optimal sales consisted of one English auction (number 1 in session 1) and four Dutch auctions (numbers 7, 8, 9 and 10 in session 2). In each case the sale was to the second highest value buyer. Using the percentage of sales that were Pareto-optimal as a measure of efficiency, the Dutch mechanism was 84% efficient, while the English was 96% efficient.

In a series of earlier experiments (Smith (1964)) one of us has compared the double oral auction for multiple units (one unit at a time is traded) of a homogeneous commodity with one-sided auctions where only buyers are permitted to make price bids or only sellers are permitted to make price offers. In the double oral auction, any buyer may freely state a price bid to buy one unit of the commodity and any seller may accept the bid of any buyer to form a contract. Similarly, any seller may freely state a price offer, and any buyer may accept such an offer. In the bid auction, buyers only may bid, and sellers are free only to accept a bid or remain silent. It was found that one-sided auctions tend to favor the silent side. Thus, with sellers making offers, buyers learned to wait until (usually) offers were somewhat below the competitive market clearing price before accepting. Our results in the Dutch auction are consistent with these earlier results in the offer auction. The two institutions have similar features although there are important differences. For example,

TABLE 3

Means and Variances of Prices, *P(t)*, in Sessions 4 and 5

Session	Auction Type, in sequence	Dutch	English	Dutch	English
5	Mean		7.08	7.83	7.688
	Variance		3.272	1.515	2.704
6	Mean	7.42	7.68	7.67	
	Variance	1.083	1.627	0.4697	

when sellers are lowering offers competitively, buyers have no way of knowing how far this process will continue; each buyer must be concerned not only with the prospect that another buyer will slip in ahead of him, but also with the possibility that sellers will stop lowering their offers. In the Dutch auction the rules of the game assure a continuous decline in the offer price until an acceptance occurs. Apparently, these differences are not significant enough to change the central result: Offer auctions and Dutch auctions, in which individual valuations are equally spaced, yield prices below the competitive (or English) price.

B. Sessions 5-6. The results of sessions 5 and 6, designed to test the more specific hypotheses H_1 and H_2 suggested by the Vickrey homogeneous expectations case, are shown in Tables 2 and 3, and in Chart 3. As seen in Chart 3, these sessions, in which values are drawn randomly from the interval [.1, \$10], do *not* show the marked tendency of Dutch auction prices to be below English auction prices that was exhibited in sessions 1-4 with equally spaced valuations. It would appear, comparing charts 1 and 2 with 3, that the method of assigning valuations may be an important treatment variable in Dutch auctions, but not for English auctions which in all sessions show a more pronounced tendency to the optimal price. This conclusion is further strengthened by comparing the mean price differences in sessions 1-4 with those in sessions 5 and 6 in Table 2. Using the pooled mean and variance of the price differences to test H_0 gives $t_d = 0.81$ and $t_e = 0.07$. In neither institution do actual prices differ from the optimal price by a significant amount.

Table 3 contains the data necessary for testing H_1 and H_2. Note the tendency for the mean Dutch price to be about the same as the mean English price, and the rather strong consistent tendency for the variance of Dutch prices to be less than the variance of English prices. Learning is suggested by the tendency of the English and Dutch means to converge as we compare the two sessions across the three-block sequences with the English and Dutch means almost coincident in the third block of auctions. The pooled variance of the Dutch prices in Table 3 is $S_d^2 = 0.994$

and of English prices is $S_e^2 = 2.444$. The difference is significant, and in the right direction to support the Vickrey model. But more interesting is a χ^2 test of H_2 and a t-test of H_1. Since $N = 8$ and valuations are random on the interval [.1, \$10] in sessions 5 and 6, we have $V_d = \frac{(N-1)^2 (10)^2}{N(N+1)^2 (N+2)} = 0.7562$ and $V_e = \frac{2(N-1)(10)^2}{(N+2)(N+1)^2} =$ 1.7284. The pooled Dutch price variance is not significantly different than the theoretical prediction, V_d (i.e., $\frac{fS_d^2}{0.7562} = 46 < \chi^2_{0.975} = 53$). Similarly, the pooled variance of English auctions is not significantly different than V_e ($fSe^2/1.7284 = 48 < \chi^2_{0.975}$). In both cases however, the difference is close to being significant ($\alpha = .05$) with the sample variances higher than the theoretical variances.

H_1 is tested using the theoretical Dutch and English price mean, $m = \frac{10(N-1)}{N+1} = 7.78$, applying to the conditions of sessions 5 and 6. The pooled mean of Dutch prices from Table 3 is $\overline{P}_d = 7.639$, which is not significantly different from 7.78 ($t_d = -0.83$). The pooled mean of English prices is $\overline{P}_e = 7.496$, which is also not significantly different from 7.78 ($t_e = -1.06$). These results are remarkably supportive of Vickrey's Nash equilibrium model of homogeneous Dutch and English auctions.

In 28 of the 36 Dutch auctions in sessions 11 and 12, the allocation was to the Pareto-optimal highest value bidder implying an efficiency of 77.8%. However, 35 of the 36 English auctions were Pareto-optimal giving an efficiency of 97.2%.

IV. SEALED-BID AUCTIONS: THEORY AND HYPOTHESES

As in our discussion of English and Dutch auctions the contributions of Vickrey (1961) and Cassady (1976) constitute the richest and most provocative references on sealed-bid auctions. Vickrey (1961, p. 20) suggests that "... the usual practice of calling for the tender of bids on the understanding that the highest ... bid ... will be accepted and executed in accordance with its own terms is isomorphic with the Dutch auction ... The motivations, strategies, and results of such a procedure can be analyzed in exactly the same way as was done above with the Dutch auction." Vickrey then inquires as to the existence of a sealed-bid procedure that is logically isomorphic to the Pareto-optimal English auction, and argues (p. 20-21) in favor of the following: Bids are to be tendered on the understanding that the award will be made to the highest bidder, but at a price equal to the second highest bid. In this procedure it is easy to see that bidding full value is a dominant strategy equilibrium, since it maximizes the probability of winning the award while the gain obtained depends only on the bid of an independent bidder.

It turns out that Vickrey's ingenious "second price" procedure was anticipated many years earlier by Jacob Marschak,[5] but in a somewhat different form. The Marschak procedure was to have the seller enter a secret bid on his own article with the understanding that the item is awarded to the (single) buyer if and only if the buyer's bid is higher than the seller's bid. Using the Vickrey line of reasoning it would appear that Marschak's version generalizes to the case of N buyers, i.e. each of N buyers would have an incentive to bid full value to maximize the probability of bidding in excess of the seller's unknown bid. The item would then be awarded to the highest bidder at the seller's asking price.

The Marschak-Vickrey sealed-bid auction is very close to being a "synthetic institution".[6] Cassady's thorough survey reveals only one institution, called "book bidding" (Cassady, (1976, pp. 152-153)) that can, in special cases, reduce to a second-price sealed-bid auction. In some English auctions (e.g. in the London stamp auction), a buyer not present can register a maximum written bid in advance with the auctioneer; the auctioneer then advances any lower oral bid from the floor by a standard increment (e.g. \$1). In the special case in which the two highest book bids exceed the highest floor bid, the auctioneer awards the item to the highest bidder, at \$1 over the second highest book bid. However, in reference to the Marschak procedure, it is sometimes an auction market rule (Cassady (1976, p. 31)) that a seller cannot bid on his own article.

Vickrey's analysis of sealed-bid auctions suggests three basic hypotheses. Let P_1 be the price in a First-Price (highest bid) auction, P_2 be the price in a Second-Price (next to the highest bid) auction, and P^o be the optimal (English) theoretical price as before. Then, if $p_1 = P_1\text{-}P^o$, $p_2 = P_2\text{-}P^o$, we state

$$H_0': p_1^* = 0, \quad p_2^* = 0, \quad \text{where } p_1^* = E(P_1 - P^o), p_2^* = E(P_2 - P^o)$$

$$H_1': P_1^* = P_2^* = m, \quad \text{where } P_1^* = E(P_1), P_2^* = E(P_2)$$

$$H_2': \text{Var } P_1 = V_1 < V_2 = \text{Var } P_2, \text{where } V_1 = V_d, V_2 = V_e.$$

If the Dutch and First-Price auctions are isomorphic, and the English and Second-Price auctions are isomorphic, then given the results of our experimental sessions 5-6 we should be unable to reject any of the hypotheses H_0', H_1' and H_2'. If these Vickrey isomorphisms fail to hold, a possible explanation may be in the divergence between the informational characteristics of the Dutch and First-Price auctions, and of the English and Second-Price auctions. Thus, in the First-Price written auction an

5. Marschak proposed his procedure for inducing full-value bidding in informal discussion with some graduate students during a visit to Harvard. Smith, who was present at the time, recently wrote him to confirm the incident and the year. The reply (Marschak (1976)): "Forgive me to have delayed my answer to your query about the happy days in 1953 at Harvard. Not 1952, but still we were young enough! Thank you for your generous reminder of that significant encounter."

6. Charles Plott has suggested the term "synthetic institution" for processes proposed by social scientists which are not based on any known historical practice.

TABLE 4

Number of Auctions (and Number of Bidders) for Each Session by Auction Type

Session	Valuation Assignment Procedure	Auction Type, in sequence (except 7)			
		First Price	Second Price	First Price	Second Price
7*	I	10 (6)			
7*	I		10 (6)		
8	II	10 (5)	10 (5)	5 (5)	
9	III	10 (5)	10 (5)	10 (5)	
10	III		10 (5)	10 (5)	10 (5)
11	II		12 (5)	12 (5)	12 (5)
12	II	12 (5)	12 (5)	12 (5)	

*This session also included a Marschak "Seller Price" auction.

agent must commit himself to a bid, under the rules, based only on a priori information on the valuations and/or bidding strategy of others. But in the dutch oral (or clock) auction, beginning with the first price offer and each successive lowering of the price, each agent is accumulating sample information viz. that at each decrement in the price no bidder has, as yet, entered an acceptance. Theoretically this information would not make any difference under the Vickrey assumptions. That is, if each agent assumes that all values come from a rectangular probability density, and is a Bayesian information processor, then, at some price, the information that no bidder has as yet entered an acceptance is not new information since no bidder has (on average) expected an acceptance. But these conditions may fail to approximate behavior.

Similarly, in the English oral auction each agent accumulates information on whether he is still an active buyer by observing the level of the ascending bids. This information may *induce* him to bid near full value. But in the Second-Price written auction an agent places only one bid, which will be a full-value bid only if he is able to *reason* (or learn) that this is a dominant strategy.

Potentially, these informational differences could yield behavioral differences that belie the isomorphisms underpining the Vickrey analysis.

V. SEALED-BID AUCTIONS: EXPERIMENTAL DESIGN

The series of sealed-bid auction experiments that are to be reported here consists of the 6 sessions catalogued in Table 4. The results of sessions 7-12 are reported in section 6 in connection with testing hypotheses H_0' to H_2', i.e. for comparing the First-Price and Second-Price treatment rules in auctions for a single unit, and for examining the alleged isomorphisms between the First-Price and Dutch auctions and between the Second-Price and English auctions.

Session 7 was the only session in which subjects simultaneously bid for an item sold under each auction method in each bidding period. Sessions 8-12 used either the First-Price rule or the Second-Price rule, then switched after several auctions from one rule to the other and then back. In sessions 9 and 10 the presentation of instructions to subjects, the recording of bids and the calculation of winning bids and prices were all done on the PLATO computer system.

Several different procedures were used for assigning valuations to individual subjects in the experimental sessions. The objective was to examine the sensitivity of results to different valuation conditions, and to vary subject knowledge of the valuation procedure.

I. In session 7 for each auction, the highest value was a random digit between \$4 and \$9; then the second highest value was chosen randomly to be \$.5, \$1.0 or \$1.5 below the highest value. The remaining four values were chosen arbitrarily (i.e. subjectively) at various values below the second highest. Values were then assigned randomly among the six subjects.

II. All 5 subjects for each auction in session 8 received valuations chosen randomly (i.e. with equal probability) from the 100 element set (\$0.1, 0.2, . . . \$9.9, \$10.0). Furthermore, subjects were fully informed of this method of assigning values.

III. In the PLATO computer sessions (9 and 10), for each auction the subjects receive a random assignment of two digit values chosen from an interval whose (random) width was between \$2.5 and \$5.5, and which begins at a random level between 0.1 and \$10 (but constrained so that the range of values do not exceed \$10). Subjects were provided with no information on this method of assigning values.

After sessions 7-10 were finished we replicated the homogeneous case (session 8 using type II valuation assignments) by running sessions 11 and 12 with 12 auction sequences. As in the Dutch-English sessions 5 and 6 the purpose was to test the more specific Vickrey hypotheses H_1' and H_2', and to further examine the Vickrey isomorphisms.

VI. SEALED-BID AUCTIONS: PRICE RESULTS

A. *Tests of H_0'*. Charts 4-7 plot the price differences $p_1(t)$ and $p_2(t)$ for the six sessions 7-12. These data support the conclusion that (a) the First and Second-Price auctions are distinct institutions, and (b) the First-Price auction produces a relatively higher selling price than the Second-Price

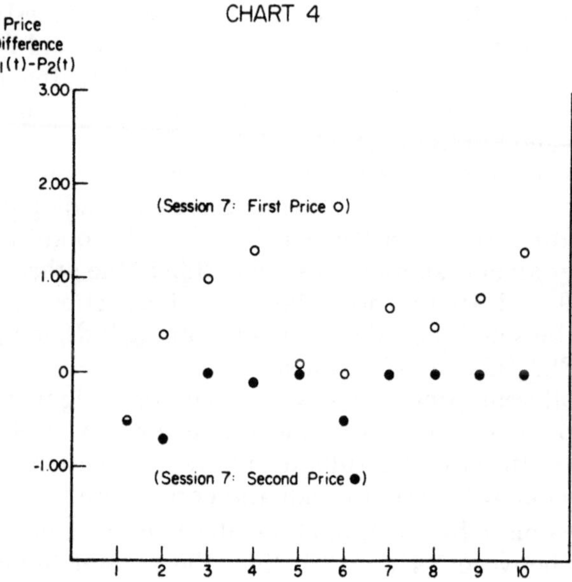
CHART 4
Price
Difference
P1(t)-P2(t)
3.00
2.00
1.00
0
-1.00
(Session 7: First Price o)
(Session 7: Second Price ●)
1
2
3
4
5
6
7
8
9
10

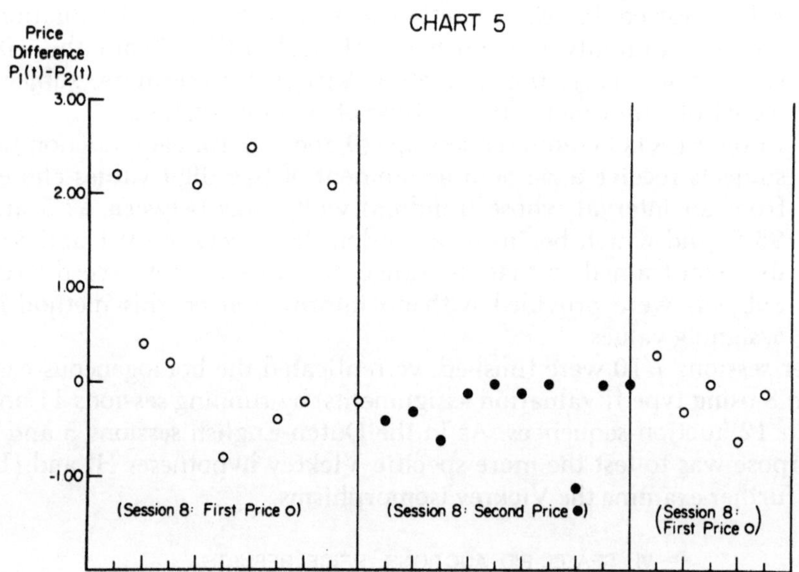
CHART 5
Price
Difference
P1(t)-P2(t)
3.00
2.00
1.00
0
-1.00
(Session 8: First Price o)
(Session 8: Second Price ●)
(Session 8: First Price o)

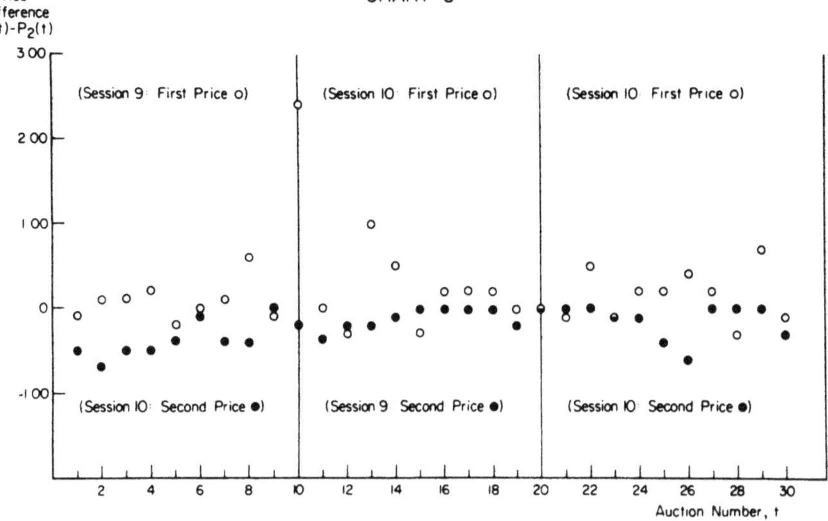
CHART 6
Price
Difference
P1(t)-P2(t)
3.00
2.00
1.00
0
-1.00
(Session 9: First Price o)
(Session 10: First Price o)
(Session 10: First Price o)
(Session 10: Second Price ●)
(Session 9: Second Price ●)
(Session 10: Second Price ●)
2
4
6
8
10
12
14
16
18
20
22
24
26
28
30
Auction Number, t

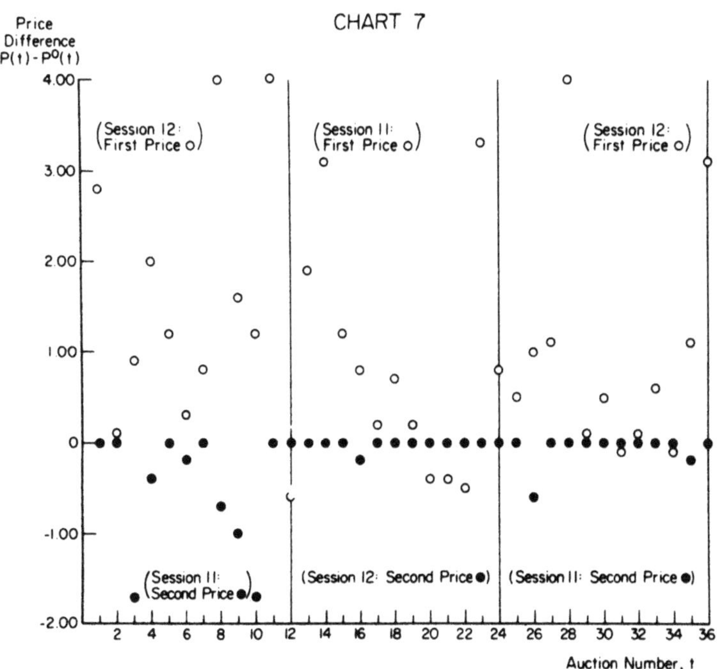
CHART 7
Price
Difference
P(t)-P0(t)
4.00
3.00
2.00
1.00
0
-1.00
-2.00
(Session 12: First Price o)
(Session 11: First Price o)
(Session 12: First Price o)
(Session 11: Second Price ●)
(Session 12: Second Price ●)
(Session 11: Second Price ●)
2
4
6
8
10
12
14
16
18
20
22
24
26
28
30
32
34
36
Auction Number, t

TABLE 5

Means and Variances of Differences
$p_1(t) = P_1(t) - P^o(t)$ and $p_2(t) = P_2(t) - P^o(t)$

Session	Auction Type in Sequence	First Price	Second Price	First Price	Second Price
7	Mean	0.56	−0.18		
	Variance	0.338	0.075		
8	Mean	0.79	−0.26	−0.14	
	Variance	1.639	0.129	0.113	
9	Mean	0.31	−0.11	0.16	
	Variance	0.588	0.019	0.098	
10	Mean		−0.37	0.15	−0.15
	Variance		0.045	0.147	0.045
11	Mean		−0.52	0.91	−1.24
	Variance		0.433	1.643	0.0315
12	Mean	1.59	−0.017	1.08	
	Variance	2.508	0.003	2.351	

auction. Since the results reported in section 3 support the conclusion that Dutch auction prices tend to be equal to or less than English auction prices, one or the other of the Vickrey isomorphisms must be called into question. Comparing the Dutch auctions in charts 1-3 with the First-Price auctions in charts 4-7 it appears that these two auction types may not be isomorphic. However, the English and Second-price auctions appear to generate similar price differences except that the latter appear to be somewhat below, while those in the former are somewhat above, the optimal level. But after several successive Second-Price auctions there is a suggestion of asymptotic convergence to the theoretical price especially in chart 4 (session 7), chart 6 (auctions 11-20, session 9, and 1-10 in session 10), and chart 7 (auctions 25-36 in session 11, and 13-24 in session 12).

Table 5 lists the means and variances of the price differences $p_1(t)$ and $p_2(t)$. With the exception of the final block of five auctions under the First-Price rule in session 8, the mean difference is positive in the First-Price auctions and negative in the Second-Price auctions (even in session 8 the mean is less negative than in the previous block of ten Second-Price auctions). A possible explanation of the tendency of Dutch auction price differences to be below First-Price auction differences is purely technical: In the Dutch auction procedure we dropped the price in 50 cent incre-

TABLE 6

t-tests of H_0'
(All two-tailed tests)

Session	Valuation Assignment Procedure	$t_1(p_1^* = 0)$	$t_2(p_2^* = 0)$
7	I	2.89[a]	−1.97
8	II	1.4	−2.16[a]
9 and 10	III	2.03[a]	−5.74[b]
11 and 12	II	2.74[b]	−0.329

[a]Significant for $\alpha < .05$

[b]Significant for $\alpha < .01$

ments, while in the First-Price auction the subjects were not constrained to submit written bids divisible by 50 cents. Since the mean price differences in the First-Price auctions for sessions 8, 11 and 12 (the homogeneous cases) tend to be considerably in excess of 50 cents, this explanation does not appear compelling.

Table 6 summarizes the results of a t-test of H_0'. The calculations for these tests are based on means and variances computed by pooling the data for the two First-Price auctions in session 8; and pooling the First-Price, and pooling the Second-Price, auction data in sessions 9 to 12 (refer to Table 5).

The pooled data for all sessions 7-12 of Table 6 show that all First-Price auctions yield prices above, while Second-Price auctions yield prices below the optimal price. It should be noted in these tests that we pool only those data for the same auction method and using the same procedure for assigning subject valuations. We do not pool sessions 7, 9 or 10, with 8, 11 or 12 as this would combine price differences based on non-comparable valuation assignments.

B. Tests of H_1' and H_2'. Table 7 provides the means and variances of prices in those sessions using random valuation assignments from the interval [.1, \$10]. Except for the second block of First-Price auctions in session 8 the mean price in Second-Price auctions is below the mean in First-Price auctions, although only slightly in session 12. Since $N = 5$ the theoretical variance in the First-Price auction is $V_1 = \dfrac{(N-1)^2(10)^2}{N(N+1)^2\,(N+2)} = 1.27$. The pooled First-Price variance in sessions 8, 11 and 12 is $S_1^2 = 2.41$, which is quite significantly different from the theoretical prediction (i.e., $\dfrac{fS_1^2}{1.27} = 95 > \chi^2_{0.999} = 86.7$). The

TABLE 7

Means and Variances of Prices, P(t), in Sessions 8, 11, and 12

Session	Auction Type, in sequence	First	Second	First	Second
8	Mean	7.03	5.96	5.26	
	Variance	1.639	2.058	1.278	
11	Mean		5.98	7.58	6.60
	Variance		3.149	1.167	2.778
12	Mean	7.19	7.16	7.18	
	Variance	1.856	4.593	3.367	

theoretical variance in Second-Price auctions is $V_2 = \frac{2(N-1)(10)^2}{(N+2)(N+1)^2} = 3.17$, while the pooled variance in sessions 8, 11 and 12 is $S_2^2 = 3.31$. This difference is not significant ($\frac{fS_2^2}{3.17} = 36.5 < \chi^2_{.90} = 63.2$). The theoretical mean price in both auctions is $m = \frac{(N-1)\,10}{N+1} = 6.67$. The pooled First-Price mean is $\bar{P}_1 = 7.06$ giving $t_1 = 1.8$ which is just short of being significant for $\alpha = 0.05$. The pooled Second-Price mean is $\bar{P}_2 = 6.44$ which is not significantly different from the theoretical mean ($t = -0.86$).

These results imply that we are unable to reject the dominant strategy model of Second-Price auctions, but that the Nash equilibrium model of First-Price auctions is open to question. Since our Dutch and English auction results were consistent with these Vickrey models it appears that only the First-Price sealed-bid auction is out of line with the theory.

VII. SEALED-BID AUCTIONS: INDIVIDUAL BEHAVIOR

All of our experiments consist of a series of many (see Table 4) auctions of a given type conducted in sequence, with only valuations and the assignment of values to individual subjects varying in this sequence. This design permits us to study individual choices for evidence of learning. Although the Second-Price auction provides an "obvious" incentive for full value bidding based on a simple dominance criterion, real people may not perceive this property except through learning, reflection, or perhaps even training or conditioning (Marschak, 1964). We do not regard this aspect of behavior as peculiar to laboratory studies, since we

TABLE 8

Net Value (Value-Bid), For Selected Trials in Second-Price Auctions

Experimental Session	Subject	Zero Trial (No payoff)	First Trial	Last Trial
	1	.9	.5	0
	2	.2	.4	0
7	3	.5	0	0
	4	0	0	0
	5	.5	.5	1.6
	6	.7	.3	0
	1		0	0
	2		.1	0
8	3		.1	.1
	4		1.1	2.2
	5		.4	0
	1		.1	.1
	2		.2	0
9	3		.4	0
	4		.1	0
	5		0	0
	1		.3	0
	2		.5	0
10	3		.4	.3
	4		.9	.1
	5		.4	.1
	1		.2	0
	2		0	.2
11	3		.5	0
	4		0	0
	5		0	0
	1		0	0
	2		.1	.1
12	3		0	0
	4		0	1.5
	5		.2	0

think of economic rationality in both field and laboratory as a behavioral mode acquired by a process of trial-and-error learning in situation-specific cases.

The importance of a learning experience to rational behavior is illustrated in Table 8. For each subject and session we list here the first trial and last trial (also the zero practice trial in session 7) observation of $V_i^2(\cdot) - B_i^2(\cdot)$ in each Second-Price auction sequence, where $V_i^j(t)$ is the value to individual i of the item in auction t under auction method j and $B_i^j(t)$ is i's bid for that item. Now think of each of these series of observations as constituting the results of a different experiment. In session 7, the

TABLE 9

t-test of Bid Deviations from First-Price Nash Equilibrium

Session \ Subject	1	2	3	4	5	Number of Bids
8	−1.88	3.33[a]	1.98[a]	5.35[b]	.99	15
11	7.13[b]	5.30[b]	6.26[b]	.05	.648	10
12	7.62[b]	5.45[b]	2.06[a]	5.00[b]	5.88[b]	24

[a]Significant $\alpha < .07$.
[b]Significant $\alpha < .01$.

zero trial column provides data on an "experiment" without learning or monetary motivation: Only one of the six subjects behaves according to the principle of rationality applied to the Second-Price Institution. The First-Trial column yields data on experiments with monetary reinforcement, but without learning: In session 7 some "improvement" appears in that now we observe two of six subjects whose behavior is consistent with the theory. Across all First-Trial "experiments" only ten of thirty-one subject responses were consistent with the theory. The Last-Trial column yields observations on an "experiment" with monetary reinforcement and an opportunity to learn from trial-and-error experience: Twenty-one of the thirty-one subjects now yield responses consistent with the theory. Based on the first two columns of data only, a researcher would have to conclude that violations of simple dominance criteria in decision making was widespread in the population of subjects.

We think these results and our interpretation of them suggest the importance of structuring experiments so that subjects have an adequate opportunity to learn the consequences of their decisions, and to adjust accordingly. It appears that most individuals are very unlikely to recognize, in situation-specific decisions, which of a series of alternatives it is in their self interest to choose. An analogue of what we have in mind is the optical illusion, e.g. a mirage, to which people properly adjust by some kind of principle of learned rationality in which one discovers that the self-interest is not served when a certain visual phenomenon is taken at its initial "face value".

Motivated by the failure of mean prices in the First-Price auction to satisfy the predictions of the Nash equilibrium model, we examined individual subject choices for this auction in sessions 8, 11 and 12. Let $B_i^t(t)$ be subject i's bid in auction t. If $V_i^t(t)$ is subject i's randomly drawn valuation on trial t, then his Nash bid strategy is $\frac{(N-1)V_i^t(t)}{N}$ on auction t (Vickrey, p. 16). If subject i's bids approximate such a strategy then we will be unable to reject the null hypothesis that the observations $\beta_i(t) =$

$B_i^l(t) - \frac{(N-1)V_i^l(t)}{N}$ come from a distribution with zero mean. Table 9 lists the t values by session and subject under this null hypothesis. Only subject I in session 8 entered bids on the average less than the Nash strategy, indicating the strong preponderance of bids above the Nash bid. The bids of nine out of fifteen subjects very significantly ($\alpha < .01$) exceeded the Nash bid. In the face of these results it is difficult to hold to the hypothesis that bidding behavior in First-Price auctions is approximated by the Nash equilibrium model.

VIII. SUMMARY

Based on the results of twelve experiments, our tentative conclusions can be summarized as follows:

(1) The Dutch oral auction tends to yield prices equal to or below the optimal price. When valuations are drawn from a rectangular distribution the mean and variance of Dutch prices are not significantly different from the mean and variance predicted by Vickrey's Nash equilibrium model.

(2) English auction prices in all experiments tend to be slightly, but not significantly, above the optimal price. This is because bids are raised progressively in noninfinitesimal amounts causing some (though not always) overbidding of the next-to-the highest valuation. When valuations are drawn from a rectangular distribution the mean and variance of prices do not differ significantly from the predictions of Vickrey's theory.

(3) Second-Price sealed-bid auction prices tend to be below (but not significantly) the optimum price. This is because not all subjects realize that bidding full value is a dominant strategy (or they hope by signaling to induce a lowering of the bids). Individual bidding sequences reveal important learning effects for the majority of subjects. We question whether any meaningful one-shot observations can be made on processes characterized by a dominant strategy equilibrium. So-called "simple dominance" is not immediately transparent to most people. When valuations are drawn from a rectangular distribution Second-Price auctions result in prices with mean and variance not significantly different from the mean and variance expected from the Vickrey analysis.

(4) The English and Second-Price auctions appear to be isomorphic if one allows for learning effects in the latter and some technical overbidding, due to discrete bid increments, in the former.

(5) Prices in the First-Price sealed-bid auctions tend to be significantly above the optimal price. When valuations are drawn from a rectangular distribution both the mean and the variance of auction prices differ from the Nash equilibrium model. Hence, the First-Price auction does not fit the consistent pattern established in the other three auction institutions.

(6) In particular the Dutch and First-Price auctions do not appear to be isomorphic. We think this may be due to information differences in the two types of auctions. However, we cannot, based on the experimental evidence to date, rule out other possible explanations. For example the discrepency might be due to sampling variability although we believe our auction sequences are large enough to make this unlikely. Another possibility is that Dutch auction prices are lower than First-Price auction prices because of the discrete increment (50 cents) by which price was progressively lowered in the Dutch experiments.

(7) If efficiency is measured by the percentage of sales that are Pareto-optimal, the English auction is the most efficient (96%, 97.2%). The English auction is essentially free of strategic considerations, and of the four institutions requires the least bidder sophistication. The Second-Price auction is next most efficient (95.7%) and, with learning, probably would be at least as efficient as the English. The First-Price auction is third in efficiency (90.2%), while the Dutch is the least efficient (84%, 77.8%).

(8) From the seller's point of view the First-Price sealed-bid auction would be preferred since it tends to provide the highest prices.

Current plans are to replicate the Dutch, First-Price and Second-Price experiments under the condition that valuations are rectangularly distributed. As a means of achieving closer control over procedures, experimenter effects, information conditions and technical considerations in the different auction mechanism, each mechanism will be programmed on the PLATO computer system. This means that a computerized version of the clock device used in the produce auctions (Cassady (1967, pp. 193-196)) in Holland will become the experimental Dutch auction. In the computer version it will be possible to study the effect of different time and distance increments between successive price bids.

REFERENCES

Battalio, R., J. Kagel, R. Winkler, Fisher, E., Basmann, R., and Krasner, L., "A Test of Consumer Demand Theory Using Observations of Individual Consumer Purchases," *Western Economic Journal*, Dec. 1973, *11*, 411-428.

Boulding, Kenneth, *Economic Analysis*. New York, N.Y.: Harper, Revised Edition, 1948.

Cassady, Ralph, *Auctions and Auctioneering*. Berkeley and Los Angeles, California: University of California Press, 1967.

Frahm, D., and Schrader, L., "An Experimental Comparison of Pricing in Two Auction Systems," *American Journal of Agricultural Economics*, Nov. 1970, 52, 528-534.

Loeb, M., "Alternative Versions of the Demand-Revealing Process," *Public Choice*, Supplement to Spring, 1977, *29(2)*, 15-26.

Marschak, Jacob, "Actual Versus Consistent Behavior," *Behavioral Science*, April 1964, 9, 103-110.

Smith, Vernon, "Effect of Market Organization on Competitive Equilibrium," *Quarterly Journal of Economics*, May 1964, *78*, 181-201.

Vickrey, W., "Counterspeculation, Auctions, and Competitive Sealed Tenders," *Journal of Finance*, May 1961, *16*, 8-37.

Marschak, Jacob, personal correspondence, June 29, 1976.

THEORY AND BEHAVIOR OF SINGLE OBJECT AUCTIONS

James C. Cox, Bruce Roberson and Vernon L. Smith

I. INTRODUCTION

This paper addresses the subject of the relation between the predictions of economic theory and bidder behavior in the Dutch auction, the English auction, the first-price sealed-bid auction, and the second-price sealed-bid auction of a single item. The four types of auction market are defined as follows.

1. *Dutch:* In this auction the offer price starts at an amount believed to be higher than any bidder is willing to pay and is lowered by an auctioneer or a clock device until one of the bidders accepts the last price offer (Cassady, 1967, p. 67). The first and only bid is the sales price in the Dutch auction.

2. *English:* This is the ". . . progressive auction, in which bids are freely made and announced until no purchaser wishes to make any further higher bid" (Vickrey, 1961, p. 14). The last bid is the sales price in the English auction.
3. *First-price:* This auction corresponds to ". . . the usual practice of calling for the tender of bids on the understanding that the highest . . . bid . . . will be accepted and executed in accordance with its own terms" (Vickrey, 1961, p. 20). In the first-price auction, the auctioned object is awarded to the highest bidder at a (sales) price equal to his bid.
4. *Second-price:* Under this auction procedure, bids are tendered on the understanding that the item will be awarded to the highest bidder, but at a price equal to the second highest bid (Vickrey, 1961, pp. 20–21). Cassady's (1967, pp. 152–153) description of how "book bids" are handled in the London stamp auction corresponds to the second-price auction.[1]

The Dutch and English auctions are commonly referred to as "oral" auctions, as distinct from the "written-bid" (i.e., sealed-bid) auctions. In fact, the feature that distinguishes the Dutch and English auctions from the sealed-bid auctions is the "real-time" element of the former auctions, not that bids are actually made orally. Thus, during the conduct of the Dutch and English auctions a bidder is able to observe some bidding behavior of his rivals. In the absence of collusion in a sealed-bid auction, a bidder is not able to make any observations of his rivals' bidding behavior.

In developing the economic theory of these four auction markets, we will be concerned with the implications of the expected utility hypothesis and the Nash equilibrium condition. The theory and the experimental design in this paper apply to the case where each bidder knows with certainty the monetary value that he places on the auctioned object but does not know the values that his rivals place on the auctioned object.

II. IMPLICATIONS OF THE EXPECTED UTILITY HYPOTHESIS

We understand the expected utility hypothesis to be the assumption that a bidder chooses his bid as if his objective were to maximize his expected (von Neuman–Morgenstern) utility of the money income gained from participating in an auction. In the present section of the paper, we explore the implications of the expected utility hypothesis for bidding behavior.

Define N as the number of bidders participating in the auction. Let the strictly increasing concave function u_i, i = 1, 2, . . ., N, be the utility function for money income for the ith bidder. Adopt the normalization that $u_i(0)$ equals 0 for all i and that the utility of not bidding equals 0 for all bidders. Further assume that there is no utility or disutility associated with participating in the auction other than the utility of the monetary gain from the auction. The monetary value to bidder i of the auctioned object is denoted by v_i. Assume that v_i is known with certainty by bidder i and that v_i is positive for each i. The bid of the ith bidder is denoted by b_i and the auction market rules require b_i to be nonnegative.

Now consider the first-price sealed-bid auction. If the ith bidder submits the highest bid, then he obtains the money income $(v_i - b_i)$. If he does not submit the highest bid, then his monetary gain from participating in the auction is zero. Let $F_i(b_i)$ be the ith bidder's subjective probability that he can win the auction with a bid in the amount b_i. Thus the expected utility to bidder i of a bid in the amount b_i in the first-price auction is

$$U_i(b_i) = F_i(b_i)u_i(v_i - b_i). \tag{2.1}$$

Assume now, for simplicity, that the amount bid is a continuous variable and that the interval $[\underline{X}_i, \overline{X}_i]$ is the support of the probability distribution function F_i. Further assume that the expected utility function (2.1) is pseudoconcave and that there exists a unique positive expected utility-maximizing bid b_i^o. Then b_i^o will satisfy the following first-order condition:

$$0 = U_i'(b_i^o) = F_i'(b_i^o)u_i(v_i - b_i^o) - F_i(b_i^o)u_i'(v_i - b_i^o). \tag{2.2}$$

Also assume that b_i^o satisfies the second-order condition for a maximum,

$$\begin{aligned} 0 > U_i''(b_i^o) &= F_i''(b_i^o)u_i(v_i - b_i^o) \\ &\quad - 2F_i'(b_i^o)u_i'(v_i - b_i^o) \\ &\quad + F_i(b_i^o)u_i''(v_i - b_i^o). \end{aligned} \tag{2.3}$$

If $U_i''(\cdot)$ is negative on an interval subset of the domain of $U_i(\cdot)$, then statements (2.2) and (2.3) and the implicit function theorem imply that there exists a differentiable function ψ_i such that

$$\begin{aligned} b_i^o &= \psi_i(v_i) \\ &= v_i - u_i^{-1}(u_i'(v_i - b_i^o)\, F_i(b_i^o)/F_i'(b_i^o)) \end{aligned} \tag{2.4}$$

and

$$\psi_i'(v_i) = [F_i(b_i^o)u_i''(v_i - b_i^o) - F_i'(b_i^o)u_i'(v_i - b_i^o)]/U_i''(b_i^o), \tag{2.5}$$

where u_i^{-1} is the inverse of the utility of money income function. The function ψ_i is called the ith bidder's strategy function or his bid function.

The implications of the expected utility hypothesis for bidding behavior in the first-price sealed-bid auction follow immediately from statement

(2.4). First, the expected utility-maximizing bid is less than the value of the auctioned object. Therefore, the first-price sealed-bid auction is not a demand-revealing allocation mechanism. Secondly, the amount by which the object value exceeds the optimal bid depends on u_i and F_i; that is, it depends on the bidder's risk preferences and expectations about his rivals' bids. Since risk preferences and expectations can differ over individual bidders, the highest bid will not necessarily be submitted by the bidder who places the highest value on the auctioned object. Thus the first-price auction does not, in general, yield Pareto-efficient allocations. However, we can identify a set of conditions under which this auction would yield efficient allocations. Concavity and monotonicity of u_i and statements (2.2), (2.3), and (2.5) imply that the bid function ψ_i is increasing. If we now assume that all N bidders have the same risk preferences and expectations about their rivals' bids, then they will all have the same increasing bid function. In that special case, the first-price sealed-bid auction will yield Pareto-efficient allocations. However, if all bidders are not identical, then the conclusion that the first-price auction is efficient has been shown by the discussion in this paragraph to be untenable. We will consider this point again in Section III below.

Consider next the second-price sealed-bid auction. In that auction the highest bid is the winning bid but the price paid for the auctioned object by the winning bidder is the amount of the second highest bid. In the absence of perfect collusion among the bidders, an individual bidder will not know with certainty the bids of his rivals before he must decide on the amount of his own bid. Thus let the random variable y be the highest bid of any of the rivals of a particular bidder i. Let the ith bidder's expectations about y be represented by the cumulative distribution function G_i, with support $[\underline{Y}_i, \overline{Y}_i]$. If the ith bidder submits the highest bid, then he obtains the money income $(v_i - y)$. If he does not submit the highest bid, then his monetary gain from participating in the auction is zero. Thus the expected utility to bidder i of a bid in the amount $b_i \in [\underline{Y}_i, \overline{Y}_i]$ in the second-price auction is

$$V_i(b_i) = \int_{\underline{Y}_i}^{b} u_i(v_i - y)\, dG_i(y). \tag{2.6}$$

Consider the interesting case where $v_i \in [\underline{Y}_i, \overline{Y}_i]$ and, for simplicity, assume that the expected utility-maximizing bid of bidder i, b_i^*, satisfies the following first-order condition:

$$0 = V_i'(b_i^*) = u_i(v_i - b_i^*)G_i'(b_i^*). \tag{2.7}$$

Statement (2.7) and the normalization $u_i(0) = 0$ imply

$$b_i^* = v_i. \tag{2.8}$$

Thus the bidder's strategy function in the second-price auction is the identity map.

The implications of the expected utility hypothesis for bidding behavior in the second-price sealed-bid auction follow immediately from statement (2.8). The expected utility-maximizing bid is equal to the value of the auctioned object. Furthermore, it does not depend on the bidder's risk preferences or his expectations about his rivals' bids. Therefore, the outcome where each of the N bidders submits a bid equal to his object value is a dominant strategy equilibrium in the second-price auction. Thus the second-price auction is a demand-revealing allocation mechanism that will, in general, yield Pareto-efficient allocations. Furthermore, the winning bid will equal the largest of the values v_i, and the sales price will equal the second highest of those values.

An additional question of interest for comparison of alternative auction markets is the effect of auction market structure on the distribution of seller's revenue. The question is often posed in terms of a comparison across auction markets of the first two moments of the probability distribution of seller's revenue. Thus it is a matter of some interest whether one auction can be shown to yield a higher expected revenue and/or a lower revenue variance than another. The preceding analysis informs us that, for a given set of individual object values, each bidder will bid lower in the first-price auction than in the second-price auction where his bid equals his value. But this does not permit a comparison of the expected sales prices in the two auctions. An attempt to make such a comparison would involve comparison of the second highest object value with a bid that is *less than* the highest object value. No such comparison can be made without a stronger set of assumptions than we now have. We will return to this question in Section III below.

The expected utility hypothesis does have testable implications for the mean sales price and the variance of sales prices in the second-price auction because it implies that the bidding strategy function for that auction is the identity map (2.8). Thus the predicted sales price for that auction is the second highest of the individual object values. If each individual object value is drawn independently from a known distribution, then the implied probability distribution of the sale price is that for the (N − 1)th-order statistic for a random sample of size N from that distribution.

The experimental design which we explain in Section IV incorporates the feature that each individual object value is drawn from the uniform distribution on the interval $[\underline{v}, \bar{v}]$. The probability distribution function for the (N − 1)th-order statistic for a random sample of size N from that distribution is

$$F(p) = N[(p - \underline{v})/(\bar{v} - \underline{v})]^{N-1} - (N - 1)](p - \underline{v})/(\bar{v} - \underline{v})^{N}. \quad (2.9)$$

Thus the predicted mean $\bar{p}_2$ and variance V_2 of the sales price are:

$$\bar{p}_2 = \int_{\underline{v}}^{\bar{v}} p\, dF(p) = \frac{(N-1)(\bar{v}-\underline{v})}{N+1} + \underline{v}; \tag{2.10}$$

$$V_2 = \int_{\underline{v}}^{\bar{v}} (p-\bar{p}_2)^2\, dF(p) = \frac{2(N-1)(\bar{v}-\underline{v})^2}{(N+1)^2(N+2)}. \tag{2.11}$$

Now consider the Dutch auction and let t denote the length of time the auction has been in progress. The bid "on the clock" at time t is b(t). Since the Dutch auction is a decreasing price auction, we have

$$b(t_1) > b(t_2), \qquad \text{for all } t_1, t_2 \text{ such that } t_1 < t_2. \tag{2.12}$$

Let $H_i(b(t))$ be the ith bidder's subjective probability at the beginning of the auction ($t = 0$) that he can win the auctioned object by accepting the bid b(t). If the ith bidder accepts the bid b(t), he gains the money income $v_i - b(t)$. The utility of that income is $u_i(v_i - b(t))$. Thus the expected utility at the beginning of the auction of planning to accept the bid b(t) is

$$W_i(b(t)) = H_i(b(t))u_i(v_i - b(t)). \tag{2.13}$$

Therefore, an optimal bidding plan for the ith bidder in the Dutch auction will be to plan to accept the bid $b(t_i^o)$ that maximizes (2.13).

The immediately preceding planning model of bidder behavior in the Dutch auction ignores the fact that that auction is a "real-time" auction in which bidders can make their decisions over time. However, given the standard behavioral assumptions that we are now using, a real-time model of bidder behavior can be shown to lead to the same conclusions about bidding in the Dutch auction as does the preceding planning model. But in order to prepare for the analysis in Section VIII that involves a real-time model of Dutch auction bidder behavior that incorporates some nonstandard behavioral assumptions, we now develop a real-time model with standard behavioral assumptions.

Suppose that the auction is in progress at time t and bidder i must decide whether to accept the bid b(t) or let the auction continue. If he accepts the bid b(t), he gains the money income $v_i - b(t)$ with utility $u_i(v_i - b(t))$. If he does not accept b(t), he has a chance to obtain the auctioned object at a lower price. Suppose that the bidder does not accept b(t) but rather lets the auction continue for one more tick of the auction clock to time $t + \Delta t$, where $\Delta t > 0$. Let $H_i(b(t + \Delta t)|b(t))$ be the ith bidder's probability that he can win the auction by accepting the bid $b(t + \Delta t)$, given the observation that the auction is still in progress at time t [and thus that he could have won the auction by accepting the bid b(t)]. Then the expected utility at time t of planning to accept the bid $b(t + \Delta t)$ is $H_i(b(t + \Delta t)|b(t))u_i(v_i - b(t + \Delta t))$. Thus the change in expected utility at time t from not accepting b(t) and planning to accept $b(t + \Delta t)$ is

$$\Delta Y_i(t) = H_i(b(t + \Delta t)|b(t))u_i(v_i - b(t + \Delta t)) - u_i(v_i - b(t)). \quad (2.14)$$

With $\Delta t > 0$, we have $H_i(b(t)|b(t + \Delta t)) = 1$; therefore, Bayes' rule and (2.14) imply

$$\Delta Y_i(t) = \frac{H_i(b(t + \Delta t))}{H_i(b(t))} u_i(v_i - b(t + \Delta t)) - u_i(v_i - b(t)). \quad (2.15)$$

We will now proceed, as in our analysis of the first-price auction, to assume differentiability of the objective function. Thus, using (2.15), we find

$$\begin{aligned} Y_i'(t) &= \lim_{\Delta t \to 0^+} \left(\frac{\Delta Y_i(t)}{\Delta t}\right) \\ &= \{[u_i(v_i - b(t))H_i'(b(t))/H_i(b(t))] - u_i'(v_i - b(t))\}\, b'(t). \end{aligned} \quad (2.16)$$

Assume that the auction begins at $t = 0$ and ends at $t = T$. Thus if the optimal time for bidder i to stop the auction is some t_i^o such that $t_i^o \in (0, T)$ then t_i^o will satisfy the following first-order condition.

$$\begin{aligned} 0 &= Y_i'(t_i^o) \\ &= \{[u_i(v_i - b(t_i^o))H_i'(b(t_i^o))/H_i(b(t_i^o))] - u_i'(v_i - b(t_i^o))\}\, b'(t_i^o). \end{aligned} \quad (2.17)$$

Note that (2.17) implies the first-order condition for maximization of (2.13) on (0, T) since $b'(t_i^o) < 0$. Therefore, the two models of bidder behavior in the Dutch auction imply the same bidding behavior: accept the bid $b(t_i^o)$ that maximizes (2.13).

We now proceed, as in the preceding analysis of the first-price auction, to assume that the bid $b(t_i^o)$ satisfies the first- and second-order conditions for a maxmium of (2.13). Also assume that $[\underline{Z}_i, \overline{Z}_i]$ is the support of the probability distribution function H_i and that the expected utility function, (2.13), is pseudoconcave. Then the preceding analysis of the first-price sealed bid auction can be interpreted so as to apply to the Dutch auction. Simply replace F_i with H_i and U_i with W_i in the appropriate equations and then the preceding analysis of the first-price auction yields the following conclusions for the Dutch auction. A bidder's expected utility-maximizing bid is less than the value to him of the auctioned object. Thus the Dutch auction is not a demand-revealing allocation mechanism. Furthermore, the amount by which the bidder's object value exceeds his optimal bid depends on his risk preferences and his expectations about his rivals' bids. Thus the Dutch auction will not generally yield Pareto-efficient allocations.

A further result of interest can be simply derived as follows. Suppose that the ith bidder believed that each of his rivals would employ the same bidding strategy in the Dutch auction as he did in the first-price auction. Then F_i and H_i would be identical and the ith bidder would be led by expected utility maximization to employ the same bidding strategy in the Dutch auction that he did in the first-price auction. Thus if every bidder believed that each of his rivals would employ the same bid function in the Dutch auction that he did in the first-price auction, then every bidder would find it in his interest to do the same. In that case the Dutch and first-price auctions would have identical quantitative characteristics as well as the common qualitative characteristics discussed above. It is in this sense that the Dutch and first-price auctions are isomorphic.

Now consider the English auction. An individual bidder will obtain a positive income from participating in the auction if and only if he can win the auction with a bid that is less than his value for the auctioned object. Thus a utility-maximizing bidder will drop out of the bidding only when the bid "on the floor" equals or exceeds his value for the object. Therefore, the strategy of remaining in the bidding competition as long as the bid on the floor does not exceed the bidder's value for the object, and of dropping out as soon as it does exceed that value, is a dominant strategy. Thus the English auction is a demand-revealing allocation mechanism that will, in general, yield Pareto-efficient allocations. Furthermore, the sales price for the auctioned object will equal the second highest of the bidders' object values plus, perhaps, a minimum bid increment. The similarity of the predicted allocations of the English auction and the second-price sealed-bid auction is the reason why those auctions are said to be isomorphic.

III. IMPLICATIONS OF THE EXPECTED UTILITY HYPOTHESIS AND THE NASH EQUILIBRIUM CONDITION

The preceding analysis has explored the implications of the expected utility hypothesis for bidder behavior. We now add to that hypothesis the additional assumption that the bidders' strategy functions satisfy a Nash equilibrium condition. That condition can be explained as follows. Let S_i be the strategy function of the ith bidder where, as above, $i = 1, 2, \ldots, N$. Now suppose bidder j knows that all bidders $i \neq j$ bid in accordance with these strategy functions and that, given this information, individual j can find no way of changing his own strategy function S_j so as to increase his expected utility. If this condition holds for $j = 1, 2,$

. . ., N, then the strategy functions S_j, j = 1, 2, . . ., N, satisfy the Nash equilibrium condition.

In Section II we found that the second-price sealed-bid and English auctions have dominant strategy equilibrium bid functions. All dominant strategy functions satisfy the Nash equilibrium condition. Therefore, our assumption here of the Nash equilibrium condition is redundant for the second-price and English auctions; it has no testable implications for bidding behavior in those auctions. In contrast, the first-price sealed-bid and Dutch auctions do not have dominant strategy equilibria. Thus, our assumption here of the Nash equilibrium condition does have testable implications for bidding behavior in those auctions.

Consider the strategy functions ψ_i, i = 1, 2, . . ., N, for the first-price auction derived in Section II above. As in statement (2.4), these functions relate the expected utility-maximizing bids b_i^o to the object values v_i. Now suppose that we can define vectors θ_i, i = 1, 2, . . ., N, that represent all individual bidder characteristics that affect the utility of money income. Thus, if $u_i(y)$ is the utility of money income y to bidder i, then we can define the utility function u as follows:

$$u_i(y) = u(y, \theta_i), \qquad i = 1, 2, \ldots, N. \tag{3.1}$$

Suppose that bidder i knows his own characteristic vector θ_i but does not know the characteristic vectors of his rivals. Further assume that bidder i believes that the characteristic vectors of his rivals are drawn independently from a known probability distribution. Finally, assume that these assumptions hold for every bidder. Then one can attempt to derive a bidding strategy function ψ, such that

$$\psi_i(v) = \psi(v, \theta_i), \qquad i = 1, 2, \ldots, N, \tag{3.2}$$

where ψ maximizes the expected utility of every bidder in the first-price auction. Such a function, if it exists, will satisfy the Nash equilibrium condition and is referred to as an equilibrium strategy function and as a Nash equilibrium bid function.

Finding equilibrium strategy functions for auctions (such as the first-price sealed-bid auction) which do not have a dominant strategy equilibrium is a considerably more ambitious undertaking than is the expected utility maximization in Section II. In order to make it tractable, authors of papers on bidding theory have assumed that all bidders have the same risk preferences; that is, they have assumed that $\theta_i = \theta$, i = 1, 2, . . ., N. In the seminal paper on equilibrium bidding theory by William Vickrey (1961), all bidders are assumed to be risk-neutral. Vickrey further assumes that each individual's value for the auctioned object is drawn from the uniform distribution on the interval, [0, 1]. Finally each individual is assumed to know his own value for the auctioned object but to know only the distribution from which his rivals' values are drawn. Using these assumptions, and letting the number of bidders be denoted by N, Vickrey shows that the noncooperative equilibrium bid function for the first-price auction is

$$b_i = \frac{N-1}{N} v_i, \qquad 1 = 1, 2, \ldots, N. \tag{3.3}$$

An immediate generalization of Vickrey's analysis is provided by allowing values to be drawn from a uniform distribution on any nonempty interval, $[\underline{v}, \overline{v}]$, such that $\underline{v} \geqq 0$. In that case, the equilibrium bid function is

$$b_i = \underline{v} + \frac{N-1}{N}(v_i - \underline{v}), i = 1, 2, \ldots, N. \tag{3.4}$$

Finally, we want to note the following about the Vickrey model. Given that the highest possible value drawing is $\overline{v}$, the highest bid that satisfies (3.4) is

$$\overline{b} = \underline{v} + \frac{N-1}{N}(\overline{v} - \underline{v}). \tag{3.5}$$

The assumption that all bidders are risk-neutral, or alternatively that they all have the same strictly concave utility function, is very restrictive. In the present paper we build on suggestions by John Ledyard to construct an equilibrium bidding model (which we will call the "Ledyard model") that permits individual bidders to differ in their attitudes towards risk. We begin by assuming that each bidder is drawn from a population of economic agents with utility of money income functions of the form

$$u_i(y) = y^{r_i}, \tag{3.6}$$

where r_i is a random variable with probability distribution Φ on [0, 1]. Note that $(1 - r_i)$ is the Arrow-Pratt constant relative risk aversion parameter for utility function (3.6).[2] Each bidder is assumed to know his own risk aversion parameter r_i, but to know only that the risk aversion parameter for each of his rivals is drawn from the probability distribution Φ. Since Φ is *not* assumed to have a density function, it can have a mass of probability of 1. Therefore, the Ledyard model includes both risk-neutral and risk-averse bidders. Included as special cases are models where all bidders are risk-neutral and all bidders are equally (constant relative) risk-averse.

The other definitions and assumptions used in the model are as follows. The number of bidders is denoted by N and the value to bidder i of the auctioned object is denoted by v_i, as in the preceding paragraphs. For each bidder i, v_i is assumed to be drawn from the uniform probability distribution on the nonempty interval $[\underline{v}, \overline{v}]$, where $\underline{v} \geqq 0$. Each bidder knows his own object value before he submits his bid but knows only the probability distribution from which his rivals' values are drawn. We also assume that the bidders do not cooperate (i.e., collude) with each other. Finally, we assume that every bidder behaves as if the assumptions contained in this paragraph and in the immediately preceding paragraph are true.

The equilibrium bidding strategy function for this model has two parts. For bids that do not exceed $\overline{b}$, as defined in statement (3.5), the equilibrium bid function is

$$b_i = \underline{v} + \frac{N - 1}{N - 1 + r_i}(v_i - \underline{v}), i = 1, 2, \ldots, N. \tag{3.7}$$

This will be verified as follows. Suppose that bidder j believes that the bid of each of his rivals satisfies bid function (3.7) when it does not exceed $\overline{b}$. Then we will demonstrate that bidder j's optimal bid satisfies the same function when it does not exceed $\overline{b}$.

The v inverse of bid function (3.7) is

$$v_i = g(b_i, r_i) = \frac{N - 1 + r_i}{N - 1} b_i - \frac{r_i}{N - 1}\underline{v}. \tag{3.8}$$

Now the probability that the bid of bidder i will be less than some amount b in the range of (3.7) is the probability of drawing values of v_i and r_i which when substituted in (3.7) will yield a bid less than b. Note that statements (3.5) and (3.8) imply that $g(b_i, r_i) \leqq \overline{v}$, for all $b_i \in [\underline{v}, \overline{b}]$, for all $r_i \in (0, 1]$. Therefore, using (3.8) and the density function for v_i, we find that the probability that bidder i will bid less than b is

$$\begin{aligned} F(b) &= \int_0^1 \int_{\underline{v}}^{g(b,r_i)} [\overline{v} - \underline{v}]^{-1} \, dv_i \, d\Phi(r_i) \\ &= \frac{[N - 1 + E(r)][b - \underline{v}]}{[N - 1]\,[\overline{v} - \underline{v}]}, \end{aligned} \tag{3.9}$$

where E(r) is the expected value of r_i.

Recall that $v_1, \ldots, v_N, r_1, \ldots, r_N$ are drawn independently. Therefore, the probability that all (N − 1) rivals of bidder j will bid less than some amount b in the range of (3.7) is $[F(b)]^{N-1}$. Let γ represent the constant bid density $[N - 1 + E(r)][(N - 1)(\overline{v} - \underline{v})]^{-1}$ in (3.9). Then $[F(b)]^{N-1}$ can be written simply as $\gamma^{N-1}[b - \underline{v}]^{N-1}$.

Now recall that bidder j has the utility of money income function y^{r_j}. If he wins the auction, he receives the money income $(v_j - b_j)$. Thus his (pseudoconcave) expected utility function of the bid b_j and the object value v_j can be written as

$$U(b_j) = \gamma^{N-1}(b_j - \underline{v})^{N-1}(v_j - b_j)^{r_j}. \tag{3.10}$$

The derivative of U is

$$U'(b_j) = \gamma^{N-1}(b_j - \underline{v})^{N-2}(v_j - b_j)^{r_j-1}$$
$$[(N - 1)(v_j - \underline{v}) - (N - 1 + r_j)(b_j - \underline{v})]. \tag{3.11}$$

Assume that $v_j > \underline{v}$; then $U(b_j)$ is positive on $(\underline{v}, v_j)$. Also, $U'(b_j)$ changes sign only once on $(\underline{v}, v_j)$ and the change in sign is from positive to negative. Thus the unique bid b_j^o that maximizes (3.10) is the value that equates the square bracket term in (3.11) to zero:

$$b_j^o = \underline{v} + \frac{N-1}{N-1+r_j}(v_j - \underline{v}). \tag{3.12}$$

Thus, if bidder j believes that each of his rivals will use bid function (3.7) for bids that do not exceed $\bar{b}$, then his best strategy is to use the same bid function for bids that do not exceed $\bar{b}$. Therefore, (3.7) satisfies the Nash equilibrium condition.

The equilibrium bidding strategy function (3.7) implies that the truncated probability distribution function on p, the winning bid and sales price, is the following.

$$G_T(p) = [\gamma(p - \underline{v})]^N, \forall p \in [\underline{v}, \bar{b}], \tag{3.13}$$

where

$$\gamma = [N - 1 + E(r)][(N - 1)(\bar{v} - \underline{v})]^{-1}. \tag{3.14}$$

Thus the truncated mean $\bar{p}_T$ of the sales price is

$$\bar{p}_T = \int_{\underline{v}}^{\bar{b}} p\, dG_T(p) = \left[\frac{N-1+E(r)}{N}\right]^N \left[\frac{(N-1)(\bar{v}-\underline{v})}{N+1} + \underline{v}\right] \tag{3.15}$$

Even in the absence of an explicit solution for the bid function for bids which exceed $\bar{b}$, the Ledyard model of the first-price auction has several testable implications in addition to the ones which follow from the expected utility hypothesis. Given that the Dutch auction is isomorphic to the first-price auction, these same implications apply to the Dutch auction. The testable implications of the model can be divided into the implications for individual bids which follow from (3.7) and the implications for the distribution of sales prices which follow from (3.3) – (3.5). We will focus on the latter.

The Vickrey model is the special case of the Ledyard model in which the entire mass of the probability distribution Φ is concentrated at $r = 1$, which implies $E(r) = 1$. Let $G_V(\cdot)$ be the probability distribution for the sales price and $\bar{p}_V$ be the mean sales price for the Vickrey model of the first-price auction. Setting $E(r) = 1$ in statements (3.13) – (3.15) yields:

$$G_V(p) = \left[\frac{N}{(N-1)(\bar{v}-\underline{v})}(p-\underline{v})\right]^N; \tag{3.16}$$

$$\bar{p}_V = \frac{(N-1)(\bar{v}-\underline{v})}{N+1} + \underline{v}\,. \tag{3.17}$$

Statements (3.16) and (3.17) can be used to calculate the variance of the sales price in the Vickrey model as follows:

$$\begin{aligned} V_V(p) &= \int_{\underline{v}}^{\underline{v}+1/\gamma} (p-\bar{p}_V)^2\, dG_V(p) \\ &= \frac{(N-1)^2(\bar{v}-\underline{v})^2}{N(N+1)^2(N+2)}\,. \end{aligned} \tag{3.18}$$

The strict risk-averse Ledyard model is the special case of the Ledyard model which excludes the Vickrey model; in other words, the strict risk-averse Ledyard model requires that $\Phi\,(r) > 0$ for some $r < 1$ although Φ can have a mass of probability at $r = 1$. Let $G_L(\cdot)$ be the probability distribution for the sales price and $\bar{p}_L$ be the mean sales price for the strict risk-averse Ledyard model. In the following paragraphs we will derive the relation between $G_L(\cdot)$ and $G_V(\cdot)$ and the relation between $\bar{p}_L$, $\bar{p}_V$, and $\bar{p}_2$.

Inspection of statements (3.13), (3.14), and (3.16) reveals a strong first-order stochastic dominance ordering of $G_T(\cdot)$ over $G_V(\cdot)$; that is

$$G_T(p) < G_V(p)\,\forall\, p \in (\underline{v}, \bar{b}]. \tag{3.19}$$

Furthermore, $G_L(\cdot)$ is identical to $G_T(\cdot)$ on $[\underline{v}, \bar{b}]$. Therefore, $G_L(\cdot)$ dominates $G_V(\cdot)$ on $[\underline{v}, \bar{b}]$. Since $G_L(\cdot)$ is a probability distribution function, it must be nondecreasing on $[\bar{b}, \underline{v}]$. Furthermore, since $G_L(\bar{b}) < 1$, we must have $G_L(p) > G_L(\bar{b})$ for some $p \in (\bar{b}, \bar{v}]$. Therefore, there is a strong first-order stochastic dominance ordering of $G_L(\cdot)$ over $G_V(\cdot)$ on $[\underline{v}, \bar{v}]$. This result will be used in Sections V and VI below.

Since $G_L(\cdot)$ agrees with $G_T(\cdot)$ on $[\underline{v}, \bar{b}]$ and increases somewhere on $(\bar{b}, \bar{v}]$, we must have $\bar{p}_L > \bar{p}_T$. Inspection of (3.15) and (3.17) reveals that $\bar{p}_T > \bar{p}_V$. Finally, inspection of (2.10) and (3.17) reveals that $\bar{p}_2 = \bar{p}_V$. Therefore, $\bar{p}_L > \bar{p}_V = \bar{p}_2$. This result will be used in Sections V and VI below.

IV. EXPERIMENTAL DESIGN

The design and execution of the experiments are shaped by the following objectives:

A. Control the procedures for conducting each experiment so that all experiments—insofar as is possible—are conducted in the same way.

This is the standard design objective of minimizing extraneous "noise" in experimental outcomes. However, this consideration becomes of amplified importance when two institutions, such as the Dutch and first-price auctions, are being compared which theoretically produce identical outcomes. In this situation in order to identify any true behavioral difference in the two auctions, the variability within first-price replications and within Dutch replications may have to be relatively small. We have attempted to achieve this by using the PLATO computer system to present programmed experimental instructions and practice examples to each subject bidder, to record all data, inconspicuously, and to enforce the appropriate market rules uniformly across replications.

B. Provide an experimental design that permits paired comparisons of the treatment effects of the different auction institutions and uses different treatment switchover sequences on paired subject groups.

Again, this is the common scientific objective of attempting to reduce error. Paired comparisons increase the power of the test while switchovers increase the credibility of the claim that any measured differences are attributable to differences in the auction institutions and not to differences in particular subject groups. But these considerations increase in importance if we encounter small, and subtle, differences among the Dutch and first- and second-price auction institutions. Consequently, all experiments consist of 30 sequential auctions: 10 Dutch (first), followed by 10 first (Dutch), and finally 10 Dutch (first) auctions. Table 1 lists all the first and Dutch switchover experiments, and Table 2 lists all the Dutch and second switchover experiments. For example, in Table 1, experimental session dfd3, representing one member of the third pair of experiments, using three bidders, consists of a 30-auction sequence of 10 Dutch, 10 first, and 10 Dutch auctions. The values v_i, for each of the three bidders in dfd3, are drawn with replacement from a uniform distribution on the interval $[\underline{v}, \overline{v}]$ for each of the 30 auctions. Session dfd3 is matched with fdf3′, the latter using a different group of three subject bidders in a first-Dutch-first 30-auction sequence but using the identical value sequences drawn randomly for the three subjects in dfd3. In Table 1 any two pairs such as 3 and 3′, 10 and 10′, and 5 and 5′ are "matched" only with respect to the value sequences applying to the different sets of N subjects in each pair. An x denotes that the subjects were experienced, i.e., had participated in a previous such experiment. For example dfd8x and fdf8'x are matched pairs of experienced subjects (N = 4).

C. Vary N *systematically across experiments so that the Vickrey and Ledyard models of noncooperative equilibrium bidding can be tested for auction markets with various numbers of rival bidders.*

For each N, we want to test some implications of the (null) Vickrey risk-neutral hypothesis against the (alternative) strict risk-averse Ledyard hypothesis.[3] In Section VI we report a Kolmogorov–Smirnov test of the hypothesis that, for each N, the frequency distribution of winning bids came from the distribution function $G_V(\cdot)$ in statement (3.16). Also reported in Section VI is a binomial test, for each N, which compares observed and risk-neutral theoretical prices in first-price auctions.

D. Hold constant the expected gain per bidder as N *increases so that motivation is approximately the same for any given bidder independently of the size of the bidding group in which he/she is a participant.*

It is well known that any market (or other) decision task may have significant subjective costs of thinking, calculating, deciding and transacting (Siegel, 1961; Marschak, 1968; Smith, 1976). The greater is the explicit monetary (or other) reward relative to this subjective transactions cost, which is obtained as an outcome of the decision, the more likely will maximization of this reward be the predominating influence in determining the decision. Since subjective transactions cost is not normally observable, but may be a contaminating factor in testing a theory, it can be important to attempt to control for this contamination.

That motivation may be a problem in the larger groups follows most directly from the Vickrey model. From the Vickrey bid function (3.4), if v is the highest value drawn among N bidders, then the price is

$$p = \left(\frac{N-1}{N}\right)(v - \underline{v}) + \underline{v},$$

determined by the bid of the highest bidder. Profit to the highest bidder is thus

$$\pi = v - p = \frac{p - \underline{v}}{N - 1}.$$

From the mean Vickrey price in (3.17) it follows that expected profit per bidder is

$$\frac{\bar{\pi}_V}{N} = \frac{\bar{v} - \underline{v}}{N(N + 1)}. \tag{4.1}$$

Table 1.

Experimental Session	*Number of Bidders N*	*Statistic*	*Mean and Variance of Ten Prices, by Institution, in Sequence* Dutch	First	Dutch	First
*dfd3	3	Mean	1.30	2.40	1.32	
		Variance	.098	.162	.235	
*fdf3′	3	Mean		2.66	3.32	2.02
		Variance		1.092	.297	1.166
fdf10	3	Mean		2.74	2.72	2.22
		Variance		.203	1.017	.268
dfd10′	3	Mean	2.62	2.84	2.36	
		Variance	.260	.827	.436	
dfd10x	3	Mean	2.42	2.22	2.40	
		Variance	.500	.402	.420	
fdf8	4	Mean		6.06	5.46	4.74
		Variance		.956	.996	5.256
dfd8′	4	Mean	5.70	5.46	3.78	
		Variance	1.10	.916	3.764	
dfd8x	4	Mean	5.43	6.03	5.64	
		Variance	1.329	.669	1.596	
fdf8′x	4	Mean		5.91	5.97	5.64
		Variance		1.361	.969	1.636
dfd9	5	Mean	7.75	9.52	8.83	
		Variance	3.565	.724	2.649	
fdf9′	5	Mean		8.62	9.58	9.31
		Variance		2.804	2.104	1.481
fdf9x	5	Mean		9.07	7.66	9.70
		Variance		.769	1.766	.260

Table 1. (Continued)

Experimental Session	*Number of Bidders N*	*Statistic*	*Mean and Variance of Ten Prices, by Institution, in Sequence*			
			Dutch	*First*	*Dutch*	*First*
dfd9′x	5	Mean	9.04	8.62	9.82	
		Variance	1.216	2.204	1.104	
*dfd2	6	Mean	12.72	12.48	13.60	
		Variance	3.231	6.20	3.896	
*fdf2′	6	Mean		13.60	13.44	13.96
		Variance		2.207	6.356	3.716
*dfd4	6	Mean	12.86	13.22	12.38	
		Variance	1.26	4.651	5.086	
*fdf4′	6	Mean		13.18	13.42	12.86
		Variance		2.846	5.548	6.238
*dfd5	9	Mean	31.30	30.40	29.50	
		Variance	2.56	6.26	4.00	
*fdf5′	9	Mean		31.78	30.16	30.88
		Variance		4.064	6.196	4.404

Notes:
* Initial series of experiments.
All variances are maximum likelihood estimates.

Hence, expected profit per bidder declines inversely with N^2, and motivation may decline rapidly. We attempt to control for this with the following variable reward design: For given $\underline{v}$, use (4.1) to choose $\bar{v}$ as a function of N such that expected profit per bidder is a constant v_0 under replication with different N. This requires

$$\bar{v} = N(N + 1)\, v_0 + \underline{v}\,. \tag{4.2}$$

The parameter values $v_0 = \$.40$ and $\underline{v} = \$.10$ are used in the experiments reported here. The corresponding values of $\bar{v}$, $\bar{\pi}_v$, and $\bar{p}_v$ for each N are shown in Table 3. With expected profit per bidder set at \$.40, the expected earnings of a subject in any 30-auction sequence is \$12.00. Since

Table 2.

Experimental Session	*Number of Bidders N*	*Statistic*	*Mean and Variance of Ten Prices by Institution, in Sequence*			
			Dutch	*Second*	*Dutch*	*Second*
sds7	3	Mean		2.06	2.22	1.84
		Variance		1.35	.668	.427
dsd7′	3	Mean	3.16	2.02	2.82	
		Variance	.392	.50	.304	
dsd1	6	Mean	12.78	11.66	11.94	
		Variance	2.028	12.638	3.065	
sds1′	6	Mean		11.74	13.10	10.30
		Variance		6.949	7.831	8.720
dsd3x	6	Mean	14.62	11.14	13.54	
		Variance	.571	4.487	2.674	
dsd4	9	Mean	25.90	27.10	28.72	
		Variance	10.08	12.32	7.684	
sds4′	9	Mean		27.16	29.98	26.80
		Variance		19.716	11.664	23.94

Note: All variances are maximum likelihood estimates.

subjects receive $3 for volunteering and arriving on time for an experiment, total expected earnings is $15.00 per subject per session. A session requires about 1 hour to complete.

We do not argue that making v_0 a design constant guarantees equal motivation across experiments in which N varies from 3 to 9. Rather, we argue that this procedure should yield more uniform motivation than if we ignored the issue. Ideally we want the utility of the monetary rewards relative to that of nonmonetary factors to be invariant across experiments, but neither utility nor the nonmonetary factors are observable.

In our experimental design we planned to conduct experiments for N = 3, 6, and 9 and to use these observations to test the Vickrey and Ledyard models. As explained in Section V, as the research developed it became important for additional experimental observations to be obtained for N = 4 and N = 5 (see Tables 1 and 3).

Table 3. Experimental Design Parameters: Dutch and Sealed-Bid Auctions (v_0 = \$.40, $\underline{v}$ = \$.10)

N	*3*	*4*	*5*	*6*	*9*
$\bar{v} = .4N(N+1) + .1$	4.90	8.10	12.10	16.90	36.10
$\bar{\pi}_v = .4N$	1.20	1.60	2.00	2.40	3.60
$\bar{p}_v = .4N(N-1) + .1$	2.50	4.90	8.10	12.10	28.90
$\bar{v} - \bar{p}_v = .8N$	2.40	3.20	4.00	4.80	7.20
$p_0 - \bar{v} = 2\delta$*	.40	.60	.60	.80	1.20
δ (\$/tick)	.20	.30	.30	.40	.60
τ* (seconds/tick)	2	2	2	2	2

Note:
* These entries apply to the Dutch auction only.
All other entries apply to the first, second and Dutch auctions.

E. Control for the effect of certain technical differences between Dutch and sealed-bid auctions that might account for differences in behavior other than that which would be attributable to the informational and incentive differences among the various auction institutions.

The Dutch auction requires three technical parameters to be specified which are not part of any theory of Dutch auctions and which represent typical features of an institution that are usually ignored (perhaps justifiably) in economic modeling. These parameters, which could conceivably affect behavior, are as follows:

1. The distance between the starting price and the highest possible value that might exist among the bidders. If p_0 is the starting price this distance is $p_0 - \bar{v}$ in the experiments, where distance is measured in dollars.
2. The delay time τ between price decrements, or successive "ticks" of the digital clock.
3. The decrement, δ, by which price falls with each "tick" of the clock.

If any of these parameters of the Dutch auction affect behavior, then there is not one Dutch institution but many depending upon the values of these parameters. In our initial design with experimental groups of size 3, 6, and 9, we elected to set δ at the corresponding values \$.20, \$.40, and \$.60, and clock speed ($1/\tau$) constant with τ = 2 seconds per tick (see Table 3). With these parameter values the distance $\bar{v} - \bar{p}_v$ from the greatest value to the mean Vickrey price is 12 ticks or price decrements. With similar motivation we elected to make each starting price 2 ticks or price decrements above $\bar{v}$, as shown in Table 3 for N = 3, 6, and 9. Later when we decided to conduct experiments for N = 4 and 5, some of this modular-3 symmetry could not be maintained except as an approximation. For example, δ had to be divisible by 0.10, which was the atomic measure of value chosen for the computer program.[4] Thus for both N = 4 and N = 5 we set δ = 0.30 (instead of 26.67 and 33.33, respectively, which would have preserved the modular-3 symmetry).

In the Dutch auction the price change decrement δ also defines the distance between adjacent feasible discrete bids, and therefore the prices, that can result.[5] It follows that if strict technical comparability among the experimental Dutch and sealed-bid auctions is to be maintained, it is essential that all adjacent feasible sealed-bids also be separated by the same distance δ that applies in the Dutch auction. Our computerized first- and second-price auction experiment accomplishes this by rounding each subject's bid to the nearest δ bid node, except that bids of $\underline{v}$ and of zero are always admissible. Consequently, in an auction with N = 3, since δ = .20 and values range from $\underline{v}$ = .10 to $\bar{v}$ = 4.90 (see Table 3), a bid of $4.54 would be rounded to $4.50, then displayed to the subject along with a message asking him/her to either confirm and enter this bid or press a key to alter it. Hence, each subject in first- or second-price sealed-bid auctions always had the opportunity to verify his/her rounded bid before it was entered into the market. Except for the starting price and clock speed parameters, all other design parameters in Table 3 apply also to the first- and second-price auctions.

Before each session begins, the experimenter executes an initialization procedure to define the experiment. In this procedure one chooses the auction sequence, say 10 Dutch, 10 first, and 10 Dutch auctions. Then the vector of parameters ($\underline{v}$, $\bar{v}$, δ, N, p_0, τ) is selected. The parameters (p_0, τ) apply only to the Dutch sequences. All other parameters apply to both the Dutch and first-price (also the second-price when appropriate) auctions. Consequently, it is impossible to do experiments in which the set of Dutch auction price outcomes is distinct from the set of first-price (or second-price) outcomes in paired comparison treatments. The PLATO instructions for a Dutch followed by a first experiment are reproduced in the Appendix to this chapter.

V. OVERVIEW OF EXPERIMENTAL RESULTS

A. Previous English and Dutch Oral Auction Experiments

Coppinger, Smith and Titus (1980, pp. 6–10) have reported the results of six English and/or Dutch oral auction experimental sessions with N =

8 bidders. In the first four of these sessions individual valuations were equally spaced, with adjacent values separated by $1.50, but randomly assigned to individual bidders. The mean deviation of English auction prices from the second highest valuation was only $.0124, which was insignificantly different from zero (t_e = .096). The Dutch oral auctions, in this context, yielded a mean deviation, from the second highest valuation, of −$1.14, which was quite significantly below zero (t_d = −5.09). In sessions 5 and 6 the valuation assignments were drawn (with replacement) from the interval [$.10, $10.0] (using $.10 increments). In neither auction was the mean price significantly different from the Vickrey mean given by Equation (3.17) (t_e = −1.06, t_d = −.83). Similarly, the English and Dutch price variances were not significantly different from the predictions of Equations (2.11) and (3.18). In these sessions 97.2% of the English auction awards, but only 77.8% of the Dutch auction awards, were Pareto-optimal.

In the Dutch experiments, the experimenter lowered the price in decrements of $.50 every 7 seconds, while in the English auctions the subjects named the amount of any increase over the previous bid, which was typically $.25. This technical difference could have affected the results, which is why this factor was computer controlled in the Dutch and first- and second-price comparisons reported here.

B. Dutch, First-Price, and Second-Price Auction Results

The means and maximum-likelihood variances for the individual Dutch-first experiments are contained in Table 1. A comparative examination of the means suggests that Dutch auction prices tend to be lower than prices in first-price sealed-bid auctions. Several of the paired experiments illustrate the importance of a paired comparison design which uses the same random sequence of valuations. Thus in fdf8 the final series of first-price auctions has a lower mean (4.74) than the middle sequence of Dutch auctions (5.46). But if we compare means using the more relevant paired experiment, dfd8′, it is seen that the final series of Dutch prices has a mean (3.78) considerably below the mean of the final first-price sequence in fdf8. In this particular matched pair, the random sequence of valuations for auctions 21 to 30 happened to be particularly low. Similarly, the mean price in first (8.62) is below both Dutch means in dfd9′x, but it is well above its matched Dutch mean (7.66) in fdf9x. Again the same phenomenon is illustrated in dfd5 and fdf5′. One cannot overemphasize the importance of a suitably controlled paired-comparison design when comparing different exchange institutions, particularly when the theory, or other a priori considerations such as exploratory experiments, allege that the institutions are equivalent.

The means and maximum-likelihood variances for the individual Dutch-

Table 4. Theoretical and Pooled Means and Variances: All Auctions

N	Statistic	Dutch, Observed	First, Observed	First, Dutch, Theoretical*	Second: Observed	Second: Theoretical
3	Mean	2.42	2.44	2.5	1.97	2.5
	Variance	.421	.589	.384	.759	.96
4	Mean	5.33	5.64	4.9		
	Variance	1.63	1.80	.96		
5	Mean	8.78	9.14	8.1		
	Variance	2.06	1.37	1.83		
6	Mean	13.12	13.22	12.1	11.21	12.1
	Variance	3.77	4.31	3.0	8.20	6.4
9	Mean	29.26	31.02	28.9	27.02	28.9
	Variance	7.03	4.91	8.38	18.66	18.85

Note:
* These are the means and variances implied by the Vickrey hypothesis; they are calculated from (3.17) and (3.18).

second experiments are shown in Table 2. A pronounced tendency for prices in the second-price sealed-bid auction to be below those in the Dutch auction seems evident.

The pooled mean and variance of prices across all experiments for Dutch and first- and second-price auctions is shown in Table 4. For all N, the observed means are ordered $m_2 < m_d < m_1$. The theoretical prediction under the Vickrey assumptions is $m_2 = m_d = m_1$ and under the Ledyard assumptions is $m_2 < m_d = m_1$. Hence, the data appear to be consistent with the assumption that bidders are risk-averse, but inconsistent with the hypothesis that the Dutch and first-price institutions are isomorphic. These results are generally consistent with those reported by Coppinger, Smith and Titus (1980, pp. 21–22) for their less rigorously controlled experiments.

VI. TESTING THE VICKREY AND LEDYARD MODELS

Initially our research design for the Dutch and first-price auctions consisted of the eight experimental sessions indicated by an asterisk in Table 1. The remaining experiments listed in Table 1 were conducted after examining the data from the first-price auctions in this initial series. Our reasons for scheduling the additional 11 experiments will be made clear

Table 5. The Kolmogorov-Smirnov Statistic D_n^+ for Dutch, First- and Second-Auction Price Distributions

N	First-Price Auctions, $D_n^+ = -sup[G_n^f(p) - G(p)]$	Dutch Auctions, $D_n^+ = -sup[G_n^d(p) - G(p)]$	Second-Price Auctions, $D_n^+ = -sup[F_n^s(p) - F(p)]$
3	.09 (n = 70)	.11 (n = 120)	.33 (n = 30)*
4	.42 (n = 60)*	.37 (n = 60)*	
5	.30 (n = 60)*	.25 (n = 60)*	
6	.38 (n = 60)*	.26 (n = 110)*	.19 (n = 60)
9	.40 (n = 30)*	.19 (n = 60)	.24 (n = 30)

Note:
* Reject hypothesis that G or F is the appropriate distribution (Pr = .005).

as we examine the test results for the first-price auction reported in Tables 5 and 6.

A. Risk Aversion and Bidding Behavior in the First-Price Auction

Table 5 shows the results of a one-tailed Kolmogorov–Smirnov test, for each N, of the hypothesis that first-price auction prices came from a population with distribution given in (3.16). We reject the null hypothesis (Pr. = 0.005) in favor of the risk-averse alternative for N = 6 and 9. In applying this test to the data from the first series of N = 3 experiments we were not able to reject the null hypothesis.

The tests in Table 5 do not make use of the fact that the assigned valuations $v_i(t)$ are controlled and observed in the experiments. An alternative (and more powerful) test making use of this information involves

Table 6. Binomial Test Comparing Observed and Predicted Risk-Neutral Prices in First-Price Auctions

N	Total Number of Auctions	Number of Auctions for which $\delta(t) > 0$*	Unit Normal Deviate, U_p
3	70	43	1.91 (P = .06)
4	60	54	6.20 (P < .0001)
5	60	60	7.75 (P < .0001)
6	60	52	5.68 (P < .00001)
9	30	30	5.48 (P < .0001)

Note:
* $\delta(t) = [p(t) - \underline{v}] - \left(\frac{N-1}{N}\right) \max_i [v_i(t) - \underline{v}]$

an examination of the distribution of the difference between the observed normalized price $p(t) - \underline{v}$ and the predicted risk-neutral normalized price from (3.17), namely

$$\left(\frac{N-1}{N}\right)[\max_i v_i(t) - \underline{v}] .$$

Table 6 reports the results of a binomial test, for each N, of the null hypothesis that in first-price auctions the difference

$$\delta(t) = [p(t) - \underline{v}] - \left(\frac{N-1}{N}\right)[\max_i v_i(t) - \underline{v}]$$

is equally likely to be positive or negative (risk-neutral) against the one-tailed alternative that the difference is more likely to be positive (risk-averse). From the values of U_p (the unit normal approximation to the binomial) we are able to reject the null hypothesis at very high levels of significance for N = 6 and 9. In applying this test to the data from the first series of N = 3 experiments we were not able to reject the null hypothesis at any level of significance approaching that of the N = 6 and 9 tests.

The apparent divergence of the N = 3 results from the N = 6 and 9 results in both the Kolmogorov–Smirnov and binomial tests led to three provisional hypotheses:

(1) The Ledyard model is superior to the Vickrey model, except that for N = 3 the assumption of noncooperative (Nash) behavior fails.
(2) The Ledyard model is superior to that of Vickrey for values of N larger than 4 or 5, i.e., the assumption of noncooperative behavior breaks down somewhere between N = 3 and N = 6, to be determined.
(3) The Ledyard model is superior to the Vickrey model for all values of N, with the apparent failure for N = 3 attributable to sampling error in our first two experiments.

On the basis that there is considerable experimental evidence in the context of oligopoly competition (Shubik 1975, p. 282; Fouraker and Siegel, 1963) to suggest that the assumption of noncooperative behavior is supported for N ≥ 3, we conjectured that the additional experimental observations would support (1). However, on this same prior evidence we could not rule out the possibility that (3) would be supported. At this critical juncture the additional experiments were conducted. These experiments included sixteen sequences of ten first-price (and seventeen Dutch) auctions and are recorded in Table 1 without asterisks.

The test results in Tables 5 and 6 allow us to reject the null hypotheses for N = 4 and 5 at the same levels of significance at which we were able to reject the null hypotheses for N = 6 and 9. The theoretical and empirical distributions for the Kolmogorov–Smirnov test for N = 5 are presented in Chart 1. On the basis of these tests, for N > 3, we reject the risk-neutral in favor of the risk-averse model of Nash equilibrium behavior.

The same tests applied to data from all of the N = 3 experiments reveal, in Tables 5 and 6, that we cannot reject the risk-neutral hypothesis. However, since there is no reason to suppose that individuals in groups of size N = 3 are any less risk-averse than those in groups of size N > 3, we interpret the results as also supporting the subsidiary hypothesis that the assumption of noncooperative behavior fails to apply when N = 3. We can think of no alternative explanation.

B. Risk Aversion and Bidding Behavior in the Dutch Auction

Table 5 reports the results of a one-tailed Kolmogorov–Smirnov test for each N, of the hypothesis that Dutch auction prices came from a

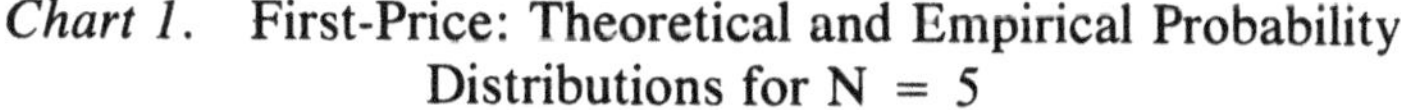

Chart 1. First-Price: Theoretical and Empirical Probability Distributions for N = 5

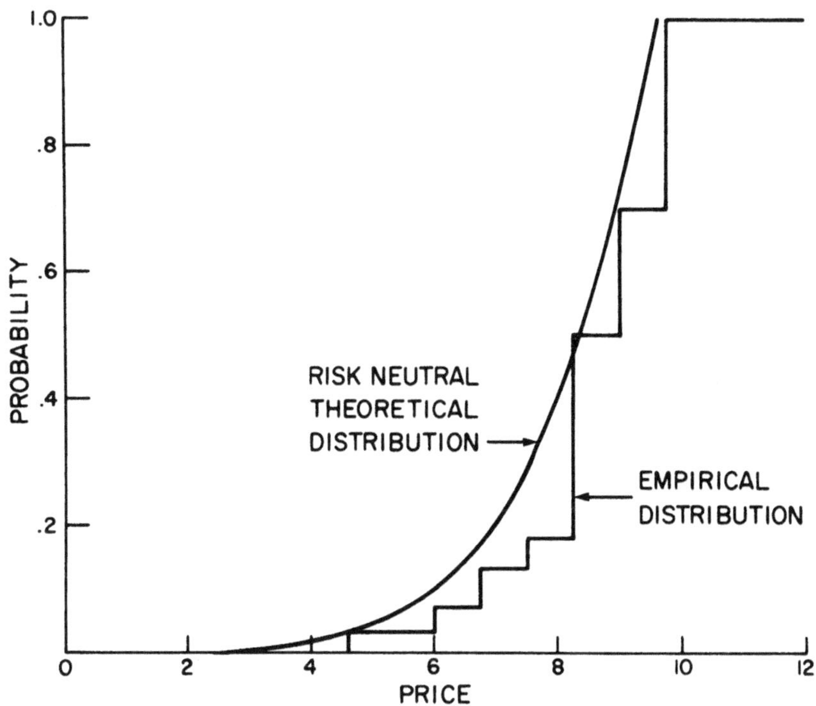

population with distribution given in (3.16). We are able to reject the null hypothesis (Pr. = 0.005) in favor of the risk-averse alternative for N = 4, 5, and 6 but are not able to do so for N = 3 and 9. The N = 3 Dutch auction results are consistent with the N = 3 first auction results. But the Dutch auction test results for N = 9 are not consistent with the pattern of test results for the first-price auction. However, one must keep in mind that $G_V(\cdot)$, for the Vickrey hypothesis, or $G_L(\cdot)$, for the Ledyard hypothesis, is the distribution function for sales price in the Dutch auction only if it is isomorphic to the first-price auction. Thus the Dutch auction test results in Table 5 are for a joint test for the effects of risk aversion and the first/Dutch isomorphism. Our rejection of this isomorphism in the next section of the paper will clarify the Dutch auction test results for N = 9 in Table 5.

C. Bidding Behavior in the Second-Price Auction

Now consider the second-price auction and note that the pooled mean price in second-price auctions reported in Table 4 is below the theoretical mean in Equation (2.10). Results of the Kolmogorov–Smirnov test of the hypothesis that second-price winning bids came from a population with distribution given by (2.9) are shown in Table 5. The hypothesis is rejected for N = 3, but not for N = 6 and 9. Coppinger, Smith and Titus (1980) also report mean prices below the dominant strategy expected price in second-price auctions (with varying significance in different experiments). They also report considerable learning effects in that some subjects in second-price auctions converge to the dominant strategy over successive auctions.

VII. PRICE AND EFFICIENCY COMPARISONS IN THE DUTCH, FIRST-PRICE AND SECOND-PRICE AUCTIONS

The paired sample comparisons listed in Table 7 show that the Dutch and first-price auctions are not behaviorally isomorphic. In every paired comparison the mean price is higher in the first than in the Dutch auction. Using the nonparametric sign test, we reject the null hypothesis that the mean price difference $m_l - m_d$ is as likely to be positive as negative in favor of the alternative that Dutch prices tend to be below those in the first-price auction ($Pr < .001$).

These Dutch auction findings not only call into question the theoretical equivalence of Dutch and first-price auctions; they also provide clear evidence against the proposition that Dutch prices will be among the highest obtainable on the grounds that any buyer will tend to "stop the clock" as soon as the price is slightly below that buyer's reservation

Table 7. Dutch-First Paired-Sample Mean Price Differences

Experiment	*N*	*First Price*	*Dutch Price*	$m_l - m_d$
dfd 3, fdf 3′	3	2.36	1.98	.38
fdf 10, dfd 10′	3	2.60	2.57	.03
fdf 8, dfd 8′	4	5.42	4.98	.44
dfd 8x, fdf 8′x	4	5.86	5.68	.18
dfd9, fdf 9′	5	9.15	8.72	.43
fdf 9x, dfd 9′x	5	9.13	8.84	.29
dfd 2, fdf 2′	6	13.35	13.25	.10
dfd 4, fdf 4′	6	13.09	12.89	.20
dfd 5, fdf 5′	9	31.02	30.32	.70

value (Boulding, 1948, p. 42; Cassady, 1967, p. 67). The opposite behavior is evident. On a more impressionistic level it is worth noting in this regard that many subjects report that they enjoy the "clock experiment" more than the others because of the "suspense of waiting." In this sense they seem to perceive the Dutch auction as a "waiting game," in which lower bids are entered than in the first-price sealed-bid auction.

The Dutch and second-price paired sample comparisons are shown in Table 8. In each paired comparison the mean price is higher in the Dutch than in the second-price auction. This is consistent with the risk-averse model of Dutch auction bidding and the dominant strategy model of second-price auction bidding. It is also consistent with the more limited, indirect, empirical results reported by Coppinger, Smith and Titus (1980, pp. 9–10, 13–18) in which Dutch prices are above English auction prices and the latter do not differ significantly from prices in the second-price auction. Using the sign test, the positive difference between the Dutch auction mean and the second-price mean is significant (Pr = .06).

If we let V_N (t) be the highest value drawn among N bidders in auction t, and $W_N(t)$ be the value drawn by the winning bidder in auction t, then the efficiency of auction t is measured by

$$E_N(t) = 100\ W_N(t)/V_N(t).$$

Table 8. Dutch-Second Paired-Sample Mean Price Differences

Experiment	*N*	*Mean Dutch Price,* m_d	*Mean Second Price,* m_2	$m_d - m_2$
sds7, dsd7′	3	2.73	1.97	.76
dsd1, sds1′	6	12.61	11.23	1.37
dsd4, sds4′	9	28.20	27.02	1.18

Table 9. Mean Efficiency (and Percent Pareto-Optimal Allocations) by Institution and Number of Bidders

Institution \ *Number of Bidders*	*3*	*4*	*5*	*6*	*9*	*Over All Groups*
Dutch	97.32 (81.82)	96.25 (76.67)	98.48 (81.67)	98.89 (83.64)	98.44 (71.67)	97.95 (80.00)
First Price	97.61 (82.86)	99.62 (95.00)	99.80 (93.33)	98.26 (83.33)	99.77 (83.33)	98.88 (87.86)
Second Price	99.28 (93.33)			99.89 (96.67)	99.54 (90.00)	99.65 (94.00)

Efficiency is 100% if and only if the winning bidder drew the highest value, which is a Pareto-optimal allocation. Unrealized gains from exchange will characterize any auction which is less than 100% efficient. Table 9 reports the mean efficiency of all auctions classified by institution and group size. The most efficient institution is the second-price auction with mean efficiency 99.65% over all groups, followed by the first-price auction (98.88%), with the Dutch auction being the least efficient (97.95%). Table 9 also reports (in parentheses) the percent of total auctions that were Pareto-optimal allocations.

VIII. TWO BIDDING MODELS THAT ARE CONSISTENT WITH BIDDING BEHAVIOR IN THE DUTCH AND FIRST-PRICE AUCTIONS

In Section II we showed that standard behavioral assumptions imply that the Dutch and first-price auctions are theoretically isomorphic. Therefore, if one is to construct a bidding theory that is consistent with the observation that these auctions are *not* behaviorally isomorphic, he must incorporate some nonstandard behavioral assumptions in the model. We will in this section provide two possible explanations of the failure of the predicted isomorphism. One explanation will be based on the utility of playing the Dutch auction "waiting game." The other explanation will be based on bidder violation of Bayes' rule.

We have adopted the "utility of playing the game" approach to modeling the Dutch auction because of the comments made by some experimental subjects. They reported that they especially enjoyed the "clock experiment" more than the others because of the "suspense of waiting." We inferred from these comments that the Dutch and first-price auctions may not be behaviorally isomorphic because of a property that follows from the real-time aspect of the Dutch auction: bidder utility from playing the waiting game.

We have two reasons for adopting the approach to the Dutch auction that is based on bidder violation of Bayes' rule. First, there is independent evidence that behavior is not consistent with Bayes' rule (Grether, 1980). Secondly, the only predicted comparison of bidding behavior across auctions that depends on Bayes' rule is the predicted isomorphism between the Dutch and first-price auctions, and that prediction is the one that is clearly inconsistent with our observations.

Now consider bidding models that include utility from playing the game. Assume that in the first-price auction an active bidder i gets the nonnegative utility a_i from playing the first-price auction game. That is, we now replace the expected utility function (2.1) with

$$U_i(b_i) = a_i + F_i(b_i)u_i(v_i - b_i), \tag{8.1}$$

where $a_i \geq 0$. We now proceed, as we did with (2.1), to assume that (8.1) is pseudoconcave and has a unique interior maximum at b_i^o. Then b_i^o will satisfy the first-order condition,

$$\begin{aligned} 0 &= U_i'(b_i^o) \\ &= F_i'(b_i^o)u_i(v_i - b_i^o) - F_i(b_i^o)u_i'(v_i - b_i^o). \end{aligned} \tag{8.2}$$

Now consider the Dutch auction and assume that the bidder gets utility $\alpha_i(t)$ from playing a Dutch auction game of length t. Assume that α_i is a positive, increasing function; that is, assume that the bidder enjoys playing this "waiting game" and that he gets more utility from playing a longer game. Suppose that the auction is in progress at time t and bidder i must decide whether to accept the bid b(t) or let the auction continue. If he accepts the bid b(t) he gains the money income $v_i - b(t)$ with utility $u_i(v_i - b(t))$. In addition, he gains the utility $\alpha_i(t)$ from playing a Dutch auction game of length t. If bidder i does not accept b(t), he will be able to play a longer auction game and will have a chance to obtain the auctioned object at a lower price. Suppose that the bidder does not accept b(t) but rather lets the auction continue for one more tick of the auction clock to time $t + \Delta t$, where $\Delta t > 0$. By doing so, he obtains the utility $\alpha_i(t + \Delta t)$ of playing a longer game and the probability $H_i(b(t + \Delta t)|b(t))$ of obtaining the utility $u_i(v_i - b(t + \Delta t))$ of the monetary gain $v_i - b(t + \Delta t)$. Thus the change in expected utility at time t from not accepting b(t) and planning to accept $b(t + \Delta t)$ is

$$\begin{aligned} \Delta X_i(t) = {} & \alpha_i(t + \Delta t) - \alpha_i(t) \\ & + H_i(b(t + \Delta t)|b(t))u_i(v_i - b(t + \Delta t)) - u_i(v_i - b(t)). \end{aligned} \tag{8.3}$$

Assume (for now) that bidder i believes that his rivals will use the same bidding strategies in the Dutch and first-price auctions. Given Bayes' rule, this assumption implies

$$H_i(b(t + \Delta t)|b(t)) = F_i(b(t + \Delta t))/F_i(b(t)). \tag{8.4}$$

We now proceed, as in Section II, to assume differentiability of the objective function. Thus, using (8.3) and (8.4), we find

$$\begin{aligned} X_i'(t) &= \lim_{\Delta t \to 0^+} \frac{\Delta X_i(t)}{\Delta t} \\ &= \alpha_i'(t) + \{[u_i(v_i - b(t))\, F_i'(b(t))/F_i(b(t))] \\ &\qquad - u_i'(v_i - b(t))\}\, b'(t). \end{aligned} \tag{8.5}$$

Suppose that the optimal time for bidder i to stop the Dutch auction is some t_i^{**} such that $t_i^{**} \in (0, T)$. Then, using (8.5), we have

$$\begin{aligned} 0 &= X_i'(t_i^{**}) \\ &= \alpha_i'(t_i^{**}) + \{[u_i(v_i - b(t_i^{**}))F_i'(b(t_i^{**}))/F_i(b(t_i^{**}))] \\ &\qquad - u_i'(v_i - b(t_i^{**}))\}\, b'(t_i^{**}). \end{aligned} \tag{8.6}$$

We have $\alpha_i'(t_i^{**}) > 0$ and $b'(t_i^{**}) < 0$; therefore the curly bracket term in (8.6) must be positive. But this implies that the derivative of (8.1) is positive at $b(t_i^{**})$. Therefore, since (8.1) is pseudoconcave, we have $b(t_i^{**}) < b_i^o$, that is, for a given object value v_i, bidder i's optimal stopping time for the Dutch auction yields a bid that is less than his bid in the first-price auction.

If bidder i will bid less in the Dutch auction than in the first-price auction, then he might believe that his rivals will behave in the same way. Suppose that is the case; specifically, assume that

$$H_i(b(t + \Delta t)|b(t)) = [F_i(b(t + \Delta t))/F_i(b(t))]^{\theta_i}, \tag{8.7}$$

where $\theta_i < 1$. Statement (8.7) implies a first order stochastic dominance ordering of the two distributions. Let $\hat{t}_i$ be the ith bidder's optimal stopping time for the Dutch auction when his expectations satisfy (8.7) rather than (8.4); then we have

$$\begin{aligned} 0 = \alpha_i'(\hat{t}_i) + \{[\theta_i u_i(v_i - b(\hat{t}_i))\, F_i'(b(\hat{t}_i))/F_i(b(\hat{t}_i))] \\ - u_i'(v_i - b(\hat{t}_i))\}\, b'(\hat{t}_i). \end{aligned} \tag{8.8}$$

We have $\alpha_i'(\hat{t}_i) > 0$ and $b'(\hat{t}_i) < 0$; therefore the curly bracket term in (8.8) must be positive. But this implies that the derivative of (8.1) is positive at $b(\hat{t}_i)$ and therefore that $b(\hat{t}_i) < b_i^o$ since (8.1) is pseudoconcave. Thus, bidder i will bid less in the Dutch auction than in the first-price auction.

Now consider the model of bidder behavior in the Dutch auction that includes bidder violation of Bayes' rule. Consider again the "real-time" model of behavior in the Dutch auction that was developed in Section II. Observation of rivals' bidding behavior in the Dutch auction is *not* informative (in the specific sense in which that term is used in statistics). In fact, recognizing that the Dutch auction is not informative is one avenue for understanding the isomorphism between the Dutch and first-price auctions that holds under conventional assumptions.

Now, however, assume that our representative bidder i behaves as if his observations of his rivals' bidding behavior in the Dutch auction were informative. Specifically, assume that bidder i violates Bayes' rule in the following way. Given the observation that none of his rivals has accepted a bid that is greater than or equal to b(t), the expected utility-maximizing bidder will utilize the probability $G_i(b(t + \Delta t)|b(t))$ that none of his rivals will accept a bid that is greater than or equal to $b(t+\Delta t)$, where $\Delta t > 0$. Assume that bidder i violates Bayes' rule in a way such that

$$\begin{aligned} G_i(b(t + \Delta t)|b(t)) &= [H_i(b(t + \Delta t)|b(t))]^{\pi_i} \\ &= [H_i(b(t + \Delta t))/H_i(b(t))]^{\pi_i}, \qquad \pi_i < 1. \end{aligned} \tag{8.9}$$

Statement (8.9) implies a first order stochastic dominance ordering of the ith bidder's conditional probability distribution $G_i(b(t + \Delta t)|b(t))$ and the conditional probability distribution implied by Bayes' rule, $H_i(b(t + \Delta t))/H_i(b(t))$. Thus (8.9) implies that, having observed that none of his rivals has accepted a bid that is greater than or equal to b(t), the bidder underestimates the risk he bears by continuing to let the auction clock run.

We could now proceed to show that if we incorporate (8.9) into the "real-time" model of bidder behavior in the Dutch auction, then the optimal bid in the Dutch auction is less than the optimal bid in the first-price auction. This conclusion follows in the case where the representative bidder believes that his rivals will use the same bidding strategies in the Dutch and first-price auctions and in the case where he believes that his rivals will bid less in the Dutch auction, as in (8.7). The reasoning that leads to these conclusions will not be reproduced here because it is essentially the same as the preceding argument that includes statements (8.7) and (8.8).

Given two theories, each predicting Dutch prices to be lower than prices in the first-price sealed-bid auction, one would like to be able to design an experiment that would provide a test of the two models of behavior. The simplest such experiment that we can suggest is to replicate an existing set of dfd and fdf experiments, with all parameters unchanged with the exception that the monetary reward level is doubled. If the utility-of-"suspense" model is a correct interpretation of the Dutch auction results, then doubling the reward level should cause Dutch prices to increase toward the level of prices in the first-price auction. If the probability-miscalculation model is appropriate, the price discrepancy in the two auction systems should remain unchanged.

IX. SUMMARY AND CONCLUSIONS

A. Our theoretical analysis of Dutch and English "oral" auctions and of first- and second-price sealed-bid auctions, generalizing and extending the work of Vickrey (1961), can be summarized as follows:

1. Implications of the expected utility hypothesis: In first-price auctions the optimal individual bid is less than the value of the auctioned item. The amount by which value exceeds the optimal bid depends upon an individual's risk preference u_i and expectations F_i about rival bidding behavior. Because of differing risk preferences and expectations among individuals, bids need not be ranked in the same order as individual values, and thus allocations need not be Pareto-efficient. A sufficient condition for allocations to be Pareto-optimal is that all individuals have identical strictly increasing bid functions. This requires the untenable assumption that all bidders have the same utility function.

Bayes' rule implies that the conclusions from the analysis of the first-price auction apply to the Dutch auction. This is because individual Bayesian expectations about rival bidding behavior will not be affected by the "knowledge" that at any given time in the auction no bidder has as yet "stopped the clock." Such expectations are completely determined by the prior probability that a given bid will win, and the Dutch clock process itself is noninformative.

In the second-price auction the optimal bid is equal to the value of the auctioned object independent of risk preference and expectations about rival bids (a bid equal to value is a dominant strategy). The optimal bid is thus higher in the second-price auction than in the first-price auction for any given valuation. The allocations are Pareto-efficient, and the probability distribution of price is that for the $(N - 1)$th-order statistic for a random sample of size N from the probability distribution of values. A similar calculation is not possible for the first-price auction without imposing additional behavioral assumptions.

In the English auction, an expected utility-maximizing bidder will drop out of the bidding only if the outstanding bid is not less than his/her value. This is a dominant strategy, and in this sense the English and second-price auctions are isomorphic.

2. Implications of the expected utility and Nash equilibrium hypotheses: By adding the assumption of Nash equilibrium bidding behavior and specializing the expected utility hypothesis to the class of utility functions with constant relative risk-aversion, we can deduce the optimal bid as a linear function of object value in the first-price auction for bids which do not exceed the risk-neutral maximum bid, $\bar{b}$. The resulting model does not imply Pareto-optimal allocations but does make possible derivation of the truncated probability distribution of selling price. The Vickrey risk-neutral model of the first-price auction is the limiting case in which all bidders have a zero coefficient of relative risk aversion.

B. From the results of 780 Dutch, first- and second-price auction experiments we offer the following conclusions concerning the market price behavior, and Pareto-efficiency of these three institutions:

1. Pooling across all experiments, the mean price in second-price auctions is less than the mean Dutch price, which is in turn less than the mean in first-price auctions. This is consistent with the weak (qualitative) implications of the expected utility hypothesis, but not the hypothesis of Bayes' rule used in the analysis of Dutch auctions.
2. In first-price auctions for groups of size N = 4, 5, 6, and 9, but not for N = 3, we reject the null hypothesis of risk-neutral Nash equilibrium bidding behavior in favor of our version of the Ledyard risk-averse model of Nash bidding behavior. This conclusion is supported by Kolmogorov–Smirnov tests on the frequency distribution of prices and by binomial tests comparing observed and risk-neutral theoretical prices.
3. The Dutch and first-price sealed-bid auctions are not isomorphic. This conclusion receives its strongest support from experiments carefully designed for paired comparison, in which mean Dutch prices are consistently and significantly below mean first-prices. We have offered two theoretical explanations for the lower observed prices in the Dutch auction. One theory postulates a utility for the "suspense of waiting" in the real-time Dutch auction. The second theory postulates a systematic underestimate of the Bayes' rule risk of loss from allowing the Dutch clock to continue. The second theory is consistent with the results of independent experiments testing Bayes' rule, while the first theory is consistent with the reported impression of subjects that they like the "suspense of waiting" associated with Dutch auctions.
4. For N = 3, but not for N = 6 and 9, we reject the hypothesis that prices in second-price auctions came from a population with distribution defined by the (N − 1)th-order statistic of values, which is implied by the dominant strategy model of bidding behavior.
5. It is conjectured that the deviant results for the case N = 3 in both first- and second-price auctions are due to failure of the assumption of noncooperative behavior which underlies both the Nash and dominant-strategy models of bidding.

6. Efficiency, measured by the percentage of the theoretical total gains from exchange that are actually realized, is greatest in second-price auctions, next highest in first-price auctions, and lowest in Dutch auctions. These results are inconsistent with the hypothesis, underlying most bidding models, that individuals have identical utility functions.

This report has concentrated on the behavior of market price and allocations and the consistency of such data with the predictions of bidding theory in the three institutions studied. Questions of individual bidding behavior, including learning with experience, will be examined in a separate paper.

APPENDIX

The instructions to follow are for a PLATO Dutch auction experiment followed by a first price sealed bid auction experiment.

Program written by Bruce E. Roberson.
Consulting provided by Vernon L. Smith.

INSTRUCTIONS

This is an experiment in the economics of market decision making. The National Science Foundation has provided funds for the conduct of this research. The instructions are simple, and if you follow them carefully and make good decisions you may earn a CONSIDERABLE AMOUNT OF MONEY which will be PAID TO YOU IN CASH at the end of the experiment.

In this experiment we are going to create a market in which you will be buyers of a fictitious commodity in a sequence of auctions. The PLATO computer will act as the "auctioneer," but it is completely passive in the sense that it is used solely to store and transmit information on decisions made by the participants in the market.

Please type in your LAST NAME after the arrow then press -NEXT-.
(Use the EDIT key if you make a typing error.)
This information is used solely to aid in the distribution of the cash earnings at the end of the experiment.

→ Testor

Thank-you, participant Testor.

Auction Number	Resale Value	Market Price	Profit
1	8.50		
2	6.00		
3	8.10		
4	12.00		
5	15.90		
6	4.70		
7	3.60		
8	13.00		
9	12.70		
10	9.50		
		Total Profit:	

This is your personal record sheet for the market experiment. Notice that the column labeled "RESALE VALUE" has been filled in with dollar and cents amounts. This indicates the value to you of purchasing a unit of this commodity. This value to you may be thought of as the amount you would receive if you were to resell the unit.

Notice that you have a resale value of $8.50 for the first auction, a resale value of $6.00 for the second auction, a resale value of $8.10 for the third auction, and so on. These resale values are assigned randomly. You have an equally likely chance of receiving any resale value between $0.10 and $16.90, inclusive. That is, you are equally likely to receive $0.10, $0.50 .... $16.50, $16.90.
Furthermore, the chance of you being assigned any particular value in this range, for example $8.50 is not changed if that value was assigned earlier to you or to another participant. It is therefore possible for you to get the same resale value for different auction periods or for two participants to have the same value in the same auction. All participants will have their resale values assigned in this manner.

If you are able to make a purchase (we'll describe the buying process soon) you will receive the difference between your resale value and the price you pay.

TO SUM UP:

resale value − price paid = profit

Note that your cash profits depend upon your ability to buy a unit at a price below the resale value given on your personal record sheet. Also note that if you buy a unit at a price equal to its resale value your profit will be zero.

Your earnings will be automatically entered in your record sheet at the close of each auction. Earnings (profits) are accumulated over several auctions, with your total profit at the end of the experiment being the summation of your profits over all auctions. But, you may ask, "How do I purchase this commodity?" Good question. Press "NEXT" for the answer.

Auction Number	Resale Value	Market Price	Profit
1	8.50		
2	6.00		
3	8.10		
4	12.00		
5	15.90		
6	4.70		
7	3.60		
8	13.00		
9	12.70		
10	9.50		
		Total Profit:	

8.90

confirm

This is the starting price of the auction, in this example. It will be $17.70 in the experiment.

This is how your screen will look during the experiment. The "clock" will act as an auctioneer.

Notice that there is a dollar and cents amount inside the clock. This is the price the auction will start at. Every 2 seconds the price in the clock will decrease by $0.40.
When all of the participants are ready to begin the price in the "clock" will start to decrease. Press "NEXT" to see what this will look like.

Auction Number	Resale Value	Market Price	Profit
1	8.50		
2	6.00		
3	8.10		
4	12.00		
5	15.90		
6	4.70		
7	3.60		
8	13.00		
9	12.70		
10	9.50		
		Total Profit:	

8.50

confirm

During the experiment the price in the ""clock'' will change automatically, you will not have to press any keys. Press "NEXT" to see what this will look like.

Auction Number	Resale Value	Market Price	Profit
1	8.50		
2	6.00		
3	8.10		
4	12.00		
5	15.90		
6	4.70		
7	3.60		
8	13.00		
9	12.70		
10	9.50		
		Total Profit:	

7.30

confirm

If you wish to buy the commodity at the price shown inside the clock press the key marked "LAB" on your keyboard. Suppose you wish to accept the price which is showing right now. You would press "LAB" to accomplish this. Press the key labeled "LAB" now to see what happens.

Auction Number	Resale Value	Market Price	Profit
1	8.50		
2	6.00		
3	8.10		
4	12.00		
5	15.90		
6	4.70		
7	3.60		
8	13.00		
9	12.70		
10	9.50		
		Total Profit:	

7.30

Please confirm bid.

confirm

Notice that upon accepting you must then confirm the contract to ensure that you have not touched the "LAB" key by mistake. To confirm the contract tap the box under the clock labeled "CONFIRM." The touch panel acts like pressing a key. IN THE ACTUAL EXPERIMENT YOU MUST DO THIS WITHIN 3 SECONDS OR THE CONTRACT WILL NOT BE CONFIRMED. If you fail to confirm your clock will continue to run as before, and you may "LAB" again if no one else has purchased the unit being auctioned. Tap the confirm box now!

Auction Number	Resale Value	Market Price	Profit
1	8.50	7.30	1.20
2	6.00		
3	8.10		
4	12.00		
5	15.90		
6	4.70		
7	3.60		
8	13.00		
9	12.70		
10	9.50		
		Total Profit:	1.20

7.30

confirm

THE FIRST PERSON TO BOTH "LAB" AND CONFIRM WILL BE THE ONLY ONE TO RECEIVE THE UNIT BEING AUCTIONED! Notice that upon confirming the contract your personal record sheet was filled in for you. This will be done for you at the close of each auction period. If someone else confirms before you, stars will be entered in the column labeled "PROFIT." The winning price will be entered under "MARKET PRICE" so that you will have a record of all winning prices. Press "NEXT" to continue.

Let's review the important items. (1) You have an equally likely chance of receiving any resale value between $0.10 and $16.90 inclusive. (2) Your bid MUST be less than or equal to your resale value. (3) You may accept the "auctioneers" offer by pressing "LAB." (4) You must confirm your acceptance within 3 seconds to make a contract. (5) The first person to "LAB" and confirm will receive the unit. (6) The starting price in each auction will be $17.70.

This is the end of the instructions. If you wish to go back and examine all the instructions over again press "HELP". For a quick review press "BACK". If you wish to see the auction example and the instructions which follow press "LAB". If you feel you now understand the instructions and are prepared to proceed with the actual experiment press "NEXT". If you have a question that you feel was not adequately answered by the instructions please raise your hand and ask the monitor before proceeding. YOUR EARNINGS MAY SUFFER IF YOU PROCEED INTO THE MARKETPLACE WITHOUT UNDERSTANDING THE INSTRUCTIONS!!

Are you sure you understand the instructions? You will not be able to return to them if you proceed beyond this point. Press "NEXT" to continue or "BACK" to return to the instructions.

After 10 Dutch auctions are completed, the following instructions are administered.

In the auction periods to follow we will have different bidding rules. The highest bidder will still be the winning buyer of the unit of the commodity for sale, but the method of entering bids will change. We will use this new bidding procedure for several more auctions. Profits accumulated using this new procedure will be added to those you have already accumulated.

On your screen your table will again be displayed, and your (and everyone else's) resale values will still be selected by the same random process. The method of figuring your profit will also remain unchanged. If you are the winning bidder you will still receive the difference between your resale value and the price you bid.

Auction Number	Resale Value	Market Price	Profit
1	8.50		
2	16.50		
3	0.10		
4	4.40		
5	8.70		
6	12.90		
7	16.60		
8	0.30		
9	3.80		
10	4.20		
		Total Profit:	

Please enter your bid for auction #1
(rounded automatically to the nearest .40)

(Press "NEXT" to enter it, or edit to change it)
This is how your screen will look during the next few auction periods. Instead of the clock appearing on your screen, you will now see the above message. Your job is to attempt to purchase the unit of commodity in each auction by entering a bid for it. The highest bidder in each auction period will be awarded the unit.

Let's go through a sample auction. Given your first period resale value of $8.50 you will enter a bid for this unit. Your bid will be automatically rounded to the nearest multiple of $.40 below the value of $17.70. That is, your bid will be rounded to the nearest value such as 17.30, 16.90, 16.50, etc. Suppose you wanted to bid 7.30 for this unit. To do so type in 7.30 and then press "NEXT". Try this now. (Use the "EDIT" key if you make a typing error.)

Please enter your bid for auction #1
(rounded automatically to the nearest .40)
(Press "NEXT" to enter it, or edit to change it)
> 7.30

Press "NEXT" to confirm your bid of 7.30 or press -BACK- to change it.

Notice that upon selecting a bid you may either confirm it or enter a new bid. Suppose you are satisfied with your bid and wish to confirm it. Press "NEXT" to do this.

Auction Number	Resale Value	Market Price	Profit
1	8.50	7.30	1.20
2	16.50		
3	0.10		
4	4.40		
5	8.70		
6	12.90		
7	16.60		
8	0.30		
9	3.80		
10	4.20		
		Total Profit:	1.20

If you are the highest bidder your personal record sheet will be filled in as above. As before, if you do not receive the unit, the column labeled "PROFIT" will have stars entered into it.

The winning bid will be displayed in the column labeled "MARKET PRICE" so that you will have a record of all contract prices. In the event that two or more bidders tie for the highest bid, PLATO will select the winner at random.

Let's review the important items. (1) Your bid MUST be less than or equal to your resale value. (2) You can change your bid if you have not yet confirmed it already. (3) The highest bidder will be the only person to receive the unit.

This is the end of the instructions. If you wish to go back and examine all the instructions over again press "HELP". For a quick review press "BACK". If you wish to see the auction example and the instructions which follow press "LAB". If you feel you now understand the instructions and are prepared to proceed with the actual experiment press "NEXT". If you have a question that you feel was not adequately answered by the instructions please raise your hand and ask the monitor before proceeding. YOUR EARNINGS MAY SUFFER IF YOU PROCEED INTO THE MARKETPLACE WITHOUT UNDERSTANDING THE INSTRUCTIONS!!

Are you sure you understand the instructions? You will not be able to return to them if you proceed beyond this point. Press "NEXT" to continue or "BACK" to return to the instructions.

ACKNOWLEDGMENTS

We are grateful to the National Science Foundation for research support and to John Ledyard for suggesting the use of a constant relative risk-averse model of bidding behavior. However, in this acknowledgment we do not intend to implicate Ledyard in our particular version or application of this model. In addition, we want to express our gratitude to Charles A. Holt for pointing out an error in a previous draft and to an anonymous referee for helpful comments.

NOTES

1. In correspondence (to Smith, February 21, 1980), Michael Darby has noted that, based on his personal experience, the application of second-price procedures to "book bids" is standard practice in American auctions.

2. In other words, for utility function (3.6) one has $[-yu_i''(y)/u_i'(y)] = (1 - r_i)$. On the basis of this familiar equation, we have decided to label (3.6) as a constant relative risk-averse utility function even though the interpretation does not follow when the utility function is defined on income rather than terminal wealth.

3. The risk-neutral case will be referred to as the null or Vickrey hypothesis, whereas strict risk aversion in which not all bidders are risk-neutral and $E(r) < 1$ will be called the Ledyard hypothesis. Vickrey (1961) was well aware of what would be the effect of risk aversion, but did not formally treat this case.

4. The limiting factor here was the response limits of the display screen in the Dutch auction. The PLATO (or any other) system cannot display digital changes at anything approaching a speed which is "fast" by electronic standards. For example, a grid 10 times as fine as our $.10 unit coupled with a 10-fold increase in clock speed would vastly exceed the screen's display capability (as well as the discerning power of the eye and brain).

5. That is, if at time t seconds after the beginning of the auction the clock price reads p_t, then at time $t + 2$ seconds the clock will tick down to a price $p_{t+2} = p_t - \delta$. If within the next 2 seconds a subject depresses an "accept" key and then is the first person to touch the sensitive "confirm" area on the computer screen, the clock stops at the price $p_t - \delta$, which is the winning bid.

REFERENCES

Boulding, Kenneth, *Economic Analysis*. New York: Harper, Revised Edition, 1948.

Cassady, Ralph, *Auctions and Auctioneering*. Berkeley and Los Angeles: University of California Press, 1967.

Coppinger, Vicki, Vernon L. Smith, and John Titus, "Incentives and Behavior in English, Dutch, and Sealed-Bid Auctions." *Economic Inquiry* 18(January):1–22, 1980.

Fouraker, L., and S. Siegel, *Bargaining Behavior*. New York: McGraw-Hill Book Co., 1963.

Grether, David M., "Bayes Rule as a Descriptive Model: The Representiveness Heuristic." *Quarterly Journal of Economics* 95(November):537–57, 1980.

Marschak, Jacob, "Economics of Inquiring, Communicating, Deciding." *American Economic Review* 58(May):1–18, 1968.

Shubik, Martin, "Oligopoly Theory, Communication, and Information." *American Economic Review* 65(May):280–83, 1975.

Siegel, Sydney, "Decision Making and Learning Under Varying Conditions of Reinforcement." *Annals of the New York Academy of Science* 89:766–83, 1961.

Smith, Vernon L., "Experimental Economics: Induced Value Theory." *American Economic Review* 66(May):274–79, 1976.

Vickrey, William, "Counterspeculation, Auctions and Competitive Sealed Tenders." *Journal of Finance* 16(May):8–37, 1961.

A TEST THAT DISCRIMINATES BETWEEN TWO MODELS OF THE DUTCH–FIRST AUCTION NON-ISOMORPHISM

James C. COX, Vernon L. SMITH and James M. WALKER*

University of Arizona, Tucson, AZ 85721, USA

Previous experiments reject the hypothesis that the Dutch and first auctions are isomorphic. Two alternatives to the standard normal form analysis of the Dutch auction are formalized: (1) bidders violate Bayes' rule, (2) bidders experience a utility of suspense that is additive with the utility of monetary reward. Paired comparisons of bidding behavior between groups in which the treatment is to triple the payoff of the baseline group yields no significant effect of this treatment. We therefore reject the utility of suspense model.

1. Introduction

The isomorphism of the Dutch and first price auctions was a standard part of received bidding theory beginning with the 1961 paper by Vickrey.[1] This isomorphism follows from the assumption that bidding theory can be based on the normal forms of bidding games, rather than on their extensive forms. Cox, Roberson and Smith (hereafter CRS) presented the results of experiments which showed that the Dutch and first price auctions are not behaviorally isomorphic. Hence, this testable implication of the normal form representation is inconsistent with empirical observations.

CRS also provided two possible explanations of the failure of the predicted isomorphism. One explanation was based on the utility of playing the Dutch auction 'waiting game'. The other explanation was based on bidder violation of Bayes' rule. The present paper reports the results of experiments that discriminate between the two competing explanations.

2. Bidding theory

2.1. The standard derivation of the isomorphism

The standard derivation of the isomorphism is based on the observation

*We are grateful to the National Science Foundation for research support.

[1]The first price and Dutch auctions are single unit auctions. The first price auction is the sealed bid auction in which the auctioned object is awarded to the highest bidder at a price equal to his bid. The Dutch auction is the decreasing price 'oral' auction in which the offer price is decreased over time by an auctioneer or a clock device until one of the bidders accepts the last price offer.

that the 'normal' or 'strategic' forms of the bidding games for the Dutch and first price sealed bid auctions are identical. Hence, the two auctions are said to be 'strategically equivalent' or 'isomorphic'. The fact that the Dutch auction is a 'real time' auction and the first price auction is not, and therefore that the extensive forms of the bidding games for the two auctions are different, is viewed as being irrelevant to bidding theory. It is assumed that only the strategic forms matter. Therefore, since the strategic forms of the bidding games for the Dutch and first price auctions are identical, it follows that the equilibrium bid functions for the two auctions are identical.

2.2. A real time model of the Dutch auction and the isomorphism

CRS present a real time model of the Dutch auction that yields insights into the Dutch/first isomorphism that are not provided by the usual strategic game model. The model is developed in the context of the information structure where each bidder knows with certainty the value to him of the auctioned object but knows neither his rivals' object values nor their bids. The real time model assumes that bidders make their decisions over time while observing some bidding behavior of their rivals. It is further assumed that bidders use their observations of their rivals' bidding behavior to revise their expectations of rival bids according to Bayes' rule. Finally, it is assumed that there is no utility or disutility associated with bidding in the (real time) Dutch auction other than the (expected) utility of the monetary reward.

Using the preceding assumptions, CRS show that the Dutch auction has the same qualitative properties as the first price auction; that is, the Dutch auction is not demand-revealing and will not generally yield Pareto efficient allocations. Finally, CRS explain how the Dutch auction can have the same quantitative properties as the first price auction. If a bidder believes that his rivals will employ the same bidding strategies in the Dutch auction as they do in the first price auction then he will be led by expected utility maximization to also employ the same bidding strategy in the Dutch auction as he does in the first price auction.

2.3. Explaining the failure of the predicted isomorphism

The experiments reported in CRS indicate that the Dutch and first price auctions are not behaviorally isomorphic: Dutch auction mean prices were consistently less than first auction mean prices for all values of N (number of bidders) that were studied ($N=3$, 4, 5, 6, 9). Since standard assumptions imply that the auctions are theoretically isomorphic, construction of a bidding theory that is consistent with observed bidding behavior requires the incorporation of some non-standard assumptions. Two bidding models of the Dutch auction are constructed by CRS that are consistent with the observation that Dutch auction prices are lower than first auction prices.

One model incorporates an assumption that bidders systematically violate Bayes' rule. The other model is based on the assumption that there is a positive utility of 'suspense' associated with playing the real time Dutch auction 'waiting game' which is additive with the expected utility of the monetary reward from the auction. The Bayes' miscalculation model is adopted for two reasons. First, there is a considerable body of earlier independent experimental evidence, from the work of Kahneman, Tversky, Grether and others [see Grether (1980)], showing that subject probability learning behavior is not consistent with Bayes' rule. Secondly, as explained in CRS, the only predicted comparison of bidding behavior across the four familiar single unit auction institutions that uses Bayes' rule is the predicted isomorphism between the Dutch and first price auctions.[2] The second model is adopted because a hypothesized utility of 'suspense' is an instance of the possible failure of the dominance precept in experimental economics [Smith (1982, p. 934), Wilde (1980)]. This precept requires the reward structure to dominate any non-monetary subjective values associated with participation in the activities of an experiment (market). The classic paper demonstrating that such non-monetary utility can be significant is that of Siegel (1961) in which the reward level was systematically varied in the Bernoulli trials experiment. The results were consistent with a model of choice in which the monetary and non-monetary utilities from subject choices were assumed to be *additive*. Based on this evidence the second model postulates additivity of the two components of utility.

We will now develop the special cases of the Dutch and first price auction models in CRS for which the utility of money income function has the constant relative risk averse (CRRA) form. [CRS and Cox, Smith and Walker (1983) have presented tests showing that bidding behavior is consistent with a CRRA model of bidding in the first price auction.] Let $v_i \in [\underline{v}, \bar{v}]$ be the value assigned to bidder i and b_i be the amount bid by i. Then if i wins the auction the monetary reward is $\beta(v_i - b_i)$, where $v_i - b_i$ is the outcome in 'experimental dollars', and β is a factor which converts this outcome into U.S. currency. We here explicitly introduce the parameter β because it is the primary treatment variable in the experiments reported below. In the analysis of the first price and Dutch auctions to follow, this monetary reward is assumed to provide CRRA utility $[\beta(v_i - b_i)]^{r_i}$, where $(1 - r_i)$ is i's Arrow–Pratt measure of constant relative risk aversion and $0 < r_i \leqq 1$.

Now consider models of the first price and Dutch auctions that include a non-monetary utility of 'suspense' from playing the auction game. In the first price auction, assume that bidder i gets utility $a_i \geqq 0$ from the auction game.

[2]The four single unit auctions are the Dutch and English oral auctions and the first price and second price sealed bid auctions.

Assuming additivity of the monetary and non-monetary utilities, the expected utility to i is

$$U_i(b_i) = a_i + [\beta(v_i - b_i)]^{r_i} F_i(b_i), \tag{1}$$

where $F_i(b_i)$ is the subjective probability that a bid of b_i will win. Now assume that U_i is pseudo-concave and has a unique interior maximum at $b_i^0 < v_i$ satisfying

$$\begin{aligned} 0 &= U_i'(b_i^0) \\ &= \beta^{r_i}\{(v_i - b_i^0)^{r_i - 1}[(v_i - b_i^0)F_i'(b_i^0) - r_i F_i(b_i^0)]\}. \end{aligned} \tag{2}$$

In (2) it is seen that b_i^0 is independent of β. Thus if β is increased, say from 1 to 3 as in the experimental comparisons reported below, this should have no significant effect on the bids, and therefore the prices, in the first price auction.

In the Dutch auction, assume that bidder i gets utility $\alpha_i(t)$ from a Dutch auction game of length t, where $\alpha_i(t)$ is a positive increasing concave function (bidder i gets more 'suspense' utility from playing a longer game). At t bidder i must decide whether to accept the bid $b(t)$ or let the Dutch clock continue. If i accepts the bid $b(t)$ he receives the monetary payment $\beta(v_i - b(t))$ with CRRA utility $[\beta(v_i - b(t))]^{r_i}$, and the non-monetary utility $\alpha_i(t)$ from playing a Dutch game of length t. If bidder i lets the auction continue for one more tick of the auction clock to time $t + \Delta t$, $\Delta t > 0$, this yields the non-monetary utility $\alpha_i(t + \Delta t)$ and the probability $H_i(b(t + \Delta t) | b(t))$ of obtaining the monetary utility $[\beta(v_i - b(t + \Delta t))]^{r_i}$. Hence the change in expected utility from continuing the auction is

$$\begin{aligned} \Delta X_i(t) = \alpha_i(t + \Delta t) - \alpha_i(t) + H_i(b(t + \Delta t) | b(t)) \\ \times [\beta(v_i - b(t + \Delta t))]^{r_i} - [\beta(v_i - b(t)]^{r_i}. \end{aligned} \tag{3}$$

If bidder i assumes that his rivals will use the same bidding strategies in the Dutch as in the first price auction, then Bayes' rule implies

$$H_i(b(t + \Delta t) | b(t)) = F_i(b(t + \Delta t))/F_i(b(t)). \tag{4}$$

Assuming differentiability, from (3) and (4),

$$\begin{aligned} X_i'(t) &= \lim_{\Delta t \to 0^+} (\Delta X_i(t)/\Delta t) \\ &= \alpha_i'(t) + \beta^{r_i}\{[(v_i - b(t))^{r_i} F_i'(b(t))/F_i(b(t))] - r_i(v_i - b(t))^{r_i - 1}\} b'(t), \end{aligned} \tag{5}$$

where $b'(t)$ is a negative constant determined by the speed of the Dutch auction.

If the optimal time for bidder i to stop the Dutch auction is t_i^*, then $X_i'(t_i^*) = 0$ and from (5) we can write

$$0 = \alpha_i'(t_i^*)\beta^{-r_i} + \{[(v_i - b(t_i^*))^{r_i} F_i'(b(t_i^*))/F_i(b(t_i^*))] - r_i(v_i - b(t_i^*))^{r_i - 1}\} b'(t_i^*). \tag{6}$$

Since $\alpha_i'(t_i^*)\beta^{-r_i} > 0$ and $b'(t_i^*) < 0$, the curly bracket term in (6) must be positive. But this implies that the derivative of (1) is positive at $b(t_i^*)$. Since (1) is pseudo-concave, it follows that $b(t_i^*) < b_i^0$ and the optimal Dutch auction bid is less than the optimal bid in the first price auction. Furthermore, since $\alpha_i'(t)\beta^{-r_i}$ is decreasing in β, it follows that an increase in β, say from 1 to 3, will increase the optimal Dutch auction bid.

The above qualitative properties of bidding behavior in the two types of auctions is not affected if we assume that i believes that his rivals will also bid less in the Dutch auction than in the first price auction, in the sense of a first order stochastic dominance ordering of the distribution functions [*CRS* (1982, p. 30)].

The testable implications of the above utility of suspense models for price behavior in the first price and Dutch auctions are as follows:

(A.1) An increase in β will have no effect on prices in the first price auction.
(A.2) An increase in β will increase Dutch auction prices.
(A.3) In paired comparisons between the two types of auctions, an increase in β will reduce the difference between prices in the first price and corresponding paired Dutch auctions.

Hypothesis (A.1) has been tested by Cox, Smith and Walker (1983). They report the result that tripling the value of β from 1 to 3 has no significant effect on prices in the first price auction. Tests of hypotheses (A.2) and (A.3) are reported in the next section.

Now consider the alternative model of bidding behavior based on bidder violation of Bayes' rule. Since the first price auction is not a real time auction, a bidder is not able to observe any of his rivals' bidding behavior before submitting a bid. Hence, Bayes' rule does not enter the theory. The special case of the above model of bidding in the first price auction, with $a_i = 0$ in eq. (1), applies here. In contrast, during a Dutch auction a bidder is able to observe some bidding behavior of his rivals and therefore has an opportunity to revise his prior expectations about their bids. Given the observation that none of his rivals has accepted a bid that is greater than or equal to $b(t)$, let $G_i(b(t+\Delta t) | b(t))$ be a bidder's probability that none of his rivals will accept a bid that is greater than or equal to $b(t+\Delta t)$, where $\Delta t > 0$

and $b(t+\Delta t)<b(t)$. Assume that a bidder violates Bayes' rule in a way such that

$$G_i(b(t+\Delta t)|b(t))=[\psi_i(b(t+\Delta t)|b(t))]^{\pi_i}=[\psi_i(b(t+\Delta t))/\psi_i(b(t))]^{\pi_i},$$
$$\pi_i<1, \qquad (7)$$

where $\psi_i(b(t))$ is the bidder's probability at the beginning of the auction that he can win the auction by accepting the bid $b(t)$. Eq. (7) implies a first order stochastic dominance ordering of the bidder's conditional probability distribution, $G_i(b(t+\Delta t)|b(t))$, and the Bayes' rule conditional probability distribution, $\psi_i(b(t+\Delta t))/\psi_i(b(t))$. Hence, having observed that none of his rivals has accepted a bid that is greater than or equal to $b(t)$, the bidder using eq. (7) underestimates the risk he bears by continuing to let the auction clock run.

If bidder i assumes that his rivals will use the same bidding strategies in the Dutch as in the first price auction, then

$$\psi_i(b(t+\Delta t))/\psi_i(b(t))=F_i(b(t+\Delta t))/F_i(b(t)). \qquad (8)$$

Proceeding analogously to statements (3), (5), and (6) above, we find that the optimal time for the bidder to stop the Dutch auction is $\tilde{t}_i$ such that

$$0=\beta^{r_i}[v_i-b(\tilde{t}_i)]^{r_i-1}\{\pi_i F_i'(b(\tilde{t}_i))[v_i-b(\tilde{t}_i)]$$
$$-r_i F_i(b(\tilde{t}_i))\}b'(\tilde{t}_i)/F_i(b(\tilde{t}_i)). \qquad (9)$$

Since $v_i>b(\tilde{t}_i)$, the curly bracket term in (9) must equal zero. But $\pi_i<1$; hence the derivative of (1) must be positive at $b(\tilde{t}_i)$. Since (1) is concave, it follows that $b(\tilde{t}_i)<b_i^0$ and the optimal Dutch auction bid is less than the optimal bid in the first price auction. Furthermore $\tilde{t}_i$ is independent of β; that is, an increase in β, say from 1 to 3, will not affect the optimal Dutch auction bid.

The above qualitative properties of bidding behavior in the two types of auctions are not affected if we assume that i believes that his rivals will also bid less in the Dutch auction than in the first price auction, in the sense of a first order stochastic dominance ordering of the distribution functions [CRS (1982, p. 30)].

The testable implications of the above probability miscalculation model for price behavior in the first price and Dutch auctions are as follows:

(B.1) An increase in β will have no effect on prices in the first price auction.
(B.2) An increase in β will have no effect on prices in the Dutch auction.

(B.3) In paired comparisons between the two types of auctions, an increase in β will have no effect on the difference between prices in the first price and corresponding paired Dutch auctions.

Statements (A.1) and (B.1) are identical. However, statements (A.2) and (B.2) are contradictory, as are (A.3) and (B.3). Therefore, an experimental design that incorporates an increase in β can provide a test that discriminates between the two models.

3. Experimental design and results

3.1. Experimental design

The eight experiments reported in this paper consist of four experiments conducted by CRS, along with four new experiments. Each of the four new experiments is a paired comparison with one of the four experiments drawn from CRS, except that subjects' payoffs for each auction period have been tripled.

All experiments were conducted using the Plato computer system which allows for control over several experimental design features. First, the Plato system facilitates the accounting process which occurs in each auction, and allows for the incorporation of the 'real time' technical characteristics of the Dutch auction. Secondly, use of the system reduces experimenter–subject interaction and facilitates the subjects' task, i.e., recording decisions and recalling information from previous auctions. Finally, Plato allows all subjects, within a given experimental design, to see identical programmed instructions.[3]

The experimental implementation of the Dutch and first price auctions can be summarized as follows. First, we induce monetary value on the imaginary auctioned object by promising to pay each subject a multiple of the difference between the value randomly assigned to the subject and the subject's bid, if (and only if) the bid wins. That multiple is $\beta=1$ in the CRS (control) experiments and $\beta=3$ in the new 'treatment' experiments conducted for this study. Each subject's randomly assigned value is known with certainty by the subject before an auction period begins. Subjects do not know with certainty the resale values assigned to other subjects. They are informed (using non-technical language) that all subject valuations are drawn each period, with replacement, from a uniform distribution with specified parameters (see below). Secondly, the institutional rules for the Dutch and first price auctions are explained to each subject through the use of Plato programmed instructions. In order to implement the Dutch auction, it is

[3]See Cox, Roberson and Smith (1982) for a detailed discussion of the experimental design including an appendix which reproduces Plato instructions to subjects.

necessary to specify three technical parameters: (1) the distance between the starting price on the clock and the highest possible resale value, (2) the time between ticks of the digital clock, and (3) the amount by which the price falls with each tick of the clock. These technical parameters are explained to subjects using programmed examples. Rules for the first price auction are also explained using example auctions. Finally, to ensure strict comparability between the Dutch and first price auctions, acceptable bids in the first price auctions are restricted to those bids which are feasible in the paired Dutch auctions. This is accomplished by having Plato round each bid in the first price auction to the closest feasible bid in the Dutch auction. Subjects then have the opportunity to confirm this rounded bid or resubmit an alternative bid.

The first three columns of table 1 list the primary design parameters for the experiments. The label for each experimental session (column 1) identifies an auction sequence; for example, DFD8x consists of 30 sequential auctions; 10 Dutch, followed by 10 first, followed by 10 Dutch auctions. The '8' in DFD8x denotes design 8, which uses 4 subject bidders (column 2). Design 9 uses 5 bidders. The valuations for each subject and each auction were drawn (with replacement) from a discrete uniform distribution contained in the interval $[\underline{v}, \bar{v}]$. In all experiments $\underline{v}=\$0.10$. In the original CRS experiments $\bar{v}$ varied between designs for different N in such a way as to hold constant the expected (risk neutral) profit per bidder per auction. This design feature was used to hold constant the per capita (or bidder) level of monetary motivation. Otherwise, the theory itself predicts that bidders will earn less in groups with larger N. This rule applied to designs 8 and 9 led to the values of $\bar{v}$ shown in column 3 of table 1.

All experiments with a given design number are 'paired' with respect to the subjects' resale values. For example, in the tth auction of all four design 8 experiments, the same set of resale values is randomly assigned to the (distinct) subject. The 'x' in DFD8x denotes that the subjects were 'experienced', which means that they had participated in previous Dutch and first price auction experiments. An asterisk, as in DFD8x*, denotes those experiments having triple payoffs, i.e., $\beta=3$ in the above models. In these experiments Plato computed each subject's payoff in 'experimental dollars'. The experimenters then multiplied these 'dollars' by 3 to obtain cash dollar payoffs. All subjects in the experiments marked with an asterisk were informed in advance that their Plato earnings would be multiplied by 3 to obtain their cash payoffs. This procedure made it possible for us to examine the hypothesized effect of changing β from 1 to 3 on Dutch and first price bidding behavior while holding constant all other parameters in the experimental design.

Some further discussion of our approach to increasing monetary rewards by tripling payoffs may be helpful. The clock speed in paired Dutch auctions with and without triple payoffs was the same. Therefore the 'experimental

Table 1

Experimental session	Number of bidders N	$\bar{v}$	Statistics	Dutch	Mean and variance of 10 prices by institution, in sequence First	Dutch	First
DFD8x	4	\$8.10	Mean	5.43	6.03	5.64	
			Variance	1.329	0.669	1.596	
FDF8′x	4	8.10	Mean		5.91	5.97	5.64
			Variance		1.361	0.969	1.636
DFD8x*	4	8.10	Mean	5.76	6.21	5.73	
			Variance	1.416	0.781	1.609	
FDF8′x*	4	8.10	Mean		6.03	5.76	5.46
			Variance		0.809	1.096	1.436
DFD9	5	\$12.10	Mean	7.75	9.52	8.83	
			Variance	3.565	0.724	2.649	
FDF9′	5	12.10	Mean		8.62	9.58	9.31
			Variance		2.804	2.104	1.481
DFD9*	5	12.10	Mean	6.76	8.41	8.20	
			Variance	0.716	1.361	0.500	
FDF9′*	5	12.10	Mean		8.95	9.55	9.52
			Variance		3.485	1.345	1.564

dollar' price decrease per tick of the Dutch auction clock was the same in paired triple and non-triple payoff Dutch auctions. However, the cash dollar price decrease per tick in a triple payoff Dutch auction was three times the cash dollar price decrease per tick in a paired non-triple payoff Dutch auction. This consideration might be relevant for interpreting the Dutch–Dutch* auction price comparisons that follow. But it is not relevant for interpreting the Dutch–first auction price comparisons that are of central importance to the isomorphism. The reason for this is the way in which Dutch auctions are paired with first price auctions. As explained above, admissible bids in a first price auction are restricted to those that are feasible in its paired Dutch auction. This aspect of the experimental design simultaneously preserves comparability of paired Dutch and first price auctions in *both* experimental and cash dollar terms.

3.2. Experimental results

Table 1 provides summary price data from the four control experiments ($\beta = 1$) and the four treatment ($\beta = 3$) experiments. Displayed are the mean and variance of prices for each 10 auction sequence of a given institution. Comparison of the mean prices in table 1 for paired triple and non-triple payoff experiments suggests no systematic effect of payoff tripling.

For a more rigorous examination of the effect of tripling payoffs on the Dutch prices, we will refer to results displayed in tables 2 and 3. If the utility of 'suspense' model is a correct interpretation of previous Dutch auction results, then Dutch prices when $\beta=3$ should be higher than the paired comparison Dutch prices when $\beta=1$. This suggests the null hypothesis H_0: $D-D^* \geqq 0$, where D^* represents Dutch prices for $\beta=3$, and D refers to Dutch prices for $\beta=1$. A statistical test that rejects H_0 would mean that the data are consistent with the utility of 'suspense' model, while failure to reject H_0 would imply empirical observations consistent with the 'probability-miscalculation' model.

Table 2
Price comparisons Dutch–Dutch*.

Paired experimental sessions	Mean price difference	Paired t-statistics	T
DFD8x–DFD8x*	−0.33	−1.071	10
	−0.09	−0.487	10
FDF8′x–FDF8′x*	+0.21	+1.413	10
DFD9–DFD9*	+0.99	+2.532	10
	+0.63	+1.716	10
FDF9′–FDF9′*	+0.03	+0.176	10

Table 3
Pooled results.[a]

Design	Constant	B_1	B_2	B_3	T	F	R^2
8	−0.460	−0.070	−0.270	−0.120	60	0.74	0.038
	(−2.959)	(−0.450)	(−1.418)	(−0.630)			
9	+0.190	+0.550	−0.780	−1.860	60	23.102	0.553
	(0.956)	(2.824)	(−3.270)	(−7.978)			

[a]t-statistics shown in parentheses.

One method of testing H_0 is to compare the mean price results when $\beta=3$ with its paired control experiment. Note that any difference in price could not be attributable to sampling variation in resale values using this form of analysis. The results of t tests comparing paired sequences of Dutch auctions are presented in table 2. In no ten-auction sequence are we led to a rejection of H_0. Thus this mode of analysis leads to rejection of the utility of 'suspense' model.

In the paired comparison set DFD9 and DFD9* we obtain significantly *lower* Dutch prices in DFD9*. This is strongly inconsistent with the utility of 'suspense' model. Examining both the Dutch and first price auctions in experiment DFD9* we find this group of bidders tended to bid lower in both first price and Dutch auctions than the other groups in design 9 (see table 1). This strongly suggests an individual group effect (due to subject sampling variation) and not a perverse effect due to tripling the payoff level.

An alternative method for analyzing the effect of tripling payoffs is to pool our results on Dutch auctions over all experiments within a given design, and test H_0 by treating triple payoffs as a treatment variable in a classical linear regression model. We tested the following linear model:

$$D_{RN}-D=A+B_1(D3)+B_2(SQ1)+B_3(SQ2)+\varepsilon, \quad \text{where} \tag{10}$$

D_{RN} = the Nash equilibrium theoretical sales price, given the sampling realizations of v_i, for risk neutral bidders in a Dutch (or first price) auction,[4]

D = the observed Dutch auction price,[5]

$D3$ = 1 if $\beta=3$, and 0 if $\beta=1$,

$SQ1$ = 1 if the auction was in the third sequence of a three sequence auction and 0 otherwise,

$SQ2$ = 1 if the auction was in the second sequence of a three sequence auction and 0 otherwise,

ε = a random error term with the standard classical properties.

The estimated parameters and *t*-statistics of eq. (10) for designs 8 and 9 are presented in table 3. The results of this method of analysis are consistent with our previous tests which led to a failure to reject H_0. That is, the results are inconsistent with the utility of 'suspense' model. In the results for design 9 we do see an effect of tripling payoffs which implies a *lowering* of Dutch price. Again, we attribute this to a group effect in experiment DFD9*.

As a final comparison we examine the effect of triple payoffs on the theoretical isomorphism between Dutch and first price auctions. The results of this analysis are presented in table 4. It is clear from the results shown in table 4 that the tendency for market prices in first price auctions to dominate those generated in the Dutch auctions is upheld regardless of the level of payoff. Comparing the differences in means of first versus Dutch auctions with triple and non-triple payoff experiments reveals no significant effect of

[4]Under the maintained hypothesis of the Dutch–first auction isomorphism, D_{RN} is the predicted sales price for risk neutral Nash equilibrium bidders in a Dutch auction with the given resale values. Using the appropriate Nash equilibrium bid function derived in Vickrey (1961) and Cox, Roberson and Smith (1982), we find that $D_{RN}=\underline{v}+[(N-1)/N][v_h-\underline{v}]$, where N is the number of bidders, v_h is the highest resale value for all bidders in the experiment, and $\underline{v}$ is the lowest possible resale value in the experiment.

[5]Note that using the dependent variable $D_{RN}-D$ means that the observed prices are normalized with respect to the risk neutral Nash price for the particular values of v_i assigned. This controls for sampling variation in the v_i, and thus reduces 'noise' in the regression model.

Table 4
Effect of triple payoff on price differences First–Dutch.[a]

Paired experiments	Mean difference	Difference due to triple payoffs	T
DFD8x, FDF8′x	0.18		30
		0.03 (0.688)	
DFD8′x*, FDF8′x*	0.15		30
DFD9, FDF9′	0.43		30
		−0.36	
DFD9*, FDF9′*	0.79	(−0.985)	30

[a]Comparisons are triple payoff experiments. *t*-statistics shown in parentheses.

level of payoff. Thus the lack of support for the theoretical isomorphism of Dutch and first price auctions is not altered by the triple payoff treatment.

4. Summary and conclusions

On the basis of several tests, using data generated by 780 Dutch, first price, and second price auctions, CRS concluded that mean prices are consistently lower in Dutch auctions than in corresponding first price auctions with identical auctioned object values, and the same number of bidders. This behavior is inconsistent with the theoretical isomorphism of the Dutch and first price auctions. CRS offered two new models of bidding in the Dutch auction that provide alternative explanations of why Dutch auction prices might be less than first auction prices. One model was based on a postulated utility of ‘suspense’ in the Dutch auction game that is additive to the expected utility of the monetary reward from bidding in the auction. The other model was based on a postulated systematic bidder violation of Bayes’ rule.

The present paper reports on a test that discriminates between the two models of the Dutch auction and of the Dutch–first auction non-isomorphism. The test is based on data from experiments that replicate a set of experiments reported in the CRS paper with all parameters unchanged except that the monetary reward level is multiplied by 3. If the additive utility of ‘suspense’ model were a correct interpretation of the Dutch auction results, then increasing the reward level would cause Dutch auction prices to approach the prices in the paired first price auctions. If the probability miscalculation model is appropriate then the price discrepancy in the two auction institutions should remain unchanged.

Our conclusions are based on the following results. (1) Comparison of the mean prices in table 1 for paired triple and non-triple payoff auction experiments suggests no systematic effect of payoff tripling. (2) Tests reported in table 2 of the null hypothesis that Dutch auction mean prices are not increased by payoff tripling consistently fail to reject the null hypothesis. (3) Estimated parameters reported in table 3 for a linear regression model that includes a dummy variable for payoff tripling finds no significant effect of payoff tripling that is consistent with the additive utility of 'suspense' model of the Dutch auction. (4) Tests reported in table 4 find that the triple payoff treatment provides no significant reduction in the magnitude of the differences between mean prices in paired Dutch and first price auctions.

The results in (1)–(4) above are uniformly consistent with the probability miscalculation model of the Dutch auction and uniformly inconsistent with the additive utility of 'suspense' model of that auction. Therefore, we reject the latter model in favor of the former model of the Dutch auction (and of the Dutch–first non-isomorphism).

Clearly, other models of the Dutch auction may be formulated that are consistent with the Dutch-first non-isomorphism. Design and implementation of tests that discriminate between the probability miscalculation model and any new alternative models is a matter for further research. However, some brief comments on this topic may be of interest now.

Referees of an earlier draft of this paper stated some conjectures about models of the Dutch auction that might be formulated as alternatives to the probability miscalculation model. One such conjecture was based on the hypothesis that bidders follow Bayes' rule in updating their probabilities during the Dutch auction but that '— calculation takes time'. Such a model was developed in Cox (1978) where it was assumed that bidders follow Bayes' rule in updating but that they lag behind the auction clock in doing so. It is shown in that paper that this 'slow Bayesian' model of the Dutch auction implies that bidders will bid *higher* in the Dutch auction than in the first price auction. That theoretical result is clearly inconsistent with the experimental data in CRS and the present paper, and this is why we did not further explore that model. This example illustrates the principle that if one allows theory to be subjected to the discipline of data, fewer theories survive to see the light of day.

A more promising conjecture advanced by the referees involves the assumption that the utility of 'suspense' of the Dutch auction is '— enhanced by the stakes'. We have developed a model of the Dutch auction that includes this assumption and is based on an adaptation of the class of constant relative risk averse utility functions used in the Nash equilibrium model developed in CRS and above. This is a log-additive utility of 'suspense' model. It can be shown that a test which discriminates between this model and the probability miscalculation model can be based on a set of experiments that multiply the highest possible value ($\bar{v}$) by, say, 3 rather than multiplying payoffs $(v-b)$ by 3 as is done in this paper. Such a test and perhaps other tests based upon alternative, fully articulated, models are fruitful topics for further research.

The point of these comments is the following. Given a standard rational model of choice that is found to be inconsistent with certain experimental observations, it is not difficult to think of intuitively plausible *a posteriori* variations on the model which allow one to conjecture that the new models are consistent with these observations. The more difficult research task is to (1) fully articulate these models within the framework of the maintained hypotheses (for example, expected utility maximization, homogeneous expectations, the Nash equilibrium principle), (2) verify that the conjectured implications are correct (our own *a priori* intuition here has not always proved reliable, as in the 'slow Bayesian' model), (3) develop those testable implications, if any, of the new models which predict dictinct observable outcomes, and (4) design and execute the appropriate experiments. An important constraint on such a program of long-term research is the need to maintain consistency, where possible, with other independent, ostensibly related, experimental studies. It is this coherence constraint that led us to choose an additive specification for the utility of 'suspense' model, in the spirit of Siegel (1961), and to propose a Bayesian miscalculation model in the spirit of Grether (1980), as a test alternative.[6] This constraint may provide a useful selection criterion, since particular specification assumptions may not be otherwise compelling.

A more difficult research decision problem arises when independent studies suggest alternative coherence constraints. Thus the work of our colleague, Chew (1981), suggests that weighted utility maximization accounts for many of the well-known inconsistencies between von Neuman–Morgenstern expected utility maximization and direct experimental observations of decision behavior. This consideration introduces a class of models generically different, and more general, than those we have considered in the present paper. Ultimately a research program on auctions must attempt to examine the implications of these alternative coherence constraints.

[6]Our Bayesian miscalculation model assumes that miscalculation is independent of the stakes. One can conjecture that the propensity to miscalculate might decrease with the stakes. In fact Grether (1980, p. 555) reports some evidence on the effect of financial incentives on the accuracy of Bayes' rule predictions and concludes 'Finally, and to the author the most surprising, the evidence that financial incentives affect the behavior is far from compelling.' Since our data show no significant increase in Dutch auction prices due to the triple payoff treatment, our results coordinate with that of Grether.

References

Chew, Soo Hong, 1981, A generalization of the quasilinear mean with applications to the measurement of income inequality and decision theory resolving the Allais paradox, University of Arizona, Tucson, AZ, Econometrica, forthcoming.

Cox, James C., 1978, A theory of sealed-bid and oral auctions, unpublished paper, University of Arizona, Tucson, AZ, preliminary draft, Aug.

Cox, James C., Bruce Roberson and Vernon L. Smith, 1982, Theory and behavior of single object auctions, in: Vernon L. Smith, ed., Research in experimental economics, Vol. 2 (JAI Press, Greenwich, CT).

Cox, James C., Vernon L. Smith and James M. Walker, 1983, Tests of a heterogeneous bidders theory of first price auctions, Economics Letters 12, 207–212.

Grether, David M., 1980, Bayes' rule as a descriptive model: The representativeness heuristic, Quarterly Journal of Economics 95, Nov., 537–557.

Siegel, Sydney, 1961, Decision making and learning under varying conditions of reinforcement, Annals of the New York Academy of Science 89, 766–783.

Smith, Vernon L., 1982, Microeconomic systems as an experimental science, American Economic Review 72, Dec., 923–955.

Vickrey, William, 1961, Counterspeculation, auctions, and competitive sealed tenders, Journal of Finance 16, May, 8–37.

Wilde, Louise, 1980, On the use of laboratory experiments in economics, in: Joseph Pitt, ed., The philosophy of economics (Redel, Dordrecht).

Theory and Behavior of Multiple Unit Discriminative Auctions

JAMES C. COX, VERNON L. SMITH, and JAMES M. WALKER*

ABSTRACT

This paper reports the results of controlled experiments designed to test the Harris-Raviv generalization of the Vickrey theory of bidding in multiple unit discriminative auctions. The paper also discusses further development of the theory—in a way suggested by the experimental results—to include bidders with distinct risk preferences.

IN A WELL-KNOWN PAPER, Vickrey [20] formulated a Nash equilibrium model of bidding by risk neutral economic agents in single unit auctions. This analysis was subsequently extended in numerous papers. Vickrey [21] generalized his original model to include multiple unit auctions in which each of N risk neutral bidders can bid on one out of a total of Q homogeneous items up for auction, where $1 \leq Q < N$. In both of the Vickrey papers, individual values for the auctioned object(s) were assumed to be drawn from a uniform distribution. Holt [12] and Riley and Samuelson [19] for single unit auctions and Harris and Raviv [11] for multiple unit auctions have extended the Vickrey model to the case in which valuations are from a general distribution function and all agents have identical concave utility functions.[1]

This paper reports the empirical properties of individual bidding behavior and seller revenue for a group of 28 laboratory experiments designed to test the Harris-Raviv generalization of the Vickrey (hereafter, VHR) model of Nash equilibrium behavior in multiple unit discriminative auctions. In Section I, we summarize briefly the theoretical results of the VHR model which form the basis for the hypotheses that we test. Section II describes the experimental design that we use. Section III describes the experimental results and various tests based on the bidding behavior of individual subjects and on aggregate market (seller revenue) data. The results from six of the ten (N, Q) parameter designs reported

* All authors from the Department of Economics, University of Arizona. We are grateful to the National Science Foundation for research support and to an associate editor of this *Journal* for helpful comments and suggestions.

[1] Other important extensions of Vickrey's original work have been provided by Matthews [16], Maskin and Riley [15], Myerson [18], Milgrom and Weber [17], and others. Since these extensions have involved institutions with information or valuation conditions that have not yet been examined experimentally, they are not directly germane to the objectives of this paper. For example, Matthews [16] has modeled single unit auctions in which the seller selects a reservation price, whereas in all of the experimental studies to date the seller passively offers the item(s) for sale. Similarly, Milgrom and Weber [17] have extended auction theory to allow valuations to be positively dependent for risk neutral bidders.

in Section III are consistent with VHR predictions of seller revenue and levels of individual bids, but not with the implication that bidders have the same bid function. In another paper (see [7], which is further generalized in [5]), we offer a parametric theory of Nash equilibrium bidding behavior in which individuals are assumed to exhibit differing degrees of constant relative risk aversion. This theory "accounts" for the results from six of the ten (N, Q) parameter designs. However, neither our parametric model nor that of VHR is consistent with the observed bids (and resulting revenues) for four of the (N, Q) parameter designs. In the present paper, this evidence is remarkably stable, replicable, and internally consistent, as is indicated by the various procedural and internal validity tests that we describe in Section IV.

I. The Vickrey-Harris-Raviv Theory of Nash Bidding Behavior

Let $Q \geq 1$ units of a homogeneous good be offered in perfectly inelastic supply to $N > Q$ bidders. Each bidder submits a bid for a single unit with the understanding that each of the Q highest bidders will be awarded a unit of the good at a price equal to his bid; i.e., the institution is a discriminative sealed-bid auction. Let v_i be the monetary value of a unit of the good to bidder i, where $i = 1, 2, \cdots, N$. Assume that each v_i is drawn (with replacement) from a distribution with density $h(\cdot)$ and probability distribution function $H(\cdot)$ whose support is the interval $[0, \bar{v}]$. If bidder i bids b_i, and this bid is accepted, he gains the monetary surplus, $v_i - b_i$, with utility $u(v_i - b_i)$. If b_i is *not* accepted, bidder i's monetary gain is zero. Assume that $u(\cdot)$ is increasing, concave, and differentiable and that $u(0) = 0$. Suppose that bidder i expects each of his rivals to bid according to the differentiable bid function

$$b_j = b(v_j) \tag{1}$$

Let $b(\cdot)$ be increasing on $[0, \bar{v}]$ and denote by π the inverse of (1); i.e.,

$$\pi(b(v_j)) = v_j \tag{2}$$

The probability, $\psi(b)$, that any one of the $N - 1$ rivals of bidder i will bid less than some amount b in the range of (1) is the same as the probability, $H(\pi(b))$, that the rival will draw a value less than that v corresponding to b given by $\pi(b)$. Hence, the probability that a bid b by i will win is the probability, $G(\pi(b))$, that at least $N - Q$ of the values drawn by i's rivals are less than $\pi(b)$. This probability is given by the distribution function of the $(N - Q)$th order statistic for a sample of size $N - 1$ from the distribution H:

$$G(\pi(b)) = \frac{(N-1)!}{(N-Q-1)!(Q-1)!} \int_0^{\pi(b)} [H(v)]^{N-Q-1}[1 - H(v)]^{Q-1} h(v)\, dv \tag{3}$$

Now let bidder i choose $b_i = b_i^0$ to maximize $u(v_i - b_i)G(\pi(b_i))$. The function $b(\cdot)$ is a Nash equilibrium bid function only if $b_i^0 = b(v_i)$. Let $b_n(\cdot)$ be the special case of (1) where all bidders are known to be risk neutral and let $b_a(\cdot)$ be the special case of (1) where all bidders are known to have the same strictly concave utility function. Harris and Raviv [11] prove the following result for these Nash equilibrium risk neutral and risk averse bid functions:

$$b_n(v) = \frac{1}{G(v)} \int_0^v x \, dG(x) < b_a(v) < v \quad \text{for all} \quad v \in (0, \bar{v}] \tag{4}$$

If the density function $h(\cdot)$ is the constant density $(\bar{v})^{-1}$, the result (4) can be expressed in terms of the following Beta integrals, which for computational purposes can be written in terms of the indicated finite polynomials (see [6]):

$$b_n(v) = \frac{\bar{v} \int_0^{v/\bar{v}} Y^{N-Q}(1 - Y)^{Q-1} \, dY}{\int_0^{v/\bar{v}} Y^{N-Q-1}(1 - Y)^{Q-1} \, dY}$$

$$= \frac{\bar{v} \sum_{k=0}^{Q-1} \dfrac{(-1)^k (v/\bar{v})^{N-Q+k+1}(Q-1)!}{(N-Q+k+1)k!(Q-1-k)!}}{\sum_{k=0}^{Q-1} \dfrac{(-1)^k (v/\bar{v})^{N-Q+k}(Q-1)!}{(N-Q+k)k!(Q-1-k)!}} < b_a(v) \tag{5}$$

In Figure 1, we plot $b_n(\cdot)$ for the parameter values, $\bar{v}$ = \$2.24, $N = 10$, and $Q = 4$. Note that the risk neutral bid function defines the boundary below which any individual's observed bids are inconsistent with the VHR theory, while bids equal to or greater than $b_n(v_i)$ but less than v_i are consistent with the theory. Thus, in Section III, if b_i^* is agent i's observed bid corresponding to the observed value v_i^*, then we test the null hypothesis that $\Pr[b_i^* < b_n(v_i^*)] \geq \frac{1}{2}$ for each i. The VHR theory will be called into question, if not falsified, if we are unable to reject this null hypothesis.[2]

However, rejection of this null hypothesis is insufficient to allow us to conclude that (with high probability) VHR stands as a nonfalsified theory of bidding behavior in discriminative auctions. This is because each subject's bids might be consistent with the inequality (5) but be inconsistent with the VHR theory's implication that all subjects bid according to the same equilibrium bid function. (This property of the theory implies that the allocations will be Pareto optimal.) Accordingly, in Section III, we report a direct test of the null hypothesis that individuals are homogeneous in their bidding behavior.

Typically in economics, when one tests the implications of a theory, the data are at best macromarket observations based on aggregation rather than observations on individual agents. Since a great variety of theories of individual behavior can yield qualitatively equivalent aggregate implications, such tests are extremely weak.[3] We have both individual and macromarket observations from

[2] Our test situation corresponds to the usual one in economics wherein there is only one formal theory. In this situation the classical falsification methodology does not articulate guidelines. The test procedure we use in Section III adopts a "naive" alternative theory to VHR, in which it is assumed that individual bids are at least as likely to be below the risk neutral bid function as above it. This naive theory becomes the null alternative to VHR, which states that bids are less likely to be below the risk neutral boundary.

[3] Macromarket tests are weak in the sense that if the observations fail to falsify the theory this

Footnote 3 continues on next page.

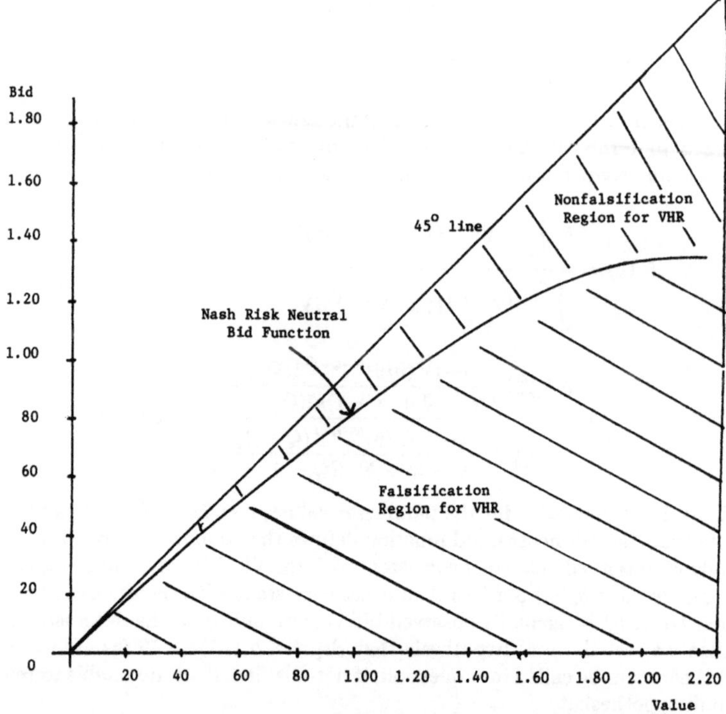

Figure 1. Critical Regions for VHR Bidding Theory for $(\bar{v}, N, Q) = (2.24, 10, 4)$

our laboratory experiments and, for purposes of summary comparisons, we also provide tests of the macromarket implications of the VHR theory.

From the ordering theorem in (4), it follows that seller revenue for risk neutral bidders (R_n) is less than seller revenue for risk averse bidders (R_a); i.e., if bidders are indexed so that $b_1 \leq b_2 \leq \cdots \leq b_N$, then

$$R_n = \sum_{j=N-Q+1}^{N} b_n(v_j) < R_a = \sum_{j=N-Q+1}^{N} b_a(v_j) \tag{6}$$

Consequently, in Section III, we report tests of the macromarket null hypothesis that

$$R_n^* = \sum_{j=N-Q+1}^{N} b_n(v_j^*) > R^* = \sum_{j=N-Q+1}^{N} b_j^* \tag{7}$$

where R^* is observed seller revenue and R_n^* is the theoretical risk neutral seller revenue conditional on the observed values, v_j^*, from a particular experimental realization. Reports of the seller revenue results will provide an overview of the

provides weaker support for the theory than if similar results had been obtained from tests of indivdual behavior. However, if the aggregate observations are inconsistent with the theory, this result is sufficient to falsify the theory.

experiments across all the parameter values studied, and allow us conveniently to integrate into the discussion the results of a large number of single unit auctions reported previously [4, 8].

II. Experimental Design

In a previous paper [6], we reported the results of 16 multiple unit auction experiments designed to make paired comparisons of the seller revenue properties of discriminative and uniform price sealed-bid auctions. Bidding data for the discriminative auction treatment in eight of these experiments (those for which the subjects were experienced) are included in this paper along with the results of 20 new discriminative auction experiments using experienced subjects. (By "experienced" we mean a subject who has been in a previous sealed-bid auction experiment of the type reported here.)

The complete experimental instructions given to all subjects are presented in [6]. Due to the length of the instructions, we will summarize here only the key points developed in the instructions and other significant experimental design features.

The experiments reported in this study were conducted using subjects drawn from a population of undergraduate students at the University of Arizona. The students were currently enrolled in lower level economics courses. All subjects were volunteers who had received a brief explanation that in our economics experiments the earnings resulting from their decisions would be paid to them in cash.

All experiments were conducted using the PLATO computer system. This approach to laboratory experiments enables us to ensure that all subjects are given identical market instructions with minimal experimenter/subject interaction. The computer system also facilitates the accounting process needed for each auction as well as curtailing subject transaction costs in bidding and obtaining information. No communication was allowed between subjects except that specified in the bidding process under 4 below.

Some important characteristics of the experiments can be summarized as follows.

1. Upon arriving at the PLATO computer site, each subject received $3.00 for keeping his/her appointment. The experimenter then assigned the subjects randomly to computer terminals at which time each subject reviewed, at his/her own pace, a set of instructions explaining the types of choices that subjects would encounter in the experiment.

2. In the instructions, subjects were informed (primarily with examples) of key properties of the discriminative auction institution in which they would be participating. Monetary values for the abstract objects being auctioned were induced on subjects using the concept of "resale values." That is, it was explained to each subject that for any winning bid the bidder would receive a profit equal to his/her resale value minus the amount bid. Each subject had one bid per auction and was informed in advance of each auction of his/her resale value for that auction.

3. Each bidder was informed (in nontechnical language) that all resale values assigned to each individual were drawn (with replacement) from a discrete uniform distribution contained in the interval $[0, \bar{v}]$. As required by the theory, subjects were informed of their own (certain) valuations for a specific auction, but were only informed of the distribution from which other subjects' values were drawn. Subjects also were informed that values were drawn independently for each auction.

4. At the end of each auction period, each subject was provided with a table of information on the outcome of that period's auction. In experiments 2′, 3′, and 6′, the only information in the table was the subject's own bid, resale value, and profit in that auction. In all of the other experiments, the table displayed the highest accepted bid and highest rejected bid in that auction as well as the subject's own bid, resale value, and profit for that auction.[4] At the subject's discretion a table was provided which summarized the available information for all preceding auctions.

5. The only restriction on a subject's bids was that they had to be in the interval $[0, \bar{v}]$. Hence, a subject could bid in excess of his/her value, which would imply a loss if the bid was accepted. An occasional subject in the inexperienced groups bid in excess of value on more than a single occasion (see [6], Table 6). All such subjects were screened out of further experiments; i.e., they were excluded from the "experienced" subject pool. In this sense all "experienced" subjects were individually rational as well as having "practiced" familiarity with the discriminative auction institution.

6. Before making any bids in the experiment, subjects were reminded of pertinent summary market parameters such as number of bidders, number of units offered, and maximum and minimum possible resale values. Subjects were also endowed with $1.00 in "working capital." This was to compensate for any loss resulting if an individual were to bid in excess of his/her value and have the bid accepted. Subjects were informed in advance that there would be many auctions but were not informed of the specific number. After a predetermined number of auctions, subjects were informed that the experiment had ended, and were then payed privately the full amount of their earnings. Experimental sessions lasted approximately one and a half to two hours.

7. The expected gain to a risk neutral bidder can be calculated (see [6], Equation (3.6)) to yield $[(Q(Q+1)\bar{v})/(2N(N+1))]$. In order to provide some uniformity of subject motivation across experiments with different values of (N, Q), we chose $\bar{v}$ as a function of (N, Q) so that the expected salient reward for a VHR risk neutral bidder would be approximately the same ($10) in all experiments except the enhanced payoff experiments (subjects also receive $3 up front for keeping the session appointment).[5] The specific design parameters which were used are shown in Table I.

[4] The highest accepted bid and highest rejected bid are revealed (after the auction) to bidders in the primary auction for U.S. Treasury bills.

[5] Exercising this control over the general level of payoffs across treatments has both empirical and theoretical justifications that are particularly important to understand. Empirically, this control serves to immunize against the risk that, *a posteriori*, a critic may correctly argue that the interpretation of deviant results (if they occur) are confounded: The results may be accounted for by variation in payoff levels, and are not necessarily attributable to the scheduled "treatment." Also it should be

Table I

Design Parameters

Design Number	Maximum Resale Value, $\bar{v}$	Number of Bidders, N	Units Offered, Q	$E(R_n)$[d]	Number of Replications (Experiments)	Number of Discriminative Auctions per Experiment[e]
1	$0.80	10	7	$1.53	4	20
2	$2.24[a]	10	4	$4.89	6	20
2′	$2.24[a]	10	4	$4.89	2	30
2″	$6.72[a]	10	4	$14.66	1	30
3	$2.70[b]	5	2	$2.70	2	30
3′	$2.70[b]	5	2	$2.70	2	30
4	$3.78	6	2	$4.32	2	30
5	$5.04	7	2	$6.30	1	30
6	$6.48[c]	8	2	$8.64	2	30
6′	$6.48[c]	8	2	$8.64	2	30
7	$9.90	10	2	$14.40	1	30
8	$2.52	7	3	$3.78	1	30
9	$3.24	8	3	$5.40	1	30
10	$4.05	9	3	$7.29	1	30

[a] In one experiment (2DE2*) using this design, the payoffs were tripled. In two others (2′DE1BLK; 2′DE2BLK), the highest rejected and highest accepted bid information was blocked. In another (2″DE2), $\bar{v}$ was tripled.

[b] In two experiments (3′DE1BLK; 3′DE2BLK) using this design, the highest rejected and highest accepted bid information was blocked.

[c] In two experiments (6′DE1BLK; 6′DE2BLK) using this design, the highest rejected and highest accepted bid information was blocked.

[d] The calculation of theoretical risk neutral revenue is based on the expression derived in Cox, Smith, and Walker ([6], Statement 4.1)),

$$E(R_n) = \frac{Q(N - Q)\bar{v}}{N + 1} < E(R_a)$$

[e] Designs 1 and 2 incorporated a sequencing of auctions that included a uniform price auction. (See [6]). However, in one experiment (2DE1) we replicated the earlier design 2 in a 30 discriminative auction sequence. (Actually designs 1 and 2 consisted of 23 auctions, and designs 3–10 of 33 auctions, but we omitted the first three auctions in all of our analyses to control for "start-up" variability).

III. Experimental Results

A. *Levels of Individuals' Bids*

From the theory of individual bidding behavior presented in Section I, the following null hypothesis can be proposed.

$$H_0^B\colon b_i^* < b_n(v_i^*) \quad \text{for all} \quad i \tag{8}$$

---

noted that the theory itself predicts that the expected gain becomes negligible for given Q and large enough N. Hence, for given Q, as N increases the "demand" parameter $\bar{v}$ must be expanded so as not to alter the relative importance of each bidder. This phenomenon is of course recognized in general equilibrium theory when, in examining large economies, the size of the economy is increased in the same proportion as the number of agents (in each characteristic class), so as not to bias the effect of increases in the number of agents. In Section IV we address the empirical and theoretical implications of the possibility that $\bar{v}$ or the reward level may itself be a "treatment" in accounting for the experimental outcomes.

Table II

Individual Bidding Results

Design	Number of Subjects	Observations per Subject	A	B (Percent)	C (Percent)
1	40	20	2	11 (28)	29 (72)
2	60	20[a]	11	31 (52)	29 (48)
2′	20	30	2	8 (40)	12 (60)
2″	10	30	1	3 (30)	7 (70)
3	10	30	10	10 (100)	0 (0)
3′	10	30	10	10 (100)	0 (0)
4	12	30	11	11 (72)	1 (8)
5	7	30	4	7 (100)	0 (0)
6	16	30	14	16 (100)	0 (0)
6′	16	30	16	16 (100)	0 (0)
7	10	30	7	10 (100)	0 (0)
8	7	30	1	6 (86)	1 (14)
9	8	30	1	5 (63)	3 (37)
10	9	30	6	9 (100)	0 (0)

Note: A, Subjects for whom H_0^B is rejected ($p = 0.05$). B, Subjects for whom sign of test statistic is consistent with VHR. C, Subjects for whom sign of test statistic is inconsistent with VHR.

[a] In experiments 2DE1 and 2DE2* there were 30 observations per subject.

Our test procedure for H_0^B is to apply the nonparametric Wilcoxon signed-ranks test [10] to the hypothesis that $\Pr[b_i^* - b_n(v_i^*) < 0] \geq \frac{1}{2}$. This is a paired sample test; thus, for each bid b_i^* corresponding to the value v_i^* for individual i, there is a paired risk neutral theoretical bid $b_n(v_i^*)$ computed from (5). The Wilcoxon procedure does not require us to impose any assumptions on the distribution of the difference, $b_i^* - b_n(v_i^*)$.

The results of the Wilcoxon test for individual subjects are summarized in Table II. At this level of analysis, we begin to see the previously mentioned dichotomy between those experimental designs which support the theory and those which do not. In design 1, 29 (72%) of 40 subjects submitted bids that are too low to be consistent with VHR theory, while in design 2, 29 (48%) of 60 subjects were inconsistent with the theoretical predictions (see Column 6, Table II). In design 2′, where the highest rejected and highest accepted bid information was blocked (i.e., not revealed to the subjects), 12 (60%) of 20 subjects submitted bids that are too low to be consistent with VHR theory. Also, in design 2″, where $\bar{v}$ had been tripled to increase expected subject profits, seven (70%) of 10 subjects bid too low to be consistent with the theory, thus suggesting no effect on the level of bids from tripling the range of payoffs. Of the eight subjects in design 9, three (37%) bid at a level too low to be consistent with VHR. In designs 4 and 8, we observe only one bidder in each design bidding too low relative to the theory. However, in design 4, we find 11 of 12 bidders bidding significantly above the risk neutral predicted level, while in design 8 we find only one of seven does so. In contrast to these results, we find 0 of the 78 subjects in designs 3, 3′, 5, 6, 6′, 7, and 10 submitting bids at a level inconsistent with the predictions of the VHR theory. In summary, at the individual bidding level, VHR is strongly supported in designs 3, 3′, 5, 6, 6′, 7, and 10; it is weakly supported in designs 4, 8, and 9; and it fails decisively to receive support in designs 1, 2, 2′, and 2″.

It is particularly instructive to examine the bidding patterns of one or two representative subjects from some of the experimental designs. Figures 2–10 show plots of individual bids at corresponding assigned values for nine subjects. The risk neutral bid function, computed from the polynomial expression in (5) for the defining experimental parameters, is shown on the same scale for each bidder. Figures 2–10 all exhibit a nonlinear bid-value relationship which resembles the graphed concave form of the risk neutral VHR bid function. In many cases, as in Figures 5 and 7–10, the individual bids form a very tight nonlinear relationship. However, some individuals differ markedly in their bid-value behavior for the same experimental design parameters. This is illustrated by comparing Figures 2 and 3 for design 1 and Figures 4 and 5 for design 2. Figures 2 and 4 are typical of the bidding pattern for the great majority of bidders in the design 1 and 2 experiments. Initially the bids increase with value approximately as does the risk neutral equilibrium bid function; then they tend to cross under and remain below this bid function. Consequently, at the lower values the bids are relatively consistent with VHR equilibrium bidding, but at the higher values the bids are inconsistent with any form of the VHR noncooperative model. In contrast, as seen in Figures 6–10, individual bidders are quite consistent with the risk averse form of the VHR model over the entire range of values sampled in designs 3–7.

B. Bidder Heterogeneity

Although we find the level of individual bids strongly consistent with the VHR theory for designs 3, 3′, 5, 6, 6′, 7, and 10, and weakly consistent for designs 4,

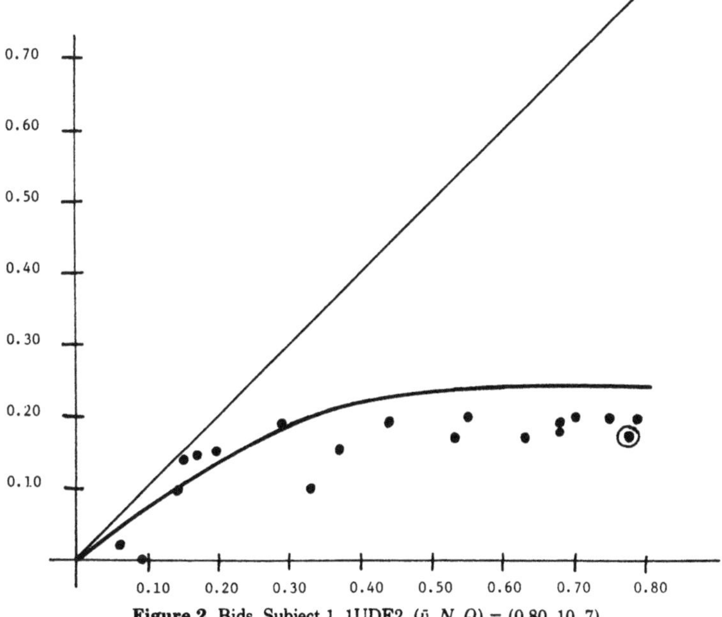

Figure 2. Bids, Subject 1, 1UDE2, $(\bar{v}, N, Q) = (0.80, 10, 7)$

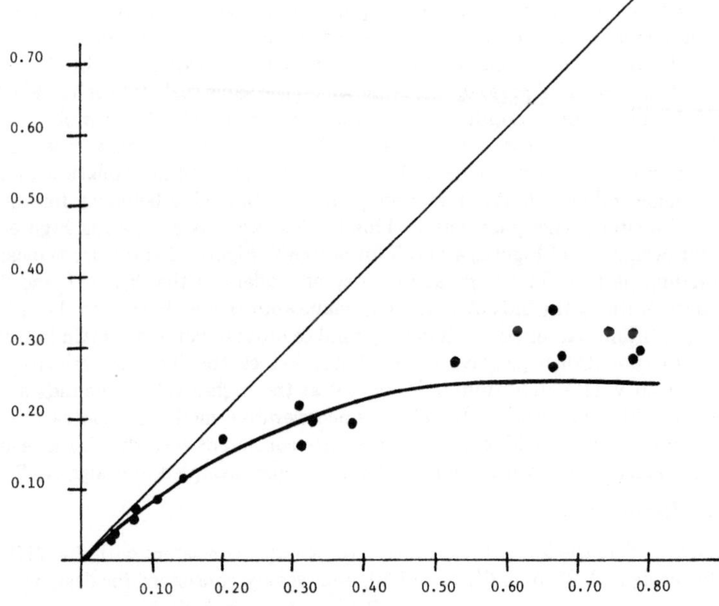

Figure 3. Bids, Subject 3, 1DUE1, $(\bar{v}, N, Q) = (0.80, 10, 7)$

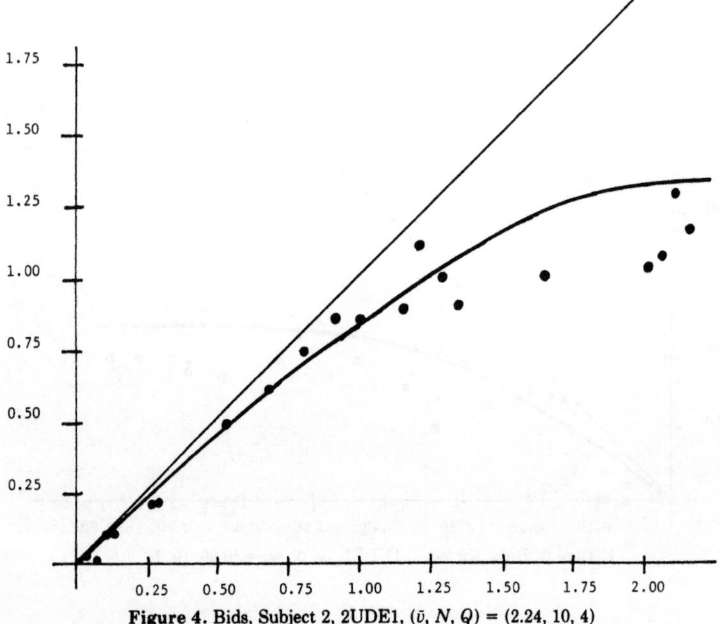

Figure 4. Bids, Subject 2, 2UDE1, $(\bar{v}, N, Q) = (2.24, 10, 4)$

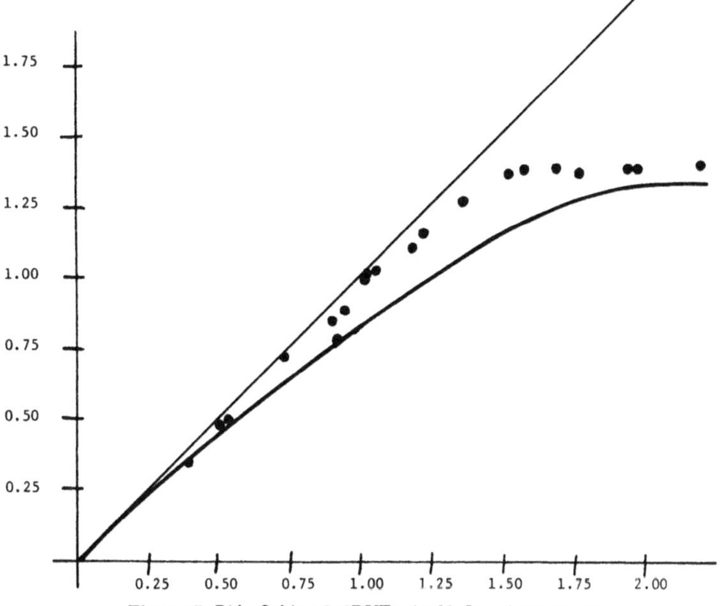

Figure 5. Bids, Subject 5, 2DUE1, $(\bar{v}, N, Q) = (2.24, 10, 4)$

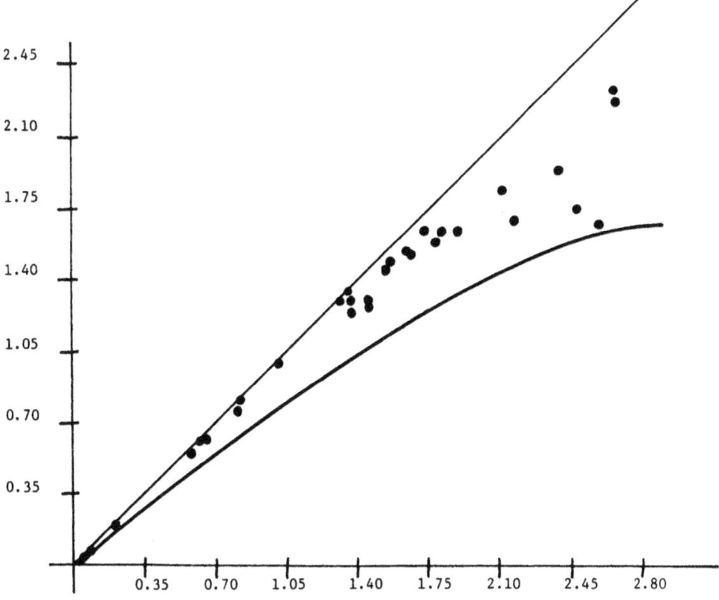

Figure 6. Bids, Subject 5, 3DE1, $(\bar{v}, N, Q) = (2.70, 5, 2)$

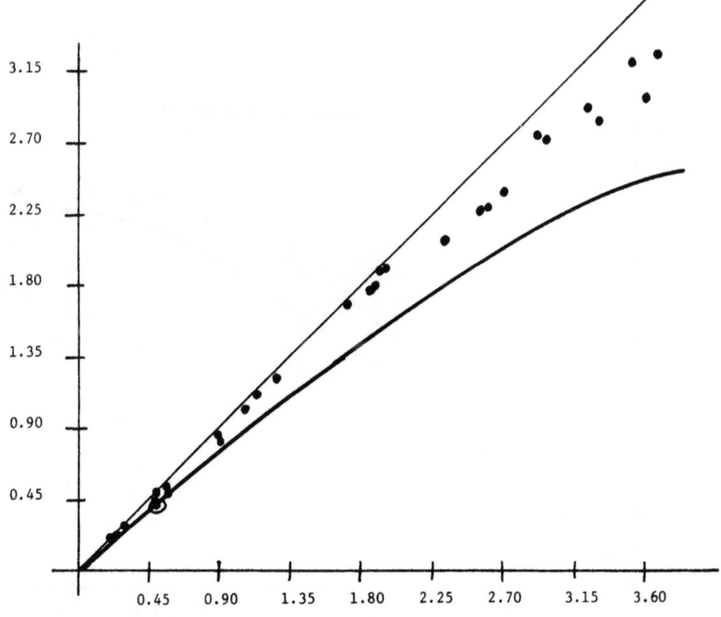

Figure 7. Bids, Subject 1, 4DE1, $(\bar{v}, N, Q) = (3.78, 6, 2)$

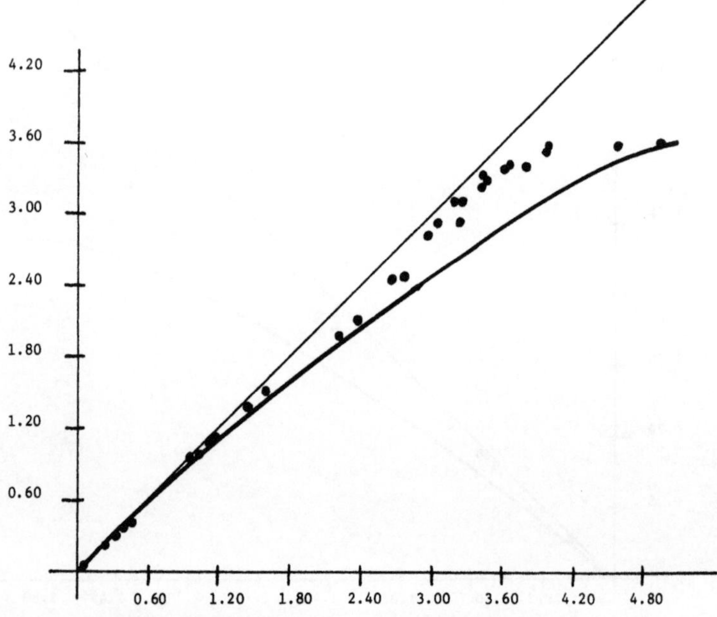

Figure 8. Bids, Subject 4, 5DE1, $(\bar{v}, N, Q) = (5.04, 7, 2)$

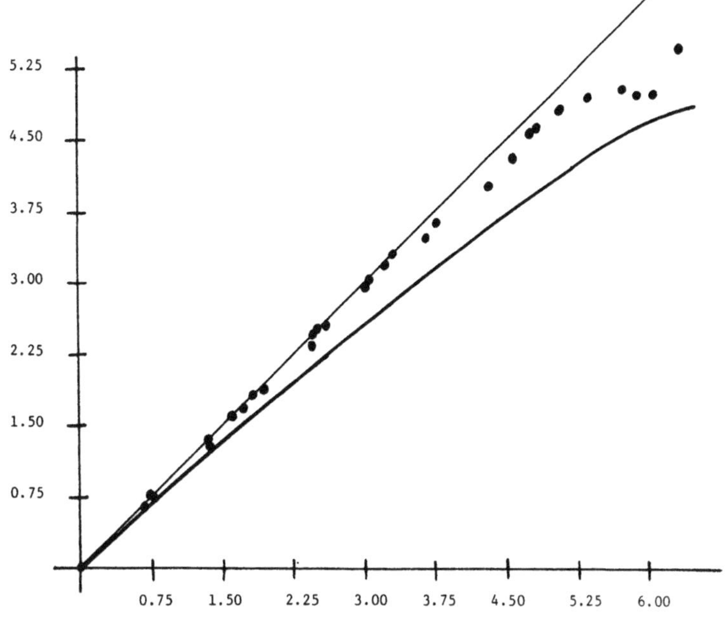

Figure 9. Bids, Subject 2, 6DE1, $(\bar{v}, N, Q) = (6.48, 8, 2)$

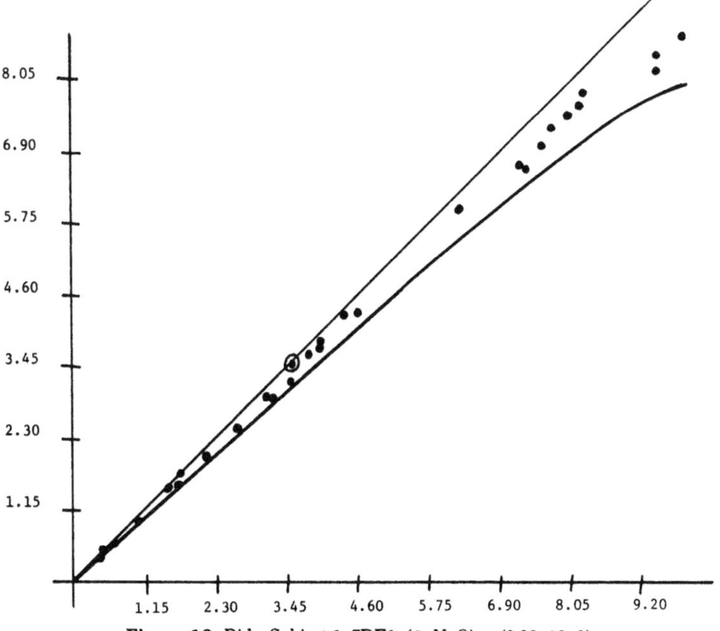

Figure 10. Bids, Subject 1, 7DE1, $(\bar{v}, N, Q) = (9.90, 10, 2)$

Table III

H-Test of Heterogeneity of Individual Bids

Session	Q	N	H-Statistic for $b_i^* - b_n(v_i^*)$
1UDE1	7	10	17.3[a]
1UDE2	7	10	30.9[a]
1DUE1	7	10	20.6[a]
1DUE2	7	10	39.2[a]
2UDE1	4	10	14.5
2UDE2	4	10	44.8[a]
2DUE1	4	10	31.2[a]
2DUE2	4	10	33.9[a]
2DE1	4	10	11.3
2DE2*	4	10	39.4[a]
2′DE1BLK	4	10	22.7[a]
2′DE2BLK	4	10	27.4[a]
2″DE2	4	10	17.5[a]
3DE1	2	5	34.5[a]
3DE2	2	5	2.7
3′DE1BLK	2	5	29.3[a]
3′DE2BLK	2	5	27.0[a]
4DE1	2	6	23.3[a]
4DE2	2	6	28.7[a]
5DE1	2	7	42.9[a]
6DE1	2	8	16.8[a]
6DE2	2	8	51.2[a]
6′DE1BLK	2	8	15.1[a]
6′DE2BLK	2	8	19.8[a]
7DE1	2	10	51.3[a]
8DE1	3	7	41.3[a]
9DE1	3	8	13.9
10DE1	3	9	22.5[a]

[a] Significant, $p = 0.05$.

8, and 9, such results are insufficient to conclude that VHR theory is supported (nonfalsified) in these designs. This is because the bidding behavior of individuals may depart from the common equilibrium bid function implied by the VHR model.

A direct statistical test of the null hypothesis, that the bids of individuals in each experiment are from the same distribution as opposed to the alternative that they are from different distributions, is reported in Table III. The first three columns of Table III identify the treatment conditions for each experiment. Thus, the experiment designated 1UDE1 indicates the following. The first "1" denotes that design 1 parameters of Table I were used. "U" indicates that the first sequences of auctions were conducted under uniform price rules and the following "D" indicates the next sequence of auctions were under discriminative price rules. The "E" represents experienced subjects and the final "1" indicates this was the first experiment of this type. One should note that the experiments using designs 3–10 and experiments 2DE1, 2DE2*, 2′DE1BLK, 2′DE2BLK, and 2″DE2 consist only of discriminative price auctions. Reported in Table III is the Kruskal-Wallis [13] nonparametric H-test applied to the deviations of individual bids from the predicted risk neutral bids, $b_i^* - b_n(v_i^*)$, for each subject in each experiment. Across all designs, in 24 of 28 experiments the null hypothesis is rejected. We conclude from these tests that individual bids are inconsistent with the VHR theory's implication that all bidders use the same bid function.[6]

C. Revenue Results

Even though the emphasis of this paper is the analysis of individual bidding behavior, it is also instructive to consider the impact of the previously summarized individual results on macro level revenue data for these sealed-bid auctions. For example, suppose all unaccepted but only some accepted individual bids were consistent with VHR theory. Then the tests on the individual data might show consistency with VHR, while the revenue data, based on the accepted bids only, might be inconsistent with VHR. Alternatively, if all unaccepted but only some accepted bids were inconsistent with VHR, the tests on the individual data could show inconsistency with VHR, while the revenue data might be consistent with VHR. Hence, tests on the revenue data are capable of yielding results that differ from the tests on individual bids.

A summary of revenue results from the discriminative auctions of all experiments using experienced subjects is given in Table IV. The fourth column of Table IV reports the observed mean (variance) of discriminative auction revenues for each experiment. In the fifth column appears the difference between the observed mean and the VHR predicted revenue (and its variance) in the discriminative auctions under the assumption of risk neutrality. From the VHR theory of bidding, the following null hypothesis can be proposed:

$$H_0^R\colon R^* - R_n^* = \textstyle\sum_{j=N-Q+1}^{N} b_j^* - \sum_{j=N-Q+1}^{N} b_n(v_j^*) < 0 \tag{9}$$

If the distribution of $R^* - R_n^*$ in successive auctions is approximately normal, and we observe an experimental sample of size T with mean $\bar{R}^* - \bar{R}_n^*$ and standard deviation S_δ, then a one-tailed paired sample t-test based on

[6] Given the traditional emphasis of economics on postulated differences in individual preferences, it is tempting, *ex post*, to be "not surprised" upon learning that in most of our groups the bidders do not behave as if they all use the same bid function. But when a theorist postulates homogeneous bidders, we assume that this postulate and the resulting theory is to be taken seriously as an approximation that could well be consistent with observation. If our subjects had not been such consistent bidders (in particular see Figures 3, 5, 7, 8, and 9) and had exhibited more noise in their empirical bid functions, then the null hypothesis could easily have failed to be rejected in most experiments. The conclusion would then have been that in terms of bidding behavior based on random value assignments, bidders are indeed homogeneous. We think that we would have attached a nonnegligible prior positive probability to this prospect. Once one has seen the data, it is of course impossible to assign credible prior probabilities. The fact that in four of the 28 experimental groups (14%) reported in Table III the null hypothesis could not be rejected suggests that the homogeneous bidders assumption is not meritless. Some subject samples do have this property. (We would expect to reject the null hypothesis in 5% of the samples even if it were true.)

Table IV

Comparison of Observed and VHR Revenues for Risk Neutral Bidders

Session	Q	N	$\bar{R}^*$ ($V_{\bar{R}}^*$)	$\bar{R}^* - \bar{R}_n^*$ (V_δ)	T	Paired Sample t-Statistic
1UDE1	7	10	1.282 (0.029)	−0.254 (0.032)	20	−6.311
1DUE1	7	10	1.444 (0.053)	−0.070 (0.037)	20	−1.630
1UDE2	7	10	1.375 (0.018)	−0.162 (0.010)	20	−7.103
1DUE2	7	10	1.484 (0.017)	−0.031 (0.008)	20	−1.575
2UDE1	4	10	4.695 (0.386)	+0.002 (0.182)	20	+0.021
2DUE1	4	10	4.467 (0.095)	−0.347 (0.150)	20	−4.000
2UDE2	4	10	4.216 (0.145)	−0.477 (0.124)	20	−6.060
2DUE2	4	10	4.592 (0.126)	−0.222 (0.149)	20	−2.572
2DE1	4	10	4.593 (0.132)	−0.142 (0.088)	30	−2.619
2DE2*	4	10	4.499 (0.138)	−0.226 (0.092)	30	−4.094
2′DE1BLK	4	10	4.310 (0.114)	−0.428 (0.116)	30	−6.092
2′DE2BLK	4	10	4.698 (0.134)	−0.048 (0.066)	30	−1.018
2″DE2	4	10	12.588 (2.734)	−1.651 (3.534)	30	−4.810
3DE1	2	5	3.204 (0.149)	+0.456 (0.038)	30	+12.808
3DE2	2	5	3.134 (0.093)	+0.386 (0.038)	30	+10.787
3′DE1BLK	2	5	3.138 (0.176)	+0.378 (0.105)	30	+6.390
3′DE2BLK	2	5	2.950 (0.068)	+0.189 (0.070)	30	+3.980
4DE1	2	6	4.932 (0.507)	+0.518 (0.210)	30	+6.195
4DE2	2	6	4.552 (0.282)	+0.137 (0.095)	30	+2.436
5DE1	2	7	6.893 (0.317)	+0.418 (0.075)	30	+8.356
6DE1	2	8	9.036 (0.669)	+0.447 (0.162)	30	+6.090
6DE2	2	8	9.314 (0.127)	+0.725 (0.206)	30	+8.747
6′DE1BLK	2	8	9.668 (1.474)	+1.082 (0.155)	30	+15.072
6′DE2BLK	2	8	9.108 (0.757)	+0.522 (0.216)	30	+6.155
7DE1	2	10	14.910 (0.759)	+0.512 (0.430)	30	+4.275
8DE1	3	7	3.680 (0.106)	−0.181 (0.120)	30	−2.860
9DE1	3	8	5.162 (0.129)	−0.234 (0.183)	30	−3.002
10DE1	3	9	7.384 (0.528)	+0.262 (0.145)	30	+3.766

$\bar{R}^*$ = Mean of observed revenue for T auctions $= \frac{1}{T} \sum_{t=1}^{T} R^*(t)$

$= \frac{1}{T} \sum_{t=1}^{T} \sum_{j=N-Q+1}^{N} b_j^*(t)$

$V_{\bar{R}}^*$ = Variance of observed revenue $= \frac{1}{T-1} \sum_{t=1}^{T} [R^*(t) - \bar{R}^*]^2$

$\bar{R}_n^*$ = Mean revenue predicted by VHR theory for risk neutral bidders, conditional on realized experimental values, v_j^*, $= \frac{1}{T} \sum_{t=1}^{T} R_n^*(t)$

$= \frac{1}{T} \sum_{t=1}^{T} \sum_{j=N-Q+1}^{N} b_n(v_j^*(t))$

V_δ = Variance of revenue difference

$= \frac{1}{T-1} \sum_{t=1}^{T} [(R^*(t) - R_n^*(t)) - (\bar{R}^* - \bar{R}_n^*)]^2$

$t = (T)^{1/2}(\bar{R}^* - \bar{R}_n^*)/S_\delta$ is appropriate. The resulting t-values for each experiment are shown in the last column of Table IV.

From these t-values the test results are unequivocal: We reject the null hypothesis in favor of the risk averse Nash equilibrium model for designs 3–7 and 10, but we cannot reject the null hypothesis for designs 1, 2, 8, and 9.

These revenue results are plotted in Figure 11, together with corresponding data for single unit auctions from experiments reported by Cox, Roberson, and Smith [4].[7] In the single unit auctions (based on "first price" rules, where the winning bidder pays the amount bid), the above null hypothesis is rejected for $N = 4$, 5, 6, and 9 but not for $N = 3$ (see [4]). In Figure 11 mean observed revenue less the mean predicted revenue for risk neutral bidders (conditional on the sample values actually drawn) from VHR theory is plotted against the proportion of rejected bids. The revenue data from all experiments are pooled for each (N, Q) treatment condition except for those replications in which payoffs were tripled, $\bar{v}$ was tripled, or between auction information was blocked.

From the information presented in Table IV and Figure 11, one can clearly see the dichotomy of the results reported earlier. It is important to note that the results reported do not suggest a sort of random behavior where the experiments support the theory part of the time and fail to do so at other times. In those designs in which the bid and revenue level implications of the theory are supported, they are consistently supported. Yet in those designs in which the experiments do not support the theory, the theory is consistently called into question by both the individual and revenue data. Furthermore, this dichotomy is not affected if we triple payoffs, triple $\bar{v}$, or block the feedback of information on the highest accepted and rejected bids.

IV. Experimental and Theoretical Issues in the Research Program for Testing VHR Theory

The multiple unit sealed-bid auction experiments reported in the previous section have been part of a continuing research program by the authors (and other associates) in which the investigation has been constantly influenced by an interplay between our development and execution of the experiments and our efforts to further develop the theory. The form and direction of this investigation has been conditioned by a methodological perspective which recognizes that whenever a new confrontation between theory and experimental evidence suggests the existence of one or more inconsistencies, this could be due either to inadequacies in the theory or to inadequacies in the generation of the observa-

[7] There is a procedural difference between the Cox, Roberson, and Smith [4] first price sealed-bid auctions and the multiple unit discriminative auctions reported here. In the former, after each auction, subjects were informed of the market price (the highest, and only, accepted bid), but were not informed of the highest rejected bid. This procedure was used in single object auctions as an information control for comparing the first price sealed-bid auction with the Dutch auction. In the Dutch auction, where price falls until an acceptance occurs, one can never know what the highest rejected bid would have been. These alternative information conditions for discriminative multiple unit auctions have been examined in [22]. Of course the VHR theory predicts no difference in bidding behavior between these alternative information conditions.

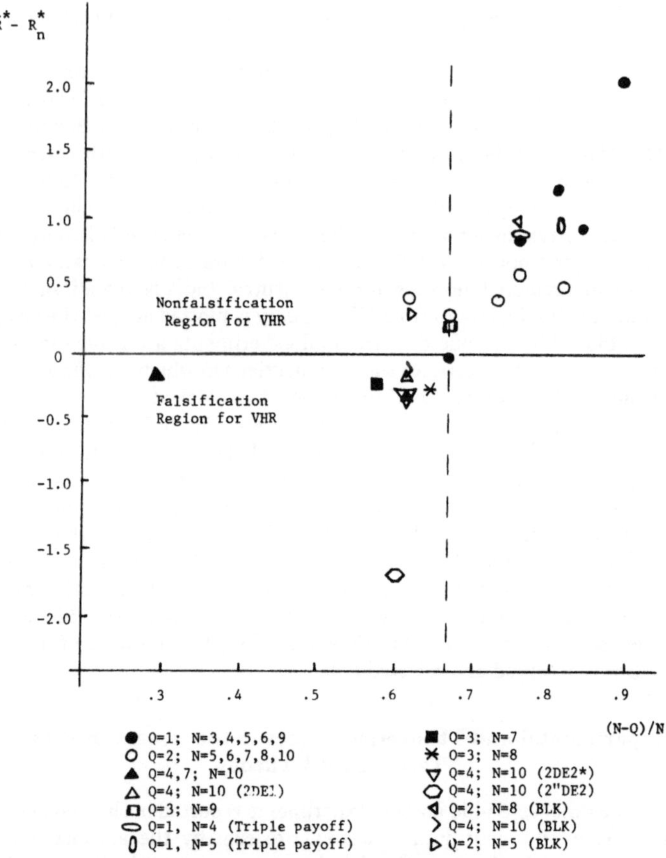

Figure 11. Critical Regions for VHR Revenues

tions—in this case the experimental test procedures. According to this perspective, any discrepancies between the observations and the implications (predictions) of the theory lead one, provisionally, to question both the theory and the observations for the purpose of taking research steps designed to resolve this inconsistency. Although no such thing as a final resolution can likely ever be asserted, our view is that before a theory can be considered to have been "falsified" by evidence, two conditions must be fulfilled. First, one must be satisfied, on the basis of an in-depth empirical examination of the sensitivity of the observations to variations in the experimental procedures, that the interpretation of the "falsifying" portion of the evidence is a defensibly correct interpretation. Second, one must be satisfied that there exists at least one other theory which does at least as well as the incumbent theory in accounting for the nonfalsifying observations, while at the same time accounting for some of the falsifying evidence.

This perspective is perhaps the dominant characteristic of the practice of science as it has been interpreted by Lakatos [14].

Our choice of the design parameters contained in Table I, the particular sequence in which the experiments based on these designs were conducted, the number of times each experimental design was replicated with different subjects, and our sensitivity tests of possible artifactual subject and level-of-reward effects on the results were all motivated and conditioned by the above considerations. In this section, we provide a detailed discussion of the questions and conjectures in our minds at the time we elected to run the particular experiments which constitute the series reported in Tables I–IV.

A. *Initial Choice of Design Parameters Influenced by First Price Auction Results*

Sometimes it is an arbitrary decision as to where in the parameter space one begins a program of new experimental research. Thus, the choice of some parameters may more likely be influenced by conjectures about where one might get the most informative observations for the money spent, than by considerations derivable from formal theory. In this case, multiple unit auction theory does not provide any guidelines as to where to begin a testing program in the parameter space defined by $N > Q \geq 2$. But in 1979, when we initiated our continuing series of multiple unit experiments, the first price (single object) auction experiments subsequently reported by Coppinger, Smith, and Titus [3] and by Cox, Roberson, and Smith [4] (hereafter CRS) had been completed, and these results strongly influenced our choice of the design parameters (N, Q) in the first several multiple unit experiments that we scheduled. These single object results also provided some guideline characteristics as to what to expect in the pattern of results from the multiple unit experiments. From the CRS experiments, we had the following conclusions: (1) The risk averse model of Nash equilibrium bidding behavior was strongly supported in all replications for $N = 4$, 5, 6, and 9. (2) For $N = 3$, CRS report some replications consistent with the risk averse model and some that are not. Pooling the revenue results across all replications for $N = 3$, CRS [4, p. 25] note that one cannot reject the risk neutral model. But since the subjects in the groups of size $N = 3$ were from the same subject pools as those in the groups of size $N > 3$, there was no basis for concluding that the deviant behavior when $N = 3$ was due to subject risk preferences (risk neutral, risk averse, or risk preferring) *independently of group size.*

These first price auction results suggested that the noncooperative model fails when group size is sufficiently small. This led us to conjecture that in the multiple unit auctions the noncooperative model might fail when group size was sufficiently small relative to the number of units offered. In the single unit auctions, the model failed only when the proportion of rejected bids was as low as two-thirds. This is seen in Figure 11 if one focuses on those mean revenue deviations that are plotted as solid circles. These five points, showing inconsistency with the model only when $(N, Q) = (3, 1)$, represented the state of our empirical knowledge when we undertook the first sequence of multiple unit auction experiments.

B. The First Series of Results for (N, Q) = (10, 7) and (10, 4)

Tentatively, we adopted the empirical hypothesis that when $\left(\frac{N-Q}{N}\right) \leq 0.67$ inconsistencies between the outcomes and VHR predictions might be expected. Consequently, we undertook a series of 16 experiments, each consisting of 23 discriminative auctions followed by 22 uniform price auctions, or vice versa, in which $\left(\frac{N-Q}{N}\right) < 0.67$. For eight of these experiments $(N, Q) = (10, 7)$, and for another eight $(N, Q) = (10, 4)$. One purpose of this series was to compare the revenue properties of the discriminative and uniform price auctions. These revenue results and comparisons are reported in Cox, Smith, and Walker [6] (hereafter CSW [6]). Since behavior may change with increased familiarity, practice, and the opportunity to reflect by experimental subjects, we also investigated "experience" as a treatment variable in this initial series of experiments.

In the first 14 of these experiments, consisting of four inexperienced and three experienced groups run under each of the two (N, Q) parameter conditions, two conclusions characterized the revenue outcomes in the discriminative auctions:

1. Subject experience had a pronounced, consistent effect on the revenue results in those sessions for which $(N, Q) = (10, 7)$. Three of the four inexperienced groups were consistent with VHR theory, while *none* of the three experienced groups were consistent with VHR theory. Consequently, we decided to run "practice" experiments and concentrate our multiple unit auction analysis on the use of experienced subjects in all subsequent experiments. This increased our research program costs, but allowed us to control for transient effects in subject behavior. In this design in which 70% of the bids are accepted, it may be that experienced subjects learn that there is minimal risk in bidding "cooperatively" since "low" bids are still likely to be accepted.
2. None of the seven experimental sessions for $(N, Q) = (10, 4)$—four using inexperienced subjects and three using experienced subjects—yielded revenue results consistent with VHR theory.

C. Effect of Screening for Noncooperative Behavior in the Uniform Price Auction

In the uniform price auction, it is a dominant strategy to bid one's value. Hence, noncooperative behavior in this auction can be identified independently of risk aversion (utility is required only to be increasing in monetary surplus). Suppose we screen for those subjects who adopt, or learn to adopt, the dominant strategy in a uniform price auction, and then use those subjects in the discriminative auction designs in which the VHR noncooperative model has been failing. If this result is reversed, it suggests that the observed tendency of VHR theory to fail in these designs is not exclusively a characteristic of the designs, but is also, in part, an identifiable characteristic of the subjects. If the results are not affected by this screening procedure, this outcome reinforces the conclusion that the failure of VHR theory in these designs is due to the parameter values. The revenue results for the two experiments using subjects screened for their tendencies to use the noncooperative strategy in uniform price auctions are reported in Table IV as experiments 1DUE2 and 2DUE2 (reported as "super experienced" experiments 1DU8′Sx and 2DU7′Sx, in CSW [6]). Clearly, these experiments yield results that do not differ significantly from those with the same parameter design, but using the experienced, unscreened subjects.

In Figure 11 the pooled revenue results for each of the parameter values $(N, Q) = (10, 7)$ and $(10, 4)$ are plotted as solid triangles. At this juncture, the combined results of the single unit auctions and the two sets of multiple unit auctions supported the hypothesis that the VHR model fails when the proportion of rejected bids was two-thirds or less.

D. *Effect of Further Tests of the Proposed "Proportion-of-Rejected Bids" Hypothesis*

If it is the proportion of rejected bids that is driving the separation of the parameter space into VHR falsifying and nonfalsifying sets of experiments, then since the model fails to be supported when $(N, Q) = (10, 4)$, it should also fail to be supported when $(N, Q) = (5, 2)$. Further, if this proportion is specifically two-thirds, the failure of the model when $(N, Q) = (3, 1)$ should extend to the first such multiple unit case, $(N, Q) = (6, 2)$. Finally, by this reasoning, the model should not fail when $Q = 2$ and $N > 6$. Based on these considerations, we scheduled the series of eight experiments listed under designs 3–7 in Tables I–IV. As we have seen in the previous section, both the revenue and the individual bid data for all eight of these experiments support the VHR model. The hypothesis that some simple "proportion-of-rejected-bids rule" would account for the falsifying cases appeared to be effectively refuted by these new experimental results. The pooled revenue deviations for designs 3–7 (excluding 3′ and 6′) are plotted in Figure 11 as open circles.

E. *Testing Again for Artifactual Subject Effects*

We wanted to be quite sure that these new experimental outcomes and their interpretation had internal validity. We therefore asked ourselves whether there might be any differences, other than the treatment parameters, between the experiments in designs 1 and 2 and those in designs 3–7. Since the experiments in designs 3–7 were conducted using a new pool of experienced subjects, recruited specifically for this new experimental series, it was conceivable that some unknown difference in the two subject pools might account for the results. This seemed unlikely, since we have long and repeated experience in finding that experimental market behavior is robust with respect to wide variations in subject groups with comparable experience. But this robustness might fail to extend to this new experimental market paradigm, and any such extension must proceed on a case-by-case empirical basis. Also, since we were getting a discrete bifurcation in the empirical support for the theory, we could not ignore the possibility that we were dealing with phenomena that were uncommonly sensitive to subject differences. This was easy to check; we replicated design 2 using a sample of 10 subjects from the pool of experienced subjects used in designs 3–7. This experiment is reported as 2DE1 in Tables III and IV. The outcome is clearly in the falsification region for the VHR model along with the other experiments in design 2. The revenue result for this experiment is plotted in Figure 11 as an open triangle. We reject, as unlikely, the hypothesis that differences in the behavior of the design 1 and 2 and design 3–7 experiments are attributable to subject differences.

F. Is $\bar{v}$ or the Level of Cash Rewards a Treatment Parameter Affecting Observed Outcomes?

Recall from Section II that each experimental design is defined by the 3-tuple, $(\bar{v}, N, Q)$, and that initially we decided to choose $\bar{v}$ as a function of (N, Q) so as to hold constant the per capita theoretical risk neutral expected earnings of subjects across experiments with differing values for (N, Q). Since actual earnings may deviate from risk neutral expected earnings if subjects are risk averse (or risk-preferring), or for other reasons, the procedure can only provide some approximate control over per capita realized earnings. Up to this point in the research program, we had not probed the internal empirical issues that relate to this experimental procedure. Two questions arise concerning our *a priori* justification for this procedure. First, since $\bar{v}$ varies with (N, Q) across designs as a by-product of holding risk neutral per capita earnings constant, could this parameter be an artifactual "treatment" that accounts for those designs that so consistently yield falsifying outcomes? Thus, it might be reasonable to conjecture that controlling for reward level across designs is of minor importance so long as rewards are "adequate" in the sense of being above some unknown threshold motivational level. Second, is the reward level itself a treatment variable in the sense that the observed behavior in any of the designs is changed if we effect a substantial increase in the reward level? If we let α be the factor that converts "experimental dollars" into U.S. currency payments to subjects, then the utility to bidder i of the experimental outcome, $v_i - b_i$, is the utility of the monetary amount, $\alpha(v_i - b_i)$, which is $u[\alpha(v_i - b_i)]$ in the VHR model. If $u(\cdot)$ is strictly concave, then the argument summarized in Section I now requires bidder i to choose $b_i = b_i^0$ so as to maximize $u[\alpha(v_i - b_i)]G(\pi(b_i))$, and this leads to a risk averse equilibrium bid function $b_a(v_i, \alpha)$ containing the conversion factor α. Hence, the VHR model generally predicts a shift in the risk averse bid function if α is changed, and in all the experiments discussed up to now we have $\alpha = 1$.

In [7] (also see [4, 5, 8]), we have extended the VHR model to allow bidders to have different constant relative risk averse (CRRA) utility functions for monetary outcome; i.e., $u_i = u[\alpha(v_i - b_i); r_i] = [\alpha(v_i - b_i)]^{r_i}$. Since in this model α affects only the scale of utility, it leads to an equilibrium bid function that is independent of the α reward parameter. Also, note that the risk neutral version of the VHR model is the special case of the CRRA model where $r_i = 1$ for all i.

These considerations led us to conduct two new experiments with design 2. In the first experiment, session 2DE2* in Tables III and IV, we tripled the experimental earnings of all subjects to obtain their payoffs in U.S. currency (i.e., $\alpha = 3$). From the revenue results in Table IV it is seen that this "treatment" has no effect on the outcomes (a result that is predicted by the CRRA model). In Figure 11 note that the revenue deviation for experiment 2DE2* (plotted as the inverted open triangle) coincides exactly with the pooled revenue deviation for the design 2 experiments which did not triple subject payoffs.

In the second new experiment, session 2″DE2, we tripled all subject value assignments; i.e., each sequence of values assigned to some subject in session 2DE2* was tripled and then assigned to a corresponding subject in 2″DE2. From Table IV it is seen that the effect is to nearly triple revenues, but the outcome is still significantly below the risk neutral predicted revenue. Also see Figure 11 where the revenue deviation for experiment 2″DE2 is plotted as a hexagon.

In Figure 11 we also plot the pooled revenue deviations from two sets of first price auctions reported in [8] in which payoffs were tripled in comparison with their corresponding control experiments. The parameter values for these experiments correspond to $(N, Q) = (4, 1)$ and $(5, 1)$. The new single and multiple unit experiments strongly reinforce the conclusion that in both the VHR-consistent and the VHR-inconsistent designs the results are due to the parameters (N, Q) and not to any effect attributable to the payoff level or to $\bar{v}$. The results are also consistent with the CRRA utility function model of Nash equilibrium bidding in [7]. Since CRRA utility is the only utility function for which individual bids are independent of the payoff scale, and for which a scaler change in $\bar{v}$ leads to the same scaler change in v_i, b_i, and payoffs, these results are particularly important in narrowing the range of models that are supported by the bidding data.[8]

G. *Effect of Between Auction Information on Highest Rejected and Highest Accepted Bids*

At this point in our experimental procedure, all experiments had involved sequences of auctions where the between auction information available to subjects included the highest rejected and highest accepted bids in the previous auctions in a sequence. (See the fourth paragraph in Section II above.) Our intention in providing this information was to create an information setting similar to those in field discriminative auctions such as the U.S. Treasury bill auction. However, from the theoretical development of Section I, it can be seen that this information is not required by bidders in the Nash equilibrium model. Hence, one might conjecture that the between auction information on highest rejected and highest accepted bids could influence subject bidding behavior and thereby affect our tests of the theory. Furthermore, if the effect of between auction bid information was different in the designs that support VHR theory than in the designs that do not support the theory then some insight might be gained into the reasons for the experimental bifurcation of the (N, Q) parameter space.

[8] Let $\mu_i = b_i/\bar{v}$ be i's normalized bid (measured as a proportion of $\bar{v}$) when i's normalized value is $\nu_i = v_i/\bar{v}$. Then the probability that a bid of μ_i or less will win is $G(\mu_i)$ and CRRA expected utility is $[\bar{v}(\nu_i - \mu_i)]^{r_i} G(\mu_i)$. If we apply the derivation procedures reported in [7] (also see the CRRA examples in [5]), the result is a normalized equilibrium bid function of the form $\mu_i = b(\nu_i, r_i)$. Therefore, $\bar{v}$ affects only the scale of utility, bids, values, and payoffs. With CRRA utility, tripling $\bar{v}$ is indistinguishable from tripling the payoff conversion factor, α, and the theory predicts that neither parameter has any effect on *normalized* bidding behavior.

To test for possible bid information effects, we conducted six new experiments in which the highest rejected and highest accepted bid information was not provided to the subjects. These experimental designs are listed as 2′, 3′, and 6′ in Tables I and II. The bidder heterogeneity and market revenue tests for these experiments are reported in Tables III and IV as the six experimental sessions labeled with the letters "BLK." The market revenue deviations for these experiments are also plotted in Figure 11. The results are clear. The levels of individual bids and market revenues observed for design 2′ are too low to be consistent with VHR theory, as they are in designs 2, 2*, and 2″. In contrast, for designs 3′ and 6′ the levels of individual bids and market revenues are consistent with VHR theory, as they are in designs 3 and 6.[9]

V. Summary and Discussion

The primary implications of VHR bidding theory that are tested using the experimental data reported in this paper are: (1) all bidders use the same increasing bid function (bidders are homogeneous in their bidding behavior); (2) no bidder will bid below the risk neutral theoretical bid function; and (3) observed auction market revenue will not be less than the corresponding risk neutral theoretical revenue. Statistical tests of hypotheses derived from these implications, using the experimental data reported in this paper, lead to the following conclusions. (1) Within our experimental designs there is a bifurcation of the results into two distinct sets defined by a corresponding partition of the (N, Q) parameter space. The levels of individual bids and market revenues are consistent with the VHR model for one group of (N, Q) parameter designs, but inconsistent with the VHR model for another group of parameter designs. This bifurcation into Group I (inconsistent) and Group C (consistent) is illustrated in Figure 12, which includes a large number of single unit auction experiments reported earlier [4, 8]. These results are internally consistent, replicable, and remarkably robust under several experimental probes attempting to uncover artifactual and subject sample effects. (2) Across all designs, the hypothesis of bidder homogeneity (that the bids of the N individuals in a given experiment all come from the same distribution) is rejected in 24 of 28 experiments.

What are the implications of these results for the VHR model? We begin by noting that given the complexity and mathematical sophistication of the theory, the VHR model does remarkably well. In Figure 12 two-thirds (10 of 15) of the parameter designs studied to date are consistent with the revenue (and individual bid level) predictions of the model. Second, we note that the VHR model assumes the following: (1) maximization of expected utility; (2) general concave utility; (3) Nash strategic behavior; (4) identical utility functions; and (5) zero subjective

[9] When this research program was initiated, we did not consider it to be conceivable that subjects would exhibit Nash equilibrium behavior without some learning adjustment over time, perhaps in response to the feedback of this bid information. Therefore, it seemed natural to provide this information even though it was redundant for a *calculating* Nash bidder. But as noted in [6] we have not identified any characteristic, replicable trends over time in the revenue data. This suggests that the feedback of bid information may not be of any significance, which is reinforced with the results from these six "BLK" experiments.

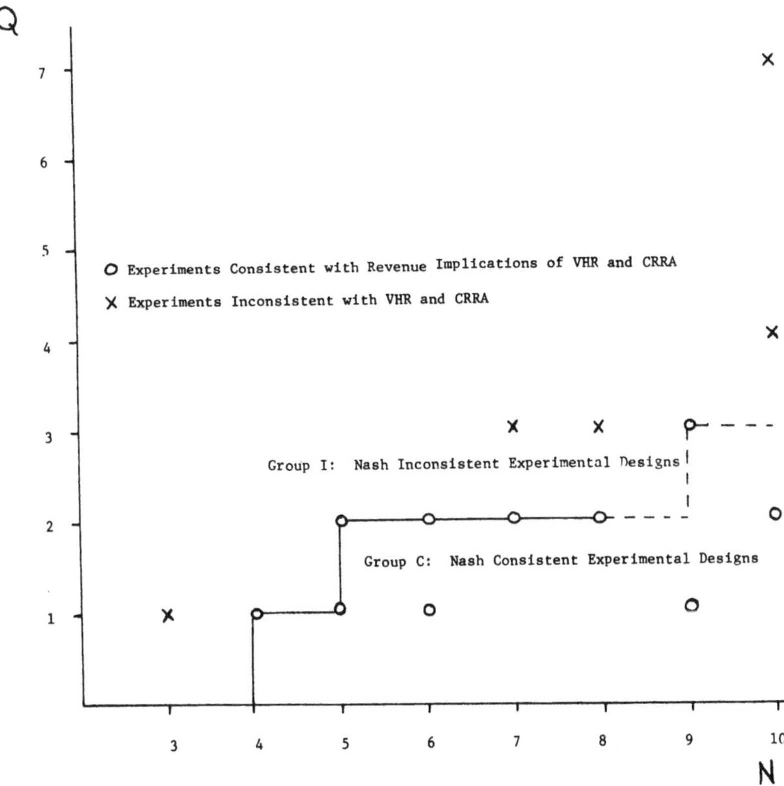

Figure 12. Bifurcation of the (N, Q) Parameter Space

cost of transacting (thinking, deciding, and acting; i.e., only $v - b$ is an argument of utility). When a theory is inconsistent with some observations, this suggests that the theory together with any or all of its assumptions is in question. But the pattern of failure of the theory may suggest "clues" as to how the theory might be modified to account for the falsifying observations, *given those ingredients of the theory that one chooses not to abandon.*[10] This criterion would seem to require us to retain assumptions (1) and (3); i.e., expected utility maximization and Nash

[10] Lakatos [14] refers to the "hard core" of a scientific research program as consisting of those assumptions which the scientist or the scientific community is unwilling to abandon in the face of falsifying evidence. Thus in the Newtonian research program, 17th and 18th century physicists did not abandon Newton's postulate of the inverse square law of mass attraction in the face of clear evidence that the planets did not move in perfect ellipses. Instead, what was modified, were the special forms (or models) of the "general" theory based on special simplifying assumptions, such as that the sun's mass is concentrated at a point, that the mass of each planet is concentrated at a point, that the mass interaction of the planets can be ignored, and so on. Thus the "hard core" was

Footnote 10 continues on next page.

strategic behavior appear to be essential if we are not going to abandon the basic concept of noncooperative equilibrium.[11] It is our position that the performance of the VHR model is sufficiently satisfactory to readily justify attempts to improve and extend it in directions disciplined by the above evidence, and that it would be quite premature at this stage to abandon its noncooperative, expected utility, foundations.

Accordingly, we have elsewhere developed heterogeneous bidder Nash models [4, 5, 7]. The multiple unit auction model developed in [7] (which generalizes the single unit auction model in [4]) replaces assumptions (2) and (4) with the specific assumption that bidders have distinct CRRA utility for monetary surplus. The CRRA model dominates the VHR model in that the former does as well as VHR in accounting for the Group C observations in Figure 12, while accounting for other evidence that is inconsistent with VHR. In particular the CRRA model is consistent with the rejection of the hypothesis that bidders bid as if they had a common bid function. It is also consistent with the experimental result that tripling payoffs has no significant effect on bidding behavior, and that tripling $\bar{v}$ effectively triples the level of individual bids.

But at this juncture in the research program we have no explanation of the Group I experiments in Figure 12 that are inconsistent with both the CRRA and VHR models. The Group I experiments are characterized by a pronounced tendency of individuals to bid below the risk neutral Vickrey bid function. It is natural to conjecture that this is due either to cooperative behavior, as suggested by CRS [4] in single unit auctions when there are only three bidders, or to strictly convex (risk-preferring) preferences for monetary outcome. However, it is one thing to conjecture that risk-preferring bidders might bid below the risk neutral bid function, but quite another matter to show that the presence of bidders with strictly convex utility can be consistent with the existence of Nash equilibrium bid functions. In [5] we have generalized the CRRA Nash equilibrium model to include a rich class of bidders in which some bidders can be risk-preferring.[12] Whether some such model can account for the Group I experiments remains an open question. Clearly, since both the Group I and Group C experiments used

surrounded by a "protective belt" of auxiliary hypotheses subject to change. Such marginal adjustments enabled Newtonian mechanics to better "account" for the observations; but anomalies remained, such as the perturbation in the orbit of the planet Mercury, which could not be accounted for by fiddling with the implementational postulates of Newton's laws. Hence, physicists simply lived with this and other anomalies until the 20th century when relativity theory accounted for some of these anomalies (such as the Mercury orbit), while at the same time also accounting for those observations which were consistent with Newton's system.

[11] An interesting and challenging alternative might be to retain Nash strategic behavior but replace expected utility maximization with Chew's weighted utility maximization [1, 2]. In effect, this approach abandons homogeneous subjective expectations. Although this alternative is worth exploring, it would appear that the more conservative line of defense should first include the more traditional expected utility calculus.

[12] It has been suggested that the failure of designs 1 and 2 to be consistent with the VHR or CRRA Nash theory could be due to the lower maximum payoff resulting from the lower value for $\bar{v}$ (see Table I) in these designs. This suggestion is most directly refuted by the results of designs 2′ and 2″, in which tripling payoffs or $\bar{v}$ did not affect the tendency of subjects to bid below the risk neutral level.

individuals from the same pool of experienced subjects, the difference in results cannot be due to differences in the risk characteristics of the subjects *independently* of the parameters (N, Q). This leaves open the possibility that there may be some interaction between the parameters (N, Q) and the presence of risk-preferring bidders that could account for the Group I outcomes without simultaneously losing consistency with the Group C outcomes. For example, the presence of only one risk-preferring bidder might lower all bids when there are only three bidders. We expect to continue our theoretical examination of these questions, and to employ direct experimental techniques for manipulating risk attitude as a means of constructing more robust tests of the effect of risk attitude on bidding behavior.

REFERENCES

1. Soo Hong Chew. "A Generalization of the Quasilinear Mean with Applications to the Measurement of Income Inequality and Decision Theory Resolving the Allais Paradox." *Econometrica*, Forthcoming.
2. ———. "Weighted Utility Theory, Certainty Equivalence, and General Monetary Lotteries." Discussion paper, University of Arizona, 1982.
3. Vicki M. Coppinger, Vernon L. Smith, and Jon A. Titus. "Incentives and Behavior in English, Dutch, and Sealed-Bid Auctions." *Economic Inquiry* 18 (January 1980), 1–22.
4. James C. Cox, Bruce Roberson, and Vernon L. Smith. "Theory and Behavior of Single Unit Auctions." In Vernon L. Smith (ed.), *Research in Experimental Economics*, Vol. 2, Greenwich: JAI Press, 1982.
5. James C. Cox and Vernon L. Smith. "Equilibrium Bidding Theory When Some Bidders May Be Risk-Preferring." Discussion paper, University of Arizona, 1983.
6. James C. Cox, Vernon L. Smith, and James M. Walker. "Expected Revenue in Discriminative and Uniform Price Sealed-Bid Auctions." In Vernon L. Smith (ed.), *Research in Experimental Economics*, Vol. 3, Greenwich: JAI Press, 1984 (in press).
7. ———. "Auction Market Theory of Heterogeneous Bidders." *Economics Letters* 9 (1982), 319–25.
8. ———. "Tests of a Heterogeneous Bidders Theory of First Price Auctions." *Economics Letters* 12 (1983), 207–12.
9. ———. "A Test That Discriminates Between Two Models of the Dutch-First Auction Nonisomorphism." *Journal of Economic Behavior and Organization* 4 (June–September 1983), 205–19.
10. Morris H. Degroot. *Probability and Statistics*. Reading: Addison-Wesley, 1975.
11. Milton Harris and Artur Raviv. "Allocation Mechanisms and the Design of Auctions." *Econometrica* 49 (November 1981), 1477–99.
12. Charles A. Holt, Jr. "Competitive Bidding for Contracts Under Alternative Auction Procedures." *Journal of Political Economy* 88 (June 1980), 433–45.
13. William H. Kruskal and W. Allen Wallis. "Use of Ranks in One-Criterion Analysis of Variance." *Journal of the American Statistical Association* 47 (December 1952), 583–621.
14. Imre Lakatos. *The Methodology of Scientific Research Programs*. Edited by John Worrall and Gregory Currie. Cambridge: Cambridge University Press, 1978.
15. Erik Maskin and John G. Riley. "Auctioning an Indivisible Object." Discussion paper no. 87D, JFK School of Government, Harvard University, 1980.
16. Steven Matthews. "Risk Aversion and the Efficiency of First- and Second-Price Auctions." CCBA Working paper no. 586, University of Illinois, 1979.
17. Paul R. Milgrom and Robert J. Weber. "A Theory of Auctions and Competitive Bidding." *Econometrica* 50 (September 1982), 1089–1122.
18. Roger B. Myerson. "Optimal Auction Design." *Mathematics of Operations Research* 6 (February 1981), 58–73.

19. John G. Riley and William F. Samuelson. "Optimal Auctions." *American Economic Review* 71 (June 1981), 381–92.
20. William Vickrey. "Counterspeculation, Auctions, and Competitive Sealed Tenders." *Journal of Finance* 16 (March 1961), 8–37.
21. ———. "Auction and Bidding Games." In *Recent Advances in Game Theory.* (Conference proceedings.) Princeton, Princeton University Press, 1962, pp. 15–27.
22. James M. Walker, Vernon L. Smith, and James C. Cox. "Bidding Behavior in Sealed Bid Discriminative Auctions: An Experimental Analysis of Multiple Sequence Auctions with Variations in Auction Information." Discussion paper: University of Arizona, 1983.

Theory and Individual Behavior of First-Price Auctions

JAMES C. COX
University of Arizona

VERNON L. SMITH
University of Arizona

JAMES M. WALKER
Indiana University

Key words: auctions, bidding theory, experiments

Abstract

First-price auction theory is extended to the case of heterogeneous bidders characterized by *M*-parameter log-concave utility functions. This model, and its specific two-parameter constant relative risk averse special case, is generally supported by the results of 47 experiments. The one-parameter special case that comprises most of the theoretical literature is not supported by the experiments. One anomaly for the two-parameter model is that too many of the subjects exhibit positive (or negative) intercepts in their linear estimated bid functions. Accordingly, we develop a specific three-parameter model, which introduces a utility of winning, and a threshold utility of surplus. The new model, tested directly by introducing lump-sum payments or charges for winning, is not falsified by the new experiments.

We develop a generalization of noncooperative equilibrium models of bidding in the first-price sealed-bid auction (hereafter, the *F* auction).[1] In our model, individual bidders can differ from each other in any way that can be represented by a finite number (*M*) of parameters (and satisfies certain regularity conditions). Our model, which we call the log-concave model, permits bidder preferences for monetary payoff to be risk averse, risk neutral, or risk preferring, although every bidder's utility function for monetary payoff must be less convex than the exponential function. Special cases of this model include the one-parameter linear (risk neutral) and concave (risk neutral or risk averse) utility models and the two-parameter

Financial support by the National Science Foundation (grants SES-8205983, SES-8404915, and SES-8608112) and the Sloan Foundation is gratefully acknowledged. We wish to thank Shawn LaMaster for capable assistance with computer graphics and data analysis.

constant relative risk averse model, all of which have been analyzed in the literature.[2]

There are two reasons why our extension of bidding theory to agents with heterogeneous risk preferences is important: (1) some such extension is demanded by the bidding data, since these data are highly inconsistent with all identical bidders models; (2) a recent comprehensive survey of over 50 bidding theory papers (McAfee and McMillan, 1987) lists only one contribution that is *not* based on the assumption that bidders have identical risk preferences (Cox, Smith, and Walker, 1982).

We also present the results of 47 F auction experiments, which are designed to discriminate among the various noncooperative equilibrium models of bidding that are contained in the general M-parameter model. These results do not support either the linear or the one-parameter concave model. The results do support important features of the constant relative risk averse model (CRRAM), such as linearity of bid functions and invariance of bidding behavior to a multiplicative transformation of payoffs. However, the homogeneity property of CRRAM bid functions is violated by 22% of the subjects. In addition, subject bids are generally inconsistent with the predictions of the conjunction of CRRAM and square or square root transformations of payoffs. We develop a specific three-parameter model, CRRAM*, based on a utility of winning and a threshold utility of surplus, to account for the observed nonzero bid function intercepts. Five new experiments (30 subjects) yield results that are consistent with the testable implications of CRRAM*.

1. The log-concave equilibrium model of bidding in the first-price auction

Consider an F auction where the seller's reservation price is zero and, therefore, no nonpositive bid can be a winning bid. Let there be $n \geqslant 2$ bidders. Each bidder's monetary value, v_i, $i = 1, \ldots, n$, for the auctioned object is independently drawn from the probability distribution with *cdf* $H(\cdot)$ on $[0,\bar{v}]$. $H(\cdot)$ has a continuous density function that is positive on $(0,\bar{v})$. Bidders are assumed to know their own v_i but to know only the distribution from which their rivals' values are drawn.

The utility to any bidder i of a winning bid in the amount b_i is the von Neumann-Morgenstern utility $u(v_i - b_i, \theta_i)$, where θ_i is an $M - 1$ vector of parameters that is independently drawn from the probability distribution with integrable *cdf* $\Phi(\cdot)$ on the convex set Θ. Each bidder knows his or her own θ_i but knows only that his or her rivals' θ's are drawn from the distribution $\Phi(\cdot)$. Thus, a bidder is represented by (v_i,θ_i), where v_i is his or her (scalar) auctioned object value and θ_i is his or her $M - 1$ vector of other individual characteristics that affect bidding behavior in this M-parameter log-concave model. Assume that $u(y,\theta)$ is twice continuously differentiable and strictly increasing in monetary payoff y and normalized such that $u(0,\theta) = 0$, for all $\theta \in \Theta$. Finally, assume that $u(y,\theta)$ is strictly log-concave in y, for each $\theta \in \Theta$; that is, assume that $u_1(y,\theta)/u(y,\theta)$ is strictly decreasing in y for each $\theta \in \Theta$ (where $u_1(y,\theta)$ is the derivative of $u(y,\theta)$ with respect to y). This means that bidder preferences for risky monetary payoff can be risk averse, risk neutral, or risk preferring, but they must be less convex than e^y.

Assume that bidder i believes that each of his or her rivals will use the differentiable bid function, $b(v,\theta)$, that is strictly increasing in v and has the property $b(0,\theta) = 0$ for all $\theta \in \Theta$. The bid function $b(v,\theta)$ has a v-inverse function $\pi(b,\theta)$ that is differentiable and strictly increasing in b. The probability that any randomly selected bidder using $b(v,\theta)$ will bid some amount less than or equal to b is

$$F(b) = \int_{\Theta} H(\pi(b,\theta))\, d\Phi(\theta) \tag{1}$$

and the probability that all $n - 1$ rivals of bidder i will bid amounts less than or equal to b is

$$G(b) = [F(b)]^{n-1} \tag{2}$$

Thus, if bidder i believes that his or her rivals will use bid function $b(v,\theta)$, with v-inverse function $\pi(b,\theta)$, then the expected utility to bidder i of a bid in the amount b_i is given by Equations (1), (2), and

$$U(b_i|v_i,\theta_i) = G(b_i)\, u(v_i - b_i,\theta_i) \tag{3}$$

If $\pi(b,\theta)$ is to be the v-inverse of an equilibrium bid function, then it must be a best reply for bidder i. The first order condition for $b_i > 0$ to maximize Equation (3) is

$$0 = U'(b_i|v_i,\theta_i) = G'(b_i)\, u(v_i - b_i,\theta_i) - G(b_i)\, u_1(v_i - b_i,\theta_i) \tag{4}$$

Substituting $\pi(b_i,\theta_i)$ for v_i in Equation (4) yields

$$0 = G'(b_i)\, u(\pi(b_i,\theta_i) - b_i,\theta_i) - G(b_i)\, u_1(\pi(b_i,\theta_i) - b_i,\theta_i) \tag{5}$$

Equation (5) implies

$$\frac{d}{db_i}(G(b_i)\, u(\pi(b_i,\theta_i) - b_i,\theta_i)) = G(b_i)\, u_1(\pi(b_i,\theta_i) - b_i,\theta_i)\, \pi_1(b_i,\theta_i) \tag{6}$$

where $\pi_1(\cdot)$ is the derivative of $\pi(\cdot)$ with respect to its first argument. Integration in Equation (6) yields

$$G(b_i)\, u(\pi(b_i,\theta_i) - b_i,\theta_i) = \int_0^{b_i} G(x)\, u_1(\pi(x,\theta_i) - x,\theta_i)\pi_1(x,\theta_i)\, dx + C \tag{7}$$

Evaluation of Equation (7) for $b = 0$ yields $C = 0$; hence

$$G(b_i)\, u(\pi(b_i,\theta_i) - b_i,\theta_i) = \int_0^{b_i} G(x)\, u_1(\pi(x,\theta_i) - x,\theta_i)\pi_1(x,\theta_i)\, dx \tag{8}$$

We will now show that bidder i will maximize his or her expected utility by bidding b_i, when his or her value is $\pi(b_i,\theta_i)$, for any $b_i > 0$ in the domain of $\pi(\cdot,\theta_i)$. Hence, $\pi(b,\theta)$ given by Equation (8) is the υ-inverse of an equilibrium bid function. First note that the way in which Equation (8) was derived implies that $(b_i,\pi(b_i,\theta_i))$ satisfies the first order condition shown in Equation (4). (Alternatively, differentiate Equation (8) with respect to b_i and get Equation (5); then note that Equation (5) implies that $(b_i,\pi(b_i,\theta_i))$ satisfies Equation (4)). Next, note that Equations (3) and (8) imply that $U(b_i\,|\,\pi(b_i,\theta_i),\theta_i) > 0$, for $b_i > 0$, because the integrand in Equation (8) is positive for all $x > 0$.

Next, define

$$\rho(b) = \frac{G'(b)}{G(b)} \tag{9}$$

and

$$\mu(\upsilon - b,\theta) = \frac{u_1(\upsilon - b,\theta)}{u(\upsilon - b,\theta)} \tag{10}$$

Equations (3), (4), (9), and (10) imply

$$U'(b_i|\upsilon_i,\theta_i) = U(b_i|\upsilon_i,\theta_i)[\rho(b_i) - \mu(\upsilon_i - b_i,\theta_i)] \tag{11}$$

Differentiation of Equation (11) yields

$$\begin{aligned} U''(b_i|\upsilon_i,\theta_i) &= U'(b_i|\upsilon_i,\theta_i)[\rho(b_i) - \mu(\upsilon_i - b_i,\theta_i)] \\ &\quad + U(b_i|\upsilon_i,\theta_i)[\rho'(b_i) + \mu_1(\upsilon_i - b_i,\theta_i)] \end{aligned} \tag{12}$$

Since $U(b_i\,|\,\pi(b_i,\theta_i),\theta_i) > 0$, for $b_i > 0$, Equations (4) and (11) imply that, for $b_i > 0$,

$$\rho(b_i) = \mu(\pi(b_i,\theta_i) - b_i,\theta_i) \tag{13}$$

Differentiation of Equation (13) yields

$$\pi_1(b_i,\theta_i)\, \mu_1(\pi(b_i,\theta_i) - b_i,\theta_i) = \rho'(b_i) + \mu_1(\pi(b_i,\theta_i) - b_i,\theta_i) \tag{14}$$

Substitution from Equations (13) and (14) into Equation (12) yields

$$U''(b_i|\pi(b_i,\theta_i),\theta_i) = U(b_i|\pi(b_i,\theta_i),\theta_i)\, \pi_1(b_i,\theta_i)\mu_1(\pi(b_i,\theta_i) - b_i,\theta_i) \tag{15}$$

Since $U(b_i \mid \pi(b_i,\theta_i),\theta_i) > 0$ and $\mu_1(\cdot) < 0$, Equation (15) implies that $U''(b_i \mid \pi(b_i,\theta_i),\theta_i) < 0$ if and only if $\pi_1(b_i,\theta_i) > 0$, as was initially assumed.

We next show that $(b_i,\pi(b_i,\theta_i))$ yields a global maximum of Equation (3). Suppose the contrary that $(\bar{b},\pi(\hat{b},\theta_i))$ maximizes Equation (3) for $\bar{b} \neq \hat{b}$. Then it must satisfy the first order condition. If $\bar{b} > \hat{b}$, then the first order condition for $(\bar{b},\pi(\hat{b},\theta_i))$ and the strictly increasing property of $u(\cdot)$ and $-\mu(\cdot)$ in $\pi(\cdot)$ and of $\pi(\cdot)$ in b imply

$$
\begin{aligned}
0 &= U'(\bar{b} \mid \pi(\hat{b},\theta_i),\theta_i) && (16)\\
&= G(\bar{b})\, u(\pi(\hat{b},\theta_i) - \bar{b},\theta_i)[\rho(\bar{b}) - \mu(\pi(\hat{b},\theta_i) - \bar{b},\theta_i)]\\
&< G(\bar{b})\, u(\pi(\bar{b},\theta_i) - \bar{b},\theta_i)[\rho(\bar{b}) - \mu(\pi(\bar{b},\theta_i) - \bar{b},\theta_i)]
\end{aligned}
$$

But Equation (16) contradicts the fact that $(\bar{b},\pi(\bar{b},\theta_i))$ satisfies the first order condition. Alternatively, let $\bar{b} < \hat{b}$. Then, the first order condition for $(\bar{b},\pi(\bar{b},\theta_i))$ and the monotonicity properties of $u(\cdot)$, $-\mu(\cdot)$, and $\pi(\cdot)$ imply

$$
\begin{aligned}
0 &= U'(\bar{b} \mid \pi(\bar{b},\theta_i),\theta_i) && (17)\\
&= G(\bar{b})\, u(\pi(\bar{b},\theta_i) - \bar{b},\theta_i)[\rho(\bar{b}) - \mu(\pi(\bar{b},\theta_i) - \bar{b},\theta_i)]\\
&< G(\bar{b})\, u(\pi(\hat{b},\theta_i) - \bar{b},\theta_i)[\rho(\bar{b}) - \mu(\pi(\hat{b},\theta_i) - \bar{b},\theta_i)]
\end{aligned}
$$

But Equation (17) contradicts the fact that $(\bar{b},\pi(\hat{b},\theta_i))$ must satisfy the first order condition if it is to maximize Equation (3). We conclude that $(b_i,\pi(b_i,\theta_i))$ is the best reply for bidder i. Therefore, $\pi(b,\theta)$ given by Equation (8) is the v-inverse of an equilibrium bid function. Since $\pi(b,\theta)$ is strictly increasing in b, it has a b-inverse $b(v,\theta)$, which is the equilibrium bid function.

One interesting question is the effect of risk attitude on equilibrium bids. Let θ^N, θ^A, and θ^P be the characteristic vectors of bidders who are risk neutral, risk averse, and risk preferring. Then, $u(v - b, \theta^N)$ is linear; $u(v - b, \theta^A)$ is strictly concave; and $u(v - b, \theta^P)$ is strictly convex in $(v - b)$. We will show that $b(v, \theta^A) > b(v, \theta^N) > b(v, \theta^P)$ for all positive v in the domain of $b(\cdot)$. Suppose that $b(\breve{v},\theta^A) \leqslant b(\breve{v}, \theta^N)$ for some $\breve{v} > 0$. Since $b(\cdot)$ is increasing in v and $b(0,\theta) = 0$ for all $\theta \in \Theta$, there exists $\hat{v} \leqslant \breve{v}$ such that $b(\hat{v}, \theta^N) = b(\breve{v}, \theta^A) = b$. Then Equation (4), linearity of $u(\cdot,\theta^N)$ and strict concavity of $u(\cdot, \theta^A)$, imply

$$
\hat{v} - b = \frac{u(\hat{v} - b,\theta^N)}{u_1(\hat{v} - b,\theta^N)} = \frac{G(b)}{G'(b)} = \frac{u(\breve{v} - b,\theta^A)}{u_1(\breve{v} - b,\theta^A)} > \breve{v} - b \tag{18}
$$

But Equation (18) implies $\hat{v} > \breve{v}$, a contradiction. Therefore, we cannot maintain the supposition that there exists $\breve{v} > 0$ such that $b(\breve{v}, \theta^A) \leqslant b(\breve{v}, \theta^N)$. A similar argument, using the strict convexity of $u(\cdot, \theta^P)$, shows that we cannot maintain the supposition that there exists $\breve{v} > 0$ such that $b(\breve{v}, \theta^P) \geqslant b(\breve{v}, \theta^N)$. Hence, we conclude that $b(v, \theta^A) > b(v, \theta^N) > b(v, \theta^P)$, for all $v > 0$ in the domain of $b(\cdot)$.

We will now consider three special cases of the log-concave bidding model. First, consider the single parameter model where $M = 1$ (and, hence, each bidder i is characterized only by v_i). Then Equation (1) becomes

$$F(b) = H(\pi(b)) \tag{1a}$$

and Equation (8) becomes

$$[H(\pi(b_i))]^{N-1} u(\pi(b_i) - b_i) = \int_0^{b_i} [H(\pi(x))]^{N-1} u_1(\pi(x) - x)\, \pi'(x)\, dx \tag{8a}$$

This is the Holt (1980), Riley-Samuelson (1981), and Harris-Raviv (1981) identical bidders model of the F auction, generalized from concave to strictly log-concave preferences.

Next, assume in addition that $u(\cdot)$ is linear and that $H(\cdot)$ is the uniform distribution on $[0,\bar{v}]$. Then Equation (1) becomes

$$F(b) = \pi(b)/\bar{v} \tag{1b}$$

and Equation (8) becomes

$$\pi(b_i)^{n-1}[\pi(b_i) - b_i] = \int_0^{b_i} [\pi(x)]^{n-1}\, \pi'(x)\, dx = \frac{1}{n}[\pi(b_i)]^n \tag{8b}$$

Hence,

$$\pi(b_i) = \frac{n}{n-1} b_i \tag{19}$$

or

$$b(v_i) = \frac{n-1}{n} v_i \tag{20}$$

This is the Vickrey (1961) risk neutral bidders model of the F auction.

Finally, let $M = 2$, which implies that θ_i is now a scalar. Let θ_i be replaced by r_i. Assume that $r_i \in (0, \bar{r}]$, where $\bar{r} > 1$. Assume that $H(\cdot)$ is the uniform distribution on $[0,\bar{v}]$. Let $u(v_i - b_i, r_i) = (v_i - b_i)^{r_i}$. Then, for $b < (n-1)\bar{v}/(n-1+\bar{r})$, Equation (1) becomes[3]

$$F(b) = \underset{r}{\mathrm{E}}\left[\frac{\pi(b,r)}{\bar{v}}\right] \tag{1c}$$

and Equation (8) becomes

$$\left[\underset{r}{\mathrm{E}}\,(\pi(b_i,r))\right]^{n-1}[\pi(b_i,r_i) - b_i]^{r_i}$$

$$= \int_0^{b_i}\left[\underset{r}{\mathrm{E}}\,(\pi(x,r))\right]^{n-1} r_i[\pi(x,r_i) - x]^{r_i-1}\,\pi_1(x,r_i)dx \tag{8c}$$

with solution

$$\pi(b_i,r_i) = \frac{n - 1 + r_i}{n - 1}\,b_i \tag{21}$$

or

$$b(v_i,r_i) = \frac{n - 1}{n - 1 + r_i}\,v_i \tag{22}$$

This is the constant relative risk averse model (CRRAM) in Cox, Roberson, and Smith (1982), generalized from concave to strictly log-concave preferences.

2. Experimental designs

The empirical results presented in the next section are drawn from 690 F auctions conducted in 47 experiments. These experiments fall into three design categories (see Table 1):

I. Experiments with ten F auctions, where the F auctions were preceded and followed by sequences of ten Dutch autions.[4]
II. Experiments with 20 F auctions (in ten auction sequences), where the two sequences of F auctions were separated by a ten auction sequence using the Dutch auction.
III. Experiments consisting of 20 or 25 F auctions only. These experiments are listed as series 1′ and 4 in Table 1.

The complete instructions given to all subjects are presented in Cox, Roberson, and Smith (1982) for designs I and II and in Cox, Smith, and Walker (1985b) for design III. Due to their length, we will summarize here only the key points developed in the instructions and other significant experimental design features.

The experiments were conducted using the PLATO computer system. This system allows us to ensure that all experiments are conducted in the same manner and that experimenter–subject interaction is minimized. The PLATO system also facilitates the accounting process required for each auction and reduces subject transaction costs in bidding and obtaining information.

All experiments used volunteers from populations of undergraduate students at Indiana University and the University of Arizona. The subjects were enrolled in undergraduate economics courses. Before enlisting volunteers, the recruiter gave the students a brief explanation of what it meant to be in an economics experiment, including a short discussion describing the opportunity for subjects to earn cash from participating in the experiment.

Other important characteristics of the experiments can be summarized as follows:

1. Upon arrival at the site of the experiment (at the scheduled time) each subject received a $3.00 payment, which had been promised during the recruiting procedure.
2. After all subjects arrived, each was assigned randomly to one of the PLATO terminals. At this time, each subject received, at his or her own pace, PLATO video screen instructions explaining the key properties of the auction institution in which he or she would be participating.
3. In experiments involving either design I or II, the 30 auctions of each experiment were divided into 3 ten-auction segments, using a classical ABA experimental design. Thus experiments were of the form: *F*-Dutch-*F* or Dutch-*F*-Dutch. Initial instructions explained only the rules of the first institution to be implemented. After the initial ten auctions, the subjects were informed by PLATO of the change to alternative auction rules and received a brief description of the change in procedures. Subjects were not informed ex ante of the total number of auctions or that the auction procedures would change during the experiment. However, at the beginning of each ten-auction segment, subjects were informed that there would be ten auctions using the currently applicable institution. In experiments using design III, subjects knew there would be many *F* auctions but not the exact number.
4. The monetary values of the abstract objects being auctioned were induced using a concept commonly referred to as *resale values*. In this procedure, each subject is informed that for any winning bid the bidder will receive a profit equal to his or her resale value, v_i, minus the amount bid.
5. Using nontechnical language, each bidder was informed that his or her resale value would be: (a) drawn from a finite set contained in the interval $[\underline{v},\bar{v}]$; and (b) drawn randomly (with replacement) for each auction with each possible value having an equal probability of being chosen. Subjects were also informed that the resale values for the other bidders would be drawn independently (with replacement) and in the same manner. In designs I and II, subjects were informed that resale values would be drawn in multiples of $0.10 and with $\underline{v}$ = $0.10, while in design III the values were drawn in $0.01 increments and with $\underline{v} = 0$.
6. In designs I and II, each subject knew in advance his or her own resale values for all ten auctions of a given experimental segment. Bids were limited to the range $[\underline{v}, v_i]$, with each subject having one bid per auction. Alternatively, in

design III each subject learned his or her resale value in auction t prior to bidding in auction t but did *not* know resale values for auctions to follow. Further, bids were limited to the range $[\underline{v}, \bar{v}]$. Again, each subject had one bid per auction.

7. Subjects were informed of the number of other bidders participating in the auctions.
8. If all bidders were to adopt the Vickrey (1961) risk neutral equilibrium bid function for the F auction, then the expected gain to a bidder would be the amount $E[g] = \$[(\bar{v} - \underline{v})/n(n + 1)]$ per auction (Cox, Roberson, and Smith, 1982, Equation 4.1). To provide some uniformity in expected profits with variations in n, we chose $\bar{v}$ as a function of n so that $E[g]$ would remain approximately constant across experiments within a given design. In designs I and II, this amount was \$0.40 per auction per bidder or \$12.00 per experiment, and in design III, where the experiments were run after those of designs I and II, we increased the amount to \$0.50 per auction per bidder. There were also several experiments (to be discussed later) where we enhanced substantially the expected payoffs. Experiments lasted approximately one and one-half hours. The first three columns of Table 1 summarize the design parameters of our basic series of F auction experiments. In series 1′ and 4, we increased the payoffs to adjust for inflation since the earlier experiments were conducted.

3. Experimental results: tests for discriminating among nash models

From the development in Section 1, we have two noncooperative equilibrium bidding models that postulate identical bidders: (1) the Vickrey risk neutral (linear utility) model, and its generalization (2) the Holt-Riley-Samuelson-Harris-Raviv risk averse (concave utility) model. In Subsections 3.1 and 3.2, we provide data and tests designed to determine whether bidding behavior is consistent with the risk neutral or risk averse models (or neither). In Subsection 3.3, we examine the hypothesis that (relative to the "noise" in individual bidding) the n bidders in each experiment exhibit distinct bidding behaviors as against the null alternative that individuals are not so distinguishable. If individuals bid as if they used distinct bid functions, this would be inconsistent with both the risk neutral and risk averse models, (1) and (2), but consistent with the general log-concave model. However, if bidding behavior is to be consistent with the log-linear model, CRRAM, individual bids also must be linear homogeneous functions of values. In Subsection 3.4, we present a report of the results of linear bid-value regressions for all subjects and some representative charts of individual bids as functions of corresponding realized values. In Subsection 3.5, we ask whether, and how, bidding behavior is affected by the lumpiness of bids. Since CRRAM also implies that increasing payoffs by any multiplicative constant will have no effect on (linear) bidding behavior, we also report comparison tests between experiments in which payoffs were tripled relative to experiments in which payoffs were not tripled for each subject.

3.1. Are winning bids (prices) consistent with risk neutral or risk averse bidding?

Vickrey's risk neutral model predicts the normalized price,

$$[p_n(t) - \underline{v}] = \left[\frac{n-1}{n}\right]\left[\max_i v_i^*(t) - \underline{v}\right] \tag{23}$$

where $v_i^*(t)$ is bidder i's realized value from the constant density on $[\underline{v},\bar{v}]$. Table 1 lists the characteristics of each series of experiments including n, the number of bidders (column 1), T, the number of auctions conducted (column 2), and $\bar{v}$, the maximum possible value (column 3). The pooled mean observed price for each series is reported in column 4 and the mean deviation of observed prices $p(t)$ from the risk neutral predicted price $p_n(t)$ is reported in column 5. These deviations are all significantly above zero (by the usual t test criterion, column 6), with the excep-

Table 1. Pooled t Tests of Price Deviations from Risk Neutral Predictions

Series (No. of Bidders)	Total Number of Auctions, T	Max Value, $\bar{v}$	Mean Observed Price	Mean Deviation from Risk Neutral Price[a]	Paired t Statistic[b]
1 (3)	70	4.90	2.44	.033	0.6
1′ (3)	100	6.00	3.69	.800	20.4*
2 (4)	60	8.10	5.64	.796	15.0*
3 (4)	30	8.10	5.90	.848	14.3*
4 (4)	250	10.00	6.90	1.044	24.1*
5 (5)	60	12.10	9.14	1.096	20.4*
6 (5)	30	12.10	8.96	.924	6.0*
7 (6)	60	16.90	13.22	.944	7.3*
8 (9)	30	36.10	31.02	2.031	13.1*

a. Mean deviations computed relative to the risk neutral price applying to the realized values (i.e.,

$$\frac{1}{T}\sum_{t=1}^{T}\delta(t),$$

where

$$\delta(t) = [p^*(t) - \underline{v}] - \left(\frac{n-1}{n}\right)[\max_i v_i^*(t) - \underline{v}],\ p^*(t)$$

is the observed price, and $v_i^*(t)$ the realized value for subject i in auction t. In series 4, the lowest possible value $\underline{v} = 0$, and in the others, $\underline{v} = 0.10$.

b. Two-tailed test of null hypothesis that the mean price deviations are zero ($p < 0.05$). *indicates rejection of the null hypothesis

tion of the series 1 deviations for $n = 3$. The deviant results for $n = 3$, and the fact that Kagel and Levin did not get deviant results for this case, led us to schedule the series 1′ experiments *without* the switchover treatment in designs I and II discussed in section 2.[5] In Table 1, it is clear that the series 1′ results for $n = 3$ do not exhibit any qualitative differences from the results for $n > 3$. These new results require correction of our earlier reported claim that the data for $n = 3$ were inconsistent with Nash risk averse bidding (Cox, Roberson, and Smith, 1982; Cox, Smith, and Walker, 1984). With the exception of series 1′, all the results in Table 1 have been reported previously by Cox, Roberson, and Smith (1982) or by Isaac and Walker (1985). Both earlier studies were confined to the analysis of auction market prices. We turn now to the analysis of all individual bids.

3.2. Are individual bids consistent with risk neutral or risk averse bidding?

More extensive than the price results of Table 1, showing that winning bids are inconsistent with the linear model and consistent with the concave model, are the results in Table 2 of the analysis of all bids submitted by each subject. In series 1 through 8 and 1′ we have data on the bidding behavior of 166 subjects. The baseline controls used in the additional experiments (series 9 and 10) reported in Section 4 (and in series 11 to be reported elsewhere) applied the same conditions as in series 1 through 8 and provide data on an additional 36 subjects. Since many groups were composed of experienced subjects (those denoted with an "x" in Table 2 who had participated in a previous experiment), not all of the subjects in Table 2 are distinct.

In Table 2, subjects are classified according to bidding group size (n) in column 1, inexperienced or experienced in column 2, and number of sequential auctions (observations) for each group in column 3. Column 4 lists the number of subjects bidding as if risk averse (i.e., the number of subjects for whom the sign of the Wilcoxon statistic) computed for the deviations

$$b_i^*(t) - \underline{v} - \frac{(n-1)}{n}(v_i^*(t) - \underline{v}) \tag{24}$$

is positive. Similarly, column 5 lists the number of subjects bidding as if risk preferring (the Wilcoxon statistic is negative). In both columns 4 and 5, the subset of subjects for whom the test statistic indicates that the deviations are significantly different from zero (different from risk neutral) are shown in parentheses (two-tail tests, $p < .05$). For example, in series 2, the experiments used subjects in groups of $n = 4$ bidders. The second row under series 2 shows that four subjects participated in an experiment with 20 auctions, of which three subjects showed risk averse bidding behavior (two of these were significantly risk averse) and one showed risk preferring behavior.

With the exception of series 1, in most of the experiments reported in Table 2 all

Table 2. Subjects Classified by Results of Wilcoxon Test That Bids are Risk Neutral[a]

Series (No. of Bidders)	Total Number of Subjects	Observations per Subject	Risk Averse Subjects (No. for which H_0 is rejected)[b]	Risk Preferring Subjects (No. for which H_0 is rejected)[b]
1(3)	6	10	2	4
	6	20	4	2
	3x	10	2	1
1′(3)	6	20	5(5)	1(1)
	9x	20	9(9)	0
2(4)	4	10	4(2)	0
	4	20	3(2)	1
	4x	10	3(2)	1
	4x	20	4(4)	0
3(4)	4x	10	4(3)	0
	4x	20	4(3)	0
4(4)	40	25	39(37)	1
5(5)	5	10	5(3)	0
	5	20	5(5)	0
	5x	10	5(4)	0
	5x	20	5(4)	0
6(5)	5	10	3	2
	5	20	5(4)	0
7(6)	12	10	8(3)	4(1)
	12	20	11(8)	1
8(9)	9	10	9(3)	0
	9	20	9(7)	0
9(4)	4x	12	4(2)	0
	8x	20	8(7)	0
10(4)	12	25	12(10)	0
11(4)	12x	20	12(11)	0
Total	202(62x)		184(138)	18(2)

a. Two-tailed test of the null hypothesis that individual subject bids do not differ from the risk neutral Nash equilibrium bid

$$b_i^*(t) - \underline{v} - \left(\frac{n-1}{n}\right)(v_i^*(t) - \underline{v}).$$

b. Subjects for whom the sign of the Wilcoxon statistic is positive (negative) are classified as risk averters (preferrers). Where the sign is ambiguous, depending upon how ties are counted in the Wilcoxon test, we use the t statistic to classify subjects (seven cases).

x denotes experienced subjects.

of the subjects bid as if risk averse, and in most cases their bids were significantly greater than risk neutral bids. Across all experiments, excluding series 1, 94% of the subjects exhibited risk averse behavior.

3.3. Do the n *bidders in each experiment exhibit distinct bidding behavior?*

Tables 1 and 2 provide strong support for the hypothesis that the overwhelming majority of individuals bid as if they are risk averse. This is consistent with the risk averse, identical bidders, Nash model. But does individual bidding behavior enable us to distinguish among individuals? Clearly, if each individual's bids are highly variable or noisy relative to value, then the bids of the n individuals in a particular experiment might not be distinguishable, and the assumption of identical bidders might be an empirically justifiable (as well as useful) simplifying assumption. Table 3 uses the nonparametric Kruskal-Wallace H test (an n-sample generalization of the Wilcoxon test) to test the null hypothesis that the $n \times T$ bid deviations from the risk neutral prediction,

$$b_i^*(t) - \underline{v} - \frac{n-1}{n}(v_i^*(t) - \underline{v}), t = 1,2, \ldots, T; i = 1,2, \ldots, n \tag{25}$$

represent n samples of size T from the same population. In this interpretation the research hypothesis is represented by any nonidentical bidders model (such as the log-concave model of Section 1), and the null hypothesis is represented by the risk averse, identical bidders model. Note that in applying a nonparametric test we eschew here any commitment to the special (linear) properties of CRRAM, which will be examined in the next two Subsections. Table 3 reports the H test χ^2 statistic for 47 experiments. The null hypothesis is rejected in 28 of the 47 (60%) of the experiments. Thus, the assumption of identical bidding behavior appears not to be tanable, although 40% of the bidding groups do bid as if composed of identical individuals. Bid function diversity is a prominent, but not extreme, characteristic of our subject pool.

3.4. Tests and empirical results of CRRAM

We find strong support for the hypothesis that individuals bid as if they are risk averse and as if they have distinct attitudes toward risk. The qualitative results reported earlier suggest that sharper tests based on CRRAM are in order.

The implication of CRRAM is that each agent's bids will be a homogeneous linear function of the corresponding values for bids that do not exceed

$$\bar{b} = \underline{v} + (n-1)(\bar{v} - \underline{v})/(n - 1 + \bar{r}) \tag{26}$$

Table 3. *H* Test of H_0 That Bidders Have Identical Bid Functions

Experiment No. by Series	Number of Bidders (No. of Auctions)	*H* Statistic for $b_i^*(t) - b_n(v_i^*(t))$	Experiment No. by Series	Number of Bidders (No. of Auctions)	*H* Statistic for $b_i^*(t) - b_n^*(v_i(t))$
1.1	3 (10)	0.5	4.6	4 (25)	10.2†
1.2	3 (20)	6.3†	4.7	4 (25)	9.6†
1.3	3 (20)	6.2†	4.8	4 (25)	41.7†
1.4	3 (10)	3.8	4.9	4 (25)	8.3†
1.5x	3 (10)	3.2	4.10	4 (25)	11.8†
1′.1	3 (20)	22.6†	5.1	5 (10)	4.4
1′.2	3 (20)	3.3	5.2	5 (20)	15.4†
1′.3x	3 (20)	1.5	5.1x	5 (20)	9.2
1′.4x	3 (20)	0.1	5.2x	5 (10)	12.4†
1.5x	3 (20)	1.2	6.1	5 (10)	9.6†
2.1	4 (20)	18.5†	6.2	5 (20)	10.5†
2.2	4 (10)	3.6	7.1	6 (10)	24.4†
2.3x	4 (10)	20.1†	7.2	6 (20)	20.5†
2.4x	4 (20)	3.4	7.3	6 (10)	6.8
3.1x	4 (10)	7.3	7.4	6 (20)	17.2†
3.2x	4 (20)	3.8	8.1	9 (20)	34.6†
4.1	4 (25)	7.0	8.2	9 (10)	19.6†
4.2	4 (25)	0.3	9.1x	4 (12)	7.7†
4.3	4 (25)	3.1	9.2x	4 (20)	27.4†
4.4	4 (25)	2.9	9.3x	4 (20)	22.3†
4.5	4 (25)	13.0†	10.1	4 (25)	7.9†
			10.2	4 (25)	2.0
			10.3	4 (25)	26.2†
			11.1x	4 (20)	11.3†
			11.2x	4 (20)	8.3†
			11.3x	4 (20)	11.5†

x denotes experienced subjects.
†χ^2 test rejects H_0 ($p < 0.05$) that individual bid deviations from risk neutral predictions are from the same population.

the maximum bid that would be entered by the least risk averse agent in the population. If $\bar{r} = 1$, the regression hypothesis is that

$$b_i(t) = \alpha_i + \beta_i v_i(t) + \varepsilon_i(t), \text{ for } v_i(t) \leq \bar{v}_i = \left(\frac{n-1+r_i}{n-1}\right)\bar{b} = \left(\frac{n-1+r_i}{n}\right)\bar{v} \tag{27}$$

where the b_i, v_i, $\bar{b}$, and $\bar{v}$, are measured (normalized) relative to $\underline{v}$, $\varepsilon_i(t)$ is a random error term with mean zero, $\alpha_i = 0$, and $\beta_i = (n-1)/(n-1+r_i)$. If we estimate the parameters for each i, CRRAM predicts that the resulting sample estimates of α_i should vary symmetrically around zero (i. e., positive values of $\hat{\alpha}_i$ are as likely as negative values). Hence, any pronounced tendency for the $\hat{\alpha}_i$ to be either positive or negative can be interpreted as a result that is inconsistent with CRRAM. Also, CRRAM implies that the estimates $\hat{\beta}_i$ provide estimates of the risk parameters $\hat{r}_i = (n-1)(1-\hat{\beta}_i)/\hat{\beta}_i$. These estimates are not unbiased because $\hat{r}_i$ is nonlinear in $\hat{\beta}_i$. For this reason, the statistical tests reported in this Subsection concentrate on the estimates of β_i and α_i.

In Table 4, a summary of the regression estimates $(\hat{\alpha}_i, \hat{\beta}_i)$ for Equation (27) are reported for a total of 156 subjects; 33 of the 156 subjects participated in two different experiments with the same n, and the results from each subject's two experiments are pooled in Table 4. Also, for these 33 subjects, we estimated the regression coefficients $(\hat{\alpha}_i^1, \hat{\beta}_i^1)$ and $(\hat{\alpha}_i^2, \hat{\beta}_i^2)$ for each of the two experiments and computed the F test of the null composite hypothesis H_0: ($\alpha_i^1 = \alpha_i^2$ and $\beta_i^1 = \beta_i^2$) that the

Table 4. Summary of Regression Estimates of $\hat{\alpha}_i$, $\hat{\beta}_i$

Number of Bidders, n	Total Subjects	Number of $\hat{\alpha}_i$ Significantly* Different from Zero (percent)	Number of $\hat{\beta}_i$ Significantly* Different from $(n-1)/n$ (percent)	Number of $\hat{\alpha}_i < 0$ (percent)	Number of $\hat{\beta}_i > (n-1)/n$ (percent)
3	27	5(18.5)	15(55.6)	15(55.6)	23(85.2)
4	67	12(17.9)	51(76.1)	36(53.7)	64(95.5)
5	20	6(30.0)	14(70.0)	14(70.0)	19(95.0)
6	24	3(12.5)	13(54.2)	18(32.7)	19(79.2)
9	18	8(44.4)	16(88.8)	15(83.3)	18(100)
Total	156	34(21.8)	109(69.9)	98(62.8)	143(91.7)

*Two-tailed t-tests. The $\hat{\alpha}_i$ are all normalized by subtracting $\underline{v} > 0$ where appropriate. Letting v_i, $\bar{v}_i$, and $\bar{v}$ be similarly normalized, all regressions deleted those observations for which $v_i > \bar{v}_i = (n-1+r_i)\bar{v}/n$, the nonlinear domain of the normalized bid function. The regressions were run both with and without the deletion of nonpositive profit bids (bids of zero and bids equal to or greater than value, when $v_i > 0$). The deletion had no (or a minor) effect in most of the cases. For example, 25 of the 40 subjects in series 4 had none of their bids affected by this deletion. All regression results reported here are for the data excluding these bids.

two regression lines come from a population with the same linear parameters. We interpret this as a test of bidder consistency in separate experiments with the same number of bidders. The empirical probability distribution of the resulting values of the F statistic is shown in Figure 1. Note that for about 80% of the subjects (26 individuals), the null hypothesis cannot be rejected. A nonparametric Wilcoxon test (used in Table 3 to compare different individuals in the same group) of each bidder's consistency failed to reject the null hypothesis for 88% of the subjects. This contrasts with the results in Table 3, where for 40% of the bidding groups we could not reject the null hypothesis that individuals in the same group use identical bid functions. Thus, the bidding behavior of the same individuals in different experiments is much less distinguishable than the bidding behavior of different individuals in the same group.

Figure 2 plots the distribution of the R^2 statistic (unadjusted for degrees of freedom) for the 156 regressions summarized in Table 4. The independent variable $v_i(t)$ accounts for less than 91% of the variation in bids for only about 6% of the subjects. For about 80% of the subjects, v_i explains over 96% of the bid variation. Thus, individual subject bids tend to exhibit a remarkably strong linear relationship with values.

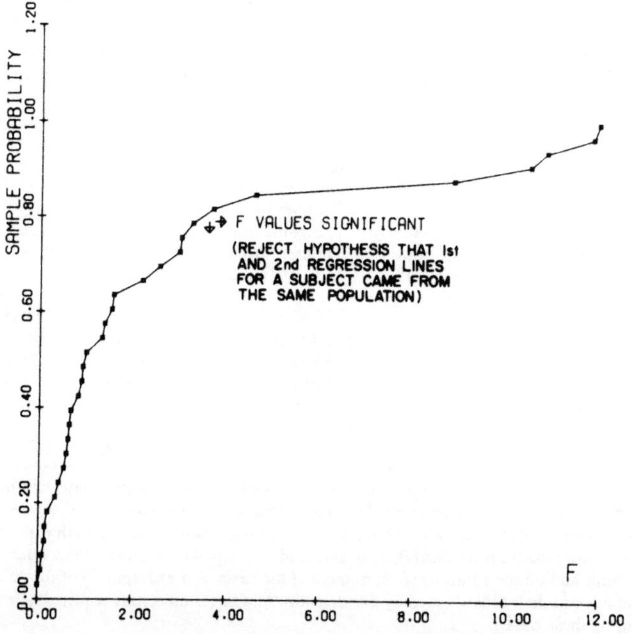

Fig. 1. Distribution of F values for tests of subject consistency

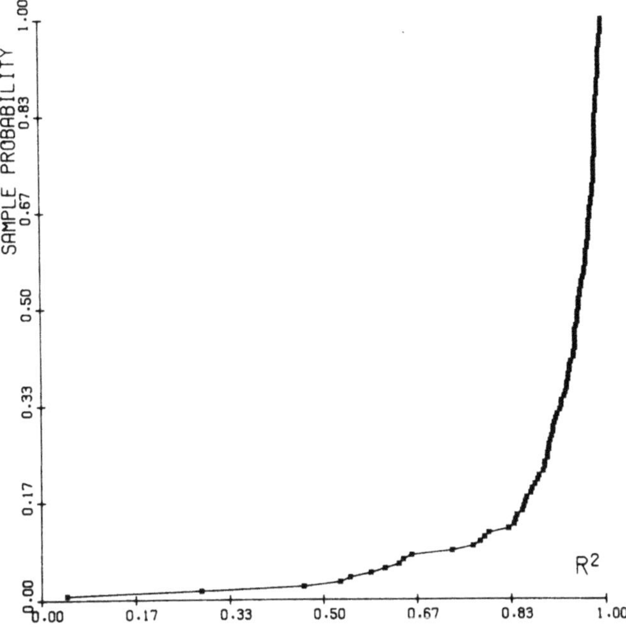

Fig. 2. Distribution of *R* squared for bid-value regressions

Returning to Table 4 (column 6) we note that, for all n, about 92% of the slopes of the estimated bid functions are consistent with risk averse bidding. Approximately 70% (column 4) of the $\hat{\beta}_i$ are significantly above the risk neutral level. But 21.8% of the intercepts are significantly different from zero, with a strong tendency for the $\hat{\alpha}_i$ to be negative (62.8%). The binomial test easily rejects the hypothesis that this many negative $\hat{\alpha}_i$ could be due to chance if α_i in the population is as likely to be positive as negative. This tendency of the estimated linear bid functions to be non-homogeneous is inconsistent with CRRAM.

In Figures 3 through 9, we provide representative bid-value plots for several individual subjects. In each figure, the plotted bids and values have been normalized on the unit interval. These charts provide visual illustrations of the statistical findings from the 156 regressions summarized earlier. Figures 3, 4, 5, 6, and 7 provide typical plots of subject bidding behavior from groups of size n = 3, 4, 5, 6, and 9, respectively. Each subject's bids tend to be contained within the cone defined by CRRAM when $r_i \in (0,1]$. As n gets larger, this cone shrinks, but the model does well in tracking the consequent changes in bidding. Figure 8 illustrates the "throw away" bid phenomenon, which is one source of the tendency for the intercepts to be negative. Some subjects bid a much smaller proportion (sometimes zero) of

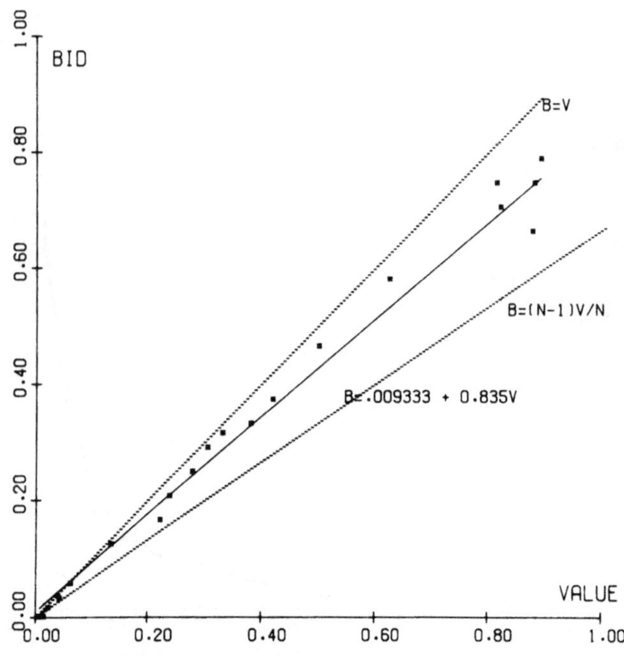

Fig. 3. Bidding behavior: Series 1′, Exp. 3, n = 3, Subject 3

their value when the realized value is at the low end of the $[\underline{v}, \bar{v}]$ interval than when the value is high enough to be likely to yield a winning bid. In Figure 8, several zero bids were entered, all of which occurred when the value realization was below $1.60. But at other values the subject bid more nearly a constant fraction of value. Figure 9 illustrates a less frequent but clearly identifiable bidding pattern, in which the subject quite consistently submits bids equal to or greater than value. One subject who did this commented that he knew such bids risked a loss if they were accepted, but that bidding in this way was like "playing Russian roulette." As illustrated in Figure 9, such bidding behavior can lead to a large and significantly positive $\hat{\alpha}_i$.

3.5. Further results: does the degree of discreteness matter? Does tripling payoffs matter? Are bid functions linear? Are bid functions stationary over successive auctions? Do the bid function slopes increase with n?

Series 2 and 3 used n = 4 subjects per bidding group and bids were required to be at discrete 30-cent subintervals on the interval [0.10, 8.10]. This was accomplished

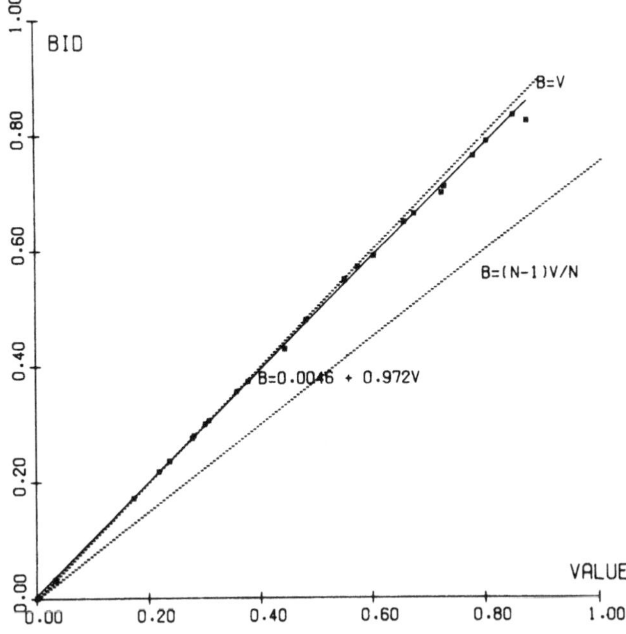

Fig. 4. Bidding behavior: Series 4, Exp. 5, $n = 4$, Subject 3

by rounding the subject's bid to the nearest 30-cent node, displaying the result to the subject, then asking the subject to either select a new trial bid for rounding or to enter (finalize) the current trial bid. Series 4 also used $n = 4$ subjects per bidding group, but bids could be entered at any one-cent node on the interval [0, 10.00]. Does this discreteness make a difference in the linear estimated bid function? Let $(\bar{\alpha}_{30}, \bar{\beta}_{30})$ be the pooled means of the estimates $(\hat{\alpha}_i, \hat{\beta}_i)$ for all i using 30-cent bid nodes and $(\bar{\alpha}_1, \bar{\beta}_1)$ be the means using one-cent nodes. We compute $\bar{\alpha}_{30} = -0.0952 < \bar{\alpha}_1 = 0.0307$, and the difference $d_\alpha = \bar{\alpha}_{30} - \bar{\alpha}_1 = -0.1259$ is significantly different from zero ($n = 56$, $t = 2.52$). We compute $\bar{\beta}_{30} = 0.9044 > \bar{\beta}_1 = 0.8784$, but the difference $d_\beta = \bar{\beta}_{30} - \bar{\beta}_1 = 0.026$ is not significantly different from zero ($n = 56$, $t = 1.44$). We conclude that the degree of discreteness matters in the sense that making the bid intervals smaller tends to increase (significantly) the mean of the estimated intercepts. However, discreteness does not matter in the sense that it has no significant effect on the mean of the estimated slopes of the bid functions. Thus, the tendency toward negative values of the $\hat{\alpha}_i$ reported in Table 4 may be an artifactual consequence of bid discreteness in experimental series 1–3 and 5–8. However, this does not eliminate the problem that some bidders bid a zero or a smaller frac-

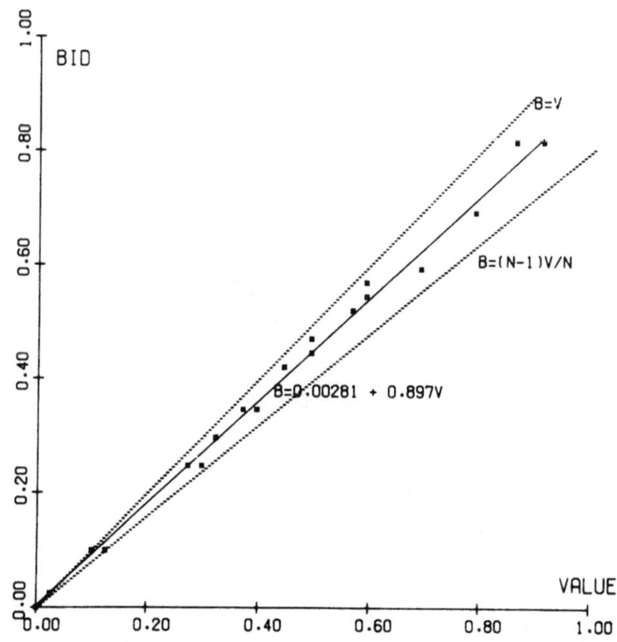

Fig. 5. Bidding behavior: Series 5, Exp. 2, $n = 5$, Subject 4

tion of value at low values or that a few bidders bid consciously and deliberately in excess of value. Both of these bidding patterns occurred in series 4 (see Figures 8 and 9) where the bid nodes were at one-cent intervals. These subjects clearly violate CRRAM.

A unique implication of CRRAM is that multiplying the profit of a winning bid $(v_i - b_i)$ by any factor $\lambda > 0$ affects only the utility scale $u_i = \lambda^{r_i}(v_i - b_i)^{r_i}$ and has no effect on the equilibrium bid. The series 6 experiments ($n = 5$) replicated the first two experiments in series 5, using the same sequences $v_i(t)$ but different subjects who were given the additional instruction that all PLATO computed earnings would be multiplied by three to determine their payoffs in U.S. currency. Eight of these subjects were then recruited to return to participate in the two series 3 experiments ($n = 4$). The latter replicated the first two experiments in series 2 except that payoffs were tripled. In series 3 (experienced subjects), let $(\bar{\alpha}_3, \bar{\beta}_3)$ be the mean regression parameters when $\lambda = 3$ and $(\bar{\alpha}_1, \bar{\beta}_1)$ be the means when $\lambda = 1$. We find $\bar{\alpha}_3 = -0.102$, $\bar{\alpha}_1 = -0.108$, and the difference is not significantly different from zero ($n = 16$, $t = 0.05$). Similarly, $\bar{\beta}_3 = 0.920$, $\bar{\beta}_1 = 0.892$, and the difference is not significant ($n = 16$, $t = 1.25$). In series 6, $\bar{\alpha}_3 = -0.200$, $\bar{\alpha}_1 = -0.281$, and the dif-

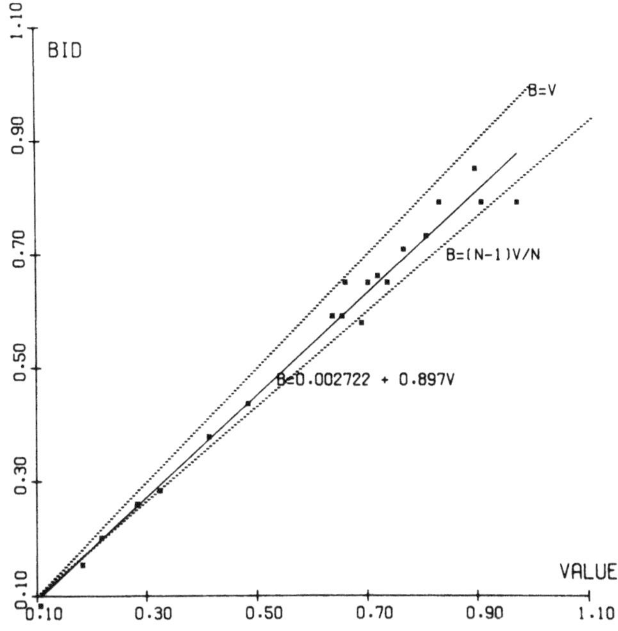

Fig. 6. Bidding behavior: Series 7, Exp. 2, $n = 6$, Subject 2

ference is not significant ($n = 20, t = 0.22$). Finally, $\bar{\beta}_3 = 0.892$, $\bar{\beta}_1 = 0.937$, and this difference is not significant ($n = 20$, $t = 1.17$). We conclude that for both experienced subjects ($n = 4$) and inexperienced subjects ($n = 5$), the effect of tripling payoffs on the estimates ($\hat{\alpha}_i$, $\hat{\beta}_i$) is minute compared with the sampling variability among individual subjects. This finding is consistent with CRRAM and inconsistent with any model that excludes log-linear preferences.

Within the class of log-concave preferences, any deviation from the log-linear utility assumption of CRRAM implies a nonlinear equilibrium bid function. Suppose we approximate such a bid function by the first three terms of its polynomial expansion. Then a test of CRRAM against the general log-concave model can be constructed by estimating the cubic equation,

$$b_i(t) = A_i + B_i v_i(t) + C_i v_i(t)^2 + D_i v_i(t)^3 + \eta_i(t) \tag{28}$$

If the null joint hypothesis H_0: $C_i = D_i = 0$ is not rejected by an F test, then CRRAM is supported over other log-concave preferences. We estimated Equation (28) for the 40 inexperienced subjects that participated in series 4 ($n = 4$). The

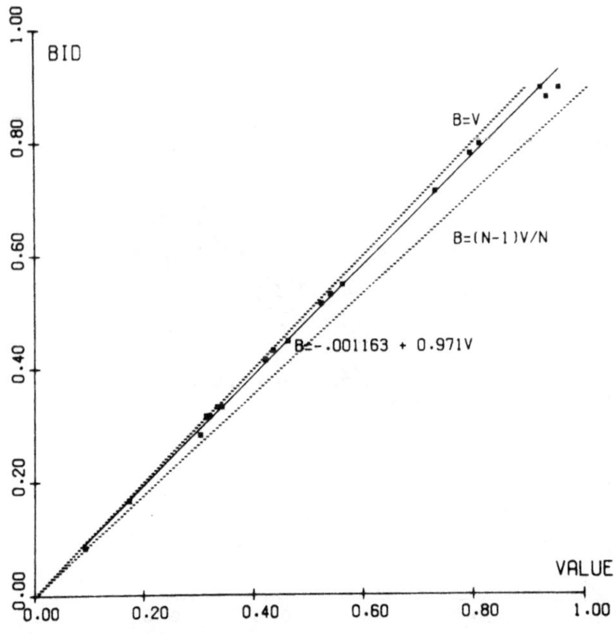

Fig. 7. Bidding behavior: Series 8, Exp. 1, $n = 9$, Subject 5

results of the F test cause us to reject H_0 for 15 (37.5%) of the subjects, but for 9 of these subjects neither $\hat{C}_i$ or $\hat{D}_i$ was significantly different from zero by the t test, suggesting only modest deviations from linearity. Also, 12 of these 15 nonlinear bid functions were concentrated in four experiments, each exhibiting at least two nonlinear bidders. This nonrandom "bunching" within experiments is implied by the log-concave model (i.e., an otherwise linear CRRAM bidder, i, will bid nonlinearly if any $j \neq i$ bids nonlinearly).[6] We conclude that 62.5% of these subjects are consistent with CRRAM, and it appears that most of the remaining subjects are consistent with the log-concave model.

Next, we ask whether individual bid functions are stationary over successive auctions by estimating the linear equation,

$$b_i(t) = A_i' + B_i'v_i(t) + C_i't + \mu_i(t) \tag{29}$$

Estimating Equation (29) for the series 4 experiments, we reject H_0: $C_i' = 0$ for eight (20%) of the subjects. The estimate of C_i' is negative for four and positive for four of these subjects, revealing no systematic learning trends.

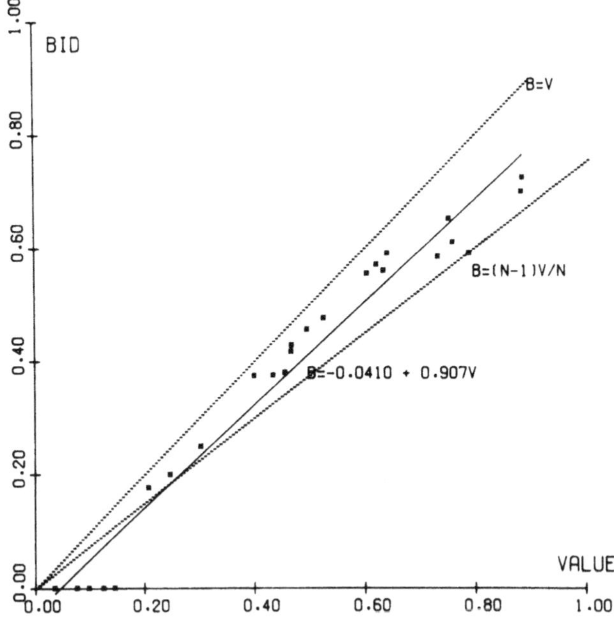

Fig. 8. Bidding behavior: Series 4, Exp. 3, $n = 4$, Subject 2

Finally, CRRAM predicts that the slope of individual bid functions is increasing in n. The sample means of these slopes across all subjects in each group size class ($\bar{\beta}$;n) are (0.765;3), (0.904;4), (0.925;5), (0.897;6), (0.999;9). The predicted ordering is satisfied except for the sample of subjects for which $n = 6$. However, no pair of the means for $n = 4$, 5, and 6 are significantly different from each other, so that resolution among them is not high, at least for the sample sizes we are using.

4. Tests of CRRAM that attempt to manipulate risk attitude

An implication of CRRAM is that if we apply the power transformation $\lambda(v_i - b_i)^q$ to the profit $v_i - b_i$ from a winning bid, the equilibrium bid function is independent of λ, but q enters the bid function as a multiplier of r_i. Thus, utility to agent i is $u_i = [\lambda(v_i - b_i)^q]^{r_i} = \lambda^{qr_i}(v_i - b_i)^{qr_i}$, and the normalized equilibrium bid function is $b_i = (n - 1)\, v_i/(n - 1 + qr_i)$ for all $b_i \in [0,\bar{b}]$, where $\bar{b} = (n - 1)\bar{v}/(n - 1 + q\bar{r})$ and $r_i \in (0,\bar{r}]$. If $q > 1$, the effect is to lower all equilibrium bids (i.e., subjects bid as if they are less risk averse). If $q < 1$, the effect is to raise all equilibrium bids, as if subjects become more risk averse.

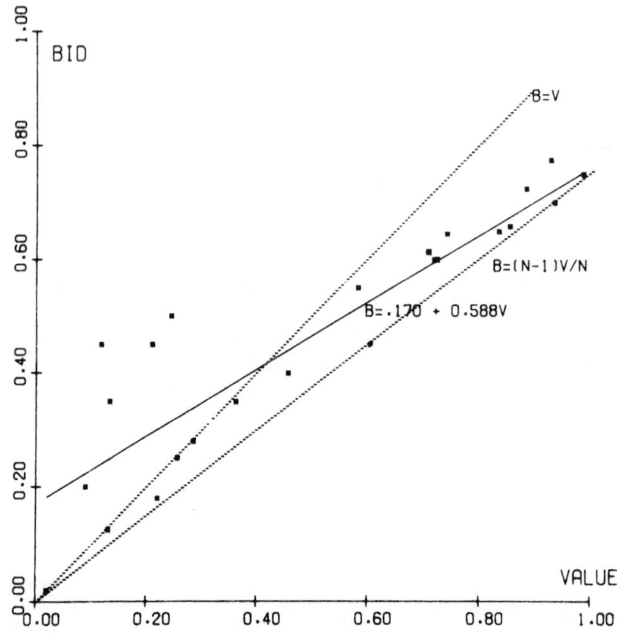

Fig. 9. Bidding behavior: Series 4, Exp. 10, n = 4, Subject 1

In this section, we report the results of two series of experiments in which q is manipulated as a treatment variable. In series 9, twelve subjects (all experienced in a previous experiment with $n = 4$ bidders) participated in three experiments, each with $n = 4$ bidders. Each experiment consisted of a baseline sequence (12 auctions in experiment 1 and 20 auctions in experiments 2 and 3) in which each subject earned one cent in cash for each PLATO cent obtained in each auction. This baseline was followed by a sequence of 20 auctions in which the cash earnings in each auction used the transformation (cash cents) = 0.02 (PLATO cents)^2. In the PLATO instructions for the squared payoff treatment, tables and graphs were used to inform the subjects of the profit implications of this transformation. However, a byproduct of these instructional materials was to make it evident that there existed a break-even profit, $\pi = 50$ cents, below which one earned less cash in the transformation experiment than in the baseline, and vice versa for profits above 50 cents (the break-even profit solves $0.02\pi^2 = \pi$). After completion of the first three experiments, 4 of the 12 subjects were recruited for a retest experiment consisting of 20 auctions using only the squared payoff treatment.

In these experiments $q = 2$ in the transformation sequence, and the weak prediction of CRRAM is that for all bidders we will observe a decrease in $\hat{\beta}_i$ relative to the baseline where $q = 1$. The strong prediction is that the slope of each i's estimated bid function is $\hat{\beta}_i = (n - 1)/(n - 1 + 2r_i)$ if $\hat{r}_i$ is the estimated risk parameter from the baseline sequence of auctions. As an alternative to the CRRAM predictions, in advance of the experiments we conjectured that a *satisficer* might bid lower in a transformation experiment when the potential profit is less than 50 cents, but higher if the potential profit is in excess of 50 cents. This bidding behavior would enable satisficers to maintain their baseline profit performance in the transformation experiment.

The results of linear regressions of bids on values for experiments 1 through 3 in series 9 and the retest experiment 4 are shown in Table 5. The subjects from one or more of the first three experiments who participated in the retest experiment 4 are indicated in the parentheses in column 1. The last column in Table 4 indicates whether the slope of the bid function increased (more risk averse) or decreased (less risk averse) from baseline to squared transformation. Note that 7 of the 12

Table 5. Series 9, Bid Functions for Baseline and Transformation

Experiment No. Subject No.	Baseline[b]			(Payoff)^2 Transformation[c]			Change in Risk Aversion Baseline to Transformation
	R^2	$\hat{\alpha}$	$\hat{\beta}$	R^2	$\hat{\alpha}$	$\hat{\beta}$	
1.1	.997	−.110	.959*	.998	−.320*	.966*	+
1.2	.981	−.672*	.989*	.951	−.524*	.877*	−
1.3	.996	.029	.962*	.994	−.005	.920*	−
1.4	.994	.140	.887*	.993	−.007	.915*	+
2.1	.981	.398	.846*	.996	−.077	.927*	+
2.2	.989	.115	.829*	.991	−.174	.902*	+
2.3	.998	−.028	.971*	.986	−.297	.925*	−
2.4	.948	−.408	.864	.981	−.673*	.946*	+
3.1	.961	.011	.806	.935	.021	.799	−
3.2	.996	−.035	.929*	.987	−.524*	.946*	+
3.3	.991	−.156	.976*	.996	−.415*	.976*	0
3.4	.983	.086	.865*	.990	−.408*	.946*	+
4.1(1.2)[a]	.981	−.672*	.989*	.971	−.833*	.971*	−
4.2(1.4)	.994	.140	.887*	.995	.063	.876*	−
4.3(1.3)	.996	.029	.962*	.967	.089	.805	−
4.4(2.3)	.998	−.028	.971*	.985	−.284*	.896*	−

a. Experiment 4 used previous subjects (e.g., subject 4.1 was 1.2 in experiment 1). All subjects experienced.

b. The baseline sequence in experiment 1 consisted of $T = 12$ auctions, while in experiments 2 and 3 there were $T = 20$ auctions in the baseline sequence.

c. All experiments consisted of $T = 20$ auctions in the sequence in which payoffs were squared.

*α significantly different from zero ($p < 0.05$, two-tailed test). β significantly different than risk neutral Nash value, 0.75 ($p < 0.05$, two-tailed test).

subjects' bids moved in the direction *opposite* to the predictions of CRRAM. However, in the retest all four subjects showed less risk averse bidding relative to the baseline, and three of the four subjects (4.2, 4.3, and 4.4) showed less risk averse bidding in the retest than in their first transformation sequence. These results suggest that CRRAM is not providing good predictions, although the retest showed some improvement. But a closer examination of the data is needed.

In particular, note in Table 5 that the estimate $\hat{\alpha}_i$ is lower in transformation than baseline for 10 of the 12 subjects. Also, only one $\hat{\alpha}_i$ was significantly different from zero in the baseline, but six showed this property in the transformation. The reason for this is revealed by the calculations presented in Table 6. This table records the change in bids (normalized by subtracting the risk neutral bid, $b_n(v_i^*)$) from baseline to square transformation where the bids imply a profit request of 50 cents or less (column 2) and the change in bids where the profit request exceeds 50 cents (column 3). This partitioning of the observations for each subject above and below the 50-cent break-even point allows us to separate the effect of the square transformation treatment according to this partition. A positive entry in column 2 means that the normalized bids in transformation were lower than in baseline,

Table 6. Series 9, Bids Above and Below 50-Cent Profit[a]

Experiment No. Subject No.	Change in Bids Below 50¢ Profit $R_{1i} = \bar{D}^B_{1i} - \bar{D}^T_{1i}$	Change in Bids Above 50¢ Profit $R_{2i} = \bar{D}^B_{2i} - \bar{D}^T_{2i}$	Comparison $R_{1i} - R_{2i}$
1.1	0.113	−0.290	0.403*
1.2	0.449*	−0.210	0.659*
1.3	0.742*	−0.150	0.892*
1.4	0.230	−0.280	0.510*
2.1	0.120	0.080	0.040
2.2	0.030	−0.880*	0.910*
2.3	0.712*	0.460	0.252
2.4	0.060	−0.392	0.452*
3.1	0.130	−0.480	0.610
3.2	0.188	−0.035	0.223*
3.3	0.530*	0.454	0.076
3.4	0.437*	−0.270	0.707*
4.1 (1.2)	0.284	−0.630	0.914*
4.2 (1.4)	0.063	0.060	0.003
4.3 (1.3)	0.655*	0.140	0.515*
4.4 (2.3)	0.925*	0.520	0.405*

a. $\bar{D}^B_{1i}$ = mean $[b_i^* - b_n(v_i^*)]$ in baseline data for profit requests < 50¢.
$\bar{D}^B_{2i}$ = mean $[b_i^* - b_n(v_i^*)]$ in baseline data for profit requests > 50¢.
If v_i^{MAX} = maximum value at which subject bid for profit < 50¢, then $\bar{D}^T_{1i}$ = mean $[b_i^* - b_n(v_i^*)]$ in transformation data for $v_i < v_i^{MAX}$ and $\bar{D}^T_{2i}$ = mean $[b_i^* - b_n(v_i^*)]$ in transformation data for $v_i > v_i^{MAX}$

* Significant, $p < 0.05$ (two-tailed test).

which is consistent with CRRAM, but is also consistent with satisficing. A positive difference in column 3 is consistent with CRRAM but inconsistent with satisficing and vice versa if the difference is negative. For the 12 subjects in the three initial experiments, all differences are positive in column 2, while for 10 subjects the differences are negative in column 3. Even where the difference is positive in column 3, it is smaller than in column 2 (see column 4). Thus, contrary to CRRAM, above the break-even 50-cent profit all but two subjects were bidding as if more, not less, risk averse. Satisficing outperforms the predictions of CRRAM where the two hypotheses are distinguishable. However, the retest results are less compelling. Three of the four subjects lowered their bids in retest transformation relative to the initial transformation, but the sample is too small to be reliable.

Clearly, the conjunction of CRRAM with the transformation model is brought into question by these results. In view of the overall good performance of CRRAM in the previous experiments, our provisional interpretation (Cox, Smith, and Walker, 1985a) of these results was that perhaps the experimental design had strongly tilted subject behavior toward the satisficing outcome. When CRRAM does well it is hardly credible to say that this is because our subjects are Nash calculating agents. It may be fairly easy to introduce perceptual distortions that alter bidding behavior. Such distortions may be a consequence of our experimental design, which first exposed the subjects to a baseline linear payment scheme, then the quadratic payment scheme, which invited comparisons in terms of the 50-cent break-even profit point. In fact, the instructional graph brought visual attention to the intersection point of the cents versus 0.02 $(\text{cents})^2$ reward schedules. Furthermore, the retest, which ran a transformation sequence only, without a preceding baseline, seemed to weaken the conjunctive evidence against CRRAM. These considerations suggested the need for further experiments.

Accordingly, we ran the two experiments in series 10 ($n = 4$). In these experiments, eight subjects were first given experience in a 25-auction sequence with linear payoffs (cash cents) = (PLATO cents). In experiment 1, four subjects returned for an experiment consisting of 20 auctions using the square root transformation, (cash cents) = 5 $(\text{PLATO cents})^{1/2}$, followed by 20 auctions using the squared transformation, (cash cents) = 0.04 $(\text{PLATO cents})^2$. In experiment 2, four subjects returned to participate in a 20-auction sequence using the squared transformation followed by 20 auctions using the square root transformation. In both experiments, note that the break-even level at which the baseline and the two transformations yield the same earnings is now only 25 cents (obtained by solving $\pi = 5\sqrt{\pi} = 0.04\ \pi^2$). We also removed all instructional materials that facilitated comparison among the different payoff transformations and which directed attention to the fixed break-even point. Finally, the baseline was conducted in a session that was separated by several days from the two transformation sequences.

Each subject's regression results for the baseline and two transformation sequences are shown in Table 7. Again there is a strong tendency for the $\hat{\alpha}_i$ to decrease from baseline to square transformation (seven of eight subjects). But there is not a corresponding tendency for $\hat{\alpha}_i$ to increase from baseline to square root transformation (three of eight subjects). The last column compares the change in

Table 7. Series 10, Bid Functions for Square Root and Square Transformations[a]

Experiment No. Subject No.	Baseline R^2	Baseline $\hat{\alpha}$	Baseline $\hat{\beta}$	(Payoff)$^{1/2}$ Transformation R^2	(Payoff)$^{1/2}$ Transformation $\hat{\alpha}$	(Payoff)$^{1/2}$ Transformation $\hat{\beta}$	(Payoff)^2 Transformation R^2	(Payoff)^2 Transformation $\hat{\alpha}$	(Payoff)^2 Transformation $\hat{\beta}$	Change in Risk Aversion Base to Square Root (square)
1.1	.995	.103	.942*	.996	.130	.917*	.999	.050	.964*	− (+)
1.2	.949	.279	.902*	.986	−.235	.985*	.991	−.302*	1.00*	+ (+)
1.3	.952	−.040	.805	.979	−.403*	.968*	.980	−.210	.935*	+ (+)
1.4	.979	−.030	.877*	.977	.150	.850*	.990	−.296*	.978*	− (+)
2.1	.842	−.599	.892	1.000	−.248*	1.00*	.990	−.382*	.955*	+ (+)
2.2	.852	.780	.685	.938	−.009	.905*	.990	−.091	.968*	+ (+)
2.3	.997	−.066	.982*	.995	−.293*	.994*	.993	−.302*	.950*	+ (−)
2.4	.941	.191	.790	.921	.046	.855	.991	.093	.876*	+ (+)

a. All subjects experienced. All experiments consisted of T = 25 auctions under the baseline. The baseline was conducted in earlier sittings by the subjects. In experiment 1, the square root transformation was used in the first 20 auctions, followed by 20 squared payoff auctions. In experiment 2, this sequence was reversed.

* See Table 5.

risk aversion as measured by the change in the $\hat{\beta}_i$ from baseline to each transformation. From baseline to square root, six of the eight subjects bid as if they had become more risk averse, which is consistent with CRAAM. From baseline to square, seven of eight subjects bid as if they had become more risk averse, which is inconsistent with CRRAM. Further, from square root to square (comparing columns 7 and 10), the $\hat{\beta}_i$ show that, contrary to CRAAM, five of the eight subjects bid as if they had become more risk averse.

We conclude that CRRAM does not dependably track changes in individual bidding behavior when the payoff transformation parameter q is manipulated as a treatment variable. However, the retest results in series 9 suggested the possibility that more support for CRRAM might develop with increased experience, but this is not solidly documented.

5. What have we learned from these experiments?

The constructive purpose of tests capable of "falsifying" a theoretical model is to improve the theory in the light of the test results, and to delineate new testable implications of the modified theory. As emphasized by Lakatos (1978, p. 35), it is written large in the history of science that "there is no falsification before the emergence of a better theory." An important part of the process of increasing the valid empirical content of a theory is to establish the ways in which existing models fail to predict accurately. Our experiments provide the following information about the performance of three models, each of which is a tractable special case of the M-parameter, log-concave model.

(1) The great majority of subjects bid as if risk averse, while some bid as if risk neutral or risk preferring (Tables 1, 2, and 4). This is inconsistent with the linear model and with the one-parameter concave model but consistent with CRRAM.

(2) In 28 of 47 experiments, we reject the hypothesis that the bids of the n bidders in the experiment come from the same population, that is, from a common bid function (Table 3). This is inconsistent with all one-parameter models, including the linear and concave models, but consistent with CRRAM.

(3) The bids of individuals exhibit tight linear relationships to independently drawn individual values, with 80% of the linear regressions yielding an R^2 in excess of 0.96 (Figure 2). This is consistent with CRRAM.

(4) As n is varied from 3 to 9, CRRAM tracks the resulting changes in individual bidding behavior except for $n = 6$.

(5) If all subjects' cash profits are tripled relative to control experiments that do not triple the earnings of a winning bidder, this produces no significant effect on the average intercept or average slope of the estimated linear bid functions of individual subjects (Section 3.5). This is consistent with CRRAM and inconsistent with any model that excludes log-linear (constant relative risk averse) preferences for monetary payoff.

(6) Upon retest, 80% of the subjects exhibit linear bidding behavior that is indistinguishable from that which was observed in their first bidding session. This supports the interpretation that the consistency of bidding behavior with CRRAM is not ephemeral or fragile.

(7) The linear estimated bid functions of individuals are not generally homogeneous. About 63% of the intercepts are negative (Table 4). However, the intercepts are significantly lower in those experiments in which bids are rounded to the nearest discrete bid node and bidding more than value is prohibited, compared with experiments in which all bids could be entered in integer cents (comparison for $n = 4$ only), and the latter are about evenly split between negative and positive intercept values. This suggests that the preponderance of negative intercepts might disappear as we approach bid continuity. But it is questionable whether, if this were so, it would rescue CRRAM, since a larger than expected percentage of the intercepts (17.9%), even in the case $n = 4$ (Table 4), are significantly above or below zero (we would expect to reject the null hypothesis in 5% of the cases if it were true). Consequently, CRRAM is not consistent with the incidence of large positive *and* negative intercepts, nor the apparent predominance of negative intercepts.

(8) The conjunction of CRRAM with quadratic and square root transformations of subject payoffs is not consistent with the experimental evidence (i.e., the relatively good predictive performance of CRRAM outlined earlier does not extend when we set $q = 2$ or $q = \frac{1}{2}$, where the cash payoff to winning bidder i is $(v_i - b_i)^q$ for a bid in the amount b_i and object value v_i. Yet the implications of the conjunction of CRRAM with the transformations is derived from the same core Nash-Harsanyi equilibrium bidding theory as is CRRAM. However, since experienced subjects were more consistent with CRRAM under the q transformation of profits, we leave open the possibility that our conclusions will be modified with a larger sample of experienced subjects.

6. Extensions of CRRAM that incorporate nonhomogeneous bid functions

CRRAM generally performs well in predicting bidding behavior in F auctions. One exception is the significant incidence of nonzero intercepts of the estimated bid functions. This suggests the question of whether CRRAM can be extended to incorporate such bidding behavior. In this section, we develop extensions of CRRAM that imply linear, but not necessarily homogeneous, bid functions.

Equation (13) and the assumption that preferences are strictly log-concave imply that $\mu(\cdot, \theta_i)$ has a first argument inverse function, $\mu^{-1}(\cdot, \theta_i)$, and hence the inverse equilibrium bid function can be written as

$$\pi(b_i, \theta_i) = b_i + \mu^{-1}(\rho(b_i), \theta_i) \tag{30}$$

Equations (1), (2), and (9) show that $\rho(b_i)$ generally depends on the distribution of agent characteristics in the population $\Phi(\theta)$. Hence, $\pi(b_i, \theta_i)$ and its b-inverse, the equilibrium bid function, generally depend on an agent's own characteristics θ_i and on the distribution of characteristics in the population $\Phi(\theta)$. CRRAM is a partial exception. It is clear from inspection of Equation (22) that (for bids less than $\bar{b}$) an agent's bid depends on his or her own risk attitude parameter r_i, but is independent of the distribution of risk attitudes in the population.[7] This theoretical separation of the effects on equilibrium bids of an agent's own characteristics from his or her expectations about his or her rivals is a significant advantage for empirical research. This property of CRRAM is lost if another parameter is introduced in a symmetric way to incorporate nonhomogeneous bid functions into the model. In order to retain the separation in subsequent experiments, we will control bidders' expectations about their rivals by simulating homogeneous linear bidding behavior for the rivals. This will permit us to test the individual bid implications of the extended models without confounding them with a possible expectation effect. We now proceed to develop the extended models.

Assume that each of the $n - 1$ (simulated) rivals of bidder i chooses his or her bid such that

$$b_j = \beta_j v_j \tag{31}$$

where $1/\beta_j$ is drawn from the distribution with *cdf.* $\Phi(1/\beta)$ on the support $(1, n/(n-1)]$ and v_j is drawn from the uniform distribution on $[0, \bar{v}]$. Then, for $b \leq \bar{v}(n-1)/n$, the probability that any simulated rival will bid some amount less than or equal to b is

$$F(b) = \int_1^{n/(n-1)} \int_0^{b/\beta} (1/\bar{v}) dv \, d\Phi(1/\beta) = (b/\bar{v}) E\,(1/\beta) \tag{32}$$

The probability that all $n - 1$ simulated rival bidders will bid amounts less than or equal to b is

$$G(b) = F(b)^{n-1} \tag{33}$$

We consider two models that incorporate a (monetary equivalent of a) utility of winning the auction, w_i, and an income threshold, t_i. Utility of monetary payoff is continuous in the first model and it is discontinuous, at $w_i - t_i$, in the second model. For money income, y_i, the utility function for CRRAM* is

$$u_i(y_i) = \begin{cases} -[-(y_i + w_i - t_i)]^{r_i} & \text{for } \; y_i + w_i - t_i < 0 \\ (y_i + w_i - t_i)^{r_i} & \text{for } \; y_i + w_i - t_i \geq 0 \end{cases} \tag{34}$$

The utility function for CRRAM** is

$$u_i(y_i) = \begin{cases} -[-(y_i + w_i - t_i)]^{r_i} & \text{for} \quad y_i + w_i - t_i < 0 \\ (y_i + w_i)^{r_i} & \text{for} \quad y_i + w_i - t_i \geqslant 0 \end{cases} \tag{35}$$

Note that if $t_i = 0$ then $w_i > 0$ is a (monetary equivalent of a) utility of winning that is independent of the surplus from winning $v_i - b_i$. Alternatively, if $w_i = 0$, then $t_i > 0$ is the (threshold) minimum level of surplus from winning necessary to generate positive utility.[8]

Consider CRRAM*. For $v_i < w_i - t_i$, $u_i(v_i - b_i) < 0$ for all $b_i > 0$; hence, the optimal bid is zero. For $v_i > w_i - t_i$, the optimal bid satisfies the first order condition,

$$\frac{G(b_i)}{G'(b_i)} = \frac{u_i(v_i - b_i)}{u_i'(v_i - b_i)} \tag{36}$$

Equations (32), (33), (34), and (36) imply that, for $b_i \leqslant \bar{v}(n-1)/n$, one has

$$b_i = \frac{n-1}{n-1+r_i}(v_i + w_i - t_i) \tag{37}$$

Since the optimal bid is zero when $v_i < w_i - t_i$ and is given by Equation (37) when $v_i > w_i - t_i$, the graph of the bid function depends on the relative sizes of w_i and t_i. Figure 10 illustrates two representative cases where $w_1 < t_1$, $w_2 > t_2$, and $r_1 = r_2 = r$.

Note the CRRAM* and its implied bid function shown in Equation (37) accounts for both the positive and the negative intercepts reported in Section 3. But CRRAM* does not account for cases like the one illustrated in Figure 8, which suggests a discontinuity in the bid function at some value $v_1 = t_1 - w_1$. For such cases, consider CRRAM**. For $v_i < w_i - t_i$, the optimal bid is zero. For $v_i > w_i - t_i$, the optimal bid satisfies Equation (36). Equations (32), (33), (35), and (36) imply that, for $b_i \leqslant \bar{v}(n-1)/n$, one has

$$b_i = \frac{n-1}{n-1+r_i}(v_i + w_i) \tag{38}$$

Figure 11 illustrates two representative cases where $w_1 < t_1$, $w_2 > t_2$, and $r_1 = r_2 = r$, with the first case corresponding to the behavior illustrated in Figure 8.

7. Using CRRAM* to interpret behavior when rival bids are simulated

We have independently reported experiments (66 subjects) comparing each subject's bidding behavior when his or her rivals were human bidders, with bidding behavior when his or her rivals' bids were simulated using homogeneous linear

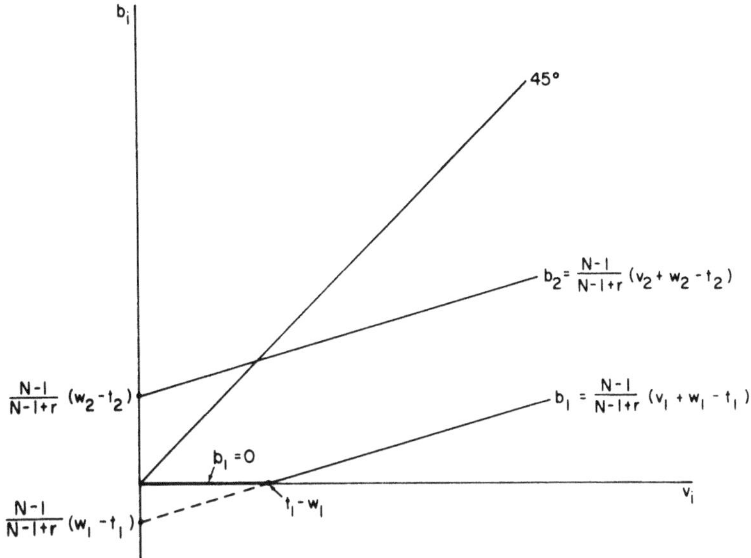

Fig. 10. Optimal bid functions for CRRAM*

bid functions (Walker, Smith, and Cox, 1987). In the simulation experiments, each subject bids against $n - 1$ simulated bidders in a sequence of 20 auctions. Each simulated competitor bids a fixed proportion of value. Value for each bidder in each auction is determined by an independent draw from a rectangular distribution, as earlier, in the same way that values are generated for human subjects. The bid-value proportion is the same across all auctions for each simulated competitor and is determined by a single independent draw from the interval $[(n - 1)/n,1)$. These proportions are drawn from the *actual* empirical distribution of estimated $\hat{\beta}_i$ coefficients for the 143 subjects reported in Table 2 for which $\beta_i \in [(n - 1)/n,1)]$. Consequently, each bidder faced simulated bidders whose behavior was similar to that of human bidders (except that each simulated bidder used a *homogeneous* linear bid function). In this manner, we seek to control each subject's *expectations* of the bidding behavior or his or her rivals by informing him or her about the simulation rules for the $n - 1$ rivals.

With the development of CRRAM*, we are now able to interpret these data in terms of bidding theory. From CRRAM*, we expect each bidder i with simulated rivals to reveal bid functions with intercepts depending only on that bidder's own $(w_i - t_i)$ characteristic. However, we expect each bidder i with human rivals to reveal bid function intercepts depending on both i's $(w_i - t_i)$ characteristic and the

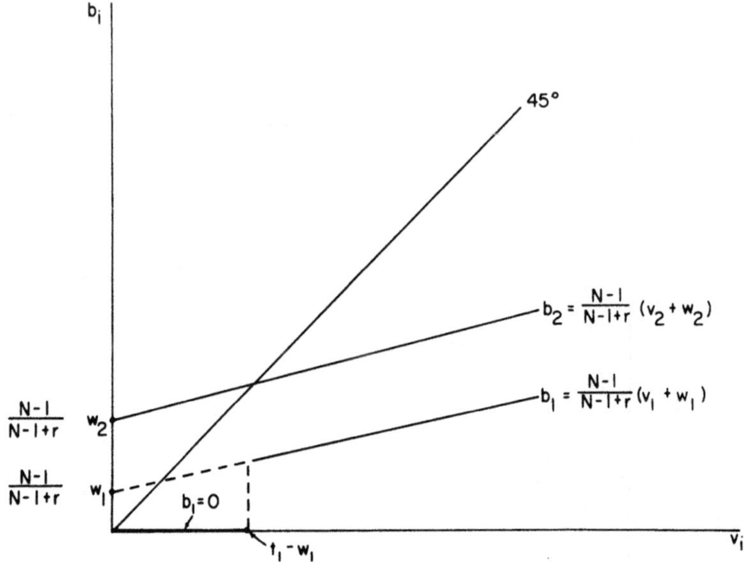

Fig. 11. Optimal bid functions for CRRAM**

distribution of this characteristic among the population of rivals. It follows that simulation is expected to eliminate sources of variability in intercept bidding behavior, and the prediction is that across subjects this treatment should reduce the variance of estimated intercepts. Data making these comparisons for groups of size $n = 3, 4$, and 6 all show the same results: the variance across subjects of the estimated intercepts is higher when there are human rivals than when there are computerized rivals. This variance ratio is statistically significant (F test) for $n = 4$ and 5, but not for $n = 3$ (Walker, Smith, and Cox, 1987, Table 1).

8. New experiments motivated by CRRAM*

In CRRAM*, the characteristic $(w_i - t_i)$ for i is unobservable and not directly manipulable. However, if subject i is paid w_i' dollars conditional on winning (in addition to the earned surplus, $v_i - b_i$), this characteristic becomes $(w_i + w_i' - t_i) > (w_i - t_i)$ and we predict an increase in i's intercept estimate, $\hat{\alpha}_i$. Similarly, if subject i is charged w_i' dollars for winning, we predict a decrease in i's intercept estimate. Consequently, using such lump sum payments (or charges) we can induce an increased utility of winning (or increased threshold utility of surplus), and the predicted outcomes are straightforward if, as hypothesized, CRRAM* characterizes individual bidding behavior.

In Table 8, we report the estimated intercepts from five experiments, using 30 subjects, for $n = 4$ and 6 (3 and 5 simulated) bidders. In experiments 11 and 12, each subject was run under baseline ($w' = 0$), lump sum payments for winning ($w' = 25$ cents), and lump sum charges for winning ($w' = -25$ cents). In experiments 13, 14, and 15, subjects were run only under the baseline and charge conditions, except that in experiment 15 the charge was $w' = -50$ cents. From CRRAM* we predict $\hat{\alpha}_i(w' = -25 \text{ cents}) < \hat{\alpha}_i(w' = 0) < \hat{\alpha}_i(w' = 25 \text{ cents})$. In experiment 11, we observed 4 of 14 instances in which one of these inequalities was violated. Since the violations (three of them) were concentrated on the charge treatment, we ran five

Table 8. Bid Function Intercepts for Different Payments or Charges, w'

$n = 4$

	Experiment 11, $\hat{\alpha}_i$				Experiment 13, $\hat{\alpha}_i$	
Subject	$w' = -25¢$	$w' = 0$	$w' = 25¢$	Subject	$w' = -25¢$	$w' = 0$
1	−0.419*	−0.517	−0.314	1	−0.264	0.067
2	−0.079*	−0.183	−0.010	2	−0.170*	−0.681
3	−0.586	−0.099	−0.121*	3	−0.404	−0.041
4	−0.255	−0.230	−0.069	4	−0.250	−0.007
5	−0.201	−0.124	−0.001	5	−0.346	−0.307
6	0.134*	−0.272	−0.045			
7	−0.285	−0.170	−0.036			

$n = 6$

	Experiment 12, $\hat{\alpha}_i$		
Subject	$w' = -25¢$	$w' = 0$	$w' = 25¢$
1	−0.169	−0.025	0.120
2	0.026	0.438	0.489
3	−0.091	0.089	0.258
4	−1.63	−0.429	−0.150
5	−0.372	0.065	0.223
6	−0.250*	−0.648	0.162
7	−0.586	−0.411	0.161
8	−0.167*	−0.210	−0.095

	Experiment 14, $\hat{\alpha}_i$	
Subject	$w' = -25¢$	$w' = 0$
1	−0.111	−0.111
2	−0.155*	−0.326
3	0.625*	0.046
4	−0.124*	−0.262

	Experiment 15, $\hat{\alpha}_i$	
Subject	$w' = -50¢$	$w' = 0$
1	−0.396	−0.305
2	−0.548	0.199
3	−0.429	−0.224
4	−0.601	−0.086
5	−0.775	−0.257
6	−0.027	0.525

*Instances in which left or right side of the inequality $\hat{\alpha}_i(w' = -25¢ \text{ or } -50¢) < \hat{\alpha}_i(w' = 0) < \hat{\alpha}_i(w' = 25¢)$ is violated.

more subjects in experiment 13 applying the charge ($w' = -25$ cents) only in addition to the baseline ($w' = 0$). Combining experiments 11 and 13, we have 5 of 19 violations of the predicted ordering. Using the sign test, we reject the null hypothesis that the intercepts are equal under the three treatments ($p = 0.05$). In experiment 12, we observed 2 of 16 instances in which the predicted inequality was violated, and both violations were under the charge treatment. Because of this asymmetry, we ran four more subjects in baseline and under the charge condition only. This yielded three violations and a tie. Since one-half of the intercepts under baseline, when $n = 6$, were larger than the treatment charge ($w' = -25$ cents), we suspected that this charge might be too small when $n = 6$ to have a strong effect on lowering the intercept. Therefore, in experiment 15, we ran six more subjects under the baseline and charge conditions, with the latter increased to $w' = -50$ cents. This yielded no violations. Overall for $n = 6$, we get 5 of 26 cases violating the inequality, and we reject the null hypothesis of no differences among the treatments.

9. Conclusions

The results of our tests of the one-parameter linear and concave models and of CRRAM are summarized in Section 5. These tests show that subject behavior in F auctions is decisively inconsistent with the one-parameter (identical bidders) models that comprise most of the theoretical literature. In contrast, our two-parameter model, CRRAM, survives the tests reasonably well. We find strong evidence of linear bidding behavior, with high subject retest reliability, that is invariant to multiplicative transformations of payoffs. This behavior is implied by the log-linear risk preferences that characterize CRRAM and is inconsistent with any bidding model that excludes such preferences. Further, in multiunit discriminative auctions, CRRAM predicts strictly concave (rather than linear) bid functions, and the results of earlier experiments have indicated that subjects do use strictly concave bid functions in such auctions (Cox, Smith, and Walker, 1982, 1984).[9] Together, the F auction and the multiunit discriminative auction experiments provide strong support for CRRAM: when it predicts linear bidding, that is what we have observed; when it predicts strictly concave bidding, observations support this prediction.

Other results are not so favorable for the model. The conjunction of CRRAM with quadratic and square root transformations of subject payoffs is not in general consistent with the experimental evidence, although support for CRRAM is stronger for the small sample of *experienced* subjects that we report. Furthermore, CRRAM is not consistent with the observed incidence of nonzero bid function intercepts. This inconsistency led us to develop two extensions of CRRAM. The first extension, CRRAM*, provides an ex post hoc explanation of the positive and negative intercepts of the estimated linear bid functions of 156 subjects based on the assumption that subject utility functions contain a parameter, $(w_i - t_i)$, where w_i is a monetary measure of the utility of winning and t_i is a threshold income level.

The second extension, CRRAM**, explains the apparently infrequent anomaly (illustrated in Figure 8) in which a subject exhibits a discontinuous drop in his or her bid function below some small value of v. Since the latter extension cannot explain negative intercepts (62.8% of the subjects), we concentrate on the testability of CRRAM*. A comparison of the bidding behavior of subjects whose competitors are other subjects, with their behavior when bidding against Nash equilibrium computerized robot bidders, is consistent with CRRAM*. However, CRRAM* can be tested directly since it predicts that if subjects are paid (charged) a lump sum for winning, the intercepts of their respective linear estimated bid functions will increase (decrease). A test of this hypothesis using 12 subjects with $n = 4$ and 18 subjects with $n = 6$ tends to support (overall 35 of 45 pairwise comparisons) these predictions of CRRAM*.

Notes

1. The first-price sealed-bid auction is the market in which the auctioned object is awarded to the bidder who submits the highest bid at a price that is equal to his or her bid. Bids may be literally sealed (in envelopes), but that is not essential. It is an essential property of this auction that it is *not* a real-time market; hence, noncollusive bidders are not able to observe the bidding behavior of their rivals.

2. Vickrey (1961) analyzes the linear model. The one-parameter concave model is developed in Holt (1980), Riley-Samuelson (1981), and Harris-Raviv (1981). A more general form of the one-parameter concave model is analyzed in Maskin and Riley (1984). The two-parameter constant relative risk averse model is developed in Cox, Roberson, and Smith (1982) and Cox, Smith, and Walker (1982).

3. There is no closed form solution for $b > (n-1)\bar{v}/(n-1+\bar{r})$. In statements (1c) and (8c), $E_r(\cdot)$ denotes expected values over the random variable r.

4. The Dutch auction is a real-time market. In this auction, the seller or his or her agent starts the offer price at an amount believed to be higher than any bidder is willing to pay. The offer price is then lowered by an auctioneer or a clock until one of the bidders accepts the last price offer. The first and only bid is the sales price in this auction. Although the Dutch and F auctions are theoretically isomorphic, 11 paired comparisons, each consisting of 30 auctions, all show mean Dutch prices below mean F prices (Cox, Roberson, and Smith, 1982; Cox, Smith, and Walker, 1983).

5. John Kagel reported to us in private conversation that they did not get deviant results for $n = 3$.

6. If i has CRRA preferences and the v_i are drawn from the uniform distribution on $[0,\bar{v}]$, then Equations (1), (2), (9), (10), and (13) imply

$$v_i = b_i + r_i \int_{\Theta} \pi(b_i,\theta)d\Phi(\theta)/(n-1) \int_{\Theta} \pi_1(b_i,\theta)d\Phi(\theta)$$

This will be nonlinear in b_i if $\pi(\cdot)$ is nonlinear in b for any subset of Θ with positive probability. We should also note that our estimates of Equation (28) are weighted against CRRAM and in favor of other log-concave models. This is because the regressions include those observations above $\bar{v}_i$ (see Table 4 footnote) in the nonlinear domain of the CRRAM bid function.

7. This quasidominance characteristic of CRRAM and of Vickrey's original risk neutral bid function is counterintuitive, since one expects noncooperative equilibrium strategy functions to be sensitive to the strategy functions (or expectations thereof) used by competitors. This unusual property follows from the assumption that values are drawn from a uniform distribution, so that $F(b)$ in Equation (1) is linear in b and that (in the range below $\bar{b}$) $\rho(b)$, the relative marginal probability of winning, is inde-

pendent of the linear bidding strategies of the other bidders. This property is also unique to single object auctions; it does not carry over to the extension of CRRAM to multiple unit auctions, with $n > q > 1$ (Cox, Smith, and Walker, 1982, 1984).

8. Note that if $r_i < 1$, then the CRRAM* and CRRAM** utility functions are strictly convex for $y_i + w_i - t_i < 0$ and strictly concave for $y_i + w_i - t_i > 0$. This is consistent with the evidence provided by experimental psychologists (see, for example, Tversky and Kaheman, 1986) that people behave as if they are risk preferring for losses and risk averse for gains. Actually, in the present application, the curvature properties of $u_i(\cdot)$ for $y_i + w_i - t_i < 0$ are irrelevant. The implications for optimal bidding are the same for all utility functions $u_i(y_i) = h_i(y_i + w_i - t_i)$, for $y_i + w_i - t_i < 0$, given that $h_i(\cdot)$ is increasing and $h(0) = 0$.

9. The multiunit discriminative auction is the market in which $q > 1$ homogeneous objects are simultaneously auctioned and each accepted bid is filled at the prices specified by the bidder. It is the multiunit version of the *F* auction. The discriminative auction is distinguished from the uniform price (or competitive) multiunit auction in which all accepted bids are filled at a common price (usually the lowest accepted or highest rejected bid). The U.S. Treasury bill auction is a multiunit discriminative auction.

References

Cox, James C., Roberson, Bruce, and Smith, Vernon L. "Theory and Behavior of Single Object Auctions." In: Vernon L. Smith, ed., *Research in Experimental Economics,* Vol. 2. Greenwich, CT: JAI Press, 1982.

Cox, James C., Smith, Vernon L., and Walker, James M. "Auction Market Theory of Heterogeneous Bidders," *Economics Letters* 9, (1982), 319–325.

Cox, James C., Smith, Vernon L., and Walker, James M. "A Test That Discriminates Between Two Models of the Dutch-First Auction Non-Isomophism," *Journal of Economic Behavior and Organization* 4, (1983), 205–219.

Cox, James C., Smith, Vernon L., and Walker, James M. "Theory and Behavior of Multiple Unit Discriminative Auctions," *Journal of Finance* 39, (1984), 983–1010.

Cox, James C., Smith, Vernon L., and Walker, James M. "Experimental Development of Sealed-Bid Auction Theory; Calibrating Controls for Risk Aversion," *American Economic Review,* Papers and Proceedings, 75, (1985), 160–165.

Cox, James C., Smith, Vernon L., and Walker, James M. "Expected Revenue in Discriminative and Uniform Price Sealed Bid Auctions." In: Vernon L. Smith, ed., *Research in Experimental Economics,* Vol. 3. Greenwich, CT: JAI Press, 1985.

Harris, Milton, and Raviv, Artur. "Allocation Mechanisms and the Design of Auctions," *Econometrica* 49, (1981), 1477–1499.

Holt, Charles A. "Competitive Bidding for Contracts Under Alternative Auction Procedures," *Journal of Political Economy* 88, (1980), 433–445.

Issac, R. Mark, and Walker, James M. "Information and Conspiracy in Sealed Bid Auctions," *Journal of Economic Behavior and Organization* 6, (1985), 139–159.

Lakatos, Imre. *The Methodology of Scientific Research Programs.* Edited by John Worrall and Gregorie Currie. Cambridge: Cambridge University Press, 1978.

Maskin, Eric, and Riley, John. "Optimal Auctions with Risk Averse Buyers," *Econometrica* 52, (1984), 1473–1518.

McAfee, R. Preston, and McMillan, John. "Auctions and Bidding," *Journal of Economic Literature* 25, (1987), 699–738.

Riley, John G., and Samuelson, William F. "Optimal Auctions," *American Economic Review* 71, (1981), 381–392.

Tversky, Amos, and Kahneman, Daniel. "Rational Choice and the Framing of Decisions," *Journal of Business* 59, (1986), S251–S278.

Vickrey, William. "Counterspeculation, Auctions, and Competitive Sealed Tenders," *Journal of Finance* 16, (1961), 8–37.

Walker, James M., Smith, Vernon L., and Cox, James C. "Bidding Behavior in First Price Sealed Bid Auctions: Use of Computerized Nash Competitors," *Economics Letters* 23, (1987), 239–244.

A combinatorial auction mechanism for airport time slot allocation

S.J. Rassenti*

V.L. Smith**

and

R.L. Bulfin***

A sealed-bid combinatorial auction is developed for the allocation of airport time slots to competing airlines. This auction procedure permits airlines to submit various contingency bids for flight-compatible combinations of individual airport landing or take-off slots. An algorithm for solving the resulting set-packing problem yields an allocation of slots to packages that maximizes the system surplus as revealed by the set of package bids submitted. The algorithm determines individual (slot) resource prices which are used to price packages to the winning bidders at levels guaranteed to be no greater (and normally smaller) than the amounts bid. Laboratory experiments with cash motivated subjects are used to study the efficiency and demand revelation properties of the combinatorial auction in comparison with a proposed independent slot primary auction.

1. The problem of allocating airport slots

■ In 1968 the FAA adopted a high density rule for the allocation of scarce landing and take-off slots at four major airports (La Guardia, Washington National, Kennedy International, and O'Hare International). This rule establishes slot quotas for the control of airspace congestion at these airports.

Airport runway slots, regulated by these quotas, have a distinguishing feature which any proposed allocation procedure must accommodate: an airline's demand for a take-off slot at a flight originating airport is not independent of its demand for a landing slot at the flight destination airport. Indeed, a given flight may take off and land in a sequence of several connected demand interdependent legs. For economic efficiency it is desirable to develop an airport slot allocation procedure that allocates individual slots to those airline flights for which the demand (willingness to pay) is greatest.

Grether, Isaac, and Plott (hereafter, GIP) (1979, 1981) have proposed a practical market procedure for achieving this goal. Their procedure is based upon the growing body of experimental evidence on the performance of (1) the competitive (uniform-price) sealed-bid auction and (2) the oral double auction such as is used on the organized stock and commodity exchanges. Under their proposal an independent primary market for slots at each airport would be organized as a sealed-bid competitive auction at timely intervals. Since the primary market allocation does not make provision for slot demand interdependence, a computerized form of the oral double auction (with block transaction ca-

---

* Bell Laboratories.

** University of Arizona.

*** Auburn University.

We are grateful to the National Science Foundation for research support under a grant to the University of Arizona (V.L. Smith, principal investigator).

pabilities) is proposed as an "after market" to allow airlines to purchase freely and sell primary market slots to each other. This continuous after market exchange would provide the institutional means by which individual airlines would acquire those slot packages which support their individual flight schedules. Thus, an airline that acquired slots at Washington National which did not flight-match the slots acquired at O'Hare could either buy additional O'Hare slots or sell its excess Washington slots in the after market. Although GIP's proposed after market permits airlines to exchange slots freely and thereby acquire the appropriate slot packages, it suffers from two disadvantages.

(1) Individual airlines may experience capital losses and gains in the process of trading airport slots in the after market. Thus, an airline with an excess of A slots and a deficiency of B slots may discover in the after market that the going price of B slots is unprofitably high (for that particular airline), while excess A slots can be sold only at a loss.
(2) It costs resources to trade in the after market. Hence, to the extent that slots are not allocated to the appropriate packages in the primary market, the cost of participating in the combined primary-after market mechanism is increased.

Ideally, the primary market would allocate slots in the appropriate packages initially with the after market performing only two functions (i) marginal corrections in primary market misallocations, and (ii) slot allocation adjustments due to new information not available at the time of the primary auction. Thus, a sudden grounding of all DC-10 aircraft would leave Continental Airlines with a surplus of O'Hare runway slots, which could be sold in the after market to airlines not affected by the DC-10 grounding.

In this article, we address the problem of designing a "combinatorial" sealed-bid auction to serve as the primary market for allocating airport slots in flight-compatible packages for which individual airlines would submit package bids. The objective is to allocate slots to an individual airline *only* in the form of those combinations and subject to those contingencies that have been prespecified by the airline.

2. The auction optimization mechanism

■ To increase the overall efficiency of the slot allocation mechanism suggested by GIP (1979), and to decrease its reliance on an after market, we have developed an optimization model with the following features for use in a computer-assisted primary sealed-bid auction market: (a) direct maximization of system surplus in the criterion function; (b) airport coordination through consideration of resource demands in logically packaged sets; (c) scheduling flexibility through contingency bids on the part of airlines.

Consider the following integer programming problem:

$$(P)\quad \begin{cases} \text{Maximize} & \sum_j c_j x_j \\ \text{Subject to:} & \sum_j a_{ij} x_j \le b_i \; \forall\, i, \\ & \sum_j d_{kj} x_j \le e_k \; \forall\, k, \\ & x_j \in \{0, 1\}; \end{cases}$$

where

$i = 1, \ldots, m$ subscripts a resource (some slot at some airport);
$j = 1, \ldots, n$ subscripts a package (set of slots) valuable to some airline;
$k = 1, \ldots, l$ subscripts some logical constraint imposed on a set of packages by some airline;

$$a_{ij} = \begin{cases} 1 \text{ if package } j \text{ includes slot } i, \\ 0 \text{ otherwise;} \end{cases}$$

$$d_{kj} = \begin{cases} 1 \text{ if package } j \text{ is in logical constraint } k, \\ 0 \text{ otherwise;} \end{cases}$$

e_k = some integer ≥ 1,

c_j = the bid for package j by some airline.

The contingency bids expressed in the set of logical constraints have one of two format types: "Accept no more than p of the following q packages." or "Accept package V only if package W is accepted." The first type is identical in format to any of the resource constraints. For example, suppose an airline bids c_a on package a, c_b on package b, and specifies either a or b, but not both. The added constraint is then written $x_a + x_b \leq 1$. The second type can be converted to this format through a simple variable transformation. For example, suppose an airline bids as in the previous example, but specifies b only if a. By creating the package ab with $c_{ab} = c_a + c_b$, package b can be eliminated from consideration. The added constraint becomes $x_a + x_{ab} \leq 1$.

In a manner analogous to the parallel independent slot auctions suggested by GIP (1979), sealed bids (c_j) for packages (j) and the contingency constraints (k) specified by each airline are used to parameterize the model and determine an "optimal" primary allocation. The problem which results is recognized as a variant of the set packing problem with general right-hand sides. It can be solved, as was done for the experiments reported in Section 3, with a specialized algorithm developed by Rassenti (1981). A problem of the enormous dimensions dictated by even a four-city application (perhaps 15,000 constraints and 100,000 variables) will present a significant challenge for the finest configuration of hardware and software available. Fortunately, a practicable solution within 1 or 2% of the linear optimum, and very often the optimum itself in the discrete solution set, is almost assuredly achievable in a reasonable amount of time.

Given the solvability of P and its potential for ensuring an efficient primary allocation, there remain several questions: how to induce bidding airlines to reveal their true values; how to price allocated slots; and how to divide income among the participating airports. We suggest a resolution of these concerns with the following procedure: (1) Determine a complete set of marginal (shadow) prices, one for each slot offered. (2) Charge any airline whose package j was accepted in the solution to P a price for j equal to the sum of the marginal prices for the slots in that package. This provides the uniform price feature that has demonstrated good demand revelation behavior in single commodity experiments (GIP, 1979). (3) Return to any airport whose slot i was included in some accepted package j an amount equal to the marginal price for i. Such a scheme will guarantee that the price paid for an accepted package is less than (or rarely equal to) the amount bid for that package.

If problem P were a linear program, the determination of the suggested set of shadow prices would be a trivial and well-solved matter. Discrete programming problems, however, present special difficulties with respect to shadow pricing. Consider, for example, a discrete project selection problem with a single resource constraint:

$$(K)\begin{cases} \text{Maximize} \quad 5X_1 + 3X_2 + 6X_3 + 5X_4 + 6X_5 + 3X_6 + 4X_7 + 3X_8 + 2X_9 + X_{10} = Z; \\ \text{Subject to:} \quad 3X_1 + 2X_2 + 6X_3 + 7X_4 + 9X_5 + 5X_6 \\ \qquad + 8X_7 + 8X_8 + 6X_9 + 4X_{10} \leq 24; \qquad X_j \in \{0, 1\} \; \forall j = 1, \ldots, 10. \end{cases}$$

If the choice space for X_j is relaxed to its linear programming equivalent, $0 \leq X_j \leq 1$, then the solution is trivially given by $(Z, X_1, X_2, \ldots, X_{10}) = (23, 1, 1, 1, 1, .66, 0, 0, 0, 0, 0)$. The critical return rate, $\lambda = 6/9$ for project 5, is the optimal Lagrangian multiplier or shadow price for the resource. But the discrete problem has the optimal solution (21, 1, 1, 1, 0, 0, 1, 1, 0, 0, 0), and obviously no critical ratio exists which separates projects that are chosen from those that are not. Figure 1 illustrates these solutions.

In the traditional sense, Lagrangian multipliers for an integer program may not exist;[1] that is, no set of prices will support the optimal division of packages into accepted and rejected categories. Therefore, it is possible that a package bid that is greater than its shadow resource cost will be rejected, while another package bid that is also greater than its shadow cost is accepted. In the experiments reported in Section 3, we provided subject bidders with a guideline explanation of these cases. This allows subjects to select strategic or best reply (Cournot) responses if they wish.

With this problem in mind, the following two pseudo-dual programs to P were developed to define bid rejection prices (problem D_R) and acceptance prices (problem D_A) that will serve as bidding guidelines for individual agents.

$$(D_R)\begin{cases} \text{Minimize} & \sum_R y_r \\ \text{Subject to:} & \sum_i w_i a_{ij} \le c_j \ \forall\, j \in A, \\ & y_r \ge c_r - \sum_i w_i a_{ir} \ \forall\, r \in R, \\ & y_r \ge 0, \qquad w_i \ge 0; \end{cases}$$

where

the optimal solution to P is $\{x_j^*\}$;
the set of accepted packages is $A = \{j | x_j^* = 1\}$;
the set of rejected packages is $R = \{r | x_r^* = 0\}$;
the set of lower bound slot prices (prices charged) to be determined is $\{w_i^*\}$;
the amount by which a rejected bid exceeds the market price (if at all) is y_r.

$$(D_A)\begin{cases} \text{Minimize} & \sum_A y_j \\ \text{Subject to:} & \sum_i v_i a_{ir} \ge c_r \ \forall\, r \in R, \\ & y_j \ge \sum_i v_i a_{ij} - c_j \ \forall\, j \in A, \\ & y_j \ge 0, \qquad v_i \ge 0; \end{cases}$$

FIGURE 1

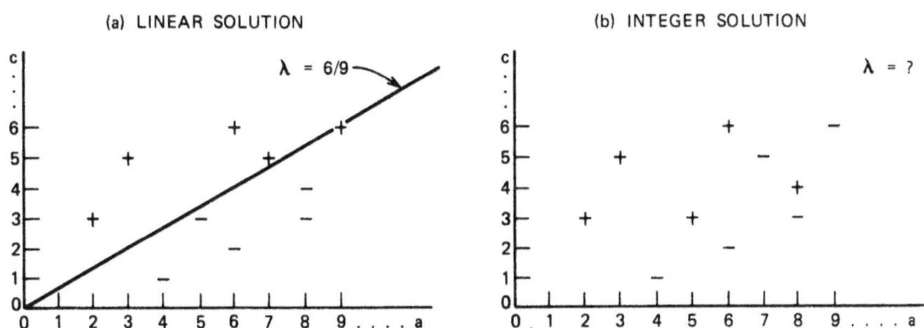

[1] Wolsey (1981) presents a "state of the art" discussion of price functions in integer programming.

where

the set of upper bound slot prices to be determined is $\{v_i^*\}$;
the amount by which an accepted bid is below the upper bound slot prices (if at all) is y_j.

Problem D_A is the complement of D_R with respect to the accept-reject dichotomy. If unambiguous separating prices exist, the solutions to D_A and D_R coincide. In Figure 2 the analogous pseudo-dual problems for the project selection problem K above are schematically solved for the obvious upper and lower bound return ratios.

The following categorization of bids can now be made. (i) If a bid was greater than the sum of its component values in the set $\{v_i^*\}$, it was definitely accepted. (ii) If a bid was less than the sum of its component prices in the set $\{w_i^*\}$, it was definitely rejected. (iii) All bids in between were in a region where acceptance or rejection might be considered independent of relative marginal value and determined by the integer constraints on efficient resource utilization. The bids in category (iii) correspond to the core of the integer programming problem P. They comprise a small percentage of all bids and are known to decrease in relative number as problem size increases. Figure 3 gives the regions analogous to (i), (ii), and (iii) for the project selection example.

What can be said about the theoretical incentive properties of this proposed computer assisted sealed-bid auction? Certainly it is *not* generally incentive compatible; that is, if any bidder desires to acquire multiple units of any given package or multiple units of the same slot, then the door is open to the possibility of strategically underbidding the true value of certain packages (Vickrey, 1961). However, strategic behavior is fraught with risks for the individual, even in simple multiple unit auctions for a single commodity, because individuals do not know the bids and the true valuations of their competitors.[2]

FIGURE 2

(a) ACCEPTANCE RATIO DETERMINED BY x_7

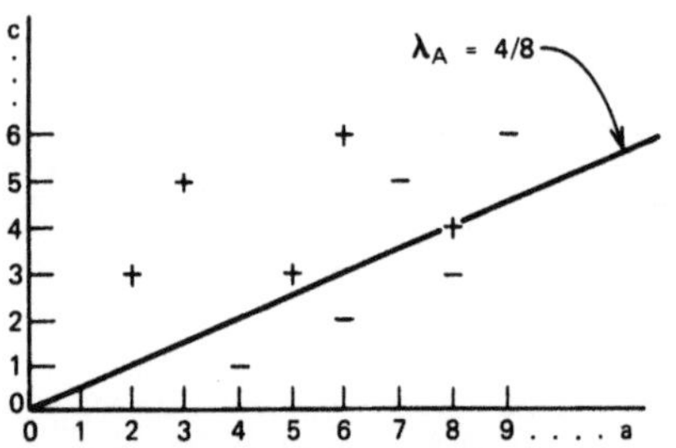

(b) REJECTION RATIO DETERMINED BY x_4

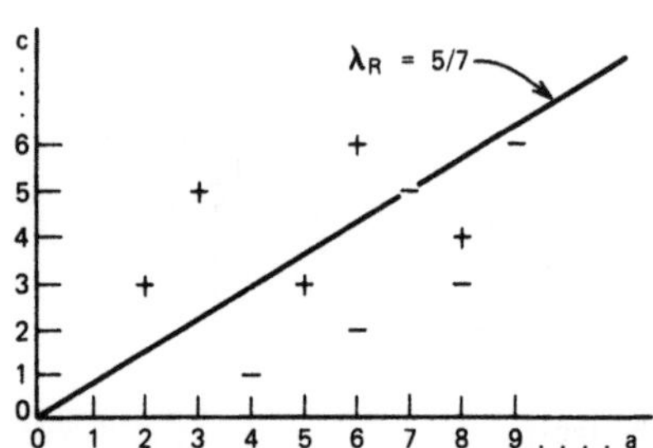

[2] A referee suggests that "if this mechanism were implemented, it would be used over a long period of time with substantial sums at stake and one would expect some investment in learning about the use of strategic maneuvers." Some comment on this view is important because it represents a widely shared belief among economists. We think it is at least as likely—the evidence seems to suggest that it is more likely—that the airlines would compete away any rents which they now capture from airport slot resources. In fact, a very reasonable hypothesis, given the immense uncertainty as to what airport slot combinations are actually worth (these are well defined in our experiments), might be that airline bids would actually exceed those levels that would sustain long-run profitability. If the recent, and continuing, vigorous price competition among airlines in passenger ticket sales is any indication, then this last hypothesis is quite likely to be supported. Braniff Airlines has just filed for Chapter 11 bankruptcy in an environment in which "it has been widely asserted that part of Braniff's financial ills stemmed from steep fare cuts to raise ridership—at the expense of profit" (*Wall Street Journal*, May 17, 1982, p. 4). In less than a week after Braniff's collapse, Midway Air announced entry and "set the fare between Chicago and Dallas-Fort Worth at a cut rate of $89 one way, despite industry hopes that the collapse of Braniff would end extensive fare wars" (*Wall Street Journal*, May 17, 1982, p. 1). These field observations of noncooperative behavior are consistent with the results of several hundred experiments in which

FIGURE 3

CATEGORIZATION FOR PROBLEM K

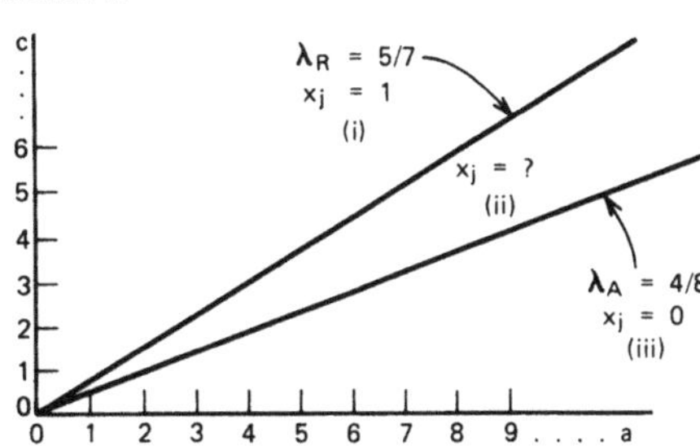

We conjecture that this is why GIP do not observe significant underrevelation of demand in laboratory experiments with one commodity auctions.

Since the combinatorial auction we suggest for the airport slot problem is far more complex than any of the single commodity auctions that have been studied, we would expect to observe at least as much demand-revealing behavior in our auction as in the others. Since this is both an open and a behavioral question, we devised a laboratory experimental design to compare our combinatorial auction procedure with the procedure proposed in GIP (1979).

3. Experimental results

■ Eight experiments were conducted using students with economics and engineering backgrounds. Each experiment consisted of a sequence of market periods in which objective economic conditions remained constant in successive periods for the six participants. The first period was always considered a learning period (no payoff), and the number of periods completed was time dependent (3-hour limit). Individual subjects were paid the difference between the assigned redemption value of packages and the prices paid for packages in the market (Smith, 1976). Subjects' earnings varied between \$8 and \$60, depending on individual endowed valuations and subject and group bidding behavior.

A 2 × 2 × 2 experimental design was employed. The three factors were: (1) GIP (control) versus our RSB (treatment) primary auction; (2) subjects "experienced" versus "inexperienced;" (3) combinatorial "complexity" (easy versus difficult) of resource utilization.

The GIP mechanism employed copied that suggested and used by GIP (1979). The first two RSB experiments used marginal package pricing and the "easy" combinatorial design, while the second two used the marginal item pricing scheme described in Section 2 and the "difficult" combinatorial design.[3] The term "experience" indicates previous participation in either a control or treatment version of an experiment, but even "inexperienced" subjects generally had some experience with other less complicated decisionmaking experiments such as a single commodity auction. Combinatorial "complexity" refers to the degree of difficulty a subject would encounter in attempting to shuffle

---

two to four sellers compete away all except competitive rents in a variety of distinct pricing institutions. In the experiments reported here subjects were quite active in attempting manipulative strategies early in each experiment. These strategies tended to be abandoned over time, as indicated by the tendency for resource prices (Table 3) to increase in successive periods.

[3] Appendix A contains the instructions and forms used in the experiments in which the primary market priced items marginally. The instructions and forms used in our GIP experiments and in the two RSB experiments that priced packages marginally can be obtained by writing Smith at the University of Arizona. Appendix B contains the contrasting package valuation designs used in the "easy" and "difficult" combinatorial treatment.

slots from one package use to another for the purpose of making a redemption claim or a purchase or sale in the after market. It has two components: the amount of package repetition among various agents and the amount of item repetition within any agent's packages.

Table 1 gives the observed efficiency after primary and secondary markets for each cell of the design. The trial (zero) period results are not listed. Efficiency is defined as total subject payoff (realized system surplus) divided by total theoretical payoff (system surplus computed by assuming full demand revelation). The data support several important hypotheses. The overall efficiency of the RSB mechanism is generally greater than that of the GIP mechanism. It is achieved without the uniformly strong dependence on the secondary market displayed by the GIP mechanism. The ability of subjects to include contingency bids in appropriate situations, though not included in the experiments conducted, should serve to accentuate this effect. Market experience seems a significant factor in determining the efficiency of either mechanism. Learning is in evidence during the multiperiod course of each experiment. The RSB mechanism, however, seems to require less learning and displays quicker achievement of high efficiency. This fact suggests that the RSB mechanism will adapt more efficiently to changing economic conditions—an important criterion in judging the performance of any mechanism.

The sample size is too small, with one observation per cell, to test for the significance of each "treatment." But by aggregation across all treatments except the bidding mechanism, we can report a nonparametric sign test of the null hypothesis that the fourth period difference in efficiency between RSB and GIP is equally likely to be positive or negative, as against the research hypothesis that there is a positive difference. From Table 1, for the primary market, all four paired differences are positive, and the null hypothesis is rejected at $p = .0625$. In the after market, three of the four paired differences are positive, and the null hypothesis can be rejected only at $p = .25$. This is consistent with our prior expectation that the principal advantage of RSB over GIP is to improve primary market allocation sufficiently to make after market exchange unnecessary. Thus, comparing after market efficiency with primary market efficiency in period 5 across all RSB experiments, we observe no difference.

The more detailed breakdown of surplus presented in Table 2 adds further support to these observations. Uniformly more agents were in debt after the GIP primary market. On several occasions, an agent who needed to participate in multilateral trades for gains in the GIP secondary market was caught short of completion (e.g., GIP-inexperienced-easy period 1). This is a difficulty to be reckoned with in any independent slot marketing scheme.

Speculation is defined as the purchase of a package by an individual for whom the package has no redemption value. Such a purchase can be profitable only through resale at a higher price in the after market. Because of the extremely high efficiency realized in the primary RSB allocation, speculative behavior is very risky (e.g., RSB-inexperienced-easy period 5 and difficult period 4). Primary prices and allocations are too near optimal to yield much speculative profit, and combinatorial problems are encountered with after market multilateral trade. Table 2 also reinforces the notion that experience is less important in the RSB mechanism. Under the more incentive-compatible conditions of RSB, there was 95% demand revelation for nonspeculative bids in the final period.

The difficulty with determining item values by independent auctions is emphasized by Table 3, which traces prices by period. The absolute deviation from theoretical values is much larger for the GIP mechanism. In fact, the task of estimating item value from package redemption value proved too much for inexperienced GIP subjects under difficult conditions where a market collapse occurred. Unless there is demand overrevelation (bidding in excess of value), it is impossible for this situation to occur in the RSB mechanism, where the optimization routine makes an "intelligent" pricing decision.

TABLE 1 **Efficiency, by Period and Treatment Condition, in the Primary and After Market**

	GIP						RSB					
	Period	Primary Market, *P*	After Market, *A*	Period	Primary Market, *P*	After Market, *A*	Period	Primary Market, *P*	After Market, *A*	Period	Primary Market, *P*	After Market, *A*
Experienced Subjects	1	0.904	0.974	1	0.609	0.730	1	0.832	0.923	1	0.986	0.986
	2	0.871	0.920	2	0.695	0.864	2	0.898	0.944	2	0.978	0.987
	3	0.871	0.953	3	0.709	0.851	3	0.935	0.973	3	0.985	0.985
	4	0.907	0.983	4	0.752	0.903	4	0.971	0.971	4	0.985	0.985
				5	0.804	0.919	5	0.986	0.986	5	0.986	0.986
				6	0.795	0.969				6	0.991	0.993
Inexperienced Subjects	1	0.853	0.861	1	0.721	0.917	1	0.884	0.923	1	0.951	0.965
	2	0.778	0.942	2	0.726	0.831	2	0.918	0.951	2	0.860	0.940
	3	0.650	0.865	3	0.602	0.798	3	0.936	0.977	3	0.976	0.979
	4	0.685	0.911	4	0.408	0.829	4	0.967	0.977	4	0.931	0.931
	5	0.763	0.907	5	0.463	0.923	5	0.869	0.870	5	0.984	0.984
				6	0.465	0.902						
		Easy			Difficult			Easy			Difficult	

TABLE 2 **Breakdown of Surplus by Market, Period, and Treatment Condition (no. agents in debt/negative agents' surplus/positive agents' surplus)**

	GIP		RSB			
Period	Primary	After	Primary	After		
1	1/ −.17/36.11	0/ 0.00/45.20	1/−1.18/33.66	0/ .00/44.57	Experienced Subjects	Easy
2	1/ −4.15/33.64	1/ −.63/36.70	0/ .00/40.69	0/ .00/46.86		
3	4/ −5.11/10.70	1/ −1.77/18.24	1/−1.83/43.64	0/ .00/46.79		
4	3/ −352/15.55	0/ .00/21.32	0/ .00/41.75	0/ .00/41.75		
5			0/ .00/43.04	0/ .00/43.04		
6						
1	0/ .00/18.95	1/ −3.71/23.66	1/ −.39/27.18	0/ .00/31.92	Inexperienced Subjects	
2	3/−10.54/ 6.99	2/ −2.99/21.19	0/ .00/32.02	0/ .00/36.39		
3	3/−30.00/ 3.06	3/ −9.54/11.18	0/ .00/30.12	0/ .00/35.66		
4	4/−34.30/ 2.86	3/ −5.84/ 4.31	0/ .00/31.83	0/ .00/33.22		
5	4/−15.90/ 3.57	2/ −6.36/13.13	1/−5.17/25.13	1/−5.17/25.29		
6						
1	5/−11.18/ 1.86	3/ −4.63/10.36	0/ .00/34.52	0/ .00/34.52	Experienced Subjects	Difficult
2	4/ −7.65/ 7.54	1/ −1.19/32.44	0/ .00/28.46	0/ .00/29.58		
3	4/ −8.84/11.84	1/ −.13/20.80	0/ .00/21.56	0/ .00/21.56		
4	2/−12.30/14.43	1/ −2.70/23.52	0/ .00/19.53	0/ .00/19.53		
5	2/ −2.75/ 9.38	2/ −.41/21.28	0/ .00/18.94	0/ .00/18.94		
6	3/−10.27/ 9.71	0/ .00/21.02	0/ .00/15.04	0/ .00/15.21		
1	3/−31.20/ 1.67	3/ −7.39/ 2.04	1/ −.71/26.72	0/ .00/27.78	Inexperienced Subjects	
2	4/−37.68/ .00	4/−27.07/ 2.32	3/−6.29/ 7.28	1/−1.93/12.79		
3	5/−60.51/ .00	5/−36.69/ .34	0/ .00/11.30	0/ .00/11.59		
4	5/−87.40/ .00	5/−35.27/ .00	1/−6.51/13.74	1/−6.51/13.74		
5	4/−77.05/ .00	3/−23.13/ 3.09	0/ .00/15.21	0/ .00/15.21		
6	3/−18.82/19.26	0/ .00/54.65				

TABLE 3 **Market Prices by Period under Difficult Conditions (using marginal item pricing in RSB mechanism)**

	GIP						RSB						
	Item Prices						Item Prices						
Period	*A*	*B*	*C*	*D*	*E*	*F*	*A*	*B*	*C*	*D*	*E*	*F*	
1	2.30	2.50	2.00	2.10	1.00	2.00	2.27	2.56	2.11	2.39	1.06	1.73	
2	2.31	2.75	2.00	2.26	1.00	2.00	3.07	2.58	2.24	2.67	.94	1.93	
3	2.50	2.76	2.00	2.01	1.00	2.00	3.10	3.03	2.78	2.63	.95	1.88	Experienced Subjects
4	3.00	3.00	2.00	2.26	.50	2.26	3.35	2.90	2.95	2.70	1.15	1.60	
5	3.00	3.05	2.00	2.50	.25	2.50	2.56	3.19	2.98	2.74	1.17	1.81	
6	3.00	3.25	2.50	2.76	.50	2.00	2.88	3.13	3.23	2.57	1.63	1.97	
Theoretical Prices	2.66	3.16	3.09	2.66	2.51	2.49	2.66	3.16	3.09	2.66	2.51	2.49	
1	3.00	2.75	2.50	3.00	2.75	3.00	1.96	3.64	2.44	2.29	.71	2.08	
2	3.20	3.20	3.00	3.10	2.90	3.00	2.25	3.80	2.50	3.32	1.25	2.13	
3	3.50	4.00	3.30	3.50	2.00	2.90	3.24	3.93	2.78	2.97	1.29	1.47	Inexperienced Subjects
4	4.00	5.00	4.00	3.30	1.50	2.50	2.89	3.78	2.73	3.03	1.59	1.58	
5	4.51	5.00	4.51	3.20	1.00	1.00	2.76	3.49	2.80	2.95	1.86	1.39	
6	4.51	.01	3.50	.01	.01	.01	2.78	3.47	2.77	2.79	2.02	1.97	
Theoretical Prices	2.66	3.16	3.09	2.66	2.51	2.49	2.66	3.16	3.09	2.66	2.51	2.49	

Finally, combinatorial complexity seems to lower GIP mechanism efficiency by a significant amount, while the performance of the RSB mechanism appears not to deteriorate and perhaps even to improve. This is to be expected if we are correct in our conjecture that the decision costs potentially associated with this factor are borne by the computer in the RSB mechanism.

4. Alternatives for implementing an airport slot auction

■ To our knowledge, this study constitutes the first attempt to design a "smart" computer-assisted exchange institution. In all the computer-assisted markets known to us in the field, as well as those studied in laboratory experiments, the computer passively records bids and contracts and routinely enforces the trading rules of the institution. The RSB mechanism has potential application to any market in which commodities are composed of combinations of elemental items (or characteristics). The distinguishing feature of our combinatorial auction is that it allows *consumers* to define the commodity by means of the bids tendered for alternative packages of elemental items. It eliminates the necessity for producers to anticipate, perhaps at substantial risk and cost, the commodity packages valued most highly in the market. Provided that bids are demand revealing, and that income effects can be ignored, the mechanism guarantees Pareto optimality in the commodity packages that will be "produced" and in the allocation of the elemental resources. The experimental results suggest that: (a) the procedures of the mechanism are operational, i.e., motivated individuals can execute the required task with a minimum of instruction and training; (b) the extent of demand underrevelation by participants is not large, i.e., allocative efficiencies of 98–99% of the possible surplus seem to be achievable over time with experienced bidders. This occurred despite repeated early attempts by inexperienced subjects to manipulate the mechanism and to engage in speculative purchases.

The problem of allocating airport time slots requires improved methods (GIP, 1981), and the problem has grown from bad to worse in the aftermath of the recent strike attempt by the air traffic controllers. We think the RSB mechanism, or some variant that might be developed from it, has potential for ultimate application to the time slot problem. But as we view it, before such an application can or should be attempted, at least two further developments are necessary. First, at least two additional series of experiments need to be completed. Another series of laboratory experiments should be designed, using larger numbers of participants, resources, and possible package combinations. The subjects in these new experiments should be the appropriate operating personnel of a group of cooperating airlines. Depending on the results of such experiments, the next step might be to design a limited scale field experiment with only a few airports and airlines.

Second, there should be extensive discussion and debate within the government, academic, and airline communities concerning alternative means of implementing the combinatorial auction. There is a wide range of choice here. Our discussion, as well as the reported experiments, were based on the assumption that airline bids would be denominated in U.S. currency and that the revenue would be allocated to the airports. There are, however, other alternatives; we offer just a few to stimulate discussion. (1) If it is believed that airport revenue should not be based on the imputed rents from scarce time slots, then bids in the combinatorial auction could be denominated in "slot currency" or vouchers issued in fixed quantities to each airline. These vouchers could be freely bought and sold among the airlines but would only be redeemable in time slots. (2) Alternatively, each airline could continue to be given some "historical" allocation of slots, with the RSB mechanism modified to become a two-sided sealed bid-offer combinatorial auction. In such an auction each airline would submit package bids for slots to be purchased, and package offers of slots to be sold. Under this form of implementation, the rent imputed to airport slots would of course be retained as "revenue" by the airlines.

(3) An important question not addressed in either the GIP or RSB procedures is the pricing of airline seats, which directly affects the willingness-to-pay for airport slots. We would suggest that the idea of a computerized continuous double (bid-offer) auction of seats be considered along with the combinatorial auctioning of slots. All the major airlines are computerized down to the boarding gate, so that the computerized trading of seats may be technically feasible, and could provide a more flexible means of increasing airline revenue while lowering passenger cost through improved load factors. (4) Finally, we should note that we think there may be an inherent contradiction in the attempt to allow free (deregulated) entry by the airlines, but not permit free entry by airports. Ultimately, a pricing system for airport slots, which returns revenue to the airports, could allow not only for package bids from the airlines, but slot price offers from the airports, with each airport subject to competition from new regional, suburban, and national airports.

Appendix A

Instructions

RSB instructions. This is an experiment in the economics of market decisionmaking. Various research organizations have provided funds for the conduct of this research. The instructions are simple, and if you follow them carefully and make good decisions, you might earn a considerable amount of money, which will be paid to you in cash after the experiment. In this experiment we are going to conduct two kinds of markets to distribute six distinct items among you in a sequence of periods or market days. The six distinct items are represented by the letters: *A*, *B*, *C*, *D*, *E*, *F*. At the end of the experiment we shall redeem (that is, buy) certain packages of items you have acquired during each period. The amounts to be paid to you as an individual can be determined from your payoff sheet included with the instructions. The payoff tables may differ among individuals. This means that the patterns of payments differ and the monetary amounts may not be comparable. The first market is the primary market and is of the sealed-bid type. In this market each of you may bid to buy items offered in fixed quantities. The second market will be a secondary market of the oral-bid-offer type. In this market you may buy or sell items obtained in the primary market to one another if you wish. Alternatively, you may simply keep what you have for the experimenters to redeem. In all sales, whether to the experimenters or to other participants, you may keep any profits you earn. For each sale you make, your profits are computed as follows: your earnings = sale price − purchase price.

□ **Redemption values.** In your folder there is a sheet labelled "Redemption Values." This sheet indicates the amount the experimenter will pay you for given packages of items at the end of the period. Suppose for example you ended the period with 2*A*, 2*C*, and 2*F* items, and your redemption values were as follows:

package	items included						value
	A	*B*	*C*	*D*	*E*	*F*	
1	1	1	1				1.20
2	1		1				.40
3	1		1			1	1.20
4	1					1	.72
5			1			1	.70
6	1					1	.60.

Since you may claim each item in only one package, you may legitimately claim for the set [*AC*, *CF*, *AF*] which will redeem .40 + .70 + .72 = $1.82. But the set [*ACF*, *CF*] with one leftover item *A* is a better claim since it redeems 1.20 + .70 = $1.90. In this case your period profit may have been increased by previously selling off the leftover item *A* in the secondary market.

□ **Primary market.** Each period there will be a limited number of units of each kind of item available. As a buyer you purchase packages of one or more units by submitting bids which may be accepted or rejected. You will decide each period how many bids to submit for which packages in what amounts. Suppose you wish to bid for packages *AF* at .72, *AF* at .48, and *AC* at .37. Then your bid sheet for the primary market should look like this:

package	items included						value
	A	*B*	*C*	*D*	*E*	*F*	
1	1					1	.72
2	1					1	.48
3	1		1				.37.

Bids are accepted or rejected each period as follows. The bid sheets are collected from all buyers. All bids are fed into a computer program which selects the set of bids which are most valuable without violating any constraint on the number of units of each item available. The program also gives two sets, low and high, of item unit values. Each accepted bid represents the purchase of one package at a total price equal to the sum of its low item values. Your purchase price will always be less than or equal to your bid price, since any bid less than the sum of its low item values was definitely rejected. Any bid greater than the sum of its high item values was definitely accepted. Consider the above set of bids. Suppose the low and high item unit values for *A*, *C*, and *F* were given as (.25, .10, .32) and (.25, .16, .34). Then package 1 was definitely accepted since .72 > .25 + .34. The market price for the package *AF* was .25 + .32 = .57. Package 2 was definitely rejected since .48 < .57. Package 3 might have been rejected or accepted since .25 + .10 < .37 < .25 + .16. At the close of the primary market bid sheets will be returned to each buyer indicating which of his bids were accepted. The low and high sets of item values will be posted.

□ **Secondary market.** The secondary market provides an opportunity to buy additional units or sell units from the inventory acquired in the primary market. This is an oral auction. You may announce a bid (offer) to buy (sell) any package of one or more items for a specified amount. This bid (offer) will be placed on the board until it is accepted by some other participant or you cancel it. You are free to make as many bids and offers as you wish. Many may remain unaccepted but you are free to keep trying. *Note*: You may not sell what you do not have in inventory. Each purchase or sale in which you participate should be recorded on a separate line in the sequence of occurrence on your secondary market balance sheet. From your final inventory at the end of the secondary market, you specify a set of item packages that you want to redeem for cash.

□ **Profits.** Period profit is calculated as: profit = redemption revenue + sales revenue from secondary market − purchase costs from both markets. After each period has ended, make the appropriate entries on your payoff sheet. The experimenters will pay you all you have earned during all periods at the conclusion of the experiment.

Primary Market Agent #1 Period #1

Agent's Bids for Packages

Package	Items Included						Bid	Accepted Yes or No	Market Price
	A	*B*	*C*	*D*	*E*	*F*			
1									
2									
⋮									
8									
# Units								Total Cost	
	Totals for Auction Accepted Bids Only								WWW

Secondary Market Agent # 1 Period # 0

Note: Before the secondary market begins, copy the # of units of each item bought in the primary market into the spaces labelled inventory for transaction 0.

Transaction	Package Dealt: Items Included						Sold For	Bought At	Inventory: # Units Each Item					
	A	*B*	*C*	*D*	*E*	*F*	$	$	*A*	*B*	*C*	*D*	*E*	*F*
0	X	X	X	X	X	X								
⋮														
6														
Total Sales YYY								X	X					
Total Costs XXX							X		X					
Final Inventory							X	X						

Redemption Values Agent # 1 Period # 0

Note: Before claiming redemptions, copy your final inventory from the secondary market into the following table. Make sure all packages you intend to redeem are covered by this inventory. Remember that any unit of a given item can only be used in one package.

Item	*A*	*B*	*C*	*D*	*E*	*F*
# Units						

Package	Items Included: *A*	*B*	*C*	*D*	*E*	*F*	Value	Claimed Yes or No
1	1	1					6.27	
2			1	1			5.77	
3	1				1		5.06	
4	1		1			1	8.25	
5		1	1		1		8.34	
Total Value of Redemptions =								ZZZ

Payoff Sheet Agent # 1

Your profit from each period is calculated as follows:
Period Profit = Redemption Value (*ZZZ*) + Sales in Secondary Market (*YYY*)
− Costs in Secondary Market (*XXX*) − Costs in Primary Market (*WWW*)
After each period concludes, make the proper entries in the following table:

Period	Red. Value *ZZZ*		Sales Sec. *YYY*		Costs Sec. *XXX*		Costs Pri. *WWW*		Profit
0		+		−		−		=	
1		+		−		−		=	
2		+		−		−		=	
⋮		+		−		−		=	
6		+		−		−		=	
	Total Profit Over All Periods						*PPP*		

I acknowledge receipt of the above amount (*PPP*) from the experimenters:

Appendix B

Agent value information

■ Easy resource utilization design.

Agent	Package	Value	Item *A*	Item *B*	Item *C*	Item *D*	Item *E*	Item *F*
1	1	5.98	1	1				
1	2	9.46	1	1	1			
1	3	5.17		1	1			
2	4	6.32	1			1		
2	5	6.63		1	1			
2	6	9.51	1	1	1			
3	7	8.77	1	1				1
3	8	5.95	1		1			
3	9	5.15		1	1			
3	10	8.85	1	1	1			
4	11	5.46	1		1			
4	12	9.83	1		1			1
4	13	5.69	1	1				
4	14	6.03		1	1			
5	15	6.42	1	1				
5	16	4.50	1				1	
5	17	4.98		1	1			
5	18	9.13	1		1		1	
5	19	4.76	1		1			
6	20	5.76	1		1			
6	21	8.02		1	1	1		
6	22	4.39		1	1			
6	23	9.45	1		1			1
6	24	6.17	1		1			
6	25	5.20	1	1				
# Units Demanded			18	15	18	2	2	3
# Units Available			13	11	15	1	2	3

□ **Difficult resource utilization design.**

Agent	Package	Value	Item *A*	Item *B*	Item *C*	Item *D*	Item *E*	Item *F*
1	1	6.27	1	1				
1	2	5.77			1	1		
1	3	5.06	1				1	
1	4	8.25	1		1			1
1	5	8.34		1	1		1	
2	6	5.31	1	1				
2	7	5.56			1	1		
2	8	5.76	1		1			
2	9	6.44		1			1	
2	10	5.84			1		1	
2	11	8.86	1				1	1
3	12	5.17	1	1				
3	13	5.76			1	1		
3	14	8.87	1		1		1	
3	15	9.40		1	1			1
4	16	5.98	1	1				
4	17	6.27			1	1		
4	18	5.78	1					1
4	19	5.78		1		1		
4	20	5.56				1		1
4	21	8.61		1			1	1
5	22	5.60	1	1				
5	23	5.82			1	1		
5	24	5.65		1				1
5	25	8.34		1		1	1	
5	26	7.82	1			1		1
6	27	5.07	1	1				
6	28	5.65			1	1		
6	29	8.33		1		1		1
6	30	9.59	1			1	1	
# Units Demanded			14	14	12	12	9	9
# Units Available			7	7	7	7	7	7

References

GRETHER, D., ISAAC, M., AND PLOTT, C. "Alternative Methods of Allocating Airport Slots: Performance and Evaluation." CAB Report. Pasadena, Calif.: Polynomics Research Laboratories, Inc., 1979.

———, ———, AND ———. "The Allocation of Landing Rights by Unanimity among Competitors." *American Economic Review*, Vol. 71 (May 1981), pp. 166–171.

RASSENTI, S. "0–1 Decision Problems with Multiple Resource Constraints: Algorithms and Applications." Unpublished Ph.D. thesis, University of Arizona, 1981.

SMITH, V. "Experimental Economics: Induced Value Theory." *American Economic Review*, Vol. 66 (May 1976).

VICKREY, W. "Counterspeculation, Auctions, and Competitive Sealed Tenders." *Journal of Finance* (March 1961).

"Midway Air Sets Chicago-Dallas Ticket at $89." *Wall Street Journal* (May 17, 1982), pp. 1, 4.

WOLSEY, L. "Integer Programming Duality: Price Functions and Sensitivity Analysis." *Mathematical Programming*, Vol. 20 (1981), pp. 173–195.

DESIGNING 'SMART' COMPUTER-ASSISTED MARKETS

An Experimental Auction for Gas Networks

Kevin A. McCABE, Stephen J. RASSENTI and Vernon L. SMITH*

Economic Science Laboratory, University of Arizona, Tucson, AZ 85721, USA

We study a sealed bid–offer auction market for simultaneously pricing natural gas at each delivery outlet, source, and on all pipelines that connect sources with delivery points. Wholesale buyers submit location-specific bid schedules for amounts of delivered gas at corresponding prices. Wellhead owners submit location-specific offer schedules for amounts of produced gas they are willing to sell at corresponding offer prices. Pipeline owners submit leg-specific schedules of transportation capacity they are willing to commit at corresponding prices. A computer algorithm maximizes total gains from exchange based on the submitted bids and offers and determines allocations and non-discriminatory prices at all nodes.

As a consequence of technological economies of scale in pipeline transportation, natural gas has been considered a classic case of natural monopoly. But entry, growth and development in the industry in the United States has yielded more than one pipeline in most producing fields. Similarly most wholesale markets are served by at least two pipelines [Norman (1987)]. The concept of natural monopoly is a static concept; i.e. given any level of demand, declining long run marginal planning cost implies that one pipeline – a very large one, if demand is high – yields the least-cost solution to satisfying that demand. But in fact demand is cyclical and tends to grow over time, and new gas wells and gas fields develop over time. Consequently, the first pipelines were of modest size, with parallel larger lines laid as demand grew. The result is multiple supply sources just as in other industries such as steel, automobiles and electrical appliances. This raises the question of whether prices and allocations in the industry could not be disciplined

*This study was supported under grants to the Economic Science Laboratory, University of Arizona, from the Federal Energy Regulatory Commission and the Energy Information Administration. The results and conclusions contained in this report are the responsibility of the authors, and not of these sponsoring agencies. We are indebted to Shawn LaMaster for computing, charting and other valuable assistance and to Praveen Kujal and Joe Campbell for research assistance and help in recruiting subjects and running the experiments. We also wish to thank Daniel Alger of the FERC for many helpful comments and suggestions as the research project developed.

satisfactorily by competitive forces as a replacement for some of the public regulatory apparatus.

Historically, in the United States federal regulation of the industry strengthened the monopoly power of gas pipelines. In the early years natural gas was an undeveloped by-product of the search for oil. Therefore it was felt that the industry needed protection from supply and demand risk to encourage pipeline construction. Consequently, before a construction permit was issued to serve a new market, the pipeline company was required to demonstrate that it had sufficient gas reserves under contract. With supplies required to be adequate, the demand side was then protected by limiting access by new pipelines. This created a regulatory system in which wholesale buyers had to purchase all wellhead gas from pipelines. The resulting pipeline monopoly was further strengthened by a requirement that imposed minimum charges (independent of quantity taken), and sole supplier conditions on the local distribution companies who were the wholesale purchasers of pipeline gas. Thus 'regulation' under the old Federal Power Commission actually took the form of government promotion of the natural gas industry [Stalon (1985)].

All this began to change because of the Natural Gas Policy Act (NGPA) of 1978. This legislation initiated a process of phased deregulation of wellhead gas by removing from the Federal Energy Regulatory Commission (FERC) the role of making judgments about the adequacy of price incentives to produce gas. The NGPA together with FERC Order 436, issued in 1985, facilitated a process whereby wholesale buyers could directly contract for, or purchase spot, gas from wellhead producers, and then buy their pipeline transportation. Thus the historic 'bundling' of gas production and transportation started to come apart. Although the regulatory process helped to insure pipeline monopoly, and this probably explains their historically high rate of return on investment compared with other industries [Norman (1987, tables 3 and 4, fig. 1)], the new competitive forces, strengthened by NGPA and the FERC Order 436, are helping to produce many changes in the industry.

It is against this background that we were asked by the FERC to develop, and examine the feasibility and properties of, an auction market for the sale and transportation of natural gas. In this article we report our initial research design and experiments based on this objective.

1. Gas auction net: Motivation and distinguishing features

The gas and transport pricing mechanism we examine in this study has been motivated in part by the following potentially desirable properties.

(1) *Self regulation*; i.e. ultimately we seek to explore the feasibility of substituting a satisfactory market mechanism for rate of return and other

regulatory constraints. The wide application of competitive sealed auctions in financial markets suggests that a suitable extension and modification of this institution may have desirable properties in gas network applications.

(2) *Non price-discrimination*; i.e. all pricc differences among wholesalers, producers and pipelines in any given pricing period are justified only on the basis of marginal costs and opportunity costs. It is our interpretation that current law favors this property.

(3) *Priority-responsive pricing for curtailments*; i.e. in the event of restrictions in pipeline capacity (say due to cold weather) there is an automatic restriction of deliveries to those wholesalers that have the highest consumption priorities (and a corresponding restriction of production schedules to those wellhead producers that have the highest production priorities) as expressed in the bids (offers) each submits to the auction-dispatch center.

(4) *Value responsive investment incentives.* A good mechanism should provide incentives for increases in production and transportation capacity where such increases have the highest value.

(5) *Simplicity and decentralization.* Although network systems may have inherent physical complications, it is desirable to have a price mechamism in which the participants can understand what is required of them and can readily fulfill these requirements. One of the advantages of a decentralized mechanism is that the participants can concentrate on judgments and actions based on the private information each is most directly informed about. Computer assistance is used where it is most appropriate and needed: to generate non-discretionary, consistent, best, but strictly routine results based on the willingness-to-pay and willingness-to-accept judgments of dispersed individual participants.

(6) *Compatibility with existing institutions.* Present institutions emphasizing contract precomitments for gas and/or transportation could continue to function simultaneously with a network auction. This could be accomplished by applying the auction to available capacities above the flows precommitted by contract. Consequently the extent of the use of the auction would be determined by the decisions of the participants, and could grow in response to increased use without the necessity of a possible disruptive discontinuous switchover. When the auction is used for spot trades holders of long gas could resell spot those quantities not needed for current consumption. In this case the auction would supplement and increase the efficiency of current institutions.

This paper reports our findings from 9 laboratory experiments designed to study the efficiency and price performance characteristics of a sealed bid–offer auction mechanism for the simultaneous allocation of gas and pipeline capacity rights among buyers of delivered gas, transporters, and sellers of wellhead gas. This computer-assisted mechanism will be called *Gas Auction Net*.

Some of the salient features of our Gas Auction Net mechanism are as follows.

(1) Consumption centers (consisting of primary gas buyers such as local distribution companies and industrial consumers) are connected to producing gas fields (consisting of primary gas sellers) by a capacity-constrained pipeline network. The network we study experimentally is thin, and weakly competitive. In this sense it is intended as a worst-case example for any price mechanism.

(2) The auction market uses 'smart' computer support to process location-specific bid schedules from gas buyers, location-specific offer schedules from wellhead producers, and segment-specific offer schedules of transfer capacity from pipeline owners. This means that each of the three types of participants is required to make judgments that reflect only their own private circumstances. That is, their willingness to buy gas, sell gas or sell transportation on each pipeline segment.

(3) The resulting prices are non-discriminatory; i.e. all sellers at the same location (or line haul pipeline input point) receive the same price, all buyers at the same location (line haul output point) pay the same price, and all pipelines connecting a given source location with a given receiving location obtain the same price. Other pricing mechanisms, such as double auction and posted pricing do not yield non-discriminative prices except in full equilibrium.[1] Gas Auction Net yields non-discriminatory prices in each price period.

(4) Differences in the price of gas between any two (production or consumption) locations reflect differences in the marginal supply price of transportation and/or pipeline capacity restrictions.

(5) The allocation of delivered gas among buyers, of produced gas among sellers, and of the resulting transportation requirements among pipelines maximizes the total system aggregate gains from exchange (surplus) given the schedules of buyer bids, seller offers and pipeline offers. In this sense Gas Auction Net guarantees a maximally efficient, or no waste, competitive market given the submitted bids and offers of all participants. Its first priority is to consume gas from the lowest cost wells, and deliver it to the highest value wholesale user using the lowest cost transportation routes.

The experiments we report evaluate the price and efficiency characteristics

[1]See Ketcham, Smith and Williams (1984) for a comparison of the double auction and posted price exchange institutions.

of Gas Auction Net as a mechanism for the exchange of rights. The rights themselves are not labelled or interpreted in terms of particular possible implementations in the gas industry. Thus the rights actually traded in an implementation of Gas Auction Net might be for spot gas commitments, hourly, monthly or weekly, or for forward commitments next winter (firm or interruptible). Our primary research task is to evaluate Gas Auction Net as a price mechanism applied to any well-defined set of contractual rights.

Technically, Gas Auction Net is an extension and generalization of the *competitive* (uniform price) sealed bid, and double sealed bid–offer, auctions. As a price mechanism its distinguishing feature is that all accepted bids to buy are filled at a price less than or equal to the lowest accepted bid price of buyers – a price that just clears the market by making the total number of units offered equal to the number demanded. This contrasts with the *discriminative* sealed bid auction where Q units are offered for sale and the Q highest bids are accepted, but each accepted bid is filled at a price equal to the amount bid. Consequently, different buyers pay different prices for the same commodity. Also, the discriminative auction provides an incentive for *strategic underbidding* of full willingness-to-pay as each bidder attempts to avoid having to pay more than the minimum necessary amount (the lowest accepted bid). This incentive is reduced in the competitive auction, and in special cases is in theory eliminated.

There is now a considerable theoretical literature on competitive auctions [see the survey by McAfee and McMillan (1987)] stimulated by Vickrey's (1961) original contribution, and generalizing the second price sealed bid auction for a single unit to the competitive multiple unit auction. There are also several experimental studies [in chronological order, Smith (1967), Belovicz (1979), Coursey and Smith (1984), Miller and Plott (1985), Cox, Smith and Walker (1985)] of competitive auctions often with empirical comparison to discriminative auctions. The first field experiments comparing competitive and discriminative auctions of long-term bonds were conducted by the U.S. Treasury in the early 1970s.

Also of particular importance to Gas Auction Net as an extension of the competitive sealed bid auction is the fact that variations on this institution have received wide acceptance as price-allocation mechanisms in financial markets. We are therefore considering the extension of an institution that has been thoroughly time-tested for over a decade and found increasing application.

2. Overview of experimental design and procedures

The research design underlying this paper is based on three series of experiments using a simplified gas transmission network. The first series uses parameters which we call Design I, and consisted of three experiments using inexperienced subjects, two using experienced subjects and one using 'super' (or twice) experienced subjects. The second series, Design II, (in addition to the inexperienced training sessions) consisted of two experiments using experienced subjects and one using super experienced subjects. Design II further differs from Design I in that in the former the cost and capacity parameters provide a more contestable and potentially more competitive network than Design I. By comparing the results from Design II with those from Design I we are able to measure the effect of increased network contestability. A third series, Design III, again consisted of two experiments using experienced and one experiment using twice experienced subjects. Design III was based on the same parameters used in Design II. But in Design II each pipeline owner also owned one of the producer wells served by the pipeline, while in Design III no pipeline transported gas from a well owned by that pipeline. By comparing the results of Design II with those of Design III we obtain a measure of the effect of vertical integration on the ability of pipelines to compete for rents with independent producers.

Subjects were recruited from the undergraduate population at the University of Arizona. They were paid three dollars upon arrival for an experiment as an incentive to arrive on time. At the end of each experiment subjects were paid their profit earnings in U.S. dollars. These payouts varied from six dollars to sixty dollars, U.S. currency. All experimental earnings are denominated in what are called 'pesos', which are then converted into U.S. dollars at a fixed specified rate – one (for experienced subjects) U.S. dollar per hundred pesos depending upon the parameter design. Using a conversion rate facilitates approximate uniformity in individual rewards across experiments with different parameter designs.

All experiments were run on the Plato Computer system. This system was used: to instruct subjects in the experimental institution; to enforce the message rules which define the institution (and thus coordinate subject interaction); and to record profits. Experimenters were on hand both to assist subjects who had difficulty in understanding the rules and to enforce privacy.

After everyone had arrived they were assigned randomly an agent type (as defined in our 'design' subsections below). Subjects then went through the instructions at their own pace. When everyone had finished reading the instructions, and all questions were answered, inexperienced subjects were then put through a one-period trial run of the experiment. When the trial period was concluded they were asked to verify their understanding of their profit page in light of their market decisions. After all questions were answered the experiment was begun.

Experience with human subjects suggests that fatigue problems may arise if one runs an experiment for more than two consecutive hours. This constraint prevented the experiments in our inexperienced treatment from lasting more than 15 periods. But experienced players finished the instructions more

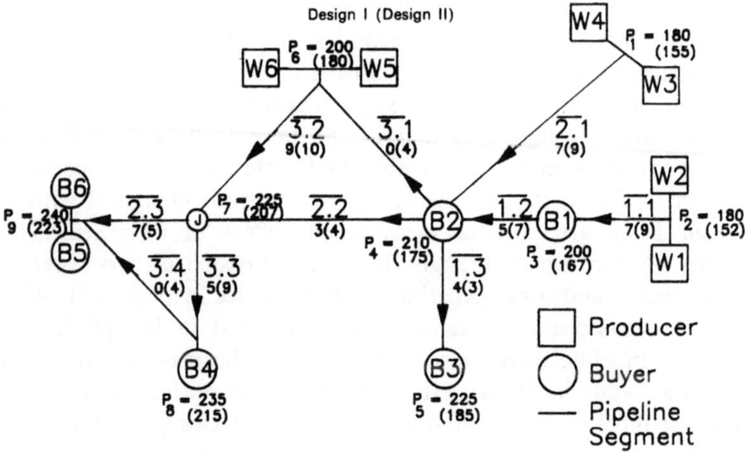

Fig. 1. Pipeline system and predicted equilibrium for market network environments.

quickly allowing us to run up to 30 or more periods. To minimize 'end play' in all experiments, subjects were not informed as to the actual number of periods.

3. Parameters: Network design I

The physical layout of our network system is shown in fig. 1. Each pipeline is identified by owner and segment. Thus 2.2 refers to line owner 2, segment 2. Line owners 1 and 2 each own three segments of the system and owner 3 owns four segments.

The top panel of table 1 lists the valuations and capacities of the six buyers. These are intended to represent opportunity costs faced by bulk buyers. The columns labelled $V1$, $Q1$ and $V2$, $Q2$ in table 1 show the unit values and corresponding quantities at which our experimental buyers can 'redeem' their purchases from the experimenter. For example buyer 1 can redeem 2 units/period at a price of 300 pesos/unit and an additional 2 units at 200 pesos/unit. Each buyer has a two-part marginal valuation schedule defined in this manner. The second panel of table 1 lists the cost and output capacities of each of the six producers in the columns labelled WC and Q. For example Well 1 can deliver up to 5 units/period at an out-of-pocket cost of 150 pesos/unit. Note that each pipeline owner is also an owner of one well; lines 1, 2, and 3 own wells $W2$, $W4$ and $W6$ respectively. This is intended to reflect the current condition in the industry in which there are

Table 1

A competitive equilibrium solution with all bids equal to values and all offers equal to costs.
Network Design I

Buyer	$V1$	$Q1$	$V2$	$Q2$	Consumption	Buyer price	(Node i.d.)	Profit
1	300	2	200	2	2	200	(P3)	200
2	255	3	245	2	5	210	(P4)	205
3	310	2	230	2	4	225	(P5)	180
4	275	3	260	2	5	235	(P8)	170
5	320	2	225	2	2	240	(P9)	160
6	285	2	260	3	5	240	(P9)	150
								1065 (59.2%)

Well	WC	Q	Production	Well price	(Node i.d.)	Profit
1	150	5	5	180	(P2)	150
2	180	4	2	180	(P2)	0
3	150	5	5	180	(P1)	150
4	180	4	2	180	(P1)	0
5	160	5	5	200	(P6)	200
6	190	4	4	200	(P6)	40
						540 (30.0%)

Line	$LC1$	$Q1$	$LC2$	$Q2$	Shipment	Line price	(Node diff.)	Profit	Ceiling price
1.1	15	7	25	3	7	20	(P3–P2)	35	30
1.2	10	5	15	3	5	10	(P4–P3)	0	20
1.3	10	3	15	2	4	15	(P5–P4)	15	20
2.1	25	7	35	4	7	30	(P4–P1)	35	40
2.2	15	6	25	3	3	15	(P7–P4)	0	30
2.3	10	6	15	3	7	15	(P9–P7)	30	20
3.1	15	5	25	2	0	10	(P6–P4)	0	30
3.2	15	8	25	3	9	25	(P7–P6)	80	30
3.3	10	8	15	3	5	10	(P8–P7)	0	20
3.4	15	6	25	2	0	5	(P9–P8)	0	30
								195 (10.8%)	

$E_B = 59.2\%$ $E_P = 27.8\%$
$E_L = 10.8\%$ $E_{PL} = 2.2\%$ Total surplus, 1800 pesos.

both independent wellhead owners and 'captive' wells owned by, or under contract with, the serving pipeline.

The bottom panel of table 1 lists the two-part marginal cost schedule for each owner-segment of pipeline in the columns labelled $LC1$ $Q1$ and $LC2$, $Q2$. The last column lists the ceiling price on each line segment. For example pipeline segment 2.2 can transport up to 6 units at 15 pesos/unit and an

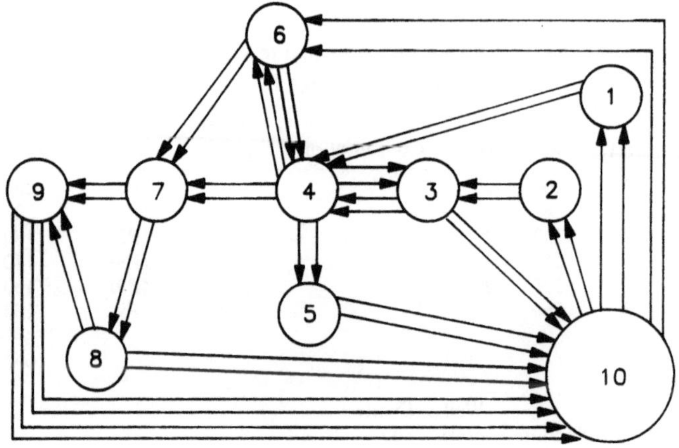

Fig. 2. Logical auction network.

additional 3 units at 25 pesos/unit.[2] His regulated ceiling price on all 9 units is 30 pesos/unit. The first 6 units constitute his 'official' or normal FERC-approved capacity, while the next 3 units represent additional higher cost capacity. The idea is that 'capacity' is not rigidly fixed, and that some abnormal capacity can be obtained at higher cost. This network is not intended to represent any particular network in the field. However, it does capture some aspects of reality such as the fact that most gas is sold in markets which are served by two or more pipelines.

4. Gas Auction Net: Mathematical representation and optimization procedures

Fig. 2 provides a schematic diagram corresponding to fig. 1 that illustrates the mathematical representation used to solve the network optimization problem. Nodes 1–9 represent the real production, consumption and junction locations in the network of fig. 1. Node 10 is artificial, and allows us to balance physical flow with payment flow in the network, and input the bids and offers of buyers and producers. Think of node 10 as completing a circular flow system which allows a return flow of monetary payments from

[2]Marginal pumping cost is an increasing, approximately quadratic, function (up to capacity) of gas throughput in a pipeline [Vincent-Genod (1984, pp. 42–43)]. We approximate this function with a two-part step function, but this approximation can be made as precise as one pleases with an *n*-part step function.

buyers to producers in exchange for the gas flowing on modes 1–9 from producers to buyers.

Each are i in the network is represented by the vector $(s_i, e_i, l_i, u_i, c_i)$ with:

s_i its starting point
e_i its end point
l_i the least permissible flow on that arc (zero in our applications)
u_i the greatest permissible flow on that arc (as determined by the bid or offer quantity entered by a buyer or a producer)
c_i the offer price (bids are signed negative) per unit of flow on that arc.

Each arc represents one bid or offer. If a buyer makes a two-part bid, then it is represented by two parallel arcs. Two-part offers by pipeline owners are represented similarly. Where gas is to be allowed to flow in either direction on a pipeline a two-part offer is represented by four arcs – two arcs in each direction, as in the arcs connecting nodes 3 and 4.

Example 1: Buyer 4 bids 300/unit for 3 units and 200/unit for 2 more units. Since buyer 4 is at location 8 (fig. 1 and tables 1 and 2) his bids would be represented by 2 arcs labelled as:

(8, 10, 0, 3, –300); and

(8, 01, 0, 2, –200).

Each arc is defined by its own identifying number from 1 to 42 so there is no problem with parallel arcs between the same nodes.

Example 2. Producer 4 offers to produce 5 units for 95/unit. Then the appropriate arc would be labelled (10, 1, 0, 5, 95).

Example 3. The owner of segment 2.2 offers to carry 6 units at 45/unit and an additional 3 unit at 55/unit. Then the appropriate arcs are labelled (4, 7, 0, 6, 45) and (4, 7, 0, 3, 55).

After all arcs are labelled using the bids and offers of the agents, the revealed surplus in the network is maximized using the following formulation:

$$\text{maximize: } -\sum_i c_i f_i \quad \text{(total surplus)};$$

$$\text{subject to: } \sum_{i \in E_j} f_i - \sum_{k \in S_j} f_k = 0 \quad (\forall \text{ nodes } j); \qquad \text{I}$$

$$l_i \leqq f_i \leqq u_i \quad (\forall \text{ arcs } i); \qquad \text{II}$$

where f_i is the flow on arc i, and for each node j. E_j is the set of arcs which end at j, and S_j is the set of arcs which begin at j. Note that constraint set I maintains the balance of flow at each node j. Constraint set II ensures that the flow on each arc does not exceed the stated bounds.

Solving the linear program yields not only the optimal flows (and production and consumption pattern) but also the set of shadow prices π_j for all nodes in the network.

Since the shadow prices are relative to one another, the difference in shadow prices at the start and end nodes of an arc gives us the value of the marginal unit of flow on that arc, hence the price associated with that flow. For example:

(a) If $\pi_{10}-\pi_8=-250$ then buyer 4 (who resides at location 8) pays 250 pesos/unit to receive delivered gas at location 8. It is clear that if two buyers reside at the same location they pay the same price.
(b) If $\pi_7-\pi_4=50$ then the owner of pipeline segment 2.2 receives 50 pesos/unit to transport between locations 4 and 7.
(c) If $\pi_6-\pi_{10}=105$ then both producers 5 and 6 who reside at location 6 receives the same price, 105 pesos/unit, to produce gas at that location.

With this linear programming formulation the budget is always balanced since the physical flow on each segment represents an activity which is exactly compensated.

A sample solution of the linear program is displayed on the right hand side of table 1 beginning with the columns labelled Consumption, Production and Shipment. The solution prices at each node, and flows on each arc, are also entered on fig. 1. This solution is based on full revelation of demand by buyers and of supply by producers and transporters, and is achieved by applying the linear program with all bids at marginal redemption value and all offers at marginal cost. Our parameters for this design imply that in a competitive equilibrium (*ce*) solution buyer surplus is 1065 (59.2%), producer surplus is 500 (27.8%) for independent wellhead owners, and 40 (2.2%) for pipeline owned wells, pipeline transportation surplus is 195 (10.8%), and total surplus is 1800 (100%), all measured in experimental pesos. These ideal surplus figures will be used to evaluate the overall efficiency of each experimental market as well as the division of the total surplus among the three constituents. Note that with these particular parameters there are no *ce* flows on segments 3.1 and 3.4. In effect, Network Design I is less connected than that displayed in fig. 1. Below, in Network Design II, this condition is relaxed by using parameters such that there are *ce* flows on all legs. Design I was our basic 'trainer' for building up a pool of experienced network subjects. Design I provides a measure of the gross behavioral 'rationality' of our mechanism in that we should not observe persistent flows on segments 3.1 and 3.4, since these segments do not provide close cost contestability with the alternative path segments with which they compete.

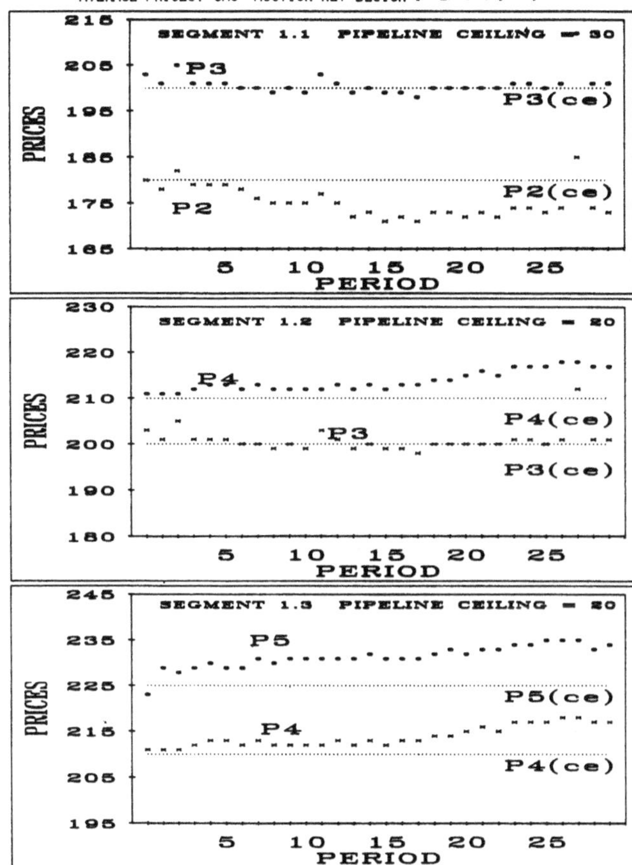

Fig. 3

5. Experimental results: Gas Auction Net Design I

The principal results of experiments 4*e*, 5*e* and 6*ee* (the inexperienced sessions 1*i*, 2*i* and 3*i* are not reported) are provided in the accompanying charts of average prices and average efficiency.

Average prices

Average prices are charted by period at the head and tail of each pipeline segment in figs. 3–5. The priuces at the top of each chart, plotted as solid 'dots', apply to the node at the end point or head to which the pipeline segment is delivering gas. The prices at the bottom, plotted as 'xs', refer to the tail node from which the segment is receiving gas. For example, in segment 1.1 delivery is to *B*1 (fig. 1), so the upper prices are observations on

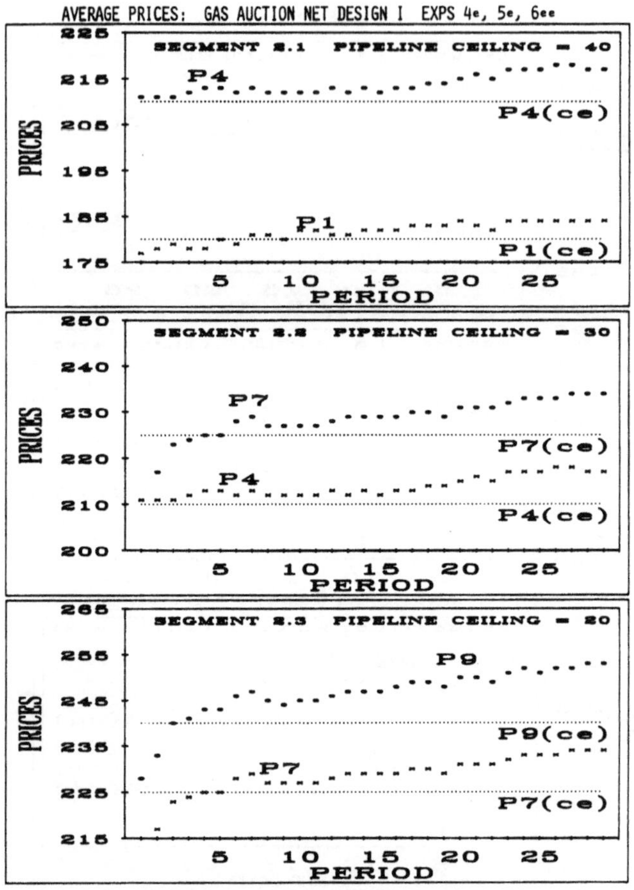

Fig. 4

P_3 (note 3, figs. 1 and 2), while the lower prices, P_2, are for wells *W*1 and *W*2 served by segment 1.1; in segment 2.3 the gas is delivered to a buyer node, at price P_9 (buyers *B*5 and *B*6), but the gas source is the junction, *J*, where price is denoted P_7. The price at the output node on the line segment is higher than the price at the input node because gas flows from lower to higher prices (just as electricity flows from low potential nodes to high potential nodes). Price differentials are required to overcome the resistance to (costs of) transporting commodity. The difference between the two series of prices is the observed line segment transportation price, P_L. The *ce* prices are represented by the dotted parallel lines, whose difference is the *ce* pipeline prices on the indicated segment. Charts are not provided for segments 3.1

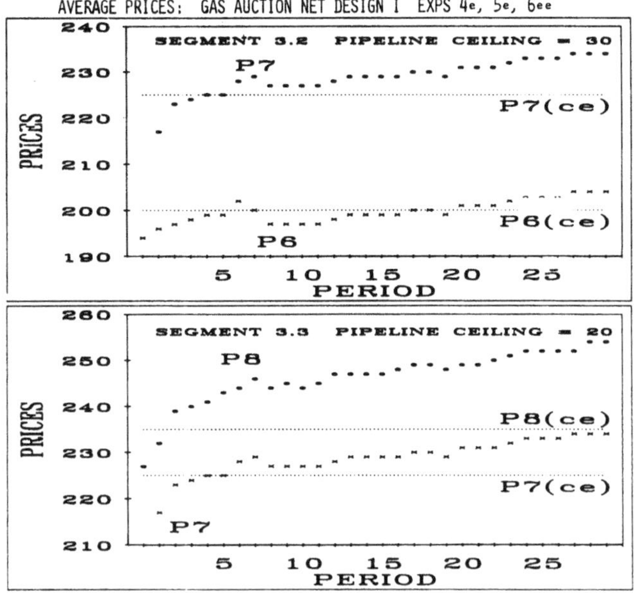

Fig. 5

and 3.4 since, as expected in Design I, the predominant observation was zero flows on these segments in all experiments.

Several characteristics of these price observations should be emphasized.

(1) Except for the first few period in the case of some nodes, prices tend to be quite stable, or to change slowly, from period to period. This is *not* due to averaging across the three experiments; it is also a characteristic of each individual experiment. This result is a consequence of the bid–offer behavior of the subjects. Over time they tend to settle into a pattern in which bids to buy delivered gas are at, or somewhat above, their respective node prices. Similarly producers offer at, or somewhat below, their node prices, while pipelines offer at, or somewhat below, their transport prices on each segment. Consequently, a small reduction in a buyer's bid or slight increase in a seller's offer, is likely to cause the agent to be cut out of the market, or at least have his allocation reduced, but this will have a relatively small effect on prices given this bid–offer pattern. The primary impact is on allocations and therefore efficiency and the distribution of surplus, as will be discussed below.

(2) Buyer *B*1 typically pays approximately the *ce* price and consumes the *ce* allocation. However, producers *W*1 and *W*2 who serve *B*1 tend to receive

less than the *ce* price. We think this is due in part to the downstream competition between pipelines 1 and 2 to serve buyers *B*2 to *B*6. (Because of the transport cost on segment 3.1, pipeline 3 is not in effective competition for buyers *B*2 and *B*3.) To be effective in this downstream competition pipeline 1 must resist letting the price of gas flowing into *B*1 rise much above the *ce* price. Since well *W*2 (owned by pipeline 1) is a marginal producer, this means that pipeline 1 must forgo any positive profit on *W*2. In fact it is typical to observe zero flows and profit for *W*2 in all three experiments. Instead, we observe the owner of pipeline 1 quoting a transportation price on segment 1.1 that is above the *ce* price. This leads *W*1 to accept a wellhead price below the *ce*. It should be noted that the owner of *W*1 has no other revenue source whereas the owner of pipeline 1 has other revenue sources on segments 1.2 and 1.3.

(3) Buyers *B*2 and *B*4–*B*6 are primarily supplied by wells *W*3–*W*6 both in a *ce* and in the realizations recorded in experiments 4*e*, 5*e* and 6*ee*. Consequently, this part of the network is potentially more contestable than the rest of the network. However, the cost advantage on segment 3.2, with a cost of 25, compared with that on 2.1 plus 2.2, with a combined cost of 45 allows 3.2 to change the ceiling price while 2.1 and 2.2 must offer transportation at prices nearer to cost.

(4) Therefore the net delivered price of gas to buyers *B*2–*B*6 tends to exceed the *ce* price. But the gas flows to these buyers, particularly to buyers *B*2 and *B*4, are close to the *ce* allocations. The deliveries to *B*5 and *B*6 appear to be short of the *ce* because 2.3 is uncontested in supplying two competing buyers. (Notice from table 1 that the high combined cost on segments 3.3 and 3.4, compared with segment 2.3 precludes effective competition from pipeline 3). *B*3 and *B*4 receive close to their *ce* allocation by *B*4 pays the transport ceiling price, and *B*3 pays a transport price closer to cost than to the ceiling. We attribute this difference to the fact that the difference between marginal value and the *ce* pice for *B*3 (230 minus 225) is much smaller than for *B*4 (260 minus 235), as can be seen in table 1. Consequently, *B*3 is likely to be more resistant to increases in pipeline charges than *B*4.

Efficiency and the distribution of surplus

The accompanying chart (fig. 6) labeled 'Average efficiency' plots the percentage (averaged across experiments 4*e*, 5*e*, and 6*ee*) of the *ce* total surplus (1800 pesos) actually realized by the participants in each period. An efficiency of 100% means the market realized the maximum possible surplus based on the costs and values listed in table 1. The division of this realized average surplus among buyers, pure producers, pipeline transportation and pipeline owned wells is also plotted in each period. The top line (solid) plotted in fig. 6 is the average realized total efficiency. The second line (long

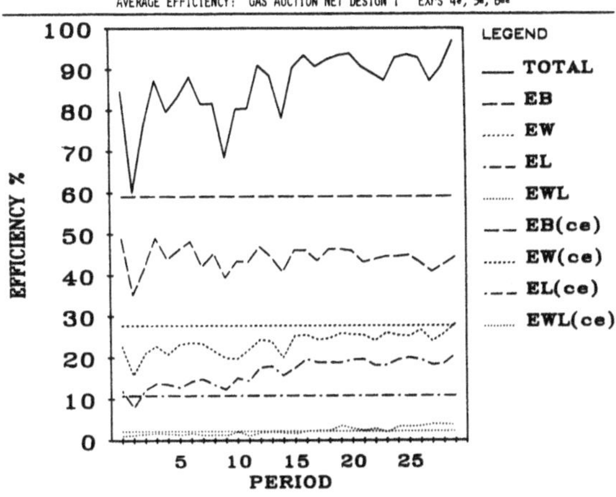

Fig. 6

dashes) plots the average surplus realized by buyers as a percentage of the total, *EB*. The third line (short dashes) plots the average percentage surplus obtained by the independent wells, *EW*. The fourth line (short and long dashes) represents the average percentage surplus obtained in pipeline transportation, *EL*. The last line (dotted) near the bottom of the chart is the average percentage surplus obtained from production capacity owned by pipelines, *EWL*. The horizontal lines, broken to match their corresponding observed values, represent the theoretical percentage surplus, *EB*(*ce*), *EW*(*ce*), *EL*(*ce*) and *EWL*(*ce*).

Note the following general characteristics of these observations.

(1) Total efficiency tends to rise over time.
(2) Buyer surplus is fairly constant over time, but below the *ce* prediction.
(3) The independent producer surplus rises, approaching the *ce* prediction over time.
(4) Pipeline transportation surplus rises over time and stabilizes above the *ce* prediction.
(5) Wells owned by pipelines show some uptrend in surplus but this surplus is little different than the *ce* prediction.

6. Parameters: Network Designs II and III

A second set of Network parameters is provided in table 2. The corresponding *ce* solution is also shown in table 2. Note that in this parameterization the *ce* solution requires flows on every pipeline segment, although profits are not always positive (segment 3.1). In a *ce* buyer surplus

Table 2

A competitive equilibrium solution with all bids equal to values and all offers equal to costs. Network Design II and III

Buyer	$V1$	$Q1$	$V2$	$Q2$	Consumption	Buyer price	(Node i.d.)	Buyer profit
1	207	2	165	2	2	167	(P3)	80
2	197	3	182	2	5	175	(P4)	80
3	230	2	185	2	3	185	(P5)	90
4	244	3	217	2	5	215	(P8)	91
5	267	2	225	2	4	223	(P9)	92
6	262	2	228	3	5	223	(P9)	93
								526 (45.7%)

Well	WC	Q	Production	Well price	(Node i.d.)	Well profit
1	131	5	5	152	(P2)	105
2	144	4	4	152	(P2)	32
3	134	5	5	155	(P1)	105
4	148	4	4	155	(P1)	28
5	157	5	5	180	(P6)	115
6	180	4	1	180	(P6)	0
						385 (33.4%)

Line	$LC1$	$Q1$	$LC2$	$Q2$	Shipment	Line price	(Node diff.)	Line profit	Ceiling price
1.1	10	8	15	3	9	15	(P3–P2)	40	24
1.2	5	6	8	3	7	8	(P4–P3)	18	13
1.3	6	3	11	2	3	10	(P5–P4)	12	17
2.1	14	7	20	3	9	20	(P4–P1)	42	32
2.2	29	4	36	3	4	32	(P7–P4)	12	57
2.3	11	4	16	3	5	16	(P9–P7)	20	24
3.1	5	4	8	3	4	5	(P6–P4)	0	13
3.2	19	7	27	3	10	27	(P7–P6)	56	42
3.3	4	7	8	3	9	8	(P8–P7)	28	13
3.4	5	4	9	3	4	8	(P9–P8)	12	16
								240 (20.9%)	

$E_B = 45.7\%$ $E_P = 28.2\%$
$E_L = 20.9\%$ $E_{PL} = 5.2\%$ Total surplus, 1151 pesos.

is 526 (45.7%), producer surplus is 325 (28.2%) for independent wellhead owners and 60 (5.2%) for pipeline owned wells, pipeline transportation surplus is 240 (20.9%) and total surplus is 1151 (100%). Again we use these ideal states to evaluate the efficiency of our experimental markets and the division of surplus among the three agent classes. In comparing Designs I and II we note that, in the latter, segments 3.1 and 3.4 have costs that actively contest alternative pathways for delivering gas. In general the pipeline parameters in Design II yield greater potential contestability than Design I. Thus in table 2 all the *ce* pipeline segment prices are at or near their respective second step marginal costs. An important research question is whether this tighter contestability will alter the marked tendency, observed in the Design I experiments, for buyers to do poorly relative to both producers and pipeline owners.

In Design III all value, cost and capacity parameters were identical to those in Design II. The only difference was that in Design III no pipeline owner was allowed to own a well in a field that the pipeline served. Our objective was to measure the allocative effect of 'captive' well ownership by pipelines. When pipelines own wells in the fields they serve, are they able to leverage prices to their advantages relative to the independent producers?

7. Experimental results: Gas Auction Net Designs II and III

Average prices

As in section 5, the accompanying charts for experiments 1*e*, 2*e*, 3*ee* (figs. 7–10) plot the delivery and source prices on each pipeline segment for each period. As in Design I, the period-by-period inertia characterizing these prices is again evident.

In contrast with the results for the Design I parameters, the new results substantially reverse the earlier finding that buyers perform poorly relative to producers and pipelines. Network competition in Design II yields buyer prices that hover more closely to the *ce* prices. Likewise, observed producer prices and pipeline prices are closer to the theoretical *ce* prices. An exception is pipeline 1, particularly on segment 1.1 (fig. 7). But this segment is the least contested in network 1, Design II. It makes strategic sense for pipeline owner 1 to price high on segment 1.1, pick off surplus from *B*1 (or P_1), then low on segment 1.2 where he/she is forced to be competitive with 2.1 in the contest for *B*2 and the long distance customers on the left side of the network. This puts pressure on 2.1 either to price near *ce* or to exercise some monopsony power against producer P_3. As shown in fig. 8 the latter tendency dominates slightly. Pricing high on 1.3 is possible since this segment is the sole source of supply for *B*3. But this pattern is not uniform across the three experiments because there are significant bilateral negotiation elements in the transportation of gas from *B*2 to *B*3.

A similar situation is observed for pipeline 3. That is, on segment 3.3, a price approximately equal to the *ce* price often prevails as indicated in fig. 9 for average prices on segment 3.3. Consequently prices at the junction, *J*, which are slightly above the *ce* price, are reflected in an average delivered price to *B*4 somewhat above the *ce* price. But the average transportation price on segment 3.4 is *below* the *ce* price because of competition with

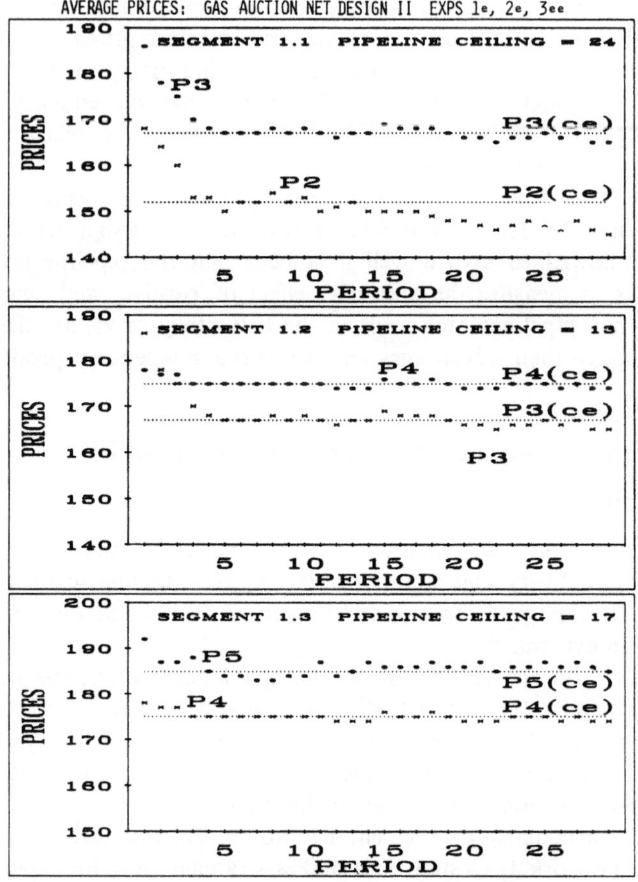

Fig. 7

segment 2.3 for the business of buyers *B*5 and *B*6. As a result, the average delivered price of gas to *B*5 and *B*6 is precisely at the *ce* price for 18 of 30 pricing periods.

Efficiency and the distribution of surplus

Although the average efficiency plotted in fig. 11 shows some modest improvement over time, efficiency is punctuated with abrupt drops and, especially on experiment 3*ee*, cycles. The cycles in 3*ee* were largely due to the 'bargaining' action of buyers *B*1 and *B*5 whose offers were repeatedly at or just below the prices at their respective nodes causing deliveries to drop sporadically to one or zero units.

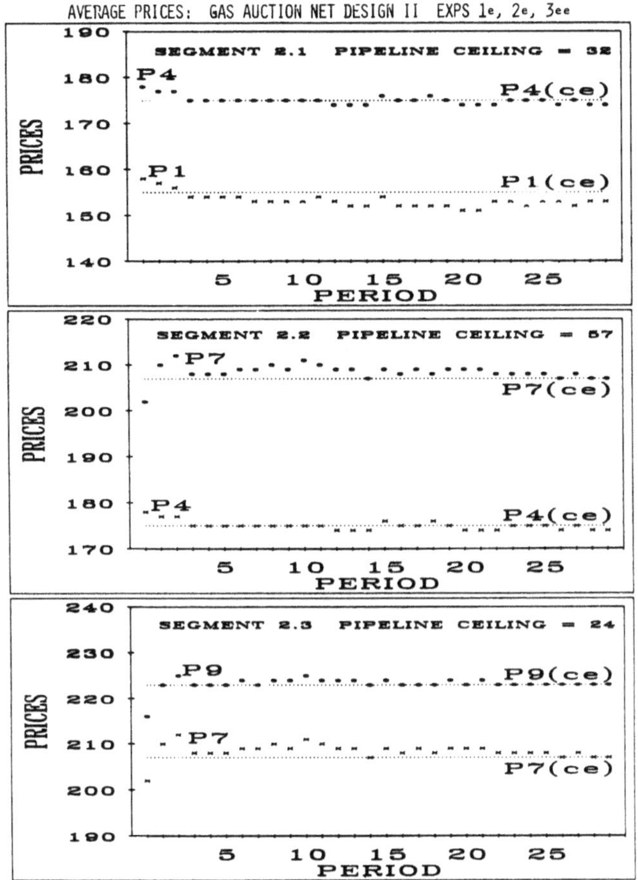

Fig. 8

We call attention to the following characteristics of the average efficiency shares graphed in fig. 11.

(1) Buyer surplus, *EB*, tends to approach the predicted *ce* share of surplus over successive periods.
(2) The surplus from the independent wells, *EW*, stabilizes much below its predicted *ce* share.
(3) Pipeline transportation efficiency, *EL*, stabilizes over time at approximately its predicted *ce* share.
(4) The wells owned by pipelines realize an efficiency level, *EWL*, tending to decline steadily over all periods.

We conclude that the greater contestability among pipelines in Design II

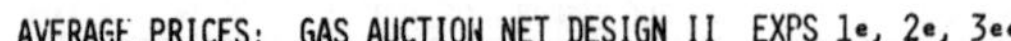

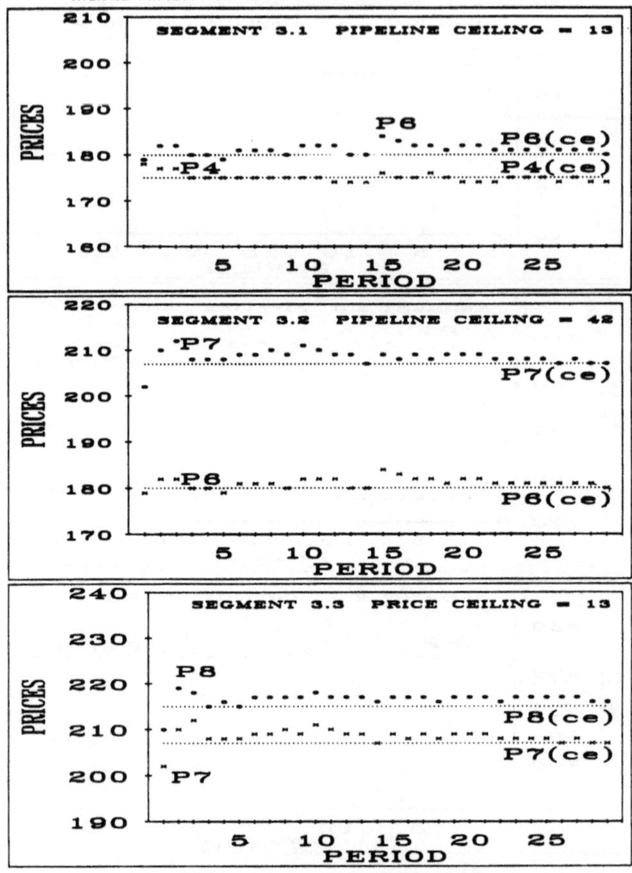

Fig. 9

AVERAGE PRICES: GAS AUCTION NET DESIGN II EXPS 1e, 2e, 3ee

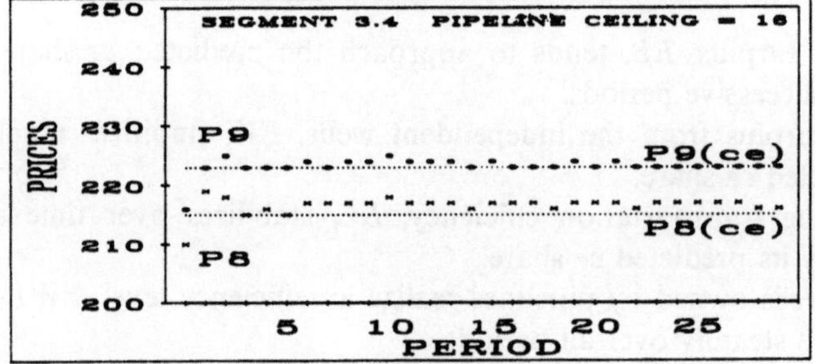

Fig. 10

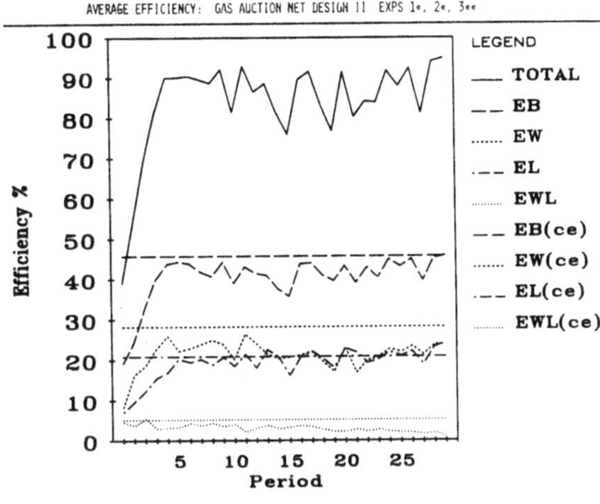

Fig. 11

relative to I results in a considerable transfer of surplus from pipelines and producers to buyers.

Since the prices results in the Design III experiments are similar to those in Design II, only the average efficiency results are reported (fig. 12) for Design III. Comparing figs. 11 and 12 it is evident that when pipelines do not transport for their own wells, as in Design III, this has no important effect on total efficiency nor on the buyer and independent producer efficiencies. But pipeline transportation profits tend to increase, while the

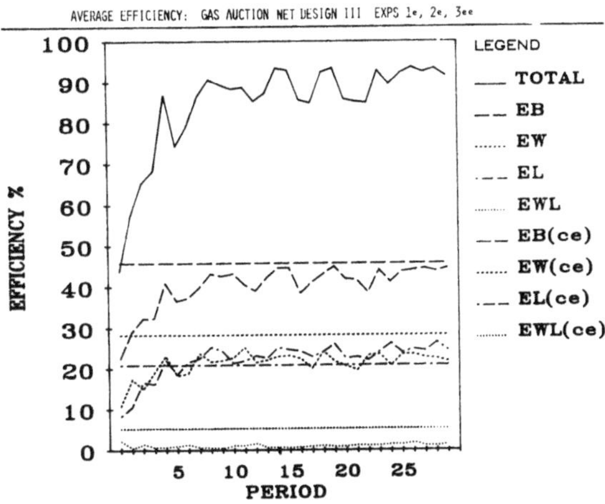

Fig. 12

profits on their own production decreases. Consequently, when pipelines transport their own gas they are able to get better prices for the gas but at the cost of lower prices for line haul transportation.

Efficiency comparisons, Design III versus Design I

In Table 3 we provide a summary observation of each measure of efficiency for each experiment. This summary measures of efficiency is the mean efficiency across all periods of each experiment,

$$\bar{E} = \sum_{t=1}^{T} E^t/T,$$

where E^t is the period t efficiency as defined by each of the measures (ET^t, EB^r, EW^t, EL^t, EWL^t) for each experiment.

Comparing Designs I and II we observe a small but insignificant decline in total efficiency. But the greater contestability of Design II causes a significant increase in the fraction of optimal surplus realized by buyers, even with our small sample size. Well owners experience a decline in their relative share. Both as transporters and as well-owners pipelines realize a significantly lower relative surplus in Design II. As transporters their share falls as much as 50 percent, and a producers by more than 50 percent. Their combined profit share efficiency, ELT, averages less than 90 percent of its predicted value in Design II.

Efficiency comparisons, Design III versus Design II

Table 3 also provides mean efficiency comparisons with (Design II) and without (Design III) pipeline ability to transport their own gas. Moving from Design II to III we find n important change in ET, EB and EW. Pipeline profit efficiency increases somewhat, but profits on pipeline-owned wells decline considerably although the decline is not statistically significant. The net effect is to increase total pipeline profits, ELT. Thus pipelines actually perform somewhat better when they do not transport their own gas.

8. Summary

The high rate of return on investment in gas pipelines, the historical imperatives of a regulatory system that strengthened any inherent monopoly power in pipeline systems, and the increased potential contestability in U.S. natural gas pipeline networks together imply the need to reevaluate federal U.S. regulation of the natural gas industry. In this maiden effort, we propose a new auction market institution for gas pipeline networks. This institution

Table 3

Mean efficiency: Total and shares.[a]

Efficiency measure	Design I Optimal efficiency	Design I Experiment	Design I $\bar{E}$	Design II Optimal efficiency	Design II Experiment	Design II $\bar{E}$	Design III Optimal efficiency	Design III Experiment	Design III $\bar{E}$	t Comparison $t_{I\text{-}II}$ (Prob)	t Comparison $t_{II\text{-}III}$ (Prob)
ET, Total	1.00	4*e*	0.868	1.00	1e	0.850	1.00	1e	0.904	3.61	−0.19
		5e	0.881		2e	0.875		2e	0.859	(0.069)	(0.87)
		6ee	0.885		3ee	0.870		3ee	0.846		
EB, Buyers	0.5917	4*e*	0.685	0.4570	1*e*	0.895	0.4570	1*e*	0.971	−4.52	0.20
		5*e*	0.718		2*e*	0.929		2*e*	0.911	(0.05)	(0.86)
		6*ee*	0.816		3*ee*	0.912		3*ee*	0.825		
EW, Producers	0.2778	4*e*	0.883	0.2824	1*e*	0.768	0.2824	1*e*	0.750	2.98	0.20
		5*e*	0.968		2*e*	0.842		2*e*	0.778	(0.096)	(0.86)
		6*ee*	0.753		3*ee*	0.723		3*ee*	0.783		
EL, Pipeline transportation	0.1083	4*e*	1.76	0.2085	1*e*	0.897	0.2085	1*e*	1.14	6.47	−2.11
		5*e*	1.43		2*e*	0.838		2*e*	1.04	(0.023)	(0.169)
		6*ee*	1.66		3*ee*	1.13		3*ee*	1.14		
EWL, Wells owned by pipelines	0.0222	4*e*	1.16	0.0521	1*e*	0.716	0.0521	1*e*	0.218	4.50	2.16
		5*e*	1.45		2*e*	0.726		2*e*	0.113	(0.046)	(0.163)
		6*ee*	0.600		3*ee*	0.250		3*ee*	0.215		
ELT, Pipeline total[b]	0.1305	4*e*	1.65	0.2606	1*e*	0.861	0.2606	1*e*	0.956	8.01	−1.65
		5*e*	1.43		2*e*	0.816		2*e*	0.855	(0.015)	(0.241)
		6*ee*	1.47		3*ee*	0.954		3*ee*	0.955		

[a]All mean efficiencies measured as a percentage of the optimal efficiency. E.g. $\bar{E}_B = 0.685$ in Design I, experiment 4*e*, means 68.5% of the optimal (competitive equilibrium) value, 0.592, was realized.

[b]*ELT* is the combined efficiency for transportation and pipeline owned or 'captive' well production. E.g. in Design I, experiment 4*e*

$$ELT = \frac{(1.76)(0.1083) + (1.16)(0.0222)}{0.1083 + 0.0222} = 1.65.$$

requires computer support. Specifically, the task of the computer is to provide node prices and pipeline flows that maximize the total gains from exchange in the network conditional upon the location-specific bid schedules of all wholesale buyers and the location-specific offer schedules of all gas and pipeline sellers.

Based on laboratory experiments with reward-motivated subjects, our major conclusion is that, where alternative pipeline transportation paths have comparable costs, and capacity is adequate, gas pipeline networks using Gas Auction Net yield substantially competitive outcomes. Gas Auction Net appears to discipline the behavior of the three types of agents, and we find nothing inherently monopolistic about pipelines except in those parts of the networks served by only one pipeline. Even in these cases bargaining appears to be sufficiently symmetric to yield outcomes that do not disadvantage buyers.

References

Belovicz, M.W., 1979, Sealed-bid auctions: Experimental results and applications, in: V.L. Smith, ed., Research in experimental economics, Vol. 1 (JAI Press, Greenwich, CT) 279–338.

Coursey, Don and Vernon L. Smith, 1984, Experimental tests of an allocation mechanism for private, public or externality goods, Scandinavian Journal of Economics 86, no. 4, 468–484.

Cox, James C., Vernon L. Smith and James Walker, 1985, Expected revenue in discriminative and uniform price sealed-bid auctions, in: V.L. Smith, ed., Research in experimental economics, Vol. 3 (JAI Press, Greenwich, CT) 183–232.

Ketcham, Jon, Vernon L. Smith and Arlington W. Williams, 1984, A comparison of posted offer and double auction pricing institutions, Review of Economic Studies 51.

McAfee, R. Preston and John McMillan, 1987, Auctions and bidding, Journal of Economic Literature 25, 699–738.

Miller, Gary and Charles R. Plott, 1985, Revenue-generating properties of sealed-bid auctions, in: V.L. Smith, ed., Research in experimental economics, Vol. 3 (JAI Press, Greenwich, CT) 159–181.

Norman, Donald A., 1987, Competition in the natural gas pipeline industry, Western International Economic Association meetings (Vancouver, B.C.).

Smith, Vernon L., 1967, Experimental studies of discrimination versus competition in sealed-bid auction markets, Journal of Business 40, 56–84.

Stalon, Charles A., (Commissioner, Federal Energy Regulatory Commission), 1985, The diminishing role of regulation in the natural gas industry, Seventh Annual North American Conference, The International Association of Energy Economists (Philadelphia, PA).

Vickrey, William, 1961, Counterspeculation, auctions and competitive sealed tenders, Journal of Finance 16, 8–37.

Vincent-Genod, Jacques, 1984, Fundamentals of pipeline engineering (Gulf, Houston, TX).

PART V

Industrial Organization

Introduction

Vickrey's contributions to bidding and auctioning theory and to incentive compatibility in his influential 1961 paper have tended to overshadow and to obscure somewhat the general motivating research question in that paper: Where markets are imperfectly competitive can a state agency, through "counterspeculation," create the conditions whereby efficient resource allocation is maintained? Vickrey acknowledges that it was A. P. Lerner who originally posed the question. Today we might rephrase the question in the form: Can one find property-right institutions with the characteristic that market efficiency will be achieved in a wide variety of environments without the state having to engage in discretionary interventionist policies, or – as Hayek would put it – so that people would be guided to take the right actions without a central authority having to tell them what to do?

This is of course precisely the problem of institutional design – an art form in which Vickrey is surely the leading past master. I didn't read Vickrey's paper until around 1975, after I had completed most of my Groves-Ledyard public good experiments. That event spawned the experimental research program in auctions with my honors undergraduate students, Vicki Coppinger and John Titus, and also the experiments that culminated in the first paper (number 32) reprinted in this section. In this paper I return to the original Lerner-Vickrey theme except that I ask the question in the following form: Can the price advantage of monopoly be neutralized or countervailed by an institution that underreveals demand to the monopolist? Although six of the experiments reported in paper 32 had also been completed before I had read Vickrey's paper (see note 1), it was his paper that galvanized those experiments and three new ones into a coherent theme.

Although the basic idea behind the concept of contestability goes back at least to J. B. Clark's writings at the turn of the century, it was not transformed into a coherent and testable theory until the work of W. Baumol, J. Panzer, and R. Willig. I and my coauthors were aware of the potential empirical support for the theory, because we recognized that the convergence properties of experimental supply-and-demand markets could be interpreted as being the result of the forces analyzed in contestable market theory. In these markets extra marginal demand and supply units contest with intramarginal units at nonequilibrium prices tending to cause equilibrating adjustments. Viewed in this way contestable market theory provides a new perspective on opportunity costs. Our research problem was to focus more specifically on the environment and the institution postulated by the theory: a declining marginal cost environment, two firms contesting for a ''natural'' monopoly market, and the posted-offer price mechanism. Our first series of market experiments, reported in paper 33, imposed a zero sunk cost of entry. A second series of experiments (with Don Coursey, R. Mark Isaac, and Margaret Luke), introducing modest sunk entry costs, has been reprinted in *Schools of Economic Thought: Experimental Economics.*

When Mark Isaac and I (paper 34) began our experimental study of predatory pricing behavior, our research plan was to try to identify environmental (''structural'') conditions that would yield predatory pricing phenomena. Then we would replicate those experiments and do variations on them in an attempt to isolate the elements that produce predatory behavior. But our best efforts failed to yield predatory phenomena. In this design-testing process we found the literature dealing with predatory conditions to be insufficiently precise to provide clear criteria for the design of the appropriate experiments. From the perspective of experimental testing, a fundamental deficiency in industrial organization theory is its failure to delineate the environmental and institutional conditions under which the various kinds of conjectured pricing behaviors are predicted to occur: competitive, collusive, dominant firm, predatory, limit pricing, and so on. We lack coherent general theories that provide a mapping from market ''structure'' into these various alleged pricing behaviors.

The most serious deficiency in predatory theory (a deficiency shared by our experimental design) is the failure to take account of predation on the value of a prey's specialized stock of capital. An incumbent predator who forces a new entrant into bankruptcy may indeed establish a reputation for predatory pricing. But this merely lowers the value of the prey's capital stock below replacement cost. Therefore any entrant can acquire this capital at a price that discounts the price-cutting reputation of the predator. The result is a new entrant whose costs make him competitively profitable at predatory prices. A viable theory of predatory reputations and any new experimental tests must both come to terms with this argument.

An Empirical Study of Decentralized Institutions of Monopoly Restraint

Vernon L. Smith

Several decades ago, Abba Lerner (1944) suggested the possibility that where markets are imperfectly competitive, due, for example, to there being too few sellers (or buyers), a central authority or marketing agency might by "counterspeculation" create the conditions whereby efficient resource allocation could be achieved. However, it remained for Vickrey (1961) to propose a scheme for operationalizing Lerner's concept of "counterspeculation"; this scheme has since been recognized as an example of an incentive compatible mechanism conceptually akin to the Clarke (1971) and Groves (1973) mechanism for demand revelation in public-good decision making. Vickrey's mechanism (pp. 9–14), using a marketing agency to process individual reported supply and demand curves, provided no direct incentives for misrepresentation of supply and demand, but because it was thought by Vickrey (perhaps correctly) to be impractical, he turned (pp. 14–29) to an analysis of various auctioning methods which represented realized or realizable institutions. His analysis showed that the English oral auction and the second-price sealed-bid auction (in which the high bidder wins, but pays a price equal to the second highest bid) were examples of decentralized price mechanisms which created incentives for efficient (Pareto-optimal) resource allocation even where numbers were few. In contrast, the Dutch descending bid and first-price sealed-bid auction (the high bidder wins and pays what he bids) were examples of decentralized mechanisms which created incentives for misrepresentation of demand and for Pareto-inefficient resource allocation.

Independently of Vickrey's work, Groves and Ledyard (1977) developed a quadratic cost allocation mechanism for solving the "free-rider" problem in public-good decisions that can be interpreted as a generalization of Vickrey's analysis of auctions. Both the Vickrey auctions and the Groves-Ledyard mechanism require agents to communicate points in ordinary Euclidean space, whereas the Vickrey-Clarke-Groves demand-revealing process requires agents to communicate functions (reported willingness to pay).

Contemporaneously with the work of Vickrey, Clarke, and Groves-Ledyard, but independently, experimental research in decentralized market mechanisms has studied the behavioral properties of several alternative pricing institutions. This research has documented, in numerous experimental replications (Smith, 1962, 1976b), the high efficiency and rapid convergence properties of the oral double-auction mechanism. Furthermore, this experimental research has identified alternative pricing institutions that differ behaviorally in terms of efficiency and convergence properties.

For example, Smith (1967) has compared discriminative with competitive sealed-bid auctions for multiple units of a commodity. Under the discriminative auction rules, all accepted bids are filled at their bid prices. Under the competitive auction rules, all accepted bids are filled at the lowest accepted bid price (as noted by Vickrey, the strictly correct procedure is to fill all bids at the first rejected bid price). The competitive rules provide an incentive for revealing demand, while the discriminative rules provide an incentive to understate demand. The experimental results are consistent with this and establish that the mean bid under discrimination is significantly less than the mean bid submitted under the competitive rules. Tsao and Vignola (1977) have shown that these results also hold in the primary market for U.S. Treasury bonds.

Smith (1964) compared the double oral auction with one-sided auctions—the oral offer and the oral-bid auction—and found that prices in the oral offer auction tended to be below those in the double auction, which in turn tended to be below those in the oral-bid auction. Williams (1973) compared the posted-bid and posted-offer institution, and found that posted-offer prices tended to be significantly above posted-bid prices. Plott and Smith (1978) compared the oral-bid auction with the posted-bid institution (similar to, but not the same as, the discriminative sealed-bid procedure) and found that posted-bid prices tended to be below the market clearing price (this replicated the results of Williams), while oral-bid contract prices tend to be above the competitive price.

Since the oral-offer auction and the posted-bid (discriminative) institution bias prices downward to the disadvantage of sellers by underrevealing demand, this raises the question of whether such institutions might function viably as decentralized mechanisms for monopoly control. Can the price advantage of monopoly be neutralized or countervailed by an institution that underreveals demand to the monopolist? Can the Pareto inefficiency of monopoly be improved by such an institution? This line of reasoning brings us back to the Lerner-Vickrey problem,[1] except that we ask not whether there is a centralized procedure for "counterspeculation" in the presence of monopoly, but is there a decentralized institution that can approximate the objectives of this "counterspeculation"? The "power" of a monopolist derives entirely from his ability to withhold production, and, in the absence of alternative sources of supply, obtain a higher price. But buyers have this same "power," that is, the ability to withhold purchase. Are some institutions more effective than others in enabling buyers to express this "power" against a single seller? The effectiveness of monopoly may be reduced or eliminated where the institution of contract promotes behavior that does not allow an increase in price sufficient to offset the reduction in sales. Recall that the monopoly price is inefficient; some gains from exchange are left unrealized. Are there institutions that allow fuller realization of these gains from trade?

This paper reports the results of eight monopoly experiments, using four contracting institutions for price determination. Two additional experiments, designed for the purpose of making certain comparisons discussed below, consisted of one "large group" competitive market experiment and one duopoly experiment.

EXPERIMENTAL DESIGN

The experimental design is standardized for all the monopoly experiments reported below. Each of five buyers has a capacity to buy a maximum of two units. The seller has a capacity to sell ten units. Table 1 lists the seller's

Table 1
Normalized Marginal Cost and Demand

Quantity	Seller (Subject No. 1) Marginal Cost (¢)	Resale Value (¢)	Buyer No.
0	0		
1	60	150	2
2	60	140	3
3	60	130	4
4	60	120	5
5	65	110	6
6	70	100	6
7	75	90	5
8	80	80	4
9	85	70	3
10	90	60	2

marginal cost for each of ten units, and each buyer's resale value (buyer marginal revenue) for each of two units. The corresponding monopoly marginal cost (competitive market supply), market demand, and monopoly marginal revenue are shown on the left of chart 1. These schedules represent flows per trading period, since all costs and values applied only to those units traded each period, as in a market where production is to order. The costs and values in table 1 and the vertical scales on all the charts to follow are normalized with a range of 60–90 for marginal cost and a range of 150–60 for demand. The actual experiments varied by an additive, constant from these normalized levels, in order to control the state of incomplete information more effectively. If the same marginal cost and demand had been used in all experiments, there was some slight possibility of this becoming known to a subject who had heard about an earlier experiment.

Chart 1
Double Auction 1
Monopoly

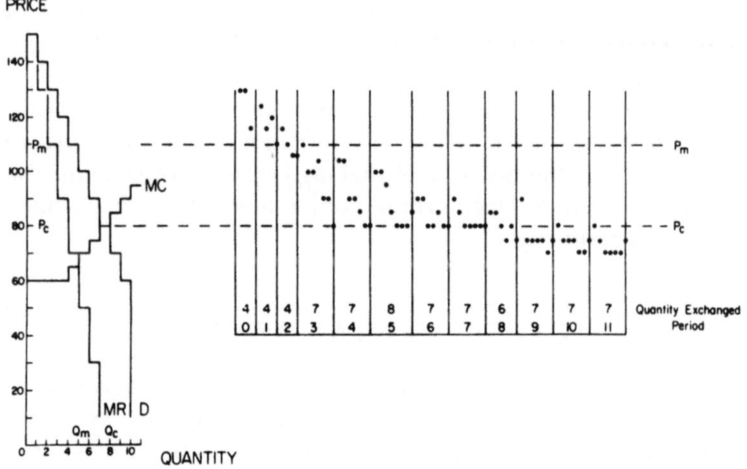

Since the ten experiments to be reported here were conducted at five different universities over a four-year period, this possibility is indeed remote.

Appendices 1–4 contain the instructions and recordkeeping forms used in the monopoly and duopoly experiments. A total of 48 subjects participated in the 8 monopoly experiments. The competitive market experiment used 10 subjects, the duopoly experiment used 12. The subjects were graduate or advanced undergraduate students in economics at Cal Tech, USC, UCLA, the University of Arizona, and Texas A. & M. The emphasis on relatively sophisticated subjects was intended to minimize the possibility of "uninformed" monopoly behavior. For the same reason, the seller position was not a random assignment among the subjects. In each experiment an effort was made to preselect a subject to be the seller—someone who was thought not likely to be "easy on the buyers." But in each experiment the remaining five subjects were assigned randomly to the five buyer valuation conditions shown in table 1. In all experiments the subjects were instructed, and were seated in a manner that would protect the privacy of individual cost or valuation assignments.

At the end of the experiment each buyer was paid in cash the difference between the assigned resale value and the purchase price, plus a 5-cent "commission" for every unit purchased from the seller. Similarly, the seller received a cash payment equal to the difference between the selling price and the assigned marginal cost, plus 5 cents for every unit sold to a buyer. The 5-cent "commission" was for the purpose of providing some minimum inducement to trade a unit at its cost or resale value, that is, to compensate for subjective transaction cost (Smith, 1976a). Consequently, there was some motivation to trade the marginal units.

The total number of trading periods varied among the experiments, but was always at least ten. In no case was this number known in advance by the subjects. If a seller were to achieve the monopoly price ($1.10) and quantity (5), his total earnings, including commission, in a ten-period experiment would be $27. If a seller were to achieve the competitive price ($.80) and quantity (8), total corresponding earnings would be $15. Hence the seller has a strong incentive to find and maintain the monopoly price-quantity exchange, if this is possible. Of course, the seller has no "true" demand information—only the bid, or offer, or contract information forthcoming in the market under the governing institution prescribed by the instructions of a particular experiment. Similarly, no seller in the economy can have "true" demand information—only the information generated by the pricing process that is the practice in a particular industry or market.

This experimental design allows an unambiguous measure of efficiency to be computed. If we omit the commissions, efficiency in any trading period is the ratio of total earnings by all subjects to the earnings that would result from the competitive price and quantity. If eight units trade at the competitive price ($.80), total earnings net of commission would be $3.90, which is just consumer plus producer surplus in the diagram on the left of chart 1. At the monopoly price and quantity, this total surplus would be $3.45. Hence, the theoretical monopoly equilibrium is 88.5 percent efficient. The actual efficiency of the experimental markets will be an important measure for comparing the different institutions.

DOUBLE-AUCTION EXPERIMENTS

Three monopoly experiments and one "large group" competitive experiment were conducted under the double-auction institution. Appendix 1 contains the instructions and recordkeeping forms for the monopoly experiments. The same procedures were used in the competitive market experiment. Each trading period in these experiments was timed to run four minutes, with an announced warning at the beginning of the final minute. Additional time was provided if there were delays, as sometimes occurred in recording bids, offers, and contracts, or if two buyers tied in the acceptance of an offer, and a coin toss was used to determine the winner. The institution was that of a relatively unstructured, double auction: any buyer could make a bid price for a single unit at any time without restriction; that is, it could be the same, higher, or lower than the last bid. The seller could make a price offer at any time, also without restriction. A bid or offer was outstanding (and binding) only for as long as it was not superseded by another bid or offer, or was accepted. A bid or offer that was accepted was a binding contract, and the seller and buyer recorded the contract price on his or her record sheet. At the end of each period the subjects were given a few minutes to compute and record their earnings for that period.

On the right of chart 1 is plotted the chronological sequence of contract prices for the first double-auction monopoly (DA1). Period 0 was a practice trial and was not counted in determining the cash payments. Price behavior in this market experiment does not inspire confidence in the proposition that a seller with imperfect information will achieve a monopoly equilibrium in double-auction trading. Buyers managed to lower prices progressively to an average level below the competitive price in the final three periods. The seller was able to sell at the monopoly price or higher only in trading period 1, but this was accomplished by not selling the fifth marginal monopoly unit. One measure of monopoly price effectiveness is to compare actual prices in each period with the quantity-conditional monopoly price. That is, since the seller does not know Q_m, the sales quantity required to support the monopoly price P_m, a different quantity, say $Q(t)$, may be, and normally is, supplied in any particular period. We ask what is the monopoly price, $P[Q(t)]$, conditional upon $Q(t)$ being the quantity actually supplied in period t. If the seller is monopoly price effective, but is not effective in determining the level at which to restrict output, we would expect actual prices in period t to be near $P[Q(t)]$.[2] Inspection of chart 1 reveals that only in periods 3, 4, and 5 did this seller's prices tend to be above $P[Q(t)]$. For example, in periods 10 and 11, $P[Q(10)] = P[Q(11)] = P[7] = \$0.90$, and in these periods every price was below \$0.80. Table 2 lists the difference

$$\delta(t) = \frac{1}{Q(t)} \sum_{q=1}^{Q(t)} P_q(t) - P[Q(t)]$$

for each period t, where $P_q(t)$ is the qth contract price in period t, and

$$\frac{1}{Q(t)} \sum_{q=1}^{Q(t)} P_q(t)$$

is the mean price in period t.

A second double-auction experiment (DA2) is exhibited in chart 2. Although the price pattern of contracts is much smoother than in DA1, the tendency of prices to erode to the benefit of buyers is strong. The number of trading periods (19) in this experiment was increased over DA1 to see if this declining price trend might be reversed through learning. In all periods, except the last, the mean price was below the conditional monopoly price (that is, $\delta < 0$ in table 2).

Similarly, experiment 3 (DA3) consisted of 16 trading periods (see chart 3). In this case, the pattern of steadily eroding prices up to period 7 was abruptly reversed in period 8. Note that sales were reduced from 7 units in period 7 to 4 units in period 8. Again, the pattern of price decline from period 8 to 16 was renewed, but much less strongly. Of the three experimental sellers, this one was the most effective (from periods 8–16) in holding prices nearer to the monopoly price than the competitive price.

One way of comparing the price effectiveness of the three sellers is to compute the mean difference between the quantity conditional monopoly

Table 2
Price-Quantity Performance

	Double Auction, Monopoly						Posted-Offer Price				Offer Auction		Posted-Bid Pricing, Monopoly					
	DA1		DA2		DA3		Monopoly		Duopoly		Monopoly		PB1		PB2		PB3	
Trading Period, t	Q	δ	Q	δ	Q	δ	Q	δ	Q	δ	Q	δ	Q	δ	Q	δ	Q	δ
1	4	−.025	2	−.25	6	+.075	7	+.35	14	−.032	2	−.125	4	−.375	6	−.20	4	−.3
2	4	−.1125	4	−.125	7	+.0643	5	0	15	+.042	6	−.0083	7	−.0886	1	−.60	7	−.0329
3	7	+.0643	4	−.1375	6	−.1083	4	−.20	14	−.05	6	−.2517	7	−.0757	0	0	8	+.0675
4	7	+.007	4	−.15	6	−.15	6	0	14	−.061	5	−.398	7	−.0714	6	−.1	7	−.0829
5	8	+.08125	4	−.15	7	−.1143	5	0	14	−.066	6	−.3	7	−.0714	4	−.2875	7	−.0914
6	7	−.0643	4	−.15	5	−.33	5	0	14	−.076	7	−.1071	7	−.0771	6	−.1083	7	−.0194
7	7	−.0786	5	−.07	7	−.1357	5	0	14	−.032	7	−.0971	7	−.0871	6	−.1167	7	−.0929
8	6	−.2	5	−.1	4	−.1625	5	0	14	−.066	7	−.09	6	−.185	6	−.13	8	+.005
9	7	−.1357	5	−.1	5	−.07	5	0	14	−.05	7	−.08	7	−.0971	6	−.1184	8	+.0075
10	7	−.1571	5	−.1	6	+.0167	5	0	14	−.05	7	−.0486	7	−.1014	7	−.03	7	−.0871
11	7	−.1714	5	−.1	5	−.05	5	0	14	−.032	7	−.0114	7	−.1	7	−.0371	7	−.08
12			5	−.13	6	+.0333					7	−.0071	7	−.0971			7	−.07
13			5	−.15	6	0							7	−.0886			7	−.07
14			5	−.15	6	0											5	−.27
15			4	−.25	6	−.0083											7	−.07
16			6	−.05	6	−.025											7	−.06
17			5	−.15													7	−.06
18			6	−.05													7	−.06
19			7	+.02													7	−.06
Means, Periods 5–10																		
$\overline{Q}$		7		4.74		5.67		5		14		6.83		6.83		5.83		7.33
$\overline{\delta}$		−.0924		−.1117														
$\overline{\delta}$		−.0924		−.1117		−.1326		0		−.0567		−.1205		−.1032		−.1318		−.0584
$\overline{Q}$, Pooled				*5.78*				*5*		*14*		*6.83*				*6.66*		
$\overline{\delta}$, *Pooled*				*−.1122*				*0*		*−.0567*		*−.1205*				*−.0978*		
Means, All Periods																		
$\overline{Q}$		6.45		7.47		5.9		5.18		14.09		6.17		6.69		4.64		7.00
$\overline{\delta}$		−.0683		−.1118		−.0553		+.0026		−.043		−.1174		−.1069		−.1345		−.0559
$\overline{Q}$, Pooled				*5.54*				*5.18*		*14.09*		*6.17*				*6.12*		
$\overline{\delta}$, *Pooled*				*−.0789*				*+.0026*		*−.043*		*−.1174*				*−.096*		

price and actual prices across all (or a portion) of the trading periods for each experiment. Let this mean difference be

$$\bar{\delta} = \frac{1}{T} \sum_{t=1}^{T} \delta(t)$$

for any experiment consisting of T trading periods. For the three DA monopoly experiments, these mean differences across all periods are $\bar{\delta}_{DA1} = -.0683$, $\bar{\delta}_{DA2} = -.1118$, and $\bar{\delta}_{DA3} = -.0553$. Under this control over the

Chart 2
Double Auction 2
Monopoly

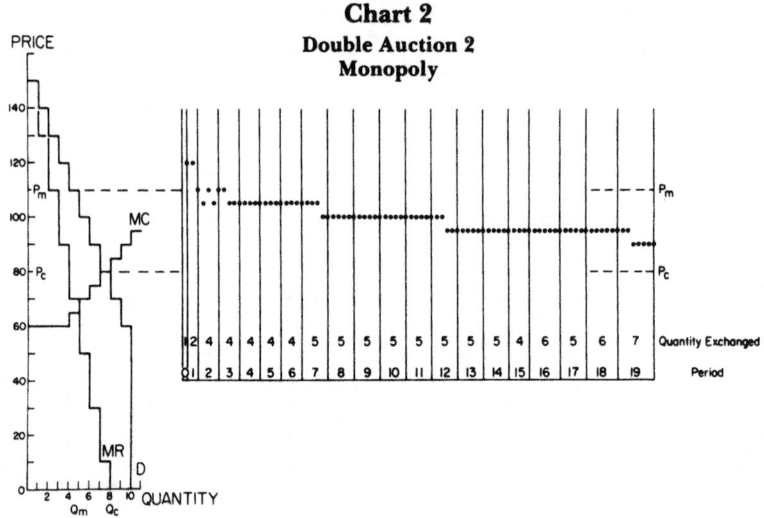

effect of supply, it is seen that the seller in DA3 was slightly more price effective than the seller in DA1, with the seller in DA2 being the least price effective. The seller in DA2 was the most effective in restricting supply ($\bar{Q} = 4.74$), but this did not lead to a corresponding increase in prices. It appears that in the double-auction institution, the more a monopoly seller restricts supply the stronger may be the bargaining resistance of buyers.

In comparison with previous experiments with the double-auction mechanism, where there are several sellers and several buyers, the most characteristic feature of these monopoly experiments is the remarkable bargaining resistance of the buyers. In double-auction trading with a single seller, buyers appear to have a capacity for tacit collusion against the seller that has not appeared before in nonmonopolistic experiments. To test this conjecture, it was decided to conduct a double-auction competitive market experiment with five buyers and five sellers, using the same demand (normalized resale values) as in the monopoly experiments. However, the assigned marginal costs (supply) only correspond to the normalized monopolist's MC function up to a quantity of five, then jump to the highest demand value. This configuration is shown on the left of chart 4. Hence, we "rig" the supply curve for five sellers so that it must effectively reproduce a monopolist's

Chart 3
Double Auction 3
Monopoly

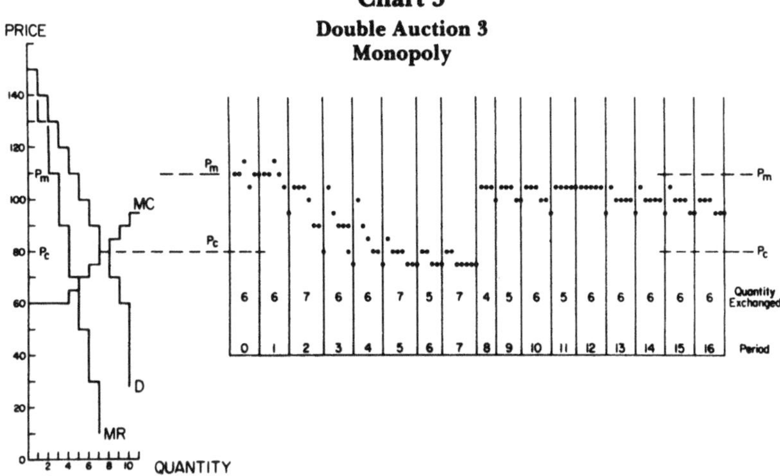

restriction of quantity to the level $Q_m = 5$. In substance, the only difference between this experiment and a monopoly experiment in which the seller is perfectly quantity effective is that we have five sellers instead of one. If our conjecture is true—namely, that buyers bargain more effectively against one seller than against several—then the five buyer–five seller experiment should produce prices near $P_m = \$1.10$.

On the right in chart 4 is shown the contract sequence for the "large group" experiment DA4. These results are typical of such experiments,

Chart 4
A Multi-Seller Auction

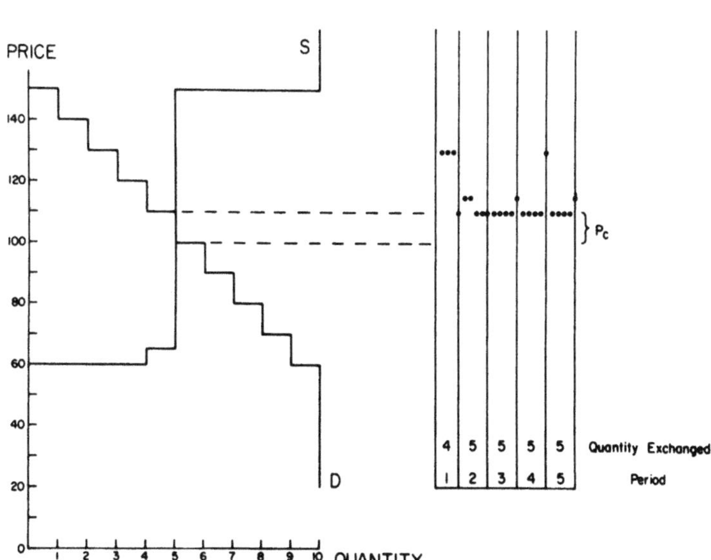

except that convergence is more commonly from below (Smith, 1976b) when producers' surplus is substantially in excess of consumers' surplus. Note the sharply higher level of prices in all periods of chart 4, compared with periods 7 to 14 in chart 2, in which the seller limited deliveries to five units per period. These results tend to support the hypothesis that in the double-auction institution, buyers bargain more effectively against a single seller than against several.

POSTED-OFFER EXPERIMENTS

Two posted-offer experiments will be reported in this section—one monopoly and one duopoly. The posted-offer institution operates as follows (see Plott and Smith, 1978, for a fuller discussion of the symmetrical posted-bid institution). Each seller independently selects a written offer price, with the understanding that each must be willing to sell at least one unit at the price quoted. These prices are collected and posted on the blackboard. The buyers are then ordered randomly in a sequence, and the first chooses one of the prices and states the quantity he is willing to buy at that price. The seller moves last by stating how much (but at least one unit) of this quantity will be accepted. If not all the buyer's bid for units is accepted, he may go to another seller to fill his unsatisfied demand. When the first buyer is finished, the second buyer in the random sequence states his quantity bid, and so on through the last buyer. Appendix 2 provides complete instructions for the monopoly and the duopoly experiments.

Based on the results reported in Plott and Smith (1978), we would expect this institution to work to the advantage of sellers. Of the four pricing mechanisms studied in this paper, this would be the one most likely to enable a single seller to achieve the monopoly price-quantity equilibrium. In this institution, a buyer's only recourse is to withhold purchase, denying himself short-run surplus, in the hope of getting more favorable subsequent price offers. Buyers are faced with a take-it-or-leave-it price offer, over which no bargaining is permitted under the rules of the experimental institution. This procedure approximates the pricing process in most large retail firms in which the separation of clerk and management functions makes it infeasible to permit price negotiations at the customer-clerk level.

The results of the posted-offer monopoly experiment are plotted on the right of chart 5. There was not a single instance of strategic behavior on thepart of a buyer. Each buyer in each period simple-maximized by buying the optimal short-run quantity at the monopolist's stated price (except that in period 1 buyer 3 purchased his second unit at a loss). In five periods the seller identified the profit maximizing price and proceeded to quote this price for the next seven periods. In postexperiment discussion, several buyers commented that they felt there was nothing else they effectively could do. In spite of the fact that strategic purchase behavior is possible, the buyers in this experiment perceived that they had no effective recourse but to

Chart 5
Posted Offer 1
Monopoly

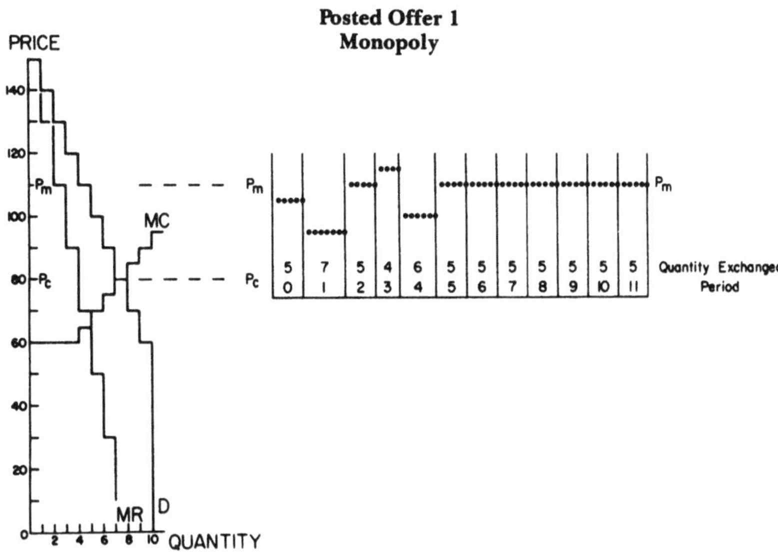

accept a take-it-or-leave-it price. Consequently, the experiment was behaviorally mechanical, even boring. This is in sharp contrast with the double-auction experiments in which buyers vigorously bargained under the procedures of that institution, and obviously perceived that they could influence the terms of trade.

Chart 6 exhibits the results of the posted-offer duopoly experiment. The procedures were identical to those in the previous monopoly experiment except that two sellers, each independently, selected a price which was then posted. Each seller had the same MC schedule as the single seller in the monopoly experiment, and there were two buyers with the same valuations as each single buyer in the monopoly experiment. Hence, the duopoly experiment exactly replicated the cost-value structure of the monopoly experiment, but doubled the size of the market (Shubik, 1975).

In chart 6, for each trading period the two posted offer prices are charted in increasing order and identified by seller number (1 or 2). The quantity exchanged at each price is represented by the length of the price bar. In every period, price was in the range \$.80–\$.90, determined by the competitive marginal demand unit and the next higher demand unit. Cooperative signals (price increases) by one or both duopolists occurred in periods 2, 3, 5, 7, 9, and 11; competitive signals occurred in periods 2, 3, 4, 5, 6, and 8. In every period, prices are above P_c but nearer to P_c than P_m. In no case did either of the two sellers strategically withhold sales to the buyers. In each case the low-priced seller sold his marginal unit at that price, while the sales of the high-priced seller were determined by the residual or contingent (Shubik, 1959, pp. 82–84) demand left by the low-priced seller. Table 3

Chart 6

Posted Offer 2
Duopoly

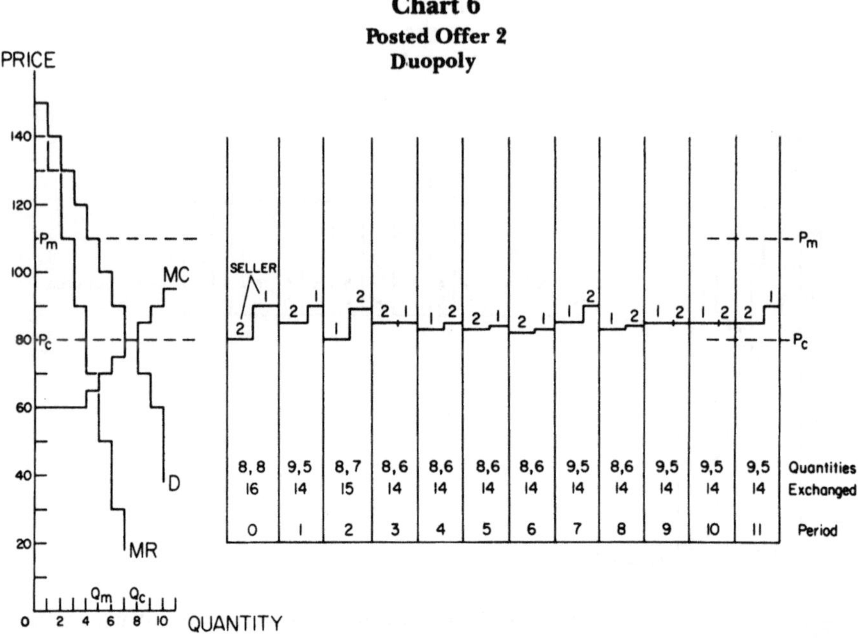

Table 3
Efficiency

	Double Auction			Posted Offer			Posted Bid		
Trading Period, t	1	2	3	Monopoly	Duopoly	Offer Auction	1	2	3
1	76.9	41.0	96.2	97.4	97.4	41.0	46.2	66.7	100.0
2	76.9	66.7	91.0	88.5	100.0	96.2	82.1	23.1	100.0
3	97.4	74.4	83.3	76.9	100.0	80.8	100.0	0	100.0
4	100.0	74.4	96.2	96.2	100.0	93.6	100.0	82.1	100.0
5	98.7	74.4	84.6	88.5	100.0	83.3	100.0	57.7	100.0
6	95.0	74.4	74.4	88.5	100.0	100.0	100.0	75.7	100.0
7	97.4	83.3	100.0	88.5	97.4	100.0	100.0	89.7	100.0
8	96.2	83.3	69.2	88.5	100.0	100.0	80.8	85.9	100.0
9	95.0	83.3	88.5	88.5	97.4	100.0	100.0	84.7	100.0
10	100.0	83.3	96.2	88.5	97.4	100.0	82.1	100.0	100.0
11	95.0	83.3	88.5	88.5	97.4	100.0	82.1	90.3	100.0
12		83.3	96.2			100.0	82.1		100.0
13		83.3	96.2				100.0		83.3
14		83.3	96.2						100.0
15		66.7	97.4						100.0
16		96.2	96.2						100.0
17		78.2							100.0
18		96.2							100.0
19		89.7							
$\overline{E}$(Periods 5–10)	97.05	80.33	85.5	88.5	98.7	97.22	93.82	82.28	100.0
Pooled $\overline{E}$ (Periods 5–10)		87.63		88.5	98.7	97.22		92.03	

shows that the duopoly experiment was never less than 97.4 percent efficient in any period.

These results confirm the expectation that the posted-offer institution favors sellers. In the case of a single seller, it allows the monopoly price to be attained. The bias in favor of sellers persists with the introduction of a second seller, but the bias is not strong enough to significantly reduce efficiency below the competitive optimum.

AN OFFER-AUCTION EXPERIMENT

In the one-sided oral offer auction (Smith, 1964) any seller may freely make a price offer for a single unit, while buyers either accept or remain silent. This institution tends to operate to the advantage of buyers. Essentially, as sellers lower prices to attract buyer acceptances, buyers learn to wait for favorable prices. In experiments with many sellers, the offer competition of sellers, combined with waiting by buyers, tends to depress prices to a level below the competitive equilibrium. This section reports the results of one such experiment with a single seller. The instructional materials for the experiment are included in Appendix 3.

Chart 7 reports all of the seller's offers in sequence. The open circles represent unaccepted offers and the solid circles indicate contracts. The pattern of successive reductions in the offers, in response to buyers' waiting

Chart 7
Offer Auction 1
Monopoly

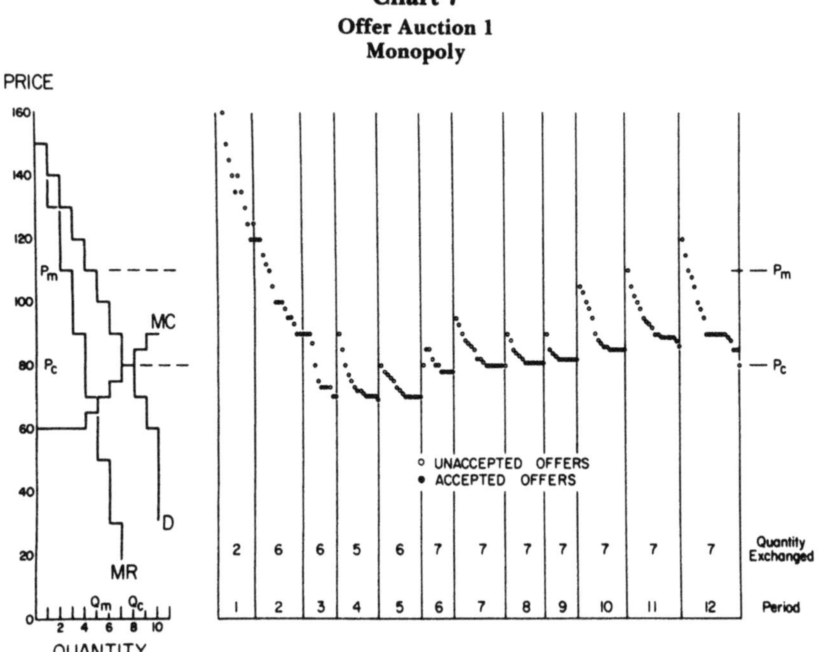

for more favorable terms, is typical of earlier reported experiments with more than one seller. In periods 3, 4, and 5, for example, buyers strategically wait for offers as low as $.70. This appears to be a clear "counterspeculative" form of restraint. The seller, perhaps realizing that the offer terms might be too soft, changed the offer concession strategy in period 6 so as to begin higher and concede less. Consequently, the seller succeeded in gradually raising contract prices from periods 6 through 12. This trend suggests the possibility that the seller might eventually have been able to approach the monopoly price. The important test would come at a price of $.90 and above, and again at $1 and above, where the corresponding marginal demand units are excluded. Would buyer bargaining resistance have significantly stiffened? In period 12, it appears that this is what was happening as the seller made several offer concessions in order (apparently) to pick up the seventh contract. (Period 12 was not known to be the final period, so we do not have a "doomsday" problem influencing behavior.)

POSTED-BID EXPERIMENTS

In the posted-bid institution, each buyer independently chooses a price with the understanding that he or she must be willing to purchase at least one unit at the price quoted. The bids are then posted publicly. The seller then chooses a buyer and price and makes a quantity offer. The buyer moves last, stating how much of the quantity offer he or she will purchase. The seller then chooses another buyer and price, makes a quantity offer, and so on. The seller may stop making quantity offers at any time and may refuse all buyers. The instructions for the three posted-bid experiments are contained in Appendix 4.

Since, in this institution, buyers have to pay what they bid, that is, buyers know that the seller will discriminate down the posted-bid array of prices, each has an incentive to avoid being among the highest bids accepted. The ideal bid for each buyer is a bid just slightly above the highest rejected bid. Hence, there are strong individual incentives that support the posting of low bids with a small variance. If this is the case, the seller will be confronted with a considerably underrevealed, relatively elastic, demand.

Charts 8, 9, and 10 plot the posted bids and corresponding sales at each bid in decreasing order, from the highest bid to the lowest, for each trading period. The circles represent bid prices that were rejected by the seller; that is, no quantity was offered to buyers who posted these bids. All three experiments show a strong tendency for buyers to underreveal demand. In experiments 1 and 3, the dispersion of bids narrows very sharply after the first two or three trading periods. In each of these experiments the seller stabilized early, with a delivery quantity of approximately seven units. In each case the seller was faced with price bids very little above the competitive price. In experiment 2 (chart 9), the seller aggressively rejected bids. After selling six units in period 1, the seller rejected all but the highest bid in period 2. This resulted in a very insignificant increase in the period 3 bids. The seller then rejected all bids in period 3, resulting in a somewhat higher

Chart 8
Posted Bid 1
Monopoly

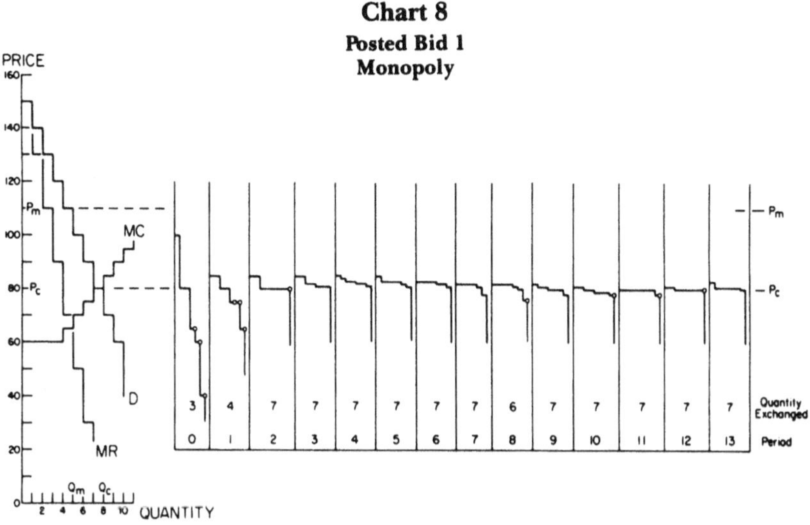

Chart 9
Posted Bid 2
Monopoly

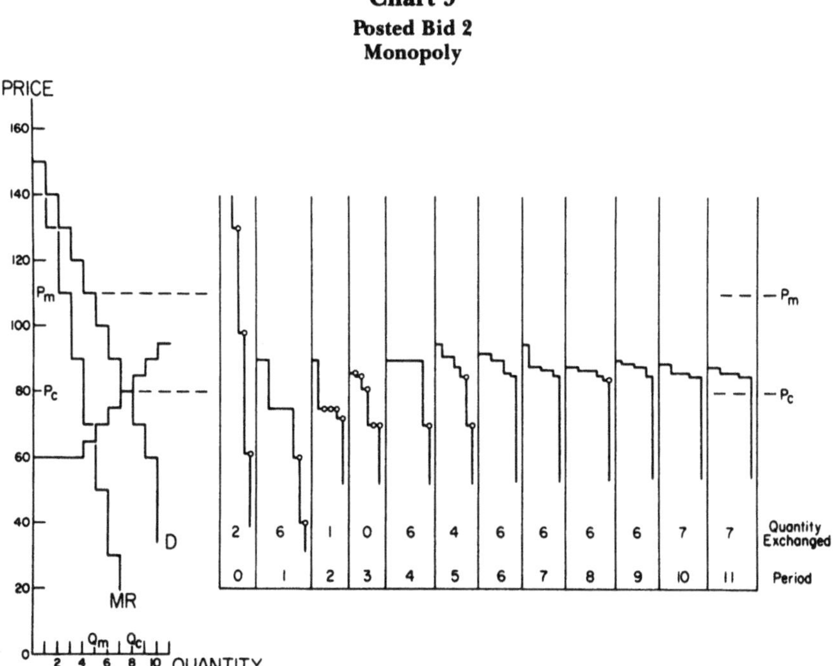

Chart 10
Posted Bid 3
Monopoly

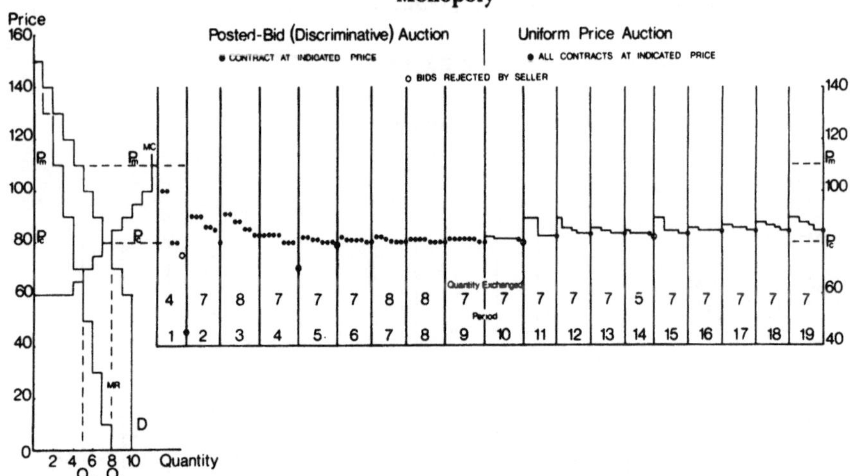

level of bids in period 4. Except for period 5, the seller then stabilized in the sale of 6 or 7 units in the remaining periods, with the result that the bids tended to drift lower and lower. These results suggest that the posted-bid institution operates very beneficially to the buyers. Even where the seller is particularly aggressive in restricting output, this action is not very effective, at least in the short run, in raising the bids. Hence, it is very costly to the seller to induce an increase in the bids by restricting sales.

In table 2 it will be noted that among the three sellers, across all periods, the seller in the second experiment (PB2) was the most effective in restricting output ($\overline{Q}$ = 4.64) but the least effective in obtaining the quantity conditional monopoly price, that is, $\bar{\delta}_{PB1} = -.1069$, $\bar{\delta}_{PB2} = -.1345$ and $\bar{\delta}_{PB3} = -.0559$. The seller in experiment 3 was the least effective in restricting output, but the most (quantity-conditional) price effective. As in the double auction, it seems that in the posted-bid institution the more a single seller restricts supply, the less is that seller's price effectiveness.

The theory that the discriminative feature of posted-bid pricing is a significant element in the underrevealing of demand was tested in the third posted-bid experiment (PB3). At the beginning of trial 10 it was announced that, henceforth, all bids accepted by the seller would be executed at the same price, and that the procedure would be as follows. After the bids are posted (as before), the seller will first announce the cutoff bid price, that is, the price below which all bids will be rejected by the seller. The seller then selects a buyer (as before), makes a quantity offer, the buyer responds with the amount he will buy, and so on, but with the understanding that all contracts will be at the cutoff bid price announced by the seller. The results are plotted in chart 10 in periods 10 through 19. Immediately with period

11, the effect was to increase the level of the posted bids, with the seller obtaining an increase in profit. The bids continued to rise (not monotonically) through the last period, with seller profit tending to rise, except for period 14, when the seller delivered only 5 units. Hence, buyers benefit by allowing bid-price discrimination, while the seller benefits from the uniform-price auction rule. This result is largely attributable to the change in buyer bidding behavior resulting from the change in the price determining rule, since the seller continued to supply substantially the same quantity. However, the exception in period 14 is interesting. The posted bids in that period were not as high as in periods 11–13. The seller reduced deliveries from 7 units to 5 units, and an increase in the bids ensued which continued through the final trading period.

COMPARISON OF THE INSTITUTIONS

Since the posted-offer monopoly experiment resulted in the monopoly price-quantity equilibrium from periods 5 through 11, and since the posted-bid rules were used in PB3 for only the first 10 periods, it is natural to compare all experiments across the block of six periods from 5 through 10. This is done for price-quantity comparisons in table 2 and for efficiency comparisons in table 3.

From table 2, comparing the pooled means for periods 5–10, sellers in double-auction experiments were more effective in restricting output than sellers in the offer auction or in post-bid experiments. Mean quantity-conditional price effectiveness was slightly better in posted-bid pricing, and slightly worse in the offer auction by comparison with the double auction, but essentially, on average, the three institutions are comparably effective in restraining a seller relative to the posted-offer institution. The compatibility of the posted-offer institution with monopoly pricing is further evidenced by the fact that adding a second seller is less effective in monopoly restraint than changing the institution. In table 2, $\bar{\delta} = -.0567$ for posted-offer duopoly, periods 5–10. The only experiment that is more price effective is posted-offer monopoly. All other pooled values of $\bar{\delta}$ are nearly twice that of the duopoly experiment. Under all three institutional alternatives to posted-offer pricing, buyers countervail monopoly pricing better than does a second competing posted-offer seller.

But institutional restraint of monopoly does not imply an increase in efficiency. This is clear in table 3. Pooled average efficiency, $\bar{E}$, for periods 5–10, in the double-auction experiments is less ($\bar{E}_{DA} = 87.63$) than for perfect monopoly ($E_m = 88.5$). Average efficiency is better in the posted-bid experiments ($\bar{E}_{PB} = 92.03$) and quite good in the offer auction ($\bar{E}_{QA} = 97.22$), but highest under posted-offer duopoly. The efficiency of posted-offer monopoly, and duopoly, effectively bracket the range of efficiency for monopoly under the three other institutions. In substance, there is an efficiency cost to the institutional restraint of monopoly. If efficiency is the objective, then a second seller under posted-offer pricing is better than a change in the institution.

CONCLUSIONS

Our conclusions must be stated with considerable qualification:

1. The sample is very small. Ten experiments are few indeed for covering the study of four different price adjustment mechanisms.
2. Many of the experiments fail to exhibit evidence that an equilibrium state was reached in the number of periods that were allowed; longer sequences are definitely called for. Also, the effect of increasing the number of buyers confronting the seller needs exploration. Murnighan and Roth (1977), in a simplified game context, find that a monopolist's effectiveness increases with the number of players.

Subject to these qualifications, the following conclusions are supported by the data.

1. The posted-offer institution is the pricing mechanism most supportive of the monopoly price.
2. The double-auction, offer-auction, and posted-bid institutions are effective in constraining a single seller's attempt to obtain the monopoly price. In terms of the measure, $\bar{\delta}$, of monopoly price effectiveness, the four institutions are ordered as follows, from most to least effective:
$$\bar{\delta}_{PO} > \bar{\delta}_{PB} > \bar{\delta}_{DA} > \bar{\delta}_{OA}$$
3. Using the measure $\bar{Q}$ of quantity effectiveness, the institutions are ordered as follows, from most to least effective in output restriction:
$$\bar{Q}_{PO} < \bar{Q}_{DA} < \bar{Q}_{PB} < \bar{Q}_{OA}$$
4. In terms of average allocational efficiency, $\bar{E}$, the institutions are ordered from lowest to highest efficiency, as follows:
$$\bar{E}_{DA} < \bar{E}_{PO} < \bar{E}_{PB} < \bar{E}_{OA}$$
5. In terms of price advantage for buyers, posted-offer duopoly is inferior to monopoly under any of the other institutions.
6. In terms of efficiency, posted-offer duopoly is superior to monopoly that uses any of the four institutions.
7. A monopoly seller is more effective in increasing price and profits under the posted-bid uniform price rule than under the discriminative posted-bid pricing rule.

APPENDIX 1

Instructions (For Monopoly Double Auction)

This is an experiment in the economics of market decision making. Various research foundations have provided funds for this research. The instructions are simple, and if you follow them carefully and make good decisions you may earn a considerable amount of money which will be paid to you in cash.

In this experiment we are going to conduct a market in which some of you will be buyers and one of you will be a seller in a sequence of trading periods. Attached to the instructions you will find record and information sheets labeled "Buyer" # or "Seller" #. You are not to reveal this information to anyone. It is your own private information.

BUYER INSTRUCTIONS. A buyer can purchase from the seller at most two units of a fictitious good per trading period. For the first unit that you buy, you will be paid the amount listed in the row marked *1st Unit Resale Value.* If you buy your second unit, you will receive the amount in the column marked *2nd Unit Resale Value.* The profits (which are yours to keep) are computed by taking the difference between the resale value and the purchase price of the unit bought. In addition to this profit you will receive a 5-cent commission for each purchase. That is, (resale value) – (purchase price) + (5-cent commission) = PROFIT.

The three rows following the resale value are provided to allow you to compute your total profits at the end of each period. Please list the purchase price as soon as a contract is made in the row marked "Purchase Price." *Under no condition should you buy a unit for a price which exceeds the resale value.*

SELLER INSTRUCTIONS. Each seller can sell as many units as you wish to the buyers. For the first unit that you sell, you will be paid the amount listed in the row marked *Selling Price* for unit 1; for the second unit that you sell, you will receive the amount in the row marked *Selling Price* for unit 2; and so on for as many units as you sell. The profits for all units sold (which are yours to keep) are computed by taking the difference between selling price and the indicated cost of the unit sold. In addition to this profit you will receive a 5-cent commission for each sale. That is,
(selling price) – (cost of unit sold) + (5-cent commission) = amount earned

The three rows following the selling price are provided to allow you to compute your profit at the end of each period for all units. Please list the selling price as soon as a contract is made in the row for the unit selling price. *Under no condition should you sell a unit below the cost of that unit.*

MARKET ORGANIZATION. The market for this commodity is organized as follows. We open the market for a trading period (the length of a single period will be ______ minutes). The seller is free at any time to raise his hand and make an offer to sell one unit as long as the stated price is *not below* the cost on your sheet for that unit. Any buyer is free at any time to raise his hand and make a bid to buy one unit as long as the stated price is *not above* the resale price on your sheet for that unit. When a bid or offer is made, I will write the price on a data sheet and repeat it. At this point a new bid or offer may be made *which always supersedes the previous bid or offer* whether the new price is higher or lower than the previous price. Anyone wishing to accept a bid or offer may say "I'll take it" or "Sold." When a bid or offer is accepted it is a binding contract, and the buyer and seller will record the transaction price to be included in their profit calculation.

There are likely to be many bids and offers that are not accepted. You are free to keep trying, and make your profits as large as you can. Except in the bids and offers, you are not to speak to any other subject. Trading will take place over very many market periods. *Each column* in your table applies to *one* trading period. Trading period 0 will be a trial period to familiarize you with the procedure and will not count toward your cash earnings.

Are there any questions?

Record Sheet, Buyer

____

Record of Purchases and Profits

	Trading Period Number	0	1	2	3	4	5	6	7	8	9	10	11	12	13	14	15
1	1st unit resale value																
2	Purchase price																
3	Profit (row 1-row 2)																
4	Profit + 5¢ commission (row 3 + .05)																
5	2nd unit resale value																
6	Purchase price																
7	Profit (row 5-row 6)																
8	Profit + 5¢ commission (row 7 + .05)																
9	Total Profit (row 4 + row 8)																

Note: Record sheets are the same for all experiments.

Record Sheet, Buyer

____

Record of Purchases and Profits

	Trading Period Number	16	17	18	19	20	21	22	23	24	25	26	27	28	29	30	31
1	1st unit resale value																
2	Purchase price																
3	Profit (row 1-row 2)																
4	Profit + 5¢ commission (row 3 + .05)																
5	2nd unit resale value																
6	Purchase price																
7	Profit (row 5-row 6)																
8	Profit + 5¢ commission (row 7 + .05)																
9	Total Profit (row 4 + row 8																

Total profit, all trading periods ______________

Name ______________

Note: Record sheets are the same for all experiments.

Record of Sales and Profits, Seller #____________________

Unit Sold	Trading Period Number		0	1	2	3	4	5	6	7	8	9	10
	1	Selling Price											
	2	Cost of 1st Unit											
1	3	Profit (row 1-row 2)											
	4	Profit + 5¢ Commission											
	5	Selling Price											
	6	Cost of 2nd Unit											
2	7	Profit (row 5-row 6)											
	8	Profit + 5¢ Commission											
	9	Selling Price											
	10	Cost of 3rd Unit											
3	11	Profit (row 9-row 10)											
	12	Profit + 5¢ Commission											
	13	Selling Price											
	14	Cost of 4th Unit											
4	15	Profit (row 13-row 14)											
	16	Profit + 5¢ Commission											

Note: Record sheets are the same for all experiments.

APPENDIX 2

Instructions (For Monopoly-Posted Offer)

Substitute the following in Appendix 1

MARKET ORGANIZATION. The market for this commodity is organized as follows. We open the market for a trading period. The seller decides on a selling price, which will be written on one of the cards provided. The seller will have two minutes to submit a price offer. The card will be collected and the price written on the blackboard. A buyer will be chosen at random, and if he wishes to make a purchase will offer the quantity (up to 2) he will buy. The seller may accept any number of the units offered by the buyer. However, when a seller posts a price it is with the understanding that you are willing to deliver *at least one unit* to *a* buyer at that price. When the seller accepts units offered by the buyer it is a binding contract, and the buyer and seller will record the transaction prices to be included in their profit calculation. After the first buyer has made his contract, a second buyer will be selected to offer a purchase quantity, and so on, until each buyer has had an opportunity to make a purchase. The market will then be closed, and reopened for a new trading period.

Except in the offers and their acceptance you are not to speak to any other subject. You are free to make your profits as large as you can. Trading will take place over very many market periods. *Each column* in your table applies to *one* trading period. Trading period 0 will be a trial period to familiarize you with the procedure and will not count toward your cash earnings.

Are there any questions?

Instructions (For Duopoly-Posted Offer)

Substitute the following in Appendix 1

MARKET ORGANIZATION. The market for this commodity is organized as follows. We open the market for a trading period. Each seller decides on a selling price which will be written on one of the cards provided. The sellers will have two minutes to submit a price offer. The cards will be collected and the prices written on the blackboard. A buyer will be chosen at random, and if he wishes to make a purchase will select a seller and offer the quantity (up to 2) he will buy. The seller may accept any number of the units offered by the buyer. However, when a seller posts a price it is with the understanding that you are willing to deliver *at least one unit* to *a* buyer at that price. When the seller accepts an offer of units by the buyer it is a binding contract, and the buyer and seller will record the transaction prices to be included in their profit calculation. If the buyer is unable to buy all he wishes from the first seller, he may make an offer to buy from the second seller any additional units that he wants. After the first buyer has made all his contracts, a second buyer is chosen at random who then chooses a seller, makes an offer to buy, and so on, until each buyer has had an opportunity to make a purchase. The market will then be closed, and reopened for a new trading period.

Except in the offers and their acceptance, you are not to speak to any other subject. You are free to make your profits as large as you can. Trading will take place over very many market periods. *Each column* in your table applies to *one* trading period. Trading period 0 will be a trial period to familiarize you with the procedure and will not count toward your cash earnings.

Are there any questions?

APPENDIX 3

Instructions (For Monopoly Offer Auction)

Substitute the following in Appendix 1

MARKET ORGANIZATION. The market for this commodity is organized as follows. We open the market for a trading period (the length of a single period will be ________ minutes). The seller is free at any time to make an offer to sell one unit by stating a price offer. When an offer is made I will write the price on a data sheet and repeat it. If any buyer wishes to accept the offer he may say "I'll take it" or "Sold." If no buyer accepts the offer, the seller may, if you wish, make a new price offer *which always supersedes the previous offer* whether the new price is higher or lower than the previous price. When an offer is accepted it is a binding contract, and the buyer and seller will record the transaction price to be included in their profit calculation.

There are likely to be many offers that are not accepted. The seller is free to keep trying, and as a buyer or a seller you are free to make your profits as large as you can. Except in the offers and their acceptance, you are not to speak to any other subject. Trading will take place over very many market periods. *Each column* in your table applies to *one* trading period. Trading period 0 will be a trial period to familiarize you with the procedure and will not count toward your cash earnings.

Are there any questions?

APPENDIX 4

Instructions (For Monopoly Posted Bid)

Substitute the following in Appendix 1

MARKET ORGANIZATION. The market for this commodity is organized as follows. We open the market for a trading period. Each buyer decides on a buying price which will be written on one of the cards provided. Buyers will have two minutes to submit a price bid. The cards will be collected and the prices written on the blackboard. The seller will then choose a buyer and state the quantity he is willing to sell to that buyer. The buyer may accept any number (up to 2) of the units offered by the seller. However, when a buyer posts a price it is with the understanding that you are willing to accept *at least one unit* from the seller at that price. When a buyer accepts units offered by the seller it is a binding contract, and the buyer and seller will record the transaction prices to be included in their profit calculation. After the first buyer has made his contract the seller will choose a second buyer, state the quantity he is willing to sell, and so on, until the seller has made all the sales he wishes to make. The market will then be closed, and reopened for a new trading period.

Except in the offers and their acceptance, you are not to speak to any other subject. You are free to make your profits as large as you can. Trading will take place over very many market periods. *Each column* in your table applies to *one* trading period. Trading period 0 will be a trial period to familiarize you with the procedure, and will not count toward your cash earnings.

Are there any questions?

NOTES

Support by the National Science Foundation is gratefully acknowledged. I wish to thank A. Williams, who conducted the experiment reported in chart 4, for permission to report these results, and M. Korody, who conducted a pilot monopoly experiment (not discussed here) in the Plott-Smith seminar in experimental economics at Cal Tech, spring quarter, 1974.

1. This monopoly study was motivated directly by the Plott-Smith (1978) study of the posted-bid and oral-bid auction institutions, and the author's earlier studies of one-sided auctions (Smith, 1964, 1967). The finding that certain institutions tended to favor buyers as against sellers led to the conjecture that if these performance characteristics were strong enough, they might provide a form of decentralized control over monopoly. Six of the experiments reported below had been conducted before I had read Vickrey's remarkable precursory contribution to the literature on incentive compatibility.

2. An alternative measure of the seller's monopoly effectiveness is to compare his actual profit in period t with the profit that would result from the quantity-conditional price, $p[Q(t)]$.

REFERENCES

Clarke, E. H. "Multipart Pricing of Public Goods," *Public Choice*, 2 (Fall 1971), pp. 17–33.

______. "A Market Solution to the Public Goods Problem," University of Chicago, Urban Economics Reports, 1968.

Groves, T. "Incentives in Teams," *Econometrica*, 41 (July 1973), pp. 617–633.
———. "The Allocation of Resources under Uncertainty: The Information and Intensive Roles of Prices and Demands in a Team," Technical Report 1, Center for Research in Management Science, U.C. Berkeley, 1969, pp. 71–73.
Groves, T., and Ledyard, J. "Optimal Allocation of Public Goods: A Solution to the Free-Rider Problem," *Econometrica*, 45 (May 1977), pp. 703–809.
Lerner, A. P. *Economics of Control*. London: Macmillan, 1944.
Murnighan, J. K., and Roth, A. E. "Results in Small and Large Group Characteristic Function Games Where One Player Is a Monopolist," Public Choice Society Meetings, New Orleans, Mar. 10–13, 1977.
Plott, C., and Smith, V. "An Experimental Examination of Two Exchange Institutions," *Review of Economic Studies*, 45 (Feb. 1978), pp. 133–153.
Shubik, M. *Strategy and Market Structure*. New York: John Wiley and Sons, 1959.
———. "On the Role of Numbers and Information in Competition," *Revue Economique*, 26 (1975), pp. 605–621.
Smith, V. L. "An Experimental Study of Competitive Market Behavior," *Journal of Political Economy*, 70 (Apr. 1962), pp. 111–137.
———. "Effect of Market Organization on Competitive Equilibrium," *Quarterly Journal of Economics*, 78 (May 1964), pp. 181–201.
———. "Experimental Studies of Discrimination versus Competition in Sealed-Bid Auction Markets," *Journal of Business*, 40 (Jan. 1967), pp. 56–84.
———. "Experimental Economics: Induced Value Theory," *American Economic Review*, 66 (May 1976a), pp. 274–279.
———. "Bidding and Auctioning Institutions: Experimental Results," chap. 6 in Y. Amihud, ed., *Bidding and Auctioning for Procurement and Allocation*. Studies in Game Theory and Mathematical Economics. New York: New York University Press, 1976b.
Tsao, C., and Vignola, A. "Price Discrimination and the Demand for Treasury's Long Term Securities," 1977. To appear in *Research in Experimental Economics*, vol. 2. Greenwich, Conn.: JAI Press.
Vickrey, W. "Counterspeculation, Auctions and Competitive Sealed Tenders," *Journal of Finance*, 16 (Mar. 1961), pp. 8–37.
Williams, F. "Effect of Market Organization on Competitive Equilibrium: The Multi-Unit Case," *Review of Economic Studies*, 40 (Jan. 1973), pp. 97–113.

NATURAL MONOPOLY AND CONTESTED MARKETS: SOME EXPERIMENTAL RESULTS*

DON COURSEY
University of Wyoming

R. MARK ISAAC and VERNON L. SMITH
University of Arizona

I. Introduction

THE concept of natural monopoly is one of the most familiar in economics. Most textbook descriptions are similar to that of Mansfield:

> . . . [A] firm may become a monopolist because the average cost of producing the product reaches a minimum at an output rate that is big enough to satisfy the entire market at a price that is profitable. In a situation of this sort, if there is more than one firm producing the product, each must be producing at a higher-than-minimum level of average cost. Each may be inclined to cut the price to increase its output rate and reduce its average costs. The result is likely to be economic warfare—and the survival of a single victor, the monopolist.[1]

Many supposed natural monopolies are the object of widespread state, local, and federal regulation. It was in addressing issues of public utility regulation that Demsetz laid the foundation for an alternative scenario for decreasing cost markets.[2] In a model of rivals offering goods or services through a bidding process, Demsetz says:

> Economies of scale in production imply that the bids submitted will offer increasing quantities at lower per unit costs, but production scale economies imply nothing obvious about how competitive these prices will be. If one bidder can do the job at less than two or more, because each would then have a smaller output rate, then the bidder with the lowest bid price for the entire job will be awarded the

* We wish to thank Dennis Carlton, Dan Alger, and an anonymous referee for helpful comments. Financial assistance provided by the NSF is gratefully acknowledged.

[1] Edwin Mansfield, Microeconomics: Theory and Application 255 (1970).

[2] Harold Demsetz, Why Regulate Utilities? 11 J. Law & Econ. 55 (1968).

contract, whether the good be cement, electricity, stamp vending machines, or whatever, but the lowest bid price need not be a monopoly price.[3]

Demsetz's article promoted a debate over whether a formal auction system might provide a practical approach to monopoly control. This literature is rich in examining the practical difficulties of implementing such an institution.[4] Recent work in the Demsetz tradition is embodied in what has been called the "contestable markets" theory. This literature argues that the forces Demsetz saw as disciplining price in a "natural monopoly" depend only on entry and do not require the implementation of a formal auctioneering mechanism. As Bailey has argued:

> [I]ts [the theory's] most dramatic results relate to natural monopoly. The theory pertains to markets which have substantial attributes of natural monopoly, but which are characterized by free and easy entry and exit. For such markets, the cost-minimizing market structure calls for a single seller, yet the theory asserts that these sellers are without monopoly power. In the case of contestable markets, potential entry or competition *for* the market disciplines behavior almost as effectively as would actual competition *within* the market. Thus, even if operated by a single firm, a market that can be readily contested performs in a competitive fashion.[5]

In the typical description of the dynamics of natural monopoly theory, the single survivor of price cutting in a scale-economies environment operates as a true monopolist because the survivor gains the protection of alleged barriers to entry.[6] Yet, several of the advocates of contestable markets hypotheses argue that it is not the economies of scale per se that pose an entry barrier. They suggest that only if the cost curves reflect

[3] *Id.* at 57.

[4] See, for example, Oliver E. Williamson, Franchise Bidding for Natural Monopolies—in General and with respect to CATV, 7 Bell J. Econ. 73 (1976); and Martin Loeb & Wesley A. Magat, A Decentralized Method for Utility Regulation, 22 J. Law & Econ. 399 (1979).

[5] Elizabeth E. Bailey, Contestability and the Design of Regulatory and Antitrust Policy, 71 Am. Econ. Rev. Papers & Proc. 178 (1981). See also Elizabeth E. Bailey & John C. Panzar, The Contestability of Airline Markets during the Transition to Deregulation, 44 Law & Contemp. Prob. 125 (1981); William J. Baumol & Robert D. Willig, Fixed Costs, Sunk Costs, Entry Barriers, and Sustainability of Monopoly, 96 Q. J. Econ. 405 (1981); William J. Baumol, John C. Panzar, & Robert D. Willig, Contestable Markets and the Theory of Industry Structure (1982); and William J. Baumol, Contestable Markets: An Uprising in the Theory of Industry Structure, 72 Am. Econ. Rev. 1 (1982).

[6] A representative example from an undergraduate text is the following quote from James P. Quirk, Intermediate Microeconomics 260 (1st ed. 1976): "Any prospective entrant faces the problem that the monopolist can squeeze him out by lowering price in the short run to the level where the entrant takes losses only to raise the price again to the monopoly level once the entrant has been bankrupted."

large sunk fixed costs already borne by the incumbent can the incumbent firm even be assumed to be advantaged over potential entrants.[7]

The important characteristic of the contestable markets hypothesis, as we interpret it, is that at least two firms bid, in the sense of Demsetz, directly for buyer purchases. Note that we do *not* mean that at least two firms bid for the alienable right to supply a particular market as a monopolist. In this latter case, monopoly is cast in the concrete of law, and bidding merely permits the owner of the auctioned right (the city, U.S. Treasury, and so on) to capture all the monopoly rents. Under our bidding interpretation we refer (as does Demsetz) to a free and open right to supply, with the market's being won by the lowest price bidder. This bidding could occur within a formal auction process or through the unstructured price announcements of firms who are actual or potential rivals.

Much of the research in the area of contestable markets deals explicitly and directly with the applicability of the contestable markets hypothesis to questions of public regulatory policy.[8] The current economic and political climate suggests that questions relating to the deregulated performance of currently or historically regulated markets are of continuing concern. The acceptability and/or applicability of the contestable markets hypothesis may play an important role in the regulatory future of industries such as trucking, communications, and banking. For example, the chairman of the Interstate Commerce Commission (ICC) is reported to favor a requirement that truckers relinquish any unused operating permits.[9] The existence of unused permits in any particular market, however, is essential if the market is to be contested with a minimum of regulatory delay. The purpose of our research is to examine both the natural monopoly and the contestable markets hypotheses using appropriately designed laboratory experiments.

In Section IV we report four experiments, each with a single seller (the "monopoly" case), in which the effective cost of entry for a second firm is infinite and six experiments, each with two potential sellers (the "duopoly" case), whose cost of entry is zero. Originally we planned to do

[7] See, for example, Bailey, *supra* note 5, at 178–79; Bailey & Panzar, *supra* note 5, at 128–29; Baumol & Willig, *supra* note 5, at 418–19. Quirk, *supra* note 6, also makes the point about sunk costs in the second edition of the textbook, at 310.

[8] Especially Bailey, *supra* note 5; Bailey & Panzar, *supra* note 5; and Baumol, *supra* note 5.

[9] Business Week, November 9, 1981, reports at 74, "ICC sources say Taylor ordered his aides to draft a position paper advocating that truckers relinquish all operating rights not being used."

only four duopoly experiments, but the results of two of our first four duopolies (posted offer experiments 37 and 48) were not as unequivocal as the other two (45 and 47). Consequently, we expanded the sample size with two additional duopoly experiments (51 and 52). In all experiments all firms have identical decreasing marginal costs to capacity, and the capacity output of any firm is sufficient to satisfy the entire market demand. The price mechanism employed is a multiperiod posted offer market (explained in the next section), in which sellers quote public offers and buyers privately select the sellers from whom units are purchased. In the duopoly experiments each seller has an equal and unrestricted right to the market with each seller's market share determined by the buyers who are free to choose between the two posted price offers.

One of the principal tasks of the research has been to state correctly and explicitly the predictions of the contestable markets hypothesis in the context of our experimental design. This hypothesis can be interpreted in both "strong" and "weak" forms. It could be interpreted as suggesting that the existence of two identical potential sellers is enough to bring forth competitive price and quantity. Or, in a slightly weaker version applicable to experimental markets, the markets might converge to the competitive outcomes across time. On the other hand, such requirements might be too strong. After all, in the more familiar realm of nondecreasing cost industries, there are innumerable nonmonopoly predictions of duopoly behavior that also differ from purely competitive outcomes. Similar "intermediate" behavior might be observed in a contested decreasing cost duopoly. Thus, both a weak and a strong version of the contestable markets hypothesis will be derived in Section IV.

We next note that the contestable markets hypothesis (in either version) is falsifiable within our experimental design. There are at least two types of observed behavior that would lead to a failure of the hypothesis. First, the duopolists might use the vehicle of price signaling to establish a tacitly coordinated "shared monopoly." In our experimental design there is a strong incentive for such coordination, since the maximum profit to be shared by such a strategy is nearly $94 over twenty-five decision periods. If the duopolists were to "take turns" charging the monopoly price, each would pocket $47. Second, the duopolists may be found to behave in a manner suggested by the earlier reported description of the more traditional natural monopoly arguments. In our design, a seller who serves the entire market may still just break even at a low competitive price with all demand revealed. If sellers post identical prices and split the market, losses may be incurred. Either firm, fearful of such losses in a contested market, could prefer zero profits with certainty by conceding the entire market to the rival. (Of course, nothing in this version of the traditional alternative to the contestable markets hypothesis predicts which firm will be the "survivor.") If either of these alternate patterns of behavior (a collusive shared monopoly or a surviving monopolist) yields outcomes different from competitive predictions, then the contestable markets hypothesis is falsifiable in our design. This raises an important subsidiary question: What is the single uncontested seller (monopoly) outcome in this decreasing cost design? Comparing the behavior of contested markets only with theoretical monopoly predictions could be misleading. It is not self-evident that a single seller or collusive sellers facing unknown demand and profit motivated buyers will in fact be able to achieve the theoretical monopoly outcomes. If the results of the duopoly experiments are significantly different from theoretical monopoly predictions, this might be caused not by the contesting of the market but rather by some other feature of this cost and demand environment, such as a strategic decision by one or more buyers to underreveal demand.

The four true monopoly experiments (34–36, 46), in which it is common knowledge that there is only one actual or potential seller, serve as the monopoly behavior standard for comparison with the contested duopoly results. It might be thought that the results of a monopoly experiment would be trivially unsurprising with price and output converging quickly to the monopoly equilibrium. Such an assumption confuses the *condition* of monopoly (one uncontested seller) with monopoly *behavior*. Actual monopolists, like our experimental monopolists, do not know their demand functions except as demand is revealed at quoted prices by the free choice of buyers. Monopoly theory assumes implicitly that all buyers reveal 100 percent of their demand and that the seller optimally restricts supply. Smith reports the results of nine increasing-cost monopoly experiments (using five buyers) conducted under the double auction, offer auction, posted bid, and posted offer pricing institutions.[10] The one posted offer experiment that was reported converged quickly to the monopoly equilibrium with no buyer's withholding demand. In all the other institutions, prices and allocations failed to achieve monopoly levels and in many cases converged to levels near the competitive equilibrium because of successful buyer signaling and underrevelation of demand. This suggests that the posted offer institution is more likely than the other institutions to achieve a monopoly equilibrium, but such a generalization from

[10] Vernon L. Smith, An Empirical Study of Decentralized Institutions of Monopoly Restraint, in Essays in Contemporary Fields of Economics in Honor of Emanuel T. Weiler (1914–1979), at 83 (James P. Quirk & George Horwich eds. 1981); and Vernon L. Smith, Reflections on Some Experimental Market Mechanisms for Classical Environments, in Research in Marketing, Supplement 1: Choice Models for Buyer Behavior 13 (L. McAlister ed. 1982).

the result of one experiment is not justified. Even if the reported result is replicable, we do not know whether it extends to the decreasing-cost case. Hence, the need for a rigorous empirical test of the single-seller monopoly hypothesis which could be falsified by persistent strategic underrevelation of demand by buyers, or a failure of the seller to price optimally, or some other unanticipated feature of this design.

Table 1 lists all possible outcome combinations in each of the two (monopoly, duopoly) market types on the assumptions that a (price, quantity) observation is counted as supporting either the theoretical monopoly or competitive predictions. For example, an outcome (price or quantity) might be counted as "competitive" support if it is closer to the competitive than monopoly predictions. (Notice that this implies that, for purposes of this table, we have ignored the distinction between the strong and weak forms of the contestable markets hypothesis.) Of the four price-quantity, monopoly-competitive combinations in each of the two market types, one (competitive quantity/monopoly price) is impossible. A necessary condition for confirming (that is, nonfalsifying) either the standard monopoly theory (in the single seller design) or the contestable markets hypothesis (in the duopoly design) is that demand be fully revealed. The standard monopoly result requires supply restriction by the single seller, while the contestable markets hypothesis requires that at least one duopolist fully serve the market at the competitive price.

II. The PLATO Posted Offer Procedure

Most retail markets are organized under what has been called the posted offer institution.[11] As we define it, in this institution each seller independently posts a take-it-or-leave-it price at which deliveries will be made in quantities elected by each individual buyer subject to seller capacity limits. These posted prices may be changed or reviewed frequently, infrequently, regularly, or irregularly, but in any case a central characteristic of this mechanism is that the posted price is not subject to negotiation.

The experiments reported here use the posted offer mechanism programmed for the PLATO computer system by Jonathan Ketcham.[12] This program allows subject buyers and sellers, sitting separately at PLATO terminals, to trade for a maximum of twenty-five market "days" or pric-

[11] Charles R. Plott & Vernon L. Smith, An Experimental Examination of Two Exchange Institutions, 45 Rev. Econ. Stud. 133 (1978).

[12] Jonathan Ketcham, Vernon L. Smith, & Arlington W. Williams, A Comparison of Posted Offer and Double Auction Pricing Institutions, 51 Rev. Econ. Stud. (1984), in press.

TABLE 1
A CLASSIFICATION OF ALTERNATIVE EXPERIMENTAL OUTCOMES AND POSSIBLE TYPES OF BEHAVIOR

Alternative	Outcome	Possible Behavior	Comment
	True Monopoly (Single Seller; Infinite Entry Cost)		
M1	Mp, Mq	B: Demand fully revealed S: Supply optimally restricted	Does not falsify traditional monopoly theory
M2	Cp, Mq	B: Demand under revealed S: Supply restricted	Falsifies traditional monopoly theory
M3	Cp, Cq	B: Demand revealed S: Supply unrestricted	Falsifies traditional monopoly theory
	Contestable Markets Hypothesis Duopoly (Two Firms, Zero Entry Cost)		
C1	Mp Mq	B: Demand fully revealed S: Supply optimally restricted by either i) tacit collusion of 2 firms, or ii) a "surviving" monopolist is ceded the market	Falsifies CMH, a "Natural Monopoly" type of outcome
C2	Cp Mq	B: Demand under revealed S: Supply restricted by either i) tacit collusion of 2 firms, or ii) a "surviving" monopolist is ceded the market	Falsifies CMH
C3	Cp Cq	B: Demand revealed S: Supply unrestricted at the competitive price by at least one firm	Does not falsify CMH

NOTE.—M_p: Price supports theoretical monopoly prediction; M_q: Quantity supports theoretical monopoly prediction; C_p: Price supports theoretical competitive prediction; C_q: Quantity supports theoretical competitive prediction; *B*: Buyers; *S*: Seller(s); CMH: Contestable markets hypothesis.

ing periods. The display screen for each subject shows his or her record sheet, which lists a maximum of five units that can be purchased (sold) in each period. For each unit, the buyer (seller) has a marginal valuation (cost) which represents the value (cost) to him or her of purchasing (selling) that unit. These controlled, strictly private unit valuations (costs) induce individual, and aggregate market, theoretical supply and demand schedules.[13] That is, in an experiment, buyers (sellers) earn cash rewards equal to the difference between the marginal value (selling price) of a unit and its purchase price (marginal cost). Sales are "to order" in the sense that there are no penalties, or carry-over inventories, associated with units not sold (or units not purchased). Consequently the assigned marginal valuations and costs induce well-defined flow supply and demand conditions.

Each period begins with a request that sellers select a price offer by typing a price into the computer keyset. This offer is displayed privately on the seller's screen. The seller is then asked to select a corresponding quantity to be made available at that offer price. The maximum number of units a seller can offer corresponds to the number of the last unit whose cost is not greater than the offer price. The minimum number of units a seller can offer corresponds to the number of the first unit whose cost is not greater than the offer price. (However, the seller is required to offer at least one unit; that is, a seller cannot post a price for zero units.) This procedure permits individual-induced marginal costs to be declining, constant, or increasing. If the seller faces declining marginal costs, as in the experiments reported below, these minimum and maximum quantity constraints prevent his choices from being such that a loss is guaranteed, but if price is below the first unit marginal cost, a loss will be taken on the first units sold that must be more than offset by profits on later units if an overall profit is to be earned in the period. Since it is costly in time and effort for a seller to calculate the profit that any given offer may provide, especially with declining costs, PLATO always informs the seller of the potential profit (loss) if all offered units are sold. When a seller is satisfied with the selected price and quantity, he presses a touch sensitive "offer box" displayed on the screen. This action places, irrevocably, that seller's offer in the market. Before touching the offer box the seller may change the price and/or quantity as many times as desired. Each seller learns his competitor's price, in the current period, only after each has entered his price into the market.

The screen viewed by the buyer displays one price box for accepting units offered by each seller. After all sellers have entered their offers, each seller's price is posted in these buyers' acceptance boxes and at the bottom of each seller's screen. PLATO then randomly orders the buyers in a buying sequence, and the first is informed that he may now purchase the good. A buyer, once selected, can purchase from any seller. To purchase a unit from a selected seller, the buyer presses the box corresponding to

[13] See Vernon L. Smith, Experimental Economics: Induced Value Theory, 66 Am. Econ. Rev. Papers & Proc. 274 (1976).

that seller, then depresses a "confirm" key on the keyset. Repeating this sequence causes a second unit to be purchased, and so on. A buyer is allowed to purchase up to his buying capacity from any seller or sellers. However, a buyer can neither purchase a unit whose price is greater than the unit's marginal valuation nor buy from a seller who has sold all of the units offered. When a seller's last available unit is sold the price appearing in the buyer's box for that seller is replaced with the message "out of stock" on the buyer's screen. After the first buyer has finished making purchases, the next buyer in random order may begin purchasing, and so on. The period ends when the last buyer completes this buying mode and price posting for the next period begins.

Thus, the posted offer mechanism captures the essential feature of the Bailey and Panzar models in that the actual allocation of sales to firms is made by the buyers themselves and not by an auctioneer or regulatory intermediary.

It is important to emphasize that buyers and sellers have only limited information. All unit values (costs) assigned to individual buyers (sellers) are strictly private, known only to the subject (and the experimenter). Each buyer sees all of the seller's price offers but not the quantities available at these prices. In the experiments reported below sellers do not see the price posted by other sellers in the current period until after each has entered his own final price selection for that period. Finally, buyers (sellers) know only their own purchases (sales) and profits. Nevertheless, something less than a perfectly noncooperative setting exists. With each seller seeing the prices posted by other sellers in all previous periods, some indirect communication (or "price signaling") can be attempted. Such signaling has been observed in previous posted offer markets but has not proven to be very successful in effecting collusion.[14]

III. Experimental Design

We report ten experiments—four with a single seller and six with two sellers. The duopoly sellers are each given marginal cost schedules identical with the schedules given to the monopoly sellers (except perhaps for a parameter-disguising constant added to all unit costs and values). The aggregate demand and individual marginal cost schedules are shown on the left of Figure 1. We define the competitive equilibrium quantity, Q_c, as the largest quantity that can be sold without loss by at least one seller (that is, where average cost is less than or equal to price, or $AC(Q_c) \leqq D(Q_c)$). Since demand is sufficient to satisfy no more than one seller at

[14] See Ketcham, Smith, & Williams, *supra* note 12.

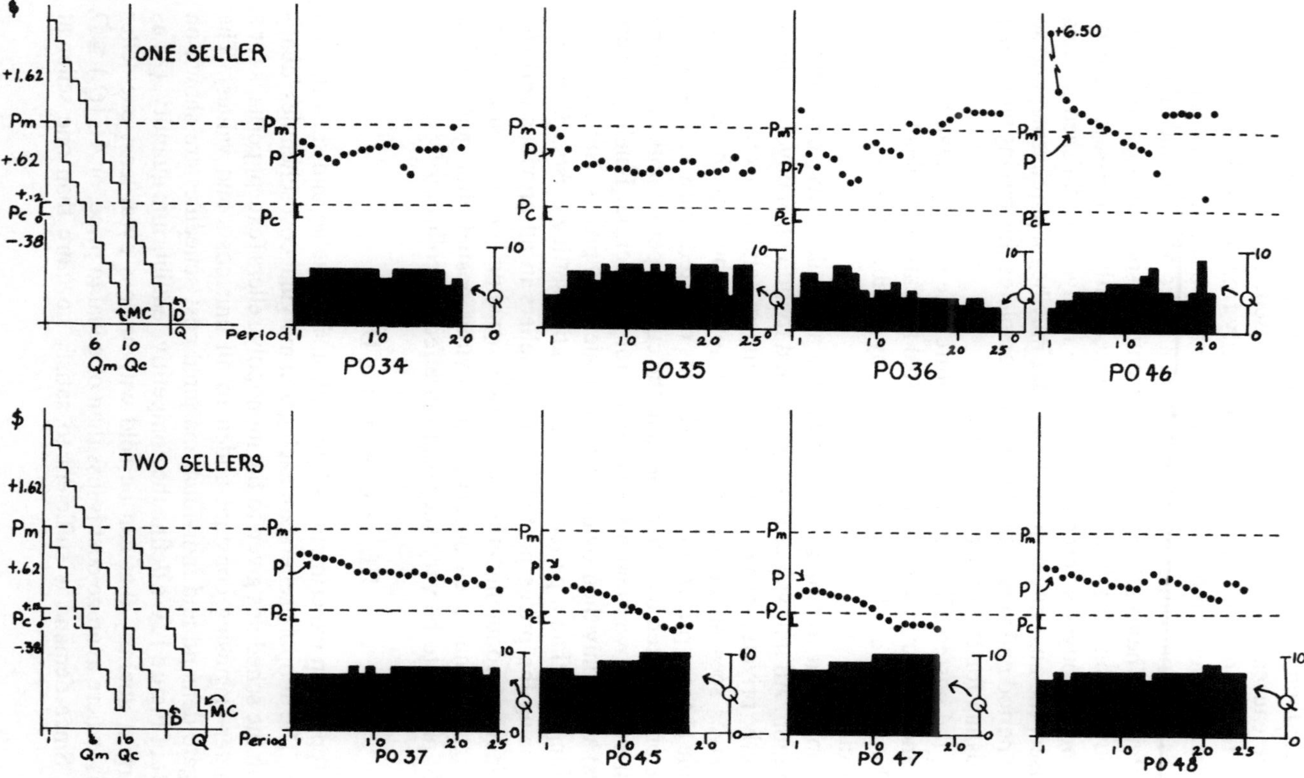

ONE SELLER
TWO SELLERS
$
+1.62
Pm
+.62
Pc
-.38
MC
D
Q
Qm Qc
Period
P
+6.50
PO34
PO35
PO36
PO46
PO37
PO45
PO47
PO48

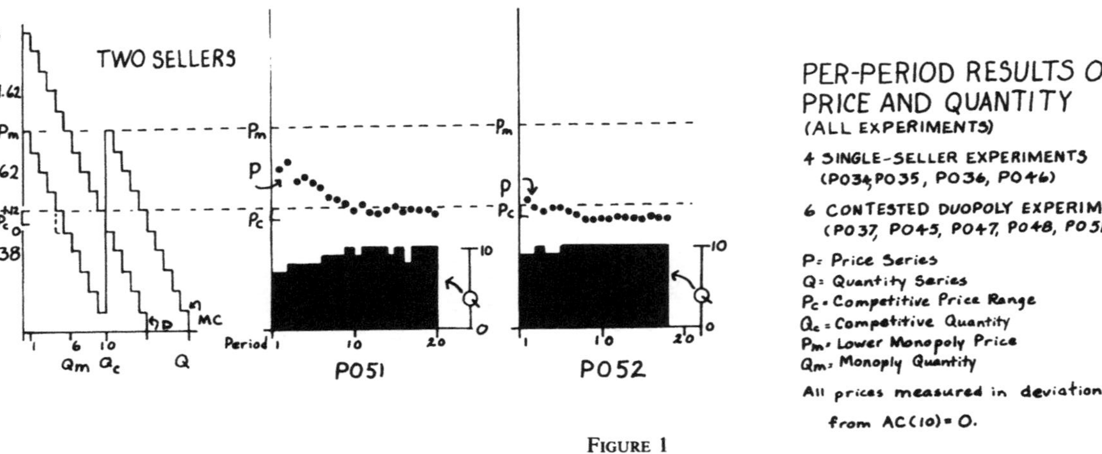

PER-PERIOD RESULTS ON PRICE AND QUANTITY
(ALL EXPERIMENTS)

4 SINGLE-SELLER EXPERIMENTS (P034, P035, P036, P046)

6 CONTESTED DUOPOLY EXPERIMENTS (P037, P045, P047, P048, P051, P052)

P = Price Series
Q = Quantity Series
P_c = Competitive Price Range
Q_c = Competitive Quantity
P_m = Lower Monopoly Price
Q_m = Monoply Quantity

All prices measured in deviations from AC(10) = 0.

FIGURE 1

capacity sales, $Q_c = 10$, whether there is one seller or two. Any price which supports Q_c is a competitive equilibrium price. In our experimental design any $P_c \in [AC(10), AC(10) + .12]$ is a competitive equilibrium price. The individual unit marginal valuations, marginal costs, and average costs are shown in Table 2, measured in deviations from $AC(10)$.

All five buyers in each experiment had participated in at least one previous posted offer experiment, but with design parameters different from the experiments reported here. Since the PLATO posted offer mechanism provides for a maximum trading capacity of five units for each agent (a screen display limitation) each monopoly experiment was initialized as if there were "two" sellers (each duopoly as if there were "four" sellers). Then each subject seller was provided two adjacent terminals. The fact that the markets actually consisted of one or two sellers (not two or four) was known to all participants.

Some of the parameter implications of this design for both monopoly and duopoly are summarized in Table 3.[15] Note that if a firm posts the monopoly price, and if it is the only firm or this is the lowest price, then the seller makes a profit of $3.75 in the period. Each seller has an incentive to post a lower price if he thinks the other seller will post any given price above $P = 0$. If the two sellers post the same price, one of the two sellers may incur a loss depending on how buyers choose to divide their purchases. If buyers are egalitarian and divide their purchases equally, then both sellers incur losses at tied prices below $0.75. Because of the scale economies, there is a social loss if either firm satisfies less than 100 percent of the demand at any ruling price.

It is worth reemphasizing at this point the methodological approach of this design. We have attempted to insure that the duopoly markets exhibit as few potential barriers to entry or competition as possible, except for those that derive from the natural monopoly nature of the cost functions of the two sellers. Bailey and Panzar report on their theory as follows:

[15] The use of two PLATO terminals required us to alter their parameters slightly under certain unusual conditions. The sellers' profits in each of the periods consisted of the sum of the profits on the first five units (left terminal) and on the next five units (right terminal). This addition was done by hand and not internally in PLATO. Because of the decreasing costs, sellers typically lost money on some early units and made money on the later ones. By a coincidence of the experimental design, prices at or below the upper bound of the competitive price range guaranteed a loss on the first five units, tripping the internal filter in the PLATO program designed to keep persons from guaranteeing themselves a monetary loss in the period. To correct this, we lowered the cost of the fifth unit by 25 cents if and only if a seller attempted to enter a price in the competitive price range. This intramarginal change in rent had only one effect on the parameters or predictions of the model: by lowering average cost, it dropped the lower bound of the competitive price range by 2.5 cents for persons trading in that range. The upper competitive price, the competitive quantity, and the monopoly price and quantity predictions were unchanged.

TABLE 2
INDUCED INDIVIDUAL VALUES AND COSTS

AGENT	UNIT									
	(1)	(2)	(3)	(4)	(5)	(6)	(7)	(8)	(9)	(10)
Buyer 1	2.37	.12	−.88	...	...	...	...	...	...	...
Buyer 2	2.12	.37	−.13	...	...	...	...	...	...	...
Buyer 3	1.87	.62	−.63	...	...	...	...	...	...	...
Buyer 4	1.62	.87	−.38	...	...	...	...	...	...	...
Buyer 5	1.37	1.12	−1.13	...	...	...	...	...	...	...
Seller 1	1.12	.87	.62	.37	.12	−.13	−.38	−.63	−.88	−1.13
Average cost	1.12	1.00	.87	.75	.62	.50	.37	.25	.12	0

NOTE.—All values and costs are stated in deviations from $AC(10)$.

TABLE 3
PARAMETER SUMMARY, MONOPOLY AND DUOPOLY

Parameter Description	Value
Number of buyers	5
Monopoly price (normalized)	1.12
Seller surplus (per period) at P = 1.12	3.75
Buyer surplus (per period) at P = 1.12	3.75
Competitive price (normalized)	[0, .12]
Seller surplus (per period) at P = 0	0
Buyer surplus (per period) at P = 0	12.50

"The theory of contestable markets has been developed to analyze the equilibrium properties of markets that may have economies of scale but that are characterized by perfectly free and easy entry and exit."[16] In testing this theory, we have attempted to reproduce these conditions specified by the theory. If the theory is falsified, we are done; that is, no further experiments are necessary. If the theory is not falsified, a wide range of questions opens about the robustness of the assumptions behind the contestable markets hypothesis. This would call for further study by theoretical, empirical, and experimental economists into the limits of contesting as a discipline against monopoly behavior.

IV. HYPOTHESES AND EXPERIMENTAL RESULTS

The contestable markets hypotheses presented in the introduction can be formalized in a manner conducive to laboratory experimentation. Define a vector (P, Q, E) as price, quantity, and market efficiency. The theoretical competitive equilibrium predictions, (P_c, Q_c, E_c), and the theoretical monopoly equilibrium predictions, (P_m, Q_m, E_m), are constant vectors given by economic theory. From the actual laboratory experiments come vectors describing laboratory monopolies, (P_s, Q_s, E_s), and duopolies (P_d, Q_d, E_d). These results could and did vary over the course of the experiments.

We define a laboratory strong version of the contestable markets hypothesis in terms of convergence of the duopoly results over time to the competitive predictions:

$$H_s: (P_d, Q_d, E_d) \rightarrow (P_c, Q_c, E_c)$$

$$\hat{H}_s: (P_d, Q_d, E_d) \not\rightarrow (P_c, Q_c, E_c).$$

[16] Bailey & Panzar, *supra* note 5, at 125.

There is also a weak interpretation of the contestable markets hypothesis. The laboratory duopolies could exhibit neither monopoly nor competitive behavior, but some intermediate outcome. While the market is not a true "closed" monopoly, the two sellers may each have some market power that is not eliminated by the contestability of the market. The following is a formal statement of a weak version of the contestable markets hypothesis:

$$H_w\colon P_d \leqslant \frac{P_m + P_c}{2}$$

$$Q_d \geqslant \frac{P_m + P_c}{2}$$

$$E_d \geqslant \frac{E_m + E_c}{2}$$

versus

$$\hat{H}_w\colon P_d > \frac{P_m + P_c}{2}$$

$$Q_d < \frac{Q_m + Q_c}{2}$$

$$E_d < \frac{E_m + E_c}{2}.$$

That is, if the weak version of the competitive markets hypothesis fails, then the duopolies will be achieving outcomes closer to the monopoly than to the competitive predictions. Such behavior could be manifested by a single monopoly survivor, by a shared monopoly, or by some kind of rotating monopoly behavior.

On the other hand, a monopolist may not be able to exercise complete monopoly power within a market. It is important to separate competitive pressure due to factors of contestability from any underlying weakness with respect to the applicability of theoretical monopoly predictions. Therefore, we next define an ordering hypothesis that requires that laboratory contestable duopoly markets actually perform more competitively than laboratory monopolies:

$$H_0\colon P_d \leqslant \frac{P_s + P_c}{2}$$

$$Q_d \geqslant \frac{Q_s + Q_c}{2}$$

$$E_d \geqslant \frac{E_s + E_c}{2}$$

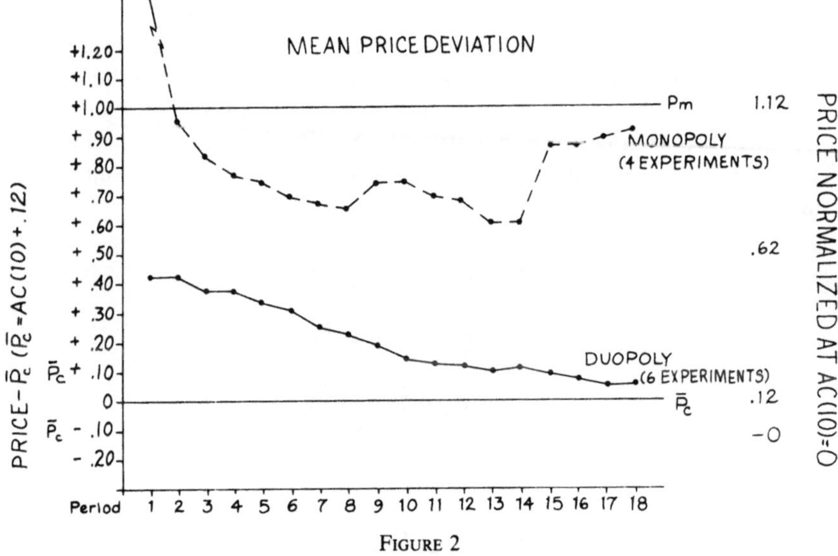

FIGURE 2

versus

$$\hat{H}_0: P_d > \frac{P_s + P_c}{2}$$

$$Q_d < \frac{Q_s + Q_c}{2}$$

$$E_d \leqslant \frac{E_d + E_c}{2}.$$

Figure 1 charts the lowest ruling price and the quantity traded in each period for the ten experiments.[17] Figure 2 charts the mean monopoly and mean duopoly prices computed for all experiments in each treatment. Table 4 summarizes the mean price, quantity, efficiency, and the index of monopoly effectiveness (the proportion of theoretical monopoly profit actually realized by the seller(s)).[18]

The most striking feature of these results is the overwhelming support they give at least to the weak version of the contestable markets hypothesis. Mean duopoly price is closer to the competitive price than the

[17] In 46, the monopolist entered a price in trading period 20 that he later said was accidentally and incorrectly $1.00 lower than he wanted.

[18] Complete copies of the data protocols for all experiments are available from the authors.

TABLE 4

MEAN QUANTITY, EFFICIENCY, AND INDEX OF MONOPOLY EFFECTIVENESS BY PERIOD

Period	Mean Quantity, Monopoly	Mean Quantity, Duopoly	Mean Efficiency Monopoly	Mean Efficiency Duopoly	Mean Monopoly Effectiveness Monopoly	Mean Monopoly Effectiveness Duopoly
1	3.50	7.70	44.67	76.67	.42	.53
2	5.00	7.70	46.00	76.67	.57	.53
3	5.75	8.20	57.50	81.67	.62	.51
4	6.00	7.80	58.00	75.50	.59	.36
5	6.25	7.80	60.50	76.00	.64	.39
6	6.75	8.20	67.50	79.30	.71	.43
7	6.50	8.30	64.50	79.30	.60	.38
8	6.75	8.80	67.50	76.50	.66	.37
9	6.25	8.70	62.50	83.80	.68	.33
10	6.25	9.00	59.00	82.15	.70	.09
11	6.25	9.00	61.50	88.70	.60	.36
12	6.25	9.30	61.00	90.30	.57	.35
13	6.75	9.20	65.50	85.50	.59	.34
14	6.75	9.30	66.50	76.90	.56	−.14
15	6.00	9.20	56.00	86.50	.69	.10
16	6.00	9.30	59.00	93.30	.77	.30
17	5.25	9.00	51.00	81.20	.59	−.06
18	5.00	9.30	49.00	85:50	.56	.02
Theoretical	6.00	10.00	60.00	100.00	1.00	(0 to .3625)

monopoly price at period 1 and tends to decay thereafter. Mean duopoly quantity follows a similar pattern after period 5. Only in efficiency are the results not so clear cut. Mean duopoly efficiency is never as low as 60 percent, and in nine of the final ten periods it is closer to the competitive than monopoly level. The efficiency time path is more erratic than the quantity dimension because of several ties in pricing in which both firms supply the market at inefficiently low output levels.

In period 18, the last period for which data are available for all experiments, the market performance vectors are as follows:[19]

	Duopoly Mean	Monopoly Mean	Competitive Theory	Monopoly Theory
Price	.182	1.0425	(0, .12)	(1.12 or 1.37)
Quantity	9.3	5.00	10.0	(6.0 or 5.0)
Efficiency	85.5	49.00	100.0	(60.0 or 50.00)

The data are almost, but not quite, as convincing with regard to the strong version of the contestable market hypothesis. We state this reservation primarily because of the bifurcated nature of the data (see Figure 1). Four duopoly experiments had price and quantity outcome that converged directly to the competitive predictions. For these, the strong version of the hypothesis clearly holds. The other two duopoly experiments never achieved the competitive outcomes, although a visual inspection suggests they were tending in that direction. To test whether these experiments actually demonstrated convergent tendencies, we estimated the following regressions:

$$\ln P_t = A_0 + A_1 t + U_t,$$

where P_t was the normalized price above the top of the competitive set in period t; A_0, and A_1 are coefficients, A_1 being a decay parameter; and U_t is the error term. Ordinary least squares on the twenty-five observations of both experiment 37 and experiment 48 yielded the following results (t-statistics in parentheses),

for 37:

$$\ln P_t = \underset{(-8.08)}{-0.3813} \quad \underset{(-8.14)}{-0.0258}\, t;$$

[19] Dan Alger of the FTC pointed out to us after work on this research had begun that there are actually two points at which monopoly profits obtained. One, the lower of the two, is the one we had designated as P_m. The other is at $P_m + .25$, which may explain the tendency of two of the monopoly experiments to evince several periods of pricing near this point.

for 48:

$$\ln P_t = \underset{(-7.54)}{-0.58} \quad \underset{(-4.88)}{-0.025\,t};$$

(48 adjusted for autocorrelation:

$$\ln P_t = \underset{(-4.55)}{-0.5836} \quad \underset{(-2.85)}{-0.0240\,t}).$$

The negative coefficient on the time variable (with significant t-statistic) in each equation suggests that price in these two experiments decayed toward the competitive range at the rate of about 2.5 percent per period, thus supporting the laboratory-markets version of the strong contestable markets hypothesis.

It is necessary to examine these results, which support the competitive markets hypothesis, in the light of the behavior of true single-seller markets. The importance of this comparison is in seeing whether our conclusions of competitive behavior stand when actual monopoly behavior is used as the benchmark. Again, the data are clear cut. Qualitatively, it can be seen that the mean duopoly price is more competitive than the mean monopoly price in eighteen out of eighteen periods; mean duopoly quantity is greater in eighteen of eighteen periods, and mean duopoly efficiency is greater in eighteen of eighteen periods.

Two nonparametric tests were used to judge the robustness of the qualitative observation that contested duopolies are more competitive than the laboratory monopolies. First, a binomial cell test over the two intervals

$$I_1: \left(P > \frac{P_m + \overline{P}_c}{2}\right)$$

and

$$I_2: \left(P < \frac{P_m + \overline{P}_c}{2}\right),$$

where $\overline{P}_c$ is .12, the maximum of the competitive price range). All four period 18 monopoly prices fell in I_1 and all six duopoly prices fell in I_2. This would occur with a probability of .00098 if generated from a random binomial process. Second, a nonparametric Mann and Whitney rank-sum test was conducted.[20] This test checks the equality of the distribution of prices between the duopoly and monopoly experiments. A total of eigh-

[20] Alexander M. Mood & Franklin A. Graybill, Introduction to the Theory of Statistics (1974).

teen observation periods in each of the ten experiments yielded a sample of 180 observations. Using this sample, the hypothesis that the experimental duopoly prices and experimental monopoly prices arise from different distributions can be accepted at the 99.99995 confidence level. In summary, the use of the observed monopoly data as a benchmark does not alter the conclusion that contestable decreasing-cost duopoly markets behave more competitively than uncontested monopoly counterparts.

Parenthetically, these competitive results occurred in spite of what might be viewed as attempts to keep prices high by means of indirect price signaling. Across the six duopoly experiments, 47 percent of all posted offers were higher than the prevailing market price in the immediately previous market period. But in only 35 percent of these signaling attempts did the signaler's competitor follow through with a next-period offer price above the signaler's price.[21] This was the anatomy of the failure of signals to yield tacit collusion.

These experiments provided a related set of observations that proved to be very interesting. Even though contested duopolies are clearly different from the single seller counterparts, these laboratory monopolists did not automatically lock on the monopoly outcomes. Experiments 34 and 35 are particularly notable in this regard (see Figure 1). We observed that a principal problem facing the monopolists was the withholding of demand by buyers. Given the decreasing-cost schedule of our monopolists, withholding of demand hits the seller at his most profitable units. Small amounts of withholding resulted in very large reductions in sellers' profits. Buyer withholding occurred at a much higher rate in the monopoly experiments than in the duopoly experiments (9.14 percent versus

[21] The following table provides these data for each experiment:

Experiment	Incidence of Price Signals (A)	Incidence of Signal Reinforcement (B)
37	25/48 = .521	6/25 = .24
45	9/26 = .346	3/9 = .33
48	25/48 = .521	8/25 = .32
47	12/34 = .353	4/12 = .33
51	20/38 = .526	8/20 = .40
52	16/34 = .471	8/16 = .50
All	107/228 = .469	37/107 = .35

Column A: Fraction of price offers by a seller which exceed the previous period's ruling price and are potentially profitable (signal). Column B: Fraction of "signals" in column A for which the signaler's competitor followed through in the subsequent period with an offer price above that of the signaler's price (signal reinforcement).

1.16 percent).[22] This tended to discipline the monopolists against attempts to increase price. This discipline appeared to weaken in three of the four experiments as the experiment progressed beyond about fifteen periods (see Figure 1). These withholding effects have important applications in addressing the question, "How tough is it to be a monopolist?" Witness the following case of two segmented air-frame markets, one a contested duopoly, the other apparently serviced by only a single seller:

> Delta and other airlines, it's known, had been pushing McDonnell Douglas to build a new plane, if only to spur price competition with Boeing. Until yesterday's announcement, just 52 of the narrow-body 757s had been purchased, as airlines held off to see whether Douglas would enter the fray. The plane Douglas has been considering is known as the DCXX, or ATMR, for Advanced Transport–Medium Range, and would compete directly with the 757.
>
> Meanwhile, Boeing's wide-body 767, which has competition in the form of the European Airbus Industrie A-310, has drawn orders for a healthy 161 aircraft. "Airlines know they get the best deal when two companies are aggressively going after their business," one industry source says.[23]

Apparently, as in our laboratory markets, buyers displayed a greater tendency to withhold demand in the monopoly market than in the duopoly market.

V. Conclusions, Interpretations, and Implications

The most significant conclusion of this research is that the behavioral predictions of the contestable market hypothesis are fundamentally correct. It is simply not true that monopoly pricing is a "natural" result of a market merely because firms in the market exhibit decreasing costs and demand is sufficient to support no more than a single firm.

The data from these experiments point toward an even stronger conclusion. There is clear evidence not only that contesting duopolies exhibit behavior more competitive than theoretical monopoly predictions, but also that they actually perform up to the standards of the competitive

22 These data include all subjects in all six duopoly experiments with the exception of the final one, 52. In that experiment, a single buyer who showed no unusual buying behavior nevertheless was causing the experiment severe problems because of his tendency to play with the PLATO terminal keys in nonprescribed ways. He was excused (in period 3, *after* the market had already entered the competitive range) and replaced with a graduate student. The replacement was instructed to refrain from withholding demand. Such behavior makes a buyer essentially a passive participant and was virtually the universal pattern observed among buyers in the first five duopoly experiments (in which only 1.16 percent of all demand was withheld). However, because this replacement was so instructed, the data reported include only the other four buyers from experiment 52.

23 Victor F. Zonana, Boeing's Sale to Delta Gives It Big Advantage over U.S. Competitors, Wall Street Journal, November 13, 1980, at 1.

model. Four of our six experiments moved rapidly to competitive outcomes; two others moved in that direction but never actually entered the competitive range. The fact that these results obtained with only two sellers is particularly convincing, since the most familiar paradigm suggests that adding more sellers (if it had any effect at all) would increase the competitive discipline of the marketplace.

As we view it, the essential feature of a contested market is that firms bid directly for the purchases of buyers. If either of two sellers can satisfy the entire market, then the posted offer pricing institution reduces, in its essential features, to a sealed-bid auction in which the seller with the ruling bid collects a price equal to his bid for the entire market.[24] Thus, given the market structure, sellers are bidding to supply a single unit, the market, as in a sealed-bid auction with two bidders competing for a single item. However, in this case the item won has a volume dimension that varies with the level of the ruling price. Also, in this case, the tie-breaking rule is discretionary, since it depends on the free choice made by each buyer. The usual tie-breaking rule in sealed-bid auctions is to make the award to one of the bidders at random (an equally likely choice). Note that such a rule is more efficient than the "buyer's discretion" rule in posted offer markets, since the random award rule guarantees the market to one seller. With increasing returns it is always better to have all sales made by one seller.

The sealed-bid interpretation also provides a possible explanation of different modes of contested market behavior. As shown by Cox, Roberson, and Smith, risk-averse buyers will bid more (sellers will bid less) than risk-neutral buyers (sellers) for an item sold (purchased) under the high (low) bid rule.[25] Hence, greater risk aversion may account for the four contesting duopoly experiments that converged quickly to the competitive equilibrium.

The comparison of our monopoly experiments with our contested market experiments suggests that the contesting of the markets (and not some other feature of our design) was responsible for the competitive tendencies in the latter. An examination of the monopoly experiment is particularly important since our experiments incorporated a finite numbr of human buyers. This could leave open the possibility that the competitive discipline of the markets is due not directly to contesting by sellers but rather to the actual (or merely anticipated) strategic withholding of de-

[24] This analogy was pointed out in Plott & Smith, *supra* note 11.

[25] James C. Cox, Bruce Roberson, & Vernon L. Smith, Theory and Behavior of Single Object Auctions, in 2 Research in Experimental Economics 1 (Vernon L. Smith ed. 1982).

mand by buyers.[26] The data presented here suggest that this is not the case. With a 9.14 percent buyer withholding of demand, the monopolists encountered some difficulty in obtaining prices at or near the monopoly level, primarily in the earlier periods. However, by the later periods of the experiment, average monopoly price was close to the predictions of the monopoly model. If this 9.14 percent rate of underrevelation did not ultimately prevent monopolists from obtaining prices at or near a monopoly level, it suggests that it is unlikely that there was any significant effect from the much lower rate of underrevelation (1.16 percent) that occurred in the contested duopolies.

Our research program on contestable markets will expand on the present study by (*a*) introducing finite nonzero entry costs, and (*b*) running some experiments in which "dummy" buyers are computer programmed to reveal demand, with this "full revelation" being known by sellers. The results of the present study indicate that experiments under *a* are needed to explore the entry cost limits of the contestable markets hypothesis. Experiments under *b* will allow us to examine further our current claim that the competitive tendencies in our duopoly experiments are indeed caused by sellers contesting the market.

[26] We wish to thank our referee for emphasizing that the contestable markets theory assumes a "large number" of buyers.

In Search of Predatory Pricing

R. Mark Isaac and Vernon L. Smith

University of Arizona

Can predatory pricing be reproduced in a laboratory environment? We report research motivated by this objective. We began with conditions that, based on the literature, appeared to combine the features this literature has suggested are favorable to the emergence of predation. Next we operationalized what was meant by predatory pricing in our design in order to compare prices with predictions from alternative theories. Of 10 experiments, none evidenced predatory behavior; most supported the dominant firm theory. The second series of experiments addresses remedies for predation and finds that the effect is to increase prices and reduce efficiency.

I. Overview of Research Procedure and Results

Is predatory pricing an observable phenomenon that can be induced in a laboratory environment? We report research motivated by the maintained hypothesis that if such behavior is a human trait we ought to be able to observe it in the laboratory. Our procedure was first to specify a set of structural conditions that appeared to us to combine those features that were favorable to the emergence of predatory behavior: (1) two firms—one large, one small; (2) scale economies, with the larger firm having a cost advantage over the smaller (but with the smaller firm's production required for market efficiency); (3) a "deep pocket" possessed by the advantaged firm; and (4) sunk entry costs tending to discourage reentry when such costs must be incurred. Next we constructed an experimental design to operationalize these conditions and to define predatory pricing within this design. In this

We gratefully acknowledge the financial support of the Federal Trade Commission and the research assistance of David Porter, Mark Olson, and Peter Knez.

design, predatory prices are distinct from several alternatives: competitive prices, the shared monopoly price, the dominant firm price, and Edgeworth-style price cycles.

Our first three experiments were conducted with attributes 1–3. The second series added feature 4. After six experiments, we still had not observed predatory pricing. A reconsideration of the literature suggested that most predatory pricing theories implicitly assumed a fifth feature: (5) firms have complete information about competitors' costs. Although we do not consider complete information a realizable field condition in most (if any) markets, we decided this condition should be included in the search for predatory pricing behavior. Our third series of experiments, incorporating conditions 1–5, still produced no evidence of predatory pricing. Because some scholars have suggested that predatory pricing, if it exists, is driven by goals other than profit maximization, we attempted, without success, to generate "cut-throat" pricing in one experiment by inducing rivalistic incentives. At this point we wondered if there were something artifactual about our experimental design that, unsuspected by us, would inhibit the small firm's being driven out of the market even if the large firm posted prices and quantities below marginal cost. For example, do subjects who are assigned the small firm's structural conditions perceive themselves as duty bound to remain in the market? If this were the case, then the predicted effect of predation would not be observed, even if we did observe predatory price levels quoted by the large firm. So we conducted one experiment in which, unknown to the small firm, the large firm was a confederate of the experimenters and was instructed to price repeatedly at predatory levels. This prompted the small firm to leave the market, and therefore we were confident of our small firm's vulnerability to being forced out of the market by a determined predator.[1]

The second part of the research program had the objective of examining proposed antitrust remedies for predatory pricing that might be imposed on an industry thought to be subject to predation. For our antitrust treatment condition, we applied a semipermanent price reduction rule (Baumol 1979) and a quantity expansion limit (Williamson 1977). We conducted seven experiments (series 6) with attributes 1–4 and with these two antitrust restrictions. Since no predation was found in the 11 experiments based on conditions 1–4

[1] While the negative results of the 11 experiments we report cannot prove that predatory pricing does not exist, we feel that they alter the burden of proof for those who would design public policy as though predation were a robust phenomenon. We invite antitrust scholars to scrutinize our experimental design, to suggest specific ways in which they would alter it, and to state the corresponding outcomes they are prepared to predict. We will take their suggestions seriously.

TABLE 1

CLASSIFICATION OF EXPERIMENTS

TREATMENT SERIES NO.	NO. OF REPLICATIONS	TREATMENT CONDITION					EXPERIMENT NUMBER(S)
		Entry Cost	Complete Information	Induced Rivalry	Confederate	Antitrust Rules	
1	3	No	No	No	No	No	129, 131, 133
2	3	Yes	No	No	No	No	135, 136, 138
3	3	Yes	Yes	No	No	No	139, 140, 141
4	1	Yes	No	Yes	No	No	142
5	1	Yes	No	No	Yes	No	143
6	7	Yes	No	No	No	Yes	145, 146, 147, 149, 150, 152, 153

alone, we interpret this series of seven experiments as a test for the existence of type 2 regulatory error, that is, whether adopting anti-predatory pricing rules might induce anticompetitive incentive effects.

Table 1 summarizes the treatment conditions underlying the experiments in each of the series 1–6.

II. Predatory Pricing: From the Literature to Experimental Design

The idea that there is a distinction to be made between the price that is low because of good competition and the price that is low because of bad predation is well established in American legal and political history. It appears in early Supreme Court decisions subsequent to the enactment of the Sherman Act (e.g., *Trans-Missouri Freight* case and *Standard Oil* case).[2]

Economists J. B. and J. M. Clark, in a book chapter subtitled "Destructive Competition," describe a process of selective price cutting that is similar to the contemporary concept of predatory pricing, and Senator Estes Kefauver, prominent in the development of modern congressional antitrust policy, has mourned the passage of the era of "independent" bakeries.[3] Private antitrust cases and threats of litigation flourish. Of course, the existence of such cases does not necessarily demonstrate the existence of predation, since there clearly are other incentives for firms to assert that they are victims of predation.[4]

[2] U.S. v. Trans-Missouri Freight Association, 166 U.S. 290, 328 (1897). The court suggested that monopolization may involve strategic price reductions that may drive out of business "the small dealers and worthy men whose lives have been spent therein and who might be unable to readjust themselves to their altered surroundings." Standard Oil Company of New Jersey v. U.S., 221 U.S. 1 (1911). In this case the court implied that predation had replaced productive forms of business behavior: "The very genius for commercial development and organization which it would seem was manifested from the beginning soon begot an intent and purpose to exclude others which was frequently manifested by acts and dealings wholly inconsistent with the theory that they were made with the single conception of advancing the development of business power by usual methods, but which on the contrary necessarily involved the intent to drive others from the field and to exclude them from their right to trade and thus accomplish the mastery which was the end in view."

[3] This chapter is contained in Clark and Clark, *The Control of Trusts* (1912). Lest anyone confuse destructive competition with healthy price rivalry, they (p. 98) call such practices "refined forms of robbery" and demand that "the illegitimate breaking of a general scale of prices must, in some way, be stopped." Sen. Kefauver states (1965, p. 139) that many independents "personally know small bakers who have been destroyed by engaging in competitive warfare with the majors."

[4] In International Air Industries et al. v. American Excelsior Company, 517 F.2d 714 (1975), *cert. denied,* 424 U.S. 943 (1975), predation was alleged in the "evaporative-cooler pad" industry. The courts rejected the claim, stating, "It would appear that [the defendant] was selling its cooler pads at a price far above even its average cost. More-

Our task in the present research was to operationalize the concept of predation into a reasonable economic design with testable predictions. Our goal was to create an economic environment that we felt would have a "best shot" at observing predatory pricing. Unfortunately, we found no single universally accepted model of predatory pricing. However, we were able to identify several important design elements to use in some or in all of our experiments.

The trading environment we chose for our investigation is that of firms producing to order a homogeneous product for sale in a posted-offer market with full demand revelation.[5] Other design features were identified from our reading of the literature in predatory pricing. These are presented in the paragraphs below. Finally, in the last seven experiments, we conducted the markets with a predatory pricing antitrust program (PPAP), which is described in paragraph 7 below.

1. *Number of firms.* Every source we consulted spoke of predation by a single predator. However, the prey may be singular (Salop 1981, p. 11) or plural (Scherer 1980, p. 335; Kreps and Wilson 1982; Milgrom and Roberts 1982; Selten 1978). Because of our previous experience with two-firm markets (Coursey, Isaac, and Smith 1984; Coursey, Isaac, Luke, and Smith 1984; hereafter CIS and CILS), we decided to continue with this design feature. In this case, however, the two firms were not symmetric in costs.

2. *Costs of the firms.* The literature appears to be in disagreement whether predator and prey are to be distinguished by costs. Some (McGee 1958, p. 140) say no. Others (Ordover and Willig 1981, p. 308; Salop 1981, p. 19) seem to suggest that while costs may be equal, they also may not. Still others build predation models explicitly around the concept of a dominant firm that has some cost advantage (Gaskins, as quoted in Scherer 1980, p. 338). Our previous experiences (CIS, CILS) with the symmetric cost case were marked by a complete absence of any success of one firm in achieving unchecked

over, the record indicates that barriers to entry in the cooler pad market were virtually non-existent." This is not to indicate that the court ignored marginal costs. They seem to be following an Areeda and Turner (1975) model in which average cost is used in certain instances as a proxy for the more important (but less observable) marginal cost. With regard to the issue of entry costs, the court estimated that "the total costs of entering the market on a scale large enough to supply the entire southwestern and far western United States" was less than $300,000.

[5] The made-to-order nature of production does not allow for carryover of stock from one period to another, and it eliminates the costs and risks of holding unsold stock. This ensures that the induced marginal cost schedules generate replicated periods with identical well-defined (flow) supply conditions. To our knowledge the literature nowhere suggests that predation is related to production for inventory.

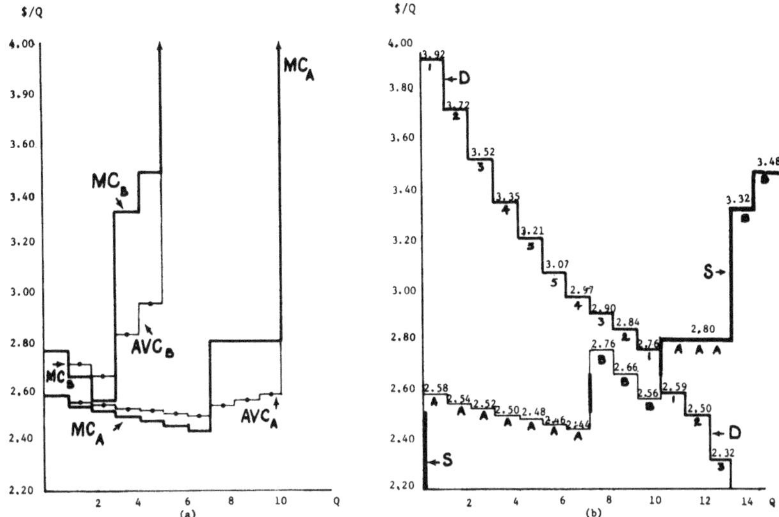

FIG. 1.—Seller costs, buyer values, and supply and demand conditions

monopoly power. Therefore, in order to create conditions more favorable to obtaining predation, we chose to give the predator an important cost advantage over the prey (hereafter called the "large" or "small" firm), but the small firm, although perhaps disadvantaged in our design, is efficient enough to be in production at a Pareto-efficient competitive equilibrium (Kefauver 1965, p. 144; Ordover and Willig 1981, p. 308).

These cost conditions were obtained via the induced seller marginal cost schedules exhibited in figure 1*a*. Figure 1*b* exhibits the market supply and demand conditions. From figures 1*a* and 1*b* several important attributes of our laboratory market can be noted. At the competitive equilibrium ($P_c \in [2.66, 2.76]$) both firms are producing. Seller A sells 7 units while seller B sells 3 units. Furthermore, there exist combinations of price and quantity for seller A ($2.60 \leqslant P_A < 2.66$; $8 \leqslant Q_A \leqslant 10$) such that seller A can exclude seller B from the market and yet earn a positive cash flow of returns from the experimenters.

3. *Deep pocket.* Many sources describe the predator as having a capital market advantage over the prey via what is popularly described as a deep pocket. The *Wall Street Journal* (1983) says of an FTC decision: "Critics of the agency say the new formula will let Borden price ReaLemon below its true costs in areas where Borden faces competition, while making up the difference in areas where ReaLemon enjoys

a monopoly." This is almost a twin argument to a hypothetical situation described by Clark and Clark (1912, p. 97).[6] Scherer (1980) quotes Edwards as saying of the predator, "the length of its purse assures it of victory." Scherer says directly of the predator, "it subsidizes its predatory operations with profits from other markets." Salop (1981, p. 11) defines the deep pocket as the case "in which an incumbent predator has superior access to financial resources." The idea is also mentioned by Kefauver (1965, pp. 146–49). We provided a deep pocket in the following manner: Since economic losses were a real possibility in our design, each seller was provided an up-front capital endowment. However, in all cases the endowment to seller A (the potential predator) was double the endowment to seller B. (Also, firm A's pocket was further deepened under treatment 4 below, which gives firm A the advantage of incumbency, as an uncontested monopolist, for the first 5 periods of each experiment.)

4. *Sunk cost entry and reentry barriers.* A common theme in the descriptions of conditions favorable to predators is the requirement that the small firm face barriers to entry or reentry. This raises the separate but related issue of what constitutes an effective barrier to entry. The contemporary debate on the contestable markets hypothesis concerns whether economies of scale alone can fulfill this requirement. If economies of scale do serve as an effective barrier, then our design features 1, 2, and 3 above might be sufficient to provide requisite hurdles. However, our previous research (CIS and CILS) suggests that scale economies alone might not provide a sufficient barrier to entry. Therefore, as an additional potential entry barrier, we add a fourth item suggested by Ordover and Willig (1981, p. 305), namely, sunk cost of entry or reentry. Furthermore, we require, at the time the small firm is making its entry decision, that the large firm should have an incumbency advantage that entails some privately held knowledge about the nature of demand and an initially irreversible commitment of already having "sunk" the entry cost. (See also Salop 1981, pp. 16–20.)

The sunk entry cost was obtained, as in CILS, by requiring sellers to purchase an entry permit before each was allowed to participate in the market. Permits cost $1.00 each and were good for only 5 consecutive periods. At $1.00 each, the permit charge represents two-thirds of the small firm's maximum 5-period earnings at competitive prices. To create the incumbency advantage, the experiments with this design feature opened with seller A required to purchase two

[6] But see Brozen (1982, pp. 330–33) for a well-documented compilation of arguments skeptical of the cross-subsidization, deep-pocket, entry barrier hypothesis. Among the quotes are two from Scherer.

permits good for periods 1–10. Seller B was not allowed the option of entering until period 6. Thus, at the point when seller B had to make an initial entry decision, seller A had irrevocably sunk enough costs to be in the market for (at least) 5 more periods. Also at the beginning of period 6, seller A had a 5-period advantage in obtaining private information about market demand and in deepening his purse.

5. *Information.* Much of the literature makes no explicit reference to the information available to the firms, yet most appear to assume implicitly that firms have complete information about each other's costs. (Exceptions are found in Salop [1981], Kreps and Wilson [1982], and Milgrom and Roberts [1982].) In most of our experiments, the firms did not know one another's cost structure and neither knew demand. However, in three experiments we introduced complete cost information. In these experiments, participants had been in a previous predatory pricing experiment (although not with one another). Each was assigned the opposite of his previous position (so as to have sellers who knew what it was like to be on the other side), and each was given a written table of the other's costs (to refresh their memory).

6. *Rivalry.* Implicit in many of the discussions of predation is the issue of intent. If we cannot distinguish predatory from healthy forms of competition on the basis of performance variables, then intent is a logical direction for attempts at a distinction to take. Unfortunately, an intent-based standard is highly subjective.

In one of our experiments, we introduced a treatment distinction between the large firm's normal desire to exclude the smaller firm (based on a presumed profit-maximizing calculus) and a desire to exclude based on a rivalistic, abnormal intent. When this rivalistic feature is in effect, the large firm is told privately that it will receive a $1.00 cash bonus for each period in which the smaller firm chooses not to enter the market. In effect we attempt to induce a direct utility to A for excluding B, which is motivated by the conjecture that predation may occur but not spring from a profit-maximizing intent.

7. *Predatory pricing antitrust program (PPAP).* Our final seven experiments were conducted with this PPAP in place. This was operationalized in two parts. First, the incumbent firm faced an output expansion limit. Whenever the smaller firm entered the market (i.e., seller B bought a permit in period t when he or she did not have a permit in period $t - 1$), seller A could not expand his or her maximum quantity offered for sale for 2 periods. Second, the incumbent faced a semipermanent price reduction regulation. During any of the periods in which seller B could be in the market, all of seller A's price reductions (if they occurred) had to be maintained for at least 5 consecutive periods.

III. The PLATO Posted-Offer Procedure

Most retail markets are organized under what has been called the posted-offer institution (Plott and Smith 1978). As we define it, in this institution each seller independently posts a take-it-or-leave-it price at which deliveries will be made in quantities selected by each individual buyer subject to seller capacity limits. These posted prices may be changed or reviewed frequently, infrequently, regularly, or irregularly, but in any case a central characteristic of this mechanism is that the posted price is not subject to negotiation.

The experiments reported here use the posted-offer mechanism programmed for the PLATO computer system by Ketcham (see Ketcham, Smith, and Williams 1984). This program allows buyers and sellers, sitting separately at PLATO terminals, to trade for a maximum of 25 market "days" or pricing periods. Each display screen shows that subject's record sheet, which lists the maximum units that can be purchased (sold) in each period. For each unit, the buyer (seller) has a marginal valuation (cost) that represents the value (cost) of purchasing (selling) that unit. These controlled, strictly private, unit valuations (costs) induce individual and aggregate market theoretical supply and demand schedules (Smith 1976). That is, in an experiment, buyers (sellers) earn cash rewards equal to the difference between the marginal value (selling price) of a unit and its purchase price (marginal cost). Sales are "to order" in the sense that there are no penalties or carryover inventories associated with units not sold (or units not purchased). Consequently the assigned marginal valuations and costs induce well-defined flow supply and demand conditions.

Each period begins with a request that sellers select a price offer by typing a price into the computer keyset. This offer is displayed privately on the seller's screen. The seller is then asked to select a corresponding quantity at that offer price. Because the essence of the predatory pricing hypotheses is that a seller may have a strategic reason for pricing below marginal cost, the program we utilized placed no restriction except for an ultimate capacity constraint on what combination of prices and quantities any seller was permitted to post.

Since it is time and effort costly for a seller to calculate the profit that any given offer may provide, especially with U-shaped costs, PLATO always informs the seller of the potential profit (loss) if all offered units are sold. When satisfied with the selected price and quantity, the seller presses a touch-sensitive "offer box" displayed on the screen. This action places that seller's offer irrevocably into the market. Before touching the offer box the seller may change the price and/or quantity as many times as desired. Each seller sees the prices posted by the other seller only after both have entered their offers by touching the offer boxes.

Because virtually all of the hypotheses regarding predatory pricing explicitly or implicitly assume that buyers act to fully reveal market demand, we needed to incorporate this feature into all 18 of our experiments. To do this, we used the computerized buyer subroutine that had proved successful in previous research (CILS 1984). After both sellers entered their offers, PLATO randomly ordered each of the five buyers in figure 1 into a buying sequence, just as with human subject buyers. However, the purchasing decisions were made by a PLATO program with the buying rule that demand was fully revealed. That this computerized response would take place, and that the buyers would purchase all that was profitable to them at the given prices, was explained to the sellers so that it was not credible for sellers to harbor even the expectation that demand might be underrevealed. A trading period ended when the last buyer completed this buying mode. Sellers were not told what the final period of the experiment would be.

There is no difference in physical surroundings or computer interaction depending on whether or not a seller has purchased an entry permit. This was done to minimize any extraneous incentives to purchase or not to purchase a permit. A seller who chooses not to purchase an entry permit remains at the terminal, watching the prices posted by the other seller. Since this is a posted-offer market, sellers with and without permits are equally passive in computer terminal responsibilities once the market has opened to the buyers.

IV. Alternative Hypotheses

Predatory pricing is a hypothesis about firm behavior under certain structural conditions, which, according to our interpretation, is represented by specifications 1–5 in Section II. However, in addition to the predatory pricing literature, an extensive oligopoly literature has identified many other hypothesized modes of pricing behavior when numbers are few. Because we could not be sure that we would observe predatory behavior, it was necessary for us to consider alternatives that we might observe under conditions thought to favor such behavior. This necessity was underlined when the first few experiments failed to yield predatory pricing, and therefore early in the search process we were motivated to specify alternative outcome hypotheses. Although the literature was helpful in suggesting alternative hypotheses we do not find it helpful in providing a coherent, clear delineation of the conditions necessary to yield each of the various modes of pricing behavior. In view of this we decided to err on the side of overspecification by assuming that any behavioral hypothesis might apply as long as it assumed that one or both firms choose prices. This seems to rule out only the Cournot quantity-adjuster model of oligopoly.

A. *Predatory Pricing*

Based on the literature summarized in Section II above there are two elements in the definition of predatory pricing. First, the price charged by the predator is lower than would be optimal in a simple myopic (short-run) pricing strategy. Second, the price has the effect of preventing entry, or driving out and preventing reentry, of the prey. In our experimental design if there is a predator we expect it to be firm A, with firm B the prey, since we assume that predatory action by firm B would be suicidal and that the agent for firm B will become aware of this assessment. Therefore, we interpret the first element to mean that $P_A(Q_A) < MC_A(Q_A)$, where $P_A(Q_A)$ is the inverse demand function, and the second element to mean that $P_A(Q_A) < \min AC_B(Q_B)$. For seller A in our design, price offers below \$2.66 are potentially predatory, depending on the quantity offer chosen by A. For example, if seller A posts a price of \$2.64 but limits the quantity offered to 7 units, then $P_A(7) > MC_A(7)$, and this strategy leaves some (contingent) excess demand in the market for firm B to satisfy at a higher price. We define a predatory action by seller A to be a posted price less than \$2.66 accompanied by the selection of a quantity of at least 8 units. Thus, a predatory action is defined by the choice ($P_A \in$ [\$2.60, \$2.65], $Q_A \geqq 8$) since this yields $P_A(Q_A) < MC_A(Q_A)$ and $P_A(Q_A) < \min AC_B(Q_B)$. Since $P_A(Q_A) > AVC_A(Q_A)$, this predatory action still generates a positive profit for firm A; our design is deliberately rigged to allow firm A to predate without imposing a loss on himself. Consequently, although there is a short-run opportunity cost of predation to the predator there is no net out-of-pocket loss.

In summary, if we observe firm A choosing predatory prices and quantities that conform to this definition followed by firm B exiting and not reentering even when firm A subsequently increases its price, we will count such an observation as supporting the predatory pricing hypothesis. However, if we observe firm B exiting the market and electing not to reenter in response to price cutting by firm A that is not predatory, we will interpret this to mean that firm B is particularly vulnerable to price-cutting actions, and we will still count such an observation as supporting the predatory pricing hypothesis. Behavior of this type would suggest that firm A had established a credible predatory threat to firm B without pricing in the defined predatory range.

B. Competitive Equilibrium

If predatory behavior is manifest, but it fails to eliminate the small firm from the market, the result may be to spoil any effective tacit cooperative coupling between the two firms. Hence, the competitive equilibrium may prevail, as a default outcome, from the failure of predatory attempts. Alternatively, price cutting may be less severe than the predation model suggests but be sufficient to lock the two firms into the competitive equilibrium. The extensive experimental evidence favoring the competitive equilibrium, under different trading institutions, when numbers are few suggests a strong a priori case for this hypothesis in the present design. In this design, competitive equilibria are defined by $Q_A = 7$, $Q_B = 3$, and prices in the interval [2.66, 2.76].

C. Dominant Firm Equilibrium

If firm B is assumed to be a price taker, or adapts to its disadvantaged position by becoming a price taker, then a possible outcome is that of the dominant firm equilibrium. This is often associated with a leader-follower argument or a minorant game institution in which firm A moves first and firm B moves last, responding with the quantity that maximizes profit given the price quoted by A. In a repeat simultaneous move game, firm B might still be regarded as moving after B, in the subsequent period, so that the leader-follower posture could still emerge.

The traditional analysis yields the dominant firm equilibrium price (P_{df} = \$2.84) and corresponding quantities $Q_A = 6$ and $Q_B = 3$. This is obtained by assuming that firm B matches any price posted by A and chooses the quantity that maximizes B's profit.

In preparing this design, we calculated the joint profit matrix for firms A and B for a subset of the feasible prices that can be posted by them. In this matrix, if firm A posts the dominant firm equilibrium price, P_{df} = \$2.84, then the best response of firm B is also to post this price. At these prices firm A offers 10 units, firm B offers 3 units, and expected profits are (π_A, π_B) = (\$1.99, \$0.51) per period. Strictly speaking, this is slightly different from the dominant firm model profit shares, based on certain demand in which the large firm cedes the residual supply to the fringe. In our design, this would require seller A to limit Q_A to 6 units, and the profit shares would be (\$1.96, \$0.54) per period.

D. *Edgeworth Price Cycles*

Inspection of the joint profit possibilities also reveals the clear potential for an Edgeworth cycle in duopoly pricing. If the two firms start at the dominant firm equilibrium (P_A, P_B) = (\$2.84, \$2.84), firm A has an incentive to cut price one cent to \$2.83. But this wipes out the profit of firm B, whose best reply is to match A's price, giving A an incentive to cut to \$2.82, and so on, until prices fall to (P_A, P_B) = (\$2.79, \$2.79). At this point, A's incentive is to raise price back to \$2.84, with B then matching this price.

E. *Shared Monopoly (Tacit Collusion)*

If firms A and B are able to effect cooperation through price signaling, this strategy will be most effective if they (1) maximize joint profits and (2) divide this profit in a manner that will sustain the tacit "agreement" (the two firms cannot communicate except through the prices they select). The largest collective profit is for all production to be allocated to firm A, who charges the monopoly price P_M = \$3.21 and sells the quantity $Q_M = 5$, yielding π_M = \$3.43 per period for firm A. But in the absence of a mechanism for agreement, including an imputation of a share of this profit to B, there is no way to effect this outcome. Through signaling, it is conceivable that the two firms might work out an alternating sequence in which A and B take turns satisfying the whole market at their respective monopoly prices. This would yield a profit that averages one-half the monopoly price for each firm. Under this scenario we would have (P_A, Q_A, π_A) = (\$3.21, 5, \$1.71) and (P_B, Q_B, π_B) = (\$3.52, 3, \$1.29). A less sophisticated form of tacit collusion would be for the firms to post the same price and then share the market according to the demands realized via the random choice of firm made by each buyer in the posted-offer mechanism. At the shared monopoly price P_M = \$3.21, joint profit is a maximum, and (π_A, π_B) = (\$1.80, \$1.21). But by defecting at a price one cent less, firm A can reap a substantial increase in profit. This is the case for all matching price strategies, and thus the maintenance of such strategies clearly requires cooperation by firm A. The same proposition holds for firm B except that the gains from defection are much smaller.

Since the CIS and CILS experiments did not yield any outcomes tending to support the attainment of a shared monopoly through tacit collusion, we doubted that such outcomes would be likely even in the present asymmetric cost design. However, we conjectured that under the PPAP treatment, tacit collusion would be more likely. Under this treatment firm A is constrained not to expand output for 2 periods after firm B enters, and any price reduction cannot be reversed for 5 periods. At a collusive high price this constraint makes it more costly for A to punish B for defection. Firm B, knowing that any cut in price by A cannot be reversed for 5 periods, may be hesitant to defect and risk being locked into a lower price pattern. Similarly, at low prices if A signals with a price increase, this action may have greater credibility under the PPAP for firm B and may increase the probability that B will follow.

F. *Relative Profitability of Alternative Outcomes*

Some of the debate on the appropriateness of predation models has centered on the profitability to the large firm of a predation strategy relative to alternative tactics. Two observations regarding this discussion relate to our experimental design. First, we note (McGee 1958) that one commonly proposed alternative to a strategy of predation is a buyout of firm B by A. This is *not* allowable in our particular design but could be incorporated into an extension of our design.[7] Second, notice that seller A makes a profit of $3.42 per period as an uncontested monopolist, $1.99 per period in expected profits as a dominant firm, from $1.10 to $1.80 per period in the competitive price range, and (at most) $0.88 per period with a predation strategy. Thus, the reader should note that firm A's estimates of the direct profitability of predation depend crucially on A's expectations about firm B's exit behavior. Firm A's decision to pursue a predatory strategy depends, furthermore, on the profitability of predation relative to the profits A expects to receive if B stays in the market. Predation will look less attractive if firm A expects that the two firms will stabilize at a collusive price level near the shared monopoly price than if A expects that having B in the market will cause prices to collapse to the competitive range.

V. Experimental Results

We report the results of 18 experiments using the six different treatment conditions shown in table 1. Series 1–5, consisting of 11 experiments, imposed alternative conditions thought to be favorable (per-

[7] An obvious question is whether our prohibition against mergers makes predation more or less likely. If a buy-out is, as suggested by McGee (1980), a relatively attractive substitute for predation, then forbidding such a substitute strategy is consistent with our goal of creating conditions in which predation is relatively likely. However, Burns (1984) has suggested that in the case of the old American Tobacco Company, buy-outs may have been an integral part of a predatory campaign.

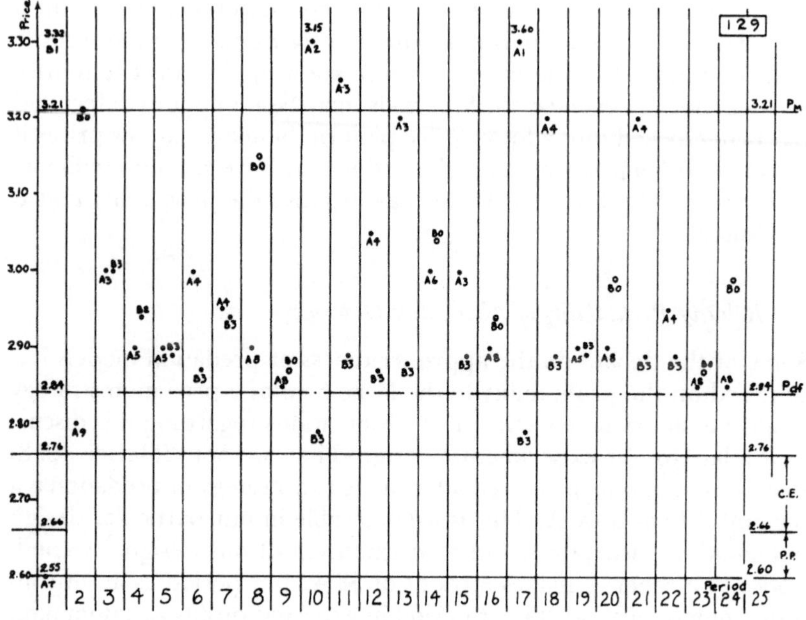

Fig. 2

haps progressively more favorable) to the emergence of predatory pricing behavior.

Figures 2–5 chart the sequential prices and corresponding sales quantities for one experiment from each of the series 1, 2, 3, and 6. Posted prices in each period are indicated by the solid and open circles. Thus in figure 2 (experiment 129) for period 8 the solid circle, denoted "A8," shows that A sold 8 units at the posted price, $2.90. The open circle, denoted "B0," indicates that B sold zero units at the posted price, $3.15. Periods such as 1–5 in figure 3 (experiment 135) show only the price posted by the incumbent seller A, indicating that seller B was not allowed to purchase a permit in periods 1–5. On all charts the monopoly price for A (3.21), the dominant firm price (2.84), the competitive interval [2.66, 2.76], and the potential predatory price range [2.60, 2.66] are marked on the far right. Finally, for experiment 153 subject to the PPAP, the heavy black arrow near the bottom of the chart denotes periods in which seller A has triggered a temporary price ceiling on himself through a reduction in price. The numbers along the arrow state the operative price ceiling.

Table 2 summarizes the performance of the 18 experiments. Each experiment is scored according to which type of pricing behavior was the plurality in the first 18 potentially contested periods: shared mo-

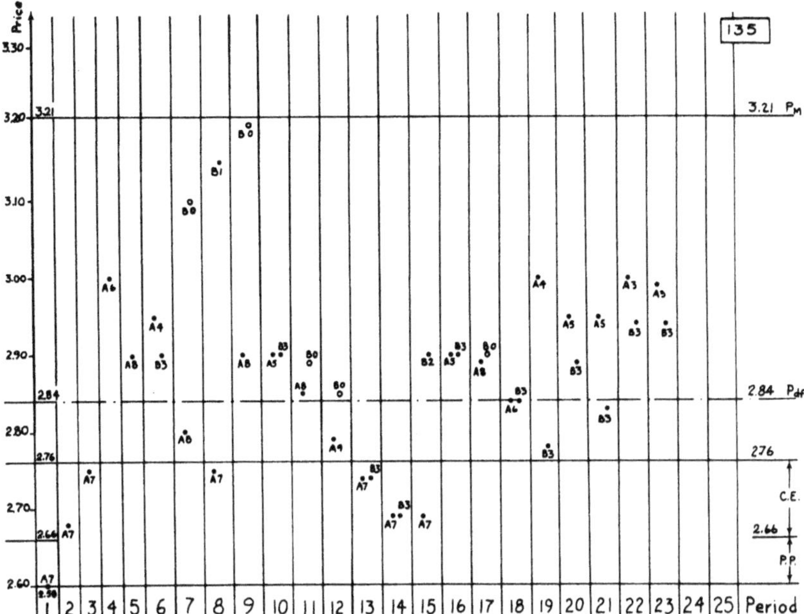

FIG. 3

TABLE 2

EXPERIMENTAL OUTCOMES
(Each Experiment Scored according to Plurality of Price Outcomes in the First 18 Potentially Contested Periods)

	PERFORMANCE HYPOTHESES			
TREATMENT SERIES	Shared Monopoly	Dominant Firm	Competitive Equilibrium	Predation: Predatory Pricing or Monopoly Pricing by a Surviving Firm
1	1 (133)	1½ (129, 131-tie)	½ (131-tie)	0
2	0	2 (135, 136)	1 (138)	0
3	1 (140)	2 (139, 141)	0	0
4	0	1 (142)	0	0
5 (confederate)	0	½ (2d half of 143)	0	½ (1st half of 143)
6 (antitrust)	5 (145, 146, 147, 149, 150, 152, 153)	2 (147, 149)	0	0
1–4 pooled	2	6½	1½	0

nopoly, dominant firm, competitive, or predatory (including both predatory pricing and monopoly pricing by a successfully predatory large firm). Since many observations are not precisely at any of those models' predictions, a simple metric was used in the scoring. Each price observation was counted as a hit for the model whose price prediction was nearest to the observation.

From table 2, there are two strongly supported general conclusions: (1) the absence of any predatory pricing behavior and (2) the radically different behavior of those markets conducted under the antitrust treatment rules. Each of these observations will be examined in more detail.

1. *The absence of predation.* We will summarize our experimental results by providing a brief narrative on each of the series 1–5, followed by a general discussion of all 10 experiments.

Series 1. We began our research with three experiments incorporating design features 1, 2, and 3. We found no evidence of what we had designated a priori as predation. The three large sellers posted 73 prices, and none satisfied our definition of predatory pricing.

There were three instances in which a large seller posted a price in the potentially predatory range. But, in each of these three cases, the large seller restricted quantity to 7 units, so the price was above both marginal and average cost. Each of these instances was in period 1, and none of the three large sellers ever repeated a price in this predatory range. It is perhaps arguable that this action can be interpreted as either (1) the early period price experimentation of a seller who does not have prior knowledge of demand or the costs of the rival or (2) a supersophisticated signal of a potential willingness to predate in the future. We are highly skeptical of the second interpretation, since all three instances occurred in period 1 and none was ever repeated. However, whether such strategic signaling behavior was in the minds of the large sellers or was capable of predatory interpretation by the small seller, the behavior does not match our interpretation of any consensus definition of predatory pricing, since price was not below average or marginal cost, and in each case the small seller picked up some residual demand and a rewarding profit.

Series 2. After our failure to observe predation in the first three experiments, we added design feature 4 (sunk entry costs) for the next three and introduced the incumbency treatment. Again, there were no predatory price-quantity pairs chosen out of the 69 observations. In this series, there were only two cases of a price posted in the potentially predatory range, and in both cases quantity was restricted so price was not less than marginal or average cost. In the experiments requiring that firms purchase an entry permit, we have a stronger test of whether large seller pricing activity can successfully signal predatory threats even if not at predatory levels. Of the 54 periods in which the small sellers could contest the market with a permit, they did so in all 54 periods.

Series 3. In these three experiments we went back to the drawing board to see what design features we might add to capture the phenomenon of predation. As described previously in Section II, we decided on design feature 5 (complete information). We speculated that if both firms were clearly aware of the advantages of the large firm, expectations might foster predation or the fear of predation leading to the exit of the small firm. We were wrong. None of the 69 decisions by large firms was predatory. Only *one* seller A's price was even potentially predatory, and it was, as before, accompanied by a quantity restriction. The small firm stayed in the market in 54 out of 54 possible periods.

Series 4 (experiment 142). Having failed to find predation in the first nine experiments, we wondered whether predation could be induced by the creation of "rivalistic" incentives having nothing to do with the underlying economic structure. To test this conjecture, we privately informed seller A that we would pay him $1.00 for each period in which seller B chose not to purchase a permit, The rivalistic seller never posted a potentially predatory price; in fact, only once did seller A post less than $2.83. The small firm never failed to purchase a permit.

Series 5. After 10 unsuccessful efforts to foster predation, we became seriously concerned that there might be some flaw in our design that was muting (what we assumed to be) the vulnerability of the small seller. Therefore, in experiment 143, we decided to push rivalry to its extreme point and choose as seller A a confederate (a graduate student), whose personal incentives were direct instructions to post predatory prices and quantities in periods 1–11. This fact was, obviously, concealed from the small firm. Seller B entered the market in period 6, was shut out in periods 6–10 (incurring the $1.00 permit loss), and refused to renew his permit in period 11. His decision not to reenter was reiterated to us at the beginning of period 12, and we signaled our confederate to begin to try to take advantage of his monopoly position. There is perhaps a strong clue to the weakness of the predatory pricing folklore in the subsequent behavior of our small seller. Despite being mercilessly pummeled by seller A, losing money, and twice deciding not to submit to such punishment again, seller B took only 1 period to look at seller A's price increase (period 12) and reentered (period 13) to capture some (perhaps transient) supernormal profits. That is, the difference in firm size and costs, economies of scale, nontrivial sunk entry costs, and an asymmetric deep pocket, combined with the actual experience of being forced out of the market due to losses, were not enough to preempt reentry when the predator attempted to take advantage of his newly established monopoly position. While we could have had seller A retaliate, in period 13 *alone* seller B earned $1.32, which more than covered his reentry cost. This poses two obvious questions for further research. First, how much punishment in the form of retaliation by seller A is necessary to keep seller B from reentering? Does this required level of retaliation so weaken seller A's profit picture that seller A would be better off coexisting with seller B? Second, what would happen if seller B had to publicly announce an intention to reenter at least 1 period before reentry could occur?

General discussion of series 1–5. Although we observe no instances in which $P_A(Q_A)$ is in accord with our strict definition of predatory pricing, there are several sequences in which firm A's pricing behavior might be interpreted by firm B as having a predatory quality. For example, in experiment 135 (fig. 3), periods 7–9, firm A ignores firm B's repeated signal to raise the price. Then in period 10, firm B matches price with firm A, whereupon in periods 11–14 firm A repeatedly undercuts firm B's previous price. Firm A eventually seems to concede that this strategy is failing and engages in (fruitless) signals to raise price in periods 19–23. Similar results obtained in another experiment (140 in fig. 4). In both these experiments we can imagine that firm B might feel that he or she had been the victim of predatory behavior and might be tempted to file suit, given triple damage legal incentives and the vagueness of marginal cost in the nonexperimental world.

But if predation is not a satisfactory hypothesis for explaining firm behavior in this market environment, then a logical followup question is to ask which (if any) of the alternative hypotheses are being supported. Refer again to table 2 and the pooled results from series 1–4. (We exclude series 5, since it incorporated a confederate.) In these nine experiments, the modal (in fact, majority) observation supported the dominant firm prediction. Of the nine experiments, six-and-a-half were best described by the dominant firm model.

More evidence of the plausibility of the dominant firm model in this design can be seen by considering the confederate experiment (143). Beginning with period 17, we signaled our confederate to begin posting the pair ($P = 2.84$, $Q = 6$), which is the large firm's dominant firm strategy. We wondered if this behavior would indeed attract seller B to his competitive fringe strategy ($P = 2.84$, $Q = 3$). The answer was yes. This suggests that the leader-follower flavor of the dominant firm model can be captured in an iterative environment in which, technically, both firms move simultaneously in any 1 period.

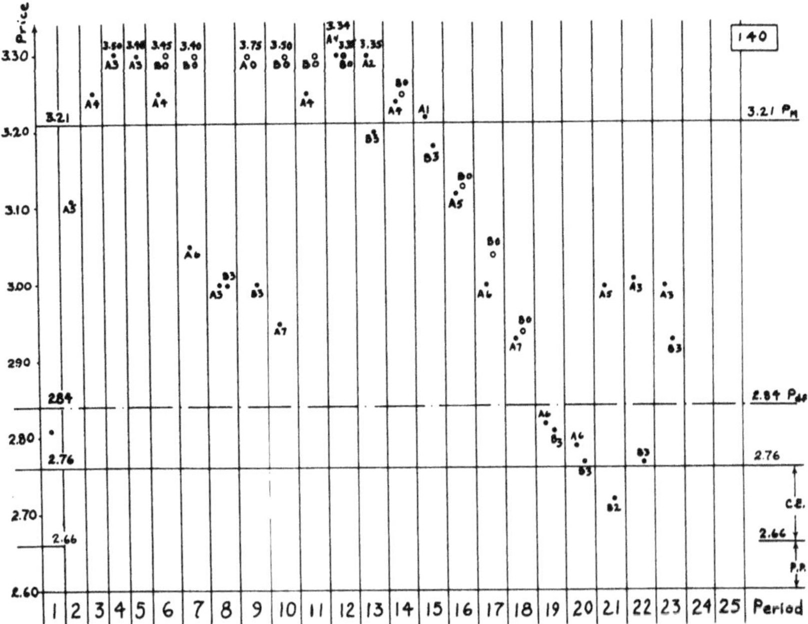

FIG. 4

One shortcoming of the mutually exclusive fourfold categorization of table 2 is that it does not account for our fifth alternative hypothesis, the Edgeworth cycle. This is because these cycle prices include \$2.84, the dominant firm price. Yet it would be useful to ask whether the eight experiments in series 1–4 that were scored either "competitive" or "dominant firm" were being driven by the dynamics suggested by the Edgeworth model. One arbitrary measure is to ask whether the runner up, or second place outcome, in the two categories (competitive, dominant firm) accounted for as many as one-third of the number of observations as the primary category. If the answer is yes, this indicates a lot of activity between the competitive and dominant firm prices, which is at least consistent with the Edgeworth model. If the answer is no, this could indicate either acyclical (equilibrated?) behavior or cycles outside the Edgeworth range (perhaps cycles of success and failure in firms' attempts to establish tacit cooperation).

Using the categorization above, one finds that only two of the first 10 experiments, 131 and 138, can be classified as Edgeworthian. The others show no single consistent pattern. For example, one experiment (141) converged very closely to the dominant firm prediction while another (129 in fig. 2) appeared more unstable. Its cycles away from the dominant firm price tended to be toward the monopoly rather than the competitive prediction.

2. *The effect of antitrust procedures in series 6.* The seven experiments incorporating our PPAP were all conducted with design features 1–4. Thus, in the absence of the antitrust rules, the treatment is that of series 2. This raises the following question. When one discusses the effects of antitrust rules, what is the appropriate control sequence? Is it just series 2, or is it the pooled results from series 1–4? Series 2 by itself is the more exact structural control, but there are only three observations. Pooling adds more information, and the results from 1, 3, and 4 seem consistent with 2. But pooling runs the risk of introducing some specification error. We therefore will report both comparisons. It happens that the qualitative results are robust with respect to the pooled or not-pooled control.

The fundamental conclusion from our series 6 experiments is the existence of a type 2 regulatory error. That is, adding rules against predation in an environment where predation might be expected to occur may not be benign. Our results show a performance that is less competitive and less efficient with the safeguards against predation in place.

This qualitative result can be seen in at least three different ways. First, the effect can be seen at a glance in the data of experiment 153 (fig. 5), which vividly demonstrates the most extreme example we observed showing how the antitrust rules can provide incentives for tacit cooperation near the monopoly price and quantity.

Second, refer again to the classification of the experiments in table 2. Suppose we combine the observations so that we count each experiment as either (i) a shared monopoly or (ii) not a shared monopoly. The proportion of shared monopolies in series 6 is .71 while in series 2 it is zero. (A χ^2 test on this difference in proportions is significant at $\alpha = .05$.) Comparing series 6 with the pooled proportion of series 1–4, one gets .71 against .20 (which is also significant at $\alpha = .05$). Thus, we can reject the hypothesis that there was no shift toward shared monopoly outcomes when the PPAP rules were applied.

Third, one can examine directly the efficiency criterion of market performance. In figure 6, we have graphed the period-by-period measure of what we call "quasi efficiency." (This measures the ratio of realized surplus obtained by the participants to the maximum possible surplus, without attempting to amortize into this ratio the cost of the entry permits where they were required.) A fully competitive market would be 100 percent efficient by this measure. A fully rationalized cartel would score 72.5 percent. Again, a comparison of the charts in figure 6 is striking. In every period, the markets with PPAP per-

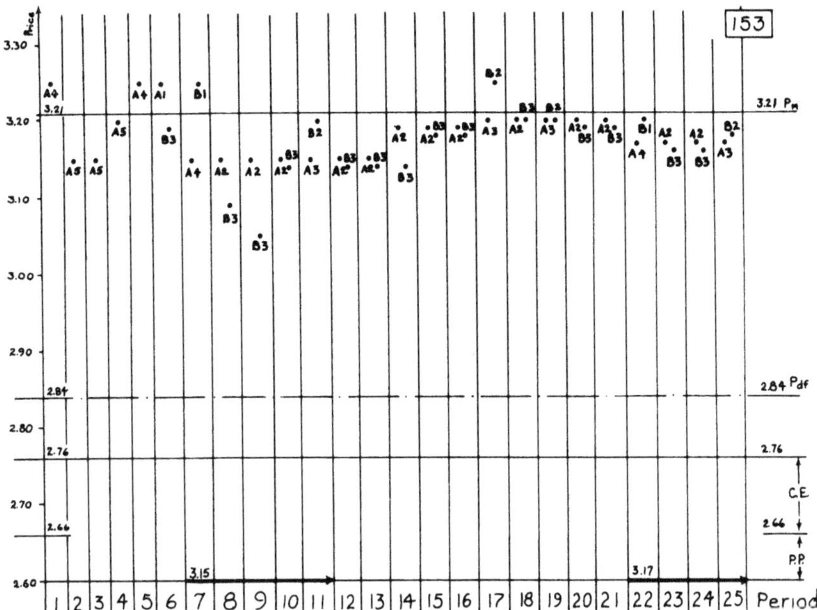

FIG. 5

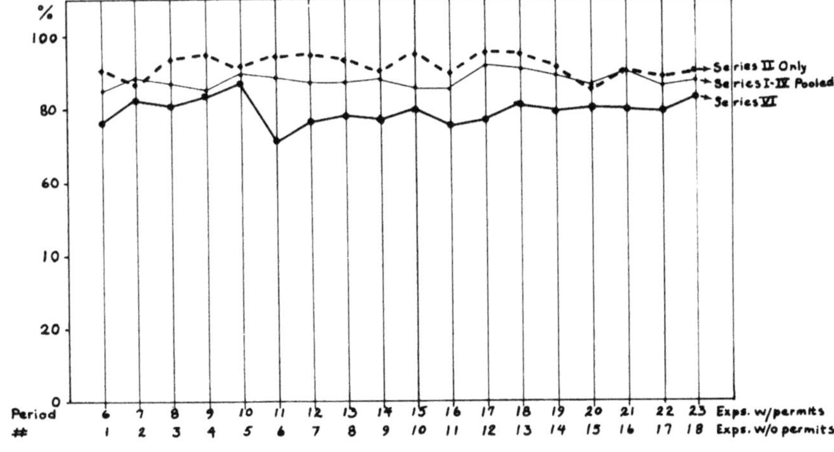

FIG. 6.—Market quasi efficiency in first 18 contested periods (i.e., does not attempt to amortize permit costs).

TABLE 3

TESTS OF MEAN EFFICIENCIES WITH AND WITHOUT ANTITRUST RULES IN EFFECT

	Based on All 18 Contestable Periods	Based on Last 5 periods
Control is series 2 alone	Difference = −12.17% t = −2.00*	Difference = −8.25% t = −1.57
Control is pooled series 1–4	Difference = −7.91% t = −1.89*	Difference = −7.37% t = −2.056*

NOTE.—Negative numbers indicate reduced efficiency with antitrust rules.
* Significant, α = .05.

formed less efficiently, on average, than the markets without this treatment (using either series 2 or pooled series 1–4 as the control). A statistical test of the significance of this difference is presented in table 3. We present four t-tests on the difference in efficiencies in 2×2 dimensional form. Two of these tests use series 2 data as the control; two use pooled data from series 1–4. On the second dimension, two tests use the mean of all 18 potentially contested periods as the base and two use the mean of only the last five (this latter was a measure introduced in CILS). In all four cases the direction of the difference shows lower market efficiency with the antitrust rules. In three of the four tests, the difference is significant using a one-tailed t-test at α = .05.

VI. Conclusions

Based on the results of 11 predatory pricing experiments, our principal conclusion is that, so far, the phenomenon has eluded our search. We are unable to produce predatory pricing in a structural environment that, a priori, we thought was favorable to its emergence. The predominant outcome is that of the dominant firm equilibrium. These results would appear to be consistent with Selten's (1978) game-theoretic analysis of predation in which such a strategy is inconsistent with the perfect equilibrium solution concept. By backward induction at each stage, predation does not pay. At each stage an entrant knows that if it enters and is preyed on it would have been better not to enter. But this expectation is offset by the potential prey's also knowing that with actual entry the incumbent is better off not to predate. Thus it is rational throughout the history of the market for the incumbent not to predate and for the potential prey to enter.

Where next in the parameter space should one look for predatory pricing? We suspect that more work on rivalistic behavior might be fruitful. Although our one attempt to introduce rivalistic incentives failed to yield a predatory outcome, we still think this is a direction of search that might have good results. This direction abandons the concept of rational predatory action and is contrary to the mainstream economic theory exercise. It also abandons the objective of asking whether predatory behavior will arise "naturally," as a human trait, in the laboratory. To deliberately induce rivalistic behavior is to assume that such behavior exists in the field but for some reason has not been manifest in the laboratory. This calls for harder evidence on the mainsprings of behavior in alleged predatory cases in the field than we have been able to discern in the literature.

A second potentially promising direction is suggested by the game-theoretical literature on reputation (Kreps and Wilson 1982; Milgrom and Roberts 1982). In this literature Selten's paradox (the inconsistency of predation with perfect equilibria) is resolved by an imperfect information assumption—either that agents are uncertain of the payoffs of their fellows (Kreps and Wilson 1982) or that they are uncertain whether such payoffs are uncertain (absence of common knowledge) (Milgrom and Roberts 1982). These assumptions lead to models of rational predation in which it pays an incumbent to predate following entry because the resulting reputation deters future entrants and these future benefits outweigh the earlier short-term losses. Of course, the imperfect information assumptions were part of our experimental design, and reputation effects did not arise naturally. However, our use of a confederate in one experiment could be expanded to attempt consciously to create reputations of the type investigated in these models. Again, this involves a departure from the search for naturally occurring behavior that is predatory, and the justification for this raises methodological issues that have not been examined in any depth.

We think there is a sense in which all of the existing predatory models, as well as our experimental design, are deficient. Entry requires capital investment, exit implies divestiture, and (with the exception of general purpose broadly marketable capital, like trucks) the value of an entrant's capital stock should not be assumed to be independent of whether predatory pricing occurs. If the capital stock is specialized (e.g., railroad track), an exiting prey will surely not be able to recover more than a fraction of replacement cost from any potential new entrant. But this means that a new entrant can buy in as a competitor at a capital cost that has already discounted the expectation of predation. Hence some profitability is assured a new entrant, while if predation is discontinued, supranormal profits will be enjoyed. Unless the predator buys the discounted capital stock of the prey (Burns 1984), predation merely bankrupts the prey firm but fails to eliminate the existence of a competitor. Bankruptcy gets rid of incumbent management, not capital assets, which are reallocated to new managers.

The results from our seven experiments with the predatory pricing antitrust rule form the basis for our second major conclusion. We have evidence for the existence of a type 2 regulatory error. The antitrust regulations imposed on a market that might be thought to be susceptible to predatory pricing caused the market to perform less competitively and less efficiently than in the absence of any regulations against predation. We cannot say that any regulations against predatory pricing would have this effect, although these results graphically display the potential for efficiency losses from programs providing for output expansion limits combined with rules requiring semipermanence of price reductions. More generally, we believe that these results emphasize the necessity for public policymakers to realize that any remedies designed to correct alleged market deficiencies may provide counterproductive incentives. Their task may become one of evaluating various proposals on the basis of which one might result in the largest net benefit, not which one corrects a particular defect.

References

Areeda, Phillip, and Turner, Donald F. "Predatory Pricing and Related Practices under Section 2 of the Sherman Act." *Harvard Law Rev.* 88 (February 1975): 697–733.

Baumol, William J. "Quasi-Permanence of Price Reductions: A Policy for Prevention of Predatory Pricing." *Yale Law J.* 89 (November 1979): 1–26.

Brozen, Yale. *Concentration, Mergers, and Public Policy.* New York: Macmillan, 1982.

Burns, Malcolm R. "The Effects of Predatory Price Cutting on the Acquisition Cost of Competitors." Mimeographed. Lawrence: Univ. Kansas, Dept. Econ., March 1984.

Clark, John Bates, and Clark, John Maurice. *The Control of Trusts.* New York: Macmillan, 1912.

Coursey, Don; Isaac, R. Mark; and Smith, Vernon L. "Natural Monopoly and Contested Markets: Some Experimental Results." *J. Law and Econ.* 27 (April 1984): 91–114.

Coursey, Don; Isaac, R. Mark; Luke, Margaret; and Smith, Vernon L. "Market Contestability in the Presence of Sunk Costs." *Rand J. Econ.* 15 (Spring 1984): 69–84.

Kefauver, Estes. *In a Few Hands: Monopoly Power in America.* New York: Pantheon, 1965.

Ketcham, J.; Smith, Vernon L.; and Williams, A. W. "A Comparison of Posted-Offer and Double-Auction Pricing Institutions." *Rev. Econ. Studies* 51 (1984): 595–614.

Kreps, David M., and Wilson, Robert. "Reputation and Imperfect Information." *J. Econ. Theory* 27 (August 1982): 253–79.

McGee, John S. "Predatory Price Cutting: The Standard Oil (N.J.) Case." *J. Law and Econ.* 1 (October 1958): 137–69.

———. "Predatory Pricing Revisited." *J. Law and Econ.* 23 (October 1980): 289–330.

Milgrom, Paul R., and Roberts, John. "Predation, Reputation, and Entry Deterrence." *J. Econ. Theory* 27 (August 1982): 280–312.

Ordover, Janusz A., and Willig, Robert D. "An Economic Definition of Predatory Product Innovation." In *Strategy, Predation, and Antitrust Analysis*, edited by Steven C. Salop. Washington: FTC Bur. Econ., 1981.

Plott, Charles R., and Smith, Vernon L. "An Experimental Examination of Two Exchange Institutions." *Rev. Econ. Studies* 45 (February 1978): 133–53.

Salop, Steven C. "Strategy, Predation, and Antitrust Analysis: An Introduction." In *Strategy, Predation, and Antitrust Analysis*, edited by Steven C. Salop. Washington: FTC Bur. Econ., 1981.

Scherer, Frederic M. *Industrial Market Structure and Economic Performance*. 2d ed. Chicago: Rand McNally, 1980.

Selten, R. "The Chain-Store Paradox." *Theory and Decision* 9 (1978): 127–59.

Smith, Vernon L. "Experimental Economics: Induced Value Theory." *A.E.R. Papers and Proc.* 66 (May 1976): 274–79.

Wall Street Journal. "F.T.C. to Relax 1978 Order against Borden on Pricing Practices for ReaLemon Juice." March 2, 1983.

Williamson, Oliver E. "Predatory Pricing: A Strategic and Welfare Analysis." *Yale Law J.* 87 (December 1977): 284–340.

PART VI

Perspectives on Economics

Theory, Experiment and Economics

Vernon L. Smith

It is now over thirty years since research was initiated in the laboratory experimental study of market behavior and performance.[1] This essay provides my interpretation of what the implications of this type of work are for the study of economics. The essay is not intended as a systematic survey of the field, although examples will be cited where appropriate and necessary. The reader can find the associated references in more general surveys (E. Hoffman and M. Spitzer, 1985; C. Plott, 1979, 1982, 1986a, 1986b; V. Smith, 1976, 1980, 1982a, 1982b, 1986).

Experimentation and Economics

Economics as currently learned and taught in graduate school and practiced afterward is more theory-intensive and less observation-intensive than perhaps any other science. I think the statement that "no mere fact ever was a match in economics for a consistent theory" accurately describes the prevailing attitude in the profession (Milgrom and Roberts, 1987, p. 185). This is because the training of economists conditions us to think of economics as an *a priori* science, and not as an observational science in which the interplay between theory and observation is paramount. Conse-

[1]My first supply and demand experiment was done in January 1956, but others were involved at about the same time or earlier. Among the pioneering contributors to experimental economics were a number of scholars in the United States and Germany, many of whom were working quite independently without knowledge of each other's almost simultaneous work: E. Chamberlin (Harvard), A. Hoggatt (Berkeley), H. Sauermann and R. Selton (Germany), M. Shubik (Yale), S. Siegle and L. Fouraker (Pennsylvania State) and J. Friedman (Yale).

quently, we come to believe that economic problems can be understood fully just by thinking about them. After the thinking has produced sufficient technical rigor, internal coherence and interpersonal agreement, economists can then apply the results to the world of data.

But experimentation changes the way you think about economics. If you do experiments you soon find that a number of important experimental results can be replicated by yourself and by others. As a consequence, economics begins to represent concepts and propositions capable of being or failing to be demonstrated. Observation starts to loom large as the centerpiece of economics. Now the purpose of theory must be to track, but also predict new observations, not just "explain" facts, *ex post hoc*, as in traditional economic practice, where mere facts may be little more than stylized stories. The professional problem is for the theorist to recognize and respond to this purpose, and to undertake the arduous and challenging task of theory development disciplined by ongoing empirical studies. As Einstein put it, "[T]his theory is not speculative in origin; it owes its invention entirely to the desire to make physical theory fit observed fact as well as possible... the justification for a physical concept lies exclusively in its clear and unambiguous relation to facts that can be experienced." But this process is not tautological so long as every time new data motivates an extension in theory, the new theory can be confronted with new field or laboratory observations, and this confrontation yields at least some victories some of the time.

In any confrontation between theory and observation the theory may work or fail to work. When the theory works it becomes believable in proportion to its predictive "miracle," instead of only respectable in proportion to its internal elegance or its association with authority. But when it works, you lean mightily upon the theory with more challenging "boundary" experiments designed to uncover the edges of validity of the theory where certainty gives way to uncertainty and thereby lays the basis for extensions in the theory that increase its empirical content. When the theory performs well you also think, "Are there parallel results in naturally occurring field data?" You look for coherence across different data sets because theories are not specific to particular data sources. Such extensions are important because theories often make specific assumptions about information and institutions which can be controlled in the laboratory, but which may not accurately represent field data generating situations. Testing theories on the domain of their assumptions is sterile unless it is part of a research program concerned with extending the domain of applications of theory to field environments.

When the theory fails to work in initial tests, the research program is essentially the same. This is because all theories can be expected to be more or less improvable, and statistical tests of theories, whether the results are initially "falsifying" or not, are simply the means to motivate extensions in theory. Better theory that narrows the distance between theory and observation is always welcome.

From the perspective of experimental methodology, this scenario is what the profession of economics is all about. But it is not always what we economists do very well as a profession, because our publishing incentives are not always compatible with this research paradigm.

What Is There in a Theory to Test?

As is well known, when economists test a theory we make direct comparisons between observations and the predictions of the theory. But what precisely among the elements of a theory do we test when we make these comparisons? To answer this underlying question, it is instructive to distinguish among the following three ingredients of a theory: environment, institution and behavior.

The *environment* consists of the collection of all agents' characteristics; that is, tastes and technology, which in traditional economics are represented by utility or preference functions, resource endowments and production or cost functions. In reduced form these characteristics are the individual demand (willingness-to-pay) and supply (willingness-to-accept) schedules. The *institution* defines the language (messages or actions) of communication; examples include bids by buyers, offers by sellers, acceptances by either, and the characteristics of the commodity. The institution also specifies, either formally as on an organized exchange or informally by tradition, the order in which economics agents move, or that there is no order (moves are free form), and the rules under which messages become contracts and thus allocations. For example, in most retail markets the sellers first post their offer prices, then buyers scan, search and perhaps accept offers for stated quantities. The organized commodity and stock markets use variations on the oral double auction; buyers and sellers freely announce price-quantity bids and offers. A contract occurs when a buyer accepts a seller's offer or a seller accepts a buyer's bid. Consequently, the institution specifies the rules, terms or conditions under which components of market demand make contact with components of market supply to produce binding allocations.

Finally, *behavior* is concerned with agent choices of messages or actions given the agent's characteristics (environment) and the practices (institutional rules) relating such choices to allocations. Theories introduce assumptions about agent behavior: that agents maximize utility, profit or expected utility, that common information yields common expectations, that agents make choices as if they are risk averse, that expectations adjust using Bayes rule, that transactions costs (the cost of thinking, deciding, acting) are negligible.[2] Theories of behavior make predictions about messages—the bid(s) that an agent will submit at a sealed bid auction, the price that will be posted by an oligopolist, the reservation price below which a price searching agent will buy, and so on. Messages are not outcomes; they translate into outcomes depending upon the allocation and cost imputation rules of the institution.

[2]The distinction between that which we label "behavior" and that which is called an "agent's characteristic" (environment) will not, nor need it be, *a priori*. Part of the function of experiments is to increase our understanding of the issues involved in being or not being able to make this distinction. For example, is risk aversion an agent characteristic or an element of behavior embedded in his choices? It is both, but can we separate them in the context of experiments? It is yet to be shown empirically that we can operationalize this separation. See Cedric Smith's proposal (discussed below) to risk neutralize subjects by paying them in lottery tickets.

In laboratory market experiments, we test the theory's assumptions about agent behavior. How? Laboratory market experiments begin with an experimental design which seeks to control the environment using the techniques of induced valuation, and to control the institution by defining the language and the rules under which experimental subjects will be allowed to trade.[3] With these controls we narrow the interpretation of inconsistency between predictions and observations so that the burden of inconsistency is borne by the behavioral assumptions of the theory. When the experimental observations are consistent with a theory we have our first evidence that the theory—as implemented by the particular environment and institution that was used—has predictive power. If the theory was explicit about the institution (for example, specified a sealed-bid discriminative auction), but made very general assumptions about the environment (for example, Q units offered to $N > Q$ unit bidders), then it is natural to direct the research exercise to variations on the original experimental environment. If the theory was not explicit about the institution (the strong interpretation is that the theory claims to be institution-free, but more likely the demands of tractability led the theorist to make simplifying institutional assumptions), then a reasonable research objective is to explore experimental designs that vary the institution. In this way one lays a foundation of empirical results that can motivate accommodating extensions in the original theory.

The above interpretation of experimental tests of a theory can be contrasted with tests based only on field data. In the latter case the economist has no independent control over the environment and the institution; as a result, the process is a *composite test* of the theory's assumptions about the environment, the institution and agent behavior. If the theory passes the test, it may be because all elements of the theory are "correct," or because "incorrect" elements of the theory had offsetting effects that could not be identified by the test. If the theory fails, the economist cannot know which of its elements accounted for the falsifying outcome.

When various operational forms of a theory are not falsified by laboratory data, we can say that the theory's assumptions about behavior are supported given the environment and institution posited by the theory and the experiment. But we are not finished. Often the theory will specify a particularly simple artificial institution which may fail to coincide with any that we observe in the field: for example, that firms choose price and/or quantities, and that buyers fully reveal demand. These institu-

[3]Value is induced on buyer i by assigning him/her values $V_i(1) \geq V_i(2) \geq \cdots \geq V_i(Q_i)$ for successive units $1, 2, \ldots, Q_i$, and guaranteeing to i that he/she will be paid in cash the difference between the assigned value, and the corresponding realized price paid in the market, $V_i(q_i) - Pq_i$, for each unit purchased, q_i. If $U_i(\cdot)$ is i's unobserved monotone increasing utility of money, then i is motivated to buy an additional unit at any price below its assigned value. The valuation schedule thus becomes the individual's maximum willingness-to-pay for the item. Similarly, a supply schedule is induced upon sellers by assigning them individual "costs" for successive units and paying in cash the difference between the realized prices received and the assigned costs. This procedure easily generalizes to induce utility $U_i[V^i(X_i, Y_i)]$ on two "commodities" (X_i, Y_i) with the dollar valuation function $V^i(X_i, Y_i)$. The environment is defined and controlled by the collection of all assigned value (cost) schedules. The institution is controlled by defining the manner in which individuals interact to yield exchange prices and contracts.

tional assumptions can be reproduced in the laboratory, with real reward-motivated people as firms and simulated demand-revealing buyers. But it is a one-sided partial equilibrium theory of the firm and its market. This modelling tradition has carried over into contemporary game-theoretic theories of behavior in industrial organization.[4] In recent extensions of search theory it is assumed that firms quote prices, knowing search behavior, and this generates an equilibrium-predicted price distribution. These models can be tested using artificial institutions that impose the conditions postulated by the theories. But the observed institution is free-form so that firms may quote prices while learning about the search behavior of buyers, and simultaneously the latter may choose their search behavior while learning about the prices set by firms. In these examples the experiments are constrained by the (message space) *limitations of the theories* that are tested, *not by limitations in the experimental methodology*. In fact, the easiest experiment is to put no restrictions on the price setting-searching process.

Much of the experimental literature is guided by nothing more sophisticated than the static theory that markets will clear. However, this body of literature has sought to break through the boundaries created by the current limitations of theory, and to establish a less restrictive empirical foundation for theory improvement. One such example is the large literature on the double "oral" auction trading institution, various forms of which are used in the organized stock, commodity, currency and interest rate futures markets. In this institution the messages are bids by buyers, offers by sellers and acceptances by either. There are some rules, such as that all-or-none bids are prohibited, and that a new bid must provide better terms than a standing bid. But beyond these the institution is free-form and is similar to modelling a *two-sided* search equilibrium market. Sellers announce and modify offer prices, while learning about the acceptance behavior of buyers. Simultaneously, the latter choose their acceptance behavior while learning about the prices announced by sellers. Buyers also announce bid prices, and sellers are free to accept such prices. Until recently (in the work of Easely and Ledyard, Wilson and Friedman) this institution has been beyond our analytical efforts. Yet to date no other trading institution studied in the laboratory has exceeded its capacity to exhaust the gains from exchange, or exceeded its speed of convergence to competitive equilibria.

Although this discussion has emphasized laboratory experiments, what I say applies also to field empirical research. Natural experiments occur all the time, and it would be desirable to develop a professional readiness to seize upon these occasions. When Mt. St. Helens started to quiver, it was quickly peppered with geologists and instruments collecting the data that can only be generated during the reactivation of a volcano. By comparison, the tradition of direct observation in economics appears weak; our training does not seem to include the techniques, nor develop the alertness, to respond to contemporary or historical empirical opportunities. One need not romanticize the techniques of other sciences, or exaggerate their applicability to

[4]Several experimental studies suggest that market behavior may be different when there are real buyers than when one simulates a revealed demand schedule in response to seller decisions.

economics, to recognize that economists could benefit from a stronger passion and curiosity for the microeconomics of how things work.[5]

Experiments, Institutions and Economic Theory

Since it is impossible to test a theory using experimental market data without specifying an institution, the experimental study of allocation processes forces an institutional and informational mode of thinking into every research design. People have to know what the message space is, who can move when, (as in posted price institutions), or that moves are unrestricted (as in oral double auction institutions), who knows what, when, and how their message decisions generate allocations, cost imputations and net returns. Experimentalists were therefore primed to welcome, and their research has been much influenced by, the *institution-specific theory* that began to develop about 1960.

The important thing we have learned from these theories, and from many of the experiments testing them, is that *institutions matter*.[6] This is because agent incentives in the choice of messages (like bids) are affected by the institutional rules that convert messages into outcomes (like whether the high bidder wins an auction and pays the amount of the high bid or the amount of the second highest bid). In pre-1960 theory, by contrast, allocations were derived directly from the environment using ad hoc assumptions about demand revelation, or "price taking" behavior, by agents. Figure 1 illustrates the different ways of thinking. Experiments now address the question of how different institutions affect the incentive to reveal demand and supply. Thus the double oral auction elicits effective full revelation of demand and supply, but everyone in the market is a price maker as well as a price taker. Pre-1960 economic theory was totally unprepared for this kind of result.

Several questions can be raised concerning this dichotomy between institution-free and institution-specific theory. For example: doesn't the above definition of an institution preclude the possibility that any theory be institution-free? The answer is that a theory can be considered institution-free if it can be shown that the allocations it predicts are the same for all members of some class of institutions. An example is the theory of the four standard auctions: the English ascending price auction, in which the prices increase until only one bidder is left; the Dutch descending price auction, in

[5]An example of what I mean is the opportunistic response of Deacon and Sonstelie (1985) to an unusual natural experiment in which federal regulations temporarily constrained a few California stations to sell gasoline at prices less than those at other stations. Of course queues formed at the lower price stations. The authors put together a survey research program which was applied to both the high-price and low-price outlets which enabled them to measure the characteristics of respondents in the two situations, estimate the welfare cost of a market-wide ceiling on gasoline prices, and estimate the value of time spent in queues.

[6]The influential early contributions to this new conception of theory include Vickrey's (Nash-Harsanyi) models of the four standard auctions, Hurwicz's more abstract "mechanism" theory, and Shubik's emphasis on the extensive form game representation of microeconomics. Since that time there has been an increased development (particularly in bidding, information, and price search theory) of models that show how prices and allocations can or might be generated out of the internal processes of an institutionally mediated information exchange system. These theories have allowed institutions to slip unannounced back into economics, but now as an integral part of theorizing.

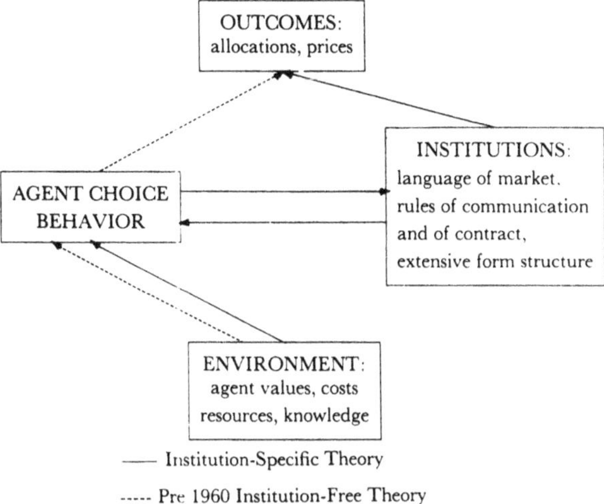

Fig. 1. Institutions in economic theory

which prices fall until some bidder bids; the first price sealed bid auction, in which the high bidder wins and pays his bid; and the second price sealed-bid auction, in which the high bidder wins but pays the amount of the second highest bid. These institutions are all equivalent if the environment is one in which all agents are risk neutral. The English and second price auctions are equivalent and the outcomes are all the same regardless of the risk attitude of agents. The Dutch and first price auctions are equivalent whatever the risk attitude of agents, but the outcomes (except in the risk neutral case) are distinct from those in the English and second price auctions. The experimental data tend to support the equivalence between English and second price auctions; do not support the equivalence of all four auctions (people do not behave as if risk neutral), and do not support the equivalence of Dutch and first price auctions.

Experimental methods can be used to test hypotheses about why certain institutions survive in the economy. Laboratory experiments enable economists to evaluate the performance characteristics of alternative institutions in controlled value-cost environments. These performance measures include: efficiency, speed of convergence, price stability, extent of price discrimination, responsiveness to changes in the environment, and so on. Dutch auctions are less efficient but faster (as implemented in the field), than English, first price, or second price auctions. This difference may account for the tendency to use Dutch auctions for selling perishables such as cut flowers, produce and fish. Posted price institutions are less efficient and yield higher selling prices than oral double auction institutions; but in the former price policy can be centralized, negotiation (a transactions cost) avoided and the products vended do not have to be standardized. These data can provide the basis for more complete theories of markets in which the institution is a variable and whose predictions can be tested with field observations across markets organized under different institutions of exchange.

There now exist many examples of continuing research programs in which theory has been sufficiently institution-rich to allow direct tests of the behavioral assumptions of the theory. I will discuss the first of two such examples in some detail to illustrate how a dialogue between testing and theory development can proceed using the trichotomy: environment, institution and behavior.

The first example involves Vickrey's risk neutral Nash equilibrium model of the first price sealed bid auction, which has stimulated an extensive study of bidding behavior in private value auctions by Cox, Smith and Walker (1988). (In a private value auction, each agent has a distinct value for the item.) Vickrey's theory assumes that each of N bidders, i, derives utility $u = v_i - b_i$ if i is the high bidder with bid b_i and i's value for the auction objective is v_i. Note that all bidders are identical except for their values, v_i. Vickrey also assumed that the v_i are distributed as a rectangular distribution. Each bidder knows N and his/her own value, but only the distribution of all others values. Given this environment Vickrey deduced the equilibrium bid function $b_i = (N - 1)v_i/N$; that is, all individuals are predicted to bid the same fraction, $(N - 1)/N$, of their respective values.

We first found that about 92 percent of the subjects bid too high to be consistent with the Vickrey model; that is, they bid on the risk averse side of Vickrey's linear bid function. I often encounter the argument that the amounts of money used in laboratory experiments are "too small" for subjects to show risk averse behavior. But there is no theorem stating how small is "locally" in the phrase "locally linear." A lot of data from quite different experimental markets shows systematic deviations from risk neutral predictions. These data are given coherence by the hypothesis that subjects are risk averse.

Our experiments also found that the relationship between bids and values tends to be systematic for each individual, but to differ across individuals. This result is inconsistent with the hypothesis that individuals have identical risk aversion.[7] Given these empirical results, we derived a new theoretical model based on the assumption that each bidder has constant relative risk averse utility from winning the auction with a particular bid given a particular private value of the prize. This model was consistent with the highly linear distinct bidding behavior of subjects. It can be shown that this is the *only* utility model which predicts that bids in relation to value will not be affected if the payoffs are increased by any multiple. We reran some of the

[7]A comprehensive survey of bidding theory (McAfee and McMillan, 1987) contains only one paper which admits of an environment in which agents may have differing nonlinear utility functions. Yet here is a critique of the above experimental results: "Of course, we don't have to go to an experimental situation to refute the hypothesis that individuals have the same degree of risk aversion!" Two comments are in order. First, if there is a widespread consensus on this "stylized fact" how come so many bidding models assume it away? I would suggest that the requirements of tractability, and the incentive to publish, loom large in charting this "low-apple-picking" course of least resistance. Otherwise, why do theory that assumes to be true that which we "know" to be false? Second, our auction experiments reject the hypothesis that people have the same degree of risk aversion, but a valuable field study by Binswanger (1980, p. 395), framed within the context of choice among uncertain prospects, found that "at high payoff levels, virtually all individuals are moderately risk-averse with little variation according to personal characteristics. Wealth tends to reduce risk aversion slightly, but its effect is not statistically significant."

experiments but tripled the payoffs, and observed no significant change in the relationship between an individual's bid and his/her value.[8]

Our model, however, implies linear homogeneous bid functions, and some 22 percent of the fitted linear individual bid functions had intercepts significantly different from zero. We hypothesized that the positive intercepts were due to a utility of winning in addition to the utility of the surplus won, while the negative intercepts were due to a threshold income necessary to provide positive utility. Does our *ex post facto* attempt to explain these nonzero intercepts increase empirical content? Yes; the new model is testable in that it implies that paying winning subjects a cash lump sum in addition to the auction surplus will increase their estimated linear bid function intercepts. Similarly, charging winning subjects a lump sum is predicted to decrease these intercepts. These new implications are not falsified by the indicated new experiments.

Despite this deepening chain of empirical successes, like *all* theory, this class of models is not without some unresolved empirical anomalies. For example, many years ago it was pointed out (C. Smith, 1961, pp. 13–14) that one could induce risk neutral behavior on risk averse expected utility maximizing agents. Instead of paying them cash for the outcomes of their decisions you give them chances, or lottery tickets, on a fixed reward if they win, and a smaller amount if they lose. This makes expected utility linear in outcomes whatever the utility of money function, and subjects are predicted to bid as if risk neutral in lottery tickets. However, this prediction is clearly falsified by auction experiments using this environment. It seems likely that it is the compound probability axiom of expected utility theory that fails in this application.[9]

[8]I have been asked: "How do you react to criticisms which say that from market data we can reject the assumption of constant relative risk aversion? We can look at how individuals change their portfolio with wealth, and it does not conform even to a much looser specification of the utility function? Why test a theory which has been rejected by market data?" Here are my reactions: (1) We can't reject the theory from this kind of market data. That data tells us how portfolios change with some measure of "wealth," confounded with changes in time, income, expectations, information, unmeasured probability assessments, and so on *ad infinitum*. We can't learn what we want to know from this sort of exercise independently of more rigorous tests, although market evidence and experimental evidence can illuminate each other. (2) Constant relative risk averse utility has been reported to do well in accounting for U.S. Treasury bill dealers' behavior (Wolf and Pohlman, 1983) both as elicited and as observed in bidding, but the constant relative risk averse coefficient shows greater risk aversion for actual bids than for the (Kahneman and Tversky) hypothetical assessments. (3) Non-constant relative risk averse utility cannot account for first price auction bidding behavior because the latter appears not to change when we triple payoffs. (4) Constant relative risk averse utility need not be valid over the entire interval of positive income to yield predictive accuracy over the relevant range of observations. Probably no functional form will be satisfactory everywhere.

[9]This interpretation raises the question, "If the compounding axiom fails, what does it imply about individual behavior? You can't have an important prediction of the theory rejected and still accept the theory." It is correct to say that not all observed behavior is consistent with expected utility maximization, but it is incorrect to say that you cannot therefore accept the theory. You can accept it, indeed you have little choice, until a better theory emerges. Theories are not accepted because all tests have failed to refute them. Lakatos (1978, pp. 4–5) wrote, "...scientists talk about anomalies, recalcitrant instances, not refutations... When Newton published his *Principia* it was common knowledge that it could not properly explain even the motion of the moon; in fact, lunar motion refuted Newton. Kaufman, a distinguished physicist, refuted Einstein's relativity theory in the very year it was published." People accept theories, in spite of anomalies, because they account for some evidence, and in particular are able to predict novel, even

In any case these results should alert scholars to the hazards of applying this procedure and assuming that their subjects are rendered neutral to risk. Any test of a theory which applies this procedure is necessarily a joint test of Smith's hypothesis and the theory; if the hypothesis fails to test out, the test of the theory is open to doubt. But even if C. Smith's hypothesis had been consistent with these tests, the exercise has limited transfer value in natural field and laboratory environments if real people are risk averse in the rewards that mediate their choices. If this is the case one must sooner or later confront the empirical demand for theories based on heterogeneous risk averse agents.

The second example is one in which the demand for new theory requires more than modifications that introduce individual differences in risk aversion. This is the extensive study of common value auctions by J. Kagel and D. Levin (1986) showing that subjects generally do not satisfy the predictions of a particular risk neutral Nash model of bidding. In this environment (see Thaler in the Winter 1988 issue of this journal for a discussion and a different interpretation) subjects do not know the common value of the item when they bid; but they each have an independent unbiased sample ("signal") which is positively related to true value. Unless one's bid is suitably discounted, as in this Nash model, the high bidder tends to be the one with the most optimistic sample estimate of value, and is said to be a victim of the "winner's curse." In small groups (3–4) experienced subjects make consistently positive profits and bid closer to the Nash prediction than the "winner's curse" prediction. (Profits are about 65 percent of the Nash prediction so that even here there appears to be room for theory improvement by appropriately introducing risk aversion). However, bids are found to increase with the number of bidders in larger groups (6–7), and contrary to this theory, experienced subjects suffer losses and bankruptcies. These data suggest that, *ceteris paribus*, the theory needs extensions that make the number of active bidders endogenous, and which predict equilibrium adjustment over time through some exit (entry) survival process. This is implied by the fact that the endogenous forces tending to vary N frustrated the Kagel-Levin attempt to fix N as a treatment variable in the larger groups. But the theory under test assumes that N is given. The data suggest an alternative zero profit market clearing model (it might be formulated as a Nash model) with N as a variable, in which entry would occur for $N = 3$ or 4 and exit when $N = 6$ or 7, yielding an equilibrium industry size, $N^* = 5$, for the parameters used by Kagel and Levin. One would seek a model in which N^* is a function of parameters characterizing the environment and, in

---

stunning, facts that cannot be accounted for by alternative theories. Newton's theory enabled Halley to make the stunning prediction that a certain comet would return in seventy-two years, as indeed it did, and Einstein's theory made the stunning prediction that a star's light was bent by the gravitational pull of the sun. Vickrey's model, suitably modified for heterogeneous risk averse bidders, rather astoundingly, I would say, accounts for and predicts the behavior of naive reward-motivated subjects in a first price auction. What alternative theory shows a comparable capacity to organize this immense data set?

addition to explaining the Kagel-Levin results, would lead to new testable implications.

Noncooperative Equilibrium Theory and Experiment

Two prevailing criticisms about noncooperative (Nash) equilibrium theory require modification in the light of experimental evidence.

First, it is widely believed that the concept of a noncooperative Nash equilibrium is "inherently" unsatisfactory because of its strong (or unrealistic) information requirements that each agent must know the preferences of all other agents.

Second, noncooperative equilibrium concepts are of questionable value because there are so many different such concepts leading to distinct theoretical implications; even with any given concept, such as Nash-Harsanyi, there are sometimes multiple solutions that leave open the question of a criterion for choosing among them.

The first criticism does not reflect the experimental results from many different environments which support noncooperative theory. The second criticism reflects a mode of thinking that excludes the prospect that a theory might be taken seriously enough to test it.

There are now numerous experimental studies based on noncooperative equilibrium concepts in which the results support the proposition that such equilibria are *more* likely to obtain under the minimal information requirement that no agent knows the preferences (or in an experiment, the payoffs used to induce preferences) of any other agent, and are *less* likely to obtain, or take longer to obtain, under the complete information conditions that critics argue are needed for equilibrium.

Fouraker and Siegel provided the first evidence on this point a quarter of a century ago in their classic work on bargaining behavior. Their bilateral bargaining, repeat transaction experiments were run under both complete and incomplete information. In these experiments, the seller chooses a price message, followed by the buyer choosing a quantity message, so that the noncooperative message equilibrium corresponds to the monopoly price and quantity. With incomplete information, eight of nine observations support a Nash outcome, and one supports the competitive equilibrium. With complete information 11 of 21 observations support a Nash noncooperative equilibrium, while 10 support competitive. Similarly, in their Cournot quantity message triopoly markets, support for Nash was 15 of 33 under complete information, 20 of 33 under incomplete. Finally, in their Bertrand price message markets, Nash was supported in 17 of 17 duopoly pairs under incomplete information, but only 11 of 17 under complete information. Another example based on large group double auction markets is discussed in the next section.

Two rudimentary fallacies underlie the criticism that the Nash equilibrium is not useful because it requires full information. First, *theorists* have to assume complete information in order to calculate a noncooperative equilibrium. But it does not follow that agents either require such information, or would know how to make the calculations if they had the information. An equilibrium is a state, and analysts can ask whether a market tends to settle upon that state independently of the process used to calculate the state.

The second fallacy is that if agents have complete information, why should they use it to identify a noncooperative equilibrium? With complete information one can also identify more lucrative cooperative outcomes, and this is precisely the way real people deviate from Nash in most of the above experiments. Subjects are not so irrational as to satisfy "rational" models of behavior when it is contrary to their self-interest!

As theorists, we have been lax in the assumptions we make as to what follows from the state of common knowledge. First, what can objectively exist—say, in an experiment—is a state of common information, which is not the same thing as common knowledge or *expectations*. Real people have their own diverse ideas as to the knowledge implications of common information. Second, people have their own agenda as to what it is rational to expect and do given common information, and their presuppositions need not accord with economists' presumptions about rational behavior.

The second major criticism of the concept of noncooperative equilibrium, that there are so many such concepts all with different theoretical implications, is symptomatic of a research program which attempts to answer scientific questions independently of observations. The obvious criterion in most sciences for selecting among alternative theoretical predictions is empirical, not *a priori*. One can design experiments capable of yielding results that may support any of the theoretical predictions, then see if the data "select" (are closer to) one among the competitors. Multiple theoretical predictions are exactly what the experimentalist likes to see in any science.

Concepts of noncooperative equilibrium have performed well in a large number of experimental markets—better than they have had a right to perform given that they were never intended to be tested, and that their acceptability is judged on internal rather than empirical criteria. Furthermore, the nonuniqueness of Nash equilibrium concepts (and even of equilibria) is a strength, not a weakness. When one concept fails empirically (as in common value auctions with N fixed and certain) there may be other formulations that do not contradict observation.

Laboratory Experiments, Psychology and Economics

The considerable literature that has developed using experimental methods has examined many of the mainstream issues in microeconomic theory and is helping to illuminate an increasing number of applied economic questions. If one seeks common general themes in this literature, particularly concerning behavior, I see three such empirical propositions, with far-reaching implications for how economists think about economics and how we interpret, and perhaps do, theory. The first proposition is that economic agents do not solve decision problems by thinking about them and calculating in the same way as economists. Second, from this first proposition it should not be presumed that economic agents will fail to get the "right" answers in the context of markets: namely, the answers that are predicted by market theories. The experimental evidence is often consistent with the predictions of market theories. Third, economists have little in the way of formal understanding of how people are able to get the "right" answers without consciously performing our logic and calculations.

Experimentalists in both psychology and economics have provided overwhelming evidence in market experiments, in informal subject debriefing, and in choice surveys, that supports the first proposition. The second receives support from hundreds of supply and demand, oligopoly, bargaining and other experiments stretching back three decades in the work of many experimental economists and the psychologist S. Siegel. The third proposition calls attention to the lack of a satisfactory analytical-empirical integration of two bodies of evidence: one relating to the introspective and sometimes actual cash motivated responses of people in surveys soliciting choices among alternatives; the other to cash motivated choices in the context of repetitive market exchange.

Several psychologists (Edwards, Kahneman, Lichtenstein, Slovic, Tversky) and economists (Allais, Ellsberg) have pioneered the development of experimental designs for collecting evidence on hypothetical and actual individual choice behavior. This evidence generally tends to be inconsistent with expected utility theory, and with some of the fundamental behavior hypotheses in the theory of demand (Kahneman, Knetsch and Thaler, 1986; Knetsch and Sinden, 1984), such as the opportunity cost principle, and the implication of demand theory that there should exist only "small" differences between willingness-to-pay and willingness-to-accept. Some of this work has been replicated using cash payoffs and the conclusions (preference or demand theory is violated) are not changed. Although replication using cash payoffs (where this has not been done) is certainly needed, I think it is a mistake to assume that the economist's paradigm will somehow be rescued in the context of these particular experimental designs, if experimenters would just pay money.

Given the high replicability of most of these studies, I think further such replications are of marginal value. What would be of much greater value is research directed at closing two gaps: the gap between decision theory and decision behavior, and the gap between evidence concerning how people think about economic questions and evidence concerning how people behave in experimental markets. Closing these gaps is crucial if we are not to get stuck on a research plateau. This is because it is clear from the work of Lakatos and other philosopher-historians of science that "there is no refutation without a better theory" (Lakatos, 1978, p. 6). Scientists in all disciplines simply ignore falsifying evidence until new and better theory emerges. Theory selection is based on opportunity cost, not absolute falsificationist standards.

There are two distinct paths whereby the distance between decision theory and behavior can be narrowed. The first lies in the empirical interpretation of expected utility theory: What are the prizes as perceived by the decision maker?

Almost uniformly we economists have assumed *a priori* that the objects to which the axioms of utility theory "should" apply are different amounts of wealth. Psychologists have followed this tradition in their empirical interpretation of data on choice behavior. For example, Kahneman and Tversky have a class of decision problems in which the observations are consistent with expected utility theory if the utility function is S-shaped and is applied not to wealth, but to changes in wealth (income) from a reference point representing the individual's current wealth state. This curve describes risk seeking behavior below the reference point, and risk averse behavior above. But this result does not violate the theory. The axioms of the theory do not tell us what the prizes are. The theory simply postulates objects that can be preference ordered. It is an extra-theoretical subsidiary hypothesis to assert that these objects are amounts of final wealth measured in some particular way. Empirical evidence going back 35 years to H. Markowitz has suggested that the theory does much better if the prizes are changes in wealth, not absolute wealth. Selecting among hypotheses that are subsidiary to the axioms of a theory, but essential to its empirical interpretation, ought to be one of the more important functions of experimental methods.

In our application of utility theory to a risk averse model of the first price auction discussed earlier, we explicitly apply it to income because subjects participate in a sequence of auctions, with each auction representing a potential increment of wealth for each bidder. It is this form of the theory that organizes the data. This interpretation is consistent with other experimental evidence, and with the observed tendency of gamblers to make repetitive small stakes bets, as against a single bet wagering one's entire gambling budget.

Also in the auction example, notice that when we encountered linear empirical bid functions with nonzero intercepts, instead of dumping all utility theory forthwith, we asked whether it was possible to redefine the prizes so as to account for this contrary evidence, but in a way that was testable. The modified utility function has the Kahneman-Tversky S-shape, but with a "reference point" whose position varies with individual characteristics. The point to be emphasized is not that we have shown that prize reinterpreting extensions of expected utility theory will always work, but that they work in the context of auctions. Furthermore, such extensions in one context may be applicable in others, increasing coherence.

The second path in bringing together decision theory and behavior is to modify the axioms. Chew and Machina have done this expertly with various modifications of independence. These modifications account for some but not all of the violations. The Chew-Machina modifications accommodate Allais-type violations, and under certain conditions, preference reversals[10]; they provide new testable propositions not deducible from expected utility theory, and thereby yield an increase in empirical content. For a comprehensive discussion of these developments, see Machina (1987).

The fact that expected utility theory is consistent with some of the empirical evidence, especially when reinterpreted in terms of the prizes, and when extended along more fundamental Chew-Machina lines, argues strongly against any serious

[10]A preference reversal occurs when a subject says that he prefers *A* to *B* (or *B* to *A*) and that his willingness-to-pay (or willingness-to-accept) for *A* is less (greater) than that for *B*. A great many subjects' choices exhibit such reversals when *A* and *B* are different gambles (or different dividend paying assets). It should be added that the Chew-Machina modifications can accommodate preference reversals if they are the result of violations of the independence axiom. This is implied by the contributions of Holt and Karni and Safra. However the experimental tests by Cox and Epstein (1987) support the proposition that preference reversals are not due to violations of independence.

proposal to abandon it. At this juncture there is no alternative so that to abandon it is to substitute the void for a foundation of sand. The predictions of the theory and its extensions are noncontroversial, and it provides a powerful problem solving heuristic (Lakatos, 1978). Without this theory we have several empirical regularities whose predictive power in new situations is a function of the experience and opinion of the observer. There is a world of difference between having a theory whose predictions for all parameterizations are noncontroversial and having names to assign to certain empirical regularities.

How do we close the second gap, between the psychology of choice and agents' economic behavior in experimental exchange markets? The introspective empirical results make it clear that people's choices violate such basic tenets of demand theory as opportunity cost considerations and the approximate equality between willingness to accept and willingness to pay.[11] I think we economists need to accept these replicable empirical results as providing meaningful measures of *how people think about economic questions*. For their part, psychologists need to accept the dominating message in experimental research on the performance of a wide variety of bidding, auctioning and customer (posted price) markets: markets quite often "work" in the sense that over time they converge to the predictions of the economist's paradigm.[12] The few studies that simultaneously measure what people *say* (as questionnaire respondents), and what people subsequently *do* in experimental markets, confirm both kinds of evidence (Coursey, Hovis and Schulze, 1987; Knez and Smith, 1987). That is, the introspective responses of those subjects replicate the similar results of psychologists, but the responses are not necessarily consistent with the subjects' own subsequent market convergence behavior over time.[13] I suggest that we assume that these two bodies of evidence correctly measure the thoughtful choices and revealed actions of

[11]It should be emphasized that what is at stake here is the traditional utility-based theory of excess demand functions whose validity or falsity is separable from the theory of markets. The observation that willingness-to-accept exceeds willingness-to-pay, and that this is due to "loss aversion," implies that excess demand functions are discontinuous at the initial endowment. This means that gains from exchange are predicted to be lower than the prediction of the standard utility analysis. But market theory begins with postulated demand functions, which need not come from a utilitarian theory of demand. The Swedish economist Gustav Cassel argued that market theory should only begin with market demand and supply because the utilitarian derivation of market behavior was doomed to fail. Markets can be doing their thing whether or not demand theory is of any relevance to expressed demand.

[12]A new example of the discrepancy between behavior in one-shot choice experiments and behavior in markets is in the study of experimental markets for insurance by C. Camerer and H. Kunreuther (1987). Choice experiments often show evidence of violating expected utility theory when low probability significant loss events are involved. Camerer and Kunreuther study double auction markets for insurance contracts with these characteristics, and conclude that there is nothing special about risky losses in the range of parameters they study using this particular trading institution.

[13]In Knez and Smith (1987) we solicited willingness-to-pay and willingness-to-accept responses from potential buyers and sellers for two assets with known probability distributions of dividends. In subsequent double auction trading of these assets 40 percent of the buyers and 34 percent of the sellers announced bids or offers that violated their earlier stated responses. Furthermore, the stated preferences of subjects between the two assets changed considerably after experiencing market trading in them. From these results one should not conclude that the original hypothetical measures were wrong, but that people adapt their beliefs in the light of market experience. Here the incidence of "irrationality" is fairly common in the measures of what people think, but rare in their actual transactions. Only 3 of 146 transactions violated rational principles.

human subjects in these contexts. Reconciling these two sets of observations might be accomplished along the following lines.

People have their own homegrown beliefs about how markets work, or should work. (This is why economic concepts are difficult to teach to beginners.) Their questionnaire responses reflect these beliefs, which are often couched in terms of "fairness" criteria. Also, their initial behavior in a market may reflect these beliefs. But over time their behavior adapts to the incentive properties of markets as often (but certainly not always) represented in the standard economic analysis or its extensions.

It seems to me that we are confronted with two experimental research programs both of which have weak theoretical underpinnings. The economist's maximizing paradigm often performs well in predicting the equilibrium reached over time in experimental markets, but this theory is not generally able to account for short-run dynamic behavior, such as the contract price paths from initial states to final steady states. Similarly, the psychologist's "reference frame" descriptive paradigm performs well in explaining subject introspective responses, and their short-run, or initial, decision behavior, but it provides no predictive theory of reference frame adjustment over time. In fact, the statement (Kahneman, Knetsch and Thaler, 1986, p. 731) "that they (people) adapt their views of fairness to the norms of actual behavior" can be interpreted as a description of what is observed in experimental markets.

Initial choices may reflect all manner of beliefs and expectations, but if these choices are not sustainable in a market clearing or a noncooperative equilibrium, subjects adapt their expectations and behavior until they attain such an equilibrium. For example, it has been demonstrated that in an experimental design in which all the exchange surplus is captured by the buyers, convergence to the competitive equilibrium is slower and more erratic under complete (all values and costs are common knowledge) than under incomplete (values and costs are private) information (C. Smith, 1982, pp. 945–946). The condition of complete information gives the freest play to expectations based on social norms and beliefs. The latter are often inconsistent with equilibrium and retard full convergence until traders learn to adapt their beliefs about what they think "ought" to occur to what is attainable and can be sustained. Real people abandon their *a priori* beliefs when they find that their interest is poorly served by such beliefs. Under incomplete information people have little contextual basis for applying their *a priori* beliefs, and can be presumed to be more accepting of the behavior that sustains equilibrium. For the theorist, perhaps one way to model these phenomena in common information environments is to introduce agent *uncertainty about the behavior* of other agents.[14] Now the theory will no longer predict that agents will come off the blocks straight into full rational expectations equilibrium. But as people adapt, and behavioral uncertainty is reduced, the theory can account for equilibrium convergence under some learning scenarios. This accords with observed price bubbles in experimental asset markets. With increasing subject experience

[14] For example, in the various decision problems presented to subjects (see Kahneman, Knetsch and Thaler (1986) and the literature they cite) about 20 to 40 percent of the subjects respond with answers consistent with standard economic reasoning, while the majority responds contrarily, using "fairness" or other "nonrational" criteria.

the incidence of bubbles decreases and prices tend to converge to intrinsic dividend value.

The proposition that people adapt their beliefs about markets to the incentives of markets may also apply to disparate bodies of evidence on opportunity cost and sunk cost. Survey instruments show that, contrary to standard economic analysis, people do not ignore sunk costs and do not treat opportunity costs as equivalent to out-of-pocket costs. These concepts have not been generally examined in experimental markets. However, in my joint work with A. Williams and J. Ledyard in double auction trading with three commodities and two markets, the results fail to falsify the opportunity cost principle. In this environment each demand function depends on the prices of both commodities, and therefore willingness-to-pay in each market is based on foregoing the opportunity to buy an additional unit in the alternative market. These markets converge to the competitive equilibrium, supporting the effectiveness of opportunity cost in this context.

In general, one might think of changes in the reference frame or norms of behavior over time as being induced by the invisible reality of opportunity costs, entry or exit, and the irrelevance of sunk costs. Adaptation, where it is observed, may therefore be forced and agents need not have a cognitive grasp of the causes that are driving changes. Such a model implies sluggish nonoptimal intertemporal adjustment. If some agents (20 to 40 percent) are aware of the effects of opportunity cost, the effects of entry and exit, and the irrelevance of sunk costs, they may approximate optimal adjustment over time, and expedite the adjustment of the less perceptive agents.

Postscript

Experimentalists in economics frequently encounter an argument that proceeds roughly as follows: (a) If a theory is well articulated with clearly stated assumptions, and if there are no errors in the logic and the mathematics; then, (b) certain correct conclusions follow from the theory. So (c), what is there in a theory to test? The punch-line (c) often comes out in other forms without the conditionals (a) and (b) being stated. For example, when the data are consistent with the predictions of a theory, it is sometimes said that the results are not interesting because they merely confirm what economists already knew (or teach?), which seems to suggest that "truly" authoritative theory cannot be doubted seriously. When the data are inconsistent with the predictions of theory it is not uncommon to assert that there must be "something" wrong with the experiments.

Such objections are not without precedent in the history of any science. They tend to impose a double standard: if your theory says that the world is flat, then the tendency of some travelers to be "lost" (they never return home) is taken as evidence that they fell off the edge, while the fact that other travelers return home is interpreted to imply that they did not travel far enough to fall off the earth's edge. Similarly, my experience has been that questions about experimental procedure are more likely to be raised when the results appear to disconfirm accepted theory than when they appear to confirm such theory. However, if one wants to gain a greater understanding of economic phenomena, the most productive knowledge-building attitude is to be skeptical of *both the theory and the evidence*. This is likely to cause you to seek improvements in both the theory and the methods of testing.

One often hears it said that there is "too much theory spinning" or "not enough empirical work" in economics. Neither of these complaints adequately targets our professional weaknesses. Empirical studies would certainly benefit from more theory built directly on observed institutional processes. But not every testable theory may be worth laboratory testing. We need to think ahead to the domain of applicability of such efforts to field environments and institutions. Similarly, we could benefit from an increase in the kind of empirical research, both laboratory and field, that identifies and collects new data sources under the control and responsibility of the scientist; research that seeks to establish, rigorously, those empirical regularities worthy of stimulating deeper theoretical treatment. But we are particularly weak in ongoing research programs in which there is a progressive dialogue between theory development and particular results from laboratory and field tests; that steadily increase the empirical content of theory; and that build usable knowledge and a deeper understanding of things. The process will sometimes yield lags in empirical research, but just as often lags in theory. As the physicist Steven Weinberg described a similar situation in particle physics recently: "[T]here is not one iota of direct experimental evidence for supersymmetry, yet we study it because it looks so much like the sort of theory we would like to believe in. This is symptomatic of the terrible state we are in... The salvation of elementary particle physics is, at least for the moment, in the hands of the experimentalists."

In economics the tendency of theory to lag behind observation seems to be endemic, and, as theorists, few of us consider this to be a "terrible state." But as noted by Lakatos (1978, p. 6), "where theory lags behind the facts, we are dealing with miserable degenerating research programmes."

Theory should be ever more demanding of our empirical resources. Simultaneously, data should be ever more demanding of the empirical relevance of theory and of the theorist's expertise in working imaginatively on problems of the world, rather than on stylized problems of the imagination.

■ *I am grateful for research support from the National Science Foundation and from the Sloan Foundation to the University of Arizona, Economic Science Laboratory. I wish also to express my thanks to J. Cox, D. Kahneman, M. Machina, D. McCloskey, C. Shapiro, J. Stiglitz, T. Taylor and R. Thaler for dozens of pages of commentary on earlier drafts of this essay. I have attempted to incorporate their many valuable comments into the final version. That the final result is an improvement is as certain as is my failure to do as well as I would have liked. Words, pictures and formulas cannot convey a lifetime of experiences under the able tutoring of one's experimental subjects.*

References

Binswanger, Hans P., "Attitudes Toward Risk: Experimental Measurement in Rural India," *American Journal of Agricultural Economics*, August 1980, *62*, 395–407.

Camerer, Colin, and Howard Kunreuther, "Experimental Markets for Insurance," Department of Decision Sciences, University of Pennsylvania, July 1987.

Coursey, Don, John Hovis, and William Schulze, "On the Supposed Disparity Between Willingness-to-Accept and Willingness-to-Pay Measures of Value," *Quarterly Journal of Economics*, August 1987, *102*, 679–690.

Cox, James, Vernon Smith, and James Walker, "Theory and Individual Behavior of First Price Auctions," *Journal of Risk and Uncertainty*, March 1988, *1*, 61–99.

Cox, James C., and Seth Epstein, "Preference Reversals Without the Independence Axiom," Department of Economics, University of Arizona, Discussion Paper No. 87-10, Sept. 1987.

Deacon, Robert, and Jon Sonstelie, "Rationing by Waiting and the Value of Time: Results from a Natural Experiment," *Journal of Political Economy*, August 1985, *93*, 627–647.

Hoffman, Elizabeth, and Matthew L. Spitzer, "Experimental Law and Economics," *Columbia Law Review*, June 1985, *85*, 991–1036.

Kagel, John, and Daniel Levin, "The Winner's Curse and Public Information in Common Value Auctions," *American Economic Review*, December 1986, *76*, 894–920.

Kahneman, Daniel, Jack Knetsch, and Richard Thaler, "Fairness as a Constraint on Profit Seeking: Entitlements in the Market," *American Economic Review*, September 1986, *76*, 728–741.

Knetsch, Jack, and John Sinden, "Willingness to Pay and Compensation Demanded: Experimental Evidence of An Unexpected Disparity in Measures of Value," *Quarterly Journal of Economics*, August 1984, *99*, 507–521.

Knez, Marc, and Vernon Smith, "Hypothetical Valuations and Preference Reversals in the Context of Asset Trading." In Roth, Alvin, ed., *Laboratory Experiments in Economics: Six Points of View*. Cambridge: Cambridge University Press, 1987, pp. 131–154.

Lakatos, Imre, *The Methodology of Scientific Research Programmes*. Vol 1. Worrall, J., and G. Currie, eds. Cambridge: Cambridge University Press, 1978.

Machina, Mark J., "Choice Under Uncertainty: Problems Solved and Unsolved," *Journal of Economic Perspectives*, Summer 1987, *1*, 121–154.

McAfee, R. Preston, and John McMillan, "Auctions and Bidding," *Journal of Economic Literature*, June 1987, *25*, 699–738.

Milgrom, Paul, and John Roberts, "Information Asymmetries, Strategic Behavior, and Industrial Organization," *American Economic Review*, May 1987, *77*, 184–193.

Plott, Charles R., "The Application of Laboratory Experimental Methods to Public Choice." In Russell, C. S., ed., *Collective Decision Making: Applications from Public Choice Theory*. Baltimore: Johns Hopkins University Press, 1979, pp. 137–160.

Plott, Charles R., "Industrial Organization Theory and Experimental Economics," *Journal of Economic Literature*, December 1982, *20*, 1485–1527.

Plott, Charles R. (a), "Laboratory Experiments in Economics: The Implications of Posted-Price Institutions," *Science*, 9 May 1986, *232*, 732–738.

Plott, Charles R. (b), "Rational Choice in Experimental Markets," *Journal of Business*, October 1986, *59*, S301–S327.

Smith, Cedric, "Consistency in Statistical Inference and Decision," *Journal of the Royal Statistical Society*, Ser. B, 1961, *23*, 1–25.

Smith, Vernon L., "Bidding and Auctioning Institutions: Experimental Results." In Amihud, Y., ed., *Bidding and Auctioning for Procurement and Allocation*. New York: New York University Press, 1976, pp. 43–64.

Smith, Vernon L., "Relevance of Laboratory Experiments to Testing Resource Allocation Theory." In Kmenta, J., and J. Ramsey, eds., *Evaluation of Econometric Models*. New York: Academic Press, 1980, pp. 345–377.

Smith, Vernon L. (a), "Reflections on Some Experimental Market Mechanisms for Classical Environments." In McAlister, L., ed. *Choice Models for Buyer Behavior*. Greenwich: JAI Press, 1982, pp. 13–47.

Smith, Vernon L. (b), "Microeconomic Systems as an Experimental Science," *American Economic Review*, December 1982, *72*, 923–955.

Smith, Vernon L., "Experimental Methods in the Political Economy of Exchange," *Science*, 10 October 1986, *234*, 167–173.

Thaler, Richard H., "Anomalies: The Winner's Curse," *Journal of Economic Perspectives*, Winter 1988, *2*, 191–201.

Wolf, Charles, and Larry Pohlman, "The Recovery of Risk Preferences from Actual Choices," *Econometrica*, May 1983, *51*, 843–850.

Experimental Economics: Behavioral Lessons for Microeconomic Theory and Policy

It is an honor on this occasion and by this means to pay tribute to the memory of Nancy Schwartz. Although Nancy's work was that of an accomplished theorist, and not of an experimentalist, she had an interest in experimentalism that was born of her natural curiosity about all economic matters. It is also a pleasure, once again, to visit my many friends at Northwestern.

Almost everyone wants to know if things work, and experimental economics asks whether and under what circumstances our models work. Over the past 30-odd years, this intellectual effort has developed a methodology for providing experimental answers to this question, integrating them with field observations and, where appropriate, for modifying our models in response to the resulting evidence. In this address I want to talk about what we have learned and the consequences of this learning for how we do theory. I will also have something to say about the potential implications of our learning for microeconomic policy.

For economic theory there is both good news and bad news. The good news is that we are on the right track, generally, in modeling the relationship among institutional rules, individual incentives, and market performance. Institutions clearly matter. The lesson here can be said to provide a perspective on the biblical imperative (slightly reinterpreted from Romans): For rules are not a terror to good works, but to bad. That perspective is the following: Rules determine incentives, and incentives determine the performance of markets by encouraging desirable behavior and discouraging undesirable behavior in a way that is self-regulating. As much of the non-Western world, outside China, now realizes, if you do not rely on self-regulating rules, your economic system cannot be made to work.

Furthermore, our models of noncooperative behavior are fairly good; they often are able to do a credible job of predicting observations, even in quite complex environments, although it is plain that there is room for improvement and, of course, interpretation. The bad news for theory is that we can't seem to get our interpretation of the information and environmental conditions right for these models, so that the models correctly correspond to both the conditions and the results of the experiments. We need more institution-specific theory, whose rigorous development is guided by comparably rigorous empirical learning. The good news is that, by and large, markets work the way we think they should to coordinate the dispersed actions of economic agents. The bad news is that, in the meantime, as theorists, we have been less than successful in showing how our concepts of incentive compatibility and strategy-proofness can be implemented beyond the impossibility theorems suggesting that the world can't work the way we observe it working in the laboratory. As a consequence, our scientific advance is handicapped by our failure to pursue the exciting implications of the fact that things sometimes work better than we had a right to expect from our abstract interpretations of theory.

Information and Noncooperative Equilibria

It is widely believed and repeated that noncooperative equilibria are attainable only under the condition of complete and common information on preferences, i.e., where each agent knows the utility values for all agents. Indeed, these presumed strong information requirements are often cited as "the weakness of the Nash (noncooperative) equilibrium concept" (Sonnenschein 1983, 16). In a parallel vein, neoclassical economists from Jevons to Samuelson have assumed that competitive equilibria also required complete information on (or "perfectly foreseen") supply and demand. These assumptions have scarce empirical support in the context of single-decision games. But in the less artificial context of repeated games, these assumptions do not just fail to be supported by decades of experimental data. Rather, the data support the opposite proposition that noncooperative and competitive equilibrium concepts are best able to predict behavior under private incomplete information; that under complete information conditions, these concepts either fail, or do less well, in predicting behavior than under private information conditions. These experimental results have come from a wide spectrum of institutions: posted-price, bilateral-bargaining games; oligopoly markets; a variety of sealed bid auctions; continuous double auctions (see McCabe, Rassenti, and Smith 1989(a) for a partial summary); and many more. This is very encouraging in that our experimental observations tell us that the well-known embarrassment of multiple equilibria in repeated games of complete information is largely a cockpit problem for the theorist, not a behavioral problem for real, motivated people.

The economics of incentives is alive and well in the laboratory; the stuck zippers are in the profession, not in our behavioral data. The theoretical charge is to develop formulations showing that noncooperative equilibria are sustainable under private incomplete information; that under complete information, agents can identify more attractive states than the noncooperative outcomes and can attempt to achieve these states; that these attempts are more likely to be successful when the number of competitors is only two, but become less likely to be successful as the number increases above two.

In some very long oligopoly games under full information on own-demand, cooperation is increased, but still declines as N increases above two (Friedman and Hoggatt 1980). I should note also that the incidence of tacit cooperation where numbers are low occurs in experiments in which buyers' behavior is *simulated* to be fully demand revealing as assumed in currently tractable theory. But where oligopoly experiments have used human buyers as well as sellers, the results show that the strategic behavior of buyers is important in helping to countervail seller cooperation (Kruse 1988). To my knowledge, we have no complete oligopoly models of the behavior of both buyers and sellers. Duopoly games with simulated buyers are really just bilateral bargaining games for the division of surplus.

But why is it so natural and commonplace to suppose that complete information is necessary for noncooperative equilibria? I think it is because we cannot imagine, untutored by observation, how agents might achieve an equilibrium except by rational cognition and, as theorists and experimentalists, *we* have to have complete information to *calculate* such an equilibrium. It is important here to distinguish theory from the casual assertions of theorists. For, in fact, the condition of complete information is not a formal part of the theory of how an equilibrium is achieved, and lacking such a process theory, we have simply tacked on to the formal theory the ad hoc assertion that agents have to know what we have to know. But if noncooperative states, in truth, possess an equilibrium property, it is conceivable that agents could grope around and find it without calculation, just as a marble thrown into a bowl will find the bottom without knowledge of Newtonian mechanics.

Although I have emphasized noncooperative theory, these comments also apply to the Nash model of cooperative bargaining. Roth and Malouf (1979) summarize experimental data that support (often with very low variance) the Nash model under private information, but which strongly contradict the model under complete information.

Finally, let me report the best news of all. Theorists are increasingly becoming concerned with these long-standing discrepancies between theory and experiment. D. Easely, J. Ledyard, D. Friedman, M. Satterthwaite, S. Williams, R. Wilson (see Wilson 1990), and others have all made important contributions to the analysis of the exceptionally challenging problem of modeling double auctions; Kalai and Lehrer (1990) have an important theorem providing conditions under which incompletely informed players in a bimatrix game converge to a noncooperative equilibrium (also see Canning 1990). Selten's (1989) Schwartz lecture is a magnificent essay on the mutual dependence between theory and experiment. These are exciting scientific developments, as they portend significant methodological changes in the way that we do, and think, about economic theory. Deeper experiments are sure to follow breakthroughs in theory.

Common Information and Common Knowledge or Expectations

The theoretical problem that an equilibrium of a model might be approximated without agent knowledge or understanding of the model has important implications for the concept of common knowledge that allegedly underlies contemporary game theory. I avoid using the term "common knowledge," preferring instead to use two distinct and more appropriate terms, "common information" and "common expectations." This is because all that one can achieve, operationally, in a given experimental or field situation is a state of common information. All subjects in an experiment can receive a public rendition of the instructions and payoffs for all participants; then all see the situation and all see that all see it. But it does not follow from such common information alone that "knowledge" in the sense of expectations, or knowing what others will do, will be common. I could give everyone in this room common, complete information, and yet each of you would face uncertainty concerning how others will behave, given this information.

Empirically, common expectations are achieved through shared experience. By all observing what all do, over time groups come to have common expectations. This has been the result in an immense variety of different experiments: in simple repeated games, in rich *n*-person markets, in fiat money experiments, and in laboratory stock markets. The assumption of common knowledge in game theory models, while enabling us to "defend" game theory solutions, also has limited severely our progress by begging the key question of the processes whereby agents come to have common knowledge. This is where the action — the dynamics — is to be found; where we discover how it is that groups learn their way from initial states to equilibrium states.

In the stock market experiments, fundamental share value is derived from dividends whose per-period probability distribution is common information. Since expected share value in any period is just expected single-period value times the number of trading (or dividend) periods remaining, fundamental value declines linearly from period one to the final period. Capital gains are necessarily zero-sum across all traders. But common information is not sufficient to induce common expectations. Inexperienced subjects produce large volume price bubbles that deviate substantially from intrinsic dividend value. When the subjects return for a second session, volume is reduced and the price bubble is less pronounced relative to dividend value. Where subjects return for a third session, volume is thinner at prices much closer to intrinsic value as the wellsprings of hope for capital gains finally run dry. Through this sequential experience subjects acquire the common expectation that exchange value is near dividend value. Having experienced it, they believe it, and we have not been successful in reinflating a bubble with twice-experienced subjects using similar environments.

What is incorrect in both the rational expectations and game theory models is the assumption that common information eliminates behavioral or strategic uncertainty. In the stock market context, this uncertainty is resolved through shared experience in a stationary environment. This expectations interpretation is supported by the observation that in finite horizon-price search experiments (Cox and Oaxaca 1989), individual subjects behave in accordance with the predictions of a rational backward-induction model. But this is a game against nature in which subjects have only to anticipate their own behavior later in the game, not the behavior of others.

The problem that common information on payoffs is not sufficient to yield common expectations is recognized by those game theorists who argue that common knowledge must include knowledge of the model itself (Aumann 1987, 473). This means that the predictions of the model apply only to those who agree as to the game being played and how to analyze it. Therefore, my conclusion was that game theory was a predictive science only to the extent that it applied to game theorists or their cognitive equivalents.

But my colleague Kevin McCabe has corrected me by noting that game theorists disagree on solution concepts and the analysis of games. Thus, the requirement that the model be common knowledge simply substitutes an unspecified process of pregame agreement for the experiential process by which agents arrive at common expectations, and the disagreement among game theorists suggests that no logical agreement process exists — at least not yet. All the important theoretical action is relegated to an unmodeled pregame process. The same considerations apply to Nash-Muth rational common expectations theory, which has found support in hundreds of double-auction experiments under incomplete information.

Concerning common "knowledge," the lesson here for economics, as in other sciences, is that theorists vitally need the assistance of data (and vice versa, as any experimentalist can tell you) and that speculative theory that goes too far beyond observation, although entertaining, incurs the hazard of becoming entangled in its own bootstraps.

But let me return to the experimental stock markets. Economists living on both coasts had trouble believing the first 30 experiments. Others felt that the results corresponded to what they expected, but their expectations came from intuition, not from formal models. The problem, I was assured by the first group, was that the subjects could not sell short, that transactions cost was virtually zero (you trade electronically by pressing buttons), or that the subjects were students, not business persons. Everybody had his (they were all males) own pet explanation of what was wrong with the first set of experiments, but none of these explanations was theory-based. Of course, each of these suggestions had merit, but the important point is that there was little consensus. When widely accepted models fail, the best and the brightest grasp for straws.

Some 50 experiments later we had answers to these questions and many others. Briefly, the bubble propensities summarized above are not eliminated when subjects have the right to sell short or buy on margin or are required to pay a transactions fee; nor do they go away when we use business persons or stock traders as subjects. On the contrary, the bubbles are somewhat worse with margin buying, which lends credence to the widespread imposition of margin limits by the brokerage industry as well as by regulators. Bubbles are also, if anything, worse with business persons, though not with stock traders.

Furthermore, the widely recommended use of limit price change rules in the wake of the October 1987 worldwide stock market crash is not found by experiment to be efficacious. Limit price rules actually intensify bubbles. We think this is because the limit on price declines in each period induces a perception of reduced downside risk, causing the boom to carry further and longer before a crash occurs.

But on the positive side, we find that the introduction of a futures contract that expires at the midpoint of the horizon does help to dampen bubbles by focusing traders' initial attention on their expectations of share value at mid-horizon. A futures market appears to reduce myopia in the spot market by giving subjects an advance reading on their expectations at mid-horizon. A reasonable interpretation is that the function served by the institution of futures markets is not so much to predict the future, but to allow the market to achieve common expectations; to resolve behavioral uncertainty — in advance of an event.

This consensus building function is also served in the context of other asset trading environments (Forsythe, Palfrey, and Plott 1982) and in simple extensive form bargaining games (Harrison and McCabe 1988). In the bargaining games, subjects acquire the common expectations needed to backward-induct properly by first playing the last two rounds of a three-round sequence before playing the full three-round sequence. Thus, each subject plays the "future" in advance, discovers what to expect of her opposite, and is then able to solve correctly the three-round game, which of course cannot be solved without compatible expectations.

Practice and Institutions in Market Learning

Many years of experimental research have made it plain that real people do not solve decision problems by thinking about them in the way that we do as economic theorists. Only academics learn primarily by reading and thinking. Those who run the world, and support us financially, tend to learn by watching, listening, and doing. Try learning to operate a computer by merely reading one of those horrible instructional manuals. When experiments approximate the predictions of theory, it is because subjects experience the choices of others and then choose based on what they have learned to expect. This feedback process can be realized in repeated market games, with each decision disciplined by the social interaction of people through the rules of the trading institution. Just as the computer and the piano are human tools that we learn to use almost exclusively by practice, so the set of rules of an institution, such as those of the oral double-auction, is a social tool that can guide the collective to achieve outcomes that are individually and — if the rules are right — socially optimal.

In fact, people tend to perform poorly when they must rely completely on their unaided and untutored cognitive powers in stating how they would choose in simple games against nature, e.g., in selecting among gambles. This is shown in the instructive opinion choice surveys of Kahneman and Tversky (1979), which may tell us little about the equilibrating forces whose effects we observe in experimental markets, but much about the untrained thinking processes of humans isolated from each other and from institutions. Moreover, there are many cases in which behavioral convergence to noncooperative states in repeated games does not require Cournot convergent theory designs.

By Cournot convergent, I refer to a strategy sequence that converges to a noncooperative equilibrium when each agent on round $t+1$ chooses her best response on the assumption that all other agents will simply repeat their previous choices on round t. The robustness of empirical convergence in Cournot divergent designs was first shown by John Carlson (1967) in the context of his "Cobweb Theorem" experiments. These results have been extended by Wellford (1989). Similar findings were obtained in my Groves-Ledyard public good experiments (Smith 1979) and in countless Cournot oligopoly experiments, which appear likely to be unstable, theoretically, under the adaptive expectations hypothesis (Szidarovszky and Okuguchi 1987). These cases suggest that the structural form of expectations, not just their parameterization in a fixed form, is adaptive. Such adaptation appears to be stimulated when people find that their current myopic responses are serving them poorly.

Experimenter Induced Fair Outcomes?
Experimenters must be alert to the possibility that their experimental procedures constitute an unintended treatment, which contaminates their interpretation of the experimental results. Experimentalists often do supplementary experiments designed to check for such artifactual elements. A long-respected scientific rule in experimentalism is that important variables likely to affect observations should either be controlled as treatments or their effects randomized to reduce systematic error bias. For example, initial endowments, agent roles, and rights to act are commonly assigned at random among individual subjects. The objective is to avoid introducing any systematic correlation between such assignments and the personal characteristics of subjects.

Like all good rules, this one should be applied with sensitivity to the possibility of exceptions. This is particularly important in experimental economics, where our methods, techniques, and subject matter often differ from those of other experimental sciences. Since we are only at the beginning, much is yet to be learned about shaping the technology of experiment in economics.

Apparently, the idea that one should randomize effects that are not controlled comes from biology, where you randomize treatments among plots of land to prevent differences in soil quality from being attributed accidentally to the treatments. But human subjects are not plots of land, and the method of assignment may not have a neutral affect on behavior. This lesson has been clearly demonstrated in the bargaining experiments of Hoffman and Spitzer (1985). Subject pairs in these experiments bargain over the division of surplus under different property right arrangements. Under one arrangement, the agent whose productive activity causes harm to the other agent has the right to inflict this harm. This is the "polluter's" rights model. Under the alternative arrangement, the harmed agent has a right to be compensated for damage. This is the "pollutee" rights model.

According to the so-called Coase (1960) theorem, the creation of social surplus, or the gain from exchange, is not altered by the property right arrangement, although certainly the distribution of the surplus between the two parties may be altered. The Hoffman-Spitzer experiments provide strong support for this proposition. All pairs bargain to the solution that maximized their combined gains from exchange. But in every case, the person designated as the "controller" who was endowed with the privileged right failed to take advantage of this right. The controller, instead of extracting her individually rational share of the gains, agreed to an equal split of the gains. This outcome is commonly reported in bargaining experiments and is interpreted to be the result of a "fairness" ethic.

In Hoffman-Spitzer, all bargaining was face-to-face and was monitored by the experimenters, who had the impressionistic suspicion that this outcome might be influenced by the fact that the assignment of the controller right was determined by flipping a coin. Thus, they replicated their experiments, but assigned the role of "controller" to the winner of a pregame contest. The instructions emphasized that the winner had *earned* the right to be the controller. The effect of this new treatment on outcomes was dramatic: two-thirds of the bargaining pairs now negotiated individually rational outcomes. This is particularly impressive under face-to-face bargaining where lack of anonymity might be thought to increase the pressure on the controller to be accommodative.

The random assignment of rights is widely perceived to be a fair method of allocation; for example, hunting rights, student basketball tickets, and tied trades on stock exchanges are allocated by lottery. Consequently, when you flip a coin to select which of two persons is to be assigned an advantageous endowment, or right, the subjects are likely to believe that you are doing this to be fair. So if you are being fair to them, why should they not be fair to each other? These results call into question the interpretation of data from the large literature in bilateral bargaining that is characterized by a first-mover, or other asymmetric advantage, randomly assigned. The point is not that fairness criteria are unimportant. I believe they are. Rather, the question is whether inducing fair behavior is the appropriate way to frame the test of a bargaining theory that assumes self-interested agents whose interests conflict, as with management and labor.

Now, if one were to replicate all the asymmetric bargaining experiments, assigning privileged rights only to those who earned them, and still observed fair outcomes, then this would call into question the relevancy of the theory. Since that has not been done, I do not believe that the current state of experimental testing is adequate to support rejection of the theory in its present form. Fairness considerations are important — too important to be slipped in artifactually as an inadvertent product of a procedure intended for a different purpose.

Reward Motivation and Decision Cost

I first learned the full significance of reward saliency in experiments from the psychologist, Sidney Siegel (1961). The context was the very simple Bernoulli trials experiment. On each trial the subject's task was to predict which of two independent events would occur. The more frequent event occurred with probability π (say, 70%) and the less frequent event with probability $(1-\pi)$, where π is usually not known by the subject. For two decades before Siegel's 1961 paper, psychologists had been doing these experiments, always instructing the subject to "do your best" to predict correctly on each trial. The standard observed outcome was probability matching in which the proportion of times the more frequent event is chosen, is $p=\pi$. Of course if your objective is to maximize the number of correct predictions, then as soon as you have determined which is the more frequent event, you should predict it 100% of the time. Consequently, the typical conclusion from the data was that the model of rational maximizing behavior had to be rejected. Syd Siegel thought that this was a curious conclusion because subjects had no incentive to maximize the number of correct predictions other than perhaps the homegrown satisfaction of being correct.

Siegel argued that, from the subject's point of view, the task was excruciatingly boring, and hypothesized that the subject's diversification of his prediction strategy was a means of reducing this boredom. Specifically, he hypothesized that the subject's choice criterion was composed of two additive subjective utilities: the utility of a correct prediction and the utility of variability, where the latter was proportional to $p(1-p)$, which is the variance of outcomes in a Bernoulli process with parameter p. This assumption has the property that the utility of variability was greatest when $p=1/2$; i.e., when diversification, or boredom relief, was greatest. Siegel then deduced two propositions: first, the optimal response is $p^*=\pi$ (probability matching) if the marginal utility of a correct response is equal to the marginal utility of variability, and second, the optimal response p^* would increase with an increase in the marginal utility of being correct.

An obvious way of increasing p^* was to introduce monetary rewards for a correct prediction. He conducted experiments in which subjects were run under three motivation treatments: no payoff ("do your best"); payoff (reward for each correct prediction); and payoff-loss (a reward for a correct, and a charge for an incorrect, prediction). Siegel's model predicted:

$\pi=p$ (no payoff) $<p$ (payoff) $<p$ (payoff-loss).

Siegel (see Siegel, et al. 1964) reported only the mean observed values of p, but the standard error for each treatment is computed from his raw data, and reported in Table 1 as decision error:

Table 1
Prediction Results, Final Block of 20 Trials for $\pi=0.70$

Treatment	No Payoff	Payoff	Payoff-loss
No. of subjects	12	12	12
Mean value of p	0.70	0.77	0.93
Decision error	0.069	0.062	0.058

As the stakes are increased, decisions approach the monetary maximizing strategy and decision error declines. These results strongly support the Siegel hypothesis, that the phenomenon of probability matching was actually the exception that proved the utility maximizing rule. But he went further; he showed that estimating the parameters for one value of π allowed predictions of behavior to be made at another level of π, that the model worked for children as well as adults, and that the choice proportion p could also be increased by a treatment that afforded subjects a means of relieving boredom without having to vary their prediction.

Although Siegel could not have known it at the time, in retrospect we now know that he developed perhaps the first formal model of decision opportunity cost that explicitly modeled the individual's subjective cost of transacting. Economists often make reference to transactions costs in post hoc explanations of observed deviations from optimality, but the topic is rarely treated at the theoretical-empirical depth illustrated by this example.

It is worth mentioning as a footnote in the history of ideas that as inspiration for his model Siegel cites Herbert Simon (1956, *271*): "To predict how economic man will behave, we need to know not only that he is rational, but also how he perceives the world — what alternatives he sees and what consequences he attaches to them." Siegel interpreted Simon's argument as suggesting that the rational model is essentially correct, but more or less incomplete. To make it complete, it was necessary to examine decision problems carefully from the utilitarian point of view of the decision maker (not just from the point of view of the experimenter/theorist). Note that this interpretation differs from the "satisficing" and "bounded rationality" constructions that were later put on Simon's original idea, constructions that were critical of the very foundation of rational behavior as conventionally defined. In Siegel's implementation, actions differ from the predictions of the standard model because of decision cost. Since the latter is necessarily part of the problem of realizing rational outcomes, the result is not just a better descriptive/predictive model. It is a better normative model of action as experienced by the individual. Thus, the distinction between the descriptive and the normative model of behavior becomes clouded; neither is cast in objective reality independent of experience. I believe this is the right way, although certainly not the easiest way, to approach the problem of modeling rational behavior.

Over the past three decades there have been many investigations of the effect of payoffs on outcomes in simple games and in market experiments. The most common effect of increased payoffs is to reduce decision error, but the central tendencies in the data can also shift with increased reward. Recent research in first-price auctions has varied the conversion rate of "tokens" into money among the five levels 0, 1, 5, 10, and 20 times the normal earnings in laboratory experiments. At a 20 to 1 conversion rate, subjects can easily earn $125 per hour.

In the figure below, we chart the marginal means that result from summing over four experience levels at each of the indicated five payoff multiples. The top chart shows decision error plotted against payoffs. Decision error is measured by the standard error of the estimated (linear) equilibrium bid function, where the auction is modeled as an incomplete information game. In the lower chart we provide a measure of risk aversion (the slope of the bid function, which increases directly with constant relative risk aversion) plotted against payoffs. Contrary to claims sometimes made in the literature, the predictions of the risk-neutral model are not supported as payoff (and payoff opportunity cost) increases; if anything, subjects become more risk averse at higher payoff conversion rates.

Figure 1

Effect of Payoff Level
in First Price Auction Experiments

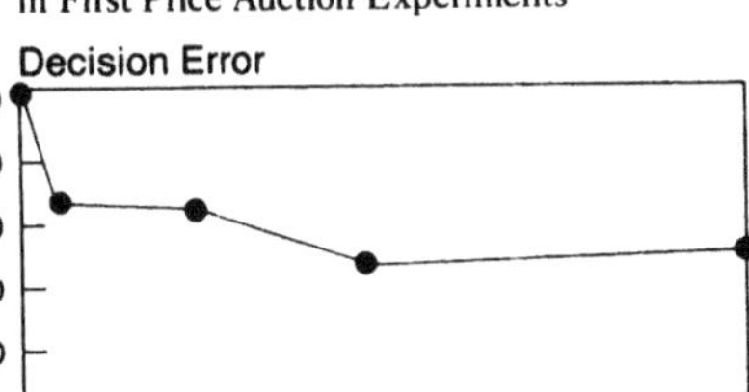

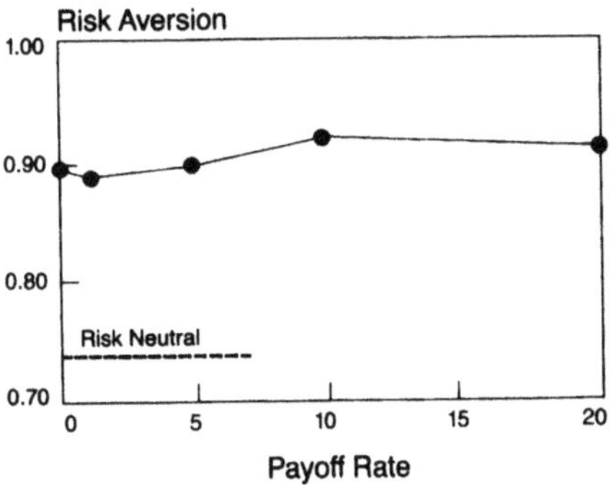

Strategy-Proofness in Theory and Behavior: An Example

It has long been recognized that it would be desirable if the rules of a market institution were such that the market was strategy-proof. This worthy objective has been elusive and has held theoretically only under limited conditions. Since mechanism theory informs us that almost any price-allocation institution can be strategically manipulated by a sufficiently sophisticated agent (Satterthwaite 1987), it is important to ask how motivated agents actually behave in a situation that is not theoretically strategy-proof.

Figure 2 provides an example of what happens in the competitive, or uniform price, sealed bid-offer (two-sided) auction. The induced market demand and supply schedules are depicted by the solid step functions. There are four buyers and four sellers, each with a capacity to buy (or sell) six units. All value (cost) information is private. The institution is one in which buyers submit a limit demand price for each unit they desire to buy and sellers submit a limit supply price for each unit they desire to sell. The limit buy prices are arranged from highest to lowest, while the supply prices are ordered from lowest to highest. Where the resulting arrays cross determines the market price and volume exchanged. In the example, these arrays are shown as dotted step functions. Since each buyer and seller is assigned multiple units on the market demand and supply schedules, it follows that those who are assigned induced values and costs near to the competitive market price are in a position to influence the price. Thus, if all buyers (and sellers) were to bid at their respective values (costs), a buyer with a marginal demand unit can lower the market price by underbidding her value for that unit. This would raise the profits earned on that buyer's higher-valued units.

But this conventional manipulation argument poses the wrong question. The actual situation is one in which *all agents* have some opportunity to manipulate price by concealing their true demand or supply. In this situation, do subjects work out some sort of equilibrium that is efficient, in the sense of maximizing their collective gain, and which is behaviorally strategy-proof? The answer is yes, and the character of that equilibrium is illustrated in Figure 2.

Figure 2

Example of Bid-Offer Array Crossing

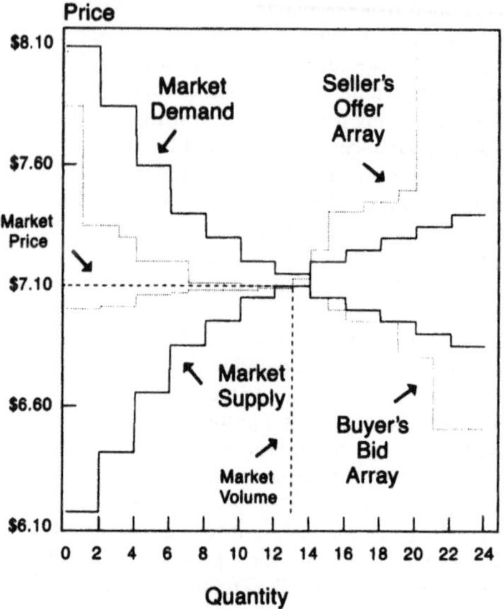

Notice that most of the bids and offers are close to the market price with many ties, or near ties, at this price. Consequently, if any buyer lowers her bid or any seller raises his offer in the next period, the likely result is that the agent's unit will not trade, will be displaced by another agent's unit, and the market price will be unaffected. This unconscious group equilibrium has the property that each side is protected from price manipulation by the other side and simultaneously punishes the other side for attempted manipulation. Behaviorally, this equilibrium is strategy-proof.

This example, which represents a typical outcome in uniform-price, sealed-bid-offer auctions, shows that concealment is not inimical to efficient outcomes. In this case, 99.1 percent of the gains from exchange were realized, while revelation was only 31.9 percent of the true demand and supply. The strategy is unconscious because none of the subjects have the global information shown in Figure 2 and therefore have no awareness of the collective ends achieved by their strategies. But in repeat interaction they discover what works. Extant theory is unable to predict, or come to terms with, this kind of strategy-proof behavioral equilibrium.

Experimental Microeconomic Policy

Perhaps the most important new direction for experimental economics in the last decade has been defined by the demands of the deregulation and denationalization movement that pervades much of the world. Here is the challenge. Can we design self-regulating market institutions to replace the regulatory procedures traditionally employed in public utility industries such as natural gas and electric power transmission networks? Or, where command systems are likely to continue being used, as in the U.S. space station and space shuttle programs, can market mechanisms be used to improve resource allocation (Banks, Ledyard, and Porter 1989)? In researching these questions, we use the experimental laboratory as a test-bed to evaluate the efficiency and price performance of proposed new institutions of exchange.

The traditional decentralized property right arrangements are problematic in gas pipeline and power transmission networks characterized by highly interdependent delivery technologies. Computerized central dispatch over large regions is essential if economies of coordination are to be fully captured and the full power of network competition is to discipline prices. My colleagues and I have proposed a "smart" computer-assisted market institution to solve this problem (McCabe, Rassenti, and Smith 1989b).

For example, in the natural gas case, wholesale buyers of gas submit location-specific bids for gas delivered to their city gates, wellhead owners submit location-specific offers of gas into the pipeline system, and pipeline owners submit leg-specific offers of transportation capacity. A computerized dispatch center applies linear programming algorithms to these decentralized bids and offers to compute prices and allocations so that the reported gains from exchange are maximized. The dispatch center itself would be a joint venture of all users governed by a cotenancy contract of the kind used for the co-ownership of pipelines, power lines, and power plants.

The objective is to combine the information advantages of decentralized ownership with the coordination advantages of central processing. Laboratory experiments show that even thin networks can achieve high efficiencies and competitive pricing. In effect we offer a solution to the Lange-Lerner-Hayek controversy of the 1930s in which Hayek argued that centralism could not be made to work by following marginal cost pricing rules; that only decentralized agents had the information and incentives needed to fuel the pricing system.

Government-specified property right systems offer the potential for providing a private market solution to the general problem of natural monopoly price regulation. Suppose a single capital facility (such as a pipeline or transmission line) is adequate to supply the needs of a community. The American model is to give legal monopoly status to a single owner of the facility, and then to regulate this monopoly with prices determined by cost plus a specified profit rate of return. As a consequence, the incentives to control cost are weak, as is made plain by the staggering cost overruns in nuclear power.

An alternative to this regulatory mechanism is the following: the government specifies that such natural monopoly facilities be governed by a competitively ruled cotenancy property right regime. Under this mechanism, the facility and its operations are held in a separate management company with multiple co-owners who compete to supply services using the common facility. Many precedents now exist using this mechanism: specialized printing facilities co-owned by morning and evening newspapers, shopping malls, power generators, and pipelines. The shopping mall is a superb example of a contractual institution providing economies of scale and scope under one roof in which firms produce competing and complimentary services, while they share common parking, walkway, security, utilities, and custodial services. Power generators are typically built to exhaust scale economies; then capacity drawing rights are allocated among several co-owners in proportion to the fixed capital cost borne by each. Each user has a small condominium package of capacity, and each benefits from the low unit cost of a large facility.

But existing, naturally occurring, cotenancy contracts are not competitively ruled. For example, it is common for such contracts to specify that capacity cannot be expanded except through agreement by all the cotenants. This would be replaced by a free entry property right rule permitting any cotenant, or any outsider, to expand capacity unilaterally and to thereby obtain new capacity rights equal to the expansion.

These are only a few of the exciting current challenges to our ability to design new self-regulating institutions for solving problems of contestability, or poor performance, in product and financial markets. The proposed institutions are based on what we have learned from theory and past experiments about the economics of incentives; on field experience with component building blocks, such as the cotenancy contract; on the enormous power of the computer to construct new forms of exchange never before imagined or imaginable; and on the experimental laboratory where our incentive design errors can be corrected at low cost before the proposals are tried elsewhere.

Syd Siegel would be proud to know that the field of experimental economics that he helped to found has flourished so vigorously, but I suspect he would emphasize that we have learned little relative to that which is yet to be learned. After 30 years we are, indeed, only just getting started.

REFERENCES

Aumann, Robert. 1987. Game theory. In *The new Palgrave*, vol. 2, edited by J. Eatwell, M. Milgate, and P. Neuman, 460-79. London: The Macmillan Press.

Banks, Jeffrey, John O. Ledyard, and David Porter. 1989. Allocating uncertain and unresponsive resources: an experimental approach. *Rand Journal of Economics* 20: 1-25.

Canning, David. 1989. Convergence to equilibrium in a sequence of games with learning. London School of Economics and Political Science, Discussion Paper, TE/89/190, March 1989.

Carlson, John. 1967. The stability of an experimental market with a supply-response lag. *Southern Economic Journal* 33: 305-21.

Coase, Ronald. 1960. The problem of social cost. *Journal of Law and Economics* 3: 1-44.

Cox, James C., and Ronald Oaxaca. 1989. Laboratory experiments with a finite horizon job search model. *Journal of Risk and Uncertainty* 2: 301-29.

Forsythe, Robert, Thomas R. Palfrey, and Charles R. Plott. 1982. Asset valuation in an experimental market. *Econometrica* 50: 537-67.

Friedman, James W., and Austin C. Hoggatt. 1980. *An experiment in noncooperative oligopoly*. Greenwich, Conn: JAI Press.

Harrison, Glenn W., and Kevin A. McCabe. 1989. Testing bargaining theory in experiments. University of Arizona. Working paper.

Hoffman, Elizabeth, and Matthew L. Spitzer. 1985. Entitlements, rights, and fairness: an experimental examination of subjects' concepts of distributive justice. *Journal of Legal Studies* 14: 259-97.

Kahneman, Daniel, and Amos Tversky. 1979. Prospect theory: an analysis of decisions under risk. *Econometrica* 47: 263-91.

Kalai, Ehud, and Ehud Lehrer. 1990. Learning by rational players. Paper delivered at the Public Choice/Economic Science Assocation Joint Meetings, Tucson, Arizona, March 1990.

Kruse, Jamie. 1988. Contestability in the presence of an alternative market: an experimental examination. University of Colorado. Working paper.

McCabe, Kevin A., Stephen J. Rassenti, and Vernon L. Smith (a). 1989. Lakatos and experimental economics. Discussion Paper No. 89-24, Economics Science Laboratory, University of Arizona.

McCabe, Kevin A., Stephen J. Rassenti, and Vernon L. Smith (b). 1989. Designing 'smart' computer-assisted markets: an experimental auction for gas networks. *Journal of Political Economy* (North-Holland) 5: 259-83.

Roth, A. E., and M. K. Malouf. 1979. Game theoretic models and the role of information in bargaining. *Psychological Review* 86: 574-94.

Satterthwaite, Mark A. 1987. Strategy-proof allocation mechanisms. In *The new Palgrave*, vol. 4, edited by J. Eatwell, M. Milgate, and P. Newman, 518-20. London: The Macmillan Press.

Selten, Reinhard. 1989. Evolution, learning, and economic behavior. 1989 Nancy L. Schwartz Memorial Lecture, J. L. Kellogg Graduate School of Management, Northwestern University.

Siegel, Sidney. 1961. Decision making and learning under varying conditions of reinforcement. *Annals of the New York Academy of Science* 89:766-83.

Siegel, Sidney, Alberta Siegel, and Julia Andrews. 1964. *Choice, strategy, and utility*. New York: McGraw-Hill.

Simon, Herbert. 1956. A comparison of game theory and learning theory. *Psychometrica* 21: 267-72.

Smith, Vernon L. Incentive compatible experimental processes for the provision of public goods. 1979. In *Research in experimental economics*, vol. 1, edited by V. Smith. Greenwich, Conn: JAI Press: 59-168.

Sonnenschein, Hugo. 1983. The economics of incentives: an introductory account. 1983 Nancy L. Schwartz Memorial Lecture, J. L. Kellogg Graduate School of Management, Northwestern University.

Szidarovszky, Ferenc, and Koji Okuguchi. 1987. Notes on the stability of quadratic games. *Keio Economic Studies* 24:33-45.

Wellford, Charissa P. 1989. A laboratory analysis of price dynamics and expectations in the cobweb model. Discussion Paper No. 89-15, Department of Economics, University of Arizona.

Wilson, Robert. 1990. Strategic analysis of auctions. Stanford Business School, February 19, 1990.

For EU product safety concerns, contact us at Calle de José Abascal, 56–1°, 28003 Madrid, Spain or eugpsr@cambridge.org.

www.ingramcontent.com/pod-product-compliance
Ingram Content Group UK Ltd.
Pitfield, Milton Keynes, MK11 3LW, UK
UKHW012158180425
457623UK00018B/270